PAGE 52

ON THE ROAD

and insider tips

Kaliningrad Region p282
St Petersburg p162
Northern European Russia p299
Moscow p54
Golden Ring p137
Western European Russia p238
Volga Region p346
The Urals p383
Western Siberia p450
Eastern Siberia p492
Russian Far East p563
Russian Caucasus p406

PAGE 697

SURVIVAL GUIDE

VITAL PRACTICAL INFORMATION TO HELP YOU HAVE A SMOOTH TRIP

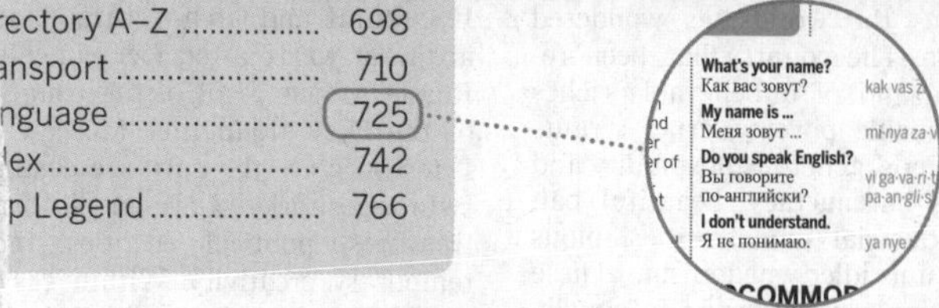

THIS EDITION WRITTEN AND RESEARCHED BY
Simon Richmond
Marc Bennetts, Greg Bloom, Marc Di Duca, Anthony Haywood, Tom Masters,
Leonid Ragozin, Tamara Sheward, Regis St Louis, Mara Vorhees

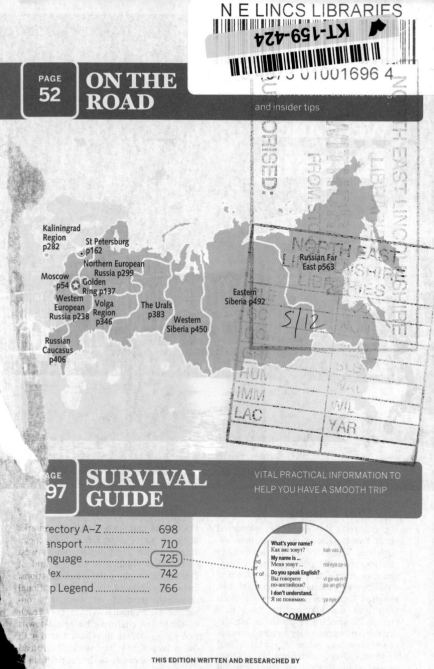

welcome to Russia

Eternal Russia

For centuries the world has wondered about Russia. The country has been reported as a land of unbelievable riches and indescribable poverty, cruel tyrants and great minds, generous hospitality and meddlesome bureaucracy, beautiful ballets and industrial monstrosities, pious faith and unbridled hedonism. These eternal Russian truths coexist in equally diverse landscapes of icy tundra and sun-kissed beaches, dense silver-birch and fir forests, deep, mysterious lakes, snow-capped mountains and swaying grassland steppes. Factor in ancient fortresses, luxurious palaces, swirly-spired churches and lost-in-time wooden villages and you'll begin to see why Russia is simply amazing.

Urban & Rural

If cultural and architectural landmarks are what you're after, focus on European Russia, which is all of the country west of the Ural Mountains. Moscow and St Petersburg are the must-see destinations, twin repositories of eye-boggling national treasures, political energies and contemporary creativity. Within easy reach of either are charming historical towns and villages where the vistas dotted with onion domes and lined with gingerbread cottages measure up to the rural Russia of popular imagination.

To get the most from Russia, howev make your way off the beaten track. T nation's vast geographical distances a

MARTIN MOOS / LONELY PLANET IMAGES ©

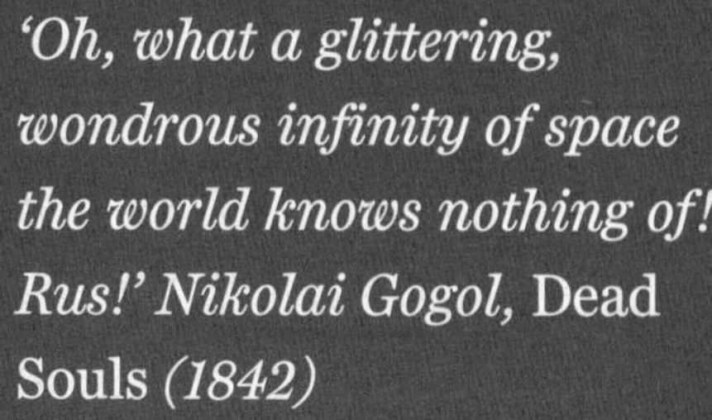
'Oh, what a glittering, wondrous infinity of space the world knows nothing of! Rus!' Nikolai Gogol, Dead Souls *(1842)*

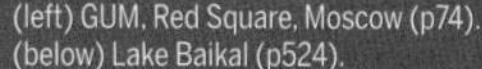
(left) GUM, Red Square, Moscow (p74).
(below) Lake Baikal (p524).

IMAGEBROKER / ALAMY ©

cultural differences mean you don't tick off its highlights in the way you might those of a smaller country. A more sensible approach is to view Russia as a collection of countries, each one deserving exploration. Rather than transiting via Moscow, consider flying direct to a regional centre such as Irkutsk or Yekaterinburg.

A Riddle Worth Solving

It would be a fib to say that travel here is all plain sailing. Russia's initial face can be frosty. Tolerating bureaucracy, corruption and occasional discomfort, particularly away from the booming urban centres, remains an integral part of the Russian travel experience. However, a small degree of perseverance will be amply rewarded and one of the great joys of Russian travel is being swept away by the locals' boundless hospitality.

In 1978, in his commencement address at Harvard, Aleksandr Solzhenitsyn talked about Russia's 'ancient, deeply rooted autonomous culture…full of riddles and surprises to Western thinking'. From the power machinations of the Kremlin and a resurgent Russian Orthodox Church to the compelling beauty of its arts and the quixotic nature of its people, whose moods can tumble from melancholy to indifference or exuberance in the blink of an eye, Russia is a fascinating creation that will perplex, delight and ultimately seduce you.

› Russia

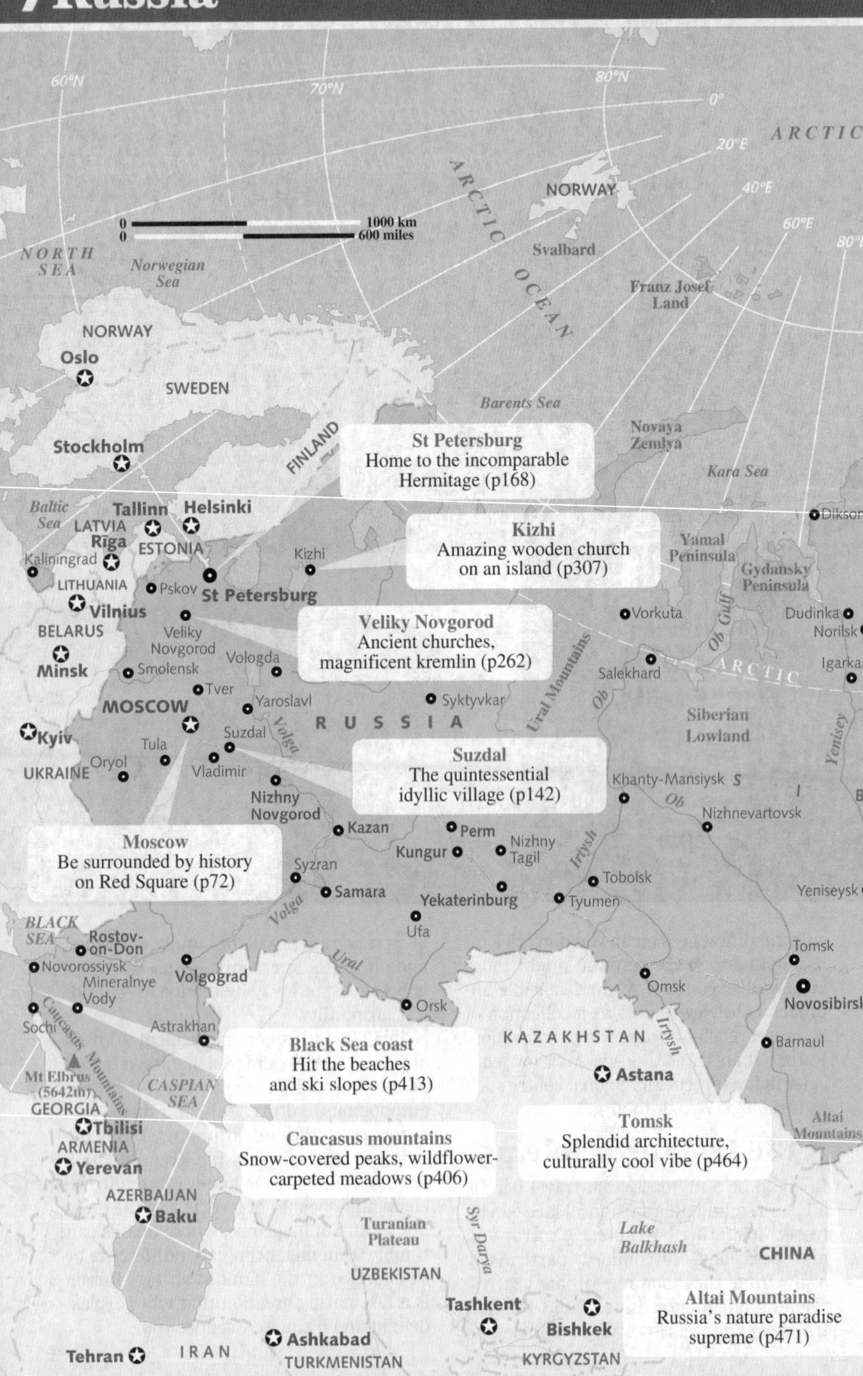
St Petersburg
Home to the incomparable Hermitage (p168)
Kizhi
Amazing wooden church on an island (p307)
Veliky Novgorod
Ancient churches, magnificent kremlin (p262)
Suzdal
The quintessential idyllic village (p142)
Moscow
Be surrounded by history on Red Square (p72)
Black Sea coast
Hit the beaches and ski slopes (p413)
Caucasus mountains
Snow-covered peaks, wildflower-carpeted meadows (p406)
Tomsk
Splendid architecture, culturally cool vibe (p464)
Altai Mountains
Russia's nature paradise supreme (p471)
0 1000 km
0 600 miles
60°N
70°N
80°N
0°
20°E
40°E
60°E
80°E
ARCTIC OCEAN
NORTH SEA
Norwegian Sea
Barents Sea
Kara Sea
Baltic Sea
BLACK SEA
CASPIAN SEA
NORWAY
Svalbard
Franz Josef Land
Novaya Zemlya
Oslo
SWEDEN
Stockholm
FINLAND
Tallinn
Helsinki
LATVIA
Rīga
ESTONIA
Kaliningrad
LITHUANIA
Vilnius
BELARUS
Minsk
Kyiv
UKRAINE
Pskov
St Petersburg
Kizhi
Veliky Novgorod
Smolensk
Vologda
Tver
Yaroslavl
MOSCOW
Tula
Oryol
Suzdal
Vladimir
Volga
RUSSIA
Syktyvkar
Nizhny Novgorod
Kazan
Perm
Kungur
Nizhny Tagil
Syzran
Samara
Yekaterinburg
Ufa
Ural
Orsk
Ural Mountains
Vorkuta
Salekhard
Ob
Ob Gulf
Yamal Peninsula
Gydansky Peninsula
Dikson
Dudinka
Norilsk
Igarka
ARCTIC
Siberian Lowland
Yenisey
Khanty-Mansiysk
Nizhnevartovsk
Irtysh
Tobolsk
Tyumen
Yeniseysk
Tomsk
Omsk
Novosibirsk
Barnaul
Rostov-on-Don
Novorossiysk
Mineralnye Vody
Volgograd
Sochi
Astrakhan
Caucasus Mountains
Mt Elbrus (5642m)
GEORGIA
Tbilisi
ARMENIA
Yerevan
AZERBAIJAN
Baku
KAZAKHSTAN
Astana
Altai Mountains
Turanian Plateau
Syr Darya
UZBEKISTAN
Lake Balkhash
CHINA
Tashkent
Bishkek
Ashkabad
TURKMENISTAN
KYRGYZSTAN
Tehran
IRAN

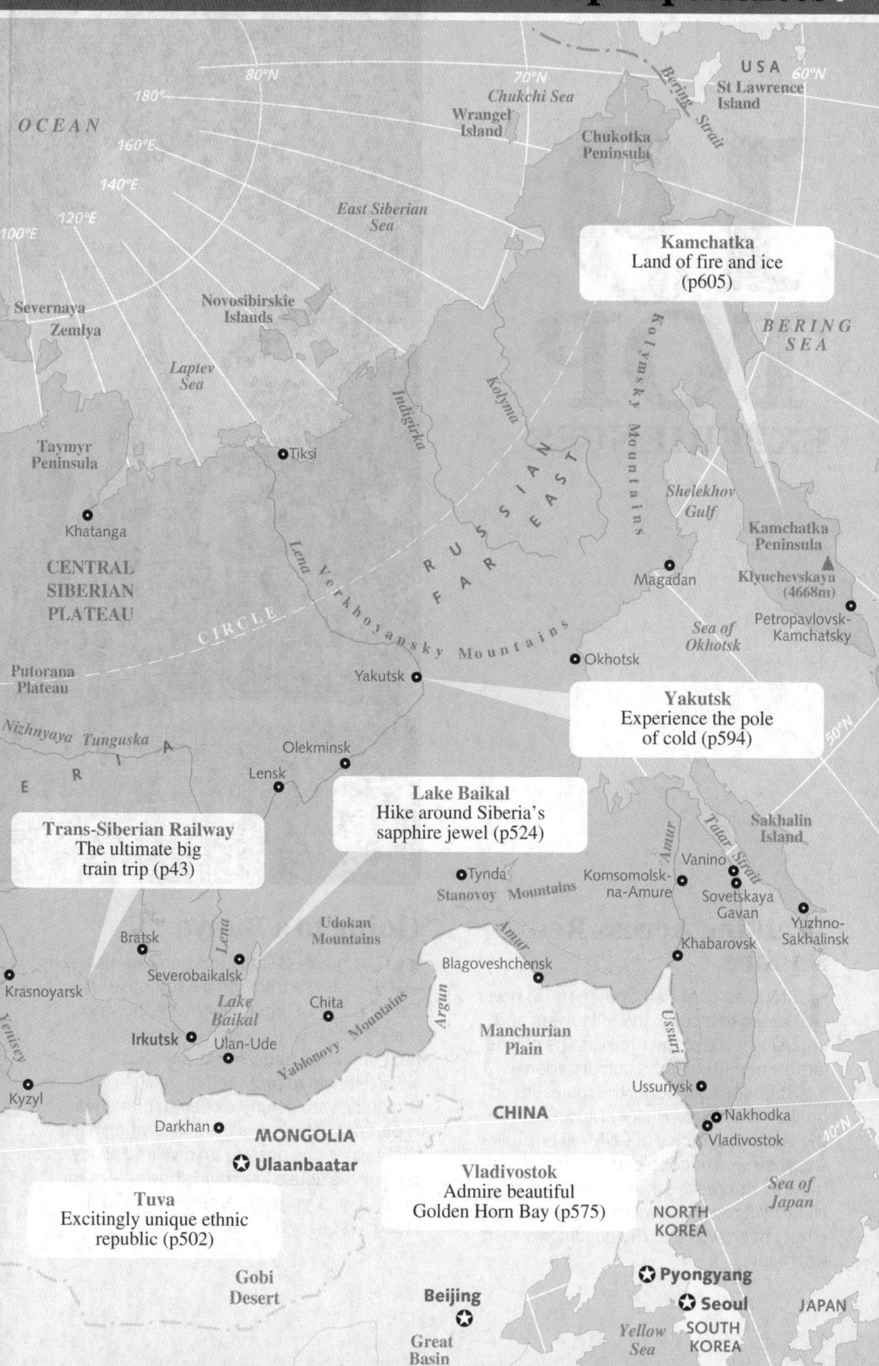
Kamchatka
Land of fire and ice
(p605)
Yakutsk
Experience the pole
of cold (p594)
Lake Baikal
Hike around Siberia's
sapphire jewel (p524)
Trans-Siberian Railway
The ultimate big
train trip (p43)
Vladivostok
Admire beautiful
Golden Horn Bay (p575)
Tuva
Excitingly unique ethnic
republic (p502)
OCEAN
Chukchi Sea
Wrangel Island
Chukotka Peninsula
USA
St Lawrence Island
Bering Strait
East Siberian Sea
BERING SEA
Severnaya Zemlya
Novosibirskie Islands
Laptev Sea
Taymyr Peninsula
Tiksi
Khatanga
CENTRAL SIBERIAN PLATEAU
RUSSIAN FAR EAST
Kolymsky Mountains
Shelekhov Gulf
Kamchatka Peninsula
Magadan
Klyuchevskaya (4668m)
Petropavlovsk-Kamchatsky
Sea of Okhotsk
Okhotsk
Verkhoyansky Mountains
Yakutsk
Putorana Plateau
Nizhnyaya Tunguska
Olekminsk
Lensk
Sakhalin Island
Tatar Strait
Vanino
Komsomolsk-na-Amure
Sovetskaya Gavan
Yuzhno-Sakhalinsk
Tynda
Stanovoy Mountains
Udokan Mountains
Bratsk
Severobaikalsk
Krasnoyarsk
Khabarovsk
Blagoveshchensk
Lake Baikal
Chita
Irkutsk
Ulan-Ude
Yablonovy Mountains
Manchurian Plain
Kyzyl
Ussuriysk
Nakhodka
Vladivostok
Darkhan
MONGOLIA
CHINA
Ulaanbaatar
Sea of Japan
NORTH KOREA
Pyongyang
Seoul
SOUTH KOREA
JAPAN
Gobi Desert
Beijing
Great Basin
Yellow Sea

19 TOP EXPERIENCES

Walking Across Red Square

1 Stepping onto Red Square (p63) never ceases to inspire: the tall towers and imposing walls of the Kremlin, the playful jumble of patterns and colours adorning St Basil's Cathedral, the majestic red bricks of the State History Museum and the elaborate edifice of GUM, all encircling a vast stretch of cobblestones. Individually they are impressive, but the ensemble is electrifying. Come at night to see the square empty of crowds and the buildings awash with lights.

Going to a Banya

2 The quintessential Russian experience is visiting a traditional bathhouse, or *banya* (p657). Forget your modesty, strip down and brave the steam room. As the heat hits you'll understand why locals wear felt hats to protect their hair. A light thrashing with a bundle of birch branches is part of the fun, as is the invigorating blast that follows the poststeam dive into an icy pool or the douse in a frigid shower – as the locals say *'S lyogkim parom!'* (Hope your steam was easy!).

1

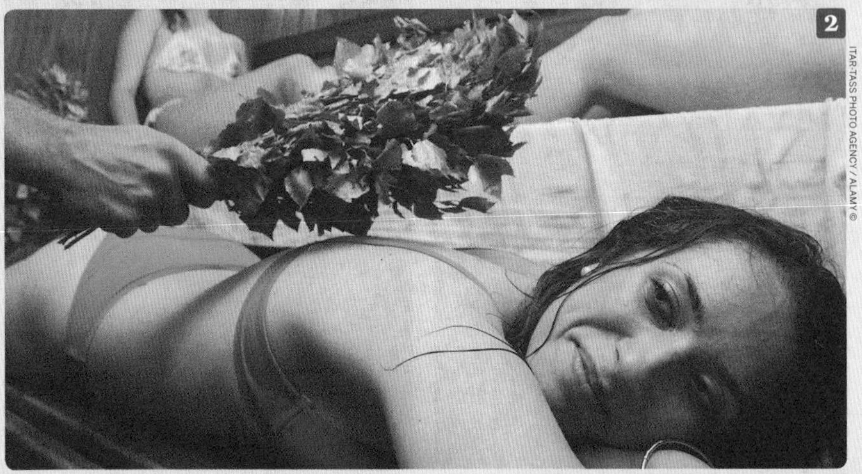

2

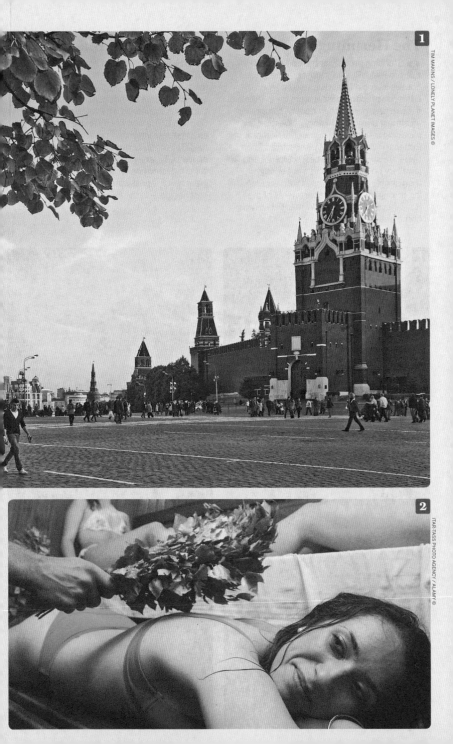

The Hermitage

3 Standing proudly at the end of Nevsky prospekt, Russia's most famous palace houses its most famous museum (p168). Little can prepare most visitors for the scale of the exhibits, nor for their quality, comprising an almost unrivalled history of Western art, including a staggering number of Rembrandts, Rubens, Picassos and Matisses. In addition, there are superb antiquities, sculpture and jewellery on display. If that's not enough, then simply content yourself with wandering through the private apartments of the Romanovs, for whom the Winter Palace was home until 1917.

Exploring the Black Sea

4 The serene Black Sea coast has long been a favourite of Russian holidaymakers for its seaside towns, easy-going ambience and magnificent inland scenery in the nearby Caucasus mountains. The gateway to it all is Sochi (p415), a vibrant city reinventing itself as a first-rate international resort and host of the 2014 Winter Olympics. The looming peaks of nearby Krasnaya Polyana (p424) make a superb destination for ski lovers, while there's great hiking – past waterfalls and up to eagles'-nest heights – in the Agura Valley (p422).

3

HOLGER LEUE / LONELY PLANET IMAGES ©

4

MKS / IMAGEBROKER ©

5
MARK NEWMAN / LONELY PLANET IMAGES ©

6
ESTEA / SHUTTERSTOCK ©

Kamchatka

5 It seems almost trite to describe Kamchatka (p605) as majestic. To many Kamchatka is, quite simply, the most beautiful place in the world. It's Yellowstone and Rotorua and Patagonia rolled into one, and it teems with wildlife free to frolic in one of the world's great remaining wildernesses. Traditionally the domain of well-heeled tourists who can afford helicopter rides to view its trademark volcanoes, geysers and salmon-devouring bears, Kamchatka has finally loosened up a bit for the independent traveller. Now if only they could fix that weather...

Veliky Novgorod's Kremlin

6 In the town that considers itself Russia's birthplace stands one of the country's most impressive and picturesque stone fortresses (p262). Within the kremlin's grounds rise up the Byzantine 11th-century Cathedral of St Sophia and a 300-tonne sculpture celebrating 1000 years of Russian history. Climb the Kokui Tower for an overview of the complex, then enter the Novgorod State United Museum to see one of Russia's best collections of iconographic art. A pleasant park and riverside beach also fringe the magnificent brick walls.

JANE SWEENEY / LONELY PLANET IMAGES ©

MARTIN MOOS / LONELY PLANET IMAGES ©

ROBERTO GEROMETTA / LONELY PLANET IMAGES ©

Suzdal's Idyll

7 Ding-dong ring the bells of a few dozen churches as you ride your bike through the streets of Suzdal (p142), lined with wooden cottages and lush gardens. This is Russia as it would have been, if not for the devastating 20th century – unpretentious, pious and very laid-back. Some of the best religious architecture is scattered around, but you can just as well spend all day lying in the grass and watching the river flow before repairing to a *banya* for the sweet torture of heat, cold and birch twigs. Nativity of the Virgin Cathedral, Suzdal.

Spending the Night on a Train

8 Daylight gradually fades, light illuminates the carriage, windows turn opaque and reflect life inside the train. One of the pleasures of travelling Russia is to board an overnight train (p42) and alight in a different city the following morning. This may be inside a deluxe carriage from St Petersburg; most likely it's in a four-berth compartment as you travel across Siberia on Russia's 'track of the camel', or perhaps hurtle through a Siberian night in third-class to the snores, silences and groans of more than 50 fellow travellers.

Kizhi

9 Old buildings made from logs may not usually be synonymous with 'heart-stopping excitement', but Kizhi's (p307) collection of wooden masterpieces is enough to spike the blood pressure of those weary of even the most glorious architecture. The first glimpse of the heavenly Transfiguration Church, viewed from the approaching hydrofoil, causes such a ripple that the boat practically bounces: *is it... it is!* Up close, the church is a miracle of design and construct: legend has it that the unnamed builder destroyed his axe upon its completion, correctly assuming that its glory could not be matched. Transfiguration Church, Kizhi.

Going to the Ballet

10 What could be more Russian than a night at the ballet, dressed to the nines, watching *Swan Lake* or *Romeo & Juliet*? St Petersburg's famed Mariinsky Theatre (p219) and the Bolshoi Ballet (p120) in Moscow both offer the ultimate in classical ballet or operatic experiences, and now with a contemporary twist as the Mariinsky's long-awaited second stage finally opens in 2012, while the Bolshoi is looking better than ever after a long renovation. Tickets are no longer cheap, but the experience will stay with you forever. Ballet in Moscow.

Hiking the Great Baikal Trail

11 Already one of Russia's most successful environmental projects, the Great Baikal Trail has the ambitious aim of encircling Lake Baikal with marked hiking trails (p537). That's still a long way from being achieved, but where trails have been etched into the landscape, donning boots for a trek along Baikal's shores is all the rage. Whichever section you choose, Baikal's gob-smacking vistas and the tough going will leave you breathless as you pass through virgin taiga, along isolated beaches and through cold, flowing rivers.

10

ITAR-TASS PHOTO AGENCY / ALAMY ©

11

YUI / SHUTTERSTOCK ©

Tomsk

12 Closed to foreigners during the Soviet period, Tomsk (p464) is today very much open – both literally and metaphorically. A university city with a massive student population, the 'cultural capital of Siberia' is vibrant, friendly and home to a lively art scene. After you've finished exploring its many restaurants, cafés and bars, take a wander through the city's side streets, home to some eye-catching examples of carved wooden facades and architecture. Then head to the riverbank to find out how the city took its revenge on playwright Anton Chekhov.

Olkhon Island

13 Sacred of the sacred to the shamanist western Buryats, who attach a legend or fable to every rock, cape and hillock, enchanted Olkhon (p541) sits halfway up Lake Baikal's western shore. It's obvious why the gods and other beings from the Mongol *Geser* epic chose to dwell on this eerily moving island, though today it's more likely to be a bunch of backpackers you meet emerging from a cave. The island's landscapes are spellbinding, Baikal's waters lap balmiest on its western shore and if you're after some Siberia-inspired meditation, there's no better spot.

Exploring the Altai

14 Misty mountain passes, standing stone idols, tranquil lakes and empty roads that stretch on forever. Welcome to the Altai Republic, Russia's supreme natural paradise (p471), almost twice the size of Wales but with less than one-tenth of the population. You can travel for hours here without seeing another soul – unless you count the wild horses and goats. From snow-capped peaks to the lunar landscapes of Kosh-Agach, desolation has never been quite so appealing. But be warned – the Altai and its mysteries possess a magnetic pull, drawing travellers back year after year.

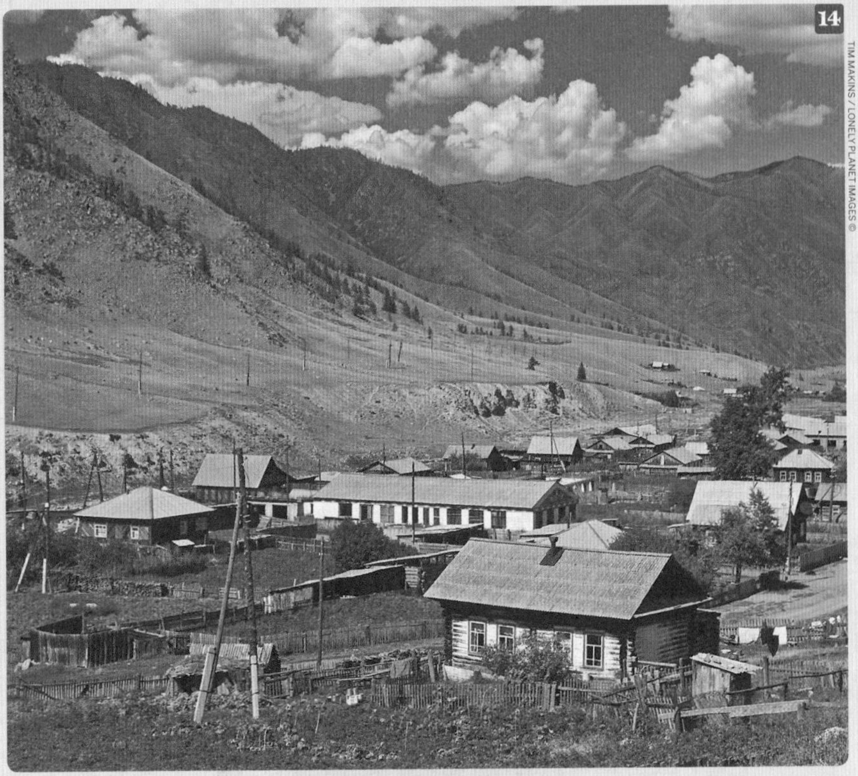

14

The Caucasus Mountains

15 Photos simply don't do them justice: the astonishing beauty of the Caucasus mountains is best appreciated on a trek among the jagged peaks. You can take short hikes through meadows, past waterfalls and up into alpine heights from the villages of Dombay (p435) and Arkhyz (p441). Those seeking to conquer Europe's highest mountain set their sights on Elbrus (p443), the twin-peaked overlord that tops out at 5642m – one of Russia's most rewarding mountain adventures. Wherever you plan to go, be sure to arrange permits well in advance. Mt Elbrus.

15

16

IMAGES & STORIES / ALAMY ©

17

ITAR-TASS PHOTO AGENCY / ALAMY ©

Tuva

16 Throat-singers zing and burp under upturned eaves, nomads' yurts pimple the dust-bare grasslands, a hoard of Scythian gold gleams in the National Museum and a clipped Turkic tongue stutters on the dusty streets – this is Tuva (p502), a republic isolated from the rest of Russia by the Yergaki Mountains (at least until the new railway is built), where Slavic influence has all but faded. You'll long remember a tour of this incredible country, not least for its wildernesses peppered with petroglyph-etched standing stones and its excitingly unique traditional music.

Pole of Cold

17 Some people just want cold. Bone-tingling, mind-numbing, nostril-hair-freezing cold. And there's no better place in the world to be cold than in the Sakha Republic (p593), home of the self-proclaimed 'pole of cold'. Yakutsk, the capital, is the world's coldest city of any decent size. But the actual pole of cold – the coldest inhabited place on earth – is in Oymyakon (p600), where temperatures have dropped to −71°C. A festival here celebrates cold every February. Yakutsk street.

MARTIN MOOS / LONELY PLANET IMAGES ©

RICHARD I'ANSON / LONELY PLANET IMAGES ©

Golden Horn Bay

18 Vladivostok (p575), capital of Russia's east, has a swagger in its step after being remade for an economic summit in 2012. No longer a remote satellite of Moscow, Vladivostok is Asia's rising star; Golden Horn Bay is its heart and soul. Take it in from one of the city's myriad viewpoints or join the frenzy of activity on the bay with a ferry cruise. Check out the impressive new suspension bridge spanning the bay. Suddenly those San Francisco comparisons don't seem quite so preposterous.

Buying Souvenirs at Izmaylovo Market

19 It's a fine line between shopping and fun at the kremlin in Izmaylovo (p105). Cross the footbridge and walk through the gate to enter a Disney-like medieval village, complete with wooden church, white-washed walls and plenty of souvenir shops. Just as in times of yore, the best shopping is in the trade rows outside the kremlin walls. Wander among the stalls of the sprawling market to find an endless array of traditional handicrafts, as well as art and antiques, Central Asian carpets, Soviet paraphernalia and more. Matryoshki dolls.

need to know

Currency

» Russian rouble (R)

Language

» Russian

When to Go

High Season (Jun–Sep)

» Protect against disease-carrying ticks.

» Book all forms of transport in advance.

» Prices can rise in St Petersburg, particularly during White Nights in June and July.

Shoulder (May & Oct)

» Late spring and early autumn see the country bathed in the fresh greenery or russet shades of the seasons.

Low Season (Nov–Apr)

» Snow falls and temperatures plummet, creating the wintery Russia of the imagination.

» Best time for skiing (although resorts charge higher prices) and visiting museums and galleries.

Your Daily Budget

Budget Less than

R1500

» Dorm bed: R700–800

» Café or street-stall meal: R200–500

» Travel on buses and metro: R10–20

Midrange

R1500–6000

» Double room in a midrange hotel: R2000–3000

» Two-course meal: R500–1000

» Museum entry fee: R100–300

» City-centre taxi ride: R200–300

Top End Over

R6000

» Double room in a top-end hotel: R5000+

» Two-course meal with wine: R2000+

» Ballet tickets: R3200

» First-class train ticket, Moscow–St Petersburg: R5200–6000

Money

» Credit and debit cards accepted. ATMs plentiful. Euro or US dollars best currencies for exchange.

Visas

» Required by all; apply at least a month in advance of your trip.

Mobile Phones

» Prepaid SIM cards readily available. International roaming OK.

Transport

» Trains and flights between regions. There are also many buses, and, in summer, cruises and ferries on rivers.

Websites

» **Lonely Planet** (www.lonelyplanet.com/russia) Greatest website for preplanning.

» **The Moscow Expat Site** (www.expat.ru) Mine expat knowledge of Russia.

» **Russia Beyond the Headlines** (http://rbth.ru) News, views and cultural features.

» **Way to Russia** (www.waytorussia.net) Comprehensive online travel guide.

Exchange Rates

Australia	A$1	R31
Canada	C$1	R29
Europe	€1	R41
Japan	¥100	R38
New Zealand	NZ$1	R25
UK	UK£1	R47
US	US$1	R29

For current exchange rates see www.xe.com.

Important Numbers

ambulance	☎03
country code	☎7
fire	☎01
international access code	☎8
police	☎02

Arriving in Russia

» **Sheremetyevo Airport, Moscow** (p130)
Trains – business/standard R550/320; about 35 minutes
Taxis – R1000 to R1500; at least an hour

» **Domodedovo Airport, Moscow** (p130)
Trains – business/standard R550/320; about 45 minutes
Taxis – R1000 to R1500; at least an hour

» **Pulkovo Airport, St Petersburg** (p226)
Buses – R21 to R27; about 15 minutes
Taxis – R600 to R800 to the centre

Independent Travel

Outside the major cities, your odds of meeting anyone who speaks English are slim. With limited language skills, everything you attempt will likely be more costly and difficult. However, it's far from impossible; if you really want to meet locals and have a flexible itinerary, independent travel is the way to go.

To help things along, it's a good idea to consider using a specialist travel agency to arrange your visa, make any key transport and accommodation bookings, and/or hire guides; see p713 for a list of reputable agents.

Using a tour agency to buy only train tickets, though, will be more expensive than if you were to do it yourself in Russia: check prices carefully and consider doing this only if you absolutely must travel on certain dates and want a specific class of ticket. There are also websites through which you can book train tickets directly (see p43).

first time

Everyone needs a helping hand when they visit a country for the first time. There are phrases to learn, customs to get used to and etiquette to understand. The following section will help demystify Russia so your first trip goes as smoothly as your fifth.

Language

Russian is the common language, although dozens of other languages are spoken by ethnic minorities. It's relatively easy to find English speakers in the big cities, but not so easy in smaller towns and the countryside. Learning Cyrillic and a few key phrases will help you enormously in being able to decode street signs, menus and timetables. For more on language see p725.

Booking Ahead

Book a night or two of accommodation in advance for big cities such as Moscow and St Petersburg; it's rarely necessary elsewhere. Reserve tickets for certain popular trains in advance also (see p42).

Hello.	Здравствуйте.	*zdrast*·vuy·tye
I would like to book a room.	Я бы хотел/хотела забронировать номер. (m/f)	ya bih khat·*yel*/khat·*ye*·la za·bra·*ni*·ra·vat' *no*·mir
a single room	одноместный номер	ad·nam·*yes*·nih *no*·mir
a double room	номер с двуспальней кроватью	*no*·mir z dvu·*spaln*·yey kra·*vat*·yu
My surname is...	Моя фамилия ...	ma·*ya* fa·*mi*·li·ya ...
from... to... (date)	С ... по ...	s ... pa ...
How much is it...?	Сколько стоит за ...?	*skol'*·ka *sto*·it za ...
per night	ночь	noch'
for two people	двоих	dva·*ikh*
Thank you (very much).	Спасибо (большое).	spa·*si*·ba (bal'·*sho*·ye)

What to Wear

Everyone makes an effort when they go to the theatre or a posh restaurant – you should do likewise to fit in. If you're planning on exploring on foot, a comfortable pair of waterproof walking shoes will come in handy, as will an umbrella or rain jacket.

In winter, bundle up with several layers before going out and bring a long, windproof coat to stay nicely warm. Hats and coats are always removed on entering a museum or restaurant and left in the cloakroom.

What to Pack

- » Passport
- » Credit card
- » Phrasebook or minidictionary
- » Money belt
- » Travel plug
- » Insect repellent
- » Mobile phone charger
- » Earplugs
- » Eye mask
- » Inflatable pillow
- » Painkillers (or other hangover cure)
- » Padlock
- » Medical kit
- » Sunscreen
- » Penknife
- » Torch
- » Sense of humour
- » Bucketful of patience

Checklist

» Check the validity of your passport.

» Check you have a visa.

» Check airline baggage restrictions.

» Check travel health websites (see p703).

» Tell banks and credit card providers your travel dates.

» Organise travel insurance (see p703).

Etiquette

Russians are sticklers for formality. They're also rather superstitious. Follow these tips to avoid faux pas.

» Visiting Homes
Shaking hands across the threshold is considered unlucky; wait until you're fully inside. Remove your shoes and coat on entering a house. Always bring a gift. If you give anyone flowers, make sure it's an odd number – even numbers of blooms are for funerals.

» Religion
Women should cover their heads and bare shoulders when entering a church. In some monasteries and churches it's also required for a woman to wear a skirt – wraps are usually available at the door. Men should remove their hats in church and not wear shorts.

» Eating & Drinking
Russians eat resting their wrists on the table edge, with fork in left hand and knife in the right. Vodka toasts are common at shared meals – it's rude to refuse to join in and traditional (and good sense) to eat a little something after each shot.

Tipping

» When to Tip
Customary in restaurants, cafés and bars, optional elsewhere.

» Restaurants
Leave small change or about 10%, if the service warrants it.

» Guides
Around 10% of their daily rate; a small gift will also be appreciated.

» Taxis
No need to tip as the fare is agreed either before you get in or metered.

» Hotels
Only in the most luxurious need you tip bellboys etc, and only if service is good.

Money

It's illegal to make purchases in any currency other than roubles. If prices are listed in US dollars or euros, you will still be presented with a final bill in roubles.

ATMs, linked to international networks such as Amex, Cirrus, MasterCard and Visa, are common right across Russia – look for signs that say *bankomat* (БАНКОМАТ). Credit cards are commonly accepted in the big cities but don't expect to be able to use your American Express card, for example, in more off-the-beaten-track spots and rural areas.

If you are going to rely on ATMs, make certain you have a few days' supply of cash at hand in case you can't find a machine to accept your card. Also inform your bank or credit card provider of the dates you'll be travelling in Russia and using your card, to avoid a situation where the card is blocked.

Getting Your Visa

Visa Agencies

Action-visas.com www.action-visas.com
CIBT http://uk.cibt.com
Comet Consular Services www.cometconsular.com
IVDS www.visum-dienst.de
Real Russia www.realrussia.co.uk
VisaHQ.com http://russia.visahq.com
Visalink.com.au http://visalink.com.au
ZVS http://zvs.com

Invitations can also be arranged with:
Express to Russia www.expresstorussia.com
Visa Able www.visaable.com
Way to Russia www.waytorussia.net

Cost

Minimum charge (excluding processing fees) for single-entry tourist visa for citizens of the following countries:
Australia AU$50
most EU countries €35
UK £50
USA US$140

Main Visa Types

Tourist Valid maximum of 30 days, nonextendable
Business Valid for three months, six months or one year
Transit By air for 48 hours, by train 10 days
72-Hour On Demand Only for Kaliningrad, St Petersburg and Vyborg

Starting the Process

Save for a handful of exceptions, everyone needs a visa to visit Russia. Arranging one is, generally, reasonably straightforward but can be time consuming, bureaucratic and – depending on how quickly you need the visa – costly. Start the application process at least a month before your trip.

For most travellers a tourist visa (single- or double-entry and valid for a maximum of 30 days, nonextendable, from the date of entry) will be sufficient. If you plan on staying longer than a month, it's advisable to apply for a business visa. Whatever visa you go for, the process has three main stages: invitation, application and registration.

Note that application and registration rules for trips to sensitive border regions, such as the Altai (p471), Volga Delta (p378), Caucasus (p406) and Tuva (p502), are slightly different; see each of these sections for specific details.

Invitation

To obtain a visa, you first need an invitation. Hotels and hostels will usually issue anyone staying with them an invitation (or 'visa support') free or for a small fee (typically around €20 to €30). If you are not staying in a hotel or hostel, you will need to buy an invitation – this can be done through most travel agents or via specialist visa agencies.

Application

Invitation in hand, you can then apply for a visa. Costs vary – anything from €35 to €330 – depending on the type of visa applied for and how quickly you need it. Russian consular offices apply different fees and slightly different application rules country by country (and sometimes even between consulates in the same country!). Avoid potential hassles by checking well in advance what these rules might be. For example, applications in the US and UK *must* be made using the online form of the Consular Department of the Ministry for Foreign Affairs of the Russian Federation (available at http://evisa.kdmid.ru).

We highly recommend applying for your visa in your home country rather than on the road. Trans-Mongolian travellers should note that unless you can prove you're a resident of China or Mongolia, attempting to get visas for Russia in Beijing and Ulaanbaatar can be a frustrating and ultimately fruitless exercise.

Registration

Since March 2011 every visitor to Russia must have their visa registered *within seven days of arrival,* excluding weekends and public holidays. The obligation to register is with the accommodating party – your hotel or hostel, or landlord, friend or family if you're staying in a private residence.

However, not everyone knows about this change of rule; previously, it was necessary for visitors to register within three days. If you encounter problems direct your inquisitors to the online notice of this law change on the website of law publication *Rossiyskaya Gazeta* (www.rg.ru/2011/03/23/migranty-site-dok.html).

If you're staying at a hotel, the receptionist will register you for free or for a small fee (typically around €10). Once registered, you should receive a slip of paper confirming the dates you'll be staying at that particular hotel. Keep this safe – that's the document that any police who stop you will request to see.

If staying in a homestay or rental apartment, you'll either need to make arrangements with the landlord or a friend to register you through the post office. See http://waytorussia.net/RussianVisa/Registration.html for how this can be done as well as for the downloadable form that needs to be submitted at post offices.

IMMIGRATION FORM

Prior to arrival in Russia, you'll need to fill out an immigration form; these are given out on your flight, available in the arrival halls or produced electronically by passport control (this happens at Moscow airports). Half the form is kept by passport control, while the other half you keep and surrender on exiting Russia. Take good care of your immigration form as you'll need it for registration and could face problems while travelling in Russia – and certainly will on leaving – if you can't produce it.

Depending on how amenable your hotel or inviting agency is, you can request that they register you for longer than you'll actually be in one place. Otherwise, every time you move city or town and stay for more than seven days, it's necessary to go through the registration process again. There's no need to be overly paranoid about this, but the more thorough your registration record, the less chance you'll have of running into problems. Keep all transport tickets (especially if you spend nights sleeping on trains) to prove to any overzealous police officers exactly when you arrived in a new place.

It's tempting to be lax about registration, and we've met many travellers who were and didn't experience any problems as a result of it. But if you're travelling in Russia for a while, it's worth doing for peace of mind since it's not uncommon to encounter fine-hungry cops hoping to catch tourists too hurried or disorganised to be able to explain long gaps in their registration.

Types of Visa

In addition to the tourist visa, there are other types of useful visas.

Business

Available for three months, six months or one year, and as single-entry, double-entry or multiple-entry visas, business visas are valid for up to 90 days of travel within any 180-day period. You don't actually need to be on business to apply for these visas (they're great for independent tourists with longer

VISA EXTENSIONS & CHANGES

Any extensions or changes to your visa will be handled by offices of UFMS (Upravleniye Federalnoy Migratsionnoy Slyzhby), Russia's Federal Migration Service, often just shortened to FMS. It's likely you'll hear the old acronyms PVU and OVIR used for this office.

Extensions are time consuming and difficult; *tourist visas can't be extended at all*. Avoid the need for an extension by arranging a longer visa than you might need. Note that many trains out of St Petersburg and Moscow to Eastern Europe cross the border after midnight, so make sure your visa is valid up to and including this day.

travel itineraries and flexible schedules) but to get one you must have a letter of invitation from a registered Russian company or organisation (these can be arranged via specialist visa agencies); a covering letter stating the purpose of your trip; and proof of sufficient funds to cover your visit.

Transit

For transit by air, a transit visa is usually valid for up to three days. For a nonstop Trans-Siberian Railway journey, it's valid for 10 days, giving westbound passengers a few days in Moscow; those heading east, however, are not allowed to linger in Moscow.

Visa-Free Travel

Only three destinations – St Petersburg, Vyborg and Kaliningrad – can be visited without a prearranged visa, and only for up to 72 hours. For St Petersburg and Vyborg you need to enter and exit the city on a cruise or ferry such as that offered by **St Peter Line** (www.stpeterline.com) or **Saimaa Travel** (www.saimaatravel.fi). For Kaliningrad, make arrangements in advance with locally based tour agencies; for details see p284.

what's new

For this new edition of Russia, *our authors have hunted down the fresh, the transformed, the hot and the happening. These are some of our favourites. For up-to-the-minute recommendations, see lonelyplanet.com/russia.*

Contemporary Art Boom

1 Moscow's former Red October chocolate factory has been reincarnated as the city's hottest art and entertainment centre, with the Strelka Institute for Media, Architecture and Design (p104) as the focal point. St Petersburg's Erarta (p191) and Perm's 'PERMM' (p386), in the city's former river station, both serve up the shock of the new.

Great Wooden Palace at Kolomenskoe

2 Build, demolish, repeat. This amazing piece of architectural whimsy is a painstaking reproduction of Tsar Alexey's 17th-century palace; the original was demolished by Catherine the Great. (p105)

Food & Culture in Nizhny Novgorod

3 A new National Centre of Contemporary Art and several other museums in restored mansions are complemented by a 'Food and Culture' movement, bringing together good grub and alternative culture. (p349)

Lake Manzherok

4 A slowly developing ski resort lies on the bank of tranquil Lake Manzherok amid some stunning countryside. It's a great place to unwind – even in the summer. (p481)

Tuva's National Museum

5 Worth a Scythian emperor's ransom, the gold haul from Tuva's Arzhaan I *kurgan* (burial mound), newly displayed at the National Museum in Kyzyl, ranges from impossibly intricate sequins to uber-blingy imperial torques. (p504)

Frolikha Adventure Coastline Trail

6 This 100km stretch of adventure hiking along the unpeopled northeast coast of Lake Baikal is the latest addition to the Great Baikal Trail. (p521)

Nuclear Icebreaker Tours

7 In Murmansk, clamber aboard the NS *Lenin,* the world's first nuclear icebreaker, for the chance to twiddle knobs, forage through Cold War–era documents and goggle at two massive atomic reactors. (p323)

Lake Seliger

8 Far more than a summer location for nationalist youth camps, this lovely lakeland area is best experienced on cruises from Ostashkov. (p261)

Vladivostok

9 It's more like what *isn't* new in Vladivostok: new airport, new trains, new hotels, newly developed island, *two* giant new suspension bridges downtown, all built for APEC 2012. (p575)

Olympification of the Black Sea Coast

10 Hosting the 2014 Winter Olympics is driving massive changes to Sochi, Adler and Krasnaya Polyana, including a high-speed rail link from coast to mountains. (p413)

if you like...

Epic Journeys

The 9289km trip from Moscow to Vladivostok on the Trans-Siberian Railway is the big one: the basics are covered on p42, along with those of the Baikal-Amur Mainline (BAM), the 'other trans-Sib' route. You might also want to consider getting behind the wheel of your own vehicle for a long-distance Russian road trip (p40).

Chuysky Trakt Hop in a shared taxi or hire a car to travel the 600km route through dramatic Altai landscapes, including glimpses of snowy mountain peaks and vertigo-inducing canyons. (p484)

Neryungri to Yakutsk An iron butt is required for this full-day classic jeep ride through the Sakha Republic. (p591)

Frolikha Adventure Coastline Trail Pushed through virgin territory by Great Baikal Trail volunteers, this 100km-long lakeside trail is an eight-day Siberian odyssey. (p521)

Golden Ring Circuit around Russia's oldest and cutest towns on a loop that begins and ends in Moscow. (p137)

Majestic Landscapes

From the wildflower-filled meadows of the southern Caucasus (p406), home to 200 peaks over 4000m, to the Arctic wilderness of the Kola Peninsula (p301), where you may spot the northern lights reflecting off snowbound forests and tundra, Russia offers a breathtaking range of natural landscapes.

Tunka Valley A wall of snow-capped peaks sends icy streams murmuring into this broad vale where hot springs gush in mineral-hued pools and Buddhist prayer wheels whirr in the breeze. (p543)

Barguzin Valley Isolated, virtually uninhabited and hemmed by high peaks, this is one of the most stunning Siberian landscapes in which to go astray. (p546)

Kamchatka Frozen peninsula king-like with its crown of volcanoes. (p605)

Volga Delta Where the mighty river explodes like a firecracker into myriad *raskaty* (channels). (p378)

Arts & Crafts

Art lovers should have illustrious galleries including Moscow's Tretyakov (p94) and St Petersburg's Hermitage (p224) on their to-do list, but there are plenty of other cultural storehouses scattered across the nation that warrant attention. Russia is also famous for its colourful handicrafts, such as *matryoshki* (nesting dolls), which make memorable souvenirs.

Flyonovo Crafts are still produced at the pretty riverside estate of late-19th-century art-lover Princess Maria Tenisheva, 18km southeast of Smolensk. (p257)

Novgorod State United Museum Within Veliky Novgorod's kremlin is an incredible collection of iconographic art spanning several centuries. (p262)

Kremlin in Izmaylovo A bustling market for all kinds of handicrafts, but you can also watch them being made or try your hand at making your own. (p105)

Caucasus Crafts In Nalchik buy Kabardian and Circassian crafts as well as intricate Dagestani silver jewellery. (p441)

LOU JONES / LONELY PLANET IMAGES ©

» Catherine Palace, Tsarskoe Selo (p233)

Imperial Grandeur

Russia's tsars and empresses lived the high life in fabulous palaces and estates. Moscow abounds with grand Russian Empire–style buildings since much of the city had to be rebuilt after the fires of 1812. St Petersburg is an architectural digest of baroque, rococo and neoclassical styles, and is ringed by leafy estates where the palaces are even more eye popping.

Catherine Palace The vast baroque centrepiece of Tsarskoe Selo is famed for its Amber Room, dazzling Great Hall and beautiful grounds. (p233)

Petrodvorets Gape at the Grand Cascade fronting Peter the Great's Gulf of Finland crash pad. (p227)

Yusupov Palace A canal-side mansion offering a series of sumptuously decorated rooms culminating in a gilded minitheatre. (p186)

Kolomenskoe Museum-Reserve An ancient royal country seat and Unesco World Heritage Site. (p104)

Tsaritsyno The contemporary manifestation of the exotic summer home that Catherine the Great began but never finished. (p105)

Soviet Relics

Artistic and architectural reminders of the Soviet era are scattered across Russia. Stalin's Seven Sisters towers punctuate the Moscow skyline, while cities such as Komsomolsk-na-Amure (p590) were created from scratch by heroic workers and Gulag prisoners in the 1930s. Lenin murals and statues abound, among them the giant bronze head of the Bolshevik leader in Ulan-Ude (p547) and a photogenic mosaic in Sochi (p418).

Garage Centre for Contemporary Culture Constructivist architect Konstantin Melnikov's bus depot gets a thrilling makeover and new lease of life as an arts venue. (p81)

All-Russia Exhibition Centre (VDNKh) Filled with grandiose pavilions and fabulous fountains glorifying socialism's economic achievements. (p101)

Alyosha The ever-vigilant, utilitarian concrete statue keeps an eye on Murmansk's wind-whipped and splendidly hideous Soviet architecture. (p322)

Mamaev Kurgan An astounding 72m-tall statue of Mother Russia is the memorial to those who fell in the bloody Battle of Stalingrad. (p370)

Literary Titans

Moscow and St Petersburg are stacked with small museums and memorials to Russia's men and women of letters, including Alexander Pushkin, Anton Chekhov, Nikolai Gogol, Leo Tolstoy, Vladimir Nabokov and Anna Akhmatova.

Spasskoe-Lutovinovo The family home of Ivan Turgenev, surrounded by beautiful grounds, is a short trip from the literary town of Oryol. (p249)

FM Dostoevsky House Museum The author, famously associated with St Petersburg, lived for many years in this modest, riverside home in sleepy Staraya Russa. (p268)

Pyatigorsk Visit the cottage and adjoining museum where Mikhail Lermontov spent his final days before being killed in a duel. (p428)

Mikhailovskoe Stand in the shade of Pushkin's beloved oak tree on his family's estate near the small town of Pushkinskie Gory. (p274)

Zhivago Restaurant and café in the Urals city of Perm that featured as a backdrop to classic works by Boris Pasternak and Anton Chekhov. (p387)

If you like... historical reenactments, on the first Sunday in September the museum complex at Borodino restages the 1812 battle between Russia and France. (p135)

Religious Buildings

Orthodox Christianity is resurgent and boldly evident in marvellously restored churches and monasteries across the country, including the replica of the Cathedral of Christ the Saviour in Moscow (p91). The synagogues, mosques and even Buddhist temples of the capital and St Petersburg attest to Russia's multifaith society.

Ivolginsk Datsan The centre of Russian Buddhism continues to expand into its dramatic setting. (p554)

Mystical Islands The vastly different islands of Kizhi (p307), Solovetsky (p312) and Valaam (p310) offer one thing in common: divine (literally) ancient architecture.

Kul Sharif Mosque Dominating Kazan's World Heritage–listed kremlin is this enormous mosque named after the imam who died defending the city against Ivan the Terrible's troops. (p354)

Church of the Intercession on the Nerl Revered for its exemplary perfect proportions and beautiful setting. (p142)

Sergiev Posad Russia's holiest of holies, the beautiful Trinity Monastery of St Sergius. (p160)

Quirky Places & Experiences

For connoisseurs of the strange, bizarre and offbeat, the biggest country in the world comes up trumps. Within this famous enigma wrapped up in a riddle, puzzle and smile over everything from viewing Rasputin's embalmed penis (p204) to supping tea with a yeti in the Siberian ski resort of Sheregesh (p490).

Permafrost Kingdom A never-melting pod of elaborate ice sculptures in a cocoon of permafrost and neon. (p598)

Bunker-42 A secret underground Cold War communications centre now open for exploration. (p99)

Sumarokovskaya Moose Farm Meet some friendly moose and drink their milk at this farm-cum-scientific-institute outside Kostroma. (p149)

Dancing Forest Marvel at the twisting and turning pines, sculpted by the winds that whistle across the Kurshskaya Kosa National Park. (p297)

Chess City Sit on the 12 chairs of the Ostap Bender monument in this literary fantasy come to surreal life in Elista. (p380)

Multicultural Encounters

Scores of different races and ethnic groups, big and small, inhabit Russia. One of the most ethnically complex regions is the Caucasus, where Karachay, Circassian, Kabardian and a host of other Muslim peoples live.

Tuva With its throat-singing, yurt-building, milk-fermenting traditions, this isolated republic in southern Siberia is a revelation. (p502)

Lovozero This dilapidated outpost is worth the trek for those wanting to come into contact with the reindeer-herding Sami (Lapp) people of the Kola Peninsula. (p321)

Elista The capital of Kalmykia is home to the only Buddhist national group within Europe. (p379)

Esso Make contact with Evenki and Even people in this pretty village in the hinterland of Kamchatka. (p615)

Kosh-Agach With a population made up almost entirely of ethnic Altai and Kazakhs, it's easy to forget you are still in Russia. (p485)

month by month

Top Events

1. **Easter**, March/April
2. **Victory Day**, 9 May
3. **Sadko Festival**, June
4. **White Nights**, June/July
5. **Kamwa Festival**, July/August

January

Much of Russia becomes snow- and icebound during this and subsequent winter months, but the weather rarely causes disruption to transport. Book transport tickets well in advance of the busy New Year period.

Russian Orthodox Christmas (Rozhdestvo)

On Christmas Eve (6 January) the religious fast from morning to nightfall, after which they tuck in to a feast that includes roast duck and the porridge *kutya*. Special masses are held in churches at midnight.

Hyperborea Festival

Running into February, this Karelian festival celebrates all that is wonderful about wintertime with parties, exhibitions, and an ice- and snow-sculpture competition that attracts entrants from across Russia and the world.

March

The devout deny themselves meat, milk, alcohol and sex during Lent's 40-day pre-Easter fasting period. Many restaurants offer special Lenten menus. Come prepared for wet, cold weather.

Pancake Week (Maslenitsa)

The Russian for this Shrovetide festival comes from the word *masla* (butter). Folk shows and games celebrate the end of winter, with lots of pancake eating before Lent (pancakes were a pagan symbol of the sun).

Women's Day

Celebrated on 8 March, this is like St Valentine's Day, with women getting presents of flowers, chocolates and the like, and a chance to rest up while men take care of the daily chores.

Tibetan Buddhist New Year (Tsagaalgan)

A movable feast lasting 16 days, Tsagaalgan celebrates the lunar new year and hence advances by about 10 days annually. It's mainly celebrated at family level in Buryatiya and Tuva, where it's known as Shagaa.

Golden Mask Festival

This Moscow-based festival (www.goldenmask.ru), usually held in late March and early April, involves two weeks of performances by Russia's premier drama, opera, dance and musical performers, culminating in a prestigious awards ceremony.

April

In Western European Russia melting snow makes the streets a slushy mess. However, it's a great time to brave Siberia and the far north, where winter still rules but with less savage force.

Festival of the North

A 10-day Arctic funfest (p325) kicking off in late March in Murmansk, replete with reindeer-sled races and snowmobile events. Kola's indigenous Sami (Lapp) people join the celebrations with displays of traditional culture.

Easter (Paskha)

Easter Sunday begins with midnight services. Afterwards, people eat *kulich* (traditional dome-shaped bread) and *paskha* (cheesecake), and exchange painted wooden Easter eggs. Falls on 15 April 2012, 5 May 2013 and 20 April 2014.

Alexander Nevsky Festival

The second weekend in April sees this celebration in Veliky Novgorod honouring Russia's best-known prince. Members of historical clubs dress up as knights, engage in mock battle and storm the kremlin walls.

May

The long-awaited arrival of pleasant spring weather makes this one of the best months for travel. Between International Labour Day on 1 May and Victory Day on 9 May some offices and museums have limited hours as people take advantage of the holidays for extended r'n'r.

Victory Day

On 9 May, this public holiday celebrates the end of WWII, which Russians call the Great Patriotic War. Big military parades in Moscow and St Petersburg are well worth attending.

Glinka Festival

The composer Mikhail Glinka is honoured in his home town of Smolensk with this week-long festival of classical music (p256) at the end of the month that draws in top talent.

Cossack Fairs

Held in Starocherkassk on the last Sunday of the month from May to September, with much singing, dancing, horse riding and merrymaking.

June

Popular month for *den goroda* (city day), when towns celebrate their birthdays with parades and street festivals: Veliky Novgorod has one on 12 June and Tver on 25 June. The weather is hot, but be prepared for rain too.

White Nights

As days lengthen Russia's cultural capital, St Petersburg, hosts a huge party made up of a variety of events including a jam-packed itinerary of shows at the Mariinsky Theatre and Concert Hall (p206). Events run until late July.

Sadko Festival

Held the first weekend of June in Veliky Novgorod, this event includes traditional dancing, singing and a crafts fair in the kremlin.

Ysyakh

Held around 21 June near Yakutsk (p596), this celebration of Sakha culture includes the chance to sample traditional eats while watching local sports and spectacular costumed battle reenactments.

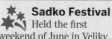

International Platanov Festival

Voronezh hosts this ambitious week-long jamboree of theatre, music and the arts (http://en.platonovfest.com) in memory of local talent Andrei Platanov, a banned Soviet-era writer.

Moscow International Film Festival

Russia's premier film festival (www.moscowfilmfestival.ru) runs for 10 days at the end of the month and includes retrospective and documentary cinema programs as well as the usual awards.

Rock on the Volga

Europe's largest one-day rock fest (p363) offers sets by top Russian outfits like DDT, Akvarium and Nochnye Snaypery, as well as international acts such as Deep Purple.

Uglich Versta

A few hundred bicyclists meet for three days of riding, singing and drinking at this annual cycle fest (www.velo.uglich.ru) in the Golden Ring town. Expect competitions, kids events, entertainment and a bicycle parade.

Perm White Nights

Inaugurated in 2011, Perm's White Nights (p387) fest runs through most of June, offering an eclectic mix of contemporary music, street art, theatre, readings and interesting side-festival events.

Sabantuy

Joking competitions and serious sport events – horse races and *koresh* (wrestling matches) – feature prominently during this holiday celebrated all over Tatarstan and beyond in the middle of June.

Kinotavr Film Festival

Running for a week in early June, Sochi's Kinotavr (p418) showcases over a dozen feature-length Russian films, with Russian filmmakers and actors on hand. Open-air screenings, too.

July

The best time to visit the Volga Delta is between late July and late September, when lotus flowers blossom. Russians head to the coast and their dachas (summer house) as the weather really heats up.

Sayan Ring International Ethnic Music Festival

Similar to the UK's Womad Festival, this large event (p502) floods the small Siberian town of Shushenskoe with almost 25,000 visitors. Tuvan throat singers usually steal the show.

El-Oiyn Festival

Held every two years on the first weekend of July, this 'folk games' festival (p484) gathers some 60,000 people for a celebration of Altai culture.

Kamwa Festival

The 'ethno-futuristic' Kamwa Festival (www.kamwa.ru), taking place from late July to early August in Perm and Khokhlovka, brings together ancient ethno-Ugric traditions and modern culture.

Solovetsky Islands Herring Festival

Head to Solovki to get your hands on some of Russia's finest fish – literally, in the case of the barehanded catch competition (p317).

August

Train prices can spike during this hot month as many people take holidays – book ahead if you want to travel on particular services along the Trans-Siberian route.

Tuvan Naadym

Naadym offers four wild days of underpants-hoicking *khuresh* wrestling, stern-faced archery contests, gravity-defying feats of steppe horsemanship, lots of croaky throat singing and fireworks bursting over the Tuvan capital Kyzyl.

Dzhangariada Festival

Held in late August or September, this Kalmyk cultural celebration (p382) takes place on the open steppe at a different location every year. It includes wrestling, archery contests and traditional singers.

November

Russia's brief, brilliantly colourful autumn in October is swiftly followed by the onset of winter – come prepared for snow flurries and plummeting temperatures.

Ded Moroz's Birthday

On 18 November, head to the attractive town of Veliky Ustyug to join the celebration for the Russian Santa Claus' birthday.

December

Short days and long nights keep people inside for most of this month. If you're prepared it's the best time to see freshly snow-covered landscapes.

December Nights Festival

Moscow's most prestigious music event, hosted at the Pushkin Fine Arts Museum, features a month of performances by high-profile musicians and accompanying art exhibits.

New Year's Eve

See out the old year with vodka and welcome in the new one with champagne while listening to the Kremlin chimes on TV.

Whether you've got six days or 60, these itineraries provide a starting point for the trip of a lifetime. Want more inspiration? Head online to lonelyplanet .com/thorntree to chat with other travellers.

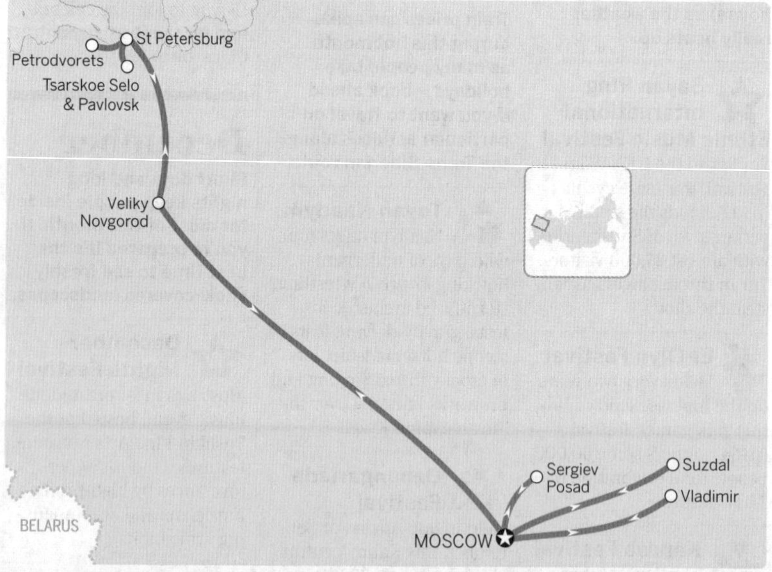

Two Weeks
Russian Capitals

The awe-inspiring cities of **Moscow** and **St Petersburg** encompass the country's turbulent past and glittering present. Moscow has its historic **Kremlin**, glorious **Red Square**, classic **Tretyakov Gallery**, renovated **Bolshoi Theatre**, exciting contemporary arts scene and extensive metro system with stations that are a sight in themselves.

In St Petersburg don't miss the incomparable **Hermitage** and the **Russian Museum**, or cruising the city's **rivers and canals**. Enjoy some of Russia's top restaurants and bars, and attend first-rate performances at the **Mariinsky and Mikhailovsky Theatres**.

St Petersburg is ringed by grand palaces set in beautifully landscaped grounds such as **Petrodvorets**, **Tsarskoe Selo** and **Pavlovsk**. From Moscow it's easy to make trips to the historic Golden Ring towns of **Sergiev Posad**, **Suzdal** and **Vladimir**, where you will be rewarded with a slice of rural Russian life far from the frenetic city pace.

Between the two big cities, tourist-friendly **Veliky Novgorod** deserves a couple of days, too. It's home to an impressive riverside kremlin, ancient churches and a wonderful open-air museum of wooden architecture.

Three to Four Weeks

Trans-Siberian Odyssey

The classic Russian adventure is to travel the **Trans-Siberian Railway**, an engineering wonder that spans and holds together the world's largest country. So you can finish up with a grand party in either **Moscow** or, better yet, **St Petersburg**, go against the general flow by commencing your journey at **Vladivostok**. Situated on a stunningly attractive natural harbour, the Pacific coast port is newly spruced up for its hosting of the 2012 APEC summit.

An overnight journey west is **Khabarovsk**, a lively city with a lingering tsarist-era charm located on the banks of the Amur River. Two more days down the line hop off the train at **Ulan-Ude**, the appealing capital of Buryatiya where Russian, Soviet and Mongolian cultures coexist; from here you can venture into the steppes to visit Russia's principal Buddhist monastery, **Ivolginsk Datsan**.

The railway then skirts around the southern shores of magnificent **Lake Baikal**. Allow at least three days (preferably longer) to soak up the charms of this beautiful lake, basing yourself on beguiling **Olkhon Island**; also check out historic **Irkutsk** on the way to the lake or back.

Flush with oil wealth, happening **Krasnoyarsk**, on the Yenisey River, affords the opportunity for scenic cruises along one of Siberia's most pleasant waterways. Detour slightly from the main Trans-Sib line to **Tomsk**, the 'cultural capital of Siberia', to hang with its lively student population and admire the city's treasure trove of wooden architecture.

Crossing the Urals into European Russia, spend a day or so in **Yekaterinburg**, a historic, bustling city well stocked with interesting museums and sites connected to the murder of the last tsar and his family. **Perm** is also doing an excellent job of reinventing itself as a cultural centre; use it as a base from which to make trips to an ice cave at **Kungur** and the Gulag labour camp **Perm-36**, preserved as a museum.

Finally, fortify yourself for the bustle of Moscow by taking a reviving break in the Golden Ring towns of **Yaroslavl** or **Vladimir**, which is also the access point for the idyllic village of **Suzdal**: all are stacked with beautiful, old, onion-domed churches.

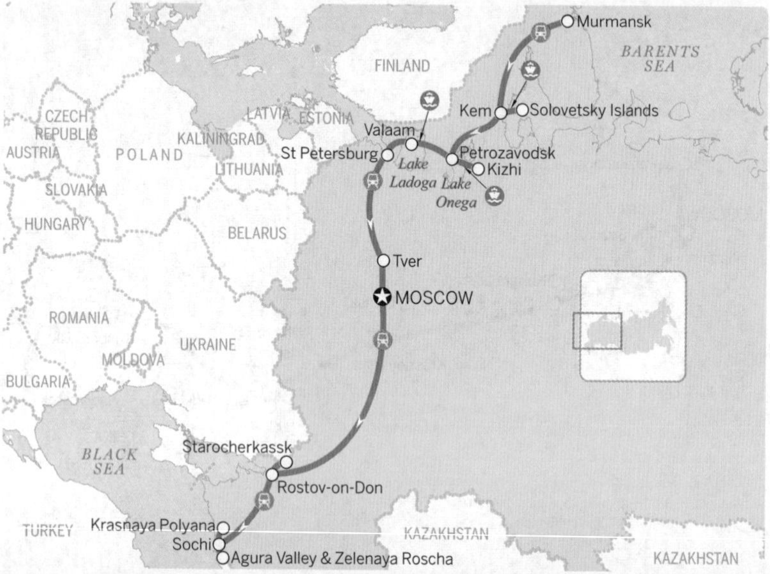

One Month
White Sea to Black Sea

This offbeat itinerary runs from the frigid climes of the Arctic Circle to the sun-kissed Black Sea lapping at the foothills of the Caucasus. Start by paying your respects to the giant concrete soldier 'Alyosha' who overlooks **Murmansk**, the world's largest Arctic city. Here you can board a decommissioned nuclear icebreaker and breathe the air that inspired the creator of Chanel No 5. In the summer, the sun never fully sets, while in winter look out for the colourful northern lights.

Take a train directly south through the Kola Peninsula, heading for **Kem**, access point for the **Solovetsky Islands**; the beautiful landscapes and monastery here were also the setting for some of the most brutal scenes in Solzhenitsyn's *Gulag Archipelago*. Back on the mainland keep south towards appealing **Petrozavodsk** where you can board a hydrofoil that will zip you across Lake Onega to another island – **Kizhi**, home to an architectural reserve that includes the astounding Transfiguration Church, a symphony of wooden domes, gables and decoration. Continuing the islands-in-lakes theme, **Valaam** in Lake Ladoga is the mystical location of a beguiling monastery and can also be reached via Petrozavodsk.

Top up on big-city culture and fun in **St Petersburg** before boarding one of the many overnight trains that head south to the Black Sea resorts. Note that several of these services skirt through Belarus, thus requiring a transit visa and Russian double-entry visa. To avoid this, make your way south via **Moscow**, perhaps pausing at **Tver**, another appealing historic town that Catherine the Great also used to pause in.

If you don't relish spending more than a couple of nights on a train, break your journey at the metropolis of **Rostov-on-Don**, from where you can make a side trip to the old Don Cossack capital of **Starocherkassk** and tour the remains of the Ataman Palace. As host of the 2014 Winter Olympics, the sprawling Black Sea coast resort of **Sochi** is where all the action is. From here, you can visit Stalin's former dacha **Zelenaya Roscha**, take in the stunning waterfalls and vistas of the verdant **Agura Valley** and relax amid the towering peaks of **Krasnaya Polyana**, where soon-to-be world-class resorts are being built for Olympians.

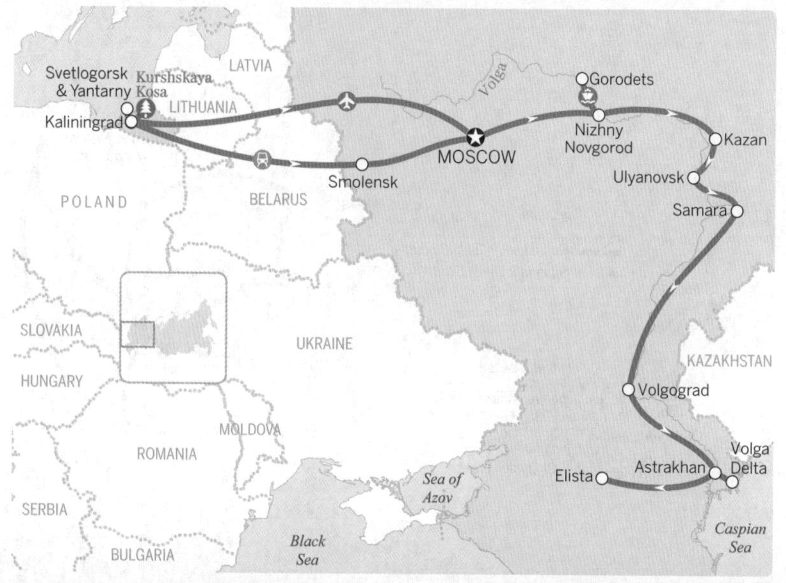

Three Weeks

The Amber–Caviar Route

Ease yourself into Russia by exploring the geographically separate Kaliningrad Region, Russia's far-west outpost that's the source of 90% of the world's amber. Four to five days is sufficient to get a taste of the historic city of **Kaliningrad**, the delightful seaside resorts of **Svetlogorsk** and **Yantarny**, and the 'dancing forest' and sand dunes of **Kurshskaya Kosa**, a World Heritage–listed national park.

With a transit visa to Belarus and a double-entry visa to Russia it's possible to take a train through Lithuania and Belarus to reenter 'big Russia' at **Smolensk**. The skyline of this historic city, partly surrounded by the impressive remains of its kremlin walls, is dominated by the Assumption Cathedral, a place of worship so grand Napoleon gave orders that his invading armies protect it from harm. From here you can connect by train or bus to **Moscow**. Alternatively, there are plenty of flights from Kaliningrad to the capital.

With its magnificent cliff-top kremlin overlooking the mighty Volga River, laid-back **Nizhny Novgorod** is your next stop. Spend a day or so here enjoying the town's museums and its 'Food and Culture' movement, and making a short trip by hydrofoil to the small town of **Gorodets**, known for its folk arts. Further along the river you'll get your first taste of East-meets-West culture at the intriguing Tatarstan capital of **Kazan**. The highlight here is the World Heritage–listed kremlin that includes an enormous mosque and small satellite branch of St Petersburg's Hermitage.

The Volga continues to guide you south past Lenin's birthplace of **Ulyanovsk** and **Samara**, from where you could go hiking in the rocky Zhiguli Hills or search out the town's several offbeat design and cultural sights.

An amazing 72m tall statue of Mother Russia wields her sword over **Volgograd**, a city entirely rebuilt after Russia's bloodiest battle of WWII. Follow the river to its mouth into the Caspian Sea and the ancient city of **Astrakhan**, jumping-off point for exploring the glorious natural attractions, including rare flamingos, of the **Volga Delta**, home to the endangered sturgeon, the source of Beluga caviar. Finally, turn west to the fascinating Buddhist enclave of **Elista**, graced with Tibetan-style temples and possibly the world's highest density of street sculpture.

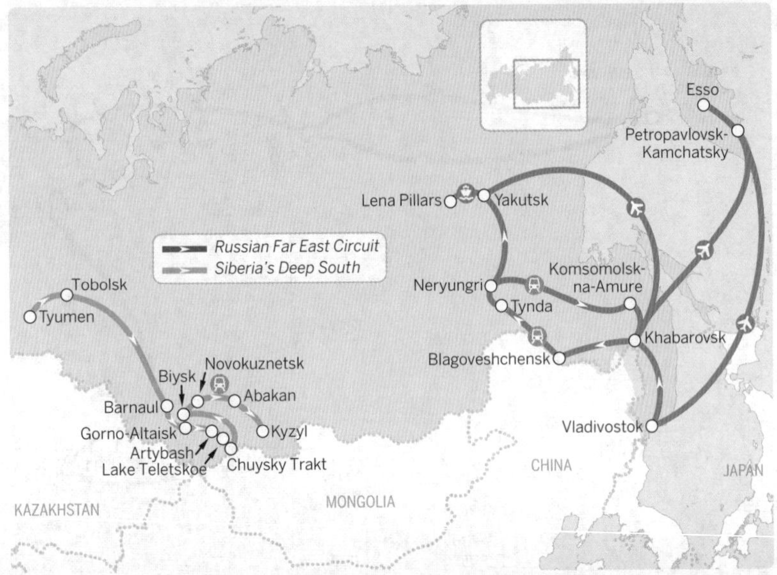

One Month
Siberia's Deep South

For a journey covering some of Siberia's lesser-known locations begin in the oil-rich city of **Tyumen**, which includes several picturesque areas of traditional architecture. Journey northeast in the footsteps of the Siberian conqueror Yermak Timofeevich, the exiled writer Fyodor Dostoevsky and the last tsar to **Tobolsk**, whose splendid kremlin lords it over the Tobol and Irtysh Rivers. Next, head south to **Barnaul**, gateway to the mountainous Altai Republic. Here you can arrange a white-water rafting expedition or plan treks out to beautiful **Lake Teletskoe** and the pretty village of **Artybash**. Drive along the panoramic **Chuysky Trakt**, a helter-skelter mountain road leading to yurt-dotted grasslands, first stopping in **Gorno-Altaisk** to register your visa. Return to **Biysk**, take a bus to **Novokuznetsk** then a train to **Abakan** to arrange onward travel to Tuva. This remote and little-visited region, hard up against Mongolia (with which it shares several cultural similarities), is famed for its throat-singing nomads and mystical shamans. **Kyzyl** has a good new National Museum and Cultural Centre and can be used as a base for expeditions to pretty villages and the vast Central Asian steppes.

One Month
Russian Far East Circuit

From the 'wild east' port of **Vladivostok** head via **Khabarovsk** to lively **Blagoveshchensk** with its splendid tsarist architecture. Take the overnight train to **Tynda**, the main hub on the Baikal-Amur Mainline (BAM), from where there's a choice. Tough-travel fanatics can train it to **Neryungri** then endure a very bumpy all-day ride in a Russian UAZ jeep to **Yakutsk**, the extraordinary permafrost-bound capital of the Sakha Republic. Alternatively, board the BAM through to the attractive city of **Komsomolsk-na-Amure** and back to Khabarovsk, from where there are flights to Yakutsk. Once in Yakutsk, visit the city's eccentric Permafrost Kingdom and Mammoth Museum. If it's the summer sailing season, cruise to the scenic **Lena Pillars** on the Lena River. Backtrack to Khabarovsk or Vladivostok from where you can fly to spectacular Kamchatka, to cap off your adventures by climbing one of the snow-capped volcanoes rising behind the rugged peninsula's capital, **Petropavlovsk-Kamchatsky**. Or make your way north to **Esso**, newly friendly to independent travellers with cheap guesthouses, public hot springs and well-mapped trails for trekking.

Russian Adventures

Top Five Adventures

Climb mountains in the Caucasus

Hike the Great Baikal Trail

Drive across Russia

Fish for wild salmon in Kamchatka

Ski at Krasnaya Polyana

Inspiring Adventure Tales

Barbed Wire and Babushkas, Paul Grogan. Kayaking down the Amur River through China and Siberia.

River of No Reprieve, Jeffrey Tayler. Sailing an inflatable raft along the Lena River, from Lake Baikal to the Arctic Ocean.

Off the Rails, Tim Cope & Chris Hatherly. Cycling 10,000km from Moscow to Beijing.

www.timcopejourneys.com Tim Cope's other Russian expeditions include rowing a boat 4500km down the Yenisey River to the Arctic Ocean.

Cycling Home from Siberia, Rob Lilwall. Rob's website (http://roblilwall.com) features original blog posts and videos.

Outdoor Adventures

From the Sahara-like sand dunes of Kaliningrad to the snow-covered volcanoes of Kamchatka, Russia offers a thrilling range of terrain for outdoor adventures. There are majestic mountains to climb, national parks to hike through and fast-flowing rivers for rafting and canoeing. Skiers can rack up bragging rights by ticking off resorts such as Abzakovo (Vladimir Putin's favourite) or Krasnaya Polyana, location of the 2014 Winter Olympics. If these activities don't spark your fancy, how about flying a supersonic MiG fighter jet or training as a cosmonaut? Both these adventures – and a lot more – are possible in Russia.

Specialist operators are listed in this and each destination chapter. While most are professional, this is Russia, so be flexible, patient and prepared for things not to go as smoothly as you may hope. There will often also be a group of enthusiasts more than happy to share their knowledge and even equipment with a visitor; you might also be able to locate guides for trekking and other activities where detailed local knowledge is essential. Provide as much advance warning as possible; even if you can't hammer out all the details, give operators an idea of your interests.

Always check the safety equipment before you set out and make sure you know what's included in the quoted price. Also, make sure you have adequate insurance – many travel insurance policies have exclusions for risky activities, including skiing, diving and even trekking.

Boating, Canoeing & Rafting

Although the pollution of many rivers discourages numerous travellers from even getting near the water, the coasts offer many canoeing and kayaking possibilities. The Altai region's pristine rivers are best for full-blown expedition-grade rafting, as well as easy, fun splashes possible on a 'turn up' basis. Kamchatka's Bystraya River is also recommended.

The Solovetsky Islands in Northern European Russia are an example of the remote and fascinating places that can be toured by boat during the summer. For details of cruises on icebreakers into the Arctic Circle see p323.

The Volga River Delta, with its fascinating flora and fauna, below Astrakhan, is an amazing place to explore by boat. In towns and parks with clean lakes, there are usually rowing boats available for rent during the warmer months. Both Moscow and St Petersburg sport active yacht clubs.

California-based agency **Raft Siberia** (☎1-916-624 5189; www.raftsiberia.com) arranges rafting trips on the Katun, Chuya, Sayan Oka and Chatkal Rivers in Siberia. One of its founders, Vladimir Gavrilov, is the author of *Rivers of an Unknown Land: A Whitewater Guide to the Former Soviet Union,* the only English-language guidebook to include detailed information about rafting rivers in Russia.

Russian agencies offering boating, kayaking and rafting trips:

Caucasus Mountains

» Masterskaya Priklucheny, Sochi (p418)

» Reinfo, Sochi (p418)

Russian Far East

» Chip Levis, Esso (p615)

» DVS-Tour, Magadan (p595)

» Kamchatintour, Petropavlovsk-Kamchatsky (p609)

» Lost World, Petropavlovsk-Kamchatsky (p609)

» Nata Tour, Komsomolsk-na-Amure (p591)

Siberia

» Alash Travel, Kyzyl (p505)

» Ak Tur, Barnaul (p471)

» **K2 Adventures** (☎03812-671 648; www.adventuretravel.ru) Omsk

» MorinTur, Ulan-Ude (p550)

St Petersburg & Petrozavodsk

» **Megatest** (☎499-126 9119; www.megatest.ru) Moscow

» **Solnechny Parus** (☎812-327 3525; www.solpar.ru) St Petersburg

» Wild Russia, St Petersburg (p446)

» Russia Discovery North-West, Petrozavodsk (p303)

Ural Mountains

» Ekaterinburg Guide Centre, Yekaterinburg (p395)

» Krasnov, Perm (p388)

» Tengri, Ufa (p401)

» Ural Expeditions & Tours, Yekaterinburg (p395)

Volga Region

» Samara Intour, Samara (p363)

» Team Gorky, Nizhny Novgorod (p353)

Cycling

Russia's traffic-clogged cities are far from a cyclists' nirvana, but off-road cyclists will find plenty of challenging terrain. Rural Russians are quite fascinated with and friendly towards long-distance riders. Just make certain you have a bike designed for the harshest conditions and carry plenty of spare parts.

Bike Rentals

» Moscow (p106)

» St Petersburg (p204)

» Suzdal (p143)

» Svetlogorsk (p293)

Organised Bike Tours

Agencies offering organised bike tours:

» Ekaterinburg Guide Centre, Yekaterinburg (p395)

» Kola Travel, Monchegorsk (p320)

» Russia Discovery North-West, Petrozavodsk (p303)

» Samara Intour, Samara (p363)

» Skat Prokat, St Petersburg (p204)

» Team Gorky, Nizhny Novgorod (p353)

ILYA GUREVICH: EXTREME CYCLING

Ilya Gurevich is one of the people behind the St Petersburg–area cycling website **VeloPiter** (www.velopiter.spb.ru), as well as **Towns.ru** (www.towns.ru), which carries reviews and pictures of charming off-the-beaten-path places around the country, many of which could be visited on a cycling tour. We met up with him to talk about some of his cycling adventures – most of which have taken place in the depths of winter when freezing conditions have allowed access to places otherwise too wet or infested with insects to visit in the summer.

Tell us about one of your more memorable cycling trips. In March 2001 I cycled with two others across a frozen Lake Baikal. [Ilya's route and a report in Russian is shown at www.velopiter.spb.ru/rep/baikal.] We started the trip by taking the BAM railway to Novy Uoyan, which is north of the lake, and cycling through the forest as far as Ust-Barguzin on the lake's eastern shore. It was very cold, down to −37°C on the lake. Obviously there's no road; we followed the tracks made by lorries that cross through the forest and over the lake in winter. It took us 19 days to travel 1019km.

Is that the coldest place you've cycled? No, that would have to be my trip from Yakutsk to Oymyakon (the Sakha Republic settlement with the lowest recorded temperatures in Russia) in 2004. There were five of us and it took two weeks to make that journey, during which I endured the coldest night of my life: −45°C.

What's the biggest challenge on these trips? Sometimes the conditions make it very difficult to judge how quickly you can go. In 2007 I planned a trip from Amderma (on the Kara Sea within the Arctic Circle) to Vorkuta. However we only managed the first 167km to the village of Ust-Kara, which took us 13 days. One day was so bad we covered just 12km.

What advice would you have for anyone wanting to undertake a similar bike ride in Russia? Bring the right equipment, especially if you're travelling across ice and snow in winter. Having ice spikes on your wheels is essential. Also do a less ambitious preliminary trip to test out what it's like to cycle in the Russian winter.

Former submarine designer Ilya Gurevich and colleagues lead cycling trips around Russia and beyond. For details contact him on spbfp@atlant.ru.

Diving

Fancy diving Lake Baikal, within the Arctic Circle or in the Baltic Sea? Such specialist trips can be arranged. Contact these agencies:

» BaikalExplorer, Irkutsk (p531)

» Demersus, Yantarny (p295)

» **Nereis** (☎812-103 0518; www.nereis.ru/eng/index.html) St Petersburg. Can arrange ice diving and diving in the White Sea.

» **RuDive** (☎495-005 7799; www.dive.ru) Moscow. A group of dive companies, with the Diving Club and School of Moscow State University at its core. They offer trips in the White and Barents Seas and the Sea of Japan, including ice diving off the live-aboard boat *Kartesh* (www.barentssea.ru/index/en.htm).

» SVAL, Lake Baikal (p539)

» Three Dimensions, Lake Baikal (p539)

Fishing

Serious anglers drool at the opportunity to fish the rivers, lakes and lagoons of the Kaliningrad Region, Northern European Russia, the Russian Far East and Siberia. Kamchatka is a particular draw, with steelhead fishing in the peninsula reckoned to be the best in the world.

Start saving up: organised fishing trips in Russia can be heart-stoppingly expensive. While it's possible to go it alone and just head off with rod and tackle, most regions have severe restrictions on fishing, so you'd be wise to at least check these out before departure. A curious alternative is ice fishing for Lake Baikal's unique *omul* (p539).

Hooked: Fly Fishing Through Russia (titled *Reeling in Russia* in the US) by Fen Montaigne charts the former Moscow-based correspondent as he spends a revealing three months casting his rod in the country's largely polluted lakes and rivers.

See p318 for details about fishing in the Kola Peninsula's Varzuga River.

Fishing agencies:

» Baltma Tours, Kaliningrad (p292)

» DVS-Tour, Magadan (p595)

» Explore Kamchatka, Yelizovo (p609)

» Kamchatintour, Petropavlovsk-Kamchatsky (p609)

» Lost World, Petropavlovsk-Kamchatsky (p609)

» Nata Tour, Komsomolsk-na-Amure (p591)

» Yug Kola, Apatity (p318)

Flying & Skydiving

If you've ever wanted to fly in a MiG-31, -25 or -29, contact **Country of Tourism** (www.bestrussiantour.com); it can arrange tourist flights in these supersonic aircraft at Nizhny Novgorod's Sokol aviation plant. It can also organise trips to see the launch of the manned Soyuz spacecraft from the Baikonur Cosmodrome in Kazakhstan and a range of activities at Star City (see p39).

For flights in MiGs (starting at US$11,300), an L-39 Albatros (US$2650) or an Su-27 Flanker (US$14,550) out of Zhukovsky Airbase, an hour's drive southeast of Moscow, contact the US-based firm **MiG-25.com** (www.mig-25.com) at least 16 days in advance of your ideal flight date so it can sort out security clearance. Flights on L-29, Yak-52, Yak-18T and TL-2000 aircraft out of St Petersburg can be arranged at much shorter notice.

Helicopter tours over St Petersburg can be arranged with **Helitour** (www.helitour.ru/ENG).

Hiking, Mountaineering & Rock Climbing

Serious hikers and mountain climbers will have the Caucasus mountains topping their wish list, particularly the areas around Mt Elbrus (p443), Dombay (p435), Krasnaya Polyana (p424) and Mt Fisht (p423). The Agura Valley (p422) is a prime location for rock climbing.

However, in early 2011, terrorist attacks in the region resulted in tightened security and the enforcement of rules regarding travel permits. For any trekking in the Caucasus check on the current situation and arrange far in advance any necessary permits – this is best done through local agencies; see p446 for some options.

In the southern Ural Mountains, Zyuratkul National Park (p401) and Taganay National Park (p402) are both beautiful places to hike. Siberia also harbours many equally fantastic hiking and mountaineering locations, principally the Altai region (p471) and around Lake Baikal, where you'll find the Great Baikal Trail (p537). In the Russian

SAFETY GUIDELINES FOR HIKING

Before embarking on a hike, consider the following:

» Be sure you're healthy and feel comfortable about hiking for a sustained period. The nearest village in Russia can be vastly further away than it would be in other countries.

» Get the best information you can about the physical and environmental conditions along your intended route. Russian 'trails' are generally nominal ideas rather than marked footpaths, so employing a guide is very wise.

» Walk only in regions, and on trails, within your realm of experience.

» Be prepared for severe and sudden changes in the weather and terrain; always take wet-weather gear.

» Pack essential survival gear including emergency food rations and a leak-proof water bottle.

» If you can, find a hiking companion. At the very least tell someone where you're going and refer to your compass frequently so you can find your way back.

» Unless you're planning a camping trip, start early so you can make it home before dark.

» Allow plenty of time.

» For longer routes, consider renting, or even buying (then later reselling), a pack horse.

Far East, look no further than Kamchatka (p605) for plentiful hiking and mountaineering possibilities, including the chance to summit active volcanoes.

Elsewhere, multiple national parks and state nature reserves exist, but don't expect them to have especially good facilities or even well-marked trails. For this reason, it's especially important to seek out local advice, information and even guides before setting off.

Reliable agencies:

Caucasus Mountains

» Dombay Tourist, Dombay (p440)

» Pyatigorsk Intour, Pyatigorsk (p432)

» Reinfo, Sochi (p418)

Siberia

» Acris, Novosibirsk (p471)

» Ak Tur, Barnaul (p471)

» Alash Travel, Kyzyl (p505)

» Alie Parusa, Novosibirsk (p471)

» Altair-Tur, Novosibirsk (p471)

» **K2 Adventures** (☎03812-671 648; www.adventuretravel.ru) Omsk. Good for tackling Mt Belukha.

» Sibir-Altai, Novosibirsk (p471)

Ural Mountains

» Ekaterinburg Guide Centre, Yekaterinburg (p395)

» Ural Expeditions & Tours, Yekaterinburg (p395)

Other Regions

» Kola Travel, Monchegorsk (p320)

» **Megatest** (☎499-126 9119; www.megatest.ru) Moscow

» Wild Russia, St Petersburg (p446). Recommended for Mt Elbrus.

Horse Riding

Many of the same areas that offer good hiking and mountaineering also offer

ADVENTURES IN SPACE

Do you have US$100 million to spare? If so, consider signing up for the first private lunar expedition, organised by US-based **Space Adventures** (☎in USA 888-85-SPACE, outside USA 703-524-7172; www.spaceadventures.com; Suite 1000, 8000 Towers Crescent Dr, Vienna, VA 22182), the same outfit that in 2001 helped US billionaire Dennis Tito spend a week at the International Space Station as the first paying customer of the Russian Space Agency. Since then several other 'spaceflight participants' (the preferred term over 'space tourists') have handed over upwards of US$20 million to join the civilian-in-space club, including Dr Charles Simonyi, the Hungarian-born computer programmer who has made two trips and documented them on www.charlesinspace.com.

For less wealthy individuals, Space Adventures offers a range of programs – while they might not actually shoot you into space, they certainly give you an idea of what it takes to be there. Running out of Zvezdny Gorodok (Star City), a once highly classified community of cosmonauts and scientists, around an hour's drive northeast of Moscow, these programs include ones that allow participants to train as a cosmonaut (US$89,500), board the Soyuz spacecraft simulator as a trainee commander (US$15,950), experience the high g-forces of a rocket launch in the world's largest centrifuge (US$9750) and, for qualified divers, enjoy spacewalk training outside a full-scale model of the International Space Station submerged in a neutral buoyancy tank (US$33,750 for two people). The least costly deal is to train for a spacewalk (US$7650), which still includes visiting Star City, trying on an Orlan spacesuit, meeting with cosmonauts and chowing down at Star City's cafeteria. A feature in *Wired* magazine (www.wired.com/techbiz/people/magazine/16-09/ff_starcity) gives the inside scoop on training to go into space at Star City.

Moscow-based Country of Tourism (p38) can also arrange similar tours to Star City, including zero-gravity flights from €5200. If you just want to visit Star City and have a look around, this is also possible. Tours of the technical area and museum can be arranged through the **Yury Gagarin Russian State Science Research Cosmonauts Training Centre** (☎495-526 3842; www.gctc.ru/eng/index.html).

horse-riding treks. Try Dombay (p439) and Arkhyz (p441) in the Caucasus, the Altai region (p471), around Lake Baikal (p524) and Kamchatka (p605). There's also the famous Georgenburg Stud Farm in Chernyakhovsk (p298).

Specific operators who can arrange horse riding:

» Baikal Naran Tour, Ulan-Ude (p550)

» EcoTuva, Kyzyl (p505)

» GTK Suzdal, Suzdal (p143)

» Krasnov, Perm (p388)

» Oleg, Teberdinsky State Natural Biosphere Reserve (p439)

» Ural Expeditions & Tours, Yekaterinburg (p395)

Skiing & Winter Sports

The 2014 Winter Olympics (see http://sochi2014.com) based in Sochi and Krasnaya Polyana are set to put Russia on winter sports enthusiasts' radars across the world.

Downhill ski slopes are scattered throughout the country, although cross-country skiing is more common, attracting legions of enthusiasts during the long winters. Given the wealth of open space, you won't have a problem finding a place to hit the trail. For off-piste adventures, try heliskiing and back-country skiing in the Caucasus and Kamchatka.

Ski resorts and areas:

Caucasus Mountains

» Mt Elbrus (p445)

» Mt Cheget (p445)

» Dombay (p437)

» Krasnaya Polyana (p425)

Siberia

» Bobrovy Log Ski Resort, Krasnoyarsk (p512)

» **Gladenkaya** (http://ski-gladenkaya.ru) Sayanogorsk, Khakassia Republic

» Lake Manzherok, Altai (p481)

» Sheregesh (p490)

St Petersburg & Northern European Russia

» Kirovsk (p319)

» **Krasnoe Ozero** (www.krasnoeozero.ru), near St Petersburg

» **Tuutari Park** (www.tyytari.spb.ru), near St Petersburg

» **Zolotai Dolina** (www.zoldolspb.narod.ru/business4.html), near St Petersburg

Ural Mountains

» Abzakovo (p404)

» **Metallurg-Magnitogorsk** (www.ski-bannoe.ru) near Bannoye, Bashkortostan

DRIVING THE TRANS-SIBERIAN HIGHWAY

For intrepid souls the challenge of driving across the vast expanse of Russia is irresistible. Ewan McGregor and Charley Boorman wrote about their Russian road adventures in *Long Way Round* (www.longwayround.com); their round-the-world route took them from Volgograd all the way to Yakutsk and Magadan via Kazakhstan and Mongolia.

The celebrity bikers had a camera crew and support team following them. For a more accurate view of what to expect read *The Linger Longer* by brothers Chris and Simon Raven, who somehow coaxed a rusty Ford Sierra from the UK to Vladivostok; *One Steppe Beyond* by Thom Wheeler, which covers a similar journey in a VW campervan; and *Travels in Siberia* by the humorist Ian Frazier, who was accompanied by two Russian guides on his 2001 drive from St Petersburg to Vladivostok in a Renault van.

Whatever your mode of transport, since the full black-top completion in September 2010 of the 2100km Amur Hwy, between Chita and Khabarovsk (previously the rockiest section of the road) driving the 11,000km from St Petersburg to Vladivostok has become a more feasible proposition. Even so, it's worth heeding the words of Prime Minister Vladimir Putin who, in August 2011, drove a 350km stretch of the Amur Hwy in a bright-yellow Lada Kalina Sport, afterwards commenting: 'It is a dependable, modern farm road, but not the Autobahn.'

For some information in Russian on this section of the road see http://amur-trassa.ru. Also, **National Geographic Adventure** (http://adventure.nationalgeographic.com) has a feature article called 'Road-Tripping the Trans-Siberian Highway' about driving the route in 2008.

For further details, go to World Snowboardguide.com (www.worldsnowboardguide.com/resorts/russia) or Onboard.ru (www.onboard.ru).

Snowmobiling & Arctic Adventures

For snowmobile safaris and activities in the Arctic contact Kola Travel in Monchegorsk (p320), **Megatest** (☎499-126 9119 www.megatest.ru) in Moscow, or Yug Kola in Apatity (p318). GTK in Suzdal (p143) also offers snowmobile rides.

For full-on Arctic expeditions contact **Vicaar** (☎812-713 2781; www.northpolextreme.com; St Petersburg).

More Unusual Adventures

If you're not up to training to be an astronaut (p39) then try the following on for size...

» Join a mineralogical (rock-hunting) tour – the geologically minded should contact Kola Travel (p320) or Yug Kola (p318) to organise one of these.

» Sample ski-climbing – first you climb up, then you ski down. Do this with the pro skiers at Go-Elbrus (p446).

» Drive off-road. Check out the options on **World 4x4 Adventures** (www.world4x4.co.uk), including the **Ladoga Trophy Raid** (www.ladoga-trophy.ru), an eight-day marathon around Lake Ladoga starting and ending in St Petersburg.

» Bungee jump over the Altai's Katun River (p482).

» Go dog sledding at the Baikal Dog Sledding Centre (p537) or in Kamchatka (p609).

Great Train Journeys

Inspirational Books

The Big Red Train Ride, Eric Newby
Through Siberia by Accident and **Silverland**, Dervla Murphy
Trans-Siberian Railway, Anne and Olaf Meinhardt
The Trans-Siberian Railway: A Traveller's Anthology, ed Deborah Manley
Journey into the Mind's Eye, Lesley Blanch
Wall to Wall: From Beijing to Berlin by Rail, Mary Morris
The Great Railway Bazaar, **Riding the Iron Rooster** and **Ghost Train to the Eastern Star**, Paul Theroux

Useful Websites

RZD (http://rzd.ru) National rail network
Man in Seat 61 (www.seat61.com) Up-to-date info and links
Trans-Siberian Railway Web Encyclopaedia (www.transsib.ru) Not updated, but still a mine of useful background detail
A Journey on the Trans-Siberian Railway (www.trans-siberian-railway.co.uk) Clive Simpson's site, based on his 2006 trip

Top Trips

Moscow–Vladivostok
Moscow–Ulaanbaatar and Beijing
Tayshet–Sovetskaya Gavan
Murmansk–Adler

Russian Railways

One of the best ways to see the country, as well as connect with Russians and gain an insight into how they tick, is to take a train journey. You may not have time for the classic trans-Siberian routes (which require a minimum of a week if done nonstop), but with over 85,200km of track – making it one of the largest networks in the world – there's a fair chance that Russian Railways (RZD or РЖД) will have a service to suit your travel plans.

A good 1st- or 2nd-class berth on a sleeper train compares favourably with similar berths in Western Europe, as they're larger and often more comfortable. Every train in Russia has two numbers – one for the eastbound train (even-numbered trains) and one for the westbound (odd-numbered trains).

The following sections set the scene and provide inspiration for your Russian rail adventure. For more general information on buying tickets and travelling on trains in Russia, see p719.

Classes

The top class of ticket is called SV (a two-berth sleeping carriage), followed by *kupe* (four-berth carriage), *platskartny* (dorm carriage) and *obshchiy* (general or seating class). For details of what to expect in each of these classes of carriage and the costs of each type of ticket see p719.

Costs

Unless otherwise specified, we quote 2nd-class *(kupe)* fares. Expect 1st-class (SV) fares to be double this and 3rd-class *(platskartny)* to be about 40% less. Children under five travel free if they share a berth with an adult; otherwise, children under 10 pay a reduced fare for their own berth.

Complicating matters is RZD's policy of varying fares by the season. At peak travel times, eg early July to early August and around key holidays such as Easter and New Year, fares can be between 12% and 16% higher than the regular fare. The inverse happens at slack times of the year, such as early January to March, when there are discounts on fares. On 9 May (Victory Day) Russian Railways has also been known to discount fares to half price. On *skory* (fast) and *firmeny* (fast – nicer class) trains it's also possible to have two grades of *kupe* fare: with or without meals.

Fares quoted in this book were collected between April and August 2011, so please take them as a general guide only.

Trans-Siberian Routes

Extending 9289km from Moscow to Vladivostok on the Pacific, the Trans-Siberian Railway and connecting routes are among the most famous and potentially enjoyable of the world's great train journeys. Rolling out of Europe and into Asia, over vast swaths of taiga, steppe and desert, the Trans-Siberian – the world's longest single-service railway – makes all other train rides seem like once around the block with Thomas the Tank Engine.

Don't look for the Trans-Siberian Railway on a timetable, though. The term is used generically for three main lines and the numerous trains that run on them. For the first four days' travel out of Moscow's Yaroslavsky vokzal (station), the trans-Siberian, trans-Manchurian and trans-Mongolian routes all follow the same line, passing through Nizhny Novgorod on the way to Yekaterinburg in the Ural Mountains and then into Siberia.

Many travellers choose to break their journey at Irkutsk to visit Lake Baikal (we recommend you do) but, otherwise, the three main services continue on round the southern tip of the lake to Ulan-Ude, another possible jumping-off point for Baikal. From here trans-Siberian trains continue to Vladivostok, while the trans-Mongolian ones head south for the Mongolian border, Ulaanbaatar and Beijing. The trans-Manchurian service continues past Ulan-Ude to Chita, then turns southeast for Zabaikalsk on the Chinese border.

For full details about the journey, read Lonely Planet's *Trans-Siberian Railway* guide.

In addition to the RZD services listed below, GW Travel (p713) offers both trans-Siberian and BAM trips on the luxurious private Golden Eagle train.

Moscow to Vladivostok

The 1/2 Rossiya train is the top Moscow–Vladivostok service. If you're planning to

BUYING TRAIN TICKETS ONLINE

You can book train tickets online with **RZD** (rzd.ru) but its interface is in Russian: **Man in Seat 61** (www.seat61.com) has a guide on how to navigate the RZD interface if you don't read Cyrillic. Otherwise, these sites are in English:

» **Bilet.ru** (☎495-246 2029; www.bilet.ru)

» **Real Russia** (www.realrussia.co.uk)

» **Russian Rails** (www.russianrails.com)

» **TrainsRussia.com** (☎in USA 1-404-827 0099, in Moscow 495-225 5012; www.trainsrussia.com/en/travels) Authorised US agent for RZD; tickets are issued in its Moscow office. They can then be picked up in Moscow, delivered for US$15 to any address in Moscow or for US$30 to any Moscow airport or rail station, or sent via international DHL delivery to your home address.

» **VisitRussia.com** (☎in USA 1-800-755 3080, in Moscow 495-504 1304; www.visitrussia.com)

stop off at Irkutsk, also consider using the 9/10 Baikal, reputed to be one of the best trains in Russia in terms of carriage standards and service.

Other good services that can be usefully included in a Moscow to Vladivostok itinerary include: the 15/16 Ural between Moscow and Yekaterinburg; 25/25 Sibiryak between Moscow and Novosibirsk; 7/8 Sibir between Novosibirsk and Vladivostok; 55/56 Yenisey between Moscow and Krasnoyarsk; and 5/6 Okean between Khabarovsk and Vladivostok.

If you'd prefer to skip Moscow in favour of St Petersburg as the start or finish of a trans-Siberian journey, the 71/72 Demidovsky between St Petersburg and Yekaterinburg is a recommended option. And if you'd like to speed things up a little there's also the high-speed 175/173 Sapsan service connecting St Petersburg and Nizhny Novgorod in just over eight hours.

Moscow to Ulaanbaatar & Beijing

The more popular of the two options running directly between Moscow and Beijing is the weekly 3/4 trans-Mongolian service, a Chinese train that travels via Ulaanbaatar and the only one to offer deluxe carriages with showers.

If you're planning to stop off in Irkutsk, there's also the less fancy daily 264/263 service to/from Ulaanbaatar.

The weekly 19/20 Vostok trans-Manchurian service is a Russian train that crosses the border into China at Zabaikalsk, and passes through Harbin before terminating in Beijing seven days after its initial departure from Moscow.

The BAM: Tayshet to Sovetskaya Gavan

Everyone knows the Trans-Siberian Railway, but there is also another trans-Sib route, the no-less-remarkable Baikal-Amur Mainline (Baikalo-Amurskaya Magistral; BAM). Stretching across almost half of Russia, the BAM begins at Tayshet, 4515km east of Moscow, curls around the top of Lake Baikal, cuts through nonstop taiga, winds around snow-splattered mountains and burrows through endless tunnels on its way east to Sovetskaya Gavan on the Tatar Strait.

The majority of towns on the line were thrown up to house construction workers and sport a functionalist 1970s look. In contrast the incredibly remote and utterly wild scenery viewed from the train window is nothing short of awe inspiring. As well as Lake Baikal's lovely northern lip, adventures on the BAM reach some very out-of-the-way places including Bratsk, Tynda and Komsomolsk-na-Amure. For more on the BAM, see p519.

Other Long-Distance Routes

A glance through RZD's timetable reveals some other intriguing services that link up far-flung corners of the country and further afield. If the east–west trans-Siberian routes don't thrill you, there are north–south routes such as the 225/226 Murmansk–Adler train that connects the Arctic Circle city with the sun-kissed shores of the Black Sea. The three-day journey passes through Kem (jumping-off point for the Solovetsky Islands), Petrozavodsk (for access to Kizhi),

BREAKING YOUR JOURNEY

There is no Russian rail pass. RZD's rules allow passengers to break their journey once (for not more than 10 days) on any route, but the bureaucracy involved is off-putting, even to those who speak good Russian and have plenty of time on their hands. Hence, if you are travelling from, say, Moscow to Vladivostok, and plan on spending a night or two in Nizhny Novgorod and Irkutsk, you'll need three separate tickets: Moscow–Nizhny Novgorod, Nizhny Novgorod–Irkutsk and Irkutsk–Vladivostok.

If you're planning to frequently hop on and off trains and want to save some money along the way, it's a good idea to avoid the premium trains and go for the regular services, which offer the cheaper *platskartny* (3rd-class) carriages. Most of these services are perfectly acceptable and take pretty much the same travelling time point to point as the premium trains.

SHE WHO MUST BE OBEYED

On any long-distance Russian train journey you'll soon learn who's in charge: the *provodnitsa*. Though sometimes male *(provodnik)*, these carriage attendants are usually women.

As well as checking your ticket before boarding the train, doling out linen and shaking you awake in the middle of the night when your train arrives, the *provodnitsa*'s job is to keep her carriage spick and span (most are very diligent about this) and to make sure the samovar is always fired up with hot water. They will have cups, plates and cutlery to borrow, if you need them, and can provide drinks and snacks for a small price; some have even been known to cook up meals and offer them around.

On long journeys the *provodnitsa* works in a team of two; one will be working while the other is resting. Charm them and your journey will be all the more pleasant.

Tver, Moscow, Voronezh, Rostov-on-Don and Sochi. If travelling this route in the winter months, apart from the glorious snow-blanketed wilderness (and little snowed-in villages pumping chimney smoke), watch out for little ice-fishing 'cities' that pop up on wide frozen lakes and the occasional glimpse of villagers playing football on said icy expanses. Train breaks are always great for running out to buy huge smoked fish (or more expensive smoked whole eels) from the babushkas on the platforms.

Even on short visits to the country it's possible to squeeze in one overnight train journey, the most popular one being between Moscow and St Petersburg. The high-speed, TGV-standard Sapsan trains may link the two metropolises in four hours, but they lack the glamour and romance of climbing aboard premium overnight RZD services such as the Krasnaya Strela (Red Arrow) or the private **Grand Express** (http://grandexpress.ru/en).

And if you really can't get enough of long-distance trains, the RZD network is just as connected to Europe's networks as it is to those of Asia's, offering direct services to, among other places, Amsterdam, Basel, Berlin, Nice, Paris, Prague and Vienna. The website **Man in Seat 61** (www.seat61.com) has full details.

On the Journey

There is nothing quite like the smell of a Russian train: coal smoke, coffee, garlic, sausage, sweat, vodka and dozens of other elements combine to form an aroma that's so distinctive it will be permanently etched in your sensual memory.

To calculate where you are while on a journey, keep an eye out for the small, black-and-white kilometre posts generally on the southern side of the track. These mark the distance to and from Moscow. In between each kilometre marker are smaller posts counting down roughly every 100m. The distances on train timetables don't always correspond to these marker posts (usually because the timetable distances are the ones used to calculate fares).

Luggage

> In Europe and America people travel in a train fully aware that it belongs either to a state or company and that their ticket grants them only temporary occupation and certain restricted rights. In Russia people just take them over.
>
> *Laurens van der Post,* Journey into Russia

Russians have a knack of making themselves totally at home on trains. This often means that they'll be travelling with plenty of luggage, causing inevitable juggling of the available space in all compartment classes.

In all but local trains there's a luggage bin underneath each lower berth that will hold a medium-sized backpack or small suitcase. There's also enough space beside the bin to squeeze in another medium-sized bag. Above the doorway (in 1st and 2nd classes) or over the upper bunks (in 3rd class) there's room to accommodate a couple more rucksacks.

Etiquette

» Smoking is forbidden in the compartments but permitted in the spaces at the ends of the cars, past the toilets.

» Sleeping compartments are mixed sex; when women indicate that they want to change clothing or get out of bed, men go out and loiter in the corridor.

» It's good manners to offer any food or drinks you bring to the fellow passengers in your compartment; Russians will always offer to share their food with you.

Toilets

Located at both ends of each carriage, toilets can be locked long before and after station stops (there's a timetable on the door). Except on a very few trains there are no shower facilities – improvise with a sponge, flannel or short length of garden hose that you can attach to the tap for a dousing.

Food & Drink

Every sleeping carriage has a samovar filled with boiling water that's safe to drink and ideal for hot drinks, instant noodles or porridge.

The quality of food in dining cars varies widely. Rather than for eating they become the place to hang out, drink beer and play cards, particularly on the long trans-Siberian trip. Note also on the trans-Mongolian and trans-Manchurian trains that the dining cars are changed at each border, so en route to Beijing you get Russian, Chinese and possibly Mongolian versions. Occasionally, between the Russian border and Ulaanbaatar there is no dining car.

A meal in a restaurant car can cost anything from R400 to R1000. If you don't fancy what's on offer, there's often a table of pot noodles, savoury snacks, chocolate, alcohol, juice and the like being peddled by the staff. They sometimes make the rounds of the carriages, too, with a trolley of snacks and drinks. Prices are typically a little more than you'd pay at the kiosks or to the babushkas at the station halts.

Shopping for supplies at the stations is part of the fun of any long-distance Russian train trip. The choice of items is often excellent, with fresh milk, ice cream, grilled chicken, boiled potatoes, home cooking such as *pelmeni* (Russian-style ravioli dumplings) or *pirozhki* (savoury pies), buckets of forest berries and smoked fish all on offer.

regions at a glance

When planning a trip to the largest country in the world, you need to have some priorities in place. The vast majority of visitors are going to want to spend time in Moscow and St Petersburg; both these historic cities deliver the goods in terms of memorable sights and comfortable facilities, and function as bases for trips further afield to locations in Western European Russia or the Golden Ring. Siberia's splendid natural attractions are pretty irresistible but you're going to need time to see this vast area, which we split into more manageable western and eastern regions. To get fully off the beaten track head to the Russian Far East, Northern European Russia or the Caucasus.

Moscow

Art ✓✓✓
History ✓✓✓
Performing Arts ✓✓✓

Glorious Galleries

The illustrious and impressive Tretyakov and Pushkin Galleries are only the beginning of the art in Moscow, where contemporary artists and their patrons are taking over former factories and warehouses, using the vestiges of industry to create, provoke and beautify.

Historical Landmarks

The Kremlin shows off the splendour of Muscovy's grand princes. St Basil's Cathedral recounts the defeat of the Tatars. On Red Square, Lenin lies embalmed. And only a few kilometres away, Yeltsin defied the army, leading to the demise of the Soviet Union.

Performing Arts

The city's classical performing arts are still among the best and cheapest in the world. Nowadays, even the most traditional theatres are experimenting with innovative arrangements and cutting-edge choreographies. Sometimes debauched and depraved, sometimes intellectual and inspiring, it is always eye-opening.

p54

Golden Ring

Churches & Icons ✓✓✓
Country Roads ✓✓
Village Life ✓

Churches & Icons

Aesthetes of the world unite to admire the quintessentially Russian images of golden cupolas and whitewashed monastery walls guarding the treasure of treasures – stunning medieval frescoes and icons encaged in richly decorated altars.

Country Roads

Starting in Vladimir and ending in Yaroslavl, the picturesque A113 skirts through dark coniferous forests, sun-filled birch-tree groves and neat villages of brightly painted log houses and dilapidated churches. Car or bike – anything goes on this quiet section of the Ring.

Village Life

Wake up late in your gingerbread cottage, plunge into the lake or river, savour your breakfast bliny and then procrastinate unashamedly for the rest of the day in a garden chair, with a book and a jar of freshly picked strawberries for company.

p137

St Petersburg

Palaces ✓✓✓
History ✓✓✓
Art ✓✓✓

Imperial Splendour

The grand palaces of the Romanovs and their favourites line the embankments of the Neva River, its tributaries and canals. Restoration over the past two decades has been painstaking; the results are breathtaking.

Revolutionary Road

Everything about St Petersburg is revolutionary: from Peter the Great's determination to forge a new Russia by opening the country to the rest of Europe, to Lenin's leadership of a coup in 1917, which led to the creation of the world's first communist state.

Staggering Collections

The Hermitage collection is unrivalled anywhere else in the country if not the entire world. The Russian Museum positively groans under the weight of its own unique collection of Russian painting from icons to the avant-garde.

p162

Western European Russia

Kremlins ✓✓✓
Architecture ✓✓✓
Literary Shrines ✓✓✓

Mighty Fortresses

Early Rus trading towns such as Veliky Novgorod, Pskov and Smolensk sought to protect their wealth and power within formidable stone fortresses. The remains stand today as majestic backdrops to historical explorations.

Mystical Churches

Enter the ancient monasteries at Pechory and Tikhvin, or the icon-crammed cathedrals of Veliky Novgorod, Smolensk and Voronezh to witness the revival of Orthodox Christianity in the region where the religion originally took root centuries ago.

Literary Shrines

The family estates of literary titans Alexander Pushkin, Ivan Turgenev and Leo Tolstoy provide insight into the country life of the gentry in the 19th century. In Staraya Russa, Fyodor Dostoevsky's home looks as if the writer has only just popped out for a stroll.

p238

Kaliningrad Region

History ✓✓✓
Museums ✓✓
Beaches ✓✓✓

Historical Roots

Physical remnants of the Germanic kingdom of Prussia, including a rebuilt Gothic cathedral and the city's gates and fortifications, provide an insight into the time when Kaliningrad was called Königsberg. Venture out into the beautiful countryside to find the remains of two castles at Chernyakhovsk.

Fascinating Museums

Learn about the region's maritime history at the Museum of the World Ocean and be dazzled by artworks carved from petrified tree resin at the Amber Museum, both in Kaliningrad. Be charmed by the sculptures and gardens at the Herman Brachert House-Museum near Svetlogorsk.

Beautiful Beaches

Discover some of Russia's best beaches at Yantarny, Zelenogradsk and in the Kurshskaya Kosa National Park where massive sand dunes and wind-sculpted pines are sandwiched between the Baltic and placid Curonian Lagoon.

p282

Northern European Russia

Great Outdoors ✓✓✓
History ✓✓✓
Museums ✓✓

Great Outdoors

Each season offers its own adventures, from swimming with human 'walruses' in winter to summertime fishing for champion salmon in rugged, yet pristine rivers.

Historical Architecture

From the wooden marvels of Kizhi and Malye Karely to the haunting stone edifices of Solovki to the nautically inspired churches of landlocked Totma, the architectural landscape of Northern European Russia is as worth traversing as its natural one.

Offbeat Museums

Northern European Russia may be sparsely populated, but it has a crowded selection of offbeat museums. The mineral-heavy towns of the Kola region rock several highbrow geology repositories, exhibitions in Kargopol and Totma offer unique glimpses into local life, and Arkhangelsk's WWII-centric museum is a destination in itself.

p299

Volga Region

Architecture ✓✓✓
Landscapes ✓✓✓
Food & Culture ✓✓

Diverse Architecture

Historic kremlins overlook the Volga River in Nizhny Novgorod, Kazan and Astrakhan, monumental Stalinist buildings rise up out of Volgograd, contrasted by simple wood cottages in towns throughout the region.

Mighty Volga

Broad like an ocean in parts, flowing lazily between low banks or racing through narrow channels near the Caspian Sea, the Volga has many different faces. The Samara Bend is perfect for hiking, and in the Volga Delta this magnificent river culminates in a spectacular wetland where boats are often the only mode of transport.

Food & Culture

Tatar culture dominates the region, especially in Kazan and Astrakhan, and here you can best sample Tatar cuisine. Buddhism and a very different culinary culture prevail in Kalmykia, while in Nizhny Novgorod a 'Food and Culture' project is thriving.

p346

The Urals

Landscapes ✓✓✓
Cities & Towns ✓✓
Museums ✓✓

Diverse Landscapes
Stretching from the steppe into the Arctic, the Ural Mountains may only be truly spectacular in the north, but they are a lush, picturesque getaway elsewhere, with Lake Zyuratkul or the ice cave of Kungur.

Cities & Towns
Yekaterinburg is the most famous of the Ural Mountains cities, but don't forget Chelyabinsk – idiosyncratic beneath its urban grit – while Perm lives the eccentric difference. Nevyansk and other Ural Mountains towns are often attractive remnants of better mining times.

Gulag & Art
Perm and its environs have two very different spaces: Perm-36, the once-horrific Gulag camp located outside town, while the modern and contemporary art space PERMM offers up the shock of the new. Yekaterinburg is home to a good variety of museums.

p383

Russian Caucasus

Skiing ✓✓✓
Trekking ✓✓✓
Scenery ✓✓

Olympic Skiing
Host to the 2014 Winter Olympics, Sochi is a gateway to fantastic skiing. The mountain resorts of Krasnaya Polyana have scores of memorable runs, with an excellent assortment of cosy guesthouses and revitalising *bani* (hot baths) when the day is done.

Terrific Trekking
The alpine backdrop of the Caucasus is a magnet for adventure seekers. You can summit majestic Mt Elbrus – Europe's highest peak – or go on multiday treks exploring some of Russia's most dramatic scenery.

Idyllic Scenery
Anapa is a peaceful spot to take in the beauty of the Black Sea coast, while pretty Mineral Waters towns like Kislovodsk and Pyatigorsk, nestled in the Caucasus foothills, are idyllic settings for scenic walks in the surrounding hills.

p406

Western Siberia

Great Outdoors ✓✓✓
Winter Sports ✓✓
Architecture ✓✓

Magnificent Nature
The Altai Republic is about as far removed from civilisation as you can get in Russia. From snow-capped mountains to remote lakes, the region is a playground for nature lovers. Tourism is massively underdeveloped here though, so be prepared to rough it.

Skiing & Snowboarding
The popular ski resort of Sheregesh may be rough around the edges, but at least you won't have to queue long for the lifts. It also enjoys a stunning location in the heart of the Siberian countryside.

Historic Buildings
Tobolsk, Siberia's old capital, sports a handsome kremlin and charmingly decrepit old town. In Siberia's 'cultural capital', Tomsk, it's easy to lose yourself in a wonderland of wooden mansions and log cabins with intricately carved facades.

p450

Eastern Siberia

Great Outdoors ✓✓✓
Landscapes ✓✓✓
Museums ✓✓

Great Outdoors
Whether you take a hike along the Great Baikal Trail, discover the impenetrable taiga on horseback, click on skis for a bit of off-piste or kayak Lake Baikal's sapphire waters, Eastern Siberia is outdoorsy bliss.

Stunning Landscapes
From the grasslands of Tuva to the rock fingers of Krasnoyarsk's Stolby Nature Reserve; from the impossibly lonely back country of the Barguzin Valley to the snow-whipped Eastern Sayan Mountains, be sure to have your camera primed to capture Eastern Siberia's show-stopping vistas.

Exceptional Museums
Russia's museums are generally fusty, dusty, underfunded affairs, but Siberia's east has some wonderful exceptions. Be rendered speechless by the intricacy of Scythian gold, take a virtual submarine to Lake Baikal's murky depths and peruse a mini Khakassian Stonehenge at the region's intriguing repositories of the past.

p492

Russian Far East

Mountains ✓✓
Adventures ✓✓✓
Indigenous Cultures ✓✓

Mountainous Scenery
Kamchatka hogs the glory with its volcanoes, but Russia's entire eastern seaboard from Vladivostok to Magadan is a riot of old-growth taiga and icy peaks that attract intrepid explorers and bears alike.

Extreme Adventures
In addition to anything mountain-related (see above), you can kayak between Kamchatka and the Kuril Islands, hitch the Chukotka highway, drive a reindeer sled across the Arctic… you're only limited by your imagination. Dress warmly: the Far East is not known for good weather.

Indigenous Cultures
The weak don't survive in the 'pole of cold,' and so it is that the Far East's native inhabitants are among the world's heartiest. Journey to their villages, where they fish and herd reindeer, or celebrate the summer solstice with the Sakha at Yakutsk's Ysyakh.

p563

Every listing is recommended by our authors, and their favourite places are listed first

Look out for these icons:

Our author's top recommendation

A green or sustainable option

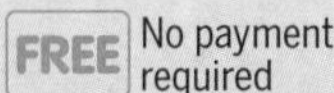

No payment required

See the Index for a full list of destinations covered in this book.

On the Road

Moscow

Includes »

Best Places to Eat

» Delicatessen (p115)
» Café Pushkin (p116)
» Khachapuri (p116)
» Volkonsky (p116)
» Barashka (p115)

Best Places to Stay

» Home from Home (p112)
» Golden Apple (p111)
» Artel (p110)
» Basilica Hotel (p113)

Why Go?

The creative energy in the capital is palpable. Former factories and warehouses are now edgy art galleries, while classic venues are experimenting and expanding. Tchaikovsky and Chekhov remain well represented at Moscow's theatres, but you can also see world premieres by up-and-coming composers and choreographers. Foodies flock to wine bars, coffee bars, sushi bars and even beer bars, while night owls enjoy a dynamic scene of exclusive nightclubs, edgy art cafés and underground blues bars.

The ancient city has always been a haven for history buffs, and new museums are broaching subjects long brushed under the carpet. The red-brick towers of the Kremlin occupy the founding site of Moscow (Москва); churches remember fallen heroes and victorious battles; and remains of the Soviet state are scattered all around.

The capital is also experiencing an unprecedented growth in birth rates. From artistry and history to recreation and procreation, Moscow is definitely a cauldron of creativity.

When to Go

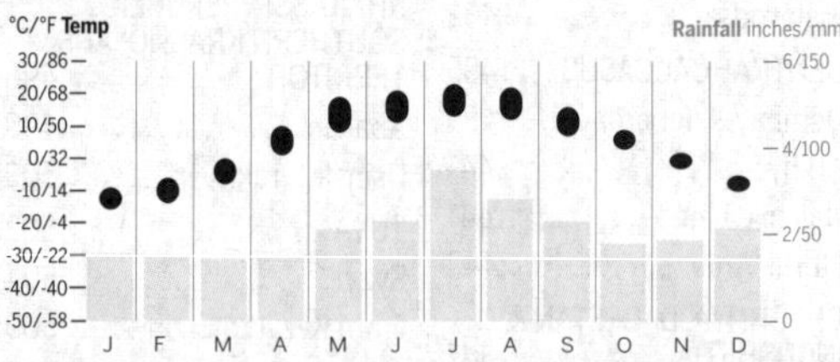

May & Jun Long hours of daylight and mild temperatures entice Muscovites outdoors.

Sep Moscow celebrates City Day, as the foliage turns the capital splendid oranges, reds and yellows.

Dec The sparkling snow-covered city hosts its premier cultural event, the December Nights Festival.

Arriving in Moscow

Most travellers arrive by air, flying into one of the city's three airports. The majority of international flights go in and out of Domodedovo and Sheremetyevo international airports. All three airports are accessible by the convenient **Aeroexpress train** (☎8-800-700 3377; www.aeroexpress.ru; business/standard R550/320) from the city centre.

If you wish to take a taxi, it is highly recommended to book in advance to take advantage of the fixed rates offered by most companies (R1000 to R1500). Note that driving times vary wildly depending on traffic.

Rail riders will arrive at one of the more central train stations – Kievsky or Belorussky vokzal if you're coming from Europe; Leningradsky vokzal if you're coming from St Petersburg; and Yaroslavsky or Kazansky vokzal if you're coming from the east. All of the train stations are located in the city centre, with easy access to the metro. Alternatively, most taxi companies offer a fixed rate of R300 to R500 for a train station transfer.

GET THE BIG PICTURE

Moscow can be overwhelming for the first-time visitor. An introductory tour can provide an overview of the city, as well as useful advice and information for the rest of your trip.

» **Moscow Free Tour** (www.moscowfreetour.com) Offers a free walking tour, led by knowledgeable and extremely enthusiastic guides. Did we mention it's free?

» **Moscow Mania** (p109) Young and enthusiastic history scholars offer the informative 'Meet Moscow' tour as an introduction to the city's history and architecture.

» **Capital Tours** (p107) Technically it's a hop-on, hop-off bus service, but it's more useful as a one-off overview of the city.

» **River Cruises** (p106) Two boat-tour companies follow the route from Kievsky vokzal or the former Hotel Ukraine in Dorogomilovo to Novospassky Monastery in Taganka. Again, you can get off and on the boat, but the 90-minute trip is a pleasant way to get the big picture.

New in Moscow

» **Red October** (p104) Formerly a chocolate factory, now an art and entertainment hot spot.

» **Ivan the Great Bell Tower** (p67) Now open for business.

» **Moscow Planetarium** (p81) Reopened after 17 years – it was worth the wait.

» **Great Wooden Palace at Kolomenskoe** (p105) The eighth wonder of the world once more.

NEED TO KNOW

Most Moscow museums are closed on Monday, but the Kremlin and the Armoury are closed on Thursday instead.

Fast Facts

» **Telephone area code** ☎495 or ☎499

» **Population** 11.5 million

» **Moscow Time** (GMT/USC + four hours)

Where to Stay

Moscow is big and filled with cars. Pay attention to the location of your hotel or hostel so you don't spend all your time commuting. Choose a place that is in the centre (preferably within the Garden Ring) and a short distance from the metro.

Resources

» **Expat.ru** (www.expat.ru) Run by and for English-speaking expats living in Moscow.

» **Moscow Business Telephone Guide** (www.mbtg.ru) A free bilingual phone book.

» **Art Guide** (www.artguide.ru) Art galleries, museum and events in the capital.

Moscow Highlights

1. Be awestruck by the assemblage of tall towers and onion domes on **Red Square** (p72)
2. Splurge on a Russian feast amid 18th-century opulence at **Café Pushkin** (p116)
3. See the ballerinas slide across *Swan Lake* at the **Bolshoi Theatre** (p121)
4. Explore the former **Red October** (p104) chocolate factory, now filled with art galleries, nightclubs and fashion boutiques
5. Ogle the icons, peruse the Peredvizhniki and contemplate the avant-garde at the **Tretyakov Gallery** (p94)

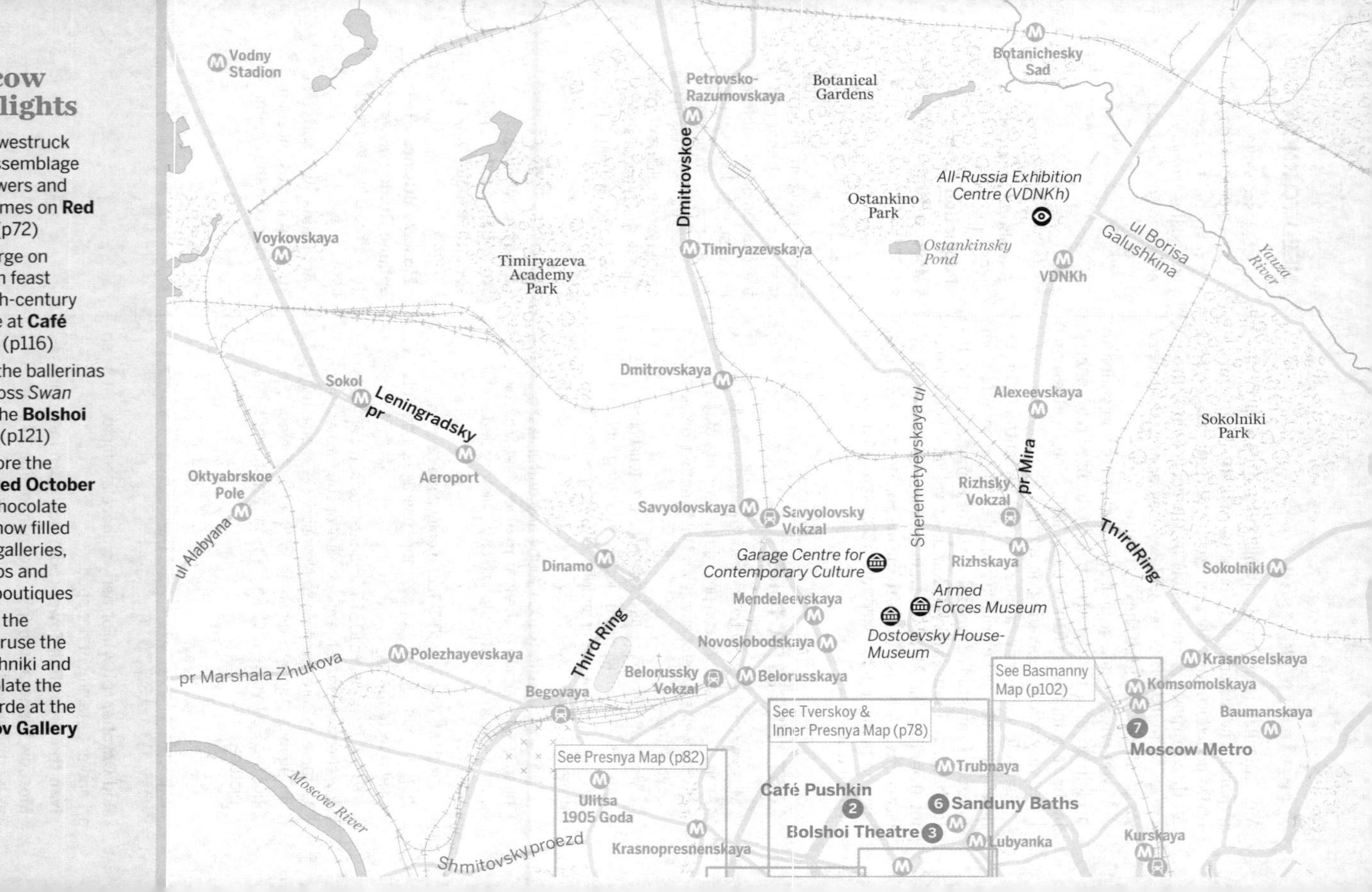

6 Steam your cares away at the luxurious **Sanduny Baths** (p106)

7 Ride the Moscow **metro** (p132) for a cheap history lesson and art exhibit all in one

8 Avoid traffic jams, feel the breeze on your face and get a new perspective on the most famous sights on board a **river cruise** (p106)

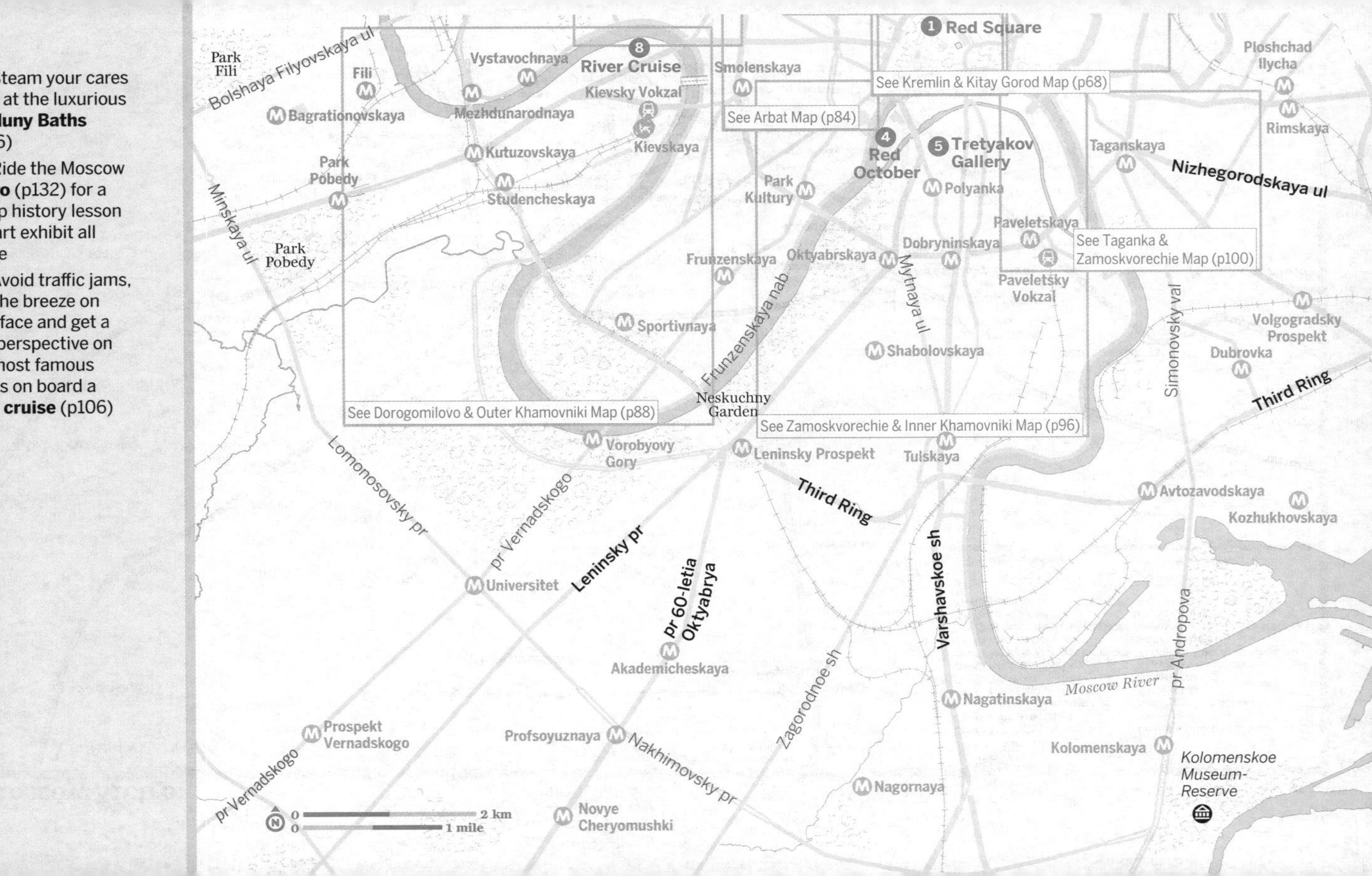

Moscow Metro

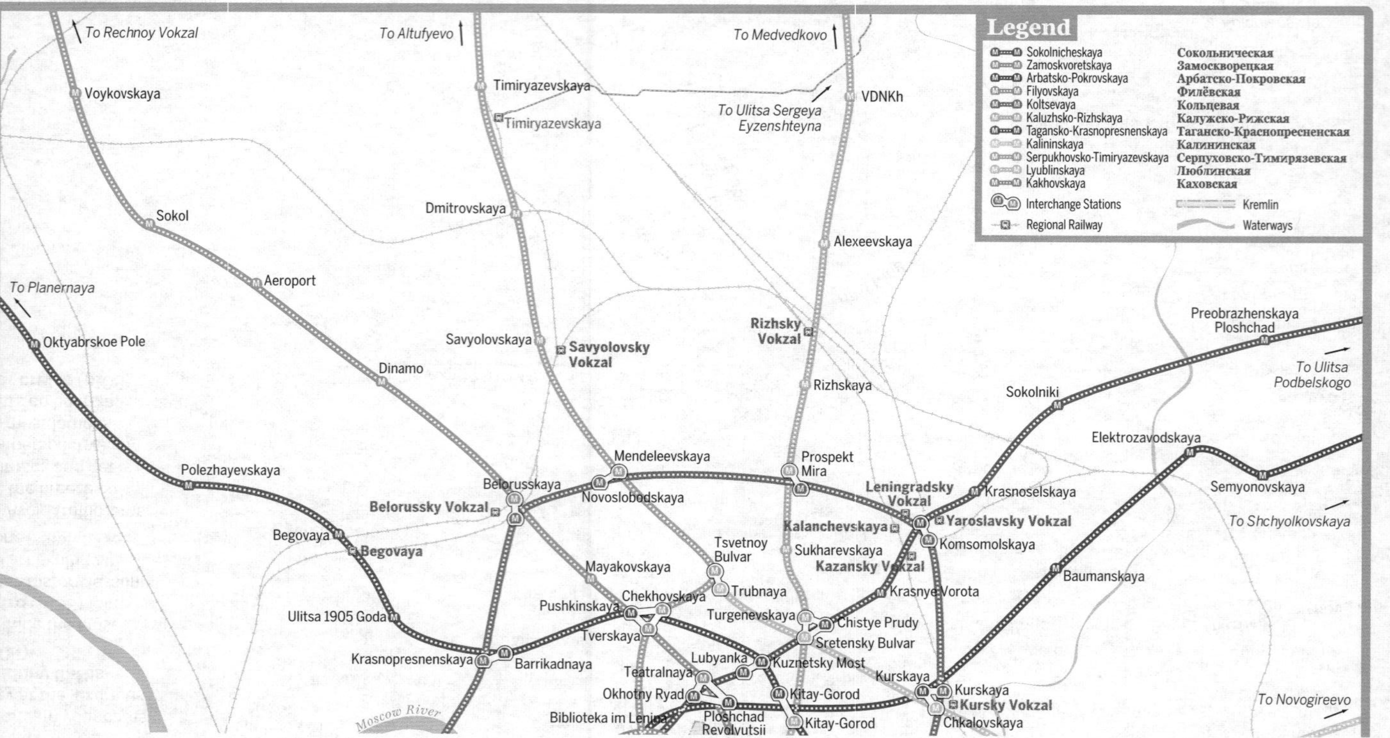

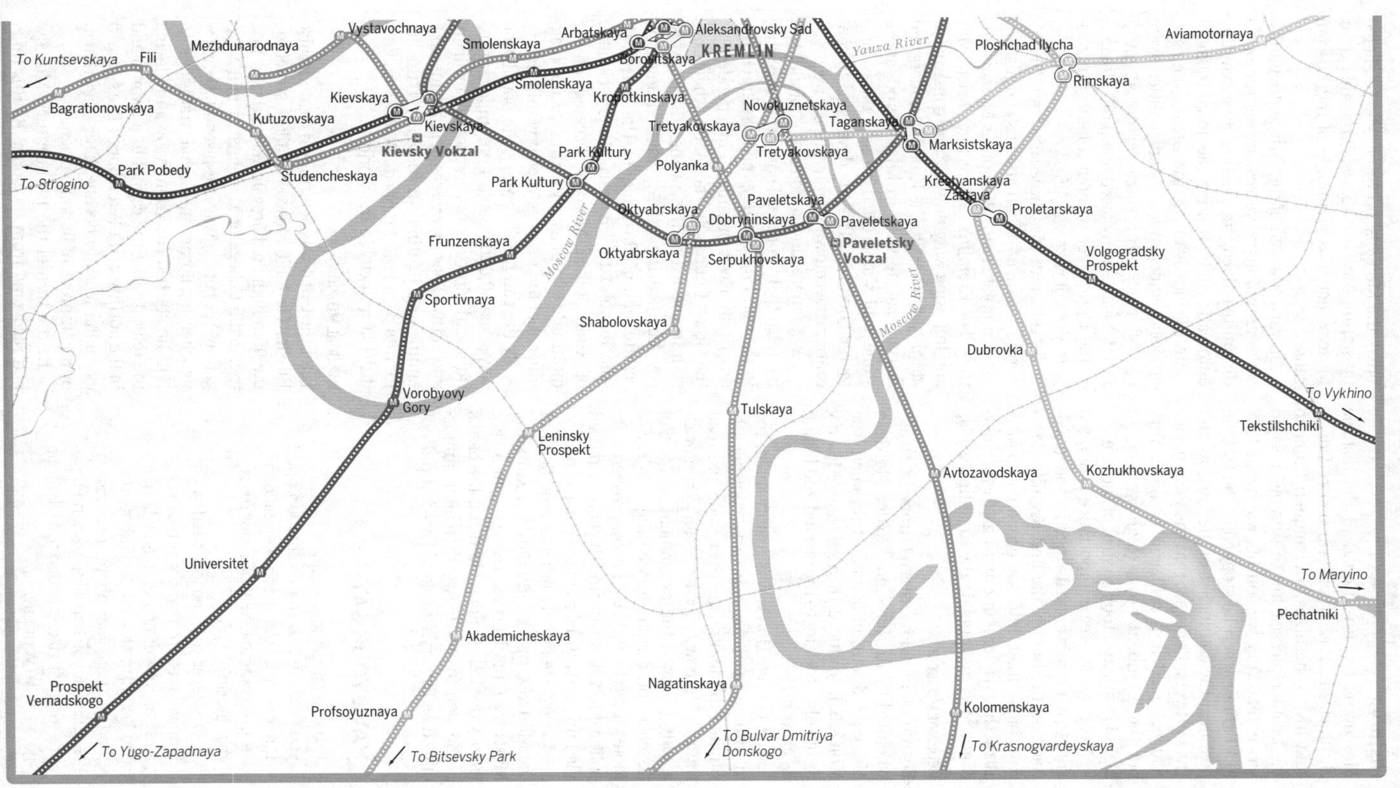
To Kuntsevskaya
Fili
Mezhdunarodnaya
Vystavochnaya
Smolenskaya
Arbatskaya
Aleksandrovsky Sad
KREMLIN
Borovitskaya
Yauza River
Ploshchad Ilycha
Aviamotornaya
Rimskaya
Bagrationovskaya
Kievskaya
Smolenskaya
Kropotkinskaya
Novokuznetskaya
Kutuzovskaya
Kievskaya
Tretyakovskaya
Taganskaya
Kievsky Vokzal
Park Kultury
Tretyakovskaya
Marksistskaya
To Strogino
Park Pobedy
Studencheskaya
Park Kultury
Polyanka
Krestyanskaya Zastava
Paveletskaya
Proletarskaya
Oktyabrskaya
Dobryninskaya
Paveletskaya
Frunzenskaya
Moscow River
Oktyabrskaya
Serpukhovskaya
Paveletsky Vokzal
Volgogradsky Prospekt
Sportivnaya
Shabolovskaya
Moscow River
Dubrovka
Vorobyovy Gory
Tulskaya
To Vykhino
Tekstilshchiki
Leninsky Prospekt
Avtozavodskaya
Kozhukhovskaya
Universitet
To Maryino
Pechatniki
Akademicheskaya
Nagatinskaya
Prospekt Vernadskogo
Profsoyuznaya
Kolomenskaya
To Yugo-Zapadnaya
To Bitsevsky Park
To Bulvar Dmitriya Donskogo
To Krasnogvardeyskaya

History

Moscow is first mentioned in the historic chronicles in 1147, when Prince Yury Dolgoruky invited his allies to a banquet: 'Come to me, brother, please come to Moscow'. Legend has it that Yury was on his way from Kyiv to Vladimir when he stopped at the trading post near the confluence of the Moscow and Yauza Rivers. Believing that the local prince had not paid him sufficient homage, Yury put the impudent boyar (high-ranking noble) to death and took control of the site.

Moscow's strategic importance prompted Yury to construct a moat-ringed wooden palisade on the hilltop, the first Kremlin. Moscow blossomed into an economic centre, attracting traders and artisans to the merchant rows just outside the Kremlin's walls.

MEDIEVAL MOSCOW

Beginning in 1236, Eastern Europe was overwhelmed by the ferocious Golden Horde, a Mongol-led army of nomadic tribesmen. The Mongols introduced themselves to Moscow by burning the city to the ground and killing its governor.

The Golden Horde was mainly interested in tribute, and Moscow was conveniently situated to monitor the river trade and road traffic. Moscow's Prince Ivan Danilovich readily accepted the assignment as Mongol tax collector, earning himself the moniker of Moneybags (Kalita). As Moscow prospered, its political fortunes rose, too. It soon surpassed Vladimir and Suzdal as the regional capital.

Moscow eventually became a nemesis of the Mongols. In the 1380 Battle of Kulikovo, Moscow's Grand Prince Dmitry won a rare victory over the Golden Horde on the banks of the Don River. He was thereafter immortalised as Dmitry Donskoy. This feat did not break the Mongols, however, who retaliated by setting Moscow ablaze. From this time, Moscow acted as champion of the Russian cause.

Towards the end of the 15th century, Moscow's ambitions were realised as the once-diminutive duchy emerged as an expanding autocratic state. Under the long reign of Grand Prince Ivan III (the Great), the eastern Slav independent principalities were consolidated into a single territorial entity. In 1480 Ivan's army faced down the Mongols at the Ugra River without a fight: the 200-year Mongol yoke was lifted.

To celebrate his successes, Ivan III imported a team of Italian artisans and masons for a complete renovation of his Moscow fortress. The Kremlin's famous thick brick walls and imposing watchtowers were constructed at this time. Next to the Kremlin, traders and artisans set up shop in Kitay Gorod, and a stone wall was erected around these commercial quarters. The city developed in concentric rings outward from this centre.

As it emerged as a political capital, Moscow also took on the role of religious centre. In the mid-15th century, the Russian Orthodox Church was organised, independent of the Greek Church. In the 1450s, when Constantinople fell to the heathen Turks, Moscow claimed the title of 'Third Rome', the rightful heir of Christendom. Under Ivan IV (the Terrible), the city earned the nickname of 'Gold-Domed Moscow' because of the multitude of monastery fortresses and magnificent churches constructed within them.

By the early 15th century, the population surpassed 50,000 people. Contemporary visitors said Moscow was 'awesome', 'brilliant' and 'filthy'. The city was resilient against fire, famine and fighting. In the early 17th century its population topped 200,000, making it the largest city in the world.

IMPERIAL MOSCOW

Peter the Great was determined to modernise Russia. He built Moscow's tallest structure, the 90m-high Sukharev Tower, and next to it founded a College of Mathematics and Navigation. Yet Peter always despised Moscow for its scheming boyars and archaic traditions. In 1712 he startled the country by announcing the relocation of the capital to a swampland in the northwest (St Petersburg). The spurned ex-capital fell into decline, later exacerbated by an outbreak of bubonic plague.

By the turn of the 19th century, Moscow had recovered from its gloom. By this time, the city hosted Russia's first university, museum and newspaper. Moscow's intellectual and literary scene gave rise to a nationalist-inspired Slavo-phile movement, which celebrated the cultural features of Russia that were distinctive from the West.

In the early 1800s Tsar Alexander I decided to resume trade with England, in violation of a treaty Russia had made with France. A furious Napoleon Bonaparte set out for Moscow with the largest military force the world had ever seen. The Russian army engaged the advancing French at the Battle of Borodino, 130km from Moscow. More than 100,000 soldiers lay dead at the end of this inconclusive one-day fight. Shortly thereafter, Napoleon entered a deserted Moscow. By some accounts, defiant Muscovites burned down their city rather than see it occupied. French soldiers tried to topple the formidable Kremlin, but its sturdy walls withstood their pummelling.

The city was feverishly rebuilt following Napoleon's final defeat. Monuments were erected to commemorate Russia's hard-fought victory, including a Triumphal Arch and the grandiose Cathedral of Christ the Saviour. In the centre, engineers diverted the Neglinnaya River to an underground canal and created two new urban spaces: the Alexander Garden and Teatralnaya pl. Meanwhile, the city's two outer defensive rings were replaced with the tree-lined Boulevard Ring and Garden Ring roads.

By midcentury, industry overtook commerce as the city's economic driving force. With a steady supply of cotton from Central Asia, Moscow became a leader in the textile industry, and was known as 'Calico Moscow'. By 1900, Moscow claimed over one million inhabitants. The Garden Ring became an informal social boundary line: on the inside were the abodes and amenities of businessmen, intellectuals, civil servants and foreigners; on the outside were the factories and flophouses of the toiling, the loitering and the destitute.

RED MOSCOW

Exhausted by three years engaged in fighting during WWI, the tsarist regime meekly succumbed to a mob of St Petersburg workers in February 1917; a few months later, Lenin's Bolshevik party stepped into the political void. In Moscow the Bolshevik coup provoked a week of street fighting, leaving more than a thousand dead. Fearing a German assault on St Petersburg, Lenin ordered that the capital return to Moscow.

In the early 1930s Josef Stalin launched an industrial revolution, instigating a wave of peasant immigration to Moscow. Around the city, makeshift work camps were erected to shelter the huddling hordes. Moscow became a centre of military industry, whose engineers and technicians enjoyed a larger slice of the proletarian pie.

Under Stalin a comprehensive urban plan was devised for Moscow. On paper, it appeared as a neatly organised garden city; unfortunately, it was implemented with a sledgehammer. Historic cathedrals and monuments were demolished, including landmarks such as the Cathedral of Christ the Saviour and Kazan Cathedral. In their place appeared the marble-bedecked metro and neo-Gothic skyscrapers.

When Hitler launched 'Operation Barbarossa' into Soviet territory in June 1941, Stalin was caught by surprise. By December the Nazis were just outside Moscow, within 30km of the Kremlin – an early winter halted the advance. In the Battle of Moscow, war hero General Zhukov staged a brilliant counteroffensive and saved the city from capture.

After Stalin's death in 1953, Nikita Khrushchev – a former mayor of Moscow – tried a different approach to ruling. He introduced wide-ranging reforms and promised to improve living conditions. Huge housing estates grew up round the outskirts of Moscow; many of the hastily constructed low-rise projects were nicknamed *khrushchoby,* after *trushchoby* (slums). Khrushchev's populism and unpredictability made the ruling elite nervous and he was ousted in 1964.

From atop Lenin's mausoleum, Leonid Brezhnev presided over the rise of a military superpower during the Cold War. The aerospace, radio-electronics and nuclear weapons ministries operated factories and research laboratories in and around the capital. By 1980 as much as one-third of the city's industrial production and one-quarter of its labour force were connected to the defence industry. As a matter of national security, the KGB secretly constructed a second subway system.

Brezhnev showed a penchant for lavish cement-pouring displays of modern architecture, such as the State Kremlin Palace. Residential life continued to move further away from the city centre. Shoddy high-rise apartments went up on the periphery and metro lines were extended outwards. By

1980 the city's population surpassed eight million.

TRANSITIONAL MOSCOW

Mikhail Gorbachev came to power in March 1985 with a mandate to revitalise the ailing socialist system; he promoted Boris Yeltsin as the new head of Moscow. Yeltsin's populist touch made him an instant success with Muscovites and he embraced the more open political atmosphere, allowing 'informal' groups to organise and express themselves in public. Moscow streets such as ul Arbat hosted demonstrations by democrats, nationalists, reds and greens.

On 18 August 1991 the city awoke to find tanks in the street and a self-proclaimed 'Committee for the State of Emergency in the USSR' in charge. They had already detained Gorbachev and ordered Yeltsin arrested. Crowds gathered at the White House to build barricades. Yeltsin, from atop a tank, declared the coup illegal. He dared KGB snipers to shoot him; when they didn't, the coup – and Soviet communism – was over. By the year's end Boris Yeltsin had moved into the Kremlin.

The first years of transition were fraught with political conflict. In September 1993 Yeltsin issued a decree to shut down the Russian parliament. Events turned violent, and a National Salvation Front called for popular insurrection. The army intervened on the president's side and blasted the parliament into submission. In all, 145 people were killed and another 700 wounded – the worst such incident of bloodshed in the city since the Bolshevik takeover in 1917.

Within the Moscow city government, the election of Yury Luzhkov as mayor in 1992 set the stage for the creation of a big-city boss in the grandest of traditions. The city government retained ownership of property in Moscow, giving Luzhkov's administration unprecedented control over would-be business ventures, and making him as much a CEO as a mayor.

While the rest of Russia struggled to survive the collapse of communism, Moscow quickly emerged as an enclave of affluence and dynamism. The new economy spawned a small group of 'New Russians', routinely derided and often envied for their garish displays of wealth. Outside this elite, Russia's transition to the market economy came at enormous social cost. The older generation, whose hard-earned pensions became practically worthless, paid the price of transition.

MILLENNIUM MOSCOW

In September 1999 a series of mysterious explosions in Moscow left more than 200 people dead. It was widely believed, although unproven, that Chechen terrorists were responsible for the bombings. This was the first of many terrorist attacks in the capital that were linked to the ongoing crisis in Chechnya.

In 2002, Chechen rebels, wired with explosives, seized a popular Moscow theatre, holding 800 people hostage for three days. Russian troops responded by flooding the theatre with immobilising toxic gas, resulting in 120 deaths and hundreds of illnesses. Over the next decade, suicide bombers in Moscow made strikes in metro stations, at rock concerts, on trains and aeroplanes, and in the international airport, leaving hundreds of people dead and injured, and reminding Muscovites that there is no end in sight to the Chechen crisis.

In 2010, long-time mayor Yury Luzhkov lost his job. After 18 years in the top seat, he was finally fired by President Medvedev, who issued a formal decree on the matter. The new boss, Sergei Sobyanin, was handpicked by the president in tandem with Prime Minister Putin (making one wonder who the new boss really was).

Sobyanin was a surprising choice, as he hails from the Siberian province of Tyumen, although he had previously been working in Moscow as the Head of the Presidential Administration. Analysts theorise that his 'outsider' status and his clean reputation made him an attractive candidate who would not offend.

Sobyanin's early initiatives included a crackdown on corruption and a slow-down of construction, both of which were welcomed by many Moscow residents. He also promised to find a way to ease the city's massive traffic problems.

As the economic rhythms of the city seem to be steadying, wealth is trickling down beyond the 'New Russians'. In Moscow, the burgeoning middle class endures a high cost of living, but enjoys unprecedented employment opportunities and a dizzying array of culinary, cultural and consumer choices.

The city continues to attract fortune seekers from the provinces, from other parts of the former Soviet Union and from around the world. And Moscow – political capital, economic powerhouse and cultural innovator – continues to lead the way as the most fast-dealing, freewheeling city in Russia.

Sights

KREMLIN & RED SQUARE

Moscow started life in the 12th century as a triangular plot of land – a smallish fort – perched atop Borovitsky Hill. Surrounded by a wall for protection, the fort contained the earliest settlement, while ceremonies and celebrations were held on the plaza outside. The fort, of course, is the Kremlin, while the ceremonial plaza is Red Square – still at the heart of Moscow historically, geographically and spiritually.

KREMLIN

The apex of political power, the **Kremlin** (Map p68; www.kreml.ru; adult/student R350/100, audio guide R200; 9.30am-5pm Fri-Wed; M Aleksandrovsky Sad) is the kernel not only of Moscow but of all of Russia. From here Ivan the Terrible orchestrated his terror; Napoleon watched Moscow burn; Lenin fashioned the proletariat dictatorship; Stalin purged his ranks; Khrushchev fought the Cold War; Gorbachev unleashed *perestroika;* and Yeltsin concocted the New Russia.

A 'kremlin' is a town's fortified stronghold, and the first low, wooden wall around Moscow was built in the 1150s. The Kremlin grew with the importance of Moscow's princes, becoming in the 1320s the headquarters of the Russian Church, which had shifted from Vladimir. The 'White Stone Kremlin' – which had limestone walls – was built in the 1360s, with almost the same boundaries as it has today.

Towards the end of the 15th century, Ivan the Great brought master builders from Pskov and Italy to supervise the construction of new walls and towers (most of which still stand), as well as the Kremlin's three great cathedrals and more. The Kremlin's walls today have 19 distinctive towers.

Before entering the Kremlin, deposit bags at the **Kremlin left-luggage office** (Камера хранения; Map p68; per bag R60; 9am-6.30pm Fri-Wed; M Aleksandrovsky Sad), beneath the Kutafya Tower near the main **Kremlin ticket office** (Кассы музеев Кремля; Map p68; 9.30am-4pm Fri-Wed; M Aleksandrovsky Sad). The ticket to the 'Architectural Ensemble of Cathedral Square' covers entry to all four churches, as well as Patriarch's Palace. It does not include Ivan the Great Bell Tower, the Armoury or the Diamond Fund Exhibition.

In any case, you can and should buy tickets for Ivan the Great and for the Armoury here. There's also an entrance at the southern **Borovitskaya Tower** (Боровицкая башня; Map p68), mainly used by those heading straight to the Armoury or Diamond Fund Exhibition.

Inside the Kremlin, police will keep you from straying into the out-of-bounds areas. Visitors wearing shorts will be refused entry. Photography is not permitted inside the Armoury or any of the buildings on Sobornaya pl (Cathedral Sq).

Visiting the Kremlin buildings and the Armoury is at least a half-day affair. If you intend to visit the Diamond Fund or other special exhibits, plan on spending most of the day here. If you are short on time, skip the Armoury and the Diamond Fund, and dedicate a few hours to admiring the amazing architecture and historical buildings around Sobornaya pl.

To really do the Kremlin justice, let the professionals show you around:

STAND ON CEREMONY

Every Saturday at noon on Sobornaya pl (Cathedral Sq), the Presidential Regiment shows up in all its finery for a ceremonial procession, featuring some very official-looking prancing and dancing, both on foot and on horseback. The price of admission to the Kremlin allows access to the demonstration. Otherwise, on the last Saturday of the month, the demonstration is repeated at 2pm for the masses on Red Square.

Kremlin Excursions Office TOURS
(Бюро экскурсий Кремля; Map p68; 495-697 0349; www.kremlin.museum.ru; Alexander Garden; M Alexandrovsky Sad) Make advanced arrangements for the 'One Day at the Kremlin' tour.

Capital Tours TOURS
(Map p68; www.capitaltours.ru; ul Ilyinka 4; adult/child R1550/750; 2-5pm; M Ploshchad Revolyutsii) Departing from the tour office in Gostinny Dvor every day that the Kremlin is open. Price includes admission.

Moscow Mania TOURS
(www.mosmania.com; adult/child R600/300) Led by an archaeologist who participated in an excavation of the Kremlin in 2007. Advance arrangements required.

Northern & Western Buildings HISTORICAL BUILDING
The main entrance is through **Kutafya Tower** (Кутафья башня; Map p68), which stands away from the Kremlin's west wall,

The Kremlin

A DAY AT THE KREMLIN

Only at the Kremlin can you see 800 years of Russian history and artistry in one day. Enter the ancient fortress through the Trinity Gate Tower and walk past the impressive Arsenal, ringed with cannons. Past the Patriarch's Palace, you'll find yourself surrounded by white-washed walls and golden domes. Your first stop is **Assumption Cathedral** 1 with the solemn fresco over the doorway. As the most important church in prerevolutionary Russia, this 15th-century beauty was the burial site of the patriarchs. The **Ivan the Great Bell Tower** 2 now contains a nifty multimedia exhibit on the architectural history of the Kremlin. The view from the top is worth the price of admission. The tower is flanked by the massive **Tsar Cannon & Bell** 3.

In the southeast corner, **Archangel Cathedral** 4 has an elaborate interior, where three centuries of tsars and tsarinas are laid to rest. Your final stop on Sobornaya pl is **Annunciation Cathedral** 5, rich with frescoes and iconography.

Walk along the Great Kremlin Palace and enter the **Armoury** 6 at the time designated on your ticket. After gawking at the goods, exit the Kremlin through Borovitsky Gate and stroll through the Alexander Garden to the **Tomb of the Unknown Soldier** 7.

MARA VORHEES

Tomb of the Unknown Soldier
Visit the Tomb of the Unknown Soldier honouring the heroes of the Great Patriotic War. Come at the top of the hour to see the solemn synchronicity of the changing of the guard.

Assumption Cathedral
Once your eyes adjust to the colourful frescoes, the gilded fixtures and the iconography, try to locate *Saviour with the Angry Eye*, a 14th-century icon that is one of the oldest in the Kremlin.

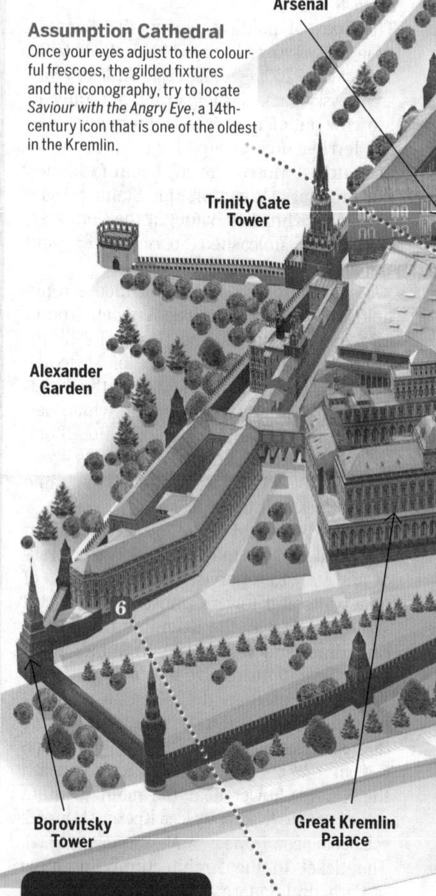

Armoury
Take advantage of the free audio guide to direct you to the most intriguing treasures of the Armoury, which is chock-full of precious metalworks and jewellery, armour and weapons, gowns and crowns, carriages and sledges.

KREMLIN PRESS OFFICE

TOP TIPS

» **Lunch** There are no eating options. Plan to eat before you arrive or stash a snack.

» **Lookout** After ogling the sights around Sobornaya pl, take a break in the park across the street, which offers wonderful views of the Moscow River and points south.

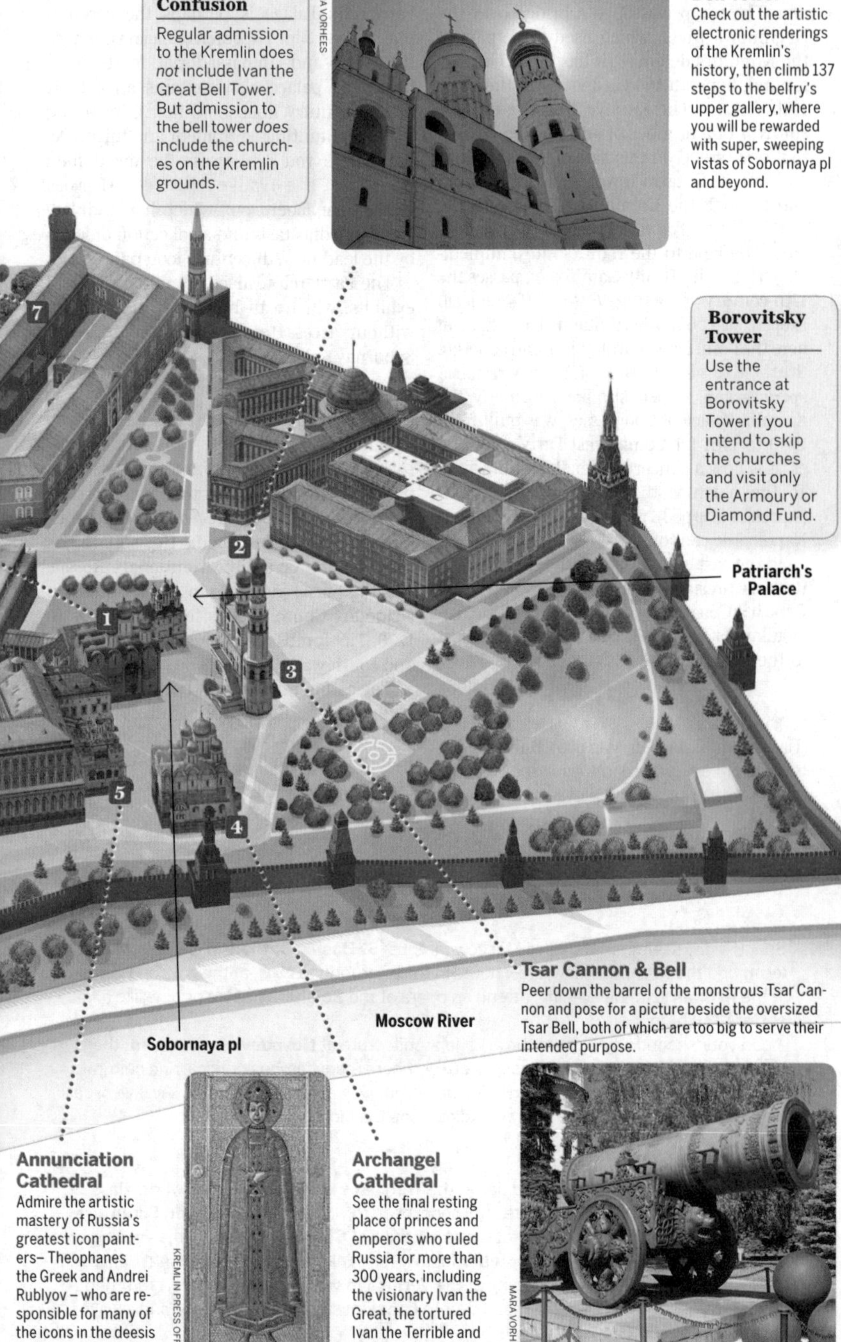
Avoid Confusion
Regular admission to the Kremlin does *not* include Ivan the Great Bell Tower. But admission to the bell tower *does* include the churches on the Kremlin grounds.
MARA VORHEES
Ivan the Great Bell Tower
Check out the artistic electronic renderings of the Kremlin's history, then climb 137 steps to the belfry's upper gallery, where you will be rewarded with super, sweeping vistas of Sobornaya pl and beyond.
Borovitsky Tower
Use the entrance at Borovitsky Tower if you intend to skip the churches and visit only the Armoury or Diamond Fund.
7
2
1
3
5
4
Patriarch's Palace
Tsar Cannon & Bell
Peer down the barrel of the monstrous Tsar Cannon and pose for a picture beside the oversized Tsar Bell, both of which are too big to serve their intended purpose.
Moscow River
Sobornaya pl
Annunciation Cathedral
Admire the artistic mastery of Russia's greatest icon painters– Theophanes the Greek and Andrei Rublyov – who are responsible for many of the icons in the deesis and festival rows of the iconostasis.
KREMLIN PRESS OFFICE
Archangel Cathedral
See the final resting place of princes and emperors who ruled Russia for more than 300 years, including the visionary Ivan the Great, the tortured Ivan the Terrible and the tragic Tsarevitch Dmitry.
MARA VORHEES

at the end of a ramp over the Alexander Garden. The ramp was once a bridge over the Neglinnaya River, which used to be part of the Kremlin's defences; it has flowed underground, beneath the garden, since the early 19th century. The Kutafya Tower is the last survivor of a number of outer bridge towers that once stood on this side of the Kremlin.

From the Kutafya Tower, walk up the ramp and through the Kremlin walls beneath the **Trinity Gate Tower** (Троицкая башня; Map p68). The lane to the right (south), immediately inside the Trinity Gate Tower, passes the 17th-century **Poteshny Palace** (Потешный дворец; Map p68) where Stalin lived. East of here the bombastic marble, glass and concrete **State Kremlin Palace** (Государственный кремлёвский дворец; Map p68), formerly the Kremlin Palace of Congresses, was built from 1960 to 1961 for Communist Party congresses. It is now a concert and ballet auditorium. To the north is the 18th-century **Arsenal** (Арсенал; Map p68), ringed with 800 captured Napoleonic cannons.

To the east of the Arsenal, the offices of the Russian president are in the yellow former **Senate** (Сенат; Map p68) building, a fine, triangular 18th-century classical edifice. Next to the Senate is the 1930s former **Supreme Soviet** (Верховный Совет; Map p68) building.

Patriarch's Palace HISTORICAL BUILDING

(Патриарший дворец; Map p68) Built for Patriarch Nikon (whose reforms sparked the break with the Old Believers) mostly in the mid-17th century, the highlight of the Patriarch's Palace is perhaps the ceremonial **Cross Hall** (Крестовая палата), where the tsar's and ambassadorial feasts were held. The palace also contains an exhibit of 17th-century household items, including jewellery, hunting equipment and furniture. From here you can access the five-domed **Church of the Twelve Apostles** (Церковь двенадцати апостолов), which has a gilded, wooden iconostasis and a collection of icons by the leading 17th-century icon painters.

The Patriarch's Palace often holds special exhibits, which can be visited individually, without access to the other buildings on Sobornaya pl.

Assumption Cathedral CHURCH

(Успенский собор; Map p68) The heart of the Kremlin is **Sobornaya ploshchad**, surrounded by magnificent buildings. Assumption Cathedral stands on the northern side, with five golden helmet domes and four semicircular gables facing the square. As the focal church of prerevolutionary Russia, it is the burial place of most of the Russian Orthodox Church heads from the 1320s to 1700. The tombs are against the north, west and south walls.

The cathedral was built between 1475 and 1479 after the Bolognese architect Aristotle Fioravanti had toured Novgorod, Suzdal and Vladimir to acquaint himself with Russian architecture. His design is based on the As-

MOSCOW IN...

Two Days

Spend a day seeing what makes Moscow famous: **St Basil's Cathedral**, **Lenin's Mausoleum** and the **Kremlin**. Allow a few hours in the afternoon to gawk at the gold and gems in the **Armoury**. In the evening, attend an opera at the **Bolshoi Theatre** or dine like a tsar at **Café Pushkin**.

On your second day, admire the art and architecture at **Novodevichy Convent**, then head next door to the eponymous **cemetery**, where many famous political and cultural figures are laid to rest. In the afternoon, make your way across the river to Kievsky vokzal, where you can hop on board a **river cruise** along the Moscow River.

Four Days

Art lovers should spend their third day at the **Tretyakov Gallery**, housing a world-class collection of Russian art. In the late afternoon, head to whimsical **Art Muzeon Sculpture Park** and fun-filled **Gorky Park**, stopping for a drink at **Chaikhona No 1**. In the evening, wander around the former **Red October** factory for drinks, dinner and late-night dancing.

Reserve the morning for shopping at the **Vernisage market** at Izmaylovo, crammed with souvenir stalls. Afterwards, head over to **Izmaylovsky Park** for a picnic and a walk in the woods.

sumption Cathedral at Vladimir, with some Western features.

In 1812 French troops used the cathedral as a stable, looting 295kg of gold and over 5 tonnes of silver, although much of it was recovered.

The church closed in 1918. However, according to some accounts, when the Nazis were on the outskirts of Moscow in 1941, Stalin secretly ordered a service in the Assumption Cathedral to protect the city from the enemy. The cathedral was officially returned to the Church in 1989, but still operates as a museum.

A striking 1660s **fresco** of the Virgin Mary faces Sobornaya pl, above the door once used for royal processions. The visitors' entrance is at the western end, and the interior is unusually bright and spacious, full of warm golds, reds and blues.

The tent-roofed wooden throne near the south wall was made in 1551 for Ivan the Terrible; it's commonly called the **Throne of Monomakh** because of its carved scenes from the career of 12th-century grand prince, Vladimir Monomakh of Kyiv.

Iconostasis

The iconostasis dates from 1652, although its lowest level contains some older icons, among them (second from the right) *Saviour with the Angry Eye* (Spas Yaroe Oko) from the 1340s. On the left of the central door, the *Virgin of Vladimir* (Vladimirskaya Bogomater) is an early-15th-century Rublyov-school copy of Russia's most revered image; the 12th-century original, *Vladimir Icon of the Mother of God,* which stood in the Assumption Cathedral from the 1480s to 1930, is now in the Tretyakov Gallery. One of the oldest Russian icons, the 12th-century red-clothed *St George* (Svyatoy Georgy) from Novgorod, is positioned by the north wall.

Murals

Most of the existing murals on the cathedral walls were painted on a gilt base in the 1640s, but three grouped together on the south wall – *The Apocalypse* (Apokalipsis), *The Life of Metropolitan Pyotr* (Zhitie Mitropolita Petra) and *All Creatures Rejoice in Thee* (O tebe Raduetsya) – are attributed to Dionysius and his followers, the cathedral's original 15th-century mural painters.

Church of the Deposition of the Robe CHURCH

(Церковь Ризположения; Map p68) This delicate little single-domed church, found beside the west door of the Assumption Cathedral, was built between 1484 and 1486 by masons from the town of Pskov. As it was the private chapel of the patriarch, it was built in exclusively Russian style, and the frescoes on the pillars depict the church metropolitans and Moscow princes over the centuries. The church now houses an exhibition of 15th- to 17th-century woodcarvings.

Ivan the Great Bell Tower LANDMARK

(Колокольня Ивана Великого; Map p68; ☎495-697 0349; www.belltower.lagutin.ru; admission R500; ⏲10am, 11.15am, 1.30pm & 2.45pm) With its two golden domes rising above the eastern side of Sobornaya pl, the Ivan the Great Bell Tower is the Kremlin's tallest structure – a landmark visible from 30km away. Before the 20th century it was forbidden to build any higher than this tower in Moscow.

Its history dates back to the Church of Ioann Lestvichnik Under the Bells, built on this site in 1329 by Ivan I. In 1505 the Italian Marco Bono designed a new belfry, originally with only two octagonal tiers beneath a drum and a dome. In 1600 Boris Godunov raised it to 81m.

The building's central section, with a gilded single dome and a 65-tonne bell, dates from between 1532 and 1542. The tent-roofed annexe, next to the belfry, was commissioned by Patriarch Filaret in 1642 and bears his name.

Ivan the Great is the site of the Kremlin's newest exhibit, a multimedia presentation of the architectural history of the complex. Using architectural fragments and electronic projections, the exhibit illustrates how the Kremlin has changed since the 12th century. Special attention is given to individual churches within the complex, including several churches that no longer exist.

The 45-minute tour ends with a 137-step climb to the top of the tall tower, yielding an amazing (and unique!) view of Sobornaya pl, with the Church of Christ the Saviour and the Moskva-City skyscrapers in the distance.

The price of a ticket to Ivan the Great includes admission to the other churches (not the Armoury), so you don't have to buy an additional ticket to the Kremlin grounds.

Tsar Bell & Cannon LANDMARK

(Map p68) Beside the bell tower, not inside it, stands the **Tsar Bell** (Царь-колокол), the world's biggest bell. Sadly, this 202-tonne monster never rang. In a 1701 fire, an earlier 130-tonne version fell from its belfry and

Kremlin & Kitay Gorod

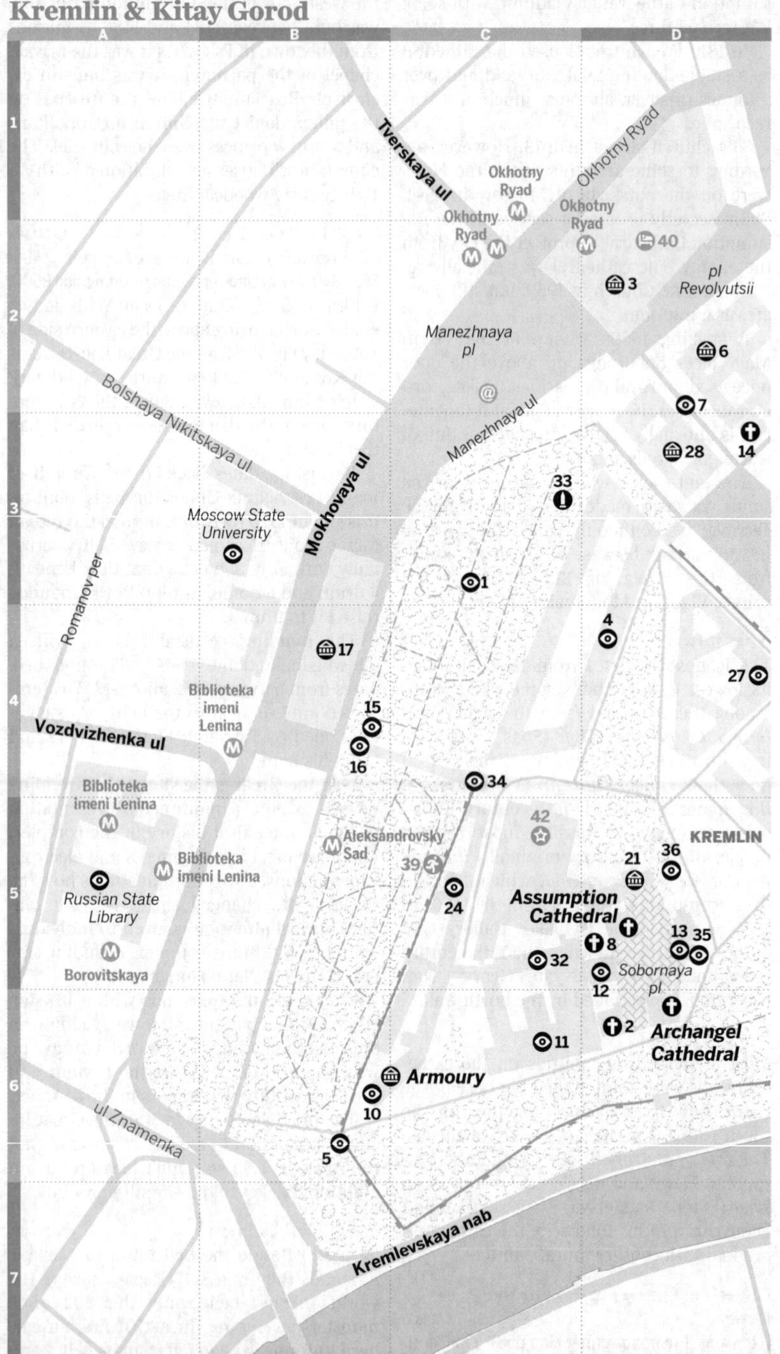

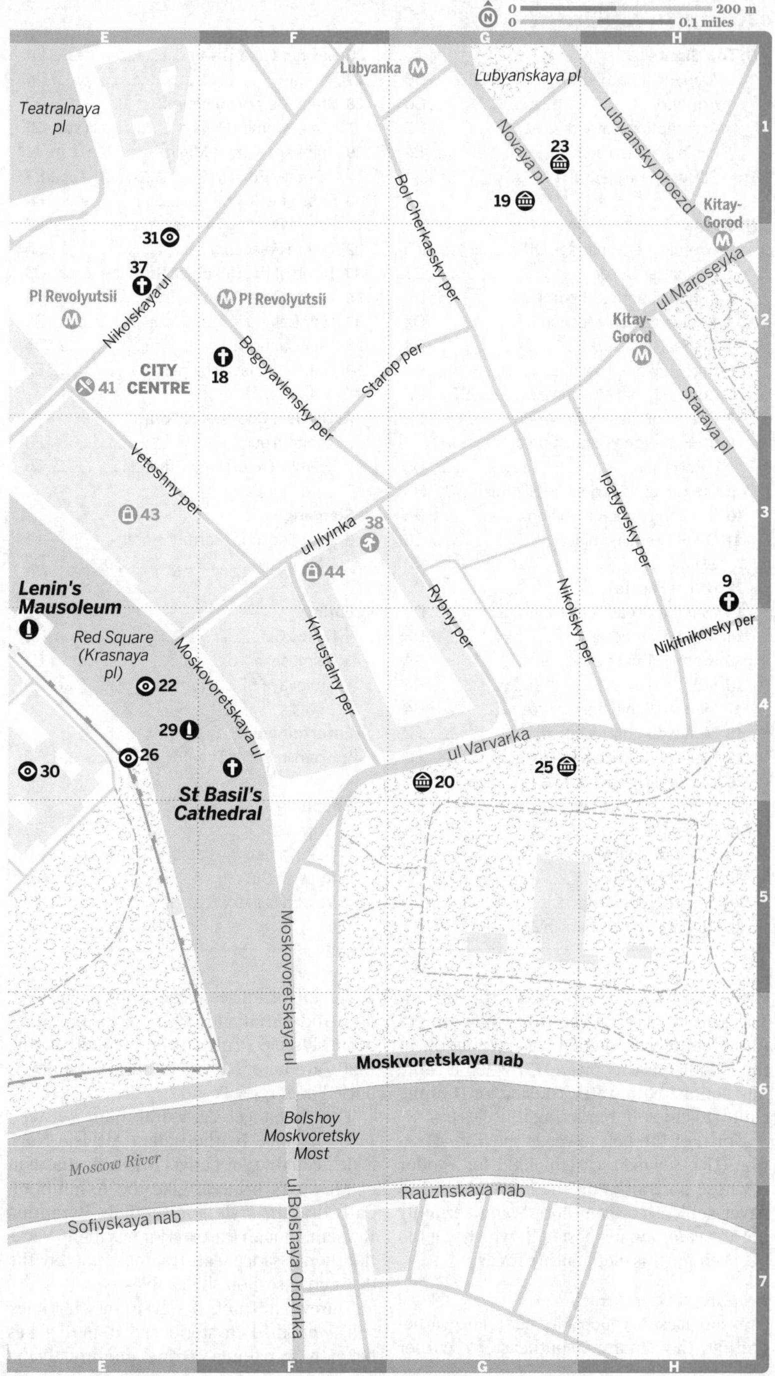

0 200 m
0 0.1 miles
E
F
G
H
Lubyanka
Lubyanskaya pl
Teatralnaya pl
Novaya pl
Lubyansky proezd
23
19
Bol Cherkassky per
Kitay-Gorod
31
37
Nikolskaya ul
Pl Revolyutsii
Pl Revolyutsii
ul Maroseyka
Kitay-Gorod
18
Bogoyavlensky per
Starop per
CITY CENTRE
41
Staraya pl
Vetoshny per
Ipatyevsky per
43
38
ul Ilyinka
44
Lenin's Mausoleum
Rybny per
Nikolsky per
9
Nikitnikovsky per
Red Square (Krasnaya pl)
Khrustalny per
Moskvoretskaya ul
22
29
ul Varvarka
26
25
30
20
St Basil's Cathedral
Moskvoretskaya ul
Moskvoretskaya nab
Bolshoy Moskvoretsky Most
Moscow River
Rauzhskaya nab
Sofiyskaya nab
ul Bolshaya Ordynka
1
2
3
4
5
6
7

Kremlin & Kitay Gorod

Top Sights
Archangel Cathedral D6
Armoury C6
Assumption Cathedral D5
Lenin's Mausoleum E4
St Basil's Cathedral F4

Sights
Kremlin Left-Luggage Office....... (see 16)
1 Alexander Garden........ C3
2 Annunciation Cathedral D6
3 Archaeological Museum D2
4 Arsenal D4
5 Borovitskaya Tower B6
6 Central Lenin Museum D2
7 Chapel of the Iverian Virgin........ D2
8 Church of the Deposition of the Robe........ D5
9 Church of the Trinity in Nikitniki........ H3
10 Diamond Fund Exhibition........ B6
11 Great Kremlin Palace C6
GUM........ (see 43)
12 Hall of Facets D5
13 Ivan the Great Bell Tower........ D5
14 Kazan Cathedral D3
15 Kremlin Ticket Office........ B4
16 Kutafya Tower B4
17 Manezh Exhibition Centre........ B4
18 Monastery of the Epiphany........ F2
19 Moscow City History Museum G1
20 Old English Court........ G4
21 Patriarch's Palace........ D5
22 Place of Skulls........ E4
23 Polytechnical Museum........ G1
24 Poteshny Palace C5
Resurrection Gate .... (see 7)
25 Romanov Chambers in Zaryadie........ G4
26 Saviour Gate Tower E4
27 Senate D4
28 State History Museum........ D3
State Kremlin Palace .... (see 42)
29 Statue of Kuzma Minin & Dmitry Pozharsky........ E4
30 Supreme Soviet........ E4
31 Synod Printing House........ E2
32 Terem Palace........ C5
33 Tomb of the Unknown Soldier C3
34 Trinity Gate Tower C4
35 Tsar Bell D5
36 Tsar Cannon D5
37 Zaikonospassky Monastery E2

Activities, Courses & Tours
38 Capital Tours F3
39 Kremlin Excursions Office C5

Sleeping
40 Four Seasons (Former Hotel Moskva) D2

Eating
Bosco Cafe........ (see 43)
41 Pelmeshka E2
Stolovaya 57 .... (see 43)

Entertainment
42 Kremlin Ballet Theatre........ C5

Shopping
43 GUM E3
Gus-Khrustalny Factory Store .... (see 44)
Russian Gift .... (see 43)
44 Vologda Linen........ F3

shattered; with these remains, the current Tsar Bell was cast in the 1730s for Empress Anna Ioanovna. The bell was cooling off in the foundry casting pit in 1737 when it came into contact with water, causing an 11-tonne chunk to chip off, rendering it useless.

North of the bell tower is the **Tsar Cannon** (Царь-пушка), cast in 1586 for Fyodor I, whose portrait is on the barrel. Shot has never sullied its 89cm bore – and certainly not the cannonballs beside it, which are too big even for this elephantine firearm.

Archangel Cathedral CHURCH
(Архангельский собор; Map p68) The cathedral at the square's southeastern corner was – for centuries – the coronation, wedding and burial church of tsars. The tombs of all Muscovy's rulers from the 1320s to the 1690s are here, bar one – Boris Godunov is buried at Sergiev Posad.

The Archangel Cathedral, built between 1505 and 1508 by the Italian Alevisio Novi, is dedicated to Archangel Michael, guardian of Moscow's princes. Like the Assumption Cathedral, its style is essentially Byzantine Russian, though the exterior has many Venetian Renaissance features, most notably the distinctive scallop-shell gables.

Tsarevitch Dmitry – Ivan the Terrible's son, who died mysteriously in 1591 – lies beneath a painted **stone canopy**. Ivan's own tomb is out of sight behind the iconostasis, along with those of his other sons: Ivan (whom he killed) and Fyodor (who succeeded him). From Peter the Great onwards, emperors and empresses were buried in St Petersburg; the exception was Peter II, who died in Moscow in 1730 and is buried here.

During restorations in the 1950s, 17th-century **murals** were uncovered. The south wall depicts many of those buried here, and on the pillars are some of their predecessors, including Andrei Bogolyubsky, Prince Daniil and his father, Alexander Nevsky.

Annunciation Cathedral CHURCH

(Благовещенский собор; Map p68) Dating from 1489, the Annunciation Cathedral at the southwest corner of Sobornaya pl contains the celebrated icons of master painter Theophanes the Greek. Built by Pskov masters, the cathedral was the royal family's private chapel. Originally, it had just three domes and an open gallery around three sides. Ivan the Terrible added six more domes and chapels at each corner, enclosed the gallery and gilded the roof.

Ivan's fourth marriage disqualified him under Orthodox law from entering the church proper, so he had the southern arm of the gallery converted into the **Archangel Gabriel Chapel**, from which he could watch services through a grille. The chapel has a colourful iconostasis dating from its consecration in 1564, and an exhibition of icons.

Many of the murals in the gallery date from the 1560s. Among them are the *Capture of Jericho* in the porch, *Jonah and the Whale* in the northern arm, and the *Tree of Jesus* on the ceiling.

The cathedral's small central part has a lovely jasper floor, and the 16th-century frescoes include Russian princes on the north pillar and Byzantine emperors on the south, with Apocalypse scenes above both.

Iconostasis

The real treasure is the iconostasis, where restorers in the 1920s uncovered early-15th-century icons by three of the greatest medieval Russian artists.

Theophanes likely painted most of the six icons at the right-hand end of the *deesis* row, the biggest of the six tiers of the iconostasis. Left to right are the *Virgin Mary, Christ Enthroned, St John the Baptist,* the *Archangel Gabriel,* the *Apostle Paul* and *St John Chrysostom*. Theophanes' icons are distinguished by his mastery at portraying visible pathos in facial expressions.

Archangel Michael is ascribed to Andrei Rublyov, who may also have painted the adjacent *St Peter*. Rublyov is also reckoned to be the artist of the first, second, sixth and seventh (and probably the third and fifth) icons from the left of the festival row, above the *deesis* row. The seven at the right-hand end are attributed to Prokhor of Gorodets.

Archaeology Exhibit

The basement – which remains from the previous 14th-century cathedral on this site – contains a fascinating exhibit on the **Archaeology of the Kremlin**. The artefacts date from the 12th to 14th centuries, showing the growth of Moscow during this period.

Hall of Facets & Terem Palace HISTORICAL BUILDING

(Map p68) On the western side of the square, named after its facing Italian Renaissance stone, is the square **Hall of Facets** (Грановитая палата). Its upper floor housed the tsar's throne room, the scene of banquets and ceremonies, and was reached by external staircases from the square below.

The 16th- and 17th-century **Terem Palace** (Теремной дворец) is the most splendid of all the Kremlin palaces. Catch a glimpse of its sumptuous cluster of golden domes and chequered roof behind and above the Church of the Deposition of the Robe.

Both the Hall of Facets and Terem Palace are closed to the public.

Saviour Gate Tower HISTORICAL BUILDING

(Спасская башня; Map p68) The Saviour Gate Tower is the Kremlin's 'official' exit onto Red Square. The current clock dates from the 1850s. Hauling 3m hands and weighing 25 tonnes, the clock takes up three of the tower's 10 levels. Its melodic chime sounds every 15 minutes across Red Square and across the country (on the radio).

Great Kremlin Palace HISTORICAL BUILDING

(Большой Кремлёвский дворец; Map p68) Between the Armoury and the Annunciation Cathedral stretches the 700-room Great Kremlin Palace, built as an imperial residence between 1838 and 1849. Now it is an official residence of the Russian president and is used for state visits and receptions. It's not open to the public.

Armoury MUSEUM

(Оружейная палата; Map p68; adult/student R700/250; ⌚10am, noon, 2.30pm & 4.30pm;

WANT MORE?

For in-depth information, reviews and recommendations at your fingertips, head to the Apple App Store to purchase Lonely Planet's *Moscow City Guide* iPhone app.

Alternatively, head to **Lonely Planet** (www.lonelyplanet.com/russia/moscow) for planning advice, author recommendations, traveller reviews and insider tips.

Ⓜ Aleksandrovsky Sad) In the Kremlin's southwestern corner is the Armoury, a numbingly opulent collection of treasures accumulated over centuries by the Russian state and Church. Tickets – which specify a time of entry – can be purchased 45 minutes in advance.

Here you can see the renowned **Fabergé eggs** made from precious metals and jewels by the St Petersburg jewellers. The tsar and tsarina traditionally exchanged these gifts each year at Easter. Most famous is the Grand Siberian Railway egg, with gold train, platinum locomotive and ruby headlamp, created to commemorate the completion of the Moscow–Vladivostok line.

The **royal regalia** includes the joint coronation throne of boy tsars Peter the Great and his half-brother, Ivan V (with a secret compartment from which Regent Sofia prompted them), as well as the 800-diamond throne of Tsar Alexey, Peter's father. The gold Cap of Monomakh – jewel-studded and sable-trimmed – was worn for two centuries of coronations until 1682.

Among the **coaches** is the sleigh that Elizabeth rode from St Petersburg to Moscow for her coronation, pulled by 23 horses at a time.

Diamond Fund Exhibition MUSEUM

(Алмазный фонд России; Map p68; www.almazi.net; admission R500; ⌚10am-1pm & 2-5pm Fri-Wed; Ⓜ Aleksandrovsky Sad) If the Armoury doesn't sate your diamond lust, there's more in the separate Diamond Fund Exhibition; it's in the same building as the Armoury. The lavish collection shows off the precious stones and jewellery garnered by tsars and empresses over the centuries, including the largest sapphire in the world. The highlight is the 190-carat diamond given to Catherine the Great by her lover Grigory Orlov. It is possible to check out the Diamond Fund without paying for a ticket to enter the Kremlin. Head to Borovitskaya Tower at the far southern end of the Alexander Garden: the guards look intimidating but they should let you through if you insist you are going to the Diamond Fund. Purchase tickets at the entrance to the exhibition.

Alexander Garden GARDEN

(Александровский сад; Map p68) The first public park in Moscow, Alexander Garden sits along the Kremlin's western wall. Colourful flower beds and impressive Kremlin views make it a favourite strolling spot for Muscovites and tourists alike.

At the north end is the **Tomb of the Unknown Soldier** (Могила неизвестного солдата; Map p68), where newlyweds bring flowers and have their pictures taken. The tomb contains the remains of a soldier who died in December 1941 at km41 of Leningradskoe sh (the nearest the Nazis came to Moscow). The inscription reads, 'Your name is unknown, your deeds immortal', along with an eternal flame and other inscriptions listing the Soviet hero cities of WWII, honouring 'those who fell for the motherland' between 1941 and 1945. The changing of the guard happens every hour.

RED SQUARE

Immediately outside the Kremlin's northeastern wall is the celebrated **Red Square** (Красная площадь; Map p68; Krasnaya pl; Ⓜ Ploshchad Revolyutsii), the 400m-by-150m area of cobbles that is at the very heart of Moscow. Commanding the square from the southern end is St Basil's Cathedral. This panorama never fails to send the heart aflutter, especially at night.

Red Square used to be a market square adjoining the merchants' area in Kitay Gorod. It has always been a place where occupants of the Kremlin choose to congregate, celebrate and castigate for all the people to see. Soviet rulers chose Red Square for their military parades; and nowadays it's the location for concerts, festivals and cultural events.

Incidentally, the name 'Krasnaya ploshchad' has nothing to do with communism: *krasny* in old Russian meant 'beautiful' and only in the 20th century did it come to mean 'red', too.

Enter Red Square through the **Resurrection Gate** (Ворота Воскресеня; Map p68). Rebuilt in 1995, it's an exact copy of the original completed on this site in 1680, with its twin red towers topped by green tent spires.

The first gateway was destroyed in 1931 because Stalin considered it an impediment to the parades and demonstrations held in Red Square. Within the gateway is the bright **Chapel of the Iverian Virgin** (Map p68), originally built in the late 18th century to house the icon of the same name.

St Basil's Cathedral CHURCH

(Собор Василия Блаженного; Map p68; www.saintbasil.ru; adult/student R250/50; 11am-5pm; M Ploshchad Revolyutsii) No picture can prepare you for the crazy confusion of colours and shapes that is St Basil's Cathedral, technically Intercession Cathedral. This ultimate symbol of Russia was created between 1555 and 1561 (replacing an existing church on the site) to celebrate the capture of Kazan by Ivan the Terrible. Its design is the culmination of a wholly Russian style that had been developed building wooden churches.

The cathedral's apparent anarchy of shapes hides a comprehensible plan of nine main chapels: the tall, tent-roofed one in the centre; four big, octagonal-towered ones, topped with the four biggest domes; and four smaller ones in between.

The misnomer 'St Basil's' actually refers only to the northeastern chapel, which was added later. It was built over the grave of the barefoot holy fool, Vasily (Basil) the Blessed, who predicted Ivan's damnation. Vasily, who died while Kazan was under siege, was buried beside the church that St Basil's soon replaced. He was later canonised.

The interior is open to visitors: besides a small **exhibition** on the cathedral itself, it contains lovely frescoed walls and loads of nooks and crannies to explore.

Out the front of St Basil's is a **statue** of Kuzma Minin and Dmitry Pozharsky (Памятник Минину и Пожарскому), the butcher and the prince who together raised and led the army that ejected occupying Poles from the Kremlin in 1612. The round, walled **Place of Skulls** (Лобное место) was reputedly used for public executions. Most famously, this is apparently where Peter the Great executed the traitorous Streltsy, the sharpshooting guardsman who revolted against him in 1682.

FREE **Lenin's Mausoleum** HISTORICAL SITE

(Мавзолей Ленина; Map p68; www.lenin.ru; 10am-1pm Tue-Thu, Sat & Sun; M Ploshchad Revolyutsii) The embalmed body of Vladimir Lenin has lain in the granite tomb on Red

LENIN UNDER GLASS

Red Square is home to the world's most famous mummy, that of Vladimir Lenin. When he died of a massive stroke (on 22 January 1924, aged 53), a long line of mourners patiently gathered in winter's harshness for weeks to glimpse the body as it lay in state. Inspired by the spectacle, Stalin proposed that the father of Soviet communism should continue to serve the cause as a holy relic. So the decision was made to preserve Lenin's corpse for perpetuity, against the vehement protests of his widow, as well as his own expressed desire to be buried next to his mother in St Petersburg.

Boris Zbarsky, a biochemist, and Vladimir Vorobyov, an anatomist, were issued a political order to put a stop to the natural decomposition of the body. The pair worked frantically in a secret laboratory in search of a long-term chemical solution. In the meantime, the body's dark spots were bleached, and the lips and eyes sewn tight. The brain was removed and taken to another secret laboratory, to be sliced and diced by scientists for the next 40 years in the hope of uncovering its hidden genius.

In July 1924 the scientists hit upon a formula to successfully arrest the decaying process, a closely guarded state secret. This necrotic craft was passed on to Zbarsky's son, who ran the Kremlin's covert embalming lab for decades. After the fall of communism, Zbarsky came clean: the body is wiped down every few days, and then, every 18 months, thoroughly examined and submerged in a tub of chemicals, including paraffin wax. The institute has now gone commercial, offering its services and secrets to wannabe immortals for a mere million dollars.

Every so often, politicians express intentions to heed Lenin's request and bury him in St Petersburg, but it usually sets off a furore from the political left as well as more muted objections from Moscow tour operators. It seems that the mausoleum, the most sacred shrine of Soviet communism, and the mummy, the literal embodiment of the Russian revolution, will remain in place for at least several more years.

Square since 1924 (apart from a retreat to Siberia during WWII).

From 1953 to 1961 Lenin shared the tomb with Stalin. In 1961 at the 22nd Party Congress, the esteemed and by then ancient Bolshevik Madame Spiridonova announced that Vladimir Ilych had appeared to her in a dream, insisting that he did not like spending eternity with his successor. With that, Stalin was removed, and given a place of honour immediately behind the mausoleum.

Before joining the queue at the northwestern corner of Red Square, drop your camera and backpack at the left-luggage office in the State History Museum, as you will not be allowed to take them with you. After trouping past the embalmed, oddly waxy figure, emerge from the mausoleum and inspect the burial places along the Kremlin wall of Stalin, Brezhnev and other communist heavy hitters.

State History Museum MUSEUM

(Государственный исторический музей; Map p68; www.shm.ru; Krasnaya pl 1; adult/student R250/80, audio guide R130; ⏲10am-6pm Wed-Sat & Mon, 11am-8pm Sun; Ⓜ Ploshchad Revolyutsii) At the northern end of the square, the State History Museum has an enormous collection covering the whole Russian empire from the Stone Age on. The building, dating from the late 19th century, is itself an attraction – each room is in the style of a different period or region, some with highly decorated walls echoing old Russian churches.

GUM HISTORICAL BUILDING

(ГУМ; Map p68; www.gum.ru; Krasnaya pl 3; ⏲10am-10pm; Ⓜ Ploshchad Revolyutsii) The elaborate 19th-century facade on the northeastern side of Red Square is the Gosudarstvenny Universalny Magazin (State Department Store). GUM once symbolised all that was bad about Soviet shopping: long queues and empty shelves, bar a few drab goods. A remarkable transformation has taken place since *perestroika* and today GUM is a bustling place with more than 1000 fancy shops.

FREE **Kazan Cathedral** CHURCH

(Казанский собор; Map p68; Nikolskaya ul 3; ⏲8am-7pm; Ⓜ Ploshchad Revolyutsii) Opposite the northern end of GUM, the tiny Kazan Cathedral is a 1993 replica. The original was founded in 1636 in thanks for the 1612 expulsion of Polish invaders; for two centuries it housed the *Virgin of Kazan* icon, which supposedly helped to rout the Poles. Three hundred years later the cathedral was completely demolished, allegedly because it impeded the flow of celebrating workers in May Day and Revolution Day parades.

Central Lenin Museum HISTORICAL BUILDING

(Центральный музей Ленина; Map p68; pl Revolyutsii 2; Ⓜ Ploshchad Revolyutsii) Part Russian Revival, part neo-Renaissance, this red-brick beauty was built in the 1890s as the Moscow City Hall. It's better known by its later role, the big daddy of all the Lenin museums, which was closed in 1993 after the White House shootout. Nowadays, it is sometimes used for special exhibits or simply as a backdrop for rows of souvenir kiosks.

Archaeological Museum MUSEUM

(Музей археологии Москвы; Map p68; www.mosmuseum.ru; Manezhnaya pl 1; admission R60; ⏲10am-5.30pm Tue-Sun; Ⓜ Okhotny Ryad) An excavation of Voskresensky most (Voskresensky Bridge), which used to span the Neglinnaya River and commence the road to Tver, uncovered coins, clothing and other artefacts from old Moscow. The museum displaying these treasures is situated in a 7m-deep underground pavilion that was formed during the excavation itself. The entrance is at the base of the Hotel Moskva.

Manezh Exhibition Centre ART GALLERY

(ЦВЗ Манеж; Map p68; Manezhnaya pl; exhibits R200-300; ⏲11am-8pm Tue-Sun; Ⓜ Biblioteka im Lenina) The long, low building on the southwestern side of the square is the Manezh Exhibition Centre, housing local art exhibitions.

KITAY GOROD

The narrow old streets east of Red Square are known as Kitay Gorod. It translates as 'Chinatown', but the name actually derives from *kita*, meaning 'wattle', and refers to the palisades that reinforced the earthen ramp erected around this early Kremlin suburb. Kitay Gorod is one of the oldest parts of Moscow, settled in the 13th century as a trade and financial centre.

From the 16th century Kitay Gorod was exclusively the home of merchants and craftsmen, as evidenced by the present-day names of its lanes: Khrustalny (Crystal), Rybny (Fish) and Vetoshny (Rugs). Ul Varvarka has Kitay Gorod's greatest concentration of interesting buildings. They were long dwarfed by the gargantuan Hotel Rossiya, which was finally demolished in 2006. At the time of research, it was still a mystery what would be built in its place.

Starye Polya RUINS

(Старые поля; Map p78; Teatralny proezd; Ⓜ Teatralnaya) Along Teatralnaya proezd, archaeologists uncovered the 16th-century fortified wall that used to surround Kitay Gorod, as well as foundations of the 1493 Trinity Church. Coins, jewellery and tombstones were also excavated at the site. The gated walkway of Tretyakovsky proezd leads into Kitay Gorod.

Lubyanka Prison NOTABLE BUILDING

(Лубянка; Map p78; Lubyanskaya pl; Ⓜ Lubyanka) For several decades the broad square at the top of Teatralny proezd was a chilling symbol of the Komitet Gosudarstvennoy Bezopasnosti (Committee for State Security), better known as the KGB.

In the 1930s the Lubyanka Prison was the feared destination of thousands of victims of Stalin's purges, but today the grey building is the headquarters of the KGB's successor, the FSB (Federal Security Service). The building is not open to the public.

From 1926 to 1990 Lubyanskaya pl was known as Dzerzhinskogo pl, after Felix Dzerzhinsky, founder of the Cheka (the KGB's ancestor). A tall statue of Dzerzhinsky that dominated the square was memorably removed by angry crowds when the 1991 coup collapsed. Now you can see the statue in all its (somewhat reduced) glory in the Art Muzeon Sculpture Park, where it stands among others fallen from grace. The much humbler **Memorial to the Victims of Totalitarianism** (Памятник жертвам тоталитарного режима) stands in the little garden on the square's southeastern side. This single stone slab comes from the territory of an infamous 1930s labour camp on the Solovetsky Islands in the White Sea.

Zaikonospassky Monastery MONASTERY

(Заиконоспасский монастырь; Map p68; Nikolskaya ul 7-9; Ⓜ Ploshchad Revolyutsii) This monastery was founded by Boris Godunov in 1600, although the church was built in 1660. The name means 'Behind the Icon Stall', a reference to the busy icon trade that once took place here. On the orders of Tsar Alexey, the Likhud brothers – scholars of Greek – opened the Slavonic Greek and Latin Academy on the monastery premises in 1687.

Monastery of the Epiphany MONASTERY

(Богоявленский монастырь; Map p68; Bogoyavlensky per 2; Ⓜ Ploshchad Revolyutsii) This monastery is the second oldest in Moscow; it was founded in 1296 by Prince Daniil, son of Alexander Nevsky. The current **Epiphany Cathedral** was constructed in the 1690s in the Moscow baroque style.

Synod Printing House HISTORICAL BUILDING

(Печатный двор Синод; Map p68; Nikolskaya ul 15; Ⓜ Ploshchad Revolyutsii) The ornate green-and-white building at No 15 is the old Synod Printing House. It was here in 1563 that Ivan Fyodorov reputedly produced Russia's first printed book, *The Apostle*. (The first Russian newspaper, *Vedomosti*, was also printed here, in 1703.)

Romanov Chambers in Zaryadie MUSEUM

(Палаты Романовых в Зарядье; Map p68; ul Varvarka 10; admission R150; ⏲10am-5pm Thu-Mon, 11am-6pm Wed; Ⓜ Kitay-Gorod) The small, though interesting, Romanov Chambers in Zaryadie is devoted to the lives of the Romanov family, who were mere boyars before they became tsars. The house was built by Nikita Romanov, whose grandson Mikhail later became the first tsar of the 300-year Romanov dynasty. Enter from the back.

Church of the Trinity in Nikitniki CHURCH

(Церковь Троицы в Никитниках; Map p68; Ipatyevsky per; Ⓜ Kitay-Gorod) Opposite St George's Church, Ipatyevsky per leads to the 1630s Church of the Trinity in Nikitniki, one of Moscow's finest. The church's onion domes and lovely tiers of red-and-white spade gables rise from a square tower, while the interior is covered with 1650s gospel frescoes by Simon Ushakov and others.

Old English Court MUSEUM

(Палаты старого Английского двора; Map p68; www.mosmuseum.ru; ul Varvarka 4a; admission R40; ⏲11am-6pm Tue-Sun; Ⓜ Kitay-Gorod) The reconstructed 16th-century Old English Court, white with peaked wooden roofs, was the residence of England's first diplomats and traders sent to Russia.

Moscow City History Museum MUSEUM

(Музей истории города Москвы; Map p68; www.mosmuseum.ru; Novaya pl 12; admission R60; Ⓜ Lubyanka) The little Moscow City History Museum shows how the city has spread from its starting point at the Kremlin.

Polytechnical Museum MUSEUM

(Политехнический музей; Map p68; www.polymus.ru; Novaya pl 3/4; adult/child R150/70; ⏲10am-6pm Tue-Sun; Ⓜ Lubyanka) Across the street from the Moscow City History Museum, the huge Polytechnical Museum covers the history of Russian science, technology and industry. Descriptions are in Russian only.

TVERSKOY DISTRICT

The streets around Tverskaya ul comprise the vibrant Tverskoy district, characterised by old architecture and new commerce. Small lanes such as Kamergersky per and Stoleshnikov per are among Moscow's trendiest places to sip a coffee or a beer and watch the big-city bustle. Now restored to its prerevolutionary fashionable status, ul Petrovka constitutes Moscow's glossiest central shopping area.

Teatralnaya ploshchad SQUARE

(Театральная площадь; Map p78; Ⓜ Teatralnaya) 'Theatre Sq' opens out on both sides of Okhotny Ryad. The northern half of the square is dominated by the historic **Bolshoi Theatre** (Большой театр), where Tchaikovsky's *Swan Lake* premiered – unsuccessfully – in 1877. Across ul Petrovka from the 'big' Bolshoi is the 'small' Maly Theatre, a drama establishment, while on the southern half of Teatralnaya pl is the tiled, sculptured facade of the luxurious Hotel Metropol.

Upper St Peter Monastery MONASTERY

(Петровский монастырь; Map p78; cnr ul Petrovka & Petrovsky bul; ⌚8am-8pm; Ⓜ Chekhovskaya) The Upper St Peter Monastery was founded in the 1380s as part of an early defensive ring around Moscow. The grounds are pleasant in a peaceful, near-deserted way. The loveliest structure is the brick **Cathedral of Metropolitan Pyotr** (Собор Митрополита Петра) in the middle of the grounds, restored with a shingle roof. (When Peter the Great ousted the Regent Sofia in 1690, his mother was so pleased she built him this church.)

Moscow Museum of Modern Art MUSEUM

(ММОМА, Московский музей современного искусства; Map p78; www.mmoma.ru; ul Petrovka 25; adult/student R150/100; ⌚noon-8pm; Ⓜ Chekhovskaya) A pet project of the ubiquitous Zurab Tsereteli, the Moscow Museum of Modern Art is housed in a classical 18th-century merchant's home. It contains 20th-century paintings, sculptures and graphics, including some works by Marc Chagall, Natalia Goncharova, Vasily Kandinsky and Kasimir Malevich. Don't bypass the whimsical sculpture garden in the courtyard.

Tverskaya ploshchad SQUARE

(Тверская площадь; Map p78; Ⓜ Okhotny Ryad) A **statue** (Памятник Юрию Долгорукому) of the founder of Moscow, Yury Dolgoruky, presides over this prominent square near the bottom of Tverskaya ul. So does Mayor Sergei Sobyanin, as the buffed-up five-storey building opposite is the **Moscow mayor's office**. Many ancient churches are hidden in the backstreets, including the 17th-century **Church of SS Cosmas & Damian** (Церковь святых Косьмы и Дамиана) and **Church of the Resurrection** (Церковь Воскресения).

Church of the Nativity of the Virgin in Putinki CHURCH

(Церковь Рождества Богородицы в Путинках; Map p78; ul Malaya Dmitrovka 4; Ⓜ Pushkinskaya) When this church was completed in 1652, the Patriarch Nikon responded by banning tent roofs like the ones featured here. Apparently, he considered such architecture too Russian, too secular and too far re-

MAMONTOV'S METROPOL

The **Hotel Metropol** (Гостиница Метрополь; Map p78), among Moscow's finest examples of art nouveau architecture, is another contribution by famed philanthropist and patron of the arts, Savva Mamontov. The decorative panel on the hotel's central facade, facing Teatralny proezd, is based on a sketch by the artist Mikhail Vrubel. It depicts the legend of the Princess of Dreams, in which a troubadour falls in love with a kind and beautiful princess and travels across the seas to find her. He falls ill during the voyage and is near death when he finds his love. The princess embraces him, but he dies in her arms. Naturally, the princess reacts to his death by renouncing her worldly life. The ceramic panels were made at the pottery workshop at Mamontov's Abramtsevo estate.

The ceramic work on the side of the hotel facing Teatralnaya pl is by the artist Alexander Golovin. The script was originally a quote from Nietzsche: 'Again the same story: when you build a house you notice that you have learned something'. During the Soviet era, these wise words were replaced with something more appropriate for the time: 'Only the dictatorship of the proletariat can liberate mankind from the oppression of capitalism'. Lenin, of course.

moved from the Church's Byzantine roots. Fortunately, the Church of the Nativity has survived to grace this corner near Pushkinskaya pl.

Vasnetsov House-Museum MUSEUM
(Дом-музей Васнецова; www.tretyakovgallery.ru; per Vasnetsova 13; admission R100; ⌚10am-5pm Wed-Sun; Ⓜ Sukharevskaya) Viktor Vasnetsov (1848–1926) was a Russian-revivalist painter and architect famous for his historical paintings with mystical and fairy-tale subjects. Fronted by a colourful gate, his self-designed home is in neo-Russian style, still filled with the original wooden furniture, tiled stove and many of the artist's paintings. The attic studio, where he once painted, is now hung with paintings depicting Baba Yaga and other characters from Russian fairy tales. From Sukharevskaya metro station, walk three blocks west along the Garden Ring, turn right on Meshchanskaya ul and left on per Vasnetsova.

Glinka Museum of Musical Culture MUSEUM
(Музей музыкальный культуры Глинки; Map p78; www.museum.ru/glinka; ul Fadeeva 4; admission R200; ⌚noon-7pm Tue-Sun; Ⓜ Mayakovskaya) Musicologists will be amazed by the massive collection of musical instruments at the Glinka Museum of Musical Culture. The museum holds over 3000 instruments – handcrafted works of art – from the Caucasus to the Far East. Recordings accompany many of the rarer instruments (there is no info in English, but at least visitors can experience what the instruments sound like).

Gulag History Museum MUSEUM
(Государственный музей истории ГУЛАГа; Map p78; www.museum-gulag.narod.ru; ul Petrovka 16; adult/student R100/20, tour R800; ⌚11am-7pm Tue-Sat; Ⓜ Chekhovskaya) In the midst of all the swanky shops, an archway leads to a courtyard strung with barbed wire and hanging with portraits of political prisoners. This is the entrance to the Gulag History Museum. Guides dressed like camp guards describe the vast network of labour camps that existed in the former Soviet Union and recount the horrors of camp life. The museum also serves as a memorial to the millions of victims of the system.

Contemporary History Museum MUSEUM
(Музей современной истории России; Map p78; www.sovr.ru; Tverskaya ul 21; adult/student R100/70; ⌚10am-6pm Tue-Sun; Ⓜ Pushkinskaya) North of Pushkinskaya pl, the Contemporary History Museum provides an account of Soviet history from the 1905 and 1917 revolutions up to the 1980s. The highlight is the extensive collection of propaganda posters, in addition to all the Bolshevik paraphernalia.

Armed Forces Museum MUSEUM
(Центральный музей Вооруженных Сил; Map p56; www.cmaf.ru; ul Sovetskoy Armii 2; admission R75; ⌚10am-4.30pm Wed-Sun; Ⓜ Novoslobodskaya) Covering the history of the Soviet and Russian military since 1917, the Armed Forces Museum occupies 24 exhibit halls, plus open-air exhibits. It houses more than 800,000 military items, including uniforms, medals and weapons. Among the highlights are remainders of an American U2 spy plane (brought down in the Urals in 1960) and the victory flag raised over the Reichstag in 1945. Unfortunately, descriptions are in Russian only, but you can book an English-language tour for R1500. Take trolleybus 69 (or walk) 1.25km west from the Novoslobodskaya metro.

Dostoevsky House-Museum MUSEUM
(Дом-музей Достоевского; Map p56; ul Dostoevskogo 2; admission R50; ⌚11am-6pm Thu, Sat & Sun, 2-7pm Wed & Fri; Ⓜ Novoslobodskaya) Although Dostoevsky is more closely associated with St Petersburg, the renowned author was actually born in Moscow. On the grounds of the Marinsky Hospital, his family lived in an apartment, which is now the Dostoevsky House-Museum. The family's flat has been re-created according to the written descriptions of Fyodor's brother.

Museum of Decorative & Folk Art MUSEUM
(Всероссийский музей декоративно-прикладного и народного искусства; Map p78; www.vmdpri.ru; Delegatskaya ul 3 & 5; admission R200; ⌚10am-6pm Wed-Sun; Ⓜ Tsvetnoy Bulvar) Just beyond the Garden Ring, the Museum of Decorative & Folk Art has a good two-room *palekh* (painted lacquerwork) collection, as well as lots of regional folk art.

PRESNYA DISTRICT

Presnya is Moscow's largest administrative district, encompassing some of the capital's oldest neighbourhoods as well as its newest development. Inside the Garden Ring, Presnya includes lovely residential areas, chock full with evocative architecture, historic parks and fantastic drinking and dining spots. The area around Patriarch's Ponds has emerged as a dining hot spot, with restaurants lined up along Spiridonovsky per.

Tverskoy & Inner Presnya

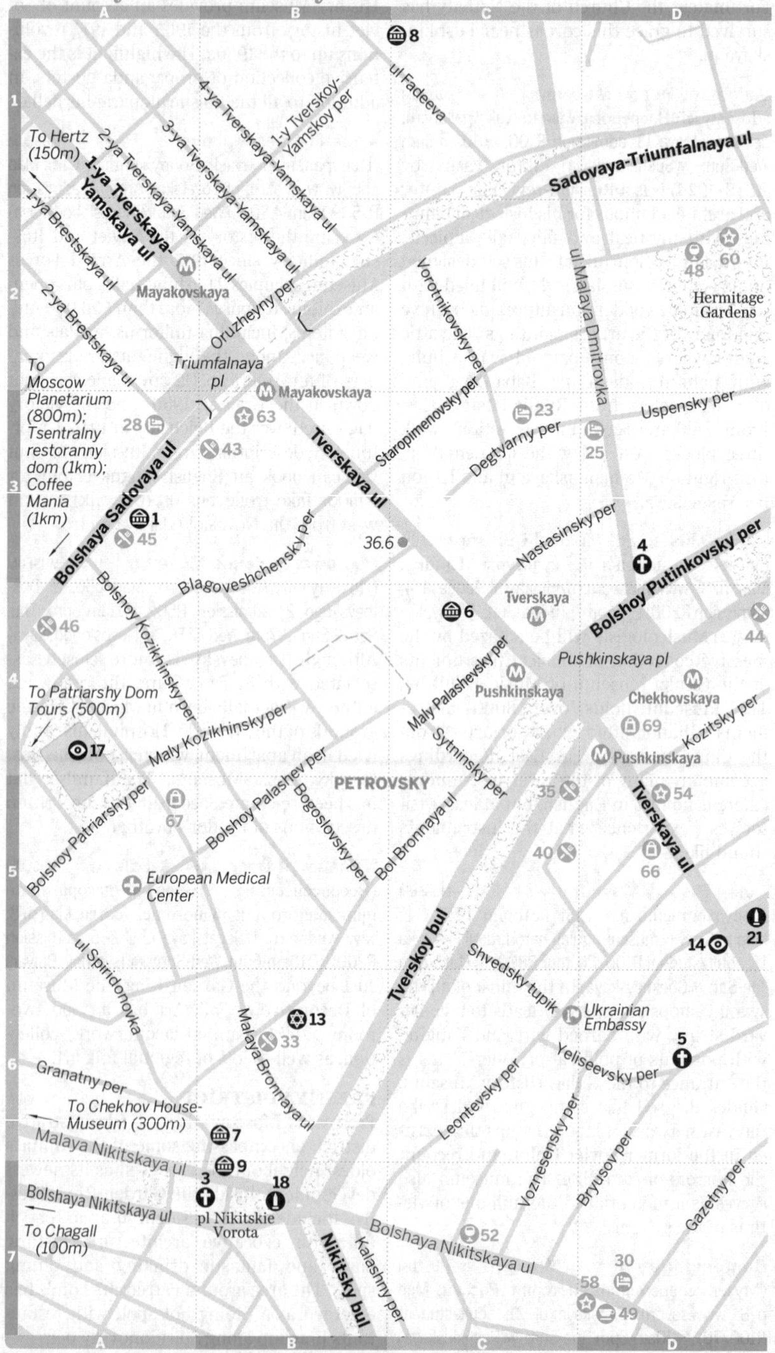

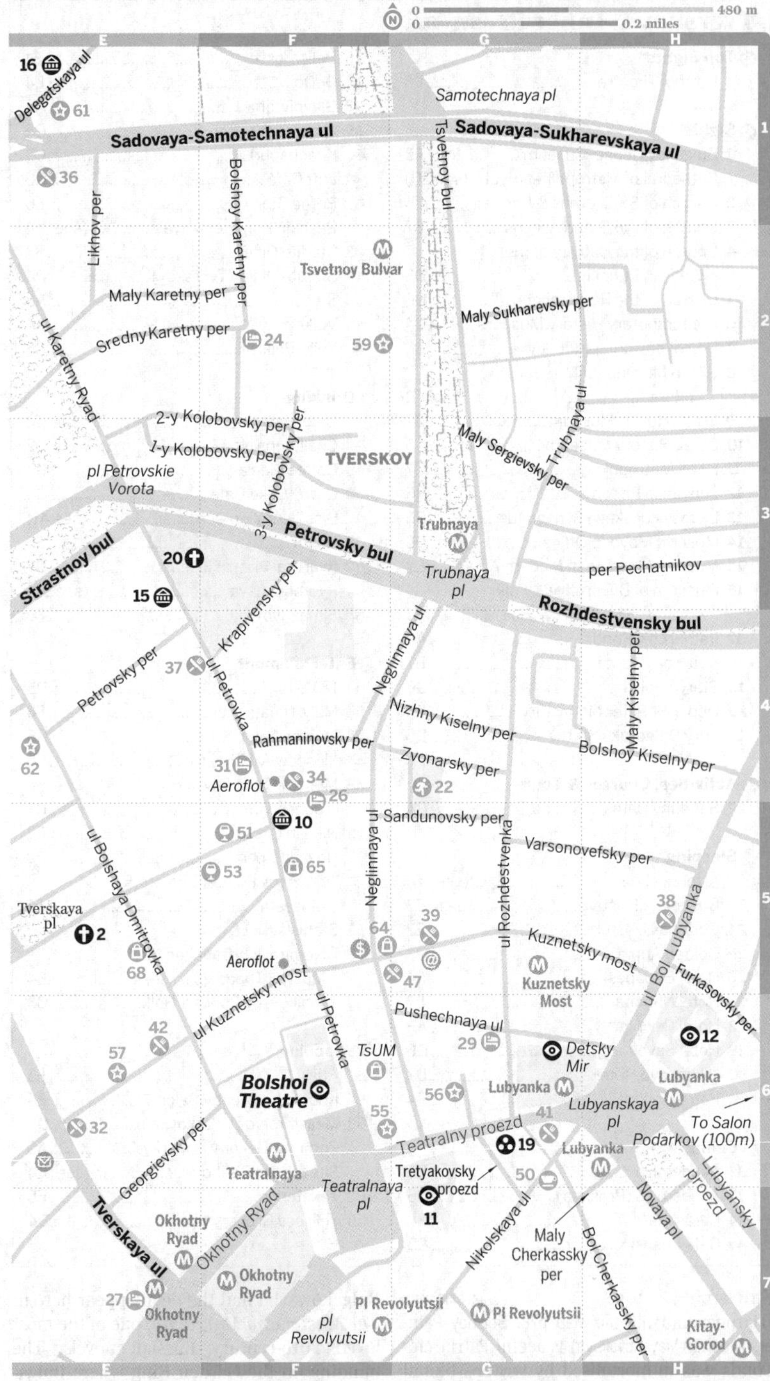

0 480 m
0 0.2 miles
Samotechnaya pl
Sadovaya-Samotechnaya ul
Sadovaya-Sukharevskaya ul
Delegatskaya ul
Tsvetnoy bul
Bolshoy Karetny per
Likhov per
Tsvetnoy Bulvar
Maly Karetny per
Sredny Karetny per
Maly Sukharevsky per
ul Karetny Ryad
2-y Kolobovsky per
1-y Kolobovsky per
3-y Kolobovsky per
TVERSKOY
Maly Sergievsky per
Trubnaya ul
pl Petrovskie Vorota
Strastnoy bul
Petrovsky bul
Trubnaya
Trubnaya pl
per Pechatnikov
Rozhdestvensky bul
Krapivensky per
Petrovsky per
ul Petrovka
Neglinnaya ul
Maly Kiselny per
Nizhny Kiselny per
Bolshoy Kiselny per
Rahmaninovsky per
Zvonarsky per
Aeroflot
Sandunovsky per
ul Rozhdestvenka
Varsonofefsky per
ul Bolshaya Dmitrovka
Tverskaya pl
ul Bol Lubyanka
Kuznetsky most
Furkasovsky per
Aeroflot
ul Kuznetsky most
ul Petrovka
Kuznetsky Most
Pushechnaya ul
Detsky Mir
TsUM
Bolshoi Theatre
Lubyanka
Lubyanka
Lubyanskaya pl
To Salon Podarkov (100m)
Teatralny proezd
Georgievsky per
Lubyanka
Lubyansky proezd
Tretyakovsky proezd
Teatralnaya
Teatralnaya pl
Novaya pl
Okhotny Ryad
Okhotny Ryad
Tverskaya ul
Nikolskaya ul
Maly Cherkassky per
Bol Cherkassky per
Okhotny Ryad
Okhotny Ryad
Pl Revolyutsii
Pl Revolyutsii
pl Revolyutsii
Kitay-Gorod
MOSCOW

Tverskoy & Inner Presnya

Top Sights

Bolshoi Theatre ... F6

Sights

1 Bulgakov House-Museum ... A3
Cathedral of Metropolitan Pyotr . (see 20)
2 Church of SS Cosmas & Damian ... E5
3 Church of the Grand Ascension ... B7
4 Church of the Nativity of the Virgin in Putinki ... D3
5 Church of the Resurrection ... D6
6 Contemporary History Museum ... C4
7 Dom Ikony on Spiridonovka ... B6
8 Glinka Museum of Musical Culture ... C1
9 Gorky House-Museum ... B7
10 Gulag History Museum ... F5
11 Hotel Metropol ... G7
12 Lubyanka Prison ... H6
13 Lyubovicheskaya Synagogue ... B6
14 Moscow Mayor's Office ... D5
15 Moscow Museum of Modern Art ... E3
16 Museum of Decorative & Folk Art ... E1
17 Patriarch's Ponds ... A4
18 Rotunda Fountain ... B7
19 Starye Polya ... G6
20 Upper St Peter Monastery ... E3
21 Yury Dolgoruky Statue ... D5

Activities, Courses & Tours

22 Sanduny Baths ... G4

Sleeping

Artel ... (see 56)
23 Chocolate Hostel ... C3
24 Godzillas Hostel ... F2
25 Golden Apple ... D3
26 Hotel Budapest ... F4
27 Hotel National ... E7
28 Hotel Peking ... A3
29 Hotel Savoy ... G6
30 Nikitskaya Hotel ... D7
31 Petrovka Loft ... F4

Eating

32 Akademiya ... E6
33 Akademiya (Presnya) ... B6
34 Barashka ... F4
35 Café Pushkin ... C5
36 Delicatessen ... E1
37 DoDo ... E4
38 Glavpivtorg ... H5
39 Jagannath ... G5
40 Khachapuri ... C5
41 Loft Café ... G6
42 Prime Star ... E6
Pushkin Konditerskaya ... (see 35)
43 Starlite Diner ... B3
44 Starlite Diner (Tverskoy) ... D4
45 Stolle ... A3
46 Volkonsky ... A4
47 Yolki-Palki ... G5

Drinking

Cafe Mart ... (see 15)
48 Chaikhona No 1 ... D2
49 Coffee Mania ... D7
50 Cup & Cake Cafe ... G6
Dissident Vinoteca ... (see 41)
51 Gogol ... F5
52 Kvartira 44 ... C7
Ryumochnaya ... (see 52)
53 Simachyov ... F5

Entertainment

54 12 Volts ... D5
55 Maly Theatre ... F6
56 Masterskaya ... G6
57 Moscow Art Theatre ... E6
58 Moscow Tchaikovsky Conservatory ... D7
59 Nikulin Circus ... F2
60 Novaya Opera ... D2
61 Obraztsov Puppet Theatre & Museum ... E1
62 Stanislavsky & Nemirovich-Danchenko Musical Theatre ... E4
63 Tchaikovsky Concert Hall ... B3

Shopping

64 Atlas ... F5
65 Khudozhestvenny Salon ... F5
66 Ministerstvo Podarkov ... D5
67 Podarky, Dekor y Podarky ... A5
Simachyov Boutique ... (see 53)
68 Yekaterina ... E5
69 Yeliseev Grocery Store ... D4

Patriarch's Ponds HISTORIC PARK

(Патриаршие пруды; Map p78; Bolshoy Patriarshy per; Ⓜ Mayakovskaya) Peaceful Patriarch's Ponds was immortalised by writer Mikhail Bulgakov, who had the devil appear here in *The Master and Margarita,* one of the most loved 20th-century Russian novels. The building on the Garden Ring where Bulgakov wrote the novel and lived up until his death now contains the **Bulgakov House-Museum** (Дом Булгакова; Map p78; www.dombulgakova.ru; Bolshaya Sadovaya ul 10; admission free; ⏲1-11pm Sun-Thu, to 1am Fri & Sat; Ⓜ Mayakovskaya). The flat itself used to be a hang-out for dissidents and hooligans, but is now off limits. Instead, there is a small exhibition and a funky café on the 1st floor. A black cat hangs out in the courtyard.

White House NOTABLE BUILDING

(Белый дом; Map p82; Krasnopresnenskaya nab 2; Ⓜ Krasnopresnenskaya) The Russian White House was the scene of two crucial episodes in recent Russian history. It was here that Boris Yeltsin rallied the opposition to confound the 1991 hard-line coup, then two years later sent in tanks and troops to blast out conservative rivals. These days, things are relatively stable around the White House, where Prime Minister Putin has his office.

Moskva-City NEIGHBOURHOOD

(Москва-сити; Map p88; Ⓜ Delovoi Tsentr) This strip along the Moscow River is the site of one of Moscow's largest ongoing urban projects, known as Moscow-City. The neighbourhood is truly up-and-coming, with an emphasis on 'up'. Skyscrapers of glass and steel tower 20 stories over the rest of the city, shining like beacons to Moscow's wheelers, dealers and fortune seekers. The 302m Moscow Tower of the 'City of Capitals' building is supposed to be the tallest skyscraper in Europe.

Ice Sculpture Gallery MUSEUM

(Галерея лёдовой скульптуры; Map p88; www.posuda-ice.ru/gallery; Krasnaya Presnya Park; adult/child R470/250; ⏲11am-8pm; Ⓜ Ulitsa 1905 Goda) Ice sculpture has a long history in Russia, but it's not usually a year-round attraction. Until now. Cool off in the first-ever year-round Ice Sculpture Gallery. The price includes a special down vest and warm fuzzy foot-covers to protect you from the −10°C climate. The changing exhibit is small but spectacular – the frozen masterpieces enhanced by colourful lights and dreamy music.

Moscow Planetarium PLANETARIUM

(Планетарий Москвы; off Map p78; www.planetarium-moscow.ru; ul Sadovaya-Kudrinskaya 5; exhibits R350-500; ⏲museum 10am-9pm, theatre 10am-midnight Wed-Mon; Ⓜ Barrikadnaya) The new planetarium shines bigger and brighter than before, expanding in area by more than three times and incorporating all kinds of high-tech gadgetry, interactive exhibits and educational programs. The centrepiece is the Big Star Hall (the biggest in Europe!), with its 25m silver dome roof, a landmark which is visible from the Garden Ring. There are two observatories, the larger of which (aka the Big Observatory) employs Moscow's largest telescope. In addition to the traditional planetary attractions, the new facility includes an innovative interactive exhibit called the Lunarium, where visitors can perform experiments and witness the laws of nature in action.

DON'T MISS

GARAGE CENTRE FOR CONTEMPORARY CULTURE

Pet project of Dasha Zhukova (supermodel and girlfriend of billionaire Roman Abramovich), the **Garage Centre for Contemporary Culture** (GCCC; Map p56; www.garageccc.com; ul Obratsova 19a; admission R200-300; ⏲11am-9pm Mon-Thu, to 10pm Fri-Sun; Ⓜ Novoslobodskaya) is an old bus depot that has been converted into Moscow's largest exhibition hall. It's an incredible space, originally designed in 1926 by constructivist architect Konstantin Melnikov. Since its opening in 2008, the centre has hosted a wide variety of Russian and international artists, including Ilya and Emilia Kabakov, Francesco Vezzoli, Carsten Höller, Mark Rothko and David Lynch. The GCCC stretches the definition of the word 'exhibit', showcasing interior design, performance art, films and fashion. It's two blocks north and two blocks east from Novoslobodskaya or Mendeleevskaya metro station.

Church of the Grand Ascension CHURCH

(Церковь Большого Вознесения; Map p78; Bolshaya Nikitskaya ul; Ⓜ Arbatskaya) In 1831 the poet Alexander Pushkin married Natalya Goncharova in the Church of the Grand Ascension on the western side of pl Nikitskie Vorota. The couple are featured in the **Rotunda Fountain** (Фонтан Ротунда), erected in 1999 to commemorate the 200th anniversary of the poet's birthday. Pl Nikitskie Vorota, where Bolshaya Nikitskaya ul crosses the Boulevard Ring, is named after the Nikitsky Gates in the city walls, which the ring has replaced.

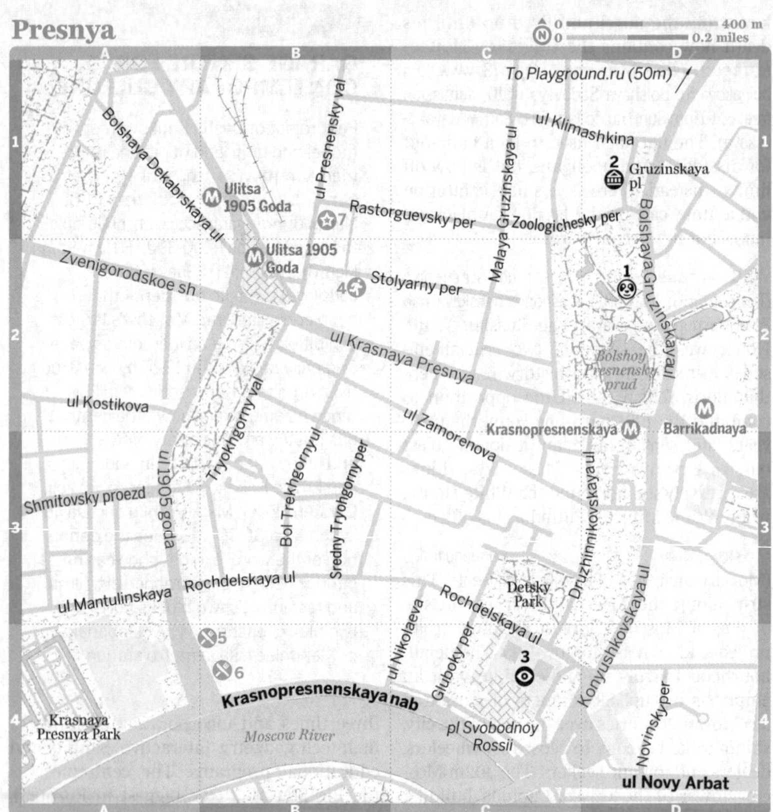

Presnya

Sights

1 Moscow Zoo D2
2 Tsereteli Studio-Museum D1
3 White House C4

Activities, Courses & Tours

4 Krasnopresnenskie Bani B2

Eating

5 Barashka B4
6 Shinok B4

Entertainment

7 Sixteen Tons B1

FREE **Gorky House-Museum** MUSEUM
(Дом-музей Горького; Map p78; Malaya Nikitskaya ul 6/2; ⏲11am-6pm Wed-Sun; Ⓜ Pushkinskaya) Also known as the Ryabushinsky house, the fascinating 1906 art nouveau Gorky House-Museum was designed by Fyodor Shekhtel. Gifted to Maxim Gorky in 1931, the house is a visual fantasy with sculpted doorways, ceiling murals, stained glass, a carved stone staircase and exterior tile work. Besides the fantastic decor, it contains many of Gorky's personal items, including his extensive library.

Dom Ikony on Spiridonovka MUSEUM
(Дом Иконы на Спиридоновке; Map p78; www.dom-ikony.ru; ul Spiridonovka 4; admission R150; ⏲noon-10pm Tue-Sun; Ⓜ Pushkinskaya) The collection of more than 2000 items here includes pieces from the 15th to the 20th century, with many countries represented. The prize is perhaps the 15th-century icon of the Mother of God – Odigitria. Other pieces were part of the collection of the last Russian tsar, Nicholas II.

Tsereteli Studio-Museum MUSEUM
(Музея-мастерская Зураба Церетели; Map p82; www.mmoma.ru; Bolshaya Gruzinskaya ul 15;

admission R150; Ⓜ Belorusskaya) You can't miss this place, for the whimsical characters that adorn the front lawn. That gives just a tiny hint of what's inside: a courtyard crammed with bigger-than-life bronze beauties and elaborate enamel work. The highlight is undoubtedly Putin in his judo costume, although the huge tile Moscow cityscapes are impressive. Indoors, there are three floors of the master's sketches, paintings and enamel arts.

Chekhov House-Museum MUSEUM
(Дом-музей Чехова; off Map p78; ul Sadovaya-Kudrinskaya 6; admission R100; ⏲11am-6pm Mon, Wed & Sat, 2-8pm Tue & Thu; Ⓜ Barrikadnaya) 'The colour of the house is liberal, ie red', Anton Chekhov wrote of his house on the Garden Ring, where he lived from 1886 to 1890. Appropriately, the house now contains the Chekhov House-Museum, with bedrooms, drawing room and study intact. One room is dedicated to Chekhov's time in Melikhovo, showing photographs and manuscripts from his country estate.

Moscow Zoo ZOO
(Московский зоопарк; Map p82; www.moscowzoo.ru; cnr Barrikadnaya & Bolshaya Gruzinskaya uls; adult/child R200/free; ⏲10am-7pm Tue-Sun May-Sep, to 5pm Oct-Apr; Ⓜ Barrikadnaya) Behind Kudrinskaya pl is the main entrance to the big Moscow Zoo. Popular with families, highlights include big cats and polar bears, as well as special exhibits featuring animals from each continent.

Lyubovicheskaya Synagogue SYNAGOGUE
(Любавическая синагога; Map p78; Bolshaya Bronnaya ul 6; Ⓜ Pushkinskaya) Converted to a theatre in the 1930s, the Lyubovicheskaya Synagogue was still used for gatherings by the Jewish community throughout the Soviet period.

ARBAT DISTRICT

Ul Arbat is a 1.25km pedestrian mall stretching from Arbatskaya pl on the Boulevard Ring to Smolenskaya pl on the Garden Ring. Moscow's most famous street, it's something of an art market, complete with instant portrait painters, soapbox poets, jugglers and buskers. The evocative names of nearby lanes identify the area as an old settlement of court attendants, who were eventually displaced by artists and aristocrats. Bound by the Moscow River on both sides, this district includes the area south of ul Novy Arbat.

Museum of Oriental Art MUSEUM
(Музей искусства народа востока; Map p84; www.orientmuseum.ru; Nikitsky bul 12a; admission R300; ⏲11am-7pm Tue-Sun; Ⓜ Arbatskaya) This impressive museum on the Boulevard Ring holds three floors of exhibits, spanning the Asian continent. Of particular interest is the 1st floor, dedicated mostly to the Caucasus, Central Asia and North Asia (meaning the Russian republics of Cukotka, Yakutia and Priamurie). One unexpected highlight is a special exhibit on Nikolai Rerikh, the Russian artist and explorer who spent several years travelling and painting in Asia.

LEAVING A MARK ON MOSCOW

As the chief architect of the Okhotny Ryad shopping mall and the massive Cathedral of Christ the Saviour, Zurab Tsereteli has been criticised for being too ostentatious, too gaudy, too overbearing and just too much.

The most controversial of Tsereteli's masterpieces is the gargantuan **statue of Peter the Great**, which now stands in front of the Red October chocolate factory. At 94.5m (that's twice the size of the *Statue of Liberty*, without her pedestal), Peter towers over the city. Questions of taste aside, Muscovites were sceptical about the whole idea: why pay tribute to Peter the Great, who loathed Moscow and even moved the capital to St Petersburg? Some radicals even attempted – unsuccessfully – to blow the thing up. After that, a 24-hour guard had to stand watch.

Mixed reactions are nothing new to Zurab Tsereteli. An earlier sculpture of Christopher Columbus was rejected by five North American cities, before finally finding a home in Puerto Rico. Despite his critics, who launched a 'Stop Tsereteli' website, this prolific artist does not stop. He launched the Moscow Museum of Modern Art and took over the Russian Academy of Arts. He then opened the aptly named Tsereteli Gallery, which houses room after room of the artist's primitive paintings and elaborate sculptures. His latest venue is the Tsereteli Studio-Museum, with a courtyard crammed with bronze beauties.

Arbat

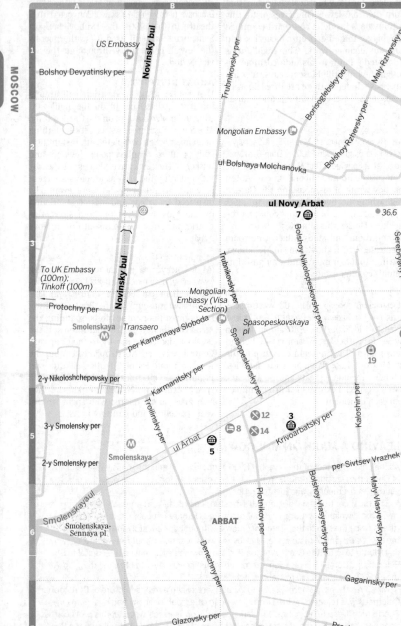

A
B
C
D
1
2
3
4
5
6
7
US Embassy
Novinsky bul
Bolshoy Devyatinsky per
Trubnikovsky per
Borisoglebsky per
Maly Rzhevsky per
Bolshoy Rzhevsky per
Mongolian Embassy
ul Bolshaya Molchanovka
ul Novy Arbat
7
36.6
Bolshoy Nikolopeskovsky per
Serebryany per
To UK Embassy (100m); Tinkoff (100m)
Mongolian Embassy (Visa Section)
Protochny per
Smolenskaya
Transaero
per Kamennaya Sloboda
Spasopeskovskaya pl
Spasopeskovsky per
17
19
2-y Nikoloshchepovsky per
Karmanitsky per
Troilinsky per
Kaloshin per
12
3
8
14
Krivoarbatsky per
3-y Smolensky per
ul Arbat
5
Smolenskaya
2-y Smolensky per
per Sivtsev Vrazhek
Bolshoy Vlasyevsky per
Maly Vlasyevsky per
Plotnikov per
Smolenskaya ul
Smolenskaya-Sennaya pl
ARBAT
Denezhny per
Gagarinsky per
Glazovsky per
Prechistensky per
Ruzheyny per

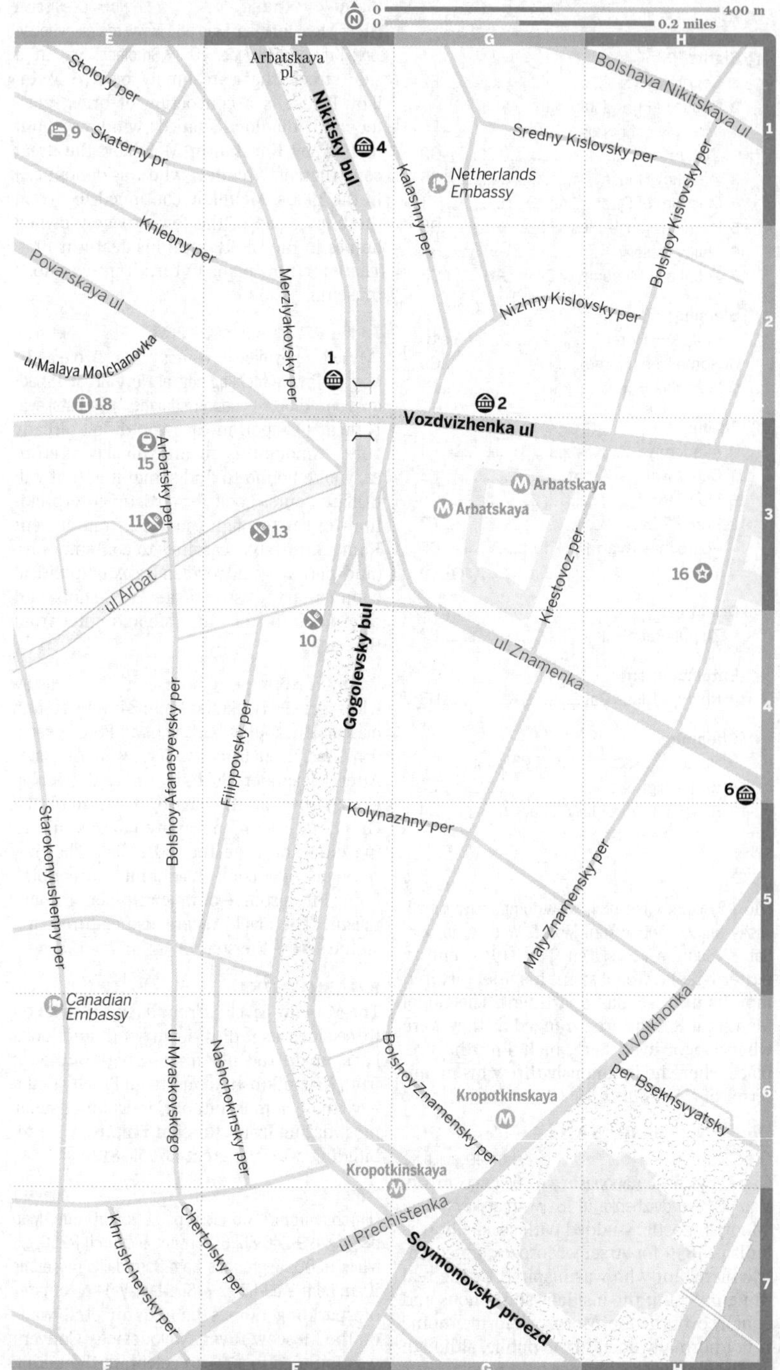

0 400 m
0 0.2 miles
Arbatskaya pl
Stolovy per
Skaterny pr
Nikitsky bul
Bolshaya Nikitskaya ul
Sredny Kislovsky per
Netherlands Embassy
Kalashny per
Bolshoy Kislovsky per
Khlebny per
Povarskaya ul
Merzlyakovsky per
Nizhny Kislovsky per
ul Malaya Molchanovka
Vozdvizhenka ul
Arbatsky per
Arbatskaya
Arbatskaya
Krestovoz per
ul Arbat
Gogolevsky bul
ul Znamenka
Bolshoy Afanasyevsky per
Filippovsky per
Kolynazhny per
Starokonyushenny per
Maly Znamensky per
Canadian Embassy
ul Volkhonka
per Bsekhsvyatsky
ul Myaskovskogo
Nashchokinsky per
Bolshoy Znamensky per
Kropotkinskaya
Kropotkinskaya
ul Prechistenka
Chertolsky per
Khrushchevsky per
Soymonovsky proezd

Arbat

Sights

1 Gogol House....F2
2 House of Friendship with Peoples of Foreign Countries....G2
3 Melnikov House....C5
4 Museum of Oriental Art....F1
5 Pushkin House-Museum....B5
6 Shilov Gallery....H4
7 Tochka-G Museum of Erotic Art....C3

Sleeping

Bulgakov Hotel....(see 8)
8 Home from Home....C5
9 Melodiya Hotel....E1

Eating

10 Akademiya....F4
11 Genatsvale on Arbat....E3
12 Moo-Moo....C5
13 Prime Star....F3
14 Vostochny Kvartal....C5
Yolki-Palki....(see 15)

Drinking

15 Zhiguli Beer Hall....E3

Entertainment

16 Rhythm Blues Cafe....H3

Shopping

17 Bukle....D4
18 Dom Knigi....E2
19 Russian Embroidery & Lace....D4

FREE **Gogol House** MUSEUM
(Дом Гоголя; Map p84; www.domgogolya.ru; Nikitsky bul 7; noon-7pm Mon & Wed-Fri, to 5pm Sat & Sun; M Arbatskaya) The 19th-century writer Nikolai Gogol spent his final tortured months in this small apartment. The Gogol Memorial Rooms are arranged as they were when Gogol lived here, including the fireplace where he infamously threw his manuscript of *Dead Souls*.

House of Friendship with Peoples of Foreign Countries NOTABLE BUILDING
(Дом дружбы с народамн зарубежных стран; Map p84; Vozdvizhenka ul 16; M Arbatskaya) The 'Moorish Castle', studded with seashells, was built in 1899 for Arseny Morozov, an eccentric merchant who was inspired by the real thing in Spain; the inside is sumptuous and equally over the top. Morozov's former home is not normally open to the public, although exhibitions are sometimes held here.

Melnikov House NOTABLE BUILDING
(Дом Мельникова; Map p84; www.melnikovhouse.org; Krivoarbatsky per 10; M Smolenskaya) In a side street, the refreshingly bizarre Melnikov House is a concoction of brick, plaster and diamond-shaped windows built in 1927 by Konstantin Melnikov, the great constructivist architect who was denounced in the 1930s. Melnikov continued to live in the house, one of the few privately owned homes in the USSR, until his death in 1974. There are now plans to turn it into a public museum.

Tochka-G Museum of Erotic Art MUSEUM
(Музей эротического искусства "Точка-G"; Map p84; www.tochkag.net; ul Novy Arbat 15; admission R500; noon-midnight; M Arbatskaya) It means G-spot, in case you didn't already guess. Among this gigantic display of erotica, you're bound to find something that will titillate yours. Look for 'artistic' interpretations of sex through the ages, from ancient Kama Sutra–style carvings to contemporary (and perhaps controversial) sexual-political commentary. Also on-site: sex shop and café! Look for the Om Cafe and enter from the back.

Pushkin House-Museum MUSEUM
(Дом-музей Пушкина; Map p84; www.pushkinmuseum.ru; ul Arbat 53; admission R80; noon-9pm Wed, 10am-6pm Thu-Sun; M Smolenskaya) After Alexander Pushkin married Natalya Goncharova at the nearby Church of the Grand Ascension, they moved to this charming blue house on the old Arbat. The museum provides some insight into the couple's home life, a source of much Russian romanticism. (The lovebirds are also featured in a statue across the street.)

KHAMOVNIKI

The Moscow River surrounds this district on three sides, as it dips down south and loops back up to the north. Heading southwest from Kropotkinskaya metro, ul Prechistenka is virtually a museum of classical mansions, most dating from Russian Empire–style rebuilding after the great fire of 1812.

Novodevichy Convent CONVENT
(Новодевичий монастырь и кладбище; Map p88; 499-246 8526; convent & church R250, exhibits R200; grounds 8am-8pm daily, museums 10am-5pm Wed-Mon; M Sportivnaya) A cluster of sparkling domes behind turreted walls on the Moscow River, Novodevichy Convent was founded in 1524 to celebrate the taking

of Smolensk from Lithuania, an important step in Moscow's conquest of the old Kyivan Rus lands. Novodevichy was later rebuilt by Peter the Great's half-sister Sofia, who used it as a second residence when she ruled Russia as regent in the 1680s.

When Peter was 17, he deposed Sofia and confined her to Novodevichy; in 1698 she was imprisoned here for life after being implicated in the Streltsy rebellion. Sofia was joined in her retirement by Yevdokia Lopukhina, Peter's first wife, whom he considered a nag.

Enter the convent through the red-and-white Moscow-baroque **Transfiguration Gate-Church** (Преображенская надвратная церковь), built in the north wall between 1687 and 1689. The first building on the left contains an Exhibition Room. Yevdokia Lopukhina lived in the **Lopukhin Building** (Лопухинский корпус) against the north wall, while Sofia probably lived in the chambers adjoining the **Pond Tower** (Напрудная башня).

The oldest and most dominant building in the grounds is the white **Smolensk Cathedral** (Смоленский собор), its sumptuous interior covered in 16th-century frescoes. The huge iconostasis – donated by Sofia – has icons from the time of Boris Godunov. The **tombs** (Могилы Софийские и Лопухинские) of Sofia, a couple of her sisters and Yevdokia Lopukhina are in the south nave.

The **bell tower** (Колокольня), against the convent's east wall, was completed in 1690 and is generally regarded as the finest in Moscow. Other churches on the grounds include the red-and-white **Assumption Church** (Успенская церковь; 1685 to 1687), and the 16th-century **St Ambrose's Church** (Амбросиевская церковь).

Boris Godunov's sister Irina lived in the building adjoining the latter church. Today, the **Irina Chambers** (Ирининские палаты) hold a permanent exhibit of 16th- and 17th-century religious artwork such as icons and embroidery.

FREE **Novodevichy Cemetery** CEMETERY
(Новодевичье кладбище; Map p88; ⌚9am-5pm; Ⓜ Sportivnaya) Adjacent to the Novodevichy Convent, Novodevichy Cemetery is among Moscow's most prestigious resting places – a veritable 'who's who' of Russian politics and culture. You will find the tombs of Anton Chekhov, Nikolai Gogol, Vladimir Mayakovsky, Konstantin Stanislavsky, Sergei Prokofiev, Sergei Eisenstein, Andrei Gro-

ARBAT, MY ARBAT

Arbat, my Arbat, You are my calling
You are my happiness and my misfortune.

Bulat Okudzhava

For Moscow's beloved bard Bulat Okudzhava, the Arbat was not only his home, it was his inspiration. Although he spent his university years in Georgia dabbling in harmless verse, it was only upon his return to Moscow – and to his cherished Arbat – that his poetry adopted the freethinking character for which it is known.

He gradually made the transition from poet to songwriter, stating that, 'Once I had the desire to accompany one of my satirical verses with music. I only knew three chords; now, 27 years later, I know seven chords, then I knew three.' While Bulat and his friends enjoyed his songs, other composers, singers and guitarists did not. The ill feeling subsided when a well-known poet announced that 'these are not songs. This is just another way of presenting poetry.'

And so a new form of art was born. The 1960s were heady times – in Moscow as elsewhere – and Okudzhava inspired a whole movement of liberal-thinking poets to take their ideas to the streets. Vladimir Vysotsky and others – some political, some not – followed in Okudzhava's footsteps, their iconoclastic lyrics and simple melodies drawing enthusiastic crowds all around Moscow.

The Arbat today – crowded with souvenir stands and overpriced cafés – bears little resemblance to the hallowed haunt of Okudzhava's youth. But its memory lives on in the bards and buskers, painters and poets who still perform for strolling crowds on summer evenings.

Dorogomilovo & Outer Khamovniki

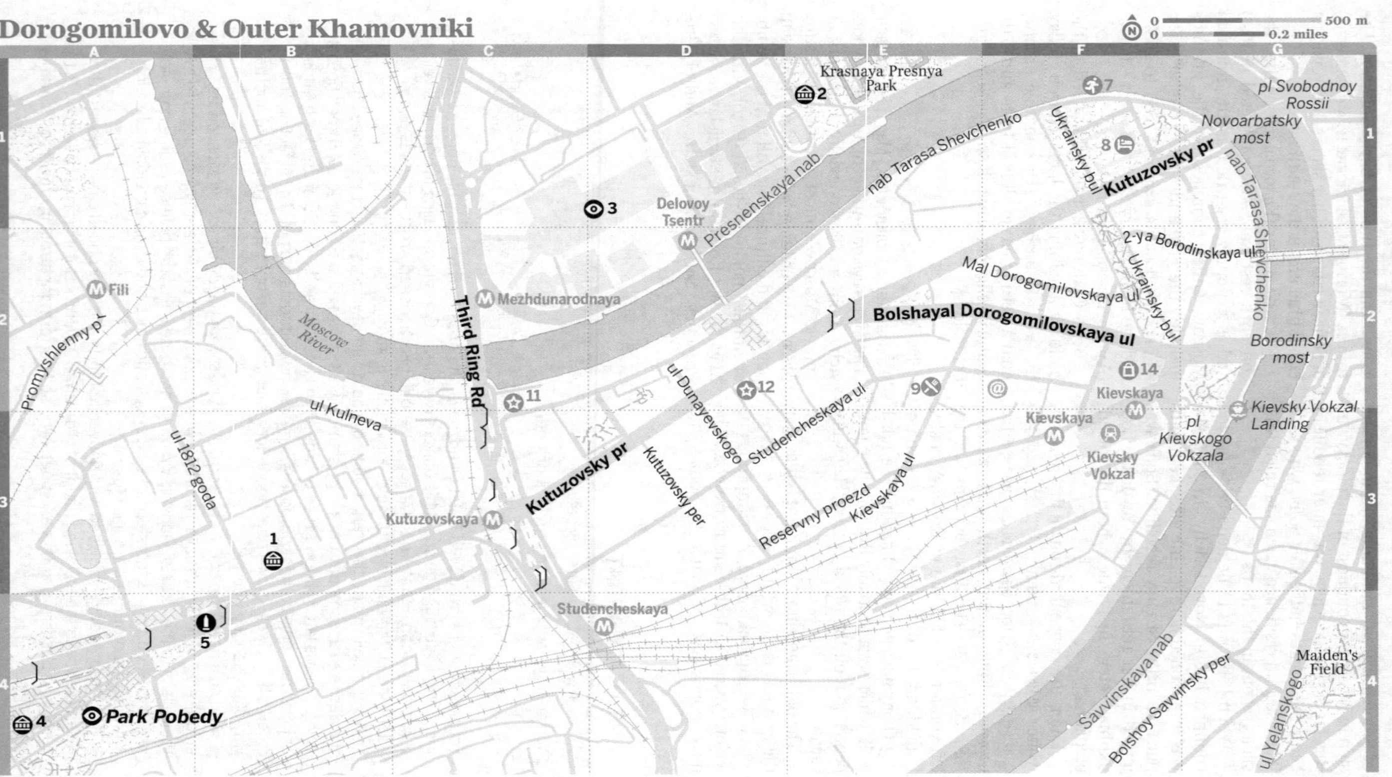

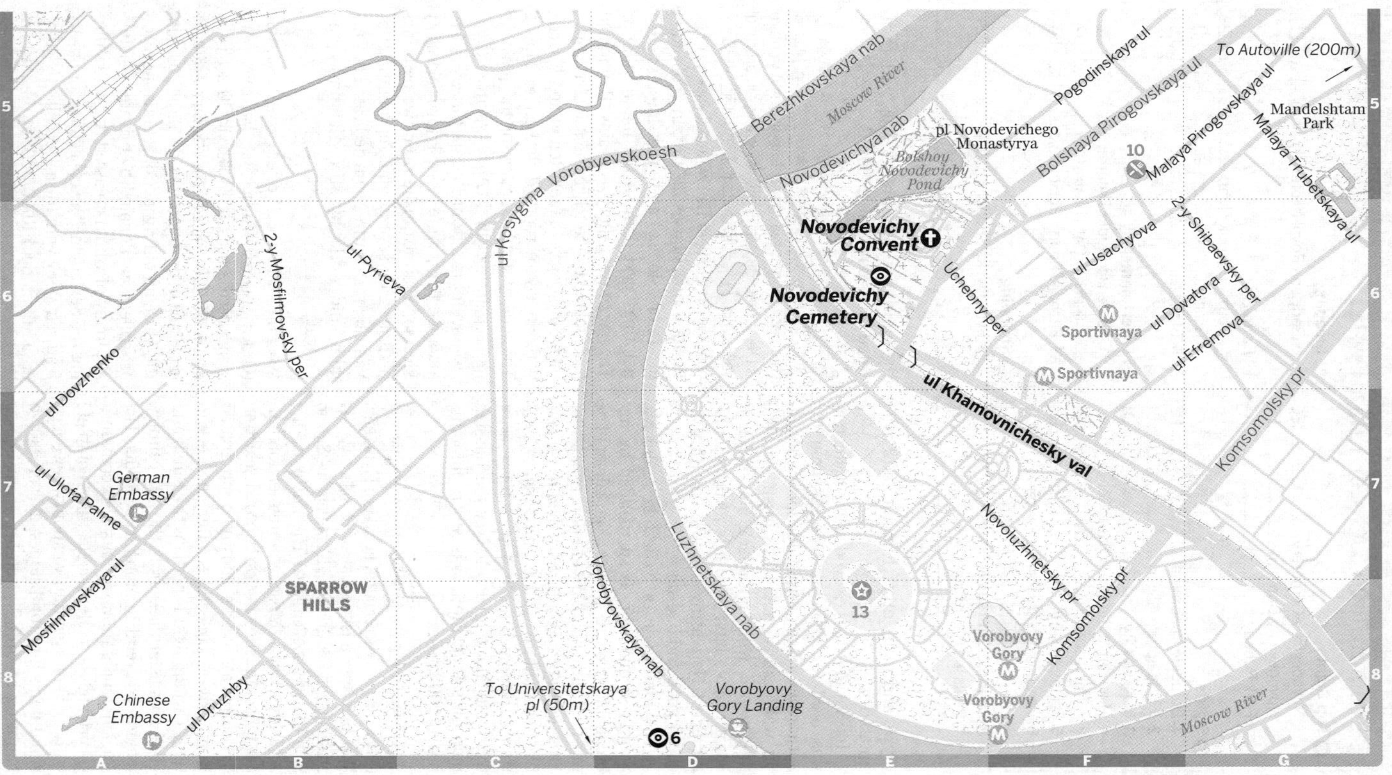
To Autoville (200m)
Mandelshtam Park
Malaya Trubetskaya ul
Malaya Pirogovskaya ul
Pogodinskaya ul
Bolshaya Pirogovskaya ul
10
pl Novodevichego Monastyrya
Berezhkovskaya nab
Moscow River
Novodevichya nab
Bolshoy Novodevichy Pond
Novodevichy Convent
Novodevichy Cemetery
ul Usachyova
2-y Shibaevsky per
ul Dovatora
ul Efremova
Uchebny per
Sportivnaya
ul Khamovnichesky val
Komsomolsky pr
Novoluzhnetsky pr
Komsomolsky pr
Vorobyovy Gory
Vorobyovy Gory
13
Luzhnetskaya nab
Vorobyovskaya nab
Vorobyovy Gory Landing
To Universitetskaya pl (50m)
6
ul Kosygina
Vorobyevskoesh
ul Pyrieva
2-y Mosfilmovsky per
ul Dovzhenko
ul Ulofa Palme
German Embassy
SPARROW HILLS
Mosfilmovskaya ul
Chinese Embassy
ul Druzhby
A
B
C
D
E
F
G
5
6
7
8

Dorogomilovo & Outer Khamovniki

Top Sights

Novodevichy Cemetery E6
Novodevichy Convent E6
Park Pobedy A4

Sights

1 Borodino Panorama B3
2 Ice Sculpture Gallery E1
3 Moskva-City D1
4 Museum of the Great Patriotic War A4
5 Triumphal Arch B4
6 Vorobyovy Gory Nature Preserve D8

Activities, Courses & Tours

7 Radisson River Cruises F1

Sleeping

8 Radisson Royal (Hotel Ukraine) F1

Eating

9 Dorogomilovsky Market E2
Grably .... (see 14)
10 Stolle F5

Entertainment

11 Fomenko Studio Theatre C2
12 Kuklachev Cat Theatre D2
13 Luzhniki Sports Palace E8

Shopping

14 Evropeysky Shopping Centre F2

myko, and many other Russian and Soviet notables.

In Soviet times Novodevichy Cemetery was used for eminent people, whom the authorities judged unsuitable for the Kremlin wall – most notably, Khrushchev. The intertwined white-and-black blocks round Khrushchev's bust were intended by sculptor Ernst Neizvestny to represent Khrushchev's good and bad sides.

The tombstone of Nadezhda Alliluyeva, Stalin's second wife, is surrounded by unbreakable glass to prevent vandalism. The most recent notable addition is former President Boris Yeltsin, who died of congestive heart failure in 2007. The cemetery's entrance is on Luzhnetsky proezd. If you want to investigate it in depth, buy the Russian map on sale at the kiosk, which pinpoints nearly 200 graves.

Pushkin Fine Arts Museum — MUSEUM

(Музей изобразительный исскуств Пушкина; Map p96; www.artsmuseum.ru; ul Volkhonka 12; adult/student R300/150; ⌚10am-6pm Tue-Sun, to 9pm Thu; Ⓜ Kropotkinskaya) The Pushkin Fine Arts Museum is Moscow's premier foreign-art museum, showing off a broad selection of European works mostly appropriated from private collections after the revolution. The highlight is perhaps the Dutch and Flemish masterpieces from the 17th century, including several Rembrandt portraits. The Ancient Civilisation exhibits also contain a surprisingly excellent collection, complete with ancient Egyptian weaponry, jewellery, ritual items and tombstones, as well as two haunting mummies. Another room houses the impressive Treasures of Troy, with excavated items dating to 2500 BC.

Gallery of European & American Art of the 19th & 20th Centuries — MUSEUM

(Галерея искусства стран Европы и Америки XIX-XX веков; Map p96; www.newpaintart.ru; ul Volkhonka 14; adult/student R300/150; ⌚10am-6pm Tue-Sun, to 9pm Thu; Ⓜ Kropotkinskaya) The Pushkin now houses its amazing collection of Impressionist and post-Impressionist paintings next door to the main building. The separate gallery contains the famed assemblage of French Impressionist works, including Degas, Manet, Renoir and Pisarro, with an entire room dedicated to Monet. The gallery displays many of the most famous paintings by Matisse, such as *Goldfish;* sculptures from Rodin's *Gates of Hell,* among others; some lesser-known pieces by Picasso; a few exquisite primitive paintings by Rousseau; several amazing paintings by Van Gogh; an entire room dedicated to Gauguin; and works by Miró, Kandinsky and Chagall.

Museum of Private Collections — MUSEUM

(Отдел личных коллекций; Map p96; www.artprivatecollections.ru; ul Volkhonka 10; adult/student R300/150; ⌚noon-7pm Wed-Sun; Ⓜ Kropotkinskaya) On the opposite side of the Pushkin, the Museum of Private Collections shows off art collections donated by private individuals, many of whom amassed the works during the Soviet era. The collectors/donors are featured along with the art. A collective ticket (adult/student R500/300) to the Pushkin

Fine Arts Museum, the Gallery of European & American Art and the Museum of Private Collections is available at any site.

FREE **Cathedral of Christ the Saviour** CHURCH
(Храм Христа Спасителя; Map p96; www.xxc.ru; ⌚10am-5pm; Ⓜ Kropotkinskaya) Now dominating the skyline along the Moscow River, the gargantuan Cathedral of Christ the Saviour sits on the site of an earlier and similar church of the same name. The original church was built from 1839 to 1860 to commemorate Russia's victory over Napoleon, but it was destroyed during Stalin's orgy of explosive secularism. Stalin planned to replace the church with a 315m-high 'Palace of Soviets' (including a 100m statue of Lenin) but the project never got off the ground – literally. Instead, for 50 years the site served an important purpose: as the world's largest swimming pool.

This time around, the church was completed in a mere two years, in time for Moscow's 850th birthday in 1997, and at an estimated cost of US$350 million. Much of the work was done by former Mayor Luzhkov's favourite architect Zurab Tsereteli, and it has aroused a range of reactions from Muscovites, from pious devotion to abject horror. Muscovites should at least be grateful they can admire the shiny domes of a church instead of the shiny dome of Lenin's head.

Multimedia Art Museum ART GALLERY
(Мультимедиа Арт Музей; Map p96; www.mdf.ru; ul Ostozhenka 16; admission R200; Ⓜ Kropotkinskaya) Formerly the Moscow House of Photography (MDF), this slick modern gallery is home to an impressive photographic library and archives of contemporary and historic photography. The facility usually hosts several simultaneous exhibits, often featuring works from prominent photographers from the Soviet period, as well as contemporary artists. The complex also hosts several month-long festivals, Photobiennale and Fashion & Style in Photography (held in alternating years).

Tolstoy Estate-Museum MUSEUM
(Усадьба Толстого 'Хамовники'; off Map p96; www.tolstoymuseum.ru; ul Lva Tolstogo 21; adult/student R200/50; ⌚10am-6pm Wed-Sun, 1-9pm Thu; Ⓜ Park Kultury) Leo Tolstoy's winter home during the 1880s and 1890s now houses the interesting Tolstoy Estate-Museum. See the salon where Sergei Rachmaninov and Nikolai Rimsky-Korsakov played piano, and the study where Tolstoy himself wove his epic tales.

At the south end of ul Lva Tolstogo, the beautiful **Church of St Nicholas of the Weavers** (Церковь Николы в Хамовниках) vies with St Basil's Cathedral as the most colourful in Moscow. It was commissioned by the Moscow weavers' guild in 1676.

Rerikh Museum MUSEUM
(Музей Рериха; Map p96; www.icr.su; Maly Znamensky per 3/5; adult/student R220/110; ⌚11am-5pm Wed-Sun; Ⓜ Kropotkinskaya) Nikolai Rerikh (known internationally as Nicholas Roerich) was a Russian artist from the late 19th and early 20th centuries, whose fantastical artwork is characterised by rich, bold colours and mystical themes.

Burganov House MUSEUM
(Дом Бурганова; Map p96; www.burganov.ru; Bolshoy Afansyevsky per 15; admission R180; ⌚11am-7pm; Ⓜ Kropotkinskaya) Part studio, part museum, the Burganov House comprises several interconnected courtyards and houses, where the works of sculptor Alexander Burganov are artfully displayed alongside pieces from the artist's private collection.

Glazunov Gallery MUSEUM
(Галерея Глазунова; Map p96; www.glazunov.ru; ul Volkhonka 13; adult/student R160/80; ⌚11am-6pm Tue-Sun; Ⓜ Kropotkinskaya) Ilya Glazunov is famous for huge, colourful paintings that depict hundreds of people and places and events from Russian history in one monumental scene.

Tsereteli Gallery MUSEUM
(Галерея Церетели; Map p96; www.tsereteli.ru; ul Prechistenka 19; admission R200; ⌚noon-7pm Tue-Sat; Ⓜ Kropotkinskaya) Another endeavour of the tireless Zurab Tsereteli is the aptly named Tsereteli Gallery, housed in the 18th-century Dolgoruky mansion. The **Russian Academy of Arts** (Российская академия художеств; Map p96; www.rah.ru; ul Prechistenka 21; admission R80; ⌚11am-8pm Tue-Sun; Ⓜ Kropotkinskaya) holds rotating exhibits next door.

Shilov Gallery MUSEUM
(Галерея Шилова; Map p84; www.shilov.su; ul Znamenka 5; adult/student R160/80; ⌚11am-7pm Fri-Wed; Ⓜ Biblioteka im Lenina) Contemporary Russia's most celebrated portrait painter, Alexander Shilov is known for his startling realism. His fans claim that the artist provides

MOSCOW FOR CHILDREN

Filled with icons and onion domes, the Russian capital might not seem like an appealing destination for kids; but you'd be surprised. In Moscow, little people will find museums, parks, theatres and even restaurants that cater especially to them.

Sights & Activities

They may not appreciate an age-old icon or a Soviet hero, but Moscow still has plenty to offer the little ones.

PARKS

For starters, the city is filled with parks that offer playgrounds and plenty of room to run around. Among the parks listed in this chapter, Patriarch's Ponds (p80) has a playground and plenty of room to run around. Gorky Park (p94) and Vorobyovy Gory Nature Preserve (p93) are good for older kids who can ride bikes. Izmaylovsky Park (p105) also has bikes, as well as paddle boats, a Ferris wheel and other amusements.

Even when the weather is cold, your kids can frolic in the waves at Kva-Kva Water Park (p106).

MUSEUMS

Most sights and museums offer reduced-rate tickets for children up to 12 or 18 years of age. Admission for children less than five years old is often free. Look out for family tickets, which allow the whole family to enter for one price.

Most of Moscow's art museums have special programs and activities geared towards kids over the age of five. They mostly take place in Russian, so the language barrier may be an issue. Other kid-friendly sites include Moscow Zoo (p83), Moscow Planetarium (p81) and the Armed Forces Museum (p77).

Eating

Many restaurants host 'children's parties' on Saturday and Sunday afternoons, offering toys, games, entertainment and supervision for kids while their parents eat. Top eating recommendations for children:

great insight into his subjects, with some high-level political figures among them.

Tolstoy Literary Museum MUSEUM
(Литературный музей Толстого; Map p96; www.tolstoymuseum.ru; ul Prechistenka 11; adult/student R200/100; 11am-6pm Tue-Sun; M Kropotkinskaya) This mansion contains Leo Tolstoy's manuscripts, letters and sketches, with a focus on literary influences and output, as opposed to the author's personal life.

Pushkin Literary Museum MUSEUM
(Литературный музей Пушкина; Map p96; www.pushkinmuseum.ru; ul Prechistenka 12/2; admission R120; 10am-5pm Tue-Sun; M Kropotkinskaya) The Pushkin Literary Museum is one of the most beautiful examples of the Moscow empire architectural style; the exhibit inside is devoted to Pushkin's life and work.

Autoville MUSEUM
(Автовиль; off Map p88; www.autoville.ru; ul Usachyova 2; admission R300; 10am-10pm; M Sportivnaya) This impressive facility brings together under one roof dozens of exquisite automobiles from around the world and over the years. It's certainly a sort of art exhibit, which presents the vehicles as objects of great beauty as well as functionality.

DOROGOMILOVO & SPARROW HILLS

West of the centre, these overlapping districts occupy a sort of peninsula formed by a loop in the Moscow River. This was the route taken by armies attacking from (and retreating to) the west – in 1812 and again in 1944. The district's sights commemorate these events.

Park Pobedy SQUARE
(Парк Победы; Map p88; Kutuzovsky pr; admission free; dawn-dusk; M Park Pobedy) Also known as Victory Park, this huge memorial complex celebrates the Great Patriotic War. The park includes endless fountains and monuments, and the memorial **Church of St George** (Церковь св Георгия). The dominant monument is a 142m obelisk (each 10cm represents a day of the war).

» Starlite Diner (p116)
» American Bar & Grill (p117)
» Chaikhona No 1 (p118)
» Il Patio (p117)
» Tinkoff (p119)

Children's Theatre

Cultural instruction starts at a young age in Moscow, with many companies and performances geared specifically towards young kids. Performances are usually in the afternoons.

Obraztsov Puppet Theatre & Museum (Театр кукол Образцова; Map p78; www.puppet.ru; Sadovaya-Samotechnaya ul 3; adult R300-1000, child R200-600; ⏲box office 11am-2.30pm & 3.30-7pm; Ⓜ Tsvetnoy Bulvar) The country's largest puppet theatre performs colourful Russian folk tales and adapted classical plays. Kids can get up close and personal with the incredible puppets at the museum, which holds a collection of over 3000.

Kuklachev Cat Theatre (Театр кошек Куклачёва; Map p88; www.kuklachev.ru; Kutuzovsky pr 25; tickets R200-800; ⏲noon, 2pm or 4pm Thu-Sun; Ⓜ Kutuzovskaya) At this unusual theatre, acrobatic cats do all kinds of stunts for the audience's delight.

Moscow Children's Musical Theatre (Театр Сац; www.teatr-sats.ru; pr Vernadskogo 5; tickets R50-500; ⏲Wed, Fri & Sun Sep-Jun; Ⓜ Universitet) All performances staged here are highly entertaining and educational, as actors appear in costume before the show and talk with the children.

Transport

The metro might be fun for kids, but be careful during rush hour, when trains and platforms are packed. **Detskoe Taxi** (Детское такси; ☎495-765 1180; www.detskoetaxi.ru; R500 per 10km) company will look out for your kids, offering smoke-free cars and child seats upon request.

At the far end of the park, the Memorial Synagogue at Poklonnaya Hill houses the **Museum of Jewish Legacy History and Holocaust** (Мемориальная синагога; ☎495-148 1907; www.poklonnaya.ru; Minskaya ul; admission free; ⏲10am-6pm Tue-Thu, noon-7pm Sun; Ⓜ Park Pobedy). Admission is with a guide only, so you must make arrangements in advance, especially if you want a tour in English.

Museum of the Great Patriotic War MUSEUM
(Центральный музей Великой Отечественной войны; Map p88; www.poklonnayagora.ru; ul Bratiev Fonchenko 10; adult/child R100/40; ⏲10am-5pm Tue-Sun Nov-Mar, to 7pm Apr-Oct; Ⓜ Park Pobedy) The huge complex contains two impressive memorial rooms, as well as an exhibit of dioramas of every major WWII battle involving Soviet troops. Exhibits highlight the many heroes of the Soviet Union, as well as weapons, photographs, documentary films, letters and many other authentic wartime memorabilia.

Borodino Panorama MUSEUM
(Бородинская битва; Map p88; Kutuzovsky pr 38; adult/student R150/50; ⏲10am-5pm Sat-Thu; Ⓜ Park Pobedy) Following a vicious but inconclusive battle at Borodino in August 1812, Moscow's defenders retreated along what are now Kutuzovsky pr and ul Arbat, pursued by Napoleon's Grand Army. Today, this pavilion along the route contains a giant 360-degree painting of the Borodino battle. Standing inside this tableau of bloodshed – complete with sound effects – is a powerful way to visualise the event.

The **Triumphal Arch** (Триумфальные ворота) celebrates Napoleon's eventual defeat. Demolished at its original site outside Belarus Station in the 1930s, it was reconstructed here in a fit of post-WWII public spirit.

FREE **Vorobyovy Gory Nature Preserve** NATURE RESERVE
(Природный заказник Воробёвы Горы; Map p88; www.vorobyovy-gory.ru; Ⓜ Vorobyovy Gory)

Following the south shore of the Moscow River, this narrow strip of land in Sparrow Hills (Воробёвы горы, Vorobyovy Gory) contains a network of wooded trails and a sandy beach. An eco-train runs along the bank of the river; you can also rent bicycles or inline skates at the southeastern entrance.

From the river, the ski lift and walking trails lead up to **Universitetskaya ploshchad** (Университетская площадь) for the best view over Moscow. Behind the square is the 36-storey spire of **Moscow State University** (Московский Государственный Университет; Universitetskaya pl; MUniversitet), one of the 'Seven Sisters' that is visible from most places in the city thanks to its elevated site.

ZAMOSKVORECHIE

Zamoskvorechie (meaning 'Beyond the Moscow River') stretches south from opposite the Kremlin, inside a big river loop. The Vodootvodny canal slices across the top of Zamoskvorechie, preventing spring floods in the city centre and creating the sliver of Bolotny Island. The atmosphere of 19th-century Moscow lives on in the low buildings, crumbling courtyards and clusters of onion domes along narrow ul Bolshaya Ordynka, which runs 2km down the middle of Zamoskvorechie. The many churches here make up a scrapbook of Muscovite architectural styles, making Zamoskvorechie a varied, intriguing area.

State Tretyakov Gallery — MUSEUM

(Третьяковская галерея; Map p96; www.tretyakovgallery.ru; Lavrushinsky per 10; adult/student R360/220; 10am-7.30pm Tue-Sun; MTretyakovskaya;) Nothing short of spectacular, the State Tretyakov Gallery holds the world's best collection of Russian icons, as well as an outstanding collection of other pre-revolutionary Russian art, particularly from the 19th-century Peredvizhniki movement (known as the Wanderers).

The original part of the Tretyakov building is a likeness of an old boyar castle, and was created by Viktor Vasnetsov between 1900 and 1905. The collection is based on that of the 19th-century industrialist brothers Pavel and Sergei Tretyakov (Pavel was a patron of the Peredvizhniki).

Within the museum grounds, the **Church of St Nicholas in Tolmachi** (Церковь св Николая в Толмачах; noon-4pm) is the church where Pavel Tretyakov regularly attended services. It was transferred to the museum grounds and restored in 1997, and now functions as an exhibit hall and working church. The exquisite five-tiered iconostasis dates back to the 17th century. The centrepiece is the revered 12th-century *Vladimir Icon of the Mother of God,* protector of all of Russia.

It's worth showing up early in order to beat the queues. The entrance to the gallery is through a lovely courtyard; the **Engineer's Building** (Инженерный корпус; Map p96; Lavrushinsky per 12) next door is reserved for special exhibits.

Gorky Park — HISTORIC PARK

(Парк Горького; Map p96; www.propark.ru; ul Krymsky val; 10am-10pm; MPark Kultury) Amusement park no longer, Gorky Park is still one of the most festive places in Moscow – a perfect way to escape the hubbub of the city. Officially the Park Kultury (Park of Culture), it's named after Maxim Gorky. The park stretches almost 3km along the river, upstream of Krymsky most. This place is undergoing a major overhaul: the rides and games and beer tents have been cleared out, leaving a pleasant and peaceful green space to rent bikes or have a picnic. Apparently the park has been bought out by billionaire Roman Abramovich, who is working with the city of Moscow to revamp the whole place.

In winter the ponds are frozen for ice skating and tracks are made for cross-country skiing. Skis and skates are also available for rental.

New Tretyakov — ART GALLERY

(Третьяковская галерея на Крымском валу; Map p96; ul Krymsky val; adult/student R360/220; 10am-7.30pm Tue-Sun; MPark Kultury) The premier venue for 20th-century Russian art is the State Tretyakov Gallery on ul Krymsky val, better known as the New Tretyakov. This place has much more than the typical socialist realist images of muscle-bound men wielding scythes and busty women milking cows (although there's that too). The exhibits showcase avant-garde artists such as Malevich, Kandinsky, Chagall, Goncharova and Lyubov Popova.

In the same building as the New Tretyakov, the **Central House of Artists** (Центральный дом художников; Map p96; admission R100-200; 11am-7pm Tue-Sun; MPark Kultury) is a huge exhibit space used for contemporary art shows.

A TOUR OF THE TRETYAKOV

Duration: Two Hours

The Tretyakov's 62 rooms are numbered and progress in chronological order from rooms 1 to 48 (starting on the 2nd floor). Rooms 1 through 7 display painting and sculpture from the 18th century, with many portraits and official-looking commissioned paintings. Things start to get more interesting in rooms 8 through 15, which display landscapes, character paintings and more portraits from the first half of the 19th century.

The real gems of the collection, however, are from the second half of the 19th century and the early 20th century, which you'll find starting with room 16. It was the 1870s when daring artists started to use their medium to address social issues, thus founding the Peredvizhniki.

2ND FLOOR

Room 17 is dedicated to Vasily Perov, one of the original founders of the Wanderers movement. Look for his famous portrait of Dostoevsky and the moving painting *Troika,* with its stark depiction of child labour. Ivan Kramskoi was another of the original Wanderers, and his work is on display in room 20. In room 25, Ivan Shishkin is a landscape painter who is closely associated with the same movement.

Viktor Vasnetsov is in room 26, with fantastical depictions of fairy tales and historical figures. His painting *Bogatery* (Heroes) is perhaps the best example from the revivalist movement, although *A Knight at the Crossroads* is more dramatic. By contrast, Vasily Vereshchagin – in room 27 – is known for his harsh realism, especially in battle scenes. *The Apotheosis of War,* for example, is not subtle.

Vasily Surikov was also skilled at large-scale historical scenes, as you'll see in room 28. Most famously, *Boyarina Morozova* captures the history of the schism in the Orthodox Church and how it tragically played out for one family.

Author of the works in rooms 29 and 30, Ilya Repin is perhaps the most beloved Russian realist painter. *Ivan the Terrible and His Son Ivan* is downright chilling. Room 31 has a few masterpieces by Nicholas Ge, another founder of the Peredvizhniki movement.

Rooms 32 to 34 are dedicated to Mikhail Vrubel, a symbolist-era artist who defies classification. One entire wall is covered with his fantastic art nouveau mural *The Princess of the Dream*. The melancholy *Demon Seated* is also provocative.

1ST FLOOR

A selection of Isaac Levitan's landscapes is in room 37, while Mikhail Nesterov – in room 39 – combines symbolism with religious themes. *The Vision of the Youth Bartholomew* depicts an episode from the childhood of St Sergius of Radonezh (patron saint of Russia), when he was blessed by a monk in the woods. In rooms 41 and 42, Valentin Serov was the most celebrated portraitist of his time.

Moving into the 20th century, artists began to reject the strict rules of realism. Room 43 displays Korovin's foray into Impressionism, and Alexander Golovin and Boris Kustodiev represent the art nouveau movement in room 44. Displayed in room 46, Pavel Kuznetsov was the founder of the Blue Rose, the Moscow group of symbolist artists. Georgy Sudeykin and Sapunov were primarily known for their set and costume designs. Nicholas Rerikh (Roerich) shows off his fantastical storytelling style in room 47. In room 48, Martiros Saryan is also a symbolist, although his work is strongly influenced by his Armenian heritage.

ICONS

If you still have some energy, icons are found on the ground floor in rooms 56 to 62. Andrei Rublyov's *Holy Trinity* (1420s) from Sergiev Posad, widely regarded as Russia's greatest icon, is in room 60.

Zamoskvorechie & Inner Khamovniki

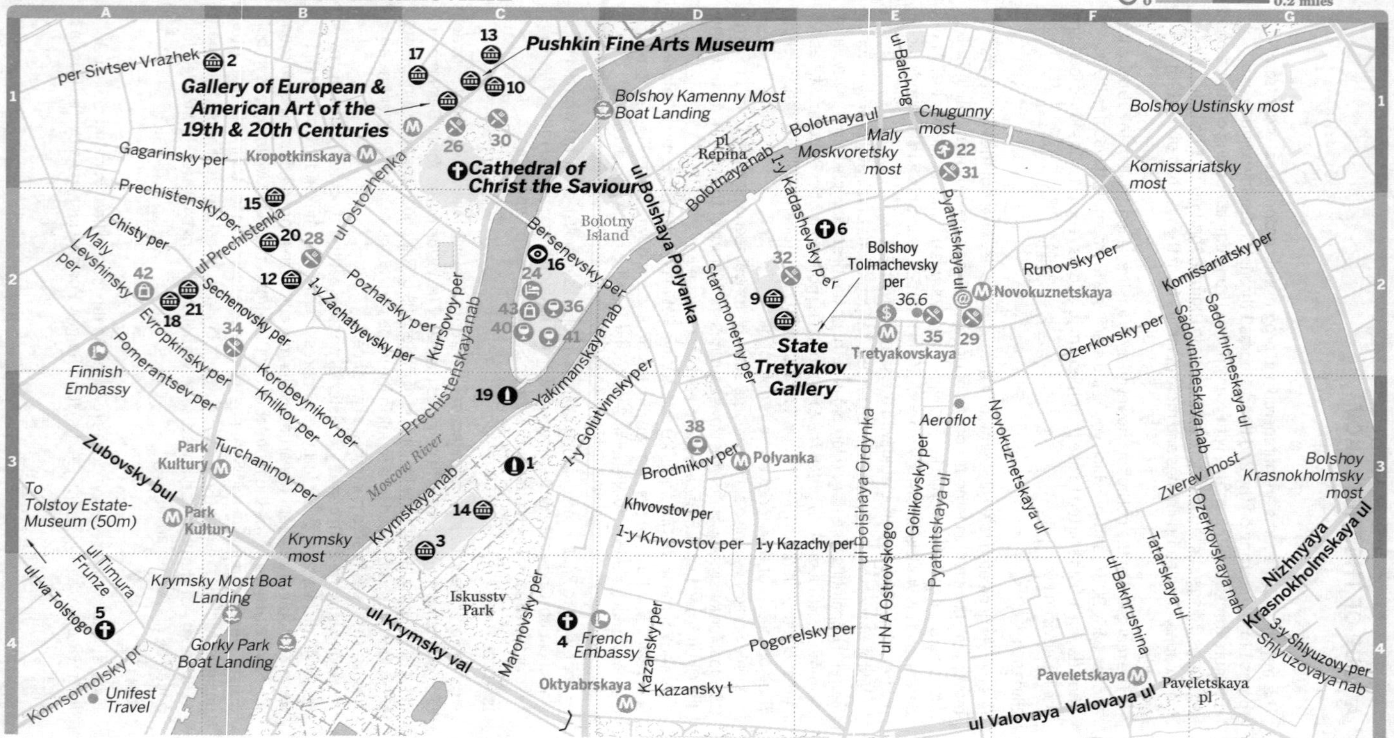

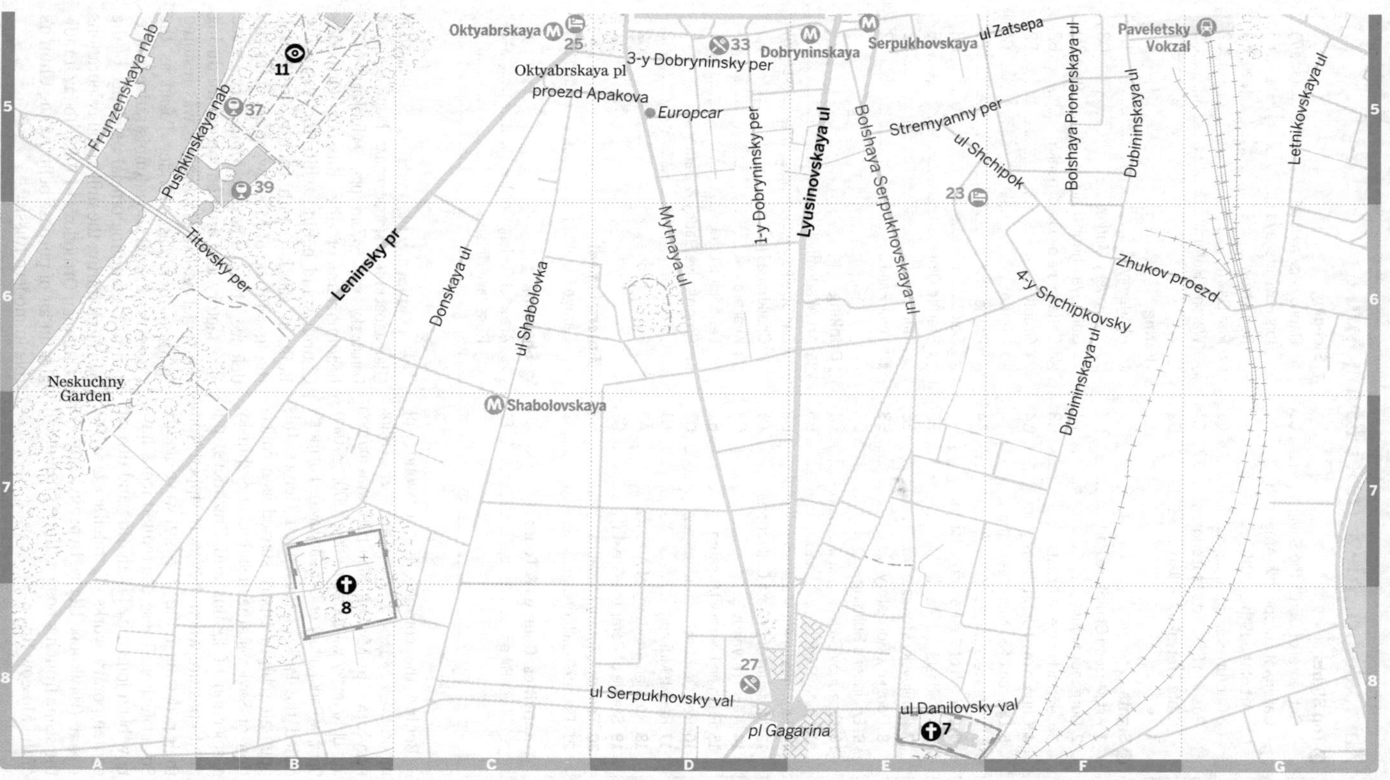

Frunzenskaya nab
Pushkinskaya nab
11
37
39
Titovsky per
Leninsky pr
Neskuchny Garden
Oktyabrskaya
25
Oktyabrskaya pl
proezd Apakova
Europcar
3-y Dobryninsky per
33
Dobryninskaya
Serpukhovskaya
ul Zatsepa
Bolshaya Pionerskaya ul
Paveletsky Vokzal
Dubininskaya ul
Letnikovskaya ul
1-y Dobryninsky per
Lyusinovskaya ul
Bolshaya Serpukhovskaya ul
Stremyanny per
ul Shchipok
23
Zhukov proezd
4-y Shchipkovsky
Dubininskaya ul
Donskaya ul
ul Shabolovka
Mytnaya ul
Shabolovskaya
8
27
ul Serpukhovsky val
pl Gagarina
ul Danilovsky val
7
A
B
C
D
E
F
G
5
6
7
8

Zamoskvorechie & Inner Khamovniki

Top Sights
- Cathedral of Christ the Saviour C1
- Gallery of European & American Art of the 19th & 20th Centuries C1
- Pushkin Fine Arts Museum C1
- State Tretyakov Gallery D2

Sights
1. Art Muzeon Sculpture Park C3
2. Burganov House B1
3. Central House of Artists C3
4. Church of St John the Warrior C4
5. Church of St Nicholas of the Weavers A4
6. Church of the Resurrection in Kadashi E2
7. Danilovsky Monastery E8
8. Donskoy Monastery B8
9. Engineer's Building D2
10. Glazunov Gallery C1
11. Gorky Park B5
12. Multimedia Art Museum B2
13. Museum of Private Collections C1
14. New Tretyakov C3
15. Pushkin Literary Museum B2
16. Red October C2
17. Rerikh Museum C1
18. Russian Academy of Arts A2
19. Statue of Peter the Great C3
20. Tolstoy Literary Museum B2
21. Tsereteli Gallery A2

Activities, Courses & Tours

22 Oliver Bikes E1

Sleeping
- Danilovskaya Hotel .... (see 7)
- 23 Ibis Paveletskaya E5
- Red Arrow .... (see 36)
- 24 Red Dawn C2
- 25 Warsaw Hotel C5

Eating
- 26 Akademiya C1
- 27 Danilovsky Market D8
- Galereya Khudozhnikov .... (see 21)
- 28 Genatsvale on Ostozhenka B2
- 29 Grably E2
- 30 Il Patio C1
- 31 Prime Star E1
- 32 Sok D2
- 33 Starlite Diner D5
- 34 Tiflis B2
- 35 Yolki-Palki E2

Drinking
- 36 Art Akademiya C2
- Bar Strelka .... (see 16)
- 37 Chaikhona No 1 .... B5
- 38 Kvartira 44 .... D3
- 39 Lebedinoe Ozero B5
- 40 Progressive Daddy & Daddy's Terrace C2
- 41 Rolling Stone C2

Entertainment
- Garage Club .... (see 38)

Shopping
- 42 Artefact Gallery Centre A2
- 43 Russkaya Ulitsa C2

Behind the complex is the wonderful, moody **Art Muzeon Sculpture Park** (Парк искусств Арт-Музеон; Map p96; www.muzeon.ru; ul Krymsky val 10; admission R100; ⏲10am-9pm; Ⓜ Park Kultury or Oktyabrskaya). Formerly called the Park of the Fallen Heroes, this open-air sculpture park started as a collection of Soviet statues (Stalin, Dzerzhinsky, a selection of Lenins and Brezhnevs) put out to pasture when they were ripped from their pedestals in the post-1991 wave of anti-Soviet feeling. These discredited icons have now been joined by fascinating and diverse contemporary works. Tsereteli's **Peter the Great** (Памятник Петру Первому) surveys the scene from his post on the embankment of the Moscow River.

FREE **Danilovsky Monastery** MONASTERY
(Даныловский монастырь; Map p96; ul Danilovsky val; ⏲7am-7pm; Ⓜ Tulskaya) The headquarters of the Russian Orthodox Church stand behind white fortress walls. Built in the late 13th century by Daniil, the first Prince of Moscow, as an outer city defence, the Danilovsky Monastery served as a factory and a detention centre during the Soviet period. However, it was restored in time to replace Sergiev Posad as the Church's spiritual and administrative centre, and to become the official residence of the patriarch during the millennial celebrations of Russian Orthodoxy in 1988. Today it radiates an air of purpose befitting the Church's role in modern Russia.

On holy days in particular, the place fills with worshippers murmuring prayers, lighting candles and ladling holy water into jugs at the tiny chapel inside the gates. Enter beneath the pink **St Simeon Stylite Gate-Church** (Надвратная церковь Симеона Столпника) on the north wall. Its bells are the first in Moscow to ring on holy days.

The monastery's oldest and busiest church is the **Church of the Holy Fathers of the Seven Ecumenical Councils** (Храм св отцов семи вселенских соборов), where worship is held continuously from 10am to 5pm daily. The yellow, neoclassical **Trinity Cathedral** (Троицкий собор), built in the 1830s, is an austere counterpart to the other buildings.

Donskoy Monastery MONASTERY
(Донской монастырь; Map p96; www.donskoi.org; Donskaya ul; MShabolovskaya) Founded in 1591, the Donskoy Monastery is the youngest of Moscow's fortified monasteries. It was built to house the *Virgin of the Don* icon (now in the Tretyakov Gallery), which was credited with bringing victory in the 1380 Battle of Kulikovo. It's also said that in 1591 the Tatar Khan Giri retreated without a fight after the icon showered him with burning arrows in a dream.

Most of the monastery, surrounded by a brick wall with 12 towers, was built between 1684 and 1733 under Regent Sofia and Peter the Great. The **Virgin of Tikhvin Church** over the north gate, built in 1713 and 1714, is one of the last examples of Moscow baroque. When burials in central Moscow were banned after a 1771 plague, the Donskoy Monastery became a graveyard for the nobility, and it is littered with elaborate tombs and chapels.

Church of St John the Warrior CHURCH
(Церковь Иоанна Воина; Map p96; ul Bolshaya Yakimanka 48; MOktyabrskaya) The finest of all Zamoskvorechie's churches mixes Moscow and European baroque styles, resulting in a melange of shapes and colours. It was commissioned by Peter the Great in thanks for his 1709 victory over Sweden at Poltava. Inside, the gilt, wood-carved iconostasis was originally installed in the nearby **Church of the Resurrection in Kadashi** (Церковь Воскресения на Кадашах; Map p96; 2-y Kadashevsky per 7). The iconostasis was moved when the latter church was closed (it now houses a restoration centre).

TAGANKA

Taganskaya pl on the Garden Ring is a monster intersection – loud, dusty and crowded. It's the hub of this district south of the little Yauza River. Taganka was the territory of the 17th-century blacksmiths' guild; later it became an Old Believers' quarter. The square's character disappeared with reconstruction in the 1970s and '80s, but traces remain in the streets radiating from it.

Bunker-42 Cold War Museum MUSEUM
(Map p100; ☎495-500 0554; www.bunker42.com; 5-ya Kotelnichesky per 11; admission R1300; ⏲by appointment; MTaganskaya) On a quiet side street near Taganskaya pl, a nondescript neoclassical building is the gateway to the secret Cold War–era communications centre. Operated by Central Telephone & Telegraph, the facility was meant to serve as the communications headquarters in the event of a nuclear attack. As such, the building was just a shell and entryway to the 7000-sq-metre space that is 60m underground.

Now in private hands, the facility has been converted into a sort of museum dedicated to the Cold War. Unfortunately, not much remains from the Cold War days. The vast place is nearly empty, except for a few exhibits set up for the benefit of visitors, such as a scale model of the facility. Visitors watch a 20-minute film about the history of the Cold War, followed by a guided tour of the four underground 'blocks'.

Rublyov Museum of Early Russian Culture & Art MUSEUM
(Музей Андрея Рублёва; off Map p100; Andronevskaya pl 10; adult/student R200/100; ⏲11am-5.30pm Thu-Tue; MPloshchad Ilycha) On the grounds of the former Andronikov Monastery, the Rublyov Museum exhibits icons from days of yore and from the present. Unfortunately, it does not include any work by its acclaimed namesake artist. It is still worth visiting though, not least for its romantic location. Andrei Rublyov, the master of icon painting, was a monk here in the 15th century. He is buried in the grounds, but no one knows quite where.

In the centre of the monastery grounds is the compact **Saviour's Cathedral** (Спасский собор), built in 1427, the oldest stone building in Moscow. The cluster of *kokoshniki,* or gables of colourful tiles and brick patterns, is typical of Russian architecture from the era. To the left is the combined rectory and 17th-century Moscow-baroque **Church of the Archangel Michael** (Церковь Архангела Михаила); to the right, the old monks' quarters house the museum.

Taganka & Zamoskvorechie

Taganka & Zamoskvorechie

Sights

1 Bunker-42 Cold War Museum B1
2 Novospassky Monastery C3

Sleeping

3 Ozerkovskaya Hotel A2

Eating

4 Yolki-Palki.. B2

Drinking

5 Vysotsky B1

Entertainment

6 Moscow International House of Music.. B2
7 Taganka Theatre B1

Novospassky Monastery MONASTERY
(Новоспасский монастырь; Map p100; www.spasnanovom.ru; Verkhny Novospassky proezd; 7am-7pm; Proletarskaya) Novospassky Monastery is a 15th-century fort-monastery, which is located about 1km south of Taganskaya pl. The centrepiece of the monastery, the **Transfiguration Cathedral** (Собор Преобразования), was built by the imperial Romanov family in the 1640s in imitation of the Kremlin's Assumption Cathedral.

Under the river bank, beneath one of the towers of the monastery, is the site of a mass grave for thousands of Stalin's victims. At the northern end of the monastery's grounds are the brick **Assumption Cathedral** and an extraordinary Moscow-baroque **gate tower**.

BASMANNY

Chistye Prudy PARK
(Чистие пруды; Chistoprudny bul; Map p102; Chistye Prudy) Chistye Prudy (Clean Ponds) refers to the lovely little pond that graces the Boulevard Ring at the ul Pokrovka intersection. The Boulevard Ring is always a prime location for strolling but the quaint pond makes this a desirable address indeed. Paddle boats in summer and ice skating in winter are essential parts of the ambience. Pick a café and sip a beer or coffee while watching strollers or skaters go by.

Hidden behind the post office is the famous **Menshikov Tower** (Башня Меньшикова; Map p102; Krivokolenny per; Turgenevskaya), built from 1704 to 1706 by the order of Alexander Menshikov (PTG's right-hand man) at his newly founded estate. The tower was the tallest building in Moscow at the time of its construction (originally 3m taller than the Ivan the Great Bell Tower in the Kremlin) and was one of Moscow's first baroque buildings.

Choral Synagogue SYNAGOGUE
(Хоральная синагога; Map p102; Bolshoy Spasoglinishchevsky per 10; ⏲9am-6pm; ⓂKitay-Gorod) The building of a synagogue was banned inside Kitay Gorod, so Moscow's oldest and most prominent synagogue – the Choral Synagogue – was built just outside the city walls, not far from the Jewish settlement of Zaryadye. Construction started in 1881, but it dragged on for years due to roadblocks by the anti-Semitic tsarist government. It was finally completed in 1906 and was the only synagogue that continued to operate throughout the Soviet period, in spite of Bolshevik demands to convert it into a workers' club.

Andrei Sakharov Museum MUSEUM
(Музей Сахарова; Map p102; www.sakharov-center.ru; Zemlyanoy val 57; ⏲11am-7pm Tue-Sun; ⓂChkalovskaya) South of Kursky vokzal is a two-storey house in a small park, which contains the Andrei Sakharov Museum. Its displays cover the life of Sakharov, the nuclear-physicist-turned-human-rights-advocate, detailing the years of repression in Russia and providing a history of the dissident movement. Temporary expositions cover current human-rights issues. Look for a piece of genuine Berlin Wall in front of the building.

MGU Botanical Garden GARDEN
(Ботанический сад МГУ; Map p102; www.hortus.ru; pr Mira 26; day/evening admission R100/150; ⏲10am-10pm May-Sep, to 5pm Oct-Apr; ⓂProspekt Mira) When you need an escape from the city's hustle and bustle, the MGU Botanical Garden offers a wonderful retreat. Established in 1706, the garden was owned by the Moscow general hospital to grow herbs and other medicinal plants. These days, it is operated by the university. Visitors can wander along the trails, enjoy an exhibition of ornamental plants and explore three greenhouses containing plants from various climate zones.

MOSCOW OUTSKIRTS

All-Russia Exhibition Centre PARK
(Всероссийский Выставочный Центр; Map p56; www.vvcentre.ru; ⏲pavilions 10am-7pm, grounds 8am-10pm; ⓂVDNKh) No other place sums up the rise and fall of the Soviet dream quite as well as the All-Russia Exhibition Centre. The old initials by which it's still commonly known, VDNKh (ВДНХ), tell half the story – in Russian they stand for Exhibition of Achievements of the National Economy.

Originally created in the 1930s, VDNKh was expanded midcentury to impress upon one and all the success of the Soviet economic system. Two kilometres long and

WORTH A TRIP

OLD BELIEVERS' COMMUNITY

One of Russia's most atmospheric religious centres is the **Old Believers' Community** (Старообрядческая Община; ⏲9am-6pm Tue-Sun; ⓂPloshchad Ilycha), located 3km east of Taganskaya pl. Old Believers split from the main Russian Orthodox Church in 1653 when they refused to accept certain reforms. They have maintained old forms of worship and customs ever since.

In the late 18th century, during a brief period free of persecution, rich Old Believer merchants founded this community, among the most important in the country. To get here, take trolleybus 16 or 26, or bus 51, east from Taganskaya pl; get off after crossing a railway. The tall, green-domed 20th-century bell tower of **Rogozhskoe Cemetery** (Рогожское кладбище) is clearly visible to the north.

The yellow, classical-style **Intercession Church** (Церковь Заступничества) contains one of Moscow's finest collections of icons, all dating from before 1653, with the oldest being the 14th-century *Saviour with the Angry Eye* (Spas Yaroe Oko), protected under glass near the south door. The icons in the *deesis* row (the biggest row) of the iconostasis are supposed to represent the Rublyov school, while the seventh, *The Saviour*, is attributed to Andrei Rublyov himself.

Visitors are welcome at the church, but women should take care to wear a long skirt (not trousers) and headscarf.

Basmanny

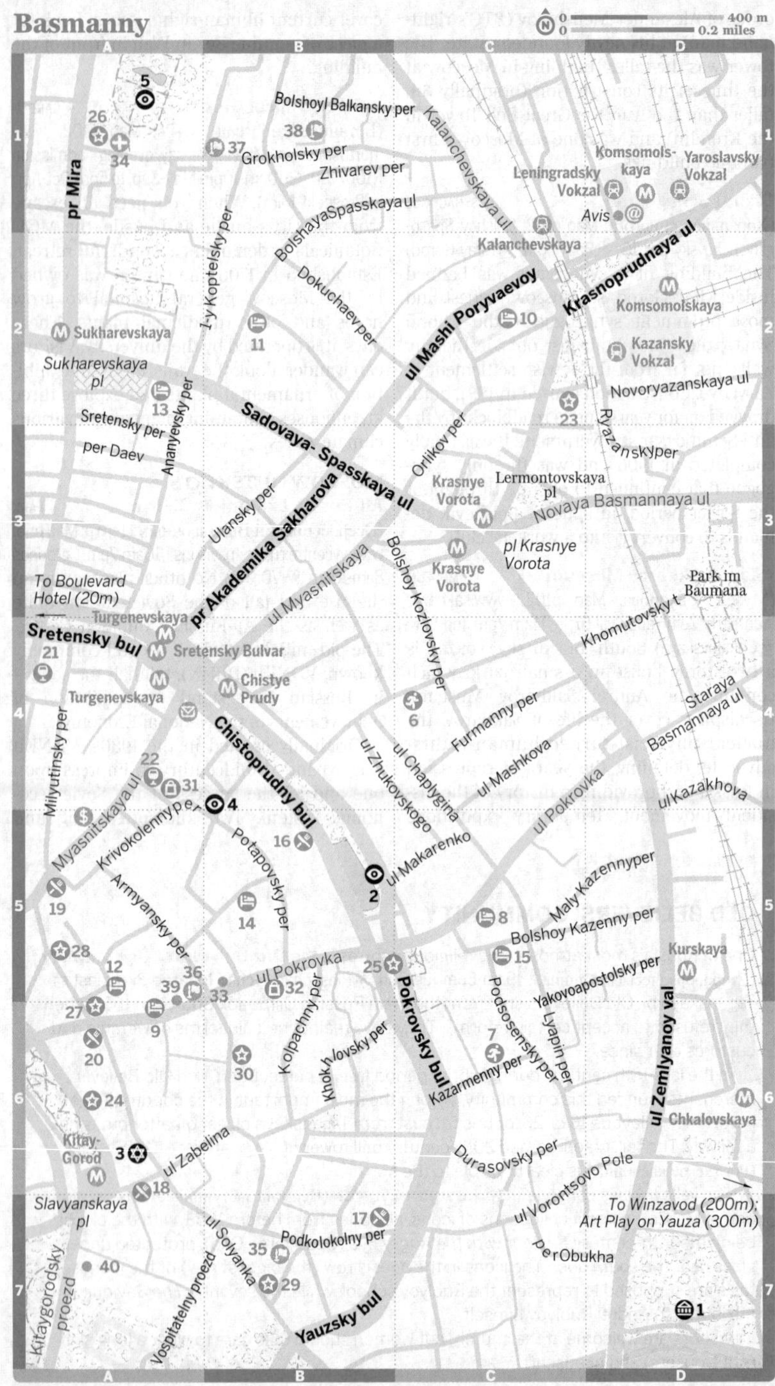
0 400 m
0 0.2 miles
Bolshoyl Balkansky per
Grokholsky per
Zhivarev per
Kalanchevskaya ul
BolshayaSpasskaya ul
Komsomols-kaya
Yaroslavsky Vokzal
Leningradsky Vokzal
Avis
Kalanchevskaya
Krasnoprudnaya ul
pr Mira
1-y Koptelsky per
Dokuchaev per
ul Mashi Poryvaevoy
Komsomolskaya
Kazansky Vokzal
Sukharevskaya
Sukharevskaya pl
Novoryazanskaya ul
Sretensky per
per Daev
Ananyevsky per
Sadovaya- Spasskaya ul
Orlikov per
Ryazanskyper
Krasnye Vorota
Lermontovskaya pl
Novaya Basmannaya ul
Ulansky per
pr Akademika Sakharova
Bolshoy Kozlovsky per
pl Krasnye Vorota
To Boulevard Hotel (20m)
ul Myasnitskaya
Park im Baumana
Turgenevskaya
Sretensky bul
Sretensky Bulvar
Chistye Prudy
Khomutovsky t
Furmanny per
Staraya Basmannaya ul
Milyutinsky per
Chistoprudny bul
ul Zhukovskogo
ul Chaplygina
ul Mashkova
ul Pokrovka
ul Kazakhova
Myasnitskaya ul
Krivokolenny per
Potapovsky per
ul Makarenko
Maly Kazennyper
Armyansky per
Bolshoy Kazenny per
Kurskaya
ul Pokrovka
Pokrovsky bul
Podsosensky per
Yakovoapostolsky per
Kolpachny per
Khokhlovsky per
Lyapin per
Kazarmenny per
ul Zemlyanoy val
Chkalovskaya
Kitay-Gorod
ul Zabelina
Durasovsky per
ul Vorontsovo Pole
Slavyanskaya pl
ul Solyanka
Podkolokolny per
To Winzavod (200m); Art Play on Yauza (300m)
per Obukha
Kitaygorodsky proezd
Vospitatelny proezd
Yauzsky bul

Basmanny

Sights
1 Andrei Sakharov Museum D7
2 Chistye Prudy B5
3 Choral Synagogue A6
4 Menshikov Tower B4
5 MGU Botanical Garden A1

Activities, Courses & Tours
6 CREF Language Centre C4
7 Taste of Russia C6

Sleeping
8 Bentley Hotel C5
9 Comrade Hostel A6
10 Hilton Moscow Leningradskaya C2
11 Hotel Volga B2
Kitay-Gorod Hotel .... (see 24)
12 Napoleon Hostel A5
13 Suharevka Mini-Hotel A2
14 Sverchkov-8 .... B5
15 Trans-Siberian Hostel C5

Eating
16 Avocado B5
17 Dacha on Pokrovka B7
18 Liudi Kak Liudi A6
19 Moo-Moo A5
20 Volkonsky A6

Drinking
21 Liga Pap A4
22 Petrovich A4

Entertainment
23 Central Station MSK C2
24 Chinese Pilot Dzhao-Da A6
25 Krizis Zhanra B5
26 Madam Galife A1
27 PirOGI on Maroseyka A6
28 Propaganda A5
29 Solyanka B7
30 Zapasnik Art Garbage B6

Shopping
31 Bookhunter A4
32 Tricotage Club B5

Information
33 36.6 Pharmacy B5
34 American Medical Center A1
35 Australian Embassy B7
36 Belarusian Consulate A5
37 Irish Embassy B1
38 Japanese Embassy B1
39 Maria Travel Agency A5
40 RosOkhranKultura A7

1km wide, it is composed of wide pedestrian avenues and grandiose pavilions, glorifying every aspect of socialist construction. The pavilions represent a huge variety of architectural styles, symbolic of the contributions from diverse ethnic and artistic movements to the common goal. Here you will find the kitschiest socialist realism, the most inspiring of socialist optimism and, now, the tackiest of capitalist consumerism.

VDNKh is a vast place, covering over 200 hectares with gargantuan statues, flamboyant fountains and distinctive architecture. These days, the attraction is less the exhibitions themselves – although you may happen upon a business or cultural event of interest – and more the elaborate environs, a curious vestige of Soviet paradise gone awry.

Cosmonautics Museum MUSEUM
(Мемориальный музей космонавтики; www.space-museum.ru; admission R200; ⏲10am-7pm Tue-Sun; Ⓜ VDNKh) The soaring 100m titanium obelisk outside the All-Russia Exhibition Centre is a monument 'To the Conquerors of Space', built in 1964 to commemorate the launch of Sputnik. In its base is the Cosmonautics Museum, featuring cool space paraphernalia and an inspiring collection of space-themed propaganda posters. In addition to the historical exhibits, there are some excellent displays about the science of space exploration.

Ostankino Estate-Museum PALACE
(Музей-усадьба Останкино; www.ostankino-museum.ru; admission/excursion R80/150; ⏲10am-6pm Wed-Sun mid-May–Sep; Ⓜ VDNKh) The pink-and-white Ostankino Palace was built in the 1790s as the summer pad of Count Nikolai Sheremetev. The lavish interior, with hand-painted wallpaper and intricate parquet floors, houses the count's art treasures. Along with the Italian Pavilion and the Egyptian Hall, the centrepiece is the oval theatre-ballroom built for the Sheremetev troupe of 250 serf actors. These days, the theatre hosts a **summer music festival** ('Шереметевские сезоны' музыкальный фестиваль; ☎495-683 4645; tickets R200-750; ⏲Jun-Sep), featuring intimate concerts.

MOSCOW'S WHITE-HOT CONTEMPORARY ART SCENE

The Garage Centre for Contemporary Culture isn't the only place to take the pulse of Moscow's vibrant contemporary art scene. In addition to visiting the following recommended spots, set your travel plans to coincide with the Moscow Biennale of Contemporary Art.

Red October (завод Красный Октябрь; Map p96; Bersenevskaya nab; Ⓜ Kropotkinskaya) The red-brick buildings of this former chocolate factory now host **Pobeda Gallery** (http://pobedagallery.com; bldg 4, Bolotnaya nab 3; ⏰1-8pm), **Lumiere Brothers Photography Centre** (www.lumiere.ru; bldg 1, Bolotnaya nab 3; ⏰noon-9pm Tue-Sun) and **Igor Kormyshev** (bldg 1, Beresenevsky per 2; www.kormyshev.ru), plus the centrepiece **Strelka Institute for Media, Architecture and Design** (www.strelkainstitute.ru).

Winzavod (Винзавод; off Map p102; www.winzavod.ru; 4 Siromyatnichesky per 1; ⏰noon-8pm Tue-Sun; Ⓜ Chkalovskaya) A former wine factory has morphed into this postindustrial complex of prestigious galleries, shops, a cinema and a trendy café.

Proekt_Fabrika (www.proektfabrika.ru; 18 Perevedenovsky per; ⏰10am-8pm Tue-Sun; Ⓜ Baumanskaya) A still-functioning paper factory is the location for this nonprofit set of gallery and performance spaces enlivened by arty graffiti and creative-industry offices.

Art Play on Yauza (off Map p102; www.artplay.ru; Nizhnyaya Syromyaticheskaya ul 10; ⏰noon-8pm Tue-Sun; Ⓜ Chkalovskaya) The 'design centre' is home to firms specialising in urban planning and architectural design, as well as furniture showrooms and antique stores.

To reach the Ostankino Palace, walk west from VDNKh metro (across the car parks) to pick up tram 7 or 11 or trolleybus 13, 36, 69 or 73 west along ul Akademika Korolyova. Note that the palace is closed on days when it rains or when humidity is high.

Ostankino TV Tower LANDMARK
(Останкинская башня; ☎8-800-100 5553; www.nashabashnya.ru; weekday/weekend R550/850; ⏰10am-8pm Tue-Sun; Ⓜ VDNKh) When the Ostankino TV Tower was built in 1967, it was the tallest free-standing structure in the world (surpassing the Empire State Building). At 540m, it is now third on the list (though not for too much longer). The observation deck has recently reopened after a decade-long closure. Tours must be booked in advance; bring your passport.

FREE **Kolomenskoe Museum-Reserve** MUSEUM
(Музей-заповедник Коломенское; Map p57; www.mgomz.ru; ⏰grounds 8am-9pm; Ⓜ Kolomenskaya or Kashirskaya) Set amid 4 sq km of parkland, on a bluff above a Moscow River bend, Kolomenskoe Museum-Reserve is an ancient royal country seat and Unesco World Heritage Site.

Ethnographic Centre
(Bolshaya ul; Ⓜ Kolomenskoe) Located on one of the original roads from Kolomenskoe village, the ethnographic centre is a work in progress. For starters, historians have reconstructed a peasant's farm and a blacksmith's compound, as well as a three-domed wooden church. Further south, there is a working stable yard and apiary. The idea is to make this a living museum, where visitors can witness 17th-century village life first hand.

Churches & Gates
From Bolshaya ul, enter the grounds of the museum-reserve through the 17th-century **Saviour Gate** (Спасские ворота) to the star-spangled **Our Lady of Kazan Church**. Ahead, the whitewashed, tent-roofed 17th-century **Front Gate** – guarded by two stone lions – was the main entrance to the royal palace.

Wooden Buildings
Among the old wooden buildings on the grounds is the **cabin** where Peter the Great lived while supervising ship- and fort-building at Arkhangelsk. There are also a few handsome structures that were brought from other regions, specifically the **Bratsk fortress tower** and the **gate-tower of St Nicholas Monastery** from Karelia.

Ascension Church
Outside the front gate, overlooking the river, rises Kolomenskoe's loveliest structure, the Ascension Church, sometimes called the 'white column'. Built between 1530 and 1532

for Grand Prince Vasily III, it probably celebrated the birth of his heir, Ivan the Terrible. As the first brick church with a tent-shaped roof (previously found only on wooden churches), it represents an important development in Russian architecture. This break with the Byzantine tradition would pave the way for St Basil's Cathedral, which was built 25 years later. There is an **exhibit** on Milestones in Kolomenskoe History in the tent-roofed gatehouse nearby.

Great Wooden Palace
(Дворец царя Алексея; ⏲10am-6pm; Ⓜ Kashirskaya) In the mid-17th century, Tsar Alexey built a palace so fab it was dubbed 'the eighth wonder of the world'. This whimsical building was famous for its mishmash of tent-roofed towers and onion-shaped eaves, all crafted from wood and structured without a single nail. Unfortunately, the legendary building had fallen into disrepair and was demolished in 1768 by Catherine the Great.

Some 230 years later, architects and builders managed to construct a replica of the palace based on an existent model of the original. Now, the wooden palace of Tsar Alexey stands about 1km south of its original location. This lack of historical accuracy has raised some eyebrows, but the masterpiece is open for visitors to admire its exquisite 17th-century interiors. In total, 24 rooms have been replicated, based on the records of the original architects and decorators.

Tsaritsyno PALACE
(Музей-заповедник Царицыно; www.tsaritsyno-museum.ru; grounds admission free; ⏲grounds 6am-midnight, exhibits 11am-6pm Tue-Fri, to 8pm Sat & Sun; Ⓜ Tsaritsino) On a wooded hill in far southeast Moscow, Tsaritsyno Palace is a modern-day manifestation of the exotic summer home that Catherine the Great began in 1775 but never finished. Architect Vasily Bazhenov worked on the project for 10 years before he was sacked. She hired another architect, Matvey Kazakov, but the project was eventually forgotten as she ran out of money. For hundreds of years, the palace was little more than a shell, until the government finally decided to finish it in 2007.

Nowadays, the **Great Palace** (Большой дворец; admission R150) is a fantastical building that combines old Russian, Gothic, classical and Arabic styles. Inside, exhibits are dedicated to the history of Tsaritsyno, as well as the life of Catherine the Great. The nearby kitchen building, or **khlebny dom** (Хлебный дом; admission R100), also hosts rotating exhibits, sometimes culinary and sometimes on less-tantalising topics such as icons and art. The *khlebny dom* is a pleasant place to hear classical **concerts** (☎499-725 7291; tickets R150-300; ⏲5pm Sat & Sun) in summer.

The extensive grounds include some other lovely buildings, including the **Small Palace**, the working **Church of Our Lady Lifegiving Spring**, the cavalier buildings and some interesting bridges. A pond is bedecked by a fantastic fountain set to music. The English-style wooded park stretches all the way south to the **Upper Tsaritsynsky Pond**, which has rowing boats available for hire in summer, and west to the Tsaritsyno Palace complex.

Kremlin in Izmaylovo THEME PARK
(Кремль в Измайлово; www.kremlin-izmailovo.com; Izmaylovskoe sh 73; ⏲10am-8pm; Ⓜ Partizanskaya) The famous flea market is only part of a big theme park that includes shops, restaurants, museums and monuments, all contained within a mock 'kremlin' (complete with walls and towers that make a great photo op). Within the kremlin walls, the place re-creates the workshops and trade rows of an old settlement.

A concept long overdue, the **Vodka History Museum** (www.vodkamuseum.ru; ⏲10am-6pm) is just three rooms, with the all-important *traktir* (tavern) attached. Other museums in the complex include the **Russian Costume & Culture Museum** and a small **Toy Museum**.

Izmaylovsky Park & Royal Estate HISTORIC PARK
(Усадьба Измайлово; www.izmailovsky-park.ru; Izmaylovskoe sh; admission free; ⏲11am-9pm; Ⓜ Partizanskaya) This former royal hunting reserve, 10km east of the Kremlin, is the nearest large tract of undeveloped land to central Moscow. Its 15 sq km contain a recreation park at the western end and a much larger expanse of woodland (Izmaylovsky Lesopark) east of Glavnaya alleya, the road that cuts north–south across the park. On a small moated island to the northwest, the royal estate has only a few buildings remaining, including the 1679 **Intercession Cathedral** and the nearby triple-arched, tent-roofed **Ceremonial Gates** (1682).

Stalin's Bunker MUSEUM
(Бункер Сталина; www.cmaf.ru; Sovietskaya ul 80; Ⓜ Partizanskaya) A branch of the Armed

Forces Museum, this secret bunker was built under a sports stadium in the late 1930s in anticipation of the conflict with Germany. You must make advanced arrangements for a group tour of this facility, which includes the command room, dining room, an elegant marble meeting hall, and Stalin's office and living area. Tours are in Russian, but tour companies occasionally bring groups here for English tours.

Activities

TOP CHOICE Sanduny Baths BANYA
(Сандуновские бани; Map p78; private 495-628 4633, general 495-625 4631; www.sanduny.ru; Neglinnaya ul 14; private cabins per 2hr R3000-6000, general admission per 2hr R1000-1800; 8am-midnight; M Chekhovskaya) Sanduny is the oldest and most luxurious *banya* (hot bath, a bit like a sauna) in the city. From the moment you disrobe in one of the richly carved wooden dressing stalls, to your final plunge in the column-lined swimming pool, you will be surrounded by exoticism and extravagance.

Krasnopresnenskie Bani BANYA
(Краснопресненские бани; Map p82; www.banina presne.ru; Stolyarny per 7; general admission per 2hr R850-1000; 8am-10pm; M Ulitsa 1905 Goda) Lacking the old-fashioned, decadent atmosphere of the Sanduny Baths, this modern, clean, efficient place nonetheless provides a first-rate *banya* experience.

Capital Shipping Co BOAT TRIPS
(CCK, Столичная Судоходная Компания; 495-225 6070; www.cck-ship.ru; adult/child R400/150; M Kievskaya) Ferries ply the Moscow River from May to September between Kievsky vokzal and Novospassky Monastery. Traditionally, this was simply a way to get from point A to point B, but visitors to Moscow realised that riding the entire route (1½ hours) was a great way to see the city. Alternatively, you can buy a ticket for the full day (adult/child R800/200), which allows you to get on and off at will. CCK also offers boat excursions out of Moscow, such as to the Nikolo-Ugreshsky Monastery in the eastern suburb of Dzerzhinsky.

Radisson River Cruises BOAT TRIPS
(Map p88; www.radisson-cruise.ru; adult/child R800/600; M Kievskaya) The Radisson operates big riverboats that cart 140 people up and down the Moscow River from the dock near the former Hotel Ukraine. In summer, ferries depart twice a day from Monday to Thursday and five times on Saturday and Sunday. Boats are enclosed (and equipped with ice cutters) so the cruises run year-round, albeit less frequently in winter.

Oliver Bikes CYCLING
(Оливер Байкс; Map p96; www.bikerentalmoscow.com; Pyatnitskaya ul 2; 1/24hr R200/700; noon-10pm Mon-Fri, from 10am Sat & Sun; M Novokuznetskaya) Oliver rents all kinds of two-wheeled vehicles, including cruisers, mountain bikes, folding bikes and tandem bikes, all of which are in excellent condition. The place is conveniently located for bike rides along the Moscow River, in Gorky Park, Neskuchny Garden and Vorobyovy Gory Nature Preserve. Ride carefully!

Kva-Kva Water Park WATERSPORTS
(www.kva-kva.ru; XL Shopping Centre, Yaroslavskoe sh; adult/child from R830/480; 10am-10pm; M VDNKh) This huge complex features seven long and winding water slides, a terrific tsunami water ride, waterfalls and wave pools, not to mention a fabulous *banya*. From VDNKh metro station, take bus N333 to the shopping centre, which is about 1km past MKAD.

Courses

Taste of Russia COOKING
(Map p102; 495-916 3708; www.tasterussia.ru; bldg 4, Kazarmenny per 3; 3hr course R2800, market tour R1300; M Kurskaya) If you love Russian food, you can learn to make it yourself. This operation offers courses (in English), as well as market tours, wine tastings and special children's classes. Courses take place in the evening, when you prepare the meal, then eat it together.

Centre for Russian Language & Culture LANGUAGE
(495-431 3051; www.ruslanguage.ru; Moscow State University; 20hr course €120; M Universitet) Caters mostly to students, offering semester-long courses and dormitory lodging. Special weekly courses for expats (lodging not included) also available.

Ziegler & Partner LANGUAGE
(495-939 0980; www.studyrussian.com; Moscow State University; 2-/4-week course €1110/1990; M Universitet) A Swiss group offering individually designed courses from standard conversation to specialised lessons in business, law, literature etc. Price includes 20 to 24 hours of lessons per week as well as dorm lodging.

GAY & LESBIAN MOSCOW

Moscow is the most cosmopolitan of Russian cities, and the active gay and lesbian scene reflects this attitude. Newspapers such as the *Moscow Times* feature articles about gay and lesbian issues, as well as listings of gay and lesbian clubs.

Resources

Gay.ru (www.gay.ru/english) Includes updated club listings, plus information on gay history and culture in Russia.

Gayrussia (www.gayrussia.ru) An advocacy group that is also involved with the organisation of Gay Pride.

GayTours (www.gaytours.ru) Dmitry is a gay-friendly face in Moscow and his site is still a wealth of information about gay life in the city.

Lesbi.ru (www.lesbi.ru) An active site for lesbian issues.

Gay & Lesbian Venues

12 Volts (12 Вольт; Map p78; ☎495-933 2815; www.12voltclub.ru; bldg 2, Tverskaya ul 12; meals R400-600; ⊙6pm-6am; ⓂMayakovskaya) Enter from the courtyard and buzz for admission. Once you're in, you'll find both gays and lesbians socialising together in a cosy environment, enjoying great drink specials and listening to pop music.

Central Station MSK (Центральная Станция МСК; Map p102; www.centralclub.ru; Yuzhny proezd 4; ⊙restaurant from 7pm, club from 9pm; ⓂKomsomolskaya) The Moscow branch of St Petersburg's biggest gay club. The downstairs lounge holds a gay cabaret featuring some of Moscow's loveliest ladies, while the masses get their groove on upstairs on the main dance floor. Enter through the yellow gate.

Secret (bldg 8, Nizhny Susalny per 7; cover R0-250; ⓂKurskaya) The 'sliding scale' cover charge and cheap drinks attract a young, student crowd. The earlier you arrive, the cheaper the admission, but if you're a male aged 18 to 22 it's free any time.

Moscow Pride

Gay Pride Parades have been held in Moscow every year since 2006, despite bureaucratic obstacles, popular protests and sporadic violence. **Moscow Pride** (www.moscowpride.ru) takes place in May.

In 2010, the European Court of Human Rights fined the government of Russia for human-rights violations related to previous Pride Parades. Nonetheless, in 2011, officials refused yet again to grant the right to assemble (even though antigay protesters were able to obtain permits for their counter-rally on the same day).

The event went forward as planned, even without permits. After only a few minutes, the parade was interrupted by a group of religious protestors, some of whom wore T-shirts that said 'God is with us' as they attacked the peaceful marchers. A few dozen people were arrested, including three high-profile gay-rights activists from the US and France.

CREF Language Centre LANGUAGE
(КРЕФ Центр Изучения Иностранных Языков; Map p102; ☎495-545 4745; www.cref.ru; Malaya Lubyanka ul 16; 40hr course R18,800-23,500; ⓂLubyanka) Also offers individual courses and short-term courses that include lodging.

Liden & Denz Language Centre LANGUAGE
(☎495-254 4991; www.lidenz.ru; Gruzinsky per 3; 20hr course from €280; ⓂBelorusskaya) These more-expensive courses service the business and diplomatic community, with less-intensive evening courses.

Russian Village LANGUAGE
(☎495-225 5001; www.rusvillage.com; weekend-/week-/month-long course from €790/1750/4590) An upscale 'country resort' language school located in the village of Pestovo, north of Moscow. Prices include lodging and meals.

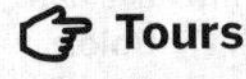

Tours

Capital Tours WALKING TOURS
(Map p68; ☎495-232 2442; www.capitaltours.ru; ul Ilyinka 4; ⓂPloshchad Revolyutsii) This spin-off of Patriarshy Dom in Gostiny Dvor offers a daily Kremlin tour (adult/child R1550/775, 2pm

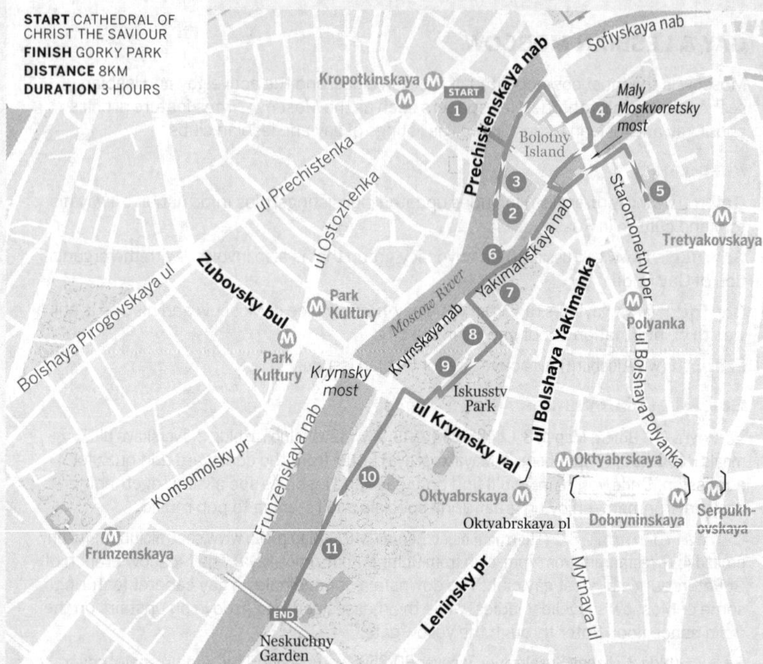

Walking Tour

River Route

Spanning from the Cathedral of Christ the Saviour to Gorky Park, this riverside walking route passes architectural gems, fast-changing neighbourhoods and peaceful parks. In case of tired feet, riverboats ply this route from the Cathedral of Christ the Saviour to Vorobyovy Gory.

Start at the 1 **Cathedral of Christ the Saviour**, from where a pedestrian bridge leads across the Moscow River to Bolotny Island. The Patriarshy most offers a fantastic panorama of the Kremlin towers and of the cathedral itself.

South of the bridge on Bolotny Island is the old 2 **Red October** chocolate factory, now housing a cluster of galleries, shops, clubs and cafés, as well as the centrepiece 3 **Strelka Institute**. This is Moscow's hottest spot for art and entertainment, so poke into any place that looks interesting.

Make a detour north along Sofiyskaya nab. The centrepiece of the little park 4 **Bolotnaya ploshchad** is an intriguing sculpture by Mikhail Shemyakin, *Children are Victims of Adults' Vices* (with all the vices depicted in delightful detail).

Walk across the Maly Kamenny most. The 5 **State Tretyakov Gallery** is a few blocks to the east, but if you don't want to be sidelined for the rest of the day, head south along Yakimanskaya nab, passing Zurab Tsereteli's unmistakable sculpture of 6 **Peter the Great**, or 'Peter the Ugly' according to some sources.

From the embankment, along Krymskaya nab, enter the 7 **Art Muzeon Sculpture Park**, an art museum and history lesson all in one. From here, you can enter the 8 **New Tretyakov**, the branch dedicated to 20th-century art, and the 9 **Central House of Artists**, which is filled with galleries and exhibitions.

Cross ul Krymsky val using the underground passageway. You will reappear at ground level at the entrance to 10 **Gorky Park**. Stroll across the fun-filled theme park, stopping to eat ice cream or ride the Ferris wheel. At the southern end, you can have a drink at 11 **Chaikhona No 1** or stroll across the pedestrian bridge to Frunzenskaya metro station.

Friday to Wednesday), among other walking tours. Also operates a hop-on, hop-off bus service (adult/child R1000/500; 10.30am, 1.30pm and 3.30pm) that departs from the Bolshoi, with 13 stops around the city.

Moscow Mania HISTORY TOURS
(☎8-903-234 9540; www.mosmania.com) Young and enthusiastic history scholars have organised more than 50 walking routes around Moscow, covering the top sights and many lesser known destinations.

Patriarshy Dom Tours CULTURAL TOURS
(Патриарший Дом Туры; off Map p78; ☎495-795 0927; http://russiatravel-pdtours.netfirms.com; Moscow school No 1239, Vspolny per 6; Ⓜ Barrikadnaya) Provides unique English-language tours on just about any specialised subject.

Festivals & Events

Winter Festival CULTURAL
An outdoor fun-fest for two weeks in December and January, for those with antifreeze in their veins. Admire the elaborate ice sculptures on Red Square, stand in a crowd of snowmen on ul Arbat and ride the troika at Izmailovsky Park.

Moscow Forum MUSIC
(www.mosforumfest.ru) This contemporary music festival – usually held in March – features avant-garde musicians from Russia and Europe performing at the Moscow Tchaikovsky Conservatory.

Fashion Week in Moscow FASHION
(www.fashionweekinmoscow.com) The capital's premier fashion event is the chance for Russia's top designers to show the world their sexiest stuff in the age-old halls of Gostiny Dvor. Shows takes place in March and October.

Golden Mask Festival THEATRE
(www.goldenmask.ru) This festival involves two weeks of performances by Russia's premier drama, opera, dance and musical performers, culminating in a prestigious awards ceremony. The event brightens up the otherwise dreary March and April.

Russian Fashion Week FASHION
(www.mercedesbenzfashionweekrussia.com) This fashion event attracts top-name Russian and international fashion designers to unveil their new collections on Moscow runways. The event takes place at the World Trade Centre in April and again in October or November.

Moscow International Film Festival FILM
(www.moscowfilmfestival.ru) This 10-day event in June/July attracts filmmakers from the US and Europe, as well as the most promising Russian artists. Films are shown at theatres around the city.

City Day CULTURAL
City Day, or *den goroda* in Russian, celebrates Moscow's birthday on the first weekend in September. The day kicks off with a festive parade, followed by live music on Red Square and plenty of food, fireworks and fun.

Moscow Biennale of Contemporary Art ART
(www.moscowbiennale.ru) This month-long festival, held in odd-numbered years (and sometimes in different months but most recently in October), has the aim of establishing the capital as an international centre for contemporary art. Venues around the city exhibit works by artists from around the world.

December Nights Festival ART, MUSIC
(www.museum.ru/gmii) Perhaps Moscow's most prestigious music event, this annual festival in December is hosted at the Pushkin Fine Arts Museum, with a month of performances by high-profile musicians and accompanying art exhibits.

Sleeping

With the world's most expensive average hotel rates, Moscow is not a cheap place to stay. The city is flush with international luxury hotels, but more affordable options are few and far between. Fortunately, a slew of hostels have opened in Moscow, so budget travellers have plenty of options. And, slowly but surely, more midrange options are also appearing, usually in the form of 'minihotels'. Prices listed include the 20% VAT (value-added tax) but not the 5% sales tax that's charged mainly at luxury hotels.

» **Budget** For the purposes of this chapter, budget accommodation is less than R3000. Budget accommodation is usually dorm-style, although there are a few private rooms available in this range.

» **Midrange** Midrange accommodation falls between R3000 and R8000 per night. This wide-ranging category includes privately owned minihotels, which usually occupy one or two floors in an apartment building. The rooms have been renovated to comfortably accommodate guests, but the hotel itself (which might have a dozen rooms or less) does not usually offer other facilities. Considering the shortage of midrange options, minihotels are some of the best-value accommodation in the city.

» **Top End** Top end starts at R8000 and goes all the way up.

KITAY GOROD

Hotel Metropol HISTORIC HOTEL **$$$**

(Гостиница Метрополь; Map p78; ☎499-501 7800; www.metmos.ru; Teatralny proezd 1/4; s/d from R9700/10,700; Ⓜ Teatralnaya) Nothing short of an art nouveau masterpiece, the historic Metropol brings an artistic touch to every nook and cranny, from the spectacular exterior to the grand lobby and the individually decorated rooms. The place dates to 1907, so rooms are small by today's standards; if you need space, upgrade to a suite. Prices vary widely by season and day: call the reservations department for the best price.

Kitay-Gorod Hotel MINIHOTEL **$$**

(Отель Китай-Город; Map p102; ☎495-991 9971; www.otel-kg.ru; Lubyansky proezd 25; s R3500-4500, d R5500; Ⓜ Kitay-Gorod) Ever since the demolition of the old Hotel Rossiya, it has been impossible for budget-conscious travellers to stay this close to the Kremlin. We're pleased to see that capitalism has brought us full circle, with this privately owned minihotel on the edge of Kitay Gorod. This place has tiny little rooms, but they are fully and comfortably equipped. The hotel's small size guarantees a warm welcome (unlike at the Rossiya).

TVERSKOY DISTRICT

TOP CHOICE **Artel** MINIHOTEL **$$**

(Map p78; ☎495-626 9008; www.artelhotel.ru; bldg 3, Teatralny proezd 3; s/d economy from R2450/2850, s/d standard R3570/4000; Ⓜ Kuznetsky Most) Tucked into an alley behind the Bolshoi, the Artel has an unbeatable location and an awesome, offbeat atmosphere. Graffiti covers the walls in the stairwell and lobby, while various artists have taken their design skills to some of the (more expensive) rooms. The economy rooms are minute but the whole place feels very creative and cool. Note the music club Masterskaya is one floor below, so at times it may *sound* creative and cool too.

SERVICED APARTMENTS

Entrepreneurial Muscovites have begun renting out apartments on a short-term basis. Flats are equipped with kitchens and laundry facilities, and they almost always offer wireless internet access. The rental agency usually makes arrangements for the flat to be cleaned every day or every few days. Often, a good-sized flat is available for the price of a hotel room, or less. It is an ideal solution for travellers in a group, who can split the cost.

Apartments are around €100 to €200 per night. Expect to pay more for fully renovated, Western-style apartments. Although there are usually discounts for longer stays, they are not significant, so these services are not ideal for long-term renters.

» **Cheap Moscow** (www.cheap-moscow.com) Heed the disclaimers, but this site has loads of listings for apartments to rent directly from the owner.

» **Moscow Suites** (www.moscowsuites.com) Slick apartments in central locations. Services like airport pick-up and visa support are included in the price, which starts at US$200.

» **Intermark Serviced Apartments** (www.intermarksa.ru) Catering mostly to business travellers, Intermark offers four-star quality accommodation, starting at R5500 per night.

» **Rick's Apartments** (www.enjoymoscow.com) Rick's apartments are off the Garden Ring between Sukharevskaya and Tsvetnoy Bulvar metro stations. Studios start at US$135, with two-bedroom apartments about US$215.

» **Evans Property Services** (www.evans.ru) Caters mainly to long-term renters, but also offers some apartments for US$150 to US$250 per night.

» **HOFA** (www.hofa.ru) Apartments from €62 per night and a variety of homestay programs.

» **Moscow4rent.com** (www.moscow4rent.com) Most flats are centrally located, with internet access, satellite TV and unlimited international phone calls. Prices start at US$150 per night.

TOP CHOICE **Golden Apple** BOUTIQUE HOTEL $$$

(Золотое Яблоко; Map p78; ☎495-980 7000; www.goldenapple.ru; ul Malaya Dmitrovka 11; r from R12,000; ; MPushkinskaya) At 'Moscow's first boutique hotel', a classical edifice fronts the street, but the interior is sleek and sophisticated. The rooms are decorated in a minimalist, modern style – subdued whites and greys punctuated with contrasting coloured drapes and funky light fixtures. Comfort is also paramount, with no skimping on luxuries such as heated bathroom floors and down-filled duvets. Check the website for some great promotional discounts.

Hotel Savoy BOUTIQUE HOTEL $$$

(Отель Савой; Map p78; ☎495-620 8500; www.savoy.ru; ul Rozhdestvenka 3; r from R8260; ; MLubyanka) Built in 1912, the Savoy maintains an atmosphere of prerevolutionary privilege for its guests. It is more intimate and more affordable than the other luxury hotels, with 70 elegant rooms. All rooms are equipped with marble bathrooms and Italian fittings and furnishings. The state-of-the-art health club includes a glass-domed 20m swimming pool, complete with geysers and cascades to refresh tired bodies.

Hotel National HISTORIC HOTEL $$$

(Map p78; ☎495-258 7000; www.national.ru; 15/1 Mokhovaya ul; r from R9528; ; MOkhotny Ryad) For over a century, the National has occupied this choice location at the foot of Tverskaya ul, opposite the Kremlin. The handsome building is something of a museum from the early 20th century, displaying frescoed ceilings and antique furniture. Rooms have king-sized beds, flat-screen TVs, down comforters and jewel-toned decor. While the place reeks of history, the service and amenities are up to modern five-star standards.

Godzillas Hostel HOSTEL $

(Map p78; ☎495-699 4223; www.godzillashostel.com; Bolshoy Karetny per 6; dm R450-780, d/tr R1960/2600; @; MTsvetnoy Bulvar) Godzillas is the biggest and most professionally run hostel in Moscow, with 90 beds spread out over four floors. The rooms come in various sizes, but they are all spacious and light-filled, and painted in different colours. To cater to the many guests, there are bathroom facilities on each floor, three kitchens and a big living room with satellite TV. Reminder: don't leave valuables in the luggage storage facility.

Petrovka Loft MINIHOTEL $$

(Map p78; ☎495-626 2210; www.petrovkaloft.com; ul Petrovka 17/2; s & d from R3500; ; MTeatralnaya) Enter the courtyard and go straight ahead to find the entrance to this 10-room hotel (note the four-storey climb). None of the rooms has a bathroom but everything is pretty stylish and clean, and the location is brilliant.

Hotel Budapest HOTEL $$

(Гостиница Будапешт; Map p78; ☎495-925 3050; www.hotel-budapest.ru; Petrovskie linii 2/18; s/d from R5950/6900; ; MKuznetsky Most) This 19th-century neoclassical edifice is an atmospheric option to retire to after shopping on ul Petrovka or seeing a ballet at the Bolshoi. Indeed, guests have been doing exactly that for more than a century. The rooms are traditional and comfortable, though nothing fancy, unless you dish out some extra cash for a suite (from R7500).

Chocolate Hostel HOSTEL $

(Map p78; ☎495-971 2046; www.chocohostel.com; Apt 4, Degtyarny per 15; dm R700-800, tw/tr/q R2400/3000/4000; @; MPushkinskaya) Chocolate lovers rejoice – this charming, friendly hostel will soothe your craving. Bring your favourite brand from home for its collection. In return you'll get simple, friendly accommodation – colourfully painted rooms with metal furniture and old-style parquet floors. Bonus: bikes available for rent!

PRESNYA DISTRICT

Melodiya Hotel BOUTIQUE HOTEL $$

(Отель Мелодия; Map p84; ☎495-660 7178; www.melody-hotel.ru; Skaterny per 13; s/d R5100/5600; ; MArbatskaya) If you like small hotels in quaint neighbourhoods, you will love the Melody Hotel. At least you will want to love it. Service can be spotty and the rooms are rather nondescript; but the place offers good value and the location – tucked into a quiet residential street – is as lovely as a song. Get the best rates on www.booking.com.

Nikitskaya Hotel BOUTIQUE HOTEL $$$

(Никитская гостиница; Map p78; ☎495-933 5001; www.assambleya-hotels.ru; Bolshaya Nikitskaya ul 12; s/d from R7900/9900, breakfast R500; ; MOkhotny Ryad) While the building and rooms at the Nikitskaya are freshly renovated, the hotel preserves an old-fashioned atmosphere of cosiness and comfort. And you can't beat the location. Discounts are available at weekends and other low-occupancy times.

Hotel Peking HOTEL $$
(Гостиница Пекин; Map p78; ☎495-650 0900; www.hotelpeking.ru; Bolshaya Sadovaya ul 5/1; s/d from R4400/4700; ⊖❄🛜; Ⓜ Mayakovskaya) Towering over Triumfalnaya pl, this Stalinist building is blessed with high ceilings, parquet floors and a marble staircase. The rooms vary, but they have all been renovated in attractive jewel tones with modern furniture.

ARBAT DISTRICT

TOP CHOICE **Home from Home** HOSTEL, MINIHOTEL $
(Map p84; ☎495-229 8018; www.home-fromhome.com; apt 9, ul Arbat 49; dm R450-700, d R2000; ⊖@; Ⓜ Smolenskaya) Original art and mural-painted walls create a bohemian atmosphere, which is enhanced by ceiling medallions and exposed brick. For its excellent private en suite rooms, it goes by the name **Bulgakov Hotel** (www.bulgakovhotel.com). There is also a comfy, cosy common area with kitchen facilities. The building is on the Arbat but you must enter the courtyard from Plotnikov per and look for entrance No 2.

ZAMOSKVORECHIE

TOP CHOICE **Red Dawn** BOUTIQUE HOTEL $$
(Красная Заря; Map p96; ☎495-980 4774; www.red-zarya.ru; bldg 8, Bersenevsky per 3/10; r from R7000; ❄🛜; Ⓜ Kropotkinskaya) With a prime waterfront location on the edge of the Red October chocolate factory, this well-placed hotel offers lovely river views and easy access to the capital's hottest nightlife. Spacious designer rooms are done up in browns and beiges, which should be soothing for your hangover. Prices decrease significantly at the weekend.

Red Arrow MINIHOTEL $$
(Красная Стрела; Map p96; ☎8-985-928 6000; bldg 4, Bolotnaya nab 7; r R2500-4000; ❄🛜; Ⓜ Kropotkinskaya) If you can find this teeny-weeny minihotel, you'll enjoy cool, contemporary rooms in Moscow's newest and trendiest area for eating and drinking. Look for a barely marked door in the small courtyard beside Art Akademiya. The seven small rooms exude the postindustrial hipness of the surrounding Red October chocolate factory, with high ceilings, painted brick walls and modern bathrooms. Note that the place is not protected from the nightlife noise, so you might as well go out and join the party.

Danilovskaya Hotel HOTEL $$
(Даниловская гостиница; Map p96; ☎495-954 0503; www.danilovsky.ru; Bul Starodanilovsky per; s/d/ste R5500/6000/8500; ⊖❄@🛜≋; Ⓜ Tulskaya) Moscow's holiest hotel is on the grounds of the 12th-century monastery of the same name – the exquisite setting comes complete with 18th-century churches and well-maintained gardens. The modern five-storey hotel was built so that nearly all the rooms have a view of the grounds. The recently renovated rooms are simple but clean, and breakfast is modest: no greed, gluttony or sloth to be found here.

Ozerkovskaya Hotel BOUTIQUE HOTEL $$
(Озерковская гостиница; Map p100; ☎495-953 7644; www.cct.ru; Ozerkovskaya nab 50; s/d from R5900/6900; ⊖🛜; Ⓜ Paveletskaya) This comfy, cosy hotel has only 27 rooms, including three that are tucked up under the mansard roof. The rooms are simply decorated, but parquet floors and comfortable queen-sized beds rank it above the standard post-Soviet fare. Add in attentive service and a central

SLEEPING WITH STALIN'S SISTERS

Two of the Stalinist skyscrapers known as the Seven Sisters contain hotels, both of which have been renovated into four-star facilities with Western management.

Radisson Royal (Hotel Ukraine) (Рэдиссон Ройал Гостиница Украина; Map p88; ☎495-221 5555; www.ukraina-hotel.ru; Kutuzovsky pr 2/1; r from R10,000; ⊖❄🛜≋; Ⓜ Kievskaya) This bombastic beauty sits majestically on the banks of the Moscow River facing the White House. The place has retained its old-fashioned ostentation, with crystal chandeliers, polished marble and a thematic ceiling fresco in the lobby, while the guestrooms have a similar atmosphere of old aristocracy.

Hilton Moscow Leningradskaya (Map p102; ☎495-627 5550; www.hilton.com; Kalanchevskaya ul 21/40; d from R10,300; ⊖❄🛜≋; Ⓜ Komsomolskaya) Hilton has maintained the Soviet grandiosity in the lobby, but updated the rooms with contemporary design and state-of-the-art amenities. This beauty overlooks Komsomolskaya pl, in all its chaotic, commotion-filled glory.

location (convenient for the express train to Domodedovo Airport), and you've got an excellent-value accommodation option.

Ibis Paveletskaya HOTEL $$
(Map p96; ☎495-661 8500; www.ibishotel.com; ul Shchipok 22; r from R3100; ⊜❄📶; Ⓜ Paveletskaya) You know exactly what you're getting when you book a room at the Ibis: affordable, comfortable rooms and professional, reliable service. The Ibis Paveletskaya is no different. For so long, Moscow suffered from a serious deficiency of both these qualities, so the Ibis is a welcome addition.

Warsaw Hotel HOTEL $$
(Гостиница Варшава; Map p96; ☎495-238 7701; www.hotelwarsaw.ru; Leninsky pr 2/1; s R4300-5800, d R5550-6000; ⊜❄📶; Ⓜ Oktyabrskaya) The Warsaw Hotel doesn't exactly add to the aesthetics of Oktyabrskaya pl. However, the interior is fully renovated, as evidenced by the sparkling, space-age lobby, adorned with lots of chrome, blue leather furniture and spiderlike light fixtures.

BASMANNY

TOP CHOICE **Basilica Hotel** MINIHOTEL, HOSTEL $$
(☎reservations 910-420 3446, front desk 915-462 5575; www.basilicahotel.ru; Serebryanichesky per 1a; s/d from R3000/4000; ⊜❄@📶; Ⓜ Kitay-Gorod) On the grounds of the 1781 Church of Silver Trinity, this aptly named hotel offers lovely, light-filled rooms with wood floors and contemporary furnishings. In the same building, the **hostel** (www.sweetmoscow.com; dm R700, s/d without bathroom from R2300/2400) has similarly decorated four- and six-bed dorm rooms. Besides the brightly painted kitchen and lounge area, there is an inviting outdoor patio. For extra fun, guests can climb to the top of the church's belfry (which is otherwise closed to the public). Breakfast not included.

Trans-Siberian Hostel HOSTEL $
(Map p102; ☎495-916 2030; www.tshostel.com; Barashevsky per 12; dm R630-700, d R2200-3000; ⊜@📶; Ⓜ Kitay-Gorod) This tiny hostel has private rooms in addition to two dorm rooms, one with four heavy wooden bunks and one with eight. The only common space is the kitchen, but it's spacious and modern. A train-themed decor brightens the place up, starting from the moment you step off the street.

Boulevard Hotel MINIHOTEL $$
(Отель Бульвар; off Map p102; ☎495-776 7276; www.bulvar-sr.ru; ul Sretenka 1; s R3800-5100, d R4700-6050; ⊜❄📶; Ⓜ Chistye Prudy) On the 2nd floor of a lovely classical building on the Boulevard Ring, this minihotel offers simple, individually appointed rooms. They are not too fancy, but they benefit from a few artistic touches, such as boldly painted walls, period furnishings and artistic details. The lower end of the price range is for Friday and Saturday nights.

Sverchkov-8 MINIHOTEL $$
(Сверчков-8; Map p102; ☎495-625 4978; www.sverchkov-8.ru; Sverchkov per 8; s/d R4800/5200; ⊜❄📶; Ⓜ Chistye Prudy) On a quiet residential lane, this is a tiny 11-room hotel in a graceful 19th-century building. The hallways are lined with green-leafed plants, and paintings by local artists adorn the walls. Though rooms have old-style bathrooms and faded furniture, this place is a rarity for its intimacy and homey feel.

Suharevka Mini-Hotel MINIHOTEL, HOSTEL $
(Сухаревка; Map p102; ☎8-910-420 3446; www.suharevkahotel.ru; Bolshaya Sukharevskaya pl 16/18; dm/r R500/1800; ⊜@📶; Ⓜ Sukharevskaya) This place occupies two side-by-side flats in a big block on the Garden Ring. The 'hostel side' is cramped and cluttered, with no real common space. Some travellers will appreciate the relative spaciousness and serenity across the hall on the 'hotel side'. All bathroom facilities are shared.

ONCE & FUTURE HOTEL MOSKVA

The story goes that Stalin was shown two possible designs for the Hotel Moskva on Manezhnaya pl. Not realising they were alternatives, he approved both. The builders did not dare point out his error, and so built half the hotel in constructivist style and half in Stalinist style. The incongruous result became a familiar and beloved feature of the Moscow landscape, even gracing the label of Stolichnaya vodka bottles. After years of rumours, the infamous Hotel Moskva was finally demolished in 2003, one in a long list of Soviet-era institutions to bite the dust. The site was claimed by **Four Seasons** (Map p68; http://hotel-moskva.com/en/hotel), which reconstructed the old building complete with architectural quirks. The new high-class luxury hotel is expected to open in 2012.

Bentley Hotel MINIHOTEL $$$
(Map p102; ☎495-917-4436; www.bentleyhotel.ru; ul Pokrovka 28; r R7900-8400; Ⓜ Kitay-Gorod) Upstairs from a popular American-style diner, Bentley goes all out to make its guests feel right at home. Cheeseburgers aside, the minihotel is a warm and inviting place, with a dozen spacious and richly decorated rooms.

Hotel Volga HOTEL $$
(Апарт-Отель Волга; Map p102; ☎495-783 9109; www.hotel-volga.ru; Bolshaya Spasskaya ul 4; s/d R6800/7200; Ⓜ Sukharevskaya) This characterless but comfortable hotel complex, run by Moscow's city government, is on a quiet corner northeast of the centre. The location is just outside the Garden Ring and not far from the metro. Most of the rooms are actually suites with several rooms or a kitchen, making the Volga ideal for small groups or families.

Napoleon Hostel HOSTEL $
(Наполеон Хостел; Map p102; ☎495-628 6695; www.napoleonhostel.ru; 4th fl, Maly Zlatoustinsky per 2; dm R800-1000; Ⓜ Kitay-Gorod) After a four-storey climb, you'll find a friendly, up-to-date hostel. The light-filled rooms have six to 10 wooden bunks, for a total of 48 beds (but only two toilets and two showers – do the maths), plus a clean kitchen and a comfy common room that is well stocked with board games and a plasma TV. Tea and coffee are free but there's no breakfast.

AIRPORT ACCOMMODATION

Recommended for transit travellers who need to crash between flights, both hotels listed here operate free shuttle buses from their respective airports.

Aerotel Domodedovo (Аэротель Домодедово; ☎495-795 3572; www.airhotel.ru; Domodedovo Airport; s/d R6300/6900;) Small but satisfactory rooms, plus a fitness centre and billiards room.

Atlanta Sheremetyevo Hotel (☎498-720 5785; www.atlantahotel.ru; 36/7 Tsentralnaya ul, Sheremetyevsky; r from R4500;) Friendly, small and convenient, the Atlanta is an anomaly in the airport world. Reduced rates available for six- and 12-hour layovers.

Comrade Hostel HOSTEL $
(Map p102; ☎495-628 3126; www.comradehostel.com; ul Maroseyka 11; dm R500-600; @; Ⓜ Kitay-Gorod) It's hard to find this tiny place – go into the courtyard and look for entrance No 3, where you might spot a computer-printed sign in the 3rd-floor window. Inside, there is a great, welcoming atmosphere: the place is packed, but everybody seems to get along like comrades. Breakfast is not included.

Eating

In recent years Moscow has blossomed into a culinary capital. Foodies will be thrilled by the dining options, from old-fashioned *haute russe* to contemporary fusion. Daring chefs are breaking down stereotypes and showing the world how creative they can be. They're importing exotic ingredients, rediscovering ancient cooking techniques and inventing new ones. And Moscow diners are eating it up. Literally.

Many restaurants, especially top-end eateries, accept credit cards, and almost all restaurants have English-language menus. Discounted 'business lunch' specials are often available weekdays before 4pm. This is a great way to sample some of the pricier restaurants around town. Most upscale places require booking a table in advance, especially on weekends.

During Lent (the 40-day period before Orthodox Easter), vegetarians will have a plethora of eating options, as many restaurants offer special Lenten menus that feature no meat or dairy products. Only a few restaurants are exclusively vegie all year round.

KREMLIN & RED SQUARE

Stolovaya 57 CAFETERIA $
(Столовая 57; Map p68; 3rd fl, GUM, Krasnaya pl 3; meals R300-400; ⏲10am-10pm; Ⓜ Okhotny Ryad) Newly minted, this old-style cafeteria offers a nostalgic re-creation of dining in post-Stalinist Russia. The food is good – and cheap for such a fancy store. Meat cutlets and cold salads come highly recommended.

Bosco Cafe INTERNATIONAL $$
(Map p68; www.bosco.ru; GUM, Krasnaya pl 3; meals R600-1000; ⏲10am-11pm; Ⓜ Ploshchad Revolyutsii) Sip a cappuccino in view of the Kremlin. Munch on lunch while the crowds line up at Lenin's Mausoleum. Enjoy an afternoon aperitif while admiring St Basil's domes. This café on the 1st floor of GUM is the only place to sit right on Red Square and marvel at its magnificence.

FAST FOOD RUSSIAN-STYLE

There's no shortage of fast food in Moscow – and we're not talking about the invasion of McDonald's. If you're short on cash or short on time (or both), try one of these Russian fast food chains:

Moo-Moo (Ресторан Му-му; www.moo-moo.ru; 9am-11pm;) Arbat (Map p84; ul Arbat 45/24; meals R200-300; Smolenskaya); Basmanny (Map p102; Myasnitskaya ul 14; Lubyanka) Cafeteria-style service and Holstein-print decor.

Prime Star (Прайм Стар; www.prime-star.ru; meals R200-300; 7am-11pm;) Arbat (Map p84; ul Arbat 9; Arbatskaya); Tverskoy (Map p78; ul Bolshaya Dmitrovka 7/5; Teatralnaya); Zamoskvorechie (Map p96; Pyatnitskaya ul 5; Novokuznetskaya) A healthy sandwich shop, also serving soups, salads, sushi and other 'natural food'.

Yolki-Palki (www.elki-palki.ru; meals R300-500;) Arbat (Map p84; 495-291 7654; ul Novy Arbat 11; 11am-midnight; Arbatskaya); Taganka (Map p100; 495-912 9187; Taganskaya pl 2; 9am-11pm Mon-Fri, from 10am Sat & Sun; Taganskaya); Tverskoy (Map p78; Neglinnaya ul 8/10; 10am-midnight, from 11am Sat & Sun; Kuznetsky Most); Zamoskvorechie (Map p96; 495-953 9130; Klimentovsky per 14; 10am-9pm; Tretyakovskaya) This Russian chain is beloved for its country-cottage decor and its well-stocked salad bar.

KITAY GOROD

Loft Café FUSION $$

(Map p78; www.cafeloft.ru; 6th fl, Nautilus, Nikolskaya ul 25; meals R1000-1500; 9am-midnight; ; Lubyanka) On the top floor of the Nautilus shopping centre, next door to the luxury spa, you'll find this tiny, trendy café. An even smaller terrace gives a fantastic view of Lubyanka pl. Innovative, modern dishes fuse the best of Russian cuisine with Western and Asian influences.

Pelmeshka CAFETERIA $

(Пельмешка; meals R150-200;) Red Square (Map p68; Nikolskaya ul 8/1; 10am-midnight; Ploshchad Revolyutsii); Zamoskvorechie (Kozhevnicheskaya ul 1; 10am-7pm Mon-Fri; Paveletskaya) Pelmeshka is a clean, post-Soviet *stolovaya* (canteen), serving many different kinds of *pelmeni* (Russian-style ravioli) – the most filling of Russian favourites. It's packed with patrons at lunchtime, a sign that the food is tasty as well as cheap.

TVERSKOY DISTRICT

Delicatessen INTERNATIONAL $$

(Map p78; 495-699 3952; www.newdeli.ru; Savodvaya-Karetnaya ul 20; meals R800-1000; noon-midnight Tue-Sat; ; Tsvetnoy Bulvar) 'Thank you for finding us' reads the sign over the door at this casual but classy restaurant bar. It does take some finding, but it's worth the effort. The menu has an eclectic array of offerings like *salade niçoise*, shrimp ceviche and beef tartar, as well as burgers and pasta.

DoDo FUSION $$$

(Map p78; 8-903-105 1010; www.dodoproject.com; ul Petrovka 21/2; meals R1000-1500; 10am-midnight Sun-Thu, to 6am Fri & Sat; ; Chekhovskaya) Inspired cuisine in a sleek setting at affordable prices: in Moscow this concept is as rare as the dodo itself. You'll want to spend some time perusing the menu, which deftly blends flavours from all corners of the globe.

Barashka RUSSIAN $$$

(Барашка; Map p78; 495-625 2895; www.novikovgroup.ru; ul Petrovka 20/1; meals R1500-2000; ; Teatralnaya) Set in an understated Baku-style courtyard, Barashka offers a menu full of fresh tasty salads, grilled meats and slow-cooked stews, many of which feature the little lamb for which the restaurant is named. There is also a **Presnya branch** (Map p82; 495-252 2571; ul 1905 goda 2; Ulitsa 1905 Goda).

Jagannath VEGETARIAN $

(Джаганнат; Map p78; Kuznetsky most 11; meals R400-600; 10am-11pm; ; Kuznetsky Most) If you are in need of vitamins, this is a funky vegetarian café, restaurant and shop. Its Indian-themed decor is more New Agey than ethnic. Service is slow but sublime, and the food is worth the wait.

Akademiya ITALIAN $$

(Академия; Map p78; www.academiya.ru; Kamergersky per 2; business lunches R280, meals R600-1000; 9am-midnight Mon-Fri, from 11am Sat & Sun; ; Teatralnaya) Somebody at

Akademiya knows real estate. That's the only way to explain how this upscale pizzeria is able to find all the sweetest spots: you'll also find Akademiya in **Arbat** (Map p84; Gogolevsky bul 33/1; Ⓜ Arbatskaya), **Presnya** (Map p78; Bolshaya Bronnaya ul 2/6; Ⓜ Tverskaya) and in front of the **Cathedral of Christ the Saviour** (Map p96; Ⓜ Kropotkinskaya).

PRESNYA DISTRICT

Café Pushkin RUSSIAN $$$

(Кафе Пушкинъ; Map p78; ☎495-739 0033; www.cafe-pushkin.ru; Tverskoy bul 26a; business lunches R750, meals R1500-2000; ⏲24hr; Ⓜ Pushkinskaya) The tsarina of *haute-russe* dining, with an exquisite blend of Russian and French cuisines – service and food are done to perfection. The lovely 19th-century building has a different atmosphere on each floor, including a richly decorated library and a pleasant rooftop café. Go next door to **Pushkin Konditerskaya** for dessert.

Volkonsky BAKERY $

(Волконский; www.wolkonsky.com; meals R200-400) Basmanny (Map p102; ul Maroseyka 4/2; Ⓜ Kitay-Gorod); Presnya (Map p78; Bolshaya Sadovaya ul 2/46; ⏲8am-11pm; Ⓜ Mayakovskaya) The queue often runs out the door, as loyal patrons wait their turn for the city's best fresh-baked breads, pastries and pies.

Khachapuri GEORGIAN $$

(Хачапури; Map p78; www.hacha.ru; Bolshoy Gnezdnikovsky per 10; lunches R200-500, meals R500-800; ⏲10am-11pm; Ⓜ Pushkinskaya) Unassuming, affordable and appetising, this urban café exemplifies what people love about Georgian culture: in short, the warm hospitality and the fresh-baked *khachapuri* (cheesy bread). Aside from seven types of delicious *khachapuri*, there's also an array of soups, shashlyki (kebabs), *khinkali* (dumplings) and other Georgian favourites.

Stolle RUSSIAN $

(Штолле; Map p78; www.stolle.ru; Bolshaya Sadovaya ul 8/1; meals R200-600; ⏲8am-10pm; Ⓜ Mayakovskaya) This is one of Moscow's coolest places to come for coffee, although you'd be a fool to leave without sampling one of its magnificent *pirozhki* (pies). It may be difficult to decide (mushroom or meat, apricot or apple?) but you really can't go wrong. There is another outlet in **Khamovniki** (Map p88; Malaya Pirogovskaya ul 16; ⏲9am-9pm; Ⓜ Sportivnaya).

Chagall JEWISH $$

(off Map p78; www.chagall.ru; Bolshaya Nikitskaya ul 47/3; meals R800-1200; Ⓜ Barrikadnaya) Inside a Jewish community centre, this convivial kosher restaurant serves tasty, freshly made dishes. The sour-sweet beef dish *esik fleisch* is delicious, as are the latkes (potato pancakes).

Starlite Diner DINER $$

(Старлайт Дайнер; Map p78; www.starlite.ru; Bolshaya Sadovaya ul 16; meals R500-700; ⏲24hr; Ⓜ Mayakovskaya) Outdoor seating and classic diner decor make this a long-time favourite of Moscow expats. Additional outlets are in **Tverskoy** (Map p78; Strastnoy bul 8a; Ⓜ Pushkinskaya) and in **Zamoskvorechie** (Map p96; Bolotnaya pl 16/5; Ⓜ Tretyakovskaya).

Tsentralny restoranny dom CAFETERIA $

(Центральный ресторанный дом; off Map p78; Kudrinskaya pl 1; meals R200-300; ⏲10am-11pm; Ⓜ Barrikadnaya) The 'central restaurant house' is on the ground floor of the Stalinist skyscraper at Kudrinskaya pl, and the bombastic Russian Empire–style interior has been preserved. It's an odd setting for a self-service lunch but that's the charm of it. Standard Russian canteen fare for cheap.

Shinok UKRAINIAN $$

(Шинок; Map p82; ☎495-651 8101; www.shinok.ru; ul 1905 goda 2; meals R1000-1200; ⏲24hr; Ⓜ Ulitsa 1905 Goda) In case you didn't think Moscow's themed dining was over the top, this restaurant has re-created a Ukrainian peasant farm in central Moscow. As you dine, you can look out the window at a cheerful babushka while she tends the farmyard animals (they're very well taken care of, we're assured).

ARBAT DISTRICT

Genatsvale on Arbat GEORGIAN $$

(Генацвале на Арбате; Map p84; ☎495-697 9453; www.restoran-genatsvale.ru; ul Novy Arbat 11; meals R600-1000; Ⓜ Arbatskaya) Bedecked with fake trees and flowing fountains, this restaurant conjures up the Caucasian countryside – the perfect setting to feast on favourites such as *khachapuri* and lamb dishes. If you prefer a more intimate atmosphere, head to the original **Genatsvale on Ostozhenka** (Генацвале на Остоженке; Map p96; ☎495-695 0401; ul Ostozhenka 12/1; Ⓜ Kropotkinskaya).

Vostochny Kvartal UZBEK $$

(Восточный квартал; Map p84; ul Arbat 45/24; meals R400-800; Ⓜ Smolenskaya) Acting as the 'Eastern Quarter' of the Arbat, this place serves some of the best food on the block.

KHAMOVNIKI

Tiflis
GEORGIAN $$

(Тифлис; Map p96; 499-766 9728; ul Ostozhenka 32; meals R800-1200; Kropotinskaya) The name of this restaurant comes from the Russian word for the Georgian capital, Tbilisi, and when you enter this restaurant you might think you are there. Its airy balconies and interior courtyards recall a 19th-century Georgian mansion – a romantic and atmospheric setting.

Galereya Khudozhnikov
FUSION $$

(Галерея художников; Map p96; ul Prechistenka 19; meals R1000-1500; Kropotkinskaya) This fantastical restaurant inside the Tsereteli Gallery is everything that you would expect from this over-the-top artist. The place certainly lives up to its name, which means Artists' Gallery. The menu is a fusion of European and Asian influences. Though it is secondary to the art, the food is well prepared and, appropriately enough, artistically presented.

Il Patio
ITALIAN $

(Ил Патио; Map p96; www.il-patio.rosinter.com; ul Volkhonka 13a; meals R400-800; Kropotkinskaya) This ubiquitous chain has a slew of outlets, each representing a different Italian city. The most inviting one, near the Cathedral of Christ the Saviour, has a large glass-enclosed seating area, making a perfectly pleasant setting for feasting on wood-oven pizzas and fresh salads.

ZAMOSKVORECHIE

Grably
CAFETERIA $

(Грабли; Map p96; www.grably.ru; Pyatnitskaya ul 27; meals R200-300; 10am-11pm; Novokuznetskaya) The big buffet features an amazing array of fish, poultry and meat, plus breakfast items, salads, soups and desserts. After you run the gauntlet and pay the bill, take a seat in the elaborate winter-garden seating area. There's also an outlet in the **Evropeysky Shopping Centre** (Европейский Торговый Дом; Map p88).

Sok
VEGETARIAN $$

(Сок; Map p96; www.cafe-cok.ru; Lavrushinsky per 15; meals R500-800; 11am-11pm; Tretyakovskaya) Citrus-coloured walls and delicious fresh-squeezed juices are guaranteed to brighten your day. All the soups, salads, pasta and fabulous desserts are vegetarian, with many vegan options too. The menu even features a few Russian classics like beef stroganoff, made with seitan (a wheat-based meat substitute).

TAGANKA

American Bar & Grill
AMERICAN $$

(off Map p100; http://ambar.rosinter.com; ul Zemlyanoy val 59; meals R600-800; noon-2am; Taganskaya) One of Moscow's oldest expat hang-outs, this place still attracts a regular crowd for its enormous portions, its outdoor terrace and its Wild West interior. With classic fare such as big burgers and spicy chicken wings, it's always a pleasant place for cold beers. You're bound to meet some other *inostrantsy* (foreigners) who are quaffing them, too.

BASMANNY

Liudi Kak Liudi
FAST FOOD $

(Люди как люди; Map p102; www.ludikakludi.ru; Solyansky t 1/4; meals R300; 11am-10pm Mon-Sat, to 8pm Sun; Kitay-Gorod) This cute café has a few things going for it: location, warm welcome, tasty food and low prices. It's the perfect lunch stop for pretty much anyone, which explains why this is such a popular place.

Dacha on Pokrovka
RUSSIAN $$

(Map p102; www.dacha-napokrovke.ru; Pokrovsky bul 18/15; meals R500-800; Kitay-Gorod) This

TO MARKET, TO MARKET

Moscow markets *(rynky)* are busy, bustling places, full of activity and colour. Even if you're not shopping, it's entertaining to peruse the tables piled high with multicoloured produce: homemade cheese and jam; golden honey straight from the hive; vibrantly coloured spices pouring out of plastic bags; slippery silver fish posing on beds of ice; and huge slabs of meat hanging from the ceiling. Many vendors bring their products up from the Caucasus to sell them in the capital. Prices are lower and the quality of product is often higher than in the supermarkets. Bring your own bag and don't be afraid to haggle.

Danilovsky Market (Даниловский рынок; Map p96; Mytnaya ul 74; Tulskaya)

Dorogomilovsky Market (Дорогомиловский рынок; Map p88; Mozhaysky val 10; 10am-8pm; Kievskaya)

Rizhsky Market (Рижский рынок; pr Mira 94-96; Rizhskaya)

ramshackle old mansion offers a welcoming and familiar atmosphere – the perfect place to enjoy delicious and affordable Russian home-cooking.

Glavpivtorg RUSSIAN $$
(Map p78; www.glavpivtorg.ru; ul Bolshaya Lubyanka 5; business lunches R200, meals R800-1200; MLubyanka) The 'central beer restaurant No 5' re-creates an upscale apparatchik drinking and dining experience. The Soviet fare is authentic, as is the *russky* crooner music (maybe too authentic for some tastes). But the three varieties of beer brewed on-site are decidedly New Russia.

Avocado VEGETARIAN $
(Авокадо; Map p102; Chistoprudny bul 12/2; meals R200-400; 10am-11pm; ; MChistye Prudy) Meatless versions of soups and salads, pasta and *pelmeni* are all featured (although there is no English-language menu, so bring your phrasebook).

Drinking

These days, there are coffee houses and beer pubs sprouting up all over Moscow. Traditionally, ul Arbat is a prime spot for the café scene, especially as it is closed to automobile traffic. Likewise, the trendy Kamergersky per is a pedestrian-only street, which makes it a hot spot for strollers and drinkers.

Moscow temperatures occasionally call for a warming drink, so it's nice to know you're never far from a fresh brewed cup o' joe. A few of the Russian chains have followed their Western counterparts and opened up outlets on every corner. Rest assured, you will never be far from a Kofe Khaus or a Shokolodnitsa. But a few other places earn higher marks for atmosphere and artistry (not to mention coffee).

KITAY GOROD

Dissident Vinoteca WINE BAR
(Map p78; www.dissident.msk.ru; 5th fl, Nautilus, Nikolskaya ul 25; 11am-midnight; MLubyanka) Comfortable and classy, this rare Moscow wine bar offers over 200 kinds of wine by the glass, along with appropriate accompaniments such as cheese, pâté and other hors d'oeuvres. Panoramic views of Lubyanka Prison are free.

Cup & Cake Cafe CAFÉ
(Map p78; www.ginzaproject.ru; Nikolskaya ul 10/2; MLubyanka) Fronting a fancy fashion boutique, this tiny café is big on style, with plush pillows and rich fabrics strewn about. Come to indulge in coffee and sweets – and to look good while doing so.

TVERSKOY DISTRICT

Cafe Mart CAFÉ
(Map p78; www.cafemart.ru; ul Petrovka 25; meals R800-1200; 11am-midnight Sun-Wed, to 6am Thu-Sat; ; MChekhovskaya) Located in the basement of the Moscow Museum of Modern Art, this club-café is an appropriately artistic place, with warm lighting and mosaic-covered walls. The standard bar menu and decent wine list are accompanied by a selection of enticing exotic teas.

Chaikhona No 1 CAFÉ
(Чайхона No 1; Map p78; www.chaihona.com; Hermitage Gardens; from 2pm; MChekhovskaya) Housed in an inviting, exotic tent, laid with oriental rugs and plush pillows, this cool Uzbek lounge and café is one of the best chill-out spots in the city. There are other outlets around the city, including one near **Gorky Park** (Парк Культуры им Горького; Map p96; MFrunzenskaya).

Simachyov BAR
(Симачёв; Map p78; www.bar.denissimachev.com; Stoleshnikov per 12/2; from 11am; MChekhovskaya) By day it's a **boutique** and café, owned and operated by the famed fashion designer of the same name. By night, this place becomes a hip-hop-happening nightclub that combines glamour and humour. You still have to look sharp to get in here, but at least you can be bohemian about it.

Gogol CLUB
(Гоголь; Map p78; www.gogolclubs.ru; Stoleshnikov per 11; 24hr, concerts 9pm or 10pm Thu-Sat; MChekhovskaya) Fun, informal and affordable (so surprising on swanky Stoleshnikov), Gogol is great for food, drinks and music.

PRESNYA DISTRICT

Kvartira 44 BAR
(Квартира 44; Map p78; www.kv44.ru; Bolshaya Nikitskaya ul 22/2; noon-2am Sun-Thu, to 6am Fri & Sat; ; MOkhotny Ryad) Somebody had the brilliant idea to convert an old Moscow apartment into a crowded, cosy bar, with tables and chairs tucked into every nook and cranny. There's another in **Zamoskvorechie** (ul Malaya Yakimanka 24/8; MPolyanka).

Coffee Mania CAFÉ
(Кофемания; Map p78; www.coffeemania.ru; Moscow Tchaikovsky Conservatory, Bolshaya Nikitskaya ul 13; meals R600-800; 24hr; ; MOkhotny Ryad) This friendly, informal café is beloved

for its homemade soups, freshly squeezed juices and steaming (if overpriced) cappuccinos, not to mention its summer terrace overlooking the leafy courtyard of the conservatory. There is an additional outlet at **Kudrinskaya ploshchad** (off Map p78; Kudrinskaya pl 46/54; ⌚8am-midnight; ⓂBarrikadnaya).

Ryumochnaya BAR

(Рюмочная; Map p78; Bolshaya Nikitskaya ul 22/2; meals R300-500; ⌚11am-11pm; ⓂOkhotny Ryad) This is a hold-over (or a comeback?) from the days when a drinking establishment needed no special name. The *ryumochnaya* was the generic place where comrades stopped on their way to or from work to toss back a shot or two before continuing on their way.

ARBAT DISTRICT

Zhiguli Beer Hall BREWERY

(Пивной зал Жигули; Map p84; www.zhiguli.net; ul Novy Arbat 11; ½ litre beer R100-150; ⌚10am-2am Sun-Thu, to 4am Fri & Sat; ⓂArbatskaya) It's hard to classify this old-style *stolovaya* that happens to brew great beer. The minimalist decor and cafeteria-style service recall the heyday, although this place has been updated with big-screen TVs and a separate table-service dining room.

Tinkoff BREWERY

(Тинкофф; off Map p84; Protochny per 11; ½ litre beer R180, meals R600-800; ⌚noon-2am; 👪; ⓂSmolenskaya) Moscow's branch of this now-nationwide microbrewery features sport on the big screen, lagers and pilsners on draught, and a 1m-long sausage on the menu (yikes).

ZAMOSKVORECHIE

Bar Strelka BAR

(Map p96; www.strelkainstitute.ru; Bersenevskaya nab 14/5; ⓂKropotkinskaya) The Strelka Institute for Media, Architecture and Design is the focal point of the new development at the Red October chocolate factory. Aside from the course offerings and the popular bar, Strelka promises to give Moscow a healthy dose of contemporary culture, hosting lectures, workshops, film screenings and concerts.

Lebedinoe Ozero CAFÉ

(Лебединое озеро; Map p96; http://s-11.ru/lebedinoe-ozero; Neskuchny Garden; ⌚noon-2am May-Sep; ⓂFrunzenskaya) The name means 'Swan Lake' and, yes, it overlooks a little pond where resident swans float contentedly. Come to lounge in the sun, sip (expensive) fruity cocktails or take a cooling dip.

> **HOW TO GET PAST FACE CONTROL**
>
> » Dress up: skirts and heels for women, dress pants and leather shoes for men.
>
> » Arrive by car.
>
> » Arrive in a small group, preferably with more men than women.
>
> » Speak English. Foreigners are not as special as they used to be, but they're still pretty special.
>
> » Smile. Show the bouncer that you are going to enhance the atmosphere inside.
>
> » If possible, book a table. Unfortunately, at the more elite clubs this requires a sometimes hefty 'table deposit'.

Art Akademiya CAFÉ

(Арт Академия; Map p96; www.academiya.ru; Bersenevskaya nab 6/3; ⌚noon-midnight Sun-Thu, to 6am Fri & Sat; 🚭📶🍷📋👪; ⓂKropotkinskaya) The pizza chain with all the best locations has nabbed a massive space in the Red October Factory complex for this superstylish, contemporary-art-packed lounge bar-café.

Progressive Daddy & Daddy's Terrace BAR

(Map p96; www.progressivedaddy.ru; Bersenevskaya nab 6/2; ⓂKropotkinskaya) Daddy snagged the prime location in the Red October complex: at the tip of the island, on the top floor of the factory, the restaurant-bar-club has the best views in the joint (if not the city).

Rolling Stone BAR

(Map p96; Bolotnaya nab 3; ⌚noon-midnight Sun-Thu, to 6am Fri & Sat; ⌚Kropotkinskaya) Plastered with covers of the namesake magazine and lit by naked bulbs, this place has the feel of an upscale dive bar. What makes it upscale is the location – the ultratrendy Red October complex – and the clientele – they might be dressed in casual digs but they still have to look impeccable to get past the face control.

TAGANKA

Vysotsky BAR

(Map p100; ☎495-915 0434; www.club-vysotsky.ru; Nizhny Tagansky t 3; meals R800-1000;

noon-5am; Taganskaya) Named for the iconic Soviet film star, poet and music maker. Experience what it was like when there was no place to go out except your friends' flats, where you would sit around and drink cheap champagne, argue about politics and sing along while somebody played the guitar.

BASMANNY

Petrovich BAR

(Map p102; 495-923 0082; www.club-petrovich.ru; Myasnitskaya ul 24/1; meals R800-1000; Chistye Prudy) Soviet times may not have been happier; they may not have been simpler. But they were definitely funnier, according to local cartoonist and restaurateur Andrei Bilzh. See his eponymous masterpieces at this popular retro bar, which reminisces with Soviet propaganda and pop music. Book in advance and enter through an unmarked door in the courtyard.

Liga Pap BAR

(Map p102; www.ligapap.ru; ul Bolshaya Lubyanka 24; meals R500-1000; Lubyanka) It's a sports bar, but it sure is a snazzy one. The gorgeous interior features big windows, tiled floors and Gothic arched ceilings, in addition to the 20-plus flat-screen TVs. The centrepiece of the main hall is the huge screen, complete with projector and dramatic auditorium-style seating.

☆ Entertainment

The key to finding out what's on when you're in Moscow is the weekly magazine *element* and the comprehensive weekly entertainment section in Friday's *Moscow Times*.

Theatre and concert programs are displayed at venues and at ticket kiosks. Aside from the Bolshoi, you can usually purchase tickets directly from box offices on the day of the performance. Most theatres are closed between late June and early September.

Classical Music

Moscow International House of Music CLASSICAL MUSIC

(Московский международный дом музыки; Map p100; www.mmdm.ru; Kosmodamianskaya nab 52/8; tickets R200-2000; Paveletskaya) This graceful, modern, glass building has three halls, including Svetlanov Hall, which holds the largest organ in Russia. This is the usual venue for performances by the **National Philharmonic of Russia** (www.nfor.ru), a privately financed and highly lauded classical-music organisation.

Tchaikovsky Concert Hall CLASSICAL MUSIC

(Концертный зал Чайковского; Map p78; box office 495-232 0400; www.classicalmusic.ru; Triumfalnaya pl 4/31; tickets R100-1000; Mayakovskaya) Home to the famous State Philharmonic, the capital's oldest symphony orchestra, the concert hall was established in 1921. This is where you can expect to hear the Russian classics such as Stravinsky, Rachmaninov and Shostakovich, as well as other European favourites. Look out for special children's concerts.

Moscow Tchaikovsky Conservatory CLASSICAL MUSIC

(Московская консерватория Чайковского; Map p78; box office 495-629 8183; www.mosconsv.ru; Bolshaya Nikitskaya ul 13; Okhotny Ryad) The country's largest music school has two venues: the Great Hall (Bolshoy Zal) and the Small Hall (Maly Zal).

Opera & Ballet

TOP CHOICE **Bolshoi Theatre** OPERA, BALLET

(Большой театр; Map p78; 8-800-333 1333; www.bolshoi.ru; Teatralnaya pl 1; tickets R200-2000; Teatralnaya) An evening at the Bolshoi is still one of Moscow's most romantic and entertaining options for a night on the town. The glittering six-tier auditorium has an electric atmosphere, evoking more than 230 years of premier music and dance. The Bolshoi has recently undergone a much-needed renovation, reopening the doors of its main stage after several years of work. The smaller New Stage (Novaya Stsena), remodelled in 2003, also hosts performances.

Stanislavsky & Nemirovich-Danchenko Musical Theatre OPERA, BALLET

(Музыкальный театр Станиславского и Немирович-Данченко; Map p78; www.stanislavskymusic.ru; ul Bolshaya Dmitrovka 17; tickets R200-1000; box office 11.30am-7pm; Chekhovskaya) Another opera and ballet company with a similar classical repertoire and high-quality performances. This historic theatre company was founded when two legends of the Moscow theatre scene – Konstantin Stanislavsky and Vladimir Nemirovich-Danchenko – combined forces in 1941.

Kremlin Ballet Theatre BALLET

(Театр кремлевский балет; Map p68; www.kremlin-gkd.ru; ul Vozdvizhenka 1; box office noon-8pm; Alexandrovsky Sad) The Bolshoi does not have a monopoly on ballet and opera in Moscow. Leading dancers also appear with the

TICKETS FOR THE BOLSHOI

Unlike other theatres around Moscow, it is not possible to buy tickets to the Bolshoi at the *teatralnaya kassa* (ticket office). In theory, tickets can be reserved by phone or over the internet up to three months in advance of the performance. It is usually possible to purchase tickets at the Bolshoi's **box office** (499-250 7317; Main Stage 11am-3pm & 4-8pm, New Stage 11am-2pm & 3-7pm), especially if you go several days in advance. Otherwise, you can show up shortly before the show but you may have to buy tickets from a scalper. Scalpers are easy to find (they will find you); the trick is negotiating a price that is not several times the ticket's face value. Most importantly, make sure you examine the ticket and the date of the show (even the year) before money changes hands.

A limited number of reduced-price student tickets (R20) go on sale at the box office one hour before the performance. Go to window No 4 and bring your student ID.

Kremlin Ballet, which performs in the State Kremlin Theatre (inside the Kremlin).

Novaya Opera OPERA
(Новая опера; Map p78; www.novayaopera.ru; ul Karetny Ryad 3; tickets R150-1000; box office noon-7:30pm; M Tsvetnoy Bulvar) This 'New Opera' in the Hermitage Garden performs a wide variety of productions based on the choreography of founder and director Evgeny Kolobov.

Folk Music

While opera and ballet dominate the playbills at the top Moscow venues, there are also a few elaborate folk shows, with Cossack dancing, gypsy music and traditional costumes.

Russian National Dance Show CABARET
(www.nationalrussianshow.ru; pr Mira 150; tickets R1500; 7.30pm Jun-Sep; M VDNKh) The Kostroma Dance Co puts on quite a show, with 50 performers, dozens of ensembles and 300 costumes. It amounts to a history of Russian song and dance. Summer months only.

Russian Ball at Yar CABARET
(Ярь; www.sovietsky.ru; Sovietsky Hotel, Leningradsky pr 32/2; tickets R1000; M Dinamo) Everything about Yar is over the top, from the vast, gilded interior and traditional Russian menu (dinner R800 to R1200)to the Moulin Rouge–style dancing girls.

Theatre

Moscow has around 40 professional and numerous amateur theatres, with a wide range of plays – contemporary and classic, Russian and foreign – staged each year. Most performances are in Russian.

Fomenko Studio Theatre THEATRE
(Московский театр Мастерская Фоменко; Map p88; 499-249 1740; www.fomenko.theatre.ru; nab Tarasa Shevchenko 29; tickets R100-5000; M Kutuzovskaya) The theatre world is talking about Pyotr Fomenko. Ever since the founding of his drama theatre in 1988, he has been known for his experimental productions, which used to take place in a rundown old cinema house. In 2008, Fomenko moved his troupe into fancy new digs overlooking the Moscow River – a marble and glass beauty built by architect Sergei Gnedovsky.

Moscow Art Theatre (MKhT) THEATRE
(Московский художественный театр (МХТ); Map p78; http://art.theatre.ru; Kamergersky per 3; box office noon-7pm; M Teatralnaya) Often called the most influential drama theatre in Europe, this is where method acting was founded over 100 years ago, by Stanislavsky and Nemirovich-Danchenko.

Taganka Theatre THEATRE
(Театр на Таганке; Map p100; www.taganka.org; ul Zemlyanoy val 76; M Taganskaya) This legendary theatre is famous for its rebellious director, Yury Lyubimov, and the unruly actor Vladimir Vysotsky. The Taganka received attention for its exploration of 'epic theatre' – a reaction against the method acting that was pioneered across town by Stanislavsky. Lyubimov surprised the theatre world with his sudden retirement, followed by several leading actors, in 2011, at the age of 93.

Maly Theatre THEATRE
(Малый театр; Map p78; www.maly.ru; Teatralnaya pl 1/6; box office 11am-8pm; M Teatralnaya) 'Maly' means small, meaning smaller than the Bolshoi across the street. This elegant theatre, founded in 1824, mainly features performances of 19th-century works by Ostrovsky and the like, many of which premiered here back in the day.

STANISLAVSKY'S METHODS

In 1898, over an 18-hour restaurant lunch, actor-director Konstantin Stanislavsky and playwright-director Vladimir Nemirovich-Danchenko founded the Moscow Art Theatre as the forum for method acting. The theatre is known by its Russian initials, MKhT, short for Moskovsky Khudozhestvenny Teatr.

More than just providing another stage, the Art Theatre adopted a 'realist' approach, which stressed truthful portrayal of characters and society, teamwork by the cast (not relying on stars) and respect for the writer. 'We declared war on all the conventionalities of the theatre...in the acting, the properties, the scenery, or the interpretation of the play', Stanislavsky later wrote.

This treatment of *The Seagull* rescued playwright Anton Chekhov from despair after the play had flopped in St Petersburg. *Uncle Vanya, Three Sisters* and *The Cherry Orchard* all premiered in the MKhT. Gorky's *The Lower Depths* was another success. In short, the theatre revolutionised Russian drama.

Method acting's influence in Western theatre has been enormous. In the USA Stanislavsky's theories are, and have been, the primary source of study for many actors, including such greats as Stella Adler, Marlon Brando, Sanford Meisner, Lee Strasberg, Harold Clurman and Gregory Peck.

MKhT, now technically called the Chekhov Moscow Art Theatre, still stages regular performances of Chekhov's work, among other plays.

Circus

Moscow has two separate circuses, putting on glittering shows for Muscovites of all ages. The show usually mixes dance, cabaret and rock music with animals and acrobats. Performance schedules are subject to change.

Nikulin Circus CIRCUS
(Цирк Никулина; Map p78; www.circusnikulin.ru; Tsvetnoy bul 13; tickets R400-2500; ⏲box office 11am-2pm & 3-7pm; Ⓜ Tsvetnoy Bulvar) Founded in 1880, this smaller circus is named after beloved actor and clown Yury Nikulin (1921–97), who performed at the studio here for many years.

Bolshoi Circus on Vernadskogo CIRCUS
(Большой Цирк на Вернадского; www.bolshoicircus.ru; pr Vernadskogo 7; tickets R100-1000; ⏲shows 7pm Wed, 1pm & 5pm Sat & Sun; Ⓜ Universitet) This huge circus has five rings and holds 3400 spectators. The company includes hundreds of performers, from acrobats to animals.

Nightclubs

Krizis Zhanra NIGHTCLUB
(Кризис Жанра; Map p102; www.kriziszhanra.ru; ul Pokrovka 16/16; ⏲concerts 9pm Sun-Thu, 11pm Fri & Sat; 🗒; Ⓜ Chistye Prudy) Everybody has something good to say about Krizis: expats and locals, old timers and newcomers, young and old. What's not to love? Good cheap food, copious drinks and rockin' music every night, all of which inspires the gathered to get their groove on.

Propaganda NIGHTCLUB
(Пропаганда; Map p102; www.propagandamoscow.com; Bolshoy Zlatoustinsky per 7; meals R500-700; ⏲noon-6am; Ⓜ Kitay-Gorod) This long-time favourite looks to be straight from the warehouse district, with exposed-brick walls and pipe ceilings. This is a gay-friendly place, especially on Sunday nights.

Garage Club NIGHTCLUB
(Клуб Гараж; Map p96; www.garageclub.ru; Brodnikov per 8; ⏲24hr; Ⓜ Polyanka) This is the place to be on Wednesday and Sunday nights, if you want to strut your r'n'b stuff on the dance floor. It also gets packed in the early-morning hours of the weekend, when the clubbing crowd comes for the famous 'after party'. At other times, it's just a cool place to get comfortable in a car seat and have a few drinks. The bouncers exercise face control at party time.

Solyanka BAR
(Солянка; Map p102; http://s-11.ru; ul Solyanka 11; cover R300-500; ⏲noon-midnight Sun-Wed, to 5am Thu-Sat; @; Ⓜ Kitay-Gorod) Solyanka No 11 is a historic 18th-century merchant's mansion that has been revamped into an edgy, arty club. By day it's an excellent restaurant; on Thursday, Friday and Saturday nights, the big bar room gets cleared of tables and the DJ spins hip hop, techno and rave. The mu-

sic usually starts at 11pm (and so does the face control).

Discoteque NIGHTCLUB
(www.discoteque.ru; bldg 5, Nizhny Susalny per 5; cover R500; Ⓜ Kurskaya) Just one of several former-factory clubs that are pumping until early morning. DJs play house music; barely dressed girls dance in cages; and the crowd lets loose down below on the dance floor.

Live Music

Masterskaya LIVE MUSIC
(Мастерская; Map p78; http://mstrsk.livejournal.com; bldg 3, Teatralny proezd 3; cover R300; noon-6am; Ⓜ Okhotny Ryad) The eclectic and arty interior here makes a cool place to chill out and drink coffee or eat lunch during the day. Evening hours give way to a diverse array of live music acts or the occasional dance or theatre performance. Enter from the courtyard.

Zapasnik Art Garbage LIVE MUSIC
(Запасник Art Garbage; Map p102; www.art-garbage.ru; Starosadsky per 5; noon-6am; wi-fi; Ⓜ Kitay-Gorod) Enter this funky club-café through the courtyard littered with sculpture. Inside, the walls are crammed with paintings of all genres, and there are DJs spinning or live music playing every night. Is it art or is it garbage? We'll let you decide.

Madam Galife LIVE MUSIC
(Map p102; www.madamgalife.ru; pr Mira 26/1; wi-fi; Ⓜ Prospekt Mira) This funky art café was opened by a local director and playwright. Looking out to the MGU Botanical Garden, it's like an outdoor café, but you don't have to think about the weather. Also adding to the awesome atmosphere is the live music – mostly piano and some other jazzy ensembles – that plays every night.

PirOGI on Maroseyka LIVE MUSIC
(Map p102; www.ogipirogi.ru; ul Maroseyka 9/2; 24hr; wi-fi; Ⓜ Kitay-Gorod) A slick storefront invites the young, broke and beautiful to enjoy decent food, affordable beer and movies, and music every night.

Sixteen Tons LIVE MUSIC
(Шестнадцать Тонн; Map p82; www.16tons.ru; ul Presnensky val 6; cover R300-1000; 11am-6am, concerts 10pm or 11pm Thu-Sat; wi-fi; Ⓜ Ulitsa 1905 Goda) Downstairs, the brassy English pub-restaurant has an excellent house-brewed bitter. Upstairs, the club gets some of the best Russian bands that play in Moscow, including Billy's Band, Mara and Bi-2.

Chinese Pilot Dzhao-Da LIVE MUSIC
(Китайский лётчик Джао-да; Map p102; www.jao-da.ru; Lubyansky proezd 25; cover R300-500; concerts 10pm Thu, 11pm Fri & Sat; Ⓜ Kitay-Gorod) This divey basement place hosts lots of different kinds of bands from around Europe and Russia. Look out for free concerts on Monday nights.

Rhythm Blues Cafe LIVE MUSIC
(Ритм Блюз Кафе; Map p84; 499-245 5543; www.blueshouse.ru; Starovagankovsky per; noon-midnight Sun-Thu, to 5am Fri & Sat; Ⓜ Aleksandrovsky Sad) If your dog got run over by a pick-up truck, find some comfort at the Rhythm Blues Cafe, with down-and-out live music every night, plus cold beer and salty cured meats. Book a table if you want to sit down.

Sport

Russia's international reputation in sport is well founded, with athletes earning international fame and glory for their success in ice hockey, gymnastics and figure skating.

FOOTBALL

The most popular spectator sport in Russia is football (soccer), and five Moscow teams play in Russia's premier league (Vysshaya Liga). Lukoil has thrown its considerable financial weight behind **FC Spartak** (www.spartak.com), Moscow's most successful team. The team's nickname is Myaso, or 'Meat', because the team was sponsored by the collective farm association during the Soviet era. Spartak plays at **Luzhniki Stadium** (Дворец спорта Лужники) but construction is under way for a new dedicated stadium, which is expected to be complete in 2013.

Other Moscow teams in the league are two-time winner **FC Lokomotiv** (www.fclm.ru), three-time winner **Central Sports Club of the Army** (CSKA; www.pfc-cska.com), **FC Dynamo** (www.fcdynamo.ru) and **FC Moskva** (www.fcmoscow.ru).

ICE HOCKEY

The Russian Super League was disbanded after the 2007–08 season and replaced by the Continental Hockey League (KHL), which also includes non-Russian teams. Moscow's main entrant in the KHL is **HC CSKA** (www.cska-hockey.ru), or the Red Army team.

BASKETBALL

Men's basketball has dropped in popularity since its days of Olympic glory in the 1980s. But Moscow's top basketball team, **CSKA** (www.cskabasket.com), still does well in European league play.

CSKA Arena SPORTS

(Арена и Стадион ЦСКА; ☎495-225 2600; Leningradsky pr 39a; Ⓜ Aeroport) This 5500-person arena was built in the lead-up to 1980, when it hosted the Olympic basketball tournament. These days it is home to Moscow's most successful basketball and hockey teams.

Luzhniki Sports Palace SPORTS

(Map p88; www.luzhniki.ru; Luzhnetskaya nab 24; Ⓜ Sportivnaya) Home to premier-league football teams Torpedo and Spartak, Moscow's largest stadium seats up to 80,000 people.

Shopping

News flash: Moscow is an expensive city. So don't come looking for bargains. Do come looking for creative and classy clothing and jewellery by local designers; an innovative art scene; high-quality handicrafts, linens, glassware and folk art; and unusual and exotic souvenirs that you won't find anywhere else.

Now restored to its prerevolutionary fashionable status, ul Petrovka is Moscow's main shopping strip. It begins beside the Bolshoi Theatre and heads north, lined with upmarket boutiques, as well as a large department store and a fancy shopping centre. It culminates in Stoleshnikov per, a pedestrian strip given over to the most exclusive shops.

Kitay Gorod is a charming area to stroll and shop, starting with the old arcades at Gostiny Dvor. Nikolskaya ul is lined with shops, terminating at the gated fashion fantasy world inside Tretyakovsky proezd. Ul Arbat has always been a tourist attraction and so is littered with souvenir shops and stalls.

While the European fashion houses still rule the roost, Moscow designers are attracting increasing attention, thanks to designs that incorporate uniquely Russian elements, including furs, fabrics and styles. Beware of sticker shock.

Moscow's art world is developing at an exponential rate, thanks to the economic boom. Witness the creative energy first hand at the city's postindustrial art centres (see p104), and there are also many galleries within New Tretyakov at the Central House of Artists (p94). Note: if you're buying antiques – or anything vaguely arty or old – see p701 for customs details.

WORTH A TRIP

RUSSIAN GIFT

Still looking for that perfect souvenir? Then it's time to make a trip out to Moscow's enormous handicraft centre, **Russian Gift** (www.russiangifts.ru; ul Zorge 2; ⏲10am-8pm; Ⓜ Polezhayevskaya), dedicated to preserving Russian folk traditions. Interestingly, the centre is housed in a supermodern building. In the lobby, you'll likely hear some folk music and sample some *medovukha* (honey ale), before continuing on to peruse the thousands of handicrafts on display. Really crafty folks might be interested in a guided tour, while children can partake of a Russian tea party. There are smaller outlets of this store in GUM (Map p68) and in many of the upscale hotels.

KREMLIN & RED SQUARE

GUM SHOPPING MALL

(ГУМ; Map p68; www.gum.ru; Krasnaya pl 3; Ⓜ Ploshchad Revolyutsii) In the elaborate 19th-century building on Red Square, the State Department Store – better known as GUM – is a bright and bustling centre filled with shops and cafés.

KITAY GOROD

Gus-Khrustalny Factory Store SOUVENIRS

(Гусь-Хрустальный заводской магазин; Map p68; www.ghz.ru; Ⓜ Ploshchad Revolyutsii) This factory store in Gostiny Dvor carries an excellent selection of beautiful and reasonably priced crystal and glassware from the town of Gus-Khrustalny (east of Moscow).

Vologda Linen SOUVENIRS

(Вологодский лён; Map p68; www.linens.ru; Ⓜ Ploshchad Revolyutsii) Russia's cool, moist summers are ideal for producing flax, the fibre used to manufacture linen. High-quality products such as tablecloths, napkins, bed covers and even clothing are still manufactured in Russia, and sold here in Gostiny Dvor.

TVERSKOY DISTRICT

TOP CHOICE **Yeliseev Grocery Store** FOOD & DRINK

(Елисеевский магазин; Map p78; Tverskaya ul 14; ⏲8am-9pm Mon-Sat, 10am-6pm Sun; Ⓜ Pushkinskaya) Peek in here for a glimpse of prerevolutionary grandeur, as the store is set in the former mansion of the successful merchant Yeliseev. It now houses an upscale food hall selling caviar and other delicacies. It's a great place to shop for souvenirs for your foodie friends back home.

Yekaterina CLOTHING, ACCESSORIES

(Екатерина; Map p78; www.mexa-ekaterina.ru; ul Bolshaya Dmitrovka 11; Ⓜ Teatralnaya) One of Russia's oldest furriers, this place has been manufacturing *shapky* (fur hats) and *shuby* (fur coats) since 1912. While Yekaterina has always maintained a reputation for high-quality furs and leather, its designs are constantly changing and updating to stay on top of fashion trends.

Khudozhestvenny Salon ART GALLERY

(Художественный салон; Map p78; ☎495-628 4593; ul Petrovka 12; ⏲10am-8pm; Ⓜ Chekhovskaya) Although it has a rather innocuous name, this 'Art Salon' is packed with paintings, sculpture, ceramics, jewellery and handicrafts by local artists.

Atlas MAPS

(Атлас; Map p78; ul Kuznetsky most 9/10; Ⓜ Kuznetsky Most) A little shop housing an impressive collection of maps, including city and regional maps covering the whole country. The walls are plastered with most of the maps that are for sale.

PRESNYA DISTRICT

Ministerstvo Podarkov ART GALLERY

(Министерство Подарков; Map p78; www.buro-nahodok.ru; Maly Gneznikovsky per 12/27; ⏲11am-9pm; Ⓜ Pushkinskaya) For quirky, clever souvenirs, stop by this network of artists' co-operatives, with uniquely Russian gifts such as artist-designed *tapki* (slippers) and hand-woven linens. There is another outlet – **Podarky, Dekor & Podarky** (Подарки, декор и подарки; Map p78; Malaya Bronnaya ul 28/2; Ⓜ Mayakovskaya) – near Patriarch's Ponds.

ARBAT DISTRICT

TOP CHOICE **Bukle** CLOTHING, ACCESSORIES

(Букле; Map p84; www.vereteno.com; ul Arbat 27/47; Ⓜ Arbatskaya) The collection of Lyudmila Mezentsevaya, called Vereteno, is on display at this little café-cum-boutique. On sale is mostly casual wear, including T-shirts, skirts, sweaters, scarves, handbags and watches, all with an innovative twist.

Russian Embroidery & Lace SOUVENIRS

(Русская вышивка и кружево; Map p84; ul Arbat 31; Ⓜ Smolenskaya) Considering the lack of flashy signs and kitschy kitsch, it would be easy to miss this plain storefront on the Arbat. But inside there are treasures galore, from elegant tablecloths and napkins to delicate handmade sweaters and embroidered shirts.

DON'T MISS

IZMAYLOVO MARKET

The centrepiece of Izmaylovo is still the **Vernisage market** (Вернисаж в Измайлово; www.kremlin-izmailovo.com; Izmaylovskoe sh 73; ⏲10am-8pm; Ⓜ Partizanskaya), packed with art, handmade crafts, antiques, Soviet paraphernalia and just about anything you might want to bring home. Various 'trade rows' are dedicated to icons, carpets, textiles, antiques, paintings and more. There is also a functioning **blacksmith workshop**, where you can watch the smithies doing their thing. Feel free to negotiate, but don't expect vendors to come down much more than 10%.

Dom Knigi BOOKSTORE

(Дом книги; Map p84; www.mosdomknigi.ru; ul Novy Arbat 8; ⏲9am-11pm Mon-Fri, from 10am Sat & Sun; Ⓜ Arbatskaya) Among the largest bookshops in Moscow, Dom Knigi has a selection of foreign-language books to rival any other shop in the city, not to mention guidebooks, maps, reference and souvenir books.

KHAMOVNIKI

Artefact Gallery Centre ART GALLERY

(Артефакт; Map p96; ul Prechistenka 30; Ⓜ Kropotkinskaya) Near the Russian Academy of Arts, this is a sort of art mall, housing a few dozen galleries under one roof. Look for paintings, sculptures, dolls, pottery and other kinds of art that people actually buy, as opposed to the more avant-garde exhibits at other art centres.

ZAMOSKVORECHIE

TOP CHOICE **Russkaya Ulitsa** CLOTHES, ACCESSORIES

(Русская улица; Map p96; www.russian-street.ru; Bersenevskaya nab 8/1; Ⓜ Kropotkinskaya) Showcasing Moscow's burgeoning fashion industry, this little boutique 'Russian street' is crammed with cool clothes and accessories from more than 60 different Russian designers. Items run the gamut from trendy tees to sophisticated dresses.

BASMANNY

Tricotage Club CLOTHING, ACCESSORIES

(Трикотаж-клуб; Map p102; www.sviterok.ru; ul Pokrovka 4; ⏲10am-10pm Mon-Fri, from 11am Sat & Sun; Ⓜ Kitay-Gorod) Hand-knitted sweaters, socks and mittens in all shapes and sizes. But that's not all. You'll find a fun selection of toys and homemade souvenirs, as well as sleek and sexy styles of men's and women's clothing. This is not your grandmother's knitwear.

Salon Podarkov SOUVENIRS
(Салон Подарков; off Map p78; Myasnitskaya ul 5; 11am-7pm Mon-Sat; Lubyanka) This 'gift salon' is a sort of indoor souvenir market, with dozens of individual stalls selling all kinds of arts and crafts. Look for sellers dedicated to watches, glass, china, knitwear, linen, jewellery, bronze, stonework, painted folk toys and more. Located right behind Lubyanka Prison.

Bookhunter BOOKSTORE
(Map p102; www.bookhunter.ru; Krivokolenny per 9; 9am-9pm; Chistye Prudy) It's a tiny little shop, but it's stuffed with fiction and non-fiction books in English (not to mention German, French and Spanish). You'll find all sorts of art, academic and other reference books (including a good selection of travel guides) as well as Russian and foreign literature.

Information

Dangers & Annoyances

As in any big city, be on your guard against pickpockets and muggers. Be particularly careful at or around metro stations, especially at Kurskaya and Partizanskaya, where readers have reported specific incidents. Always be cautious about taking taxis late at night, especially near bars and clubs that are in isolated areas. Never get into a car that already has two or more people in it.

Some police officers can be bothersome, especially to dark-skinned or foreign-looking people. Other members of the police force target tourists, though reports of tourists being hassled about their documents and registration have declined. Always carry a photocopy of your passport, visa and registration stamp. If stopped by a member of the police force, do not hand over your passport! It is perfectly acceptable to show a photocopy instead.

Emergency

Ambulance (03)
Fire (01)
Police (02)
Universal Emergency Number (112)

Internet Access

Almost all hotels and hostels offer wi-fi, as do many bars, restaurants and cafés. It isn't always free, but it is ubiquitous. Look for the icon in the listings for hotels, restaurants, bars and cafés that offer wireless access. If you are not travelling with your own computer, there are plenty of internet cafés around the city, offering excellent, fast and generally affordable internet access. You can also look for the internet icon @ in this book's listings for general internet access in hotels.

Biblioteca Internet Lounge (Map p84; www.internet-lounge.ru; 6th fl, Novinsky bul 8; 10am-10pm; ; Smolenskaya) This lounge inside the Lotte Plaza is an internet café for fancy people, complete with face control.

Cafemax – Dorogomilovo (Map p88; Bryanskaya ul 5; per hr R100; 24hr; ; Kievskaya) Discounts available late at night and early morning.

Cafemax – Zamoskvorechie (Map p96; Pyatnitskaya ul 25; per hr R100; 24hr; ; Novokuznetskaya)

Internet Club (Map p78; Kuznetsky most 12; 9am-midnight; Kuznetsky Most)

Playground.ru (off Map p82; 495-980 1020; Tishinskaya pl 1; per hr R50; 24hr; Belorusskaya) This computer gaming club is inside the Tishinka shopping centre.

Time Online – Leningradsky vokzal (Тайм Онлайн - Ленинградский вокзал; Map p102; 495-266 8351; Komsomolskaya pl 3; per hr R70-100; 24hr; ; Komsomolskaya) Offers copy and photo services, as well as over 100 zippy computers.

Time Online – Okhotny Ryad (Тайм ОнЛайн; Map p68; www.timeonline.ru; per hr R70-100; 24hr; ; Okhotny Ryad) At the Okhotny Ryad shopping centre.

Media

All of the following English-language publications can be found at hotels, restaurants and cafés around town.

element (www.elementmoscow.ru) This oversized newsprint magazine comes out weekly with restaurant reviews, concert listings and art exhibits. It also publishes a seasonal supplement highlighting Moscow's hottest restaurants.

Moscow News (www.moscownews.ru) This long-standing Russian news weekly – now in English too – focuses on domestic and international politics and business.

Moscow Times (www.themoscowtimes.com) This first-rate daily is the undisputed king of the hill in locally published English-language news, covering Russian and international issues, as well as sport and entertainment. The Friday edition is a great source for what's happening at the weekend.

Passport Magazine (www.passportmagazine.ru) An excellent monthly lifestyle magazine that includes restaurant listings, book, music and film reviews, as well as articles on culture and business in the capital.

Medical Services

HOSPITALS Both of the international medical facilities listed here accept health insurance from major international providers.

American Medical Center (Американский Медицинский Центр; Map p102; ☎495-933 7700; www.amcenter.ru; Grokholsky per 1; Ⓜ Prospekt Mira) Offers 24-hour emergency service, consultations and a full range of medical specialists, including paediatricians and dentists. Also has an on-site pharmacy with English-speaking staff.

Botkin Hospital (Боткинская больница; ☎495-945 0045; www.botkinmoscow.ru; 2-y Botkinsky proezd 5; Ⓜ Begovaya) The best Russian facility.

European Medical Center (Европейский Медицинский Центр; Map p78; ☎495-933 6655; www.emcmos.ru; Spiridonevsky per 5; Ⓜ Mayakovskaya) Includes medical and dental facilities, which are open around the clock for emergencies. The staff speak 10 languages.

PHARMACIES A chain of 24-hour pharmacies called **36.6** (Аптека 36.6; ☎495-797 6366; www.366.ru) has many branches all around the city:

Arbat (Map p84; ul Novy Arbat 15; Ⓜ Arbatskaya)

Basmanny (Map p102; ul Pokrovka 1/13; Ⓜ Kitay-Gorod)

Tverskoy (Map p78; Tverskaya ul 25/9; Ⓜ Tverskaya)

Zamoskvorechie (Map p96; Klimentovsky per 12; Ⓜ Tretykovskaya)

Money

Banks, exchange counters and ATMs are ubiquitous in Moscow. Currencies other than US dollars and euros are difficult to exchange and yield bad rates. Credit cards, especially Visa and MasterCard, are widely accepted in upmarket hotels, restaurants and shops. You can also use your credit card to get a cash advance at most major banks in Moscow. **Alfa-Bank** (Алфа-банк; ⌚8.30am-8pm Mon-Sat) has ATMs that offer US dollars and euros in addition to roubles. There are many outlets around town:

Basmanny (Map p102; Myastnitskaya ul 13/1; Ⓜ Lubyanka)

Tverskoy (Map p78; Kuznetsky most 9/10; Ⓜ Kuznetsky Most)

Zamoskvorechie (Map p96; ul Bolshaya Ordynka 21/2; Ⓜ Tretyakovskaya)

Post

Service has improved dramatically in recent years, but the usual warnings about delays and disappearances of incoming mail apply. Note that mail to Europe and the USA can take two to six weeks to arrive.

Central telegraph office (Центральный телеграф; Map p78; Tverskaya ul 7; ⌚post 8am-10pm, telephone 24hr; Ⓜ Okhotny Ryad) This convenient office offers telephone, fax and internet services.

DHL Worldwide Express (☎495-956 1000; www.dhl.ru) Air courier services. Call for information on drop-off locations and to arrange pick-ups.

Main post office (Московский главпочтамт; Map p102; Myasnitskaya ul 26; ⌚8am-8pm Mon-Fri, 9am-7pm Sat & Sun; Ⓜ Chistye Prudy) Moscow's main post office is on the corner of Chistoprudny bul.

Telephone

Most payphones require prepaid phonecards, which are available from metro token booths and from kiosks. Cards can be used for local and domestic or international long-distance calls, and are available in a range of units; international calls require at least 100 units. The only trick is to remember to press the button with the speaker symbol when your party answers the phone.

For international calls, it's often easier to go to the central telegraph office, where you prepay for the duration of your call.

HOW TO DIAL THE TELEPHONE

It's more complicated than you would think. There are now two area codes functioning within the city: ☎495 and ☎499. Dialling patterns for the two area codes are different:

» Within the ☎495 area code, dial seven digits, with no area code.

» Within the ☎499 area code, dial 10 digits (including ☎499).

» From ☎495 to ☎499 (or vice versa), dial ☎8 plus 10 digits (including appropriate area code). Although this looks like an intercity call, it is charged as a local call.

The addition of mobile phones also complicates matters, as mobile-phone numbers have a completely different area code (usually ☎915, 916 or 926). To call a mobile phone from a landline (or vice versa) you must dial ☎8 plus 10 digits.

Travel Agencies

Maria Travel Agency (Агентство Мария; Map p102; ☎495-775 8226; www.maria-travel.com; ul Maroseyka 13; Ⓜ Kitay-Gorod) Offers visa support, apartment rental and some local tours, including the Golden Ring.

Unifest Travel (Туристическое Агенство Юнифест Тревел; ☎495-234 6555; http://unifest.ru; Komsomolsky pr 13; Ⓜ Park Kultury) Formerly Infinity Travel, this on-the-ball travel company offers rail and air tickets, visa support, and trans-Siberian and Central Asian packages. It's a great source for airline tickets.

Websites

See p126 for a list of publications that offer electronic versions of their newspapers/magazines. Other useful resources:

Art Guide (www.artguide.ru) Listings for exhibits, auctions and other arty events, as well as museum listings.

Moscow Expat (www.expat.ru) Run by and for English-speaking expats living in Russia. Provides useful information about real estate, restaurants, children in Moscow, social groups and more.

Moscow Architecture Preservation Society (www.maps-moscow.com) An energetic group of international journalists raising awareness of architectural preservation issues in Moscow.

Moscow Is My Oyster (http://moscowismyoyster.tumblr.com) A fun blog about eating, drinking, shopping and people-watching in Moscow.

Redtape.ru (www.redtape.ru) Like expat.ru but better. Forums offer inside information on just about any question you might ask.

 Getting There & Away

Air

International flights from Moscow's airports incur a departure tax, which is sometimes split between arrival and departure. In any case the taxes are included in the price of the airline ticket.

AIRPORTS Moscow has three main airports servicing international and domestic flights.

Domodedovo (Домодедово; www.domodedovo.ru) Located 48km south of the city, Domodedovo has undergone extensive upgrades and has become the city's largest and most efficient international airport.

Sheremetyevo-1 & 2 (Шереметьево; http://svo.aero) The other main international airport is Sheremetyevo-2, 30km northwest of the city centre. Nearby Sheremetyevo-1 services flights to/from St Petersburg, the Baltic states, Belarus and northern European Russia. The two terminals are across the runways from each other, but they are connected by a free shuttle bus.

Vnukovo (Внуково; www.vnukovo-airport.ru) About 30km southwest, Vnukovo serves most flights to/from the Caucasus, Moldova and Kaliningrad. This airport has also undergone substantial renovation and is expanding its services significantly, specifically catering to budget airlines like SkyExpress.

TICKETS You can buy domestic airline tickets from most travel agents, and at Aeroflot and Transaero offices all over town. Convenient ticket offices:

Aeroflot (Аэрофлот; ☎495-223 5555; www.aeroflot.ru; ⏲9am-8.30pm Mon-Sat, to 4.30pm Sun) Kuznetsky Most (Map p78; ul Kuznetsky most 3; Ⓜ Kuznetsky Most); Tverskoy (Map p78; ul Petrovka 20/1; Ⓜ Chekhovskaya); Zamoskvorechie (Map p96; Pyatnitskaya ul 37/19; Ⓜ Tretyakovskaya)

Transaero (Трансаэро; ☎495-788 8080; www.transaero.com; ⏲9am-6pm Mon-Sat) Arbat (Map p84; per Kamennaya Sloboda 8; Ⓜ Smolenskaya); Zamoskvorechie (Map p100; Paveletskaya pl 2/3; Ⓜ Paveletskaya)

Boat

Moscow is a popular start or end point for cruises that ply the Volga River.

Bus

Buses run to a number of towns and cities within 700km of Moscow. Bus fares are similar to *kupeyny* (2nd-class) train fares. Buses tend to be crowded, although they are usually faster than the *prigorodnye poezdy* (suburban trains).

To book a seat, go to the long-distance **Shchyolkovsky Bus Station** (Ⓜ Shchyolkovskaya), 8km east of the city centre. Queues can be bad, so it's advisable to book ahead, especially for travel on Friday, Saturday or Sunday.

Buses also depart from outside the various train stations, offering alternative transport to the destinations served by the train. These buses do not run according to a particular schedule, but rather leave when the bus is full. Likewise, they cannot be booked in advance.

Car & Motorcycle

Ten major highways, numbered M1 to M10 (but not in any logical order), fan out from Moscow to all points of the compass. Most are in fairly good condition near the city, but some get pretty bad further out:

M1 The main road to/from Poland via Brest, Minsk and Smolensk.

M2 Heads southwest toward Oryol and Ukraine.

M7 Heads east to Vladimir and Nizhny Novgorod.

M8 Heads northeast to Yaroslavl, via Sergiev Posad.

M10 The road to St Petersburg; dual carriageway as far as Tver.

LEAVING MOSCOW

Domestic Flights

DESTINATION	DURATION	FLIGHTS PER DAY	FARE (R)
Arkhangelsk	1hr 50min	5-6	3300-6000
Astrakhan	2hr 15min	4-5	4300-5300
Irkutsk	5½hr	3-7	12,000-15,000
Kaliningrad	2hr	10-12	5300-5500
Krasnodar	2hr	18-24	4100-5800
Murmansk	2½hr	4-5	5300-6300
Novosibirsk	4hr	13-15	6200-6800
Rostov-on-Don	1hr 45min	13-17	5200-6700
Samara	1hr 45min	9-13	5000-6400
Sochi	2hr 15min	18-21	3800-5100
Ufa	2hr	10-12	5100-5800
Vladivostok	8½hr	4-5	14,800-17,800
Volgograd	1hr 40min	7-11	5400-6000
Yekaterinburg	2½hr	13-17	6200-7000

Sample Buses

DESTINATION	DURATION (HR)	BUSES PER DAY	ONE-WAY FARE (R)
Nizhny Novgorod	9	7-8	300-350
Pereslavl-Zalessky	2½	8	270
St Petersburg	12	5	800-1000
Suzdal	4½	1	365
Vladimir	4	2-3	250

HIRE While there's little reason for the average traveller to rent a car for getting around Moscow (as public transport is quite adequate), you may want to consider it for trips out of the city. Be aware that some firms won't let you take their cars out of the Moscow Oblast.

The major international rental firms have outlets in Moscow (at either Sheremetyevo or Domodedovo Airports, as well as in the city centre). Prices start at R1700 per day, although you may be able to cut this price by reserving in advance. The major car-rental agencies will usually pick up or drop off the car at your hotel for an extra fee.

Avis (Авис-Москва; Map p102; ☎495-578 8425; www.avis.com; Komsomolskaya pl 3; ⏰10am-8pm; Ⓜ Komsomolskaya) Located at Leningradsky vokzal.

Europcar (☎495-926 6373; www.europcar.ru; 4-y Dobryninsky per 8; ⏰10am-7pm; Ⓜ Oktyabrskaya) Cars prohibited from leaving Moscow Oblast.

Hertz (off Map p78; ☎495-232 0889; www.hertz.ru; 1-ya Brestskaya ul 34; ⏰9am-9pm; Ⓜ Belorusskaya)

Thrifty (☎495-788 6888; www.thrifty.ru) Outer North (bldg 3, Leningradskoe sh 65; ⏰9am-9pm; Ⓜ Rechnoy Vokzal); Outer South (bldg 1, ul Obrucheva 27; ⏰8am-8pm; Ⓜ Kaluzhskaya) Mileage limited to 200km per day.

PETROL Moscow has no shortage of petrol stations selling all grades of fuel. Most are open 24 hours and can be found on the major roads in and out of town.

Train

Moscow has rail links to most parts of Russia, most former Soviet states, many Eastern and Western European countries, as well as China and Mongolia. See p719 for general information on train travel, fares and deciphering timetables.

STATIONS Moscow has nine main stations. Multiple stations may service the same destination, so be sure to confirm the arrival/departure station.

Belorussky vokzal (Белорусский вокзал; Map p56; www.belorusskiy.info; Tverskaya Zastava pl; Ⓜ Belorusskaya) Serves trains to/from Smolensk, Kaliningrad, Belarus, Lithuania, Poland and Germany; some trains to/from the Czech Republic; and suburban trains to/from the west including Mozhaysk, Borodino, Zvenigorod, as well as the Aeroexpress to Sheremetyevo.

Kazansky vokzal (Казанский вокзал; Map p102; www.kazansky.info; Komsomolskaya pl; Ⓜ Komsomolskaya) Serves trains to/from Kazan, Izhevsk, Ufa, Ryazan, Ulyanovsk, Samara, Novorossiysk and Central Asia; some trains to/from Vladimir, Nizhny Novgorod, the Ural Mountains, Siberia, Saratov and Rostov-on-Don; and suburban trains to/from the southeast, including Bykovo airport, Kolomna, Gzhel and Ryazan.

Kievsky vokzal (Киевский вокзал; Map p88; www.kievskiy.info; Kievskaya pl; Ⓜ Kievskaya) Serves Bryansk, Kyiv, western Ukraine, Moldova, Slovakia, Hungary, Austria, Prague, Romania, Bulgaria, Croatia, Serbia, Greece and Venice; suburban trains to/from the southwest, including Peredelkino and Kaluga, as well as the Aeroexpress to Vnukovo.

Kursky vokzal (Курский вокзал; pl Kurskogo vokzala; Ⓜ Kurskaya) Serves Oryol, Kursk, Krasnodar, Adler, the Caucasus, eastern Ukraine, Crimea, Georgia and Azerbaijan. It also has some trains to/from Rostov-on-Don, Vladimir, Nizhny Novgorod and Perm; and suburban trains to/from the east and south, including Petushki, Vladimir, Podolsk, Chekhov, Serpukhov and Tula.

Leningradsky vokzal (Ленинградский вокзал; Map p102; www.leningradskiy.info; Komsomolskaya pl; Ⓜ Komsomolskaya) Serves Tver, Novgorod, Pskov, St Petersburg, Vyborg, Murmansk, Estonia and Helsinki; and suburban trains to/from the northwest including Klin and Tver. Note that sometimes this station is referred to on timetables and tickets by its former name, Oktyabrsky.

Paveletsky vokzal (Павелецкий вокзал; Map p100; Paveletskaya pl; Ⓜ Paveletskaya) Serves Yelets, Lipetsk, Voronezh, Tambov, Volgograd and Astrakhan; some trains to/from Saratov; and suburban trains to/from the southeast, including Leninskaya and Domodedovo Airport.

Rizhsky vokzal (Рижский вокзал; Map p56; Rizhskaya pl; Ⓜ Rizhskaya) Serves Latvia, with suburban trains to/from the northwest, including Istra and Novoierusalimskaya.

Savyolovsky vokzal (Савёловский вокзал; Map p56; pl Savyolovskogo vokzala; Ⓜ Savyolovskaya) Serves Cherepovets; some trains to/from Kostroma and Vologda; suburban trains to/from the north, including Sheremetyevo Airport.

Yaroslavsky vokzal (Ярославский вокзал; Map p102; http://yaroslavsky.dzvr.ru; Komsomolskaya pl; Ⓜ Komsomolskaya) Serves Yaroslavl, Arkhangelsk, Vorkuta, the Russian Far East, Mongolia, China and North Korea; some trains to/from Vladimir, Nizhny Novgorod, Kostroma, Vologda, Perm, Urals and Siberia; and suburban trains to/from the northeast, including Abramtsevo, Khotkovo, Sergiev Posad and Aleksandrov.

SUBURBAN TRAINS When taking trains from Moscow, note the difference between long-distance and 'suburban' trains. Long-distance trains run to places at least three or four hours out of Moscow, with limited stops and a range of accommodation classes. Suburban trains, known as *prigorodnye poezdy* or *elektrichki*, run to stops within 100km or 200km of Moscow. These slow trains stop almost everywhere, and have a single class of hard bench seats. You simply buy your ticket before the train leaves, and there's no capacity limit – so you may have to stand part of the way.

Most Moscow stations have a separate ticket hall for suburban trains, usually called the Prigorodny Zal and often tucked away beside or behind the station building. These trains are usually listed on separate timetables, and may depart from a separate group of platforms.

TICKETS For long-distance trains it's best to buy your tickets in advance, especially in summer. Always take your passport along when buying a ticket.

Tickets are sold at the train stations themselves, but it is much easier to buy tickets from a travel agent or *kassa zheleznoy dorogi* (railway ticket office). Most hotels and hostels will also make arrangements for train tickets.

ℹ Getting Around

The central area around the Kremlin, Kitay Gorod and the Bolshoi Theatre is best seen on foot. Otherwise, the fastest, cheapest and easiest way to get around is almost always on the metro.

To/From the Airports

All three airports are accessible by the convenient **Aeroexpress train** (☎8-800-700 3377; www.aeroexpress.ru; business/standard R550/320) from the city centre. On some airlines, you can check into your flight (and check your luggage) at the train station no later than two hours before your flight departure time.

If you have a lot of luggage and wish to take a taxi, it is highly recommended to book in advance to take advantage of the fixed rates offered by most companies (usually R1000 to R1500 to/from any airport). Note that driving times vary wildly depending on traffic.

Domodedovo The Aeroexpress train leaves Paveletsky vokzal every half-hour between 6am and midnight for the 45-minute trip to Domodedovo.

TRAIN TRAVEL

Sample Moscow–St Petersburg Trains

NAME & NO	DEPARTURE	DURATION (HR)	FARE (R)
2 Krasnaya Strela	11.55pm	8	2600-3000
4 Ekspress	11.59pm	8	2600-3000
54 Grand Express	11.40pm	9	2700-3400
152 Sapsan	6.45am	4	1st/2nd class 5056/2612
158 Sapsan	1.30pm	4	1st/2nd class 4645/2354
162 Sapsan	4.30pm	4	1st/2nd class 5460/2870
166 Sapsan	7.45pm	4	1st/2nd class 5530/2870

Sample International Trains

DESTINATION	TRAIN	DEPARTURE (PM)	STATION	DURATION	FARE (R)
Almaty	007	10.40 (even dates)	Paveletsky	79hr	10,300
Kyiv	001	11.17 (odd dates)	Kievsky	8hr 40min	3800-4400
Minsk	001	10.25	Belorussky	10hr	3450
Rīga	001	6.59	Rizhsky	16hr	6100-6600
Tallinn	034	6.05	Leningradsky	15½hr	6500-7000
Vilnius	005	6.55	Belorussky	14hr	5000-5500

Sample Domestic Trains

DESTINATION	TRAIN	DEPARTURE	STATION	DURATION	FARE (KUPE)
Irkutsk	006	9.35pm	Yaroslavsky	74hr	R9300
Kazan	002	10.08pm	Kazanksky	11½hr	R2900-3000
Murmansk	016	1.00am	Leningradsky	35½hr	R3400-5500
Nizhny Novgorod	172 Sapsan	6.45am	Kursky	4hr	1st/2nd class R4200/1500 (seat)
Pskov	010	6.30pm	Leningradsky	13hr	R2000-2800
Samara	010	6.10pm	Kazansky	15hr	R2800-4400
Tver	162 Sapsan	4.30pm	Leningradsky	1hr	1st/2nd class R2900/1200 (seat)
Vladimir	172 Sapsan	6.45am	Kursky	1hr 45min	1st/2nd class R3500/1000
Yaroslavl	016	10.05am	Yaroslavsky	4hr	R850-1600
Yekaterinburg	008	2.50pm	Kazansky	29	R4700-5500

Sheremetyevo The slick new Aeroexpress train departs from Belorussky vokzal every half-hour from 5.30am to 12.30am for the 35-minute trip to Sheremetyevo.

Vnukovo The Aeroexpress train makes the 35-minute run from Kievsky vokzal to Vnukovo airport every hour from 6am to 11pm.

Boat

See p106 for information on ferries that ply the Moscow River.

Bus, Trolleybus & Tram

Buses, trolleybuses and trams might be necessary for reaching some sights away from the city centre. They can also be useful for a few cross-town or radial routes that the metro misses. Tickets (R28) are usually sold on the vehicle by a conductor or by the driver.

Metro

The **Moscow Metro** (Map p58; www.mosmetro.ru) is the easiest, quickest and cheapest way of getting around Moscow. Plus, many of the elegant stations are marble-faced, frescoed, gilded works of art. The trains are generally reliable: you will rarely wait on the platform for more than three minutes. Nonetheless, they do get packed, especially during rush hour.

The 150-plus stations are marked outside by large 'M' signs. Magnetic tickets (R28) are sold at ticket booths. Queues can be long, so it's

UNDERGROUND ART

The Moscow metro is justly famous for the art and design of many of its stations. Many feature marble, bas-reliefs, stucco, mosaics and chandeliers. Diversity of theme is not their strongest point – generally, it's history, war, the happy life of the Soviet people, or all of the above.

Ring Line Stops

» **Taganskaya** Features a war theme, with the heads of unknown war heroes set in luscious, floral stucco frames made of white-and-blue porcelain with gold linings.

» **Prospekt Mira** Also decorated in elegant gold-trimmed white porcelain. The bas-reliefs depict happy farmers picking fruit, children reading books, and so on.

» **Novoslobodskaya** Features brightly illuminated stained-glass panels with happy workers, farmers, artistic types and lots of flowers.

» **Belorusskaya** Mosaics on the ceiling depict yet more happy workers, along with farmers milking cows, dancing and taking oaths. All wear Belarusian national shirts for the occasion.

» **Komsomolskaya** A huge stuccoed hall, its ceiling covered with mosaics depicting past Russian military heroes: Peter the Great, Dmitry Donskoy, Alexander Suvorov and more.

» **Barrikadnaya** Done in dramatic red-and-white marble, it features bas-reliefs depicting the fateful events of 1905 and 1917.

» **Kievskaya** The hall is decorated with labelled mosaics depicting events in Ukrainian history, and goodwill between Ukrainians and Russians.

Radial Line Stops

» **Mayakovskaya** Grand Prize winner at the 1938 World's Fair in New York. It has a central hall with sky-themed mosaics on the ceiling.

» **Novokuznetskaya** Features military bas-reliefs done in sober khaki, and colourful ceiling mosaics depicting pictures of the happy life. The elegant marble benches came from the first Church of Christ the Saviour.

» **Ploshchad Revolyutsii** Life-sized bronze statues in the main hall and beside the escalators illustrate the idealised roles of common men and women. Heading up the escalators the themes, in order, are revolution, industry, agriculture, hunting, education, sport and child-rearing.

» **Park Pobedy** Commemorating the 60th anniversary of the victory in the Great Patriotic War, this is the deepest Moscow metro station. The enamel panels at either end of the hall (created by Zurab Tsereteli) depict the victories of 1812 and 1945.

» **Partizanskaya** Features floral bas-reliefs decorated with AK-47 machine guns.

useful to buy a multiple-ride ticket (10 rides for R265 or 20 rides for R520). The ticket is actually a contactless smart card, which you must tap on the reader before going through the turnstile.

Stations have maps of the system at the entrance and signs on each platform showing the destinations. The maps are generally in Cyrillic and Latin script, although the signs are usually only in Cyrillic. The carriages also have maps inside that show the stops for that line in both Roman and Cyrillic letters.

Interchange stations are linked by underground passages, indicated by *perekhod* signs, usually blue with a stick figure running up the stairs. Be aware that when two or more lines meet, the intersecting stations often have different names.

Taxi

The safest and most reliable way to get a taxi is to order one by phone. Normally, the dispatcher will ring you back within a few minutes to provide a description and licence number of the car. Most companies will send a car within 60 minutes of your call. Reliable taxi companies offering online scheduling:

Central Taxi Reservation Office (Центральное бюро заказов такси; ☎495-627 0000; www.6270000.ru; R400 per 30min)

Detskoe Taxi (Детское такси; ☎495-765 1180; www.detskoetaxi.ru; R500 per 10km) 'Children's Taxi' has smoke-free cars and car seats for your children.

Diligence Taxi Service (Дилижанс; ☎495-966 5214; www.the-taxi.ru; R500 per 40min)

New Yellow Taxi (Новое жёлтое такси; ☎495-940 8888; www.nyt.ru; R22-30 per km)

Taxi Bistro (☎495-961 0041; www.taxopark.ru; R300-400 per 20min)

Taxi Blues (☎495-105 5115; www.taxi-blues.ru; R300 per 20min)

UNOFFICIAL TAXIS Almost any car in Moscow could be a taxi if the price is right, so if you're stuck, get on the street and stick your arm out. Many private cars cruise around as unofficial taxis, known as 'gypsy cabs', and other drivers will often take you if they're going in roughly the same direction. Expect to pay R200 to R400 for a ride around the city centre.

Don't hesitate to wave on a car if you don't like the look of its occupants. As a general rule, it's best to avoid riding in cars that already have a passenger. Be particularly careful taking a taxi that is waiting outside a nightclub or bar.

AROUND MOSCOW

As you leave Moscow, the fast-paced modern capital fades from view and the slower-paced, old-fashioned countryside unfolds around you. The subtly changing landscape

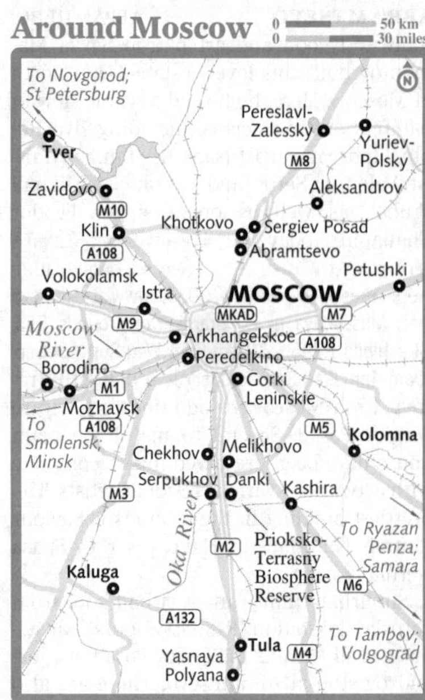

of the Moscow region (Подмосковье) is crossed by winding rivers and dotted with peasant villages – the classic provincial Russia immortalised by artists and writers over the centuries.

Most of these destinations are accessible from Moscow by *elektrichka,* or suburban train. Renting a car for a day allows much more flexibility once you arrive at your destination. That said, with patience or endurance (or both), all of these places are accessible on foot or by local bus. For more short-trip possibilities from Moscow see the Golden Ring chapter (p137).

Country Estates

Moscow's elite have long escaped the heat and hustle of city life by retreating to the surrounding regions. The quintessential aristocratic getaway is Prince Yusupov's palatial estate at Arkhangelskoe. On a more modest scale, Tchaikovsky, Chekhov and Pasternak all sought inspiration in the countryside around Moscow, not to mention the countless painters and sculptors who retreated to the artists' colony at Abramtsevo. Even Lenin maintained a country estate on the outskirts of Moscow. All of these properties are now house-museums to inspire the rest of us.

ABRAMTSEVO АБРАМЦЕВО

Railway tycoon and art patron Savva Mamontov built this lovely estate 45km north of Moscow. Here, he hosted a whole slew of painters and musicians, including Ilya Repin, landscape artist Isaak Levitan, portraitist Valentin Serov and ceramicist Mikhail Vrubel, as well as opera singer Fyodor Chaliapin. Today the **Abramtsevo Estate Museum-Preserve** (Музей-заповедник Абрамцево; ☎495-993 0033; www.abramtsevo.net; Museynaya ul 1, Abramtsevo; grounds R55, all exhibits R295; ⏲10am-6pm Wed-Sun Apr-Sep, 10am-4pm Wed-Sun Oct-Mar) is a delightful retreat from Moscow or addition to a trip to Sergiev Posad. Several rooms of the main house have been preserved intact, complete with artwork by various resident artists. The prettiest building in the grounds is Saviour Church 'Not Made by Hand' (Tserkov Spasa Nerukotvorny).

Suburban trains run every half hour from Yaroslavsky station (R150, 1½ hours). Most – but not all – trains to Sergiev Posad or Alexandrov stop at Abramtsevo. There are also regular buses between Abramtsevo and Sergiev Posad (20 minutes).

ARKHANGELSKOE АРХАНГЕЛЬСКОЕ

In the 1780s the wealthy Prince Nikolai Yusupov purchased this grand palace on the outskirts of Moscow, and turned it into a spectacular **estate** (www.arkhangelskoe.ru; admission R100; ⏲grounds 10am-8pm daily, exhibits 10.30am-4.30pm Wed-Sun). Now his palace displays the paintings, furniture, sculptures, glass, tapestries and porcelain that Yusupov accumulated over the years. In summer, the majestic colonnade is the exquisite setting for live classical music **concerts** (☎501-853 8229; ⏲5pm Sat & Sun May-Sep). There is also a popular **jazz festival** (www.usadba-jazz.ru) in June.

From Tushinskaya metro, take bus 541 or 549 or *marshrutka* (fixed route minibus) 151 to Arkhangelskoe (30 minutes).

PEREDELKINO ПЕРЕДЕЛКИНО

Boris Pasternak – poet, author of *Doctor Zhivago* and winner of the 1958 Nobel Prize for literature – lived for a long time on Moscow's southwestern outskirts, just 5km beyond the city's outer ring road, where there is now the **Pasternak House-Museum** (www.pasternakmuseum.ru; ul Pavlenko 3; admission R100; ⏲10am-4pm Thu-Sun).

Frequent suburban trains go from Moscow's Kievsky vokzal to Peredelkino (R40, 20 minutes) on the line to Kaluga-II station. From Peredelkino station, follow the path west along the train tracks past the cemetery (where Pasternak is buried) and over the bridge. After about 400m, ul Pavlenko is on the right-hand side.

GORKI LENINSKIE ГОРКИ ЛЕНИНСКИЕ

In Lenin's later years, he and his family spent time at the 1830s Murozov manor house, set on lovely wooded grounds, 32km southeast of the capital. Designed by Fyodor Shekhtel, it now houses a **Lenin museum** (www.gorki-len.narod.ru; adult/child R100/50; ⏲10am-4pm Wed-Mon), where you can see a re-creation of Lenin's Kremlin office, as well as his vintage Rolls-Royce – one of only 15 such automobiles in the world.

Bus 439 (R60, 30 minutes) leaves every 90 minutes for the estate from the Domodedovskaya metro station in Moscow. By car, follow the M4 highway (Kashirskoe sh) to 11km beyond MKAD, then turn left to Gorki Leninskie.

KLIN КЛИН

From 1885, Pyotr Tchaikovsky spent his summers in Klin, 75km northwest of Moscow. In a charming house on the edge of town, he wrote the *Nutcracker* and *Sleeping Beauty,* as well as his famous *Pathétique* Symphony No 6. After he died in 1893, the estate was converted into the **Tchaikovsky House-Museum** (www.cbook.ru/tchaikovsky; ul Chaykovskogo 48; adult/child R250/120; ⏲10am-5pm Fri-Tue); it's maintained just as when Tchaikovsky lived here. You can peruse photographs and personal effects, but only special guests are allowed to play his grand piano. Occasional concerts are held in the concert hall.

Suburban trains from Moscow's Leningradsky vokzal run to Klin (R140, 1½ hours) throughout the day. Most of these continue to Tver (R100, two hours). From the station, take *marshrutka* 5 to Tchaikovsky's estate.

MELIKHOVO МЕЛИХОВО

'My estate's not much,' wrote playwright Anton Chekhov of his home at Melikhovo, south of Moscow, 'but the surroundings are magnificent'. Here, Chekhov lived from 1892 until 1899 and wrote some of his most celebrated plays, including *The Seagull* and *Uncle Vanya*. Today the estate houses the **Chekhov Museum** (www.chekhovmuseum.com; adult/child R150/115; ⏲10am-4pm Tue-Sun), dedicated to the playwright and his work. Theatre buffs should visit in May, when the museum hosts Melikhovo Spring, a week-long theatre festival.

Suburban trains (R120, 1½ hours) run frequently from Moscow's Kursky vokzal to the town of Chekhov, 12km west of Melikhovo. Bus 25 makes the 20-minute journey between Chekhov and Melikhovo, with departures just about every hour.

Istra Истра

In the 17th century, Nikon – the patriarch whose reforms drove the Old Believers from the Orthodox Church – decided to show one and all that Russia deserved to be the centre of the Christian world. He did this by building a little Holy City right at home, complete with its own Church of the Holy Sepulchre.

Sights & Activities

New Jerusalem Monastery MONASTERY

(Новоиерусалимский монастырь; www.n-jerusalem.ru; grounds admission free, museums each R50-200; ⏲10am-4pm Tue-Sun) This grandiose complex was founded in 1656 near the picturesque Istra River (renamed the 'Jordan' by Patriarch Nikon). Unlike other Moscow monasteries, this one had no military use. After years as a museum, the monastery is now in Orthodox hands and renovation of the buildings is ongoing.

In the centre of the grounds is the **Cathedral of the Resurrection** (Воскресенский собор), modelled after Jerusalem's Church of the Holy Sepulchre. Like its prototype, it's really several churches under one roof, including the detached **Assumption Church** (Успенский церковь) in the northern part of the cathedral. Here, pilgrims come to kiss the relics of the holy martyr Tatyana, the monastery's patron saint. The unusual underground **Church of SS Konstantin & Yelena** (Константино-Еленинская церковь) has only its belfry peeping up above the ground. Patriarch Nikon was buried in the cathedral, beneath the **Church of John the Baptist** (церковь Иоанна Предтечи).

The **refectory** exhibits weapons, icons and artwork from the 17th century, including personal items belonging to Patriarch Nikon. In the monastery walls, there is additional exhibit space displaying 20th-century drawings and handicrafts from around the Moscow region. On weekends you can sample fresh-brewed tea and homemade pastries in the **tearoom**.

Museum of Wooden Architecture

(⏲May-Sep) Just outside the monastery's north wall, the Moscow region's outdoor architectural museum is a collection of picturesque peasant cottages and windmills set along the river. The museum keeps sporadic hours but the views of the river and meadows are lovely.

Getting There & Around

Suburban trains run from Moscow's Rizhsky vokzal to Istra (R130, 1½ hours, hourly), from where buses run to the Muzey stop by the monastery. A 20-minute walk from the Istra train station is a pleasant alternative.

Borodino Бородино

Borodino battlefield is the site of turning-point battles in the Napoleonic War of 1812. Two hundred years later, the rural site presents an amazing, vivid history lesson. Start at the Borodino Museum, which provides a useful overview, then spend the rest of the day exploring the 100-sq-km preserve. If you have your own car, you can see monuments marking the sites of the most ferocious fighting, as well as the headquarters of both French and Russian armies. If you come by train, you'll probably be limited to the monuments along the road between the train station and the museum (which is many).

The rolling hills around Borodino and Semyonovskoe are largely undeveloped, due to their historic status. Facilities are extremely limited; be sure to bring a picnic lunch.

Sights & Activities

In 1812 Napoleon invaded Russia, lured by the prospect of taking Moscow. For three months the Russians retreated, until on 26 August the two armies met in a bloody battle of attrition at the village of Borodino, 130km west of Moscow. In 15 hours more than one-third of each army was killed – over 100,000 soldiers in all. Europe would not know such devastating fighting again until WWI.

DON'T MISS

LIVING HISTORY

The first Sunday in September, the museum complex hosts a reenactment of the historic battle, complete with Russian and French participants, uniforms and weapons.

The French seemed to be the winners, as the Russians withdrew and abandoned Moscow. But Borodino was, in fact, the beginning of the end for Napoleon, who was soon in full, disastrous retreat.

The entire battlefield – more than 100 sq km – is now the **Borodino Field Museum-Preserve** (Бородинский музей-заповедник; www.borodino.ru), basically vast fields dotted with dozens of memorials to specific divisions and generals (most erected at the centenary of the battle in 1912). Start your tour at the **Borodino Museum** (Бородинский музей; ☎515 46; www.borodino.ru; admission R50; ⏲10am-6pm Tue-Sun), where you can study a diorama of the battle before setting out to see the site in person.

The front line was roughly along the 4km road from Borodino village to the train station: most of the monuments are close to the road. The hilltop monument about 400m in front of the museum is **Bagration's tomb** (Могила Багратиона), the grave of Prince Bagration, a heroic Georgian infantry general who was mortally wounded in the battle.

Further south, a concentration of monuments around Semyonovskoe marks the battle's most frenzied fighting; it was here that Bagration's heroic Second Army, opposing far larger French forces, was virtually obliterated. Apparently Russian commander Mikhail Kutuzov deliberately sacrificed Bagration's troops to save his larger First Army, opposing lighter French forces in the northern part of the battlefield. **Kutuzov's headquarters** (Штаб Кутузова) are marked by an obelisk in the village of Gorky. Another obelisk near Shevardino to the southwest, paid for in 1912 with French donations, marks **Napoleon's headquarters** (Штаб Наполеона).

Ironically, this battle scene was re-created during WWII, when the Red Army confronted the Nazis on this very site. Memorials to this battle also dot the fields, and WWII trenches surround the monument to Bagration. Near the train station are two WWII mass graves.

The **Saviour Borodino Monastery** (Спасо-Бородинский монастырь; ⏲10am-5pm Tue-Sun) was built by the widows of the Afghan War. Among its exhibits is a display devoted to Leo Tolstoy and the events of *War and Peace* that took place at Borodino.

Getting There & Around

Suburban trains leave from Moscow's Belorussky vokzal to Borodino (R140, two hours) at 7.15am, 10.45am and 12.40pm. Only a few trains return to Moscow in the evening, at 5pm and 8.20pm. There is more frequent transport to/from the nearby village of Mozhaysk, from where you can catch a taxi to Borodino for about R350.

Since the area is rural, visiting by car is more convenient and probably more rewarding. If driving from Moscow, stay on the M1 highway (Minskoe sh) until the Mozhaysk turn-off, 95km beyond the Moscow outer ring road. It's 5km north to Mozhaysk, then 13km west to Borodino village.

Golden Ring

Includes »

Best Places to Eat

» Dudki Bar (p155)

» Salmon & Coffee (p140)

» Plyos Temperance Society Tearoom (p147)

» Traktir na Ozernoy (p160)

» Russkoye Podvorye (p158)

Best Places to Stay

» Romanov Les (p147)

» Ipatyevskaya Sloboda (p149)

» Volzhskaya Zhemchuzhina (p153)

» Petrov Dom (p145)

» Khors (p158)

Why Go?

The Golden Ring (Золотое Кольцо) is textbook Russia of onion-shaped domes, kremlins and gingerbread cottages with cherry orchards. It is a string of the country's oldest towns that formed the core of eastern Kyivan Rus. Too engrossed in fratricide, they failed to register the rise of Moscow, which elbowed them out of active politics.

Ring is in the name because of Muscovites' famous obsession with rings. When Soviet Intourist bosses were devising a new brand for attractions accessible from the capital, they drew a loop beginning and ending in Moscow and called it the Golden Ring.

When travelling here, brace for a flow of images that are quite literally iconic. Themselves architectural icons, local churches contain Russia's oldest religious art. There is more – picturesque country roads are inviting for a bicycle adventure, while steam baths will clear your mind after mead-drinking sessions. Moose milk may also help, but science is silent on that.

When to Go

Vladimir

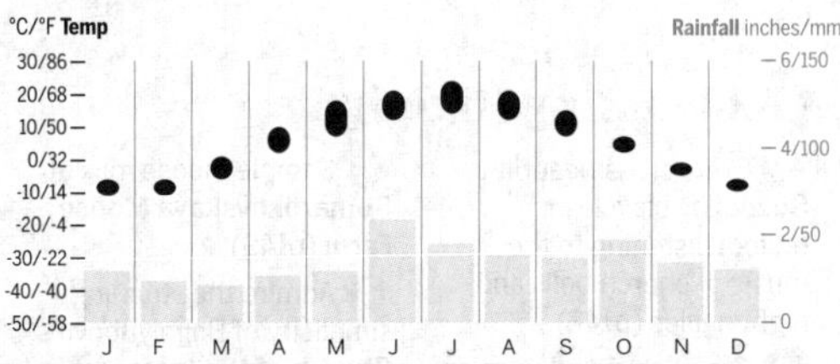

Late Jan The air is crisp, the snow is fluffy and a hot *banya* is readily available.

Jun Cyclists of the world unite for the annual Uglich Versta festival.

Aug Thousands flock into forests to pick mushrooms and wild berries.

Vladimir Владимир

☎4922 / POP 340,000 / ⌚MOSCOW

Vladimir may look like another Soviet Gotham City, until you pass the medieval Golden Gate and stop by the cluster of exquisite churches and cathedrals, some of the oldest in Russia. Hiding behind them is an abrupt bluff with spectacular views of the Oka Valley. Prince Andrei Bogolyubsky chose Vladimir as his capital in 1157 after a stint in the Holy Land where he befriended European crusader kings, such as Friedrich Barbarossa. They sent him their best archi-

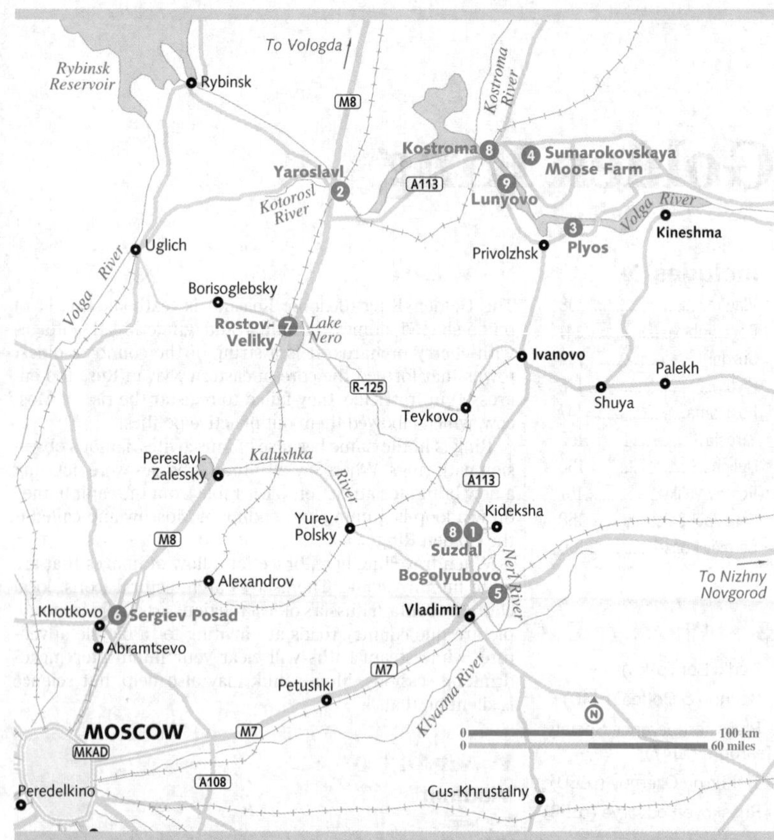

Golden Ring Highlights

1. Criss-cross beautiful **Suzdal** by bicycle or on foot, listening to the music of church bells and nightingales (p142)
2. Count church domes on a stroll in Yaroslavl, then try downing as many beers at **Dudki Bar** (p155)
3. Ponder the landscape artist's career in **Plyos** (p146)
4. Sample moose milk at **Sumarokovskaya Moose Farm** (p149)
5. Admire the stunning simplicity of Bogolyubovo's **Church of the Intercession on the Nerl** (p141)
6. See the universe reflected in Christ's eyes at Sergiev Posad's **Trinity Cathedral** (p160)
7. Take a dip in Lake Nero and watch the sun set under the pink walls of **Rostov-Veliky's kremlin** (p157)
8. Steam off church fatigue at **Goryachie Klyuchi** (p143) in Suzdal or **Azimut** (p149) in Kostroma
9. Log your Golden Ring memories in your log house at **Romanov Les** (p147) in Lunyovo

tects, who designed the town's landmarks, fusing Western and Kyivan traditions. Vladimir flourished for less than a century under Andrei's successor Vsevolovod III, until a series of devastating Tatar-Mongol raids led to its decline and dependence on Moscow. The last, a 1408 siege, is vividly if gruesomely reenacted in Andrei Tarkovsky's film *Andrei Rublyov*.

Sights

Assumption Cathedral CHURCH

(Успенский собор; Sobornaya pl; adult/under 15 yr R70/30; ⏲7am-8pm Tue-Sun, tourist time 1-4.45pm) Construction on this white-stone version of Kyiv's brick Byzantine churches began in 1158, its simple but majestic form adorned with fine carving, innovative for the time. The cathedral gained the four outer domes when it was extended on all sides after a fire in the 1180s.

Inside the working church, a few restored 12th-century murals of peacocks and prophets can be deciphered about halfway up the inner wall of the outer north aisle; this was originally an outside wall. The real treasures though are the Last Judgment frescoes by Andrei Rublyov and Daniil Chyorny, painted in 1408 in the central nave and inner south aisle, under the choir gallery towards the west end.

The church also contains the original coffin of Alexander Nevsky of Novgorod, the 13th-century military leader who was also Prince of Vladimir. He was buried in the former **Nativity Monastery** (Рождественский монастырь) east of the cathedral, but his remains were moved to St Petersburg in 1724 when Peter the Great awarded him Russian hero status.

Adjoining the cathedral on the northern side are an 1810 **bell tower** and the 1862 **St George's Chapel**. It is presumed that outside the allocated tourist time, you can only visit the cathedral for prayer.

Cathedral of St Dmitry CHURCH

(Дмитриевский собор; Bolshaya Moskovskaya ul 60; adult/under 15 yr R50/20) A quick stroll to the east of the Assumption Cathedral is the smaller Cathedral of St Dmitry, built between 1193 and 1197, where the art of Vladimir-Suzdal stone carving reached its pinnacle.

The attraction here is the cathedral's exterior walls, covered in an amazing profusion of images. The top centre of the north, south and west walls all show King David bewitching the birds and beasts with music. The Kyivan prince Vsevolod III, who had this church built as part of his palace, appears at the top left of the north wall, with a baby son on his knee and other sons kneeling on each side. Above the right-hand window of the south wall, Alexander the Great ascends into heaven, a symbol of princely might; on the west wall appear the labours of Hercules.

Chambers MUSEUM

(Палаты; Bolshaya Moskovskaya ul 58; adult/under 15 yr R150/70; ⏲10am-5pm Tue-Sun) The grand 18th-century court building between the two cathedrals is known as Palaty – the Chambers. It contains a children's museum, art gallery and historical exhibition. The former is a welcome diversion for little ones, who may well be suffering from old-church fatigue. The art gallery features art since the 18th century, with wonderful depictions of the Golden Ring towns.

History Museum MUSEUM

(Исторический музей; Bolshaya Moskovskaya ul 64; adult/under 15 yr R50/20; ⏲10am-5pm Wed-Mon) Across the small street from the Palaty, this museum displays many remains and reproductions of the ornamentation from Vladimir's two cathedrals. Reminiscent of Moscow's History Museum, the red-brick edifice was purpose-built in 1902.

Golden Gate HISTORICAL BUILDING

(Золотые ворота) Vladimir's Golden Gate, part defensive tower, part triumphal arch, was modelled on the very similar structure in Kyiv. Originally built by Andrei Bogolyubsky to guard the western entrance to his city, it was later restored under Catherine the Great. You can climb the narrow stone staircase to check out the **Military Museum** (Военный музей; adult/under 15 yr R40/20; ⏲10am-6pm Fri-Wed) inside. It's a small exhibit, the centrepiece of which is a diorama of old Vladimir being ravaged by nomadic raiders in 1238 and 1293. Across the street to the south you can see a remnant of the **old city wall** (Старая стена города) that protected the city.

Crystal, Lacquer Miniatures & Embroidery Museum MUSEUM

(Выставка хрусталя, лаковой миниатюры и вышивки; Bolshaya Moskovskaya ul 2; admission R60; ⏲10am-4pm Wed-Mon) Housed in the former Old Believers' Trinity Church, this museum features the crafts of Gus-Khrustalny and other nearby towns. The shop in the basement has a decent selection of crystal for sale.

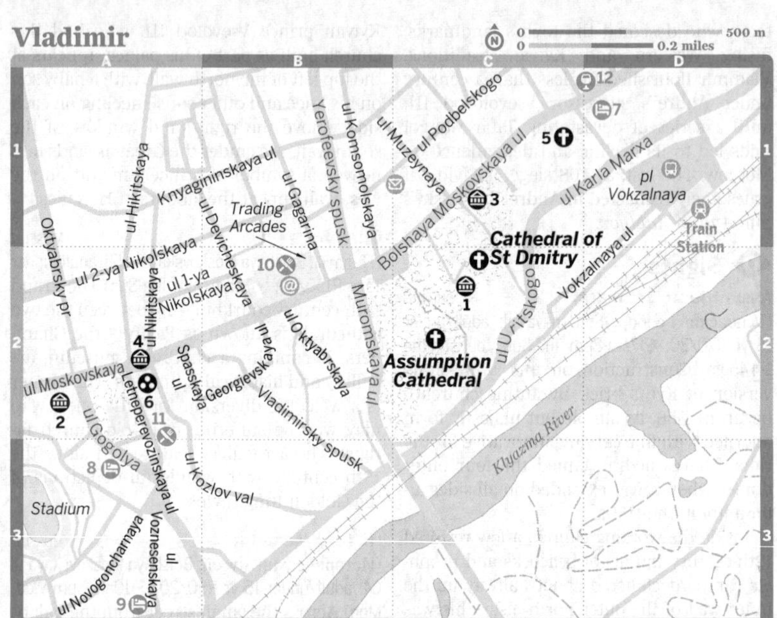

Sleeping

All hotel prices include breakfast.

Voznesenskaya Sloboda HOTEL €€€
(Вознесенская слобода; ☎325 494; www.vslobo da.ru; ul Voznesenskaya 14b; d R4600; ❄) Perched on a bluff with tremendous views of the valley, this hotel might have the most scenic location in the whole of the Golden Ring area. Outside is a quiet neighbourhood of old wooden cottages and new villas dominated by the elegant Ascension church. The interior of the new building is tastefully designed to resemble art nouveau style c 1900. The popular restaurant Krucha is on the premises.

Hotel Vladimir HOTEL €€
(Гостиница Владимир; ☎324 447; www.vladimir -hotel.ru; Bolshaya Moskovskaya ul 74; s/d from R2300/2800; @) This hotel near the train station used to be a state-run establishment, but it has successfully survived the transition to a privately owned, efficiently run hotel. All the rooms have been renovated with new bathrooms and furniture, but retain a hint of old-fashioned Soviet charm in the choice of wallpaper and draperies. It is a big place with a slew of services.

Monomakh Hotel HOTEL €€
(Мономах; ☎440 444; www.monomahhotel.ru; ul Gogolya 20; s R2300-2800, d R3500; ⊖❄@☜) Off the main drag, this newish hotel has 16 rooms that are simply decorated but fully equipped.

Eating & Drinking

Salmon & Coffee EUROPEAN, ASIAN €€
(Лосось и кофе; www.losos-coffee.ru; Bolshaya Moskovskaya ul 19a; meals R200-400) Salmon is yet to be found in the Oka, while coffee is not exactly what medieval princes had for breakfast. But instead of hinting at the city's past, this DJ café is here to give a cosmopolitan touch to the ancient town. Lots of dark wood, dim lights and magenta-coloured metal railings create a cool, intriguing atmosphere. The menu is divided in half between European and Japanese. One can only admire the chef's sense of experimentation, but some dishes seemed way too funky to our tastes.

Traktir RUSSIAN €€
(Трактир; ☎324 162; Letneperevozinskaya ul 1a; meals R300-500; ⏲11am-last guest) This wooden mega-cottage, serving a simple menu of Russian food, is about the liveliest place in town. In summer, the terrace opens up for cold beer and grilled shashlyk. With live music on weekends (8pm to 11.30pm, Thursday to Saturday), it's a popular spot for people to congregate and celebrate.

Vladimir

Top Sights

Assumption Cathedral C2
Cathedral of St Dmitry C2

Sights

1 Chambers C2
2 Crystal, Lacquer Miniatures and Embroidery Museum A2
Golden Gate .... (see 4)
3 History Museum C1
4 Military Museum A2
5 Nativity Monastery C1
6 Old City Wall A2

Sleeping

7 Hotel Vladimir D1
8 Monomakh Hotel A3
9 Voznesenskaya Sloboda A3

Eating

10 Salmon & Coffee B2
11 Traktir A2

Drinking

12 Guinness Pub D1

Guinness Pub SPORTS BAR

(Bolshaya Moskovskaya ul 67; beer R100) Here is a friendly, cheapish and blissfully unauthentic pseudo-Irish pub, its walls adorned with insignia of obscure teams from obscure leagues. Plasma screens show football or hockey nonstop, but a surprising number of regulars come here to play chess.

Information

Post & telephone office (Почтамт и переговорный пункт; ul Podbelskogo; 8am-8pm Mon-Fri)

Coffee Bean (Bolshaya Moskovskaya ul 19a, inside Torgovye Ryady shopping mall) This outlet of the best Moscow coffee chain is mostly useful for free wi-fi. Ask baristas for the key.

Getting There & Away

Vladimir is on the main Trans-Siberian line between Moscow and Nizhny Novgorod.

BUS Buses going to Kursky vokzal in Moscow depart from outside the train station hourly (R300, 3½ hours). For other destinations use the main **bus station** (Автовокзал) across the square, which serves the following:

Murom R245, 2½ hours, hourly
Nizhny Novgorod R360, 4½ hours, seven daily
Suzdal R70, one hour, half-hourly
Yuryev-Polsky R150, two hours, every three hours

Many Suzdal buses continue on to Ivanovo (R185, 2½ hours) where you can change for Plyos and Kostroma.

TAXI Taxi drivers charge R700 for a one-way trip to Suzdal.

TRAIN The cheapest train from Moscow is the high-speed *elektrichka* that departs from Kursky vokzal around 6pm (R600, 2½ hours). Sapsan high-speed trains call twice daily on the way to Moscow (R1200, two hours) and Nizhny Novgorod (R1300, two hours). Another useful Moscow–Nihzny train is Burevestnik (2½ hours in both directions). About 10 slower trains daily stop on the way to/from the Urals and beyond (*platskart* R800-1000, *kupe* from R1700, three hours), notably Perm-bound Kama and Novosibirsk-bound Sibiryak.

Getting Around

Trolleybus 5 from the train and bus stations runs up Bolshaya Moskovskaya ul.

Bogolyubovo Боголюбово

4922 / POP 3900 / MOSCOW

According to legend, when Andrei Bogolyubsky was returning north from Kyiv in the late 1150s, his horses stopped where Bogolyubovo now stands, 11km east of Vladimir. Apparently, they wouldn't go another step, so Andrei was forced to establish his capital in Vladimir and not his father's old base of Suzdal.

Whatever the reasoning, between 1158 and 1165, Andrei built a stone-fortified palace at this strategic spot near the confluence of the Nerl and Klyazma Rivers. Nearby, he built the most perfect of all old Russian buildings, the Church of the Intercession on the Nerl. Bogolyubovo is accessed most easily from Vladimir.

Sights

Palace & Monastery HISTORICAL BUILDINGS

Fragments from Andrei Bogolyubsky's palace survive amid a renovated 18th-century monastery. Driving along the Vladimir–Nizhny Novgorod road, you can't miss the monastery in the middle of Bogolyubovo.

The dominant buildings today are the monastery's 1841 **bell tower** beside the road and its 1866 **Assumption Cathedral**. Just east of the cathedral there is the arch and tower, on whose stairs – according to a chronicle – Andrei was assassinated by hostile boyars (nobles). The arch abuts the 18th-century **Church of the Virgin's Nativity**.

Church of the Intercession on the Nerl CHURCH
(Церковь Покрова на Нерли; ⌚10am-6pm Tue-Sun) The church's beauty lies in its simple but perfect proportions, a brilliantly chosen waterside site (floods aside) and the sparing use of delicate carving. Legend has it that Andrei had the church built in memory of his favourite son, Izyaslav, who was killed in battle against the Bulgars. As with the Cathedral of St Dmitry in Vladimir, King David sits at the top of three facades, the birds and beasts entranced by his music. The interior has more carvings, including 20 pairs of lions. If the church is closed (from October to April the opening hours are more sporadic), try asking at the house behind.

To reach this famous church, walk down Vokzalnaya ul, immediately east of the monastery. At the end of the street, cross the railroad tracks and follow the cobblestone path across the field. You can catch a ride in the horse-drawn carriage for R150 per person, two people minimum.

Getting There & Away

In Vladimir, take trolleybus 1 to any stop beyond the railway station turn, then catch *marshrutka* 53, 153 or 18 (R12, 15 minutes).

Drivers heading from central Vladimir should head straight out east along the main road to Nizhny Novgorod. Coming from Suzdal, turn left when you hit Vladimir's northern bypass and go 5km.

Suzdal Суздаль

☎49231 / POP 12,000 / ⌚MOSCOW

The Golden Ring comes with a diamond and that's Suzdal. If you have only one place to visit near Moscow, come here – even though everyone else will do the same. In 1864, local merchants failed to coerce the government into building the Trans-Siberian Railway through their town. Instead it went through Vladimir, 35km away. As a result Suzdal was bypassed not only by trains, but by the 20th century altogether. This is why the place remains largely the same as ages ago – its cute wooden cottages mingling with golden cupolas that reflect in the river, which meanders sleepily through gentle hills and flower-filled meadows.

As it happens, Suzdal served as a royal capital when Moscow was a mere cluster of sheds. It transformed into a major monastic centre in the times of Ivan the Terrible and an important commercial hub later on. But nowadays, it seems perfectly content in its retirement from both business and politics.

Sights

Kremlin HISTORICAL SITE
(Кремль; exhibits R30-70 each, joint ticket adult/child R400/100; ⌚10am-6pm Tue-Sun) The 1.4km-long earth rampart of Suzdal's kremlin, founded in the 11th century, encloses a few streets of houses and a handful of churches, as well as the main cathedral group on Kremlyovskaya ul.

Nativity of the Virgin Cathedral
(Рождественский собор) The Nativity of the Virgin Cathedral, its blue domes spangled with gold, was founded in the 1220s. Only its richly carved lower section is original white stone though, the rest being 16th-century brick. The inside is sumptuous, with 13th- and 17th-century frescoes and 13th-century damascene (gold on copper) on the west and south doors.

Archbishop's Chambers
(Архиерейские палаты) The Archbishop's Chambers house the **Suzdal History Exhibition** (admission R70; ⌚10am-5pm Wed-Mon). The exhibition includes the original 13th-century door from the cathedral, photos of its interior and a visit to the 18th-century **Cross Hall** (Krestovaya palata), which was used for receptions. The tent-roofed 1635 **kremlin bell tower** (Соборная колокольня) on the east side of the yard contains additional exhibits.

Torgovaya ploshchad SQUARE
Suzdal's Torgovaya pl (Market Sq) is dominated by the pillared **Trading Arcades** (Торговые ряды; 1806–11) along its western side. There are four churches in the immediate vicinity, including the **Resurrection Church** (Воскресенская церковь; admission R50). Make the precarious climb to the top of the bell tower and be rewarded with wonderful views of Suzdal's gold-domed skyline. The five-domed 1707 **Emperor Constantine Church** (Царево-Константиновская церковь) in the square's northeastern corner is a working church with an ornate interior. Next to it is the smaller 1787 **Virgin of All Sorrows Church** (Скорбященская церковь).

Saviour Monastery of St Euthymius MONASTERY
(admission R20-80 each, all-inclusive ticket R300, under 15 yr R150; ⌚10am-6pm Tue-Sun) Founded in the 14th century to protect the town's

northern entrance, Suzdal's biggest monastery grew mighty in the 16th and 17th centuries after Vasily III, Ivan the Terrible and the noble Pozharsky family funded impressive new stone buildings and big land and property acquisitions. It was girded with its great brick walls and towers in the 17th century.

Inside, the **Annunciation Gate-Church** (Благовещенская надвратная церковь) houses an interesting exhibit on Dmitry Pozharsky (1578–1642), leader of the Russian army that drove the Polish invaders from Moscow in 1612.

A tall 16th- to 17th-century **cathedral bell tower** (Звонница) stands before the seven-domed **Cathedral of the Transfiguration of the Saviour** (Спасо-Преображенский собор). Every hour on the hour from 11am to 5pm, a short concert of chimes is given on the bell tower's bells. The cathedral was built in the 1590s in 12th- to 13th-century Vladimir-Suzdal style. Inside, restoration has uncovered some bright 1689 frescoes by the school of Gury Nikitin from Kostroma. The tomb of Prince Dmitry Pozharsky is by the cathedral's east wall.

The 1525 **Assumption Refectory Church** (Успенская церковь), facing the bell tower, adjoins the old **Father Superior's chambers** (Палаты отца-игумена), which house a display of Russian icons and the excellent naïve art exhibition showcasing works by local Soviet-era amateur painters.

The old **monastery prison** (Монастырская тюрьма), set up in 1764 for religious dissidents, is at the north end of the complex. It now houses a fascinating exhibit on the monastery's prison history, including displays of some of the better-known prisoners who stayed here. The combined **hospital and St Nicholas Church** (Больничные кельи и Никольская церковь; 1669) features a rich museum of church gold treasures.

FREE Intercession Convent CONVENT

(Покровский монастырь; Pokrovskaya ul; admission free; ⌚9.30am-4.30pm Thu-Mon) This convent was founded in 1364, originally as a place of exile for the unwanted wives of tsars. Among them was Solomonia Saburova, the first wife of Vasily III, who was sent here in the 1520s because of her supposed infertility. The story goes that she finally became pregnant, but she was too late to avoid being divorced. A baby boy was born in Suzdal. Fearing he would be seen as a dangerous rival to any sons produced by Vasily's new wife, Solomonia secretly had him adopted, pretended he had died and staged a mock burial. This was probably just as well for the boy since Vasily's second wife did indeed produce a son – Ivan the Terrible.

The legend received dramatic corroboration in 1934 when researchers opened a small 16th-century tomb beside Solomonia's in the crypt underneath the **Intercession Cathedral** (Покровский собор). They found a silk-and-pearl shirt stuffed with rags, but no bones. The crypt is closed to visitors.

Museum of Wooden Architecture & Peasant Life MUSEUM

(Музей деревянного зодчества и крестьянского быта; Pushkarskaya ul; adult/under 15 yr R150/60; ⌚9.30am-7pm Wed-Mon May-Oct) This open-air museum, illustrating regional peasant life, is a short walk across the river, south of the kremlin. Besides log houses, windmills, a barn and lots of tools and handicrafts, its highlights are the 1756 **Transfiguration Church** (Preobrazhenskaya tserkov) and the simpler 1776 **Resurrection Church** (Voskresenskaya tserkov).

Activities

The rolling hills and attractive countryside around Suzdal are ideal for outdoor adventures, including horse riding and mountain biking.

GTK Suzdal CYCLING, HORSE RIDING

(GTK; ☎23 380, 20 908; ul Korovniki 45; ⌚10am-6pm) The Hotel Tourist Complex rents bicycles, snowmobiles and skis, as well as offering horse-riding tours.

Goryachie Klyuchi BANYA

(Горячие ключи; ☎24 000; www.parilka.com; ⌚11am-1am) Suzdal is a great place to cleanse body and soul in a Russian *banya* (bathhouse). Beautiful lakeside *bani* are available for rental at Goryachie Klyuchi starting at R1000 per hour for up to four people. Rooms start at single/double R2100/2500.

Dva Kolesa CYCLING

(Two Wheels; ☎8-910-186 0252; www.dvakolesa.ru; ul Tolstogo 5) This little guesthouse rents bicycles at R500 per day to those who didn't come on their own two wheels, unlike most of their guests. Owners lead bicycle excursions through villages surrounding Suzdal. Rooms go for R2000 during the week and R3000 on weekends.

Suzdal

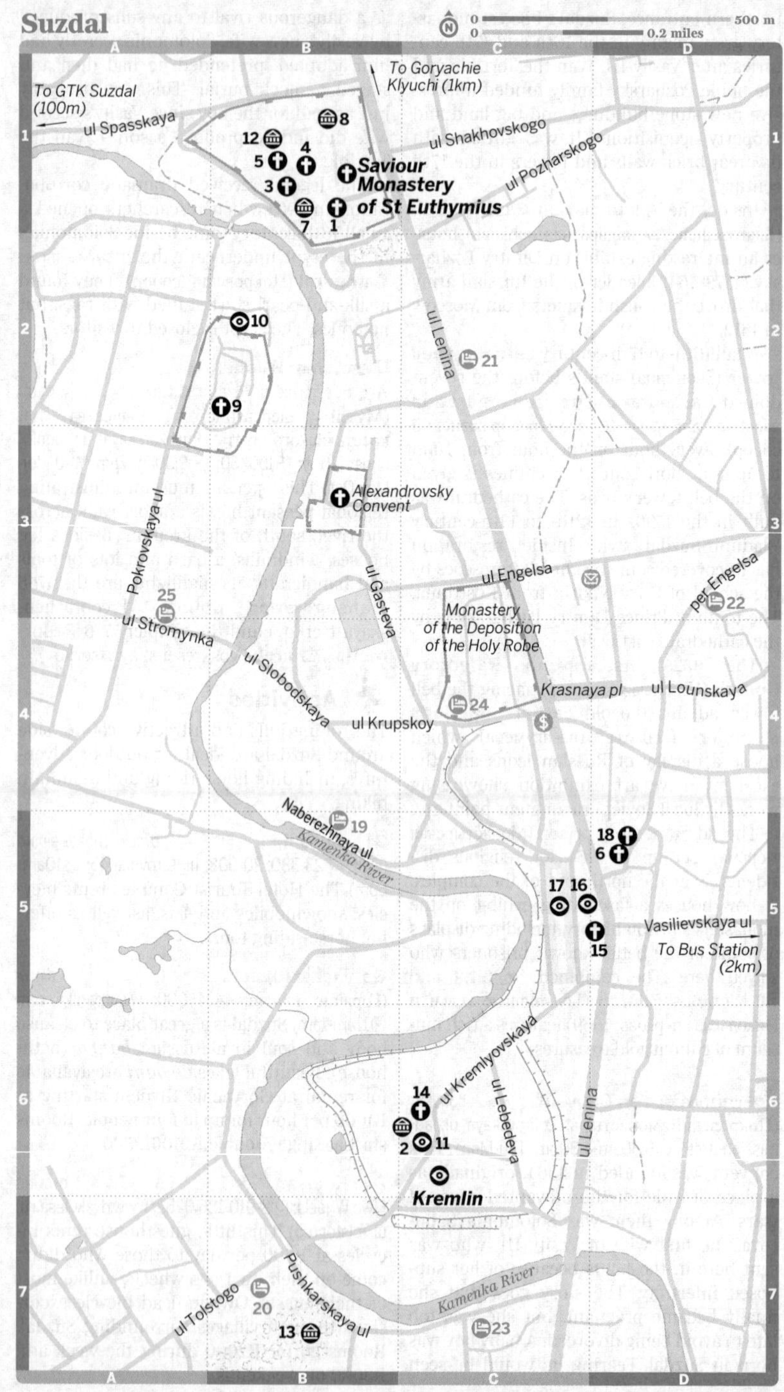

0
500 m
0
0.2 miles
To GTK Suzdal (100m)
To Goryachie Klyuchi (1km)
ul Spasskaya
ul Shakhovskogo
ul Pozharskogo
Saviour Monastery of St Euthymius
ul Lenina
Alexandrovsky Convent
Pokrovskaya ul
ul Gasteva
ul Engelsa
per Engelsa
Monastery of the Deposition of the Holy Robe
ul Stromynka
ul Slobodskaya
Krasnaya pl
ul Lounskaya
ul Krupskoy
Naberezhnaya ul
Kamenka River
Vasilievskaya ul
To Bus Station (2km)
ul Kremlyovskaya
ul Lebedeva
Kremlin
Pushkarskaya ul
ul Tolstogo

Sleeping

Suzdal is experiencing a tourist boom, which means there is plenty of choice in the mid-range and high-end bracket – from quaint two- or three-room guesthouses to vast holiday resorts. You may save up to R1000 per night if you avoid coming to Suzdal during weekends or holidays. Breakfast is included in all prices, unless otherwise stated.

Pushkarskaya Sloboda RESORT €€
(Пушкарская слобода; 23 303; www.sloboda-gk.ru; ul Lenina 45; d in inn from R2900, d in village from R3700;) This holiday village has everything you might want from your Disney vacation – accommodation in the log-cabin 'Russian inn' or the reproduction 19th-century 'Gunner's Village'; three restaurants, ranging from the rustic country tavern to a formal dining room; and every service you might dream up. It's an attractive, family-friendly, good-value option, though it might be too well-manicured for some tastes.

TOP CHOICE **Petrov Dom** GUESTHOUSE €€
(23 326, 8-919-025 8884; www.petrovdom.ru; per Engelsa 18; r weekdays R1500, weekends R2000, holidays R2500;) Vlad and Lena offer three nicely furnished and strictly non-smoking rooms in their wooden dacha-style house with a lovely garden on a quiet street (not to be confused with ul Engelsa), which makes it a great option for travellers with children. A sumptuous breakfast is included. Self-caterers are welcome to use the kitchen and garden grill.

Godzillas Suzdal HOSTEL €
(in Moscow 495-699 4223; www.godzillashostel.com/suzdal; Naberezhnaya ul 12; per person R650-750;) An affiliate of the namesake hostel in Moscow, this big log-cabin facility overlooking the river opened just a few years ago, but has already undergone a thorough renovation. Each dorm room has its own bathroom and balcony. Guests can also enjoy the blooming garden and Russian *banya*, as well as the chill-out lounge and the bar in the basement. Breakfast not included.

Stromynka 2 HOTEL €€
(25 155; www.stromynka2.ru; ul Stromynka 2; s/d from R2300/2500;) A cross between a Russian gingerbread cottage and a Swiss chalet, this medium-sized hotel prides itself in having used only natural materials in the construction. Large and airy rooms are well equipped, smell like untreated wood and offer nice views of the Kamenka River Valley. Bikes available for hire; breakfast not included.

Nikolayevsky Posad RESORT €€
(☎23 585; www.nposad.ru; ul Lenina 138; r from R3200; ⊖❄@) Another large manicured resort near St Euthymius Monastery. Accommodation is in two-storey buildings styled as merchants' mansion houses. There are a nice restaurant and a 'hangover' café on site.

Kremlyovsky Hotel HOTEL €€
(Кремлёвский Отель; ☎25 055; www.kremlinhotel.ru; ul Tolstogo 5; s/d weekdays from R2700/2900, weekends R3700/3900; ⊖❄@) This white stone hotel mirrors the tall towers of the kremlin on the opposite bank of the river. The rooms are contemporary and comfortable and they offer lovely views of the winding waterway and the rustic wooden architecture in the vicinity.

Rizopolozhenskaya Hotel HOTEL €
(☎24 314; ul Lenina; s/d/q R1200/2100/3000) Housed in the decrepit Monastery of the Deposition and destined to be grabbed by the church sooner or later, this cheapie has no intention of upgrading. Instead, it keeps its Soviet-furnished rooms clean, if poorly lit, and prices low enough to attract a steady flow of guests. Breakfast not included.

GTK Suzdal HOTEL €€
(☎21 530; www.suzdaltour.ru; r hotel from R2500, motel from R3300; ❄@≋) A former Intourist flagship, this place is low on charm but high on facilities. Accommodation is in a large hotel or in terraced houses with garage in the 1st floor and rooms in the 2nd. The complex includes a fitness centre, a bowling alley, several restaurants and a slightly more expensive hotel with upgraded rooms.

Eating

In addition to the places listed below, all of the hotels have restaurants.

Salmon & Coffee EUROPEAN €€
(Лосось и кофе; Trading Arcades, ul Lenina 63a; mains R200-450) Like its sister in Vladimir, Suzdal's S&C is about the best place for an unhurried lunch or a cup of coffee. It is, however, much quainter, with lots of aged whitewashed wood to evoke the 'Cherry Orchard' dacha ambience. Despite the name, salmon is not really prominent on the menu, which includes inventive fusion European dishes and sushi.

Graf Suvorov & Mead-Tasting Hall RUSSIAN €€
(Граф Суворов и зал дегустаций; Trading Arcades, ul Lenina 63a; tasting menu R130-350, mains R150-300) With vaulted ceilings and kitschy wall paintings depicting Russian military hero Count Suvorov's exploits in the Alps, this place serves standard Russian food and a few dozen varieties of locally produced *medovukha* (mead), a mildly alcoholic honey ale that was drunk by princes of old. Go for tasting sets, which include 10 samples each. Apart from the regular one, there are separate sets of berry- and herb-flavoured *medovukha*.

Kremlin Trapeznaya RUSSIAN €€
(Кремлевская трапезная; ☎21 763; meals R300-500; ⊙11am-11pm) The attraction here is the choice location in an old dining hall inside the Archbishop's Chambers. The menu features filling Russian favourites.

Information

Post & telephone office (Почтамт и переговорный пункт; Krasnaya pl; ⊙8am-8pm) Open 24 hours for phone calls.

Sberbank (Сбербанк; ul Lenina 73a; ⊙8am-4.30pm Mon-Fri) Exchange office & ATM.

Getting There & Away

The **bus station** is 2km east of the centre on Vasilievskaya ul. Some long-distance buses pass the central square on the way.

Buses run every half-hour to/from Vladimir (R50, one hour). Otherwise, most of the buses originate elsewhere. Buses from Vladimir go to Kostroma (R360, 4½ hours, twice daily), but it's often easier to go to Ivanovo (R120, two hours, four daily) where you can also change for Plyos. A daily bus goes directly to/from Moscow's Shchyolkovsky bus station (R365, 4½ hours).

Plyos Плёс

☎49339 / POP 3000 / ⊙MOSCOW

A tranquil town of wooden houses and hilly streets winding down to the Volga waterfront, Plyos is halfway between Ivanovo and Kostroma. Though fortified from the 15th century, Plyos' renown stems from its role as a late-19th-century artists' retreat. Isaak Levitan, Russia's most celebrated landscape artist, found inspiration here in the summers of 1888 to 1890. The playwright Anton Chekhov commented that Plyos 'put a smile in Levitan's paintings'. But he made the artist cross by depicting Levitan's love life in Plyos in the rather sexist short story 'The Grasshopper'.

Sights

Town Centre NEIGHBOURHOOD
The oldest part of town is along the river, as evidenced by the ramparts of the old fort,

which date from 1410. The hill is topped by the simple 1699 **Assumption Cathedral** (Успенский собор), one of Levitan's favourite painting subjects. From the cathedral the road winds down to the main square. The town's oldest and super-short street **ulitsa Kalashnaya** – converted into a flea market these days – descends to the embankment.

For both museums, walk down ul Kalashnaya, turn right and follow the embankment.

Levitan House-Museum MUSEUM
(Дом-музей Левитана; ul Lunacharskogo 4; admission R60; ⏲10am-1pm & 2-5pm Tue-Sun) Works by the master and his disciples are displayed against the background of the Volga. The artist moved to this dacha from a poor potter's hut when money from sold paintings started trickling in.

Landscape Museum ART GALLERY
(Музей пейзажа; admission R60; ⏲10am-2pm & 3-5pm Tue-Sun) See how the same landscapes inspire contemporary artists in this museum at the far end of the embankment. Nearby, a bronze Chekhovian lady examines the environs through the empty frame of an easel.

Sleeping & Eating

Chastny Visit GUESTHOUSE €€€
(Частный визит; ☎8-499-500 3808, 8-920-343 2998; www.pless.ru; ul Gornaya Sloboda 7; garden house with outside bathroom half-pension R4500, r half-pension R7500-12,500) Occupying a prime spot on the edge of a spectacular Volga-facing bluff, this sweet wooden cottage filled with antiques is run by a French-Russian family. Operating from here, Plyos accommodation guru Irina (☎8-910-667 5559, www.plyos.livejournal.com) will find you cheaper rooms in private houses around town and organise excursions around the area.

Fortetsia Rus RESORT €€
(Фортеция Русь; ☎43 781; www.plios.ru; ul Lenina 90; r from R3100) This riverside resort with contemporary rooms faces the Volga, 2km upstream from the centre. Full family-sized dachas are also available. Restaurant Taiga is on the premises.

TOP CHOICE **Plyos Temperance Society Tearoom** TEAHOUSE €€
(Чайная Плёсского общества трезвости; ul Sovetskaya 55; ⏲1-9pm Tue-Sun) A local legend, this recently revived riverside oldie serves various kinds of tea and pastries representing remote corners of the former Russian empire. Outgoing President Medvedev ordered Bashkir herb and honey tea when he popped in, an event the place seems to be inordinately proud of. But if your tea politics is different, you may opt for Bukhara or Turkish tea blends.

Getting There & Away

Plyos is not so easy to reach unless you have your own vehicle. There are two buses daily to/from Moscow (R430, eight hours). Travelling from Suzdal or Vladimir, change at Ivanovo where buses depart for Plyos every couple of hours (R115, two hours). Heading from Plyos to Kostroma, take a taxi to Privolzhsk (15km away), then catch a bus for Volgorechensk (every 30 minutes), where you can change for Kostroma – buses leave every hour.

WORTH A TRIP

LOG INN

Overdosed on onion domes? It's time to go rural. Golden Ring towns are surrounded by deep forests, but few travellers – apart from those infected by the Russian mushroom-picking craze – actually venture outside town walls. In the village of Lunyovo, some 20km from Kostroma off the road leading to Plyos, **Romanov Les** (☎8-495-724 5969 Moscow, 8-903-634 5222 Kostroma; www.romanovles.ru; ul Podlipayeva, Lunyovo; s/d weekdays R4200/4900, weekends R4900/6100) resort provides a perfect tree-hugging experience. Accommodation is in large, fully-equipped log-houses. There are two nice restaurants and a spa with a pool (though annoyingly even guests have to pay R200 to visit) on the vast wooded premises. The Volga is about 500m away, accessed via the nearby Soviet-style Lunyovo Resort. Transfer from Kostroma can be arranged for R120 per person.

Kostroma Кострома

☎4942 / POP 274,500 / ⏲MOSCOW

The Volga flows lazily past the mansions of tsarist-era merchants in this modest-sized city, which played a crucial role in the advent of the Romanov dynasty and hasn't achieved any prominence ever since, shunning the calls of modernity for the sake of peace and quiet. Founded by Yury Dolgoruky in 1152, Kostroma developed as a market town on the river, its former commercial glory evidenced by the enormous trading arcade on the equally huge main square. One day is probably enough to explore Kostroma museums, visit St Ipaty Monastery and down a few beers at Dudki Bar. You'll need another day if you fancy a trip to the moose farm.

Sights

Monastery of St Ipaty MONASTERY

(Ипатьевский монастырь; admission to premises free, exhibitions R100 for joint ticket; 9am-5pm) There is a bizarre similarity in the names of the Romanov dynasty's start and end points. The last tsar's family was shot in engineer Ipatyev's house in Yekaterinburg (p391), while St Ipaty Monastery in Kostroma is where a large delegation of citizens came in 1613 to insist that the young Mikhail Romanov accept the Russian throne, thus ending the Time of Troubles. The 18-year-old tsar-to-be had spent 13 years in exile, his family being chief rivals of Tsar Boris Godunov. Interestingly, the monastery is believed to have been founded by an ancient ancestor of the latter, the semilegendary Tatar prince Chet who saw a vision of St Ipaty on the spot and decided to convert.

In 1590, the Godunovs built the monastery's **Trinity Cathedral** (Троицкий собор), which contains over 80 old frescoes by a school of 17th-century Kostroma painters, headed by Gury Nikitin, as well as some 20th-century additions. The fresco in the southern part of the sanctuary depicts Chet's baptism by St Ipaty.

In the Romanov era, all successive tsars came here to visit the monastery's red **Romanov Chambers** (Palaty Romanova), opposite the cathedral, which contain a dull historic exhibition. Much more exciting is the **refectory**, which displays church treasures and old icons. Footage of Tsar Nicholas II and his family visiting Kostroma in 1913 on the occasion of the Romanov House 300-year jubilee is shown nonstop on a large screen at the entrance. The 400-year jubilee, which falls in 2013, will be marked by Russia-wide festivities – see www.romanov400.ru for details.

The monastery is 2.5km west of the town centre. Take bus 14 from the central Susaninskaya pl and get off once you cross the river.

Museum of Wooden Architecture MUSEUM

(Музей деревянного зодчества; admission R70; dawn-dusk May-Oct) Behind the monastery is an attractive outdoor museum of northern-style wooden buildings, including peasant houses, windmills and churches (one built without nails). Some of the buildings house small exhibits and the grounds are pleasant for strolling, listening to the chirping of resident frogs and admiring the handiwork of the artists.

The museum is nearly indistinguishable from the surrounding neighbourhood, which consists of storybook houses, blossoming gardens and pretty churches, including a domed wooden church directly north of the monastery.

Susaninskaya ploshchad SQUARE

Picturesque Susaninskaya pl was built as an ensemble under Catherine the Great's patronage after a fire in 1773. Its centrepiece is the immense **trading arcade** which used to house hundreds of shops selling goods shipped up and down the Volga. These days one can only imagine how this capitalist anthill might have looked like in its heyday – c 1880 or so. The opposite side of the square is graced by an imposing 19th-century **fire tower** (Пожарная каланча) and a former **guardhouse** (Здание бывшей гауптвахты).

Before the revolution, there was also a huge monument to Mikhail Romanov and national hero Ivan Susanin, who guided a Polish detachment hunting for the tsar-to-be into a swamp and subsequently to their deaths. His deed was lionized by Mikhail Glinka in the opera *A Life for the Tsar*. But although Susanin died saving Romanov's royal bum, the tsar was placed at the top of the statue and his saviour at the bottom. Bolsheviks threw the wrought-iron statue into the smelter, but the current authorities resolved to install an exact copy by 2013 – the year of the Romanov dynasty's 400-year jubilee. The tsar-less Soviet-era **Susanin monument** (Памятник Сусанину) will remain in the park between the arcades.

Art Museum & Noble Assembly MUSEUM

(Художественный музей; pr Mira 5 & 7; admission to each bldg R80; 10am-5.30pm) Standing next to each other, these museums occupy two elaborate neo-Russian buildings. The Art Museum displays collections of pictures by two outstanding 20th-century artists, Boris Kustodiev and Yefim Chestnyakov. The Noble Assembly contains several interesting historical exhibitions comprised of personal belongings left from the inhabitants of pre-revolutionary Kostroma.

Convent of the Epiphany & St Anastasia CONVENT
(Богоявленско-Анастасьинский монастырь; ul Simanovskogo 26; admission R20) The large **cathedral** in this 14th- to 19th-century complex, serving as Archbishop of Kostroma's residence, is the city's main working church. The 13th-century icon of Our Lady of St Theodore, on the right-hand side of the iconostasis, is supposedly the source of many miracles.

Church of the Resurrection CHURCH
(Церковь Воскресения; ul Nizhnyaya Debrya 37) This 17th-century church has a bright patterned exterior and was partly financed with a load of gold coins mistakenly shipped from London.

Activities

Azimut BANYA
(☎390 505, 8-800-200 0048; ul Magistralnaya 40; 2hr banya rent for up to 6 people R3000, treatments per person R900-1400; accommodation s/d R2300/2600) Right by the turn towards the centre on the main Yaroslavl road, this countryside hotel is famous for its *banya* complex, which offers a dozen treatments, from traditional to slightly left field. Most involve quick shifts between boiling-hot and ice-cold tubs and a steam master beating the hell out of you with birch-tree twigs. You'll feel heavenly afterwards, promise.

Sleeping

Whichever hotel you go to, it makes sense asking bus drivers to drop you off at Oktyabrskaya pl once you cross the Volga. You'll save yourself the trek back into town from the bus station. All prices include breakfast, unless otherwise stated.

Ipatyevskaya Sloboda HOTEL €€
(Ипатьевская слобода; ☎371 224; www.i-sloboda.narod.ru; ul Beregovaya 3a; d R1600-2000, ste R3000-4200; ⊖❄) Kostroma's most atmospheric lodging choice is this old-fashioned wooden house, opposite the monastery entrance. Wood-panelled walls and brick fireplaces lend a rustic atmosphere, which is softened by stencilled designs and floral tapestries. Alarmingly, there was a 'For Sale' sign on the house when we visited, but we've been assured the hotel will not be closing for at least another couple of years. Breakfast not included.

Hotel Mush GUESTHOUSE €€
(Гостиница Муш; ☎312 400; ul Sovetskaya 29; r R2300-2900) This tiny guesthouse has a central

WORTH A TRIP

HORNYCULTURE

Many dumbfoundingly bold experiments were set in the Soviet era. One of them was an attempt to domesticate moose for dairy farming. Moose milk is much more nutritious than cows' milk and is said to be good for ulcer treatment.

Some 25km from Kostroma, the **Sumarokovskaya Moose Farm** (☎359 433, 8-903-895 4078; www.moosefarm.newmail.ru) was created in 1963. It is essentially a science institute dedicated to one branchy-horned and clumsy-legged research object. But although local scientists insist that moose don't need domestication since they 'just love living with humans', moose farming never took off for a multitude of practical reasons. These days the focus has shifted to breeding moose for areas where this iconic taiga animal is becoming extinct. But the farm is still supplying milk to **Susaninsky Sanatorium** (☎660 384; www.sansusanin.ru; p/o Borovikovo; r R1500-2650), where it is used for medical treatments.

The farm is best visited in the first weeks of May when you get a chance to see newly-born calves, or in September when they are taken out of quarantine enclosures and you are allowed to pet them and feed them carrots. Milk is available at all times.

The moose farm makes for a pleasant half-day countryside trip if you have a car. From the centre of Kostroma, go along Kineshemskoye sh, past the bus station, to Poddubnoye. Turn left to Ikonnikovo and continue till Gridino where you'll find a signposted turn. A taxi with one-hour wait will cost around R800.

It's tougher by public transport. Take a Gushchino- or Sintsovo-bound bus (20 minutes, six daily) to the Spas stop in Gridino. From there, it is a 6km trek to the farm. In winter, the whole moose population is moved to temporary enclosures in nearby locations, so you need to inquire. Heavy snow often renders the access road impassable.

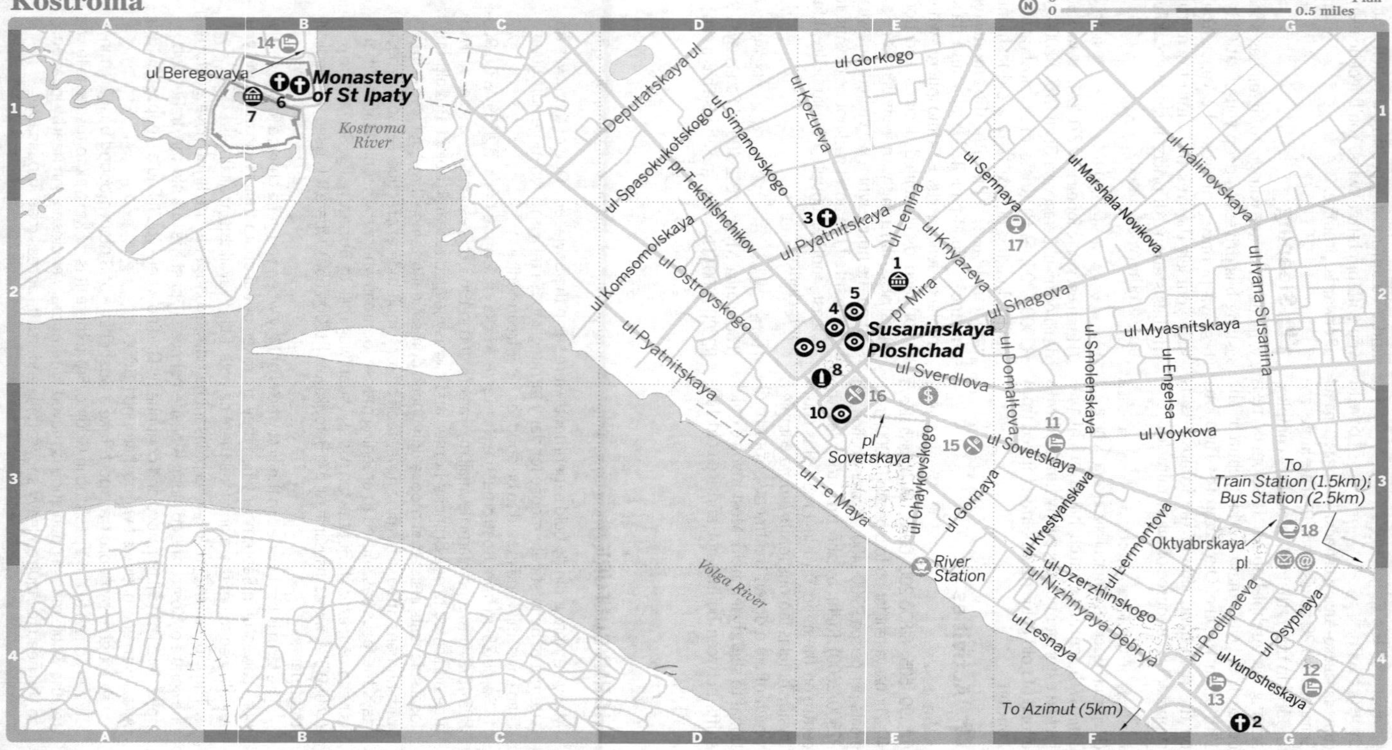
Kostroma
Monastery of St Ipaty
Susaninskaya Ploshchad
Kostroma River
Volga River
River Station
To Train Station (1.5km); Bus Station (2.5km)
To Azimut (5km)
ul Beregovaya
ul Gorkogo
Deputatskaya ul
ul Spasokukotskogo
ul Simanovskogo
ul Kozueva
pr Tekstilshchikov
ul Komsomolskaya
ul Ostrovskogo
ul Pyatnitskaya
ul Lenina
ul Knyazeva
ul Sennaya
ul Marshala Novikova
ul Kalinovskaya
ul Ivana Susanina
pr Mira
ul Shagova
ul Myasnitskaya
ul Smolenskaya
ul Engelsa
ul Sverdlova
ul Domaltova
ul Voykova
pl Sovetskaya
ul Sovetskaya
ul Chaykovskogo
ul Gornaya
ul 1-e Maya
ul Krestyanskaya
ul Lermontova
Oktyabrskaya pl
ul Dzerzhinskogo
ul Nizhnyaya Debrya
ul Lesnaya
ul Podlipaeva
ul Osypnaya
ul Yunosheskaya
1 km
0.5 miles

Kostroma

Top Sights

	Monastery of St Ipaty	B1
	Susaninskaya Ploshchad	E2

Sights

1	Art Museum & Noble Assembly	E2
2	Church of the Resurrection	G4
3	Convent of the Epiphany & St Anastasia	E2
4	Fire Tower	E2
5	Guardhouse	E2
6	Monastery of St Ipaty	B1
7	Museum of Wooden Architecture	B1
	Refectory	(see 6)
	Romanov Chambers	(see 6)
8	Susanin Monument	E2
9	Trading Arcade	E2
10	Trading Arcade	E3
	Trinity Cathedral	(see 6)

Sleeping

11	Hotel Mush	F3
12	Hotel Snegurochka	G4
13	Hotel Volga	G4
14	Ipatyevskaya Sloboda	B1

Eating

	Food Market	(see 9)
15	Horns + Hoofs	E3
16	Slaviansky	E3

Drinking

17	Dudki Bar	F2
18	Hundertwasser	G3

location (unique for Kostroma) and hospitable atmosphere, which explains why it is so often booked out. Its four rooms (two small, two big) are furnished in an old-fashioned Soviet style. Enter through the courtyard.

TOP CHOICE **Hotel Snegurochka** BOUTIQUE HOTEL €€
(Snow Maiden; ☎423 201; www.hotel-snegurochka.ru; ul Lagernaya 38/13; s/d R2200/3000;) Snow Maiden is in the name because Kostroma unilaterally declared itself the birthplace of Father Frost's (p336) companion. Expectedly, cool blue colours prevail in the modern, fully equipped rooms and you may find a Christmas tree or a pair of felt winter boots in your room even at the height of summer.

Hotel Volga HOTEL €€
(Гостиница Волга; ☎394 242; www.gkvolga.ru; ul Yunosheskaya 1; standard s/d/tr R1700/2100/2250, comfort s/d R2300/2800;) The highlight of this Intourist dinosaur is the vista: the Volga is exquisite in the morning light.

Eating & Drinking

To stock up on fresh garden produce and Caucasian *lavash* (flatbread), head to the **food market** inside the trading arcade.

Slaviansky RUSSIAN €€
(Славянский; ☎315 460; ul Molochnaya Gora 1; meals R250-500) Here is a great place for locally produced beer and various vodka-based liquors, with flavours ranging from cranberry to horseradish. That's if you can get a table, for this popular restaurant is fully booked more often than not. Sumptuous meat dishes are broadly based on traditional Russian recipes, but – another downside – service can be atrociously slow.

Horns & Hoofs EUROPEAN €
(Рога и копыта; ul Sovetskaya 2; mains R150-300; 9am-midnight) Like many similar places in Russia and Ukraine, this one is inspired by the fictional adventures of 1920s literary character Ostap Bender. Wrought-iron furniture, black-and-white photos and waiters dressed as old-world chauffeurs set the atmosphere. The menu has a good selection of soups, salads and main dishes, as well as pastries and coffee drinks.

Dudki Bar GASTROPUB €€
(Дудки бар; ☎300 003; pr Mira 18; meals R150-300) A guest from the future, this hip bar and restaurant opens new horizons of food, service and soundtrack quality in the rather backward Kostroma. Smaller than its Yaroslavl sister, this place is ruled by local hipsters, with just a few tracksuit-clad thugs looking envious and ripe for personal gentrification. Food is European and East Asian, with a tad of Indian spice. Look for the unassuming cottage at the end of pr Mira.

Hundertwasser CAFÉ €
(Oktyabrskaya pl 3; espresso R55, breakfast R280) Resembling a kaleidoscope, this large café evokes colour schemes and curving shapes favoured by Viennese vanguard architect Friedensreich Hundertwasser. Local youngsters come here to chat over a cup of coffee or a water pipe. Breakfast meals, fresh juices and smoothies dominate the menu.

Information

Post & telephone office (Почтамт и переговорный пункт; cnr ul Sovetskaya & ul Podlipaeva; 9am-9pm)

Telecom Centre (621 162; cnr ul Sovetskaya & ul Podlipaeva; per hr R60; 8am-8pm) To access the internet, buy a card at window No 5 and stick it in the slot at the computer of your choice.

Getting There & Away

The **bus station** is 4.5km east of Susaninskaya pl on Kineshemskoye sh, the continuation of ul Sovetskaya. There are buses to/from the following:

Ivanovo R210, three hours, hourly

Moscow R785, eight hours, eight daily

Nizhny Novgorod R740, 9½ hours, two to three daily

Suzdal R300, four hours, two to three daily

Vladimir R410, five hours, two to three daily

Yaroslavl R190, two hours, hourly

There are four daily suburban trains to/from Yaroslavl (R110, 2½ hours) and three long-distance trains to/from Yaroslavsky vokzal in Moscow (R1050 to R1900, 6½ hours). The **train station** is 3.5km east of Susaninskaya pl.

Getting Around

Buses 1, 2, 9, 9 Expres, 14K, 19 and others run between the bus station and Susaninskaya pl, along the full length of ul Sovetskaya. Trolleybus 2 runs between the train station and Susaninskaya pl.

Yaroslavl Ярославль

4852 / POP 604,000 / MOSCOW

Embraced by two rivers, the mighty Volga and the smaller Kotorosl, Yaroslavl's centre is dotted with onion domes like no other place in Russia. It indeed boasts a record-breaking 15-dome church. This religious zeal dates back to the times of Kyivan Rus, when the town was founded by Prince Yaroslav of Kyiv to guard his realm's northeastern flank.

The place was then known as Bear's Corner. According to the legend, Prince Yaroslav forced local Finno-Ugric people into Christendom by axing their totem bear, which now appears on the city's coat of arms.

However, most churches and houses gracing the quaint city centre are products of 17th- to 19th-century merchants competing to outdo each other in beautifying their city. Much of that beauty remains unscathed by Soviet development. These days the millennium-old Yaroslavl remains a cultured city with Russia's oldest theatre and one of the country's most renowned universities, which used to be a major destination for Western exchange students in the Soviet times.

Sights

You'll find most sights either very close to or right on the city's main attraction: the riverside promenade that runs along the Volga and the Kotorosl.

Monastery of the Transfiguration of the Saviour MONASTERY

(Спасо-Преображенский монастырь; www.yarmp.yar.ru; Bogoyavlenskaya pl 25; grounds R20, exhibits R40-50 each; exhibits 10am-5pm Tue-Sun year-round, grounds 8am-8pm daily Oct-May) Founded in the 12th century, the Monastery of the Transfiguration of the Saviour was one of Russia's richest and best-fortified monasteries by the 16th century. The oldest surviving structures, dating from 1516, are the **Holy Gate** near the **main entrance** (Главный вход) by the river and the **Cathedral of the Transfiguration** (Преображенский собор и звонница; admission R60; Thu-Mon).

Other buildings house exhibitions on history, ethnography, icons and the **'Treasures of Yaroslavl' exhibition** (admission R100), featuring works of gold, silver and precious gems.

Church of Elijah the Prophet CHURCH

(Церковь Ильи Пророка; Sovetskaya pl; admission R70; 10am-1pm & 2-6pm Thu-Tue May-Sep) The exquisite church that dominates Sovetskaya pl was built by prominent 17th-century fur dealers. It has some of the Golden Ring's brightest frescoes, done by the ubiquitous Gury Nikitin of Kostroma and his school, and detailed exterior tiles. The church is closed during wet spells.

John the Baptist Church at Tolchkovo CHURCH

(Церковь Иоанна Крестителя в Толчково; 2-ya Zakotoroslnaya nab 69; admission R50; 10am-5pm Sat-Thu) It's a shame that dingy industrial surroundings discourage most people from visiting Yaroslavl's most unique church. Protected by Unesco, the red-brick 17th-century structure boasts a staggering 15 green-coloured cupolas and some of the most extensive series of frescoes in the Orthodox world – a whole Biblical encyclopedia authored by local artists Dmitry Plekhanov and Fyodor Ignatyev. The church is located on the southern bank of the Kotorosl, by the second bridge, some 3km from the centre.

Music & Time MUSEUM
(Музыка и время; ☎328 637; Volzhskaya nab 33a; adult/child R150/100; ⏲10am-7pm) Every object has a voice in this little house containing ex-conjuror John Mostoslavsky's impressive collection of clocks, musical instruments, bells and old vinyl records. Guides, including the owner himself, turn each tour into a bit of a concert. English-language guides are available most days. Great for children.

Annunciation Cathedral CHURCH
(Kotoroslnaya nab 2a) The city's main cathedral originally dated from 1215, but was blown up by the Bolsheviks in 1937. What you see now is a modern replica erected for the city's millennium celebrations in 2010. In front of it, a stone-slab **monument** marks the spot where Yaroslav founded the city in 1010. The new **Strelka Park** stretches right onto the tip of land between the Volga and the Kotorosl Rivers where the **Yaroslavl Millennium Monument** was opened in 2010. Above the Kotorosl, the raised embankments indicate the site of Yaroslavl's old kremlin.

Ploshchad Volkova SQUARE
The massive 17th-century gate-shaped **Vlasyevskaya Watchtower** combined with the **Church of the Sign** loom over this square named after Fyodor Volkov, who founded Russia's first professional theatre in 1750 in a Yaroslavl leather store. The impressive 19th-century **Volkov Theatre** on the other side of the square remains home to one of Russia's most renowned troupes.

Old Art Exhibition ART GALLERY
(Volzhskaya nab 1; admission R50; ⏲10am-5pm Sat-Thu) The 17th-century former metropolitan's chambers showcase icons and other religious art from the 13th to 19th centuries.

Yaroslavl Art Museum ART GALLERY
(Ярославский художественный музей; http://artmuseum.yar.ru; Volzhskaya nab 23; admission R50; ⏲10am-5pm Tue-Sun) The restored former governor's mansion now showcases 18th- to 20th-century Russian art with a large hall dedicated to impressionist Konstantin Korovin.

History of Yaroslavl Museum MUSEUM
(Музей Истории Ярославля; Volzhskaya nab 17; admission R55; ⏲10am-6pm Wed-Mon) This museum is in a lovely 19th-century merchant's house. A monument to victims of war and repression in the 20th century is in the peaceful garden.

Activities

River Station BOAT TRIPS
(Речной вокзал) Summer services from the city's riverine gateway include a range of slow boats to local destinations. The best trip is to **Tolga** (one hour), where you'll find a convent with lovely buildings from the 17th century.

Sleeping

Yaroslavl suffers from a shortage of accommodation options, so you might want to make a hotel reservation beforehand, especially if you are arriving in the evening. All hotel prices include breakfast.

Volzhskaya Zhemchuzhina BOAT HOTEL €€€
(Волжская жемчужина; ☎731 273; www.riverhotel-vp.ru; Volzhskaya nab; s R2700-3300, d R4300-5200; ⊖❄📶) The floating 'Volga Pearl' is a converted river station – dozens of such floating hubs lined the Volga when boat travel was still in vogue. Polished maple furniture and plenty of natural light ensure that the place doesn't feel too cramped. Double rooms have access to a shared balcony.

Hotel Yubileynaya HOTEL €€€
(Юбилейная; ☎309 259; www.yubil.yar.ru; Kotoroslnaya nab 26; s/d from R3250/4650; ❄@) Overlooking the Kotorosl River, this is the city's largest centrally located hotel, a leftover from Soviet times. It has been thoroughly renovated, both inside and outside. Modern-looking rooms are simply decorated and comfortably furnished. The only drawback is the fluorescent blue light that illuminates the facade (and the rooms) facing the river.

Uyut APARTMENTS €€
(☎8-903-690 1879, 8-920-659 3233; www.yar-nasutki.ru; apt R1300-2000; 📶) A good alternative to Yarolslavl's expensive hotels, this agency runs 10 one- and two-room apartments in different parts of the city. It also does visa registrations.

TOP CHOICE **Ioann Vasilyevich** HOTEL €€€
(Иоанн Васильевич; ☎670 760; www.ivyar.ru; Revolyutsionnaya ul 34; r from R4600; ❄@) If you don't mind a Soviet spy, a tsar or an alien staring at you from the wall when you awake, here is your chance to immerse yourself in Russian cinema. Each large comfortable room

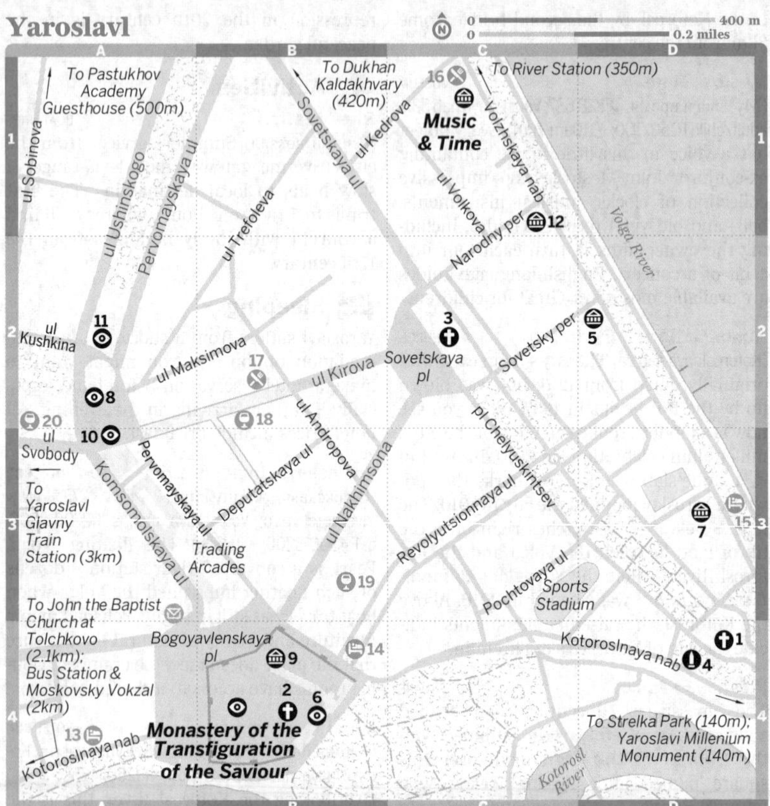

in this new hotel is themed on a popular film, with colour schemes, furniture and fixtures selected accordingly. Yes, photographic wallpaper with film scenes is over the top, but the location on a quiet boulevard near the monastery is hard to beat.

Pastukhov Academy Guesthouse HOTEL €€
(370 379; www.gapm.ru; ul Respublikanskaya 42; d R2200-2700;) This small hotel occupies a former dormitory in a grand neoclassical 19th-century building that's part of a management school. Rooms are modern, though sound protection is a problem. Cheaper ones come in a block of two with a tiny shared hallway through which you access your own private bathroom.

Eating

Note that most places listed in the Drinking section will be just as good for lunch or dinner.

Sobranie RUSSIAN €€
(Собрание; 303 132; Volzhskaya nab 33; mains R200-300) On the grounds of the museum complex Music & Time, this traditional Russian restaurant is decorated with stained glass, artwork and antiques that look like they might be part of the collection. This quaint place caters to hungry tourists in search of traditional Russian cuisine. Much of the cooking is done in the old-fashioned stone oven.

Van Gogh EUROPEAN €€
(Ван Гог; ul Kirova 10/25; mains R200-400) The menu requires some deciphering as all the choices are named after technical terms and geographic landmarks from the life of the eponymous artist. Once you figure it out though, the soups, salads and pastas are excellent and innovative. This funky café livens up on Friday and Saturday nights, with local bands and free-flowing drinks.

Dukhan Kaldakhvary CAUCASIAN €€
(Духан Калдахвары; Sovetskaya ul 21; mains R200-400) This Caucasian eatery offers an unusual mixture of Armenian, Abkhazian and Mengrel (West Georgian) dishes. Regional nuances aside, a straightforward mutton shashlyk will easily make your day. Entrance is from a small lane at the back of the building.

Trapeznaya Ioann Vasilyevich RUSSIAN €
(☎914 707; Revolyutsionnaya ul 34; meals R150-400) There's a creative take on the traditional Russian menu in this large, funky restaurant by the namesake hotel.

Drinking

TOP CHOICE **Dudki Bar** GASTROPUB
(☎330 933; ul Sobinova 33; meals R200-400) Definitely the most happening place in town, this Kostroma import is heaving during weekends, and most other days too. Brass instruments (the word 'pipe' is in the bar's name) and pictures of dogs portrayed as aristocratic ancestors adorn the walls. There is a large bar on the 2nd floor and a more intimate one downstairs. European and Asian (including some Indian) food is superb by local standards, but getting a table without reservation can be problematic.

La Gavroche CAFÉ
(ul Kirova 5; wi-fi) This friendly café on the main pedestrian drag is good for breakfasts, a cup of macchiato and catching up on your Facebook news.

Actor PUB
(Актёр; ul Kirova 5; ⏲10am-2am) Cheap beer and jazzy sounds drift through nicotine clouds in this popular theatre pub.

Afonya BAR
(ul Nakhimsona 21a) This cute retro-Soviet *pivnaya* (beer joint with stand-up tables) has an extensive choice of dried fish snacks, if you fancy drinking the Russian way.

Information

Post & telephone office (Почтамт и переговорный пункт; Komsomolskaya ul 22; ⏲8am-8pm Mon-Sat, 8am-6pm Sun)

Getting There & Away

Bus

The **bus station** (Moskovsky pr) is 2km south of the Kotorosl River, near Yaroslavl's second train station, **Moskovsky vokzal**. One or two buses go daily to/from Moscow's Shchyolkovsky station (R500, six hours), plus about five buses stopping in transit. Most of these stop at Pereslavl-Zalessky (R260, three hours), Rostov-Veliky and Sergiev Posad. Other departures include Ivanovo (R280, three hours, every two hours), Kostroma (R175, two hours, 10 daily) and Uglich (R165, three hours, 12 daily).

Train

The main **train station** (ul Svobody) is Yaroslavl Glavny, 3km west of the centre. Trains run frequently to/from Yaroslavsky vokzal in Moscow (R900 to R1600, 4¼ hours) – most en route to/from other destinations further north. The most convenient option is the fast *elektrichka* (R760, 3¾ hours, twice daily), which calls at Sergiev

Posad and Rostov. There are eastbound trains that will get you back on the main Trans-Siberian line at Perm (R1500 to R3500, 20 hours, four daily) and at least one train daily to Nizhny Novgorod (R600 to R1900, nine hours), if you are heading down south.

Getting Around

From Yaroslavl Glavny train station, head 200m to the right for the tram stop on ul Ukhtomskogo. Tram 3 goes along Bolshaya Oktyabrskaya ul to the **tram terminal** west of Bogoyavlenskaya pl; trolleybus 1 runs along ul Svobody to pl Volkova and on to Krasnaya pl. From the bus station and Yaroslavl Moskovsky train station, trolleybus 5 or 9 goes to Bogoyavlenskaya pl.

Uglich Углич

☎48532 / POP 36,500 / ⏲MOSCOW

This quaint upper Volga town was the scene of an unsolved crime that changed the history of Russia. It was here, in 1591, that the son of Ivan the Terrible, Dmitry (later to be impersonated by the string of False Dmitrys in the Time of Troubles), died in rather suspicious circumstances – officially he threw himself on a sword in a bout of epilepsy. It is, however, widely believed that he was killed on the orders of his foster father Boris Godunov.

Typically the first stop on Volga cruises after Moscow, Uglich boast 14 museums and an excellent tourist office.

Sights & Activities

Kremlin HISTORIC SITE

(joint ticket R80; ⏲9am-5pm) Within the waterside kremlin, the 15th-century **Prince's Chambers** house a historical exhibit that tells the sordid tale of Dmitry. The star-spangled **Church of St Dmitry on the Blood** (Tserkov Dmitria-na-krovi) was built in the 1690s on the spot where the body was found. The church now displays the bell that was used to call an insurrection on the murder of the *tsarevitch* in 1591. The 300kg bell was banished for many years to the Siberian town of Tobolsk (this after Godunov ordered it to be publicly flogged and have its tongue ripped out); it has since returned to its rightful location in Uglich. The impressive five-domed **Transfiguration Cathedral** (Preobrazhensky sobor) and an **Art Museum** are also in the kremlin.

Vodka Museum MUSEUM

(ul Berggolts 9; admission R60; ⏲9am-8pm) A few blocks over from the kremlin, you can learn about the history of Russia's favourite drink at the Vodka Museum. Price of admission includes samples!

Museum of City Life MUSEUM

(Uspenskaya pl 5; admission R60; ⏲9am-5pm) This interactive museum has costumes and musical instruments that are often put to use in concerts and other special programs for children.

Uglich Bells MUSEUM

(Угличские звоны; ☎29 866; ul Bakhareva 27; ⏲9am-5pm) Located in the private home of collector Alexei Kulagin. Besides the impressive collection of bells, he has also put together an assortment of whimsical papier-mâché figures depicting real and fantastical figures from Russian history and literature.

Festivals & Events

Uglich Versta CYCLING

A few hundred bicyclists meet in June for three days of riding, singing and drinking at this annual fest. The program includes various competitions, entertainment and a bicycle parade. Special events are organised for children. For details check www.velo.uglich.ru or call the tourist office.

Sleeping & Eating

Volzhskaya Riviera RESORT €€€

(Волжская Ривьера; ☎91 900; www.volga-hotel.ru; Uspenskaya pl 8; r R3150-3890, river view s/d from R3680/4410;) Opulence, we has it. The line from a British commercial featuring a Russian oligarch and his mini-giraffe springs to mind at the first glimpse of this riverside resort's colonnaded facade guarded by marble lions. Inside, there is everything you'd expect from an upscale accommodation declared Russia's best four-star hotel in 2010 – plush rooms, pool, spa, a floating piano bar and a restaurant by the name of Mon Plaisir. No minigiraffes, though.

Uspenskaya Hotel HOTEL €

(Успенская; ☎51 870; Uspenskaya pl; r R1300-1900, ste R2200-2500) A cheery place with slightly dilapidated rooms, opposite the kremlin.

Information

Uglich Tourist Office (☎23 072; visit@uglich.ru; ul Rostovskaya) Of all places in Russia, it is off-the-beaten-track Uglich that has one of the country's first foreigner-happy information offices with English-speaking staff that will quickly sort your excursions and load you with helpful brochures, maps and myriad sightseeing tips.

Getting There & Away

The easiest way to get to Uglich by bus is from Yaroslavl (R200, three hours, 12 daily). Buses to Rostov-Veliky run sporadically, so you may have to travel via Borisoglebsky.

Rostov-Veliky

Ростов-Великий

48536 / POP 33,200 / MOSCOW

Coloured in the same delicate shade of pink as the sunsets they have been watching for hundreds of years, the impregnable walls and perfectly proportioned towers of Rostov's kremlin rise magnificently above the shimmering Lake Nero. Frowning upon Moscow for its relatively young age, Rostov (first chronicled in 862) was the original capital of Kyivan princes who moved into Finno-Ugric lands, which would become known as Muscovy and Russia. Today, it is a sleepy village-like town that wakes you up with the sound of cockerels and gets eerily quiet when darkness falls, especially in winter. If you need to regain consciousness after Moscow's chaos, go no further.

Rostov is about 220km northeast of Moscow. The train and bus stations are together in the drab modern part of Rostov, 1.5km north of the kremlin.

Sights

Kremlin FORTRESS

(www.rostmuseum.ru; grounds R50, joint ticket to exhibitions R450; 10am-5pm) Rostov's main attraction is unashamedly photogenic. Though founded in the 12th century, nearly all the buildings here date to the 1670s and 1680s.

With its five magnificent domes, the **Assumption Cathedral** (Успенский собор) dominates the kremlin, although it is just outside the latter's north wall. Outside service hours, you can get inside the cathedral through the door in the church shop on ul Karla Marksa. The cathedral was here a century before the kremlin, while the belfry was added in the 1680s. Each of 15 bells in the **belfry** (Звонница; admission R100) has its own name; the largest, weighing 32 tonnes, is called Sysoy.

The west gate (the main entrance) and the north gate are straddled by the **Gate-Church of St John the Divine** (Надвратная церковь Иоанна Богослова) and the **Gate-Church of the Resurrection** (Надвратная церковь Воскресения), both of which are richly decorated with 17th-century frescoes. Enter these churches from the **monastery walls** (admission R45), which you can access from the stairs next to the north gate. Like several other buildings within the complex, these are only open from May to September. Between the gate-churches, the **Church of Hodigitria** (Церковь Одигитрии) houses an exhibition of Orthodox Church vestments and paraphernalia.

The metropolitan's private chapel, the **Church of the Saviour-over-the-Galleries** (Церковь Спаса-на-Сенях), contained within the **metropolitan's house** (Покои метрополита), has the most beautiful interior of all, covered in colourful frescoes. Other rooms in the house are filled with exhibits: the **White Chamber** (Белая палата) displays religious antiquities, while the **Red Chamber** (Красная палата) shows off *finift* (luminous enamelled miniatures), a Rostov artistic speciality.

Monastery of Saviour & St Jacob MONASTERY

(ul Engelsa 44; 10am-5pm) The restored monastery is the fairy-tale apparition you'll see as you approach Rostov by road or rail. Take bus 1 or 2 or walk alongside Lake Nero 2km west from the kremlin. English-language excursions may be available for R300 from the excursion bureau next to the gates. For a donation of R20 you can climb the wall on its lake-view side.

Activities

Zarya BOAT TRIPS

(Заря; adult/student R150/100; 11am-6pm May-Sep) For a different perspective on this panorama, board the ferry *Zarya* for a float around Lake Nero. The hour-long trip leaves from the pier near the west gate of the kremlin and cruises past both monasteries.

Dom Remyosel CRAFTS

(67 223; www.domremesel.com; Tolstovskaya nab 16; 10am-7pm) Apart from being a great shop, the 'House of Crafts' invites visitors to try their hand in making dolls, clay whistles, bark shoes, Easter eggs and other traditional souvenirs. Classes cost R55 to R350.

Sleeping

Rostov is a popular weekend destination, meaning that hotel prices are generally lower between Sunday and Thursday. All prices include breakfast unless otherwise indicated.

Khors GUESTHOUSE €
(Хорс; ☎62 483, 8-903-163 0594; www.khors.org; r weekdays R500-1200, weekends R1000-2400; @) Also containing an art gallery of the same name, this complex has a handful of tiny rooms with Soviet furniture and shared access to a bathroom and kitchen (which means you make your own breakfast). Tip: drag your mattress up onto the roof to awake to the sunrise over Lake Nero.

Usadba Podozerka GUESTHOUSE €€
(Усадьба Подозерка; ☎8-962-211 9163; www.podozerka.ru; ul Podozerka 33; q weekdays/weekends & holidays R2000/R2500) A newer guesthouse right next to Khors offers rooms in smallish purpose-built wooden bungalows with simply furnished rooms. There is a *banya* on the premises (R2000 for three hours). Breakfast not included.

Dom na Pogrebakh HISTORIC HOTEL €
(Дом на погребах; ☎61 244; www.domnapogrebah.ru; s/d/tr without bathroom R700/1000/1500, d with bathroom R2500) Right inside the kremlin near the east gate, this place has clean, wood-panelled rooms with heavy doors and colourful tapestries. The location within the building varies, but if you can snag a room with a view of the west gate it is charming indeed.

Hotel Lion HOTEL €
(Гостиница Лион; ☎64 949; www.lion-hotel.ru; ul 50-letiya Oktyabrya 9/6; r R1200-1650;) This big and basic hotel offers affordable rooms and a convenient location. The drab decor does not do much for the dark interior, but the place is clean and comfortable enough.

Usadba Pleshanova HOTEL €€
(Усадьба Плешанова; ☎76 440; www.hotelvrostove.ru; Pokrovskaya ul 34; r weekday/weekend from R2000/2300;) This 19th-century manor house, once the residence of a merchant and philanthropist family, is now a welcoming inn with a nice restaurant, cosy library and wood sauna.

Russkoye Podvorye HOTEL €
(Русское подворье; ☎64 255; ul Marshala Alexeyeva 9; s weekdays/weekends R700/1400, d weekdays/weekends R1400/1900;) This newish hotel occupies the arcaded house of 18th-century merchant Ivan Khlebnikov. Inside, however, it is all quite modern, with spirit-lifting floral ornaments in the rooms and comfy beds. Breakfasts are served in perhaps the best restaurant in town.

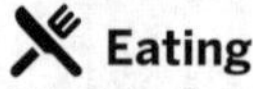

Eating

All of the hotels have restaurants or cafés on site.

Trapeznaya Palata RUSSIAN €€
(Трапезная Палата; mains R150-250; ⏰9am-5pm, later in summer) The draw to the refectory is the atmospheric location inside the kremlin, near the metropolitan's house. The grand dining room is often crowded with tour groups supping on traditional Russian fare.

Russkoye Podvorye RUSSIAN €€
(Русское подворье; ul Marshala Alexeyeva 9; mains R120-300) What claims to be a 'medieval Russian' menu is essentially a fresh and intelligent take on Russian cuisine as it was before mayo and potatoes. Mushrooms, turnips and more unusual ingredients feature in inventive dishes. There is also a good selection of porridges, which used to be the main staple in the old times.

Café Alaverdy GEORGIAN €
(Кафе Алаверды; ul Kamenny most 4; meals R150-200) A simple Georgian eatery tucked into a courtyard right by the kremlin. *Khachapuri* cheese pies and *khinkali* dumplings are as good as it gets this side of Lake Nero.

Getting There & Away

BUS The most convenient option to/from Yaroslavl is by bus, either transit or direct (R120, 1½ hours, every 90 minutes). Transit buses also pass through on the way to Moscow (R430, four to five hours, every 90 minutes); most of them go via Pereslavl-Zalessky and Sergiev Posad. One lone bus goes to Uglich (R130, three hours).

TRAIN The best option from Moscow is the Yaroslavl-bound fast *elektrichka* (R430, three hours, twice daily), which calls at Sergiev Posad en route. There are also five slow *elektrichki* daily plying the route between Yaroslavl and Alexandrov, where you can change for Moscow trains.

Pereslavl-Zalessky
Переславль-Залесский

☎48535 / POP 42,700 / ⏰MOSCOW

Another ancient lakeside town, Pereslavl is a popular dacha getaway for Muscovites. Its attractions are scattered around a large and not always interesting area, which makes it hard to explore without a car. But you'll easily find a few quiet and pretty spots once you escape from the Moscow–Yaroslavl highway cutting right through the centre.

The town's main claim to fame is as the birthplace of Alexander Nevsky. Its earthen walls and the little Cathedral of the Transfiguration are as old as the town itself. Pereslavl is also famous as the unlikely cradle of Russian naval might thanks to a holidaying teenager who went on to become Peter the Great.

Sights

TOWN CENTRE

Kremlin HISTORIC SITE

The walls of Yury Dolgoruky's kremlin are now a grassy ring around the centre of town. The 1152 **Cathedral of the Transfiguration of the Saviour** (Преображенский собор; Krasnaya pl; admission R70; ⌚10am-6pm), one of the oldest buildings in Russia, is inside this green ring. A bust of Alexander Nevsky stands out in front, while three additional churches across the grassy square make for a picturesque corner. These include the tent-roofed **Church of Peter the Metropolitan** (Церковь митрополита Петра; ul Sadovaya 5), built in 1585 and renovated in 1957, and the 18th-century twin churches fronting the road.

Trubezh River PROMENADE

The Trubezh River, winding 2km from the kremlin to the lake, is fringed by trees and narrow lanes. You can follow the northern riverbank most of the way to the lake by a combination of paths and streets. The **Forty Martyrs' Church** (Сорокосвятская церковь; Levaya nab 165) sits picturesquely on the south side of the river mouth.

BOTIK AREA

The following sights are located on the southern bank of Lake Pleshcheyevo. From the main road, turn to ul Podgornaya under Goritsky Monastery.

Goritsky Monastery MONASTERY

(Горицкий монастырь; grounds R20, exhibits R40-80 each, all-inclusive ticket R350; ⌚10am-6pm May-Oct, 9am-5pm Nov-Apr) This large monastery standing at the turn to Botik Museum (2.5km south of the centre) was founded in the 14th century, though the oldest buildings today are the 17th-century gates, gate-church and belfry. The centrepiece is the **Assumption Cathedral** (Uspensky sobor; admission R80), with its beautiful carved iconostasis. The other buildings hold art and history exhibits.

Botik Museum MUSEUM

(Ботик Петра; grounds R10, exhibitions R70 each; ⌚10am-5pm Tue-Sun) Lake Pleshcheyevo is the place where Peter the Great developed his obsession with the sea. As a young man, he studied navigation here and built a 'toy flotilla' of more than 100 little ships by age 20. You can explore some of this history at the small Botik Museum, situated in Veskovo 4km along the road past the Goritsky Monastery at the southern end of the lake. Its highlight is the sailboat *Fortuna*, one of only two of Peter the Great's boats to survive fire and neglect; the other is in the St Petersburg Naval Museum.

Kukushka.ru MUSEUM

(☎49 479; www.kukushka.ru; adult/child R100/50; ⌚10am-6pm Wed-Sun Apr-Oct, 10am-5pm Sat & Sun Nov-Mar) A further 12km along the road passing Botik Museum is the turn-off to this unique railway museum. The collection of locomotives occupies the tracks and depot that were used up until the middle of the 20th century. Don't miss the opportunity to ride on the **handcart** (adult/child R100/50). Visitors are ferried from the parking lot 1km away from the museum in vintage WWII-era cars.

Sleeping

Hotel Pereslavl HOTEL €€

(Гостиница Переславль; ☎31 559; Rostovskaya ul 27; r R2400, studio R2750, ste R3850) Despite its uninspiring exterior, this central hotel has updated its rooms – they now sport new furniture, carpeting and, most importantly, bathrooms. The rooms are crowded but they feel fresh.

Albitsky Sad Motel HOTEL €€

(Альбицкий сад; ☎31 430; as_motel_pereslavl@mail.ru; ul Kardovskogo 21; d R2500-2900, tr R3500-3900; ⊖❄) On the main road just south of the centre, 'Albitsky Garden' resembles an old manor house, its yellow exterior adorned with white trim. The motel offers about 16 tastefully decorated rooms (and at least one honeymoon suite that is not quite so tasteful), as well as an inviting restaurant.

Art Hotel APARTMENTS €€€

(☎98 130; http://arthotel.ucoz.ru; Bol Protechnaya 45; apt R6000-8000) Sure, it's pricey. But for your money, you get a fully equipped, artistically designed apartment set amid flowering gardens, with an art gallery and a *banya* on site. The two apartments (sleeping two to six people each) are lovingly decorated in a funky, contemporary style featuring original artwork by the owners. Bol Protechnaya runs parallel to the main road, on the eastern side.

Eating

Traktir na Ozernoy CAUCASIAN €€
(Трактир на Озерной; Rostovskaya ul 27; mains R200-500) Gnaw on shashlyk to your heart's desire at this Caucasian-food eatery attached to Hotel Pereslavl. Pork, chicken, lamb and sturgeon – they're all grilled up in plain view and served hot and spicy. Also go for pastry – meat-filled *chebureki* and cheese-filled *khachapuri*.

Getting There & Around

Pereslavl-Zalessky is not on the train line, but buses travel frequently to Moscow (R310, 2½ hours). Not all of these stop at Sergiev Posad (one hour, three daily). Others travel to Yaroslavl (R180 to R270, three hours, seven daily) via Rostov-Veliky (1½ hours).

Bus 1 runs up and down the main street from just south of the **bus station** (Автовокзал); heading out from the centre you can catch it just north of the river. Taxis wait at Narodnaya pl.

Sergiev Posad

Сергиев Посад

496 / POP 112,700 / MOSCOW

Blue and golden cupolas offset by snow-white walls – this colour scheme lies at the heart of the Russian perception of divinity and Sergiev Posad's monastery is a textbook example. It doesn't get any holier than here in Russia, for the place was founded in 1340 by the country's most revered saint. St Sergius of Radonezh was credited with providing mystic support to Prince Dmitry Donskoy in his improbable victory over the Tatars in the battle of Kulikovo Pole (1380). Soon after his death at the age of 78, Sergius was named Russia's patron saint. Since the 14th century, pilgrims have been journeying to this place to pay homage to him.

Although the Bolsheviks closed the monastery, it was reopened following WWII as a museum, residence of the patriarch and a working monastery. The patriarch and the church's administrative centre moved to the Danilovsky Monastery in Moscow in 1988, but the Trinity Monastery of St Sergius remains one of the most important spiritual sites in Russia.

Sergiev Posad is an easy day trip from Moscow and that's how most people visit it. If you plan to move further, consider doing it on the same day: clogged with pilgrims and traffic, the town is not a great place to overnight.

Pr Krasnoy Armii is the main street, running north to south through the town centre. The train and bus stations are on opposite corners of a wide square to the east of pr Krasnoy Armii. The monastery is about 400m north of there.

Sights

FREE **Trinity Monastery of St Sergius** MONASTERY
(Троице-Сергиева Лавра; www.stsl.ru; admission free; 10am-6pm) The monastery is an active religious centre with a visible population of monks in residence. Visitors should refrain from photographing the monks, female visitors should wear headscarves and men are required to remove hats before entering the churches.

Trinity Cathedral
(Троицкий собор) Built in the 1420s, the squat, dark Trinity Cathedral is the heart of the Trinity Monastery. The tomb of St Sergius stands in the southeastern corner, where a memorial service for St Sergius goes on all day, every day. The icon-festooned interior, lit by oil lamps, is largely the work of the great medieval painter Andrei Rublyov and his students.

Cathedral of the Assumption
(Успенский собор) The star-spangled Cathedral of the Assumption was modelled on the cathedral of the same name in the Moscow Kremlin. It was finished in 1585 with money left by Ivan the Terrible in a fit of remorse for killing his son. Outside the west door is the **grave** (Могила Бориса Годунова) of Boris Godunov, the only tsar not buried in the Moscow Kremlin or St Petersburg's SS Peter & Paul Cathedral.

Chapel-at-the-Well
(Надкладезная часовня) Nearby, the resplendent Chapel-at-the-Well was built over a spring that is said to have appeared during the Polish siege. The five-tier baroque **bell tower** (Колокольня) took 30 years to build in the 18th century and once had 42 bells, the largest of which weighed 65 tonnes.

Vestry
(Ризница; admission R200; ⌚10am-5.30pm Wed-Sun) The Vestry, behind the Trinity Cathedral, displays the monastery's extraordinarily rich treasury, bulging with 600 years of donations by the rich and powerful – tapestries, jewel-encrusted vestments, solid-gold chalices and more.

Refectory Church of St Sergius
(Трапезная церковь преподобного Сергия) The huge block with the 'wallpaper' paint job is the Refectory Church of St Sergius, so called because it was once a dining hall for pilgrims. Now it's the Assumption Cathedral's winter counterpart, holding morning services in cold weather. It is closed outside of services, except for guided tours. The green building next door is the metropolitan's residence.

Konny Dvor MUSEUM
(Конный Двор; ul Udarnoy Armii; joint ticket R140; ⌚10am-5pm Wed-Sun) Just outside the monastery wall and behind Old Lavra Hotel, the former monasterial stables house three interesting historic and traditional craft exhibitions.

Toy Museum MUSEUM
(Музей Игрушек; pr Krasnoy Armii 123; ⌚11am-5pm Wed-Sun) Come to the Toy Museum for toys from throughout history and around the world. The museum houses a particularly good collection of nesting dolls, as Sergiev Posad was the centre of *matryoshka* production before the revolution.

Sleeping & Eating

Russky Dvorik HOTEL €€
(Гостиница Русский Дворик; ☎547 5392; www.russky-dvorik.ru; ul Mitkina 14/2; s/d weekdays from R1600/2400, weekends from R1900/2800) Some of the rooms at this delightful hotel boast views of the onion domes peeking out above whitewashed walls. The place is quite modern, despite its rustic style. The fanciest room even has a jacuzzi. The affiliated **restaurant** (☎45 114; pr Krasnoy Armii 134; meals R300-900; ⌚10am to 9pm) is a charming, kitschy place decked out like a Russian dacha.

Old Lavra Hotel HOTEL €€
(Старая гостиница Лавры; ☎549 9000; pr Krasnoy Armii 133; s/d weekdays R1600/2300, weekends R1800/2600) Revived in its original capacity, this massive monastery hotel has no trappings that might distract its supposedly puritan guests from prayer and contemplation – not even TV! But despite their blandness, rooms are modern and very clean. A vast restaurant is in the premises. Expectedly, alcohol is strictly banned in the whole complex.

Art Café San Marino ITALIAN €€
(pr Krasnoy Armii 138/2; mains R220-350) Looking utterly unorthodox in front of the holy site, this little cellar café is filled with art and books. Salads and pastas with a few vegetarian options dominate the menu. Live jazz concerts happen regularly. A singing canary will keep you awake at other times.

Information

Post & telephone office (Почтамт и переговорный пункт; pr Krasnoy Armii 127a) Outside the southeastern wall of the monastery.

Getting There & Away

BUS Bus 388 to Sergiev Posad from Moscow's VDNKh metro station departs every 10 to 20 minutes from 8.30am to 7.30pm (R145, 70 minutes). Transit buses for Kostroma (R560), Yaroslavl (R400) or Rybinsk pass almost hourly; all these will take you to Pereslavl-Zalessky and Rostov-Veliky (R280) if you can get a ticket.

TRAIN The fastest transport option is the express train that departs from Moscow's Yaroslavsky vokzal (R320, one hour, at least twice daily) and continues to Yaroslavl (three hours) via Rostov (two hours). Suburban trains also run every half-hour (R130, 1½ hours); some of them continue to Alexandrov where you can change for Yaroslavl.

St Petersburg

Includes »

Best Places to Eat

» Dom Beat (p213)
» Botanika (p213)
» Kompot Café (p213)
» Teplo (p214)
» MiX in St Petersburg (p212)

Best Places to Stay

» W Hotel (p207)
» Rachmaninov Hotel (p207)
» Rossi Hotel (p207)
» Hostel Ligovsky 74 (p210)
» Casa Leto (p207)

Why Go?

Beautiful, complex and imperious, with a hedonistic, creative temperament, St Petersburg (Санкт-Петербург) is the ultimate Russian diva. From its early days as an uninhabited swamp, the 300-year-old city has been nurtured by a succession of rulers, enduring practically everything that history and nature's harsh elements could throw at her. Constantly in need of repair but with a carefree party attitude, Piter (as she's affectionately known by locals) still seduces all who gaze upon her grand facades, glittering spires and gilded domes. Such an environment has inspired many of Russia's greatest artists, including Pushkin, Gogol, Dostoevsky, Rachmaninoff, Tchaikovsky and Shostakovich.

The long summer days of the White Nights season are particularly special – the fountains flow, parks and gardens burst into colour and Piter's citizens hit the streets to party. With a little preparation, though, the icy depths of winter have their own magic, and are the perfect time for warming body and soul in all those museums and palaces.

When to Go

St Petersburg

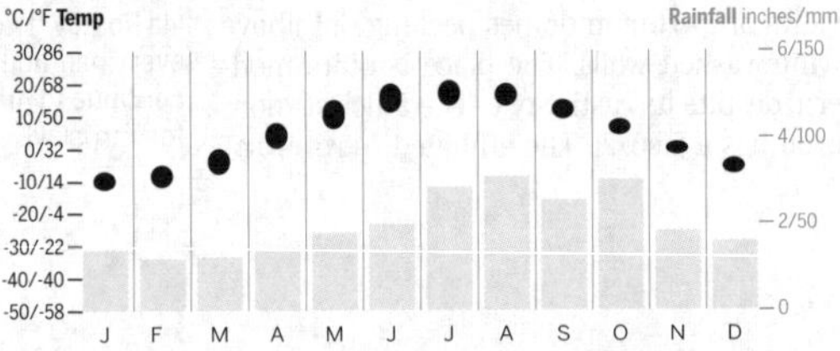

Mid-May–mid-Jul The White Nights, when the sun never truly sets, is the most popular time to visit.

May & Sep A great time to visit St Petersburg while avoiding the crowds of the peak months.

Nov-Jan Freezing, dark and blanketed in snow, winter in St Petersburg is quite magical.

Art Attack

St Petersburg, long Russia's artistic engine, has recently seen the opening of several new museums and galleries that are really putting the city on the international modern art map. As well as the incredible world-class collections at the Hermitage and the Russian Museum, the recent opening of the Erarta Museum of Contemporary Art, Russia's largest private art museum with over 2000 modern Russian works, has made St Petersburg about far more than classical art. Add to that two very interesting contemporary galleries, Loft Project ETAGI and the Rizzordi Art Foundation, and you'll find plenty to keep you occupied while you're in town.

PALACES UNDERGROUND

The St Petersburg metro isn't quite as palatial as Moscow's, but you shouldn't miss the stations on the southern half of Line 1 (that's the red line on the official metro map). Some highlights:

» **Avtovo** Don't miss the Babylonian lavishness of the marble and cut-glass columns holding up the roof, the relief of soldiers in the ticket hall and the temple-like entrance.

» **Narvskaya** A fantastic sculpted relief of Lenin and the rejoicing proletariat hangs over the escalators, and carvings of miners, engineers, sailors and teachers grace the platform columns.

» **Ploshchad Vosstaniya** Lenin and Stalin are depicted together in the roundels at either end of the platform, as well as Lenin on a tank, Lenin alone and the Kronshtadt sailors.

Bridges Up!

From the end of April to November, all bridges across the Neva River rise at around 1.30am nightly to let ships pass through the city and on to the rest of the world, or into Russia's deep interior. The spectacle is well worth seeing, but it's also well worth planning for – don't find yourself on the wrong side of the water when the bridges go up, or you'll have a long night ahead of you until they go back down again at around 5am. See p224 for times.

NEED TO KNOW

While the majority of St Petersburg's museums close on a Monday, potentially any day of the week can be their day off – always check with the listings before you head off somewhere.

Fast Facts

» **Telephone area code** ☎812

» **Population** 4.8 million

» **Number of metro stations** 65

» **Name changes** 3

» **Number of bridges** 342

» **St Petersburg Time** Moscow (GMT/USC +4 hours)

Don't Drink the Water

Tiny traces of *Giardia lamblia*, a nasty parasite that causes stomach cramps, nausea, bloated stomach, diarrhoea and frequent gas, have been found in St Petersburg's water. There's no preventative drug so the best advice is not to drink straight from the tap.

Resources

» **St Petersburg Tourist Information** (http://eng.ispb.info)

» **St Petersburg Times** (www.sptimes.ru)

» **In Your Pocket St Petersburg** (www.inyourpocket.com/russia/st-petersburg)

» **Way to Russia** (www.waytorussia.net)

St Petersburg Highlights

1 Spend a day (or more!) in the **Hermitage** (p168), one of the world's most unrivalled art collections

2 Witness the amazing kaleidoscope of colours that is the **Church of the Saviour on Spilled Blood** (p175)

3 Revel with locals during the ethereal endless daylight of the **White Nights** (p206)

4 Climb the enormous dome of **St Isaac's Cathedral** (p186) for the best view over the imperial city

5 Have the ultimate Russian experience by taking in a ballet at the **Mariinsky Theatre** (p219)

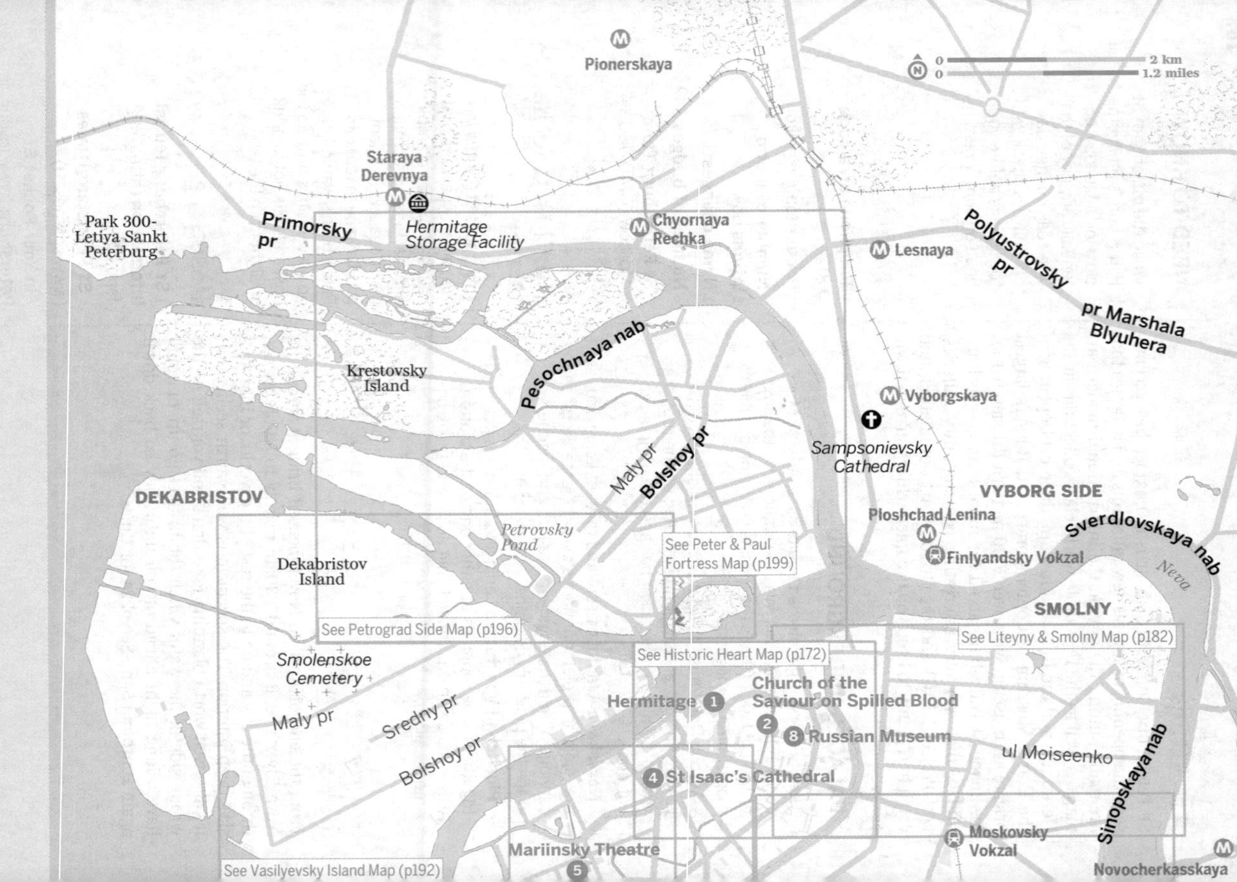

6 Cruise the **rivers and canals** (p205) for the best views of this most watery of cities – they don't call it the Venice of the North for nothing!

7 Head out of town to **Tsarskoe Selo** (p232), Catherine the Great's incredible summer palace, and see the magnificent Amber Room

8 Take in the excellent collection of art, from icons to the avant-garde, at the **Russian Museum** (p175)

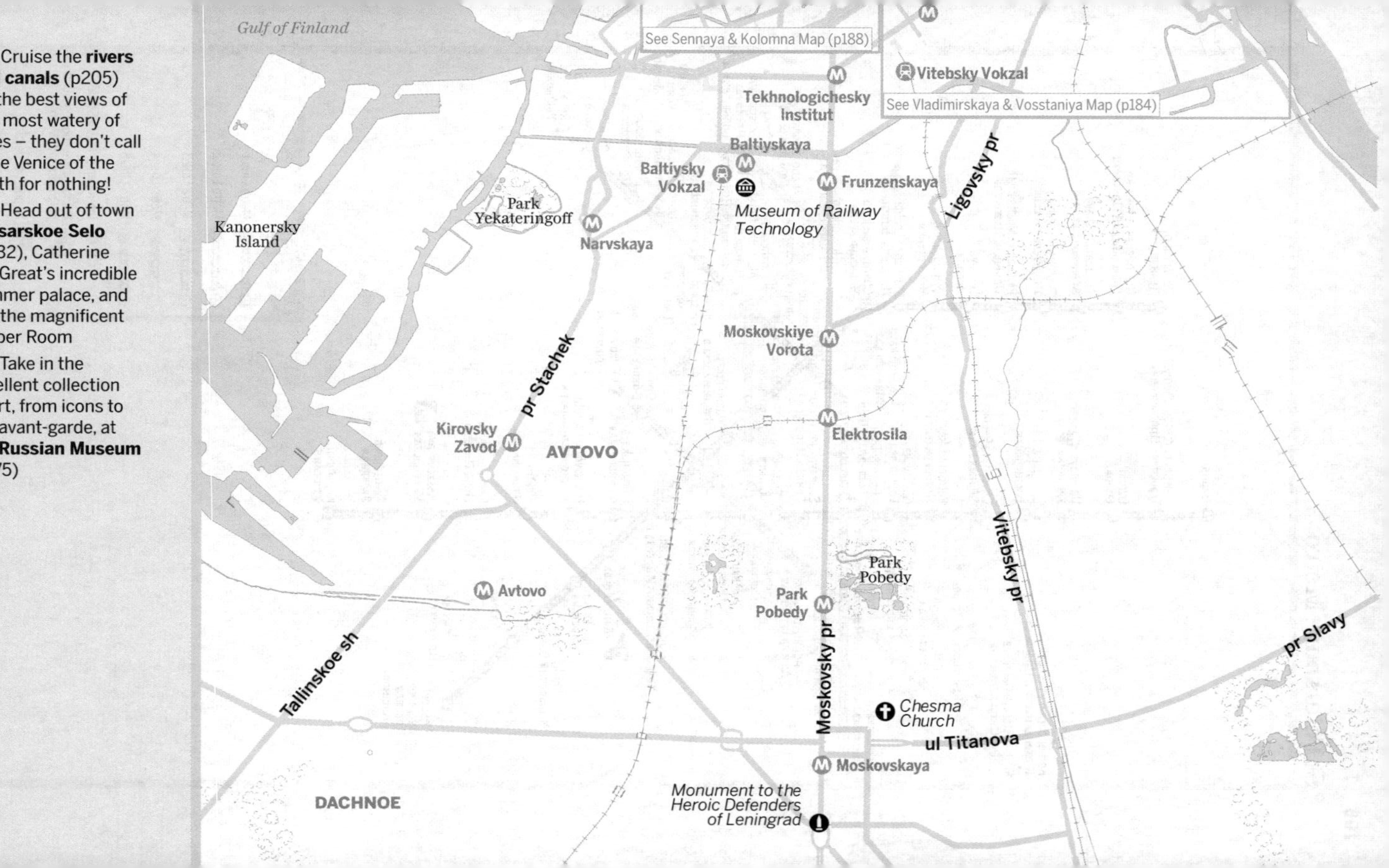

St Petersburg Metro

Parnas
Парнас
Prospekt Prosveshcheniya
Проспект Просвещения
Ozerki
Озерки
Udelnaya
Удельная
Pionerskaya
Пионерская
Chyornaya Rechka
Чёрная Речка
Petrogradskaya
Петроградская
Gorkovskaya
Горьковская
Gostiny Dvor
Гостиный Двор
Nevsky Prospekt
Невский Проспект
Sennaya Ploshchad
Сенная Площадь
Spasskaya
Спасская
Sadovaya
Садовая
Pushkinskaya
Пушкинская
Zvenigorodskaya
Звенигородская
Tekhnologichesky Institut
Технологический Институт
Frunzenskaya
Фрунзенская
Moskovskiye Vorota
Московские Ворота
Elektrosila
Электросила
Park Pobedy
Парк Победы
Moskovskaya
Московская
Zvyozdnaya
Звёздная
Kupchino
Купчино
Devyatkino
Девяткино
Grazhdansky Prospekt
Гражданский Проспект
Akademicheskaya
Академическая
Politekhnicheskaya
Политехническая
Ploshchad Muzhestva
Площадь Мужества
Lesnaya
Лесная
Vyborgskaya
Выборгская
Ploshchad Lenina
Площадь Ленина
Chernyshevskaya
Чернышевская
Ploshchad Vosstaniya
Площадь Восстания
Mayakovskaya
Маяковская
Dostoevskaya
Достоевская
Vladimirskaya
Владимирская
Ligovsky Prospekt
Лиговский Проспект
Ploshchad Alexandra Nevskogo
Площадь Александра Невского
Novocherkasskaya
Новочеркасская
Ladozhskaya
Ладожская
Prospekt Bolshevikov
Проспект Большевиков
Ulitsa Dybenko
Улица Дыбенко
Elizarovskaya
Елизаровская
Lomonosovskaya
Ломоносовская
Proletarskaya
Пролетарская
Obukhovo
Обухово
Rybatskoe
Рыбацкое
Obvodny Kanal
Обводный Канал
Volkovskaya
Волковская
Komendantsky Prospekt
Комендантский Проспект
Staraya Derevnya
Старая Деревня
Krestovsky Ostrov
Крестовский Остров
Chkalovskaya
Чкаловская
Sportivnaya
Спортивная
Admiralteyskaya
Адмиралтейская
Primorskaya
Приморская
Vasileostrovskaya
Василеостровская
Baltiyskaya
Балтийская
Narvskaya
Нарвская
Kirovsky Zavod
Кировский Завод
Avtovo
Автово
Leninsky Prospekt
Ленинский Проспект
Prospekt Veteranov
Проспект Ветеранов
Legend
Metro Line 1
Metro Line 2
Metro Line 3
Metro Line 4
Metro Line 5
Interchange Metro Station
Points where above-ground rail meets with Metro
Airport connection

History

The area around the mouth of the Neva River may have been a swamp but it's been long fought over. Alexander of Novgorod defeated the Swedes here in 1240 – earning the title Nevsky (of the Neva). Sweden retook control of the region in the 17th century – it was Peter the Great's desire to crush this rival and make Russia a European power that led to the founding of St Petersburg. At the start of the Great Northern War (1700–21), he captured the Swedish outposts on the Neva, and in 1703 he began his city with the Peter & Paul Fortress.

After Peter trounced the Swedes at Poltava in 1709, the city he named Sankt Pieter Burch (in Dutch style, after his namesake) really began to grow. In 1712 Peter moved the capital from Moscow to this uninhabited site, drafting in armies of peasants to work as forced labour. Many died of disease and exhaustion, and it's still known as the city built upon bones. Architects and artisans came to St Petersburg from all over Europe, and by Peter's death in 1725 the city had a population of 40,000; 90% of Russia's foreign trade passed through it.

Peter's immediate successors moved the capital back to Moscow but Empress Anna Ionone (1730–40) returned it to St Petersburg. Between 1741 and 1825, during the reigns of Empress Elizabeth, Catherine the Great and Alexander I, it became a cosmopolitan city with an imperial court of famed splendour. These monarchs commissioned great series of palaces, government buildings and churches, turning it into one of Europe's grandest capitals.

The emancipation of the serfs in 1861 and industrialisation, which peaked in the 1890s, brought a flood of poor workers into the city, leading to squalor, disease and festering discontent. St Petersburg became a hotbed of strikes and political violence, and was the hub of the 1905 revolution, sparked by 'Bloody Sunday' on 9 January 1905, when a strikers' march to petition the tsar in the Winter Palace was fired on by troops. In 1914, in a wave of patriotism at the start of WWI, the city's name was changed to the Russian-style Petrograd.

In 1917 the workers' protests turned into a general strike and troops mutinied, forcing the end of the monarchy in March and the establishment of a provisional government. Seven months later, Lenin's Bolshevik Party staged an audacious coup and the Soviet government came into being. Fearing a German attack on Petrograd, the new government moved the capital back to Moscow in March 1918.

Renamed Leningrad after Lenin's death in 1924, the city became a hub of Stalin's 1930s industrialisation program. By 1939 its population had grown to 3.1 million and it accounted for 11% of Soviet industrial output. Stalin feared the city as a rival power base, however, and the 1934 assassination of the local communist chief Sergei Kirov at Smolny was the start of his 1930s Communist Party purge.

When Germany attacked the USSR in June 1941, its armies took only two and a half months to reach Leningrad. As the birthplace of Bolshevism, Hitler swore to wipe the city from the face of the earth. His troops besieged the city from 8 September 1941 until 27 January 1944 – Leningrad survived and, after the war, was proclaimed a 'hero city'. It took until 1960 for the city's population to exceed pre-WWII levels.

During the 1960s and '70s, Leningrad developed a reputation as a dissidents' city with an artistic underground spearheaded by the poet Joseph Brodsky and, later, rock groups such as Akvarium. In 1989 Anatoly Sobchak, a reform-minded candidate, was elected mayor. Two years later, as the USSR crumbled, the city's citizens voted to bring back the name of St Petersburg (though the region around the city remains known as Leningradskaya Oblast).

In the anarchic post-Soviet years of the early 1990s, it often seemed like the local 'Mafia' were more in charge than the city's elected officials, who proved to be equally corrupt. Romanov ghosts returned to the city on 17 July 1998, when the remains of Tsar Nicholas II and some of his family were buried in the crypt at the SS Peter & Paul Cathedral within the fortress of the same name.

Five years later enormous sums were budgeted to spruce up the city for its tercentenary celebrations. Local boy made good Vladimir Putin didn't waste the opportunity to return to his birthplace and show it off to visiting heads of state and other dignitaries. His presidential successor Dmitry Medvedev, also a St Petersburg native, has done likewise.

Run for much of the past decade by Governor Valentina Matvienko, a staunch ally of Putin, St Petersburg was in something of

THE LENINGRAD BLOCKADE

The defining event of the 20th century for St Petersburg was the Nazi blockade of the city during WWII. Around a million people died from shelling, starvation and disease in what's often called the '900 Days' (actually 872). By comparison, the USA and UK suffered about 700,000 dead between them in all of WWII.

The Nazi plan, as indicated in a secret directive, was to 'wipe the city of Petersburg from the face of the earth'. After the Germans launched their surprise attack on the Soviet Union on 22 June 1941, many residents fled Leningrad as the Germans continued to approach the city at great speed. Art treasures and precious documents from the Hermitage and other museums were shipped out; factories were evacuated and relocated to Siberia; historical sculptures were buried or covered with sandbags. Yet no one could have predicted the suffering yet to come.

A fragile 'Road of Life' across frozen Lake Ladoga was the only (albeit heavily bombed) lifeline the city had for provisions and evacuations. Food was practically nonexistent, and at one point rations were limited to 175g of sawdust-laden bread a day. People ate their pets, rats and birds. The paste behind wallpaper was scraped off and eaten, leather was cooked until it was chewable and, eventually, the most desperate souls turned to cannibalism.

Despite the suffering and the 150,000 shells and bombs that rained down on the city, life went on. Concerts and plays were performed in candlelit halls, lectures were given, poetry was written, orphanages were opened and brigades were formed to clean up the city. The most famous concert was the 9 August 1942 performance of Shostakovich's 7th Symphony by the Leningrad Philharmonic, broadcast nationally by radio from the besieged city. According to survivors, random acts of kindness outnumbered incidents of robbery and vandalism, and lessons learned about the human spirit would be remembered for a lifetime.

For a detailed, harrowing description of the blockade, read Harrison Salisbury's *900 Days: The Siege of Leningrad*. Otherwise, a visit to one or all of the following blockade-related sites – St Petersburg History Museum, Museum of the Defence and Blockade of Leningrad, and the Monument to the Heroic Defenders of Leningrad – will greatly enrich your understanding of the city's darkest hour.

political limbo following President Dmitry Medvedev's decision to nominate Matvienko for the speakership of the Federation Council in the summer of 2011. Locals, far from used to electing their own politicians, remain stoical about whatever will come next. Rather than politics and social problems, what inspires most citizens to take to the streets are the fortunes of local football team Zenit, UEFA champions for 2008, and plans to insert contemporary architecture into the city's historic heart.

Sights

While St Petersburg is a huge and sprawling city spread over many different islands, its main sights are fairly well centred in the Historic Heart, the area broadly surrounding the main avenue, Nevsky pr. Other rich pockets of sights include those on Vasilyevsky Island and the Petrograd Side, just across the Neva River from the Historic Heart; and those further down Nevsky pr in the areas around Smolny and pl Vosstaniya.

HISTORIC HEART

State Hermitage Museum MUSEUM

(Эрмитаж; Map p172; www.hermitagemuseum.org; Dvortsovaya pl; adult/student R400/free, 1st Thu of month free; 10.30am-6pm Tue-Sat, to 5pm Sun; M Admiralteyskaya) Mainly set in the magnificent Winter Palace – a stunning mint-green, white and gold profusion of columns, windows and recesses, with its roof topped by rows of classical statues – the Hermitage fully lives up to its sterling reputation. You can be absorbed by its treasures for days and still come out wanting more.

The Hermitage's collection really began with Catherine the Great, one of the greatest art collectors of all time. Nicholas I also greatly enriched the collection, which he opened to the public for the first time in 1852. It was the postrevolutionary period that saw the collection increase threefold, as many valuable private collections were seized by the state, including those of the Stroganovs, Sheremetyevs and Yusupovs. In 1948 it incorporated the renowned collections of post-Impressionist and Impressionist paintings of Moscow industrialists Sergei Shchukin and Ivan Morozov.

Throughout the 1990s, in part thanks to partnerships with foreign museums and donors, the museum was able to renovate its heating and temperature control system, install a new fire detection system, fit its windows with UV-filtering plastic and begin a digitised inventory of its mammoth collection. Under the 'Hermitage 20/21' project, celebrating the 250th anniversary of the museum's foundation back in 1764, galleries of modern and contemporary art will be set up in the General Staff Building.

The enormous collection (over three million items) almost amounts to a comprehensive history of Western European art, and for as much as you see in the museum, there's about 20 times more in its vaults, part of which you can visit. The vastness of the buildings – of which the Winter Palace alone has 1057 rooms and 117 staircases – demands a little planning: it's well worth choosing the areas you'd like to concentrate on before you arrive. For planning help, see 176.

The State Hermitage consists of five linked buildings along riverside Dvortsovaya nab. From west to east they are the Winter Palace, the Little Hermitage, the Old and New Hermitages (or Large Hermitage), and the State Hermitage Theatre.

There are also separate sections of the museum in the east wing of the General Staff Building, the Menshikov Palace on Vasilyevsky Island, the Winter Palace of Peter I (further east along the embankment from the main Winter Palace) and the Imperial Porcelain factory. All have separate, very reasonable admission (R60) unless you purchase a ticket online for US$25.95, which gives you access to all the facilities over a two-day period.

Winter Palace

The Winter Palace was commissioned from Bartolomeo Rastrelli in 1754 by Empress Elizabeth. Catherine the Great and her successors had most of the interior remodelled in a classical style by 1837. It remained an imperial home until 1917, though the last two tsars spent more time in other palaces.

Little Hermitage

The classical Little Hermitage was built for Catherine the Great as a retreat that would also house the art collection started by Peter the Great, which she significantly expanded.

Old Hermitage

At the river end of the Little Hermitage is the Old Hermitage, which also dates from the time of Catherine the Great.

New Hermitage

Facing Millionnaya ul on the south end of the Old Hermitage, the New Hermitage was built for Nicholas II to hold the still-growing art collection. The Old and New Hermitages are sometimes grouped together and labelled the Large Hermitage.

ST PETERSBURG IN...

Two Days

Devote much of your first day to the **Hermitage**, but drag yourself away in the afternoon to see the polychromatic **Church of the Saviour on Spilled Blood** and to climb the colonnade of **St Isaac's Cathedral** for a bird's-eye view of the city. From here you're well placed to hop on a boat for an early-evening **cruise**.

Kick off day two by exploring the splendid **Russian Museum**. Follow the Fontanka River past the **Summer Garden**, walk across the **Troitsky most** and then, after lunch on the Petrograd Side, explore the **Peter & Paul Fortress**. If you have time, don't miss strolling past the beautiful **Mosque** and wandering impressive **Kamennoostrovsky prospekt**. Cap the day off with a performance at the **Mariinsky Theatre**.

Four Days

Following on from the previous two-day itinerary, spend a day exploring one of the imperial parks and palaces – **Tsarskoe Selo** is arguably the most interesting, definitely the best value for money and can be easily combined with the charming park at **Pavlovsk**. On day four, start at the **Strelka** to take in the view, visit the **Kunstkamera** and then take a bus down to the superb new **Erarta**. Ride the metro back across the river and see the **Alexander Nevsky Monastery**.

The Hermitage

A HALF-DAY TOUR

Successfully visiting the State Hermitage Museum, with its four vast interconnecting palaces, and some 365 rooms of displays, is an art form in itself. Our half-day tour of the highlights can be easily done in four hours, or can also be extended to a full day.

Once past ticket control, take a right at the end of the Rastrelli Gallery to see Room 101, the fantastic Egyptian collection. Return the way you came and then head up the incredibly grand **Jordan Staircase** 1 to the Neva Enfilade and the Great Enfilade for the impressive staterooms, the Romanov's private apartments and the **Palace Church** 2. Head back towards the Jordan Staircase via Rooms 153 and 151 for a full survey of the Romanovs in portrait form. Next visit Hidden Treasures Revealed, a superb survey of late-19th and early-20th-century French art, before proceeding to the Pavilion Hall to see the amazing Peacock Clock. Take in the Renaissance in the Italian rooms, where you shouldn't miss masterpieces by **Da Vinci** 3 and **Caravaggio** 4, and should see both the absorbing Spanish and Dutch art collections, the latter culminating in the **Rembrandt** 5 orgy of Room 254. Finally, walk through the Great Enfilade, take the staircase to the 3rd floor and end your tour with the modern collection from the impressionists, including a superb room of **Monet** 6 and two show-stopping rooms of **Picasso** 7.

Picasso
The Absinthe Drinker, Room 348
Picasso's blue period is represented in the Hermitage by four paintings, of which this is arguably the most significant. Painted when Picasso was just 22 years old, it is a stunning portrayal of human loneliness.

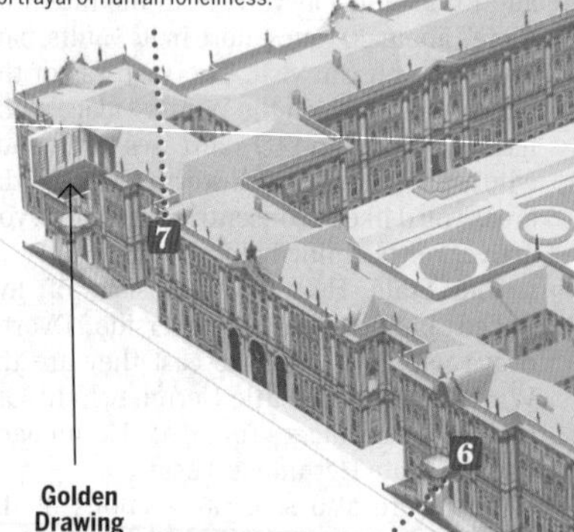

Monet
Waterloo Bridge, Effect of Mist, Room 319
The Monets in Room 319 make up a sublime ensemble, but no painting is more subtle and delicate than this one, painted from the artist's suite at the Savoy Hotel and depicting the extraordinary light during a foggy morning in London.

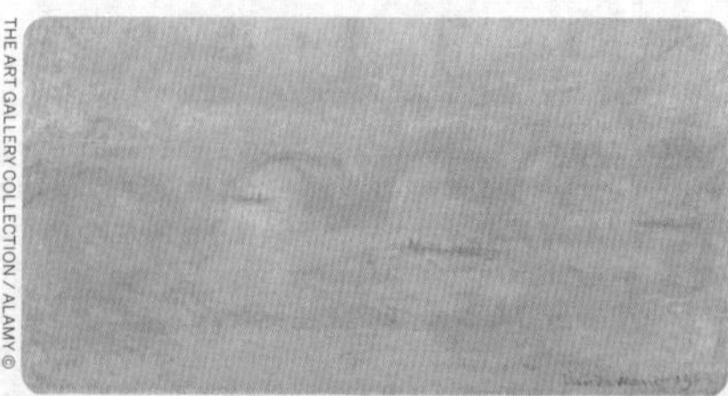

TOP TIPS

» **Queues** Reserve tickets online to skip the long lines.

» **Dining** Bring a sandwich and a bottle of water with you: the cafe is dire.

» **Footwear** Wear comfortable shoes.

» **Cloakroom** Bear in mind the only one is before ticket control, so you can't go back and pick up a sweater.

LEE FOSTER / LONELY PLANET IMAGES ©

Jordan Staircase

Originally designed by Rastrelli, this incredibly lavish staircase is named for the celebration of Christ's baptism in the River Jordan, for which the imperial family would descend the stairs annually to the Neva River.

Rembrandt

Return of the Prodigal Son, Room 254
Perhaps the most famous painting in the Hermitage is this colossal psychological masterpiece. Inspired by the Bible story, the scene of a wayward son returning to his father is a moving portrait of contrition and forgiveness.

DANITA DELIMONT / ALAMY ©

Da Vinci

Madonna and Child (Madonna Litta), Room 214
One of just a handful of paintings known to be the work of Leonardo da Vinci, the *Madonna Litta* makes an interesting counterpart to the Hermitage's other Da Vinci painting, the *Benois Madonna.*

St George's Hall

1

2

5

3

4

Hermitage Theatre

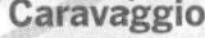

Palace Church

This stunningly ornate church within the Winter Palace was the Romanovs' private place of worship and saw the marriage of the last tsar, Nicholas II, to Alexandra Fyodorovna in 1895.

Caravaggio

Lute-Player, Room 237
The Hermitage's only Caravaggio is one of three versions of this painting in existence (the other two are in private collections). Caravaggio apparently described the work as the best piece he'd ever painted.

DAVID PARKER / ALAMY ©

IGOR GOLOVNOV / ALAMY ©

Historic Heart

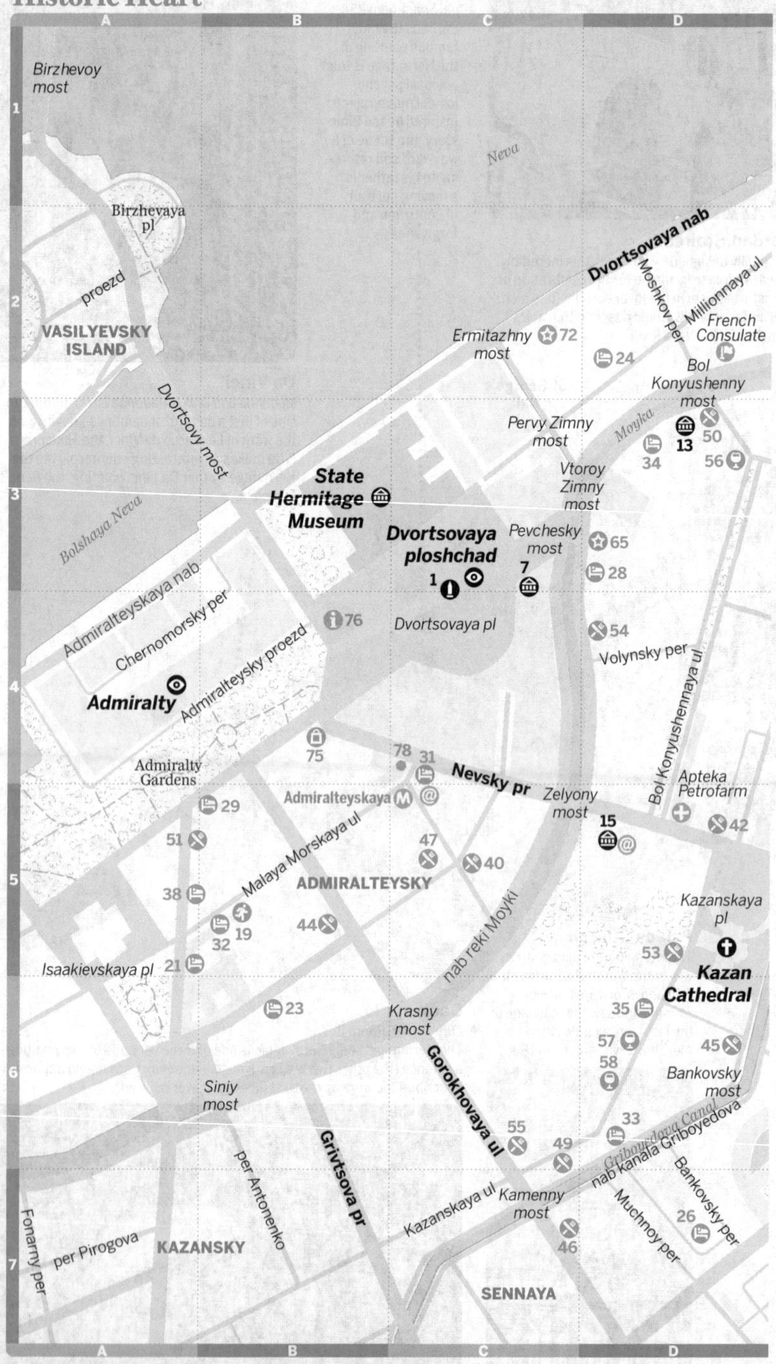

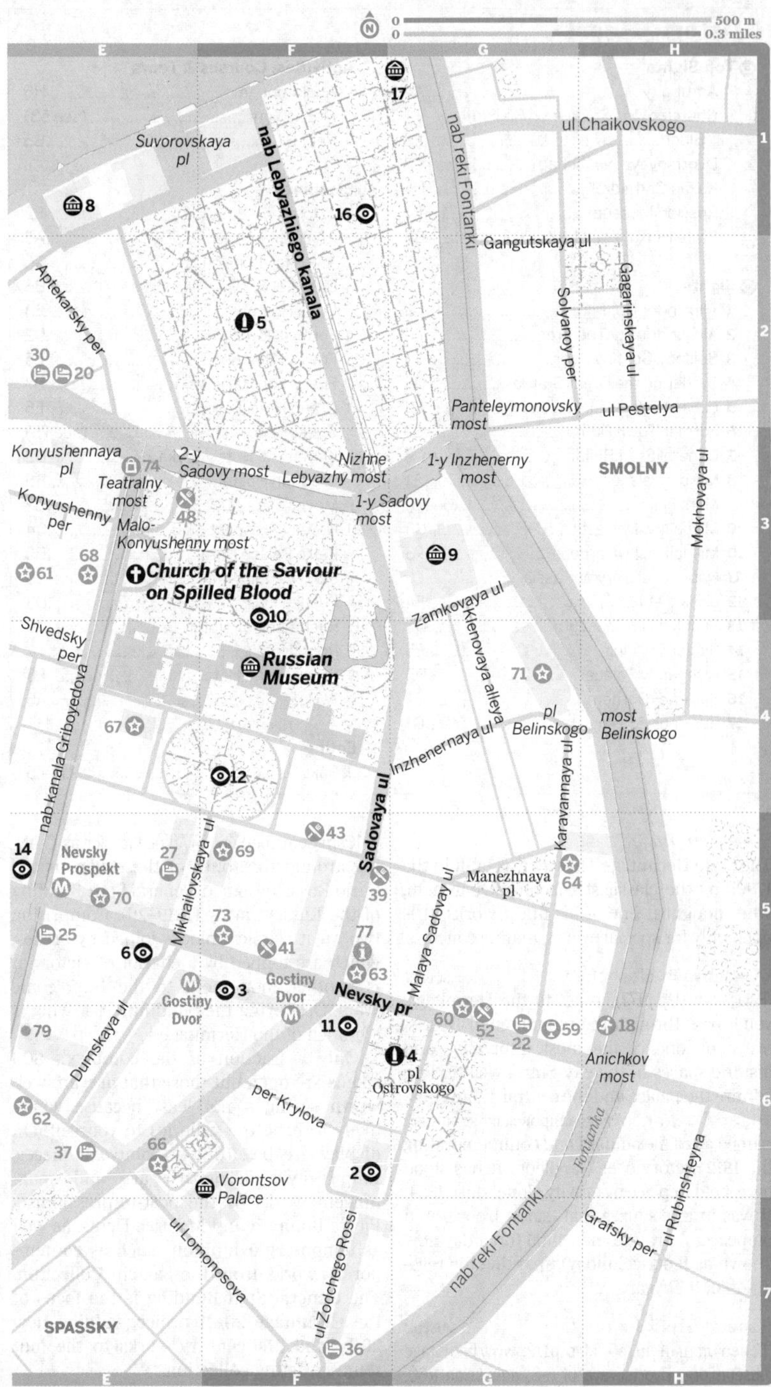
0 500 m
0 0.3 miles
Suvorovskaya pl
nab Lebyazhiego kanala
nab reki Fontanki
ul Chaikovskogo
Gangutskaya ul
Solyanoy per
Gagarinskaya ul
Aptekarsky per
Panteleymonovsky most
ul Pestelya
Konyushennaya pl
2-y Sadovy most
Nizhne Lebyazhy most
1-y Inzhenerny most
SMOLNY
Mokhovaya ul
Teatralny most
1-y Sadovy most
Konyushenny per
Malo-Konyushenny most
Church of the Saviour on Spilled Blood
Zamkovaya ul
Klenovaya alleya
Shvedsky per
Russian Museum
nab kanala Griboyedova
pl Belinskogo
most Belinskogo
Inzhenernaya ul
Karavannaya ul
Sadovaya ul
Nevsky Prospekt
Mikhailovskaya ul
Manezhnaya pl
Malaya Sadovaya ul
Gostiny Dvor
Nevsky pr
Dumskaya ul
Anichkov most
pl Ostrovskogo
per Krylova
Fontanka
Vorontsov Palace
ul Lomonosova
ul Zodchego Rossi
nab reki Fontanki
Grafsky per
ul Rubinshteyna
SPASSKY

Historic Heart

Top Sights
Admiralty A4
Church of the Saviour on Spilled Blood E3
Dvortsovaya ploshchad C3
Kazan Cathedral D5
Russian Museum F4
State Hermitage Museum B3

Sights
1 Alexander Column C3
2 Alexandrinsky Theatre F6
3 Bolshoy Gostiny Dvor F5
4 Catherine the Great Statue G6
5 Eternal Flame F2
6 Former Town Duma E5
7 General Staff Building C3
8 Marble Palace E1
Mars Field (see 5)
9 Mikhailovsky Castle G3
10 Mikhailovsky Gardens F3
11 National Library of Russia F6
12 pl Iskusstv F4
13 Pushkin Flat-Museum D3
14 Singer Building E5
15 Stroganov Palace D5
16 Summer Garden F1
17 Summer Palace G1

Activities, Courses & Tours
18 Anglotourismo H6
Fit Fashion (see 53)
19 Rent Bike B5

Sleeping
20 3MostA E2
21 Angleterre Hotel A5
22 Anichkov Pension G6
23 Casa Leto B6
Cuba Hostel (see 35)
24 Fortecia Peter D2
25 Friends Hostel E5
26 Friends on Bankovsky D7
27 Grand Hotel Europe E5
Guest House Nevsky 3 (see 75)
28 Kempinski Hotel Moyka 22 D3
29 Location Hostel B5
30 Moyka 5 E2
31 Nevsky Prospekt B&B C4
32 Petro Palace Hotel B5
33 Pio on Griboyedov D6
34 Pushka Inn D3
35 Rachmaninov Hotel D6
36 Rossi Hotel F7
37 Stony Island Hotel E6
38 W Hotel A5

Eating
39 Baku F5

State Hermitage Theatre
The State Hermitage Theatre was built in the 1780s by the classicist Giacomo Quarenghi, who thought it one of his finest works. It is open only for special events, mainly concerts.

Dvortsovaya ploshchad SQUARE
(Palace Sq; Map p172) To get to the Hermitage, you'll pass through the monumental Dvortsovaya pl, one of the most impressive and historic spaces in the city. Stand well back to admire the palace and the central 47.5m **Alexander Column** (Александровская колонна), named after Alexander I and commemorating the 1812 victory over Napoleon. It has stood here, held in place by gravity alone, since 1834. It was in this square that tsarist troops fired on peaceful protestors in 1905 (on a day now known as Bloody Sunday), sparking the revolution of that year.

General Staff Building MUSEUM
(Генеральный штаб; Map p172; www.hermitagemuseum.org; Dvortsovaya pl 6-8; admission R60; 10am-6pm Tue-Sun; M Admiralteyskaya) Curving around the south of the square is the Carlo Rossi–designed General Staff Building of the Russian army (1819–29). Comprising two great classical blocks joined by arches, which are topped by a chariot of victory, it is another monument to the Napoleonic Wars. Occupying the building's east wing is a branch of the Hermitage.

Only a fraction of the complex's 800 rooms are open but those that are, are well worth seeing – not least because you're likely to have the galleries to yourself. On display are beautiful art nouveau pieces, Empire-style decorative art and magnificent works by the post-Impressionists Pierre Bonnard and Maurice Denis, as well as temporary exhibitions such as contemporary works from the Saatchi Collection. The General Staff Building is the focus of the Hermitage 20/21 project, adding new 20th- and 21st-century works to the museum's existing collection.

40 Café King Pong C5
41 Chaynaya Lozhka F5
42 Dve Palochki D5
43 Dve Palochki F5
44 Entrecôte B5
Fiolet .... (see 36)
45 Garçon D6
46 Kilikia C7
MiX in St Petersburg .... (see 38)
47 Ne Goruy C5
48 Park Giuseppe E3
49 Soup Vino C6
50 Stolle D3
51 Tandoori Nights A5
52 Teremok G6
53 Terrassa D5
54 Troitsky Most D4
55 Zoom Café C6

Drinking
Bar with No Name .... (see 26)
Café Singer .... (see 14)
MiXup Bar .... (see 38)
56 Other Side D3
57 Radio Baby D6
58 Tinkoff D6
59 Tribunal Bar G6

Entertainment
Alexandrinsky Theatre .... (see 2)
60 Avrora G6
61 Barakobamabar E3
62 Central Station E6
63 Demmeni Marionette Theatre F5
64 Dom Kino G5
65 Glinka Capella D3
66 Maltiskaya Capella E6
67 Mikhailovsky Theatre E4
68 Mod Club E3
Rodina .... (see 64)
69 Shostakovich Philharmonia Bolshoy Zal F5
70 Shostakovich Philharmonia Maly Zal E5
71 St Petersburg State Circus G4
72 State Hermitage Theatre C2
73 Theatre Ticket Office F5

Shopping
Dom Knigi .... (see 14)
Gostiny Dvor .... (see 3)
74 Souvenir Market E3
75 Staraya Kniga B4

Information
76 City Tourist Information Booth B4
77 City Tourist Information Centre F5

Transport
78 Central Airline Ticket Office C4
79 Central Train Ticket Office E6

Church of the Saviour on Spilled Blood CHURCH
(Храм Спаса на Крови; Map p172; www.cathedral.ru; Konyushennaya pl; adult/student R250/150; ⏲10am-6pm Thu-Tue; Ⓜ Nevsky Prospekt) Officially known as the Church of the Resurrection, this multidomed dazzler, partly modelled on St Basil's in Moscow, was built between 1883 and 1907 on the spot where Alexander II, despite his reforms, was blown up by the People's Will terrorist group in 1881 (hence its gruesome name).

It's now most commonly known as the church that took 24 years to build and 27 years to restore. In August 1997, with much fanfare, it finally opened its doors after the painstaking work by over 30 artists to restore the interior's incredible 7000 sq metres of mosaics – they fully justify the entrance fee. On the very spot of the assassination is the marble bust *Shatrovy Cen,* a monument to Alexander.

Russian Museum MUSEUM
(Русский музей; Map p172; www.rusmuseum.ru; Inzhenernaya ul 4; adult/student R300/150; ⏲10am-5pm Mon, to 6pm Wed-Sun; Ⓜ Gostiny Dvor) The former Mikhailovsky Palace houses one of the country's finest collections of Russian art (see boxed text p178). After the Hermitage you may feel you've had your fill of art, but try your utmost to make some time for this gem of a museum.

The palace was designed by Carlo Rossi and built between 1819 and 1829 for Grand Duke Mikhail (brother of tsars Alexander I and Nicholas I) as compensation for not being able to have a chance on the throne. The museum was founded in 1895 under Alexander III and opened three years later.

The Benois building, now connected to the original palace, was constructed between 1914 and 1919. The building is also impressive when viewed from the back on a stroll through the lovely **Mikhailovsky**

VISITING THE HERMITAGE

The main entrance to the Hermitage is through the courtyard of the Winter Palace from Dvortsovaya pl (Palace Sq). The ticket counters are just inside, flanking a useful information booth where you can pick up free colour maps of the museum in most major European languages. Groups enter from the embankment side of the Winter Palace.

Queues for tickets, particularly from May to September, can be horrendous. The museum can also be very busy on the first Thursday of the month, when admission is free for everyone. Apart from getting in line an hour or so before the museum opens or going late in the day when the queues are likely to be shorter, there are a few strategies you can use. The best is to book your ticket online through the **Hermitage** (www.hermitagemuseum.org) website: US$17.95 gets you entry to the main Hermitage buildings, plus use of camera or camcorder; US$25.95 buys you the two-day ticket to all of the Hermitage's collections in the city (except the storage facility). You'll be issued with a voucher that allows you to jump the queue and go straight to the ticket booth.

Joining a tour is another way to avoid queuing. These whiz round the main sections in about 1½ hours but at least they provide an introduction to the place in English. It's easy to 'lose' the group and stay on until closing time. To book a tour, call the museum's **excursions office** (☎571 8446; ⏲11am-1pm & 2-4pm); the staff will tell you when they are running tours in English, German or French and when to turn up.

Also contact the excursions office if you plan to visit the **Gold and Diamond Rooms** (rooms 41–45) special collections in the Treasure Gallery. English tours of both rooms cost an extra R300 each and places are limited, so book early if you're interested. The focus is a hoard of fabulously worked Scythian and Greek gold and silver from the Caucasus, Crimea and Ukraine, dating from the 7th to 2nd centuries BC.

There is a special entrance for the physically disabled from Dvortsovaya pl (the museum also has a few wheelchairs) – call in advance if you need this. The rest of the museum is wheelchair accessible, including lifts for getting between the floors.

Highlights of the Hermitage

It would take days to fully do justice to the Hermitage's huge collection. If your time is limited, head straight to the following rooms:

» **Room 100** Ancient Egypt

» **Jordan Staircase** Directly ahead when you pass through the main entrance inside the Winter Palace

» **Rooms 143–146** Hidden treasures revealed: French late-19th-century and early-20th-century paintings taken from private collections in Germany in 1945

» **Rooms 178–98** Imperial staterooms and apartments including the Malachite Hall, Nicholas Hall, Armorial Hall and Hall of St George

» **Room 204** The Pavilion Hall

» **Rooms 207–238** Italian art, 13th to 18th centuries

» **Rooms 239–40** Spanish art, 16th to 18th centuries

» **Rooms 245–47** Flemish art, 17th century

» **Rooms 249–258** Dutch art, 17th century

» **Room 271** The imperial family's cathedral

» **Room 298–301** English art

» **Room 316–320** Impressionist and post-Impressionist art

» **Room 343–350** 20th-century art

Gardens (the main entrance is opposite the Church of the Saviour on Spilled Blood, with another on Sadovaya ul just south of the Moyka River).

The museum owns another three city palaces where permanent and temporary exhibitions are also held: the Marble Palace, the Mikhailovsky Castle and the Stroganov Palace. An adult ticket for R600 and a student ticket for R300, available at each palace, covers entrance to them all within a 24-hour period.

The museum's main entrance is through a tiny door on the far right side of the main building, off Inzhenernaya ul. You can also enter via the Benois wing off nab kanala Griboyedova. Call ☎314 3448 to book an English guided tour.

Immediately in front of the museum is the pretty **ploshchad Iskusstv** (Arts Sq), in the middle of which stands a statue of Pushkin, erected in 1957. Both the square and Mikhailovskaya ul, which joins the square to Nevsky pr, were designed by Rossi in the 1820s and '30s.

Nevsky prospekt STREET

(Map p172) Nevsky pr is and always will be Russia's most famous street, running 4km from the Admiralty to the Alexander Nevsky Monastery, from which it takes its name. The inner 2.5km to Moskovsky vokzal is St Petersburg's seething main avenue, the city's shopping centre and focus of its entertainment and street life.

Nevsky pr was laid out in the early years of St Petersburg, as the start of the main road to Novgorod, and soon became dotted with fine buildings, squares and bridges. At the beginning of the 1900s, it was one of Europe's grandest boulevards, with cobblestone footpaths and a track down the middle for horse-drawn trams. On either side of the tracks were wooden paving blocks to muffle the sound of horse-drawn carriages – an innovation that was a world first and for which the avenue was dubbed the quietest main street in Europe.

Today, things are quite a bit noisier. The traffic and crowds can become oppressive and, after a while, you'll find yourself going out of your way to avoid the street. However, walking Nevsky is an essential St Petersburg experience, and if you're here on a holiday evening (such as 27 May – City Day), the sight of thousands of people pouring like a stream down its middle is one you'll not soon forget.

Stroganov Palace MUSEUM

(Строгановский дворец; Map p172; www.rusmuseum.ru; Nevsky pr 17; adult/student R300/150;

THE CURATOR'S CHOICE *DR DMITRY OZERKOV*

'I first visited the Hermitage when I was five or six years old. At that time what I liked the most were the **Egyptian mummies** (room 100). They were displayed at a low height so I could see them well and read their names, such as Pa De Ist. I have a personal relationship with this mummy as I've known him for over 20 years – of course, for him it's nothing!

'Visitors to the Hermitage shouldn't miss **Raphael's Loggia** (room 227) – Catherine the Great commissioned Giacomo Quarenghi in the 1780s to create this copy of a gallery she admired at the Vatican. It was made exactly to scale, so not only is it a great event of art, but also of technique and design. It's actually in better shape than the original, and thus has become the major reference for the work.

'The Hermitage has lots of works by Rubens, many of them from his studio – he was like the Damien Hirst of his day presiding over a factory of artists. One piece that undoubtedly was done by his hand, though, is **Perseus and Andromeda** (room 246). It's a masterpiece. You look at Medusa's eyes and you feel afraid, and the horse looks so real you feel you could touch it.

'From the 20th-century works I recommend Matisse's **Dance** and **Music** (room 344), a magnificently vibrant pair of paintings commissioned by his patron Sergei Shchukin. Originally the genitalia of the nude male dancers were shown, but Shchukin, concerned about what polite Moscow society may say about such a scandalous work gracing a house in which his young female ward lived, had them painted over. If the light is right, it's possible to see the painting as Matisse intended. It's a dilemma for the Hermitage whether to restore it to as it was.' *Dr Dmitry Ozerkov, Chief Curator, Hermitage 20/21 Project*

HIGHLIGHTS OF THE RUSSIAN MUSEUM

Mikhailovsky Palace, 2nd floor

Room 11 The White Hall, the most ornate in the palace, with period furniture by Rossi, is where Strauss and Berlioz, as guests, performed concerts.

Room 14 Karl Bryullov's massive *Last Day of Pompeii* (1827–33), which was, in its time, the most famous Russian painting ever; there were queues for months to see it. Ivan Aivazovsky's Crimea seascapes also stand out, most frighteningly *The Wave*.

Room 15 Features a huge number of studies for Alexander Ivanov's most famous work, *The Appearance of Christ to the People*, which hangs in Moscow's Tretyakov Gallery.

Mikhailovsky Palace, 1st floor

Rooms 23–38 The Wanderers (Peredvizhniki) and associated artists, including Nikolai Ghe's fearsome *Peter I Interrogating Tsarevitch Alexey in Peterhof* (room 26); KA Savitsky's *To War* (room 31); and Vasily Polenov, including his *Christ and the Adulteress* (room 32).

Rooms 33–34 & 54 Works by Ilya Repin (1844–1930), probably Russia's best-loved artist; room 33 has portraits, *Barge Haulers on the Volga* (an incomparable indictment of Russian 'social justice') and *Zaporozhye Cossacks Writing a Mocking Letter to the Turkish Sultan*.

Benois Building, 2nd & 1st floors

Room 71 Boris Kustodiev's smug *Merchant's Wife at Tea*.

Room 72 Nathan Altman's world-famous cubist *Portrait of Anna Akhmatova*.

Room 75–76 Works by suprematist Kasimir Malevich, including his *Red Square (Painterly Realism of a Peasant Woman in Two Dimensions)* and *Black Square*.

Rooms 77–78 Constructivist works by Alexander Lebedev and Alexander Rodchenko.

Rooms 79 Kuzma Petrov-Vodkin's *Portrait of Akhmatova* and *Mother of God*.

10am-5pm Wed-Mon; MNevsky Prospekt) Next to the Moyka River, Rastrelli's baroque, salmon-pink palace houses a branch of the Russian Museum, though it will probably be forever better known for the Stroganov chef's invention of a beef dish served in a sour cream and mushroom sauce that became known to the world as 'beef stroganoff'. It's well worth going inside to see the impressively restored state rooms upstairs, where the Arabesque Dining Room, the Mineralogical Study and the Rastrelli Hall with its vast frieze ceiling are the obvious highlights. Downstairs there are temporary exhibits and an internet café.

FREE **Kazan Cathedral** CHURCH

(Казанский собор; Map p172; www.kazansky-spb.ru; Kazanskaya pl; 11am-7pm; MNevsky Prospekt) The great colonnaded arms of this neoclassical cathedral reach out towards Nevsky. Built between 1801 and 1811, its design by Andrei Voronikhin, a former serf, was influenced by St Peter's in Rome. His original plan was to build a second, mirror version of the cathedral opposite. Inside, the cathedral is dark and traditionally Orthodox, with a daunting 80m-high dome. There is usually a long queue of believers waiting to kiss the icon of Our Lady of Kazan, a copy of one of Russia's most important icons.

Marble Palace MUSEUM

(Мраморный дворец; Map p172; www.rusmuseum.ru; Millionnaya ul 5/1; adult/student R300/150; 10am-5pm Wed-Mon; MNevsky Prospekt) Between Mars Field and the Neva is another branch of the Russian Museum, built for Catherine the Great's lover, Grigory Orlov, from 1768 to 1785. Designed by Antonio Rinaldi, the palace is so named because it uses 36 different kinds of marble in its construction, both inside and out. Check out the grey-and-blue marble staircase and the fantastic Marble Hall. The art on display here ranges from exhibitions of contemporary art to a permanent display of paintings from the Ludwig Museum in Cologne that includes works by Picasso, Warhol, Basquiat and Liechtenstein. The monstrous equestrian statue outside the museum of Alexander III is by the sculptor Paolo Trubetskoy, who famously quipped that he 'simply depicted one animal on another'.

Summer Garden PARK

(Летний сад; Map p172; Ⓜ Gostiny Dvor) Central St Petersburg's loveliest and oldest park, the Summer Garden is on its own island between Mars Field and the Fontanka River (you can normally enter at the northern or southern end).

Early-18th-century architects designed the garden in a Dutch baroque style, following a geometric plan, with fountains, pavilions and sculptures studding the grounds. The ornate cast-iron fence with the granite posts was a later addition, built between 1771 and 1784. The gardens functioned as a private retreat for Peter the Great before becoming a strolling place for St Petersburg's 19th-century leisured classes. Only in the 20th century were commoners admitted.

St Petersburg's first palace is the modest, two-storey **Summer Palace** (Летний дворец Пётра Первого; Ⓜ Gostiny Dvor) in the garden's northeast corner. Built for Peter from 1710 to 1714, it is pretty well intact with little reliefs around the walls depicting Russian naval victories.

Mikhailovsky Castle MUSEUM

(Михайловский замок; Map p172; www.rusmuseum.ru; Sadovaya ul 2; adult/student R300/150; ⏲10am-5pm Wed-Mon; Ⓜ Gostiny Dvor) A much greater Summer Palace used to stand across the canal from the southern end of the Summer Garden. But Rastrelli's fairy-tale wooden creation for Empress Elizabeth was knocked down in the 1790s to make way for the bulky Mikhailovsky Castle. The pale-orange-painted building was briefly home to Paul I, who was suffocated in his bed only a month after moving into the castle. Later it became a military engineering school (hence its other commonly used name, Engineers' Castle). Inside are some finely restored state rooms, including the lavish burgundy throne room of the tsar's wife Maria Fyodorovna and some of the original statues from the Summer Garden.

Admiralty LANDMARK

(Адмиралтейство; Map p172; Admiralteysky proezd 1; Ⓜ Admiralteyskaya) The gilded spire of the old Admiralty, at the western edge of Dvortsovaya pl, is an unmistakable city landmark (it's closed to the public). It was here that the Russian navy had their headquarters from 1711 to 1917, and today the building houses the city's largest naval college. Constructed from 1806 to 1823 to the designs of Andreyan Zakharov, it's a prime example of the Russian Empire style of classical architecture, with its rows of white columns and plentiful reliefs and statuary. Check out the nymphs holding giant globes flanking the main gate.

Singer Building LANDMARK

(Дом Зингера; Map p172; Nevsky pr 28; Ⓜ Nevsky Prospekt) Opposite the Kazan Cathedral is the Singer Building, a Style Moderne beauty recently restored to the splendour of its past as the headquarters of the sewing machine company. Since Soviet times it's been the home of the Dom Knigi bookshop; there's a good coffee shop on the 1st floor with a great view over Nevsky pr.

Bolshoy Gostiny Dvor SHOPPING CENTRE

(Гостиный двор; Map p172; www.gostinydvor.ru; Nevsky pr 35; ⏲10am-10pm; Ⓜ Gostiny Dvor) One of the world's first indoor shopping malls, this impressively vast structure is another Rastrelli creation dating from 1757 to 1785. Occupying an entire block, the completely restored perimeter of the department store is over 1km long. The clock tower of the **former Town Duma**, seat of the prerevolutionary city government, stands opposite.

Ploshchad Ostrovskogo SQUARE

(Map p172; Ⓜ Gostiny Dvor) Commonly referred to as the Catherine Gardens, after the enormous **Catherine the Great statue** at its centre, pl Ostrovskogo is the scene of many a chess, backgammon and sometimes even mah-jong game. The square was designed by Carlo Rossi in the 1820s and 1830s. At the empress's heels are some of her renowned statesmen, including her lovers Orlov, Potemkin and Suvorov.

The square's western side is taken up by the lavish **National Library of Russia** (Российская национальная библиотека), St Petersburg's biggest with some 31 million items, nearly a sixth of which are in foreign languages. Rossi's **Alexandrinsky Theatre** at the southern end of the square is one of Russia's most important theatres. In 1896 the opening night of Chekhov's *The Seagull* was so badly received here that the playwright fled to wander anonymously among the crowds on Nevsky pr.

Pushkin Flat-Museum MUSEUM

(Музей квартира Пушкина; Map p172; www.museumpushkin.ru; nab reki Moyki 12; adult/student R200/80; ⏲10.30am-5.30pm Wed-Sun; Ⓜ Admiralteyskaya) Beside one of the prettiest curves of the Moyka River is this little house where the poet Pushkin died after his duel in 1837. Now the Pushkin Flat-Museum, it has been reconstructed to look as it did in the poet's time and includes (for morbid fans) Pushkin's death mask, a lock of his hair and the waistcoat worn on the day he died. You can only visit on a tour, and these are given in Russian only.

Mars Field PARK

(Марсово поле; Map p172) Once the scene of 19th-century military parades, the grassy Mars Field lies immediately west of the Summer Garden. An **eternal flame** burns at its centre for the victims of the 1917 revolution and the ensuing civil war. Don't take a shortcut across the grass – you may be walking on the graves of the communist luminaries also buried here.

LITEYNY & SMOLNY

This section covers sights east of the Fontanka Canal and north of Nevsky pr. It includes Smolny, a governmental region and one of the less-touristed areas of the city, running east from Liteyny pr towards Smolny Cathedral.

Smolny Cathedral CHURCH

(Смольный собор; Map p182; pl Rastrelli 3/1; adult/student R150/90, bell tower R100; ⏲10am-7pm Thu-Tue; Ⓜ Chernyshevskaya) The sky-blue Smolny Cathedral, one of the most fabulous of Rastrelli's buildings, is the centrepiece of a convent built mostly to the Italian architect's designs from 1748 to 1757. His inspiration was to combine baroque details with the forest of towers and onion domes typical of an old Russian monastery. There's special genius in the proportions of the cathedral (it gives the impression of soaring upward), for which the convent buildings are a perfect foil.

The cathedral is mainly used as an exhibition and concert hall and isn't worth paying to get into, but it's possible to climb up one of the 63m **belfries**, which provides sweeping views of the city. If you don't want to make the long walk from the metro station, trolleybuses 5 and 7 from Nevsky pr end up here.

Anna Akhmatova Museum at the Fountain House MUSEUM

(Музей Анны Ахматовой в Фонтанном Доме; Map p182; www.akhmatova.spb.ru; Liteyny pr 53; admission R100, audio tour R100; ⏲10.30am-6.30pm Tue-Sun, 1-9pm Wed; Ⓜ Gostiny Dvor) This touching and fascinating literary museum celebrates the life and work of Anna Akhmatova, St Petersburg's most famous 20th-century poet. Akhmatova lived here from 1924 until 1952, as this was the apartment of her common-law husband Nikolai Punin. Even if you know little about this celebrated early-20th-century poet, you will find yourself moved by the lovingly curated exhibits here. The evocative apartment on the 2nd floor is filled with mementos of the poet and her family, all of whom were persecuted during Soviet times. Outside, in a corner of the quiet garden, is a video room where you can watch Russian-language documentaries on her life.

Admission also includes the Josef Brodsky 'American Study'. The poet did not live here, but his connection with Akhmatova was strong. His office has been recreated here, complete with furniture and other 'artefacts' from his adopted home in Massachusetts.

Museum of Decorative & Applied Arts MUSEUM

(Музей прикладного искусства; Map p182; www.spbghpa.ru; Solyanoy per 15; adult/student R60/30; ⏲11am-4.30pm Tue-Sat; Ⓜ Chernyshevskaya) In 1878, millionaire Baron Stieglitz founded the School of Technical Design and wanted to surround his students with world-class art to inspire them. He began a collection, continued by his son, that includes a unique array of European and Oriental glassware, porcelains, tapestries, furniture and paintings. Between 1885 and 1895, a building designed by architect Max Messmacher was constructed to house the collection – the building itself also became a masterpiece. Each hall is decorated in its own, unique style, including Italian, Renaissance, Flemish and baroque. The Terem Room, in the style of the medieval Terem Palace of Moscow's Kremlin, is an opulent knockout.

There's no English labelling but the gorgeous objects displayed, from medieval handcrafted furniture to a rare collection of 18th-century Russian tiled stoves to the contemporary works of the students of the arts school, speak for themselves. Their surroundings merely match their magnificence.

After the revolution, the school was closed, the museum's collection redistributed to the Hermitage and Russian Museum, and most of the lavish interiors brutally painted, plastered over or even destroyed (one room was used as a sports hall). The painstaking renovation continues to the present day.

Just finding the museum can be tricky: enter through the academy building (the second entrance as you walk up Solyarnoy per from ul Pestelya). Tell the guard that you want to go to the museum *(v muzey)*, then go up the main staircase, turn right at the top, walk through two halls and then go down the staircase to your left.

Sheremetyev Palace PALACE

(Шереметьевский дворец; Map p182; www.theatremuseum.ru; nab reki Fontanki 34; admission R250; ⏲noon-7pm Wed-Sun; ⓂGostiny Dvor) Splendid wrought-iron gates, facing the Fontanka River, guard the entrance to the Sheremetyev Palace (1750–55), which houses two lovely little museums. In the palace itself is the **Museum of Music** (Музей музыки), which has a collection of musical instruments from the 19th and 20th centuries, some beautifully decorated.

The Sheremetyev family was famous for the concerts and theatre it hosted at the palace. The rooms upstairs have been wonderfully restored and you get a great sense of what cultured life must have been like here. Check the local press for notices of concerts, which are occasionally still held here.

Museum of the Defence & Blockade of Leningrad MUSEUM

(Государственный мемориальный музей обороны и блокады Ленинграда; Map p182; Solyanoy per 9; admission R200; ⏲10am-5pm Thu-Tue, closed last Thu of month; ⓂChernyshevskaya) Next door to the Museum of Decorative and Applied Arts is the grim but engrossing Blockade Museum, opened just three months after the blockade was lifted. At that time it had 37,000 exhibits, including real tanks and aeroplanes, but three years later, during Stalin's repression of the city, the museum was shut, its director shot and most of the exhibits destroyed or redistributed. It reopened in 1989 and the displays now contain donations from survivors, including propaganda posters from the time and an example of the tiny piece of sawdust-filled bread Leningraders had to survive on.

Cathedral of the Transfiguration of Our Saviour CHURCH

(Спасо-Преображенский собор; Map p182; Preobrazhenskaya pl; ⓂChernyshevskaya) The interior of this beautifully restored yellow cathedral is one of the most gilded in St Petersburg. The grand gates bear the imperial double-headed eagle in vast golden busts, reflecting the fact that Empress Elizabeth ordered its construction in 1743. This is where the Preobrazhensky Guards (the monarch's personal protection unit) had their headquarters. Rebuilt in 1829 to a neoclassical design by Vasily Stasov, the cathedral is dedicated to the victory over the Turks in 1828–29; note the captured guns in the gate surrounding the church!

Tauride Gardens & Tauride Palace PARK

(Таврический сад; Map p182; ⓂChernyshevskaya) The Tauride Gardens are a great place for a stroll, and there are some rusty rides for the kiddies. The view across the lake towards the Tauride Palace, built between 1783 and 1789 for Catherine the Great's lover Potemkin, is a fine sight. The palace (closed to the public) takes its name from the Ukrainian region of Crimea (once called Tavria), which Potemkin was responsible for conquering. Between 1906 and 1917, the State Duma, the Provisional Government and the Petrograd Soviet all met here.

VLADIMIRSKAYA & VOSSTANIYA

South of Nevsky pr and east of the Fontanka River is Vladimirskaya, dominated by the gold-domed cathedral of the same name. Further east of here, across the swathe of tracks leading up to the Moscow Station, is Vosstaniya, bordered on its far west side by the Neva River.

FREE **Alexander Nevsky Monastery** MONASTERY

(Александро-Невская Лавра; Map p184; www.lavra.spb.ru; Nevsky pr 179/2; ⏲grounds 6am-10pm; ⓂPloshchad Alexandra Nevskogo) This working monastery, where you'll find the graves of some of Russia's most famous artistic figures, is entered from pl Alexandra Nevskogo at the very far end of Nevsky pr. It was built between 1710 and 1713 on the orders of Peter the Great, who sought to link St Petersburg to a historic battle led by Alexander Nevsky against the Swedes in 1240, thus underscoring Russia's long history with the newly captured region. Even though the site of Nevsky's victory was further upstream by the mouth of the Izhora River, the monastery became the centre of the Nevsky cult and his remains were transferred here from Vladimir in 1724. In 1797 the monastery

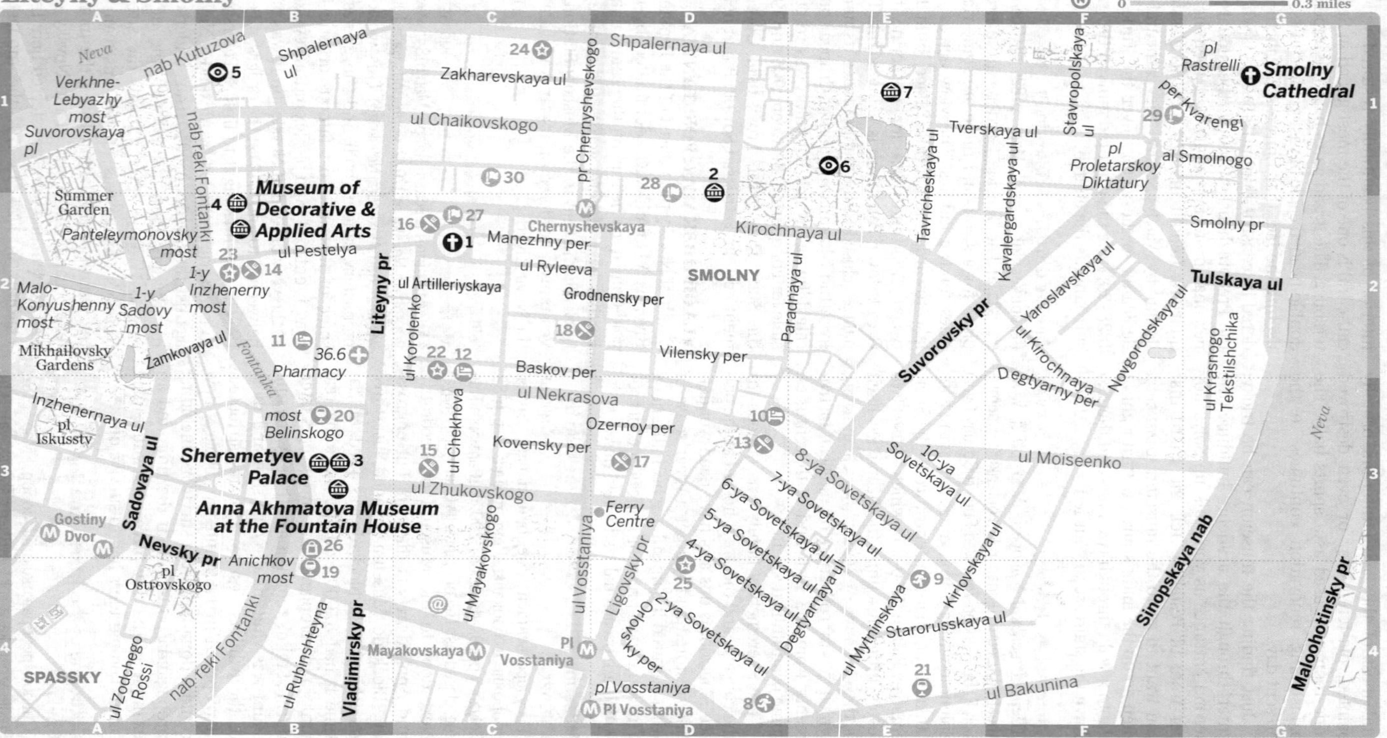
Liteyny & Smolny
0 600 m
0 0.3 miles
Smolny Cathedral
pl Rastrelli
per Kvarengi
al Smolnogo
Smolny pr
Tulskaya ul
ul Krasnogo Tekstilshchika
Neva
Malooktinsky pr
Sinopskaya nab
Novgorodskaya ul
pl Proletarskoy Diktatury
Stavropolskaya ul
Yaroslavskaya ul
ul Kirochnaya
Degtyarny per
Kavalergardskaya ul
Tverskaya ul
Tavricheskaya ul
Suvorovsky pr
ul Moiseenko
10-ya Sovetskaya ul
Kirilovskaya ul
Starorusskaya ul
ul Bakunina
ul Mytninskaya
8-ya Sovetskaya ul
7-ya Sovetskaya ul
6-ya Sovetskaya ul
5-ya Sovetskaya ul
4-ya Sovetskaya ul
2-ya Sovetskaya ul
Degtyarnaya ul
Paradnaya ul
Kirochnaya ul
SMOLNY
Vilensky per
Shpalernaya ul
pr Chernyshevskogo
Chernyshevskaya
Manezhny per
Grodnensky per
ul Ryleeva
Baskov per
ul Nekrasova
Ozernoy per
Kovensky per
Ferry Centre
Ligovsky pr
Orlovsky per
pl Vosstaniya
Pl Vosstaniya
ul Vosstaniya
Zakharevskaya ul
ul Chaikovskogo
ul Artilleriyskaya
ul Korolenko
ul Chekhova
ul Zhukovskogo
ul Mayakovskogo
Mayakovskaya
Liteyny pr
Vladimirsky pr
Shpalernaya ul
Museum of Decorative & Applied Arts
ul Pestelya
36.6 Pharmacy
most Belinskogo
Sheremetyev Palace
Anna Akhmatova Museum at the Fountain House
ul Rubinshteyna
nab reki Fontanki
Fontanka
Anichkov most
Nevsky pr
pl Ostrovskogo
ul Zodchego Rossi
nab Kutuzova
Verkhne-Lebyazhy most
Suvorovskaya pl
Summer Garden
Panteleymonovsky most
1-y Inzhenerny most
1-y Sadovy most
Malo-Konyushenny most
Zamkovaya ul
Mikhailovsky Gardens
Inzhenernaya ul
pl Iskusstv
Sadovaya ul
Gostiny Dvor
SPASSKY

Liteyny & Smolny

became a *lavra,* the most senior grade of Russian Orthodox monasteries.

For most visitors the main reason for coming here is to view the **graveyards** (admission R200; ⌚9.30am-6pm) on either side of the main entrance. The **Tikhvin Cemetery** (Тихвинское кладбище), on the right, contains the most famous tombs: Tchaikovsky, Rimsky-Korsakov (check out his wild tomb!), Borodin, Mussorgsky and Glinka all rest here. Turn right after entering and you'll reach the tomb of Dostoevsky. The **Lazarus Cemetery** (Лазаревское кладбище), on the left, contains several late, great St Petersburg architects – among them Starov, Voronikhin, Quarenghi, Zakharov and Rossi.

Across the canal just outside the main *lavra* complex, the first main building on the left is the 1717–22 baroque Annunciation Church, now the misleadingly named **Museum of Urban Sculpture** (Городской музей скульптуры; admission R100; ⌚11am-5pm Tue-Wed, Fri-Sun), which actually houses more graves, including those of imperial military heroes and minor members of the Russian royal family, including Peter the Great's infant son.

About 100m further on is the monastery's classical **Trinity Cathedral** (Троицкий собор; ⌚6am-8pm), built between 1776 and 1790. Hundreds crowd in on 12 September to celebrate the feast of St Alexander Nevsky. His remains are in the silver reliquary in the main iconostasis.

Opposite the cathedral is the St Petersburg **Metropolitan's House**, built from 1775 to 1778. On the far right of the grounds facing the canal you'll see St Petersburg's **Orthodox Academy**, one of only a handful in Russia (the main one is in Sergiev Posad). Around the back of the complex is the charming (and free) **Nikolsky Cemetery** (Никольское кладбище), with a charming stream running through it.

Dostoevsky Museum MUSEUM

(Литературно-мемориальный музей Достоевского; Map p184; www.md.spb.ru; Kuznechny per 5/2; adult/student R160/80, audio tour R170; ⌚11am-6pm Tue-Sun; Ⓜ Vladimirskaya)

Dostoevsky lived in flats all over the city (mainly in the Sennaya area) but his final residence, where he penned most of *The Brothers Karamazov,* is preserved at the engrossing Dostoevsky Museum. It all looks just as it did before the writer died in 1881. There's also a rather gloomy statue of Dostoevsky outside the Vladimirskaya metro.

Vladimirskaya & Vosstaniya

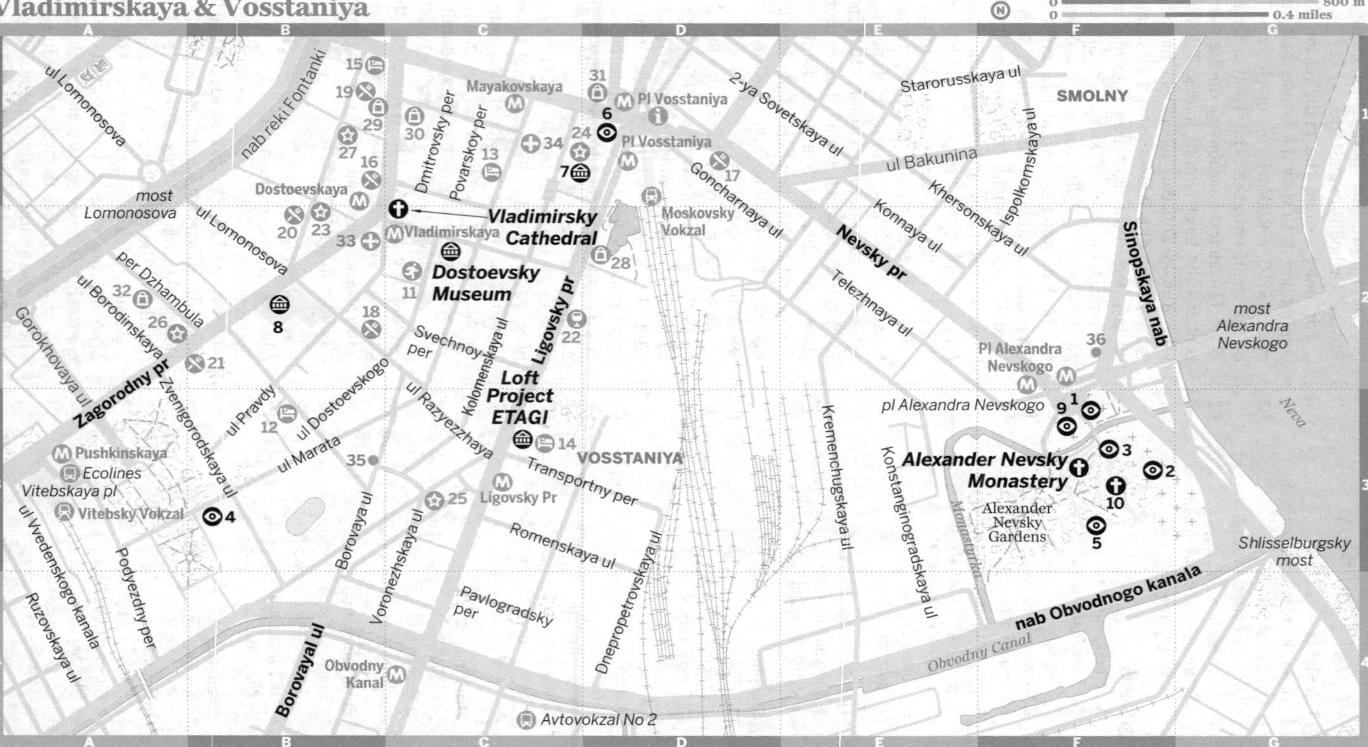

Vladimirskaya & Vosstaniya

Top Sights
Alexander Nevsky Monastery ... F3
Dostoevsky Museum ... C2
Loft Project ETAGI ... C3
Vladimirsky Cathedral ... C2

Sights
1 Lazarus Cemetery ... F3
2 Metropolitan's House ... F3
Museum of Non-Conformist Art ... (see 7)
3 Museum of Urban Sculpture ... F3
New Academy of Fine Arts Museum ... (see 7)
4 Oceanarium ... B3
5 Orthodox Academy ... F3
6 Ploshchad Vosstaniya ... D1
7 Pushkinskaya 10 ... C1
8 Rimsky-Korsakov Flat-Museum ... B2
Temple of Love, Peace & Music ... (see 7)
9 Tikhvin Cemetery ... F3
10 Trinity Cathedral ... F3

Activities, Courses & Tours
11 Coachmen's Baths ... C2
Mops Spa ... (see 19)

Sleeping
12 Brothers Karamazov ... B3
13 Helvetia Hotel & Suites ... C1
14 Hostel Ligovsky 74 ... C3
15 Life Hostel ... B1

Eating
16 Baltic Bread ... B1
17 Bistro Garçon ... D1
18 Dom Beat ... B2
Fartuk ... (see 20)
19 Mops ... B1
20 Schaste ... B2
21 Troitsky Most ... B2

Drinking
Dom Beat ... (see 18)
22 Dyuni ... C2
Terminal Bar ... (see 20)

Entertainment
23 Club ... B2
Dusche ... (see 22)
24 Fish Fabrique Nouvelle ... C1
25 Griboyedov ... C3
26 Jazz Philharmonic Hall ... A2
Jesus Club ... (see 22)
27 Maly Drama Theatre ... B1

Shopping
28 Galeria ... D2
29 Imperial Porcelain ... B1
30 La Russe ... C1
31 Nevsky Centre ... D1
32 Tula Samovars ... A2

Information
33 36.6 Pharmacy ... B2
34 Medem International Clinic & Hospital ... C1

Transport
35 Astoria Service ... B3
36 Avis ... F2

FREE **Vladimirsky Cathedral** CHURCH
(Владимирский собор; Vladimirsky pr 20; 8am-6pm, services 6pm; M Vladimirskaya) The 18th-century Vladimirsky Cathedral, designed by Quarenghi, was used as an underwear factory during Soviet times. It was reconsecrated in 1990 and is now one of the busiest churches in town. For a brilliant view of its amazing onion domes, have a drink in the 7th-floor bar of Hotel Dostoevsky across the road, part of the Vladimirsky Passage shopping mall. The church's interiors are also stunning (go upstairs to see the main body of the church).

Loft Project ETAGI ART GALLERIES
(Лофт проект ЭТАЖИ; Map p184; www.loftprojectetagi.ru; Ligovsky pr 74; noon-10pm; M Ligovsky Prospekt) Perhaps St Petersburg's most interesting and exciting artistic space, this fantastic conversion of the former Smolninsky Bread Factory has plenty to keep you interested, including many of the original factory fittings seamlessly merged with the thoroughly contemporary design. There are three galleries here, two exhibition spaces, a couple of shops, a hostel and Café Green Room, with a great summer terrace. Come by to check out what's going on in St Petersburg's contemporary art scene – go through the little entrance with the turnstile and ETAGI is in the courtyard.

Ploshchad Vosstaniya SQUARE
(Площадь Восстания; Map p184; M Ploshchad Vosstaniya) Marking the division of Nevsky pr and Stary (old) Nevsky pr is pl Vosstaniya, whose landmarks are the giant granite pillar

with the communist star, and Moskovsky vokzal. The Cyrillic on top of Hotel Oktyabrskaya across from the station translates as 'Hero City Leningrad'; several cities were designated 'hero cities' for their heroism, stoicism and losses during WWII.

FREE **Pushkinskaya 10** ART GALLERY
(Пушкинская 10; Map p184; http://en.p-10.ru; Ligovsky pr 53; ⏲3-7pm Wed-Sun; MPloshchad Vosstaniya) This legendary locale is a required stop for anyone interested in the contemporary art and music scene in St Petersburg. The former apartment block – affectionately called by its street address despite the fact that the public entrance is actually on Ligovsky pr – contains studio and gallery space, as well as the cool music clubs Fish Fabrique and Fabrique Nouvelle, the **Experimental Sound Gallery** (Галерея Экспериментального Звука 21; GEZ-21) and an assortment of other shops and galleries. It offers a unique opportunity to hang out with local musicians and artists, who are always eager to talk about their work.

The story of Pushkinskaya 10 goes back to 1988, when a group of artists/squatters took over the condemned apartment block. The decrepit building became 'underground central', as artists and musicians moved in to set up studios, others stopped by to hang out with them, and outsiders became curious about the creative activity going on inside.

The main galleries, the **Museum of Non-Conformist Art** and the **New Academy of Fine Arts Museum**, are on the 4th floor. Smaller galleries are scattered throughout the building, and the artists often open their studios to visitors, especially on Saturday afternoons. A highlight is the **Temple of Love, Peace & Music** (1st fl; ⏲6-8pm Fri). Collector Kolya Vasin (Russia's most famous Beatles' fan) has an amazing array of John Lennon paraphernalia, which he shares with other fans on designated days.

It's possible to arrange a free tour of the building in English. Call Anastasia on ☎8-911-977 3850 to book a time.

Rimsky-Korsakov Flat-Museum MUSEUM
(Мемориальный музей-квартира Римского-Корсакова; Map p184; www.theatremuseum.ru; Zagorodny pr 28; admission R100, audio guide R100; ⏲11am-6pm Wed-Sun; MVladimirskaya) The charming Rimsky-Korsakov Flat-Museum remains as it was when the composer lived here in the early 20th century. Check at the museum and on the website for details of concerts that are occasionally held here.

SENNAYA & KOLOMNA

This area, south and west of St Isaac's Cathedral, contains some interesting sights but is also fine just for casual wandering, particularly around the meandering Griboyedova Canal, which flows close to Sennaya pl, the Mariinsky Theatre and through Kolomna.

St Isaac's Cathedral CHURCH
(Исаакиевский собор; Map p188; www.cathedral.ru; Isaakievskaya pl; cathedral adult/student R250/150, colonnade R150; ⏲10am-6pm Thu-Tue; MAdmiralteyskaya) The golden dome of St Isaac's Cathedral, looming just south of pl Dekabristov, dominates the St Petersburg skyline. Its obscenely lavish interior is open as a museum, although religious services are still held here on major religious holidays.

The French architect Auguste de Montferrand won a competition organised by Alexander I to design the cathedral in 1818. It took so long to build – until 1858 – that Alexander's successor Nicholas I was able to insist on a more grandiose structure than Montferrand had planned. Special ships and a railway had to be built to carry the granite from Finland for the huge pillars. There's a statue of Montferrand holding a model of the cathedral on the west facade.

You'll need a separate ticket to climb the 262 steps up to the colonnade around the drum of the dome; the panoramic city views make the climb worth it.

Yusupov Palace PALACE
(Юсуповский дворец; Map p188; www.yusupov-palace.ru; nab reki Moyki 94; adult/child R500/380; ⏲11am-5pm; MSpasskaya) In a city of glittering palaces, the sumptuous interiors of the Yusupov Palace more than hold their own. A series of sumptuously decorated rooms, each more spectacular than the last, culminate in a gilded jewel box of a theatre, where classical music, ballet and opera performances are still held; check the website for details. Attending such a performance is recommended as it includes a tour of the palace first (minus the tour-group crowds that can descend on the place in the summer) and a viewing of the cellar room where the plot to murder Rasputin was hatched, complete with hokey waxworks of the mad monk and his nemesis, the equally bonkers Prince Felix Yusupov.

The palace is certainly one of St Petersburg's finest, but it's very overpriced for foreigners (Russians get a far better deal), and if you want to see the room where Rasputin's murder began you have to pay for an extra tour (adult/student R300/180), which takes place at 1.45pm daily except Sunday. There are only 20 tickets available each day, so come in good time to secure a place. The tour is in Russian only, so it's hard not to feel you're getting a bum deal. The admission price to the palace includes an audio tour in English and a number of other languages, but you'll need to leave a R1000 deposit per audio guide.

Ploshchad Dekabristov SQUARE

(Площадь Декабристов; Decembrists' Sq; Map p188; Ⓜ Admiralteyskaya) Between the Neva River and St Isaac's Cathedral is pl Dekabristov, named after the first attempt at a Russian revolution, the Decembrists' Uprising of 14 December 1825, which kicked off and then quickly fizzled here.

The most famous statue of Peter the Great (practically a trademark image of the city) stands at the river end of the square. The **Bronze Horseman** (Медный всадник) has Peter's mount rearing above the snake of treason and was sculpted over 12 years for Catherine the Great by Frenchman Etienne Falconet. The inscription reads 'To Peter I from Catherine II – 1782'.

Mariinsky Theatre THEATRE

(Мариинский театр; Map p188; www.mariinsky.ru; Teatralnaya pl 1; ⌚box office 11am-7pm, performances 7pm; Ⓜ Sennaya Ploshchad) The pretty green-and-white Mariinsky Theatre has played a pivotal role in Russia's cultural scene ever since it was built in 1859 as the home of the Imperial Russian Opera and Ballet companies. Tchaikovsky's *Sleeping Beauty* and *The Nutcracker* both premiered here. In 1935 the Soviets renamed it the Kirov Opera and Ballet Theatre, but the theatre reverted to its prerevolutionary name in 1992.

The Mariinsky has undergone an artistic renaissance under dynamic, workaholic artistic director Valery Gergiev. However, the 19th-century theatre is clapped out and in desperate need of renovation, with ancient equipment unable to cope with modern productions. In 2004 ambitious plans were signed off and a second stage for the theatre was constructed behind the current building.

FREE **Nikolsky Cathedral** CHURCH

(Никольский собор; Map p188; Nikolskaya pl 1/3; ⌚9am-7pm; Ⓜ Sadovaya) Its picture-perfect canalside setting, baroque spires and golden domes make the ice-blue Nikolsky Cathedral, just south of the Mariinsky Theatre, one of the city's best-loved churches. Nicknamed the Sailors' Church (Nicholas is the patron saint of sailors), it contains many 18th-century icons and a finely carved wooden iconostasis. A graceful bell tower overlooks the canal, which is crossed by the Staro-Nikolsky most (from this bridge, you can see at least seven bridges, more than from any other spot in the city).

FREE **Nabokov Museum** MUSEUM

(Музей Набокова; Map p188; www.nabokovmuseum.org; Bolshaya Morskaya ul 47; ⌚11am-6pm Tue-Fri, noon-5pm Sat & Sun; Ⓜ Admiralteyskaya) From his birth in 1899 until 1917, when his family fled Russia, Vladimir Nabokov, author of *Lolita* and arguably the most versatile and least classifiable of modern Russian writers, lived at this lovely 19th-century town house now turned into a small museum. In Nabokov's autobiography *Speak, Memory,* he refers to it as a 'paradise lost' and it's easy to imagine why after seeing the charming carved-oak interiors. There are various displays of Nabokov-related artefacts, but the museum is more of a cultural centre hosting festivals and special events.

Russian Vodka Museum MUSEUM

(Музей русской водки; Map p188; www.vodkamuseum.su; Konnogvardeysky bul 4; admission with/without tour R300/150; ⌚noon-10pm; Ⓜ Admiralteyskaya) This excellent private museum tells the story of Russia's national tipple in an interesting and fun way, from the first production of 'bread wine' to the phenomenon of the modern international vodka industry, complete with waxwork models and some very cool bottles. You can guide yourself through the exhibit, or, for twice the price, be accompanied by an English-speaking guide who'll liven things up a bit. If you'd like to taste the exhibits too, then a tour with a full tasting is R450/300 with/without a guide. There's an excellent restaurant in the same building, and if you eat there, you can visit the museum with a tasting for a very reasonable R150.

Sennaya ploshchad SQUARE

(Сенная площадь; Ⓜ Sennaya Ploshchad) The frenetic Haymarket is crowded with giant kiosks and glitzy shopping malls, and despite a massive redevelopment a decade ago it still retains the same seedy and

Sennaya & Kolomna

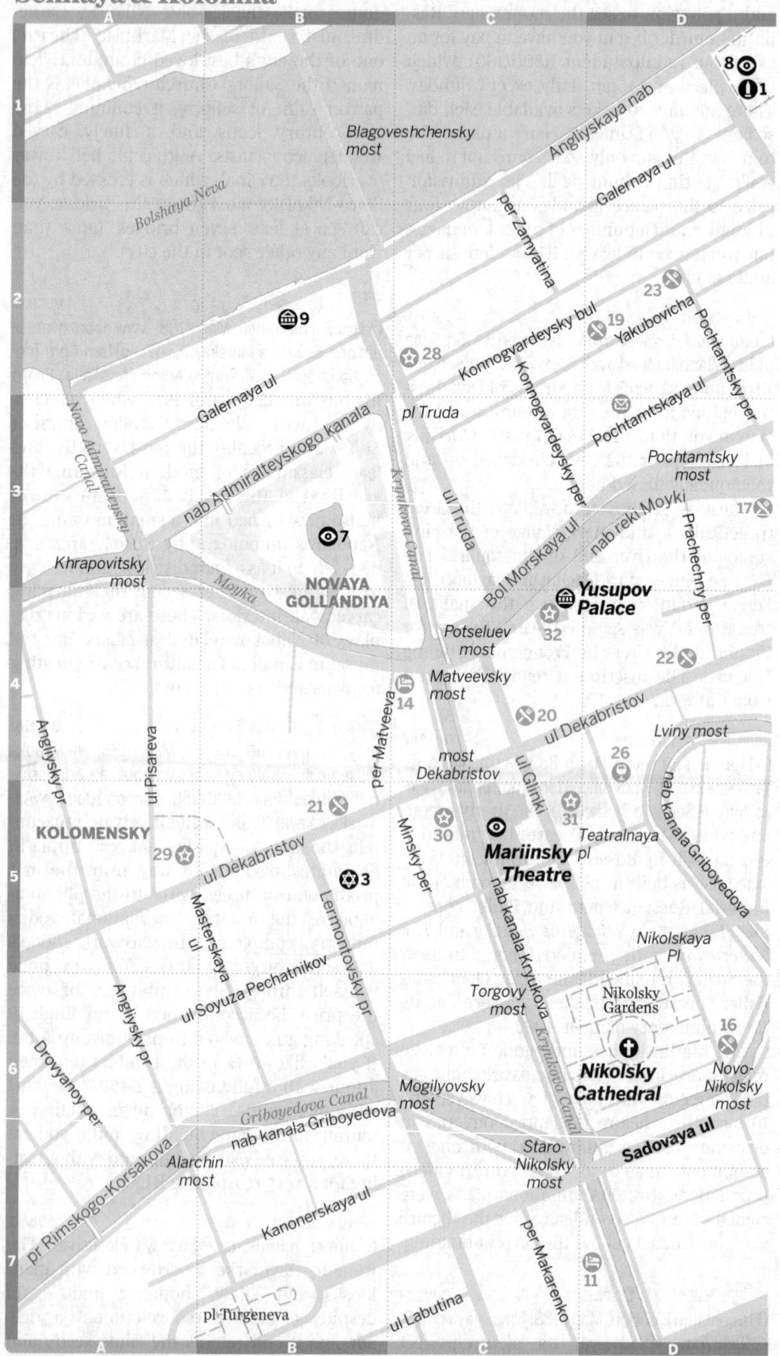

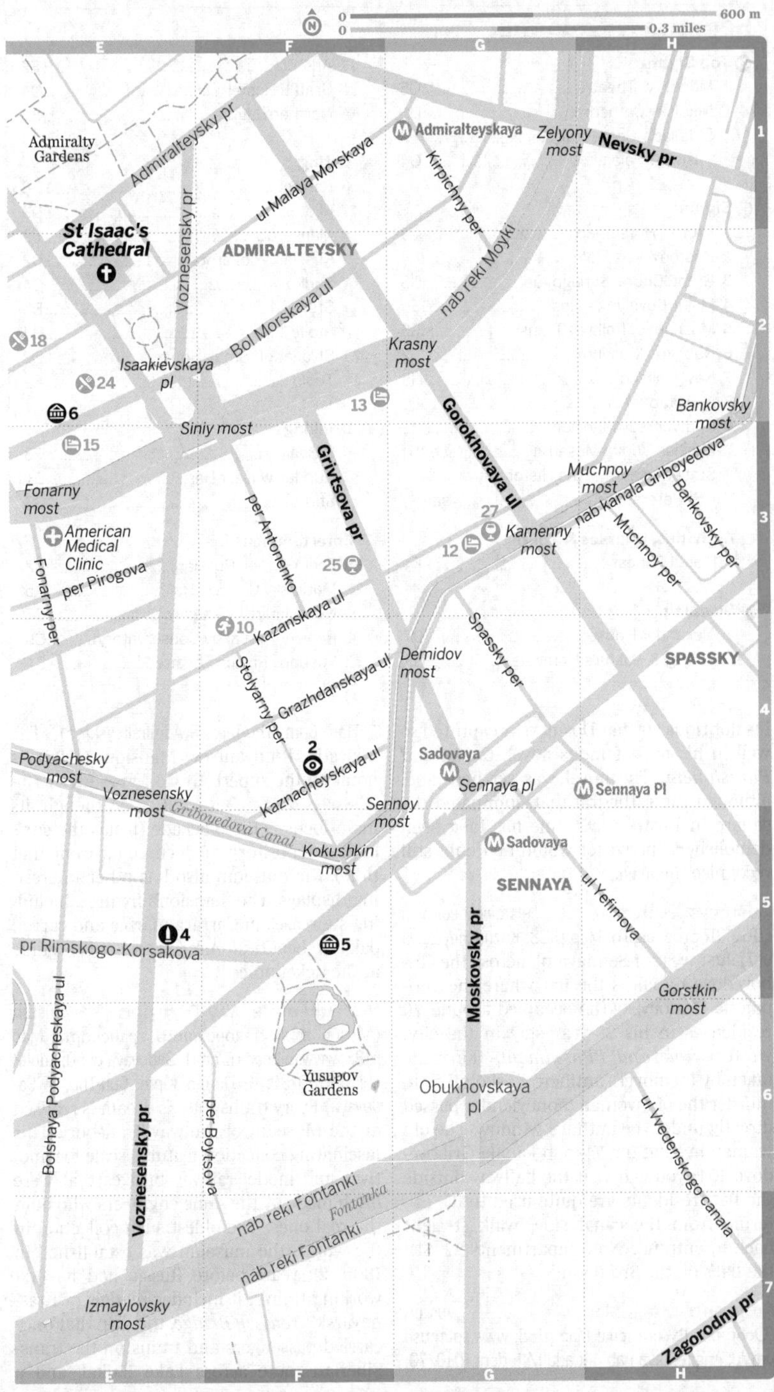
0
600 m
0
0.3 miles
E
F
G
H
1
2
3
4
5
6
7
Admiralty Gardens
Admiralteysky pr
ul Malaya Morskaya
Admiralteyskaya
Zelyony most
Nevsky pr
Kirpichny per
St Isaac's Cathedral
Voznesensky pr
ADMIRALTEYSKY
nab reki Moyki
Bol Morskaya ul
18
Isaakievskaya pl
Krasny most
24
13
6
Siniy most
Gorokhovaya ul
Bankovsky most
15
Grivtsova pr
Muchnoy most
nab kanala Griboyedova
Fonarny most
per Antonenko
27
Bankovsky per
American Medical Clinic
Kamenny most
Muchnoy per
12
Fonarny per
per Pirogova
25
Kazanskaya ul
Spassky per
10
Demidov most
SPASSKY
Stolyarny per
Grazhdanskaya ul
2
Podyachesky most
Sadovaya
Kaznacheyskaya ul
Sennaya pl
Sennaya Pl
Voznesensky most
Griboyedova Canal
Sennoy most
Sadovaya
Kokushkin most
SENNAYA
ul Yefimova
4
pr Rimskogo-Korsakova
5
Moskovsky pr
Gorstkin most
Bolshaya Podyacheskaya ul
Yusupov Gardens
Obukhovskaya pl
per Boytsova
Voznesensky pr
ul Vvedenskogo canala
nab reki Fontanki
Fontanka
nab reki Fontanki
Izmaylovsky most
Zagorodny pr
ST PETERSBURG

Sennaya & Kolomna

Top Sights

Mariinsky Theatre ... C5
Nikolsky Cathedral ... D6
St Isaac's Cathedral ... E2
Yusupov Palace ... C4

Sights

1 Bronze Horseman ... D1
2 Dostoevsky's Flat ... F4
3 Grand Choral Synagogue ... B5
4 Major Kovalyov's Nose ... E5
5 Museum of Railway Transport ... F5
6 Nabokov Museum ... E2
7 New Holland ... B3
8 pl Dekabristov ... D1
9 Rumyantsev Mansion ... B2
Russian Vodka Museum ... (see 19)
State Museum of the History of St Petersburg ... (see 9)

Activities, Courses & Tours

10 Planet Fitness ... F4

Sleeping

11 Alexander House ... D7
12 Andrey & Sasha's Homestay ... G3
13 Arkadia ... F2
14 Graffiti Hostel ... C4
15 Northern Lights ... E3

Eating

16 Entrée ... D6
17 Idiot ... D3
18 Mansard ... E2
19 Russian Vodkaroom No 1 ... D2
20 Sadko ... C4
21 Stolle ... B5
22 Stolle ... D4
23 Stroganoff Steak House ... D2
24 Teplo ... E2

Drinking

25 Bardak ... F3
26 Hundertwasser Bar ... D4
27 Stirka ... G3

Entertainment

28 Feel Yourself Russian ... C2
29 Mariinsky Concert Hall ... A5
30 New Mariinsky Theatre ... C5
31 Rimsky-Korsakov Conservatory ... C5
32 Yusupov Palace Theatre ... C4

insalubrious air that Dostoevsky captured so well in his most famous novel, *Crime and Punishment*. The novel was set here and, although the cathedral that dominated the square in Dostoevsky's time has long been demolished, the writer would no doubt still recognise the area.

Dostoevsky's Flat HISTORICAL BUILDING
(Дом Достоевского; Map p188; Kaznacheyskaya ul 7) Just west of Sennaya pl, across the Griboyedova Canal, is the flat where the peripatetic Dostoevsky (he occupied around 20 residences in his 28-year stay in the city) wrote *Crime and Punishment;* the route taken by the novel's antihero Raskolnikov to murder the old woman moneylender passed directly under the author's window. The old woman lived at flat 74, nab kanala Griboyedova 104; you can visit the hallway outside the flat (residents are quite used to it). Entering from the canal side, walk straight back to entrance No 5 (apartments 22–81); the flat's on the 3rd floor.

Rumyantsev Mansion MUSEUM
(Особняк Румянцева; Map p188; www.spbmuseum.ru; Angliyskaya nab 44; adult/student R110/70; 11am-6pm Thu-Tue; M Admiralteyskaya) The majestic Rumyantsev Mansion (1826) is home to the superb **State Museum of the History of St Petersburg**. Although its main focus is the blockade (it has the city's largest repository of documents from that time), the museum also has other interesting displays. The mansion's fixtures, including staircases in Carrara marble and carved oak, are beautiful. Ask for an English guide at the ticket office.

Museum of Railway Transport MUSEUM
(Музей железнодорожного транспорта; Map p188; www.railroad.ru/cmrt; Sadovaya ul 50; adult/child R100/30; 11am-5.30pm Sun-Thu; M Sadovaya) Every trainspotter's dream is realised at the Museum of Railway Transport. This fascinating collection features scale locomotives and model railway bridges that were often made by the same engineers who built the real ones. The oldest such collection in the world (the museum was established in 1809, 28 years before Russia had its first working train!), it includes models of Krasnoyarsk's *Yenisey Bridge,* the ship that once carried passengers and trains on the trans-Siberian route across Lake Baikal, and a

sumptuous 1903 Trans-Siberian wagon complete with piano salon and bathtub. To see full-sized vintage trains, visit the Museum of Railway Technology (p201).

FREE **Grand Choral Synagogue** SYNAGOGUE

(Большая хоральная синагога; Map p188; www.jewishpetersburg.ru; Lermontovsky pr 2; ⊙8am-8pm Sun-Fri, service 10am Sat; MSadovaya) Restored to its full Byzantine-styled glory, the Grand Choral Synagogue was designed by Vasily Stasov and opened in 1893. Its lavishness (particularly notable in the highly unusual and decorative wedding chapel to the left as you enter) indicates the pivotal role Jews played in imperial St Petersburg. All men and married women should cover their head on entering the building.

New Holland ISLAND

(Новая Голландия; Map p188; www.newhollandsp.com; cnr nab kanala Kryukova & Bolshaya Morskaya ul; MSpasskaya) This island, originally used for shipbuilding in Peter's time, has been closed to the public for the vast majority of its three centuries of existence, and it appears to be little more than a ruin at present. Its fortunes are about to change, however, as Russian billionaire Roman Abramovich acquired the island in 2010 and is planning to redevelop it into a cultural and commercial centre, which, it is hotly rumoured, will also house his own enormous contemporary art collection. If you walk by, look out for the impressive red-brick and granite arch, designed by Jean-Baptiste Vallin de la Mothe in the late 18th century, one of the city's best examples of Russian classicism.

VASILYEVSKY ISLAND

The most convenient metro station for this area is Vasileostrovskaya, but for sights around the Strelka you'd do just as well to walk over the Neva from the Hermitage or catch one of the numerous buses that run there from Nevsky pr.

Strelka VIEWPOINT

Some of the best views of St Petersburg can be had from Vasilyevsky Island's eastern 'nose' known as the Strelka (Tongue of Land). Peter the Great's plan was to have his new city's administrative and intellectual centre here. In fact, it became the focus of St Petersburg's maritime trade, symbolised by the white colonnaded Stock Exchange. The two **Rostral Columns** (Ростральные колонны; Map p192) on the point, studded with ships' prows, were oil-fired navigation beacons in the 1800s; on holidays, gas torches are still lit on them.

Menshikov Palace PALACE

(Меншиковский дворец; Map p192; www.hermitagemuseum.org; Universitetskaya nab 15; adult/student R60/free, 1st Thu of month free, audio tour R150; ⊙10.30am-6pm Tue-Sat, to 5pm Sun; MVasileostrovskaya) Another branch of the Hermitage is located in the riverside Menshikov Palace, built in 1707 for Alexander Menshikov, a close friend (and alleged one-time lover) of Peter the Great. Menshikov effectively ran Russia from here for three years between Peter's death and his own exile. The palace's impressively restored interiors are filled with period art and furniture. Fact sheets in English on each of the rooms are available.

Kunstkamera MUSEUM

(Кунсткамера; Map p192; www.kunstkamera.ru; Universitetskaya nab 3; adult/student R200/50; ⊙11am-6pm Tue-Sun, closed last Tue of the month; MAdmiralteyskaya) The city's first museum was founded in 1714 by Peter himself. It's infamous for its ghoulish collection of monstrosities, notably preserved freaks, two-headed mutant foetuses and odd body parts, all collected by Peter with the aim of educating the common people against superstitions. Most people rush to see these sad specimens, largely ignoring the other interesting (though not well-displayed) exhibits on native peoples from around the world. Here you'll also find an exhibition devoted to the scientist and renaissance man Mikhail Lomonosov (whose statue stands beside the nearby Twelve Colleges building of the city university), with a re-creation of his study-laboratory.

TOP CHOICE **Erarta Museum of Contemporary Art** MUSEUM

(Музей Эрарта; www.erarta.com; 29-aya liniya 2; adult/under 21yr R300/150, ⊙10am-10pm Thu-Tue; MVasileostrovskaya, then bus 6) This fantastic contemporary art museum has suddenly made a far-flung and otherwise totally dead area of Vasilyevsky Island a destination in itself. Opened in 2010 and housed in a superbly converted Stalinist building, the museum divides neatly into two parts. Spread over five floors on the left-hand side is the permanent collection of some 2000 works of Russian art produced between the 1950s

Vasilyevsky Island

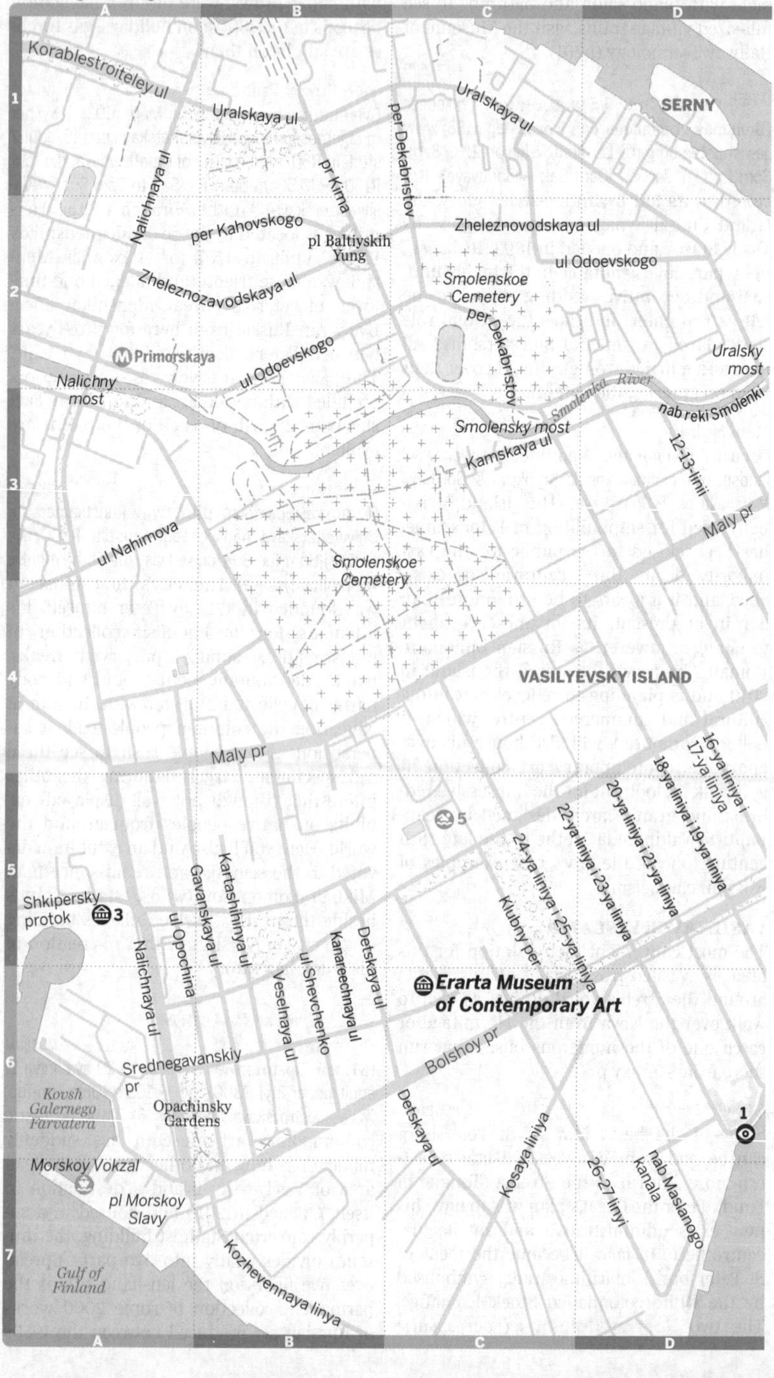

A B C D

1 2 3 4 5 6 7

Korablestroiteley ul
Uralskaya ul
Uralskaya ul
SERNY
Nalichnaya ul
pr Kirna
per Dekabristov
per Kahovskogo
pl Baltiyskih Yung
Zheleznovodskaya ul
ul Odoevskogo
Zheleznozavodskaya ul
Smolenskoe Cemetery
per Dekabristov
Primorskaya
ul Odoevskogo
Uralsky most
Nalichny most
Smolenka River
nab reki Smolenki
Smolensky most
Kamskaya ul
12-13-linii
Maly pr
ul Nahimova
Smolenskoe Cemetery
VASILYEVSKY ISLAND
Maly pr
16-ya liniya i 17-ya liniya
18-ya liniya i 19-ya liniya
20-ya liniya i 21-ya liniya
22-ya liniya i 23-ya liniya
24-ya liniya i 25-ya liniya
5
Kartashihinya ul
Gavanskaya ul
ul Opochina
Shkipersky protok
3
Nalichnaya ul
Detskaya ul
Kanareechnaya ul
ul Shevchenko
Veselnaya ul
Klubny per
Erarta Museum of Contemporary Art
Srednegavanskiy pr
Bolshoy pr
Kovsh Galernego Farvatera
Opachinsky Gardens
Detskaya ul
Kosaya liniya
1
Morskoy Vokzal
26-27 liniy
nab Maslanogo kanala
pl Morskoy Slavy
Gulf of Finland
Kozhevennaya linya

A B C D

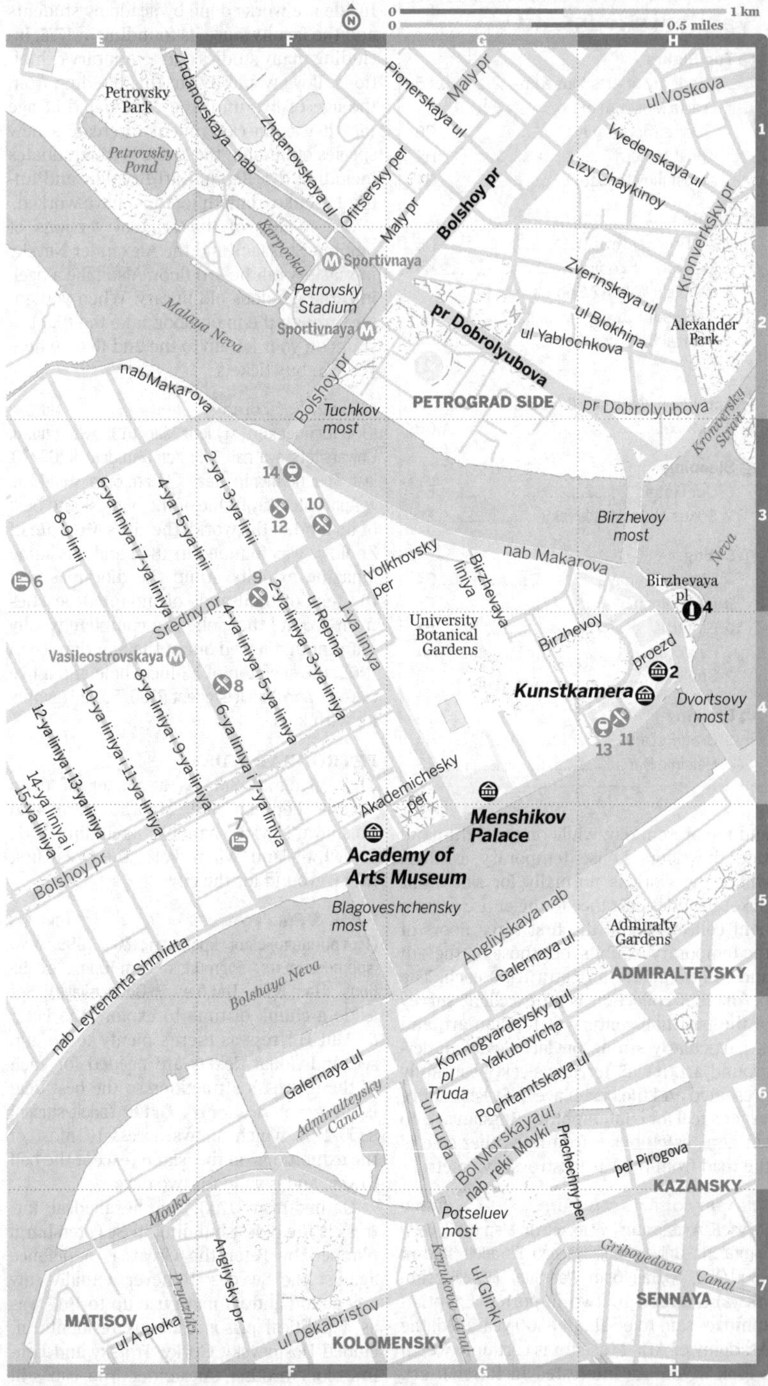

0 1 km
0 0.5 miles
E F G H
1 2 3 4 5 6 7
Petrovsky Park
Petrovsky Pond
Zhdanovskaya nab
Zhdanovskaya ul
Ofitsersky per
Pionerskaya ul
Maly pr
Bolshoy pr
ul Voskova
Vvedenskaya ul
Lizy Chaykinoy
Kronverksky pr
Karpovka
Sportivnaya
Petrovsky Stadium
Malaya Neva
Zverinskaya ul
ul Blokhina
ul Yablochkova
pr Dobrolyubova
Alexander Park
nabMakarova
Tuchkov most
PETROGRAD SIDE
Kronversky Strait
2-ya i 3-ya linii
4-ya i 5-ya linii
6-ya liniya i 7-ya liniya
8-9 linii
14 12 10 9 8 7 6
Birzhevoy most
nab Makarova
Neva
Volkhovsky per
Birzhevaya liniya
Birzhevaya pl
4
Sredny pr
2-ya liniya i 3-ya liniya
ul Repina
1-ya liniya
University Botanical Gardens
Birzhevoy proezd
2
Vasileostrovskaya
4-ya liniya i 5-ya liniya
Kunstkamera
Dvortsovy most
13 11
10-ya liniya i 11-ya liniya
8-ya liniya i 9-ya liniya
6-ya liniya i 7-ya liniya
12-ya liniya i 13-ya liniya
14-ya liniya i 15-ya liniya
Akademichesky per
Menshikov Palace
Academy of Arts Museum
Bolshoy pr
Blagoveshchensky most
Angliyskaya nab
Admiralty Gardens
Galernaya ul
ADMIRALTEYSKY
nab Leytenanta Shmidta
Bolshaya Neva
Konnogvardeysky bul
Yakubovicha
pl Truda
Galernaya ul
Admiralteysky Canal
Pochtamtskaya ul
ul Truda
Bol Morskaya ul
nab reki Moyki
Prachechny per
per Pirogova
KAZANSKY
Moyka
Potseluev most
Angliysky pr
Pryazhki
Kryukova Canal
ul Glinki
Griboyedova Canal
SENNAYA
MATISOV
ul A Bloka
ul Dekabristov
KOLOMENSKY
ST PETERSBURG

Vasilyevsky Island

Top Sights

Academy of Arts Museum F5
Erarta Museum of Contemporary Art C6
Kunstkamera H4
Menshikov Palace G4

Sights

1 Ice Breaker Krasin D6
2 Museum of Zoology H4
3 People's Will D-2 Submarine Museum A5
4 Rostral Columns H3
Zoo .... (see 2)

Activities, Courses & Tours

5 VMF C5

Sleeping

6 Our Hotel E3
7 Sokos Hotel Vasilevsky F5

Eating

8 Cheburechnaya F4
9 Dve Palochki F3
10 Gintarus F3
11 Restoran H4
12 Stolle F3

Drinking

13 Grad Petrov H4
14 Helsinki Bar F3

and the present day, while on the right-hand side the floors house temporary exhibits, where the work is normally for sale. Your ticket includes entrance to the entire permanent collection and the first three floors of the temporary exhibits, but those on the 4th and 5th floors are an extra R150 each. The permanent collection is an excellent survey of the past half-century of Russian art, and is particularly strong on late Soviet underground art. It's all terribly sleek, beautifully presented and the best place in St Petersburg to get a feel for contemporary Russian art. To get here, catch bus 6 from the other side of the road from the Vasileostrovskaya metro.

Academy of Arts Museum MUSEUM
(Музей Академии Художеств; Map p192; www.nimrah.ru; Universitetskaya nab 17; adult/student R300/150; ⏲11am-6pm Wed-Sun; Ⓜ Vasileostrovskaya) Guarded by two imported Egyptian sphinxes said to be about 3500 years old, the Academy of Arts Museum is certainly worth a look if you are interested in Russian art. Inside are works done by academy students and the faculty since its founding in 1775, including many studies and temporary exhibitions. Boys would live in this building from the age of five until they graduated at age 15 – it was an experiment to create a new species of human: the artist. With graduates including Ilya Repin, Karl Bryullov and Anton Losenko, something must have worked.

See models of the original versions of Smolny, St Isaac's and the Alexander Nevsky monastery on the 3rd floor. Also take a peek into the fabulous old library. When you enter through the main door, take the flight of stairs on your left up to the 2nd floor, where you can buy tickets.

Museum of Zoology MUSEUM
(Зоологический музей; Map p192; www.zin.ru; Universitetskaya nab 1/3; adult/student R200/70, last Thu of month free; ⏲11am-6pm Wed-Mon; Ⓜ Admiralteyskaya) One of the biggest and best of its kind in the world, the city's Museum of Zoology was founded in 1832 and has some amazing exhibits. Amid the dioramas and the tens of thousands of mounted beasties from around the globe is a complete woolly mammoth, thawed out of the Siberian ice in 1902, the skeleton of a blue whale and a live **insect zoo** (adult/student R100/50), a favourite with kids.

PETROGRAD SIDE

The Petrograd Side is a cluster of delta islands between the Malaya Neva and Bolshaya Nevka channels, including little Zayachy Island, where Peter the Great first broke ground for the city.

Peter & Paul Fortress FORTRESS
(Петропавловская крепость; Map p199; www.spbmuseum.ru; ⏲grounds 6am-10pm, exhibitions 11am-6pm Thu-Tue; Ⓜ Gorkovskaya) Set aside a chunk of time to explore the Peter & Paul Fortress as there's plenty to do and see. Individual tickets are needed for each of the fortress's attractions so the best deal is the **combined entry ticket** (adult/student R350/170), which allows access to most of the exhibitions on the island (except the bell tower) and is valid for two days.

Dating from 1703, the hexahedral fortress is the oldest building in St Petersburg, planned by Peter the Great as a defence against the Swedes. It never actually saw any action and its main use up to 1917 was as a political prison; famous residents included Dostoevsky, Gorky, Trotsky and Lenin's older brother, Alexander. You can still see their cells in the **Trubetskoy Bastion** (Трубетцкой бастион; adult/student R170/70), which remain decked out as they were in the late 19th century.

To get a sense of the scale of the place, and for wonderful river views, walk the **Nevskaya Panorama** (adult/student R150/120) along part of the battlements, then head inside the **SS Peter & Paul Cathedral** (Петропавловский собор; adult/student R200/90), whose 122m-tall, needle-thin gilded spire is one of the defining landmarks of St Petersburg. Its baroque interior is the last resting place of all of Russia's prerevolutionary rulers from Peter the Great onwards, except for Peter II and Ivan VI.

The 122.5m-high **bell tower** (adult/student R130/70; ⏲tours 11.30am, 1pm, 2.30pm & 4pm May-Sep) remains the city's tallest structure. It offers a small exhibition about the renovation of the tower, as well as an up-close inspection of the bell-ringing mechanism. The main reason to climb all these steps, of course, is for the magnificent 360-degree panorama. The bell tower is open only with an hour-long Russian-language guided tour, so arrive at least 15 minutes before the tour to get your tickets at the boathouse near the cathedral entrance.

Among the other sights within the fortress worthy of a look is the fascinating history of St Petersburg exhibition inside the **Commandant's House** (Комендантский дом; adult/student R100/60). Covering up to the 1917 revolution, there are some very good displays here including a vivid painting of the great flood of 1824 that all but swept the city away, and a model showing how the Alexander Column in Palace Sq was erected. Outside the house, look for Mikhail Shemyakin's controversial **Peter the Great statue** with its out-of-proportion head and hands: local lore has it that it's good luck to touch his right forefinger.

At noon every day a cannon is fired from the Naryshkin Bastion. **Nevsky Gate**, in the south wall, is where prisoners were loaded onto boats for execution. Note the plaques showing the water levels of famous floods. Along the walls on the **beach** on any sunny day – including the rare ones in winter and spring – you'll see standing sunbathers (standing's said to give you a *proper* tan). In winter even hardier souls come here to swim at the Walrus Club.

Mosque MOSQUE
(Соборная мечеть; Map p196; Kronverksky pr 7; ⓜGorkovskaya) This working mosque, built between 1910 and 1914, is modelled on Samarkand's Gur-e Amir Mausoleum. Although a serious place of worship, and decidedly not a tourist attraction, its fluted azure dome and minarets have emerged from a painstaking renovation and are stunning to view from outside.

Museum of Political History MUSEUM
(Музей политической истории России; Map p196; ☎313 6163; www.polithistory.ru; ul Kuybysheva 4; adult/student R200/100, English guide R700; ⏲10am-6pm Fri-Wed; ⓜGorkovskaya) Way more interesting than it sounds, the Museum of Political History occupies two elegant, connected Style Moderne palaces – one of them once belonged to Matilda Kshesinskaya, famous ballet dancer and one-time lover of Tsar Nicholas II. The Bolsheviks made it their headquarters and Lenin often gave speeches from the balcony. Although the main exhibit details Russian politics (with English captions) to the present day, you'll also come across some of the best Soviet kitsch in town and incredibly rare satirical caricatures of Lenin published in magazines between the 1917 revolutions (the same drawings a few months later would have got the artist imprisoned, or worse). Call ahead to order an English guided tour (maximum five people).

Artillery Museum MUSEUM
(Военно-исторический музей артиллерии; Map p196; www.artillery-museum.ru; Alexander

STREET NAMES

St Petersburg has two streets called Bolshoy pr: one on Petrograd Side, one on Vasilyevsky Island. The two sides of some streets on Vasilyevsky Island are known as lines *(linii)*, and are effectively different streets, thus the opposite sides of one street have different names. For example 4-ya liniya (4th line) and 5-ya liniya (5th line) are the east and west sides of the same street – but are referred to as individuals. This is due to the fact that the original plan for Vasilyevsky Island foresaw canals being built down the middle of these wide streets to please the boat-mad tsar. Following Peter's death, however, the plans were dropped, leaving locals with this strange phenomenon.

Petrograd Side

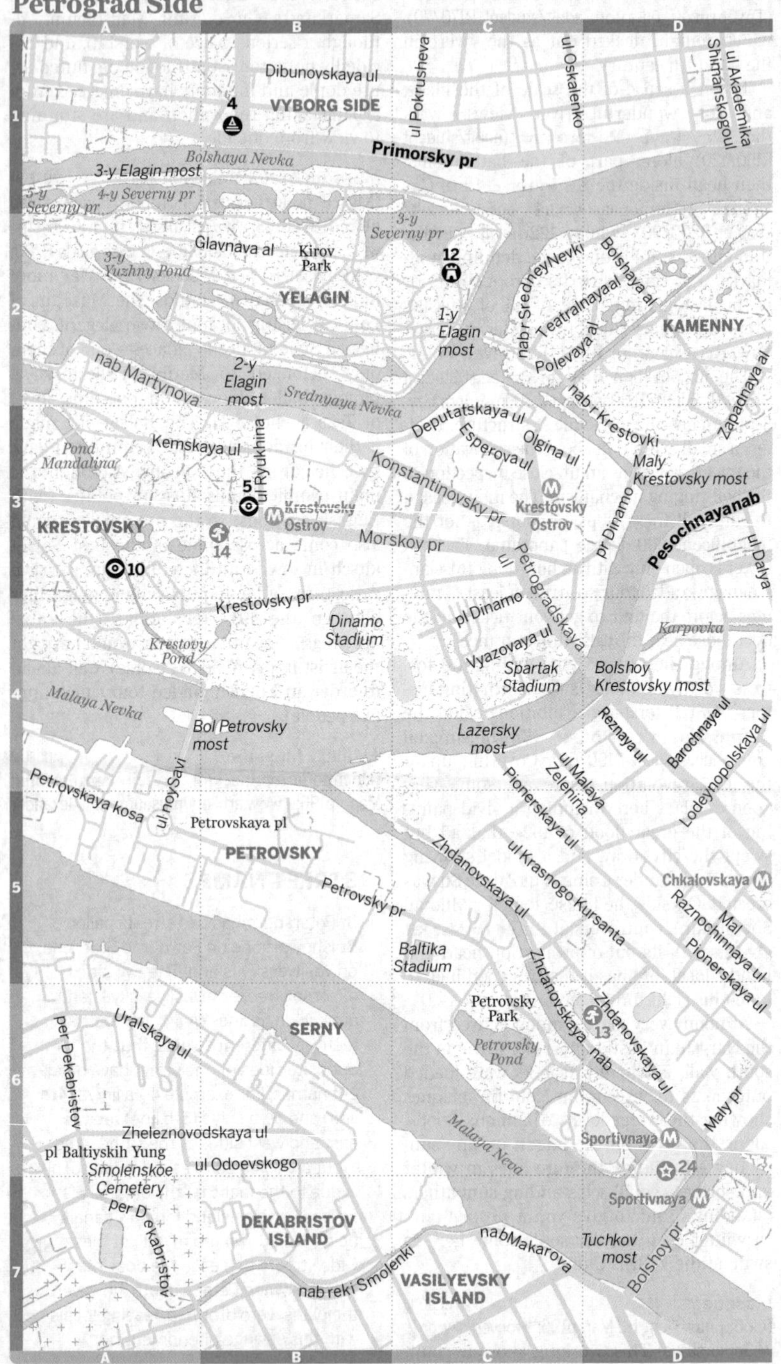

Dibunovskaya ul
VYBORG SIDE
ul Pokrusheva
ul Oskalenko
ul Akademika Shimanskogoul
Primorsky pr
Bolshaya Nevka
3-y Elagin most
4-y Severny pr
5-y Severny pr
3-y Severny pr
Glavnava al
Kirov Park
3-y Yuzhny Pond
YELAGIN
1-y Elagin most
nab r SredneyNevki
Bolshaya al
Teatralnayaal
Polevayaal
KAMENNY
Zapadnaya al
nab Martynova
2-y Elagin most
Srednyaya Nevka
Deputatskaya ul
nab r Krestovki
Esperova ul
Olgina ul
Pond Mandalina
Kemskaya ul
ul Ryukhina
Konstantinovsky pr
Maly Krestovsky most
Krestovsky Ostrov
Krestovsky Ostrov
KRESTOVSKY
Morskoy pr
pr Dinamo
Pesochnayanab
ul Dalya
ul Petrogradskaya
Krestovsky pr
pl Dinamo
Dinamo Stadium
Karpovka
Krestovy Pond
Vyazovaya ul
Spartak Stadium
Bolshoy Krestovsky most
Malaya Nevka
Bol Petrovsky most
Lazersky most
Reznaya ul
Barochnaya ul
Lodeynopolskaya ul
ul Malaya Zelenina
Petrovskaya kosa
ul noySavi
Petrovskaya pl
Pionerskaya ul
PETROVSKY
Zhdanovskaya ul
ul Krasnogo Kursanta
Chkalovskaya
Petrovsky pr
Mal Raznochinnaya ul
Pionerskaya ul
Baltika Stadium
Petrovsky Park
Zhdanovskaya nab
Zhdanovskaya ul
Uralskaya ul
SERNY
Petrovsky Pond
per Dekabristov
Maly pr
Malaya Neva
Zheleznovodskaya ul
Sportivnaya
pl Baltiyskih Yung
Smolenskoe Cemetery
ul Odoevskogo
Sportivnaya
per Dekabristov
DEKABRISTOV ISLAND
nabMakarova
Tuchkov most
Bolshoy pr
nab reki Smolenki
VASILYEVSKY ISLAND

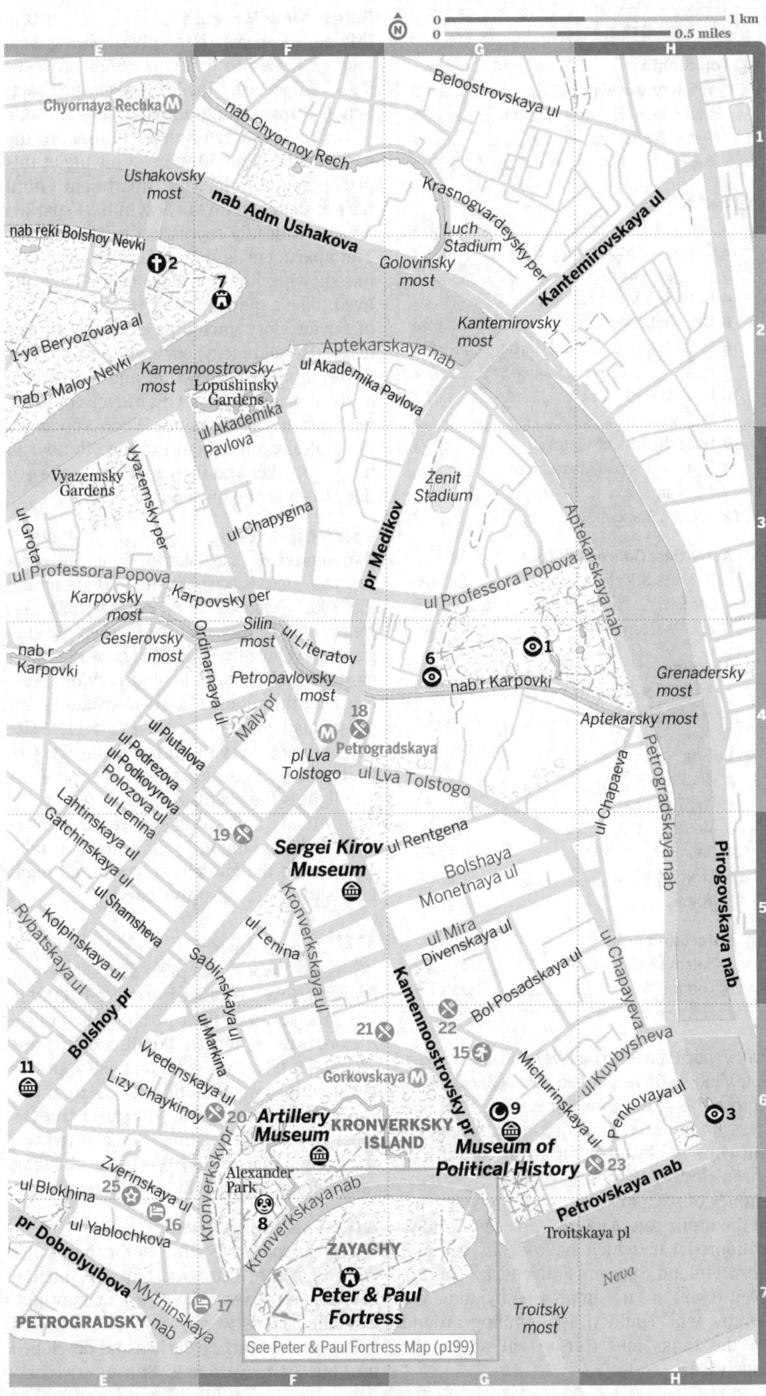

Chyornaya Rechka
Beloostrovskaya ul
nab Chyornoy Rech
Ushakovsky most
nab Adm Ushakova
Krasnogvardeysky per
Luch Stadium
nab reki Bolshoy Nevki
Golovinsky most
Kantemirovskaya ul
1-ya Beryozovaya al
Kantemirovsky most
Aptekarskaya nab
Kamennoostrovsky most
ul Akademika Pavlova
Lopushinsky Gardens
nab r Maloy Nevki
ul Akademika Pavlova
Vyazemsky Gardens
Vyazemsky per
Zenit Stadium
ul Grota
ul Chapygina
pr Medikov
Aptekarskaya nab
ul Professora Popova
Karpovsky per
ul Professora Popova
Karpovsky most
Silin most
Geslerovsky most
ul Literatov
nab r Karpovki
Ordinarnaya ul
Petropavlovsky most
nab r Karpovki
Grenadersky most
Aptekarsky most
Maly pr
ul Plutalova
Petrogradskaya
ul Podrezova
ul Podkovyrova
pl Lva Tolstogo
ul Lva Tolstogo
Polozova ul
ul Lenina
ul Chapaeva
Petrogradskaya nab
Lahtinskaya ul
Gatchinskaya ul
Sergei Kirov Museum
ul Rentgena
Bolshaya Monetnaya ul
Pirogovskaya nab
ul Shamsheva
Kronverkskaya ul
ul Lenina
ul Mira
Divenskaya ul
Kolpinskaya ul
Rybatskaya ul
Sablinskaya ul
Kamennoostrovsky pr
Bol Posadskaya ul
ul Chapayeva
Bolshoy pr
ul Markina
Vvedenskaya ul
Gorkovskaya
Michurinskaya ul
ul Kuybysheva
Lizy Chaykinoy
Artillery Museum
KRONVERKSKY ISLAND
Museum of Political History
Penkovaya ul
Alexander Park
Zverinskaya ul
ul Blokhina
Kronverkskaya nab
Kronverksky pr
Petrovskaya nab
ul Yablochkova
Troitskaya pl
pr Dobrolyubova
ZAYACHY
Neva
Peter & Paul Fortress
Mytninskaya nab
Troitsky most
PETROGRADSKY
See Peter & Paul Fortress Map (p199)
ST PETERSBURG

Petrograd Side

Top Sights

Park 7; adult/student courtyard R50/20, museum R300/150; ⌚11am-6pm Wed-Sun; Ⓜ Gorkovskaya) Across the moat from the Peter & Paul Fortress, and housed in its original arsenal, this museum is always a hit with the kids. It chronicles Russia's military history, with examples of weapons dating all the way back to the Stone Age. The centrepiece is Lenin's armoured car, which he rode in triumph from Finland Station (Finlyandsky vokzal). Even if you are not impressed by guns and bombs, who could resist climbing around on the tanks and trucks that adorn the courtyard?

Sergei Kirov Museum MUSEUM

(Музей Кирова; Map p196; www.kirovmuseum.ru; Kamennoostrovsky pr 26/28; admission R90; ⌚11am-6pm Thu-Tue; Ⓜ Petrogradskaya) Sergei Kirov, Leningrad party boss and one of the most powerful men in Russia in the early 1930s, spent 10 years of his life at this decidedly unproletarian apartment, until his murder at Stalin's behest in 1934 sparked a wave of deadly repression in the country. The apartment is now a fascinating museum showing how the Bolshevik elite really lived: take a quick journey back to the days of Soviet glory, including choice examples of 1920s technology, such as the first ever Soviet-produced typewriter and a conspicuously noncommunist GE fridge, complete with plastic food inside. When you enter the building, take the lift to the 5th floor to buy your ticket and then go down to the 4th floor to enter the museum.

Botanical Gardens GARDEN

(Ботанический сад; Map p196; ul Professora Popova 2; grounds adult/child R40/20, greenhouse R180/90; ⌚grounds 10am-6pm daily May-Sep, greenhouse 11am-4pm Sat-Thu May-Sep; Ⓜ Petrogradskaya) Once the second-biggest botanical gardens in the world, behind London's Kew Gardens, the botanical gardens contain giant dilapidated greenhouses on a 22-hectare site and, although very much faded since its glory days, it's still a pleasant place to stroll. A highlight is the 'tsaritsa nochi' *(Selenicereus pteranthus)*, a flowering cactus that blossoms only one night a year, usually in mid-June, when the gardens stay open all night for visitors to gawk at the marvel.

FREE **Cruiser Aurora** MUSEUM

(Крейсер Аврора; Map p196; www.aurora.org.ru; Petrovskaya nab; ⌚10.30am-4pm Tue-Thu, Sat & Sun; Ⓜ Gorkovskaya) Built in 1900, the cruiser *Aurora* saw action in the Russo-Japanese War and is now a museum that will appeal to naval enthusiasts and kids. It was from this ship that the shot marking the start of the October Revolution was fired. So hallowed was the cruiser that during WWII the Russians sank it to protect it from German bombs.

KIROVSKY ISLANDS

This is the collective name for the three outer delta islands of Petrograd Side – Kamenny, Yelagin and Krestovsky. Once marshy jungles, the islands were granted to 18th- and 19th-century court favourites and developed into bucolic playgrounds. Still mostly park-

Peter & Paul Fortress

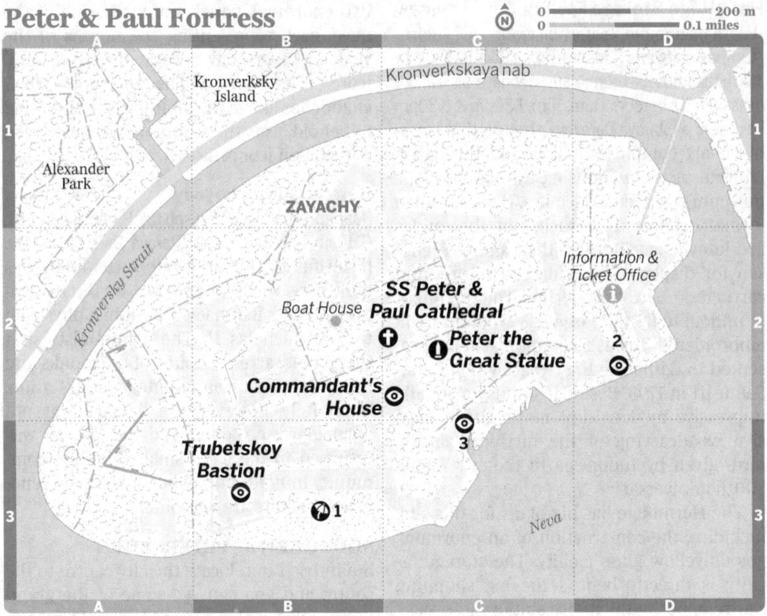

land, they remain huge leafy venues for picnics, river sports and White Nights cavorting.

Kamenny Island ISLAND

(Map p196) Kamenny Island is covered in century-old dachas (now inhabited by the wealthy), as well as winding lanes and a series of canals, lakes and ponds. At the eastern end of the island, the **Church of St John the Baptist** (Церковь Иоанна Предтечи), built between 1776 and 1781, has been charmingly restored. Behind it, the big, classical **Kamennoostrovsky Palace** (Каменноостровский дворец), built by Catherine the Great for her son, is now a weedy military sanatorium.

Yelagin Island ISLAND

(Map p196; adult/student R50/30 Sat & Sun) The centrepiece of the pedestrian-only, 2km-long Yelagin Island is the **Yelagin Palace** (Елагинский дворец; Yelagin ostrov 1; admission R200; ⌚10am-6pm Wed-Sun; Ⓜ Krestovsky Ostrov), built for his mother by Tsar Alexander I, who had architect Carlo Rossi landscape the entire island while he was at it. The palace, with beautifully restored interiors, is to your right as you cross the footbridge from Kamenny Island. The rest of the island is a lovely park, with a plaza at the western end looking out to the Gulf of Finland. You can rent rowing boats in the northern part of the island.

Peter & Paul Fortress

Top Sights

Commandant's House	C2
Peter the Great Statue	C2
SS Peter & Paul Cathedral	C2
Trubetskoy Bastion	B3

Sights

1 Beach	B3
2 Nevskaya Panorama	D2
3 Nevsky Gate	C3

Krestovsky Island ISLAND

(Map p196) The biggest of the three islands, Krestovsky Island consists mostly of the vast **Seaside Park of Victory** (Приморский Парк Победы) and, close to the metro, **Divo Ostrov** (Диво Остров; www.divo-ostrov.ru; admission free, rides R50-100; ⌚11am-8pm daily Jun-Aug, Sat & Sun Sep-May; Ⓜ Krestovsky Ostrov), an amusement park with thrill rides that kids will adore.

VYBORG SIDE

Attractions on the north bank of the Neva are few and far between – several of those that do exist, though, are worth seeing.

Hermitage Storage Facility MUSEUM

(Реставрационно-хранительский центр "Старая деревня"; Map p164; ☎340 1026; www.hermitagemuseum.com; Zausadebnaya ul 37a; admission R60; ⏰tours 11am, 1pm, 1.30pm & 3.30pm Wed-Sun; Ⓜ Staraya Derevnya) Inside this state-of-the-art complex you'll be led through a handful of rooms housing a fraction of the museum's unseen collection. This is not a formal exhibition as such, but the guides are knowledgeable and the examples chosen for display – paintings, furniture, and carriages – are wonderful. The highlight is undoubtedly the gorgeous wool and silk embroidered Turkish ceremonial tent, presented to Catherine the Great by the Sultan Selim III in 1793. Beside it stands an equally impressive modern diplomatic gift: a massive woodcarving of the mythical garuda bird, given by Indonesia to the city for its 300th anniversary.

The Hermitage has big plans for this site, including the construction of an enormous golden-yellow glass facility. The storage facility is directly behind the big shopping centre opposite the metro station.

Sampsonievsky Cathedral CHURCH

(Сампсониевский собор; Map p164; www.cathedral.ru; Bolshoy Sampsonievsky pr 41; ⏰11am-6pm Thu-Tue; Ⓜ Vyborgskaya) This fascinating light-blue baroque cathedral dates from 1740 and is a beautiful highlight of a remarkably ugly and industrial area of the Vyborg Side – it's well worth the trip out here. It is believed to be the church where Catherine the Great married her one-eyed lover Grigory Potemkin in a secret ceremony in 1774.

Today it's a delightful place, having been repainted and restored to its original glory both inside and out. The cathedral's most interesting feature is the calendar of saints, two enormous panels on either side of the nave, each representing six months of the year and every day decorated with a mini-icon of its saint(s). The enormous silver chandelier above the altar is also something to behold, as is the stunning baroque, green and golden iconostasis.

Datsan Gunzechoyney BUDDHIST TEMPLE

(Map p196; www.dazan.spb.ru; Primorsky pr 91; ⏰10am-7pm Thu-Tue; Ⓜ Staraya Derevnya) This beautiful Buddhist *datsan* (temple) was built between 1909 and 1915 at the instigation of Pyotr Badmaev, a Buddhist physician to Tsar Nicholas II. The communists shut the temple, arrested many of the monks and used the building as a military radio station. Thankfully, however, the damage was not particularly profound and the *datsan* was returned to the city's small Buddhist community in 1990, since when it has been renovated. Visitors are welcome.

SOUTHERN ST PETERSBURG

Stalin tried to relocate the city centre to the south, and you can see some of the grand Soviet master plan along Moskovsky pr and south of the Narva Gate along pr Stachek leading to the Kirovsky Zavod heavy engineering plant. Elsewhere, dotted around southern St Petersburg, there are a few other worthwhile attractions.

FREE **Monument to the Heroic Defenders of Leningrad** MONUMENT

(Памятник героическим защитникам Ленинграда; Map p165; pl Pobedy; ⏰10am-5pm Thu-Tue; Ⓜ Moskovskaya) On the way to or from the airport you won't miss the awe-inspiring Monument to the Heroic Defenders of Leningrad. Centred on a 48m-high obelisk, the monument is a sculptural ensemble of

WORTH A TRIP

RIZZORDI ART FOUNDATION

If you've visited the galleries of Ligovsky pr and Vosstaniya, and you're still looking for some more contemporary art, head out to the **Rizzordi Art Foundation** (www.rizzordi.org; Kurlyandskaya ul 49; admission free; ⏰2-8pm Tue-Sun; Ⓜ Baltiyskaya), the most exciting contemporary art venue in the city to date. Opened in summer 2011, this impressive factory conversion is worth seeing in itself – it's a huge space taking up the top two floors of a disused 19th-century brewery. Very interesting temporary exhibits from local up-and-coming artists are showcased here. Half the adventure is just getting to the site (not to mention the incredible postindustrial wasteland you have to travel through). It's a 30-minute walk from Baltiyskaya metro, or you can take bus 49 from Sennaya pl towards Dvinskaya ul and get off at Kurlyandskaya ul, the second stop after you cross the Fontanka River.

bronze statues symbolising the heavy plight of defence and eventual victory.

On a lower level, a bronze ring 40m in diameter symbolises the city's encirclement. Haunting symphonic music creates a sombre atmosphere to guide you downstairs to the underground exhibition in a huge, mausoleum-like interior, where 900 bronze lamps create an eeriness matched by the sound of a metronome – the only sound heard by Leningraders on their radios throughout the war save for emergency announcements. Twelve thematically assembled showcases feature items from the war and blockade. Ask to see the two seven-minute documentary films, played on large screens at the touch of a button.

Museum of Railway Technology MUSEUM
(Центральный музей Октябрьской железной дорогой; Map p165; nab kanala Obvodnogo 118; adult/child R200/1000; ⌚11am-5.30pm Tue-Sun; Ⓜ Baltiyskaya) Trainspotters should hasten to view the impressive collection of decommissioned locomotives at this outdoor museum behind the old Warsaw Station. Some 75 nicely painted and buffed engines and carriages dating back to the late 19th century are on display, as well as a mobile intercontinental nuclear missile launcher.

FREE **Chesma Church** CHURCH
(Чесменская церковь; Map p165; ul Lensoveta 12; ⌚10am-7pm; Ⓜ Moskovskaya) East off Moskovsky pr is the striking red-and-white striated 18th-century Gothic Chesma Church, built from 1774 to 1780 in honour of Russia's victory over the Turks at the Battle of Çesme (1770). Its relatively remote location is due to the fact that Catherine the Great was on this spot when news arrived of the victory, so that's where she ordered the church to be built.

Activities

St Petersburg offers plenty of ways to relax and enjoy yourself without spending days in museums. As with everywhere else in Russia, locals love to sweat it out in the *banya* (bathhouse) and there are plenty of great places for you to join them.

Cycling is a growing pastime in the city, as well as an increasingly popular mode of transport: avoid the major traffic-choked roads and pancake-flat St Petersburg is a great city to explore by bike. You can either rent a bike or join a Sunday-morning cycle tour. A map of safe cycle routes in the city can be found at www.i-bike-spb.ru/lanes.

When renting both bikes and skates, remember to take along your passport and a sizeable chunk of roubles (up to R7000) for a deposit.

In winter, hardy souls may want to consider joining the ice swimmers, known as *morzhi* (walruses), who meet at the Walrus Club at the southeastern corner of the Peter & Paul Fortress, where a pool is cut into the frozen Neva. Word has it that an icy plunge is good for the health and libido!

Bathhouses & Spas

Circle Baths BANYA
(Круглые бани; ☎communal 550 0985, private 297 6409; ul Karbysheva 29a; ⌚8am-10pm Fri-Tue; Ⓜ Ploshchad Muzhestva) One of the city's best baths, with a unisex heated circular open-air pool. There are private facilities, too. The *banya* is opposite the metro; look for the round building across the grassy traffic island.

Mytninskiye Baths BANYA
(Мытнинские бани; Map p182; www.mybanya.spb.ru; ul Mytninskaya 17-19; per hr R200-800; ⌚24hr by reservation; Ⓜ Ploshchad Vosstaniya) Unique in the city, Mytninskiye Baths are heated by a wood furnace, just like the log-cabin bathhouses that are still found in the Russian countryside. In addition to *parilka* (steam room) and plunge pool, the private 'lux' *banya* includes a swanky lounge area with leather furniture and a pool table.

Degtyarniye Baths BANYA
(Дегтярные бани; Map p182; www.d1a.ru; Degtyarnaya ul 1a; per hr R300-R1000; ⌚9am-midnight; Ⓜ Ploshchad Vosstaniya) These modern baths are divided into men's and women's sections, or you can book private *bani* of varying degrees of luxury. English is spoken and the website has a helpful English-language guide to how to take a *banya* for novices.

Mops Spa SPA
(Map p184; www.mopsspa.ru; ul Rubinshteyna 12; ⌚11am-11pm; Ⓜ Dostoevskaya) Run by the same Thai management as the restaurant with the same name, this wonderful retreat from the roar of traffic on nearby Nevsky is very welcome. Choose from traditional Thai massage, facials, hair treatments, aromatherapy and stone therapy just for starters.

Coachmen's Baths BANYA
(Ямские бани; Map p184; ☎312 5836; www.yamskie.ru; ul Dostoevskogo 9; Ⓜ Vladimirskaya) Recently renovated multilevel complex

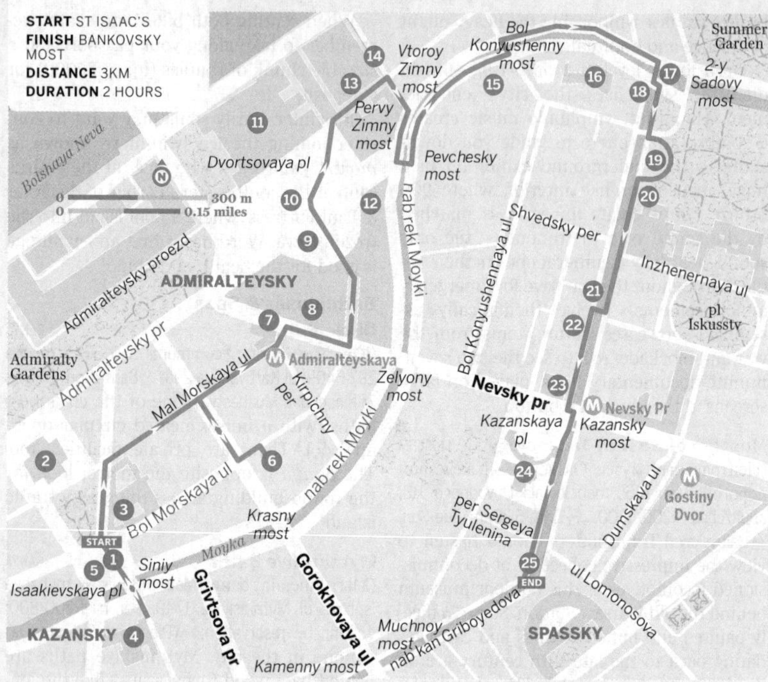

Walking Tour

Canals & Rivers

Follow this walking tour from St Isaac's Cathedral along the loop of the Moyka River and down the Griboyedova Canal.

Stand in 1 **Isaakievskaya ploshchad** and admire Montferrand's extraordinary golden-domed 2 **St Isaac's Cathedral** and the surrounding buildings, including the luxurious 3 **Hotel Astoria** and the 4 **Mariinsky Palace**, a gift from Tsar Nicholas I to his daughter Maria (hence the name), which now houses the City Legislative Council. The building is not open to the public. In the middle of the square the 5 **bronze statue** is of Tsar Nicholas I on horseback, its plinth decorated with bas-reliefs and figures representing Faith, Wisdom, Justice and Might.

From the square's northeast corner, walk down Malaya Morskaya ul; this area was one of the wealthiest during imperial times, hosting many financial institutions (several banks have now returned). At number 24 Bolshaya Morskaya ul, the famed jewellers 6 **Fabergé** is now the jewellers Yakhont. The writers Ivan Turgenev and Nikolai Gogol both lived at number 17 Malaya Morskaya ul, and Tchaikovsky died at number 13 in 1893, just days after the premiere of his Symphony No 6.

On the corner of Malaya Morskaya ul and Nevsky pr, note 7 **Wawelburg House**, a highly decorative grey stone building designed after both the Doge's Palace in Venice and Florence's Palazzo Medici Riccardi. Cross Nevsky pr here, walk 50m east and turn left (north) at Bolshaya Morskaya ul. On the way, keep an eye out for the wall of the 8 **school** at number 14, bearing a blue-and-white stencilled sign in Cyrillic maintained since WWII. It translates as 'Citizens! At times of artillery bombardment this side of the street is most dangerous!'

The most perfect way of seeing 9 **Dvortsovaya ploshchad** for the first time is to approach it via Bolshaya Morskaya ul. As you turn the corner, behold the 10 **Alexander Column**, with the 11 **Winter Palace** in the background, perfectly framed under the triumphal double arch of the 12 **General Staff Building**. Continue walking towards the square, keeping your eyes fixed on the columns and enjoy the visual magic tricks as the perspective changes the closer you get to the arches' opening.

Head northeast across the square to Millionnaya ul, and into the 13 **porch** covering the south entrance of the New Hermitage and supported by semiclad musclemen. This was the museum's first public entrance when it opened in 1852, following the tsar's visit to Munich, where he was impressed by the Bavarian city's numerous public galleries.

A favourite tourist shot from here is looking west towards St Isaac's Cathedral, past the Winter Palace – you can usually fit in a few of the Atlantes, or at least a calf or two.

You can wander first left along the 14 **Zimny Canal,** one of St Petersburg's prettiest, under the attractive arch that connects the Large Hermitage with the Hermitage Theatre and onto the dramatic Neva Embankment, where you'll have excellent views of both the Peter & Paul Fortress and the Strelka across the water. Then turn back on yourself, walk back down to the Zimny Canal to the Moyka River (glance behind you towards the Neva for another great view). This stretch of the Moyka is lovely: cross to the east bank by the Pevchesky most and admire the views as you walk past 15 **Pushkin's last home**, where the poet died in 1837 following a still-controversial duel between him and Frenchman George-Charles de Heeckeren d'Anthès. The museum itself remains preserved exactly as it was the day the poet died and is guarded zealously by an army of devoted babushkas.

Cross the river again and head east beside the water; on the opposite bank you'll see what used to be the 16 **Court Stables** (not open to the public), dating from Peter the Great's time but rebuilt in the early 19th century. Today it's a picturesque ruin, and the subject of more than a few rumours about a major renovation set to take place in the near future. One of imperial St Petersburg's flashiest streets, Bolshaya Konyushennaya ul (Big Stables St) extends south from here to Nevsky pr, and after a recent redevelopment it's once again home to big international fashion houses and a very pleasant place to stroll and shop.

Continue along the river until you come to a very picturesque ensemble of bridges where the Moyka intersects at right angles with the start of the Griboyedova Canal. While crossing over the 17 **Malo-Konyushenny most** and the pretty 18 **Teatralny most**, you'll see the Church of the Saviour on Spilled Blood across the top of the touristy souvenir market. From here you can detour over the Moyka and wander across the impressive Mars Field towards the Marble Palace or the Mikhailovsky Castle, two equally impressive restored tsarist palaces that now house collections of the Russian Museum.

Returning to the bridges, head towards the unmissable 19 **Church of the Saviour on Spilled Blood**, now St Petersburg's most recognisable icon after a huge restoration job in the 1990s following years of neglect and downright abuse by the Soviet government. Having run the gauntlet of the souvenir sellers, circle the church; to your left will be the striking Style Moderne wrought-iron fence of the 20 **Mikhailovsky Gardens**, well worth ducking into for a wander amid the beautifully restored parkland that backs onto the Mikhailovsky Castle, home to the fabulous Russian Museum. Walk south along the Griboyedova Canal until you reach the sweet footbridge that crosses it. Called the 21 **Italyansky most**, it dates from 1896 but was redesigned in 1955. Its main purpose seems to be to afford photographers a postcard-perfect view of the Church of the Saviour on Spilled Blood – join the line! Note the amazing building on the west side of the street at number 13. Originally the 22 **House of the Joint Credit Society** (not open to the public) and built in 1890, its central cupola was placed to give the appearance of a grand palace.

Continue down to Nevsky pr, where the Style Moderne 23 **Singer Building** stands regally on the corner. Now fully restored after years of being under scaffolding, this is one of the city's most delightful and whimsical buildings, and also hosts its most famous bookshop, Dom Knigi, and a great café with fantastic views over Nevsky pr.

From here admire the grand sweep of the 24 **Kazan Cathedral** opposite, cross Nevsky pr and head south along the Griboyedova Canal to the next bridge, no doubt St Petersburg's most picturesque and most photographed, the 25 **Bankovsky most**, with its gilded-winged griffins.

OFFBEAT ST PETERSBURG

Had your fill of St Petersburg's grand vistas and plethora of palaces and museums? Here are some suggestions for those who wish to swim against the tide:

» **Sniff out Major Kovalyov's nose** – the elusive character in Nikolai Gogol's celebrated story set in St Petersburg, 'The Nose', is immortalised in a **sculpture** (Map p188) on the corner of pr Rimskogo-Korsakova and Voznesensky pr.

» **Inspect Rasputin's Penis** – the mad monk's 30cm-long member is the chief attraction at the otherwise eminently missable **Museum of Erotica** (Музей Эротики; Map p182; ul Furshtatskaya 47; admission R100; ⌚8am-9pm Mon-Fri, 9am-6pm Sat & Sun; Ⓜ Chernyshevskaya) housed in a venereal disease clinic.

» **Stimulate your subconscious** – the **Sigmund Freud Museum of Dreams** (Музей сновидений Фрейда; Map p196; www.freud.ru; Bolshoy pr 18a; ⌚noon-5pm Tue & Sun; Ⓜ Sportivnaya) is housed in the Psychoanalytic Institute. The displays in the dimly lit two-room exhibition symbolise the dreams on which Freud based his theories.

» **Board an icebreaker and a sub** – tours on the hour are available at the **Icebreaker Krasin** (Ледокол Красин; Map p192; www.krassin.ru; nab Leytenanta Shmidta; admission R200; ⌚11am-6pm Wed-Sun) and **People's Will D-2 Submarine Museum** (Подводная лодка Д-2 Народоволец; Map p192; Shkipersky protok 10; adult/student R300/150; ⌚11am-6pm Wed-Sun), two workhorses from the Soviet glory days, which are sure to be a hit with the young 'uns.

» **Go mosaic crazy** – St Petersburg's hidden courtyards hold many surprises but few are as pleasant as that fronting the **Small Academy of Art** (Малая Академия Искусств; Map p182), tucked away off ul Chaikovskogo near the Fontanka River: it's been decorated in all manner of mosaic sculptures and is an enchanting place for children and adults alike.

with both ordinary and lux *bani* as well as private rooms and saunas for you to rent with up to eight friends. The attendants are friendly and the patrons take their bathing very seriously. Call ahead to check on variable times for men and women, or to book a private room.

Cycling & Skating

Skat Prokat CYCLING
(Скат Прокат; ☎717 6838; www.skatprokat.ru; Goncharnaya ul 7; per hr/day R150/500; ⌚1-8pm Ⓜ Ploshchad Vosstaniya) This tight-run outfit offers excellent Saturday- and Sunday-morning bike tours of the city (see p205). Rental bicycles are brand-new mountain bikes by the Russian company Stark, and you'll need to leave either R2000 and your passport or R7000 as a deposit. Weekend or weekly rates are also available.

Rent Bike CYCLING
(Map p172; www.rentbike.org; Malaya Morskaya ul 16; per hr/day R150/600; ⌚10am-11pm; Ⓜ Admiralteyskaya) This centrally located bike hire place offers slightly pricier bike hire than its main rival, Skat Prokat, but it may be worth paying extra if you're staying nearby.

Jet Set CYCLING
(Map p196; ☎929 1110; www.jet-set.ru.net; Tsentralnaya alleya; bike rental per hr from R250, per day R450, in-line skate rental per hr from R250; ⌚noon-11pm Mon-Fri, 11am-midnight Sat, 11am-11pm Sun; Ⓜ Krestovsky Ostrov) Also rents helmets, pads and skateboards.

Dvorets Sporta SKA SKATING
(Дворец Спорта СКА; Map p196; Zhdanovskaya nab 2; entry R300, skate rental per hr R100; ⌚noon-5am Fri-Sun; Ⓜ Sportivnaya) Has both indoor and outdoor rinks, and is open all night.

Gyms

Sports Complex GYM
(Дом физической культуры ПГУПС; Map p196; www.dfkpgups.ru; Kronverksky pr 9a; entry R300; ⌚6.30am-11pm; Ⓜ Gorkovskaya) This is the Russian version of the YMCA. It's not as shiny and new as the private clubs, but the 25m swimming pool under a glass roof is heavenly. Other facilities include weights, aerobics classes and clubs for every sport imaginable.

Fit Fashion GYM
(Map p172; www.fitfashion.ru; Kazanskaya ul 3; ⌚7am-midnight; Ⓜ Nevsky Prospekt) If you're in

town for a while, a monthly membership at this elite gym and sauna will set you back R8000 – not bad given the very high quality of the equipment and the general air of exclusiveness inside the white minimalist space.

Planet Fitness GYM
(Планета Фитнесс; Map p188; ☎315 6220; www.spb.fitness.ru; Kazanskaya ul 37; entry R1000; ⏲7am-11pm Mon-Fri, 9am-9pm Sat & Sun; Ⓜ Sennaya Ploshchad) A central branch of a major gym chain with multiple locations citywide, including a branch in the Grand Hotel Europe.

VMF SWIMMING POOL
(Бассейн ВМФ; Map p192; Sredny pr 87; entry R550; ⏲7am-10pm Mon-Sat, 8m-9pm Sun, closed 1 Jun–31 Aug; Ⓜ Vasileostrovskaya) At 50m, this is the city's largest pool, renovated in 2007.

Tours

In a city as large and foreign as St Petersburg, a lot of travellers prefer (at least initially) to be shown around on a walking tour to kick things off. There are several excellent ones on offer, as well as bike tours and a hop-on, hop-off bus that can take you around the main sights of the centre. Viewing St Petersburg from a boat is an idyllic way to tour the city, and during the main tourist season (May to October) there are plenty of boats offering to help you do this – typically found at the Anichkov most landing on the Fontanka River, just off Nevsky pr; on the Neva outside the Hermitage and the Admiralty; beside the Kazansky most over the Griboyedova Canal; and along the Moyka River at Nevsky pr. For something more private there are many small boats that can be hired as private water taxis. You'll have to haggle over rates: expect to pay around R2000 to R3000 an hour for a group of up to six people.

Peter's Walking Tours WALKING TOURS
(☎943 1229; www.peterswalk.com) Established in 1996, Peter Kozyrev's innovative and passionately led tours are highly recommended as a way to see the city with knowledgeable locals. The choice of tours available is enormous; the daily Original Peter's Walk is one of the favourites and functions as a do-it-yourself introduction to the city: you tell your guide what aspects of the city you're interested in and they improvise a tour for you then and there. Other tours include a Friday-night pub crawl, a Rasputin Walk and a WWII and the Siege of Leningrad tour.

Anglotourismo BOAT TOURS
(Map p172; ☎325 9906; www.anglotourismo.com) While there is no shortage of boat tours on the canals and rivers of St Petersburg, Anglotourismo is the only operator to run all its tours in English. You'll pay the same rate (R500) per tour as you would for a Russian-language one, so it's well worth heading down to the embarkation point at nab reki Fontanki 27 (just off Nevsky pr) to take the one-hour boat tours that leave every two hours on the hour from 11am until 7pm. Night boat tours (R700) are also available. Check the website to see if the free three-hour summer tours are operating.

Petersburg Bike Tours CYCLING TOURS
(☎943 1229; www.biketour.spb.ru) Run jointly by Peter's Walking Tours and Skat Prokat (p204), these excellent bike tours are a very popular way to cover large swathes of the city in just a few hours. Most popular is the White Night Bike Tour (R1200 including bike hire), which leaves from Skat Prokat (Goncharnaya ul 7) at 10.30pm every Tuesday and Thursday from mid-May until the end of August.

VB Excursions WALKING TOURS
(☎380 4596; www.vb-excursions) Offers excellent walking tours with clued-up students on themes including Dostoevsky and revolutionary St Petersburg. The 'Back in the USSR' tour (R1150 per person) includes a visit to a typical Soviet apartment for tea and bliny.

Liberty WHEELCHAIR-ACCESSIBLE TOURS
(www.libertytour.ru) Specialising in wheelchair-accessible tours in and around St Petersburg, this unique-in-Russia company has specially fitted vans. Can also advise on and book hotels with rooms for the disabled.

City Tour BUS TOURS
(☎718 4769; www.citytourspb.ru) The familiar red 'hop-on, hop-off' double-decker buses you'll see in most big cities in Europe have finally arrived in St Petersburg and offer a useful service for anyone unable to walk easily – the buses run along Nevsky pr from pl Vosstaniya, drop by the Russian Museum, pass the Hermitage, go over the Strelka, the Petrograd Side and then back to the Historic Heart, taking in the Church of the Saviour on Spilled Blood, the Admiralty and St Isaac's Cathedral before going back down Nevsky pr. An adult day ticket costs R450, valid for as many trips as you like.

Festivals & Events

Whether through the carnival atmosphere of White Nights or merrymaking during the freezing, dark winter days, Petersburgers love to celebrate festivals or special events.

April

Mariinsky Ballet Festival BALLET

(www.mariinsky.ru) The city's principal dance theatre hosts this week-long international ballet festival, where the cream of Russian ballet dancers showcase their talents.

Easter CHRISTIAN

(Paskha) Head to Kazan Cathedral to see Russia's most important religious festival in full Russian Orthodox style: the church (as well as many others around the city) is packed out.

May

Victory Day CELEBRATION

On 9 May, St Petersburg celebrates not only the end of WWII in 1945 but also the breaking of the Nazi blockade. The highlight is a victory parade on Nevsky pr, culminating in soldiers marching on Dvortsovaya pl and fireworks over the Neva in the evening.

City Day ANNIVERSARY

Mass celebrations are held throughout the city centre on 27 May, the city's official birthday, known as *den goroda* (city day). Brass bands, folk dancing and mass drunkenness are the salient features of this perennial favourite.

June & July

Stars of the White Nights Festival MUSIC

(www.mariinsky.ru) Held at the Mariinsky, the Conservatoire and the Hermitage Theatre, this festival from late May until July has become a huge draw and now lasts far longer than the White Nights (officially the last 10 days of June) after which it is named. You'll see ballet, opera and classical music concerts premiered and reprised.

Festival of Festivals FILM

(www.filmfest.ru) This annual international film festival held in late June is a noncompetitive showcase of the best Russian and world cinema.

September & October

Early Music Festival MUSIC

(www.earlymusic.ru) Held from mid-September until early October, this ground-breaking musical festival includes performances of forgotten masterpieces from the Middle Ages, the Renaissance and the baroque era. Musicians come from around the world to perform here.

ST PETERSBURG FOR CHILDREN

There's heaps to do with kids in St Petersburg – there are even museums your kids will like! Older children will appreciate the Kunstkamera (p191), an all-time favourite for its display of mutant babies in jars, while all age groups will like the Museum of Zoology (p194) for its stuffed animals and live insect zoo. The Artillery Museum (p195) makes for great fun climbing on its impressive collection of tanks.

Other big hitters for children include **Leningradsky Zoo** (Ленинградский зоопарк; Map p196; www.spbzoo.ru; Alexander Park 1; adult/child R350/100; ⏲summer 10am-8pm daily, winter 10am-5pm Tue-Sun; Ⓜ Gorkovskaya), which is worth visiting for its range of species, including a large number of polar bears. The **Oceanarium** (Океанариум; Map p184; www.planeta-neptun.ru; ul Marata 86; adult/child from R450/250; ⏲10am-10pm; Ⓜ Zvenigorodskaya) is home to sharks that can be seen in action at 7pm Tuesday to Sunday, and seals that perform at 11.30am and 4pm daily.

The city's parks are charming, and many have kids' playgrounds with swings, roundabouts and climbing frames: check out the Tauride Gardens (p181) and the Mikhailovsky Gardens (p175). There's also the mosaic-covered playground that's in the courtyard beside the Small Academy of Art (p204). For more high-tech amusements there's always the Divo Ostrov amusement park (p199) on Krestovsky Island. And if you need the little darlings to burn off even more energy, check out the boat, bicycle and in-line skate hiring opportunities listed on p201.

Theatres in town catering to kids include a couple offering puppet shows and, of course, the circus (p220). Several restaurants also have children's play sections, particularly good ones being at Botanika (p213), Makarov (p213), Sadko (p215), Stroganoff Steak House (p215) and Teplo (p214).

Defile on the Neva FASHION
(www.defilenaneve.ru) This major fashion event is held in mid-October at the Lenexpo Exhibition Hall on Vasilyevsky Island. A week of fashion shows, parties and symposia allows both established and up-and-coming designers to showcase their latest lines.

St Petersburg Open SPORTS
(www.spbopen.ru) Since 1995 St Petersburg has hosted this men's tennis tournament at the end of October, attracting international players to compete for a first prize of US$1 million.

December

Arts Square Winter Festival MUSIC
(www.artsquarewinterfest.ru) A musical highlight of the year, this festival held from late December to early January at the Philharmonia takes different themes each year. Both classical and contemporary opera and orchestral works are staged.

Multivision ANIMATION
(www.multivision.ru/english) This international festival of animation sees judges select the 15 best animated submissions from all over the world. The selected films are then shown locally and a winner is selected.

Sleeping

There has been a revolution in hotel accommodation in St Petersburg over the past decade and a large expansion of modern, professionally run establishments. Old Soviet fleapits have been reconstructed as contemporary and appealing hotels, some of the city centre's most desperately derelict buildings have been rebuilt as boutique luxury properties, and the overall standards of service have risen enormously. That said, most hotels are still fairly expensive, with a real lack of good, midrange places in the city centre. They do exist, however, but tend to get booked up well in advance (particularly during the summer months), so book ahead if you want to be in the Historic Heart (and let's face it, you do). There are plenty of hotels in other neighbourhoods though: Smolny, Vladimirskaya, Vasilyevsky Island and the Petrograd Side are all popular locations with relatively easy access to the rest of the city.

Rates quoted here are for the high season (generally from mid-May through to the end of August). Rates drop substantially during the November to March low season.

At the budget end of the spectrum (under R3000), more Western-style hostels have continued to open up – which is great news for cash-strapped travellers since St Petersburg remains a pricey city in which to bed down. If cost is an issue, consider homestays and apartment rentals: the latter can work out as the best deal for groups of travellers sharing or families.

HISTORIC HEART

TOP CHOICE **W Hotel** LUXURY HOTEL €€€
(Map p172; ☎610 6161; www.wstpetersburg.com; Voznesensky pr 6; r from R14,700; ❄📶🏊; Ⓜ Admiralteyskaya) When one of the world's coolest hotel brands opened its first Russian hotel in 2011, it unsurprisingly became the talk of the town, and it's not hard to see why when you walk into the dazzling reception area of this 137-room property. The rooms are all spacious and very luxuriously appointed, with marble bathrooms, iPhone docks, a Nespresso coffee maker and – what else – flatscreen TV in both the room itself and the bathroom.

TOP CHOICE **Rossi Hotel** BOUTIQUE HOTEL €€€
(Map p172; ☎635 6333; www.rossihotels.com; nab reki Fontanki 55; s/d/ste incl breakfast from R5000/9000/10,500; ❄📶; Ⓜ Gostiny Dvor) This fantastic new addition to the local hotel scene is a beautifully restored building on one of St Petersburg's prettiest squares. The 46 rooms are all individually designed, but their brightness and moulded ceilings are uniform. Antique beds, super sleek bathrooms, exposed brick walls and lots of cool designer touches create a great blend of old and new, while the very best rooms have superb views over the Fontanka River.

Casa Leto BOUTIQUE HOTEL €€€
(Map p172; ☎314 6622; www.casaleto.com; Bolshaya Morskaya ul 34; r incl breakfast R9500-12,000; ❄📶; Ⓜ Admiralteyskaya) A dramatically lit stone stairwell sets the scene for this discreet and stylish boutique hotel. With soft pastel shades and plenty of antiques, the spacious, high-ceilinged quarters are full of five-star perks, such as king-size beds, Molton Brown toiletries, heated floors and free international phone calls.

Rachmaninov Hotel BOUTIQUE HOTEL €€
(Map p172; ☎571 7618; www.hotelrachmaninov.com; Kazanskaya ul 5; r incl breakfast from R6900; 📶; Ⓜ Nevsky Prospekt) Perfectly located and run by friendly staff, the Rachmaninov is one for those in the know. Stuffed full of antiques, the rooms have been recently

renovated and feel pleasantly old world with their hardwood floors and attractive Russian furnishings.

Grand Hotel Europe LUXURY HOTEL €€€
(Map p172; ☎329 6000; www.grandhoteleurope.com; Mikhailovskaya ul 1/7; r from R15,000, ste from €25,000; ; Gostiny Dvor) One of the world's most iconic hotels, the Grand Hotel Europe lives up to its name. Since 1830, when Carlo Rossi united three adjacent buildings with the grandiose facade we see today, little has been allowed to change in this heritage building. No two rooms are the same, but all are spacious and elegant in design.

Guest House Nevsky 3 MINIHOTEL €€
(Map p172; ☎710 6776; www.nevsky3.ru; Nevsky pr 3; s/d incl breakfast R4700/5300; ; Admiralteyskaya) This tiny place has just four individually decorated rooms and gets rave reviews from guests. Each room has a fridge, TV, safe and a fan, and overlooks a surprisingly quiet courtyard just moments from the Hermitage.

Angleterre Hotel LUXURY HOTEL €€€
(Map p172; ☎494 5666; www.angleterrehotel.com; Malaya Morskaya ul 24; r from R9000; ; Admiralteyskaya) Breathtaking views of St Isaac's Cathedral can be had from the luxurious and beautifully designed rooms at this classic St Petersburg hotel. With supremely comfortable king-sized beds, huge bathrooms and a confidently understated style, it's no wonder that this luxury hotel is a firm favourite with VIPs.

Friends Hostel HOSTEL €
(Map p172; ☎571 0151; www.friendsplace.ru; nab kanala Griboyedova 20; dm/d R500/2500; ; Nevsky Prospekt) Named after the TV show, this new chain of hostels is one of the best things to have happened to St Petersburg's budget travellers for ages. All four locations are great, but our favourite is this one, just next to the Kazan Cathedral in a quiet courtyard. The newly decorated dorms are spotless; all have lockers and share good bathrooms and a kitchen. Other locations: **Friends on Bankovsky** (Map p172; ☎310 4950; Bankovsky per 3; ; Sennaya Ploshchad), **Friends on Nevsky** (☎272 7178; Nevsky pr 106; ; Mayakovskaya) and **Friends on Chekhova** (☎272 7178; ul Chekhova 11; ; Mayakovskaya).

Kempinski Hotel Moyka 22 LUXURY HOTEL €€€
(Map p172; ☎335 9111; www.kempinski.com; nab reki Moyki 22; r/ste from R10,000/19,500; ; Nevsky Prospekt) This superb hotel has a great location on the Moyka River – it's practically on the doorstep of the Hermitage – and has all the comforts you'd expect of an international luxury chain. Rooms have a stylish marine theme, with cherry-wood furniture and a handsome navy blue and gold colour scheme.

Petro Palace Hotel HOTEL €€
(Map p172; ☎571 2880; www.petropalacehotel.com; Malaya Morskaya ul 14; r from R5500; ; Admiralteyskaya) This large, superbly located midrange hotel between St Isaac's Cathedral and the Hermitage has 194 rooms and excellent facilities, including a great basement fitness centre with a decent pool, Finnish sauna and full gym. Standards are spacious and furnished in an anonymously tasteful way.

3MostA BOUTIQUE HOTEL €€
(Map p172; ☎332 3470; www.3mosta.com; nab reki Moyki 3a; s/d from R3000/5000; ; Nevsky Prospekt) This brand-new property, whose name means 'Three Bridges' in Russian, is surprisingly uncramped given its wonderful location. There are 24 rooms here, and even the standards are of a good size with tasteful furniture, minibars and TVs.

Anichkov Pension MINIHOTEL €€
(Map p172; ☎314 7059; www.anichkov.com; Nevsky pr 64, apt 4; s/d/ste incl breakfast from R5860/7200/7860; ; Gostiny Dvor) On the 3rd floor of a handsome apartment building with an antique lift, this self-styled pension has just six rooms. The standard rooms are fine, but the suites are well worth paying a little more for. The delightful breakfast room offers balcony views of the bridge from which the pension takes its name.

Pushka Inn BOUTIQUE HOTEL €€
(Map p172; ☎312 0913; www.pushkainn.ru; nab reki Moyki 14; s/d from R4500/6700, apt R10,000-15,000; ; Admiralteyskaya) On a particularly picturesque stretch of the Moyka River, this charming inn is housed in a historic 18th-century building. The rooms are decorated in dusky pinks and caramel tones, with wide floorboards and – if you're willing to pay more – lovely views of the Moyka.

Location Hostel HOSTEL €
(Map p172; ☎490 6429; www.location-hostel.ru; Admiralteysky pr; dm/d R600/1500; ; Admiralteyskaya) With a brilliant location virtually on the doorstep of the Hermitage, this arty but

small hostel is definitely a good choice for budget travellers. Dorms are quite crowded, with six to eight bunks in them, but there are also some double rooms if you need more space. There's a communal kitchen, rather tatty-looking shared bathrooms and plenty of cool art in the stairwell.

Pio on Griboyedov MINIHOTEL €€
(Map p172; ☎571 9476; www.hotelpio.ru; nab kanala Griboyedova 35, apt 5; s/d/tr/q with shared bathroom R3400/3800/4800/5400; ; MNevsky Prospekt) This excellent place overlooks the Griboyedova Canal and has six rooms, all of which share three bathrooms and toilets. It's not as hostel-like as it sounds though, much more like staying in a large apartment with friends. The communal areas are very pleasant and the rooms are comfortable and clean.

Moyka 5 MINIHOTEL €€
(Map p172; ☎601 0636; www.hon.ru; nab reki Moyki 5; s/d R5900/6800; ; MNevsky Prospekt) This hotel is part of the Nevsky Hotels chain and has a fantastic location on the Moyka River, behind the Church of the Saviour on Spilled Blood. It's a pretty slick location for a fairly simple hotel, with 24 fairly sterile but perfectly decent rooms that provide all the necessary comforts.

Nevsky Prospekt B&B MINIHOTEL €
(Map p172; ☎8-921 955 3754; www.bnbrussia.com; Nevsky pr 11, apt 8; s/d with shared bathroom incl breakfast R2500/3300; ; MAdmiralteyskaya) This delightfully decorated B&B has just five rooms and is among the city's most charming, with tiled stoves, antique furnishings and the oldest functioning radio and TV you're likely to see anywhere. The only downside is the shared bathroom facilities. Airport transfers are included in the price, but visa support is additional.

Fortecia Peter MINIHOTEL €€
(Фортеция Питер; Map p172; ☎315 0828; www.fortecia.ru; Millionnaya ul 29; r incl breakfast R4500; ; MAdmiralteyskaya) Moments from the Hermitage, this pleasant eight-room place is in a quiet courtyard. While the rooms are a little on the small side, they are perfectly comfortable and more than a little charming with their exposed brickwork and beams.

Stony Island Hotel HOTEL €€
(Map p172; ☎337 2434; www.stonyisland.com; ul Lomonosova 1; r R6500; ; MNevsky Prospekt) Right in the thick of the nightlife hot spot of Dumskaya ul, the Stony Island is for anyone who wants to be in the absolute city centre. The 17 minimalist rooms are in four different categories, and many of them are in interesting shapes thanks to the quirky historic building.

Cuba Hostel HOSTEL €
(Map p172; ☎921 7115; www.cubahostel.ru; Kazanskaya ul 5; dm R500-850, d R2600; ; MNevsky Prospekt) This fun and funky hostel has a super location behind the Kazan Cathedral. Rainbow-coloured paint covers the walls in dorm rooms that are equipped with metal bunk beds and private lockers. Rooms sleep four to 10 people and prices vary accordingly. Bathrooms are cramped, but very clean.

LITEYNY & SMOLNY

Pio on Mokhovaya MINIHOTEL €€
(Map p182; ☎273 3585; www.hotelpio.ru; Mokhovaya ul 39, apt 10; s/d/tr/q R3800/4400/5600/6400; ; MMayakovskaya) While this place lacks the perfect location and canal views of its sister property, it's actually far more spacious, stylish and comfortable than Pio on Griboyedov. It's also very child friendly, with family groups warmly welcomed and provided for.

Hotel Vera HOTEL €€
(Map p182; ☎702 6190; www.hotelvera.ru; Suvorovsky pr 25/16; s/d incl breakfast from R3600/4990; ; MPloshchad Vosstaniya) Housed in a fabulous building from 1903, this well-run option has slanted ceilings, stained-glass windows, ceramic tile stoves and ornate mouldings that remember its art deco origins. It's not all stuck in the past, however – there's satellite TV and fridges in all rooms, and bathrooms are thoroughly modern.

ACCOMMODATION AGENCIES

The following recommended agencies can help you with short-term accommodation in St Petersburg:

» **Bed & Breakfast** (www.bednbreakfast.sp.ru)
» **City Realty** (www.cityrealtyrussia.com)
» **HOFA** (www.hofa.ru)
» **Intro by Irina** (www.introbyirina.com)
» **Travel Russia** (www.travelrussia.su)

WANT MORE?

For in-depth information, reviews and recommendations at your fingertips, head to the Apple App Store to purchase Lonely Planet's *St Petersburg City Guide* iPhone app.

Alternatively, head to **Lonely Planet** (www.lonelyplanet.com/russia/st-petersburg) for planning advice, author recommendations, traveller reviews and insider tips.

Puppet Hostel HOSTEL €
(Map p182; ☎272 5401; www.hostel-puppet.ru; ul Nekrasova 12; dm/d R600/800; ; Mayakovskaya) Offering pretty basic dorms and doubles, it's also an ideal choice if you're travelling with kids because staying here usually includes free tickets to the puppet theatre next door.

VLADIMIRSKAYA & VOSSTANIYA

Helvetia Hotel & Suites HOTEL €€
(Map p184; ☎326 2009; www.helvetiahotel.ru; ul Marata 11; r incl breakfast from R6000; ; Mayakovskaya) Pass through the Helvetia's wrought-iron gates into a wonderfully private and professionally run oasis of calm and class. Guest rooms are less atmospheric, but make up for it in comfort.

Brothers Karamazov BOUTIQUE HOTEL €€
(Map p184; ☎335 1185; www.karamazovhotel.ru; Sotsialisticheskaya ul 11a; s/d from R5500/6500; ; Vladimirskaya) Pack a copy of Dostoevsky's final novel to read while staying at this appealing boutique hotel – the great man penned *The Brothers K* while living in the neighbourhood and in homage, the hotel's 28 charmingly furnished rooms are all named after different female Dostoevsky characters to help you answer that age-old question: which 19th-century fallen woman are you?

TOP CHOICE **Hostel Ligovsky 74** HOSTEL €
(Map p184; ☎329 1274; www.hostel74.ru; Ligovsky pr 74; dm/r R600/1500, design r R2500; ; Ligovsky Prospekt) The 3rd floor of Loft Project ETAGI is given over to this super-friendly hostel. Some of the dorms here are enormous (one has 20 beds in it!) but the facilities are spotless, including washing machines and a small kitchen. As well as the dorms there are three 'design rooms' that are boutique-hotel quality at budget price – reserve ahead, as these are nearly always booked up in advance.

TOP CHOICE **Life Hostel** HOSTEL €
(Map p184; ☎318 1808; www.hostel-life.ru; Nevsky pr 47; dm R800-1000, s/d R2200/2600; ; Mayakovskaya) The 15 brand-new rooms at Life Hostel range from doubles to dorms sleeping eight. There's a big kitchen, clean bathrooms, free laundry and professional English-speaking staff – all in all, a great option.

SENNAYA & KOLOMNA

TOP CHOICE **Andrey & Sasha's Homestay** HOMESTAY €
(Map p188; ☎315 3330, 8-921-409 6701; asamatuga@mail.ru; nab kanala Griboyedova 49; s/d R2400/2800; Sadovaya) Legendary hosts on the St Petersburg homestay and apartment scene, photographer Andrey and doctor Sasha have a couple of apartments they rent rooms in, including this one, which is also their delightfully decorated home.

TOP CHOICE **Alexander House** BOUTIQUE HOTEL €€€
(Map p188; ☎334 3540; www.a-house.ru; nab kanala Kryukova 27; r/ste from R9500/11,000, apt from R15,000; ; Sennaya Ploshchad) Owners Alexander and Natalya have converted this historic building opposite Nikolsky Cathedral, styling each of the 14 spacious rooms after their favourite international cities. Lovely common areas include a fireplace-warmed lounge and a vine-laden courtyard containing a guests-only restaurant.

Arkadia BOUTIQUE HOTEL €€
(Map p188; ☎571 6173; www.arkadiahotel.ru; nab reki Moyki 58; s/d from R4100/5100; ; Admiralteyskaya) Hidden away inside a quiet, flower-filled courtyard, this bright yellow hotel provides a welcome respite from the city's crowds. Warm hues, wood floors and natural lighting characterise the guest rooms.

Northern Lights MINIHOTEL €€
(Map p188; ☎571 9199; www.nlightsrussia.com; Bolshaya Morskaya ul 50; r incl breakfast without bathroom R3000; s/d incl breakfast with bathroom R4000/4300; ; Admiralteyskaya) Opposite the childhood home of Vladimir Nabokov is this very pleasant and friendly minihotel at the end of an impressive old staircase. There are just five rooms here: three have their own bathrooms and air-con, while two share facilities and are fan-cooled.

Graffiti Hostel HOSTEL €

(Map p188; ☎714 7038; www.graffitihostel.ru; nab reki Moyki 102; dm from R450, d R2000; 📶; MSennaya Ploshchad) You should have no trouble finding this new hostel, as its fabulously painted exterior sets it apart from the nearby buildings. The interior is far more simple – basic, even – but the shared bathrooms are clean enough and some even have views of St Isaac's Cathedral from their balconies.

VASILYEVSKY ISLAND

Sokos Hotel Vasilyevsky HOTEL €€

(Map p192; ☎335 2290; www.sokoshotels.com; 8-ya liniya 11-13; r from R6700; ❄📶; MVasileostrovskaya) This sleek and well-designed place is aimed at the upper end of the holiday market. The rooms are spacious, with nice design touches, while the large Repin Lounge downstairs takes care of all food and drink needs.

Our Hotel HOTEL €€€

(Nash Hotel; ☎323 2231; www.nashotel.ru; 11-ya liniya 50; s/d R8500/9400; ❄📶; MVasileostrovskaya) This very tall, beautifully remodelled building on a quiet Vasilyevsky Island side street has a striking exterior and its rooms are ablaze with colours, complete with modern furnishings and great views from the higher rooms. The odd garish touch aside, this is a smart and stylish place to stay.

PETROGRAD & VYBORG SIDE

Tradition Hotel HOTEL €€€

(Map p196; ☎405 8855; www.traditionhotel.ru; pr Dobrolyubova 2; s/d incl breakfast R8300/8900; ❄📶; MSportivnaya) Facing the Hermitage across the river, this great little hotel is a consistent traveller favourite, boasting many return guests due to its smiling and extremely helpful staff who really go out of their way for their guests.

Apart-Hotel Kronverk HOTEL €€

(Map p196; ☎703 3663; www.kronverk.com; ul Blokhina 9; r R4370, apt from R8480; ❄📶; MSportivnaya) Occupying the upper floors of a slick business centre, the Kronverk offers appealingly modern rooms with self-catering facilities. Frosted glass and streamlined black panelling create a crisp reception area where the English-speaking staff are efficient and professional.

Eating

St Petersburg has an ever-improving restaurant scene, with places to suit all budgets and tastes. It may have taken two decades since the end of communism, but finally Petersburg has become a place where good food is prized and defined not by its high price tag but rather by the talents of the chef. You certainly have to pay for quality in

THE BRIDGES OF ST PETERSBURG

Some 342 bridges span St Petersburg's network of canals and waterways. With the exception of the new Big Obukhovsky, all of the *mosty* (bridges) across the Neva are drawbridges. From the end of April to November they are raised every evening at designated times to let the ships pass, a spectacle that is worth seeing (see p224 for the schedule). Some of the most charming bridges, though, are the smaller structures that span the canals around the city. Here are a few of our favourites:

» **Anichkov most** (Map p172) Features rearing horses at all four corners, symbolising humanity's struggle with, and taming of, nature.

» **Bankovsky most** (Map p172) Suspended by cables emerging from the mouths of golden-winged griffins. The name comes from the Assignment Bank (now a university), which stands on one side of the bridge.

» **Most Lomonosova** Four Doric towers contain the mechanism that pulls up the moveable central section, allowing tall boats to pass along the Fontanka underneath.

» **Lviny most** (Bridge of Four Lions; Map p188) Another suspension bridge, this one is supported by two pairs of regal lions.

» **Panteleymonovsky most** (Map p172) At the confluence of the Moyka and the Fontanka, this beauty features lamp posts bedecked with the double-headed eagle and railings adorned with the coat of arms.

» **1-y Inzhenerny most** (First Engineer Bridge; Map p172) While there is no shortage of adornment on the cast-iron bridge leading to Mikhailovsky Castle, the highlight is the Chizhik-Pyzhik, the statue of the little bird that hovers over the Moyka.

most cases, and it's worth planning where you'd like to eat rather than leaving it to the last moment and choosing the nearest place, as the good places are rarely the most obvious, and you may have to reserve for the very best.

Many places have bargain business lunch deals for around R150 to R250 and offer 15% discounts to diners eating before 4pm, making lunch the most economical time to eat out.

HISTORIC HEART

TOP CHOICE MiX in St Petersburg INTERNATIONAL €€€
(Map p172; ☎610 6166; www.wstpetersburg.com; Voznesensky pr 6; mains R1000-1500; ⏲noon-3pm & 7pm-midnight; Ⓜ Admiralteyskaya) MiX is St Petersburg's first celebrity chef restaurant, the first Russian venture of French cookery star Alain Ducasse. Several dazzlingly glamorous rooms surround an open kitchen from which sublime yet unfussy gourmet dishes are served. Service and atmosphere are both top-notch.

TOP CHOICE Soup Vino ITALIAN €
(Суп вино; Map p172; www.supvino.ru; Kazanskaya ul 24; mains R200-500; Ⓜ Nevsky Prospekt) This cute, tiny place does exactly what it says on the label. The menu features Mediterranean-influenced soups, pasta and salads – perfect washed down with a glass of wine.

TOP CHOICE Stolle BAKERY €
(Столле; www.stolle.ru; pies R50-200; ⏲8am-10pm;) Konyushenny per (Map p172; Konyushenny per 1/6; Ⓜ Nevsky Prospekt); ul Dekabristov (Map p188; ul Dekabristov 33; Ⓜ Sadovaya); ul Dekabristov (Map p188; ul Dekabristov 19 Ⓜ Sadovaya); ul Vosstaniya (Map p182; ul Vosstaniya 32; Ⓜ Chernyshevskaya); Vasilyevsky Island (Map p192; 1-ya linii 50; Ⓜ Vasileostrovskaya) The delicious, freshly baked Saxon-style pies ('*stolle*') are legendary in St Petersburg, and a selection of sweet and savoury offerings sits on the counter, fresh from the oven any time of day. Takeaway is available.

Terrassa EUROPEAN €€
(Map p172; ☎937 6837; www.terrassa.ru; Kazanskaya ul 3a; mains R450-1000; ⏲11am-1am, from noon Sat & Sun; Ⓜ Nevsky Prospekt) Atop the Vanity shopping centre, this cool bistro boasts unbelievable views towards Kazan Cathedral. In the open kitchen, chefs busily prepare fusion cuisine, exhibiting influences from Italy, Asia and beyond.

Café King Pong ASIAN €€
(Map p172; www.kingpong.ru; Bolshaya Morskaya ul 16; mains R300-600; Ⓜ Admiralteyskaya) From the team that brings you the excellent Soup Vino and Testo comes this innovative and fun pan-Asian diner, occupying sleek and luminous premises with a retro-glamorous feel just off Nevsky. The large, good-quality menu takes in dim sum, noodles, soups and rice dishes.

Baku AZERI €€€
(Баку; Map p172; www.baku-spb.ru; Sadovaya ul 12/23; mains R300-1600; Ⓜ Gostiny Dvor) Tiled walls, arched doorways and scatter cushions whisk you away to Azerbaijan. Try famous Azeri shashlyk (kebabs) as well as delicious *kutab,* thin pancakes stuffed with different fillings. Service is deferential, and there's an upstairs room if you don't fancy the nightly live music downstairs.

Garçon FRENCH €
(Гарсон; Map p172; www.garcon.ru; nab kanala Griboyedova 25; sandwiches R200; Ⓜ Nevsky Prospekt) Finding a decent sandwich in this town can be a Herculean feat, so discovering this *boulangerie* chain's outlet just off Nevsky pr is very welcome indeed. Freshly made sandwiches in freshly baked baguettes, not to mention a great range of cakes and other treats, are all available to stay or go.

Fiolet INTERNATIONAL €€€
(Map p172; nab reki Fontanki 55; mains R500-1000; Ⓜ Gostiny Dvor) The restaurant of the excellent Rossi Hotel is a beautiful contemporary space with plush leather sofas, wooden floorboards and a popular summer terrace overlooking the Fontanka. The Asian-European menu includes such delights from fresh oysters to miso-marinated beef with *tobiko* (caviar) rolls.

Entrecôte FRENCH €€
(Map p172; www.probka.org; Bolshaya Morskaya ul 25; mains R400-700; ⏲9am-midnight; Ⓜ Admiralteyskaya) The very stylish design of this French steakhouse draws you in, with traditional white linen tablecloths under an exposed-brick interior with sleek minimalist touches. Rib-eye steaks, including *wagyu,* are the speciality here, though there's a full menu of modern French cooking and decent breakfasts too.

Dve Palochki ASIAN €€
(Две палочки; www.dvepalochki.ru; mains R200-600; ⏲11am-6pm) Bolshoy pr (Map p196; Bolshoy

pr 74; Ⓜ Petrogradskaya); Italianskaya ul (Map p172; Italianskaya ul 6; Ⓜ Nevsky Prospekt); Nevsky pr (Map p172; Nevsky pr 22; Ⓜ Nevsky Prospekt); Sredny pr (Map p192; Sredny pr 16; Ⓜ Vasileostrovskaya); ul Vosstaniya (Map p182; ul Vosstaniya 15; Ⓜ Ploshchad Vosstaniya) This local chain is one of the most sophisticated of the ubiquitous sushi bars in the city. The central branches are always packed with a trendy crowd.

Zoom Café EUROPEAN €€
(Map p172; www.cafezoom.ru; Gorokhovaya ul 22; meals R100-400; ⏲9am-midnight Mon-Sat, from 1pm Sun; Ⓜ Sennaya Ploshchad) Perennially popular café with a funky feel and an interesting menu. Zoom does everything from Japanese-style chicken in teriyaki sauce to potato pancakes with salmon and cream cheese. A great lunch spot.

Ne Goruy GEORGIAN €€
(Не горюй; Map p172; www.negoruy.ru; Kirpichny per 3; mains R200-500; Ⓜ Admiralteyskaya) The strangely named 'Don't Grieve' is actually a great little Georgian spot in the heart of the city centre where you can fill up on *khachapuri* (cheese bread) and lots of other spicy and delicious dishes from the Caucasus. No need for regret indeed.

Kilikia ARMENIAN €€
(Киликия; Map p172; www.kilikia.restoran.ru; Gorokhovaya ul 26/40; mains R200-600; ⏲10.30am-6am; Ⓜ Sennaya Ploshchad) Excellent-value tasty Caucasian dishes at this cosy Armenian place. Has live music most evenings.

Tandoori Nights INDIAN €€
(Map p172; Voznesensky pr 4; meals R350-850; Ⓜ Admiralteyskaya) Stylish Indian restaurant offering a mix of tasty traditional and modern recipes, road-tested by a top London-Indian chef.

Park Giuseppe ITALIAN €€€
(Парк Джузеппе; Map p172; www.park-restaurant.ru; nab kanala Griboyedova 2b; mains R450-1000; Ⓜ Nevsky Prospekt) Dine on crispy pizza and creamy pasta dishes at this appealing Italian restaurant overlooking the Mikhailovsky Gardens. It has a pleasant outdoor area in summer.

Chaynaya Lozhka RUSSIAN €
(Чайная ложка; Map p172; www.teaspoon.ru; Nevsky pr 44; mains R30-100; ⏲9am-9pm; Ⓜ Gostiny Dvor) This reliable Russian fast-food chain has branches all over the city. It offers very cheap bliny, fresh salads and soups.

Teremok RUSSIAN €
(Теремок; Map p172; www.teremok.ru; Nevsky pr 60; bliny R50-150; ⏲10am-10pm; Ⓜ Gostiny Dvor) Teremok serves all kinds of bliny out of kiosks and cafés. We've listed one central outlet but you can find them across the city.

LITEYNY & SMOLNY

TOP CHOICE **Botanika** VEGETARIAN €€
(Ботаника; Map p182; www.cafebotanika.ru; ul Pestelya 7; mains R200-450; Ⓜ Gostiny Dvor) Enjoying perhaps the friendliest and most laid-back atmosphere of any restaurant in St Petersburg, this vegetarian charmer wins on all counts. The menu takes in Russian, Indian, Italian and Japanese dishes, all of which are good, and service is friendly.

TOP CHOICE **Kompot Café** INTERNATIONAL €€
(Первое, второе и компот; Map p182; www.kompotcafe.ru; ul Zhukovskogo 10; mains R200-600; Ⓜ Ploshchad Vosstaniya) This new restaurant has three rooms decked out in different stylish decors. The menu stretches from breakfasts served all day long to soups, sandwiches, pies and 'funky tomato bouillabaisse'.

Makarov RUSSIAN €€
(Макаров; Map p182; ☎327 0053; Manezhny per 2; mains R500-800; ⏲9am-11pm Tue-Fri, from 11am Sat-Mon; Ⓜ Chernyshevskaya) A charming place overlooking the Cathedral of the Transfiguration of our Saviour, Makarov serves up traditional Russian dishes with a twist in a relaxed setting. Good breakfasts are served daily until noon, and until 2pm on weekends (reservations are essential).

Molokhovets' Dream RUSSIAN €€€
(Мечта Молоховец; Map p182; ☎929 2247; www.molokhovets.ru; ul Radishcheva 10; mains R1200-1600; Ⓜ Ploshchad Vosstaniya) Inspired by the cookbook of Yelena Molokhovets, the Russian Mrs Beeton, the menu at this compact, elegant restaurant covers the classics from borsch to beef stroganoff. The speciality is *koulibiaca,* a golden pastry pie of either fish or rabbit and cabbage – preorder or be prepared to wait an hour as it's cooked fresh. Whatever you have here, you can be sure it's the definitive version; book ahead for dinner.

VLADIMIRSKAYA & VOSSTANIYA

TOP CHOICE **Dom Beat** INTERNATIONAL €€
(Дом Быта; Map p184; www.dombeat.ru; ul Razyezzhaya 12; mains R300-500; Ⓜ Ligovsky

Prospekt) The sleek, retro-humorous interior, sumptuous menu and great atmosphere make this one of the best eating choices in town. As well as great breakfasts (served until 7pm!), there's a wide choice of dishes ranging from top-notch Asian cuisine to modern takes on Russian meals and international bar food.

Fartuk INTERNATIONAL €€

(Фартук; Map p184; ul Rubinshteyna 15/17; mains R200-300; Mayakovskaya) Despite its unfortunate name, Fartuk is a beautifully designed place with tiled floors and old-world-meets-industrial fittings. The crowd here is cool and the menu is interesting: wok-cooked chicken with ginger and coriander sits next to freshly made bruschetta, soups and steaks.

Schaste ITALIAN €€

(Счастье; Map p184; www.schaste-est.com; ul Rubinshteyna 15/17; mains R200-700; 8am-midnight, to 6am Fri & Sat; Mayakovskaya) 'Happiness' comes in several forms here: a multiroomed venue full of cosy nooks and crannies to huddle up in, an expansive and interesting Italian menu, delicious pastries and sweets piled up on plates around the place, and a lavish and thoroughly warm, if somewhat random, decor.

Bistro Garçon FRENCH €€

(Бистро Гарсон; Map p184; www.garcon.ru; Nevsky pr 95; mains R250-500; 10am-midnight; Ploshchad Vosstaniya) This gorgeous little bistro is smart and unpretentious, with low lighting and professional staff. Prices are reasonable given the excellent standard of the cooking. While this is the main restaurant of the group in town, you can find its bakeries, which serve up excellent sandwiches, all over St Petersburg.

Mops THAI €€

(Map p184; www.mopscafe.ru; ul Rubinshteyna 12; mains R300-700; 1pm-midnight Tue-Sun; Mayakovskaya) The first and only dedicated Thai restaurant in the city is a visual treat: the elegant dining room is all white painted floorboards and linen tablecloths, embellished with gorgeous Thai furniture. Dishes tend to be on the small side.

Troitsky Most VEGETARIAN €

(Троицкий Мост; mains R150-200; 9am-11pm) Historic Heart (Map p172; nab reki Moyki 30; Nevsky Prospekt); Kamennoostrovsky pr (Map p196; Kamennoostrovsky pr 9/2; Gorkovskaya); Zagorodny pr (Map p184; Zagorodny pr 38; Dostoevskaya) The Zagorodny pr branch is one of the nicest in this chain of vegetarian cafés, while the Moyka outlet is the most conveniently located. The Petrograd Side branch on Kamennoostrovsky pr, facing the bridge after which it is named, is the original. Whichever one you eat in, this cheap and friendly chain is great and the mushroom lasagne legendary.

Baltic Bread BAKERY €

(Балтийский Хлеб; Map p184; Vladimirsky pr 19; snacks R100-200; Dostoevskaya) This British-run bakery in the Vladimirsky Passage shopping centre is a great spot for picking up fresh bread, cakes and ready-made sandwiches on the run. You can take away or eat in the small café area provided. The **original branch** (Map p182; Grechesky pr 25; Ploshchad Vosstaniya) is on Grechesky pr.

SENNAYA & KOLOMNA

TOP CHOICE **Teplo** INTERNATIONAL €€

(Тепло; Map p188; 570 1974; www.v-teple.ru; Bolshaya Morskaya ul 45; mains R250-650; 9am-11pm, from 11am Sat, from 1pm Sun;

HISTORIC RAILWAY STATIONS

As the birthplace of Russia's railway system, it's not surprising that St Petersburg has some grand stations. The oldest and most elegant is **Vitebsky vokzal** (Vitebsk Station; Map p184; Pushkinskaya), originally built in 1837 for the line to Tsarskoe Selo. The current building dates from 1904 and is partly graced with gorgeous Style Moderne interiors.

While you're at **Moskovsky vokzal** (Moscow Station; Map p184; Ploshchad Vosstaniya), look up at the expansive ceiling mural in the main entrance hall. There's also a striking giant bust of Peter the Great in the hall leading to the platforms.

Finlyandsky vokzal (Finland Station; Map p164; Ploshchad Lenina), rebuilt after WWII, is famous as the place where, in April 1917, Lenin arrived from exile and gave his legendary speech atop an armoured car. When the progress of the revolution began to look iffy, it was from here that Lenin hightailed it off to Finland, only to return again in October to seize power. Lenin's statue, pointing across the Neva towards the old KGB headquarters, stands outside the station.

MAdmiralteyskaya) This much-fêted, eclectic and original restaurant has got it all just right. Service is friendly and fast (when it's not too busy), and the peppy, inventive menu will have something for everyone – there's a heavy Italian presence, but dishes come from all over the world. Reservations are usually essential, so call ahead.

TOP CHOICE Mansard INTERNATIONAL €€€
(Map p188; 946 4303; www.ginza-mansarda.ru; Pochtamtskaya ul 3; mains R500-1400; MAdmiralteyskaya) This extraordinary addition to St Petersburg's eating scene definitely has the best views in town: indeed, you can almost touch the dome of St Isaac's Cathedral from the beautifully designed main room. But it's no one-trick pony; the superb menu is assuredly international, and its chefs are equally adept at producing langoustine and asparagus risotto as they are a gourmet chicken Kiev. Book ahead to be sure of a table with a view.

Sadko RUSSIAN €€
(Садко; Map p188; www.sadko-rst.ru; ul Glinki 2; mains R330-650; ; MSennaya Ploshchad) This impressive restaurant's decor applies traditional floral designs to a slick contemporary style. Serving all the Russian favourites, Sadko has a great children's room and is ideal as a pre- or post-Mariinsky Theatre dining option. The waiters, many of them music students at the local conservatory, give impromptu vocal performances.

Russian Vodkaroom No 1 RUSSIAN €€
(Map p188; www.vodkaroom.ru; Konnogvardeysky bul 4; mains R450-800; ; MAdmiralteyskaya) This charming, welcoming place is the restaurant of the Russian Vodka Museum, but it's good enough to be a destination in its own right. The interior enjoys a grand old-world feel, as does the menu: leg of roast suckling pig, stewed venison tongue and whole fried Gatchina trout take you back to imperial tastes and opulence.

Entrée FRENCH €€
(Map p188; Nikolskaya pl 6; sandwiches R200, mains R400-700; MSennaya Ploshchad) Entrée comes in two parts: the café to the right has delicious cakes and sandwiches, an attractive tiled counter and, for some reason, Michael Douglas' signature scrawled on the wall. To the right is a far more formal restaurant with a classic but clever French menu and a huge wine list. Service could be a little friendlier, but otherwise this place is a great find in an otherwise barren part of town.

Stroganoff Steak House STEAKHOUSE €€
(Map p188; www.stroganoffsteakhouse.ru; Konnogvardeysky bul 5; mains R400-1000; ; MSennaya Ploshchad) Beef lovers can indulge their habit at this 12,000-sq-metre restaurant, the city's biggest. Thanks to clever design, though, it doesn't feel overwhelmingly large or impersonal. The steaks are large enough to share. There's a fun children's playroom here, making it good for young families.

Idiot VEGETARIAN €€
(Map p188; www.idiot-spb.com; nab reki Moyki 82; mains R600-900; 11am-1am; ; MSennaya Ploshchad) This long-running vegetarian café charms with its prerevolutionary atmosphere. It's an ideal place to visit for a nightcap or supper after attending the Mariinsky, as its kitchen stays open late.

VASILYEVSKY ISLAND

TOP CHOICE Restoran RUSSIAN €€
(Ресторанъ; Map p192; www.elbagroup.ru; Tamozhenny per 2; mains R300-1200; ; MAdmiralteyskaya) This beautifully designed and understated restaurant manages to combine the best of *haute-russe* cuisine with enough modern flare to keep things interesting: try duck baked with apples or traditional Russian chicken pie with pickled cep mushrooms.

Gintarus LITHUANIAN €€
(Map p192; Sredny pr 5; mains R300-600; ; MVasileostrovskaya) Sumptuously decorated in dark woods and enjoying a very homey feel, this Lithuanian restaurant is a great spot for a smart and interesting meal. If Lithuanian cuisine doesn't exactly get your mouth watering, then there are plenty of other dishes, including a range of delicious soups and lots of grilled meats.

Cheburechnaya CAUCASIAN €
(Чебуречная; Map p192; 6-ya liniya i 7-ya liniya 19; mains R100-200; MVasileostrovskaya) An authentic *stolovaya* (canteen) that continues to do what it has been doing well for decades. Go right when you enter and place your order at the cash register. Try the namesake *cheburechka,* a delicious Georgian meat-stuffed pastry.

PETROGRAD SIDE

TOP CHOICE Mesto INTERNATIONAL €€
(Место; Map p196; Kronverksky pr 59; mains R300-600; 11am-midnight; ; MGorkovskaya) This delightful place has been winning fans

for a decade now. After a recent refit it's looking better than ever, with a beautiful glass and marble counter and upholstered benches you could almost fall asleep on. The menu is eccentric but interesting and in the evening the owner will often play the piano, rounding off a great little Petrograd find.

TOP CHOICE **Chekhov** RUSSIAN €€
(Чехов; Map p196; Petropavlovskaya ul 4; mains R350-700; ; Petrogradskaya) Despite a totally nondescript appearance from the street, this Russian restaurant's charming interior perfectly recalls a 19th-century dacha, and makes for a wonderful setting for any meal. The menu (not to mention the staff's attire) is very traditional and features lovingly prepared Russian classics.

Salkhino GEORGIAN €€
(Салхино; Map p196; Kronverksky pr 25; mains R300-600; ; Gorkovskaya) An excellent Georgian restaurant, Salkhino serves big portions of delicious food in a convivial, arty setting where you feel more like a guest in someone's house than a customer.

Volna INTERNATIONAL €€
(Волна; Map p196; www.volna.su; Petrovskaya nab 5; mains R200-500; ; Gorkovskaya) This sleek and wonderfully laid-back lounge restaurant has a terrace perfect for a relaxed lunch over a bottle of wine. Inside it's a bit more upmarket, but remains unfussy. The large menu ranges from risotto, salads and pasta to a selection of Asian dishes from the wok.

Drinking

A city of midnight hedonists, St Petersburg has plenty of bars, pubs and cafés where you can enjoy a cold beer, a hot coffee or a strong cocktail at almost any time of day. Coffee culture arrived in the city a decade ago and is flourishing with numerous chains devoted to serving up fresh beans or the perfect tea infusion, although the most atmospheric places for a caffeine injection remain the independent cafés rather than the truly ubiquitous chain gang.

For drinking, you can wet your whistle almost anywhere – even in smart restaurants you're generally welcome to come in and order just a beer, while the city's best cocktail bars are truly superb. The undoubted centre of the drinking scene is Dumskaya ul and ul Lomonosova, home to dozens of bars and clubs and a sea of drunken students after midnight at the weekends. The more underground drinking scene can be found in the bars and music venues around Ligovsky pr in Vosstaniya.

HISTORIC HEART

Radio Baby BAR
(Map p172; www.radiobaby.com; Kazanskaya ul 7; 6pm-6am; Nevsky Prospekt) The barn-like bar here is divided into several different rooms, each with distinct atmospheres. There's cool lighting throughout, a 'no techno, no house' music policy, table football, a cool crowd and an atmosphere of eternal hedonism. Go through the arch at Kazanskaya ul 5, then turn left through a second arch to find this place.

Bar with No Name BAR
(Map p172; Bankovsky per 3; 6pm-6am; Sennaya Ploshchad) Follow your ears into the courtyard behind Friends Hostel: music will be coming from one of the basements – this is the bar with no name and it's hard enough to find to remain truly cool. Expect dancing, table football and a beautiful young crowd.

MiXup Bar BAR
(Map p172; www.wstpetersburg.com; Voznesensky pr 6; 1pm-midnight Sun-Thu, to 2am Fri & Sat; Admiralteyskaya) This superb new cocktail bar tops off St Petersburg's most fashionable hotel and offers fantastic city views from its Antonio Citterio–designed lounge. The rooftop is an even cooler terrace, with seating in cosy cabanas and views straight onto St Isaac's Cathedral.

Other Side PUB
(Map p172; www.theotherside.ru; Bolshaya Konyushennaya ul 1; ; Nevsky Prospekt) There's live music most nights at this fun and funky bar, as well as decent food (mains R200 to R400), but most people turn up to enjoy the seven beers on tap and other alcoholic libations.

Tinkoff BREWERY
(Map p172; www.tinkof.ru; Kazanskaya ul 7; noon-2am; Nevsky Prospekt) Set inside a microbrewery that also does a good line in German food, Tinkoff is a great place to sample one of eight beers brewed on-site and enjoy the live music in this unusual industrial space.

Tribunal Bar BAR
(Map p172; www.tribunal.ru; Karavannaya ul 26; 9pm-6am; Gostiny Dvor) This is something of a St Petersburg institution, famous for the debauchery and decadence that sets in as soon as the crowd has had enough to drink.

Scantily clad women dancing on the bar are practically guaranteed.

Café Singer CAFÉ

(Кафе Зингер; Map p172; Nevsky pr 28; 9am-11pm; Nevsky Prospekt) On the 2nd floor of the iconic Singer building, now home to the city's biggest bookshop, Dom Knigi, this great café has fantastic views of the Kazan Cathedral and the bustle of Nevsky pr through its huge windows.

LITEYNY & SMOLNY

TOP CHOICE **Zhopa** BAR

(Map p182; pr Bakunina 6; 8pm-1am Sun-Thu, to 8am Fri & Sat; Ploshchad Vosstaniya) This funky, hip and largely unknown place (the sign on the front door is just the letter Ж) is a hideaway for the cool kids. Inside it's a treasure trove of fairy lights, umbrellas hanging from the ceiling, tapestries on the walls and kitschy chandeliers.

TOP CHOICE **Probka** WINE BAR

(Пробка; Map p182; www.probka.org; ul Belinskogo 5; 1pm-1am; Gostiny Dvor) You'll feel you could almost be in Rome when you enter this charming wine bar just off Liteyny pr. Tile floors and terracotta walls recall an Italian *enoteca,* with its shelves stocked with wine bottles and liqueurs.

PIEROGI BAR

(Map p182; nab reki Fontanki 40; 24hr; ; Gostiny Dvor) The long-established Moscow chain of boho bookshop-cum-bars has now established itself in the northern capital just moments from Nevsky. It's divided into smoking and nonsmoking rooms, enjoys a very casual feel and is favoured by a young crowd.

VLADIMIRSKAYA & VOSSTANIYA

TOP CHOICE **Dyuni** BAR

(Дюны; Map p184; Ligovsky pr 50; 24hr; Ploshchad Vosstaniya) St Petersburg's hippest bar this summer (don't worry, there will be another one along shortly) is this hipster sandpit at the back of the large warehouse complex in the courtyard of Ligovsky 50. There's a cosy indoor bar and a sprawling sand-covered outside area with table football and ping pong. To find it, simply continue in a straight line from the entrance to the courtyard.

Terminal Bar BAR

(Терминал; Map p182; ul Rubinshteyna 13a; 4pm-6am; Dostoevskaya) A slice of New York bohemia on one of St Petersburg's most happening streets, Terminal is a great place for a relaxed drink with friends, who can spread out along the length of the enormous bar, while live piano from anyone who can play fills the long, arched room.

Dom Beat COCKTAIL BAR

(Дом Быта; Map p184; www.dombeat.ru; ul Razyezzhaya 12; midday-6am; Ligovsky Prospekt) The big draw at this café-bar-lounge-club-restaurant is its superb cocktails and wide drinks menu. Funky '70s interior, a cool crowd and tables cleared for dancing later on in the evening make this a great spot.

SENNAYA & KOLOMNA

Hundertwasser Bar BAR

(Map p188; www.hundertwasserbar.com; Teatralnaya pl 4; noon-11.30pm; Sadovaya) Popular with students from the Rimsky-Korsakov Conservatory across the street, and often hosting informal jam sessions, Hundertwasser Bar is a very pleasant, bohemian spot to drink, with two comfortable rooms stuffed full of old furniture. Perfect for lounging.

Stirka BAR

(Стирка; Map p188; www.40gradusov.ru; Kazanskaya ul 26; 10am-1am; Nevsky Prospekt) This friendly joint has three washing machines, so you can drop off a load and have a few beers while you wait for it to finish. A novel idea, though one few people seem to take advantage of: Stirka is mainly a casual dive bar where people drop in for drinks and the odd art show or live performance.

Bardak BAR

(Бардак; Map p188; www.bardak-bar.com; Grivtsova pr 11; noon-3am Sun-Thu, to 6am Fri & Sat; Sennaya Ploshchad) One of the few recommendable bars around insalubrious Sennaya pl, Bardak nevertheless has a fairly grizzled student clientele. The exposed brick walls plastered with photos, rickety mezzanine level and dishevelled but hip crowd explain why this groovy little bar was named after the Russian word for 'mess'.

VASILYEVSKY ISLAND

Helsinki Bar BAR

(Map p192; www.helsinkibar.ru; Kadetskaya liniya 31; noon-2am; Vasileostrovskaya) A slice of neighbouring Finland in the heart of St Petersburg, this place is hands down the coolest place to drink on Vasilyevsky Island. The vibe is retro throughout, with vinyl-spinning DJs, '70s Finnish ads on the walls, vintage furniture and Finnish home cooking on the menu.

Grad Petrov BREWERY
(Градъ Петровъ; Map p192; www.gradpetrov.com; Universitetskaya nab 5; ⏲from noon; Ⓜ Admiralteyskaya) Fresh-brewed lager, Weizen, Pilsner, Dunkel and Hefeweizen – it's reason enough to stop by this upmarket German microbrewery on Vasilyevsky Island.

☆ Entertainment

St Petersburg offers world-class classical music, ballet and opera performances, often at a fraction of the price you'd pay at home, even when there are hefty mark-ups on tickets for foreigners. As well as high culture, there's plenty of fun to be had clubbing, listening to live music and at the cinema and circus. Check the *St Petersburg Times* for current listings.

Tickets

Box offices at some of the city's venues, including the Mariinsky, Mikhailovsky and Hermitage theatres, charge higher foreigners' prices. If you can prove that you're working or studying in Russia, you'll pay the Russian price. If you purchase a Russian ticket and your cover is blown inside the theatre (an embarrassing experience), you'll be made to pay the difference by rabid babushkas. Scalpers usually sell last-minute tickets outside the theatre an hour before the show. These will be Russian tickets, and if they're for a sold-out show, there will be a hefty mark-ups. Check the ticket carefully and make sure that the date and seat position promised are correct – there are fakes around.

There are ticket-booking kiosks and offices all over the city; one of the handiest for all types of performance is the **Theatre Ticket Office** (Театральные кассы; Map p172; Nevsky pr 42; ⏲10am-9pm; Ⓜ Gostiny Dvor).

Cinemas

Check out Friday's *St Petersburg Times* for full cinema listings. Movie theatres line Nevsky pr, but practically all of the Western films played at them are dubbed.

Dom Kino CINEMA
(Дом кино; Map p172; www.domkino.spb.ru; Karavannaya ul 12; Ⓜ Gostiny Dvor) Arty Russian and foreign films, as well as some higher-brow Hollywood productions, screen here. This is also where the British Council holds its British Film Festival. In the same building you'll also find the art-house cinema **Rodina** (Родина; www.rodinakino.ru).

Avrora CINEMA
(Аврора; Map p172; www.avrora.spb.ru; Nevsky pr 60; Ⓜ Gostiny Dvor) The young Dmitry Shostakovich once played piano accompaniment to silent movies here. Today it's more about Hollywood and locally produced blockbusters.

Live Music

St Petersburg has long been the centre of Russian rock music, sprouting such influential Soviet bands as Akvarium and Kino from its legendary underground, and is still home to numerous famous groups today. Its live music scene remains exciting and vibrant, with a large selection of venues, both mainstream and – particularly – underground, to choose from. As well as rock, punk and pop, jazz remains hugely popular and the city is the best place in Russia to see it performed live.

Fish Fabrique Nouvelle LIVE MUSIC
(Map p184; www.fishfabrique.spb.ru; 1st fl, Ligovsky pr 53; ⏲3pm-6am, concerts from 8pm Thu-Sun; Ⓜ Ploshchad Vosstaniya) Here in this museum of boho, life artists, musicians and wannabes of all ages meet to drink beer and listen to music. Live bands kick up a storm from 8pm nightly.

Chinese Pilot Dzhao-Da LIVE MUSIC
(Китайский лётчик Джао Да; Map p182; www.spb.jao-da.com; ul Pestelya 7; cover R100-200 for concerts; ⏲noon-midnight; Ⓜ Gostiny Dvor) This is the Petersburg incarnation of the well-established Moscow venue of the same name, and it's one of the very best places to see live music in the city. The premises are charming – the main bar area is bathed in light with plenty of seating and a genial buzz all day, while in the back room, there's a stage and more seating for gigs.

Zoccolo LIVE MUSIC
(Цоколь; Map p182; www.zoccolo.ru; 3-ya Sovetskaya ul 2/3; cover R100; ⏲noon-midnight Sun-Thu, to 6am Fri & Sat, concerts 8pm; Ⓜ Ploshchad Vosstaniya) Zoccolo, in its urgently orange and green underground space near pl Vosstaniya, has slowly become another institution of St Petersburg's music scene. Entry is free before 5pm, when the venue functions as an arty café.

Dusche LIVE MUSIC
(Душе; Map p184; www.dusche.ru; Ligovsky pr 50; cover free-R500; ⏲8pm-2am Sun-Thu, to 6am Fri &

Sat; ⓂPloshchad Vosstaniya) Dusche is owned by members of two locally famous groups, Leningrad and Spitfire. Here you'll find nightly DJs and live music as well as a laid-back party atmosphere and the occasional art show or drama performance. To find it, go through the arch into the courtyard, take the first left, then turn right, and Dusche is on your left.

JFC Jazz Club JAZZ CLUB
(Map p182; ☎272 9850; www.jfc-club.spb.ru; Shpalernaya ul 33; cover R100-500; ⊙7-11pm; ⓂChernyshevskaya) Very small and very New York, this cool club is the best place in the city to hear modern, innovative jazz music, as well as the occasional blues, bluegrass and various other styles (see the website for a list of what's on). Table reservations are a good idea.

Jazz Philharmonic Hall JAZZ CLUB
(Филармония Джазовой Музыки; Map p184; www.jazz-hall.spb.ru; Zagorodny pr 27; cover R100-200; ⊙concerts 7pm Wed-Sun, Ellington Hall concerts 8pm Tue, Fri & Sat; ⓂVladimirskaya) Representing the traditional side of jazz, two resident bands perform straight jazz and Dixieland. Foreign guests appear doing mainstream and modern jazz.

Classical Music, Opera & Ballet

Mariinsky Theatre BALLET, OPERA
(Мариинский театр оперы и балета; Map p188; www.mariinsky.ru; Teatralnaya pl 1; ⊙box office 11am-7pm, performances 7pm; ⓂSennaya Ploshchad) Home to the world-famous Mariinsky Ballet and Opera company, a visit here is a must, if only to delight in the sparkling glory of the interior. Use the website to book and pay for tickets in advance of your visit to the theatre or to the acoustically splendid new **concert hall** (Концертный зал Мариинского театра; ul Pisareva 20), which is nearby. Don't miss (how can you?) the **New Mariinsky Theatre** (ul Dekabristov 34), across the Kryukova Canal.

Shostakovich Philharmonia Bolshoy Zal CLASSICAL MUSIC
(Большой зал филармонии Шостаковича, Grand Hall; Map p172; www.philharmonia.spb.ru; Mikhailovskaya ul 2; ⓂNevsky Prospekt) Under the artistic direction of world-famous conductor Yury Temirkanov, the St Petersburg Philharmonic Orchestra represents the finest in orchestral music. The Bolshoy Zal on pl Iskusstv is the venue for a full program of symphonic performances, while the

REIMAGINING THE CITY

Ever since Peter the Great, the St Petersburg powers-that-be have traditionally deferred to foreign architects for major construction projects, something that hasn't changed much in three centuries. Today firms such as Foster & Partners, RMJM and Diamond & Schmitt are influencing how St Petersburg transitions architecturally into the 21st century.

Canadian firm Diamond & Schmitt is the designer of the **New Mariinsky Theatre** (Map p188), behind the present theatre. The project to construct much-needed modern premises for the Mariinsky began a decade ago when an extraordinary original design by Dominique Perrault was accepted, scandalising and exciting locals in equal measure. Perrault's proposed black marble building was to be wrapped in a vast, irregular golden glass dome, and would have totally broken with St Petersburg's architectural tradition, but it fell foul of local building codes and – crucially – the Kremlin, which objected to the project's spiralling costs. After a new competition in 2009, Canadian architects Diamond & Schmitt won the €295 million tender to build a very different structure, which can at best be described as a fairly unexciting modern building – too bland to excite but too modern to fit in.

Even more controversial is the notorious **Okhta Centre**, originally to have been called Gazprom City, but given a new name following years of local opposition to St Petersburg's first high-rise building.

The Okhta Centre was originally planned to occupy the site of an abandoned factory on the Vyborg Side, just opposite Smolny Cathedral. But such was the (rare) public and international outcry at the plan that in 2010 City Hall backed down and cancelled the project, to the joy of many locals. It was later announced that the building – Europe's tallest, towering almost 400m over the Neva (that's three time higher than the spire of the SS Peter & Paul Cathedral) – would still be constructed at a new location in Lakhta, a good distance from the Historic Heart beyond the Kirovsky Islands on the Vyborg Side.

nearby **Maly Zal** (Малый зал Глинки; Small Hall; Nevsky pr 30) hosts smaller ensembles.

Mikhailovsky Theatre BALLET, OPERA
(Академический театр оперы и балета; Map p172; www.mikhailovsky.ru; pl Iskusstv 1; Ⓜ Nevsky Prospekt) Challenging the Mariinsky in terms of the standards and range of its performances is this equally historic and beautifully restored theatre.

State Hermitage Theatre BALLET, OPERA
(Эрмитажный театр; Map p172; www.hermitageballet.com; Dvortsovaya nab 34; Ⓜ Admiralteyskaya) Classic Russian ballets and gala concerts are part of the very tourist-friendly repertoire at this intimate, charming venue that's part of the Hermitage.

Yusupov Palace Theatre CLASSICAL MUSIC
(Map p188; www.yusupov-palace.ru; nab reki Moyki 94; Ⓜ Sadovaya) Housed inside the outrageously ornate Yusupov Palace, this elaborate yet intimate venue hosts charming 'Gala Evening' concerts that feature fragments of various Russian classics.

Rimsky-Korsakov Conservatory CLASSICAL MUSIC
(Консерватория Римского-Корсакова; Map p188; www.conservatory.ru; Teatralnaya pl 3; Ⓜ Sadovaya) This illustrious music school opposite the Mariinsky is worth checking out for its performances by up-and-coming musicians.

Maltiskaya Capella CLASSICAL MUSIC
(Map p172; www.maltacapella.ru; Sadovaya ul 26; Ⓜ Gostiny Dvor) Look out for one of the rare concerts here for a chance to see inside the stunning Maltese chapel that's part of the Vorontsov Palace, now used as a military school for young cadets.

Glinka Capella CLASSICAL MUSIC
(Академическая капелла Глинки; Map p172; www.glinka-capella.ru; nab reki Moyki 20; Ⓜ Admiralteyskaya) This historic hall is beautifully located on the Moyka and was constructed for Russia's oldest professional choir. These days, performances focus on choral and organ music.

Circus & Puppets

Contact the theatres to check on performance times.

St Petersburg State Circus CIRCUS
(Большой Санкт-Петербургский государственный цирк; Map p172; www.circus.spb.ru; nab reki Fontanki 3; Ⓜ Gostiny Dvor) One of Russia's leading circus companies has had a permanent home here since 1877.

Bolshoy Puppet Theatre PUPPET THEATRE
(Большой театр кукол; Map p182; www.puppets.ru; ul Nekrasova 10; tickets R100-250; Ⓜ Chernyshevskaya) This is the main venue for puppets; there are 16 different shows in the repertoire, including two for adults.

Demmeni Marionette Theatre PUPPET THEATRE
(Театр марионеток Деммени; Map p172; www.demmeni.ru; Nevsky pr 52; Ⓜ Gostiny Dvor) The oldest professional puppet theatre in Russia has been in business since 1917.

Nightclubs

Griboyedov NIGHTCLUB
(Грибоедов; Map p184; www.griboedovclub.ru; Voronezhskaya ul 2a; cover R200-400; ⏲ noon-6am, concerts 10pm; Ⓜ Ligovsky Pr; 📶) Griboyedov is the longest-standing and most respected music club in the city. This club in a bomb shelter was founded by local ska collective Dva Samolyota. It's a low-key bar in the early evening, gradually morphing into a dance club later in the night. Excellent music acts and international DJs play electronic, rock and dubstep.

Mod Club NIGHTCLUB
(Map p172; www.modclub.info; nab kanala Griboyedova 7; cover Fri & Sat R100-300; ⏲ 6pm-6am; Ⓜ Nevsky Prospekt) A popular spot for students and other indie types who appreciate the fun and friendly atmosphere, the groovy mix of music (live and spun) and added entertainment such as novus tables (a billiards-like game that is increasingly popular in Russia). Laid-back and great fun, this is a solid choice for a night out.

Tunnel Club NIGHTCLUB
(Map p196; www.tunnelclub.ru; cnr Zverinskaya ul & Lybansky per; cover R100-230; ⏲ midnight-6am Thu-Sat, to 3am Sun-Wed; Ⓜ Sportivnaya) Closed for several years, this military-themed club reopened in the bomb shelter where it was first born. The setting is still spooky but somehow appropriate for the techno and dubstep that go down here.

Barakobamabar NIGHTCLUB
(Map p172; www.barakobamabar.ru; Konyushennaya pl 2; ⏲ 6pm-6am; Ⓜ Nevsky Prospekt) In the summer months there's a great outdoor bar and dance floor, while inside there are a couple of cosy bars and a hookah lounge spread over two floors, both always full of beautiful

GAY & LESBIAN ST PETERSBURG

There's a small but vibrant gay scene in St Petersburg. The two main gay clubs are the large and mainstream **Central Station** (Map p172; ☎312 3600; www.centralstation.ru; ul Lomonosova 1/28; admission before midnight free, after midnight R100-300; ⏲6pm-6am; Ⓜ Gostiny Dvor) and the rather more exclusive but still quite cheesy **Club** (Map p184; www.the-club.fm; Scherbakov per 17; admission R300-500; ⏲11pm-6am Wed, Fri & Sat; Ⓜ Dostoevskaya). The more alternative **Blue Oyster** (Голубая устрица; www.boyster.ru; ul Lomonosova 1; ⏲6pm-6am; Ⓜ Nevsky Prospekt) is a self-styled 'trash bar' that guarantees a raucous and cheap night out for anyone; it's perhaps the most fun of all, with free entry at all times and young revellers literally hanging from the rafters. Some way out of the city centre you'll find Russia's only lesbian club, **3L** (Триэль; www.triel.spb.ru; Moskovsky pr 107-9; cover R300; ⏲10pm-5.30am Wed & Fri-Sun; Ⓜ Moskovskiye Vorota), as well as the community-minded mixed gay-lesbian club and social centre **Malevich** (Малевич; www.malevich-club.ru; Moskovsky pr 107-9; cover free-R300; ⏲11pm-6am Wed & Fri-Sun; Ⓜ Moskovskiye Vorota; 📶). The long-running Soviet-style club **Cabaret** (www.cabarespb.ru) has been around for well over a decade, with frequent changes of location, so check the website to see where its next incarnation may be.

Further information can be found on the useful local website **Excess** (www.xs.gay.ru/english).

young things. It's right at the back through the complex at Konyushennaya pl 2.

Jesus Club NIGHTCLUB
(Map p184; www.cometojes.us; Ligovsky pr 50; cover free-R200; ⏲8pm-6am Fri & Sat; Ⓜ Ploshchad Vosstaniya) A weekend destination in the Ligovsky pr 50 warehouse complex, this cool place is popular with younger clubbers, packing in the crowds at weekends to dance to techno, dubstep and other electronic styles. Most acts are local, but it occasionally gets international DJs. Walk straight down from the arch, and then turn right when you get to the open area.

Sports

Petrovsky Stadium SPORTS
(Петровский стадион; Map p196; www.petrovsky.spb.ru; Petrovsky ostrov 2; Ⓜ Sportivnaya) Petersburgers are fanatical about the fortunes of local football team **Zenit** (www.fc-zenit.ru), which usually plays here. Tickets (R100 to R1000) can be purchased at theatre ticket booths or at the stadium, three days before a game. Be sure to be wearing Zenit's light-blue colours if you want to avoid getting into any bothersome situations.

Theatre, Cabaret & Dance Shows

Drama is taken very seriously in St Petersburg and there are dozens of theatrical performances each night, all in Russian. Even if you don't speak the language, some of the theatres are visual treats in themselves. We've also included a cabaret and dance show that require littles in the way of language skills for appreciation.

Feel Yourself Russian THEATRE
(Map p188; www.folkshow.ru; Nikolayevsky Palace, ul Truda 4; ⏲show 6.30pm; Ⓜ Admiralteyskaya) Terrible title, but actually a very entertaining show of traditional Russian folk dancing and music by enthusiastic, professional troupes. Plus you get to enjoy the grand interior of the Nikolayevsky Palace.

Maly Drama Theatre THEATRE
(Малый драматический театр; Map p184; www.mdt-dodin.ru; ul Rubinshteyna 18; Ⓜ Vladimirskaya) The theatre with the best international reputation, built up under the directorship of Lev Dodin whose productions of Dostoevsky's *The Devils* and Chekhov's *Play Without a Name* have been widely acclaimed.

Alexandrinsky Theatre THEATRE
(Александринский театр; Map p172; www.alexandrinsky.ru; pl Ostrovskogo 2; Ⓜ Gostiny Dvor) The city's premier drama theatre, where Chekhov's *The Seagull* saw its premiere, is an architectural treat.

Shopping

St Petersburg's shopping scene is rather uneven. There are certainly a few charming, stand-out independent stores selling antiques, art and unique fashion, but the city is increasingly dominated by big shopping centres, which boast most of the best contemporary fashion and design boutiques.

TOP CHOICE **Udelnaya Fair** FLEA MARKET

(Удельная ярмарка; Vyborg Side; ⏰8am-5pm Sat & Sun; Ⓜ Udelnaya) St Petersburg's only well-established flea market is one shopping experience it's truly worth travelling for. It's a treasure trove of Soviet ephemera, prerevolutionary antiques and bonkers kitsch from all eras; the sheer size of the place means you'll really have to comb it to find the gems. Exit the metro station to the right and follow the crowds across the train tracks.

La Russe ANTIQUES

(Map p184; www.larusse.ru; Stremyannaya ul 3; ⏰11am-8pm; Ⓜ Mayakovskaya) This specialist in 18th- to 20th-century antiques is a real charmer, piled high with rustic old whatnots as well as more genuine antiques. You might unearth anything from a battered old samovar to an intricately painted sleigh. International shipping is no problem.

Dom Knigi BOOKSTORE

(Дом книги; Map p172; www.spbdk.ru; Nevsky pr 28; ⏰9am-midnight; Ⓜ Nevsky Prospekt) The stalwart of the city's bookshops is Dom Knigi, housed in the wonderful, whimsical Singer Building. For years, this was the only place in the city that carried a decent selection of literature, and it is still an inviting place to browse.

Staraya Kniga BOOKSTORE

(Старая книга; Map p172; Nevsky pr 3; ⏰10am-7pm; Ⓜ Admiralteyskaya) This long-established antique bookseller is a fascinating place to rummage around. The stock ranges from fancy, mint-edition books to secondhand, well-worn Soviet editions, maps and art.

Galeria SHOPPING CENTRE

(Галерия; Map p184; www.galeria.spb.ru; Ligovsky pr 30a; ⏰10am-11pm; Ⓜ Ploshchad Vosstaniya) Spread over five floors, with around 300 shops including H&M, Gap, Marks & Spencer and Zara, and an excellently stocked supermarket, this really is a one-stop shop for pretty much all your shopping needs.

Gostiny Dvor SHOPPING CENTRE

(Гостиный двор; Map p172; www.bgd.ru; Nevsky pr 35; ⏰10am-10pm; Ⓜ Gostiny Dvor) Despite a renovation for the city's tercentennial celebrations, the exterior of Russia's oldest shopping mall is already looking like it needs a serious repaint, while the interior retains a largely Soviet, if quaint, feel.

Imperial Porcelain HOMEWARES

(Императорский Фарфор; Map p184; www.ipm.ru; Vladimirsky pr 7; ⏰10am-8pm; Ⓜ Vladimirskaya) This is the convenient city-centre location of the famous porcelain factory that once made tea sets for the Romanovs. If you're determined to get a bargain, head out to the **Factory Shop** (pr Obukhovsky Oborony; 151; Ⓜ Lomonosovskaya); to get here, turn left out of the metro station and walk under the bridge. Turn left on the embankment and you'll see the factory ahead.

Souvenir Market SOUVENIRS

(Map p172; nab kanala Griboyedova 1; ⏰sunrise-sunset; Ⓜ Nevsky Prospekt) You're unlikely to find any incredible bargains at this market behind the Church on Spilled Blood, but you will find a great selection of handicrafts and other souvenirs. Haggle with the vendors – they speak enough English to barter back.

Anglia Books BOOKSTORE

(Map p182; nab reki Fontanki 38; Ⓜ Gostiny Dvor) The city's only dedicated English-language bookshop has a large selection of contemporary literature, history and travel writing. It also hosts small art and photography displays, organises book readings and is generally a cornerstone of expat life in St Petersburg.

Tula Samovars SOUVENIRS

(Тульские самовары; Map p184; www.samovary.ru; per Dzhambula 11; Ⓜ Zvenigorodskaya) This beautiful showroom is the place to buy a truly unique souvenir of your visit. The samovars range from small, simple designs to enormous and elaborate ones with precious stones and other embellishments on them.

Nevsky Centre SHOPPING CENTRE

(Невский Центр; Map p184; www.nevskycentre.ru; Nevsky pr 112; ⏰10am-11pm; Ⓜ Ploshchad Vosstaniya) Not nearly as big as Galeria on the other side of pl Vosstaniya, Nevsky Centre is perhaps slightly more glamorous and upmarket. It houses some 70 shops over seven floors, including the fabulous basement Stockmann supermarket, by far the best-stocked in the entire city.

Information

Dangers & Annoyances

CRIME & VIOLENCE Watch out for pickpockets, particularly along Nevsky pr and in crowded places such as theatres and cinemas. It's also wise to avoid crossing directly in front of Moskovsky vokzal unless you have to, since the police there have a nasty habit of trying to shake down foreigners for supposed infringements of visa registration rules.

St Petersburg is notorious for its incidence of race-related violent attacks. Precautions for non-Caucasians to take include not wandering around alone late at night or venturing out to the suburbs solo at any time of day.

ENVIRONMENTAL HAZARDS It's not just the ice on the streets that you have to look out for in winter – every year in early spring and during winter thaws, several people die when hit by child-sized, sword-shaped icicles falling from rooftops and balconies. Keep your eyes peeled to make sure one of these monsters is not dangling above your head.

From May to September mosquitoes are a nightmare. The plug-ins that slowly heat repellent-saturated cardboard pads are available everywhere in the city and are very effective. Alternatively bring repellent or cover up.

Tiny traces of *Giardia lamblia*, a nasty parasite that causes stomach cramps and diarrhoea, have been found in St Petersburg's water. There's no preventative drug so the best advice is not to drink straight from the tap. To be absolutely safe, drink only bottled water. Brushing your teeth, bathing, showering and shaving with tap water will cause no problems, however.

Emergency

All of the following numbers have Russian-speaking operators. If you need to make a police report and don't speak Russian, first contact the **City Tourist Information Centre** (Map p172; ☎310 2822; www.ispb.info; Sadovaya ul 14/52; ⊙10am-7pm Mon-Fri, noon-6pm Sat). For serious matters, contact your embassy or consulate as well (p701).

Ambulance (☎03)

Fire (☎01)

Gas leak (☎04)

Police (☎02)

Internet Access

Wireless access is increasingly ubiquitous across the city's hotels and restaurants. In nearly all cases it's free, but you'll have to ask for the password. If you don't have a smartphone or a laptop, the following internet cafés are centrally located.

Café Max (Map p182; www.cafemax.ru; Nevsky pr 90; per hr R120; ⊙24hr; ⓂMayakovskaya) A big fancy place with 150 computers, a game zone and a comfy café and beer bar. It's located on the 2nd floor. There's a second branch inside the Hermitage.

Internet Cafe (Map p172; Nevsky pr 11; per hr R80; ⊙24hr; ⓂAdmiralteyskaya) Above Subway.

Russian Museum Internet Centre (Map p172; Nevsky pr 17; per hr R150; ⊙9am-10pm; ⓂGostiny Dvor) Inside the courtyard of the Stroganov Palace.

Media

NEWSPAPERS & MAGAZINES There is a decent amount of English-language media in St Petersburg, although publications aren't regular: The *St Petersburg Times*, despite constantly slimming down and having gone from twice-weekly to once-weekly, remains the most useful listings rag in town. Russian speakers have the choice of *Afisha* and *Time Out St Petersburg*, both similar publications with excellent listings.

Afisha (www.afisha.ru) Full coverage in Russian of the city's nightlife, cultural life and eating scene with good feature writing.

In Your Pocket (www.inyourpocket.com/city/st_petersburg) Monthly listings booklet with useful up-to-date information and short features.

Pulse (www.pulse.ru) Fairly substance-free monthly magazine with features and reviews.

St Petersburg Times (www.sptimes.ru) Published every Wednesday, this plucky little newspaper has been fearlessly telling it like it really is for over 15 years. The column 'Chernov's Choice', a rundown of what's going on in the city from veteran music journalist Sergey Chernov, is especially useful.

Time Out (www.spb.timeout.ru; R50) Weekly listings magazine in Russian, particularly good on clubbing and eating out.

Medical Services

The clinics listed below are open 24 hours and have English-speaking staff.

American Medical Clinic (Map p188; ☎740 2090; www.amclinic.ru; nab reki Moyki 78; ⓂSadovaya)

Medem International Clinic & Hospital (Map p184; ☎336 3333; www.medem.ru; 6 ul Marata; ⓂMayakovskaya)

PHARMACIES Look for the sign *apteka*, or the usual green cross, to find a pharmacy.

36.6 Pharmacy (Аптека 36,6; http://spb.366.ru) A chain of 24-hour pharmacies around the city.

Apteka Petrofarm (Map p172; Nevsky pr 22; ⊙24hr; ⓂNevsky Prospekt)

Money

ATMs and currency exchange offices can be found all over the city. If you need to change money at odd times, there are lots of 24-hour exchange offices on Nevsky pr and in big hotels.

Post

Post office branches are scattered throughout St Petersburg and they vary in services, usually in proportion to size.

Central post office (Главпочтамт; Map p188; www.spbpost.ru; Pochtamtskaya ul 9; 24hr; Admiralteyskaya) The city's central post office has been sensitively renovated – you can send parcels and letters internationally from here.

Toilets

Portakabin-type toilets (R25) outside metros and the major sights are common. Shopping centres, hotels and chain cafés are the best places to look for a clean, odour-free bathroom.

Tourist Information

The English-speaking staff at the **City Tourist Information Centre** (Городской туристический информационный центр; Map p172; 310 2822; www.ispb.info; Sadovaya ul 14/52; 10am-7pm Mon-Fri, noon-6pm Sat) do their best to help with advice and information. There are also kiosks outside the **Hermitage** (Map p172; Dvortsovaya pl 12; 10am-7pm; Admiralteyskaya), on **pl Vosstaniya** (pl Vosstaniya; 10am-7pm; Ploshchad Vosstaniya) and desks at the Pulkovo-1 and Pulkovo-2 **airports** (10am-7pm Mon-Fri).

Travel Agencies

The following agencies all have English-speaking staff.

City Realty (www.cityrealty.ru) Can arrange all types of visas (tourist visas from US$25) including business ones, as well as accommodation and transport tickets. Very reliable.

Ost-West Kontaktservice (www.ostwest.com) The multilingual staff here can find you an apartment to rent and organise tours, train tickets and visa invites.

Sindbad Travel (www.sindbad.ru) A genuine Western-style discount air-ticket office, staffed by friendly, knowledgeable people. Also sells train tickets and ISIC/ITIC/IYTC cards and can book youth hostel accommodation.

Travel Russia (www.travelrussia.su) A small and very well-run company, Travel Russia organises apartments, visas, transfers and registration.

Getting There & Away

Air

Pulkovo-1 (704 3822; www.pulkovoairport.ru/eng) and **Pulkovo-2** (704 3444; www.pulkovoairport.ru/eng) serve St Petersburg. Pulkovo-2 is the main international terminal, while Pulkovo-1 handles all internal flights and those to CIS countries.

St Petersburg has direct air links with all major European capitals and many larger Russian cities. Tickets for all airlines can be purchased from travel agencies and from the **Central Airline Ticket Office** (Центральные авиакассы; Map p172; Nevsky pr 7; 8am-8pm Mon-Fri, to 6pm Sat & Sun; Admiralteyskaya), which also has counters for train and international bus tickets.

Boat

Between early April and late September, international passenger ferries connect Stockholm, Helsinki and Tallinn with **Morskoy vokzal** (Морской вокзал; Map p192; pl Morskoy Slavy 1). It's a long way from the metro, so either take bus 7 or trolleybus 10 from outside the Hermitage.

In the summer, regular river cruises depart from the **River Passenger Terminal** (Речной вокзал; pr Obukhovskoy Oborony 195; Proletarskaya) and float along the Neva to inland Russia, including cruises to Valaam, Kizhi and Moscow. Tours can be booked through most travel agents, or through the **Ferry Centre** (Паромный центр; Map p182; ul Vosstaniya 19; Ploshchad Vosstaniya).

Bus

St Petersburg's main bus station, **Avtovokzal No 2** (Автовокзал No 2; Map p184; www.avokzal.ru; nab Obvodnogo kanala 36; Obvodny Kanal) – there isn't a No 1 – has both international and European Russia services. The website has current timetables and routes. The single cheapest way to get to Helsinki is to take a *marshrutka* (fixed-route minibus) from pl Vosstaniya (R500); they leave all day when full

RAISING THE BRIDGES

From the end of April to November, all major bridges rise at the following times nightly to let seagoing ships through. The schedule (which changes every year by five minutes here or there) governs the lives of the city's motorists and nighthawks trying to get from one area to another.

» **Most Alexandra Nevskogo** (Map p184) 2.20am to 5.10am

» **Birzhevoy most** (Map p192) 2am to 4.55am

» **Blagoveshchensky most** (Map p192) 1.25am to 2.45am and 3.10am to 5am

» **Bolsheokhtinsky most** 2am to 5am

» **Dvortsovy most** (Map p192) 1.25am to 4.50am

» **Liteyny most** 1.40am to 4.45am

» **Troitsky most** (Map p196) 1.35am to 4.45am

» **Tuchkov most** (Map p196) 2am to 2.55am and 3.35am to 4.55am

from the corner of Nevsky pr and Ligovsky pr, opposite the metro station.

Other international buses are offered by a number of companies:

Ecolines (Map p184; www.ecolines.ru; Podyezdny per 3; MPushkinskaya) Daily buses from Vitebsky vokzal to Tallinn (R980), Rīga (R1250) and Kyiv (R1880), and Odesa (R2320).

Lux Express (www.luxexpress.eu; Admiral Business Centre, Mitrofanievskoe sh 2; 9am-9pm; MBaltiyskaya) Runs buses from both Avtovokzal No 2 and from outside Baltiysky vokzal. Its buses run regularly to Tallinn (from R850, 12 daily) and Rīga (from R1000, three daily).

Sovavto (www.sovavto.ru) Daily departures in very comfortable, air-conditioned buses from the Grand Hotel Europe to Helsinki (R1600, eight hours) and Turku (R2320, 11 hours).

Car & Motorcycle

See p716 for general driving information. Take it slowly; not only are there numerous speed traps (there's one just outside the city limits, towards Vyborg, where the speed limit becomes 60km/h), but also the state of some roads can easily lead you to the repair shop in no time.

Agencies offering self-drive and chauffeured vehicles:

Astoria Service (Map p184; 764 9622; www.astoriaservice.ru; Borovaya ul 11/13, office 65; MLigovsky Prospekt)

Avis (Map p184; 600 1213; www.avis-rentacar.ru; pl Alexandra Nevskogo 2; MPloshchad Alexandra Nevskogo)

Europcar (385 5202; www.europcar.ru; ul Vozrozhdeniya 20a; MKirovsky Zavod)

Hertz (326 4505; www.hertz.ru; Pulkovo-2 Airport)

Train

There are several major long-distance train stations, which also run suburban services.

Finlyandsky vokzal (Финляндский вокзал; Map p164; 768 7687; pl Lenina 6; MPloshchad Lenina) To/from Helsinki.

Ladozhsky vokzal (Ладожский вокзал; 768 5304; Zanevsky pr 73; MLadozhskaya) To/from Helsinki, the far north of Russia and towards the Urals.

Moskovsky vokzal (Московский вокзал; Map p184; 768 4597; pl Vosstaniya; MPloshchad Vosstaniya) Moscow, Siberia, Crimea and the Caucasus.

Vitebsky vokzal (Витебский вокзал; Map p184; 768 5807; Zagorodny pr 52; MPushkinskaya) Baltic states, Eastern Europe, Ukraine and Belarus.

Baltiysky vokzal (Балтийский вокзал; Map p165; 768 2859; Obvodny Kanal 120; MBaltiyskaya).

Tickets can be purchased at the train stations, the **Central Train Ticket Office** (Центральные желзнодорожные кассы; Map p172; 762 33 44; nab kanala Griboyedova 24; 8am-8pm Mon-Sat, to 4pm Sun; MNevsky Prospekt), the **Central Airline Ticket Office** (Центральные авиакассы; Map p172; Nevsky pr 7; 8am-8pm Mon-Fri, to 6pm Sat & Sun; MAdmiralteyskaya) and many travel agencies around town.

MOSCOW Around 10 daily trains to Moscow all depart from Moskovsky vokzal (see p226). Most depart between 10pm and midnight, arriving in the capital the following morning between 6am and 8am. On the more comfortable *firmeny* long-distance trains, a 1st-class *lyux* ticket (two-person cabin) runs R5200 to R6000, while a 2nd-class *kupe* (four-person cabin) is R2000 to R3000. The overnight sleepers will save a night's accommodation costs, while if you really want to save money, some services have *platskartny* (open dorm) carriages with very cheap tickets.

There are also high-speed Sapsan day trains that travel at 200km per hour to reach their destination in four hours or less. Trains depart throughout the day. Comfortable 2nd-class seats are R2300 to R2800, while super-spacious 1st-class seats run R5000 to R5600.

ELSEWHERE IN RUSSIA St Petersburg has excellent connections to the rest of European Russia, with daily trains to Murmansk, Petrozavodsk, Kaliningrad, Nizhny Novgorod, Novgorod, Pskov and Yekaterinburg. Less frequent services connect the city to Arkhangelsk and Kazan. Southern Russia and Siberia are generally reached via Moscow, although there are some direct trains to the Black Sea coast from St Petersburg. However, be aware that these don't go via Moscow and cut through Belarus, necessitating a transit visa for Belarus and a double entry visa.

FINLAND & OTHER INTERNATIONAL DESTINATIONS From Helsinki there are four daily Allegro express trains that take you from the Finnish capital to St Petersburg in an impressive 3½ hours; see www.vr.fi for prices and timetables. Services in both directions stop at Vyborg, so you can save yourself some money if you take a bus or local train there and then catch the train to Helsinki.

St Petersburg is well connected by train to lots of cities throughout Eastern Europe, including Berlin, Budapest, Kaliningrad, Kyiv, Prague and Warsaw, but all trains pass through Belarus, for which you're required to hold a transit visa. The train to Smolensk in Russia also passes through Belarus. Border guards have been known to force people off trains and back to where they came from if they don't have a visa.

Getting Around

St Petersburg can be a frustrating place to get around for visitors: the metro, while an excellent

TRAINS FROM ST PETERSBURG TO MOSCOW

TRAIN NUMBER & NAME	DEPARTURE TIME	DURATION (HR)	FARE (R)
1 Krasnaya Strela	11.55pm	8	2600-3000
3 Ekspress	11.59pm	8	2380
5 Nikolaevsk Ekspress	11.30pm	8	2750
53 Grand Express	11.40pm	9	5000-6000
151A Sapsan	6.45am	4	2612
157A Sapsan	1.30pm	4	2354
161A Sapsan	3.15pm	4	2870
165A Sapsan	7.45pm	4	2870

system, actually has relatively few stations in the centre of the city, and distances from stations to nearby sights can be long. Many visitors find buses and *marshrutky* a little daunting, as all the signage is in Russian only and you need to know where you're going, so many people just walk: bring comfortable shoes!

To/From the Airport

St Petersburg's airport is at Pulkovo, about 17km south of the centre. Domestic and CIS flights arrive at Pulkovo-1, from where you can take bus 39 (R21, every 15 minutes, 5.30am to 12.30am) from outside the terminal building. It connects you to the Moskovskaya metro station, from where you can get to anywhere in the city. Buy your ticket on the bus. Alternatively, jump into any *marshrutka*, and check with the driver that it goes to Moskovskaya (nearly all do).

International flights arrive at Pulkovo-2, from where bus K-13 shuttles you to the Moskovskaya metro station (R27, every 10 minutes, 5.30am to 12.30am). Turn left when you leave the arrivals area and the bus stop is between departures and arrivals. The bus terminates at Moskovskaya, so you don't need to worry about where to get off.

If you'd prefer to take a taxi from either terminal, there are now taxi booking stands in the arrivals area of both terminals where staff speak English. State your destination and you'll be given a slip of paper with the price on it and be taken to a taxi outside. Expect to pay R600 to R800 for a trip to the centre, depending on where exactly you're headed.

Bus, Marshrutka, Trolleybus & Tram

Tickets (R21 to R25 depending on the service) are bought inside the vehicle. Bus stops are marked by roadside 'A' signs (for *avtobus*), trolleybus stops by 'm' (representing a handwritten Russian 'T'), tram stops by a 'T', all usually indicating the line numbers too. Stops may also have roadside signs with little pictures of a bus, trolleybus or tram. *Marshrutky* stop anywhere you hail them (except on Nevsky pr, where they're banned from operating). Most transport runs from 6am to 1am.

Useful routes across the city:

Nevsky pr From Admiralty to Moskovsky vokzal, buses 7 and 22; trolleybuses 1, 5, 7, 10 and 22. Trolleybuses 1 and 22 continue to pl Alexandra Nevskogo. Trolleybuses 5 and 7 continue to Smolny.

Ligovsky pr to Petrograd Side *Marshrutka* K76, via Troitsky most and Peter & Paul Fortress.

Vitebsky vokzal to Vasilyevsky Island *Marshrutka* K124, via Sennaya pl and Mariinsky Theatre.

Hermitage to Vasilyevsky Island Bus 7; trolleybus 10.

Kirovsky Islands Bus 10 from the corner of Bolshaya Morskaya ul and Nevsky pr.

Metro

The St Petersburg metro (Map p166; www.metro.spb.ru; flat fare R25; ⏲6am-midnight) is a very efficient five-lined system. The network of some 65 stations is best used for travelling long distances, especially connecting the suburbs to the city centre.

Zhetony (tokens), valid for one ride, can be bought from the booths in the stations. You're supposed to buy an extra ticket if you're carrying a large amount of luggage. If you are staying more than a day or two, however, it's worth buying a smart card (R30), which is good for loading multiple journeys over a fixed time period. The more trips you buy, the more you save, though note, you can't share a card with a friend.

Taxi

Nearly all official taxis are unmetered (though there are plans to introduce these), so if you flag one down you'll have to go through a similar process of negotiation to that involved in catching a car (see p718), only the driver will want more money for being 'official'.

The best way to get a taxi is to order one through a company, as prices will be a lot lower than those charged if you flag a driver down on the street. Operators will usually not speak English, so unless you speak Russian you might want your hotel reception to call one of the following numbers for you:

Petersburgskoye Taxi (☎068, 324 7777; www.taxi068.spb.ru)
Taxi-4 (☎633 3333; www.taxi-4.ru)
Taxi Blues (☎321 8888; www.taxiblues.ru)
Taxi Million (☎600 0000; www.6-000-000.ru)

AROUND ST PETERSBURG

There are several grand imperial palaces and estates surrounding St Petersburg, of which Peterhof and the palace-park ensembles at Tsarskoe Selo and Pavlovsk are the best. A visit to St Petersburg is not really complete without a trip to at least one of these palaces, but be warned that at the height of summer the endless crowds of tourists can be horrific. Moreover, while Peterhof is the most impressive of them all, it's so outrageously overpriced for foreigners that at present Tsarskoe Selo makes for the best day trip when value for money is factored in.

If your time is short, or you wish to avoid the long queues, book yourself on a guided tour of either palace with a travel agency, and make sure that they prebook your entry ticket. **Peter's Walking Tours** (☎943 1229; www.peterswalk.com) in St Petersburg can do this for you.

If you have more time, several other options, most requiring an overnight stay, are outlined in the Western European Russia chapter, including the charming old Finnish town of Vyborg (p276), the sleepy village of Staraya Ladoga (p279) and the monastery town of Tikhvin (p280).

> **MOVING ON?**
>
> For tips, recommendations and reviews, head to shop.lonelyplanet.com to purchase a downloadable PDF of the Finland chapter from Lonely Planet's *Scandinavia* guide.

Around St Petersburg

Peterhof Петергоф

It's a tough call, but the gilded fountains and gardens of **Petrodvorets** (☎427 0073; www.peterhof.ru; Razvodnaya ul 2) give it a slight edge over St Petersburg's other suburban palaces. Hugging the Gulf of Finland, 29km west of St Petersburg, this 'Russian Versailles' is a far cry from the original cabin Peter the Great had built here to oversee construction of the Kronshtadt naval base. He liked the place so much he built a villa, Monplaisir, and then a whole series of palaces across an estate originally called Peterhof (pronounced Petergof), which has been called Petrodvorets (Peter's Palace) since 1944. All are surrounded by leafy gardens and a spectacular ensemble of gravity-powered fountains.

What you see today is largely a reconstruction since Petrodvorets was a major casualty of WWII. Apart from the damage done by the Germans, the palace suffered the worst under Soviet bombing raids in December 1941 and January 1942 because Stalin was determined to thwart Hitler's plan of hosting a New Year's victory celebration here.

Sights

Lower Park GROUNDS
(Нижний парк; www.peterhofmuseum.ru; adult/student R400/200; park 9am-8pm, fountains

10am-6pm) More than anything else, it's the palace grounds that make Peterhof the most popular day trip from St Petersburg for visitors. With an incredible symphony of golden fountains (all powered only by gravity), beautiful waterways and plenty of interesting historical buildings scattered about, this park will be the focus of your visit.

Whether you arrive by water or by land, you will have to purchase a ticket to enter the Lower Park to discover its fabulous fountains.

Water Avenue CANAL

Crisscrossed by bridges and bedecked by smaller sprays, the Water Avenue is a canal leading from the hydrofoil dock to the palace. It culminates in the magnificent **Grand Cascade**, a symphony of over 140 fountains engineered in part by Peter himself. The central statue of Samson tearing open a lion's jaws celebrates – as so many things in St Petersburg do – Peter's victory over the Swedes at Poltava. Shooting up 62m, it was unveiled by Rastrelli for the 25th anniversary of the battle in 1735.

Grand Palace PALACE

(Большой дворец; adult/student R500/250, audio guide R500; ⏲10.30am-6pm Tue-Sun, closed last Tue of month) Providing an amazing backdrop to the Grand Cascade, the Grand Palace is an imposing edifice, although with 30-something rooms, it is not nearly as large as your typical tsarist palace. It is open to foreign tourists only between 10.30am and noon, and again from 2.30pm until 4.15pm, so you are advised to come here immediately upon arrival if you are interested in going inside. Tickets are sold near the lobby where you pick up your *tapochki* (slippers to wear over your shoes to avoid damaging the wooden floors).

While Peter's palace was relatively modest, Rastrelli grossly enlarged the building for Empress Elizabeth. Later, Catherine the Great toned things down a little with a redecoration, although that's not really apparent from the glittering halls and art-filled galleries that are here today. All of the paintings, furniture and chandeliers are original, as everything was removed from the premises before the Germans arrived in WWII. The Chesme Hall is full of huge paintings of Russia's destruction of the Turkish fleet at Çesme in 1770. Other highlights include the East and West Chinese Cabinets, Picture Hall and Peter's study.

After WWII, Peterhof was largely left in ruins. Hitler had intended to throw a party here when his plans to occupy the Astoria Hotel were thwarted. He drew up pompous invitations, which obviously incensed his Soviet foes. Stalin's response was to preempt any such celebration by bombing the estate himself, in the winter of 1941–42, so it is ironic but true that most of the damage at Peterhof occurred at the hands of the Soviets. What you see today is largely a reconstruction; in fact, the main palace was completely gutted, as only a few of its walls were left standing.

Monplaisir VILLA

(Монплезир; adult/student R360/180; ⏲10.30am-5pm Tue & Thu-Sun May-Sep, Sat & Sun Oct-Apr) This far more humble, sea-facing villa was always Peter the Great's favourite retreat. It's easy to see why: it's wood-panelled, snug and elegant, peaceful even when there's a crowd – which there used to be all the time, what with Peter's mandatory partying ('misbehaving' guests were required to gulp down huge quantities of wine).

Also in this complex is an annexe called the **Catherine Building** (Екатерининский

TICKETS & OPENING HOURS

Inexplicably, many museums within the Peterhof estate have different closing days, although all the buildings are open from Friday to Sunday (and, with the exception of the Grand Palace, most buildings are open only at weekends between October and April). In any case, it's time-consuming and very expensive to see all of the attractions from the inside, as they each charge separate hefty admission fees, plus an extra ticket to take photographs or videos – on top of which you're paying at least 100% more than locals. All tours and posted information are in Russian, so it's worth investing in an information booklet, available at the kiosks near the entrances.

The lovely Upper Garden is free. Admission to the Lower Park is payable at the cash booths on the jetty and outside the gates leading to the Grand Cascade; hold on to your ticket when exiting this area so you can go back in later if you need to.

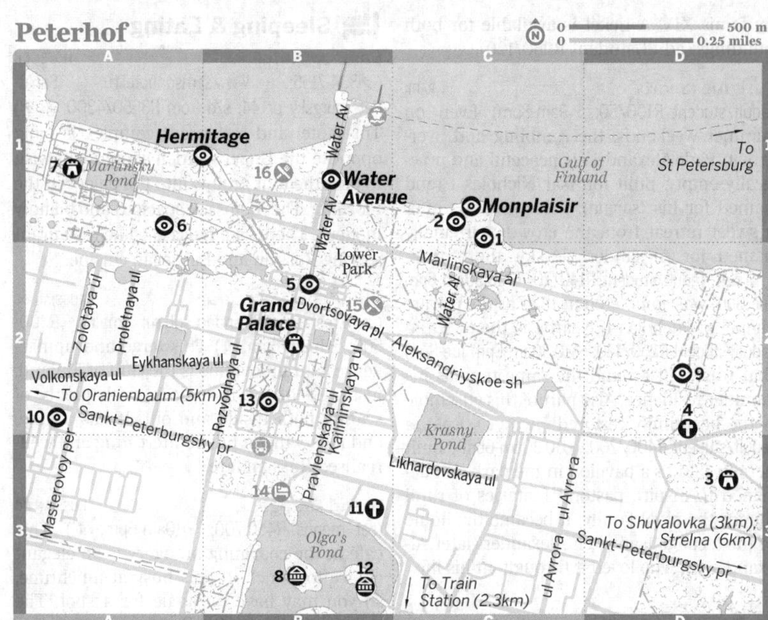

корпус; adult/student R360/180; ⊙10.30am-6pm), which was built by Rastrelli between 1747 and 1755. Its name derives from the fact that Catherine the Great was living here – rather conveniently – when her husband Peter III was overthrown. The interior contains the bedroom and study of Alexander I, as well as the huge Yellow Hall. On the right side is the magnificent **Bath Building** (Банный корпус; adult/student R360/180; ⊙10.30am-6pm Thu-Tue), built by Quarenghi in 1800, which is nothing special inside. Look out for some more trick fountains in the garden in front of the buildings. You can buy a ticket for all three buildings (adult/student R1000/500).

Hermitage VILLA

(Эрмитаж; adult/student R150/100; ⊙9am-6pm Wed-Mon) Along the shore to the west, the 1725 Hermitage is a two-storey yellow-and-white box featuring the ultimate in private dining: special elevators hoist a fully laid table into the imperial presence on the 2nd floor, thereby eliminating any hindrance by servants. The elevators are circular and directly in front of each diner, whose plate would be lowered, replenished and replaced.

Further west is yet another palace, **Marly** (adult/student R150/100; ⊙10am-6pm Tue-Sun), which was inspired by the French hunting lodge of the same name so loved

Peterhof

Top Sights

Grand Palace.......B2
Hermitage.......B1
Monplaisir.......C1
Water Avenue.......B1

Sights

1 Bath Building.......C1
2 Catherine Building.......C1
3 Farmer's Palace.......D3
4 Gothic Chapel.......D2
5 Grand Cascade.......B2
6 Lower Park.......A1
7 Marly Palace.......A1
8 Olgin Pavilion.......B3
9 Park Alexandria.......D2
10 Raketa Petrodvorets Watch Factory.......A2
11 SS Peter & Paul Cathedral.......B3
12 Tsaritsyn Pavilion.......B3
13 Upper Garden.......B2

Sleeping

14 Samson Hotel.......B3

Eating

15 Grand Orangerie.......B2
16 Shtandart Restaurant.......B1

by Louis XIV. A ticket is available for both buildings (adult/student R250/120).

Park Alexandria PARK
(adult/student R100/50; ⏲9am-8pm) Even on summer weekends, the rambling and overgrown Park Alexandria is peaceful and practically empty. Built for Tsar Nicholas I (and named for his tsarina), these grounds offer a sweet retreat from the crowds. Originally named for Alexander Nevsky, the **Gothic chapel** (adult/student R140/70; ⏲10.30am-6pm Tue-Sun) was completed in 1834 as the private chapel of Nicholas I. Nearby is the **cottage** (adult/student R250/120; ⏲10.30am-6pm Tue-Sun) that was built around the same time as his summer residence. Also part of this ensemble is the beautifully restored **Farmer's Palace** (adult/student R400/200; ⏲10.30am-6pm), built here in 1831 as a pavilion in the park and designed to inspire pastoral fantasies of rural life for the royal family; it became the home of the teenage tsarevitch Alexander (later Alexander II), who loved it throughout his life.

Petrodvorets TOWN
In case you have not had enough, there is more to see in the centre of the town of Peterhof. You'll need to leave the Lower Park grounds (and won't be able to reenter to get to the hydrofoil without buying a new ticket) in order to do this. In front of the Grand Palace is the **Upper Garden** (admission free), which backs onto the Grand Palace. It is far more manicured (and far drier) than the Lower Park, and it makes a wonderful place to stroll, occupying the grounds between the palace and the town.

Wander down Pravlenskaya ul and you'll find yourself in the middle of town. It's well worth wandering past the handsome **SS Peter & Paul Cathedral** (Петропавловский собор) and continuing around the edge of Olga's Pond (Olgin Prud) to the **Tsaritsyn & Olgin Pavilions** (adult/student R540/270; ⏲10.30am-6pm, last entry 4pm), two buildings that sit on two islands in the middle of the pond. Nicholas I had these elaborate pavilions built for his wife (Alexandra Fyodorovna) and daughter (Olga Nikolayevna) respectively. Only recently restored and reopened, they boast unique Mediterranean architectural styles reminiscent of Pompeii.

Further down Sankt-Peterburgsky pr is the **Raketa Petrodvorets Watch Factory** (www.raketa.su; Sankt-Peterburgsky pr 60; ⏲boutique 10am-5pm Mon-Fri), one of the town's biggest employers, which has an on-site shop selling *very* cool watches.

Sleeping & Eating

Samson Hotel HOTEL €€
(☎334-7155; www.samsonhotel.ru; Sankt-Peterburgsky pr 44; s/d from R3650/4300; ❄📶) This hotel and restaurant complex is bang opposite the Upper Garden should you wish to beat the tour groups into the palace in the morning. The rooms are spacious and blandly modern. There's a large cellar-like restaurant serving Russian and European cuisine.

Shtandart Restaurant RUSSIAN €€
(www.restaurantshtandart.spb.ru; mains R300-500; ⏲10am-6pm; 📋) This large and upmarket restaurant overlooks the Gulf of Finland, just west of the boat dock, with plenty of seating both inside and out. It has a large and meaty menu full of interesting and well-realised Russian fare.

Grand Orangerie RUSSIAN €€
(set menus R450-700; ⏲10am-6pm; 📋) This café in the charming orangery is an elegant choice for lunch. It gets busy at lunchtime, so you may have to queue for a spot. The menu is packed with Russian classics, and there's also a good cake selection.

Getting There & Away

It's easy and cheap to reach Peterhof by bus or *marshrutka*. *Marshrutka* 300 and 424 (R30) leave from outside the Avtovo metro station, while *marshrutka* 103 leaves from outside Leninsky Prospekt station. All pass through the town of Petrodvorets, immediately outside Peterhof. Tell the driver you want to go '*v dvaryéts*' ('to the palace') and you'll be let off near the main entrance to the Upper Garden, on Sankt-Peterburgsky pr.

There's also a reasonably frequent suburban train (R56, 30 minutes) from Baltiysky vokzal to Novy Petrodvorets, from where you can walk (around 20 minutes) or take any bus except 357 to the fifth stop, which will take another 10 minutes.

From May to September, the *Meteor* **hydrofoil** (adult single/return R500/800, student single/return R450/700) departs from the jetty in front of the Hermitage every 20 to 30 minutes from 9.30am. It's an expensive but highly enjoyable way to get to Peterhof, and you arrive right in front of the palace. The last hydrofoil leaves Peterhof at 7pm, and the trip takes 30 minutes.

Oranienbaum Ораниенбаум

While Peter was building Monplaisir, his right-hand man, Alexander Menshikov, began his own palace, Oranienbaum (Orange Tree), 5km down the coast from Peterhof.

This grand enterprise eventually bankrupted Menshikov. Following Peter's death and Menshikov's exile, the estate served briefly as a hospital and then passed to Tsar Peter III, who didn't much like ruling Russia and spent a lot of time there before he was dispatched in a coup led by his wife Catherine (later the Great).

Spared Nazi occupation and, after WWII, ruined by Soviet neglect, Oranienbaum and the surrounding town were renamed after the scientist-poet Mikhail Lomonosov. The palatial estate is once again known as Oranienbaum (though the town remains Lomonosov) and it doubles as a museum and **public park** (Музей-заповедник Ораниенбаум; www.oranienbaum.org; adult/student R140/70; ⌚9am-8pm), with boat rides on the ornamental lake. Bypassed by tour groups, it's a pleasant setting for a picnic or a tranquil walk away from the crowds.

Menshikov's impressively large **Great Palace** (Большой дворец) is closed to the public while renovations are under way, but just wandering around its exterior, peeping through the windows and glimpsing the large, sunken formal gardens that extend in front of it, is interesting enough.

One of the ground's buildings open for inspection is **Peter III's Palace** (Дворец Петра III; adult/student R140/70; ⌚10.30am-6pm Wed-Mon May-Oct), a boxy miniature palace, with rich, uncomfortable-looking interiors and some Chinese-style lacquer-on-wood paintings. It was restored in the late 1950s and early '60s, but is now in dire need of attention again: its salmon-pink walls are now flaking and chipped. It is approached through the **Gate of Honour**, all that remains of a toy fortress where Peter amused himself drilling his soldiers.

Worth a peek also is Catherine's over-the-top **Chinese Palace** (Китайский дворец), designed by Antonio Rinaldi. Rococo on the inside and baroque on the outside, the private retreat features painted ceilings and fine inlaid-wood floors and walls.

In the meadows between Peter III's Palace and the Chinese Palace is a small **Deer Park**, where you can see deer being reared for eventual release into the grounds.

Opposite the palace entrance there's a reasonably good restaurant, **Okhota** (Охота; Dvortsovy pr 65a; mains R400-800; ⌚noon-midnight; 📋), that's big on taxidermy for its hunting-themed decor.

The train from St Petersburg's Baltiysky vokzal to Petrodvorets continues to Oranienbaum (R62, one hour). Get off at Lomonosov Station, an hour from St Petersburg. From the station, walk diagonally across the little park in front, keep going up to the main road, turn right, pass the unmissable Archangel Michael Cathedral and you'll reach the park entrance on your left. *Marshrutky* to Lomonosov also run from outside metro Avtovo.

Strelna & Around

Стрельна и Окрестности Стрельны

Six kilometres east of Petrodvorets is the town of Strelna, where you'll find two more palaces originally built for Peter. The butterscotch-painted Konstantinovsky Palace was chosen by Vladimir Putin as his St Petersburg residence, underwent total renovation and reopened as the **Palace of Congress** (Дворец Конгрессов; www.konstantinpalace.ru; Beryozovaya al 3; adult/student R400/200; ⌚10am-5pm Thu-Tue). It's best to call ahead to book a tour as the palace is often used for official functions. Not a must-see sight, the palace nonetheless provides a fascinating glimpse of how a modern-day Russian leader likes to entertain his guests. There's a small collection of medals from the Hermitage's collection here and some reconstructed rooms from the time of Grand Duke Konstantin Konstanovich, the palace's last imperial owner and something of a poet and musician.

Opposite the entrance to the palace and scoring high on the modern kitsch factor is **Lindstrem's Dacha** (www.dachalindstrema.ru; ul Glinka 7; admission R200; ⌚10am-6pm), once the home of the Grand Duke's doctor Peter I von Lindstrem. Restored for the 2005 G8 summit, also hosted at the Konstantinovsky Palace, the modest-sized building was used by Putin to entertain his opposite numbers and their wives. One can only wonder what they thought of the garish *nouveau-russe* interior, which has since been supplemented by a small shrine to all things Putin, including a chance to have a three-minute audience with a life-sized hologram of the man himself.

A short walk to the west of the Palace of Congress lies the compact, and infinitely more charming, **Peter I's Palace at Strelna** (Дворец Петра I; adult/student R150/80; ⌚10.30am-5pm Tue-Sun). This is one of the first palaces that Peter the Great built out this way while supervising his far grander enterprise down the road. It has some well-furnished interiors with interesting exhibits, most notably a combined travelling chest and camp bed belonging to Alexander III.

Midway between Strelna and Petrodvorets is the tourist 'village' **Shuvalovka** (Шуваловка; www.shuvalovka.ru; Sankt-Peterburgskoe sh 111; ⌚10am-10pm Sat & Sun). The quaintly kitsch complex of traditional-style wooden buildings does have plus points, namely an excellent restaurant, a traditional *banya* and the opportunity to see Russian craftspeople in action.

All those visiting VIPs need somewhere to stay, so next to the Palace of Congress is the luxurious **Baltic Star Hotel** (☎438 5700; www.balticstar-hotel.ru; Beryozovaya al 3; r from R4500, ste/cottage R10,000/80,000; ❄📶🏊). It's a fancy enough place, but there's really no compelling reason to stay this far out of St Petersburg.

Trains and buses serving Petrodvorets pass through Strelna.

Pushkin (Tsarskoe Selo)

Царское Село

The grand imperial estate of **Tsarskoe Selo** (Tsar's Village; http://eng.tzar.ru; Sadovaya ul 7) in the town of Pushkin, 25km south of St Petersburg, is often combined on a day trip with the palace and sprawling park at Pavlovsk, 4km further south. It's a great combination, but start out early as there's lots to see: Pushkin can easily be a full-day trip in itself.

The railway that connects Pushkin and Pavlovsk with St Petersburg was Russia's first, opened in 1837 to carry the imperial family between here and the then capital. The town changed its name to Pushkin in 1937 after Russia's favourite poet, who studied here and whose school and dacha you can also visit.

Pushkin

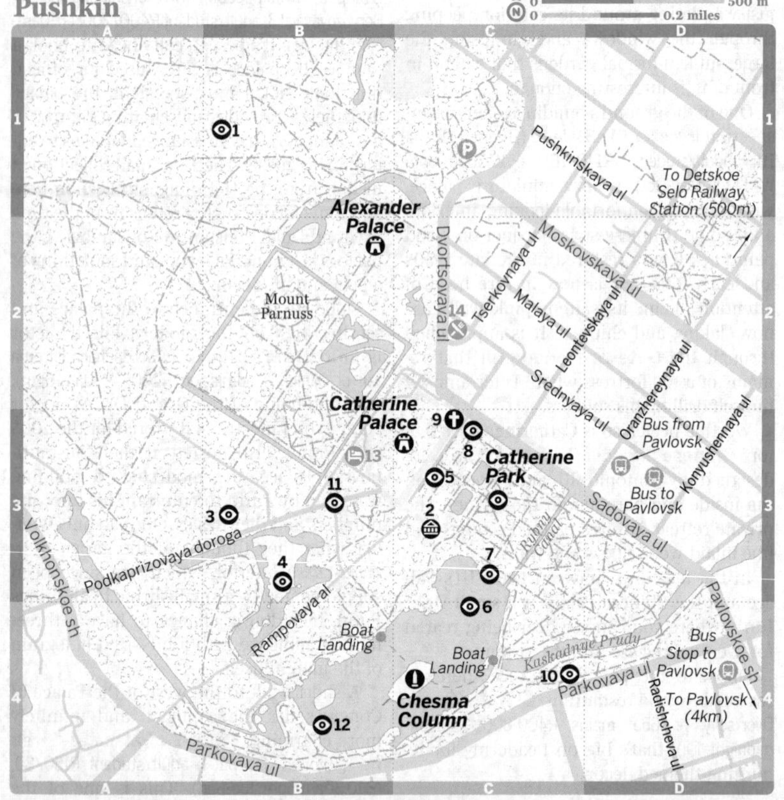

Sights

Catherine Palace PALACE

(Екатерининский дворец; www.tzar.ru; Sadovaya ul 7; adult/student R320/160; 10am-5pm Wed-Mon, open for individuals noon-2pm & 4-5pm, closed last Mon of month) The centrepiece of Tsarskoe Selo, created under Empresses Elizabeth and Catherine the Great between 1744 and 1796, is the vast baroque Catherine Palace, designed by Rastrelli and named after Elizabeth's mother, Peter the Great's second wife. As at the Winter Palace, Catherine the Great had many of Rastrelli's original interiors remodelled in classical style. Most of the gaudy exterior and 20-odd rooms of the palace have been beautifully restored – compare them to the photographs of the devastation left by the Germans.

While the palace opens for individual visitors (as opposed to groups) only at noon, it is usually necessary to queue up well in advance. All visitors are ushered into groups led by a tour guide; arrangements can sometimes be made for tours in English, but don't count on it. Everyone has to go on a guided tour here but it's easy to slip away once you're inside the palace and go around at your own pace.

Pushkin

Top Sights

	Alexander Palace	B2
	Catherine Palace	C3
	Catherine Park	C3
	Chesma Column	C4

Sights

1	Alexander Park	B1
2	Cameron Gallery	C3
3	Chinese Pavilion	B3
4	Concert Hall	B3
5	Entrance to Catherine Palace	C3
6	Great Pond	C4
7	Grotto Pavilion	C3
8	Main Entrance to Catherine Park	C3
9	Palace Chapel	C3
10	Park Entrance	C4
11	Park Entrance	B3
12	Turkish Bath	B4

Sleeping

13	Ekaterina Hotel	B3

Eating

	19th-Century Restaurant	(see 14)
14	Daniel	C2

Tours start with the white State Staircase (1860). South of here, only three rooms have been restored: the **Gentlemen-in-Waiting's Dining Room**; the dazzling **Great Hall**, the largest in the palace; and an **antechamber** with some huge blue-and-white Dutch ovens.

North of the State Staircase, you will pass through the State Dining Room, the Crimson and Green Pilaster Rooms and the Picture Gallery. The reception room of Alexander I contains portraits of his esteemed predecessors.

The highlight is Rastrelli's amazing **Amber Room**, completely covered with gilded woodcarvings, mirrors, agate and jasper mosaics (see the boxed text, p234).

Most of the palace's north end is the early-classical work of architect Charles Cameron, including the elegant Green Dining Room, the Blue Drawing Room, Chinese Blue Drawing Room and **Choir Anteroom**, whose gold silk, woven with swans and pheasants, is the original from the 18th century.

Once you finish your tour, you can head to the southern **Zubov Wing** (Zubovsky korpus; adult/student R200/100; 10am-5pm Thu-Tue), which houses special exhibitions.

Catherine Park PARK

(Екатерининский парк; adult/student R100/50; 9am-6pm) Around the Catherine Palace extends the lovely Catherine Park. The **main entrance** is on Sadovaya ul, next to the **palace chapel**. The park extends around the ornamental Great Pond and contains an array of interesting buildings, follies and pavilions.

Nearby the Catherine Palace, the **Cameron Gallery** (adult/student R100/50; 10am-5pm Thu-Tue) has rotating exhibitions. Between the gallery and the palace, notice the south-pointing ramp that Cameron added for the ageing empress to walk down into the park.

The park's outer section focuses on the **Great Pond**. In summer you can take a **ferry** (adult/child R200/100; 11am-6pm May-Sep) to the little island to visit the **Chesma Column**. Beside the pond, the blue baroque **Grotto Pavilion** (admission free; 10am-5pm Fri-Wed) houses temporary exhibitions in summer. A walk around the Great Pond will reveal other buildings that the royals built over the years, including the very incongruous-looking **Turkish Bath** with its minaret-style tower, the wonderful Marble Bridge, the **Chinese Pavilion** and a **Concert Hall** (concerts incl ferry transport R350;

⏲May-Sep) isolated on an island, where concerts take place every Saturday at 5pm.

Alexander Palace PALACE
(Dvortsovaya ul 2; adult/student R100/50; ⏲10am-5pm Wed-Mon, closed last Wed of the month) A short distance north of the Catherine Palace, and surrounded by the overgrown and tranquil **Alexander Park** (admission free) is the classical Alexander Palace. It was built by Quarenghi between 1792 and 1796 for the future Alexander I, but Nicholas II, the last Russian tsar, was its main tenant and made it his favourite residence for much of his reign. Only three rooms are open to visitors, but they're impressive, with a huge tiger-skin carpet and an extremely ropey portrait of a young Queen Victoria to boot. It's a poignant and forgotten place that doesn't get many tourists; it's a welcome contrast to the Catherine Palace.

Sleeping & Eating

Ekaterina Hotel HOTEL €€
(☎466 8042; www.hotelekaterina.ru; Sadovaya ul 5; r incl breakfast from R3500; ❄📶) Staying at this small hotel inside the palace's old servants' block not only provides great views of the building's gilded facade, but is also about your best chance of being first in line to get into the palace. The rooms lack glitz but they're modern and reasonably spacious.

Daniel INTERNATIONAL €€€
(Даниель; www.apriorico.com; Srednyaya ul 2/3; mains R700-1300; ⏲11am-11pm) Daniel offers a blow-out gastronomic feast within stumbling distance of the Catherine Palace. Swedish chef Eric Viedgård conjures culinary magic with his seasonally changing menu in an elegant contemporary space with heritage touches.

19th-Century Restaurant RUSSIAN €€
(XIX Век Ресторан; www.restaurantpushkin.ru; Srednyaya ul 2; mains R400-600) Admire the owner's impressive collection of miniature bottles of alcohol at the entrance, before choosing one of four differently decorated dining rooms in which to eat a traditional Russian meal.

Getting There & Away

From Moskovskaya metro station, take the exit marked 'Buses for the airport', and then pick up *marshrutka* 286, 299, 342 or K545 towards Pushkin (R30). These buses all continue to Pavlovsk (R32).

Suburban trains run from Vitebsky vokzal in St Petersburg, but they're infrequent except for weekends. For Pushkin, get off at **Detskoe Selo** (Детское село, R42, 30 minutes) and for Pavlovsk (R55, 40 minutes) at Pavlovsk Station (Павловск). From Detskoe Selo station *marshrutky* (R20) frequently run the 500m or so to Tsarskoe Selo.

Pavlovsk Павловск

Between 1781 and 1786, on orders from Catherine the Great, architect Charles Cameron designed the Great Palace in Pavlovsk. The palace was designated for Catherine's son Paul (hence the name, Pavlovsk), and it was his second wife, Maria Fyodorovna, who orchestrated the design of the interiors. It served as a royal residence until 1917. Ironically, the original palace was burnt down two weeks after liberation following WWII when a careless Soviet soldier's cigarette set off German mines (the Soviets blamed the Germans). As at Tsarskoe Selo, its restoration is remarkable.

THE MYSTERY OF THE AMBER ROOM

The original Amber Room was created from exquisitely engraved amber panels given to Peter the Great by King Friedrich Wilhelm I of Prussia in 1716. Rastrelli later combined the panels with gilded woodcarvings, mirrors, agate and jasper mosaics to decorate one of the rooms of the Catherine Palace. Plundered by the Nazis during WWII, the room's decorative panels were last exhibited in Königsberg's castle in 1941. Four years later, with the castle in ruins, the Amber Room was presumed destroyed. Or was it?

In 2004, as Putin and then German Chancellor Gerhardt Schröder presided over the opening of the new US$18 million Amber Room, restored largely with German funds, rumours about the original panels continued to swirl. There are those who believe that parts, if not all, of the original Amber Room remain hidden away (see www.amberroom.org). The mystery gained traction in February 2008 as attention focused on the possible contents of an artificial cavern discovered near the village of Deutschneudorf on Germany's border with the Czech Republic. Nothing conclusive has yet been unearthed here, though, so the mystery continues.

Pavlovsk

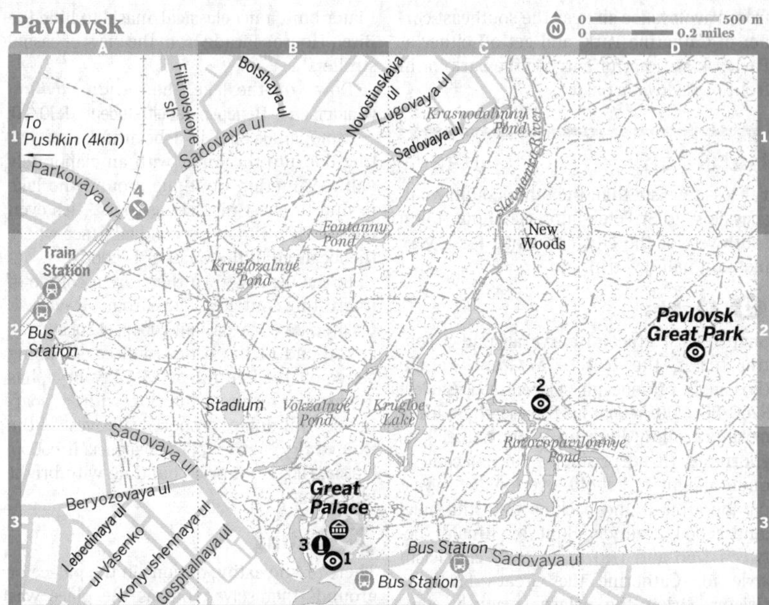

The finest rooms in Pavlovsk's **Great Palace** (Павловский дворец; www.pavlovskmuseum.ru; ul Revolutsii; adult/student R500/300; ⏲10am-5pm) are on the middle floor of the central block. Cameron designed the round **Italian Hall** beneath the dome and the **Grecian Hall** to its west, though the lovely green fluted columns were added by his assistant Vincenzo Brenna. Flanking these are two private suites designed mainly by Brenna – Paul's along the north side of the block and Maria Fyodorovna's on the south. The **Hall of War** of the insane, military-obsessed Paul contrasts with Maria's **Hall of Peace**, decorated with musical instruments and flowers.

On the middle floor of the south block are Paul's **Throne Room** and the Hall of the Maltese Knights of St John, of whom he was the Grand Master.

If you decide to skip the palace, you may simply wish to wander around the serene **Pavlovsk Great Park** (adult/student R150/80; ⏲9.30am-5pm, to 6pm Sat & Sun) – and as you'll have to pay to enter them just to access the palace, it's worth exploring and seeing what you come across. Filled with rivers and ponds, tree-lined avenues, classical statues and hidden temples, it's a delightful place to get lost. Highlights include the **Rose Pavilion** (Розовый павильон; adult/student R150/80)

Pavlovsk

Top Sights

Great Palace B3
Pavlovsk Great Park D2

Sights

1 Private Garden B3
2 Rose Pavilion C2
3 Three Graces Pavilion B3

Eating

4 Podvorye A1

and the **Private Garden** (Собственный садик; adult/student R100/50), with its beautifully arranged flowerbeds and impressive sculpture of the **Three Graces**.

Just outside the park grounds, a short walk northeast of Pavlovsk station, there's the touristy **Podvorye** (Подьворе; www.podvorye.ru; Filtrovskoye sh 16; mains R600-1000) in a traditional Russian log house on steroids. Huge portions of delicious Russian food are dished up, with a side-order of live Russian music and dancing.

Trains and *marshrutky* running from St Petersburg to Pushkin continue to Pavlovsk. *Marshrutky* (R20) frequently shuttle between Pushkin and Pavlovsk; catch one from Pavolovskoe sh near the southeast corner of Catherine Park, and get off either at Pavlovsk station (for entry to the park) or in front of Pavlovsk's palace.

Gatchina Гатчина

Far less touristy than the other country palaces close to St Petersburg, Gatchina, 45km southwest of the city, can make for a very pleasant half-day trip.

Sights

Shaped in a graceful curve around a central turret, the **Gatchina Great Palace** (Большой гатчинский дворец; adult/student R200/80; 10am-5pm Tue-Sun, closed 1st Tue of month) certainly lives up to its name – its enormous (if surprisingly plain) facade is quite a sight to behold, overlooking a vast parade ground and backing onto the huge landscaped grounds. Built by Rinaldi between 1766 and 1781 in an early classicism style for Catherine the Great's favourite Grigory Orlov, the palace curiously combines motifs of a medieval fortress with elements commonly seen in Russian imperial residences. It's hard to call it beautiful, but there's no doubt that it's extremely impressive. After Orlov's death in 1783, Catherine the Great bought the palace from his heirs and gifted it to her son Paul, who redesigned the exterior between 1792 and 1798.

Inside, the 10 **State Rooms** on the 2nd floor are impressive, including Paul I's Throne Room, hung with huge tapestries, and his wife Maria Fyodorovna's Throne Room, the walls of which are covered in paintings. Most impressive of all is the **White Hall**, a Rinaldi creation from the 1770s that was redone by Brenna in the 1790s, on the balcony of which is an impressive collection of sundials.

Gatchina Park (Гатчинский парк; admission free; dawn-dusk) is more overgrown and romantic than the other palaces' parklands. The park has many winding paths through birch groves and across bridges to islands in the large **White Lake**. Look out for the frankly bizarre **Birch House** (Берёзовый домик; adult/student R30/20; 11am-7pm Tue-Sun), which was a present from Maria Fyodorovna to Paul I. With a rough facade made of birch logs, the interior is actually very refined, with a beautiful hardwood floor made from timbers from around the world. Perhaps unsurprisingly though, Paul I later built a neoclassical 'mask' to hide the Birch House's facade from the view of casual strollers!

Down on the lake, the **Venus Pavilion** (Павильон Венеры; adult/student R30/20; 11am-7pm Tue-Sun) is a beautiful spot jutting out into the water with an elaborately painted interior. Continue around the lake to find the best picnicking spots – it's even possible to swim in a second lake (see where the locals go) if the weather is good.

In the nearby town there are a couple of interesting churches. The baroque **Pavlovsk Cathedral** (Павловский собор; ul Sobornaya), at the end of the pedestrianised shopping street off the central pr 25 Oktyabrya, has a grandly restored interior with a soaring central dome. A short walk west is the **Pokrovsky Cathedral** (Покровский собор; Krasnaya ul), a red-brick building with bright blue domes.

Eating

There are no eating options in the palace or grounds themselves, but as the place was made for picnicking, your best bet is to bring your own lunch. However, if you haven't done so, there are a couple of options in the town.

Kafe Piramida RUSSIAN €
(Кафе Пирамида; ul Sobornaya 3a; mains R150-250; 10am-11pm) Serving a wide range of traditional Russian dishes as well as delicious cakes and coffees, this cosy place is near the Pavlovsk Cathedral.

Slavyansky Dvor RUSSIAN €
(Славянский двор; ul Dostoevskogo 2; mains R200-350; 11am-midnight Mon-Thu, to 3am Fri-Sun) Housed in a restored historic building near the Pokrovsky Cathedral, this traditional Russian place (its name means 'Slavic Yard') will prepare you a filling meal at any time throughout the day.

Getting There & Away

The quickest way to get to Gatchina is by bus or *marshrutka*. *Marshrutky* K18 and 431 (R50, 45 minutes) run this route from outside Moskovskaya metro station and stop right by the park. Bus 100 (R70, one hour) also runs regularly from Moskovskaya; buses wait on ul Altayskaya and stop just short of Gatchina Park. Tell the driver you want to go to the palace ('*v dvaryéts*') – the bus turns off before you get to the park.

There are trains to Gatchina Baltiysky (R86, one hour) from Baltiysky vokzal every one to

WORTH A TRIP

REPINO РЕПИНО

Come summer, St Petersburgers stream out of the city whenever they get the chance to relax on the beaches to the north between Sestroretsk and Zelenogorsk on the Gulf of Finland. Between these two towns you'll find the village of Repino, 45km from St Petersburg. From 1918 to the end of WWII, this area was part of Finland and the village was known as Kuokkala. In 1948, back in Russian hands, the village was renamed in honour of its most famous resident, Ilya Repin.

The artist's charming house and small estate, **Penates** (adult/student R300/100; ⏲museum 10.30am-6pm Wed-Sun, grounds to 8pm), are now a museum and park, and make for a pleasant day trip any time of year. You can also visit the nearby beach and even stay in one of the area's many resort-style hotels and sanatoriums in the summer.

Repin bought land here in 1899, named the estate after a Roman household god and designed the light-flooded house in an arts and crafts style. The artist executed many of his later works here and several of his paintings still hang on the walls. The furnishings have been left just as they were during Repin's residence, which was up to his death in 1930. His grave, marked by a simple Russian Orthodox wooden cross, is in the park, along with a couple of wooden follies also designed by Repin.

Next to Penates there are a couple of decent cafés for lunch. The nearest, also called **Penates** (mains R200-450; ⏲11am-5pm), serves a range of Russian dishes including salads, soups and various shashlyks. A little further down the road towards the heart of Repino village is the far more upmarket **Skazka** (mains R400-800; ⏲11am-11pm), which offers a very meaty menu and even has rabbits in hutches scattered about the premises (though they are apparently decorative and not for eating).

The easiest way of getting to Repino is to take the frequent *marshrutky* 400 (R80, one hour) that leave from immediately outside Finlyandsky vokzal, or bus 211 (R60, one hour) from beside Chyornya Rechka metro station. Be sure to tell the driver that you want to get out at Penates.

two hours. The train station is directly in front of the palace.

Kronshtadt Кронштадт

☎812 / POP 45,100

Within a year of founding St Petersburg, Peter – desirous of protecting his new Baltic toehold – started work on the fortress of Kronshtadt on Kotlin Island, 29km out in the Gulf of Finland. It's been a pivotal Soviet and Russian naval base ever since, and was closed to foreigners until 1996.

In 1921 the hungry and poor Red Army sailors stationed here organised an ill-fated mutiny against the Bolsheviks. They set up a Provisional Revolutionary Committee and drafted a resolution demanding, among other things, an end to Lenin's harsh War Communism. On 16 March 1921 the mutineers were defeated when 50,000 troops crossed the ice from Petrograd and massacred nearly the entire naval force. The sailors' stand wasn't entirely in vain as afterwards Lenin did scrap War Communism.

Kronshtadt's key sight is the unusual and beautiful **Naval Cathedral** (Морской собор). Built between 1903 and 1913 to honour Russian naval muscle, this neo-Byzantine wonder stands on Yakornaya pl (Anchor Sq), where you'll also find an eternal flame for all of Kronshtadt's sailors, and the florid art nouveau monument of Admiral Makarov.

In the harbourside **Petrovsky Park**, 700m southwest of the cathedral, there's a statue of Peter the Great, and you can glimpse Russian warships and even some submarines: be careful about taking photographs, though. For a meal try the highly Soviet **Austeria** (ul Sovetskaya 43; mains R170-300; ⏲noon-midnight), with its curious boat-like bar and slow service.

Catch bus 510 to Kronshtadt from Staraya Derevnya metro station (R25, 40 minutes) or take *marshrutka* k-405 from Chyornaya Rechka station (R60, 40 minutes); exit the station to your left and cross the street to find the stop. In Kronshtadt, ask the driver to drop you off '*vozle sobora*' (near the cathedral). The buses back to St Petersburg depart from outside the large 'Dom Byta' on the corner of ul Grazhdanskaya and pr Lenina. From there it's about a 1km walk southeast to the Naval Cathedral.

Western European Russia

Includes »

Best Places to Eat

» 3 Etazh (p250)
» Biblioteka (p241)
» Manilov (p259)
» Dvor Podznoeva (p273)
» Nice People (p266)

Best Places to Stay

» Armenia (p241)
» Hotel Oryol (p249)
» Usadba (p256)
» Hotel Volkhov (p266)
» Letuchaya Mysh (p278)

Why Go?

The lush green countryside of Western European Russia (Западно-Европейская Россия), home to some of the nation's earliest settlements, is a crucible of Rus culture. Impressive kremlins (stone fortresses) and fairy-tale onion-domed churches rise over towns such as Veliky Novgorod, Pskov, Smolensk and Tula, offering visual history lessons and memorable vistas.

The area was the birthplace and home of many of Russia's cultural heavyweights, from author Fyodor Dostoevsky to the composer Mikhail Glinka. In Mikhailovskoe, Pushkin's ancestral estate, you can stroll along the serene lake that inspired the nation's most revered poet. The estates of Leo Tolstoy and Ivan Turgenev, near Tula and Oryol respectively, also offer serene slices of rural life.

This region is largely off most foreign travellers' itineraries. Nonetheless, you can expect to be greeted with friendliness and interest by locals, and find good-quality hotels and restaurants in which to experience that hospitality.

When to Go

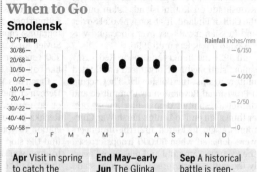

Smolensk

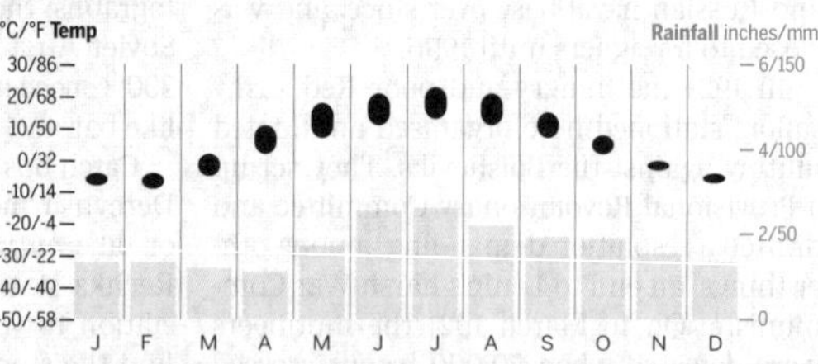

Apr Visit in spring to catch the Alexander Nevsky Festival in Veliky Novgorod.

End May–early Jun The Glinka Festival of classical music is held in Smolensk.

Sep A historical battle is reenacted at Kulikovo Pole in early autumn.

SOUTH OF MOSCOW

Tula Тула

☎4872 / POP 501,000 / ⏰MOSCOW

A town centre graced by a picturesque kremlin; a fascinating industrial history reflected in several museums; and several great restaurants: there's much to recommend in Tula. The key attraction, though, is Yasnaya Polyana, the country estate of the celebrated author Leo Tolstoy, just south of the city.

Blacksmiths, ironmongers and gunmakers have churned out everything from

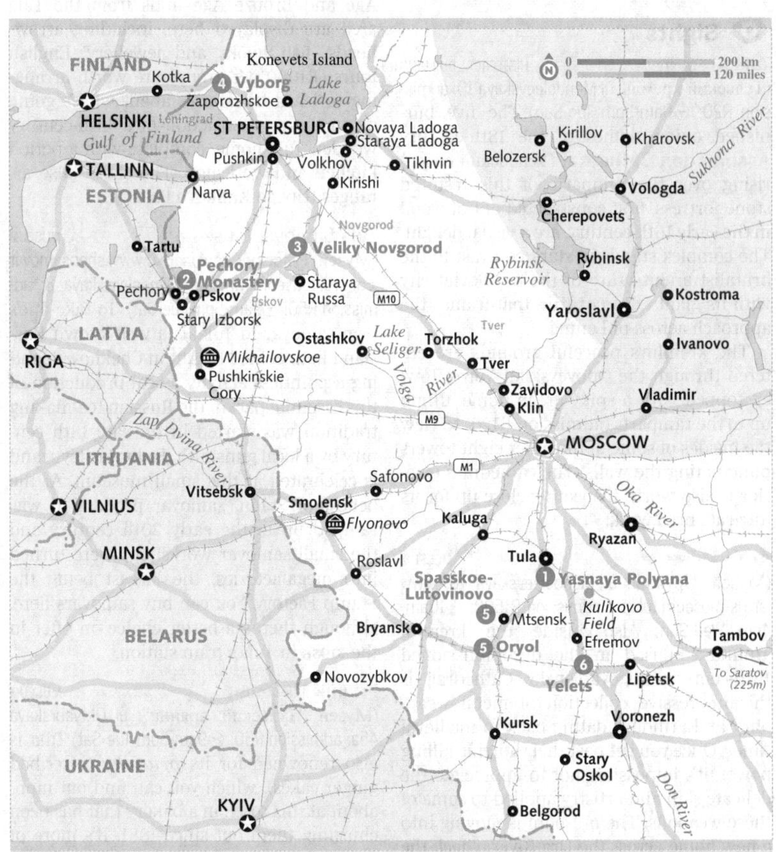

Western European Russia Highlights

1. Return to rural 19th-century Russia at **Yasnaya Polyana** (p244), the leafy estate and last resting place of Leo Tolstoy
2. Light a candle and enter the spooky underground tombs of **Pechory Monastery** (p275), where solemn monks show you their dead
3. Explore a magnificent kremlin, ancient churches and monasteries – even lounge on a riverside beach – in the tourist-friendly town of **Veliky Novgorod** (p262)
4. Stroll the romantic cobblestone streets of **Vyborg** (p276), admiring the mix of old Russian and Finnish art nouveau architecture
5. Acquaint yourself with Russia's literary talent in the charming house-museums of **Oryol** (p248), including **Spasskoe-Lutovinovo** (p249), the lovely countryside estate of Turgenev
6. Admire the beautifully decorated churches of **Yelets** (p244)

swords to small arms and samovars in Tula for centuries. The first weapons workshop was built in 1712 under the patronage of Peter the Great, and was kept busy during Peter's 21-year war with Sweden. In the 1890s mass production commenced on the Mossin-Nagant rifle, one of the world's most popular rifles for decades to come.

Sights

Tula Kremlin HISTORICAL BUILDING

(Тульский кремль; ul Mendeleevskaya 10; admission R20; 9am-5pm Tue-Sun) The five burnished onion domes of the 18th-century **Assumption Cathedral** (Успенский собор) rising over the ramparts of this restored stone fortress, first constructed out of wood in the early 16th century, are a visual delight. The complex stands in stark contrast to the brutalist architecture of the old Soviet city with its giant **Lenin statue** that frames the approach across pl Lenina.

The kremlin's peaceful grounds are entered through the Odoyevskikh Vorog Tower, topped with a spiky green dome. Climb up to the ramparts (admission R120) to view the insides of some of the other eight towers punctuating the walls. The cathedral's exterior is also worth inspecting close up for its intricate brickwork.

Arms Museum MUSEUM

(Музей Оружия; ul Mendeleevskaya 10; www.arms-museum.tula.ru; admission R1500; 10am-4pm Wed-Sun) Also inside the kremlin grounds, housed in the decommissioned 19th-century Bogoyablensky Cathedral, is this impressive collection of metal weaponry and armoury dating back to medieval times. Once you get past their horrific killing power, it's impossible not to appreciate the delicate skill and artistry applied to some of these weapons. The museum is moving into a new home across the Ura River; check the website for details.

Museum of Visual Arts MUSEUM

(Музей изобразительных искусств; ul Engelsa 66; admission R150; 11am-6pm Tue-Sun) Beside the entrance to Central Park is this exceptionally good municipal gallery charting a course from gilded icons and late-15th-century paintings from across Europe (look for a haunting image of Christ from Germany) through fascinating pieces of socialist realism from the 20th century, including animated porcelain figurines of heroic workers and explorers. The exquisite collection also includes works by Russian artists such as Ivanov, Shishkin, Ghe and Repin, as well as furniture and classical marble statues.

Antiquities Exhibition Centre MUSEUM

(Музейно-выставочный центр Тульские древности; 361 663; admission R40; pr Lenina 47; 10am-5pm, closed last Wed of month) Stone Age and Bronze Age finds from the Tula area are displayed here, including arrowheads, fish hooks and jewellery. English tours (R1000 per group) are worth arranging to learn the stories about what's going on in the reconstruction of a 19th-century wooden Tula home, complete with a period kitchen and workshop. The centre also arranges trips to Kulikovo Pole.

Tula Samovar Museum MUSEUM

(Музей Тульские самовары; www.shopsamovar.com.ru/museum.html; ul Mendeleevskaya 8; admission R50; 9am-5pm Tue-Sat) 'To take one's own samovar to Tula' is a well-known Russian idiom coined by Anton Chekhov, denoting a pointless activity. Local production of this essential part of the Russian tea-making tradition was started in the late 18th century by a local gunsmith, Fedor Lisitsyn, and is celebrated at this small museum. At the behest of Stalin, samovar production was ramped up in the early 20th century and the small samovar workshops were turned into megafactories, the largest being the Stamp Factory. You can buy samovars here, although there's a better choice on offer in the kiosk in Tula's train station.

Prianik Museum MUSEUM

(Музей "Тульский пряник"; ul Oktyabrskaya 45a; admission R50; 9am-5pm Tue-Sat) Tula is also renowned for its *prianiky* (inscribed ginger cakes), which you can find out more about at this room in a bakery that has been churning them out since 1881. It's more of a prelude to shopping and eating at the attached **shop and café** (8am-8pm) than an educational experience.

The cakes, reputedly invented in the 9th century, were a symbol of the aristocracy because the high cost of production (which required the carving of customised wooden moulds) kept it out of peasant hands. Some could well be Guinness World Record holders – check out the 16kg monster loaf. Animal themes are popular, while others denote historical events and tributes to important personalities. Plenty of *prianiky* are also sold around town.

Central Park PARK
(Центральныи парк Белоусова; http://tulagardens.ru/main2; ul Engelsa 66) Approach this large, pleasant park from pr Lenina to see the giant **Tolstoy statue** – local wags have it that the writer was on his way to the vodka factory that was once housed in the brick building opposite. Bicycles and rollerblades can be **rented** (rollerblades/bikes per hr from R80/100; noon-9pm, last rental 7.30pm) in the park.

Metal Working Museum MUSEUM
(Выставочный зал Тульский металл; ul Demidovskaya Plotina 13; admission R20; 10am-5pm Mon-Fri) Tula's long history as a centre of metalwork and gun manufacture is told through displays at this small museum on the north side of the river.

Sleeping

All of the following places include breakfast in their rates.

TOP CHOICE **Armenia** HOTEL €€
(Армения; 250 600; www.ind-garnik.ru; ul Sovetskaya 47; s/d R3600/3960;) Part of the revamped Gostiny Dvor Ind Garik business and entertainment complex, this appealing hotel offers kremlin views and spacious, pleasantly furnished rooms. There's also a sauna and pool (free to guests from 7am to 11am), a restaurant serving Armenian and Russian dishes, and a billiards club.

Hotel Moskva HOTEL €
(Гостиница Москва; 208 952; ul Puteiskaya 3; s unrenovated/renovated R750/1800, d R3100;) The convenient location opposite the train station makes up for the shabbiness of the cheapest rooms here; nevertheless they come with attached bathrooms and are fine for one night. Renovated singles and the doubles have new furnishings, far better bathrooms and a lick of paint.

Hotel Tula HOTEL €
(Гостиница Тула; 351 960; www.hoteltula.ru; pr Lenina 96; s/d/tr without bathroom R900/1600/2100, s/d R1900/2100;) Next to the bus station, and across from the impressive WWII monument in Pobedy pl, this Soviet relic offers small, well-worn unrenovated rooms. The renovated rooms are decent and much larger, the best ones even stretching to air-conditioning. From the train station, take trolleybus 5.

Eating

TOP CHOICE **Biblioteka** FRENCH €€
(Библиотека; 305 076; pr Lenina 91; meals R500-700; noon-11pm;) The svelte cutlery, rows of Russian novels, piles of magazines and clubby atmosphere lend an air of sophistication to this star performer. A perfect French onion soup, tender lamb in flaky pastry and delectable desserts are among the many appealing dishes on the Russian-only menu. At lunch there's 20% off the prices.

Skovoroda UKRAINIAN €€
(Сковорода; 364 707; pr Lenina 57; meals R400-600;) Locals swear by this convivial place, claiming it has the best borsch this side of Kyiv. It also does chicken Kiev and *vareniki* (dumplings), while those with

WORTH A TRIP

KULIKOVO POLE КУЛИКОВО ПОЛЕ

This large nature reserve and memorial complex, around 130km southeast of Tula, celebrates a crucial confrontation on 8 September 1380, when a coalition of Russian princes, under the leadership of Moscow's Dmitry Ivanovich, fought the mighty army of the Golden Horde and won. A stone column monument, erected on the site in 1850, honours the medieval soldiers who died on the Kulikovo Field, and three **museums** (Map p239; 10am-7pm daily May-Sep, to 5pm Oct, to 4pm Wed-Mon Nov-Apr) describe the history of the battle as well as local ethnography.

Each year on the third Saturday in September, historical clubs come here to reenact the battle. Other events are also held throughout the year, including a crafts fair in August. For a full listing of events, see the website of the **Kulikov Travel Department** (4872-362 834; www.kulpole.ru), based at the Tula Antiquities Exhibition Centre.

The travel department also arranges full-day tours here (R680 per person, minimum 10 people) including transport, guide and museum tickets. For extra fees, an English-speaking guide (R4500 per group) and lunch (around R200 per person) can be included.

Tula

0 500 m
0 0.25 miles

To Prianik Museum (500m)
ul Lunacharskogo
Upa River
nab Dreyera
per Oruzheyny
ul Oktyabrskaya
ul Galkina
ul Demidovskaya Plotina
ul Mosina
To Hotel Moskva (900m); Moskovsky Train Station (900m)
ul Kominterna
ul Soyfera
ul Metallistov
ul Lenina
pr Krasnoarmeysky
15
ul Soyuznaya
Tula Kremlin
11
per Denisovsky
1
Arms Museum
6
pl Lenina
3
ul Bratyev Zhabrovykh
ul Khalturina
ul Leyteyzena
ul Revolyutsii
ul Demonstratsii
7
ul Engelsa
12
14
ul Dzerzhinskaya
ul Mendeleevskaya
per Tsentralny
ul Kaminskogo
ul Sovetskaya
9
ul Pushkinskaya
16
10
ul Turgenevskaya
ul Zhukovskogo
ul Bundurina
ul Svobody
Antiquities Exhibition Centre
pr Lenina
ul Pionerskaya
ul Koletvinova
ul Staronikitskaya
ul Oboronnaya
13
ul Engelsa
ul Pervomayskaya
2
ul Gogolevskaya
ul Lva Tolstogo
Museum of Visual Arts
17
ul Petra Alekseeva
5
pr Lenina
ul Kaulya
ul Mikheeva
ul Budennogo
ul Timiryazeva
8
ul Ageeva
To Bus Station (200m); Hotel Tula (800m)

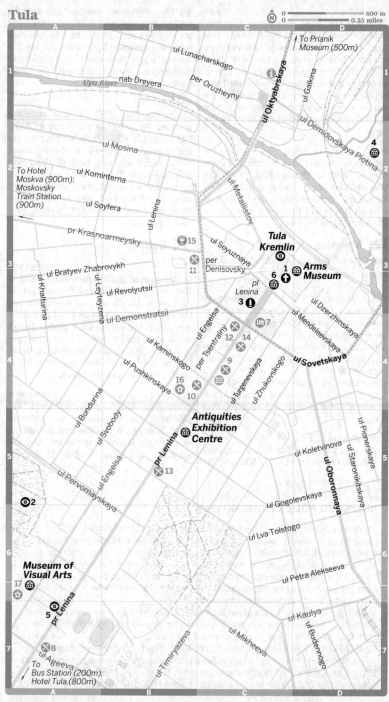

Tula

Top Sights

Sights

Sleeping

Eating

Drinking

Entertainment

more adventurous tastes can sample dishes with calves brains and chicken intestines as ingredients.

Chaikhona Izyum CENTRAL ASIAN €€
(Чайхона Изюм; ☎701 233; pr Lenina 32; ⏰11am-midnight Sun-Thu, to 3am Fri & Sat;) Samarkand comes to Tula at this exotic two-level teahouse, decked out in colourful Central Asian fabrics and comfy booths. Sample dishes such as *lagman* (noodle soup), *plov* (a meaty rice risotto) and kebabs, as well as tea with dried fruit nibbles. There's 30% off the bill from 11am to 4pm.

Vanilnoye Nebo INTERNATIONAL €€
(Ванильное Небо; pr Lenina 17; meals R500; ⏰10am-midnight) Providing a bird's-eye view of the kremlin through its floor-to-ceiling windows is this groovy café on the 4th floor of the Paradise Mall. The photo menu will tempt you into trying the food ranging from breakfast to salad, soups and a big range of creamy cakes.

Podkre Pizza PIZZA €
(Подкре Пицца; pr Lenina 12; meals R200-400; ⏰10am-10pm) Popular self-serve pizza and pasta place with views of the main square and the kremlin walls.

Egori Ebskii Centre DELI €
(Егор Ебский центр; pr Krasnoarmeysky 1; ⏰10am-10pm) Pick up fresh fruit, imported goods and deli snacks at this gleaming gourmet deli – perfect for a picnic at Yasnaya Polyana.

Café Chocolate CAFÉ €
(Кафе Шоколад; pr Lenina 31; snacks R80-150; ⏰10am-11pm) Pleasant café serving artfully designed cakes and caffeinated beverages.

Drinking

Beerlin BAR
(pr Krasnoarmeysky 4; ⏰11am-11pm Sun-Thu, to midnight Fri & Sat;) Work your way through the many fine cask-pumped ales (five/10 tasters for R240/590) from around Europe at this spacious bar and restaurant. With its wood-panelled walls, bar and furniture, it resembles a traditional English country pub.

Sovetskiy Sport PUB
(Советский Спорт; pr Lenina 57; ⏰noon-1am Sun-Thu, to 2am Fri & Sat;) This compact basement bar combines Soviet-era kitsch and propaganda with a modern-day enthusiasm for sports; watch soccer, hockey and other televised sport on one of the many flat-screen TVs.

Entertainment

Premier NIGHTCLUB
(Премьер; ☎357 606; ul Engelsa 66) This complex next to the park houses a cinema, several bars, a nightclub and a patio restaurant. While the club gets going late on weekends, the patio is a nice place for a drink on summer afternoons.

Drama Theatre THEATRE
(Тульский академический театр драмы; ☎367 332; pr Lenina 34a) It's not the Bolshoi, but the drama, dance and opera held here are well produced, with ticket prices from around R100.

Information

Post office & telephone office (Почта и круглосуточный переговорный пункт;

(☎360 287; pr Lenina 33) Also offers internet access and an ATM.

Getting There & Away

Bus

From the **bus station** (pr Lenina), services run to Moscow (one way R300, four daily, three hours), Oryol (R243, seven daily, four hours), Voronezh (R522, two daily, eight hours) and Yelets (R315, five daily, four hours).

Private minibuses (R300, three hours) connect regularly with various metro stations in Moscow, departing from the train and bus stations.

Train

Both *elektrichki* (suburban trains) and regular trains run to Moscow (*platskart/kupe* R400/850, three hours, 25 daily) from the **Moskovsky train station** (ul Puteyskaya). Other services include Oryol (R1000/2200, 25 daily, 2½ hours) and Yelets (R713/1258, six daily, 5½ hours).

Getting Around

Many buses and *marshrutky* (fixed-route minibuses; R11) run from the train station along pr Krasnoarmeysky to Lenina pl and then up pr Lenina. For the bus station and Hotel Tula, take trolleybus 5 from outside the train station.

Yasnaya Polyana
Ясная Поляна

Located 14km south of central Tula, **Yasnaya Polyana** (☎4872-393 599; www.yasnayapolyana.ru; grounds R20, Tolstoy & Kuzminsky House R150; ⏲9am-5pm Tue-Sun) is billed as a 'typical Russian estate' of the late 19th century, which it is save for one important fact: this is where Leo Tolstoy, author of *War and Peace* and *Anna Karenina*, was born, lived most of his life and is buried.

Of Yasnaya Polyana, Tolstoy wrote: 'All [my grandfather] had built here was not only solid and comfortable, but also very elegant. The same is true about the park he laid out near the house.' Beyond the addition of a few helpful signs, little has probably changed since that time.

A long birch-lined avenue leads from the entrance to the whitewashed, modestly proportioned **Tolstoy House**, where the great writer lived and worked. The rooms have been kept just as they were in 1910, with portraits, books, furniture and even some of Tolstoy's clothes laid out. Nearby in the **Kuzminsky House** is an imaginatively designed exhibition covering the range of things that inspired Tolstoy from 1851 to 1869 when he finished *War and Peace*. Deep into the estate's shady forest is **Tolstoy's grave**, unmarked except for bouquets of flowers left by admirers.

Horse riding (one hour R400, 20-minute wagon ride R150) is available on the estate grounds. Russian-language courses are also available at the estate; see the website for details. For an English-language guided trip to the estate and surrounding areas, contact **Yasnaya Polyana Tour Office** (☎4872-393 599; tour@tolstoy.ru; ul Oktyabrskaya 14; ⏲10am-6pm Mon-Fri) in Tula.

From where the bus from Tula stops on the main road, heading in the opposite direction to Yasnaya Polyana, it's a pleasant country walk for 3.5km to the historic train station at **Kozlova Zaseka** (Козлова Засека; admission R20; ⏲9.30am-4pm Tue-Sun); Tolstoy used this station many times in his life and set off for his final journey from here in 1910. It's now maintained as a one-room museum by a charming bunch of ladies.

Located 1.5km from the estate, the small, Soviet-era **Yasnaya Polyana Hotel** (☎48751-76 146; s/d R1200/1700) offers clean, comfortable rooms in peaceful surrounds. Opposite the entrance gate to the estate is **Café Preshpekt** (Кафе Прешпект; meals R200-250; ⏲8am-8pm Tue-Sun), a simple café featuring hearty home-cooked Russian fare. House specialities are said to be prepared according to recipes by Sofia Andreevna, Leo's devoted wife.

From Tula, take *marshrutka* 114 or 117 (R20, 20 minutes) from anywhere along pr Lenina; tell the driver to let you off at Yasnaya Polyana – it's a 1km walk from the main road to the estate. If you walk to Kozlova Zaseka, you can also use buses 218 or 30 to get back to Tula.

Yelets Елец

☎47467 / POP 108,400 / ⏲MOSCOW

On the tranquil Sosna River, Yelets stands out as one of the early Rus settlements to have retained some of its traditional character. The town centre is a visual delight, littered with large and small churches – some working, others undergoing restoration or still in ruins – and lined with pastel-coloured buildings and wooden cottages. The beautiful Ascension Cathedral and Znamensky Monastery are visible from kilometres around. There is also a well-stocked regional museum and a museum devoted to Soviet composer Tikhon Khrennikov.

Founded in 1146 as a fortification against the Turkic invaders from the east, Yelets became a punching bag for the Mongol Tatars, who devastated it half a dozen times during the Middle Ages. Today it's a sleepy place where most days the only thing stirring on pedestrianised ul Mira are the pigeons fluttering over Lenin's granite pate.

Yelets' centre is laid out in a grid, with ul Kommunarov connecting Hotel Yelets in the east with Ascension Cathedral in the west. Further west (downhill) lies the Sosna River. The train station and long-distance bus stop are about 3km southeast of the centre. Ul Mira, the main shopping street, runs into pl Lenina. The **Knizhni Klub** (ul Mira 92; ⌚9am-6pm) bookshop sells maps.

Sights

Ascension Cathedral CHURCH
(Вознесенский собор; ul Pushkinskaya; ⌚services 8-11am & 5-7pm) Designed by Konstantin Ton (1794–1881), the architect responsible for St Petersburg's Moscow train station and Moscow's Leningrad station, this beautiful cathedral lords it over Yelets from the foot of ul Kommunarov. Beneath the cathedral's gleaming golden dome is a fantastical, multicoloured interior, with gilt-framed iconography stacked high on each wall. There's a great view of the cathedral from the bridge crossing the Sosna, just east of town.

Znamensky Monastery MONASTERY
(Знаменский монастырь; ul Sovetskaya; ⌚6am-10pm) There are fine views across town from this early-19th-century monastery, restored in 2007. The white steeple and gold-domed church are easily recognisable from afar, and inside you'll find some fabulous frescoes. The monastery grounds are well tended with pretty flower beds, a small aviary with peacocks, and an attractive wooden chapel. At the bottom of the hill near the steps up to the monastery is a natural spring next to a blue-painted ablution hall.

Great Count's Church CHURCH
(Великокняжеская церковь; ul Sovetskaya; ⌚9am-5pm) Built during the early 1900s, this inventive piece of religious architecture has distinctly modernist, even art nouveau flair, with an exotically tiled interior of metallic hues. The cross on the top is made of crystal, supposedly donated from the local glassware factory.

Regional Museum MUSEUM
(Городской краеведческий музей; ul Lenina 99; admission R25; ⌚9.30am-5pm Tue-Sat) Amid the artefacts from the town's colourful past are a model of ancient Yelets and a collection of Russian coins from the 4th century BC to the Soviet era. A room is dedicated to the Mongol cavalry that ran roughshod over Yelets in the 13th century. Upstairs is a collection of paintings by local 19th-century artist Meshchkov and information on Yelets' devastating WWII experience.

Khrennikov Museum MUSEUM
(Дом-музей Хренникова; ul Mayakovskogo 16; admission R30; ⌚9.30am-4.30pm Tue-Sat) The successful Soviet composer grew up and first studied music in this rust-red wooden house. Original furniture, photos and artefacts are on display; the documentation is also interesting as a history of Soviet aesthetics.

Ivan Bunin Museum MUSEUM
(Дом-музей Бунина; ul Gorkogo 16; admission R15; ⌚9am-4.30pm) The writer, poet and 1933 Nobel laureate Ivan Bunin (1870–1953) spent some of his childhood in Yelets, studying at the town's gymnasium. This small museum chronicles his life and works. The man was obviously a travel fiend; check out the wall map that has pins demarking the places he visited – Mogadishu, Sri Lanka and Spain, to name a few.

City Park PARK
(ul Kommunarov) The park has a **Ferris wheel** (Колесо обозрения; ride R50) that spins during summer, a stage for concerts, kids amusements and a romantic statue of Ivan Bunin. Next to the main entrance is the antique red-brick fire station; if you're feeling confident, ask the firefighters if you can climb the **observation tower** (Пожарная каланча) to gain a bird's-eye view of the town's gilded cupolas.

Vvedenskaya Church CHURCH
(Введенская церковь; Vvedensky spusk) Downhill from the cathedral, this jewel box of a church stands near a cluster of photogenic late-17th- and early-18th-century wooden houses. At the bottom of the hill, is a riverside **beach** popular with locals who come to sunbathe and swim in the river.

Sleeping

Hotel Yelets HOTEL €€
(Гостиница Елец; ☎22 235; www.intourist-elets.ru; ul Kommunarov 14; s/d unrenovated R1200/2600, renovated R2100/3200) This nine-storey blue-painted monstrosity, the only hotel in town, offers well-worn unrenovated

rooms or better renovated ones. Both have nice views of the cupolas. The staff are friendly and there is a lobby café and a function-sized restaurant (outside and to the left).

Eating

Stary Gorod RUSSIAN €€
(Старый Город; ul Mira 100; meals R200-400; ⏲11am-4pm & 5pm-1am) The faux Greek statues and heavy emerald drapes signal this as Yelets' fanciest restaurant. The food is pretty tasty and there are plenty of dishes to choose from – which is just as well since the surly waitress will tell you some are not available.

Milano Pizzeria WESTERN €
(Милано Пиццерия; ul Mira; dishes R45-60; ⏲10am-10pm) Local fast-food place with surprisingly good pizza slices, salads and *shawarma* (chopped meat and vegies served in a pitta).

Flamingo RUSSIAN €
(Фламинго; ul Kommunarov 11; meals R250-450; ⏲11am-1am) Battleaxes, coats of arms and stone walls give the general feel of a medieval dungeon. The European-inspired menu includes Nottingham stewed beef and Irish-style meat with mushrooms (the local interpretations of these dishes, anyway).

Information

Main post office (Главный почтамт; ☎26 458; ul Lenina 83; per hr R30; ⏲8am-8pm Mon-Sat, to 7pm Sun) Has two computers for internet use. If they're unavailable, try the telephone office across the street.

Getting There & Away

Bus

There are two long-distance bus stops in Yelets: Avtostantsiya-1 is near the train station on the main highway (this is where buses from Voronezh arrive and depart), while Avtostantsiya-2 is 2.5km west of City Park off ul Kommunarov. Bus services include Moscow (one way R500, daily, 7½ hours), Oryol (R278, two daily, five hours), Voronezh (R180, six daily, three hours) and Tula (R315, five daily, four hours).

Train

Trains travel from Yelets to Moscow (*platskart/kupe* R826/1722, 11 daily, eight hours) and Tula (R713/1258, six daily, 5½ hours). To get from the train station to the centre, walk to the west end of the platform and cross the tracks to the bus stop. A taxi to Hotel Yelets from either location should cost about R100.

Voronezh Воронеж

☎4732 / POP 890,000 / ⏲MOSCOW

A stop in this industry-focused metropolis can be useful to break up the long journey between Moscow and destinations in Ukraine or the Caucasus. The city centre is pleasant, with some grand buildings, particularly around pl Lenina and up along pr Revolyutsii towards the impressive Annunciation Cathedral.

Tsar Fyodor I ordered a fort to be constructed here in the 16th century to defend the region from Tatar attack. Peter the Great expanded the city and in 1695 built a navy shipyard (the first in Russia) to raise a fleet for his assault on the Crimean khanate in the Azov campaign. Voronezh soon developed into the largest city in southern Russia, and a major centre for agriculture and manufacturing.

Destroyed in WWII, the city subsequently revived as a major industrial hub, but fell on hard times when Moscow subsidies dried up in the 1990s. Charlotte Hobson's *Black Earth City* vividly describes the year she spent studying at the local university just after the fall of the Soviet Union; the city continues to attract foreign students. The economy is now back on track, with new shopping plazas and restaurants blossoming amid the spruced-up civic buildings and churches of the city centre.

Sights

Annunciation Cathedral CHURCH
(Благовещенский кафедральный собор; Pervomaisky sad; ⏲7am-7pm) Russia's third-largest working church (after Moscow's Cathedral of Christ the Saviour and St Petersburg's St Isaac's Cathedral), this handsome 97m structure was built in Russo-Byzantine style in the late 19th century. Outside stands a statue of the early-18th-century cleric St Mitrofan surrounded by four angels. The metal fence ringing the complex is decorated with Soviet-era symbols.

IN Kramskoy Regional Fine Arts Museum MUSEUM
(Областной художественный музей Крамского; pr Revolyutsii 18; admission R100; ⏲10am-6pm Wed-Thu, Sat & Sun, from 11am Fri) Reached through a passage leading into a courtyard, this excellent regional arts museum offers up a solid collection of Russian painting and sculpture, Greek and Roman sculpture, and an Egyptian sarcophagus.

Exhibitions of modern local artists are held behind the main building.

St Alexey of Akatov Women's Monastery CONVENT
(Свято-Алексеево-Акатов Женский монастырь; ul Osvobozhdeniya Truda 1) This restored nunnery, founded in 1674, is near the river on lovely grounds, which include a tiny graveyard surrounded by colourful, lopsided cottages. The interior of the monastery church is covered entirely with frescoes.

Resurrection Church CHURCH
(Свято-Воскресенский храм; ul Ordzhonikidze 15) This attractive large green-domed church, a short walk east of pl Lenina and not far from the Art Hotel, boasts a colourful fresco-covered interior that now hosts regular choral services. View it from the nearby small Kamenny most that spans a gully.

Regional Museum MUSEUM
(Краеведческий музей; ul Plekhanovskaya 29; admission R60; ⌚11am-6pm Wed, from 10am Thu-Sun) Displays permanent exhibits on Peter the Great and the history of the region from the pre–Bronze Age to the Soviet era.

Festivals & Events

In June 2011 Voronezh hosted the first **International Platanov Festival** (http://en.platonovfest.com), a week-long jamboree of theatre, music and the arts in memory of the banned Soviet-era writer Andrei Platanov.

Sleeping

The following hotels include breakfast in their rates.

Art Hotel HOTEL €€€
(☎399 299; www.arthotelv.ru; ul Dzerzhinskogo 56; s/d from R4900/6000; 📶) Offers pleasant, modern rooms, helpful English-speaking staff and a classy Italian restaurant, Portofino. There are also a couple of sauna suites that can be hired: one with a small fitness room, the other with a billiards table and jacuzzi pool.

Petrovsky Passazh Hotel HOTEL €€€
(Отель Петровский Пассаж; ☎556 070; www.petrohotel.ru; ul 20-ti Letiya VLKSM 54a; s/d from R4000/5800; ❄📶) The owner of this boutiquey hotel is a hunter – which accounts for the stuffed bear and wild cat in the corridors. Spacious rooms are cabled for broadband internet and offer modern furnishings and big flat-screen TVs.

Azimut Hotel HOTEL €€
(☎965 249; www.azimuthotels.ru; ul Plekhanovskaya 9; s/d/apt from R1800/2950/5000; 📶) The central location, steps from pl Lenina, of this revamped Soviet-era hotel is ideal for short stays. New management has spruced it up nicely.

Eating & Drinking

Mesto Bar & Grill RUSSIAN €€
(pl Lenina 15; meals R500-600) Overlooking the leafy Koltsovsky public garden with its musical fountain, you can dine on all manner of tasty grilled foods here as well as puff on a hubble-bubble. There's a picture menu and in warmer months there's street seating. Next door and run by the same management is the appealing café and sushi bar **Chao Kakao**.

Bar Duck BAR
(ul Plekhanovskaya 23; ⌚6pm-6am) Find this cosy basement bar, its walls plastered with scrapbook cuttings, a few blocks northwest of pl Lenina.

Entertainment

Opera & Ballet Theatre THEATRE
(☎255 3927; http://theatre.vzh.ru; pl Lenina 7) Quality productions are mounted at this handsome classical-style theatre.

Spartak CINEMA
(www.kinospartak.ru; pr Revolyutsii) Multiplex with several cafés in a grand building at the northeast end of the Koltsovsky public garden.

BARak O'mama LIVE MUSIC
(http://barakomama.ru; pr Revolyutsii 35) Live music most nights from 9pm at this centrally located café-bar.

Getting There & Away

Air

The **airport** (www.voronezhavia.ru) is 10km north of the centre along Zadonskoe sh, with five flights daily to Moscow's Domodedovo Airport (R3000, one hour).

Bus

The **bus station** (Moskovsky pr 17) is 3km northwest of pl Lenina, with daily services to Moscow (one way R745, 12 hours), Saratov (R819, 12 hours) and Volgograd (R808, 13 hours). Six services a day run to Yelets (R180, three hours) and Kursk (R400, four hours).

Train

The main train station is **Voronezh 1** (pl Chernyakhovskogo), around 1.5km north of pl

Lenina, with services to Moscow (*platskart/kupe* R1100/2200, 12 daily, 10½ hours), Saratov (R1200/2450, daily, 14 hours), St Petersburg (R2000/4000, eight daily, 24 hours) and Yelets (R830/1550, 14 daily, 5½ hours).

Getting Around

From Voronezh 1 train station there are many buses, *marshrutky* and trams; to reach the centre, look for those going to **pl Lenina** (Площадь Ленина). Some long-distance trains stop at **Pridacha** (Придача) a few kilometres outside the city. If you arrive there, follow the other arrivals 300m out of the station, where you'll find a car park full of *marshrutky* to whisk you into town.

To reach the centre from the bus station, exit the station and catch buses 5a, 6 or 7 (R10) that run along ul Plekhanovskaya.

Oryol Орёл

4862 / POP 317,900 / MOSCOW

With its attractive mix of grand old buildings, riverside parks, footbridges and red-and-yellow-painted trams, Oryol (arr-*yol*) harks back to prerevolutionary Russia. The writer Ivan Turgenev was one of 12 local writers whose work is remembered at the several small house-museums, and the town is the ideal base for visiting Turgenev's beautiful estate Spasskoe-Lutovinovo.

A fortress is thought to have stood on the bluff overlooking the confluence of the Oka and Orlik Rivers since at least the 12th century. Legend has it that an eagle (*oryol* in Russian) alighted on the fortress, giving the settlement its name. Ivan the Terrible instructed that a new fortress be built here in 1566 to protect the southern edge of his empire. The city reached its peak during the 19th century, when a surprising number of gentry lived here (19,000 out of a population of 32,000 in 1853).

Sights

Literary Museums

Though you may not have heard of all of the illustrious Oryol men of letters celebrated in a cluster of literary **museums** (admission R50; 10am-5pm Sat-Thu), a few are worth visiting for the insights they provide into cultured Russian society in the 19th century.

Leonid Andreev House-Museum MUSEUM
(Дом-музей Леонида Андреева; ul 2-ya Pushkarnaya 41) The birthplace of writer and dramatist Leonid Andreev is a sweet cottage that belonged to his grandparents. Inside there is a beautiful piano and examples of Andreev's art and photography: he was an early Russian exponent of colour photography and his compositions are remarkable. Walking here from the centre of Oryol you'll pass many photogenic, tumbledown wooden cottages.

Ivan Bunin Museum MUSEUM
(Музей Бунина; Georgievsky per 1) There's a good collection of photos and other documents relating to the Nobel Prize–winning writer, plus a 'Paris Room' devoted to his years as an emigrant, including the bed in which he died. At the end of the one-hour excursion (the only way you're going to make sense of all the curious photos and yellowed books), the guide flips on a tape player and the man himself reads one of his last poems, a typed copy of which lies near his typewriter.

Turgenev Museum MUSEUM
(Музей Тургенева; 762 737; ul Turgeneva 11) Turgenev's estate, Spasskoe-Lutovinovo, may be the literary mecca, but not to be outdone, Oryol has this museum filled with old photos and notes written by the man. You will find tributes to Turgenev throughout town, including a big **statue** (Памятник Тургеневу) of him overlooking the Oka on Turgenevsky spusk, the sloping street off pl Lenina, and a **bust** (Бюст Тургенева) in the public garden.

Nikolai Leskov House-Museum MUSEUM
(Дом-музей Лескова; 763 304; ul Oktyabrskaya 9) Author and journalist Nikolai Leskov (1831–95), who wrote the book on which the opera *Lady Macbeth of Mtsensk* is based, is remembered at this turquoise-and-cream wooden house. His death mask is in one corner and in another you'll find incredible miniature silhouette cut-outs of rural scenes.

Timofey Granovsky House-Museum MUSEUM
(Дом-музей Грановского; 763 465; ul 7-go Noyabrya 24) Presents materials and memorabilia relating to the eponymous historian, as well as to other 19th-century writers and thinkers.

Other Sights & Activities

City Park of Culture and Rest PARK
(Городской парк культуры и отдыха; ul Gorkogo) Small children will enjoy the **amusement park** (аттракционы) at the northeastern end

of this leafy riverside park. You can rent **rowing boats** (Прокат лодок; ⏲9am-9pm) during the warmer months.

Ploshchad Mira SQUARE

The southern end of 'Peace Sq' is easily identified by its WWII **tank memorial**, one of the original involved in liberating Oryol from German occupation in August 1943. It's a time-honoured spot for newlyweds to pose for photos on the big day.

Opposite the square's northwest corner is the elegant **Dom Knigi**, constructed in 1955 and its exterior decorated with busts of famous writers and thinkers, including Lenin and Marx on the building's corner, now the entrance to a bank!

Regional Museum MUSEUM

(Краеведческий музей; ul Gostinaya 2; admission R50; ⏲9am-6pm Tue-Sun) Not essential viewing but hosts some good temporary exhibitions.

Sleeping

Rates for all of the following include breakfast.

TOP CHOICE **Hotel Oryol** HOTEL €€

(Гостиница Орёл; ☎550 525; www.orelhotel.ru; pl Mira 4; s/d from R2000/3000; wi-fi) A touch of grandeur remains in the public areas of this hotel offering bright, airy rooms. Staff are helpful and will sell you an access card for the wi-fi for R100.

Sarkis HOTEL €€

(Саркис; ☎544 676; www.sarkis-orel.ru; Moskovskaya ul 24a; s/d R2600/3000; wi-fi) The fluffy white towelling robes hanging in the bathrooms are a nice touch at this 14-room hotel, set back in a courtyard off the main road and above a restaurant of the same name. The rooms are all new, modern and appealing.

Atlantida HOTEL €€

(Атлантида; ☎558 333; www.atlantida-hotel.ru; ul Fomina 4a; s/d R3000/3700; wi-fi) Overlook the few nouveau riche decorative touches, such as voluminous curtain treatments and copies of old-master paintings along the corridors, and you'll find this medium-sized new hotel, restaurant, sauna and business complex is quite a decent option.

Hotel Rus HOTEL €

(Гостиница Рус; ☎552 089; www.orelhotel.ru; ul Gorkogo 37; s/d without bathroom R700/1400, with bathroom from R1500/3000; wi-fi) Sure, it's a bit of a Soviet relic, but the Rus has clean, comfortable rooms, helpful staff and a good location on pl Lenina near the park. To use the common shower costs R60.

Hotel Salyut HOTEL €

(Гостиница Салют; ☎764 207; www.salut.orel.ru; ul Lenina 36; s/d from R1300/2000) Offers similar

WORTH A TRIP

SPASSKOE-LUTOVINOVO СПАССКОЕ-ЛУТОВИНОВО

Surrounded by beautiful countryside, **Spasskoe-Lutovinovo** (Map p239; www.spasskoye-lutovinovo.ru; guided tour R150, grounds only R30; ⏲10am-5pm), 65km north of Oryol, is the family estate of Ivan Turgenev (1881–83), the place where the great 19th-century novelist completed his most famous novel, *Fathers and Sons*.

The estate was originally given to the Turgenev family by Ivan the Terrible. Though he spent much of his life in Moscow, St Petersburg, Germany and France, Turgenev thought of Spasskoe-Lutovinovo as his home and returned here many times. He was also exiled here in 1852–53 as a result of his work *A Sportsman's Sketches*, displeasing the tsar. To learn more about the writer, see www.turgenev.org.ru.

The main house, restored in the 1970s, contains some original furniture, books and Turgenev's personal effects. There's an icon hanging in Turgenev's study that was given to the family by Ivan the Terrible, and the chessboard is set ready to play (Turgenev was a masterful player).

Also on the grounds is the family church, which has been restored and holds regular services. The big oak tree planted as a sapling by Turgenev and the writer's 'exile house', where he lived in 1852–53, are both a short walk from the main house.

To get here, take one of the dozen or so daily *marshrutky* (fixed-route minibuses) that travel from Oryol to Mtsensk (R68, one hour, four per hour from 6am to 9pm), then switch at Mtsensk's bus station to a Spasskoe-Lutovinovo bus (R25, 30 minutes, hourly), or take a taxi (around R150).

Oryol

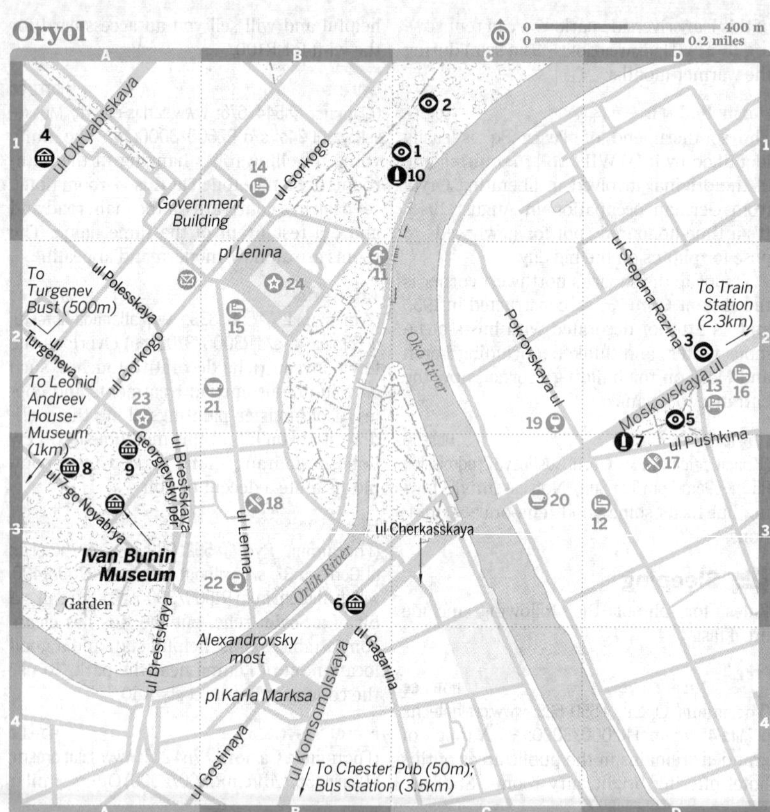

accommodation to the Rus but is a little pricier. Some rooms have been renovated with flashy pink or lime-green wallpaper.

Eating & Drinking

TOP CHOICE 3 Etazh PIZZA €€

(3 Этаж; www.3etaj.com; ul Pushkina 6; pizzas R140-390; noon-1am Sun-Thu, to 2am Fri & Sat; wi-fi) Excellent thin-crust pizzas and sandwiches are just the start of the great things about this arty café on the 3rd floor of the same building as Labirint. Cats, an octopus and a flowery world map feature in its design-savvy decor. Linger over a coffee or beer with free wi-fi, and perhaps challenge a local to a game of chess.

Labirint EUROPEAN €€

(Лабиринт; www.labirintclub.ru; ul Pushkina 6; meals R500; noon-1am Sun-Thu, to 2am Fri & Sat; wi-fi) This appealing café-lounge serves up excellent salads, pastas and meat dishes like shashlyki (meat kebabs) and pork fillets. The house speciality is marinated duck for two. Photo exhibitions decorate the walls.

Chester Pub BRITISH €€

(Честер Паб; 543 054; ul Komsomolskaya 36; meals R400-600; wi-fi) Decorated with bulldog statuettes, Union Jack flags and portraits of QEII and Churchill, this baronial-sized pub attempts to re-create a bit of England. Rounding out the picture is a tempting selection of cask ales (from R70 for 300mL) and a wide-ranging menu including several styles of sausage.

Pint House PUB €€

(Pokrovskaya ul 3; noon-2am; wi-fi) We're told that this spacious beer hall was once a public toilet. You'd be hard pressed to tell now as inside you'll find cowhide-covered columns, four house beers on tap (from R75 for ½ litre) plus several other Russian ales, to be quaffed with a wide variety of snacks and more sub-

Oryol

Top Sights
Ivan Bunin Museum A3

Sights
1 Amusement Park C1
2 City Park of Culture and Rest C1
3 Dom Knigi D2
4 Nikolai Leskov House-Museum A1
5 pl Mira D2
6 Regional Museum B3
7 Tank Memorial D3
8 Timofey Granovsky House-Museum A3
9 Turgenev Museum A3
10 Turgenev Statue C1

Activities, Courses & Tours
11 Rowing Boat Rentals B2

Sleeping
12 Atlantida D3
13 Hotel Oryol D2
14 Hotel Rus B1
15 Hotel Salyut B2
16 Sarkis D2

Eating
3 Etazh (see 17)
17 Labirint D3
18 Orlovsky Karavay B3

Drinking
19 Pint House C2
20 Santa Bin C3
21 Santa Bin B2
22 U Mosta B3

Entertainment
23 Teatr Russky Stil A2
24 Turgenev Theatre B2

stantial meals. On Saturdays a band plays in the basement space and there's a R195 business lunch deal from noon to 4pm.

U Mosta PUB €€
(У Моста; ul Lenina 13) 'The Bridge' is a mellow basement grotto with a handful of wooden tables. Pub grub is available.

Santa Bin CAFÉ €
(Санта Бин; ul Lenina 37; drinks R50-150; ⌚8.30am-10pm) A Starbucks-style coffee shop, right down to the cardboard sleeves and plastic lids. There's another branch facing pl Mira.

Orlovsky Karavay BAKERY €
(Орловский Каравай; ul Lenina 26; baked goods R20-50; ⌚8am-8pm) This bakery and snack counter offers quick, cheap bites.

Entertainment

Given Oryol's literary heritage, it's no surprise to find a number of quality theatres in town.

Turgenev Theatre THEATRE
(Театр Тургенева; ☎761 639; pl Lenina) Hosts plays and concerts. It is a clever modernist building, the facade mimicking the effect of a stage with the curtains drawn.

Teatr Russky Stil THEATRE
(Русский стиль; ☎762 024; ul Turgeneva 18) A fun, small-scale, occasionally experimental theatre. Most of the offerings are comedies.

Information

Main post office (Главный почтамт; ul Lenina 43; per hr R42) Two computers with internet access on the 1st floor.

Getting There & Away

Bus

The **bus station** (Avtovokzalnaya ul) is 4km to the south, with services to Moscow (one way R540, three daily, eight hours), Kursk (R214, three daily, three hours), Smolensk (R645, two daily, nine hours), Tula (R270, three daily, four hours), Voronezh (R310, two daily, seven hours) and Yelets (R280, one daily, five hours).

Train

The **train station** (pl Privokzalnaya) is around 2.5km north from central pl Mira. Trains run to Moscow (*platskart/kupe* R970/1900, 30 daily, 5½ hours), Kursk (R632/1200, 25 daily, two hours) and Tula (R1000/2200, 25 daily, 2½ hours).

Getting Around

From the train station, trams 1 and 2 and trolleybus 3 (all R9) stop at ul Karla Marksa, on the southeastern end of the Alexandrovsky bridge leading to ul Lenina, before continuing on to the bus station. Trolleybuses 4 and 6, which run along ul Turgeneva, also provide convenient access to the bus station. Trolleybus 5 to the train station runs along ul Gorkogo.

Taxis to the train or bus station from pl Lenina charge about R100.

Kursk Курск

☎4712 / POP 414,600 / ⏰MOSCOW

The biggest tank battle of WWII took place near Kursk in July and August of 1943. Afterwards, the ruined regional city and railway junction was rebuilt along solid Soviet lines, with only a handful of pre-20th-century structures to signify its long history, going back to at least the 11th century.

Kursk's centre is divided by ul Lenina, with Krasnaya pl at the southern end along with the giant domed Holy Sign Cathedral. Ul Dzerzhinskogo heads quite steeply downhill from the western side of Krasnaya pl to a valley, where you'll find the busy central market and the permanent circus building. **Dom Knigi** (Дом книги; ul Lenina 11) sells city maps.

Sights

There's little of major interest here save for a couple of impressive churches.

Sergievo-Kazansky Cathedral CHURCH
(Сергиево-Казаиский кафедральный совор; cnr uls Gorkogo & Zolotaya) A block east of ul Lenina on a pleasant, tree-lined street is a fine baroque building that some believe was designed by Elizabeth I's court architect, Rastrelli, in the mid-18th century. The two-level interior decoration is dazzling.

Holy Sign Cathedral CHURCH
(Знаменский кафедральный совор; ul Lunacharskogo 4) Built in the early 19th century, the Holy Sign Cathedral has been restored to its former glory; during Soviet times it was used as a cinema. Beneath its 48m cupola and neoclassical exterior, you'll find a mix of the lavishly ornate (gilded columns, an enormous chandelier) coupled with even larger paintings depicting scenes from Christ's life.

Sleeping & Eating

Hotel Tsentralnaya HOTEL €€
(Гостиница Центральная; ☎569 048; ul Lenina 2; r without bathroom R700, s/d with bathroom R1500/2000; wi-fi) This grand old place, facing onto Krasnaya pl, offers good-sized, well-maintained old-fashioned rooms with high ceilings and parquet floors. Breakfast is extra and free wi-fi is only in the lobby.

Hotel Kursk HOTEL €€
(Гостиница Курск; ☎703 059; ul Lenina 24; s/d from R1850/2100; wi-fi) The rooms at this 15-floor tower are fine, with big beds and, higher up, good views. Rates include breakfast.

Gornitsa RUSSIAN €€
(Горница; ul Lenina 2; meals R500-700) Friendly waitresses serve hearty fare, such as beefsteaks, grilled chicken and baked fish, in this re-created Russian peasant yard attached to the Hotel Tsentralnaya.

Chantal FM Cafe INTERNATIONAL €€
(ul Lenina 8; meals R150-500) If you can block out the thudding techno music, this modern café-bar serves some pretty decent food, including sandwiches, pizza and sushi, which actually looks like the dishes on the picture menu. If it's not to your fancy, there are plenty of other places to eat along ul Lenina.

Information

Post office & telephone office (Почта и круглосуточный переговорный пункт; ☎561 460; Krasnaya pl; ⏰8am-10pm Mon-Fri, 9am-6pm Sat & Sun) Internet access available.

Getting There & Away

The **train station** (ul Internatsionalnaya) is about 3km northeast of Krasnaya pl. There's also an airport with flights to Moscow and St Petersburg.

From the main **bus station** (ul 50 let Oktyabrya 114), buses run to Moscow (R730, daily, 10 hours), Oryol (R214, three daily, three hours) and Voronezh (R400, six daily, four hours). Train services include Moscow (*platskart/kupe* R1530/3200, 40 daily, eight hours) and Oryol (R632/1200, 25 daily, two hours),which can also be reached via *elektrichka* (R249, four daily, 3½ hours).

Getting Around

Numerous buses, trams and *marshrutky* (R10) ply the route between the train station and Krasnaya pl. Bus 1 and tram 2 go between the train station and the bus station. Taxis charge around R100 from either bus or train station to Krasnaya pl.

SMOLENSK REGION

The western route out of Moscow, towards Belarus, takes you through Smolensk region (Смоленская область), home to Smolensk (Смоленск), one of Russia's oldest cities.

Smolensk СМОЛЕНСК

☎4812 / POP 351,000 / ⏰MOSCOW

Set on the upper Dnepr River, this handsome city offers 16th-century fortress walls and towers to explore, onion-dome churches and well-landscaped parks. The highlight is the magnificent Assumption Cathedral, but art and music are also well represented in the home town of composer Mikhail Glinka and 19th-century arts patron Princess Maria Tenisheva, whose estate of Flyonovo makes for an interesting trip out of town.

History

Smolensk was first mentioned in 863 as the capital of the Slavic Krivichi tribe. The town's auspicious setting gave it early control over trade routes between Moscow and the west, and between the Baltic and Black Seas. By the late 1100s, Smolensk was one of the strongest principalities in Eastern Europe.

As Muscovy and Lithuania vied for power in the 13th century, Smolensk was literally caught in the middle and successively invaded from both sides. There was a big battle between the Russians and Napoleon's army outside Smolensk in 1812 (later immortalised in Tolstoy's *War and Peace*), commemorated by a couple of monuments in the town. Composer Mikhail Glinka, regarded as the founder of Russian classical music, grew up near Smolensk and performed frequently in the Nobles' Hall, facing what is now the Glinka Garden.

Heavy fighting during WWII devastated Smolensk. In a sign of Soviet favour, much of the centre was quickly rebuilt, often along original plans, resulting in the very complete feeling of the central area today. The town hit the headlines in 2010 when Polish President Lech Kaczynski and scores of other senior Polish figures died in a plane crash on the approach to Smolensk military airport in thick fog.

Sights

Assumption Cathedral CHURCH
(Успенский кафедральный собор; ul Bolshaya Sovetskaya; ⌚7am-8pm) Dominating the city's skyline is this huge green-and-white working cathedral topped by five silver domes. A church has stood here since 1101 but this one, built in the late 17th and early 18th centuries, is one of the earliest examples of the Russo-Greek revival in architecture following the Europeanisation trends of Peter the Great's reign. Its spectacular gilded and icon-encrusted interior so impressed Napoleon that, according to legend, he set a guard to stop his own men from vandalising the cathedral.

Immediately on your left as you enter, look for a small framed icon of the Virgin, richly encrusted with pearls drawn from the Dnepr around Smolensk. Further on, a cluster of candles marks a supposedly wonder-working icon of the Virgin. This is a 16th-century copy of the original, said to be by St Luke, which had been on this site since 1103 and was stolen in 1923. Also take time to stroll around the pretty grounds of the complex.

Nearby, up the hill on ul Bolshaya Sovetskaya, the pink-walled 18th-century **Trinity Monastery** (Свято-Троицкий женский монастырь) complex is under restoration: a scale model in the grounds shows what it will eventually look like.

Art Gallery ART GALLERY
(Художественная галерея; ul Kommunisticheskaya 4; admission R50; ⌚10am-6pm Tue, Wed & Fri-Sun, 11am-7pm Thu) Installed in a handsome red-and-white-decorated mansion facing the Glinka Garden, this splendid art collection includes pieces by such luminaries as Ivan Sushkin, Ilya Repin and Nikolai Rerikh, as well as a good sampling of socialist realism, 14th- to 18th-century icons and European old masters. You'll also find some portraits of Princess Maria Tenisheva, who created the Teremok estate at Flyonovo.

Smolensk Flax Museum MUSEUM
(Музей Смоленский лён; ul Tenishevoy 7/1; admission R35; ⌚10am-5pm Tue-Sun) Flax production developed from the Middle Ages as one of Smolensk's main industries, as the moderate climate sustained soil ideal for growing the plant. Exhibits here will give you an idea of how the process works and the lovely products, including beautiful traditional costumes, that can be made from the resulting cloth. The colourful, L-shaped wooden objects are *prialka* (distaffs), tools used in spinning.

Fortress Walls & Around HISTORICAL SITE
Making a circuit of the restored city walls, long sections of which boast fine towers reminiscent of the Moscow Kremlin, is a pleasant way to pass a warm summer evening, with parks and various monuments and churches to be encountered along the way. Originally built between 1596 and 1602, the impressive 6.5km-long, 5.5m-thick, 15m-high walls originally had 38 towers, with 17 still standing.

Overlooking the **Spartak Stadium** (Стадион Спартак) just outside the line of the walls on the west side of the park, the **Korolevsky Bastion** is a high earth rampart built by the Poles who captured

Smolensk

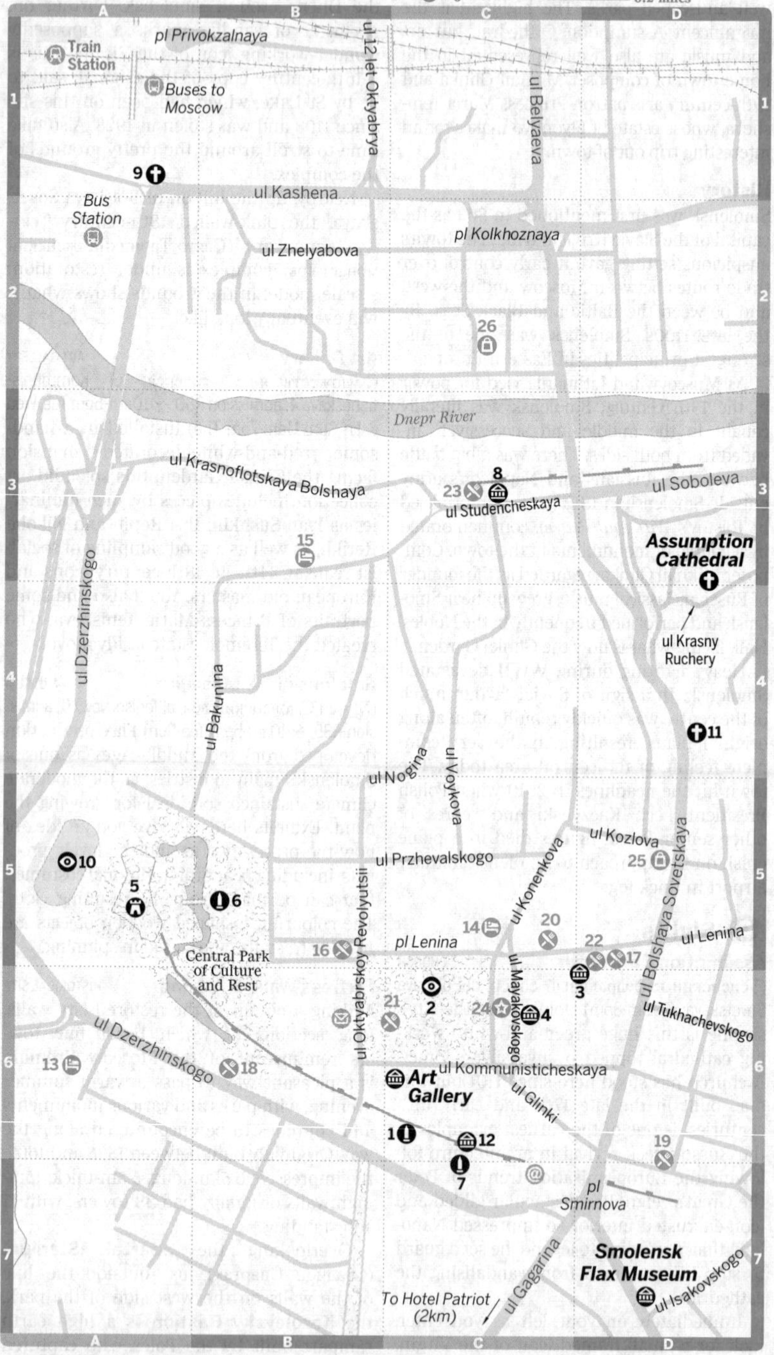

0 — 500 m
0 — 0.2 miles

A B C D
1 2 3 4 5 6 7

pl Privokzalnaya
Train Station
Buses to Moscow
ul 12 let Oktyabrya
ul Belyaeva
9
ul Kashena
Bus Station
pl Kolkhoznaya
ul Zhelyabova
26
Dnepr River
ul Krasnoflotskaya Bolshaya
8
23
ul Studencheskaya
ul Soboleva
15
Assumption Cathedral
ul Krasny Ruchery
ul Dzerzhinskogo
ul Bakunina
11
ul Nogina
ul Voykova
ul Kozlova
10
ul Przhevalskogo
25
5
6
ul Konenkova
ul Bolshaya Sovetskaya
14
20
16
pl Lenina
22
17
ul Lenina
Central Park of Culture and Rest
3
ul Oktyabrskoy Revolyutsii
21
2
24
4
ul Mayakovskogo
ul Tukhachevskogo
13
ul Dzerzhinskogo
18
Art Gallery
ul Kommunisticheskaya
ul Glinki
1
12
7
19
pl Smirnova
ul Gagarina
Smolensk Flax Museum
ul Isakovskogo
To Hotel Patriot (2km)

Smolensk

Top Sights	
Art Gallery	C6
Assumption Cathedral	D3
Smolensk Flax Museum	D7
Sights	
1 Eternal Flame Memorial	C6
2 Glinka Garden	C6
3 History Museum	D6
4 Konenkov Sculpture Museum	C6
5 Korolevsky Bastion	A5
6 Monument to the 1812 Defenders	B5
7 Monument to the Heroes of 1812	C7
8 Museum of Russian Vodka	C3
9 Peter & Paul Church	A1
10 Spartak Stadium	A5
11 Trinity Monastery	D4
12 WWII Museum	C6
Sleeping	
13 Hotel Rossiya	A6
14 Smolenskhotel	C5
15 Usadba	B3
Eating	
16 Chocolate Café	B5
17 Domino	D5
18 Domino	B6
Donna Karla	(see 22)
19 Dvoinoe Solntse	D6
French Café	(see 14)
20 Gastronom Pushkinsky	C5
21 Russky Dvor	C6
22 Samovar	D5
23 Smolenskaya Krepost	C3
Entertainment	
24 Glinka Concert Hall	C6
Shopping	
25 Dom Knigi	D5
26 Zadneprovsky Market	C2
Information	
Smolensk Travel	(see 14)

Smolensk in 1611. It saw heavy fighting in 1654 and 1812.

Backing onto a longish southwest stretch of the walls, the Central Park of Culture and Rest has a 26m-high cast-iron **monument to the 1812 defenders** (Памятник защитникам Смоленска 1812 г). At the foot of the walls southeast of the Glinka Garden you'll find an **eternal flame memorial** (Мемориал Вечный огонь) to the dead of WWII and the graves of some of the Soviet soldiers who died in Smolensk's defence, plus another **monument to the heroes of 1812** (Памятник героям 1812 г).

WWII Museum MUSEUM

(Музей "Смоленщина в годы Великой Отечественной войны"; ul Dzerzhinskogo 4a; admission R30; ⏲10am-5pm Tue-Sat) Set within the fortress walls, this museum documents the invasion and devastation of the city during WWII; it is incredible to realise just how much of old Smolensk is actually reconstruction. A collection of tanks, artillery and a MiG fighter jet are parked behind the museum.

History Museum MUSEUM

(Исторический музей; ul Lenina 8; history gallery R35, all galleries R145; ⏲10am-6pm Tue-Sun) There's a range of different display galleries here, covering natural history (R30) as well as special exhibitions. Among the interesting exhibits in the history section are fragments from the 1812 war, including a French uniform from one of Napoleon's soldiers; there's also a room devoted to local hero cosmonaut Yury Gagarin (R30), who was born in the region in 1934.

Glinka Garden PARK

(Городской сад Глинки) At the east end of this shady garden with fountains, a statue of the composer Glinka, installed in 1885, is surrounded by a fence with excerpts from his opera *A Life for the Tsar* wrought into the iron. Opposite is the concert hall in which he performed. The north side of the garden is bordered by the expansive pl Lenina, where a statue of the communist leader stands in front of the palatial city hall, once the House of Soviets.

Peter & Paul Church CHURCH

(Церковь Петра и Павла; ul Kashena) With clear Byzantine influences, this red-brick 12th-century chapel, set in a pretty walled garden, is the oldest in the city and is an architectural monument.

Konenkov Sculpture Museum MUSEUM

(Музей скульптуры Конёнкова; ul Mayakovskogo 7; admission R30; ⏲10am-6pm Tue-Sun) Contains

MOVING ON?

For tips, recommendations and reviews, head to shop.lonelyplanet.com to purchase a downloadable PDF of the Belarus chapter from Lonely Planet's *Eastern Europe* guide.

playful woodworks by Sergei Konenkov; Lenin seems to have been captured in the midst of a ballet manoeuvre. The museum also has steel, bronze and aluminium works from some of the other noted Smolensk artists.

Museum of Russian Vodka MUSEUM
(Музей Русской водки; ul Studencheskaya 4; admission R20; 9am-5pm Tue-Sat) A one-room exhibitions hall that provides a brief overview of the drink's colourful history. Guided tours (in Russian) end at the makeshift bar, where you can purchase a glass (or better yet a bottle) of some noteworthy Smolenskiy brands.

Festivals & Events

Glinka Festival MUSIC
The Glinka Festival, which usually runs between the last week of May and the first week of June, showcases Russian music. Symphony orchestras, choral groups and string quartets perform nightly in various venues, with free concerts held beside the Glinka Garden.

Sleeping

Rates for the following places all include breakfast.

TOP CHOICE **Usadba** MINIHOTEL €€
(Усадьва; 385 931; www.smolhotel.ru; ul Bakunina 2b; s/d from R2500/3100;) In a quieter residential area that's still close to the city centre, this 12-room minihotel offers comfortable rooms with good facilities. There's an attached café where breakfast and other meals are served, and a small traditional wooden sauna (R500 per hour before 4pm, R800 per hour after 4pm).

Smolenskhotel HOTEL €€
(Гостиница "СмоленскОтель"; 383 604; http://smolensk-hotel.ru; ul Lenina 2/1; s/tw/d from R3300/3900/4000;) Set on the edge of the Glinka Garden, this centrally located five-storey hotel has clean, bright rooms and polite, efficient service.

Hotel Rossiya HOTEL €€
(Гостиница Россия; 655 970; www.russia-smolensk.ru; ul Dzerzhinskogo 23/2; s/d from R2100/3120) Built to house Olympians on their way to Moscow in 1980, this place may be old-fashioned and a little rundown but has friendly service. Rooms are small and functional, with the renovated ones being on high floors and slightly smarter. There's a small gym and cinema in the complex.

Hotel Patriot HOTEL €€
(Патриот; 384 936; www.patriot-smolensk.ru; ul Kirova 22; r from R1600) This converted former apartment block, set back from the street and about 2km south of the town centre, is a possible back-up if the other places are full.

Eating & Drinking

TOP CHOICE **Russky Dvor** RUSSIAN €
(Русский Двор; www.pizzadomino.ru; Glinka Garden; meals R100-200; 10am-midnight;) Imagine a cross between St Basil's Cathedral and McDonald's and you'll start to have some idea of what this place looks like. Despite catering towards a fast-food crowd, it maintains a uniquely Russian atmosphere with decor that thrills small children. Food quality is surprisingly high, which may explain the long queues that form at lunch.

Smolenskaya Krepost RUSSIAN €€
(Смоленская крепость; 327 690; ul Studencheskaya 4; meals R500-700) Set in the old castle walls, this charming restaurant has plenty of character – from the stained-glass windows to the tiny fireplace and exposed-brick walls – with lovely views of the Dnepr from its balcony. The menu features well-prepared traditional Russian dishes.

Chocolate Café INTERNATIONAL €€
(Шоколад кафе; ul Oktyabrskoy Revolyutsii; meals R300-500; 10am-midnight;) With dark wood walls, mirrors and brown leather seating, this sophisticated place aims for a French-bistro atmosphere with a menu that is anything but. Bliny, omelettes, porridge, sushi and pasta are a few from the eclectic range of items on offer as well as decent beers, coffee and cakes.

Samovar RUSSIAN €€
(Самовар; www.pizzadomino.ru; ul Lenina 14; meals R150-300; 10am-10pm) The same company that runs Russky Dvor and Domino also has this appealing self-serve restaurant specialising in traditional savoury and sweet pies. In the same building is yet another of its themed places, **Donna Karla**, a cute café

with a tempting array of caffeinated drinks, pastries and cakes.

Domino EUROPEAN €€
(Домино; www.pizzadomino.ru; ul Dzerzhinskogo 16; meals R100-200; ⏲10am-midnight) Though the log-cabin interior borders on kitsch, the OK fast food, which includes things like pizza, bliny and salads, pulls in the crowds. The front and side patios that open in summer are good for a drink. There's also a small **branch** on ul Lenina.

French Café EUROPEAN €€
(ul Lenina 2/1; dishes R150-300; ⏲11am-11pm) Brightly lit, spacious but lacking atmosphere, this café serves coffee, small salads, caviar, sandwiches and many opportunities to satisfy your sweet tooth.

Dvoinoe Solntse TEAHOUSE €€
(Двойное Солнце; www.doublesun.ru; ul Barklaya-de-Tolli 7; meals R200-400 ⏲1pm-1am) Taking a stab at re-creating a traditional Japanese teahouse, this place has floor seating, screens and low tables. Waiters spend inordinate amounts of time sitting at your table preparing, smelling and pouring your tea. Sushi is also available.

Gastronom Pushkinsky GROCERIES €
(Гастроном Пушкинский; ul Lenina 7; ⏲24hr) The place to find delicious items for a decent picnic.

☆ Entertainment

Glinka Concert Hall CLASSICAL MUSIC
(Концертный зал Глинки; ☎32 984; ul Glinki 3; ⏲box office noon-7pm) Attending a concert is the best way to get a look at the reconstructed hall where Glinka once entertained Russian nobility and launched the history of secular art music in Russia. Tickets kick off at around R100.

Shopping

Dom Knigi BOOKSTORE
(Дом Книги; ul Bolshaya Sovetskaya 12/1; ⏲10am-7pm Mon-Sat, 11am-6pm Sun) Sells Russian-language maps.

Zadneprovsky Market MARKET
(Заднепровский рынок; pl Kolkhoznaya) Pick up fresh vegies (or colourful undergarments) at Smolensk's main market.

ℹ Information

12 Stools (Кафе 12 Стульев; ul Dzerzhinskogo 2; per hr R50; ⏲10am-8pm Mon, from 11am Tue-Thu, 24hr Fri & Sat, 11am-7pm Sun) Internet access.

Central post, telegraph & telephone office (Главный почтамт; ul Oktyabrskoy Revolyutsii 6; per hr R34; ⏲8am-8pm Mon-Sat) Internet access available.

Smolensk Travel (☎404 375; www.smolensk-travel.ru; Smolenskhotel, ul Lenina 2/1; ⏲10am-7pm Mon-Fri, 11am-3pm Sat) Can assist in buying transport tickets and booking hotels. Also arranges tours of the city and region.

ℹ Getting There & Away

Bus

Frequent buses for Moscow (one way R600, 14 daily, 5½ hours) leave from outside the main

WORTH A TRIP

FLYONOVO ФЛЁНОВО

In the late 19th and early 20th centuries, illustrious artists and musicians including Stravinsky, Chaliapin, Vrubel and Serov visited **Flyonovo** (Map p239), the pretty riverside estate of art lover Princess Maria Tenisheva, near Talashkino, 18km southeast of Smolensk. The visitors joined in applied-art workshops, which the princess organised for her peasants, and helped in building projects.

The most striking result is the almost psychedelic decoration on the exterior of the brick **Holy Spirit Church**, particularly the mural of Christ over the entrance designed by well-known landscape painter Rerikh. The ornately decorative wooden house **Teremok** (admission R35; ⏲10am-5pm Tue-Sun, closed last Thu of month), covered with peasant-style carving, is now a folk-art museum, while another large but simpler **wooden building** (admission R35) with a double-storey portico has a couple of rooms set up to resemble a school room and a long-since demolished concert hall. A smaller separate building sells crafts still produced in the workshop here.

Take *marshrutka* (fixed-route minibus) 104 from Smolensk's bus station to Talashkino (R25, 20 minutes), from where it's a pleasant 2km walk to the estate. You can hop on the same *marshrutka* at pl Smirnova.

train station and less often from the **bus station** (Автовокзал; ul Dzerzhinskogo). Other services include Oryol (R940, two daily, nine hours), Pskov (R756, three daily, eight hours) and St Petersburg (R830, daily, 15 hours).

Train

From the **train station** (ul 12 let Oktyabrya) there are around 18 daily connections with Moscow (*platskart/kupe* R800/1500, 5½ hours), including international services to Minsk, Warsaw, Prague and Berlin, Vienna, Amsterdam and Nice; tickets for these destinations are sold from window 12 in the elegant main station building.

Note that trains to St Petersburg (*platskart/kupe* R1420/2300, even days, 13 hours) go via Vitebsk in Belarus – if you take this service you will need both a multiple-entry visa to Russia *and* a Belarus transit visa.

The *elektrichka* for Bryansk (R250, daily Thursday to Sunday, five hours) leaves from the smaller station across the footbridge towards the bus station. From Bryansk there are hourly buses to Oryol.

Getting Around

From the train and bus station, you can take the bus, tram (R11) or *marshrutka* 41 to the centre of town. Taxis to the centre cost around R100.

TVER REGION

Tver Тверь

4822 / POP 403,700 / MOSCOW

On the Volga, 150km northwest of Moscow, the charming town of Tver dates back to the 12th century. Its heyday came after a fire levelled most of the town in 1763, allowing the architect Pyotr Nikitin to replan Tver's centre on a three-ray system (a style copied from Rome, Versailles and St Petersburg) and build his patron Catherine the Great a 'road palace' – now an art gallery – for her to rest in on journeys between the then Russian capital and Moscow.

Picturesque town houses and churches from the 18th and 19th centuries still line the main streets and riverbank of this mini-Petersburg on the Volga, but the Soviet period was unkind to Tver. Not only was the town renamed Kalinin (after local guy Mikhail Kalinin, Stalin's puppet president during WWII), the authorities tore down the Cathedral of the Transfiguration of our Saviour in 1935 (one had stood on the same spot since the late 13th century) and converted the mosque into a café. The latter has since been returned to the Muslim community.

Tver's thoughtful local government has erected English signboards around the city centre explaining the history of various key locations. It's a good place to break a journey between Moscow and St Petersburg, as well as an access point for historic Torzhok and the beauty spot of Lake Seliger.

Sights & Activities

Art Gallery MUSEUM

(Тверская областная картинная галерея; http://gallery.tver.ru; Sovetskaya ul 3; admission R100; 11am-5pm Tue-Sun) Fronted by a statue of Mikhail Kalinin (on the spot where Tver's cathedral once stood before the Soviets blew it up) stands what should be the town's most imposing building: Catherine the Great's 1775 Road Palace. Sadly, the ornate facade is in shocking shape. Restoration appears to be happening – slowly.

Inside, things are marginally better in the rooms exhibiting antique furniture and Russian art. The collection is not extensive, but it does feature some engaging pieces of socialist realism in the shape of paintings and pottery. Look out for the photos of the palace c 1880 to 1930 that show what it once looked like inside and out.

Museum of Tver Life MUSEUM

(Музей Тверского быта; ul Gorkogo 19/14; admission per gallery R80; 11am-5pm Wed-Sun) On the north side of the Volga, this museum is split across two adjacent houses, both once owned by members of the Arefyev family: one is set up to display the life of wealthy merchants, including displays of samovars; the other has more general exhibits including a reconstruction of a wooden dwelling typical of country folk, as well as beautiful examples of embroidery and traditional costumes.

Municipal Gardens PARK

(Sovetskaya ul) On the grounds of what once was Tver's kremlin, this park offers a funfair with a Ferris wheel and cafés, and often hosts live concerts on summer weekends. Part of the park lies on the north bank of the Volga, where a promenade provides lovely views of the old houses on the southern bank. In summer, **excursion boats** (Экскурсионный причал; 45min trip from R220; 11am-9pm) sail from the jetty.

Church of the White Trinity CHURCH

(Белая Троица церковь; pl Troitskaya) Amid this quaint neighbourhood of old wooden houses

WORTH A TRIP

TORZHOK ТОРЖОК

Hugging the Tvertsa River, the church spire and domed skyline of Torzhok seems straight out of a Russian fairy tale. An easy day trip from Tver, or a place to stop en route to Ostashkov, Torzhok was once on the main road from St Petersburg to Moscow – which explains why Pushkin passed through several times on his travels. The poet's visits are commemorated in the **AS Pushkin Museum** (Музей Пушкина; ul Dzerzhinskogo 71; admission R50; ⏲11am-5pm Wed-Sun); it's in a grey painted wooden building on the right as you enter town on the bus from Tver. It contains objects and illustrations, including doodles by Pushkin that evoke scenes along this major highway in the 19th century.

The highlight of Torzhok's many religious buildings (most in ruins) is the **Borisoglebsky Monastery** (Борисоглебский мужской монастырь; ul Staritskaya 7; grounds admission free, museum R30; ⏲10am-6pm Tue-Sun May-Sep, 9am-5pm Tue-Sat Oct-Apr), one of the oldest such complexes in Russia and which is only partly restored. Nearby, the whitewashed and blue-domed **Archangel Michael Church** (Михайло-Архангельский храм) is once again operational and has a beautifully decorated interior.

Buses (R138, 18 daily, one hour 45 minutes) and trains (R120, four daily, one hour 30 minutes) connect Torzhok with Tver as well as with Ostashkov.

with carved eaves and window frames, west of the market on ul Bragina, you'll also find Tver's oldest building, a stately stone church dating from 1564.

Regional Museum MUSEUM
(Тверской государственный объединенный музей; www.tvermuzeum.ru; Sovetskaya ul 1; admission R50; ⏲11am-5pm Wed-Sun) Provides the standard overview of Tver's history, geography and ecology.

Sleeping

The following include breakfast in their rates.

Hotel Seliger HOTEL €€
(Гостиница Селигер; ☎320 753; www.seligerhotel.ru; Sovetskaya ul 38; s/d from R2000/3000) The Seliger offers a wide range of pleasant, reasonably priced rooms in a central location. In the same complex there's a sauna, fitness club and billiards hall, as well as a popular club-restaurant next door.

Hotel Volga HOTEL €€
(Гостиница Волга; ☎348 100; www.volga-tver.ru; ul Zhelyabova 1; s/d from R2500/2800; 📶) Overlooking the Tmaka River, this revamped hotel has sharp-looking rooms, friendly service and free wi-fi. The inexpensive 24-hour self-serve bistro is also a plus.

Hotel Osnabrück HOTEL €€
(Гостиница Оснабрюк; ☎358 433; http://hotel.tver.ru; ul Saltykova-Shchedrina 20; s/d from R3200/3800; ❄📶) Named for Tver's sister city in Germany, the Osnabrück has 34 spacious rooms decorated with wood furniture and rose-toned tapestries. Its restaurant, sauna, fitness centre and business centre are all up to high standards.

Tverskaya Usadba MINIHOTEL €€
(Тверьская Усадьба; ☎331 525; ul Pushkinskaya 16; s/d from R3400/3900; ❄📶) Appealing minihotel with just eight rooms decorated with sturdy wooden furniture. There's also a sauna and restaurant in the complex.

Eating & Drinking

Pedestrianised ul Tryokhsvyatskaya is a pleasant place to stroll, shop and stop for a bite to eat, with several options.

TOP CHOICE **Manilov** RUSSIAN €€
(Манилов; Sovetskaya ul 17; meals R200-400) Step into a 19th-century-style parlour, complete with piano, at this appealing restaurant with its entrance on Studenchesky per; even the flat-screen TV on the wall screens period dramas. Dig into traditional favourites such as borsch, beef stroganoff and bliny, and sip the delicious horseradish-flavoured spirit. Different menu items are discounted daily by 20%.

TOP CHOICE **Kafe Jogolef.ru** RUSSIAN €€
(☎347 656; bul Radischeva 47; meals R400-600; ⏲10am-midnight; 📶) Set back in a courtyard, this very cool restaurant doubles as a jazz bar and art gallery. The food is well prepared, with tasty salads and soups. Business lunch is a reasonable R200.

Tver

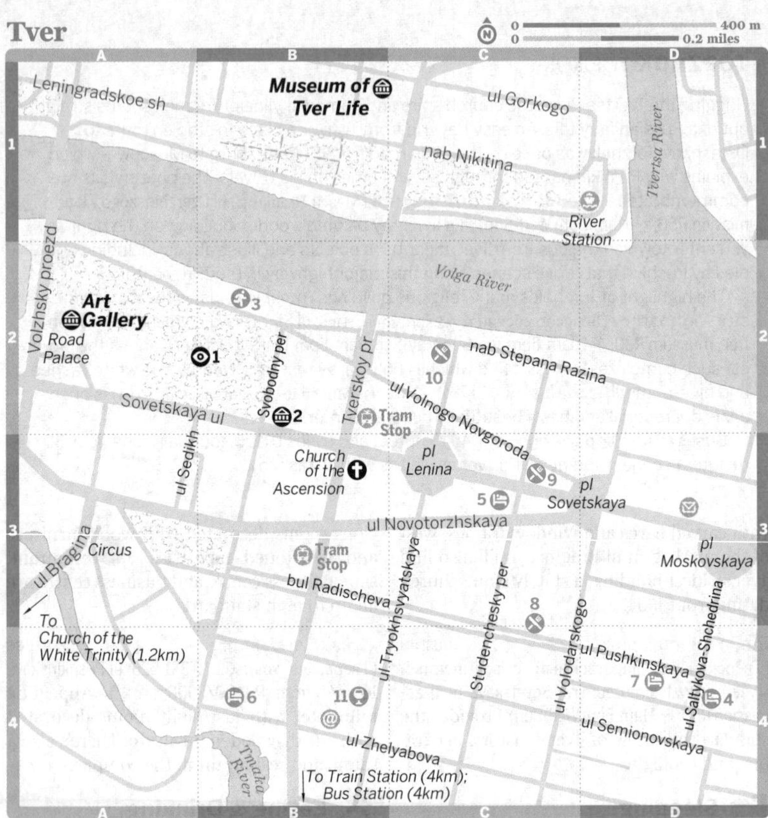

Klub Zebra INTERNATIONAL €€
(Sovetskaya ul 38; meals R400-600; noon-4am;) This dance club is also not a bad restaurant, with a great street terrace in the summer. A three-course business lunch for R250 is a great deal and it has a reasonably priced sushi bar as well as a Central Asian menu to compliment its European offerings.

Matryoshka RUSSIAN €
(Матрёшка; nab Stepana Razina 5; meals R100-300; 11am-midnight;) Supercolourful decor inspired by that of the traditional doll souvenirs sets the scene for this '*pelmeni* bar' offering no fewer than 16 types of the dumplings, plus plenty of other dishes.

Kalinin Bar BAR €€
(Калинин Бар; 357 142; ul Tryokhsvyatskaya 29/25; meals R500) Its walls plastered with Soviet-era newspapers and paintings, this retro bar is relatively tasteful, with some cool artefacts like a 1940s radio and Uralchik motorbike.

Information

Internet Club (Интернет Клуб; 8-920-157 0066; ul Zhelyabova 3; per hr R50-60; 9am-2am)

Post & telephone office (Главпочтамт; Sovetskaya ul 31; 8am-8pm Mon-Sat)

Getting There & Around

The **train station** is 4km south of the centre on ul Kominterna, with the **bus station** 300m to its east. Cruise ships and other long-distance riverboats dock at the **River Station** (Речной вокзал) on the north shore of the Volga.

Elektrichki (R265, three hours) trains stopping at Tver leave roughly every hour between 6.50am and 10pm from Moscow's Leningradsky vokzal. Long-distance trains between Moscow and St Petersburg, including the high-speed Sapsan, and between Moscow and Pskov also pause at Tver.

There are also buses (R280, three hours) to/from Moscow's Yaroslavsky vokzal.

Tver

Top Sights

Sights

Activities, Courses & Tours

Sleeping

Eating

Drinking

Trams and *marshrutky* 2, 5, 6 and 11 run from the bus and train stations up Chaykovskogo and Tverskoy pr to the town centre.

Ostashkov & Lake Seliger

Осташков и Озеро Селигер

☎48235 / POP 19,700 / ⏰MOSCOW

Ostashkov, 199km northwest of Tver, is the main base for exploring the lakes, waterways and islands around Lake Seliger. The area has become infamous in recent years because of the nationalist youth camp held along its shores each summer – so much so, that a gathering of antigovernment forces and environmentalists in the forests north of Moscow in June 2011 was dubbed 'Anti Seliger'.

Sights & Activities

The resort town, made up of tumbledown wooden cottages, decaying Soviet-era apartment blocks, rusting factories and semiderelict churches, some of which are under repair, sits on a peninsula at the southern end of the lake. Some have compared Seliger to Baikal for its beauty and diversity of nature – it's not nearly as impressive as its Siberian cousin, but is still a lovely spot, best appreciated on one of the **boat excursions** (☎51 568; www.seligerkruiz.ru; 2/4hr cruises R350/450) that run regularly between June and September.

Alternatively, relax by wandering along the town's promenades, lounging on the beaches, swimming in Seliger's clear, clean waters, and climbing the bell tower of the handsome Trinity Cathedral, now the **regional museum** (Leninsky pr 8; admission R75; ⏰11am-5pm Wed-Sun), for a brilliant vista of the surroundings.

Sleeping & Eating

It's possible to camp at the tip of the isthmus that juts out north of Ostashkov's monastery. All the following include breakfast in their rates.

TOP CHOICE **Orlovskaya Dom 1** GUESTHOUSE €€
(Орловская Дом 1; ☎8-910-830 0515; www.orlovskaja.ru; per Chaikin Bereg; s/d from R1500/2000) You couldn't wish for a better location, on the edge of the lake with the cupolas of the Trinity Cathedral right behind. Spotless rooms sport Juliet balconies. There's a café, table tennis and sauna, as well as boats and pedal boats for rental.

Epos HOTEL €€
(Эпос; ☎51 992; Leninsky pr 136; s/d from R1800/2200) Ostashkov's fanciest hotel and restaurant is a little nouveau riche with its leopard-print suite in the lobby and other dubious decorative flourishes. Still, the rooms are clean, modern and spacious, and the restaurant serves decent renditions of the usual Russian dishes – a meal is around R600.

SDL Hotel HOTEL €€
(СДЛ Отель; ☎54 983; www.sdl-tour.ru; ul Volodarskogo 187b; r from R2000; 📶) Handy for the train and bus stations at the southern end of town, this modern high-rise block harbours good-quality rooms and a café, and has friendly staff. It's part of a group that also has a luxurious resort made up of wooden chalets, 7km south of Ostashkov, facing the small Lake Sig.

Getting There & Away

Buses (R370, at least four daily, four hours) and minibuses (R355, at least three daily, three hours) connect Ostashkov with Tver; the buses run via Torzhok (R271, 2½ hours), from where there's one daily *elektrichka*. Minibuses also head to and from Moscow (R650, at least three daily, six hours), from where train 604A (*platskart/kupe* R980/1880, 11 hours) runs from early June to early September on Thursday, Saturday and Sunday. The train stops also at Tver and Torzhok.

NOVGOROD REGION

Veliky Novgorod

Великий Новгород

8162 / POP 240,000 / MOSCOW

Straddling the placid Volkhov River, Veliky Novgorod (usually shortened to Novgorod) is one of the most attractive and tourist-friendly destinations in the Novgorod region (Новгородская область). An ancient trading town, it was once the most important political and cultural centre in northwest Russia, a legacy that lives on in its impressive kremlin and numerous beautiful old churches and museums.

Novgorod is a popular weekend getaway for St Petersburg dwellers. To avoid the crowds, plan your visit on a weekday. The city is also a good base for visiting Staraya Russa, Dostoevsky's home town.

History

Much of Novgorod's early history is known through Norse sagas, as this was the first permanent settlement of the Varangian Norsemen who established the embryonic Russian state. By the 12th century the city, called 'Lord Novgorod the Great', was Russia's biggest: an independent quasi democracy whose princes were hired and fired by an assembly of citizens, and whose strong, spare style of church architecture, icon painting and down-to-earth *byliny* (epic folk songs) would become distinct idioms.

Spared from the Mongol Tatars, who got bogged down in the surrounding swamps, Novgorod suffered most at the hands of other Russians. Ivan III of Moscow attacked and annexed it in 1477, and Ivan the Terrible, whose storm troopers razed the city and slaughtered 60,000 people in a savage pogrom, broke its back. The founding of St Petersburg finished it off as a trading centre.

Sights

In addition to the following, there are scores of other old churches and monasteries around town; the helpful tourist office can provide details of which ones are open either as museums or for services.

KREMLIN

On the west bank of the Volkhov River, and surrounded by a pleasant wooded park, the **kremlin** (admission free; 6am-midnight) is one of Russia's oldest. Originally called the Detinets, the fortification dates back to the 9th century, though it was later rebuilt with brick in the 14th century (which still stands today). The complex is worth seeing with a guide; arrange one through the tourist office.

Cathedral of St Sophia CHURCH

(Софийский собор; 8am-8pm; services 10am & 6pm Sun) This working cathedral, the kremlin's focal point, was finished in 1050. It has a simple, fortress-like exterior designed to withstand attack or fire (flames had taken out an earlier, wooden church on the site). The onion domes were probably added during the 14th century – even so, they are perhaps the first example of this most Russian architectural detail. The west doors, dating from the 12th century, have tiny cast-bronze biblical scenes and even portraits of the artists. The icons inside date from the 14th century; older ones are in the museum opposite.

Novgorod State United Museum MUSEUM

(Новгородский государственный объединенный музей-заповедник; www.novgorodmuseum.ru; adult/student R140/80; 10am-6pm Wed-Mon) The highlight of this museum is its galleries of icons, one of the largest collections anywhere. Around 260 pieces have been placed in chronological order, allowing you to see the progression of skills and techniques through the centuries.

Downstairs in the history exhibition (with minimal English signs), birch-bark manuscripts are displayed, some of them 800 years old. Letters, documents and drawings on birch bark by people of all ages and social classes indicate that literacy was widespread in medieval Novgorod.

In the Russian woodcarving exhibits you can see everything from the mundane (kitchen utensils and furniture) to more detailed religious objects. In a separate exhibition are glittering pieces from Novgorod's **gold treasury** (adult/student R100/60), some dating back to the 6th century AD.

Millennium of Russia Monument MONUMENT

(Памятник Тысячелетию России) This 16m-high, 300-tonne sculpture was unveiled in 1862 on the 1000th anniversary of the Varangian Prince Rurik's arrival. A veritable who's who of Russian history over the last millennium, it depicts some 127 figures – rulers, statesmen, artists, scholars and a few fortunate hangers-on as well.

The women at the top are Mother Russia and the Russian Orthodox Church. Around the middle, clockwise from the south, are Rurik, Prince Vladimir of Kyiv (who introduced Christianity), tsars Mikhail Romanov, Peter the Great and Ivan III, and Dmitry Donskoy trampling a Mongol Tatar. In the bottom band on the east side are nobles and rulers, including Catherine the Great with an armload of laurels for all her lovers. Alexander Nevsky and other military heroes are on the north side, and literary and artistic figures are on the west.

Kokui Tower LANDMARK
(Башня Кокуй; adult/student R100/40; ⌚noon-2.30pm & 3-8pm Tue, Wed & Fri-Sun Apr-Oct) The 41m-tall Kokui Tower provides panoramic views across the complex.

Belfry LANDMARK
(admission R100/60; ⌚10am-1pm & 2-6pm Thu-Tue Apr-Oct) The Belfry, displaying enormous steel bells, also has an observation platform.

Chamber of Facets HISTORICAL BUILDING
(Грановитая палата) The Gothic Chamber of Facets is part of a palace built in 1433, and has been closed for renovation for several years.

YAROSLAV'S COURT
ЯРОСЛАВОВО ДВОРИЩЕ

Across a footbridge from the kremlin are the remnants of an 18th-century market arcade. Beyond that is the market gatehouse, an array of churches sponsored by 13th- to 16th-century merchant guilds, and a 'road palace' built in the 18th century as a rest stop for Catherine the Great.

Several of the buildings are open as museums, the best being the 12th-century **St Nicholas Cathedral** (Никольский собор; adult/student R100/60; ⌚10am-noon & 1-6pm Wed-Sun, closed last Fri of month), all that remains of an ancient palace complex from which Yaroslav's Court (Ярославово Дворище) gets its name. Inside are displays of pieces of ornate decorative tiles from churches in the region and intriguing fragments from the church's original frescoes.

Other Sights

Church of the Transfiguration of Our Saviour on Ilyina Street MUSEUM
(Церковь Спаса Преображения на Ильине улице; ul Ilina; adult/student R100/60; ⌚10am-5pm Wed-Sun, closed last Thu of month) Famous for housing the only surviving frescoes by legendary Byzantine painter Theophanes the Greek (they came close to extinction when the church served as a Nazi machine-gun nest). Restoration has exposed as much of the frescoes as possible, though they are still faint. A small exhibit upstairs includes reproductions with explanations in Russian. Note Theophanes' signature use of white warlike paint around the eyes and noses of his figures, and their piercing expressions.

Opposite is the **Cathedral of Our Lady of the Sign** (Знаменский собор; adult/student R70/40; ⌚10am-5pm Thu-Tue), a 17th-century Moscow-style complex whose interior is also festooned with somewhat more vivid frescoes.

THE SAVIOUR OF NOVGOROD

The most important icon in the Cathedral of St Sophia is that of Novgorod's patron saint, Our Lady of the Sign (Икона Знамения Божьей Матери), which, according to legend, saved the city from destruction in 1170. Accounts vary, but tend to go something like this...

The Prince of Suzdal and his large army were preparing to attack Novgorod. Things looked pretty bleak for the Novgorodians, and the bishop desperately prayed for the city's salvation. The night before the attack, he had a vision that an icon of the Virgin could save Novgorod, so he had the icon moved from the church to a pillar of the fortress. Not surprisingly, the icon was hit with an arrow shortly after the siege began. It then turned back to face Novgorod; tears were in the virgin's eyes. Darkness fell upon the land, and the army from Suzdal began attacking one another in confusion. The Novgorodians then rode out from the city and attacked, quickly dispatching their enemies.

There may be a grain of truth in all this: a close look at the icon reveals a notch over the saint's left eye, said to be where the original arrow hit. And, if you visit the Novgorod State United Museum, check out the 15th-century painting depicting three scenes from the battle. It's one of the first icons ever painted of a Russian historical event.

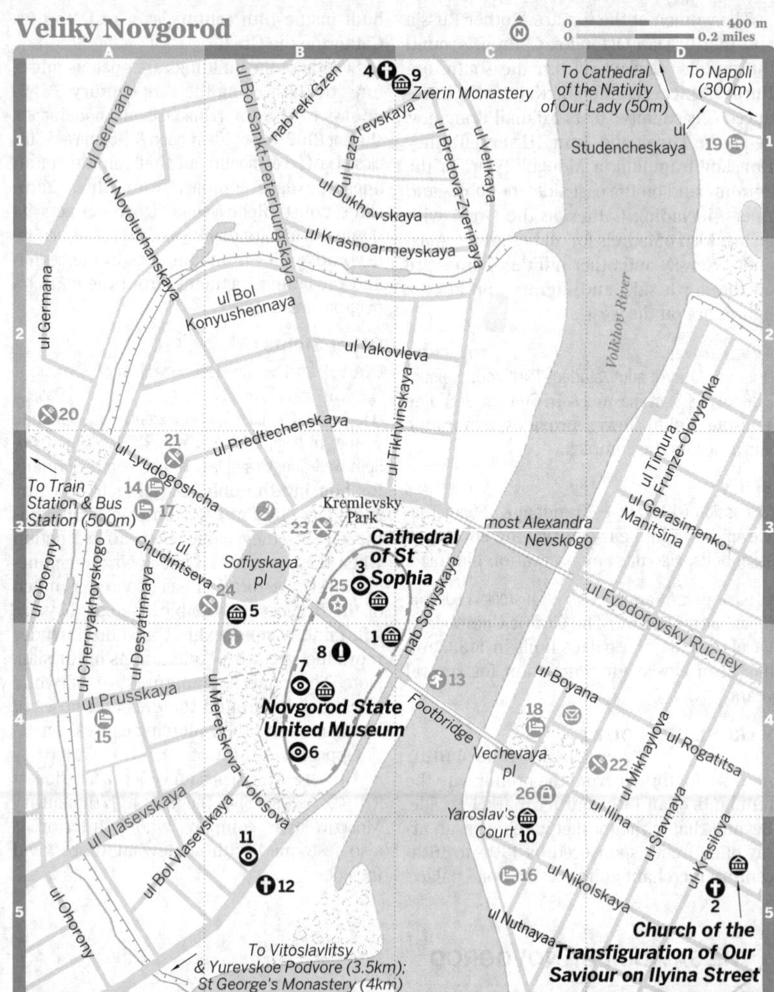

Novgorod Regional Folk Arts Centre ARTS CENTRE
(Новгородский областной Дом народного творчества; ☎739 626; ul Bredova-Zverinaya 14; ⊙noon-6pm) The folk arts centre is on the grounds of the former 15th-century Zverin Monastery (Зверин-Покровский монастырь). The craft shop sells some exquisitely woven dresses, dolls, hats and the like. Ask the tourist office to call in advance if you'd like to participate in two-hour workshops (R700 for less than six people) on producing Russian crafts, including amulet making, birch-bark crafts and textiles.

Also on the monastery grounds is the tiny **Church of St Simeon** (Церковь Симеона Богоприимца; adult/student R100/60; ⊙10am-5pm Sat-Wed, closed 1st Mon of month), its interior containing very colourful frescoes that form a religious calendar.

Fine Arts Museum MUSEUM
(Музей изобразительных искусств; www.artmus.natm.ru; pl Pobedy-Sofiyskaya 2; adult/student R140/80; ⊙10am-6pm Tue-Sun, closed last Thu of month) Offers a strong, unspectacular provincial collection, showcasing paintings by 18th- and 19th-century Russian artists, including Andropov, Bryullov and Ivanov.

Veliky Novgorod

The 3rd floor features Novgorod artists. Local crafts are among the offerings at the art shop in the lobby.

Theatre of Time HISTORICAL SITE
(Троицкий Раскоп; Troitsky ul 9; adult/student R50/35; ⌚9.30am-7pm Jun-Sep) Opposite the pink-plastered **Trinity Church** (Троицкая церковь), this is the latest of several archaeological digs that have uncovered so much about Novgorod's past. The viewing area, overlooking what are believed to be remains of a 14th-century nobleman's home, includes some English signboards. To get the most out of a visit, attend one of the **guided tours** (in Russian, adult/student R130/100; ⌚6pm Mon-Sat, 5.30pm Sun); the tourist office can assist if you need an English interpreter.

Cathedral of the Nativity of Our Lady CHURCH
(Собор Рождества Богородицы Антониева монастыря; ul Studencheskaya; ⌚10am-5pm Tue-Sun, closed 1st Wed of month) Legend has it that St Anthony sailed down Europe's rivers from Italy to Novgorod on a rock in 1106. You can view the supposed boulder in the entrance to this church on the grounds of the Antoniev Monastery, a short walk north of the Park Inn facing the river.

Festivals & Events

The tourist office website (www.visitnovgorod.ru) lists dozens of other events during the year.

Alexander Nevsky Festival HISTORICAL
The second weekend in April sees the Alexander Nevsky Festival, which honours Novgorod's best-known prince. During the festival, members of historical clubs dress up as knights, engage in mock battle and storm the kremlin walls.

Sadko Festival CULTURAL
Held the first weekend of June, this celebration includes traditional folk art, dancing, singing and a crafts fair.

City Day CULTURAL
On and around 12 June, concerts, processions and fairs attend the city's annual birthday.

Kypale CULTURAL
Held on the banks of Lake Ilmen on 2 July, this traditional St John's Day celebration combines old pagan rites with Orthodox rituals. Festival events include music, dance, food and swimming in the lake.

Sleeping

The tourist office can recommend homestays (around R1000 per person for a room). Unless otherwise noted, the rates below all include breakfast.

TOP CHOICE **Hotel Volkhov** HOTEL €€
(Гостиница Волхов; ☎225 500; www.hotel-volkhov.ru; ul Predtechenskaya 24; s/d from R1950/2900; @ wi-fi) This centrally located modern hotel runs like a well-oiled machine, with nicely furnished rooms, pleasant English-speaking staff, laundry service and free wi-fi. A sauna (extra fee) is available to guests.

Hotel Akron HOTEL €€
(Гостиница Акрон; ☎736 908; www.hotel-akron.ru; ul Predtechenskaya 24; s/d from R1550/2200; wi-fi) Similar to the Volkhov next door, but with lower prices and no elevator. Rooms have modern bathrooms, cable TV and mini-fridge. Friendly service is also a plus.

Park Inn Veliky Novgorod HOTEL €€€
(☎940 910; www.parkinn.com/hotel-velikynovgorod; ul Studencheskaya 2a; s/d R4800/5500; air-con @ wi-fi pool) This slick Radisson-group property is smoothly run and offers large, pleasant rooms in a quiet location at some remove from the town's main sights. Bus 2 stops nearby and will shuttle you to the centre in around 15 minutes, or a taxi will cost R100.

Hotel Cruise HOSTEL €
(Гостиница Круиз; ☎772 283; nsm_kruis@mail.ru; ul Prusskaya 11; dm per bed R500, d with bathroom from R2400; wi-fi) A Jekyll and Hyde operation, the Cruise is both a down-at-heel hostel *and* a spiffy boutique-style hotel. The older hostel part offers dorm rooms with three single beds that share a bathroom down the hall; if you want to stay alone in one of these rooms, pay R1000. The spacious refurbished *lyux* rooms are very stylish with limed hardwood floors and slick furnishings. There's a R100 registration charge, but wi-fi is free.

Hotel Voyage HOTEL €€
(Вояж; ☎664 166; www.hotel-voyage.ru; ul Dvortsovaya 1; r incl breakfast from R2000; wi-fi) Beside Yaroslav's Court, this small hotel offers smallish rooms that are pleasant. It also has as a sauna (extra charge).

Hotel Rossiya HOTEL €
(Гостиница Россия; ☎634 185; www.amaks-hotels.ru; nab Aleksandra Nevskogo 19/1; r from R1160) Some rooms at this older, riverside property have nice views of the kremlin. Also has a billiards hall and offers bike rental (R150 per hour).

Eating & Drinking

During summertime, several open-air cafés facing the kremlin's west side make pleasant spots for a drink.

TOP CHOICE **Nice People** INTERNATIONAL €€
(☎730 879; www.gonicepeople.ru; ul Meretskova-Volosova 1/1; meals R400-600; ⌚8am-midnight; wi-fi menu) Light floods into this appealing corner café-bar where there's a warm welcome from English-speaking staff. The menu details speciality DIY salads, with a choice of six types of lettuce, 27 toppings and seven dressings. Other tasty things and daily specials are written up on the walls.

Café Le Chocolat INTERNATIONAL €€
(☎739 009; www.cafelechocolat.ru; ul Lyudogoshcha 8; dishes R250-650; ⌚9am-11pm; menu) White leather couches, blood-red walls and black-and-white photos set the scene for this chic café. The menu features some tantalising options, including dozens of sushi platters, a range of breakfasts, desserts, creative cocktails and fruit teas.

Dom Berga RUSSIAN €€
(Дом Берга; ☎948 838; ul Bolshaya Moskovskaya 24; café/restaurant meals from R50/500; ⌚café 9am-9pm, restaurant noon-midnight) Enjoy expertly prepared Russian dishes in this handsome brick building near Yaroslav's Court – there's a choice between a simple café and fancier restaurant. Portions are a little small and pricey but it's all very palatable and elegantly done.

Ilmen RUSSIAN €€
(Ильмень; ☎178 374; ul Gazon 2; café/restaurant meals from R50/500; ⌚bistro 10am-10pm, restaurant noon-midnight) Order takeaway snacks from the deli/bakery or cheap sit-down eats from the self-serve bistro, with an outdoor area in summer. Upstairs, the more formal restaurant **Holmgard** has a menu packed with Russian dishes including freshly made kebabs.

Napoli ITALIAN €€
(Наполи; ☎636 307; www.napoli-restaurant.ru; ul Studencheskaya 21/43; meals R600-1000; ⌚noon-midnight; wi-fi) Novgorod's best Italian kitchen bakes its pizzas in a brick oven and serves tasty delicacies such as beef carpaccio and Tuscan-style pork. The dress code stipulates no shorts.

LOCAL KNOWLEDGE

OKSANA CHERNEGA

Novgorod has one of Russia's most clued-up and helpful tourist centres. Its director gives her recommendations on things to do or not to miss.

Summer Activity

Join a **cruise** (1hr cruise R300; ⏲May-Sep) along the Volkhov River – the views are really wonderful. Departures are from the dock landing below the kremlin.

Archaeological Dig

The **Theatre of Time** (p265) is one of the largest archaeological sites in Europe.

Places to Eat

Nice People is good for a range of dishes, but if you want Russian food then try **Dom Berga** or **Yurevskoe Podvore**.

Hidden Gem

The frescoes inside the **Church of the Transfiguration of Our Saviour on Ilyina Street** (p263).

Legendary Rock

The stone at the **Cathedral of the Nativity of Our Lady** (p265)on which St Anthony is said to have 'sailed' to Novgorod.

Baltysky Khleb BAKERY €
(Балтийский хлеб; pr Karla Marksa 4; meals R100; ⏲9am-9pm Mon-Fri, from 10am Sat & Sun; 📶) St Petersburg bakery Baltic Bread branches out with this rather groovily designed café where you can enjoy freshly made pastries, sandwiches, cakes and light meals in a purple and silver Austin Powersesque interior.

☆ Entertainment

Concert Hall CLASSICAL MUSIC
(Концертный зал; ☎772 777; http://filarmon.natm.ru; Kremlin 6) Novgorod's Philharmonic Concert Hall, within the kremlin grounds, often hosts live classical and popular music concerts; check the website for the schedule and ticket prices, which kick off at around R100.

Shopping

Souvenir shops are plentiful, with a prominent row of vendors near the tourist office selling woven birch boxes, miniature wooden churches, *matryoshka* nesting dolls and lacquer boxes.

Na Torgu SOUVENIRS
(На Торгу; ul Ilina 2; ⏲10am-7pm) Has one of Novogorod's best selections of arts and crafts souvenirs and includes a gallery upstairs showcasing some pieces.

ℹ Information

Main telegraph & telephone office (Главный Телеграф и Телефон; cnr ul Lyudogoshcha & ul Gazon; ⏲8.30am-10pm) Internet access available.

Post office (Почта; ul Bolshaya Dvortsovaya 2; ⏲8am-8pm Mon-Sat, 10am-4pm Sun) There are many post offices around town; this branch, just east of the bridge, has a small **internet salon** (per hr R20; ⏲9am-7pm Mon-Sat).

Tourist office (Бюро Красная Изба; ☎773 074; www.visitnovgorod.ru; Sennaya pl 5; ⏲9.30am-6pm) Friendly staff hand out Russian- and English-language maps (extensive maps available for R60) and provide comprehensive local advice. City tours in English, French or German can be arranged. A tour of the kremlin, the Cathedral of St Sophia and Yaroslav's Court will cost R1000 per group of up to five people. After hours you can contact the 24-hour hotline on ☎998 686.

ℹ Getting There & Away

The **train station** (Новгород-на-Волхове on RZD timetables) and **bus station** (Автовокзал) are next to each other on Oktyabryaskaya ul, 1.5km northwest of the kremlin.

Elektrichki run to St Petersburg's Moscow Station (R400, three daily, three hours). There's also a handy overnight train to Moscow (*platskart/kupe* R1200/2460, 7½ hours) leaving at 9.20pm.

Bus services include St Petersburg (R340, 13 daily, four hours), Pskov (R449, 8am and 4pm, 4½ hours) and Staraya Russa (R194, 14 daily, two hours).

Getting Around

From the bus and train stations, buses 4 and 20 (R14) pass in range of the Hotel Volkhov (in between the first and second stops from the stations, or a 10-minute walk) and Park Inn (get off at the stadium and cut through the park). Returning to the stations, catch bus 4 or 19 instead of bus 20.

Staraya Russa Старая Русса

81652 / POP 40,000 / MOSCOW

Set along the banks of the tranquil Polist River, Staraya Russa retains the idyllic 19th-century charm, when Dostoevsky spent summers here and wrote much of *The Brothers Karamazov* as well as other works. The town is the setting for the novel; visit the streets and churches that the characters frequented.

The town, 100km southeast of Novgorod, can easily be visited for the day. From the bus station (which is next to the train station) you can either catch a taxi (R70) to Dostoevsky's old home or take a 40-minute walk. Head under the road bridge, cross the train tracks, then continue along ul Karla Libknekhta until you hit the river; cross it, turn right and follow the riverside path south to the museum.

Sights

Dostoevsky House Museum MUSEUM

(Дом Музей Достоевского; ul Dostoevskogo 42; adult/student R70/40; 10am-5.30pm Tue-Sun) The author's family lived on the 1st floor of this riverside house, which has been lovingly maintained and still contains many original pieces. Dostoevsky's desk has copies from his mazelike drafts, and you can see his doodles on the pages. His bookcase holds books from the period, and his wife's bedroom contains her bed, chest and other personal items. An English-language handout available at the ticket office provides details of what you can see in each of the rooms.

Dostoevsky Cultural Centre ARTS CENTRE

(37 285; ul Dostoevskogo 8; adult/student R100/60; 10am-6pm Tue-Fri & Sun) A short walk north of the museum along the river will bring you to this centre which hosts temporary exhibitions and at which you can arrange Russian-language tours of the town (R500, two hours).

A little further along is the handsomely restored **Resurrection Cathedral** (Воскресенский собор) and bell tower dating from the end of the 18th century.

Regional Museum MUSEUM

(Краеведческий музей; pl Timura Frunze 6; adult/student R100/60; 10am-5pm Wed-Mon) An attractive whitewashed 12th-century monastery has become the home of this museum offering the usual historical displays and old religious relics; you can also see fragments from the church's original frescoes.

The neighbouring building houses the small **Kartinnaya Gallery** (Картинная Галерея; adult/student R70/40; 10am-5pm Wed-Mon), which has a noteworthy selection of paintings (and also a few sculptures) of artists who spent time in Staraya Russa.

Museum of the Northwest Front MUSEUM

(Музей Северо-Западного фронта; ul Volodarskogo 20; adult/student R100/60; 10am-5pm Wed-Mon) Ardent historians may want to check out this small museum dedicated to the local WWII effort.

Sleeping & Eating

Hotel Polist HOTEL €€

(Гостиница Полисть; 37 547; www.hotel-polist.ru; ul Engelsa 20; s/d from R1400/1800;) For those who want to wake up to the same morning air that once inspired the master, this well-maintained hotel is an option. It's also the location of the town's poshest restaurant – which isn't terribly fancy.

Okami INTERNATIONAL €€

(ul Karla Libknekhta 10; meals R400-600; noon-11pm) Offers a menu that mixes pizza and sushi – not an uncommon combination in Russia! The set meals of the latter from R350 are a reasonable deal – just don't expect anything too authentic.

Kafe Sadko RUSSIAN €

(Кафе Садко; ul Lenina; meals R100; 9am-9pm) Small portions of standard canteen Russian fare are served at this no-frills café facing the central square.

Getting There & Away

There are regular buses to and from Novgorod (R194, 14 daily, two hours). Going back to Novgorod, tickets tend to sell out fast, so you may want to buy your return ticket when you arrive.

WORTH A TRIP

ST GEORGE'S MONASTERY & VITOSLAVLITSY

Set amid peaceful marsh and lakelands a 15-minute bus ride south of the Veliky Novgorod town centre, these two sights make for a relaxing countryside excursion. Founded in 1030 by Yasolav the Wise, the picturesque **St George's Monastery** (Свято-Юрьев мужской монастырь; ⌚10am-8pm) functions as a theological school. It features the heavily reconstructed Cathedral of St George and a clutch of 19th-century add-ons.

About 600m up the road is **Vitoslavlitsy** (Витославлицы; adult/student R150/90; ⌚park 10am-8pm, houses to 4.30pm), an open-air museum of rustically beautiful wooden peasant houses and churches from around the region. Some of the structures date back to the 16th century, the highlight being the soaring **Church of the Nativity of Our Lady** (1531), its aspen shingles glinting in the sunlight. If you haven't bought a picnic (recommended) there's a simple café on the grounds, as well as a good souvenir shop and craft sellers plying their wares.

Opposite Vitoslavlitsy is the attractive restaurant and 16-room hotel **Yurevskoe Podvore** (Юрьевское Подворье; ☎946 060; www.tk-podvorie.ru; Yurevskoe sh 6a; s/d incl breakfast R2400/2600; 📶). The traditional Russian food (meals R600 to R1000) here includes sweet and savoury porridges that take 40 minutes to prepare. It's a comfortable place to stay if you're looking for somewhere quiet to relax.

Buses 7 and 7A (R14) from opposite the Novgorod tourist office run here. The bus route goes in a loop; it first stops at the monastery and then outside the gates to the museum before returning to town.

The **train station**, next to the **bus station** (Автостанция), is on the route between Pskov (*platskart/kupe* R1000/1500, two daily, 3½ hours) and Moscow (R1530/2320, two daily, 8½ hours); services are at inconvenient hours. On odd-numbered days there's also a train to and from St Petersburg (*platskart* R1000, 11 hours).

PSKOV REGION

Pskov Псков

☎8112 / POP 203,300 / ⌚MOSCOW

Only 30km from the Estonia border, church-studded Pskov is dominated by its mighty riverside kremlin, an enormous bulwark that has faced up to its fair share of invading armies down the centuries. Leafy lanes and parks wriggle their way round the attractive old quarter on the east bank – past weathered churches, city wall ruins and handsome 19th-century brick residences. Inside the Pogankin Chambers, a 17th-century merchant house, a great deal of the iconographic art from churches in the area has been collected and displayed in the Pskov National Museum of History, Architecture & Art.

Day trips include visiting the old fortress and beautiful countryside at Stary Izborsk; the Technicolor church and spooky cave necropolis at Pechory; and Pushkinskie Gory, location of Mikhailovskoe, the family estate and last resting place of Alexander Pushkin, Russia's poet laureate.

History

Pskov's history is saturated with 700 years of war for control of the Baltic coast. It was first mentioned in early Russian chronicles in 903 when Prince Igor of Kyiv married the future saint Olga of Pskov. German Teutonic Knights captured the town in 1240, but Alexander Nevsky routed them two years later in a famous battle on the ice of Lake Peipsi.

In the 14th century, like Veliky Novgorod, Pskov was its own sovereign republic and a member of the Hanseatic League. The Poles laid siege in the 16th century and the Swedes likewise in the following century. Peter the Great used Pskov as a base for his drive to the sea, Nicholas II abdicated at its train station, and the Red Army fought its first serious battle against Nazi troops outside the city.

Sights

Kremlin HISTORICAL SITE

(Кремль) Rising up from a high narrow cape on the banks of the Velikaya River, the mighty kremlin (also known as the Krom) is the most complete portion of a fortress that once had five layers, 37 towers, 14 gates and

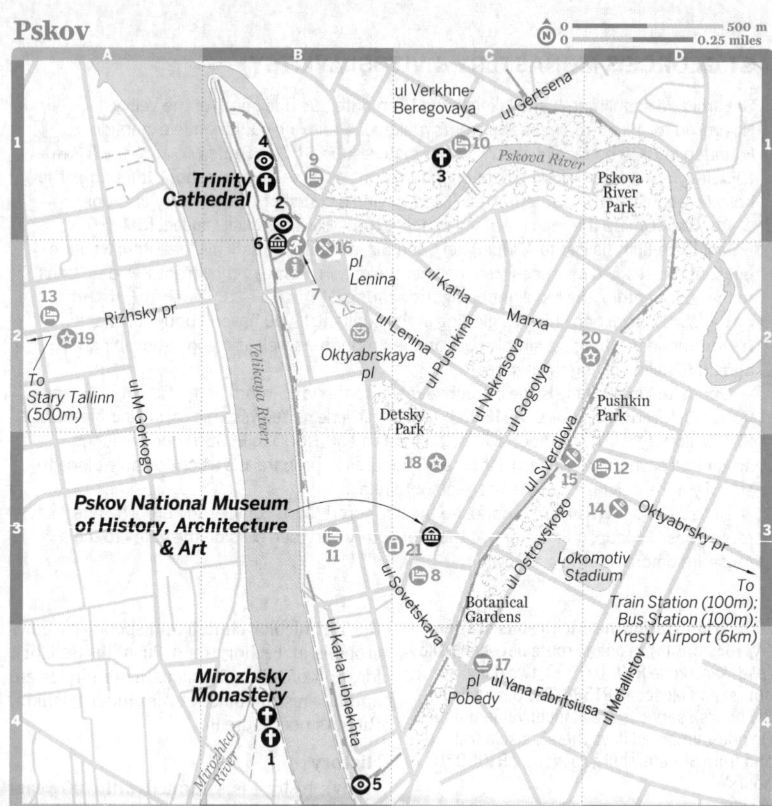

an overall length of 9.5km. In April 2010 a fire damaged the Vlasyevskaya and Rybnitskaya towers, close to Olginsky most, closing off the towers and the walkway on the river-facing side of the fortress.

The walls and towers of the 15th- to 16th-century Outer Town (Окольный город) can still be seen along ul Sverdlova, the Velikaya River embankment and across the tributary Pskova River. The largest tower – a whopping 90m in diameter and 50 metres tall – is the **Pokrovskaya Bashnya** (Покровская башня) beside Pyatidesyatiletiya Oktyabrya most.

Trinity Cathedral CHURCH

(Троицкий собор; 🕘11am-5pm) This 72m structure, which can be seen from miles away on a clear day, was consecrated in 1699. It's the fourth version of a church to have stood on this spot since the early 11th century, when a wooden one was commissioned by Princess Olga, an early convert to the Orthodox faith. Its grandeur is heightened by the simplicity of the skeletal walls surrounding it. The interior contains a large collection of bejewelled icons of the Madonna.

Pskov State Museum MUSEUM

(Псковский государственный музей-заповедник; www.museum.pskov.ru; adult/student R70/50; 🕘11am-6pm Tue-Sun) Located near the entrance to the kremlin, this museum houses a spartan collection of archaeological finds including knives, jewellery and old keys dating back to the settlement's earliest days when Scandinavian Vikings lived in the area. There are also revolving displays by local artists. A fairly dry exhibit upstairs presents old documents on the administration of Pskov during the 17th century.

Dovmont Town HISTORICAL SITE

(Довмонтов город) Named after an early Pskov prince (also known as Daumantas, who ruled the independent city between

Pskov

Top Sights

Mirozhsky Monastery ... B4
Pskov National Museum of History, Architecture & Art ... C3
Trinity Cathedral ... B1

Sights

1 Cathedral of the Transfiguration of the Saviour ... B4
2 Dovmont Town ... B1
3 Epiphany Church from Zapskovie ... C1
4 Kremlin ... B1
5 Pokrovskaya Bashnya ... B4
6 Pskov State Museum ... B2

Activities, Courses & Tours

7 Sotstourprof ... B2

Sleeping

8 Dvor Podznoeva ... C3
9 Golden Embankment Hotel ... B1
10 Heliopark Old Estate ... C1
11 Hotel Favorit ... B3
12 Hotel Oktyabrskaya ... D3
13 Hotel Rizhskaya ... A2

Eating

14 Café in the City ... D3
Dvor Podznoeva ... (see 8)
15 Kafe Epokha ... C3
16 Kafe Melnitsa ... B2
Trapeznie Palat ... (see 8)

Drinking

17 Chocolate Café ... C4
Pivnoi Dom ... (see 9)
Rublev ... (see 10)

Entertainment

18 Pskov Region Philharmonia ... C3
19 R-16 ... A2
20 TIR ... D2

Shopping

21 Menshikovikh ... C3
Russian Souvenir ... (see 7)

1266 and 1299), the preserved foundations of a dozen or so 12th- to 15th-century churches can be viewed in the walled-in area outside the Pskov State Museum.

Pskov National Museum of History, Architecture & Art MUSEUM
(Псковский государственный объединённый историко-архитектурный и художественный музей-заповедник; http://museums.pskov.ru; ul Nekrasova 7; Pogankin Chambers R200, art & history galleries R50; ⏲11am-6pm Tue-Sun, closed last Tue of month) As you can guess from its title, this museum, spread over several buildings, includes history and art exhibitions. The architecture bit comes from the museum's key block – the **Pogankin Chambers** (Поганкины палаты) – the fortress-like house and treasury of the 17th-century merchant Sergey Pogankin, with walls 2m thick.

The maze of galleries in the chambers holds 14th- to 18th-century pottery, weaving and weaponry – including the original 15th-century sword of one of Pskov's princes. A series of icons depicts the life of Christ, most from Pskov churches that have closed. It is a rare chance to thoroughly examine one particular style of iconography at close range. Note, for instance, the bulbous noses and otherwise harsh realism that characterises the Pskov school, as well as a predominance of subdued earth tones. One impressive 17th-century icon on display relates the history of Pskov's development (it looks like an ancient map of the city).

Equally impressive is the collection of silver artefacts, including beautifully crafted baroque-style silver bible covers. The largest, a 25kg beast, was originally housed at Pskov's Trinity Cathedral.

The 2nd floor of the museum's new building houses the war collection, with photos and artefacts from WWII, as well as information on more recent conflicts like Afghanistan and Chechnya. More interesting is the picture gallery, which has works from the 18th, 19th and 20th centuries, including paintings by Nikitin, Tropinin and Zhukovsky, as well as representations from the Russian avant-garde, including a couple of Petrov-Vodkins.

Mirozhsky Monastery MONASTERY
(Мирожский монастырь; ☎567 301; Mirozhskaya nab 2; grounds admission free, cathedral adult/student R300/250; ⏲11am-6pm Tue-Sun) The attraction here is the Unesco-listed, non-working **Cathedral of the Transfiguration of the Saviour** (Спасо-Преображенский собор), whose 12th-century frescoes are

MOVING ON?

For tips, recommendations and reviews, head to shop.lonelyplanet.com to purchase a downloadable PDF of the Estonia chapter from Lonely Planet's *Eastern Europe* guide.

considered one of the most complete representations of the biblical narrative to have survived the Mongols. However, unless you have a particular interest in Byzantine frescoes, you're likely to find the entry to the church overpriced.

The frescoes have been partially restored after centuries of damage from flooding, whitewashing and scrubbing; 80% of what you see today is original. The artists are unknown but were almost certainly from Greece, as the Byzantine-style of the frescoes suggests.

The cathedral was based on a 12th-century Greek model, formed around a symmetrical cross. Later additions and demolitions have altered the footprint, but you can still see traces of the original structure along exterior walls. As you walk out, note the damage above the door to the right, caused by a wayward WWII unexploded shell. The church closes often due to inclement weather: too hot, too cold or too wet; it's best to call in advance.

The monastery is also a working iconography school; ask to see any current activity. The whole complex is across the Velikaya River from the centre; take bus 2 from the vicinity of Hotel Rizhskaya.

Epiphany Church from Zapskovie CHURCH
(Церковь Богоявления с Запсковья; ul Gertsena 7) There are many more ancient churches dotted around the city. This attractive, working one, overlooking the Pskova tributary, was built in 1494 and includes a separately standing five-column belfry, its open gables and large pillars distinctive of the Pskovian style. Around the church is a lovely stretch of park, nice for strolling, picnicking or short hikes.

Tours

Sotstourprof TOURS
(723 257; www.sotstour.ru; Kremlin; 10am-6pm) Offers hour-long Russian-language kremlin tours (R650) and guided excursions further afield to Pechory Monastery and Stary Izborsk. English interpreters can be arranged.

Sleeping

Unless mentioned otherwise, the following rates include breakfast.

TOP CHOICE **Hotel Rizhskaya** HOTEL €€
(Гостиница Рижская; 562 223; www.rijskaya.ru; Rizhsky pr 25; s/tw without breakfast R1450/2600;) Overlooking a grassy square a few blocks west of the Velikaya River, this old Intourist has renovated rooms with decent furnishings, wood floors, good lighting and modern bathrooms. You'll also find friendly staff (some speak English) and a laundry. A buffet breakfast is R250 extra and registration is R50.

Heliopark Old Estate HOTEL €€€
(794 545; www.heliopark.ru; ul Verkhne-Beregovaya 4; s/d from R4700/5100;) Pskov's most upmarket option stands in a leafy street in the shadow of the Epiphany Church. Medium-sized rooms include a modern bathroom. Guests can use the spa with sauna, jacuzzi and splash pool for free between 7am and 10am (R400 afterwards).

Golden Embankment Hotel HOTEL €€
(Золотая Набережная; 627 877; www.zn-hotel.ru; Sovetskaya nab 2; s/d R2600/2900;) With a prime position in the shadow of the kremlin, this intimate hotel offers pleasant, reasonably priced rooms and a friendly welcome. Breakfast is taken in the restaurant next door.

Dvor Podznoeva HOTEL €€
(Двор Подзноева; 797 000; www.dvorpodznoeva.ru; ul Nekrasova 1; s/tw R2900/3000;) Next to the new dining complex of the same name, this hotel in a 19th-century-style building has 25 smallish but nicely decorated rooms, mainly with twin beds.

Hotel Favorit HOTEL €€
(Гостиница Фаворит; 700 631; www.favorit-pskov.ru; Detskaya ul 1b; s/d from R2700/2900;) This stand-alone building in a peaceful riverside location is within walking distance of key sights and offers small but comfortable rooms. Add R200 to rates for rooms on the upper floor.

Hotel Oktyabrskaya HOTEL €
(Гостиница Октябрьская; 664 246; okthotel@ellink.ru; Oktyabrsky pr 36; s/d without bathroom R700/1000, with bathroom R1100/2000)

Although the rates are lower than at the Rizhskaya and other similar, ex-Soviet-era midrange options, once you take the exorbitant R300 registration fee into account, this place is a lot less attractive.

Eating

TOP CHOICE **Dvor Podznoeva** RUSSIAN €€€
(Двор Подзноева; www.dvorpodznoeva.ru; ul Nekrasova 1; meals R1000-1200;) There is something for everyone at this imaginatively designed dining complex: an excellent bakery café serving tasty snacks straight from the oven; a very well-stocked wine and cheese cellar, and a relaxed beer restaurant with outdoor tables. Top of the line is **Trapeznie Palat** (Трапезные Палаты; 797 111), which re-creates the colourful interior of a 17th-century merchant's home and serves traditional local dishes. Woven strips of salmon and pike perch with a paprika sauce look lovely on the plate and taste delicious. Also sample your way through vodkas flavoured with ingredients such as ginger, horseradish, juniper and cedar.

Stary Tallinn RUSSIAN, ESTONIAN €€
(Старый Таллинн; 724 158; www.caferp.ru; Rizhsky pr 54; meals R600-800;) Tucked away in the basement of a housing block, a short walk west of the Hotel Rizhskaya, this reasonably sophisticated option compliments its Russian menu with dishes popular in neighbouring Estonia, such as *kilkis* (small fish), herring and rabbit.

Café in the City N RUSSIAN €€
(Кафе в городе Н; Oktyabrsky pr 19; meals R200; 8am-1am) 'The City N' is a bright space with high ceilings, cosy nooks and friendly staff. Breakfast (R40 to R65, served all day) includes pancakes, omelettes and tasty raisin porridge. Soups, salads and the usual range of meat and fish dishes are also available.

Kafe Epokha RUSSIAN €€
(Кафе Эпоха; www.cafe-age.ru; ul Sverdlova 45; meals R400; noon-2am) Of the two similar restaurants atop the remains of the fortress walls on either side of Oktyabrsky pr, this is the more rustic and offers a small outdoor terrace. The reasonably priced menu throws up no surprises in its list of usual Russian favourites such as salads, soups and mains.

Kafe Melnitsa RUSSIAN €
(Кафе Мелница; pl Lenina; dishes R50-100; 8am-11pm;) Bliny in all forms and flavours, plus self-serve cafeteria-style grub (schnitzel, meat patties, potato salad), are available at this low-priced eatery that's handy to the kremlin.

Drinking

Chocolate Café CAFÉ
(Кафе Шоколад; www.caferp.ru; ul Yana Fabritsiusa 2/17; 8am-11pm Mon-Fri, 11am-11pm Sat & Sun) Hip little café specialising in coffees, teas and light meals (salads, sandwiches, bliny and pastas). There's also a kid's menu with cutely styled dishes.

Pivnoi Dom BAR
(Пивной Дом; www.zn-hotel.ru; Sovetskaya nab 1/2; 8am-2am) A cooling beer or beverage on the terrace at this joint facing the kremlin is nothing short of perfect on a sunny day. If you're feeling peckish, it does dishes such as a metre-long sausage on a wooden platter and German-style pork shin.

Rublev BAR
(Рублев; www.heliopark.ru; ul Verkhne-Beregovaya 4; noon-3am;) Chunky stone walls, rustic wooden beams and furniture, and artfully distressed fragments of fresco conjure up a ye-olde-Pskov atmosphere at this hotel bar that's favoured by the city's movers and shakers.

Entertainment

TIR LIVE MUSIC
(http://tirclub.ru; ul Sverdlova 52; noon-late Mon-Fri, from 3pm Sat & Sun;) Hub of Pskov's underground and trendy music scene, TIR stages local and national bands and DJs. Groovsters hang by day in the arty, two-level interior nibbling on food and sipping drinks while tapping on their laptops.

R-16 NIGHTCLUB
(http://r-16.ru; Rizhsky pr 16; admission R200-300; 10pm-6am) Booming nightclub with a big dance floor and attached lounge. Check the website for various DJ events.

Pskov Region Philharmonia CLASSICAL MUSIC
(Псковская областная филармония; 668 920; http://filarmonia.pskov.ru; ul Nekrasova 24; tickets from R100) This ageing venue is the home of the city's classical orchestra; see the website for concert details.

Shopping

Menshikovikh SOUVENIRS
(Меншиковых; ul Sovetskaya 50; 9am-9pm) There's a huge range of gifts at this

multihalled store, in an old merchant's house, including colourful local pottery (particularly teapots and teacups), photos of Pskov's churches, books and artwork.

Russian Souvenir SOUVENIRS
(Русский Сувенир; Kremlin; ⌚9am-9pm) As well as the stalls outside the main gate of the kremlin, there's a small gift shop just inside, selling jewellery and upmarket traditional crafts including Russian dolls.

ℹ Information

Main post office (Главпочтамт; Oktyabrskaya pl; per hr R50; ⌚8am-9pm Mon-Fri, 10am-4pm Sat & Sun) In addition to postal services, you can change money here. Internet is available.

Pskov Tourist Centre (Бюро Красная Изба; ☎724 568; www.tourism.pskov.ru; pl Lenina 3; ⌚10am-8pm) English-speaking assistants can provide maps, leaflets and give advice on how to get around, including tours to places like Izborsk or Mikhailovskoe.

ℹ Getting There & Away

The **train and bus stations** are next to each other on ul Vokzalnaya. The bus is a better option to St Petersburg than the train, which leaves at 4.30am.

Air

Pskovavia (http://pskovavia.ru) has irregular passenger flights between Moscow's Domodedovo Airport and Pskov's **Kresty Airport**, 6km southeast of the city centre; check the website for details.

Bus

Bus connections from Pskov include Novgorod (one way R450, two daily, 4½ hours), Pechory (R150, 10 daily, 1½ hours), Smolensk (R756, two daily, eight to 10 hours) and Stary Izborsk (R67, six daily, 45 minutes).

Buses also run to Tallinn (R830, daily at 8.20am, six hours) and Tartu (R600, daily at 2pm, three hours), both of which pass through Izborsk and Pechory; you could pick up the bus in either place rather than backtracking to

WORTH A TRIP

MIKHAILOVSKOE МИХАЙЛОВСКОЕ

Russia's most beloved poet, Alexander Pushkin, lived several years at his family estate **Mikhailovskoe** (Map p239; ☎81146-22 321; www.pushkin.ellink.ru; admission R156; ⌚10am-5pm Tue-Sun, closed Apr, Nov & every last Tue of month), near the small town of **Pushkinskie Gory** (Пушкинские Горы; Pushkin Hills), 120km south of Pskov. He is also buried in the local monastery.

The family first came to the area in the late 1700s, when Pushkin's great-grandfather Abram Hannibal was given the land by Empress Elizabeth. The family house was destroyed during WWII and has since been rebuilt. Pushkin's writing room has also been re-created, with his comfy leather chair, portraits of Byron and Zhukovsky (Pushkin's mentor, also a poet) and a small statue of Napoleon. The thick religious book on his writing table is the one he supposedly grabbed from the family bookcase and pretended to be reading whenever he saw the local priest coming for a visit. After viewing the house, explore the surrounding 20-hectare park, which includes servants' quarters, orchards, little humped-back bridges and a wooden windmill.

At Pushkinskie Gory, about 800m north of the bus stop, is the **Svyatagorsky Monastery** (Святагорский Моиастырь), where Pushkin is buried.

Many travel agencies run excursions from Pskov, with Russian-speaking guides; enquire at the tourist office in Pskov to find one that matches your schedule.

Alternatively, catch a bus to Pushkinskie Gory from the Pskov bus station (R220, at least four daily, 2½ hours); the first bus leaves at 7.20am. The Pushkinskie Gory bus station is about 6km from Mikhailovskoe; if there is no local bus to cover the last leg, take a taxi there (R200) and return on foot – the walk is pleasant. To walk there, turn left out of the bus station and walk for 1km along the road – you'll eventually see the Svyatagorsky Monastery on your left. From there a road leads off to the right towards Mikhailovskoe, which is signposted ahead.

If you'd prefer to stay overnight, **Druzhba** (Дружба; ☎22 556; ul Lenina 8; s/d from R700/1400) has simple, pleasant rooms, odd-numbered ones offering views of the forest. To reach the hotel, walk from the bus stop along the road away from the monastery and bear right.

Pskov. Other Russian and international services can be found on the timetable at http://pskovavtotrans.ru/table/6001.

Train

Pskov is connected by train to Moscow (*platskart/kupe* R1312/2062, two daily, 13 hours), St Petersburg (R1400/2385, two daily, five hours), Rīga (R1720/2865, daily, 8½ hours) and Vilnius (R1920/2950, odd days, nine hours).

Getting Around

Buses 1, 11 and 17 run from the train station past Hotel Oktyabrskaya and through the centre (R14). Bus 2 or 17 takes you to Hotel Rizhskaya from the station (taxis charge about R100). Bus 2 also runs past Mirozhsky Monastery.

Stary Izborsk Старый Изборск

☎81148

Meaning 'old Izborsk', this sleepy village is the real deal, celebrating its 1150th anniversary in 2012. The ruins of the ancient stone fortress here are among the oldest in Russia and from its ridge location it overlooks a beautiful slice of countryside.

Sights & Activities

Fortress FORTRESS

(admission R20; ⏲9am-6pm) Inside is the 14th-century **Church of St Nicholas**, a small green-trimmed building, and a **stone tower** (Башня Луковка; R40), which has a viewing platform at the top. A path behind the fortress leads down to the tranquil **Gorodishchenskoye Lake**. The locals you'll pass toting water bottles are coming from the **Slovenian Springs** (Словенские ключи); legend has it that the water will bring love, happiness, health and good luck.

Izborsk Museum MUSEUM

(Музей Изборск; www.museum-izborsk.ru; ul Pechorskaya 39; admission R20; ⏲9am-6pm May-Sep, to 5pm Oct-Apr) On the way to the fortress from the bus stop, you'll pass this museum, a one-room display of local archaeological finds and written explanations, in Russian, of the town's rich history. Several festivals are staged in the village during the year and you can find out about them from the museum's website.

Outdoor activities HIKING, CYCLING

The surrounding countryside, threaded with trails, is ideal for gentle hiking or exploring on **horseback** (☎8-964-316 6393; per hr R400). **Bicycles** (per hr R150) are available to rent from the Izborsk Hotel. There's also a traditional **banya** (2/3hr R1800/2100), a Russian bathhouse, at the Trapeznaya Gostoyaly Dvor.

Sleeping & Eating

TOP CHOICE **Izborsk Hotel** HOTEL €€

(Гостиничный комплекс "Изборск"; ☎8112-607 031, 8-921-703 7031; www.izborsk-hotel.ru; ul Pechorskaya 13; s/d incl breakfast from R1900/2500) Some care has been taken with the decoration of this complex at the entrance to the village from the main road. Rooms have pretty wallpaper and modern furniture, and the staff are friendly. Also here is a small gift shop selling quality crafts, and a pleasant restaurant.

Gostevoy Dom GUESTHOUSE €€

(Гостевой Дом; ☎96 612; d without/with bathroom R1168/1290, ste with bathroom R3225) This appealing guesthouse overlooks the valley from beneath the back of the fortress. The two-room *lyux* suite has a broad private balcony. Guests can use the communal kitchen.

Izborsk Park RUSSIAN €€

(Изборск-Парк; www.izborsk-park.ru; ul Pechorskaya 43; meals R200-400; ⏲10am-8pm) The verandah overlooking the fortress walls at this log-cabin café is a good spot to grab a simple lunch of soup and salads, or a more filling meal such as meat-filled cabbage rolls.

Blinnaya RUSSIA €

(Блинная; bliny around R50; ⏲9am-6pm) Beyond the kremlin walls, near the Church of St Sergius, is this sweet little bliny restaurant boasting 'Izborskian' bliny. You can order them with butter, jam, condensed milk or ham. Outdoor tables and benches are ideal for an afternoon beer.

Getting There & Away

Stary Izborsk is 32km from Pskov on the road to Estonia. There are bus connections with Pskov (R67, six daily, 45 minutes) and Pechory (R41, seven daily, 20 minutes). Several of the buses from Pskov to Pechory stop in Stary Izborsk, so it's easy to combine a trip to both places.

Pechory Печоры

☎81148

This tiny town, just 2.5km from the Estonian border, is home to the photogenic **Pechory Monastery** (Псково-Печерский Свято-Успенский монастырь) with its eerie burial caves. Founded in 1473, the monastery sits in a ravine full of hermits' caves. With all the high ground outside, it's an improbable stronghold, but several tsars fortified it and depended on it. A path descends under the 1564 **St Nicholas Church** (Николская церковь) into a Disneyesque palette of colours and architectural styles, where several dozen monks still live and study.

Taking photos of the buildings is acceptable if you make a contribution at the front gate; photographing the monks is taboo. On the monastery grounds, women must wear skirts and cover their heads and shoulders (shawls and skirts to be worn over trousers are available to borrow at the entrance). Men should wear long pants.

The central yellow church comprises two buildings. At ground level is the original **Assumption Cathedral** (Успенский собор), built into the caves; upstairs is the 18th-century baroque **Intercession Church** (Покровская церковь). Below the belfry on the left is the entrance to the **caves** (10am-5pm Tue-Thu, Sat & Sun), where some 10,000 bodies – monks, benefactors and others – are bricked up in vaults.

You can wander the monastery grounds and visit most of the churches on your own. To visit the caves you'll probably have to join a tour to lead you through the dark, spooky, nearly freezing sand tunnels. Everyone carries a candle, which in places you can thrust through holes in the tunnel walls to see a few of the wooden coffins lying lopsided on top of each other. It's sometimes possible to tag onto a group that is entering, which won't cost you anything. Bring a strong torch.

On the grounds is the summer carriage of Peter the Great's daughter, the licentious Anna Ioanovna, who – as the story goes – came to have some summer fun with the monks and didn't leave until winter. Before WWII, this area was in independent Estonia, thereby avoiding the frequent stripping or destruction of churches during that time; the 16th-century bells in St Nicholas Church are original, a rarity in Russia.

There's a booth outside the monastery gates housing an **excursion office** (21 593; www.pechori.ru; 10am-5pm). The office offers tours in Russian for R550 for up to five people.

If you need a place to stay, **Hotel Planeta** (24 516; info@hotelpechory.ru; ul Mira 10; s/d R800/1600;) next to the bus station offers clean, simple rooms and a friendly welcome. It also has a restaurant.

From the bus stand there's a 9.30am bus to Tallinn (R780, five hours) and the 3pm bus to Tartu (R600, three hours). Both buses originate in Pskov. Hourly buses shuttle between Pskov and Pechory (R115, one hour) between 8am and 11pm. At least six buses a day make a stop in Stary Izborsk (R41, 20 minutes).

LENINGRAD REGION

Several places in the Leningrad region (Ленинградская область) are covered in the St Petersburg chapter; those that are likely to be more than a day trip out of the city are detailed below. For more about the region, see http://eng.lenobl.ru.

Vyborg Выборг

81378 / POP 79,224 / MOSCOW

This Gulf of Finland port and rail junction, 174km northwest of St Petersburg and just 30km from the Finland border, is a very appealing provincial town dominated by a medieval castle and peppered with beautiful Finnish art nouveau buildings and romantic cobblestone streets. There's plenty to do here to justify staying over, even though Vyborg (pronounced Vih-bork) is also an easy day trip from St Petersburg.

The border has jumped back and forth around Vyborg for most of its history. Peter the Great captured it from the Swedes in 1710. A century later it fell within autonomous Finland, and after the revolution Vyborg remained part of independent Finland. Since then the Finns have called it Viipuri. Stalin took Vyborg in 1939, lost it to the Finns during WWII, and on getting it back at the end of the war deported all the Finns. Today the Finns are back by the coachloads for sightseeing and carousing on the weekends.

Sights

With the exception of Park Monrepo, all Vyborg's main sights are neatly arranged around a compact peninsula, making it an ideal town to explore on foot.

Vyborg Castle HISTORICAL BUILDING
(Выборгский замок; Zamkovy Island; grounds admission R10; museum 11am-7pm Tue-Sun, tower 10am-10pm daily) Rising stoutly from an islet in Vyborg Bay, this castle was built by the Swedes in 1293 when they first captured

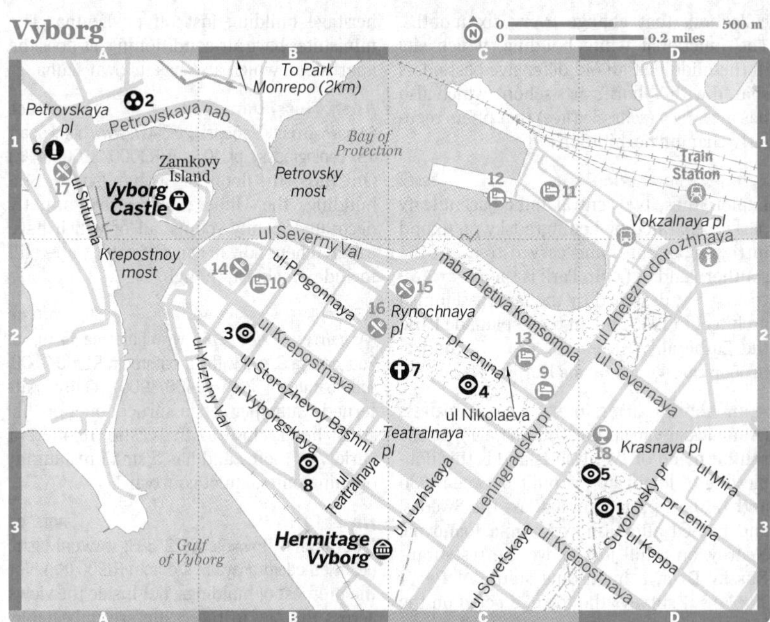

Karelia from Novgorod. Most of it now consists of 16th-century alterations. The castle contains a couple of exhibition halls, including a mildly diverting small **museum** (admission R80) on local history, but the main attraction is climbing the many steps of whitewashed **St Olaf's Tower** (admission R70) for commanding views over the town. An interesting website with history of the castle and other fortifications across northern Russia is www.nortfort.ru.

Park Monrepo PARK

(Парк Монрепо; www.parkmonrepos.org; adult/student R50/25; ⏲10am-8pm May-Oct, to 6pm Nov-Apr) A lovely place to escape the world for a few hours, if not most of the day, is this 180-hectare park facing on to tranquil Zashchitnaya Bay. It's laid out in a classical style, with various pavilions, curved bridges, arbours and sculptures. Buses 1 or 6 (R20, 15 minutes) will get you here from outside the train and bus stations.

Hermitage Vyborg MUSEUM

(Эрмитаж Выборг; ☎27 282; ul Ladanova 1; adult/student R250/150; ⏲10am-6pm) Housed in a wing of a striking building designed by Finnish architect Uno Ulberg in 1930, this small museum hosts themed exhibitions, curated from the Hermitage's massive

Vyborg

Top Sights

- Hermitage Vyborg ... B3
- Vyborg Castle ... A1

Sights

- 1 Alvar Aalto Library ... D3
- 2 Anninskie Fortifications ... A1
- 3 Clock Tower ... B2
- 4 Esplanade Park ... C2
- 5 Lenin Park ... D3
- 6 Peter the Great Statue ... A1
- Round Tower ... (see 16)
- 7 SS Peter & Paul Cathedral ... C2
- 8 Town Hall ... B3

Sleeping

- 9 Apart-Hotel Ullberg ... C2
- 10 Atlantik ... B2
- 11 Hotel Druzhba ... C1
- 12 Korolenko Boat Hostel ... C1
- 13 Letuchaya Mysh ... C2

Eating

- 14 Café Respect ... B2
- 15 Central Market ... C2
- 16 Round Tower Restaurant ... B2
- 17 Russky Dvor ... A1

Drinking

- 18 Champion ... D3

collection, that change every six months. The functional white building, which sits in the middle of an old defensive bastion, is shared with Vyborg's arts school, which also has a **gallery** (admission free) that offers regularly changing exhibitions.

Lenin & Esplanade Parks PARK

Explore these two central and adjacent leafy parks, separated by Leningradsky pr, to find intriguing statutes and carved trees. At the southern end of Lenin Park is the **Alvar Aalto Library**, designed by the famous Finnish architect in 1935 and, in the Esplanade Park, the Lutheran **SS Peter & Paul Cathedral** (Собор святых апостолов Петра и Павла).

Anninskie Fortifications FORTRESS

(Аннинские укрепленя; Ostrovnaya ul) At the southern end of Tverdysh Island is this double line of fortifications built between 1730 and 1750, as protection against the Swedes, and named after Empress Anna Ioanovna. Nearby, on a hill just above the restaurant Russky Dvor, a handsome statue of **Peter the Great** surveys the town, erected on the bicentenary of the city's capture by Russia.

Swedish Relics HISTORICAL SITE

As well as the castle, other relics of Vyborg's Swedish times are found in the squat **Round Tower** (Круглая башня; Rynochnaya pl), which now houses a restaurant; the remains of the 15th-century **Town Hall** (Башня Ратуши; ul Vyborgskaya 15), with its distinctive white tower crowned with what resembles a giant metallic wizard's hat; and the **Clock Tower** (Часовая башня; ul Krepostnaya 5), dating to 1490 – if the caretaker is around to let you in, it's worth climbing for the views of town.

Festivals & Events

In July, the town hosts the ambitious five-day **Vyborg Intelligent Performance** (www.vkontakte.ru/vbgpromenade) arts festival, which includes live music, theatre and lectures.

Sleeping

Vyborg has plenty of accommodation, but the town can get busy on weekends, so book ahead if you plan to visit then. Unless otherwise mentioned, all rates include breakfast.

TOP CHOICE **Letuchaya Mysh** HOTEL €€

(Летучая Мышь; ☎34 537; www.bathotel.ru; ul Nikolaeva 3; s/d from R2900/3600, apt s/d R5800/6400; ❄📶) This charming boutique-style hotel and restaurant occupies a small heritage building just off pr Lenina. The minisuites have air-conditioning, as does the apartment, which also has its own sauna.

Apart-Hotel Ullberg HOTEL €€

(Апарт-отель Улберг; ☎55 417; www.hotel-apart.ru; Leningradsky pr 10; s/d R3000/3200; ❄📶) On the 4th floor of a handsome 1915 building, the Ullberg offers five brightly decorated, comfy rooms, all of which have minikitchens so you can self-cater; rates still include breakfast, though.

Atlantik HOTEL €€

(Атлантик; ☎24 776; www.hotelatlantik.ru; ul Podgornaya 9; s/d without bathroom R1200/1600, with bathroom from R1600/1900) Gaily patterned wallpaper sets a spruce tone for this small hotel, close to the castle. It offers a variety of rooms and has a small restaurant opening onto a quiet courtyard.

Hotel Druzhba HOTEL €€

(Гостиница Дружба; ☎22 383; www.druvbg.ru; ul Zheleznodorozhnaya 5; s/d from R1900; 📶) Not the prettiest of buildings, but inside the views across the bay to the castle are unbeatable. The cheapest rooms are without a TV. All rates include access to the sauna in the morning.

Korolenko Boat Hostel HOSTEL €

(Гостиница Короленко; ☎/fax 34 478; dm/d R500/1500) While parts of this 1957 Volga River cruise boat have weathered time well, many of the tiny cabins with just a sink are scruffy. A twin room with its own bathroom is in better shape but still pretty cramped. Staff are friendly and it is one of the more unusual hostels you're likely to come across.

Eating & Drinking

TOP CHOICE **Russky Dvor** RUSSIAN €€

(Русский Дворь; ☎36 369; ul Shturma; meals R500-800; ⏲noon-midnight) The terrace here overlooking the castle and town is an ideal spot to enjoy some palatable traditional Russian dishes including drinks such as *kvas* (fermented rye bread water). The chef cures his own salmon and there are unusual dishes on the menu such as shark steak. The high-ceilinged castle-like interior is also impressive.

Round Tower Restaurant RUSSIAN €€

(Круглая башня; ☎31 729; wwww.roundtower.ru; Rynochnaya pl 1; meals R600-900; ⏲10am-midnight) On the top floor of the tower, this atmospheric and long-running place is a reliable option for traditional Russian cuisine, although it can sometimes be booked out by tour groups.

Café Respect RUSSIAN €€
(Podgornaya ul 10; mains R250; ⏲11am-10pm) Cosy place with only a few tables and an old-European feel, serving the usual range of dishes such as salads, soups, fish and meat main courses.

Champion BAR €€
(Чемпион; pr Lenina 10; meals R230-450; ⏲11am-2am) This modern bar, with plenty of TVs screening sports and music videos, is a good place for a cooling pint and a globe-trotting mix of international dishes for a meal or snack.

Central Market MARKET €
(Рынок, Rynok Tsentralny; Rynochnaya pl; ⏲8am-6pm) Pull together supplies for a picnic from this traditional indoor market.

Information

Vyborg Tourist Information Centre (☎34 430; www.vyborg-info.ru; Vokzalnaya ul 13; ⏲9am-5pm) Welcoming English-speaking staff can provide you with a town map and lots of other info and assistance you may need.

Getting There & Away

The **bus and train stations** are opposite each other on Vokzalnaya pl.

Boat

Saimaa Travel (www.saimaatravel.fi) arranges visa-free cruises (one/two days from €58/98 per person) from Lappeenranta in Finland to Vyborg.

Bus

Services to/from St Petersburg (either metro stations Devyatkino or Parnas) run at half-hourly intervals from 6.30am to 8pm. Although theoretical travel time is two hours, the poor road conditions and traffic can double this.

Train

Elektrichki (R265, 2½ hours, hourly) leave from St Petersburg's Finlyandsky vokzal. There are also a handful of express services (R300, 1½ hours, four daily) or the Helsinki-bound trains, all of which stop in Vyborg. Unfortunately, RZD will not sell tickets on the new Allegro service between St Petersburg and Helsinki, even though the train stops in Vyborg.

For those heading to Sortavala, take the *elektrichka* to Khiitola (R205, two hours, two daily), where you'll need to change trains.

Staraya Ladoga

Старая Ладога

☎81363 / POP 3000 / ⏲MOSCOW

Although you'd hardly guess it now, this tranquil village, 125km east of St Petersburg on the winding banks of the Volkhov River, lays claim to being Russia's first capital. Today you'll find here an ancient fortress, several churches and some prettily painted wooden cottages. It makes for a pleasant escape from St Petersburg, particularly in summer when a swim in the river adds to the charm.

The town was known simply as Ladoga until 1704, when Peter the Great founded Novaya (New) Ladoga to the north as a transfer point for the materials arriving to build St Petersburg. Protected as a national reserve, the town's basic layout has remained virtually unchanged since the 12th century, give or take a few ugly Soviet blocks.

Sights

Everything of interest lies along the main road that runs parallel to the river.

Staraya Ladoga Fortress HISTORICAL SITE
(Староладожская крепость; grounds admission free; ⏲9am-4pm Mon, to 6pm Tue-Sun) Towards the southern end of the village, and with

RUSSIA'S ANCIENT CAPITAL

Just as the origins of Rus are continually debated, so will Staraya Ladoga's status as 'Russia's first capital'. Nevertheless, its age (historians have given 753 as the village's birth date) and significance remain uncontested.

When the Scandinavian Viking Rurik, along with his relatives Truvor and Sineus, swept into ancient Russia in 862, he built a wooden fortress on the Volkhov River and made this his base. Rurik is depicted in a colourful mosaic on the side of the village school. Locals also claim that one of the **tumuli** (Урочище Сопки) at the north end of the village is the grave of Oleg, Rurik's successor.

Archaeological expeditions continue to uncover a wealth of information about the town's past. In 1997 a second 9th-century fortress was discovered 2km outside the village. Evidence of Byzantine influences in the frescoes of the village's 12th-century churches point to the town as a cultural as well as historical and commercial crossroad.

an excellent view along the river, the 7m-thick walls and stout towers of this fortress are slowly being rebuilt. Inside the grounds you'll find the small stone **St George's Church** (adult/student R50/40; ⏰May-Oct), only open May to October in order to protect the remains of the delicate 12th-century frescoes still visible on its walls, and the cute wooden **Church of Dimitry Solun**.

The Vorotnaya Tower houses the good **Historical-Architectural & Archaeological Museum** (admission adult/student R30/20), which displays an interesting retrospective of the area's history, including a scale model of how the fortress once looked, items found on archaeological digs and English explanations.

Nikolisky Monastery MONASTERY

(Николский монастырь; ⏰9am-7pm) This attractive walled complex, 500m south of the fortress, dates back to the 12th century and is still in the process of being rebuilt following its decommissioning during the Soviet years. The main church and bell tower now look quite handsome. Nearby is a pontoon from which you can swim in the river.

Church of John the Baptist CHURCH

(Церковь Рождества Иоанна Предтечи; ⏰9am-7pm) Marking the north end of the village, this blue onion-domed church dates from 1695 and is pretty as a picture with a colourful iconostasis and frescoes.

Sleeping & Eating

Mini-hotel Ladya MINIHOTEL €€

(Ладья; ☎49 555; ul Sovetskaya 3; d/ste from R1850/2100; 📶) While not looking promising from the outside, this five-room hotel, which shares the premises of the local clinic, has pleasant, contemporary-styled rooms and even a sauna. Only tea and coffee are served, so you'll have to make your own breakfast arrangements.

Knyaz Rurik RUSSIAN €€

(Князь Рюрик; ul Kultur 1; meals R300-500; ⏰10am-9pm Mon-Thu, to 11pm Fri & Sat) Rurik's family tree is painted across the brick wall of this small, nicely designed restaurant, which screens videos of the village's sights, including historical festivals at the fortress. Portions of soup, salad and shashlyk are small but tasty.

Getting There & Away

Elektrichki to Volkhov (the Volkhovstroy I station) depart from both St Petersburg's Moskovsky and Ladozhsky stations (R400, 2½ hours, 11 daily). From Volkhov, a bus (R30, 20 minutes, hourly) heads towards Novaya Ladoga from the main bus stop outside the station. Get off when you see the fortress.

Buses to and from Tikhvin also pass near the turn-off to the village, so you can combine a visit to both destinations.

Tikhvin Тихвин

☎81367 / POP 63,338 / ⏰MOSCOW

The highlight of this small, quiet town on the banks of the Tikhvinka River is a beautiful monastery established in 1560 by decree of Ivan the Terrible. There's been a community here since the 14th century and for thousands of years before that the area formed part of the hereditary lands of the Finnic Veps (also known as Vepsians). Tikhvin is also the birthplace of Nikolai Rimsky-Korsakov, whose music was inspired by the local nature, folk tunes and religious ringing of bells.

Some 200km east of St Petersburg, it's possible to see Tikhvin in a long day trip, but should you decide to linger there are a couple of accommodation options, and the town is on the rail route to Vologda and Arkhangelsk, so you could break your journey to or from either of those locations here.

The town is easy to get around by foot; either buy a map in St Petersburg bookshops before you leave or at the kiosk in the train station. The region's website is http://tikhvin.org.

Sights

FREE **Tikhvin Monastery of the Mother of God** MONASTERY

(Тихвинский Успенский монастырь; ul Tikhvinskaya 1; ⏰8am-8pm) Rising like a fairy tale across the Tabory pond, this complex is about a 1km walk from the train station straight along Sovetskaya ul. At its heart is the onion-domed **Assumption Cathedral**, established in 1510, and painted inside and partially outside with detailed frescoes. A famous icon of Mary and Jesus said to have been painted by the apostle Luke draws awed pilgrims from across Russia.

The complex's nunnery, crowned by a five-spired belfry, is where Ivan the Terrible sent his fourth wife to be confined. Within the walls you'll also find the **Tikhvin Historical Memorial and Architectural Museum** (admission R50; ⏰10am-5pm Tue-Sun), which has interesting displays on the monastery's history and examples of its religious art dating back to the 16th century. A procession is

WORTH A TRIP

KONEVETS ISLAND ОСТРОВ КОНЕВЕЦ

Around 100km north of St Petersburg, and 6km off the western shore of Lake Ladoga, this peaceful island with clean beaches and lots of forests to wander through is home to the beautiful sky-blue domed **Konevets Monastery** (www.konevps.ru), founded in 1393 by Arseny Konevetsky. Part of Finland between world wars, in Soviet times the island became an off-limits military base. The monastery reopened in the early 1990s and has since undergone massive restoration with Finnish funding.

From May to late October, tours (including transport and some meals) are organised by the monastery's St Petersburg **office** (571 8079; Zagorodny pr 7, St Petersburg; 1-/2-day tours R1650/3500; M Vladimirskaya). Two-day tours include accommodation in simple guesthouses for pilgrims (R1000 per night if you are not on a tour, also arranged via the monastery office).

By public transport, take an *elektrichka* (suburban train) from St Petersburg's Finlyandsky vokzal to Otradnoye, then a bus to Vladimirovka. Here, hire a boat to sail the 5km to the island, a total trip of around seven hours.

The monastery's website has a good map of the island. **Wandering Camera** (www.enlight.ru/camera/290/index_e.html) offers a visual preview.

held here each 9 July to celebrate the return of the icon to Tikhvin.

Rimsky-Korsakov House-Museum MUSEUM
(Государственный Дом-музей Римского-Корсакова; 51 509; ul Rimskogo-Korsakova 12; adult/student R70/50; 10am-5.30pm Tue-Sun) This early-19th-century wooden house was the composer's childhood home until the age of 12. It became a museum in 1944, the centenary of Rimsky-Korsakov's birth, and the rooms have been reconstructed to look as they would have done when his family was living there. The charming guides, who may even let you look around when it's officially closed on Monday, will point out all the original features, including a Becker grand piano on which concerts are sometimes given; call for details.

There's a stone bust of the composer on a plinth in the small park next to the house; opposite is the tiny **Church of All Saints Polkovaya** (Церковь Всех Святых "Полковая"), which also sometimes hosts concerts.

Transfiguration Cathedral CHURCH
(Спасо-Преображенский собор; pl Svobody) This attractive cathedral frames one side of Tikhvin's central square, where Lenin's statue still stands.

Sleeping & Eating

Podvorye HOTEL €€
(Подворье; 51 330; www.tikhvin-podvorye.ru; ul Novgorodskaya 35; d incl breakfast from R2200;) The interior of this small hotel emulates a log house, with spacious clean rooms that are thickly carpeted. Its adjoining restaurant is the place in town for a meal with a menu (in English) of mainly Russian dishes (R200 to R400). It also offers a business lunch deal for R250 not on the English menu.

Verizhitsa HOTEL €€€
(Верижица; 71 374; www.verizhitsa.ru; cabin from R7000) This appealing complex of wooden log cabins (each of which accommodates up to six people) has a leafy forest setting 5km east of Tikhvin. The cabins are comfortable and there's a restaurant (daily lunch deal R300) and traditional-style *banya* (extra fee). A taxi from Tikhvin costs around R150.

Chainaya CAFÉ €
(Чайная; snacks R40-150; 11am-6pm Tue-Sun) In the monastery grounds, you'll find this simple teahouse, serving delicious bliny, homemade *pelmeni* and *kvas*. In summer you can enjoy your refreshments on an outdoor terrace.

Getting There & Away

Tikhvin's **bus and train stations** are opposite each other on Vokzalny per. Trains here leave from St Petersburg's Ladozhsky vokzal (*platskart/kupe* R500/1000, 4½ to five hours, three daily). Bus 860 to/from St Petersburg (R330, four to five hours, 10 daily) is also an option.

Kaliningrad Region

Includes »

Best Places to Eat

» Dolce Vita (p290)
» Little Buddha (p290)
» Zarya (p291)
» Korvet (p295)

Best Places to Stay

» Chaika (p289)
» Pushkin Hall (p289)
» Lumier Art Hotel (p294)
» Hotel Bekker (p295)
» Loger Haus (p296)

Why Go?

Bordered by Poland, Lithuania and 148km of Baltic coastline, Russia's smallest territory, the Kaliningrad Region (Калининградская Область), is both isolated from and intimately attached to the motherland. All the traditions of the big parent can be found here, alongside plenty of fine hotels and restaurants, welcoming locals, beautiful countryside, splendid beaches and fascinating historical sights.

The Teutonic Knights ruled the Baltic in the Middle Ages from Königsberg (now the region's capital, Kaliningrad), in a land once known as Prussia. After WWII, Stalin ethnically cleansed the region of Germans, but centuries of Germanic culture and architecture were not as easily removed. From the pine forests and Sahara-style dunes of Kurshskaya Kosa National Park to charming seaside resorts such as Svetlogorsk, this 'Little Russia' is easy to get around and offers a youthful outlook.

When to Go

Kaliningrad

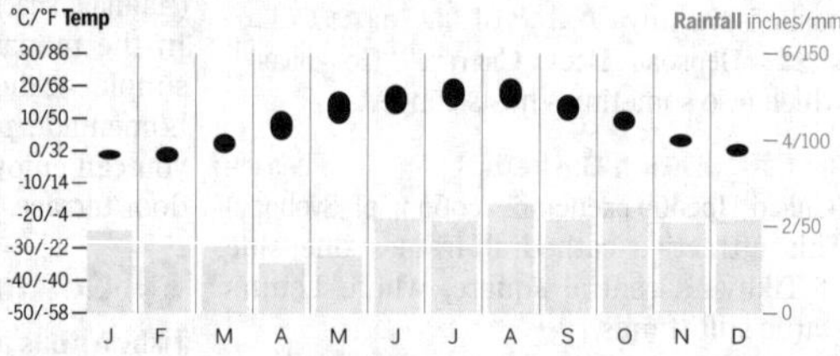

Jul Russian Navy Day – a chance to visit Baltiysk, usually off limits to tourists.

Aug Don Chento Jazz Festival in Kaliningrad.

Sep Chernyakhovsk hosts an international horse show-jumping event.

History

The region has been famous since Roman times for its amber deposits. Ruled by Teutonic Knights since the 13th century, in 1525 the area became the Duchy of Prussia, Europe's first Protestant state, with Königsberg as its capital. The city's liberal atmosphere attracted scholars, artists and entrepreneurs from across Europe; in 1697 Peter the Great visited as part of Russia's Grand Embassy and the 18th-century philosopher Immanuel Kant lived all his life there.

For four years of the Seven Years' War (1756–63), East Prussia became part of the Russian Empire and, later, during the Napoleonic Wars, Russia and Prussia were allies. After WWI, East Prussia was separated from the rest of Germany when Poland regained statehood. The three-month campaign by which the Red Army took it in 1945 was one of the fiercest of WWII; there were massive casualties on both sides and Königsberg was left in ruins.

In 1946 the region was renamed Kaliningrad in honour of Mikhail Kalinin, one of Stalin's more vicious henchmen. In a highly effective ethnic-cleansing campaign the surviving German population was relocated to far-flung corners of the Soviet Union, deported or killed. The Russian Baltic fleet was headquartered in Baltiysk, making the region a closed one to foreigners for over 40 years.

Like much of Russia, Kaliningrad struggled through extreme economic difficulties in the early 1990s. The discovery of oil off the coast and the granting of special economic zone status has helped it turn the corner. One of the venues for the 2018 FIFA World Cup, Kaliningrad is also among a handful of Russian regions permitted to develop a casino; the proposed location is near

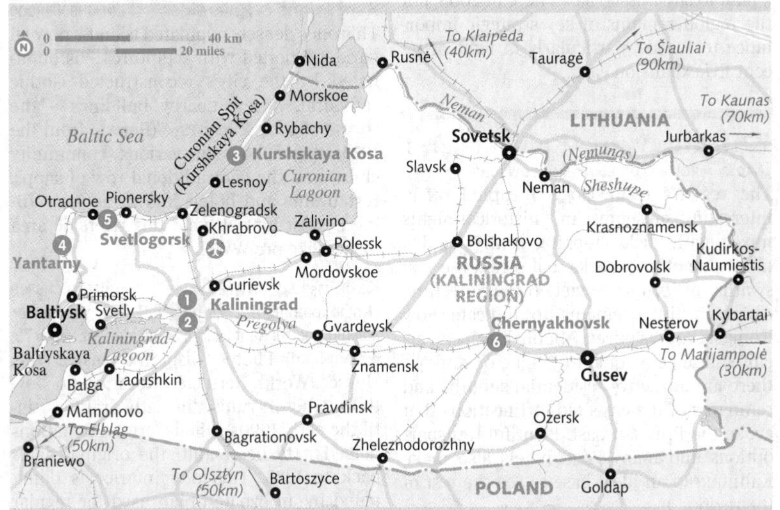

Kaliningrad Highlights

1. Pay your respects at the grave of philosopher Immanuel Kant, then listen to an organ concert in **Kaliningrad Cathedral** (p284)

2. Learn about Russian maritime history on former expedition vessels and a submarine at Kaliningrad's fascinating **Museum of the World Ocean** (p284)

3. Soak up the natural beauty of **Kurshskaya Kosa National Park** (p297), where the forest dances and the dunes roll on as far as the eye can see

4. Splash in the Baltic from the beautiful beach at **Yantarny** (p295), then visit the local amber mine

5. Stroll along shady forest lanes in the relaxing resort of **Svetlogorsk** (p293), discovering old German villas and the statues of Herman Brachert

6. Explore ruined castles and saddle up at the Georgenburg Stud Farm in **Chernyakhovsk** (p297)

VISAS

Citizens of Schengen countries, the UK, Switzerland and Japan can enter Kaliningrad with an **on-demand 72-hour tourist visa**. These need to be arranged via local tourist agencies, such as those listed on p292.

Unless you're flying, you must have either a double- or multiple-entry Russian visa (and any necessary visas for neighbouring countries) to reach the Kaliningrad Region from anywhere else in Russia.

If you have questions or problems regarding Russian visas during your stay, contact Kaliningrad's **UFMS Office** (☎563 17; ul Frunze 6).

Yantarny. President Medvedev backed off on a plan to site missile bases here in 2008, but the region remains of key strategic importance to Russia, particularly in light of recent EU expansion east.

Kaliningrad Калининград

☎4012 / POP 423,000 / ⌚MOSCOW –1HR

The region's traffic-clogged capital offers interesting museums and historical sights mixed with slick shopping centres and a multitude of leafy parks that soften the vast swaths of brutal Soviet-era architecture. Although little remains to indicate how Königsberg was once a Middle European architectural gem equal to Prague or Kraków, there are attractive residential suburbs and remnants of the city's old fortifications that evoke the Prussian past. Plentiful transport options and many good hotels also make Kaliningrad an ideal base to see the rest of the region.

History

Founded in 1255, Königsberg joined the Hanseatic League in 1340, and from 1457 to 1618 was the residence of the grand masters of the Teutonic order and their successors, the dukes of Prussia. Prussia's first king, Frederick I, was crowned in 1701 in the city's castle. For the next couple of centuries Königsberg flourished, producing citizens such as the 18th-century philosopher Immanuel Kant.

The city centre was flattened by British air raids in August 1944 and the Red Army assault from 6 to 9 April 1945. Renamed Kaliningrad on 4 July 1946, the city was rebuilt in grand Soviet concrete style, albeit tempered by parks, a network of ponds and waterways, and Kaliningrad Lagoon.

The remains of the castle were destroyed and replaced by the outstandingly ugly **Dom Sovetov** (Дом Советов, House of Soviets) in the 1960s. During the eyesore's construction it was discovered that the land below was hollow, housing a (now-flooded) four-level underground passage connecting to the cathedral. The decaying, half-finished building has never been used.

Sights

After the Kaliningrad Cathedral the most visible remains of Königsberg are its red-brick fortification walls, bastions and gates, built in stages between the 17th and 19th centuries.

Kant Island & Riverside NEIGHBOURHOOD
This once densely populated island – now all parkland dotted with sculptures – is dominated by the city's reconstructed Gothic cathedral. A few nearby buildings – the **former Stock Exchange** (Биржа) from the 1870s (now housing various community clubs) and the neotraditional row of shops, restaurants and hotels known as **Fish Village** – just hint at what this riverside area looked like pre-WWII.

Kaliningrad Cathedral MUSEUM, CHURCH
(Кафедральный собор; ☎631 705; www.sobor-kaliningrad.ru; Kant Island; adult/student R150/75; ⌚9am-5pm) Photos displayed inside this Unesco World Heritage Site attest to how thoroughly in ruins this cathedral was until the early 1990s, when German donations helped it to be rebuilt; the original dates back to 1333. The lofty interior is dominated by an ornate organ used for regular **concerts** (tickets R250-300) that are worth attending; the Russian version of the website has the schedule. Upstairs is the carved-wood Wallenrodt Library, with interesting displays of old Königsberg and objects from archaeological digs. On the top floor is an exhibition devoted to Immanuel Kant, including his death mask. The philosopher's rose-marble **tomb** (могила Канта) can be found on the outer north side of the building.

Museum of the World Ocean MUSEUM
(Музей Мирового Океана; http://world-ocean.ru/en; nab Petra Velikogo 1; adult/student R250/170, individual vessels adult/student R120/80; ⌚10am-

6pm Wed-Sun) Strung along the banks of the Pregolya River are several ships, a sub, maritime machinery and a couple of exhibition halls that make up this excellent museum. The highlight is the handsome former expedition vessel *Vityaz,* which, during its heyday, conducted many scientific studies around the world. It's moored alongside the *Viktor Patsaev,* named after one of Kaliningrad's famous cosmonauts; its exhibits relate to space research. Inside the B-413 submarine you can get an idea of what life was like for the 300 submariners who once lived and worked aboard.

A restored old storehouse building houses interesting displays on fishing and the sea-connected history of Kaliningrad, as well as a rare archaeological find: the remains of a 19th-century wooden fishing boat. There's also a pavilion with the skeleton of a 16.8m-long sperm whale and halls with small aquariums and general information about the ocean. Visits to the *Vityaz* and *Viktor Patsaev* are by guided tour (included in admission price, every 45 minutes or so); you can wander freely through the sub.

Amber Museum MUSEUM

(Музей Янтаря; www.ambermuseum.ru; pl Marshala Vasilevskogo 1; adult/student R120/90; ⌚10am-6pm Tue-Sun) Housed in the **Dohna Tower** (Башня Дона), this museum has some 6000 examples of amber artworks, the most impressive being from the Soviet period. In addition to enormous pieces of jewellery containing prehistoric insects suspended within, one of the more fascinating works is a four-panelled amber-and-ivory chalice depicting Columbus, the *Niña,* the *Pinta* and the *Santa Maria*. You can buy amber jewellery in the museum or from the vendors outside. Adjacent to the museum, the **Rossgarten Gate** (Росгартенские Ворота) now houses a restaurant.

Friedland Gate MUSEUM

(Фридландские ворота; www.fvmuseum.ru; ul Dzerzhinskogo 30; adult/student R50/20; ⌚10am-6pm Tue-Sun) The best way to see what pre-WWII Königsberg looked like is to attend the 40-minute **multimedia show** (R30; ⌚on the hour noon-5pm) that is screened in the halls of this well-organised museum occupying one of the 13 original city gates. The evocative show is made up of projections of photos taken in the city between 1908 and 1913 and some grainy footage shot in 1937 around the castle.

King's Gate MUSEUM

(Королевские ворота; ul Frunze 112; adult/student R50/30; ⌚11am-7pm Wed-Sun) Focusing on Peter the Great's Grand Embassy to the city in 1697, this revamped gate also has good models of old Königsberg and exhibits on the personalities who shaped the region's history. From Dom Sovetov follow ul Frunze about 1km east to find this gate. A little south of here, where Moskovsky pr meets Litovsky val, is the twin-towered **Sackheim Gate** (Закхаймские ворота).

Amalienau & Maraunenhof NEIGHBOURHOOD

Casual strolls through the linden-scented, tree-lined neighbourhoods of **Amalienau** (to the city's west along pr Mira) and **Maraunenhof** (at the north end of the Upper Pond) provide a further glimpse of genteel pre-WWII Königsberg. Amalienau is particularly lovely, with an eclectic range of villas, many designed by the architect Friedrich Heitmann, along ul Kutuzova and the streets connecting prs Pobedy and Mira. Maraunenhof has several appealing small hotels as well as the German consulate with its strikingly colourful building in which visas are issued.

STATUES & MONUMENTS

What do an 18th-century philosopher, cosmonauts, Woody Allen and a Soviet-era pop legend have in common? Statues and monuments celebrate them all in Kaliningrad. Königsberg's most famous son, **Immanuel Kant**, stands in front of the university named after him, tucked off Leninsky pr; the statue is a 1992 copy of the 1864 original by Christian Rauch.

Along pr Mira, the **Cosmonaut Monument** (Землякам Космонавтам) is a gem of Soviet iconography, celebrating the four Kaliningrad-born cosmonauts, including Alexey Leonov, the first man to conduct a space walk. In the lobby of the nearby Scala cinema and Zarya restaurant is a witty monument to **Woody Allen** (born Allen Konigsberg) – a pair of the film director's trademark glasses jutting from the wall. And in Central Park the hulking statue of **Vladimir Vysotsky**, a massively popular singer from the 1960s and '70s, overlooks the amphitheatre.

Kaliningrad

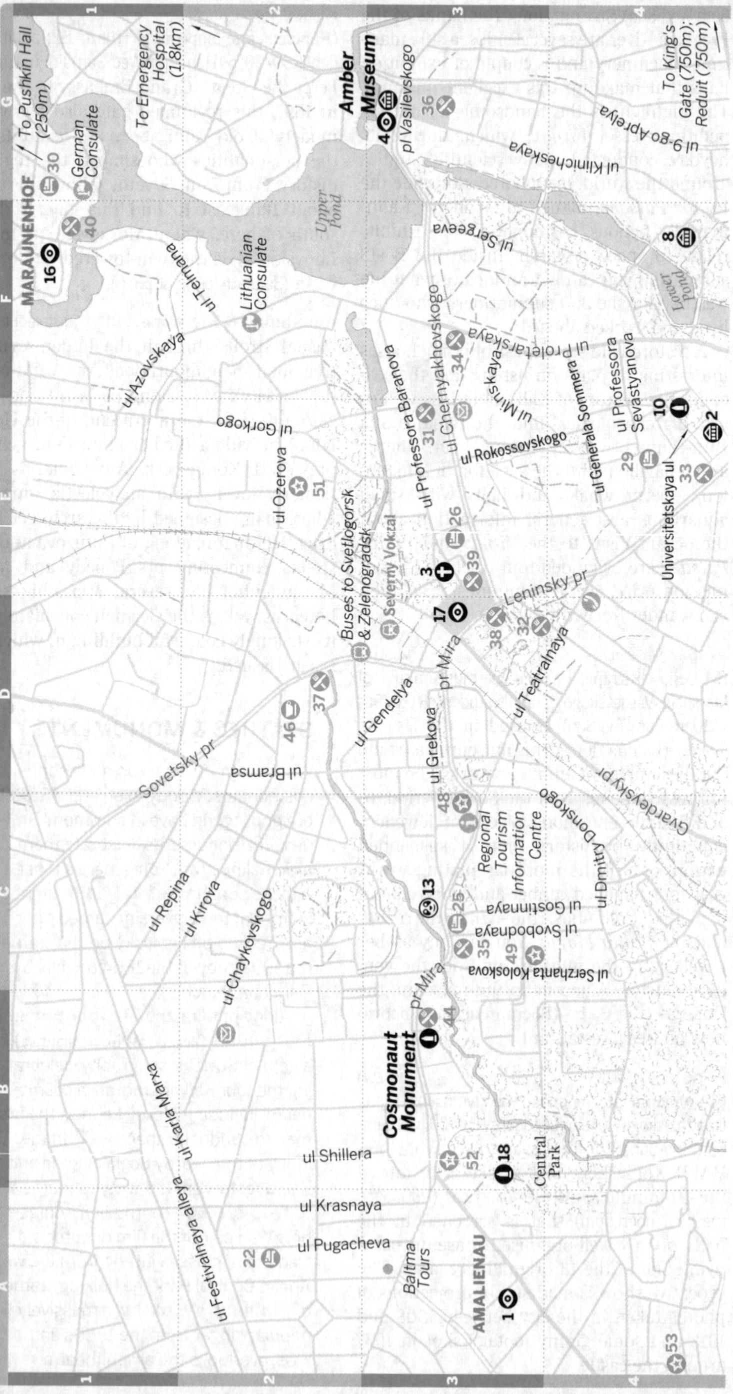

0 400 m
0 0.2 miles

A B C D E F G
1 2 3 4

MARAUNENHOF
16
To Pushkin Hall (250m)
30
40
German Consulate
To Emergency Hospital (1.8km)
ul Azovskaya
ul Telmana
Lithuanian Consulate
Upper Pond
Amber Museum
4
pl Vasilevskogo
36
ul Festivalnaya alleya
ul Karla Marxa
ul Repina
ul Kirova
ul Chaykovskogo
Sovetsky pr
ul Bramsa
46
37
ul Ozerova
51
ul Gorkogo
22
ul Pugacheva
ul Krasnaya
ul Shillera
Buses to Svetlogorsk & Zelenogradsk
Severny Vokzal
ul Gendelya
ul Professora Baranova
31
ul Chernyakhovskogo
34
Baltma Tours
Cosmonaut Monument
pr Mira
44
13
ul Grekova
48
17
3
26
39
AMALIENAU
52
1
18
Central Park
35
25
49
ul Serzhanta Koloskova
ul Svobodnaya
ul Gostinnaya
Regional Tourism Information Centre
38
32
Leninsky pr
ul Teatralnaya
ul Rokossovskogo
ul Minskaya
ul Proletarskaya
ul Sergeeva
ul Klinicheskaya
ul Dmitry Donskogo
Gvardeysky pr
ul Generala Sommera
ul Professora Sevastyanova
29
Universitetskaya ul
10
33
2
Lower Pond
8
ul 9-go Aprelya
To King's Gate (750m); Reduit (750m)
53

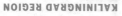

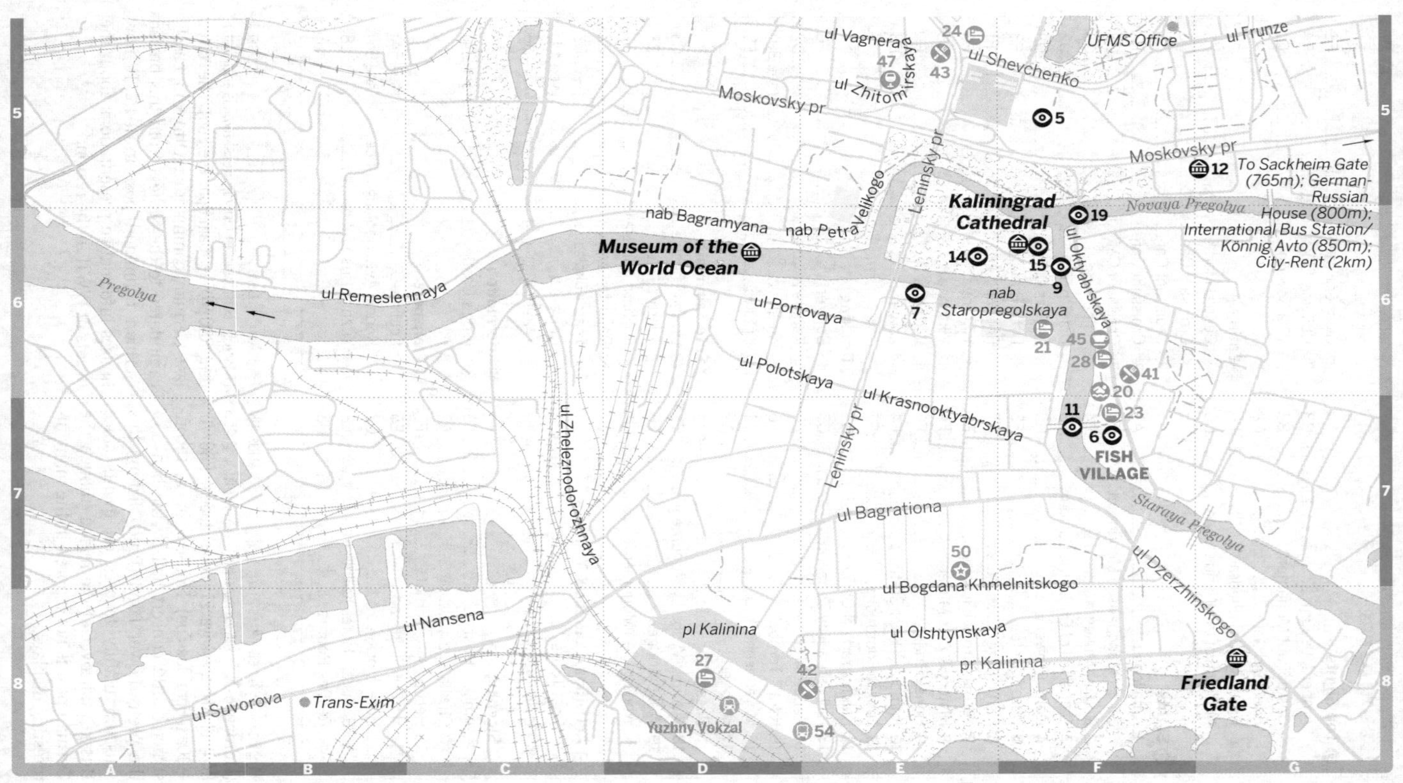

ul Vagnera
24
47
43
ul Zhitomirskaya
ul Shevchenko
UFMS Office
ul Frunze
Moskovsky pr
5
Moskovsky pr
12
To Sackheim Gate (765m); German-Russian House (800m); International Bus Station/ Könnig Avto (850m); City-Rent (2km)
Leninsky pr
nab Petra Velikogo
nab Bagramyana
Kaliningrad Cathedral
19
Novaya Pregolya
Museum of the World Ocean
14
15
9
ul Oktyabrskaya
Pregolya
ul Remeslennaya
7
nab Staropregolskaya
ul Portovaya
21
45
28
41
20
23
ul Polotskaya
ul Krasnooktyabrskaya
11
6
FISH VILLAGE
Leninsky pr
ul Zheleznodorozhnaya
ul Bagrationa
Staraya Pregolya
50
ul Bogdana Khmelnitskogo
ul Dzerzhinskogo
ul Nansena
pl Kalinina
ul Olshtynskaya
27
42
pr Kalinina
Friedland Gate
ul Suvorova
Trans-Exim
Yuzhny Vokzal
54
A
B
C
D
E
F
G
5
6
7
8

Kalininsgrad

Top Sights

Amber Museum ... G3
Cosmonaut Monument ... B3
Friedland Gate ... G8
Kaliningrad Cathedral ... F6
Museum of the World Ocean ... D6

Sights

1 Amalienau ... A3
Baron Munchausen Monument ... (see 18)
2 Bunker Museum ... E4
3 Cathedral of Christ the Saviour ... E3
4 Dohna Tower ... G3
5 Dom Sovetov ... F5
6 Fish Village ... F7
7 Former Stock Exchange ... E6
8 History & Arts Museum ... F4
9 Honey Bridge ... F6
10 Immanuel Kant Statue ... E4
11 Jubilee Footbridge ... F7
12 Kaliningrad Art Gallery ... G5
13 Kaliningradsky Zoopark ... C3
14 Kant Island ... E6
15 Kant's Tomb ... F6
16 Maraunenhof ... F1
17 pl Pobedy ... D3
Rossgarten Gate ... (see 4)
18 Vladimir Vysotsky Monument ... B3
19 Wood Bridge ... F6
Woody Allen Monument ... (see 44)

Activities, Courses & Tours

Boat Tours ... (see 45)
20 Helio Spa ... F6

Sleeping

21 Amigos Hostel ... F6
22 Chaika ... A2
23 Heliopark Kaiserhof ... F7
24 Hotel Kaliningrad ... E5
25 Hotel Moskva ... C3
26 Radisson Hotel, Kaliningrad ... E3
27 Resting Rooms ... D8
28 Skipper Hotel ... F6
29 Ubileiniy Luks ... E4
30 Villa Severin ... G1

Eating

31 Central Market ... E3
32 Croissant Café ... D3
33 Croissant Café ... E4
34 Croissant Café ... F3
35 Croissant Café ... C3
36 Dolce Vita ... G3
37 Don Chento ... D2
38 La Plas Cafe ... D3
39 Little Buddha ... E3
40 Prichal ... F1
41 Viktoriya ... F6
42 Viktoriya ... E8
43 Viktoriya ... E5
44 Zarya ... B3

Drinking

45 Bar Verf ... F6
46 Kaputsin ... D2
Kmel ... (see 39)
47 Untsiya ... E5

Entertainment

48 Drama Theatre ... C3
49 Kvartira ... C3
50 Philharmonic Hall ... E7
51 Reporter ... E2
52 Teatr Kukol ... B3
Universal ... (see 44)
53 Vagonka ... A4

Information

King's Castle ... (see 24)

Transport

Ecolines ... (see 54)
Könnig Avto Booking Office ... (see 54)
54 Yuzhny Bus Station ... E8

History & Arts Museum MUSEUM
(Историко-Художественный музей; ☎453 844; ul Klinicheskaya 21; adult/student R80/70; ⏰10am-6pm Tue-Sun) Housed in a reconstructed 1912 concert hall by the banks of the pretty Lower Pond (Prud Nizhny) this museum mainly focuses on events since Russia's takeover of the region, though the German past is not ignored in the many interesting displays.

Bunker Museum MUSEUM
(Музей Блидаж; ul Universitetskaya 3; adult/student R80/70; ⏰10am-6pm Tue-Sun) The city's last German commander, Otto van Lasch, capitulated to the Soviets from this buried German command post in 1945. It now houses informative presentations about the events of WWII in the region.

Kaliningrad Art Gallery ART GALLERY

(Калининградская художественная галерея; Moskovsky pr 60-62; adult/student R120/60; ⏲10am-6pm Tue-Sun) View modern and contemporary works by local artists, including some striking pieces from the Soviet decades, as well as various temporary exhibitions in this large municipal gallery.

Ploshchad Pobedy SQUARE

The city's centre is surrounded by shopping malls and the **Cathedral of Christ the Saviour** (Кафедральный собор Христа Спасителя), built in 2006 in the Russo-Byzantine style. Its gold domes are visible from many points in the city.

Kaliningradsky Zoopark ZOO

(http://kldzoo.ru; pr Mira 26; adult/child R100/50; ⏲9am-7pm) Bears, hippos, seals and flamingos are among the creatures that call this city-centre zoo home.

Central Park PARK

(Центральный парк; main entrance pr Pobedy 1) The forested grounds here, dotted with statuary and amusement rides, are pleasant for a stroll.

Activities

Boat Tours BOAT TRIPS

(tours up to 5 people R1000) Throughout the year, but mainly in summer, you can board small passenger boats from the promenade beside Fish Village to sail around Kant Island and down the Pregolya River (45 minutes).

Helio Spa SAUNA, SPA

(☎592 222; www.heliopark.ru; ul Oktyabrskaya 6a; admission before/after 4pm R1000/1500; ⏲7am-10pm) There are five different saunas and a medium-sized swimming pool, plus a jacuzzi and swim-up bar, at this swish spa complex attached to the Heliopark Kaiserhof hotel.

Sleeping

Kaliningrad is well served with midrange and top-end hotels, but budget accommodation is thin on the ground. Unless noted, listed rates include breakfast.

TOP CHOICE **Chaika** HOTEL €€€

(Чайка; ☎210 729; www.hotelchaika.ru; ul Pugacheva 13; s/d from R3500/4450; ❄@📶) On a leafy street near the picturesque Amalienau area, 'Seagull' is a delightful 28-room property decorated with classy heritage touches. It also has a restaurant, comfy lounge and fitness room.

Pushkin Hall HOTEL €€

(Пушкин холл; ☎365 752; http://pushkin-hall.ru; ul Dostoevskogo 19; s/d from R1800/2600; 📶) There are just seven rooms at this unsigned 'art hotel', each different and furnished with taste. The white villa is surrounded by a spacious garden and is a short walk from the tram stop on ul Telmana. Breakfast is R200 extra.

Radisson Hotel, Kaliningrad HOTEL €€€

(☎593 344; www.radisson.ru/hotel-kaliningrad; pl Pobedy 10; s/d from R5900/6350; ❄@📶) This international chain hotel keeps up top standards, offering spacious stylishly decorated rooms, some with views of the nearby cathedral. The rates drop by R2000 per night from Friday to Sunday.

Heliopark Kaiserhof HOTEL €€€

(☎592 222; www.heliopark.ru; ul Oktyabrskaya 6a; s/d from R4500/4950; ❄@📶🏊) Part of the Fish Village development, this nicely designed and furnished hotel has pleasant, light-filled rooms and a full-service spa and sauna. Rates are almost halved Friday to Sunday.

Amigos Hostel HOSTEL €

(☎8-911-485 2157; http://amigoshostel.ru; Epronovskaya ul 20-102; dm 500-600; 📶) On the 13th floor of a modern apartment block

LOCAL KNOWLEDGE

ARTYEM RYZKOV

Artyem Ryzkov is a writer, radio and TV presenter, artistic director of Scala cinema and owner of Kvartira.

Favourite Monument

I like **Baron Munchausen** in the Central Park – it's a kind of joke as the artists invented that the Baron might have visited Königsberg on his travels.

Favourite Festival

The **European Union Film Festival** held at Zarya every October.

Favourite Beach

Those along the Kurshskaya Kosa (p297) – choose a place to stop where there is no parking; that way you'll have the beach to yourself.

THE BRIDGES OF KÖNIGSBERG

The problem of Königsberg's seven bridges is one known to mathematicians the world over. The 18th-century Swiss mathematician Leonhard Euler tackled the question of whether it was possible to walk a circular route crossing each bridge once only. Euler's resulting graph theory has intrigued academics ever since. For background see http://kursinfo.himolde.no/lo-kurs/lo904/Laporte/BridgesPaper.pdf. Out of the seven bridges that formed part of the original conundrum, only the **Honey** and **Wood Bridges** remain today. The **Jubilee Footbridge** was built as part of the Fish Village development.

overlooking the cathedral and Fish Village, this welcoming place breaks new budget accommodation ground for Kaliningrad. The three dorms – one with six beds, the other two with eight – are all mixed and share one bathroom and a well-equipped kitchen.

Hotel Kaliningrad HOTEL €€
(Гостиница Калининград; ☎350 500; www.hotel.kaliningrad.ru; Leninsky pr 81; s/d from R1900/2100; 📶) Much improved following a recent facelift, the Kaliningrad has a location that can't be beat. Many of its functional rooms offer views across to the cathedral.

Streletsky GUESTHOUSE €€
(Стрелецкий; ☎391 192; www.streleckaya7.narod.ru; ul Streletskaya 7; s/d R1800/2100; 📶) In a pleasantly green area around a 10-minute bus ride from the centre is this appealing guesthouse with spacious, comfortable rooms and welcoming staff.

Villa Severin GUESTHOUSE €€
(☎365 373; www.villa-severin.ru; ul Leningradskaya 9a; s/d from R1600/1850; ❄@📶) There's a homely atmosphere at this pretty villa, set back from the Upper Pond (Prud Verkhny), with 10 comfortably furnished rooms including one simple student room (R1000 without breakfast). It also has a small sauna and café.

Resting rooms HOTEL €
(Комнаты Отдыха, komnaty otdykha; ☎586 447; 3rd fl, pl Kalinina; 12-/24-hr from R250/500) Inside the south train station, these single 'resting rooms', which come in blocks of two or three that share a bathroom, are quiet and clean. Find them by turning right down the corridor after the ticket hall and walking up to the 3rd floor.

Ubileiniy Luks GUESTHOUSE €€
(☎519 024; www.ubilejny-lux.ru; ul Universitetskaya 2; r/apt without breakfast from R2500/3800; ❄@📶) Atop a business centre, the 13 different-sized rooms here are all enormous. Most have kitchens and lounge areas, making them ideal for longer stays.

Skipper Hotel HOTEL €€
(Gastinitsa Shkiperskaya; ☎592 000; www.skipperhotel.ru; ul Oktyabrskaya 4a; r from R2500; ❄📶) Offers clean rooms with wood furnishings and river views; breakfast is taken in a café in the nearby lighthouse.

Hotel Moskva HOTEL €€
(Гостиница Москва; ☎352 300; www.hotelmoskva.info; pr Mira 19; s/d from R2100/2875; 📶) Bright spacious rooms and a good location. Breakfast is R270 extra.

Eating

Self-caterers should visit the lively **central market** (Центральный рынок; ul Chernyakhovskogo; ⏲8am-6pm) or the supermarket **Viktoriya** (Виктория; Kaliningrad Plaza, Leninsky pr 30; ⏲10am-10pm), with branches also opposite Yuzhny vokzal and near Fish Village.

TOP CHOICE **Dolce Vita** RUSSIAN, EUROPEAN €€€
(☎351 612; http://dolcevita.kaliningrad.ru; pl Marshala Vasilevskogo 2; meals R1000-1500; ⏲noon-midnight; 📶🖉) From the menu many of Dolce Vita's inventive dishes would appear overly fussy, but for the most part the competent chef makes them work. There's an excellent selection for vegetarians and luxurious takes on old Russian standards such as *pelmeni* (Russian-style ravioli) and borsch. The main dining room is plush and there's a lovely garden patio.

Little Buddha ASIAN FUSION €€€
(☎593 395; www.littlebuddhakaliningrad.com; Clover City Centre, pl Pobedy 10; meals R800-1500; ⏲noon-1am Tue-Thu, to 4am Fri & Sat; 📶) Modelled on the Parisian original, this swanky Asian-fusion restaurant, sushi bar and nightclub has spectacular interior design, dominated by a far-from-little Buddha. The food is well prepared and the cocktails, naturally, are good. Major DJs play the upstairs

club section at weekends, when there may be a cover charge if you're not dining.

Zarya RUSSIAN, EUROPEAN €
(☎213 929; pr Mira 43; meals R300-400; ⊙10am-3am; 📶) This fashionable brassiere in the lobby of the Scala cinema is beautifully decorated and also has an attractive outdoor area. The reasonably priced food is reliable – try the potato pancakes with salmon caviar or the excellent steaks from locally reared cattle.

La Plas Cafe RUSSIAN, EUROPEAN €
(pl Pobedy 1; meals R300-400; ⊙24hr) Offering big windows with views onto pl Pobedy and tasty food that actually looks as good on your plate as it does on the photo menu, this round-the-clock place is a good fit for whatever meal or snack you desire.

Prichal GEORGIAN €€
(Причал; ☎703 030; ul Verkhneozyornaya 2a; meals R500; ⊙noon-1am Sun-Thu, to 2am Fri & Sat) Private huts in a pretty garden overlooking the north end of Upper Pond make Prichal a memorable dining experience.

Croissant Café BAKERY, CAFÉ €
(Leninsky pr 63; meals R100-300; ⊙8am-11pm; 📶) Branches of this chic baked-goods heaven have proliferated around the city; you'll find others at pr Mira 23, ul Proletarskaya 79 and in the Evropa mall. Indulge in flaky pastries, quiches, muffins, biscuits and cakes, as well as omelettes and bliny for breakfast. It does a business lunch for R190 from noon to 4pm.

Don Chento PIZZA €
(Sovetsky pr 9-11; meals R200-300) Dig in at the self-serve salad bar or pick a slice of pizza at this stylish chain with several branches across the city.

Drinking

All of the following also serve food and are often good alternatives to the restaurants and cafés already recommended.

Untsiya TEAHOUSE
(Унция; ul Zhitomirskaya 22) This elegant, old-world tea shop and café serves all manner of black, green, white and fruit-flavoured teas and infusions, as well as tasty snacks such as quiches, salads and cakes.

Kmel MICROBREWERY
(Clover City Centre, pl Pobedy 10; ⊙10am-2am) Four types of beer are brewed at this appealing multilevel gastropub overlooking pl Pobedy. An interesting range of Russian and Siberian dishes (R350 to R500) are on the menu, often including unusual ingredients such as reindeer and *omul*, a fish from Lake Baikal.

Bar Verf WINE BAR
(Fish Village, ul Oktyabrskaya 4a; ⊙11am-midnight; 📶) The ambience is pleasant at this relaxed wine bar that also has outdoor tables overlooking the cathedral. It screens movies and provides coloured pencils and paper for you to doodle with.

Kaputsin CAFÉ
(Капуцин; ul Kirova 3/5; ⊙9am-10pm Mon-Sat, 10am-5pm Sun) Looking like an arts student's living room, plastered with books, maps and other knick-knacks (some for sale), this laid-back place serves nicely brewed coffee and DIY noodle and rice dishes – choose your starch, topping and sauce for around R150 a plate.

Reduit MICROBREWERY
(☎461 951; Litovsky val 27) Sample a selection of ales brewed on the premises in this vaulted bar; the restaurant upstairs offers fancier meals. Reduit is located just south of the King's Gate at the east end of ul Frunze.

☆ Entertainment

Classical music concerts are occasionally held at the cathedral. Major DJs from Russia and Western Europe jet in for gigs at

WORTH A TRIP

KVARTIRA

On the ground floor of an apartment block **Kvartira** (Квартира; ☎216 736; ul Serzhanta Koloskova 13; 📶) is tricky to classify but unquestionably one of the coolest hang-outs in Kaliningrad. Lined with a fascinating range of pop culture books, CDs, records and DVDs, all for sale or rent (as is everything else in the space, including the stylish furniture), Kvartira – which means 'apartment' – also serves drinks and snacks, but there's no menu. Movies are screened for free on several nights, while on others there may be a party or an art event; whatever's happening, you're sure to make friends with locals. It's best to visit in the early evening, but opening hours are erratic, so call before setting off.

Kaliningrad's clubs, which open around 9pm but typically don't get going until well after midnight.

Reporter LIVE MUSIC
(☎571 601; www.reporter-club.ru; ul Ozerova 18; ⊙11am-1am) Live music in a wide range of genres – from Spanish to jazz and Afrobeat – kicks off at this industrial, cool club space most nights at 9pm. It also occasionally screens films and serves food; the set lunches are R130.

Philharmonic Hall CLASSICAL MUSIC
(Филармония; ☎643 451; www.kenigfil.ru; ul Bogdana Khmelnitskogo 61a; tickets from R200) This beautifully restored neo-Gothic church, which has excellent acoustics, hosts organ concerts, chamber-music recitals and the occasional symphony orchestra.

Drama Theatre THEATRE
(Театр драмы и комедии; ☎958 188; pr Mira 4; tickets R150-200) It is mainly plays that are staged in this handsomely restored building – several are included among the annual **Baltic Season** (http://baltseasons.ru) that runs from June to November.

Universal NIGHTCLUB
(☎952 996; pr Mira 43; admission from R500) Kaliningrad's classiest club is also the location of the **Scala cinema**.

Vagonka NIGHTCLUB
(☎956 677; www.vagonka.net; Stanochnaya ul 12; admission from R500) Attracts a wide-ranging crowd with its top DJs and mix of events from live music to theme parties.

Amsterdam GAY
(www.amsterdam-club.ru; 38/11 Litovsky val; admission R1000; ⊙9am-6am Fri & Sat) This large club, found in old brick building 200m down an unnamed side street off Litovsky val, is best visited on weekends.

Teatr Kukol PUPPET THEATRE
(☎214 335; pr Pobedy 1; admission R100) Teatr Kukol is housed in a 19th-century Lutheran Queen Luisa Church. Performances typically are on Saturdays and Sundays at noon.

Information

Internet Access, Post & Telephone

As well as the post offices, you'll also find internet access at the King's Castle in Hotel Kaliningrad.

Main post office (ul Kosomonavta Leonova 22; ⊙9am-8pm Mon-Fri, 10am-6pm Sat & Sun)

Post office (Почта; ul Chernyakhovskogo 32; per hr R50; ⊙post office 10am-2pm & 3-7pm Mon-Fri, 10am-2pm & 3-6pm Sat, internet room 10am-2pm & 3-10pm Mon-Sat) Internet access and postal services.

Telekom (ul Teatralnaya 13; per hr R50; ⊙9am-7pm) For long-distance calls, fax and internet access.

Medical Services

Emergency Hospital (☎534 556; ul A Nevskogo 90; ⊙24hr)

Tourist Information

German-Russian House (☎469 682; www.drh-k.ru; ul Yaltinskaya 2a; ⊙10am-5pm Mon-Fri) A library, German classes and German cultural events.

Regional Tourism Information Centre (☎555 200; www.visit-kaliningrad.ru; pr Mira 4; ⊙9am-8pm Mon-Fri, 11am-6pm Sat Jun-Sep, 9am-6pm Mon-Fri, 11am-4pm Sat Oct-May) Helpful, English-speaking staff and lots of information on the region.

University Guides (mimoletnoe@gmail.com) Contact to arrange for a student guide to show you around town.

Travel Agencies

Baltma Tours (☎931 931; www.baltma.ru; 4th fl, pr Mira 94) The multilingual staff can arrange visas, hotel accommodation, tailored city tours and local excursions, including one to the military port city of Baltiysk (formerly Pillau), which requires a special permit to enter.

King's Castle (☎350 782; www.kaliningradinfo.ru; Hotel Kaliningrad, Leninsky pr 81; ⊙8am-8pm Mon-Fri, 9am-4pm Sat) Access the internet here and book tours, including ones to Kurshskaya Kosa.

Königsberg (www.konigsberg.ru) Web-based tour agency through which you can arrange visas and book hotels.

Getting There & Away

AIR **Khrabrovo airport** (☎610 358; http://kgd-airport.org/en) is 24km north of the city. There are daily flights to Moscow, St Petersburg and Rīga; see website for other connections.

BOAT **Trans-Exim** (☎660 470; www.transexim.ru; ul Suvorova 45) Weekly car ferries between Baltiysk and Ust-Luga, 150km west of St Petersburg. See website for the latest prices and schedules.

BUS Mainly local buses depart from the **Yuzhny bus station** (Автовокзал; ul Zheleznodorozhnaya 7), as well as international bus services run by **Ecolines** (☎656 501; www.ecolines.ru) to Warsaw and several German cities. **Könnig Avto** (☎999 199; www.kenigavto.ru) international services leave from the **international**

LEAVING KALININGRAD

Bus Services

DESTINATION	PRICE (R)	DURATION (HR)	FREQUENCY
Gdansk	950	4½	2 daily
Klaipėda	445	4	2 daily
Rīga	950	9	2 daily
Stuttgart	4100	24	2 weekly
Tallinn	1715	14	1 daily
Vilnius	920	6	1 daily
Warsaw	750	9	1 daily

Train Services

Local train services (ie those between Kaliningrad and Svetlogorsk) run on local time, but those beyond the region to Moscow, St Petersburg and Berlin have their arrival and departure times listed in Moscow time. This means if a Moscow-bound train is scheduled to depart at 10am it will leave at 9am Kaliningrad time.

DESTINATION	PRICE (R)	DURATION (HR)	FREQUENCY
Berlin	SV/*kupe* 5000/4000	14	1 daily, May-Oct
Moscow	*platskart*/*kupe* from 2500/5100	23	1 daily
St Petersburg	*platskart*/*kupe* from 2600/5300	26	1 daily
Svetlogorsk	*obshchiy* 60	1¼	at least 7 daily
Zelenogradsk	*obshchiy* 48	30min	at least 3 daily

bus station (Международный автовокзал; Moskovsky pr 184); there's a Könnig Avto booking office at Yuzhny vokzal.

The best way to Svetlogorsk (R47, one hour) and Zelenogradsk (R44, 45 minutes) is on buses that leave from next to Severny vokzal on Sovetsky pr. Services run about every 30 minutes or so until about 8pm.

TRAIN All long-distance and most local trains go from **Yuzhny vokzal** (Южный вокзал, South Station; pl Kalinina), some passing through, but not always stopping, at **Severny vokzal** (Северный вокзал, North Station; pl Pobedy).

Getting Around

Trams, trolleybuses (both R10), buses (R12) and minibuses (R12 to R17) will get you most places. For the airport, take bus 144 from the Yuzhny bus station (R30, 30 minutes). A taxi to/from the airport is R450 with **Taxi Kaliningrad** (585 858; www.taxi-kaliningrad.ru).

Car rental is available from **City-Rent** (509 191; http://city-rent39.com; Moskovsky pr 182a), which also has a branch at the airport. Rates start at €26 per day.

Svetlogorsk Светлогорск

40153 / POP 10,950 / MOSCOW –1HR

Once called Rauschen, Svetlogorsk is a pleasant, slow-placed spa town, 35km northwest of Kaliningrad. The narrow beach backed by steep sandy slopes is nothing to speak of, but the pretty old German houses, revamped sanatoriums, top-class hotels and shady forest setting make it worth a visit. Fairly untouched by WWII, Svetlogorsk has benefited from being declared a federal health resort, ie money has been spent on its infrastructure. There's also a big theatre and several new hotels under construction. However, if it's a beach you're after, the ones at Yantarny, Zelenogradsk and Kurshskaya Kosa are far nicer.

Sights

Herman Brachert House-Museum MUSEUM

(Дом-Музей Германа Брахета; www.brachert.ru; ul Tokareva 7; admission R100; 10am-6.30pm Mon-Thu, to 5pm Sat & Sun) The Herman Brachert House-Museum features the work of

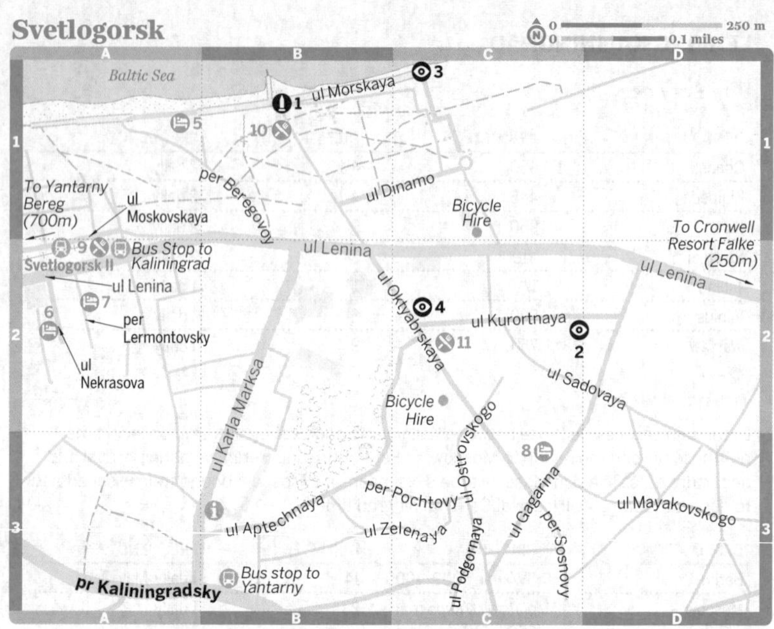

Svetlogorsk

Sights

1	Nymph Statue	B1
2	Organ Hall	C2
3	Sundial	C1
4	Water Tower	C2

Sleeping

5	Grand Palace	A1
6	Hotel Universal	A2
7	Lumier Art Hotel	A2
8	Stary Doktor	C3

Eating

9	Croissant Café	A2
10	Korvet	B1
11	Vika	C2

Brachert (1890–1972), the sculptor whose work can be spotted all around Svetlogorsk; his bronze **Nymph statue** resides in a mosaic-decorated shell on the promenade. His former home is small but the garden setting is lovely and decorated with more Brachert pieces, other works by contemporary sculptors and – looking forlorn in a corner – old statues of Lenin and Stalin. Head around 2km west along the main road from Svetlogorsk II station to reach Otradnoe.

Ul Oktyabrskaya STREET

In Svetlogorsk, the main street of ul Oktyabrskaya is lined with handsome buildings, including the striking 25m **water tower**, built in Jugendstil (art nouveau) style; take a peep inside the sanatorium beneath the water tower to see the colourful murals.

Organ Hall NOTABLE BUILDING

(Органный зал; http://organhall.ru; ul Kurortnaya 3; tickets R300) Search out the attractive, half-timbered Organ Hall, where concerts are held throughout the week.

Sundial MONUMENT

(ul Morskaya) Down on the promenade there's an impressive sundial, decorated with an eye-catching mosaic of the zodiac.

Sleeping

All rates include breakfast and are for the July/August season; prices can drop by a third or more at other times.

TOP CHOICE **Lumier Art Hotel** HOTEL €€€

(Люмьер Арт-отель; ☎507 750; www.hotellumier.ru; per Lermontovsky 2a; r from R4500; ❄🛜) With the movies as the hotel's theme, the designer clearly had a lot of fun decorating this playful boutique hotel. Even the standard rooms are stylish and come with cable TV and DVD players. Some also have balconies.

Hotel Universal HOTEL €€
(☎743 658; www.hotel-universal.ru; ul Nekrasova 3; s/d R2600/3000) Set in quiet grounds, this modern hotel is nicely designed and has a variety of spacious rooms.

Hotel Georgensvaldye HOTEL €€
(Георгенсвальде; ☎21 526; www.walde.ru; ul Tokareva 6; s/d R2600/3300) In Otradnoe, opposite the Herman Brachert House-Museum, this elegant place is ideal for those seeking peace and quiet.

Russ Hotel HOTEL €€€
(☎777 787; www.russ-hotel.ru; ul Vereshchagina 10; s/d from R4500/5200; ❄@📶) Evoking the jet-set 1970s – in a good way – the Russ is isolated at the east end of town. Shagpile carpet and silky bedspreads add a luxurious touch to the rooms. There's also a rooftop lounge bar, outdoor jacuzzi and billiards room. Signposts point to the hotel, which is about 800m east of the junction of ul Oktyabrskaya and ul Lenina.

Cronwell Resort Falke HOTEL €€€
(☎21 605; www.falke-hotel.ru; ul Lenina 16; s/d from R3300/4400; ❄@📶) With its tasteful luxury style, this hotel is a good choice for pampering. Its indoor pool, in a balmy winter garden, is big enough for a decent swim.

Stary Doktor HOTEL €€
(☎21 362; www.alterdoktor.ru; ul Gagarina 12; d with/without bathroom R3000/2400) One of Svetlogorsk's more charming options. Rooms are simple and cosy.

Grand Palace HOTEL €€€
(☎33 232; www.grandhotel.ru; per Beregovoy 2; s/d from R6400/8500; ❄@📶) Overpriced, faux-historical glitz pad, but the only one in Svetlogorsk with sea views. There are indoor and outdoor pools and a private strip of beach.

Yantarny Bereg SANATORIUM €€
(Янтарный Берег; ☎21 604; www.yantarbereg.ru; pr Kaliningradsky 79; s/d from R1400/2800) If you'd like to sample a sanatorium, this large, busy and professionally run one is the best option. You'll need to speak Russian and be prepared for a holiday-camp-meets-hospital atmosphere.

Eating & Drinking

All the reviewed hotels also have restaurants. Several pleasant open-air eating and drinking options serving pizza, shashlyk, beer and the like sprout like daisies around town during high season.

TOP CHOICE Korvet INTERNATIONAL €€
(ul Oktyabrskaya 36; meals R300-600) Specialising in pizza, this café based in the 1901 Kurhaus is a lovely place for a meal or coffee break. Lounge in comfy sofas, listening to chill-out music. On Friday and Saturday nights it morphs into party central with DJs keeping things going into the early hours.

Croissant Café INTERNATIONAL €
(ul Lenina; meals R150-300) The bakery-café that has been such a hit in Kaliningrad also has a new branch next to Svetlogorsk II train station. Offers outdoor tables to watch the world go by.

Vika RUSSIAN €€
(Вика; ul Oktyabrskaya; meals R400-600) In a newly renovated art nouveau building, this upmarket café has a good selection of salads, soups, meat and fish dishes and an unhurried ambience.

Information

Svetlogorsk Tourist Information Centre
(☎22 098; www.svetlogorsk-tourism.ru; ul Karla Marksa 7a; ⏰10am-7pm Sat, to 4pm Sun) Helpful staff who can assist with hotel bookings, tours, car rental etc. Also internet access (R35 per hour), a good gift shop and small museum about the resort's history.

Getting There & Away

From Kaliningrad take a train (R60, 1¼ hours, at least seven daily) or bus (R47, one hour, every 30 minutes). Buses arrive and depart from in front of the **Svetlogorsk II** train station. The **bus stop** for Yantarny is on pr Kaliningradsky, facing Lake Tikhoe.

Svetlogorsk is spread out but easy to navigate on foot or by bicycle: rent one from the **stall** along ul Oktyabrskaya for R50 per hour. There's another bike-rental **stall** on ul Lenina opposite a small shopping centre.

Yantarny Янтарный

⏰MOSCOW –1HR

Formerly Palmniken, this peaceful resort, 42km northwest of Kaliningrad and 24km southwest of Svetlogorsk, is the source of most of the region's stock of amber. Apart from the mine, which it's possible to visit,

THE AMBER COAST

You can hardly move in Kaliningrad without coming across shops and stalls selling souvenirs made of amber – the hard resin of coniferous trees that grew in the region approximately 45 to 50 million years ago. Ninety per cent of the world's amber hails from the region, its colour varying over more than 200 different shades, from milky white to a deep orange. Insects or plant material trapped in amber when it was still thick resin are called inclusions. At the region's sanatoriums, they even offer 'amber therapy', said to combat fatigue and other health disorders. Although a tiny percentage is recovered the traditional way from the beach, the main open-cast mine is at Yantarny, where more than 700 tonnes of amber are dug up annually.

Yantarny's long, wide sandy beach is the best in Kaliningrad.

On the headland above the beach in the centre of the small town stretches the shady **Park Bekkera**, named after Maurice Becker, the 19th-century hotelier who created the gardens and nearby hotel. Diving trips can be arranged with **Demersus** (http://demersus.ru).

Two minutes' walk from the beach, **Hotel Bekker** (☎4012-352 828; ul Sovetskaya 72; s/d incl breakfast from R2200/3600; 📶) offers spacious, pleasantly furnished rooms; some have balconies. The hotel also runs **Kafe Bekker** (meals R300-500), which has a terrace overlooking the beach.

At the time of research, **Schloss Hotel** (☎4012-931 931; http://schloss-hotel.ru; ul Sovetskaya 70; s/d from R4500/4800; ❄📶🏊), located in a restored heritage mansion, was nearing completion; it promises elegant rooms, a spa and restaurant.

There are modern beachside cabins at **Galera** (☎921-614 7441; ul Sovetskaya 1; d/tr/q R2500/3000/3500), which also has a restaurant and bar, or you could pitch a tent at the adjacent camp site **Robinson** (www.robin-camp.ru; site for 2/4 people R300/600).

Bus 120 runs to Yantarny from Kaliningrad (R60, 1½ hours, hourly). Buses 282 and 286 run to Yantarny from Svetlogorsk (R42, 45 minutes, eight daily).

Zelenogradsk Зеленоградск

☎40150 / POP 12,509 / 🕒MOSCOW –1HR

The long beach that made Zelenogradsk (formerly Kranz) a top-class resort during German times is still the town's prime attraction. It's a low-key place with a nostalgic atmosphere: crumbling Soviet eyesores, lovely old German buildings and modern villas stand side by side. Sadly, much of the promenade is off limits, as repairs to it keep dragging on. Zelenogradsk is also the gateway to Kurshskaya Kosa National Park.

Sleeping & Eating

Rates below are for high season (July and August) and include breakfast.

TOP CHOICE Loger Haus GUESTHOUSE €€
(Логер Хаус; ☎32 306; www.logerhaus.ru; ul Zheleznodorozhnaya 1; d from R2800; ❄📶) Just steps from the bus and train stations is the best of the town's several smaller guesthouses. The cream-coloured decor verges on luxurious; there are even gilt frames around the flat-screen TVs in the rooms! Also here is a fancy restaurant serving Russian and European dishes (R600 to R800), including pasta and rib-eye steak.

Koshkin Dom GUESTHOUSE €€
(Кошкин Дом; ☎775 859; www.koshkin-dom.ru; ul Gagarina 1a; s/d from R1900/2300; 🅿🏊) Cats are the design motif of this pleasant place less than a minute from the beach. There's also a sauna, a tiny swimming pool and a billiards room in the basement.

Villa Lana GUESTHOUSE €€
(☎33 410; www.villa-lana.ru; ul Gagarina 3a; s/d/apt €50/80/165; 📶) The most modest of the guesthouses along ul Gagarina offers colourfully decorated rooms, plus a separate self-catering apartment sleeping four.

Crystal Hotel HOTEL €€
(☎4012-729 333; www.crystalhotel.ru; ul Gagarina 19a; s/d R1800/2950; 📶) The cheapest in-season hotel option is also a nice place to bunk down, with decent rooms and a friendly welcome.

U Neptuna RUSSIAN €€
(У Нептуна; ul Tolstogo; meals R400-600) Offering tasty salads, soups and grilled fish. Also has sea views and an outdoor terrace.

Getting There & Away

Frequent buses run (R44, 45 minutes, every 30 minutes) from beside Kaliningrad's Severny vokzal (North Station). There are also trains to and from Kaliningrad (R48, 30 minutes, three daily) and Svetlogorsk (R35, 40 minutes, three daily).

Kurshskaya Kosa Куршская Коса

40150 / MOSCOW –1HR

Tall, windswept dunes, pristine beaches and dense pine forests teeming with wildlife lie along the 98km-long Curonian Spit, a Unesco World Heritage Site that divides the tranquil Curonian Lagoon from the Baltic Sea. The 50km of the spit within Russian territory constitutes **Kurshskaya Kosa National Park** (www.park-kosa.ru; admission per person R30, car plus driver R250). Tranquil fishing and holiday villages dot the eastern coast. From south to north they are **Lesnoy** (Лесное; formerly Sarkau), **Rybachy** (Рыбачий; formerly Rossitten) and **Morskoe** (Морское; formerly Pilkoppen).

Sights

Epha's Height VIEWPOINT
(Высота Эфа; km42) Near Morskoe, boardwalks from one side of the spit to the other provide expansive views climaxing at the 40m-high **Big Dune Ridge**. Along the way you can see the contrast between white and 'green' wooded dunes.

Dancing Forest FOREST
(Танцующий лес; km37) One of the park's most remarkable sights is this forest, where the pines have been sculpted into twisting shapes by the elements – they do indeed appear to be frozen midboogie.

National Park Museum MUSEUM
(45 119; km14; admission R50; 9.30am-4.30pm Tue-Sun May-Sep, 10am-4pm Tue-Sun Oct-April) To learn more about the park's habitat and history, drop by the museum, where you can also see deer and some cute woodcarvings by a local artist. Also call here to prearrange an excursion to the **Fringilla Field Station** (km23; tour R50; 9am-6pm Apr-Oct), a bird-ringing centre in operation since 1957, where enormous funnelled nets can trap an average of 1000 birds a day.

Sleeping & Eating

The following rates, which include breakfast, are for July and August.

Kurshskaya Kosa HOTEL €€
(Куршская Коса; 45 242; www.holiday39rus.ru; Tsentralnaya ul 17, Lesnoy; s/d from R2800/3000; @) Cheery, modern and steps from the beach, this is one of the spit's best deals. It also has a restaurant, internet access, a cash machine and rents bicycles (R100 per hour).

Traktir HOTEL €€
(Трактир; 41 290; www.rubachiy.ru; ul Lesnaya 8, Rybachy; r from R2650) At the entrance to Rybachy, this log-cabin-style hotel has small but pleasant rooms. The charm can wane if a crowd descends on the adjoining **restaurant** (mains R300-500; 10am-midnight) – a hit with locals since ex-President Putin dropped by for a meal. Solid home-cooked meals are served on rustic pottery.

Altrimo HOTEL €€
(41 139; www.altrimo.ru; ul Porganichnaya 11, Rybachy; r/apt from R3600/7000;) The most upmarket place to stay in Kurshskaya Kosa comes complete with a helipad. Its location right beside the lagoon can't be beat, the rooms are stylish and the staff are very friendly. Facilities include a pleasant open-air restaurant and a giant replica fishing boat that's part sauna, part kid's playground. You can also rent a variety of craft here for sailing or fishing trips on the lagoon.

Morskoe GUESTHOUSE €€
(Морское; 41 330; www.morskoehotel.ru; ul Dachnaya 6, Morskoe; r from R2350) Near the beach, this handsome guesthouse with English-speaking staff has 13 nicely furnished rooms, a sauna and a billiards table. Guests can rent bicycles and beach gear.

Rossiten GUESTHOUSE €€
(41 391; ul Pobedy 24, Rybachy; s/d R2600/2800) This no-frills inn, at the heart of the village, offers simple accommodation and an OK café.

Getting There & Away

Buses from Kaliningrad head up the spit en route to Morskoe (R101, two hours, four daily). All stop in Zelenogradsk, Lesnoy and Rybachy on the way there and back; Kaliningrad's Regional Tourism Information Centre has the current timetable.

Alternatively, rent a car (from around R1500) or arrange a tour (around R700) in either Kaliningrad or Zelenogradsk.

Chernyakhovsk Черняховск

40141 / POP 43,000 / MOSCOW –1HR

Founded by Teutonic Knights in 1336, the former Prussian city of Insterburg was thoroughly trashed during WWII. The two ruined castles within its boundaries indicate how important Chernyakhovsk, Kaliningrad's second-largest city, once was.

Sights

Georgenburg Castle FORTRESS

(Замок Георгенбург; ul Tsentralnaya 16; tour per person R200; 10am-5pm) This ruined fortress, 3km north of the town centre, is perched high above the Instruch River. In 1812 the castle estate was bought by a Scottish family who established the **Georgenburg Stud Farm** (32 301; www.georgenburg.com; ul Tsentralnaya 18), which continues to breed Tranken horses today. The farm is also the location of the **Georgenburg Cup**, an international show-jumping tournament, typically held on the second weekend in September. Vladimir, a potter who is also restoring parts of the castle, provides tours in Russian. Walking here from town through the beautiful countryside is a pleasure; alternatively, take bus 5 (R10) or a taxi (R100).

Insterburg Castle FORTRESS

(Замок Инстербург; ul Zamkovaya 1; admission by donation; 10am-5pm) Around 1km north of Chernyakhovsk's train and bus stations, the ruins of this castle are watched over by eccentric hippie artist Andrik Smirnov – he's set up his **studio-gallery** inside the castle's remaining structure. You'll also find a good photo and text display, in Russian and German, on the area's history. Medieval fencing matches by the local **knights' club** are held during the summer in the central courtyard and there are other events here too – for details, see the website http://instergod.ru.

St Michael's Cathedral & St Bruno's Church CHURCH

Two churches are among Chernyakhovsk's smatterings of pre-WWII architecture. The Orthodox **St Michael's Cathedral** (Св Михайловский собор; ul Suvorova) was a former Lutheran church, built between 1886 and 1890. The Catholic **St Bruno's Church** (Храм Святого Бруно; ul Lenina) was designed by Friedrich Heitmann in 1904. Both are handsome red-brick buildings.

Sleeping & Eating

Hotel Kochar HOTEL €€

(33 300; www.hotel-kachar.ru; ul Lenina 9; s/d incl breakfast R2800/3500;) Classy hotel decked out with Italian furnishings. The English-speaking staff are friendly and the restaurant (meals R600 to R800), serving European food, is Chernyakhovsk's most upmarket.

Hotel Georgenburg HOTEL €€

(32 301; http://georgenburg.com; ul Tsentralnaya 18; s/d from R1950/2550) Next to the stud farm, this 19-room hotel offers clean and pleasant accommodation, perfect if you're here for the horses. Its restaurant is also good, serving reasonably priced Russian standards with a meal costing around R500 or less. Breakfast is R250.

Pivnoy Dvor GUESTHOUSE €

(Пивной Двор; 34 628; ul Suvorova 14; r R1300) Opposite St Michael's Cathedral, this cute cottage with a pretty garden offers basic accommodation in simply furnished rooms with wooden beams. Downstairs the pub serves equally unfussy food (R400 to R500).

Aquatoria INTERNATIONAL €€

(Акватория; ul Lenina 9; meals R500; noon-midnight Sun-Thu, to 2am Fri & Sat) The set lunches (R130 to R150) here are a great deal and the crispy thin-crust pizzas it makes are on the mark. Also serves sushi and plenty of Russian food in a vaguely nautical setting.

Getting There & Away

The train and bus stations are opposite each other at the southern end of ul Lenina. *Elektrichka* (R120, 1¾ hours, three daily) make the journey to/from Kaliningrad, and long-distance services to and from Moscow and St Petersburg also pause here. Buses and minibuses (R112, 1¾ hours, every 30 minutes) to and from Kaliningrad are more frequent.

Northern European Russia

Includes »

Best Places to Eat

» Karelskaya Gornitsa (p305)
» El Fuego (p343)
» Puzatiy Patsyuk (p333)
» Traktir Zhily-Bily (p326)

Best Places to Stay

» Botel Onega (p303)
» Hotel Priyut (p316)
» Hotel Dvina (p341)
» Hotel 69 Parallel (p325)
» Hotel Angliter (p332)

Why Go?

Cold hands, warm heart? The idiom has never rung more true than in this land of polar winters and cliché-busting Russian hospitality, where those braving daunting long hauls and off-radar destinations are rewarded with a hearty reception by curious locals.

But the allure of Northern European Russia (Северно-Европейская Россия) goes deeper than vodka shots and convivial conversation: the realm that spawned the epic poetry of the *Kalevala* is home to a profound historical and scenic landscape that includes the iconic wooden architecture of Kizhi Island, the far-flung Solovetsky Islands' imposing monastery/erstwhile Gulag camp, and a vast, lush wilderness that's just beginning to recognise its tourism potential. It's also one of the best places to witness the eerie northern lights.

For all its trademark Arctic majesty, the region's short summer is also a great time to visit, perfect for making boat connections, fishing for prize salmon and frolicking beneath the midnight sun.

When to Go

Murmansk

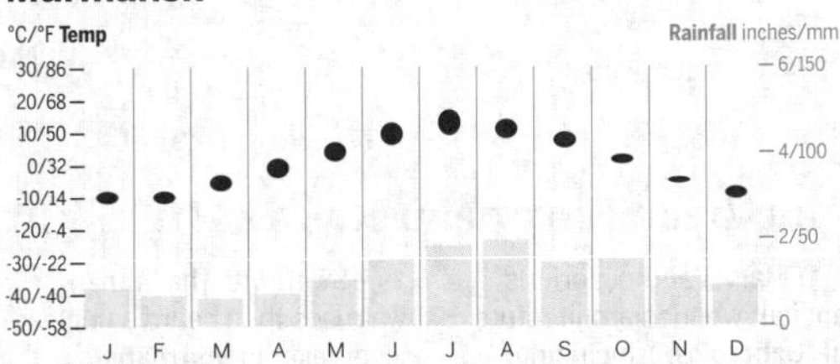

Late Apr–May Watch winter melt away as the landscape transforms almost overnight.

Late May–late Jul The fleeting summer is ideal for island access and fun in the midnight sun.

Late Nov–mid-Jan Scan the perpetually sunless skies for the gasp-inducing aurora borealis.

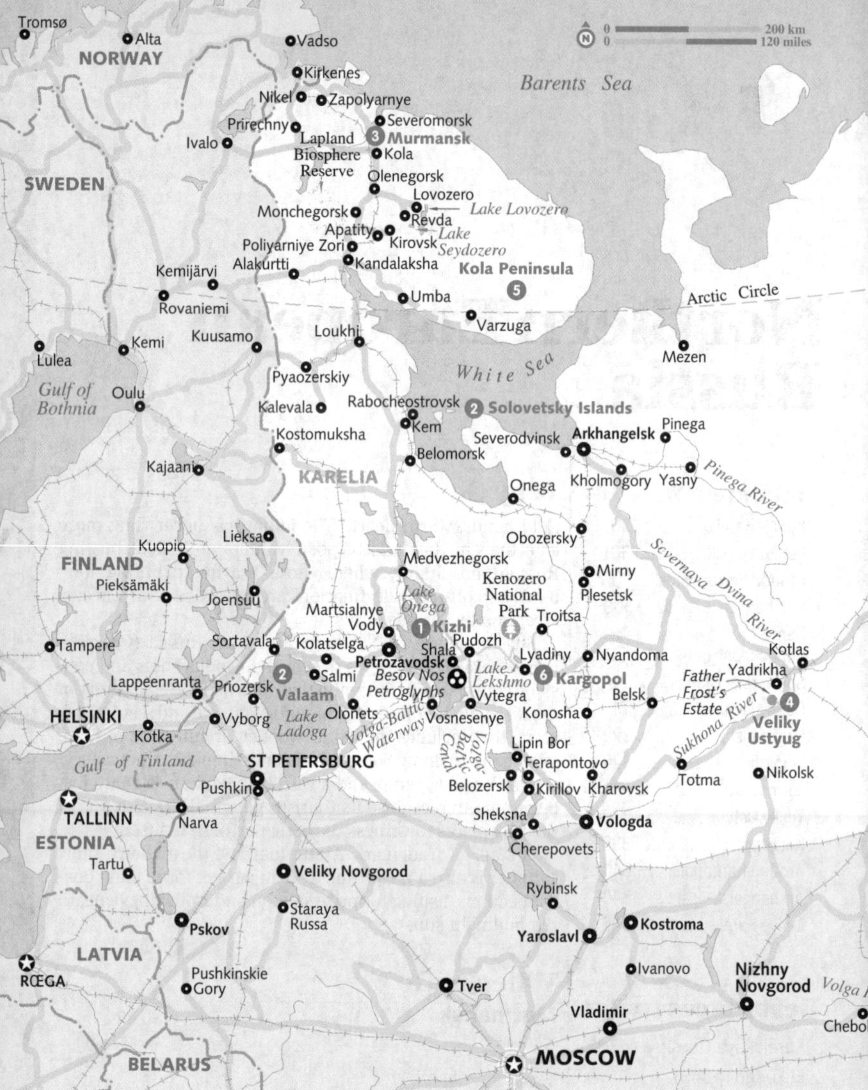

Northern European Russia Highlights

1 Marvel at the glorious ancient wooden architecture of **Kizhi** (p307), including the iconic multidomed Transfiguration Church

2 Go monastery-hopping at the sylvan retreat of **Valaam** (p310) and the ever-evocative **Solovetsky Islands** (p312)

3 Swim with the human walruses then board a nuclear icebreaker in **Murmansk** (p322), the world's biggest Arctic city

4 Stuff your stocking in **Veliky Ustyug** (p336), home to the Russian Santa, Ded Moroz

5 Hunt for the aurora borealis or bask in the midnight sun on the all-or-nothing **Kola Peninsula** (p301)

6 Try your hand at traditional folk art in the tranquil town of **Kargopol** (p338)

History

Since the last ice age, hardy northerners created petroglyphs and mysterious stone labyrinths attesting to a now-mysterious religious life that existed as early as the 3rd millennium BC.

From the 11th century AD, Russians from Novgorod made hunting, fishing and trapping expeditions to the White Sea area. Some of their seasonal camps eventually became permanent settlements, the origin of towns such as Kandalaksha, Umba and Varzuga. These Pomors (coast-dwellers) developed a distinct material culture and their own lively dialect of Russian.

Moscow grabbed the Vologda area in the early 15th century and annexed the rest of the northwest from Novgorod in 1478. Shortly after, the unexpected arrival of English sailors seeking a northeast passage to China gave Ivan the Terrible the idea of founding a port and commencing trade with the west. That port, Arkhangelsk, bloomed, as did many towns on its river supply route. All this changed, however, once Peter the Great founded St Petersburg in 1703, offering much easier access to the sea. Formerly forgotten Karelia was suddenly the supply centre for building Peter's new capital, and Petrozavodsk was founded a year later to produce armaments for his wars with Sweden.

FOUNDING MURMANSK

The northwest's biggest city, Murmansk, was founded during WWI when embattled tsarist Russia was in desperate need of supplies from its Western allies. But no sooner had the Murmansk–Moscow railway been laid than the October Revolution changed circumstances entirely. The Western allies, which opposed the new Bolshevik regime, occupied Murmansk and Arkhangelsk for two years and at one point advanced south almost to Petrozavodsk.

From the 1920s the Murmansk railway helped Soviet governments unlock the Kola Peninsula's vast mineral resources, bringing new towns like Monchegorsk and Kirovsk into existence. Gulag prisoners were part of the force that built the region's new factories and the White Sea–Baltic Canal.

WWII & AFTER

Stalin invaded Finland in 1939–40. Having been independent from Russia only since 1917, Finland allied with Germany to counter-attack along the entire Soviet-Finnish border, eventually occupying Petrozavodsk. Once again, anti-German allies fought desperately to prevent a Russian defeat, sending highly risky supply convoys from Scotland to embattled Murmansk and Arkhangelsk. Those ports held out but were both bombed to rubble by the Luftwaffe. In 1944 the Red Army fought back, pushing the Nazis out of Norway and claiming a chunk of southeastern Finland, which remains part of Russia's Republic of Karelia today. Many ethnic Finns and Karelians (a Finno-Ugric people related to Finns and Estonians) fled to Finland, and today only about 10% of the Republic of Karelia's 720,000 population is actually Karelian.

In the 1990s the Kola Peninsula's heavy industries and naval and military installations were especially hard hit by the collapse of the USSR's command economy, and cities suffered a big population decline. Recently, however, soaring global prices for minerals and timber plus the development of the Shtokman gas field have prompted a noticeable rebound. The region's major cities have an unusually progressive air for provincial Russia, helped by strong ties with Scandinavia, especially Norway, which remains sentimentally grateful for its liberation by the Red Army at the end of WWII.

KOLA & KARELIA

Best known for its cosmopolitan capital Petrozavodsk and the fairy-tale island of Kizhi, the Republic of Karelia (Карелия) is also renowned for its natural attractions. Heavily blanketed by evergreen forests, the region claims Europe's two biggest lakes, Ladoga and Onega, within its borders. Further north, the Kola (Кола) Peninsula juts out its 100,000-sq-km knob of tundra, bogs and low mountains between the White and Barents Seas. Lying almost entirely north of the Arctic Circle, its mesmerising expanses of wilderness are fabulous places to be dazzled by the aurora borealis or midnight sun. The peninsula also offers world-class, if specialist, opportunities for mineral hunters and sports fishing.

Petrozavodsk Петрозаводск

8142 / POP 263,500 / MOSCOW

Set on a bay of vast Lake Onega, Petrozavodsk (Petroskoi in Finnish) is the launching point for summer visits to Kizhi Island. The name ('Peter's factory') refers to a munitions plant founded here by Peter the Great in 1703, superseded 70 years later by the Alexandrovskiy Ironworks (still standing). But Petrozavodsk is by no means the gritty, industrial city its name would suggest. Shady promenades, a large student population and connections with Finland all make for a distinctly European atmosphere, while the centre's various neoclassical facades are rather stately – compared to Olenegorsk, anyway. Arriving from St Petersburg (420km southwest), you might be less easily impressed.

The main commercial streets are pr Lenina and pr Marksa; the latter follows the narrow, park-swaddled Lososinka River to the **hydrofoil terminal** (Водный вокзал, *vodny vokzal*).

Sights & Activities

Ploshchad Lenina SQUARE

Low-rise pl Lenina is the original heart of neoclassical Petrozavodsk, skirted by matching semicircular buildings built in 1784. In the centre of the circular 'square' is a 1933 **statue of Lenin**, who appears to be dragging himself out of a hole. Steps pass an **eternal flame** into the pretty riverside park, from which a bridge crosses to the surprisingly grand facade of the former Alexandrovskiy Ironworks, now part of the vast **Onezhskiy Tractor Factory**.

Local Studies Museum MUSEUM

(Карельский государственный краеведческий музей; pl Lenina 1; admission R100; 10am-5.30pm Tue-Sun) One of the buildings on pl Lenina houses the Local Studies Museum, with exhibitions on city and regional history plus everything you need to know about the *Kalevala*, Finland's national epic, which was pieced together in the 19th century from northern Karelian song-poems.

Arts Precinct NOTABLE BUILDINGS

At pr Marksa's eastern end, Petrozavodsk's grandest buildings include the splendid **Musical & Russian Drama Theatre** (Музыкальный и русский театр драмы; www.mrteatr.onego.ru; pl Kirova 1) and the **Fine Arts Museum** (Музей изобразительных искусств; pr Marksa 8; admission R100; 10am-6pm Tue-Sun), boasting medieval icons, folk art and works inspired by the *Kalevala*.

Akvatika WATER PARK

(Бассейн Акватика; per hr R350; 8am-10.30pm, closed Jul) The city's architectural grandeur continues along Pushkinskaya ul, where an imposing facade hides Akvatika, a swimming pool complex housing jacuzzis, *hammam* (Turkish bath), sauna and waterslide.

FREE **Pre-Cambrian Geology Museum** MUSEUM

(Музей геологии докембрия; 783 471; http://geoserv.krc.karelia.ru; Pushkinskaya ul 11) A favourite for those with rocks in their head. Nonspecialist tourists should think twice before dropping in and disturbing the busy academics who hold the keys: they're squirreled away on the Institute's 5th floor. Visits are by arrangement.

Fishermen Statue MONUMENT

(Памятник Рыбакам; Onezhskaya nab) The amble-worthy lakeside promenade is littered with sculptures presented to Petrozavodsk by its international twin cities. The most striking is the megamodern Fishermen Statue, a gift from Duluth, Minnesota.

Statue of Yury Andropov MONUMENT

(Памятник Андропову; ul Andropova) Unveiled to protests and arrests in 2005, a very youthful statue of Yury Andropov commemorates the USSR's 1982–84 supremo who had been chief of Petrozavodsk's Komsomol (Communist Party youth wing) some 50 years earlier. Andropov is best remembered as a long-term KGB director. Was the statue a sign of President Putin rehabilitating his former boss?

Statue of Peter the Great MONUMENT

(Памятник Петру I) Close to the hydrofoil terminal is a jaunty statue of Peter the Great pointing to the spot where Petrozavodsk would be founded.

Puppet House MUSEUM

(Дом кукол; www.kukla.karelia.ru; nab La Rochelle 13; admission R50; noon-5pm Tue-Sat) Cute, if occasionally creepy, collection of handmade creations by one of Russia's foremost puppet mistresses.

Tours

Intourist-Petrozavodsk TOUR COMPANY

(592 000; http://intourist.onego.ru/eng/index.html; Hotel Severnaya, pr Lenina 21) Numerous agencies can help arrange fishing, skiing and adventure tours around Karelia, including this one that's multilingual and happy to help.

Russia Discovery North-West ECOTOURS
(☎707 616; www.nwtb.ru; ul Puteyskaya 5) Specialist in adventure and ecotours.

Lukomorie TOUR COMPANY
(Лукоморье; ☎786 150; www.lukomorie.ru; ul Varlamova 13a)

Nordic Travel TOUR COMPANY
(☎560 201; www.nordictravel.ru; Kluchevskoe sh 13)

Festivals & Events

Hyperborea Festival WINTER FESTIVAL
Chase the wintertime blues away at this festival celebrating all things snow and ice. Held lakeside in January/February: see www.petrozavodsk-mo.ru for details.

Sleeping

With so many international students and businessfolk in town, Petrozavodsk is home to a diversity of accommodation unheard of in the rest of the region. Prices include breakfast, unless otherwise stated.

TOP CHOICE **Botel Onega** HOTEL €€
(Ботель "Онего"; ☎796 128; www.karelia.onego.ru; ul Rigachina 3; s R750-1800, d R1500-2200) Get your lake legs on at this fun accommodation alternative. Budget rooms are basic affairs, but it's cheap, cheerful and comes with views that leave the landlubbers for dead. Ideally located for early-morning staggers to the hydrofoil terminal.

Spa-Hotel Karelia HOTEL €€€
(Гостиница Карелия; ☎733 333; www.karelia-hotel.ru; nab Gyullinga 2; s R3960, d R4960-5960, apt/ste R6960/11,960, 📶) This bustling multistorey tower feels a little like an upmarket clinic, with a health-spa complex offering various massages, baths and beauty treatments. Many rooms have good lake views. Staff are multilingual and can assist with jaunts to Kizhi and beyond.

Hotel Severnaya HOTEL €€
(Гостиница Северная; ☎762 080, 780 703; http://severnaya.org; pr Lenina 21; s/d without bathroom R770/1100, s/d with bathroom from R1720/2570, ste R3700-6800; @) Built in the 1930s, this classically columned building is an iconic landmark on the Petrozavodsk streetscape. Rooms range from creaky cheapies with battered desks through petite but modernised en suite rooms to fancy new suites. Helpful staff speak English.

Onego Palace HOTEL €€€
(☎790 790; www.onegopalace.com; ul Kuybysheva 26; s R3800, d R4700-5200, ste R5900-7900, lyux R17,000-25,000; 📶) This spanking-new monolith looks a bit like a UFO looming over the lake it takes its name from. Thankfully, its interior is a lot less gauche, with classically styled rooms and three upmarket restaurants. Athletic types will appreciate the gym; for everyone else, there's a 24-hour lobby bar.

Hotel Maski HOTEL €€
(Гостиница Маски; ☎/fax 761 478; http://maski.onego.ru; pr Marksa 3; s/d R2800/2900, polu-lyux R3500, lyux R3900) Neat, presentable rooms shaped like pie slices in a circular building with balconies and theatrical motifs (apt, given its location in the arts precinct). Obliging staff speak English. West-facing rooms suffer road noise.

Hotel Prionezhsky BOUTIQUE HOTEL €€
(Отель Прионежский; ☎765 271; www.nikolaevskie-oteli.ru; ul Fedosovoy 46; 'First Line' s/d/ste from R2460/3300/5520, 'Second Line' d R3800-5520, ste R5520-6360; 📶) 'Second Line' rooms are sleek coffee-and-chrome affairs, while smaller 'First Line' singles are much simpler. Sing yourself sweaty at the on-site karaoke sauna (R900 per hour). To get there take trolleybus 40 along ul Kirova to 'Bolnitsa', then walk northeast through the hospital grounds.

Hotel Akvatika HOTEL €€
(Гостиница Акватика; ☎765 005; aquatika@sampo.ru; Pushkinskaya ul 7; s/tw/d R1800/3200/3700; 🏊) In one of Petrozavodsk's more palatial buildings, attached to the eponymous pool complex, the 18 rooms here are nothing to write home about but are comfortable enough and fresher than many competitors'.

Resting rooms HOSTEL €
(Комнаты отдыха, komnaty otdykha; ☎714 074; train station; 1/24hr R80/400) Typical station crash pad, up the back stairs behind the main waiting room. Showers are R50.

Eating

In addition to places listed, café-tents pop up along the waterfront and in the riverside park during summer.

For self-catering, head to the well-stocked **Lotos** (Лотос; ul Anokhina 37; ⏰8am-midnight) or **Lentorg** (Лентopг; pr Lenina 31; ⏰24hr), which is also at pl Gagarina.

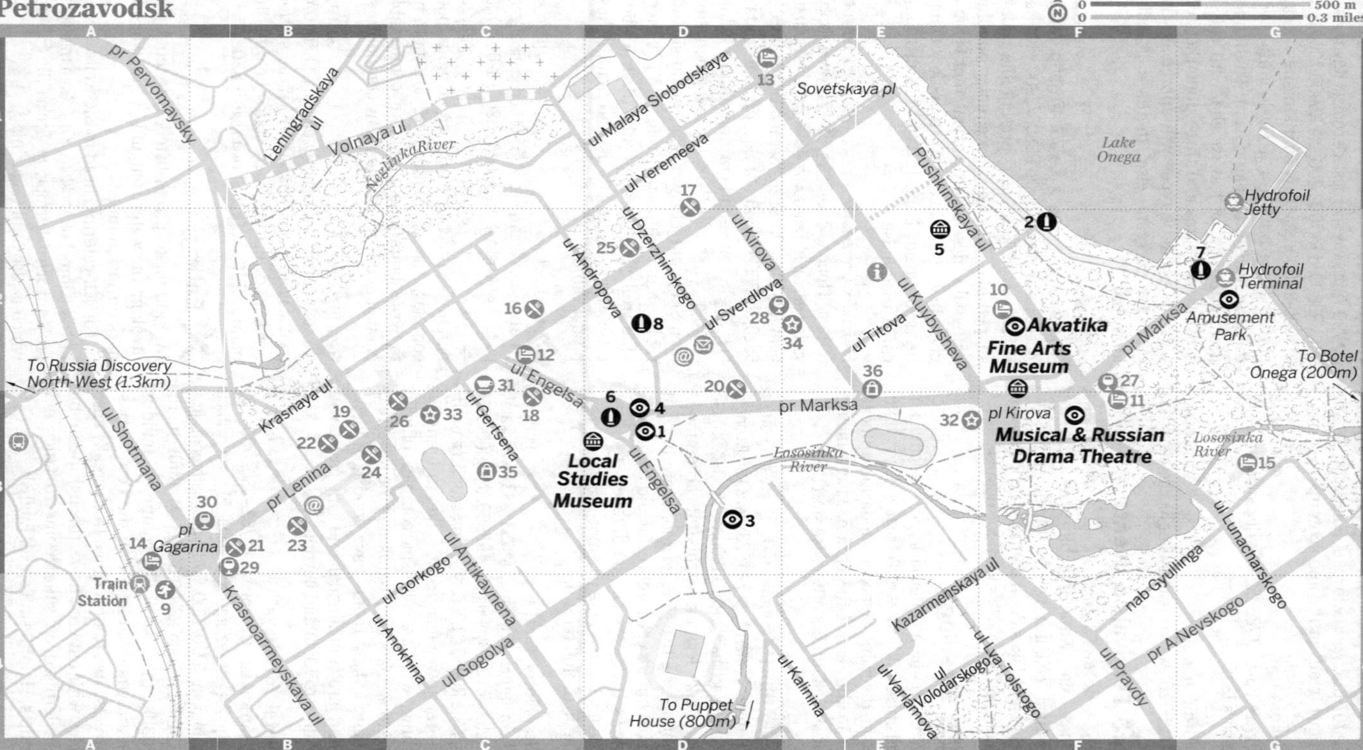
Petrozavodsk
500 m
0.3 miles
Lake Onega
Hydrofoil Jetty
Hydrofoil Terminal
Amusement Park
To Botel Onega (200m)
Akvatika
Fine Arts Museum
Musical & Russian Drama Theatre
Local Studies Museum
pl Kirova
pr Marksa
Pushkinskaya ul
Sovetskaya pl
ul Kuybysheva
ul Titova
ul Kirova
ul Sverdlova
ul Dzerzhinskogo
ul Andropova
ul Yeremeeva
ul Malaya Slobodskaya
Volnaya ul
Leningradskaya ul
Neglinka River
Lososinka River
ul Engelsa
ul Gertsena
ul Antikaynena
ul Gorkogo
ul Anokhina
ul Gogolya
Krasnoarmeyskaya ul
Krasnaya ul
pr Lenina
pl Gagarina
ul Shotmana
pr Pervomaysky
Train Station
To Russia Discovery North-West (1.3km)
To Puppet House (800m)
ul Kalinina
Kazarmenskaya ul
ul Varlamova
ul Volodarskogo
ul Lva Tolstogo
ul Pravdy
pr A Nevskogo
nab Gyullinga
ul Lunacharskogo

Petrozavodsk

Top Sights

Akvatika F2
Fine Arts Museum F2
Local Studies Museum D3
Musical & Russian Drama Theatre F3

Sights

1 Eternal Flame D3
2 Fishermen Statue F2
3 Onezhskiy Tractor Factory D3
4 Ploshchad Lenina D3
5 Pre-Cambrian Geology Museum E2
6 Statue of Lenin D3
7 Statue of Peter the Great G2
8 Statue of Yury Andropov D2

Activities, Courses & Tours

Intourist-Petrozavodsk .... (see 12)
9 Lukomorie A4

Sleeping

10 Hotel Akvatika F2
11 Hotel Maski F3
12 Hotel Severnaya C2
13 Onego Palace D1
14 Resting Rooms A3
15 Spa-Hotel Karelia G3

Eating

16 Dezhavyu C2
17 Kafe 70-ye Gody D1
18 Karelskaya Gornitsa C3
19 Kivach B3
20 La Parisienne D2
21 Lentorg B3
22 Lentorg B3
23 Lotos B3
24 Lozhka B3
25 Mak Dak D2
26 Saloon Sanches C3
Suomi .... (see 18)

Drinking

Bar Neubrandenburg .... (see 31)
27 Bar XXXX F2
28 FM-Art Kafe D2
29 Fusion B3
30 Kafe Ukuzmiya B3
31 Kaffee Haus C2

Entertainment

32 Karelian National Theatre E3
33 Klub Karelia/Cinema Pobeda C3
34 Philharmonia E2

Shopping

35 Khudozhestvenny Salon C3
36 Yuvelirnye Izdeliya E2

TOP CHOICE Karelskaya Gornitsa KARELIAN €€
(Карельская Горница; ☎785 300; www.gornica.ru; ul Engelsa 13a; mains R300-1100) Claiming to be the first Karelian restaurant in the world, this ye-olde hot spot boasts efficient costumed waiters and excellent, hearty fare including rabbit borsch and rich gamey mains. Reservations definitely recommended.

Suomi FINNISH €€
(☎785 300; http://suomi-restaurant.ru; ul Engelsa 13; mains from R300) Next door to Karelskaya Gornitsa, Suomi keeps the rustic flames a'burning with traditional Finnish dishes (miss the elk stroganoff at your peril), equally down-home surrounds and folk music performances every Friday and Saturday night.

Kafe 70-ye Gody CAFETERIA €
(Кафе 70-е годы; pr Lenina 10; snacks R20-40, mains R45-80; ⏰9am-midnight) Retro mementos including Moscow Olympics kitsch, spy-era transistor radios and a laughing Brezhnev photo make this more appealing than Petrozavodsk's other plastic-cutlery *stolovye* (canteens).

Kivach PIZZA €
(Кивач; pr Lenina 28; pizzas R95-300; ⏰7am-4am; 📶) This congenial late-night diner-style café is a favourite with the boisterous student set. Kick back in a comfy armchair, roll up your pizza (dough has never come thinner) and enjoy the show.

La Parisienne FUSION €
(http://parizhanka-cafe.ru; pr Marksa 22; mains from R120, business lunch R180; ⏰8am-midnight; 📶) This local chain's six (!) locations in Petrozavodsk are constantly packed, thanks to hip decor and enforced eclecticism: where else can you scoff sushi and sip Bosnian coffee while humming along to Edith Piaf?

Saloon Sanches MEXICAN €€€
(http://sanches.petrorest.ru; pr Lenina 26; mains R250-650, steaks R1000-1250; ⏰noon-1am) Ditch the fur hat and don a sombrero at this

incongruous yet archetypal Tex-Mex resto-bar serving R150 margaritas and wallet-and-gut-busting 300g Argentinean steaks.

Dezhavyu FUSION €
(Дежавю; pr Lenina 20; mains from R100; 9am-2am) Small but inexpensive meals served in an upbeat, youthful atmosphere where the déjà vu in question is the Eiffel Tower, a giant photo of which is echoed in ironwork motifs above the bar.

Lozhka RUSSIAN €
(Ложка; www.teaspoon.ru; pr Lenina 31; snacks from R22, lunch sets R80-140; 9am-10pm) Bright, youthful chain for bliny, salads and various teas.

Mak Dak FAST FOOD €
(pr Lenina 16; burgers R45-95; 7am-11pm) For when you really, really need a burger and fries.

Drinking

FM-Art Kafe LIVE MUSIC
(Арт Кафе; www.artcafefm.ru; ul Kirova 12; beer R60; 11am-6am Mon-Fri, from 6pm Sat & Sun) This large student-oriented basement beneath the Philharmonia offers entertainment as varied as the clientele, with revolving theme evenings ranging from jazz to folk to indie, with iPod-battles to boot. Free movies on Sundays.

Fusion BAR
(Krasnoarmeyskaya ul 33; cocktails from R150; 8.30am-2am) This super-sleek Russo-Japanese-style hang-out by the train station dishes up lethal cocktails every bit as delicious as the authentic sushi snacks (from R40). Popular with the young 'uns.

Bar XXXX BAR
(pr Marksa 3; beer from R60; noon-late) Motor-themed bar (the vintage car busting out of the front wall gives it away) that puts its pedal to the metal on Friday and Saturday nights, with live music and/or DJs (covers from R200).

Kaffee Haus CAFÉ
(Кофейный дом; pr Lenina 23; coffee R60-180, cakes R40-100; 9am-1am; wi-fi) Widely acclaimed for Petrozavodsk's best coffee and cakes, this classy nook is connected by an indoor walkway to the well-stocked, German-themed **Bar Neubrandenburg** (beers from R70).

Kafe Ukuzmiya BAR
(Укузмия; pl Gagarina; beer from R60; 10am-11pm Mon-Wed, to 1am Thu, to 3am Fri & Sat, noon-11pm Sun) If Neptune was Satan, hell would look something like this exceptionally odd-looking basement bar. Handy for the train station.

Entertainment

Musical & Russian Drama Theatre THEATRE
(Музыкальный и Русский театр драмы; 783 738 for bookings; www.mrteatr.onego.ru; pl Kirova 1) Bask in the recently renovated glory of this magnificent Parthenon pile staging light operas, plays, ballets and folk-group shows. The interior decor is a wild mixture of Ancient Greek, Roman and Soviet styles.

Klub Karelia/Cinema Pobeda CINEMA, NIGHTCLUB
(Клуб Карелия/Кинотеатр Победа; http://karelia-krc.ru/index; pr Lenina 27) Behind a pseudo-classical columned facade, the Pobeda Cinema shows movies by day but morphs into a double-level nightclub after 11pm.

Karelian National Theatre THEATRE
(Национальный театр Карелии; http://teatr.onego.ru; pr Marksa 19; ticket office 2-7pm Tue-Sun) Performances of Finnish/Karelian dramas, fairy tales, musicals and local takes on Shakespeare.

Philharmonia CLASSICAL MUSIC
(Филармония; www.philharmonia.onego.ru; ul Kirova 12) The top place for classical music and 'sympho-jazz'.

Shopping

Souvenirs are thick on the ground in Petrozavodsk, but skip the tacky stalls for these well-established retailers.

Yuvelirnye Izdeliya SOUVENIRS
(Ювелирные Изделия, Karelia-Market Mall; 10am-8pm Mon-Sat, 11am-7pm Sun) Find good-value birch-bark, woodburn and leather crafts on the 1st floor of this busy shopping complex.

Khudozhestvenny Salon SOUVENIRS
(Художественный салон; ul Gertsena 41; 10am-7pm Mon-Fri, 11am-6pm Sat & Sun) Offers the same range as Yuvelirnye Izdeliya and much more, including exquisite jewellery, in larger, dedicated surrounds.

Information

Internet Access

Free wi-fi abounds in this student city, as well as desk-based net access.

Internet-Tsentr (Интернет Центр; ul Anokhina 20; per 30min from R35; 8am-11pm) Prepay in the corridor.

Severo-Zapadny Telekom (Северо-Западный Телеком; ul Sverdlova 31; per min R1; ⏲9am-9pm Mon-Fri, 11am-7pm Sat & Sun)

Internet Resources

Karelia Cultural Tourism (http://culture.karelia.ru)

Karelia's Museums (www.museums.karelia.ru)

Karelia Tourism Portal (www.ticrk.ru/en) Extremely useful website for all things Karelia.

Komart (www.komart.karelia.ru) Handy addresses and what's-on listings.

Petromap (www.petromap.ru/map) Detailed online street map.

Post

Post office (Почта; ul Sverdlova; ⏲8am-8pm Mon-Fri, 9am-6pm Sat)

Tourist Information

Petrozavodsk tourist office (Туристический информационный центр; ☎764 835; www.ticrk.ru; ul Kuybysheva 5; ⏲9am-5pm Mon-Sat) Very obliging English-speaking staff offer loads of information and advice.

Getting There & Away

For updated transport timetables, consult http://ptz-trans.ru.

Boat

In summer, hydrofoils usually operate up to five times daily to Kizhi and at least once or twice a day across Lake Onega to Shala (R900, 1¾ hours). From Shala, buses run 40km to Pudozh, from where you could engage a taxi to Lekshmozero in the Kenozero National Park for around R3000.

Bus

The **bus station** (Автовокзал) is at ul Chapaeva 3.

Train

The 24-hour ticket office is directly north of the elegantly spired **station** (pl Gagarina 1). The ideal overnight choice for Moscow is train 17, which departs at 7pm and arrives at 9am the next day, though the 8.30pm train 381 is cheaper and arrives only two hours later. The best timed of four services to St Petersburg is the 10.55pm train (arriving at 7am). Between four and nine services run daily to/from Murmansk (*platskart/kupe* R1422/3132, 19 to 24 hours). Of these, train 22 (departing at 0.52am) is the best of a bad lot for Kem (*platskart/kupe* R828/1730, eight hours). An overnight train runs on even-numbered days to Sortavala at 7.20pm (*platskart* R636, 12 hours).

Getting Around

Trolleybuses (R12) and *marshrutky* (R15) minibuses trundle up and down pr Lenina. From the train station, trolleybus 1 is the most useful, going straight through the heart of the city and down as far as the lake. All are signed; see http://ptz-trans.ru for detailed information.

Around Petrozavodsk

Stretching north and west of Petrozavodsk, Karelia is an idyllic and accessible region for hunting, fishing and hiking. Wild camping is permitted almost anywhere unless there are signs with the words 'Не разбивать палатку'. Signs saying 'Не разжигать костры' mean 'no campfires'. Lakes and rivers offer canoeing opportunities, and some outfits offer rafting, albeit without many rapids.

By far the most rewarding day-trip destination from Petrozavodsk is Kizhi. Many travel agencies also offer excursions to **Martsialnye Vody**, touted as Peter the Great's original mineral spa, but Peter's palace is no longer standing and the trip's secondary attraction, the 10.7m **Kivach Waterfall** (Vodopad Kivach), isn't exactly Niagara.

Chartering a boat across Lake Onega to the famous but isolated **Besov Nos Petroglyphs** is likely to cost you a packet. Contact **Nordic Travel** (www.nordictravel.ru) or try asking boatmen in Shala.

KIZHI КИЖИ

This enchanting green sliver is by far the most visited of Lake Onega's 1600-plus islands, thanks to the iconic Transfiguration

SERVICES FROM PETROZAVODSK BUS STATION

DESTINATION	FARE (R)	DURATION (HR)	DEPARTURES
Kem	420	6	4.45pm
St Petersburg	580	8½	9am, 10am, 3pm
Sortavala	360	4½-5½	6 daily (more in summer)
Vologda	762	12½	7.10am daily except Wed & Thu

Church. Bubbling magnificently with 30 miniature domes, this is Russia's most instantly recognisable wooden landmark and the centrepiece of the **Kizhi Museum Reserve** (Музей-заповедник "Кижи"; http://kizhi.karelia.ru; admission R625, audio guide in English R150; ⏲8am-8pm Jun-Aug, 9am-4pm Sep–mid-Oct & 15-31 May, 10am-3pm mid-Oct–mid-May). The reserve is home to dozens more 18th- and 19th-century log buildings, some furnished in period style, which were moved here from other Karelian villages during Soviet times.

Despite numerous other tourists and the relatively high cost of a visit, Kizhi is truly one of Russia's unmissable attractions. Three hours on the island is perfect for visiting the main reserve and strolling up to Yamka village, where you'll find additional antique buildings in a more lived-in setting. Guided excursions are offered by various Petrozavodsk agencies but much of what you'll see is pretty self-explanatory and placards are in English. Stay on the marked paths: poisonous snakes like Kizhi as much as visiting humans do.

Hydrofoils dock at a landing flanked by souvenir kiosks. Tourists are expected to head south from here into the main reserve. Guards keep an eye out for those who might try to sneak north instead towards Yamka and Vasilyevo, avoiding the ticket booth.

Kizhi Museum Reserve

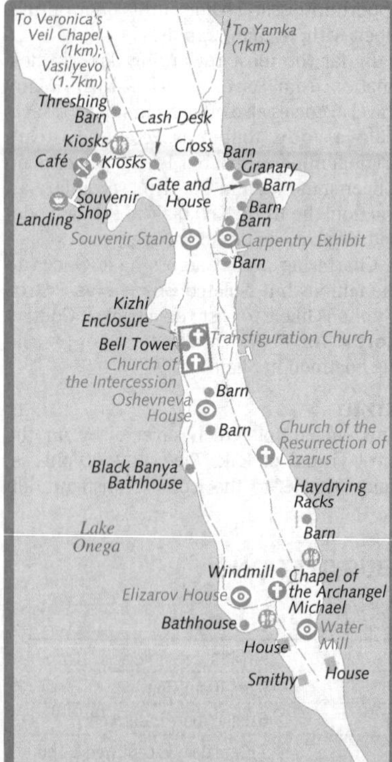

MAIN RESERVE AREA

An obvious coastal path loops around the main attractions, starting with the unmissable **Kizhi Enclosure** (Кижский погост) containing a fabulous pair of churches and an 1862 wooden **bell tower**. The world-famous 1714 **Transfiguration Church** features a chorus of wooden domes, gables and ingenious decorations to keep water off the walls. Entry isn't allowed as it's leaning slightly and held up thanks only to a steel frame. However, the lovely nine-domed **Church of the Intercession** (1764) next door hosts a rich collection of 16th- to 18th-century icons.

Directly south of the Kizhi Enclosure, the 1876 **Oshevneva House** is typical of larger historical Karelian rural homes where house and stable-barn were combined into one unit. Notice the 'bed cupboard'.

Further south is a **black banya**, a tiny wooden bathhouse hut so known because there was no chimney to allow the escape of smoke from the heater-fires.

Outside the furnished 1880 **Elizarov House**, a craftsman carves little animal figures, while within the **Chapel of the Archangel Michael**, music students often play the bells in an unusual form of busking.

The little 14th-century **Church of the Resurrection of Lazarus** from Murom monastery is the oldest structure on Kizhi: some claim it to be the oldest wooden building in Russia.

An interesting **carpentry exhibit** gives a great visual explanation of how wooden buildings were made without nails. From here you could return to the dock past a carved wooden **cross** of a type once common as a roadside waymarker in rural Karelia. Alternatively, stroll on to Yamka.

YAMKA & AROUND

Extravagantly bearded Old Believers, genuinely lived-in historic houses and a pretty east-coast setting make the hamlet of **Yamka** well worth the 15-minute walk. The reserve's seasonal staff sleep communally here in the 1905 **Pertyakov House**, with a traditional-style outdoor *banya* hut at the waterside. Two doors south, outside the **Moshikova House** is a curious blue-eyed pagan **totem** that's somewhat reminiscent of an Easter Island *moai*.

Walking west across the island towards Vasilyevo village takes you via the hilltop 17th-century **Veronica's Veil Chapel**, from which there are wonderful panoramas right across Kizhi. An alternative path from here leads back to the hydrofoil landing.

A small **café** near the pier serves (expensive) food and drinks; a little **supermarket** near the landing is a cheaper option. There's no accommodation but 7km away by chartered boat (R600 for up to four people) on a peninsula of Bolshoi Klimetskiy Island, the simple **Potanevshchina Guest House** (783 045; www.kposad.ru; full board per person per day R1800) has five double rooms (shared bathrooms) and a working *banya*.

Getting There & Away

From the end of May until August, **hydrofoils** (each way R1100) make the 1¼-hour trip from Petrozavodsk between once and five times daily according to demand and weather. The most likely departure times are at either 8.45am or 11am, and at either 11.30am or 12.15pm, with returns typically at 1pm and 4.30pm. The **Tourholding Karelia** (http://tourholding.ru/ru/trans_facil/sailings) website gives a more detailed timetable but that's not always fully observed: it's always worth double-checking (and booking) a day ahead at the Petrozavodsk **hydrofoil terminal** (Водный вокзал). Sporadic boats might run in early May and from September to mid-October, but don't count on a daily service.

In winter, some tour agencies can arrange visits to Kizhi by snowmobile or chartered helicopter from **Peski airfield**, 5km northwest of central Petrozavodsk.

Northern Lake Ladoga

The top attraction in this, Europe's largest lake, is the monastery island of Valaam. Coming from Petrozavodsk, it's most conveniently reached via Sortavala, though there's an alternative hydrofoil connection from the historic castle town of Priozersk (formerly Käkisalmi) in Leningradsky Oblast.

SORTAVALA — СОРТАВАЛА

81430 / POP 20,760 / MOSCOW

Founded by the Swedes in 1632, sleepy Sortavala became better known as Serdobol during its first Russian phase (1721 to 1812), when its quarries provided much of the stone for St Petersburg's great palaces. It was part of Finland until WWII, when, after severe bombing, its population evacuated and the area was forced into the USSR.

Sights

From the train station, walk for three minutes left along the tracks then right at the crossing. After two blocks turn left and you've found ul Karelskaya. Walking east along this main street, you'll pass Ladoga Hotel (one block), the turn for the museum (two blocks), the main bridge, ul Lenina (turn right to the port), pl Kirova, the **post office** (ul Karelskaya 19; 8am-8pm) and ul Kirova. Turn right there for **Bar Krona** (ul Kirova 6; beer R60; 9am-3am), the **bus station** (9am-6pm) and the market. Just off central pl Kirova, **Sberbank** (ul Komsomolskaya 8) has a 24-hour ATM. The Sortavala **tourist office** (ul Sadovaya 11; sortavalainfo@gmail.com) is nearby. **DiskusMedia** (wwww.touristmaps.ru) publishes road maps of southwestern Karelia (R80) including a Sortavala town plan.

Sortavala is primarily a launching point for reaching Valaam, but several century-old buildings make the charming low-rise centre worth a stroll about. Have a peek at ul Karelskaya 13, 19 and 27; the cute, wooden **firehouse** (ul Karelskaya 15); and the little **museum** (nab Ladozhskaya Flotili 5; 9am-5pm Mon-Fri, from 10am Sat & Sun), originally built in 1924 as a schoolroom. Those interested in the *Kalevala* will want to pay their respects to the *kantele*-plucking statue of bard **Petri Shemeikka** (pl Vainamoinen). Around 2km east around the lakeside is a striking **church**.

Sleeping & Eating

Consider booking accommodation ahead in summer, when all hotels tend to fill fast. As well as the following, other choices include the cheery **Hotel Scandinavia** (25 223; ul Sadovaya 28; s/d/tr with shared bathroom R1000/1800/2400) and **Hotel Ladoga** (40 244; ul Karelskaya 12; s R1800, d R3000-3050, tr R3900), Sortvala's oldest hotel (and it shows).

Hotel Piipun Pikha — HOTEL €€
(Chimney Yard; 23 240; www.kolmaskarelia.ru; ul Promyshlennaya 44; s/d/'elegant' R1900/2900/3900) Ingeniously converted from an old factory, and retaining its antique brick chimney (hence the name), this popular hotel has clean and comfy rooms, and the lakeside dining terrace (mains R180 to R330) is appealing. From the bus station, turn onto

ul Oktyabrskaya at Bar Krona, walk three blocks east, then after crossing the railway sidings, turn right and follow the road for 10 minutes. When you cross the next tracks the (unmarked) hotel is in front of you.

Hotel Kaunis HOTEL €€€
(☎24 910; www.ladogainfo.ru/page/info.php?id=22860; ul Lenina 3; s/d R3500/4650) It looks like a warehouse and the interior paintwork is a barfy green, but the Kaunis is the best portside option. Room standards are as high as the prices, with good linen and powerful showers. English is spoken and the restaurant (mains R175 to R350) has a narrow three-table balcony overlooking the port.

Getting There & Away

From Sortavala's **bus station** (ul Kirova; ⊙9am-6pm) a handful of daily buses to Petrozavodsk take four hours via Kolatselga (R310) and seven hours via Olonets (R360). Trains from Petrozavodsk arrive on even-numbered days at 7am and return on odd-numbered days at 0.18am. That's perfect timing for a one-day visit to Valaam. Trains from St Petersburg (six hours) are contrastingly poorly timed, arriving at midnight and departing Sortavala at 7.20am.

VALAAM ВАЛААМ

☎81430 / POP 200 / ⊙MOSCOW

This beautiful, mostly forested archipelago consists of around 50 isles tightly clustered around a 27.8-sq-km main island, where the **Valaam Transfiguration Monastery** (Валаамский Спасо-Преображенский монастырь; www.valaam.ru) is the main drawcard. If the crush of tourists here feels oppressive, explore a dozen other smaller churches, chapels and sketes on pretty headlands, quiet inland bays or bridged islets.

Mystics like to claim that Valaam was visited by St Andrew within a generation of Christ's crucifixion. True or not, a monastery was founded here around the late 14th century. Its dual role as fortress against Swedish invaders failed in 1611 when the Swedes destroyed it completely. Rebuilt in the 18th century with money from Peter the Great, the monastery burned down again in 1754. In the 19th century Valaam pioneered the idea of sketes, sort of halfway houses between hermitages and monasteries, where novice monks could retreat and learn from more experienced peers without the distractions of the main monastic community.

When the Soviet Union took northern Lake Ladoga from Finland in WWII, many of the monks and much of the monastery's treasure were moved to a site near Karvio, Finland, where the Uusi Valamo (New Valaam) monastery remains active. The Soviet authorities turned the original Valaam monastery into a home for war invalids. Today there's a renewed community of about 200 monks, the Transfiguration Monastery is beautifully restored and several outlying sketes have been rebuilt.

Most boats and hydrofoils from Sortavala arrive at the Monasterskaya landing, close to the main Transfiguration Monastery. However, most Priozersk hydrofoils and almost all cruise boats dock at Nikonovskaya Bay some 6km southwest along the island's unsurfaced main track. Numerous souvenir stands at both ports sell useful, if flawed, maps of the archipelago.

Sights

Map guides show various other interesting walks and attractions, but be aware that not all marked routes actually connect as shown. Do your homework before setting off on unknown paths: you're unlikely to meet many fellow walkers en route.

FREE **Transfiguration Monastery** MONASTERY
(Спасо-Преображенский монастырь; camera R50) To the left, souvenir stalls line the short road that leads via short-cut steps up to Valaam's main attraction. The monastery looks like the architectural equivalent of a nurse, all dressed up in blue and white with red crosses. With a sturdy spire and five teated domes, it appears more Catholic than Orthodox at first glance, an impression instantly dispelled upon entering. A stairway, splendidly muralled with saints, leads to an upper chapel that's a soaring masterpiece of gilt, icons and awe.

Nikonovskaya area HISTORIC BUILDINGS
Amid trees directly above the Nikonovskaya jetty, the modest red-brick **Resurrection Church** (aka New Jerusalem) isn't a real attraction but sporadic minibuses (R50) shuttle visitors to the main monastery. If none materialise, the 6km walk is blissfully peaceful. Alternatively, walk 1km west along the main track then, just beyond the pretty wooden **Gethsemane Skete**, take the forest footpath to the left, then soon after turn left again. This path winds round past the **Ascension Chapel** with lovely views down to a wood-lined bay, then curves down and back around past the **Konevsky Skete** to the Valaam **monastery farm complex**. From here you can return to Gethsemane Skete or walk

2km back to the main track near Tikhvin Bridge and hope for a passing vehicle to pick you up (not assured).

Gostiny Dvor HISTORICAL BUILDING

Directly southeast of the monastery cloister, the whitewashed Gostiny Dvor looks pretty grand from outside but the interior is far from renovated (except hotel sections).

FREE **Valaam Museum** MUSEUM

(camera R100) Of minor interest opposite the Monasterskaya dock, Valaam Museum is an old barn displaying local tools and fishing nets.

Nikolski Skete MONASTERY

For a great picnic site, stroll for about 20 minutes north of the Transfiguration Monastery to the quaint, heptagonal bell tower of Nikolski Skete.

Sleeping & Eating

In summer, booking ahead is virtually essential (25% fee). Eating options are limited and rather pricey on Valaam, with hotels holding the monopoly on restaurants and cafés.

Bring a picnic or your own snack stash. Otherwise, **stalls** at the jetties serve beer (R100), soft drinks and biscuits. There's a small **grocery** (⏲10am-2pm & 4-8pm) at the top of the monastery access steps, a **tea shack** in the 'old garden' section at the top and a tiny **bakery** window hidden deep within the northwest corner of the cloister.

Hotel Zimnyaya HISTORIC HOTEL €€

(Гостиница Зимняя, Winter; ☎38 248; http://valaam.twell.ru; Gostiny Dvor, 2nd fl; s R3000-3200, d R2000-2800, tr R2000) Don't be put off by the Gostiny Dvor building's decrepit entrance and stairways: the Zimnyaya's vaulted cell-rooms are (aptly) austere but they're clean and cosily decorated. All but three have shared bathrooms.

Hotel Letnaya HOTEL €€

(Гостиница Летняя, Summer; ☎44 593; ul Tsentralnaya; s R2400-2800, d R2800-3200) This new, completely rebuilt hotel (the original burnt to the ground in 2007) is a tasteful alternative to traditional Valaam accommodation. From the outside, it looks more like a stately home than a monks' cloister. Rooms are modest, yet comfortable.

Hotel Igumenskaya MONASTERY HOTEL €€

(Гостиница Игуменская; ☎44 543; Monastery Cloister; s/d R2180/2570) Wood-panelled rooms with simple beds and acceptable shared bathrooms come complete with an icon in a corner niche – don't forget to light the candle. From the top of the main approach stairway, enter the first lilac-scented courtyard of the main monastery, turn right and press the buzzer at the third door. There's no sign.

Getting There & Away

From June till early September it's usually possible to reach the island daily from Sortavala, though not 100% guaranteed: there's no exact timetable and trips are weather-dependent. Ask ahead at the Petrozavodsk or Sortavala tourist offices, or take a punt by simply showing up at the jetty around 8.30am. Most mornings there's at least one 9am hydrofoil (R600, 45 minutes); occasionally, you can grab a (paid) lift in a slower supply boat. Do double-check if, when and from which port boats are due to return. Booking a tour with one of many Petrozavodsk agencies is a safer bet, and Petrozavodsk's tourist office has plenty of information for the independent traveller.

In February and March a hovercraft runs from Sortavala, ice conditions allowing. With a minimum of seven passengers, tickets cost R1000 to R1500 per person.

Overnight river cruises run very regularly in summer from St Petersburg.

Kem & Rabocheostrovsk

☎81458 / POP 16,729 / ⏲MOSCOW

If you're heading for the Solovetsky Islands, the most reliable boat connection is from tiny Rabocheostrovsk, 12km northeast of Kem – a logging town in which you'll find the nearest railway station. Both Kem and Rabocheostrovsk have wooden churches and ramshackle waterfronts that are worthy of a few hours of exploration. However, most travellers get stranded here for a night or two, by which time Kem's soulless centre can feel a bit too familiar indeed.

KEM КЕМЬ

Outside Kem train station is pl Kirova where **Sberbank** (pl Kirova 3) has a 24-hour ATM. Pl Kirova continues east as pr Proletarsky passing the **post office** (pr Proletarsky 27; per hr R54; ⏲9am-6pm Mon-Fri, to 2pm Sat), where you can access the internet, after 1.5km. Some 700m beyond, pr Proletarsky meets Kemskaya Bay at a T-junction with ul Lenina. Turning left would take you to Rabocheostrovsk (12km). Alternatively, turn right and wind along the shore for 900m to find Kem's greatest attraction, the 1711 log-frame

Assumption Cathedral (Успенский собор; ul Vitsupa). Although almost constantly swathed in scaffolding, its quadruple wooden spires have a whimsical charm, as does its gentle setting amid the vegetable plots of older fishing-family homes. Across the road, the little **Museum Pomore** (ul Vitsupa 12; ⌚10am-5pm Mon-Fri, 11am-4pm Sun) has a nominal tourist information counter.

The railway dormitory (*obshchizhitye*) at pl Kirova 1 refuses tourists. That leaves just the unfriendly, overpriced **Hotel Kuzova** (Кузова; ☎22 257; ul Frunze 1; s R1800-2200, d R2400-3200, tr R4350-4650) shoved lugubriously amid semiderelict workshops some 200m south of pr Proletarsky 57 (halfway between the train station and post office). Russians pay half-price. You're better off staying the night in Rabocheostrovsk.

For those with more hunger than sense, the hotel has an uninspiring café and the station buffet is open until 11pm. If it's all too much to bear, several kiosks on pl Kirova sell beer.

At least six trains stop in Kem en route between Petrozavodsk (nine hours) and Murmansk (12 hours). However, to arrive early enough for a same-day boat connection to Solovki, the only sensible option is the overnight Vologda-bound train 373 from Murmansk (daily in summer, alternate days off-season), arriving at 6.30am. From St Petersburg (17 hours), train 22 arrives infuriatingly just too late (9am) to connect with the boat.

Returning from the islands, don't risk coronary-baiting levels of stress by hoping to catch train 21 to St Petersburg (departs Kem at 8.25pm). You'll probably fail anyway. The first day-train south to Petrozavodsk leaves at 5am.

Northbound trains are contrastingly well timed from Kem, mostly departing between 10.25pm and 1.30am, offering a good sleep en route to Murmansk.

Ticket windows are open 24 hours. Left luggage lockers are downstairs.

From the station to Rabocheostrovsk, 'Vokzal-Port' minibuses (R40, 25 minutes) run via the town centre every 20 to 40 minutes starting at 6.20am weekdays, 7am weekends. Board at the further of two unmarked 'stops' just beyond Sberbank on pl Kirova. Last service at 9pm.

A taxi to Rabocheostrovsk costs R300 to R400, or about R450 if you add a short diversion to admire the church en route.

RABOCHEOSTROVSK

РАБОЧЕОСТРОВСК

This low-rise port village sports three relatively new **wooden chapels**, one of which has an attached, ultrabasic dorm for penniless pilgrims. Boats to the Solovetsky Islands depart from behind the **Turkomplex Prichal** (☎56 060; www.prichalrk.ru/eng; Naberezhnaya 1; s R1400-2100, d R2000-3200, tr R2700-4200), whose reception desk sells the tickets. Popular with tour groups, the Prichal has pine-furnished rooms in eight chalet-style blocks. They're fairly bright and well maintained by enthusiastic staff. 'Superior' rooms have fireplaces.

Solovetsky Islands

Соловецкие Острова

☎8183590 / POP 900 / ⌚MOSCOW

Alternatively called Solovki, these distant, lake-dappled White Sea islands are home to one of Russia's most evocative and best-known monasteries. It's a holy yet haunted place: transformed by Stalin into one of the USSR's cruellest prison camps, Solovki was described in Solzhenitsyn's *Gulag Archipelago* as being so remote that a 'scream from here would never be heard'.

One day's enough to visit the main monastery site but taking two or three allows you to absorb the melancholy loneliness of the forests, bays and outer islands. Bring mosquito repellent, warm clothes and plenty of patience.

The archipelago has six main islands and over 500 lakes. By far the largest island, **Bolshoy Solovetsky** (24km by 16km) is home to the main monastery, which dominates the single low-rise **Solovetsky Village**. The ramshackle village suffers from the oppressive 'helicopter' drone of an insensitively located power station, but a short walk beyond in the virtually uninhabited hinterland you'll find profound, all-enveloping silence.

History

Many millennia ago, a now-forgotten people adorned these islands with 'labyrinths' and burial mounds, possibly considering Solovki a gateway to the spiritual world. Permanent occupation began in 1429 when monks from Kirillo-Belozersky Monastery founded a wooden hermitage at Savvatevo. Bequests and royal patronage meant the monastery rapidly grew into a rich landholder, and in the 1570s the complex became enclosed within vast fortress walls, useful as a defence against Swedish incursions. Ironically, greater damage was self-inflicted when from 1668 the monastery endured a seven-year siege for opposing the ecclesiastical reforms of Patriarch Nikon – doubly ironic as Nikon had been a young monk here (on Anzer Island).

In the early 19th century, the monastery was sliding towards decrepitude and few young men seemed interested in the harsh life of a Solovki hermit. What was needed was a good miracle. This came in 1854. In a bizarre sideshow to the Crimean War, two British frigates reportedly sailed by and bombarded the kremlin with nearly 2000 cannonballs. Somehow none did the slightest damage. This rather improbable 'divine intercession' put Solovki back into the minds of Russia's faithful. Donations rolled in and monks arrived to repopulate the monastery, which remained vibrant until the Soviet government closed it in 1921.

Two years later the islands were declared a work camp for 'enemies of the people'. At first, the prisoners were permitted to work fairly freely, keeping up the monastery's botanical garden and libraries. Many of them were scientists, writers, artists or priests. But it wasn't long until the camp was repurposed, turning into one of the USSR's most severe and dreaded Gulag camps. Prisoners were kept in intolerable conditions and tortured or killed on a whim: some experts say the Nazis adopted many inhumane practices from Solovki for their own concentration camps. The prison was closed in 1939, replaced by a naval training base.

Restoration work on the badly damaged monastery began in the 1960s. Monks started returning in the late 1980s and the islands acquired Unesco World Heritage listing in 1992. Today the monastic community is flourishing but reconstruction remains a long-term task.

PRISONERS OF THE MOTHERLAND

Billed 'the mother of the gulag' by Aleksandr Solzhenitsyn, Solovki was home to one of the USSR's first labour camps. Established in 1924, it was given the name SLON (Solovetsky Lager Osobogo Naznachenia; Solovetsky Special Purpose Camp). In Russian, 'slon' means 'elephant'; upon receiving their sentences, Solovki-bound prisoners grimly joked that they were 'off to see the elephant'.

But this wasn't the first time the monastery was used for less than pious purposes: 'undesirables' had been shipped off to the White Sea outpost since the reign of Ivan the Terrible. Prisoners of note included Count Pyotr Tolstoy – forebear of novelist and anarcho-pacifist Leo Tolstoy – and Cossack leader Petro Kalnyshevsky, who died on the island in 1803…aged 112!

Sights & Activities

Booklets and maps suggest numerous minor attractions, and the tourist office can get you to many of them if you can't face the long, lonely bicycle rides.

Solovetsky Transfiguration Monastery MONASTERY
(Спасо-Преображенский Соловецкий монастырь; ☎240; www.solovky.ru; ⏲8am-8pm, museums 10am-7pm Jun-Sep, 10am-5pm Oct-May)
This highly memorable monastery is the island's heart and soul. It's contained within a very impressive kremlin of massive boulder-chunk walls whose six sturdy fortress towers are topped with conical wood-shingle roofs. These, along with a quivering flurry of church towers and domes, reflect magnificently in Svyatoe Lake and look equally mesmerising viewed across the bay from the 1882 **Biological Station** (Соловецкая биологическая станция).

Entry to the kremlin yard and to some churches within is free. However, exhibition halls, linking corridors and fortress towers require tickets, purchased at the **Main Gate** (Святые Ворота, Svyate Vorota). In some cases, ascertaining which section requires which ticket can be slightly confusing: spot checks occur but there are no barriers. A few minor sections are limited to those on guided tours, and unannounced section closures are fairly common. Dress code is typical for active monasteries; ie skirts and headscarves for women, trousers rather than shorts for men.

The iconic 1566 **Transfiguration Cathedral** (Спасо-Преображенский собор) has distinctively powerful whitewashed walls, clusters of domes and a dazzling if very new six-level iconostasis upstairs.

With the ticket 'Raznitsa' (R100), take the corridor leading north to the majestically restored **St Nicholas Church**

Solovetsky Village

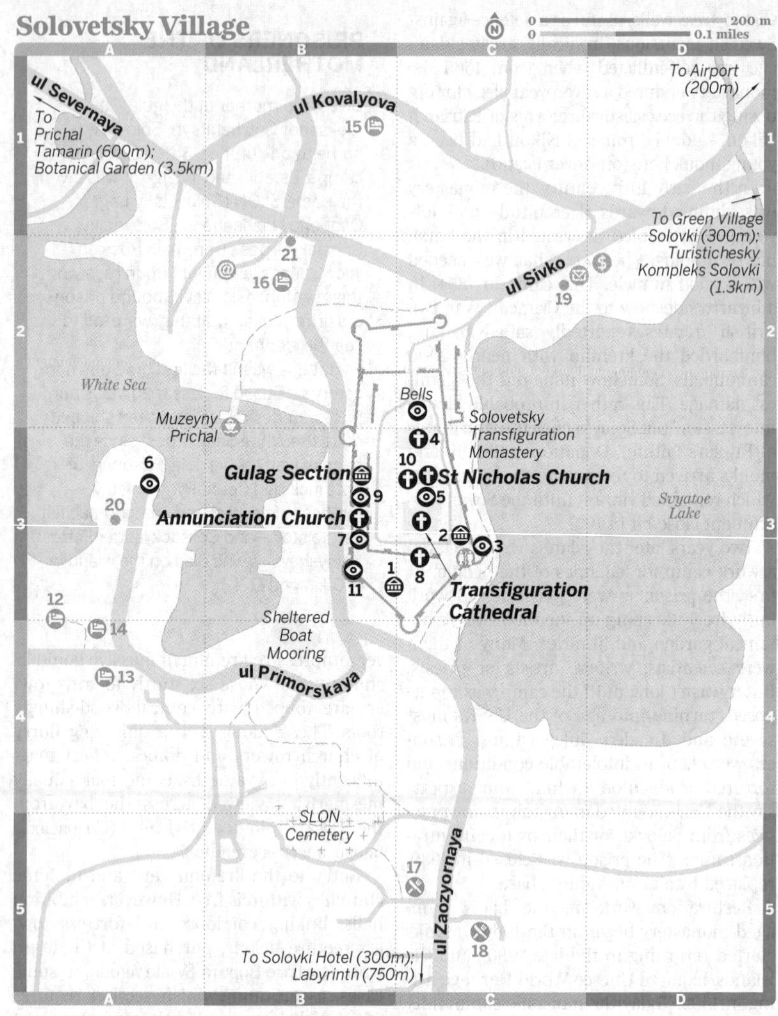

(Никольская церковь, 1832–34) and **bell tower** (Колокольня, 1777) or head to the **sacristy** where sad film footage of Stalin-era church destruction accompanies poignant exhibits of burnt and ravaged artefacts. The same ticket allows access to parts of the **Assumption Church** (Успенская церковь, Trapezny Kompleks), a cavernous former refectory with sparse photo-history boards focusing especially on the 1992 return of the relics of monastery founders Saints Zosima, Savvaty and Herman. Those revered relics were moved to the relatively plain, easy-to-miss **Filippovkaya Church** (Филипповская церковь; admission free) from the tiny but magnificently mural-covered 1601 **Annunciation Church** (Благовещенская церковь; admission free), which is entered through an unmarked door, one floor above the Main Gate. To continue down the 1st-floor **Citadel Gallery** walkway you're supposed to have the 'Gidrotekhnika' ticket (R100). This entitles visits to the cannon-decked **White Tower** (Белая Башня) and a **17th-century mill** with fascinating exhibitions explaining the monastery's medieval water and heating systems. If gates are open you can continue round to the **Arkhangelsk Tower**, descend-

Solovetsky Village

Top Sights

Annunciation Church B3
Gulag Section B3
St Nicholas Church C3
Transfiguration Cathedral C3

Sights

1 17th-Century Mill B3
2 Archaeological Exhibition C3
3 Arkhangelsk Tower C3
4 Assumption Church C3
5 Bell Tower C3
6 Biological Station A3
7 Citadel Gallery B3
8 Filippovkaya Church C3
9 Main Gate B3
10 Sacristy C3
11 White Tower B3

Sleeping

12 Hotel Priyut (Café & Check-in) A3
13 Hotel Priyut (Green House) A4
14 Hotel Priyut (Yellow House) A4
15 Hotel Solo B1
16 Peterburgskaya Hostel B2

Eating

Hotel Solo Café .... (see 15)
17 Kafe-Bar Kayut Kompania C5
18 Solovetsky Raipo C5

Information

Monastery Administration Building .... (see 2)
Tourist Office .... (see 16)

Transport

19 Nordavia C2
20 Veloprokat A3
21 Veloprokat B2

ing near the toilets to reach the **Archaeological Exhibition** (Експозиция Подземные Археологические Соловки; admission R120).

The poignant **Gulag Section** (admission R100) comprises two rooms documenting the horrors of the monastery's 20th-century history. Disappointingly, all text is in Russian; joining a tour (about R350) gives greater insight. Access is through the second door north of the Main Gate.

Labyrinths HISTORICAL SITE

Dating back around 4000 years, concentric swirls of shrub-covered stones known as labyrinths occur widely in northern Scandinavia, the Kola Peninsula and the outer Solovetsky Islands. Little **Zayatsky Island** alone has 13. A much more accessible example is just five minutes' walk south of the Solovki Hotel. Take the middle (small) woodland path where the track splits in three and the labyrinth is near the shore to your right. (This labyrinth is actually a 1960s replica but to the untutored eye it's just as good as the real thing.) The location is idyllic.

Botanical Garden GARDEN

(Ботанический сад; admission R100; ⏲8am-8pm) Around 3km northwest of the village, the botanical garden enjoys a special microclimate where monks have grown vegetables and hothouse fruits for centuries. For views, climb nearby Alexander Hill topped by the miniature **Alexander Nevsky Chapel** (1854).

Gora Sekirnaya HISTORICAL SITE

Literally translated as Hatchet Mountain, this infamous 71m hill was the site of alleged tortures in Aleksandr Solzhenitsyn's *Gulag Archipelago*. The unassuming hilltop **Ascension Church** (1857–62) was used for solitary confinement, and bodies of prisoners who died from cold and starvation were thrown down its steep stairs. At the foot of those stairs, a 1992 cross commemorates all who died on Solovki.

The site is about 10km from the village, 7km beyond the Botanical Garden towards **Savvatyevsky minor monastery**. Tours cost about R480 (minimum 15 people).

Wildlife Spotting BOAT TRIP

In early summer, white beluga whales *(belukha)* breed off Cape Beluzhy (west coast). You might spot seals when crossing from Kem. Ask at the tourist office about the possibility of organising a whale-watching trip.

Anzer Island HISTORICAL SITE

In the 1630s monks on Anzer Island broke from the jurisdiction of the main monastery. What now seem minor religious disagreements would have been forgotten long ago had not one of the monks, taking the name 'Vanquisher' (Nikon), later become Patriarch of Moscow. Nikon's church 'reforms' of the 1660s plunged the Orthodox Church into its deepest ever crisis. For Solovki, the result was a seven-year siege.

For groups of 10, visits to Anzer cost about R2000 per person including transport (enquire at the tourist office).

Tours

The tourist office has a whole slew of excursions. Thematic tours within the monastery (in English from R300) can be far more insightful than wandering around alone. Minibus trips to rural sites save exhausting pedal-power and avert the risks of getting lost in the forest. Tour pricing assumes a minimum of 10 (sometimes 15) people, but individuals can add their names to a sign-up list.

Sleeping

Most places operate only from early June to early September, sometimes closing in late August. Only Hotel Priyut stays open year round, and the http://welcome.solovky.ru/hotel.html website has a list of homestay options. Contact the tourist office about camping options.

Don't waste energy complaining about brownish, discoloured tap water: it's the same throughout the village. (It's fine for washing, though.) And please don't flush toilet paper: the sewers can't cope.

SOLOVETSKY VILLAGE

TOP CHOICE Hotel Priyut HOTEL €€
(Гостиница Приют; ☎297; shelter@atnet.ru; ul Primorskaya 11; s R2020-2600, d R2620-3450) People don't come to Solovki to loll about in their lodgings, but that's certainly a temptation at the Priyut. Family-run and heavy on the charm, it's comprised of two homely converted houses. The cheaper Yellow House (shared bathrooms) is adorably kitted out with dried flowers and endearing bric-a-brac, while the Green House's downstairs rooms have private facilities. Upstairs rooms have a communal WC but enjoy fabulous monastery views. The delightful **café** (breakfast/dinner R300/410) opens only for resident groups.

Solovki Hotel HOTEL €€€
(Соловки Отель; ☎331; ul Zaozyornaya 26; www.solovki-tour.ru; s R5000-5400, d R5700, lyux R8400-8700, VIP R9600-9800) With three double-storey log houses, a fine restaurant and woodsy setting, this is the island's poshest hotel. Standard rooms are cosy, though more expensive ones have twee pseudo-antique painted headboards and share a sitting room with a giant bearskin. Popular with tour groups despite rather dreamy service. Rates include breakfast.

Green Village Solovki HOTEL €€€
("Зелёная деревня – Соловки, Zelonaya Derevnya Solovki; ☎283; www.solovky.com; ul Sivko 20; s/d/polu-lyux/lyux/ste from R5600/5800/6600/7500/9300) Rooms in the upmarket option of Green Village Solovki have scented log walls, fine furnishings and excellent bathrooms. Unwind in the enticing lounge/library, in the (pricey) bar-restaurant or on the small balcony with perfect views across Svyatoe Lake to the monastery. Rates include breakfast.

Peterburgskaya Hostel HOSTEL €
(Петербургская; ☎321; dm/s/d/tr/q R600/1100/1600/2250/2400) Once a 19th-century inn, the Peterburgskaya Hostel is located in a large wooden building beside the monastery walls and it offers a range of spartan rooms. Showers (available 7am to 10am and 8pm to 11.30pm) and big communal washrooms are clean but the overall vibe is one of function over form.

Hotel Solo HOTEL €€
(Гостиница Соло; ☎246; solo-vky@yandex.ru; ul Kovalyova 8; s R1000-3500, d R2000-2600, tr R2850) Rooms at Hotel Solo are mostly dowdy affairs, some with small musty bathrooms and fake brick-effect wallpaper, but the café (breakfast R280, other meals from R320) is surprisingly good and has an open fire.

LAKE VARYAZHSKOE

Inconveniently located near little Lake Varyazhskoe, around 25 minutes' walk from the kremlin, are two relatively uninspiring *turbazy* (holiday camps). You're liable to end up here if you opt for cheaper Russian package tours.

Turistichesky Kompleks Solovki HOTEL €€
(☎221; www.solovkibp.ru; per person from R1700) The rickety cottages at Turistichesky Kompleks Solovki aren't especially bad, they're just not particularly thrilling.

Korpus 7 HOTEL €€
(s/d R3200/4000; ⏲from 2nd week of Jun) Korpus 7 is vastly better but hardly worth the walk-in rate.

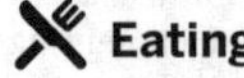

Eating

From early June, the **Solovki Hotel Restaurant & Bar** (mains from R350, beer R70; ⏲9am-10pm) and cosy **Hotel Solo Café** (mains from R150; ⏲9am-10pm) are open to nonguests.

Kafe-Bar Kayut Kompania CAFETERIA €
(Кают Компания; ul Zaozyornaya 4; meals from R80; ⏲8am-midnight Jun-Sep) The only non-hotel eatery is this passable *stolovaya* dishing up standard bellyliners.

SOLOVETSKY SOUL FOOD

While you're visiting Solovki, don't pass up the chance to sample one of Russia's most coveted culinary delights: Solovetskaya herring. A requisite dish on royal feasting tables, it was served with much fanfare to Vladimir Putin during an island visit.

The harvesting of herring began with the founding of the monastery itself in the early 1400s. Served salted, fried, in pies or – for the hardcore – raw, the humble herring is honoured each July–August with an eponymous **festival**. In addition to fishing and cooking competitions, contestants can vie for the title of best barehanded catch. Contact www.welcome.solovki.name for festival dates and details.

Solovetsky Raipo SUPERMARKET € (Соловецкий Райпо; ⏲9am-9pm, to 3am midsummer) Marked simply 'Produkty' (Продукты), this is the island's best stocked grocery.

Information

Dom Kulturni (per hr R80; ⏲10am-10pm Jun-Aug) The only internet in town.

Post office (Почта; ul Sivko 4; ⏲9am-1pm & 2-6pm Wed-Sat & Mon)

Sberbank (ul Sivko; ⏲9am-noon & 2pm-4.15pm Mon-Fri) No exchange or ATM but cash advances are theoretically possible. It's much safer to bring plenty of roubles with you to Solovki.

Tourist office (☎321; http://solovky.ru; Peterburgskaya Hostel; ⏲9am-7pm mid-May–mid-Oct) Information and a wide range of tours. Some English spoken. The office shifts into the **monastery administration building** (☎281) out of season.

Getting There & Away

Air

There are up to five weekly flights to/from Arkhangelsk in summer. Small planes should leave from Arkhangelsk-Vaskovo at 1pm every Monday, Wednesday and Friday (Wednesdays only in winter), returning at 2.15pm. You can reserve a seat directly at Solovki's minuscule **airport** (☎311) then pay on departure (from R3800, cash only). It can be easier to organise tickets on a bigger plane out of Arkhangelsk-Talagi, departing at 1.30pm on Sunday, Monday, Tuesday, Friday and Saturday in summer (Monday and Friday only in winter). They return from Solovki at 3pm. Book with **Nordavia** (☎236; www.nordavia.ru/eng; Post Office Bldg; ⏲9am-3pm Mon-Fri), either online, in Arkhangelsk or on the island. Be aware that all air transport is fraught with uncertainty, with planes unable to land in fog or strong winds. As both are common and weather can change incredibly rapidly, departures from Solovki can be confirmed only an hour before; ie once the incoming plane has actually left Arkhangelsk. Still, if Arkhangelsk is really where you want to get to, even waiting two days won't be much slower than taking the boat–train combination.

Midsummer flights to or from Petrozavodsk and tour agency charters from other cities operate sporadically.

Boat

Hydrofoils have been known to operate (summer only) to Solovetsky from Belomorsk, an area locally famed for its petroglyphs. However, the only really dependable **ferry service** (one way R800; ⏲early Jun–late Aug) leaves from Rabocheostrovsk at 8am and 10am, returning from Solovki at 4pm and 5.30pm. The crossing takes 2½ to three hours, depending on sea and weather conditions. There may be additional boats in peak season, but don't count on any. Ice usually prevents sailings in May but sporadic ferry services might continue as late as October.

Solovetsky village has several jetties *(prichaly)*. Most boats moor at **Prichal Tamarin** (Причал Тамарин), northwest of the village.

Getting Around

There are no taxis. To visit sites beyond the village, either join a tour offered by the tourist office or hire a bicycle from one of several outlets marked **Veloprokat** (Велопрокат; per hr from R50 or per day R350; ⏲mid-Jun–mid-Sep). Annoyingly, no bikes are available in early June, which would otherwise be an ideal time to visit Solovki. Island roads are bumpy, unpaved and suffer from sandy and muddy patches; it's worth paying extra for a bike with gears.

Central Kola

Rocks beneath the Khibiny and Lovozero mountains contain a freak show of exotic minerals that get the world's geologists and rock-collectors salivating. Apatity has secret museums, Kirovsk has the region's best skiing and the well-positioned Lovozero is the heart of Russia's Sami community. For all that, nonspecialist tourists may find that central Kola's attractions are rather limited, and certainly architecture here is wantonly uninspired. But for wilderness lovers, the area's understated Arctic majesty can prove addictive.

WORTH A TRIP

KOLA'S WHITE SEA COAST

With rafting, amethyst hunting, salmon fishing and petroglyph-gawking among its offerings, the Kola Peninsula's unspoilt southern shore is one of the region's offbeat delights. The **Varzuga River** is famous in angling circles for its first-class fly-fishing, with the prized Atlantic salmon found in remarkable abundance. Keen (and cashed-up) anglers can contact the UK-based **Roxtons** (www.roxtons.com) for information on all-inclusive six-day Varzuga packages. Just over 140km to the northeast, river camps near the coast's biggest town, **Umba**, also offer good, and far cheaper, spots to cast a line; **Yug Kola** (www.kolaklub.com/southkola) specialises in the Umba region. For further information on fishing the coast, visit the **Fish Pal** (www.fishpal.com/Russia) website.

Northwest of Umba, the cryptic petroglyphs (2nd to 3rd millennium BC) of **Lake Kanozero** have intrigued and bewildered experts since their discovery in 1997. Rafting tours stop at the island site. Between Umba and Varzuga, a gravel road takes rock-spotters to the **Tersky Coast**, where amethyst stones litter the coastline. Contact **Kola Travel** (www.kolatravel.com) for details on mineralogical and rafting expeditions.

The degree of welcome visitors will receive on the coast depends on the ever-changing status of regional town borders, which open and close to foreigners on a whim. Tour agencies can cut through the red tape on your behalf.

APATITY АПАТИТЫ

81555 / POP 61,300 / MOSCOW

The Kola Peninsula's second-largest town is a processing centre for Kirovsk's apatite mines (hence the name) and home to nine research institutes. Several of those have 'museums', though only the **Geological Museum** (Геологический музей; ul Fersmana 16; admission R15, full tour R50; 9am-1pm & 2-6pm Mon-Fri) is open to drop-in guests. Labelled mineral fragments are sold here as souvenirs. By appointment, more specialist visitors can arrange a guided visit to a second **Mineralogy Collection** (Минералогический музей; 79 739; root@geo.ksc.apatity.ru; ul Fersmana 14; admission free; 9am-5pm Mon-Fri by arrangement) on the top floor of the next-door Kola Scientific Centre. Friendly academics speak English but if you don't have the geological background to pose relevant questions, you're likely to feel embarrassingly out of your depth. Both museums are an easy stroll downhill from pl Lenina on Apatity's main drag, ul Lenina.

Experienced tour firm **Yug Kola** (Юг Кола; /fax 74 278; www.kolaklub.com/southkola; Room 114, Hotel Ametist; 10am-6pm Mon-Fri, 11am-5pm Sat) can get you into additional museums, including the interesting two-room **North-Russian Exploration Museum** (Музей истории изучения и освоения Европейского севера России; Akademgorodok 40a; admission R50; 10am-6pm Mon-Fri). Run by the super-enthusiastic Sergei Burenin and wife Viktoria, Yug Kola also offers tailor-made mineral-collecting, snowmobile and fishing tours on and around Kola's White Sea coast. Its office is within Apatity's conveniently central **Hotel Ametist** (Гостиница Аметист; 63 232; fax 74 118; ul Lenina 3; s R1300-1450, d R1450-1700, polu-lyux d R1950), which has basic but survivable old Soviet rooms and a bar-café. Nearby, the surprisingly stylish little **Kafe Yantar** (Кафе Янтарь; ul Kosmonavtov 8; mains from R150;) serves everything from stroganoff to sashimi. The **Druzhba supermarket** (Дружба; ul Lenina 5; 24hr) is exceptionally well stocked and also houses a bustling café.

For all transport bookings, use **MTA** (Мурманское Транспортное Агентство, Murmanskoe Transportnoe Agenstvo; ul Lenina 19; bus tickets 5.45am-1pm & 2-6pm, train tickets 10am-5pm Mon-Fri, 10am-2pm Sat), oddly hidden at the base of a residential tower block behind the street-facing shops.

Bus 130, originating in Kirovsk, runs to **Khibiny airport** (KVK; www.airkirovsk.ru), 14km south of Apatity. At research, only **Rusline** (www.rusline.aero) operates from the airport, with flights to Moscow on Tuesdays, Wednesdays, Thursdays and Saturdays (from R6525).

Apatity's **train station**, 3km west of the centre by rare bus 8 (R14), is on the main line between Murmansk (3½ to five hours) and Kem (seven to eight hours). An *elektrichka* (suburban train) to Kandalaksha (R48.20, 2¼ hours) departs at 3.40pm, returning at 10.20am.

Kirovsk-bound buses 101, 102 and 103 plus *marshrutky* (R30, 30 minutes) pick up just north of pl Lenina: pay on board. Four daily buses to Murmansk (R404, five hours) via Monchegorsk (R133, 1¼ hours) and Olenegorsk (R199, 1¾ hours) leave from the south side of pl Lenina, but tickets must be purchased in advance at MTA, often involving very lengthy queues.

KIROVSK КИРОВСК

81531 / POP 29,605 / MOSCOW

Though not exactly the Alps, Kirovsk is gaining renown as a popular ski/snowboarding destination, thanks to low prices, lack of Euro-style crowds and a season that can last as long as June. Founded in 1929 for mining the world's purest deposits of apatite (a source of phosphate for fertilisers), the town's remaining industrial detritus makes for an interesting contrast to the splendid natural surrounds. Most off-slope sights and hotels are within moseying distance from the central clock tower.

Kirovsk's derelict former train station gives crumbling testimony to Soviet antilogic. Like many of Russia's 'Potemkin villages', it was constructed only to impress visiting officials. Locals joke that its first and last passenger was Josef Stalin.

Sights

Kazan Church CHURCH

This neat church is home to the 'miraculous' Icon of St Nicholas, which apparently took the Biblical command 'heal thyself' to heart: believers allege the icon restored itself on a May night in 1994. The church is in Kukisvumchorr ('25km'): buses 1, 12, 16 and 105 (R12) run here from pr Lenina. Ask the driver to let you off.

Polar-Alpine Botanical Gardens GARDEN

(Полярно-альпийский ботанический сад; 51 436; pabgi@aprec.ru; 8.30am-4pm Mon-Fri by arrangement) From the church, walk 1.5km to a turn-off on the left and then another 1.7km from there to arrive at Russia's northernmost botanical gardens. Special hothouses nurture tropical plants and a 2km summer-only trail climbs to the alpine tundra. Keep in mind: bears are rare, but they are around.

Culture Castle THEATRE

(Дворец культуры; ul Mira; ticket office noon-6pm Mon-Fri, 11am-4pm Sat) Everything from classical concerts to Miss Kirovsk pageants are held in this impressive, pastel-yellow building next to the pool.

Activities

Bolshoy Vudyavr Ski Station SKIING

(Горнолыжный комплекс "Большой Вудъявр"; www.bigwood.ru) This is the best of Kirovsk's three ski stations, boasting modern lifts (R90 per ride) and downhill runs suitable for those of all abilities. Bring ID: you'll need it to hire equipment. It's just across the mountain east of Kirovsk but 12km away by road.

Old Ski Station SKIING

Immediately above town, a day on the slopes here is slightly cheaper and saves the R300 taxi fare.

Khibiny Mountains HIKING

Divided by deep valleys, the bald, barren Khibiny range offers keen hikers unusual summertime jaunts. Note that though the mountains only rise to 1200m above sea level, weather can be extreme and fast-changing: a guide is essential.

Delfin Swimming Pool WATER PARK

(ul Mira 9; per hr R300; 8am-2pm & 3-10pm Tue-Sun) For those who'd rather frolic indoors, this modern aqua-complex houses a jacuzzi, *hammam* and splashy water park.

Bolshoy Vudyavr Bowling Centre BOWLING

(Боулинг центр Большой Вудявр; pr Lenina 8; bowling per hr R500-700, cover after 5pm R100; 1pm-1am Wed-Sun;) Cavernous building that's also popular for its café-bar, billiards and a weekend disco (beware face control).

Sleeping & Eating

Hotel prices rise around 30% in ski season (November to May). At other times most places are half empty.

Hotel Gornitsa HOTEL €€

(Гостиница Горница; 59 111; ul Dzerzhinskogo 19; www.gornitsa.com; s R1600-1700, d R3000-3200, tr/q R4200/5200;) This unpretentious, family-style 16-room hotel is in fantastic nick, despite the hyper-colouration in some rooms. Winter visitors will appreciate the underfloor heating in bathrooms and sauna (from R600 per hour).

Hotel Severnaya HOTEL €€

(Гостиница Северная; 33 100; pr Lenina 11; s R1050-3000, d R2100-3600) This forest-green, outwardly classy neoclassical-styled hotel has 61 good-sized rooms, some of which have massive bathtubs. It's not quite as elegant as the exterior would suggest, but it's central and the staff are obliging. Cheaper 2nd-floor rooms are above the noisy restaurant.

Hotel Ekkos HOTEL €€

(Гостиница Эккос; 32 716; pr Lenina 12b; s R2350, d R2900-3300, tr/q/apt R3150/4200/5000)

This memorable 'castle' behind the Kirov statue may look a bit ramshackle from the outside, but the newly renovated rooms tell a different story. Breakfast isn't included, but there's a communal kitchen for self-caterers.

Hotel Kaskad MINIHOTEL €
(Гостиница Каскад; ☎95 603; ul Yubileynaya 14b; s & d R1300-1500) Friendly minihotel with five cosy, if not quite classy, over-colourful rooms and good location on the (oft-frozen) lake. Breakfast isn't included but there's an inexpensive on-site café.

Hotel Sport HOTEL €€
(Гостиница "Спорт"; ☎92 650; ul Dzerzhinskogo 7a; s R1000-1050, d R1500-1700, tr/polulyux R2100/2300) This drab, grey five-storey building contains utterly basic Soviet-era rooms with vinyl floors and simple shared bathrooms in all but the *polu-lyux*. Perhaps to make up for its other shortcomings, Sport offers guests discounts on ski passes and shuttles head to the slopes daily.

Kafe Vechernee CAFÉ €
(Кафе Вечернее; ul Khibinogorskaya 29; ⏰10am-10pm Mon-Sat, noon-8pm Sun) Precooked point-and-pick foods, salads and wonderful desserts sold by weight, with simple café tables at which to eat them.

Kafe Skaza CAFÉ €
(Кафе Сказка, Дворец культуры; coffee from R50; ⏰11am-7pm) Decked out in delirium-inducing colours and gigantic fake trees, this place is either a child's dream come true or a neurotic's worst nightmare.

ℹ Information

Khibiny (www.hibiny.ru/map/kirovsk.php) Interactive map.

Severo-Zapadny Telekom (Северо-Западный Телеком; pr Lenina 9; ⏰10am-9pm Mon-Sat) Public phones and internet booths (R1 per minute).

Tourist office (Туристический информационный центр; ☎55 506; pr Lenina 7; ⏰9am-1pm & 2-5pm Mon-Fri) Tucked behind the central Lenin statue.

ℹ Getting There & Away

Frequent *marshrutky* and local buses to Apatity (R30, 30 minutes) pick up along the main street.

Kola TAVS (Кола ТАВС; ul Yubileynaya 13; ⏰8.30am-7pm Mon-Fri, to 4pm Sat) sells tickets for buses to Murmansk (R374, 5½ hours) via Monchegorsk (R120, 1½ hours), leaving from outside Hotel Kaskad. It also sells train tickets ex Apatity.

MONCHEGORSK МОНЧЕГОРСК

☎81536 / POP 49,868 / ⏰MOSCOW

While Monchegorsk may not live up to its original promise ('Moncha' means 'beautiful' in Lappish), this neat, prosperous town makes a good base from which to explore the surrounding wilderness. Though still recovering from past transgressions – nickel smelting and noxious factory emissions among the worst of the offenders – Monchegorsk is attractively set between lakes and is the HQ of the **Lapland Biosphere Reserve** (http://laplandzap.ru). But wandering off into the wilds alone is neither smart nor productive: rather, get in touch with the experienced, multilingual **Kola Travel** (☎71 313; www.kolatravel.com; pr Lenina 15/2-11). This Russo-Dutch firm offers an inspiring selection of Kola adventures, including hiking, rock-hunting, snowmobile safaris and traditional hut-stays.

The town's brightly painted concrete-block architecture isn't an attraction in itself, but there's a fascinating central **Geological Museum** (Музей камня; pr Metallurgov 46; admission R50; ⏰noon-6pm Tue-Sun) that's good for a nose around, and the 1997 **Ascension Cathedral** (Вознесенский собор; Krasnoarmeyskaya ul 15) is impressive inside and out. It overlooks Bolshaya Imandra Lake, 3km southeast of town. The peculiar **Museum of Dwarves** (Музей гномов; ul Gagarina 14; admission R40) is alluring in its own creepy/kitsch way. This meticulously chronicled collection of trolls, elves, gnomes and the like is set up in the apartment of a local lore-keeper (open according to whim).

A concerted effort is being made to re-green the city, and a large lakeside **park** halfway down pr Metallurgov makes for pleasant strolling and people watching. To help you get around, an interactive city map is available at www.hibiny.ru/map/monchegorsk.php.

Hotel Sever (☎/fax 72 655; pr Metallurgov 4; s/d without bathroom R850/1200, s/d with bathroom R1300/3500) looks grand from outside but, though some rooms have been remodelled, it's not exactly swish. It's next to the congenial **Ani Kafe-Bar** (mains from R90; ⏰noon-2am) and directly across from the bright orange **Kaffe Kaffa** (⏰7.30am-11pm; 📶), which brews excellent coffees and – if you ask nicely – will whip up a mean reindeer *pelmeni* (Russian-style ravioli; R200).

Up the hill and directly overlooking the ridiculously wide central roundabout, the new **Laplandia Hotel** (☎74 551; www.laplan

dia.ru; Metallurgov 32; s R1000-2600, d R2600-3000, lyux R4500;) is a fancy, if somewhat generic, addition to Monchegorsk's limited accommodation scene.

Murmansk–Olenegorsk–Apatity–Kirovsk buses stop at Monchegorsk's dinky **bus station** (ul Komsomolskaya 25b), one block off pr Metallurgov. You can buy rail tickets here but the nearest train station is Olenegorsk.

Marshrutky 1 and 10 run between the hotels then double back past Kola Travel (an unmarked apartment, not an office), with number 10 continuing past the cathedral.

LOVOZERO & AROUND

The low cleft peak of twin mountain Karnasut–Kedikviparkh gives an appealing visual focus to this traditional reindeer-herding area, noted for its mystical Lake Seydozero. Tiny Lovozero isn't exotic but could make a decent base for hikes, enjoying the midnight sun or observing the northern lights. In Monchegorsk, **Kola Travel** (71 313; www.kolatravel.com) offers various exploratory trips to the region, including day trips to Lovozero plus Lake Seydozero.

OLENEGORSK ОЛЕНЕГОРСК

81552 / POP 23,670 / MOSCOW

To reach Lovozero, start from the Olenegorsk bus/train station on the Murmansk–Kandalaksha–Kem main line. The 80km road to Lovozero passes close to the impressively vast (but hidden) Olenegorsk open-cast iron-ore mine and right beside an antiquated if secretive tropospheric scattering watch-post for monitoring satellites. Otherwise the drive is wonderfully lonely and gives a real taste of central Kola's awesome Arctic wilderness.

If you get stranded in Olenegorsk, the unfriendly and overpriced **Hotel Gornyak** (55 281; ul Stroitelnaya 38; d without bathroom R1700-2000, s/d with bathroom R1700/3000) in the soulless city centre is a convoluted 5km (R150) taxi ride from the train/bus station. The bus station **café** (7am-8.30pm) offers consolation in the form of superb, home-made *pirozhki* (pies) for R22 a pop.

Buses to Revda (and thence Lovozero) leave daily at 11am, every day but Sunday at 6.20pm and 8pm, and at 10pm on Sundays. A ticket is R133. Monchegorsk–Murmansk buses stop here at least five times daily. There are two daily trains to Murmansk, departing at 9.50am and 6.30pm. For Kem, the perfectly timed train 373 (*platskart* R810, 10 hours) leaves Olenegorsk at 8.20pm (daily in summer, alternate days in the off-season).

REVDA РЕВДА

81538 / POP 6000 / MOSCOW

With a lovely setting close to Mt Karnasut, Revda's outer dacha/cottage area has a creaky charm but, 2km beyond, the Soviet-vintage town centre is a faceless loop of nine-storey concrete apartments entirely hiding the little cannon-fronted **museum** (ul Kuzhina 7/3) at the town's furthest end. Discussions are under way to capitalise on Revda's location by establishing it as a wilderness/ethno-tourism base, but for now it's best utilised as a miniature transport hub.

From central pr Pobedy, dusty old buses run to Olenegorsk at 5.50am and 8.30am daily, at 5pm Monday to Saturday and at 4pm Sunday. Departures to Lovozero (R44, 30 minutes) are at 8.15am, 1.20pm, 4.40pm and 7.55pm on weekdays, and 8.30am, 2.20pm and 7.55pm on weekends.

LOVOZERO ЛОВОЗЕРО

81538 / POP 2963 / MOSCOW

Under Stalin, the once-nomadic Sami (Lapp) people were brutally suppressed and forced into *kolkhozy* (collective farms). Today, of Russia's roughly 1600 Sami, close to 900 now live in the administrative village of Lovozero (Luyavvr), where a little **Sami History & Culture Museum** (Музей истории, культуры и быта кольских саамов; ul Sovetskaya 28; admission/camera/guided tour R25/50/100; 9am-1pm & 2-5pm Tue-Fri, 9am-4pm Sat) displays 2000-year-old petroglyphs and sells various Sami crafts including reindeer-fur slippers and carved bone-work. The reindeer herders are away between March and December, and outwardly the village doesn't look much different from other slowly decaying Soviet outposts. The exception is a pair of buildings nominally designed like stylised, oversized *chumy* (tepee-shaped tents). One of these is the **Sami Cultural Centre** (ul Sovetskaya 14). The other is the slightly apocalyptic-looking former Hotel Koavas, which was lying abandoned at the time of research. That leaves only the **Hotel Lovozero** (Отель Ловозеро; 30 169, 8-921-605 2020; ul Pionerskaya 6; dm per person from R700), a converted private apartment in a grim block across from the cultural centre. No English is spoken but the hospitable staff will arrange private accommodation in town (about R1000 per night) if they're booked out. For groceries, a small **produkty** (7am-midnight) is just across the way on ul Sovetskaya.

Buses to Revda (R35, 25 minutes) depart at 9.15am, 2.05pm, 5.30pm and 8.45pm on weekdays and at 9.25am, 3.30pm and 8.45pm on weekends.

LAKE SEYDOZERO ОЗЕРО СЕЙДОЗЕРО

Holy to the Sami, the beautiful 8km-long Lake Seydozero does seem to have a certain spiritual vibe. From Lovozero (22km), travel by boat (or skidoo in winter) followed by a 3km each-way walk. From Revda, drive 8km then trek 12km – rough and only possible when fords aren't too deep.

Murmansk Мурманск

8152 / POP 307,700 / MOSCOW

The world's biggest Arctic city is a bustling, rapidly modernising place set to become very wealthy as the development of the massive Shtokman gas field – one of the biggest in the world – gets under way in the Barents Sea. The majority of foreign visitors are Scandinavian businessmen paying almost Scandinavian prices. Tourism is an afterthought.

Murmansk's raison d'être is its port, kept ice-free by comparatively warm Gulf Stream waters that sweep around the Norwegian coast. Founded in 1916 as Romanov-na-Murmanye, the city developed almost overnight during WWI, and was occupied till 1920 by pro-White allies fighting the Bolsheviks. Renamed Murmansk, the 'hero city' was bombed to bits in WWII and rebuilt with stolidly uninspired Soviet-era architecture.

But it's not all just blocky buildings and businessmen up here: the city is an easily accessible base for outbound Arctic adventures and offers some unique natural attractions of its own. From late May to late July, the sun never sets – bring sunscreen and sunglasses in case the clouds clear. From 29 November to 15 January, the sun doesn't peep above the horizon, but the long winters have a singular appeal. The northern lights on the snow-covered landscape can be magical, and it's claimed that Murmansk's fresh polar air was the inspiration behind the distinctive bouquet of Chanel No 5, created by Ernest Beaux after completing a military stint nearby.

The central hub is pl Pyat Uglov (Five Corners Sq), with the main thoroughfare pr Lenina extending many kilometres south as pr Kolsky. Parallel ul Shimdta/Kominterna/Chelyuskintsev extends past Lake Semyonovskoe into the northern suburbs. For city maps, check the Murmansk phone book or download from **murmansk.aspolru** (http://murmansk.aspol.ru/maps/index.html).

Sights

Alyosha MONUMENT

By far Murmansk's most memorable sight is a gigantic concrete soldier nicknamed Alyosha. His sheer immensity and curiously placid half-smile are mesmerising. Commemorating the fighters against the devastation of the Great Patriotic War (WWII), Alyosha's hilltop perch surveys a vast sweep of Kola Inlet and snow-speckled Arctic moors beyond. To the south the city spreads out in all

TOP SECRET

During the Cold War, the Murmansk area housed the world's greatest concentration of military and naval forces. Despite drastic scale-backs, the Kola Peninsula is still home to plenty of closed military zones known as ZATOs (Zakrytye Administrativo-Territorialnye Obrazovania; Closed Administrative-Territorial Formations):

Severomorsk is headquarters of the Northern Fleet.

Shtyukozero, 8km beyond, was the scene of a potentially catastrophic near-miss in 1984 when a fire swept through silos bristling with nuclear-tipped missiles.

Polyarny and **Gadzhievo** are nuclear submarine bases, with over 50 decommissioned reactor compartments stored at nearby Sayda-Guba.

Vidyaevo and **Zaozersk** nuclear submarine bases are west of the Kola Inlet. Vidyaevo was the home port of the ill-fated *Kursk*.

Ostrovnoy on the Kola Peninsula's remote eastern coast is a former submarine base that's now a dumping and recycling centre for dismantled submarines and radioactive waste.

Don't even think about entering any closed city or zone without special permission and the paperwork to prove it. For foreigners without high-level contacts, arranging such permits is virtually impossible.

BREAKING THE ICE

It should come as no surprise that the Russians were the inventors – and perfectors – of the ice-faring vessel. The northern Pomors constructed the first ice-clearing ships (called *kochy*) in the 11th century, built with ice-resistant hardwood and used for the exploration of Arctic waters. The boats' round shape propelled them onto the ice when squeezed by floes.

Fast-forward 900 years, where the development of nuclear icebreakers has literally cleared the way for northern-bound cargo ships, scientific voyages and tourist expeditions with a force hitherto thought impossible with diesel-powered predecessors. Today's vessels – mammoth double-hulled constructs comprising steel bows and two onboard reactors – power their way through ice up to 3m thick at speeds reaching 10 knots. Nuclear icebreakers are stationed at Murmansk's Atomflot base at Kola Bay.

If a tour of the decommissioned NS *Lenin* isn't enough for you, try a two-week visit to dramatic Franz Josef Land and on through the ice to the North Pole. Packages start at around US$22,000. Don't expect to arrange things at the last minute. Berths are presold way ahead through (often foreign) adventure-tour operators, including **Blue Water Holidays** (www.cruisingholidays.co.uk), **Nordic Travel** (www.nordictravel.ru), **Quark Expeditions** (www.quarkexpeditions.com) and **Poseidon** (www.northpolevoyages.com). Quark and **Arcturus** (www.arcturusexpeditions.co.uk) also offer Northeast Passage cruises to/from Alaska.

its magnificent pastel-concrete dreariness. The icy air carries a distant soundtrack of clanking cranes and rail wagons from the romantically bleak port. Walking to the statue from one of the Ozero bus stops (trolleybus 4, bus 10) takes 20 minutes.

Oceanarium ZOO
(Океанариум; adult/child R400/300; ⌚shows 11am, 3pm & 5pm Wed-Sun) After bidding farewell to Alyosha, walk clockwise around Lake Semyonovskoe to arrive at this little bubble-domed building, home to the cutest seal shows this side of the North Pole. A sweet funfair beside it is a treat in summer and lies splendidly abandoned in winter.

Church of the Saviour on the Waters CHURCH
(Храм Спас-на-Водах; ⌚11am-7pm) Walking anticlockwise from Alyosha will take you along a footpath to this gold-domed church built in 2002 from public donations.

Lighthouse Monument MONUMENT
(Памятник Маяк; ⌚11am-5pm Wed-Sun) Just below the church, this evocative memorial commemorates lost sailors including the 118 crew of the *Kursk* nuclear submarine that sank in the Barents Sea in 2000.

Nuclear Icebreaker BOAT
(Атомный ледокол; Murmansk Port; admission R110; ⌚tours noon Wed-Fri, noon, 1pm & 2pm Sat & Sun) Give in to your wildest seafaring/Arctic explorer/Cold War spy fantasies with a nose around the 1957 NS *Lenin*, the world's first nuclear-powered icebreaker. Tours are in Russian only but the chance to press vaguely sinister-looking red buttons and rifle through old Soviet map rooms is worth every rouble. However, not everyone will appreciate the Atomflot-sponsored 'nuclear energy is awesome' presentation at the end. It's at the port, behind the blue Passenger Terminal Building.

Museum of the Northern Fleet MUSEUM
(Военно-морской музей Северного флота; www.severnyflot.ru; ul Tortseva 15; admission R150; ⌚9am-1pm & 2-5pm Thu-Mon) It's not just naval buffs that will thrill to this museum's 65,000 exhibits covering the founding of Russia's first navy in Arkhangelsk, the Murmansk convoys of WWII and the modern fleet. The museum is 5km north of the centre within a turquoise, somewhat crumbling three-storey cultural centre fronted by anchors. Take bus 10 to the penultimate stop ('Nakhimova', opposite ul Admirala Lobova 43), walk on for 300m, then turn left and it's 80m up ul Tortseva.

Regional Studies Museum MUSEUM
(Краеведческий музей; pr Lenina 90; admission R50; ⌚11am-6pm Sat-Wed) Murmansk's oldest museum features geology, natural history and oceanography on the 2nd floor. Kola Peninsula history, including the fierce defence of the north during the Great Patriotic War,

Murmansk

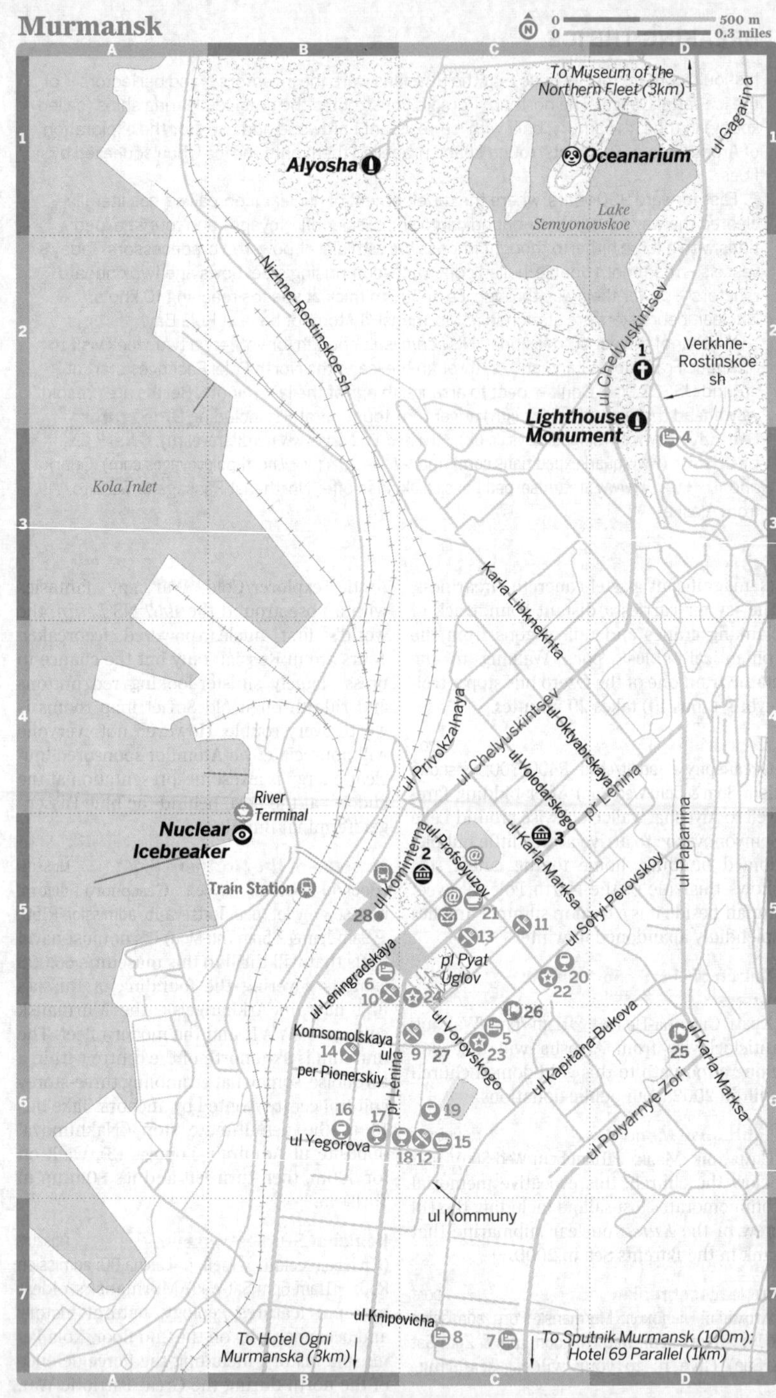
0 500 m
0 0.3 miles
To Museum of the Northern Fleet (3km)
ul Gagarina
Alyosha
Oceanarium
Lake Semyonovskoe
Nizhne-Rostinskoe sh
ul Chelyuskintsev
1
Verkhne-Rostinskoe sh
Lighthouse Monument
4
Kola Inlet
Karla Libknekhta
ul Privokzalnaya
ul Chelyuskintsev
ul Oktyabrskaya
ul Volodarskogo
pr Lenina
ul Papanina
River Terminal
Nuclear Icebreaker
3
ul Kominterna
2
ul Profsoyuzov
ul Karla Marksa
ul Sofyi Perovskoy
Train Station
28
21
11
13
ul Leningradskaya
pl Pyat Uglov
20
22
6
10
24
26
Komsomolskaya ul
14
per Pionerskiy
9
27
ul Vorovskogo
5
23
ul Kapitana Bukova
25
ul Karla Marksa
pr Lenina
16
17
19
ul Polyarnye Zori
ul Yegorova
18
12
15
ul Kommuny
ul Knipovicha
8
7
To Hotel Ogni Murmanska (3km)
To Sputnik Murmansk (100m); Hotel 69 Parallel (1km)

Murmansk

Top Sights
Alyosha ... B1
Lighthouse Monument ... D2
Nuclear Icebreaker ... B5
Oceanarium ... C1

Sights
1 Church of the Saviour on the Waters ... D2
2 Fine Arts Museum ... C5
3 Regional Studies Museum ... C5

Sleeping
4 Hotel Arktik-Servis ... D3
5 Hotel Gubernskiy ... C6
6 Hotel Meridian ... B5
7 Hotel Moryak ... C7
8 Park Inn Hotel Polyarnye Zori ... C7

Eating
9 Baltiyskiy Khleb ... C6
10 Chaynaya Lozhka ... B5
Fresh ... (see 9)
11 Kafe-Bar Sever ... C5
12 Mama Mia ... C6
13 Supermarket ... C5
Torro ... (see 6)
14 Traktir Zhily-Bily ... B6

Drinking
15 Café La Vita ... C6
16 Churchill ... B6
17 Fusion ... B6
18 Leto ... C6
19 Pinta Pub ... C6
20 Pivnoi Dom ... C5
21 Yunost ... C5

Entertainment
Marrakech ... (see 16)
22 Murmansk Puppet Theatre ... C5
23 Philharmonia ... C6
24 Philharmonia Ticket Office ... C5

Information
25 Finnish Consulate ... D6
Flait ... (see 6)
26 Norwegian Consulate ... C6
Swedish Consulate ... (see 26)

Transport
27 Gulliverrus ... C6
Rossiya ... (see 8)
28 Train Ticket Windows ... B5

is covered on the 3rd floor. There's a reasonable souvenir shop too.

Fine Arts Museum MUSEUM
(Художественный музей; ul Kominterna 13; admission per exhibit R60; ⌚11am-6pm Wed-Sun) The 1927 Fine Arts Museum hosts temporary exhibitions of varying quality.

Festivals & Events

Festival of the North SPORTS
(Праздник Севера) The annual 10-day Festival of the North in late March to early April includes a 'Polar Olympics' with reindeer-sled races, ski marathons, ice hockey and snowmobile contests. Many events are held at Dolina Uyuta (Cosy Valley), 25 minutes south of the train station by bus 1. Book well in advance, as hotels fill up fast.

Sleeping

With the vast Hotel Arktika in pl Pyat Uglov under seemingly endless reconstruction, Murmansk has a serious shortage of hotel beds. Given the endless stream of business travellers arriving to gas about gas, booking is very wise despite most hotels enforcing a reservation fee (usually 25% of one night's room rate). Most prices rise 30% during the trade exhibitions of May–June and mid-November.

TOP CHOICE **Hotel 69 Parallel** HOTEL €€
(☎253 700; www.69parallel.ru; proezd Lizhny 14; s R1200-1800, d R1800-2500, ste R2500-3000) Clean, bright, simple rooms with wooden floors and an unexpectedly classy 'boutique'(ish) vibe sorely lacking in northern Russia. The same can't be said for the two-room suite, which is a pink nightmare awaiting its Barbie. A particularly good spot if you're coming for Festival of the North.

Park Inn Hotel Polyarnye Zori HOTEL €€€
(Отель Полярные Зори; ☎289 500; www.parkinn.com/hotel-murmansk; ul Knipovicha 17; s R3600-4900, d R4400-5900, ste R8500-19,500; 📶) An understandable favourite for Westerners and Russian wheelers and dealers, this spotless business hotel has efficient English-speaking staff, a pub, restaurant, nightclub, saunas, business centre and

big buffet breakfasts. Most rooms are international business-style with cable, flat-screen TVs and underfloor heating in the bathrooms.

Hotel Arktik-Servis HOTEL €€
(Гостиница Арктик-Сервис; ☎312 659; Verkhne-Rostinskoe sh 1; 2/3-room apt R3000/4000) Within a rather gruesome-looking high-rise tower block, this is not really a hotel at all: each simple, spacious serviced apartment could sleep a football team. All this and breakfast too. Astoundingly good value compared to anything else in Murmansk. Bus 18 passes by.

Hotel Moryak HOTEL €
(Гостиница Моряк; ☎688 702; hotel_seaman@msco.ru; ul Knipovicha 23; s/d from R600/1200) The nearest Murmansk gets to budget accommodation, the Moryak enjoys a good location and sports decent, well-maintained rooms. The folks at reception suffer occasional mood swings, but are otherwise helpful. Frequently full.

Hotel Ogni Murmanska HOTEL €€
(☎554 000; www.ognimurmanska.ru; Sankt-Peterburgskoe sh km8; s R3000-3900, d R3900-4900, polu-lyux R4200-6300, lyux R4800-9800; 📶🏊) Overlooking the city from the eastern hills, this fairly classy place offers reasonable value, and while the location isn't very convenient for town, the hotel does have its own ski slope. Not for those with *The Shining*-inspired neuroses.

Hotel Meridian HOTEL €€€
(Отель Меридиан; ☎288 650; www.meridian-hotel.ru; ul Vorovskogo 5/23; s R3200-4900, tw R5900-6800, ste R7300-21,900; 📶) The Meridian sees itself as a top business hotel. It's tidy and wonderfully central, but beds are narrow and furnishings rather lacklustre given the price. There's in-house bowling, free breakfast, a boisterous disco and scary-looking security guys in the lobby at night.

Hotel Gubernskiy HOTEL €€
(Губернский; ☎459 237; ul Sofyi Perovskoy 3; s/d/tw/apt from R900/2200/1800/4000) Nostalgia trippers and Soviet-era enthusiasts will enjoy this throwback, replete with fading nature-wallpapered smoking rooms and bedrooms á la Brezhnev. That said, it's comfortable enough, staff are cooperative and the buffet breakfasts are big enough to feed a (red) army.

Black Belt MINIHOTEL €€
(Гостиница Черный Пояс; ☎277 500; http://black-belt.ucoz.ru; proezd Svyazi 16; s/d/tw from R1300/2000/3000) This modest spot offers simple rooms with shared bathrooms and good views over the city from its vantage point in Murmansk's hilltop residential area. Some English is spoken, but staff go out of their way to help however they can.

Eating

TOP CHOICE **Traktir Zhily-Bily** RUSSIAN €
(Once Upon a Time; ul Samoylovoy 5; mains from R180; ⏲11am-11.30pm) Hyper-rustic fun with home-style Russian cooking dished up beneath pastoral scenes in incongruous shades of fluoro. You will be seated in novelty wooden chairs shaped like wagons whether you like it or not.

THE BIG CHILL *TAMARA SHEWARD*

'*Vy morzh!*' I cried. 'You're a walrus!' The chubby pink babushka nodded, beaming and not a bit insulted by my having essentially called her a blubbery sea creature. Of course she was a walrus: why else would she be prancing about in her swimsuit in -7°C?

I'd stumbled across the Murmansk 'school of winter swimming and cold hardening' by accident, following an unmarked path across the road from the Church of the Saviour on the Waters just for the hell of it. It's here where self-confessed *Morzhy* plunge into winter waterholes cut into the icy Lake Semyonovskoe for health benefits including increased blood flow, immune system boosting and sex-life enhancement. Not that my Walrus was citing the specifics: 'I feel amazing every time I swim here,' she said, clutching me with a hand as smooth and cool as marble. 'I will live to 100.' I asked if many young people joined her in her daily dips. 'No,' she said, lowering herself back into the slate-grey water for another fix. 'They're soft. But I will outlive them all because they are just people and I am a *Morzh*.'

It's not often updated, but you can check out the doings of Murmansk's Walruses at www.murman.ru/morzh.

Fresh SUSHI €€
(ul Samoylovoy 6; sushi sets from R400; ⌚11am-midnight) Murmansk is in the grip of sushi mania, with anything even notionally aquatic being wrapped in seaweed to sate demand. Fresh, thankfully, lives up to its name, delivering top-quality rolls and sushi sets in superhip surrounds.

Torro STEAK €€€
(☎451 700; pr Lenina 80; mains from R400; ⌚noon-midnight; 📋) This ultraelegant restaurant seems out of place with the rough-and-tumble street corner it's perched on, but one look at its exceptional steak menu is enough to make one forget about things like 'the real world'. A special-occasion treat if you've got roubles to char-grill. Reservations recommended.

Mama Mia ITALIAN €€
(Мама Миа; ☎takeaway 478 247; ul Yegorova 14; mains R117-395, pizzas from R200, beer R70; ⌚noon-midnight) Cosy, understated and understandably popular, Mama Mia specialises in great, large pizzas and regional meat-and-berry dishes. Taste both by ordering reindeer *(olenina)* pizza.

Kafe-Bar Sever CAFÉ €
(Кафе-бар Север; ul Profsoyuzov 20; light meals from R50; ⌚10am-9pm) Sip coffee from straws and tuck into prawn salad or bain-marie sangas in this old-school Soviet canteen, complete with red carpeted walls and requisite babushkas who may or may not have been sitting at the same table for the last 50 years.

Chaynaya Lozhka RUSSIAN €
(Чайная ложка; pr Lenina 80; lunch sets R80-140; ⌚9am-10pm) Reliable, youthfully bright-orange chain café serving bliny, tea and salads cafeteria-style.

Baltiyskiy Khleb BAKERY €
(Балтийский Хлеб; ul Samoylovoy 6; ⌚9am-10pm) For self-catering, there's this tempting European-style bakery.

Supermarket SUPERMARKET €
(pr Lenina 71; ⌚7am-midnight) Grocery with huge variety and premade food.

🍷 Drinking

Pinta Pub PUB
(ul Yegorova 13a; beer from R80, ⌚noon-midnight Mon-Thu & Sun, to 5am Fri & Sat) With its Germanic facade, Scottish decor and Merry Old England bathroom tiles, geography mightn't be the Pinta's strongest point, but who cares when it has its own on-site microbrewery? A quiet eatery by day, this two-level pub morphs into a wild party palace by night, with regular live gigs by everyone from Irish folk singers to jazz troupes.

Black Cat BAR
(Черный кот; ul Burkova 17a; beers R50; ⌚11am-late) Fun local hang-out tucked away in the housing blocks overlooking Murmansk. Entertainment is provided by burly locals singing karaoke odes to the Kola wilderness.

Red Pub PUB
(Ред Паб; Molodyozhny proezd 12; ⌚noon-2am) Fun if out-of-centre Soviet-nostalgia pub. It's 10 minutes' walk from the trolleybus 6 route along pr Kolsky.

Yunost CAFÉ
(Юность; pr Lenina 86; desserts from R40, ⌚10am-midnight) Colourful café the sweet-toothed won't want to miss, with good coffee and dreamy cakes.

Leto BAR
(Лето; pr Lenina 61; espresso R95, margarita R250; ⌚noon-11pm Sun-Thu, to midnight Fri & Sat) Fast-paced and hip, with lime-green, blood-red and apricot-orange decor dangling with long conical funnel-lamps. Serves coffee, cocktails and nibbles.

Fusion BAR
(pr Lenina 72; ⌚10am-midnight) Get your pout on and hang with the mojito maniacs posing at glowing ice-blue tables in this minimalist-chic cocktail bar.

Pivnoi Dom SPORTS BAR
(Пивной Дом; ul Sofyi Perovskoy 25; ⌚11am-2am) Smoky but characterful local sports bar with a long list of imported and inexpensive beers.

Café La Vita CAFÉ
(ul Yegorova 13; coffee R54-130; ⌚8am-1am Mon-Fri, 11am-1am Sat & Sun) Tasteful, gently upmarket coffeehouse with old piano and typewriters as wall decor.

Churchill PUB
(ul Samoylovoy 10a, ⌚noon-1am Sun-Thu, to 3am Fri & Sat) Anglo-pub decked out with photos of Winston and other cigar aficionados. When the embers start to cool, head next door to late-night club **Marrakech**.

☆ Entertainment

In addition to venues listed here, most of the better hotels have their own nightclubs on the premises.

Philharmonia LIVE MUSIC
(Филармония; ul Sofyi Perovskoy 3; ⏲most shows 7pm Sep-Jun) For opera, folk music or classical concerts, buy tickets in advance from the **ticket office** (pr Lenina 67; ⏲noon-2.30pm & 3.30-6pm Tue-Sat).

Murmansk Puppet Theatre PUPPET THEATRE
(Мурманский областной театр кукол; www.murmanpuppet.ru; ul Sofyi Perovskoy 21a; tickets R30-50; ⏲shows usually 11.30am & 2pm Sat & Sun)

Pilot Club NIGHTCLUB
(www.pilotclub.ru; Kolsky pr 154; admission Thu-Sun from R150; ⏲10pm-5am) Industrial-design techno/house/pop club popular with teenagers. Pilot and several other large nightclubs, including Sfera, are located far south of the centre (trolleybus 6).

MJ Club NIGHTCLUB
(ul Halatina 2a; admission from R100; ⏲9pm-late Thu-Sun) The MJ – yes, as in 'Michael Jackson' – experience starts as soon as you put hand to white-glove door handle. 'Off the Wall', indeed.

Sfera BOWLING, NIGHTCLUB
(Сфера; Kolsky pr 27) Entertainment complex located far south of the centre (trolleybus 6) including bowling (from R600), billiards and two nightclubs.

ℹ Information

Akvatoriya (Акватория; ul Profsoyuzov; per hr R60 plus per MB R3; ⏲9am-10pm) Internet access in a roadside outbuilding of the Sever Stadium.

Barents Observer (www.barentsobserver.com) Regional news portal with many informative links.

Flait (Флайт, Flight; ☎289 551; www.russia-media.ru; Hotel Meridian; ⏲10am-6pm Mon-Fri, to 2pm Sat) Professional, multilingual agency offering travel bookings, visa help, translation and business-support services. A few self-drive cars are available for hire, and it organises additional to-order car and minibus transfers.

Main post office (Почта; pr Lenina 82a; ⏲9am-2pm & 3-7pm Mon-Sat, 11am-2pm & 3-6pm Sun)

Murman (www.murman.ru) News, weather, flights and other useful service listings.

Murmanout (http://murmanout.ru/places) Wide-ranging listings with customer comments. See http://murmanout.ru/events for what's on.

Murmansk Tourism Portal (www.murmantourism.ru)

Severo-Zapadny Telekom (Северо-Западный Телеком; ul Leningradskaya 27; ⏲9am-8pm Mon-Fri, 10am-6pm Sat & Sun) Modern public call office with internet booths (R1 per minute).

ℹ Getting There & Away

TsAVS (ЦАВС; ul Knipovicha 18; ⏲8am-7pm Mon-Sat, to 5pm Sun) sells train and air tickets for a R150 commission.

Air

Some of the airlines using Murmansk's **airport** (MMK; www.airport-murmansk.ru):

Finnair (www.finnair.com) Three weekly flights (summer only) between Murmansk and Helsinki.

Nordavia (☎449 644; www.nordavia.ru/eng) Flies thrice daily to Moscow and once daily direct to St Petersburg. On Wednesdays and Sundays also flies to Arkhangelsk (from R7660, two hours) and Tromsø, Norway (from R9160).

Rossiya (www.rossiya-airlines.com/en; foyer, Park Inn Hotel Polyarnye Zori; ⏲9am-7pm) Daily to St Petersburg (from R5200, 1¾ hours) and Moscow Vnukovo (from R6000, 2¾ hours).

Sky Express (www.skyexpress.ru) Daily budget flights to Moscow Vnukovo.

Bus

From Murmansk's **bus station** (Автовокзал; ul Kominterna 16) buses at 8am, 3pm, 4.40pm, 5.15pm and 5.50pm run to Kirovsk (R434, 5½ hours) via Olenegorsk (R205, three hours), Monchegorsk (R271, 3½ hours) and Apatity (R404, five hours).

FINLAND On Monday, Wednesday and Friday a bus runs to Rovaniemi (R3580, 12 hours) via Ivalo (R2200, 6½ hours, 8.30am) from the bus station.

NORWAY Two daily minibuses run to Kirkenes (4½ to six hours). **Sputnik Murmansk** (Спутник Мурманск; ☎443 333; www.sputnikmur.ru; ul Polyarnye Zori 12) charges R1000/1200 to Kirkenes town/airport. The minibus leaves the Park Inn Hotel Polyarnye Zori at 7am (noon on Sunday), collecting from the Hotel Meridian 15 minutes later.

Gulliverrus (Гулливеррус; ☎454 542; www.gulliverrus.ru; ul Vorovskogo 13; ⏲10am-6pm Mon-Fri, 1-5pm Sat) charges R1000/1100 for the run to Kirkenes. Its minibus departs from outside its office at 7am, and returns at 5pm (Moscow time).

Returning from Kirkenes, both minibuses depart from near Rica Arctic Hotel. For either, book through **Pasvikturist** (☎+47-7899 5080; www.pasvikturist.no; Dr Wesselsgate 9, Kirkenes; ⏲8.30am-4pm Mon-Fri), two short blocks away on Kirkenes' central pedestrian street.

Train

From the **train station** (ul Kominterna 14) at least two daily trains run to both St Petersburg (*platskart/kupe* R1803/4036, 26¾ to 28 hours) and Moscow Oktyabrskaya (*platskart/kupe* from R2092/4730, 34½ to 39½ hours). All go via Apatity (*platskart* from R558, 3½ to 4¾ hours) and Petrozavodsk (*platskart/kupe* R1422/3132, 19 to 24 hours).

Train 373 bound for Vologda (*platskart/kupe* R1744/3910, 37 hours) departs at 5.24pm on even-numbered days (or daily during some summer periods). It's ideally timed for Kem (*platskart/kupe* R941/2000), arriving with 1¼ hours to spare before the boat to the Solovetsky Islands. Or there's an attached coach bound for Arkhangelsk (*platskart/kupe* R1397/3089, 29½ hours), which arrives much less conveniently at 11pm.

The **ticket windows** (Железнодорожные кассы; 7am-6pm Mon-Fri, 8am-5pm Sat) are in a separate building across the street.

Getting Around

Murmansk airport is 27km southwest of the city at Murmashi, 40 minutes by bus/*marshrutka* 106, which departs from directly opposite the bus station (twice or thrice hourly). Frequent trolleybus 6 covers the vast length of Kolsky pr, crosses the city centre on pr Lenina then swings left on ul Karla Libknekhta. For Lake Semyonovskoe and beyond, switch at ul Chelyuskintsev onto trolleybus 2 or 4, coming up from the train station, and alight at Ozero 1 or Ozero 2 bus stops. (There's no other intermediate stop.)

Useful bus 10 (R15) follows Kolsky pr, bypasses the centre on ul Polyarnye Zori and ul Papanina, rejoins the main drag near Lake Semyonovskoe and continues to the naval museum.

VOLOGDA & ARKHANGELSK REGIONS

The vast, seemingly endless regions of Vologda (Вологодская область) and Arkhangelsk (Архангельская область) are given character by a scattering of ancient monasteries, the tattered charm of once-grand towns…and the Russian Santa Claus. Some highlights, like Kargopol, are places that time forgot once railways supplanted river transport and St Petersburg replaced Arkhangelsk as Russia's outlet to the sea. Others, like friendly little Totma, are only now starting to realise their tourism potential, while Veliky Ustyug has become a wintertime theme park in itself.

Vologda Вологда

8172 / POP 293,000 / MOSCOW

This enjoyable provincial city has a remarkable concentration of old (if often bedraggled) churches and a fair scattering of 18th- and 19th-century wooden houses.

Having taken Moscow's side against all comers seemingly from its inception, Vologda was rewarded by Ivan the Terrible, who considered the quaint city perhaps worthy of his living there. Vologdians remain steadfast in their belief that the city was a contender for Russian capital.

Until the 17th century, Vologda was an important centre of industry, commerce and arts, with Vologda lace becoming renowned as a luxury item. However, with the development of St Petersburg, Vologda was pushed into the background. At the start of the 20th century, political undesirables like Josef Stalin and religious philosopher Nikolai Berdyaev were exiled here. Nonetheless, for just a few months in 1918, Vologda became the diplomatic capital of Russia, an aspect of its history that is further explained in the Museum of Diplomatic Corps.

Vologda straddles the Vologda River, with the city centre on the southern side and ul Mira as its main axis. **Dom Knigi** (Дом книги; ul Mira 38; 10am-7pm Mon-Fri, to 6pm Sat & Sun) sells regional and detailed city maps, including a useful R90 double street map that also covers Veliky Ustyug.

Sights & Activities

Where pr Pobedy and ul Mira meet is a commercial district of attractive neoclassical buildings surveyed by a **Lenin statue** in an odd 'Hey buddy, wanna buy a watch?' pose. A mini-Lenin near the **Church of St John the Baptist** (Церковь Иоанна Предтечи, 1710–17), on equally grand pl Revolyutsii, was reputedly the first ever erected in the USSR (1924). Vladimir Ilyich does not, however, make an appearance in the happening (and decidedly capitalistic) new pedestrian area wedged between ul Mira and ul Batyushkova.

St Sofia's Cathedral CHURCH
(Софийский собор; admission/camera R100/50; 10am-6pm Wed-Sun, service 9am) Powerful five-domed St Sofia's Cathedral has a soaring interior smothered with beautiful 1680s frescoes. The astonishingly tall iconostasis is filled with darkly brooding saintly portraiture.

The cathedral is said to have been built on the direct orders of Ivan the Terrible. Ivan's ruthlessness at Novgorod (where he sacked his own city and fried citizens alive in large pans made especially for the occasion) was

Vologda

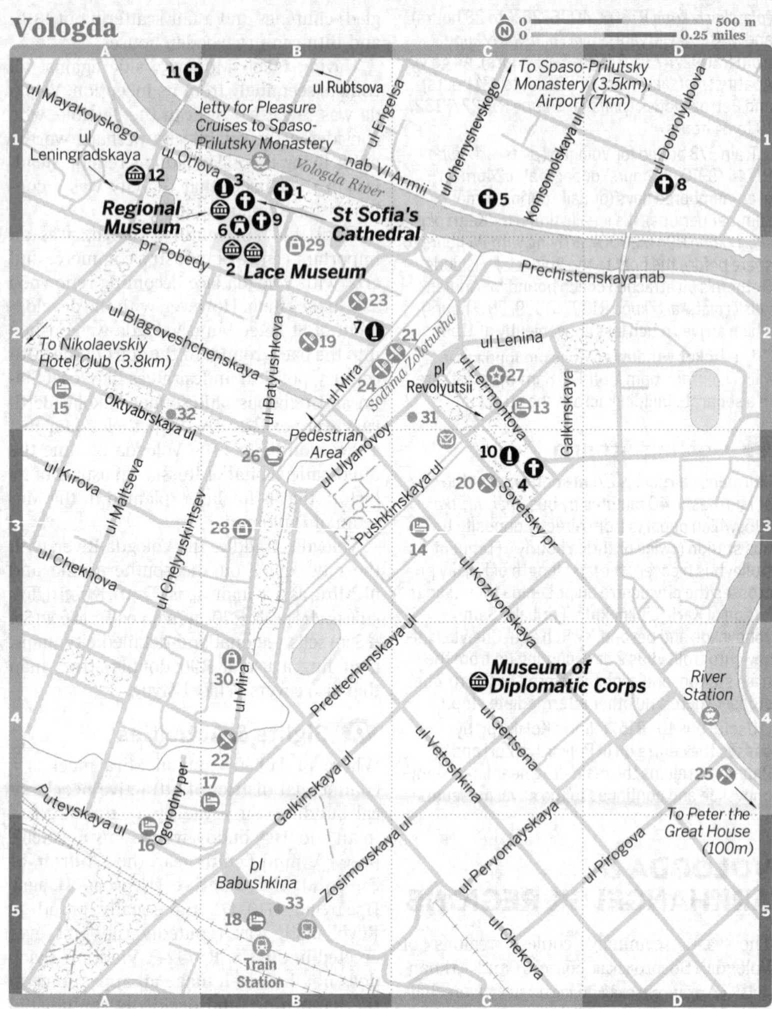

known and feared throughout Russia. So the Vologda workers jumped: the massive stone cathedral Ivan wanted was erected in just two years (1568–70). And they worked only in summer.

But haste, of course, makes waste. Local legend has it that Ivan, upon walking into St Sofia's for the first time, was struck on the head by a tile that had been grouted to the ceiling without due care. Ivan stormed out, never to return, and the cathedral was consecrated only after the Terrible One's death.

Climbing St Sofia's separate 78.5m, gold-topped **bell tower** (Колокольня; admission/camera R100/50; ⌚10am-4.30pm Wed-Sun) offers breathtaking, photogenic views down upon the cathedral's grand onion domes. Mind your own dome on the way up: the ceilings get low.

FREE **Kremlin** HISTORICAL SITE
(Архиерейский двор, Archbishop's Courtyard; ⌚9am-5.30pm) Vologda's modest but attractive kremlin is the city's historical centrepiece, a 17th-century fortified enclosure built as a church administrative centre to accompany St Sofia's next door. Several of the sub-buildings now house **museums**

Vologda

Top Sights

Lace Museum B2
Museum of Diplomatic Corps C4
Regional Museum B1
St Sofia's Cathedral B1

Sights

1 Alexander Nevsky Church B1
Art Gallery .... (see 9)
2 Art Section B2
3 Bell Tower B1
4 Church of St John the Baptist C3
5 Dmitry Prilytskogo Church C1
6 Kremlin B1
7 Lenin Statue B2
8 Nikolaya Church D1
9 Resurrection Cathedral B1
10 Small Lenin Statue C3
11 Stretenskaya Church A1
12 World of Forgotten Things A1

Sleeping

13 Hotel Angliter C2
14 Hotel PVO C3
15 Hotel Spasskaya A2
16 Hotel Sputnik A5
17 Hotel Vologda B4
18 Resting Rooms B5

Eating

19 Central Market B2
20 Kafe Lesnaya Skazka C3
21 Kamenny Most C2
22 Oasis Supermarket B4
23 Ogorod B2
24 Pirozhkova B2
25 Puzatiy Patsyuk D4
Restoran Spassky .... (see 15)

Drinking

26 Arbat Café Grand B3
Kafe Juventa .... (see 22)

Entertainment

27 Philharmonia C2
TNT .... (see 15)

Shopping

28 Dom Knigi B3
29 Dom Suvenirov B2
30 Vologodskie Suveniry B4

Information

31 Vologda Regional Academic Library C2

Transport

32 Trolleybus 1 .... A2
33 Trolleybuses 1 & 4 .... B5

(⏲10am-5pm Wed-Sun). Most compelling of these is the extensive **Regional Studies Museum** (Краеведческий музей; admission R50), in the 17th-century Gavriilovsky Korpus. Beyond all the dramatically posed stuffed mammals (including a lonely cub-under-glass mournfully watching his bear family from across the room) is a rich prehistory section, including a 3500-year-old lady skeleton clasping at her modesty.

On the eastern side of the main courtyard, the **Art Section** (Художественный отдел Кремля; admission R50) starts with an odd collection of Muppet-style dolls before getting down to business with some truly first-class icons.

The sparklingly modern **Lace Museum** (Музей кружева; admission R70) in the northeast corner includes some large examples of this archetypal Vologda craft, with fun communist-era examples incorporating tractors, hammer-and-sickle symbols and an intricate piece celebrating Russia's exploration of the cosmos. Some lace-crafters work as guards in the museum.

Just outside the Kremlin enclosure, the spired pale-blue **Alexander Nevsky Church** (Храм Александра Невского) and the amply domed 1776 **Resurrection Cathedral** (Воскресенский собор; ul Kremlevskaya 3) add photogenic foreground to kremlin views. The latter houses an **art gallery** (Художественная галерея; admission R50) of regularly changing exhibits.

FREE **Spaso-Prilutsky Monastery** MONASTERY
(Спасо-Прилуцкий монастырь; Zheleznodorozhnaya ul; ⏲9am-5pm Mon-Sat, from 11am Sun) Don't miss this active 14th-century monastery built in a splendid cacophony of architectural styles. Painted in circustent stripes, its powerful fortress towers are photogenically reflected in the river, best viewed from the nearby railway bridge. Visitors may explore the western half of the compound, including a partial rampart walk

and entry to parts of the five-domed 16th-century **Transfiguration Cathedral** (Спасо-Преображенский собор). Behind is the single-spired wooden **Dormition Church** (Uspenskaya tserkov) built in 1519.

The site is 4km north of town. Many buses pass nearby, including bus 75, 84, 88 and 91 from the stations via the Kameny Most stop (ul Mira) and buses 101 to 103 from the Ribnoryadskiy Most stop. In summer, pleasure cruises meander up the river (R450 return) from central Vologda, departing at noon, 3pm, 6pm and 9pm.

Museum of Diplomatic Corps MUSEUM
(Музей дипломатического корпуса; ul Gertsena 35; admission R40; ⏲8.30am-5.30pm Mon-Fri, 9am-4pm Sat) This unusual two-room museum chronicles a little-known blip in WWI history. In February 1918, with the Germans approaching Petrograd, Allied ambassadors were ordered to evacuate. US ambassador David Francis suggested simply relocating. Studying a map, he chose Vologda. Other embassies followed his lead, with the French, Italian and Serbian ministries sharing a luxury rail carriage parked in Vologda station. That proved handy given that, come July, all the embassies decamped again to Arkhangelsk. The eclectic and impressively researched exhibit has some notes in English and is housed in the former US embassy, a tired if once-grand timber house.

World of Forgotten Things MUSEUM
(Мир Забытых Вещей; ul Leningradskaya 6; admission R40, with tour in Russian R50; ⏲10am-5pm Wed-Sun) One of several enchanting old wooden buildings at the northern end of ul Leningradskaya houses this lovable little museum evoking the life of a 19th-century, 17-child middle-class family. Amid portraits and old dolls is a very whimsical gramophone that still plays. A selection of beautiful photos showcase other examples of Vologda's historic wooden architecture.

Peter the Great House MUSEUM
(Дом-Музей Петра I; Sovetsky pr 47; admission R40; ⏲10am-1pm & 2-5pm Wed-Sun) Vologda's oldest museum (1885) is a tiny late-17th-century stone house that supposedly hosted Tsar Peter I during his visits to Vologda. Exhibits include Peter's death mask and red tunic, underlining his remarkable height.

North Bank HISTORICAL SITE
The Vologda River's little-visited north bank has a patchy minor charm. **Dmitry Prilytskogo Church** (Храм Дмитрия Прилуцкого; nab VI Armii 121) has pretty star-spangled domes, and the splendid 1669 **Nikolaya Church** (Церковь святителя Николая на Горе; ul Gogolya 110) has oversized domes that almost seem to grow together. Several other potentially fabulous old churches lie in various stages of neglect, notably the derelict 1731 **Stretenskaya Church** (Стретенская церковь; nab VI Armii 85) with kremlin views through the cow parsley.

Semenkovo MUSEUM
(Семенково; admission R150; ⏲10am-5pm) This open-air museum featuring historical wooden architecture is 12km up the Vytegra road (bus 107). Many buildings were scaffolded at research time but remaining displays of traditional peasant life and fine craftsmanship make it worth having a peek around.

Sleeping

Accommodation in Vologda has no grey areas: hotels are either swish or they're stuck in 1974.

TOP CHOICE **Hotel Angliter** BOUTIQUE HOTEL €€€
(Гостиница Англитер; ☎762 436; www.angliter.ru; ul Lermontova 23; s/d/apt/lyux from R3100/4100/7300/7900; 📶) With tirelessly helpful multilingual staff and a supercentral location, this very comfortable boutique hotel is Vologda's top choice, even if the crystal lamps, marble toilets and pseudo-antique walnut-inlay furniture are more splashy than classy. Breakfast is included.

Hotel Spasskaya HOTEL €€
(Гостиница Спасская; ☎720 145; www.spasskaya.ru; Oktyabrskaya ul 25; s R1700-3100, d R2500-3500, ste R4000-8500; 📶) The mammoth Spasskaya wins on entertainment, amenities and location, with 9th-floor rooms enjoying fine views towards the kremlin. Standard rooms don't hide their Soviet pedigree but are larger and more pleasant than many equivalents elsewhere. Some English is spoken, and a decent buffet breakfast is included.

Nikolaevskiy Hotel Club HOTEL €€
(☎512 299; http://hotel.nikolaevskiy.ru; Kostromskaya ul 14; s/d R2700/3510; 📶) Utterly neutral rooms are instantly forgettable, but the service is impeccable and the restaurant is quite grand. However, charging R3000 per hour to use the sauna-gym may be pushing the

friendship. Buffet breakfast is included. It's 4km out of the centre: get off trolleybus 1 at Kostromskaya stop (89/91 ul Leningradskaya), then walk eight minutes west.

Hotel Sputnik HOTEL €€
(Гостиница Спутник; ☎722 752; Puteyskaya ul 14; s R900-1400, d R1200-1850) Reconstruction work continues slowly on this oldie-but-adequate'y. Some of the rooms have had facelifts and are fine for a night or two, but there's no mistaking the hallmarks of the typical USSR-era hotel: clashing decor and harrumphing staff.

Hotel Vologda HOTEL €€
(Гостиница Вологда; ☎723 079, 560 515; ul Mira 92; s/d without bathroom from R528/816, Kat 1 s/d from R938/1396, renovated s/d from R1970/2788, lyux s/d from R3650/4540) Behind what appears to be a neatly modernised facade beats a very Soviet heart with disdainful administrators and (much jollier) floor ladies prowling nondescript corridors. Rooms are a mixed bag: ultra-cheapies and Kat 1 rooms border on the woebegone but are comfortable enough for hardy types, while midrange versions are quite liveable.

Hotel PVO HOTEL €€
(Гостиница правительства области, Hotel Pravitelstva Vologodskoi Oblast; ☎720 732; ul Kozlyonskaya 8; s/d from R1595/2880, polu-lyux/lyux R3405/5970) Central but institutional and often full of travelling bureaucrats.

Resting rooms HOSTEL €
(комнаты отдыха, komnaty otdykha; ☎798 238; 2nd fl; 12-/24-hr R400/700) Neat, clean dorm beds on the train station's 2nd floor (out the main entrance and up the stairs at the left). Six-hour stays cost half the rate.

Eating

TOP CHOICE **Puzatiy Patsyuk** UKRAINIAN €€
(Пузатый Пацюк; Sovetsky pr 80; mains from R250; ⌚9am-4am) This adorable rustic-effect nostalgia restaurant serves top-notch food including duck in a wonderfully tart apple-and-cowberry sauce *(kachka s yablykami)*. The menu (in Ukrainian with Russian translations) is a well-crafted take on a tsarist-era police report. At weekend evenings there's a R50 cover charge and occasional live entertainment.

Kamenny Most FUSION €€
(ul Chelyuskintsev 47; mains from R200; ⌚9am-midnight Mon-Thu & Sun, to 2am Fri & Sat) Tasteful and tasty split-level restaurant, with posh pastas, fresh fish dishes and attentive service. Comprehensive wine list and buzzing ambience help make this central Vologda's top nosh spot.

Pirozhkova CAFETERIA €
(Пирожкова; ul Mira 9; pastries from R20; ⌚7am-7pm) Stand-and-scoff joint offering fresh-baked fillers that are literally cheaper than chips. Swarms of clamouring locals can't be wrong.

Ogorod RUSSIAN €€
(Огород; pr Pobedy 10; mains R90-300; ⌚8.30am-11.30pm) Warmly attractive café that keeps prices low by serving meals cafeteria-style. There's a second branch beneath a 24-hour supermarket at ul Gertsena 20.

Restoran Spassky BUFFET €
(Hotel Spasskaya; mains from R250) Good-value weekday lunch buffets (R270) at this otherwise pricey hotel restaurant include seven main courses, a salad bar and help-yourself juices.

Kafe Lesnaya Skazka CAFÉ €
(Кафе Лесная сказка; Sovetsky pr 10; mains R90-200; ⌚11am-3am) Basic but quite acceptable meals are the go in this modest café, set in a fetching little 1911 ex-chapel. Business lunches run from R100 and a bar out the back serves huge beers for R80.

Central Market MARKET €
(Центральный рынок; ul Batyushkova 3a; ⌚7.15am-7pm Tue-Sun, to 4pm Mon) Indoor/outdoor bazaar.

Oasis Supermarket SUPERMARKET €
(Oasis Mall, ul Mira; ⌚9am-10pm) Large and very Western.

Drinking & Entertainment

Kafe Juventa CAFÉ
(4th fl, Oasis Mall; espresso R60; ⌚9am-6pm; 📶) Hipsters in Vologda? The indie crew at Juventa (accordingly, 'youth') is friendly, fashionable and, most importantly, grinds mayhaps the best brew in town.

Arbat Café Grand CAFÉ, BAR
(cnr ul Mira & ul Batyushkova; espresso R80, beer R100; ⌚noon-2am Mon-Thu & Sun, to 5am Fri & Sat; 📶) A chatty hang-out by day, this café transforms into a pop-walloping bar once the sun goes down (and sometimes before). Its huge verandah is ideal for gawking at the goings-on in the pedestrian mall below.

TNT NIGHTCLUB
(Hotel Spasskaya; ⌚8pm-5am) Different ambiences on different nights (cover charge varies) with separate billiards room, beer-pub and tenpin bowling for R500 per lane per hour (open 11am to 5am).

Philharmonia LIVE MUSIC
(Филармония; www.volfilarmonia.ru; ul Lermontova 21) As well as its vibrant program of mostly classical music (October to May), the Philharmonia also organises a two-week 'Summer at the Kremlin' festival of open-air concerts (June to July).

Shopping

The best *kruzhevo* (Vologda lace), colourful lacquerware, painted wooden trays and carved birchwood items can be found at **Dom Suvenirov** (Дом Сувениров; Kremelskaya pl 8; ⌚10am-7pm Mon-Sat) and **Vologdskie Suveniry** (Вологодские Сувениры; cnr ul Mira & ul Chekhova; ⌚10am-7pm Mon-Fri, to 5pm Sat & Sun).

Information

Main post office (Почта; Sovetsky pr 4; ⌚8am-10pm Mon-Fri, 9am-6pm Sat & Sun) Internet R54 per hour.
Vologda Lace (www.artrusse.ca/lace.htm) Background info on the city's claim to fame.
Vologda Oblast (www.vologda-oblast.ru) Government-run site.
Vologda Regional Academic Library (Областная библиотека; ul Ulyanovoy 1; ⌚10am-5pm) For internet (per hour R50) turn right as you enter this grand old building.

Getting There & Away

Bus

The **bus station** (Автовокзал) is at pl Babushkina 10.

Train

From the **train station** (pl Babushkina 8) around seven daily services run to Moscow (8½ to 9½ hours), of which train 59 at 9.15pm (*platskart/kupe* R1267/2760) is the best-timed overnighter. Day-train 375 departing at 6.42am is much cheaper (*obshchiy/platskart* R810/1215) and offers the best value of numerous options for reaching Yaroslavl (*obshchiy/platskart* R306/593, 4½ hours).

In summer up to five trains run overnight to St Petersburg (*platskart/kupe* from R1300/2849, 12 to 13 hours).

For Arkhangelsk, train 16 (*platskart/kupe* R1018/2175) leaves at 7pm, arriving at 6.50am. Train 374 to Murmansk (*platskart/kupe* R1744/3910, 37 hours) leaves at 2.40pm on even-numbered days (daily in summer). Kotlas train 376 (*platskart/kupe* R897/1360, 12½ hours) leaves at 10pm and arrives at Yadrikha (for Veliky Ustyug) at 9am.

Getting Around

From the train station, trolleybuses 1 and 4 run up ul Mira; number 4 continues north while number 1 turns left on Oktyabrskaya ul, doubling back down ul Leningradskaya near the Spasskaya Hotel. Minibus 84 runs frequently to the airport from outside the bus station, passing very close to the monastery. Bus 6 takes Zosimovskaya ul then heads west along ul Gertsena.

Totma Тотьма

☎81739 / POP 10,000 / ⌚MOSCOW

Totma was founded prior to 1137 (about a decade before the first mention of Moscow) and makes an intriguing short stop along the Vologda–Veliky Ustyug route. Though landlocked, this beautiful, church-heavy town revels in a rich marine heritage, an anomaly explained in two attractive museums.

From the bus station the town centre is four blocks south down ul Belousovskaya. Turn right halfway along ul Kirova to begin sightseeing from the Seafarers' Museum.

Sights

Seafarers' Museum MUSEUM
(Музей Мореходов; ul Kirova; admission R60; ⌚10am-5pm Tue-Sun) Located within the

SERVICES FROM VOLOGDA BUS STATION

DESTINATION	FARE (R)	DURATION (HR)	DEPARTURES
Cherepovets	260	2½	hourly, passing Cherepovets airport
Petrozavodsk	762	12½	8.10am daily except Wed & Fri
Totma	367	4½	9 daily
Veliky Ustyug	702	10	9.15am & 6.20pm, 7am (Wed, Sat & Sun), 3.30pm (Fri)
Yaroslavl	378	4½	11.35am, 2.20pm & 5.10pm (Fri & Sun only)

WORTH A TRIP

KIRILLOV-BELOZERSKY MONASTERY
КИРИЛЛО-БЕЛОЗЕРСКИЙ МОНАСТЫРЬ

The small lakeside town of Kirillov, 130km northwest of Vologda, may not ring many bells now, but in the 16th and 17th centuries, its main attraction – the **Kirillov-Belozersky Monastery** (www.kirmuseum.ru/en) – was the largest monastery in northern Russia and one of the most powerful in the country.

Founded in 1397 by a monk from Moscow, the monastery's first incarnation was a cave dug in the ground. From these inauspicious beginnings, it grew to encompass 12 hectares, upon which still stand 12 churches, mighty three-storey fortress walls and the centrepiece Assumption Cathedral, home to a glorious 17th-century iconostasis.

The wealth of the monastery was made possible by wealthy patrons including the Romanovs and Ivan the Terrible. Ivan had a personal room within the monastery, planning to take his own vows here. However, things did not go quite as planned, with the tsar becoming disenchanted with what he saw as the 'lecherous' goings-on within the cloister. A prolific and polemic letter-writer, Ivan penned a no-holds-barred epistle to the abbot of the time, blasting the lack of asceticism within its walls: 'Today in your cloister Sheremetyev sits in his cell like a tsar; Khabarov and other monks come to him and drink and eat as though they were laymen, and Sheremetyev – whether from weddings or births, I don't know – sends sweets and cakes, and other spiced delicacies around to all the cells, and behind the monastery is a courtyard, and in it are supplies for a year.'

The monastery today suffers from a different form of excess, coming in the form of endless coach-loads of cruise-boat tourists. But a trip here during the off-season or early morning should allow you at least an hour or two of relative solitude.

Entry is free, but many exhibition rooms and churches charge their own admission prices, starting from R50.

Buses between Kirillov and Vologda (R190, 2¾ hours) run at least six times daily (last leaving Kirillov at 9.40pm). Hotel accommodation is available in Kirillov; see the monastery website for details.

Church of the Entry into Jerusalem (tserkov Vhoda v Iersusalim), this homey museum features exhibitions highlighting Totma's unlikely contributions to marine exploration (one-fifth of all Russian mid-18th-century expeditions originated here) and the discovery of strategic islands off Alaska. The church itself was built from donations from returning Totma-based seamen and is constructed to give the odd sensation of being at sea.

Kuskova Museum MUSEUM
(Дом-музей Кускова – музей Русской Америки в России; Chkalovskiy per 10; admission R60; ⏲10am-5pm Tue-Sun) A block south down ul Lenina beyond the beautifully proportioned Church of the Nativity of Christ (Церковь Рождества Христова), this museum occupies a small log house, the birthplace of Ivan Kuskov (1765–1823), a wooden-legged explorer of Alaska, who went on to found Fort Ross, California. Fort Ross remained a thriving Russian settlement until sold in 1841.

Saviour-Sumorin Monastery MONASTERY
(Спасо-Суморин монастырь) Though partly derelict and littered with debris, the evocative remains of this monastery are enough to give a taste of its former grandeur. Its neoclassical **Ascension Cathedral** (Вознесенский собор) has a fine columned portico but has yet to be fully restored. To get here, start at the Seafarers' Museum then curve west along unpaved ul Babushkina for 15 minutes, then cross the small bridge.

Sleeping & Eating

Hotel Varnita HOTEL €€
(☎24 288; s/d from R1700/2000) With fresh modern rooms with light pine furniture and private bathrooms, this is Totma's best option, though it can get loud. It's on the 3rd floor of the pink and yellow building beside the bus station. Downstairs you'll find a supermarket and Totma's top restaurant, the pseudo-rustic **Pechki-Lavochki** (mains R100-270; ⏲11am-midnight).

Hotel Rassvet HOTEL €€
(☎23 154; ul Kirova 12; s/d from R1200/1800) Right beside the Church of the Entry into Jerusalem, the two-storey Rassvet looks more like an ageing office building than a

hotel. Most of the cosmetically repapered rooms have a tap. Better rooms have showers and water heaters. Toilets are shared but very clean.

Turbaza Monastyrskie Keli MONASTERY €
(☎22 796; Saviour-Sumorin Monastery; s/d/tr/q R400/500/700/900) Predominantly occupied by local students, this thick-walled old monastery building has very simple rooms sharing basic bathrooms (shower R25). It opens and closes with regular irregularity: call ahead to be sure.

Kafe Lyubava CAFÉ €
(ul Belousovskaya 16; mains R35-100; ⏲11am-4pm daily, 6pm-midnight Wed-Sat) Offers cheap eats in simple surrounds.

Kafe Fort Ross CAFÉ €
(ul Vologodskaya 11; mains from R60; ⏲9am-9pm) This nautical-themed café is inside the Totma Youth Centre.

Getting There & Away

Buses to Vologda (R367, 4½ hours) leave at least nine times daily between 6am and 3.30pm. There's at least one daily afternoon bus for Veliky Ustyug (R420, 4¾ hours).

Veliky Ustyug

Великий Устюг

☎81738 / POP 31,784 / ⏲MOSCOW

This attractive historical town was a forgotten backwater till 1998 when, for obscure reasons, then-Moscow Mayor Yury Luzhkov declared Veliky Ustyug to be the official home of Ded Moroz. He gave the town a large sum of money, and said 'Make it so.' Ded Moroz (Father Frost) is the Russian equivalent of Santa Claus.

Father Frost festivals create several 'high seasons', notably around his 'birthday' (18 November), 5 July, the weeks leading up to New Year, and other Russian holidays. Book ahead at such times.

Ustyug was founded in 1147 at a key river junction, making it an important transport and trade port in the days before railways. In the latter part of the 17th century, its importance was underlined with the 'honour' of being called 'Veliky' (great). Bypassed by the railway, it declined rapidly in the 19th century but, until the 1917 revolution, four monasteries and 27 churches still pricked its skies with spires. Most were desecrated during the Soviet era and, despite limited restoration, many are still used for banal civic purposes today.

Dotted with historic buildings, main streets ul Naberezhnaya, ul Krasnaya and Sovetsky pr (Uspenskaya) parallel one another and the wide Sukhona River.

Sights & Activities

Father Frost's Estate THEME PARK
(Вотчина Деда Мороза; www.dom-dm.ru/en; adult/child R180/140; ⏲10am-5pm) This low-budget theme park for Russian kids is a hilarious festival of kitsch. It's supposedly Father Frost's forest-bound home, and costumed staff somehow manage to keep a remarkably straight face as they play along with the farcical premise. Visits start with a forest stroll through the **Trapa Skazok**, where a witty bunny-girl leads you through 'wishes', little games and exercises: great fun for children but all in Russian. Then there's **Dom Deda Moroza** (Дом Деда Мороза; tours per person R130, photos R60). This large wooden house attempts a 'fairy-tale atmosphere', but the reality stumbles somewhere between museum and silly glitz-fest where guests must endure over-lengthy tours of all 12 rooms. Gasp at DM's Liberace-style wardrobe! Observe the pyramid of seven, progressively smaller pillows on his bed (one for each day of the week)! Dutifully admire the presents he's received (shouldn't he be giving?). Finally, a fanfare announces the arrival of Ded Moroz himself, very tall, red-clad and as luxuriantly white-whiskered as you'd hope. He proceeds to hand out presents and hugs to kids; adult males receive nothing more than a nutcracker handshake, while lucky ladies get a very beardy smooch.

Full-entry package tickets (adult/child R450/260) include all of the above plus the right to be photographed with Father Frost.

The 'estate' also has a hotel, a children's camp, a reasonably priced café and a small but expanding zoo. It's 12km west of Veliky Ustyug, R200 by taxi. At 2pm you could head back to town on bus 122 (R21).

Father Frost residence MUSEUM
(Sovetsky pr 85; ⏲9am-6pm) A good central starting point for exploring the town's historic centre is Ded Moroz's part-time 'residence' where the Russian Santa shows up at festival times. There's a **'throne room'** (admission R20) and a vaguely interesting **exhibition room** (admission R10). Tours in Russian are given by slightly unhinged

volunteers still incensed over DM's knock-back as a potential Sochi Olympics mascot.

Father Frost Post Office NOTABLE BUILDING
(Пота Деда Мороза; per Oktyabrsky 1a; ⏲8am-8pm Mon-Fri, 10am-6pm Sat, 10am-5pm Sun) Ever wondered why you never got that bike? You were probably sending your Santa letters to the North Pole instead of to this adorable log cabin. Here, sacks and boxes overflow with letters from children all over Russia (and beyond) that are all sorted and dutifully answered. Wags have suggested it's the most efficient post office in the country.

Churches HISTORICAL BUILDINGS
Built in 1658, the **Dormition Cathedral** (Успенский собор; Sovetsky pr 84) is attached to a disproportionately tall **bell tower** (admission R40; ⏲10am-5pm Tue-Sun summer only); clamber up for terrific views. Next door, **St Procopio's Cathedral** (Собор Прокопия Праведного; ul Naberezhnaya 57) has a stone purported to grant your wish if you sit on it, clear your mind, and look at the church complex across the wide, unbridged river. About 500m down, Veliky Ustyug's oldest original structure, the 1648 **Ascension Church** (Вознесенская церковь; admission R100; ⏲10am-noon & 1-5pm Tue-Sat) sports a riot of small gables, arches and domes. A glorious iconostasis is within.

State Historical, Architectural & Art Museum-Reserve MUSEUM
(Дом Усова, Dom Usova; ul Naberezhnaya 64; ⏲10am-5pm Tue-Sun) Numerous other historic buildings throughout the old centre can be visited on guided excursions (R200 per person) organised through the State Historical, Architectural & Art Museum-Reserve, headquartered in a pale-pink, 18th-century riverside mansion.

Sleeping

In addition to the places reviewed here, there are several out-of-town hotels for visitors who are driving or on a tour.

Hotel Veliky Ustyug HOTEL €€
(☎26 766; ul Krasnoarmeyskaya 15; s R900-1200, d/tr/polu-lyux R2000/2700/3000, lyux R4000-5000) Central Veliky Ustyug's most appealing option has very professional staff. There's an attractive pseudo-olde lobby, and rooms are smart if unexotically furnished, though occasionally graced by the presence of Ded Moroz dolls. Single rooms share bathrooms between pairs. The hotel is between ul Krasnaya and Sovetsky pr, one block north of Krasny per.

Hotel Iceberg HOTEL €
(☎24 343; ul Uglovsky 3; s & d R550-1300) The town's newest accommodation option is sparkling and staffed by a chirpier bunch than usual. Some economy rooms adhere to the tried and tested 'must clash' school of decorating, but most are sunny and comfortable enough.

Hotel Dvina HOTEL €€
(☎20 348; www.hotel-dvina.ru; ul Krasnaya 104; s/d/tr R1500/1800/2250) Friendly and fairly cosy despite hypnotically over-patterned wallpaper, most of the Dvina's rooms are decent-sized and almost all have water heaters (in other hotels centralised hot water is

SANTA CLAUS VS DED MOROZ

Bearded and benevolent they may both be. But the similarities end there for the Western Santa Claus and Russia's Ded Moroz. Who will you be asking for a puppy this Christmas?

SANTA	DED MOROZ
Lives at the North Pole with wife and elves	Hails from Veliky Ustyug, also home to his brother Aquarius
Delivers presents in secret, via chimney	Hands over goodies in person
Has a close working relationship with nine flying reindeer	Kicks it with Snow Maiden (Snegurochka), his attractive granddaughter
Wears a red suit	In Soviet times, Stalin issued a decree stating that Ded Moroz had to wear blue robes, to distinguish him from the 'bourgeois' Santa
Based on St Nicholas, much-loved for his gift-giving to the poor	Early tales have DM freezing people solid and kidnapping children for ransom money

turned off in June). A handful of cheaper singles share bathrooms.

Hotel Sukhona HOTEL €
(☎22 552; fax 21025; Krasny per 12; s/d without bathroom from R500/825, s/d with bathroom from R1200/1600) Dismiss the lobby's chemical smells (a hair salon is attached) and the jarring animal-print bedspreads – this is a decent and very central base. It's also right across from the 18th-century Spaso-Preobrazhensky Cathedral. Ring the black bell to call the *dezhurnaya* (floor lady) for your key.

Eating

Hotel Dvina's pub-style café is pleasant, while Hotel Veliky Ustyug's fancy-looking restaurant (occasional R50 cover) is surprisingly reasonable if you don't mind karaoke.

Pogrebok FUSION €€
(Погребок; Sovetsky pr 121a; mains from R130; ⏲noon-midnight) Pogrebok offers meat dishes, pizzas, kebabs and even curry (sometimes), washed down with excellent home-brewed ales in an attractive vaulted basement wallpapered with old newspapers and furnished with heavy wooden benches. There's a brilliant billiards room too. It's directly behind Sovetsky pr 121, but access is from a side alley.

Shopping

Berendey SOUVENIRS
(Берендей; Sovetsky pr 115; ⏲10am-6pm Mon-Fri, to 3pm Sat & Sun) Has affordable Niello metalwork and some decent birch craft.

Deda Moroza Suveniri SOUVENIRS
(Sovetsky pr 85; ⏲9am-6pm Mon-Fri, to 5pm Sat & Sun) Also has good-quality handicrafts plus some classy doll versions of Veliky Ustyug's head honcho.

Information

With freaky dino-decor, **Kafe Vodoley** (☎23 478; Krasny per 13; per hr R60; ⏲11am-midnight Mon-Thu & Sun, to 2am Fri & Sat) is an internet café that, for once, really is a café (mains from R100, beer R60). It sells soft toys too.

There are ATMs at the **Prestizh supermarket** (ul Krasnaya 110; ⏲7am-11pm) and **Sberbank** (ul Krasnaya 128), which changes euros and US dollars.

Getting There & Away

Air

Veliky Ustyug has an airport about 5km west of town, but flights are very sporadic. Kotlas airport, 65km north, is better connected.

Bus

The **bus station** (ul Transportnaya) is 2.5km north of the centre. Buses leave for Arkhangelsk (R980, 11 hours) at 4am and for Kotlas (R125, 1¾ hours) 11 times daily, almost all via Yadrikha (R90, 70 minutes). Vologda (R702, 10 hours) buses via Totma (R380, 4¾ hours) depart at 5pm daily plus at 5.10am (apart from Wednesday and Saturday) and 7pm Monday, Thursday and Sunday. Hotels also organise minibuses to Vologda and Totma.

Train

The nearest operative railway station is in the tiny village of Yadrikha, from which there are at least four daily trains to Moscow (19 to 21 hours) via Vologda (12 to 13 hours), one to Arkhangelsk (19 hours) and one to St Petersburg (25 hours). Veliky Ustyug–bound buses wait for arriving trains.

For Vyatka/Kirov on the Trans-Siberian main line, there's a train at 1.40pm from Kotlas Yuzhny station (not Yadrikha). It continues to Nizhny Novgorod on even-numbered days.

In Veliky Ustyug, train tickets are sold at **Zh/D Kassy** (Ж/Д; ul Krasnaya 100; ⏲8am-1pm & 2-6pm Mon-Fri, 8.30am-4pm Sat & Sun).

Getting Around

Taxis within town cost about R70. Bus 1 (R12) runs down ul Vinogradova from the bus station then turns southeast along ul Krasnaya. Bus 3 runs along ul Krasnaya and on to the airport.

Kargopol Каргополь

☎81841 / POP 10,148 / ⏲MOSCOW

Gently attractive Kargopol was one of Russia's richest cities in the 16th and 17th centuries, when it commanded the Onega River route to the White Sea, then Muscovy's only coastline. Once Russia had gained access to the Baltic, Kargopol lost its raison d'être and faded into obscurity, hardly helped by a devastating 1765 fire. Today it's a peaceful, if out-of-the-way historical town known for its naive-style painted clay figurines *(Kargopolskiye igrushki)* and for a local yeti/bigfoot-style myth.

Pr Oktyabrsky and parallel ul Lenina run southwest past the hotels, pl Lenina and grassy pl Sobornaya. Turning right here, ul Leningradskaya is paralleled by ul Gagarina, ul Bolotnikova and ul Sergeeva.

Sights

Ploshchad Sobornaya SQUARE
This large grassy square houses three fine churches and a sturdy 1778 **bell tower**

(Kolokolnya; admission R50; ⌚10am-1pm & 2-5pm Tue-Sun), whose sweeping views justify the somewhat claustrophobic climb.

The five-domed, 1562 **Nativity Cathedral** (Христорождественский собор; admission R60; ⌚10am-1pm & 2-5pm Tue-Sun) has intriguing timber-encased corner buttresses and contains a splendid, if poorly lit, iconostasis. On a pillar, the superb **Starshni Sud icon** is a Who's Who of saints on what looks like a heavenly snakes-and-ladders board.

The 1751 **John the Baptist Church** (Церковь Иоанна Предтечи) has an impressively Gothic bulk with unusual octagonal windows and distinctive double domes on long cylindrical towers.

Less visually exciting but historically important, the 1809 **Vvedenskaya Church** (admission R50; ⌚10am-1pm & 2-5pm Tue-Sun) stored the hidden chattels of the Russian royals during Napoleon's 1812 attack on Moscow. Now the upstairs interior hosts a small but eclectic collection of whimsical knick-knacks.

Krasnoarmeyskaya ploshchad SQUARE

A second trio of historic churches lies between ul Lenina and pr Oktyabrsky at ul Sergeeva. The most impressive is the disused 1692 **Annunciation Church** (Благовещенская церковь; pr Oktyabrsky) with some unusually intricate window mouldings. The active 1680 **Rozhdenstva Bogooroditsy Church** (ul Lenina) is elegant despite the discordant metallic gleam of its multiple domes.

Shevelyov Museum MUSEUM

(Дом-музей Шевелевых; ul Gagarina 30) Although it's unmarked and opening hours vary, a steady stream of summer tourists winds its way to this small workshop where Kargopol's best-known toy-making family does hands-on 'masterclasses' showing how to make traditional pottery and archetypal *Kargopolskiye igrushki* figures. The very popular gift shop also sells various items of woven birch bark.

Museum Administration Building CULTURAL HERITAGE

(www.kargopolmuseum.narod.ru; pr Oktyabrskaya 50) The ethno-fun continues here with low-key musical, dance and **folklore events** (admission R40-100; ⌚9pm Fri-Sun, mid-Jun–Aug) held outside most weekend evenings in summer.

Zosimy & Savvatiya Church CHURCH

(кЦерковь Зосимы и Савватия; pr Oktyabrsky 18; admission R50; ⌚10am-1pm & 2-5pm Tue-Sun) At the southwestern end of town, this 1819 church has a small collection of local crafts, costumes and icons, plus Saturday recitals.

Bereginya Centre HISTORICAL BUILDING

(Центр Берегиня; ul Arkhangelskaya; ⌚9am-noon & 1-5pm Mon-Thu, 9am-noon & 2-4pm Fri) Bereginya Centre displays and sells a range of crafts in an 18th-century house that was once the town jail.

Activities

Lache Tur TOURS

(☎22 056; www.lachetur.ru; Hotel Kargopol; ⌚9am-6pm Mon-Sat) This very accommodating tour agency rents bicycles, canoes and rafts, and organises rural accommodation and interesting tours. Some English spoken.

Sleeping

If both hotels are full, **Lache Tur** (☎22 056; www.lachetur.ru; Hotel Kargopol; ⌚9am-6pm Mon-Sat) can arrange homestay beds for around R500.

Hotel Kargopol HOTEL €€

(☎21 165; www.solovkibp.ru/kargopol/hotel; ul Lenina 60; s/d/polu-lyux/lyux R2350/2950/3550/4650) From a squeaking-floor lobby, attractively appointed corridors lead through to sensibly equipped modern rooms, all with fridge and good bathrooms (with underfloor heating in the *lyux* suites). Staff are very obliging.

Hotel Kargopolochka HOTEL €

(☎21 264; karhotel@atnet.ru; ul Lenina 83; dm/s/d/tr/q without bathroom R650/780/1020/1300/1750, s/d with bathroom R800/1600) Most rooms share toilets and hot water is turned off in June, but overall this simple, renovated Soviet hotel is more pleasant than many equivalents elsewhere.

Eating & Drinking

Both hotels have cafés.

Zakusochnaya FAST FOOD €

(Закусочная; ul Gagarina 8; snacks & salads R15-45; ⌚8am-8pm Mon-Fri, to 6pm Sat & Sun) The very basic Zakusochnaya offers surprisingly passable pastries and precooked meals.

Tsentralny Magazin SHOP €

(ul Lenina 57; ⌚24hr) Make like a local with a beer bought from Tsentralny Magazin and swilled beside the shiny white Lenin statue.

Information

The **post office** (ul Leningradskaya 10; ⌚8am-8pm Mon-Fri, to 7pm Sat, 9am-6pm Sun) is on ul Leningradskaya.

Kargopol's only public internet computer is within the **Dom na Pyatnitskoy** (ul Sergeeva 1; per hr R60; 9am-6pm): part chess hang-out, part handicapped-persons' retreat.

Sberbank (ul Pobedy 12) facing pl Sobornaya has an ATM around the side.

Kargopol Town (www.kargopol.ru) has a useful English-language website. Map-guide pamphlets sold at the hotels (R50) are in Russian but have photos.

Getting There & Away

There are daily buses to Arkhangelsk (R870, 13 hours) at 7am but no bus service to Pudozh nor Kirillov/Lipin Bor. The road to Lipin Bor has a messy 40km mud section that is passable only by sturdy 4WD. Virtually all visitors arrive by train at Nyandoma, 80km east of Kargopol on the Vologda–Arkhangelsk train line. Four daily buses (R138, 1½ hours) are loosely timed to fit with rail timetables while faster shared taxis (R700 to R850 per car, one hour) await each train.

Arriving at 10.15am on train 316 from Moscow, you could see all of Kargopol's sights in a day then continue to Arkhangelsk on train 16 at 00.30am. Southbound from Arkhangelsk, slow train 671 runs cheaply (*platskart* R680) and conveniently overnight, departing at 9.52pm and arriving at 6.48am. There are night trains from Nyandoma to Kotlas (at 00.33am) for Veliky Ustyug and to Vologda (at midnight alternate days) but there's no convenient night train *from* Vologda.

Around Kargopol

Several villages in Kargopol district have historic log churches.

The region's most accessible is just 5km north of Kargopol (R240 return by taxi) in **Saunino** village, 1.7km west of the Troitsa road.

The most impressive ensemble of wooden churches is beside the Pudozh road in the archetypal log-cottage village of **Lyadiny** (aka Gavrilovskaya), 35km west of Kargopol. Here the 1693 Bogoyavlenskaya and 1761 Vlasevskaya churches form a photogenic ensemble with an 1820 wooden bell tower. They're clearly visible from the window of the Lekshmozero bus.

KENOZERO NATIONAL PARK

КЕНОЗЕРСКИЙ НАЦИОНАЛЬНЫЙ ПАРК

The gateway to this delightful patchwork of forests and lakes is the quaint village of **Lekshmozero** (aka Morschihinskaya) that sits idyllically on the unbanked shores of large Lake Lekshmo. From where the bus terminates, walk back 30m to a *zhurval* (shadoof-style lever-well) and turn left along ul Zapadnaya to find the picturesque if battered lakeside brick **church**. A footpath to the left brings you round to a striking yellow building that's both a **hotel** (31 697; d R1760) and the national park visitor centre. Nearby, the **Fisherman's Hut Hotel** offers woodsy double rooms for R1360. Book on the above number or through www.kenozero.ru.

Lekshmozero is also the launching point for the popular **Ecological Route**, a one-day open-boat trip to a reconstructed traditional mill via a series of lakes and tiny linking canals: be prepared to get wet feet! Your best bet is to book through an agency: Lache Tur in Kargopol can help.

Buses from Kargopol to Lekshmozero (R140, 1¾ hours) via Lyadiny (R70, 50 minutes) depart at 5.15pm on Tuesday, Friday and Sunday, and at 6.15am Tuesday and Friday. They return two hours later.

Arkhangelsk Архангельск

8182 / POP 356,000 / MOSCOW

In the 17th century Arkhangelsk was immensely important as Russia's only seaport. Sadly, few historic buildings remain and, with only minor exceptions, the cityscape is a grey expanse of concrete. However, the riverfront does have a certain insidious charm, and strong links with Scandinavia give the disarmingly friendly populace a cosmopolitan openness. The main reason that most tourists pass through is to use the (infamously weather-dependent) flights to the Solovetsky Islands.

In 1693 Peter the Great began shipbuilding operations here, launching the Russian navy's tiny first ship, the *Svyatoy Pavel*, the following year. The founding of St Petersburg in 1703 pushed Arkhangelsk out of the limelight but it later became a centre for Arctic exploration, a core of the huge northern lumber industry and a crucial supply point during the 20th-century world wars.

The main thoroughfares, Voskresenskaya ul and Troitsky pr, intersect at pl Lenina. This soulless central square is guarded by a 22-storey tower topped by a thistle of communication spires that's known to all as 'Vysotka' (the skyscraper). Mostly pedestrianised pr Chumbarova-Luchinskogo is an up-and-coming shopping street with several restored historical timber houses.

Sights

Gostiny Dvor HISTORICAL BUILDING
(Гостиный Двор, Merchants' Yard; nab Severnoy Dviny 85/86) In the 17th and 18th centuries, Arkhangelsk's heart and soul was this, a grand, turreted brick trading centre built between 1668 and 1684. Luxurious European textiles, satin and velvet arrived here while flax, hemp, wax and timber for ships' masts were exported. The once-huge complex is now only a shadow of its former self and is under almost constant renovation, but some partly restored sections host **exhibition rooms** (per exhibition R50; ⏲10am-5pm Tue-Sun) that usually have a couple of worthwhile historical and/or art displays.

Regional Studies Museum MUSEUM
(Архангельский областной краеведческий музей; pl Lenina 2; admission R60-100; ⏲10am-6pm Tue-Sun) The historical section upstairs in this compelling museum has strikingly presented sections on the Soviet-era timber industry, Gulag camps and notably WWII, when the city was pounded by 2100 German bombing runs. Hours could be lost simply studying the photo albums and personal effects of fallen local soldiers. Downstairs, the Nature Section's weirdly arranged taxidermy collection induces guilty chuckles.

Fine Arts Museum MUSEUM
(Музей изобразительных искусств; pl Lenina 2; admission R100; ⏲10am-5pm Wed-Mon) Arkhangelsk's most compelling art gallery hosts regularly changing exhibitions that range from modern reflections on Soviet propaganda to nude studies. Upstairs are impressive icons, bone carvings and decorative art displays. The building's sombre exterior gives no clue to the treasures within.

Prospekt Chumbarova-Luchinskogo HISTORICAL SITE
Work is in progress to restore the limited collection of traditional timber houses that still survive on this, Arkhangelsk's one vaguely atmospheric central street. Should it live up to its potential, this could be one hip strip indeed. In the fine Marfin Mansion, the **Lair of Art Gallery** (Марфин Дом; http://marfin.wmsite.ru; pr Chumbarova-Luchinskogo 38; admission R60; ⏲11am-8pm) hosts occasional concerts, but is best visited for its furnished interior and large model of how Arkhangelsk looked a century ago.

Naberezhnaya Severnoy Dviny PARK
Given the first hint of warm summer weather, Arkhangelskians emerge to stroll this broad promenade and loiter in any of its many seasonal beer-and-shashlyk tents. As the June sun slowly declines, reflected in the 2km-wide river, the sky's colours grow ever less believable.

House-Museums MUSEUMS
(admission R70; ⏲10am-5pm Wed-Mon) The century-old former homes of three local poet-artists are open as mildly interesting museums. Noted for its period interior furnishings is that of **EK Plotnikova** (Усадебный Дом Плотникова; Pomorskaya ul 1), whose paintings feature prominently at the Fine Arts Museum. For imaginative presentation, visit the home of **SG Pisakhov** (Дом-Музей Писахова; Pomorskaya ul 10), whose passion for the Arctic scenery of Novaya Zemlya was shared by AA Borisov. The latter's works are shown at the **AA Borisov Museum** (Музей Борисова; Pomorskaya ul 3), an unmarked brick house.

Assumption Church CHURCH
This whitewashed modern church overlooks the wide beach at nab Severnoy Dviny.

Eternal Flame MONUMENT
A very Soviet memorial honouring the fallen of the Great Patriotic War.

Nikolsky Church CHURCH
(Teatralny per 3) Slightly kitsch, this little church was built in 1904.

Peter I Statue MONUMENT
This windswept take on PTG and the unexotic River Terminal building both feature on Russia's R500 banknotes.

Tours

Kompaniya Solovki TOURS
(Компания Соловки; ☎655 008; www.solovkibp.ru; pr Chumbarova-Luchinskogo 43) Good range of tour options, but the Solovetsky 'hotel' (Turistichesky Kompleks Solovki) is one of those islands' least appealing options.

Pomor Tur TOURS
(Помор Тур; ☎202 720; www.pomor-tur.ru; Voskresenskaya ul 99; ⏲10am-6pm Mon-Fri) City and regional excursions including themed tours to the Solovetsky Islands and one-week paddle-steamer cruises to Kotlas/Veliky Ustyug.

Sleeping

TOP CHOICE **Hotel Dvina** HOTEL €€
(Гостиница Двина; ☎288 888; www.hoteldvina.ru; Troitsky pr 52; s/d R2300/2600, business s/d

Arkhangelsk

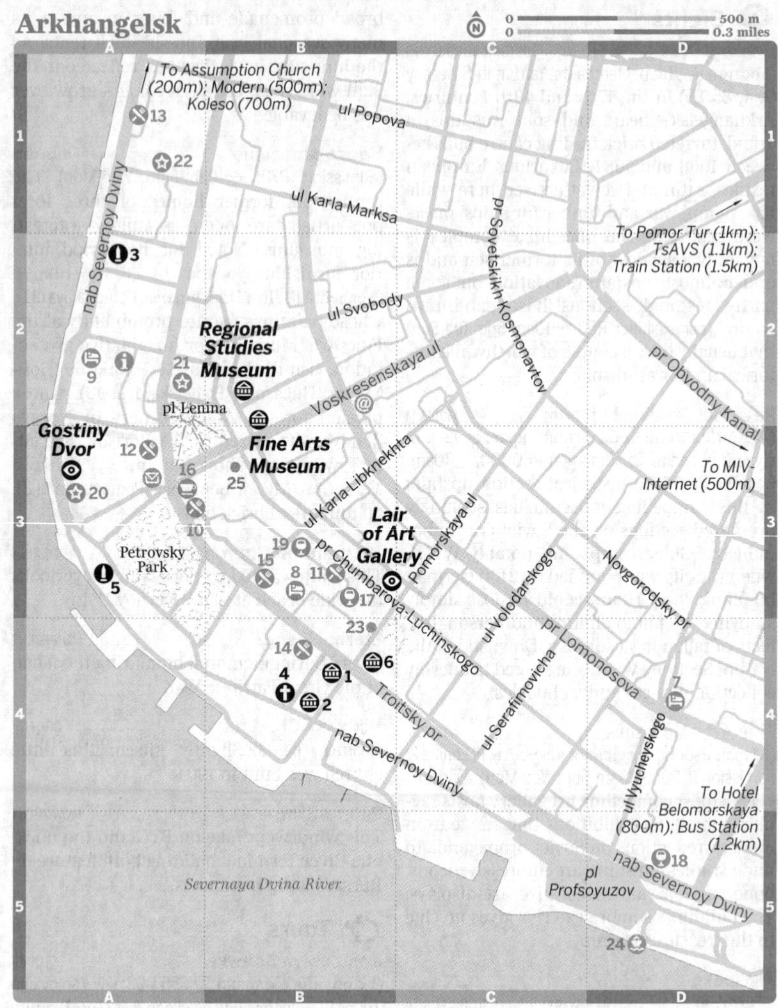

R2500/3125, lyux R3000-7000; 📶) Don't be put off by 13 storeys of peeling pink exterior paintwork: within, the super-central Dvina has been tastefully refurbished with quality linens, tiled bathrooms and a delightful (if prim) restaurant. 'Business' and 'standard' rooms are virtually indistinguishable. Very helpful desk staff speak English.

Pur Navolok Hotel HOTEL €€
(Пур Наволок Отель; ☎217 200; www.purnavolok.ru; nab Severnoy Dviny 88; s R2800-3000, d/polu-lyux R3300/3700, lyux R5900-8300; 📶) Probably northern Russia's best-value business hotel, the professionally run Pur Navolok offers bright international-style rooms (some with beach views) accessed by glass elevator from an airy modern atrium. Rates include extensive buffet breakfasts. Staff are multilingual.

Hostel Lomonosov HOSTEL €
(Ломоносов; ☎285 294; www.hostellomonosov.com; ul Lomonosov 84; dm R400-480; 📶) Spanking-new hostel that's positively futuristic when compared to many other (and more expensive) northern options. Enthusiastic staff offer discounts for students and long-termers: ask when booking.

Arkhangelsk

Hotel Belomorskaya HOTEL €€
(Беломорская; ☎661 600; www.belhotel.ru; ul Timme 3; s/d/polu-lyux/lyux from R1700/2000/2200/2600) But for the occasional mattress sag and long-suffering sighs on reception, this is a decent and inoffensive sleeping option. On the bus 1 route between the train station and town.

Eating

TOP CHOICE **El Fuego** STEAKHOUSE €€€
(pr Chumbarova-Luchinskogo 39; steak from R900; ⊙noon-2am) Top-notch dining for the discerning carnivore. Extremely knowledgeable waitstaff, an exemplary steak menu and chefs of international calibre make for a special night out. Its grill-scented, dark, brick surrounds feel especially cosy during winter.

Restoran Bobroff RUSSIAN €€
(Ресторан Боброфф; nab Severnoy Dviny; mains R200-420; ⊙11.30-2am) This jolly tavern-restaurant opens into a small period-style dining room with formal portraits and Dutch-style tiled fireplace. Its home-brewed ales are the perfect complements to dishes ranging from the hearty (beef in bilberries) to the sublime (cod in langoustine sauce).

Restoran Pomorsky RUSSIAN €€
(Ресторан Поморский; Troitsky pr; mains R220-850; ⊙noon-midnight) Set in log-cabin-effect alcoves, this local favourite serves imaginatively named dishes like Bride of Three Bridegrooms (salmon caviar bliny) and the Herder Bag (pork stuffed with cheese). It's oddly hidden on the rear 3rd floor of the office building above the Polina Café.

Barkhat RUSSIAN €€
(Бархат; pr Chumbarova-Luchinskogo 49; mains from R160, ⊙noon-midnight) Downstairs from the Shyolk café, the Barkhat restaurant has a slightly stiff vibe but the food is excellent and sensibly priced.

Nulevaya Versta CAFETERIA €
(Нулевая Верста; Troitsky pr 45; mains R40-75; ⊙10am-8pm) Cheap but unusually presentable subterranean cafeteria.

Bingo FUSION €
(Troitsky pr 64; mains R130-365, beer R65-120; ⊙noon-7am) Armenian food and toasted sandwiches in a modest French-themed basement bar-café.

Sigma SUPERMARKET €
(Troitsky pr 52; ⊙9am-10pm) A well-stocked supermarket next to the Dvina.

Drinking

Biblio-Café CAFÉ
(pl Lenina 3; coffee from R60; ⏰8am-11pm; 📶) Smart and sunny hideaway brewing strong cuppas behind the Arkhangelsk library.

Shyolk CAFÉ
(Шёлк; pr Chumbarova-Luchinskogo 46; coffee from R50; ⏰10am-midnight) Upbeat tea- and coffeehouse with understated oriental touches and mouth-watering pastries.

Lock Stock PUB
(nab Severnoy Dviny 30; beer from R100; ⏰11-1am) Anglo-pub with authentic local boozer decor and hugely comprehensive beer list.

Bierfest PUB
(Hotel Dvina approach lane; beer R135-180; ⏰noon-midnight) Pseudo-German beer cellar charging Germanic prices.

Entertainment

TOP CHOICE **Koleso** LIVE MUSIC
(Wheel; www.arkoleso.ru; ul Gaydara 4/1; ⏰5pm-late) This Arkhangelsk institution hosts knees-up rock, folk, rockabilly and country gigs from local and visiting acts on weekends and some weeknights. Check the regularly updated website to see what's on while you're in town. Bus 6 will get you there.

Jazz Klub Artel LIVE MUSIC
(☎209 215; www.aokm.ru/programs/en; nab Severnoy Dviny 86; ⏰8pm-late Sat) Jazz fans in town on a Saturday night shouldn't miss the almost-legendary jam sessions at this cavern-club hidden within the Gostiny Dvor. Call first to confirm.

Philharmonia LIVE MUSIC
(Филармония; pl Lenina 1; ⏰ticket office noon-7pm Mon-Sat) The Philharmonia hosts orchestral concerts and operas, while its **Maly Zal** (Филармония Малый Зал; ul Karla Marksa 3; ⏰ticket office 1-7pm Tue-Sun) stages organ and chamber music in the 1768 Lutheran church of St Catherine. There's a busy White Nights program in June.

Modern CINEMA, NIGHTCLUB
(Модерн; pr Lomonosova 269) Cinema with weekend nightclub.

Information

Dom Knigi (Дом Книги; pl Lenina 3; ⏰10am-8pm Mon-Fri, to 6pm Sat & Sun) Stocks good city and regional maps plus a few guidebooks.

MIU-Internet (МИУ-Интернет; pr Obvodny Kanal 8-10; per hr R50; ⏰24hr) Excellent connection and friendly student staff.

Post office (Почта; Voskresenskaya ul 5; ⏰8am-9pm Mon-Fri, 9am-6pm Sat & Sun)

Severo-Zapadny Telekom (Северо-Западный Телеком; pr Lomonosova; ⏰8am-9pm Mon-Fri, to 8pm Sat & Sun)

Tourist office (Туристический информационный центр; ☎214 082; www.pomorland.info; ul Svobody 8; ⏰9am-1pm & 2-5.30pm Mon-Thu, to 4pm Fri) Enthusiastic, well-informed, English-speaking staff are an inspiring source of information for the city and the whole of Arkhangelsk region. Extensive website.

Getting There & Away

TsAVS (ЦАВС; ☎238 098; Voskresenskaya ul 116; ⏰9am-7pm Mon-Fri, 10am-5pm Sat & Sun) and a handy ticket desk in Hotel Dvina both sell rail and air tickets.

Air

Arkhangelsk's main airport, **Talagi** (ARH; ☎211 560), is 12km northeast of the centre.

Most flights are operated by **Nordavia** (☎655 776; www.nordavia.ru/eng; Pomorskaya ul 7; ⏰9am-8pm Mon-Fri, 10am-7pm Sat & Sun) and **Rossiya** (☎635 898 www.rossiya-airlines.ru/en; pl Lenina 4; ⏰9.30am-7pm Mon-Fri, 10am-4pm Sat & Sun).

FLIGHTS FROM TALAGI AIRPORT

DESTINATION	FARE (FROM R)	DURATION (HR)	DEPARTURES
Kotlas	3000	1½	Mon, Wed & Thu
Moscow SVO	4900	1¾	3-4 daily
Murmansk	5760	2	Mon, Wed & Sat
Solovetsky Islands	3810	1	Sun-Tue & Fri-Sat in summer (Mon & Fri in winter)
St Petersburg	4000	1½	2-3 daily
Tromsø, Norway	11,850	5	Wed & Sat

Weather permitting, further Solovetsky Islands flights leave in small planes from **Vaskovo airport** (ULAH; ☎450 926), 20km southwest of the city centre.

Bus

From the **bus station** (Автовокзал; ul 23-y Gvardeyskoy Divizii 13), daily services run to Veliky Ustyug (R980, 11½ hours, 8am) and Kargopol (R870, 13 hours, 7.30am).

Train

From the **station** (pl 60-letia Oktyabrya 2), two or three trains daily run to Moscow's Yaroslavsky station (*platskart/kupe* from R1517/3363, 21 to 24 hours) via Vologda (R1018/2175, 14 to 15 hours) and Yaroslavl (R1232/2468, 18 to 20 hours). There's one train daily each to St Petersburg (*platskart/kupe* from R1483/3293, 26 hours, departs 8.43pm) and Kotlas (R1049/2259, 19 hours, 3.40pm). On even-numbered days (daily during most of summer) carriages bound for Murmansk (*platskart/kupe* R1397/3089, 30 hours) via Kem (R854/1796, 16 hours) are attached to train 671. This train departs at 9.52pm daily to Nyandoma (R680, 8½ hours) and is ideal for reaching Kargopol.

Getting Around

Appearing as 'MR Vokzal' (МР Вокзал) on destination boards, the **River Terminal** (Морской-речной вокзал; nab Severnoy Dviny 26) is a major hub for city buses and *marshrutky*. From here the rare bus 110 runs to Vaskovo airport and frequent route 12 runs every few minutes to Talagi airport via pl Lenina and northern Troitsky pr.

Bus 54 starts at the **bus station**, picks up at the train station, runs down Voskresenskaya ul then turns east along Troitsky pr at pl Lenina. *Marshrutka* 62 also runs down Voskresenskaya ul but crosses pl Lenina, stops outside the post office then meanders east along nab Severnoy Dviny.

Route 1 from the train station curls south on ul Timme and ul Uritskogo past the Belomorskaya and CentrIN hotels, then turns west along nab Severnoy Dviny and takes Troitsky pr north.

Two versions of route 75 make banana-shaped loops around the city centre. Both use ul Gagarina, pr Obvodny Kanal and ul Uritskogo but in opposite directions: blue-sign 75 runs clockwise closing the loop via Troitsky pr, green-sign 75 runs anticlockwise using pr Lomonosova.

Malye Karely

Малые Карелы

Set in pretty rolling dales 25km southeast of Arkhangelsk's centre, this delightful open-air **Wooden Architecture Museum** (Музей деревянного зодчества; admission R200; ⏲10am-7pm Jun-Sep, to 5pm Oct-May) is Arkhangelsk's foremost attraction. Featuring dozens of 16th- to 19th-century wooden buildings relocated here from rural villages during the 1970s, its authentic surrounds have been used as a film set on local and international productions. Allow around two hours to see the site, more on national holidays when there are costumed presentations of historic crafts (and prices rise 30%).

You enter past a series of **windmills**, in the largest of which you can admire the complete interior workings. Cut across to the impressive 1669 **Ascension Church** (Вознесенская церковь) with its top-knot of wooden domes and forest-scented, icon-plastered interior. The 19th-century **Tretyakov House** displays curious furnishings of the era, while the quaint little **Miracle Worker's Chapel** (Часовня Макария Унженского, Chasovnya Makariya Unzhenskogo) has retained intact its eight-panelled octagonal ceiling paintings.

To reach the village-like **Mezensky Sector** from here, take the steep steps down to a bog-crossing boardwalk, then back up again. That's tough going for the infirm but worth the effort. Notice the hay barns from Khornema and the *chyornye izby* (black cottages), so called because their lack of a chimney resulted in smoke-stained walls. The much larger 19th-century **Elkino House** has an exhibition on Pomor fishing and boat-building. But the sector's centrepiece is the splendid 1672 **St George's Church** (Георгиевская церковь), displaying a small but valuable selection of remarkable wayside crosses including one gigantic example that virtually fills the nave.

Just 200m from the museum entrance in this otherwise rural backwater is the self-contained holiday-hotel complex **Turisticheskaya Derevnya Malye Karely** (☎462 472; www.karely.ru; d R2500-2900, apt R3900-4900, cottage from R13,100). Bowling, billiards and fishing excursions are available, making the modern timber cottages and apartments a fun getaway alternative to central Arkhangelsk. The restaurant has an olde-Russia theme.

Every 20 to 30 minutes, little bus 104 from Troitsky pr in central Arkhangelsk runs all the way to Malye Karely (R38, 45 minutes), terminating opposite the hotel complex. Taxis want around R400 each way: returning from Malye Karely you'll generally need to phone for one.

Volga Region

Includes »

Best Places to Eat

» Bezukhov (p352)
» Priyut Kholostyaka (p357)
» Staraya Kvartira (p365)
» Art & Fact (p365)
» Tatarskaya Kukhnya (p377)

Best Places to Stay

» Jouk-Jacques (p352)
» Hotel Giuseppe (p356)
» Procosta (p379)
» Bristol-Zhiguli Hotel (p364)
» Stary Stalingrad (p372)

Why Go?

The Volga (Волга), one of Europe's great rivers, winds for some 3530km through Russia's heartland and has been a part of the continent's longest 'highway' since time immemorial. The stretch of the Volga covered in this chapter – between Nizhny Novgorod and the Caspian Sea – forms a rich and varied cultural region with over a dozen different ethnic groups, most notably the Volga Tatars. Travelling along or alongside the river you encounter spectacular hilltop kremlins in Nizhny Novgorod, Kazan and Astrakhan, bombastic architecture in Volgograd, numerous lively provincial capitals, as well as picturesque stretches such as the Samara Bend. This natural beauty culminates in the magnificent Volga Delta south of Astrakhan, a vast region of reeds and waterways. West of the Volga River, Kalmykia takes in a windswept area of steppe that is home to the Buddhist Kalmyks, who originate from western Mongolia.

When to Go

Astrakhan

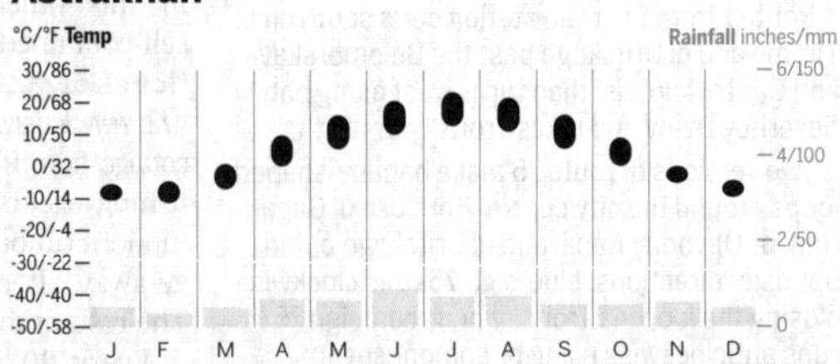

Feb Much of the Volga River is frozen over and draped in a winter landscape.

Late Apr–late May Spring sun warms the air and accommodation is plentiful.

Late Jul–Sep The navigation season is in full swing and the lotus flowers are blooming in the delta.

History

Since ancient times, the Volga has supported agricultural settlements and served as a main link in transcontinental commerce. More than a thousand years ago, the Vikings plied its waters, establishing a trade route between Baghdad and the Baltic.

MEDIEVAL VOLGA

In the Middle Ages, the Lower Volga was dominated by the Khazars, a Turkic tribe whose leaders converted to Judaism. The Khazar capital stood at Itil (present-day Astrakhan). The Middle Volga was the domain of another Turkic tribe, the Bulgars.

Volga Region Highlights

1. Explore the waterways of the **Volga Delta** (p378)
2. Climb the stairs and paths of **Mamaev Kurgan** (p370), Volgograd's magnificent memorial to the Battle of Stalingrad
3. Explore the culinary and cultural scenes in historic **Nizhny Novgorod** (p352), brought together in an interesting 'Food and Culture' movement
4. Sail the **Volga River** (p353) on a short excursion or a fully fledged cruise ship, taking in the major stops and sights
5. Stroll through multicultural **Kazan** (p354), one of Russia's most dynamic cities and home to a picturesque kremlin
6. Rattle in a *marshrutka* across the grassy steppe to **Elista** (p379), capital of Europe's only Buddhist republic
7. Stroll along the **Volga-Don Canal** (p371) on the fringes of Volgograd and relax in the baroque town square of **Sarepta**

Descendants of the Huns and distant relatives of the Balkan Bulgarians, they migrated eastwards, mixed with local Finno-Ugric tribes and adopted Islam in the 10th century. Their feudal state was northeastern Europe's most advanced economic and cultural centre at that time. The forests of the Upper Volga were originally settled by Finno-Ugric tribes, who were partly displaced by the Turkic and Slavic migration. The river was also a vital conduit in the lucrative fur trade for Novgorod's merchants.

THE GOLDEN HORDE

In the 13th century, the entire Volga region was conquered by the heirs of Chinggis (Genghis) Khaan, the Mongol-led Golden Horde, who made Saray (near present-day Volgograd and Astrakhan) their capital. For the next 200 years, the Volga's Slavic and Turkic communities swore allegiance and paid tribute to the great khan, or suffered his wrath. Challenged by the marauder armies of Timur (Tamerlane) in the south and upstart Muscovite princes in the north, the Golden Horde eventually fragmented into separate khanates: Kazan, Astrakhan, Crimea and Sibir. In the 1550s Ivan the Terrible razed Kazan and Astrakhan, and claimed the Middle and Lower Volga for Muscovy (modern-day Moscow), the capital of the new Russian state.

COSSACKS

While the river trade was a rich source of income for Muscovy, it also supported gainful bandit and smuggling ventures. Hostile steppe tribes continued to harass Russian traders and settlers, and the region remained an untamed frontier for many years.

In response, the tsar ordered the construction of fortified outposts at strategic points on the river. Serfs, paupers and dropouts fled to the region, organising semi-autonomous Cossack communities (p629). The Cossacks elected their own atamans (leaders) and pledged their swords in service to the tsar and the Church. The Cossacks not only defended the frontier for the tsar but also operated protection rackets, plundered locals and raided Russia's southern neighbours.

Cossacks conducted large-scale peasant uprisings. In 1670 Stepan Razin led a 7000-strong army of the disaffected, which moved up the Lower Volga before meeting defeat at Simbirsk (Ulyanovsk). In 1773 Yemelyan Pugachev declared himself tsar and led an even larger contingent of Cossacks and run-away serfs on a riotous march through the Middle Volga region. The bloody revolt was forever romanticised by Alexander Pushkin in his novel *The Captain's Daughter*.

GERMANS IN THE VOLGA REGION

Astounded by the scale of rebellion, Catherine the Great sought to bolster the economic development of the region by inviting Germany's peasants to settle here from 1763. The largest concentration of German Lutherans was near Saratov. By the end of the 19th century, the population had reached over 1.5 million ethnic Germans.

In the 1920s a German autonomous republic was established along the Lower Volga. Hitler's 1941 blitzkrieg across the USSR's western border prompted a wave of persecution against the Volga Germans, who were branded 'enemies of the state'. The German autonomous republic was eliminated, residents were forced into exile and their citizenship was revoked. After Stalin's death, nearly a million survivors were liberated from Siberian labour camps, but were not allowed to return to their old villages.

SOVIET DEVELOPMENT

The USSR harnessed the mighty Volga for its ambitious development plans. Eight complexes of dams, reservoirs and hydroelectric stations were constructed between the 1930s and 1960s. A network of canals connected Russia's heartland to Moscow and the Baltic and Black Seas. Smoke-stacked factories, sulphurous petrochemical plants, sprawling collective farms and secret military complexes sprang up along its shores. Provincial trading towns, such as Nizhny Novgorod and Samara, grew into urban industrial centres and were closed to outsiders. The river continues to convey as much as two-thirds of all Russia's overland cargo freight.

AFTER COMMUNISM

After the collapse of the USSR, each of the Volga regions went its own way. Some, like Ulyanovsk, resisted change, while others such as Samara, Saratov and Tatarstan moved quickly to liberalise markets and politics. When in 2004 the system of electing regional governors was changed to give Moscow direct control over the appointment, pluralism and dissent all but vanished from the region.

NIZHNY NOVGOROD REGION

Nizhny Novgorod
Нижний Новгород

☎831 / POP 1.25 MILLION / ⏰MOSCOW

A glorious setting is not something most Russian cities can boast, but Nizhny (as it is usually called) is a lucky exception. The mighty cliff-top kremlin overlooking the confluence of two wide rivers – the Volga and the Oka – is the place where merchant Kuzma Minin and Count Dmitry Pozharsky (men commemorated in a monument in front of St Basil's Cathedral, Moscow) rallied a popular army to repel the Polish intervention in 1612.

Nizhny has been a major trading centre since its foundation in 1221. In the 19th century when the lower bank of the Oka housed the country's main fair – *yarmarka* – it was said that 'St Petersburg is Russia's head; Moscow its heart; and Nizhny Novgorod its wallet.' During Soviet times the city was named Gorky, after the writer Maxim Gorky, born here in 1868. Closed to foreigners by the Soviets, Gorky was chosen as a place of exile for the dissident physicist Andrei Sakharov.

Nizhny is often called Russia's 'third capital', but it is markedly quieter than the other two, with a laid-back ambience characteristic of the Volga cities downstream. Walking along riverside promenades, drinking beer in an outdoor café by the kremlin or taking a boat ride to the painters' town of Gorodets are all excellent cures for nerves damaged by Moscow's crowds and traffic.

Sights

The shop on the 2nd floor of the Nizhegorodsky State Art Museum sells an excellent *Walk Around Nizhny Novgorod* book (R170) in English, German and Russian with 10 illustrated routes.

Kremlin HISTORICAL BUILDINGS

(Кремль; www.ngiamz.ru) Built upon remnants of an earlier settlement, Nizhny Novgorod's magnificent kremlin dates back to 1500–15 when the Italian architect Pyotr Fryazin began work on its 13 towers and

NIZHNY NOVGOROD'S STATE MUSEUMS

Nizhny Novgorod has an excellent ensemble of museums inside and around the kremlin. Inside the kremlin, the **Nizhegorodsky State Art Museum** (Нижегородский государственный художественный музей; www.museum.nnov.ru/art; admission R100; ⏰11am-6pm Wed-Mon) focuses on Russian artists, beginning (on the left after you enter) with 16th-century icons. The entire collection is chronological, so you can see by Room 6 how rudimentary landscape perspectives creep into 17th-century icons. After the icons comes the large collection of mostly oil-on-canvas paintings by Russian masters, including Vasily Surikov and lots by Nikolai Rerikh (room 20), culminating in Soviet art. The English descriptions are excellent.

Situated in the former arsenal located on the right after you enter the main gate, the new **National Centre of Contemporary Art** (Государственный центр совеременного исткуства; www.ncca.ru; admission R100; ⏰noon-8pm Tue-Sun) has changing exhibitions of international and Russian contemporary artists.

Outside the kremlin and just a short walk along the attractive Verkhne-Volzhskaya nab, lined with restored 19th-century buildings, you find the **Western European Art Collection** (Собрание Западноевропейское искусство; Verkhne-Volzhskaya nab 3; admission R120; ⏰11am-6pm Wed & Fri-Mon, noon-8pm Thu), with its collection of mostly anonymous or lesser-known European painters who, despite their modest credentials, produced some remarkable works.

A few houses along, inside a 19th-century mansion once belonging to the Rukavishnikov merchant family, is the **Rukavishnikov Mansion** (Усадьба Рукавишникова; Verkhne-Volzhskaya nab 7; tours R300; ⏰10am-5pm Tue-Fri, noon-7pm Sat & Sun). This is visited on 40-minute tours in Russian and English leaving every 1½ hours from 10am to 4pm weekdays and half-hourly weekends from noon to 6pm. Furniture and the illustrious interior of the unusual mansion are the threads running through all excursions in this museum, and these are complemented by changing exhibitions – often with a focus on household furnishing and objects.

Nizhny Novgorod

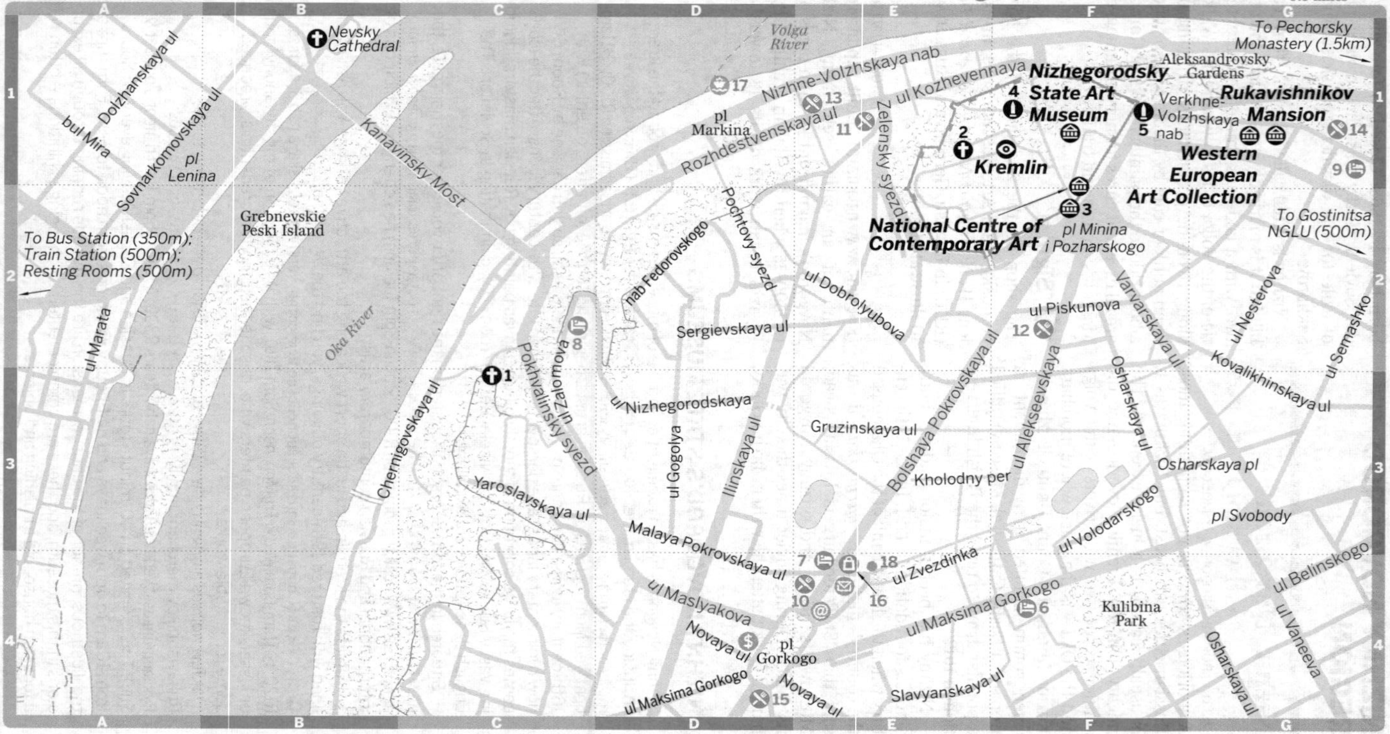

0 — 1 km
0 — 0.5 miles

Nevsky Cathedral
Volga River
To Pechorsky Monastery (1.5km)
Aleksandrovsky Gardens
Nizhne-Volzhskaya nab
ul Kozhevennaya
Nizhegorodsky State Art Museum
4
Rukavishnikov Mansion
Verkhne-Volzhskaya nab
5
14
17
13
11
pl Markina
Rozhdestvenskaya ul
Zelensky syezd
2
Kremlin
Western European Art Collection
9
Dolzhanskaya ul
bul Mira
Sovnarkomovskaya ul
pl Lenina
Kanavinsky Most
Grebnevskie Peski Island
To Bus Station (350m); Train Station (500m); Resting Rooms (500m)
National Centre of Contemporary Art
3
pl Minina i Pozharskogo
To Gostinitsa NGLU (500m)
nab Fedorovskogo
Pochtovy syezd
ul Dobrolyubova
ul Piskunova
ul Nesterova
ul Semashko
ul Marata
Oka River
8
Sergievskaya ul
12
Varvarskaya ul
Kovalikhinskaya ul
1
Pokhvalinsky syezd
ul Zalomova
ul Nizhegorodskaya
Bolshaya Pokrovskaya ul
ul Alekseevskaya
Osharskaya ul
Chernigovskaya ul
Gruzinskaya ul
ul Gogolya
Ilinskaya ul
Kholodny per
Osharskaya pl
Yaroslavskaya ul
pl Svobody
ul Volodarskogo
Malaya Pokrovskaya ul
7
18
ul Zvezdinka
ul Belinskogo
16
10
ul Maslyakova
ul Maksima Gorkogo
6
Kulibina Park
Novaya ul
pl Gorkogo
ul Vaneeva
Osharskaya ul
ul Maksima Gorkogo
15
Novaya ul
Slavyanskaya ul

Nizhny Novgorod

Top Sights
Kremlin F1
National Centre of Contemporary Art F1
Nizhegorodsky State Art Museum F1
Rukavishnikov Mansion G1
Western European Art Collection G1

Sights
1 Annunciation Monastery C3
2 Cathedral of the Archangel Michael E1
3 Dmitry Tower F2
4 Monument to Heroes of WWII F1
5 Pilot Valery Chkalov Monument F1

Sleeping
6 Ibis Hotel F4
7 Jouk-Jacques E4
8 Nizhegorodsky Hotel Complex C2
9 October Hotel G1

Eating
10 Angliiskoe Posolstvo E4
11 Bezukhov E1
Biblioteka (see 16)
12 Moloko F2
13 Restoratsia Pyatkin E1
14 Tiffani G1
15 Vesyolaya Kuma D4

Shopping
16 Dirizhabl E4

Transport
17 River Station D1
18 Turbyuro E4
Volga-Flot Tour Office (see 17)

12m-high walls. Even before the kremlin was finished the Khan of Kazan made his first attempt to take it and failed.

Inside, most of the buildings are government offices. The small 17th-century **Cathedral of the Archangel Michael** (Собор Михаила Архангела) is a functioning church. Behind it, an eternal flame burns near a striking **monument** (Памятник героям Отечественной войны) to the heroes of WWII. The main entrance to the kremlin is at the **Dmitry Tower** (Дмитриевская башня; admission R70; ⏲10am-5pm, closed Mon), which has changing exhibitions on local history.

Annunciation Monastery MONASTERY
(Благовещенский монастырь; ul Garshina) The proliferation of onion domes and golden spires is a ubiquitous reminder of the city's rich history. The 13th-century Annunciation Monastery, above Chernigovskaya ul, is located among the city's oldest buildings.

Pechorsky Monastery MONASTERY
(Печерский Вознесенский монастырь; Privolzhskaya sloboda 108) The 17th-century Pechorsky Monastery, overlooking the Volga, houses a small **Museum of the Nizhny Novgorod Diocese** (Музей Нижнего Новгородского епархий; admission R20; ⏲10am-5pm), which includes a moving exhibition on Bolshevik repressions against the church. Beneath the monastery is the **Rowing Canal**, with sandy banks that have become the city's main beach, sprinkled with beach restaurants. Take any *marshrutka* or bus from pl Minina i Pozharskogo to pl Sennaya.

Museum of Volga People's Architecture & Culture MUSEUM
(Музей архитектуры и быта народов Нижегородского Поволжья; www.ngiamz.ru; Gorbatovskaya ul 41; admission R40; ⏲10am-5pm Sat-Thu, closed mid-Oct–mid-May) The open-air Museum of Volga People's Architecture & Culture has a pleasant woodland setting and a collection of traditional wooden buildings from Russian and Mordva (a Finno-Ugric people) villages. The museum is located in the remote Shchelokovsky Khutor Park, which is the final stop of bus 28 (30 minutes, every hour), which passes ul Belinskogo in the centre. *Marshrutka* 62 also stops close.

Sakharov Museum MUSEUM
(Музей Сахарова; pr Gagarina 214; admission R50; ⏲9am-5pm Sat-Thu) A reminder of more repressive times, the Sakharov Museum is located in the flat where the dissident scientist spent six years in exile. The Nobel laureate was held incommunicado until 1986, when a KGB officer came to install a telephone. When it rang, it was Mikhail Gorbachev at the other end, informing Sakharov of his release. The phone is a highlight of the exhibition. To get there take bus 1 from pl Minina i Pozharskogo or *marshrutka* 3 or 19 from pl Gorkogo to the stop Muzey Akademika Sakharova.

Tours

Team Gorky TOUR COMPANY
(☎278 9404; www.teamgorky.ru; ul 40 let Oktyabrya 1a) Canoe and bicycle tours in the

Nizhny Novgorod region and beyond. Three-day adventure canoe trips start at R6300.

Sleeping

TOP CHOICE Jouk-Jacques BOUTIQUE HOTEL €€€
(Жук-Жак; ☎433 0462; www.jak-hotel.ru; Bolshaya Pokrovskaya ul 57; s R3750-6825, d R6825, ste R9375; ❄📶) This cosy boutique hotel is one of the best in town. The cheapest rooms are a bit cramped but they're neat, and breakfasts are superb by Russian standards.

Nizhegorodsky Hotel Complex HOTEL €€
(Нижегородский Гостиничный Комплекс; ☎430 5387; www.hotel-nn.ru; ul Zalomova 2; s R2660-4250, d R3200-4250; ⊖📶) This ugly concrete eyesore has good refurbished rooms, and the embankment underneath has been converted into a lovely terraced park. The more expensive rooms have fabulous river views. Steps just to the left as you exit lead directly to the Rozhdestvenskaya bus stop.

Ibis Hotel HOTEL €€
(Ибис Отель; ☎233 1120; www.ibishotel.com; ul Maksima Gorkogo 115; r without breakfast from R3100) Nizhny's Ibis is a relative newcomer and offers a high standard of rooms and comforts, with the advantage that it is large enough to cope with busy periods.

October Hotel HOTEL €€€
(Гостиница Октябрьская; ☎432 8080; www.oktyabrskaya.ru; Verkhne-Volzhskaya nab 9a; s R4000-5000, d R6100, ste R10,000-14,000; 📶@⊖) The rooms here have been renovated but overall it retains a hint of post-Soviet kitsch.

Gostinitsa NGLU HOTEL €
(Гостиница НГЛУ; ☎436 5945; Bolshaya Pecherskaya ul 36; dm R480, s/d without bathroom R880/1440, tw apt with bathroom R2520; ⊖) This is part of the Linguistic University dormitory; it doesn't register visas.

Resting rooms HOSTEL €
(Железнодорожные комнаты отдыха, komnaty otdykha; ☎244 2110; dm R750, s/d without breakfast R1550/3300) Located in a separate building on your right as you *exit* the train station.

Eating & Drinking

The cheap and cheerful summer cafés by the city's main hang-out near the **Pilot Valery Chkalov monument** (Памятник летчику Чкалову) are a great place to mingle with locals. Rozhdestvenskaya ul east of the river station also has clusters of places to eat and drink.

TOP CHOICE Bezukhov RUSSIAN, INTERNATIONAL €€
(Безухов; www.bezuhov.ru; Rozhdestvenskaya ul 6; mains R375; ⏲24hr; ✍📶) This literary café with antique furnishings, stucco ceiling and the feel of a living room is part of a project in Nizhny Novgorod called 'Eda i Kultura' (Food and Culture), which brings food and culture together into a delicious whole. The menu is overflowing with salads, pastas and fish, poultry and red-meat dishes, and augmented by good breakfasts and sushi rolls.

Restoratsia Pyatkin RUSSIAN €€
(Ресторация Пяткин; Rozhdestvenskaya ul 23; mains R350; ⏲noon-midnight) This place makes you feel like a merchant back in his mansion after a great trading day at the fair. The menu is full of Volga fish specialities; it also brews the unusual apple *kvas* (fermented rye bread water) and has a children's menu.

Moloko RUSSIAN, BAR €€
(Молоко; ul Alekseevskaya 15; mains R200-300, coffee R100; ⏲noon-2am; 📶✍) Also part of the Food and Culture project – more upmarket in style but with very similar food to Bezukhov – 'Milk' exudes a sleek lounge feel beyond its sofas and aged wooden panelling. Pl Minina i Pozharskogo is your best transport stop.

Angliiskoe Posolstvo PUB €€
(Английское Посольство; ul Zvezdinka 12; mains R500; ⏲8am-midnight Mon-Fri, 8am-2am Sat & Sun; ⊖) Set on two levels, the 'English Consulate' is a convivial place for that familiar pub atmosphere (or Russian interpretation of it). A selection of English beers is available and fish and chips costs R260.

Tiffani INTERNATIONAL, CAFÉ €€€
(Тиффани; ☎436 3542; Verkhne-Volzhskaya nab 8; mains R370-950; ⏲breakfast-late; 🗐✍) This upmarket all-rounder is a restaurant during the day and evening, a café at any time and has well-known DJs some nights. The views across the Volga to the forest are spectacular and kids love it because they can loll on plush sofas beneath the black marble ceiling. Dress up in the evening.

Vesyolaya Kuma UKRAINIAN €€
(ul Kostina 3; mains R400; ⏲noon-midnight; ⊖🗐) Set among a row of lesser restaurants, the 'Happy Godmother' merrily serves hearty borsch and other Ukrainian fare.

Biblioteka ITALIAN €

(Библиотека; Bolshaya Pokrovskaya ul 46; dishes R180-300; ⌚11am-10pm; 🚭📋🍴) Upstairs from the Dirizhabl bookshop with generic but tasty Italian dishes in an informal, quirky atmosphere.

Shopping

Dirizhabl BOOKSTORE

(Дирижабль; Bolshaya Pokrovskaya ul 46; ⌚10am-9pm Mon-Sat, 11am-8pm Sun) A good selection of maps and local guidebooks, and some books in foreign languages.

Information

Central post office (Центральный почтамт; pl Gorkogo; per hr R40; ⌚8am-8pm)

Ellips Bank (Эллипс Банк; pl Maksima Gorkogo 4/2) ATM, accepts major cards.

Volga Telecom (Волга Телеком; pl Gorkogo; per 30min R40; ⌚24hr) Internet terminals.

Getting There & Away

Air

The Nizhny Novgorod International Airport is 15km southwest of the city centre. S7 flies six times a week from Moscow (from R4000, one hour) and **Lufthansa** (☎275 9085) flies directly to/from Frankfurt five times a week (return €600, 3½ hours). Airline tickets are available at agencies around the city, including the **Turbyuro** (Турбюро; ☎439 3260; ul Zvezdinka 10b; ⌚8am-8pm, closed Sun).

Boat

The **river station** (Речной вокзал) is on Nizhne-Volzhskaya nab, below the kremlin. A **Volga-Flot Tour Office** (Волжский флот; ☎461 8030; www.vftour.ru; ⌚9am-7pm Mon-Fri, 10am-4pm Sat, 10am-3pm Sun) inside the station building and the cash office on the embankment sell mostly weekend day trips departing 9am to the ancient **Makaryev Monastery** (R1440) at the village of Makaryevo, 60km to the east. Book ahead. Food and an excursion are included. Hydrofoils to Gorodets leave from their own pier.

Bus

Buses to Vladimir (R400, 4½ hours, eight daily), Kostroma (R750, eight hours, daily) and Gorodets (R120, 1½ hours, almost every half-hour) depart from the small Kanavinskaya **bus station** (Автостанция). Private operators run minibuses to Moscow (R600, six hours, at least six daily), which depart across the road from the train station; others start from the bus station.

Train

Nizhny Novgorod **train station** still goes by its old name of Gorky-Moskovsky vokzal, so 'Gorky' appears on some timetables. It is on the western bank of the Oka River, at pl Revolyutsii. The **service centre** at the train station is helpful for buying rail tickets and also has internet.

WESTBOUND The high-speed Sapsan runs to Moscow's Kursky vokzal (seat R1490, four hours, two daily). One service continues to St Petersburg (seat R4200, 8½ hours, one daily). Over a dozen other trains also serve Moscow (*platskart* R1123, seven hours), via Vladimir (*platskart* R872, three hours).

EASTBOUND A good service to Perm (*platskart* R1716, 14½ hours, daily) is the flagship No 18; for Kazan (*platskart* R822, nine hours, daily) the No 41 is a good choice. Other trains go to Yekaterinburg (*kupe* R3800, 21 hours, six daily) and beyond.

Getting Around

The three major hubs for public transport are the train station (Московский вокзал), pl Minina i Pozharskogo (пл Минина и Пожарского) near the kremlin, and pl Gorkogo (пл Горкого) south of this. Change for either pl Gorkogo or the kremlin at the stop on the city side of the bridge, Kanavinsky most. At pl Minina i Pozharskogo, transport heading back to the train station picks up from the kremlin side of the road.

The city's metro might be extended across the river in the lifetime of this book, providing a useful link between pl Gorkogo and the train station.

Gorodets Городец

This neat little town, famous for its distinct style of folk art, has been spruced up to appeal to day trippers arriving in hydrofoils or by bus from Nizhny. At the time of the schism in the Russian Orthodox Church (1660), Gorodets became home to a population of Old Believers seeking religious sanctuary (see the boxed text, p624). They became skilful craftsmen, artists and wealthy tradesmen.

In a largely illiterate society, Gorodets oil-on-wood paintings played the role of glossy magazines, informing people of 'high-society' lifestyles and even political events, like wars. The craft is alive and kicking, so it's highly likely that you'll come away from your trip carrying a picture (from R150) or a whole piece of furniture, painted in Gorodets style. The town's other speciality is *pryaniki* – hard honey-rich cakes sold in most shops.

Sights

Countess Panina's House HOUSE-MUSEUM

(ul Rublyova 16; admission R20; ⌚10am-4pm, Tue-Sun) This house-museum has exhibits of irons and old costumes.

Museum of Samovars MUSEUM
(nab Revolyutsii 11; admission R30; ⏲9am-5pm Tue-Fri, 10am-4pm Sat & Sun) All types of the quintessential Russian tea-making equipment are on display here.

Local Studies Museum MUSEUM
(ul Lenina 11; admission R30; ⏲10am-4pm Tue-Sun) This museum includes the Virgin of Feodorovo icon – a curious three-dimensional depiction of Jesus creating a holographic effect.

Children's Museum MUSEUM
(ul Lenina 12; admission R20; ⏲10am-4pm Tue-Sun) This replica of a 19th-century schoolroom offers classes in making Gorodets-style clay animal-shaped pennywhistles (R20).

Getting There & Away

Several hydrofoils leave daily from Nizhny Novgorod's river station (R150, one hour). Volga-Flot Tour in Nizhny runs excursions for around R600. Buses run from Nizhny Novgorod's bus station (R120, 1½ hours, almost half-hourly).

REPUBLIC OF TATARSTAN

Kazan Казань

☎843 / POP 1.1 MILLION / ⏲MOSCOW

Kazan (meaning a cooking pot in Tatar) is the Istanbul of the Volga – a place where Europe and Asia curiously inspect each other from the tops of church belfries and minarets. It is about 150 years older than Moscow and the capital of the Tatarstan Republic (Республика Татарстан) – the land of the Volga Tatars, a Turkic people commonly associated with Chinggis Khaan's hordes, although they prefer to identify themselves with the ancient state of Volga Bulgaria, which was devastated by the Mongols.

Tatar autonomy is strong here and is not just about bilingual street signs. It also ensures that Tatarstan benefits greatly from vast oil reserves in this booming republic. The post-Soviet cultural revival, manifested by the popularity of modern Muslim fashions and Tatar-language literature, characterises Kazan's self-confidence.

Although Tatar nationalism is strong, it is not radical, and the local version of Islam is supermoderate. Slavic Russians make up about half of the population, and this cultural conflux of Slavic and Tatar cultures makes Kazan all the more an interesting city.

History

Kazan was founded as a northeastern outpost of Volga Bulgaria around 1000 AD. After the Tatar Mongols flattened Great Bulgar, it became the capital of the region and was incorporated into the Golden Horde. The independent Kazan khanate was created in 1438. It was ravaged in 1552 by Ivan the Terrible's troops and Tatar allies, and the collapse of Kazan caused such unease further east in the surviving khanate of Sibir (in Western Siberia), that Sibir nominally began paying tribute to Ivan. Kazan's collapse also cleared the way for Slavic Russians to move into the Urals region around Perm.

Tsar Ivan was quick to build a new – Russian – city on the ruins. Architects responsible for St Basil's Cathedral in Moscow (which honours the seizure of Kazan) were employed to plan the kremlin. Tatars were banished from the northern side of the Bulak Canal (about 500m east of the Volga shoreline) until the enlightened age of Catherine the Great. But the division of the city into the Russian and Tatar parts is still quite visible – the only centrally located mosque north of the canal is Kul Sharif, inside the kremlin.

Kazan grew into one of Russia's economic and cultural capitals, with the country's third university opening here in 1804. Its alumni include Leo Tolstoy and Vladimir Ulyanov (ie Lenin), who stirred up political trouble and was expelled. In Soviet times, Kazan became the capital of the Tatar Autonomous Republic and a major centre of the aviation industry.

Sights

Kremlin HISTORICAL BUILDINGS
A Unesco World Heritage Site, Kazan's striking kremlin (Кремль) is the focal point of the city's historic centre. It is home to government offices, pleasant parks and several functioning religious buildings. Some of the white limestone walls date from the 16th and 17th centuries.

At the entrance to the kremlin is the striking bronze figure of a man tearing barbed wire: the **Musa Dzhalil monument** (Памятник Мусе Джалилю). This was erected to honour the Tatar poet who was executed by the Nazis in Berlin's Moabit Prison in 1944, leaving a notebook full of poems to a Belgian friend.

After you enter the main gate, an alley leads past the enormous **Kul Sharif Mosque** (Мечеть Кул Шариф), completed in 2005, which is named after the imam who died defending the city against the troops of Ivan the Terrible in 1552. In front of this is the former cadet school building, housing the **Hermitage Centre** (Эрмитаж-Казань; admission R120; ⏲10am-5pm Tue-Sun), running rotating exhibitions from the collection of St Petersburg's Hermitage. The building also houses the **Tatarstan Museum of Natural History** (Музей естественной истории Татарстана; admission R100; ⏲10am-5pm Tue-Sun), with exhibits on the cosmos and dinosaurs. Both museums have English-language labelling.

Further along is the **Annunciation Cathedral** (Благовещенский собор) – built on the foundations of a razed eight-minaret mosque by Postnik Yakovlev, who is also responsible for St Basil's Cathedral in Moscow. Beside the cathedral, the 59m-high leaning **Syuyumbike Tower** (Башня Сююмбике) is the subject of the most romantic of Kazan's legends.

National Museum of the Republic of Tatarstan MUSEUM
(Национальный музей Республики Татарстан; Kremlyovskaya ul 2; admission R100; ⏲10am-6pm Tue-Sun) Opposite the kremlin's main entrance, the National Museum occupies an ornate 1770 building and has a large archaeology collection as well as jewellery, weapons and exhibits on the history of the Tatar people and its literary figures.

Tatarstan National Library LIBRARY
(Национальная библиотека Республики Татарстан; ☎238 7910; ul Kremlevskaya 33; tours in groups of three in English R300; ⏲9am-6pm) This small but highly unusual library dates from 1919, when several mid-19th-century houses were united and restyled to give each room its own art nouveau theme. Call ahead for English tours, or drop by for one in Russian (R50).

SS Peter & Paul Cathedral CHURCH
(Петропавловский собор; ul Musy Dzhalilya 21) This is Kazan's most attractive Orthodox church, built between 1723 and 1726 to commemorate Peter the Great's visit in 1722.

Soltanov Mosque MOSQUE
(Мечеть Солтанов; ul Gabdully Tukaya 14) Many of the mosques are clustered in the dumpy southwest corner of town. Near the central market is the Soltanov mosque, dating from 1867.

Nurullah Mosque MOSQUE
(Мечеть Нурулла; ul Moskovskaya 74) The Nurullah mosque, one of the most historic of the 41 surviving mosques in Kazan, has been rebuilt several times since 1849.

Festivals & Events

Sabantuy FESTIVAL
Joking competitions and serious sport events – horse races and wrestling (*koresh*) matches – feature prominently during Sabantuy, the main Tatar holiday celebrated all over Tatarstan and beyond in the middle of June. The winner of the wrestling competition is named Batyr and has to lift an overweight ram onto his shoulders for the cheering crowd.

THE TRUE STORY OF THE DEFIANT PRINCESS

On a guided tour of Kazan's kremlin, you'll likely hear this legend about the Syuyumbike Tower. When Ivan the Terrible seized Kazan, the tale goes, he planned to marry Syuyumbike, the beautiful niece of the deposed khan. Nobody wants an ugly, paranoid dictator as a husband, so out of sheer desperation she agreed to marry him only if he built a tower higher than anything either of them had ever seen. Once the construction was complete, she ascended the tower and threw herself off in front of the bewildered Ivan.

A neat little tale, but residents of the small town of Kasimov, hidden in the forests of the Ryazan region on the banks of the Oka, have a different story. In medieval times, Kasimov was a Tatar stronghold and a major rival of Kazan. Therefore its khan, Shakh-Ali, was all too keen to accept Tsar Ivan's invitation to join the expedition against Kazan, especially since he was promised Syuyumbike as a trophy. When he met the captured princess, Shakh-Ali disliked her from first sight, but he eventually succumbed to Ivan's dynastic manipulations and married her. The newlyweds went to Kasimov and avoided each other for the rest of their long lives, with Syuyumbike transforming from a tiny Eastern beauty into a bulky matriarch keen on political intrigue.

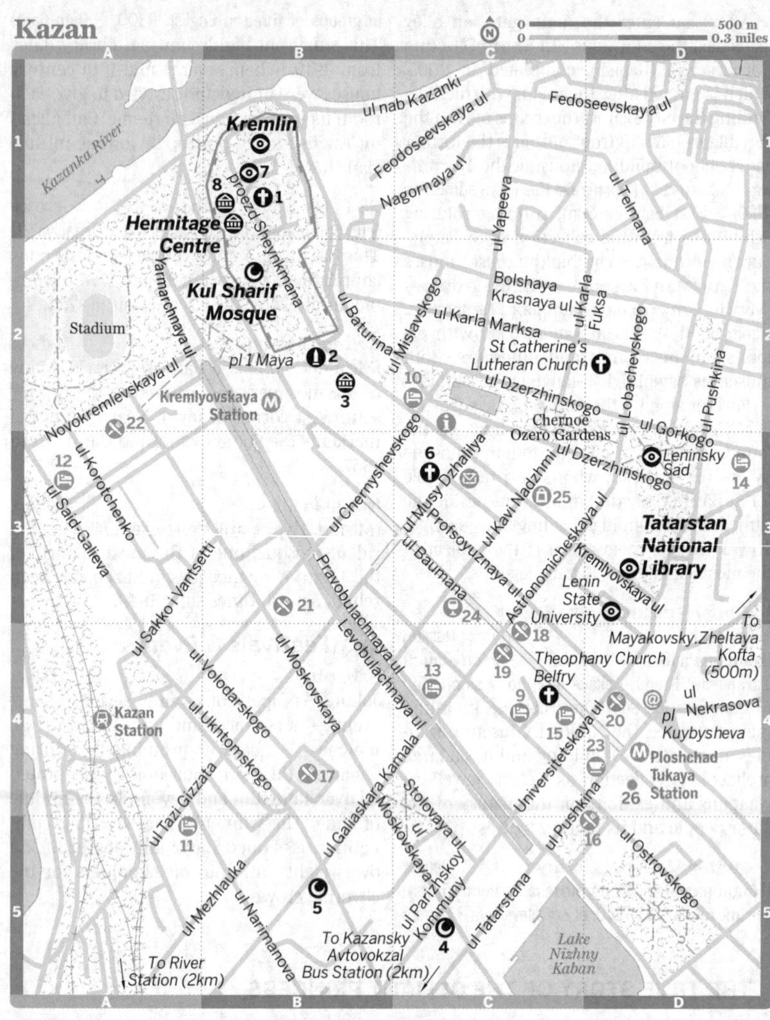

Sleeping

TOP CHOICE Hotel Volga HOTEL €€

(Гостиница Волга; ☎231 6349; www.volga-hotel.ru; ul Said-Galieva 1; s from R1400, d R1600-4900) The furbishing can be a little tired in some of the rooms and breakfast is a meagre affair, but the Volga is clean, welcoming and convenient to the train station and kremlin. The street is busy but the windows are well soundproofed.

Hotel Giuseppe HOTEL €€€

(Гостиница Джузеппе; ☎292 6934; www.giuseppe.ru; Kremlyovskaya ul 15/25; s R3100-5500, d R4030-7150, ste R8000-23,000; ❄📶) Above the Giuseppe pizzeria, this Italian-run place has spacious, comfortable rooms; corridors are decorated tastefully to give the atmosphere of a Venetian villa.

Shalyapin Palace Hotel HOTEL €€€

(☎238 2800; www.shalyapin-hotel.ru; Universitetskaya ul 7/80; s R3000-5500, d R5500-6800, ste R7300-30,000; ❄📶🏊) Named after Russia's greatest opera singer, whose statue greets you at the door, this large hotel has comfortable rooms, a fitness centre, sauna and 25m pool. Wi-fi is free in the lobby but costs per MB R5 in the rooms.

Kazan

Top Sights

Sights

Sleeping

Eating

Drinking

Shopping

Transport

Ibis Hotel HOTEL €€
(Ибис Отель; 567 5800; www.ibishotel.com; Pravobulachnaya ul 43/1; s without breakfast from R2200;) This centrally located chain hotel offers excellent value.

Hotel Art HOTEL €€€
(567 3003; www.hotelart-kazan.ru; ul Ostrovskaya 33; s R3500-4000, d R4500-5700, ste R5700-7600;) This central design hotel is close to the action on ul Baumana. Sleek with modern rooms.

Hotel Milena HOTEL €€
(Отель Милена; 292 9992; www.milenahotel.ru; ul Tazi Gizzata 19; r R1950-2400, ste R3450-3680, apt R9200-10,500;) Inexpensive and close to the train station. Ask for a quiet room as there's a flour mill nearby.

Mikado Hostel HOSTEL €
(Хостел Микадо; 253 2293; www.mikadootel.com; ul Gorkogo 6a; 9-bed dm from R500;) One of the cheapest options in town, this place is located one block east of the park, Leninsky Sad. Book online.

Eating & Drinking

The Bahetle (Бахетле) supermarket on the 1st floor of the **TsUM Shopping Mall** (ЦУМ; ul Moskovskaya 2; 9am-10pm) sells excellent Tatar pastries and anything you might need on the road. The colourful, sprawling **central market** (Рынок; ul Mezhlauka) is good for stocking up on snacks or simply for browsing.

TOP CHOICE **Priyut Kholostyaka** INTERNATIONAL €€
(Приют холостяка; 292 0771; ul Chernyshevskogo 27a; mains R350-600; 11am-midnight Mon-Fri, 11am-2am Sat & Sun) What a relief to escape the train station's dingy neighbourhood by sneaking into the 'Bachelor's Shelter', a rabbit hole which opens into a spotlessly white oasis of style with surrealist glass painting and coat-hangers shaped like wild garlic flowers. International food, including the inevitable sushi, is on the menu, and it has got the best latte this side of the Volga.

Giuseppe ITALIAN €
(Пиццерия Джузеппе; Kremlyovskaya ul 15; pizza R200; 9.30am-11.30pm;) A lively place for pizza and pasta, cappuccino and cannoli (Sicilian filled-pastry desserts). Order at the counter. There is a pricier but excellent restaurant upstairs in Hotel Giuseppe for formal dining (mains R500).

Kazan Askhane-Chai Yorty TATAR €
(Дом чая, кафе "Казанская ашхане"; ul Baumana 64; mains R80, pastry R30; 9am-7pm) This cheap eatery serves hearty Tatar food. Go for pastry – *echpohmak* with meat, *bekken* with cabbage, *kystyby* with mashed potatoes or *gubadiya* with sweet rice and raisins.

Dom Tatarskoy Kulinarii TATAR €€
(Дом Тартарской кулинарии; ☎292 7070; ul Baumana 31/12; mains R800-900; ⏲lunch & dinner) Despite the hefty price on many of the mains, you can find horsemeat with stewed vegetables here for R560 and a few cheaper dishes such as the *manti* (steamed dumplings) for R450.

Art Café CAFÉ, INTERNATIONAL €€
(Арт-кафе; ul Ostrovskogo 38; mains R400; ⏲8am-6am; 📶🗒) This stylish café and restaurant is a multipurpose place for breakfast, lunch and dinner, but it's also nice to linger around here over a cup of coffee or glass of wine.

Myasnoy Udar STEAKHOUSE €€
(Мясной удар; Profsoyuznaya ul 9; meals R500-700; ⏲7.30am-11pm; 🚭📶🗒) Besides the sought-after salad bar, 'Meat Kick' offers Western-style steakhouse fare in a comfortable, pseudo-rustic setting.

Capital Coffee House CAFÉ €
(Кофейня Капитал; ul Pushkina 5; coffee R120; ⏲8am-midnight Mon-Thu, 8am-2am Fri, 11am-midnight Sat & Sun; 🚭@📶🗒) Apart from making good coffee and nice international food (breakfast R150), these people promise to fix any cocktail according to your recipe. It has a slightly retro feel, and there are three PCs with internet access (R60 for half an hour).

Baker Street PUB €€
(ul Kremlevskaya 25; mains R450, business lunch R250-300; ⏲10am-1am; 📶🗒) A designer pub with tasteful decor and musical accompaniment.

Cuba Libre BAR €
(Куба Либре; ul Baumana 58; mains R350, cuba libre R220; ⏲noon-2am Sun-Thu, noon-5am Sat-Fri) A convivial drinking den where you can chat to friendly bartenders and other visitors while sipping Kazan's best mojitos. Wild Latin dancing may erupt at any moment.

WORTH A TRIP

BOLGAR – BACK TO THE ROOTS

It might be the smallest town in Tatarstan, but Bolgar (Болгар) shares its name on equal terms with the country of Bulgaria. The word 'Volga' is most likely a Slavic corruption of the same name. Bolgar is the descendant of Great Bulgar, the capital of one of the most powerful states of early medieval Eastern Europe. Ruins of that city, on the outskirts of the modern town, have been turned into an open-air museum, which has become a major place of pilgrimage for Tatars in search of their roots.

The Bulgars were a Turkic tribe based south of the Don when they came under pressure from the Khazars and had to migrate. One branch headed west and occupied the eastern Balkans, but it was soon assimilated by local Slavs, leaving no trace but the name. The eastern branch settled on the Volga and mixed with local Finno-Ugric tribes. Sunni Islam became the official religion in 921.

The **Great Bulgar Museum** (ul Nazarovykh 67; admission R100; ⏲8am-5pm) is located 1km east of the town on the high bank of the Volga. The site comprises several ruins scattered around a vast expanse of grassland on top of a high cliff above the Volga. It's dominated by the minaret, which was restored in 2005, and the Russian 18th-century Assumption Church, which stands right next to it and houses an interesting archaeological museum.

Sleeping

Hotel Regina (Отель Регина; ☎84347-310 44; www.hotelregina.ru; ul Gorkogo 30; s R1050-1400, d R1250-3000)

Transport

Kazan–Bolgar by Boat The main pier, located a few kilometres upstream from the museum, is used by daily hydrofoils (R180, 2½ hours), leaving Bolgar at 6am and Kazan at 6pm. Check at Kazan's river station for occasional boats docking at the tourist pier near the museum.

Bus Departs Kazan Yuzhny (southern) bus station at 10am and 5pm daily, and from Bolgar at 7am and 2pm (R270, five hours).

Taxi Hotel Regina can arrange a shared taxi back to Kazan (from R350 per person).

Entertainment

Mayakovsky.Zheltaya Kofta NIGHTCLUB
(Ресторан-клуб "Маяковский.Желтая кофта; www.zheltaya-kofta.ru; ul Mayakovskogo 24a; cover R300) It can be Tatar rap or punk bands singing covers of Soviet soundtrack faves, or something even more experimental in this club with a youthful crowd and decor inspired by artist Kasimir Malevich. Take tram 9 from pl Tukaya towards KGSA and ask for ul Mayakovskaya.

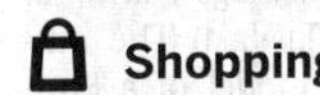

Shopping

Dom Knigi BOOKSTORE
(Дом киниги; ul Kremlevskaya 25; ⌚9.30am-7.30pm) Come here for maps and books in Russian.

Information

Kazan tourist office (Казанский туристско-информационный центр; ☎292 3010; http://gokazan.com; Kremlyovskaya ul 15/25; ⌚9.30am-6.30pm Mon-Fri, 9.30am-3.30pm Sat) One of the few city tourist offices in Russia, staff here are knowledgeable and keep an excellent sheet map of town (also available in many hotels).

Main post & telephone office (Почта и телеграф; Kremlyovskaya ul 8; ⌚8am-8pm Mon-Fri, 9am-6pm Sat, 9am-2pm Sun)

Tattelekom (Таттелеком; ul Pushkina 15; per hr R30; ⌚24hr)

Getting There & Away

The **Aviakassa** (☎238 1555) booth inside **Hotel Tatarstan** (Гостиница Татарстан; ul Pushkina 4) is convenient for both air and railway tickets.

AIR **Kazan International Airport** (☎267 8807; www.airport.kazan.ru), located 30km south of the city, has good connections with the rest of Russia, including Khabarovsk, Krasnoyarsk, Novosibirsk, Moscow and St Petersburg. There are also flights to Frankfurt in Germany (four hours, four weekly) and Istanbul in Turkey (four hours, two weekly).

BOAT Boats depart Kazan at 8.45am for Sviyazhsk and leave Sviyazhsk at 4.30pm (R91, two hours, daily); excursions boats leave Kazan at 10am (R350, Saturday and Sunday). Boats for Sviyazhsk and Bolgar (p358) leave from the **river station** at the end of ul Tatarstan. It's best to buy tickets from the river station well in advance.

TRAIN The beautifully restored original train station on ul Said-Galieva now serves as a waiting room. Long-distance tickets are sold in a building adjacent to the new sleek suburban train station. Queues are smaller at ticket counters on the 2nd floor, where the service centre is also located. Heading west, frequent trains connect Kazan with Moscow (R2165, 13 hours). Heading east, the daily No 16 to Yekaterinburg (R2442, 13½ hours) is the best service but its departure time is less convenient than several others.

KAZAN'S BUS STATIONS

Kazan has two bus stations, each serving different destinations. The **Kazansky Avtovokzal** (Казанский автовокзал; www.avtovokzal-kzn.ru; Devyataeva 15), also known locally as the 'Stolichny Avtovokzal', is located near the river station and has online summer (Расписание лето межгород) and winter (Расписание зима межгород) timetables. Most long-distance destinations depart from here, including those for Ulyanovsk (R400, five hours, nine daily) and Samara (R800, seven hours, two daily). **Yuzhny Avtovokzal** (Южный автовокзал; ☎261 5636; Orenburgsky trakt 207) is located up to an hour away (allowing for traffic jams) from pl Tukaya by bus 37. This station serves Bolgar.

Getting Around

Bus 97 (every half an hour, 5am to 11pm) connects the airport with Kazan's centre, passing metro Prospekt Pobedy at the end of the city's only metro line. Stations **Kremlyovskaya** and **Ploshchad Tukaya** are located at either end of ul Baumana. Tram 7 and buses 53 and 6 link the train, bus and river stations. Tram 2 and bus 8 go from the river station to pl Tukaya.

Sviyazhsk Свияжск

A favourite escape for Kazan's artists, this island has some of the oldest architecture in the region and a fascinating history.

When Ivan the Terrible decided to end the Kazan khanate, he first ordered a base to be built for the coming onslaught on top of Mt Kruglaya at the mouth of the Sviyaga River. Its wooden kremlin was built 700km upstream in the town of Myshkin near Yaroslavl. When finished, the builders marked each log, disassembled the fortress and sent it floating down the river to Sviyazhsk, where it was reassembled. Immediately after the Tatar defeat, Ivan's favourite architect Postnik Yakovlev (cocreator of Moscow's St Basil's Cathedral and Kazan's Annunciation

Cathedral) embarked on the construction of churches and monasteries here.

The Bolsheviks destroyed about half of Sviyazhsk's churches – wooden crosses now mark their location – but several highlights were spared by the atheist zealots. These include the **Assumption Monastery**, whose **St Nicolas Church** is used for exhibitions of local artists, and **John the Baptist Monastery**, whose wooden **Trinity Church** looks like a modern dacha and is the only edifice inside the monastery from the original Myshkin-built fortress (though it doesn't look anything like the original, having been rebuilt in 2002).

Boats depart Kazan at 8.45am for Sviyazhsk, and leave Sviyazhsk at 4.30pm (R91, two hours, daily); excursions boats leave Kazan at 10am (R350, Saturday and Sunday). Some trains from Kazan (one way R46, 1¼ hours, 16 daily) go via Staroye Arakhchino, where you can view the **Temple of All Religions**, an offbeat temple with cupolas, minarets and spires representing 12 religions. It is the brainchild of the Tatar artist-cum-alternative-healer Ildar Khanov.

ULYANOVSK & SAMARA REGIONS

Ulyanovsk Ульяновск

8422 / POP 614,000 / MOSCOW

The view of the Volga from the Venets promenade is arresting, but turn around and what you'll see is less inspiring. Welcome to the communist Bethlehem, the birthplace of Lenin.

Founded as Simbirsk in the 17th century, the city was dubbed the Nobles' Nest as many young aristocrats spent summers here dreaming of great endeavours while resting on a couch between noon-time breakfast and late-afternoon nap, their lifestyle epitomised by Simbirsk native Ivan Goncharov in his novel *Oblomov*. Ulyanovsk is better known now, however, as the birthplace of the revolutionaries Alexander Kerensky and the more famous Vladimir Ulyanov (aka Lenin).

Today it's a grey-ish city with sights dedicated to Lenin and a cluster of museums presenting the town in the light of 'old Simbirsk'.

Sights

TOP CHOICE **Lenin Memorial Centre** MUSEUM

(Ленинский Мемориальный Центр; www.lenin-memorial.ru; pl 100-Letiya Lenina 1; admission to exhibition halls R200; 10am-5pm Tue-Sun) This sprawling memorial centre dedicated to Ulyanovsk's famous son is built around two family houses and a large exhibition building that contains permanent and changing exhibits. It has space dedicated to Lenin, old Simbirsk and changing exhibitions.

Museum of Ulyanovsk Architecture MUSEUM

(Градостроительство и архитектура Симбирска-Ульяновска; ul Tolstogo 24a & 43; admission R100; 9am-5pm Tue-Sun) The museum contains a full-size model of a Simbirsk wooden fortress watchtower and an exhibition about architects responsible for the town's best buildings, both at ul Tolstogo 43. The building at ul Tolstogo 24a contains a moving exhibition dedicated to the city's architectural heritage that was destroyed by the communists.

Lenin's Motherland Museum-Reserve MUSEUMS

Recently a movement has sprung up to push ahead the revival of old Simbirsk by turning historic houses mostly on and around ul Lenina and ul Tolstogo into museums. The list of all 13 is available at www.ulzapovednik.ru/museum. They include **Simbirsk in the Late 19th and Early 20th Centuries** (Симбирск конца XIX-начала XX вв; ul Lenina 90; admission R150; 9am-5pm Tue-Sun), the **Museum of Ulyanovsk Photography** (Музей 'Симбирская фотография'; ul Engelsa 1b; admission R150; 10am-4.30pm Tue-Sun) and the **Regional Art & Local Studies Museum** (Художественный и краеведческий музей; bul Novy Venets 3; admission R50; 10am-6pm Tue-Sun).

Lenin Flat-Museum MUSEUM

(Квартира-музей Ленина; ul Sovetskaya; admission R200; 9am-5pm, closed Thu & Sat) A must-see for Lenin addicts – this is where Lenin grew up. It's part of the memorial centre.

Goncharov Museum MUSEUM

(Музей Гончарова; ul Lenina 134; admission about R60-100) Closed for restoration in 2011, this historic house is where the writer Ivan Goncharov grew up. Exhibition space was being enlarged on our last visit.

Sleeping & Eating

At the time of research, a Hilton hotel was being built on ul Goncharova, just south of the Venets.

Ulyanovsk

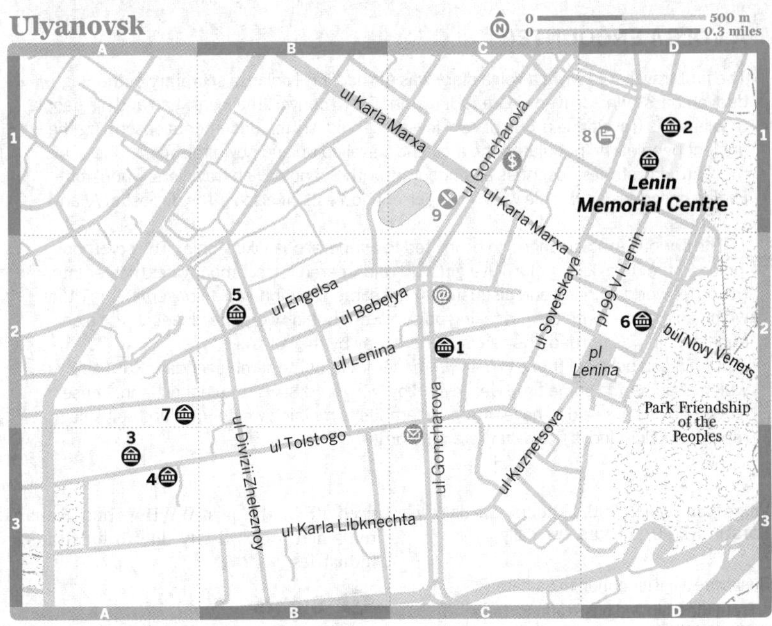

Hotel Venets HOTEL €€
(Гостиница Венец; ☎394 576; ul Sovetskaya 15; with breakfast s R2400-3580, d R3000-5700, ste R6200-9500; 📶) This formidable piece of Soviet hotel architecture in a towering block opposite the memorial centre has meagre breakfasts but stunning views in all directions. The bar on the top floor has good views. Registration is a hefty €10.

Maxi Pizza PIZZA €
(Макси Пицца; ☎421 465; ul Goncharova 21; slice of pizza R75; ⏰10am-11pm) This cafeteria-style place is almost always packed with students and other young 'uns. You can't go wrong with cheap pizza and beer; the salads are also good.

Information

Internet Salon (Интернет-салон; ☎420 911; ul Bebelya 22; per MB R2; ⏰8am-10pm) Enter through the courtyard.

Getting There & Around

The **long-distance bus station** (www.avtovokzal73.ru) is 4km from the centre and is served by tram 2 from Hotel Venets. Several buses run to Kazan (R420, five hours), Samara (R370, five hours) and Syzran (R201, three hours, hourly).

Ulyanovsk-Tsentralnaya train station is 4.5km from the centre and is served by *marshrutka* 94 or 95 or tram 4. Trains run to the following destinations:

Kazan *platskart* R550, six hours, frequent
Moscow *platskart* R1600, 15 hours, four daily
Ufa *platskart* R457, 14 hours, three daily

Ulyanovsk

Top Sights

Lenin Memorial Centre D1

Sights

1 Goncharov Museum C2
2 Lenin Flat Museum D1
3 Museum of Ulyanovsk Architecture A3
4 Museum of Ulyanovsk Architecture A3
5 Museum of Ulyanovsk Photography B2
6 Regional Art & Local Studies Museum D2
7 Simbirsk in the Late 19th and Early 20th Centuries A2

Sleeping

8 Hotel Venets D1

Eating

9 Maxi Pizza C1

A VOLGA ENCOUNTER

The first traveller to write a Volga diary was Ahmed ibn-Fadlan, a secretary of the Baghdadi embassy who arrived in Great Bulgar in 922 to convert the local khan and his people to Islam. His travelogue is one of very few preserved written documents describing the ancient people who populated the area and travelled up and down the Volga. One of his most striking stories describes an encounter with Scandinavian travellers, whom ibn-Fadlan describes as 'people with most perfect bodies', but also as 'the dirtiest of Allah's creatures'.

The curious Arab arranged to be invited to a funeral of a Viking chief. The ceremony included the ritual killing of a slave girl who volunteered to accompany her master into the other world. Thrilled and disgusted at the same time, ibn-Fadlan observed the ritual, which culminated with the girl taking poison. Both bodies were then loaded onto a ship and the ship was burned, the ashes carried away by the Volga.

Ibn-Fadlan believed these Vikings were members of the semi-legendary Rus tribe, which at about the same time was invited by Novgorod Slavs to rule their land. These Novgorodians are said to have uttered a famous complaint, which Russians still enjoy repeating: 'Our land is rich, but there is no order.'

Volgograd *kupe* R2900, 19 hours, two daily, via **Saratov** R1220, 11 hours, two daily

Buses are a better option to Samara.

From the train and bus stations, **taxis** (☎494949) to the centre costs about R250. Haggle.

Samara Самара

☎846 / POP 1.16 MILLION / ⏰MOSCOW

'Oh, Samara, the little town, I am so restless – give me some rest.' The quintessential drinking song is now only partly true: this city of over a million is little no more, and in recent years has focused on drawing visitors to the city. Not without justification, for Samara is a pleasant place to visit. On a summer day, the riverbanks are packed with bathing beauties, in-line skaters and beer drinkers. It has a couple of interesting museums and a small but lively arts scene. Samara also serves as the base for excursions into the nearby Zhiguli Hills.

Samara grew up where the Volga meets the Samara River, at a sharp bend across from the Zhiguli Hills. Founded as a border fortress in 1568, it saw the local governor drowned by Stepan Razin's Cossacks in 1670 and another governor flee Yemelyan Pugachev's peasant army in 1774. The Russian Civil War began in Samara, when a unit of Czechoslovakian prisoners of war commandeered their train and seized control of the city, turning it into a stronghold for the emerging White Army. During WWII a bunker was built here for Stalin but he never used it; in the post-WWII period Samara remained a closed city due to its strategic industries.

Sights

As well as visiting the key sights, take the time to stroll along the banks of the Volga River, which is flanked by lush parks and sandy beaches.

TOP CHOICE Samara Art Museum ART GALLERY
(Художественный музей; www.artmus.ru; ul Kuybysheva 92; admission R100; ⏰10am-6pm) Easily the most important cultural attraction in the city, the Samara Art Museum exhibits mainly Russian art, including works by those artists who came to the region to paint. Look for *Boyarishina,* given by Surikov to a local doctor who treated him when he fell ill. The museum also holds an impressive collection of early Kazimir Malevich works.

Zhiguli Brewery BREWERY
(Жигулёвское пиво; www.samarabeer.ru; Volzhsky pr 4) This unlikely highlight of Samara is best enjoyed either on a warm day or when the Volga is frozen over. The eastern side was built by Austrian aristocrat Alfred von Wakano in 1881. Here you can take your plastic bottle out of the rucksack and fill it up at the kiosk that sells the amber gold from the tap. You'll also find a row of stalls selling smoked and salted fish. Fill up, grab some fish and stroll down to the Volga to enjoy the meal before walking back along the embankment into the centre. To get out here, take any *marshrutka* east from Len-

ingradskaya ul along ul Kuybysheva, asking the driver to stop at Pivzavod.

Stalin's Bunker HISTORICAL BUILDING
(Бункер Сталина; ☎333 3571; ul Frunze 167; ⏲prebook group tours) Stalin's Bunker, built nine storeys below the Academy of Culture and Art, never actually served its intended purpose, as Stalin decided to stay in Moscow to direct events. Unfortunately, it is almost impossible to get in without booking a group tour with a tour company. Samara Intour can organise one, but it costs R2000 per individual or group, so it's best to share costs with travel companions.

Synagogue SYNAGOGUE
(Синагога; ul Sadovaya 49) This turreted building from 1903 was turned into a bread factory during Soviet times and is closed but now being restored to its original striped-brick 'rainbow' style.

Alabin Museum MUSEUM
(Музей Алабина; www.alabin.ru; Leninskaya ul 142; admission R100; ⏲10am-6pm Tue-Sat) Come here for exhibits on regional palaeontology and archaeology, including dinosaur fossils found in the Zhiguli Hills.

Children's Art Gallery ART GALLERY
(Детская художественная галерея; ul Kuybysheva 139; adult/child R70/50; ⏲9am-5.30pm) Housed in the landmark **Engineer Klodt's House** (Дом инженера Клодта), which resembles a fairy-tale castle and contains a collection of children's art and art for children.

Tours

Samara Intour TOUR COMPANY
(Самара Интур; ☎279 2040; www.samaraintour.ru; Samarskaya ul 51/53; ⏲9am-7pm Mon-Fri, 10am-5pm Sat) This highly professional travel agency has some staff who speak English and German. They can combine you with a group to get you into Stalin's bunker at discount rates, organise rafting (€50 per day) or mountain-bike trips (about €20 per day), as well as horse riding and other activities such as the *zhigulyovskaya krugosvetka* boat trip in the Samara Bend. They also book flights and train tickets.

Festivals & Events

Rock on the Volga MUSIC
(www.rocknadvolgoi.ru) This festival is held annually in mid-June on the fields of the Krasny Pakhar (Red Ploughman) collective farm, 20km north of Samara. It's a remote location for Europe's largest one-day festival and, as well as long-standing Russian outfits like DDT, Akvarium (Aquarium) and Nochnye Snaypery (Night Snipers), it has featured the likes of Deep Purple and Skunk Anansie.

Sleeping

TOP CHOICE **Azimut Hotel** HOTEL €€
(Гостиница Азимут; ☎277 8080; www.azimuthotels.ru; ul Frunze 91/37; s R2500-3100, d R2700-5300; ⊖☜) This historic hotel offers some of the best value in town. Rooms are comfortable, breakfast is in the pleasant restaurant and staff are helpful and knowledgeable.

OFFBEAT IN SAMARA

Below its provincial urban surface, Samara has several small but interesting design and culture places. Out just beyond pl Slavy, **Salon-Atelye SaXara** (салон Ателье SaXara; www.saxara.ru; ul Polevaya 54; ⏲10am-7pm Mon-Sat, 11am-5pm Sun) has upmarket women's clothing and accessories with pronounced retro fin-de-siècle nuances. **Vse Drugoe** (Все другое; per Vysotskogo 10; ⏲10am-8pm) has lots of interesting designer knick-knacks and accessories like handbags and cameras along with more-standard 'design' items like Moleskin notebooks. Vse Drugoe often supports cultural events such as those held in the cultural centre for young Samarians, **KZ Art-Propaganda** (КЦ Арт Пропаганда; www.art-propaganda.ru; ul Kuybysheva 68; ⏲10am-9pm Mon-Fri, 4-9pm Sat & Sun). This has a small room upstairs where exhibitions are sometimes held; just hang out and ask anyone who happens to be there about events if you want to make contact with the scene in Samara. Occasional recent flyers are also put up there.

Podval (Подвалъ; ul Nekrasovskaya 63; admission about R100; ⏲7pm-3am) is true to its name ('The Basement') and has live rock, metal, gothic and other acts every night. Also popular is **Skvoznyak** (Сквозняк; www.skvoznyak.ru; ul Novo-Sadovaya 106g; cover R200; ⏲5pm-3am). Trams going east along ul Galaktionovskaya then pr Lenina take you there. Ask for the entertainment centre Zvezda; it's opposite.

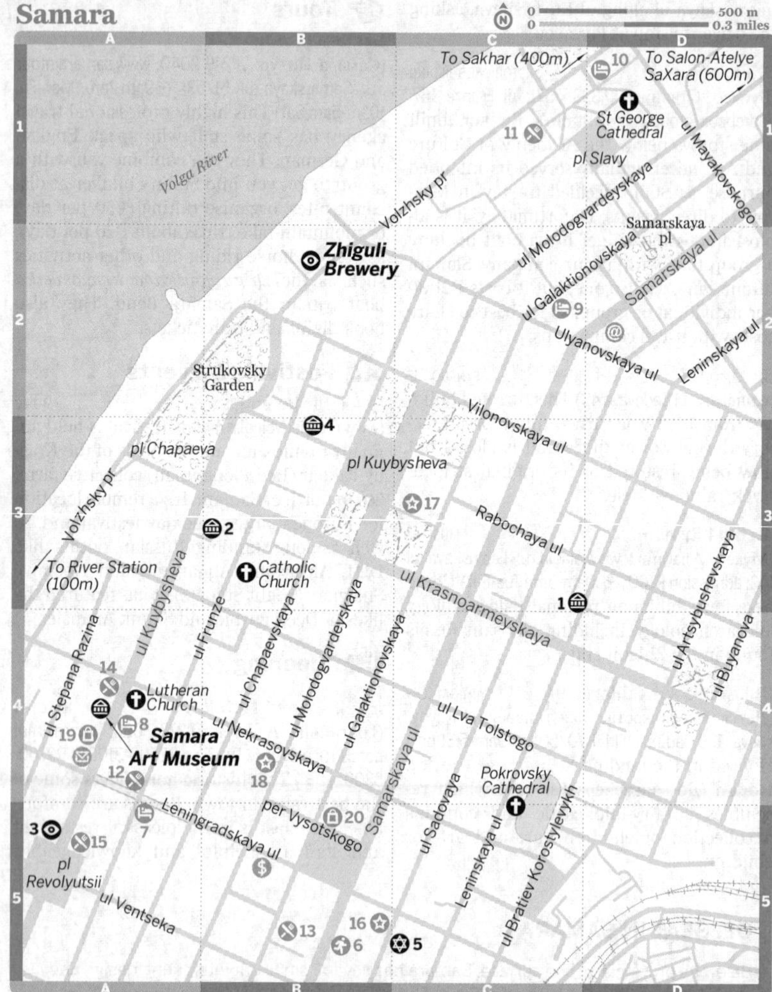

The doors could be a little heavier to reduce sound from the corridors, but otherwise it's excellent.

Bristol-Zhiguli Hotel HOTEL €€€
(Гостиница Бристоль-Жигули; ☎332 0655; www.bristol-zhiguly.ru; ul Kuybysheva 111; s R2500, d R4400-4700, ste R5000-7900; ⊜@☜) The most expensive room in this hotel inside an ornate 19th-century building is the one where opera singer Fyodor Chaliapin once stayed, using the balcony as a stage to sing for a crowd of adoring fans. Cheaper rooms without bathrooms are available.

Hotel Europe HOTEL €€€
(Гостиница Европа; ☎708 631; www.hoteleurope.ru; Galaktionovskaya ul 171; with breakfast s R3300-3900, d R4290-6370, apt R7670; ⊜❄@☜☒) Housed in a lovely 1902 mansion, this hotel has 20 simple guest rooms and a highly rated restaurant. The decor is comfortable and modern, if nondescript.

Volga Hotel HOTEL €€
(Гостиница Волга; ☎242 1196; Volzhsky pr 29; s R700-2600, d R1200-3600; ☜) Located at the northern end of the embankment, the Volga has the cheapest rooms in town. Although it maintains a staid, Soviet ambience, it's fine

Samara

Top Sights
- Samara Art Museum ... A4
- Zhiguli Brewery ... B2

Sights
- 1 Alabin Museum ... C3
- 2 Children's Art Gallery ... B3
- 3 KZ Art-Propaganda ... A5
- 4 Stalin's Bunker ... B3
- 5 Synagogue ... C5

Activities, Courses & Tours
- 6 Samara Intour ... B5

Sleeping
- 7 Azimut Hotel ... A5
- 8 Bristol-Zhiguli Hotel ... A4
- 9 Hotel Europe ... C2
- 10 Volga Hotel ... D1

Eating
- 11 Art & Fact ... C1
- 12 Kipyatok ... A4
- Staraya Kvartira ... (see 6)
- 13 Troitsky Market ... B5
- 14 U Palycha ... A4
- 15 Zhili-Byli ... A5

Entertainment
- 16 Bumazhnaya Luna ... B5
- 17 Opera & Ballet Theatre ... C3
- 18 Podval ... B4

Shopping
- 19 Chakona ... A4
- 20 Vse Drugoe ... B5

for short stays. Rooms with bathrooms are more expensive; wi-fi costs R100 per 100MB.

Eating & Drinking

TOP CHOICE **Staraya Kvartira** RUSSIAN €€

(Старая квартира; www.oldflat.ru; Samarskaya ul 51/53; mains R400-600; noon-midnight) Easily one of the most interesting restaurants in Samara, the 'Old Flat' is literally a rabbit warren of rooms accessed via the souvenir shop (downstairs from Samara Intour). The food is excellent, especially the lamb casserole *(zharkoye razboynichye)* with eggplant, garlic and peppers.

Kipyatok RUSSIAN €€

(Кипяток; 333 2720; Leningradskaya ul 40; mains R300; 10am-midnight;) This funky restaurant re-creates the golden age of the Russian culinary arts in the early 20th century. Creative dishes are complemented by homemade *kvas* (fermented rye bread water) and freshly produced cranberry *mors* (fruit drink).

Art & Fact INTERNATIONAL, BAR €€

(www.artfact-samara.ru; Volzhsky pr 19; mains R650-1100, pizza R300, soups R150-300; noon-11pm Mon-Thu, noon-3am Fri, 3pm-3am Sat, 3-11pm Sun) This restaurant and bar, complete with a stage and dance space on the ground floor, is relaxed and convivial, especially in the upstairs Whisky Bar, where you have a panorama of the writhing below. A glass of Australian Jacob's Creek wine costs R220.

Zhili-Byli RUSSIAN €

(Жили-были; ul Kuybysheva 81; mains R250; 11am-midnight) This is a good-value chain restaurant with rustic decor.

U Palycha RUSSIAN €€

(У Палыча; http://palich.ru; ul Kuybysheva 100; meals R500-800) Highly recommended for its Russian cuisine, including its *pelmeni* (Russian-style ravioli). There's live Russian folk music most nights.

Troitsky Market MARKET €

(Троицкий рынок; ul Galaktionovskaya; 7am-7pm Mon-Sat, 10am-6pm Sun) Stalls full of fresh fruit and vegies, lots of fresh and smoked fish, as well as breads, meats and cheeses.

Sakhar CAFÉ, BAR

(Сахар; Volzhsky pr 39; 6pm-3am) Sleek lounge near pl Slavy with a devoted following among a young, fashionable set. For something more relaxed, head down to the river where there are other bars and restaurants. Sakhar is one block east of pl Slavy near the circus (Цирк).

Entertainment

Opera & Ballet Theatre THEATRE

(Театр оперы и балета; 322 509; www.opera-samara.ru; pl Kuybysheva 1; ticket office 11am-7pm) The main venue for classical dance and musical performances.

Bumazhnaya Luna NIGHTCLUB, BAR

(Бумажная луна; Leningradskaya ul 77; mains R300; noon-2am) The 'Paper Moon', an artsy club-bar-restaurant with funky design, attracts Samara's bohemians. Concerts and readings take place almost daily.

Shopping

Chakona BOOKSTORE

(Чакона; www.chaconne.ru; ul Kuybysheva 84; 10am-9pm) Come here for books (mostly

Russian) and maps; it's located on the 3rd floor.

Information

Post office (Почтамт; ul Kuybysheva 82; ⌚9am-7pm Mon-Fri, 9am-5pm Sat & Sun)
Sberbank (Leningradskaya ul 63)
Vizit Internet Centre (Визит интернет центр; Samarskaya ul 199; per MB R4; ⌚9am-5pm Mon-Fri, 9am-3pm Sat)

Getting There & Away

Air and rail tickets are available at Samara Intour.

Air

Lufthansa, Aeroflot and Czech Airlines regularly serve Frankfurt in Germany (return R17,000) and Prague (return R14,000). S7, UTAir and Aeroflot fly to Moscow (R7000, 2½ hours).

Boat

The **river station** (Речной вокзал) is at the west end of the embankment, in front of Hotel Rossiya. Long-distance cruises operate to various destinations along the Volga. Several cruise agencies run kiosks here. **Infoflot** (276 7491; www.infoflot.com) sells return cruises to Kazan (from R6900, three days), Ulyanovsk (from R4300, three days) and Volgograd (from R10,400, five days). There are also boats to closer destinations, including Shiryaevo (R70, 2½ hours, two daily).

Bus

The central bus station is 6km southeast of the centre. It has connections to the following:
Saratov Kazan R650, 10 hours, daily
Syzran R231, four hours, five daily
Tolyatti R135, two hours, hourly
Ulyanovsk R370, five hours, hourly

Train

Samara has good connections with Moscow (*kupe* R2560, 17 hours), Saratov (*kupe* R1170, 11 hours) and Volgograd (*kupe* R1760, 19 hours). For Kazan bus is better, and for Astrakhan book via Volgograd as direct trains pass through Kazakhstan.

Getting Around

Most bus and *marshrutky* routes run straight as a nail in the central part of town, so it's easiest just to walk to the major street to grab one (eg ul Kuybysheva to go east to pl Slavy, or ul Samarskaya for pl Samarskaya).

To/From the Bus & Train Stations

Trolleybuses 2, 4, 12, 16 and 17 run between the train and bus stations. From pl Revolyutsii, take bus 37, 46, 47 or *marshrutky* 257d, 94, 247, 47, 37, 269 or 259.

Haggle **taxis** (☎302 0202) down to R300 or less from the bus station to the centre (the more 'honest' drivers hang out on the right as you leave the bus station building). The price is about R100 to R150 from the train station to anywhere on the map in this book.

Samara Bend

Самарская Лука

Samara sits on the left bank of the Volga, while the right bank is dominated by the rocky Zhiguli Hills. The river loops around the hills creating a peninsula, encompassing 32,000 hectares of national forest reserve. The **Samara Bend National Park** (Samarskaya Luka in Russian) is a prime area for hikes along rocky ledges and grand Volga vistas. The peaks – the highest being Strelnaya Mountain at 370m – are in the northwest corner of the reserve. These hills were the hideout of peasant rebel Stepan Razin in the 17th century.

The easiest way to reach the reserve in summer is to take a boat to any of the villages on the right bank, such as Shiryaevo.

NICK CAVE & THE VOLGA

The connection between rock musician Nick Cave, The Seekers – a popular Australian folk band of the 1960s – and the Volga River would seem tenuous, but one of the most popular songs by The Seekers, and a classic cover that any Nick Cave fan will know, is the mournful 'The Carnival Is Over'. In fact, this classic dirge is a Volga folk song about the ataman Stepan Razin, who threw a kidnapped Persian princess overboard from a pirated ship on the Volga to prevent his men from dallying with her (probably not the best solution for such circumstances, but anyway). Songwriter Tom Springfield (brother of 1960s singer Dusty, for trivia freaks) wrote the English lyrics to the Seekers' version, and this obscure Volga song popular in the late 19th century acquired a double-bass backing and a slightly de-Russified folk edge, eventually landing high among the top 50 best-selling records of all time. You can check out the three versions on YouTube.

WORTH A TRIP

TOLYATTI – HOME OF THE LADA

If you're an antitourist like Daniel Kalder (see p619), it's hard to think of a better destination than Tolyatti (Тольятти). Welcome to Lada-land, the place where one of the world's most ridiculed vehicles is produced. The city is a particularly depressing Soviet urban sprawl, where the quality of the roads matches that of Lada cars. That said, it is strategically placed by the giant Kuybyshev reservoir dam, with the Zhiguli Hills starting right across the water. Besides, an embryonic sports and tourism industry is emerging here.

The **Technical Museum** (Yuzhnoye sh 137; admission R30; 9am-5pm), in the New Town (Novy Gorod) and opposite the VAZ plant that makes Ladas, has a vast collection of mostly military hardware, including a nuclear submarine. While here, you can also knead your muscles at the **Spin Park** (8482-489 120; www.spin-sport.ru; Portposyolok, Komsomolskoye sh 22; mountain bikes 1hr R500; 8am-7pm), with its 20km of bicycle lanes in a forested area and a swimming pool for chilling out after the exercise.

If you're staying overnight **Zhiguli** (8482-223 311; www.lada-gam.ru; ul Mira 77; s R1200-2100, d R1500-3500, apt R6400; restaurant 9am-2am; mains R400;) is simple but adequate.

Buses go to/from Samara (R135, two hours, hourly), Ulyanovsk (R310, four hours, at least hourly) and Kazan (R400, 6½ hours, three daily). Tolyatti has three districts. Expect to pay about R200 for trips between these, less for just one district. **Novoe Taxi** (8482-310 000, 777 600) is a reliable company.

If you want to explore the area by public transport or bicycle, local hubs Tolyatti and Syzran come into the equation. Together with Samara, they form an almost equilateral triangle and often have better connections with adjacent regions than the provincial capital.

The traditional way to experience the Samara Bend is by boat. Every year, thousands of locals raft *zhigulyovskaya krugosvetka,* which translates as 'Zhiguli round-the-world trip'. The route follows the loop in the river, then cuts back up north via a channel on the west side of the park. Samara Intour organises these trips (R11,500 for a 10-day trip).

Shiryaevo Ширяево

In the 1870s, Ilya Repin spent two years in this village just north of Samara on the west bank of the Volga. Here he completed sketches for his famous painting *Barge Haulers on the Volga,* which is now in St Petersburg's Russian Museum.

Today, this pleasant village welcomes art lovers and day trippers. The **Repin Museum** (ul Sovetskaya 14; admission R100; 11am-4pm, closed Mon) has a nice selection of Volga River paintings, including some Repin reproductions. The appeal lies less in seeing the art, however, than in experiencing this quintessential Volga village.

Regular boat from Samara (R70, 2½ hours, two daily) is the best way to reach Shiryaevo. You can reach it more easily by bus from Tolyatti (R101, two hours, four daily).

SARATOV & VOLGOGRAD REGIONS

Saratov Саратов

8452 / POP 831,000 / MOSCOW

Another town, another song. 'So many golden lights on the streets of Saratov, so many bachelors around, but I'm in love with a married guy' goes the 1950s superhit. Lamps are indeed golden-coloured along the riverside promenade, where the tune is chimed on the hour.

Saratov lacks major tourist attractions, but it's a laid-back place and has a bit of a seaside resort atmosphere. The former name of ul Kirova is Nemetskaya (German), a sure sign that Saratov was once at the heart of the Volga German region. Wartime deportations spared few Volga Germans and only a handful returned here from exile, but their presence can be felt in the city's distinctly Central European ambience.

The first man in space, cosmonaut Yury Gagarin, lived in Saratov and studied at the local university, which now bears his name.

Sights

Sokolovaya Gora PARK

The strategic Sokolovaya Gora (Соколовая гора) overlooking the city and the river bending around it is a popular getaway for Saratovians. The main attraction here is the **Victory Park**, its lanes packed with

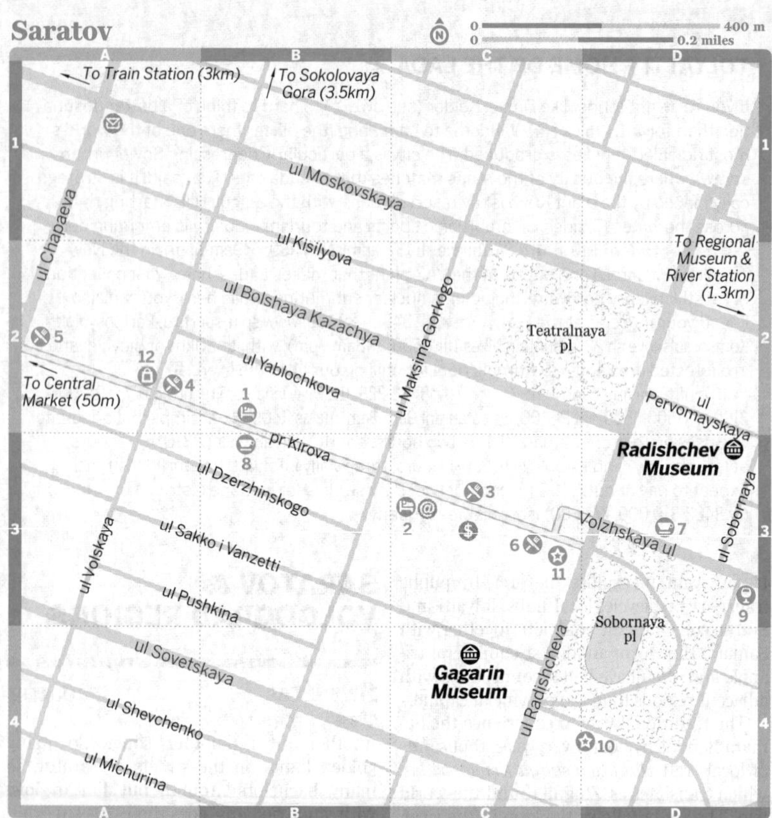

military hardware – from an armoured train and fighter planes to a funny-looking minisubmarine. The main park lane eventually leads you into the **Ethnic Village**, with houses representing numerous ethnic groups that inhabit Saratov Oblast – including German, Dagestani, Mordva, Tatar and Korean. To get to Sokolovaya Gora take *marshrutka* 72 from the train station or 72k from ul Radishcheva.

Regional Museum MUSEUM
(Саратовский областной музей краеведения; ul Lermontova 34; admission R100; ⏲10am-5pm Tue-Sun) The Regional Museum is located in the ancestral house of British actor Peter Ustinov, who was descended from a local merchant's family. There's an exhibition on Volga Germans – which dodges uncomfortable issues such as the deportation – and a plane in which Gagarin learned to fly. Descriptions are in Russian only.

FREE **Gagarin Museum** MUSEUM
(Музей Гагарина; ul Sakko i Vanzetti 15; admission free; ⏲9am-4pm Mon-Fri) A museum dedicated to the cosmonaut who not only lived and studied in Saratov, but also landed (crashed?) his rocket nearby after his much-lauded flight. The landing site, 40km out of town near the village of Kvasnikovka, is marked by a commemorative monument.

Radishchev Museum ART GALLERY
(Музей Радищева; ul Pervomayskaya 75; admission R200; ⏲10am-6pm Tue-Sun) This is the main branch of the city's Fine Arts Museum. It contains a good selection from the 18th to the 20th centuries.

Sobinov Conservatory NOTABLE BUILDING
(Консерватория Собинова; pr Kirova 1) This concert hall is one of Saratov's architectural landmarks. It's located at the eastern end of pr Kirova.

Saratov

Sleeping

TOP CHOICE Hotel Volga HOTEL €€

(Гостиница Волга; ☎263 645; www.astoria.saratov.ru; pr Kirova 34; s R2650, d R3100-3600, ste R4100-5100) Statues of black knights and naked runners observe you from the roof as you enter this art nouveau masterpiece. Rooms are Soviet-style but clean, and high ceilings give them an attractive, prerevolutionary air.

Hotel Slovakia HOTEL €€

(Гостиница Словакия; ☎237 618; www.hotelslovakia.ru; ul Lermontova 30; s R2600-4000, d R3000-5800, apt R8400-10,200; ❄@📶) A towering Soviet block on the Volga waterfront, Hotel Slovakia is the most common option for visiting businesspeople. There's a sauna and wi-fi in most parts of the building. Take trolleybus 1 or 9 east along ul Moskovskaya.

Pioner Lyux Bohemia HOTEL €€€

(Отель Пионер-Люх Богемия; ☎454 501; www.bohemiahotel.ru; pr Kirova 15/1; r R4200-5700, ste R8000; 🚭📶) This hotel with 30 rooms is upstairs in a courtyard alongside Café V and the Pioner Cinema complex. Rooms are spacious, have large windows and are nicely decorated in postmodern tones.

Hotel Volna HOTEL €€

(Гостиница Волна; ☎280 885; nab Kosmonavtov 7a; s R1000-2000, d R2000-5000) With its superb location inside the river-station building and reasonable prices, this place is popular with Russian travellers but only takes foreigners for one night (without registration). It has some very cheap rooms without bathrooms for R1000 per room. Take trolleybus 1 or 9 east along ul Moskovskaya.

Eating

House of Culinary Julienne RUSSIAN €

(Дом кулинарии Жюльен; ul Chapaeva 64; meals R250; ⏰8am-8pm) This Soviet-styled cafeteria with loud colours sells ready-made food, which you can also eat at stand-up tables on the premises. Another one is located a block along on pr Kirova that's open till 9pm and sells pastries as well.

Buratino RUSSIAN €€

(Буратино; pr Kirova 10; mains R300-400; ⏰11am-midnight; 📋) This is a quintessential Saratovian café-restaurant themed on 'Red Count' Alexey Tolstoy's version of Pinocchio. Beneath it, there is a funky basement restaurant called Misteria Buff – after Mayakovsky's futurist show. Buratino also runs a summer terrace next to writer Konstantin Fedin's monument on the embankment.

Pivnoy Zavod MICROBREWERY €

(Пивной завод; pr Kirova 5; mains R170-300; ⏰11am-11pm; 📶📋) Beer brewed on the premises, sausages and other hearty fare are on the food and drinks menu here. Servings are not large, though – the Caucasian lamb sausage is quite decent if you don't eat pork. It also has fresh *mors* (juice from berries).

Central Market MARKET €

(Центральный рынок; pl Kirova; ⏰8am-7pm) Head to the market for fresh fruit and art nouveau elegance.

Drinking

Café Coupe CAFÉ €

(Volzhskaya ul 34; coffee R120; ⏰10am-11pm) This elegant café in a former burgher house evokes fin-de-siècle Paris and serves a few inexpensive light dishes such as soup.

Café et Chocolat CAFÉ €

(Кафе и Шоколад; pr Kirova 21-23; coffee R110, omelette or crepe R150-185; ⏰9am-11pm; 📶📋)

One of several across town, this branch has free wi-fi and is the most central. The omelette is brilliantly disguised on the English menu as fried eggs.

Opium CAFÉ, BAR €€
(☎230 730; Volzhskaya ul 27b; drinks R120; ⏱24hr; 📶) A diminutive DJ-café with red sofas, cocktails, *kalyan* (hookah) and free wi-fi.

☆ Entertainment

Schnittke Philharmonic Theatre CONCERT HALL
(Филармония Шнитке; ☎224 871; Sobornaya pl 9) This hall remains true to the ideology of polystylism fostered by home-grown composer Alfred Schnittke, so jazz is as much at home here as classical music.

Sobinov Conservatory CLASSICAL MUSIC
(Консерватория им Собинова; ☎230 652; pr Kirova 1) One of the best in Russia, holding frequent performances by resident and visiting musicians in an architectural highlight in Saratov.

Shopping

Dom Knigi BOOKSTORE
(Дом Книги; ul Volskaya 81; ⏱9am-9pm) This bookstore has a fine collection of maps and reference books.

ℹ Information

Pioner Kino (Пионер кинотеатр; pr Kirova 15; R40 for 30min; ⏱11am-11pm) Internet on the left as you enter the cinema complex, next to the hotel Pioner Lyux Bohemia.

Post office (Почтамт; cnr ul Moskovskaya & ul Chapaeva; ⏱8am-8pm)

ℹ Getting There & Around

BOAT Inside the **river station** at the eastern end of ul Moskovskaya, **Volga-Heritage** (☎280 874; www.volga-nasledie.ru; nab Kosmonavtov 7a) sells cruises in the navigation season to destinations along the Volga, such as Astrakhan (return from R10,000, five days) and Samara (return from R5000, three days).

TRAIN The **train station** (Privokzalnaya pl) is at the western end of ul Moskovskaya. The No 17 (*kupe* R3550, 16 hours, daily) is the best (but most expensive) of the frequent trains to Moscow. Others go to Samara (*kupe* R1220, 9½ hours) and Volgograd (*platskart* R685, eight hours).

GETTING AROUND Trolleybuses 2 and 2A stop at the market at the western end of pr Kirova. Trolleybuses 1 and 9 ply ul Moskovskaya from the train station to the river station. Trolleybus 15 connects the train station and the central market, called 'Pytny Rynok'. *Marshrutka* 79 from the train station stops there too. For a taxi, call ☎603 333 or 606 044.

Volgograd Волгоград

☎8442 / POP 1.01 MILLION / ⏱MOSCOW

Volgograd is a grandiose city in all senses. It was founded in 1589 as Tsaritsyn, but it made history during a 36-year period when it appeared on maps as Stalingrad. In 1942, this city became the scene of an epic battle that changed the course of WWII (see p643). The number of soldiers and citizens that died in this battle is almost twice the current population of the city. Volgograd had to be rebuilt from scratch, which explains the Stalinesque grandeur of public buildings and broad avenues, all of which is Soviet baroque at its most eloquent or hideous, depending on your architectural taste.

In the far corner of this sprawling city, you can marvel at a feat of Soviet engineering – the first lock of the Volga-Don canal. Nearby is the partially restored town square of Tsaritsyn's German district.

Sights & Activities

Mamaev Kurgan MONUMENT
Known as Hill 102 during the Battle of Stalingrad, Mamaev Kurgan (Мамаев курган) was the site of four months of fierce fighting. It's now a memorial to all who died in this bloody but victorious fight. The complex's centrepiece is an extraordinarily evocative 72m statue of **Mother Russia** wielding a sword extending another 11m above her head. The *kurgan* (mound) is covered with statues, memorials and ruined fortifications; it also has a church these days. The Pantheon is inscribed with the names of 7200 soldiers – over one million Russian soldiers died here in battle in WWII. It can be reached by taking the high-speed tram to the Mamaev Kurgan stop, 3.5km north of the centre.

Museum of the Defence of Stalingrad MUSEUM
(Музей обороны Сталинграда; http://panorama.volgadmin.ru; ul 13-ya Gvardeyskoy Divizii; admission R200; ⏱10am-6pm Tue-Sun) This museum has dozens of exhibits on the Battle of Stalingrad and the soldiers who fought in it. The model of the ruined city (postbattle) is a moving display of the human capacity for both destruction and rebuilding. Upstairs

VOLGOGRAD RIVER STATION & TOURS

Once one of the grandest on the river, Volgograd's **river station** (речной вокзал; Rechnoy vokzal) is today among the tackiest, mostly given over to average bars, clubs and restaurants. At the time of research the upstairs area was getting a new Coffee House chain restaurant, though, augmented by a sprinkling of useful services. As a rule, all Volga excursions except to/from Moscow are return.

Gostinitsa Rechnoy Vokzal (Гостиница речной вокзал; ☎900 896; 4th fl, Rechnoy vokzal; r R1200) Upstairs via a separate staircase, this hotel has basic but perfectly acceptable rooms.

Only Body (☎900 572; www.onlybody.pro34.ru; 2nd fl, Rechnoy vokzal; ⌚by appointment only) Offers 30-minute face and one-hour body massages for R600 and R1400 respectively. It also does waxing and has a solarium. Book ahead.

Piligrim-Tur (Пилигрим-Тур; ☎264 838; www.piligrimtur.ru; 1st fl, Rechnoy vokzal) One of a couple of kiosks offering tour services and return journeys for Volgograd and major ports between Nizhny Novgorod (R22,500 to R46,000, 10 days) and Astrakhan (R7000 to R14,500, four days). Other three-day return cruises to Astrakhan cost R9000 to R11,000. See the website for dates.

Volga-Tur (Волга-Тур; ☎383 568; www.volga-tur.run; Rechnoy vokzal) A booth inside the river station with frequent return tours to Astrakhan from late May to late September (return R6000 to R12,000). Expect to pay anything between R12,000 and R28,000 per person one way starting in Moscow or Volgograd, depending on season and cabin class.

is the **Battle of Stalingrad Panorama** (Панорама 'Сталинградская битва'; admission R200), a 360-degree illustration of the battle as it might have been seen from atop Mamaev Kurgan. Viewers can relive the battle experience in the midst of the chaos and carnage. Despite the two-tier admission price, captions are in Russian only.

The complex is two blocks east of the Ploshchad Lenina high-speed tram stop; otherwise, a 20-minute stroll through the river park from alleya Geroyev gets you here.

Old Sarepta Museum MUSEUM
(Музей Старая Сарепта; ☎673 302; ul Vinogradnaya 6; admission R175; ⌚8.30am-4.30pm Mon-Fri, 10am-2pm Sun) An hour by *marshrutka* from the centre, what is currently known as the Krasnoarmeysk district was once the German colony of Sarepta. The original settlers were German Catholic missionaries from Moravia (in the Czech Republic) who arrived here in 1765 with the aim of proselytising the Kalmyks. Failing that, they became the mustard tycoons of Russia.

The repressions of the 1930s, WWII and the deportation of Volga Germans left precious little of the old Sarepta except a few buildings on a peaceful square, including a Lutheran church. The museum here houses permanent exhibitions on the history of the colony plus changing exhibitions featuring artists from the Volgograd region. To get here, take the *marshrutka* 15a from pr Lenina and ask the driver to stop at Vinogradnaya.

Volga-Don Canal CANAL
After visiting Old Sarepta Museum, take the 15a or any of the many *marshrutky* across the bridge to the Yubileyny (Юбилейный) stop and walk back to the canal and along the road in the direction towards the huge Stalinesque neoclassical arch. This marks the first lock in the Volga-Don Canal. Built in 1952, it forms the grandiose gateway of an aquatic avenue that now connects the White and the Black Seas via the Volga to the Don Rivers. A million people, including 236,000 Axis prisoners of war and Russian Gulag inmates, took part in the construction. Directly across from a shashlyk restaurant – you can't miss the Aeroflot jet out front – is the revamped **Museum of the Volga-Don Canal** (Музей Волго-Донского канала; ul Fadeyeva 35a; admission free; ⌚10am-noon & 1-4pm Tue, Wed & Fri). These are core hours but if you drop by during Russian office hours and ring the bell, staff will gladly let you in. The interesting exhibition tells the story of the canal and gives insight into water transportation in Europe. Captions are in Russian and English.

From the museum, continue walking along the street and parkland paths for

Volgograd

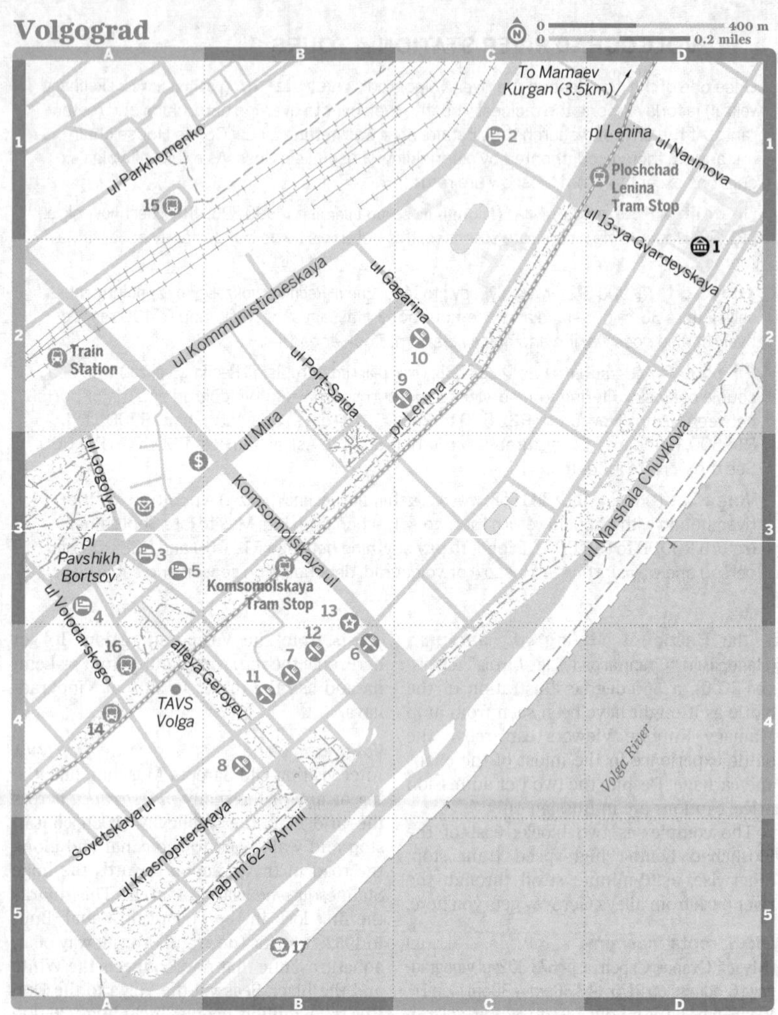

about 1km to a square and gigantic **Lenin statue** presiding over the beginning of the canal at the Volga. In summer, the square and boulevard are popular places for hanging out for a snack or drink.

Sleeping

For budget sleeps, head to Gostinitsa Rechnoy Vokzal in the river station.

Hotel Volgograd HOTEL €€
(Гостиница Волгоград; 408 030; www.hotelvolgograd.ru; ul Mira 12; s R2600-2900, d R2500-4500, tr R3300, ste R4000-8500;) South across pl Pavshikh Bortsov, this hotel has clean and comfortable rooms. It occupies one of the few buildings remaining from Tsaritsyn times, although it was considerably altered after the war.

TOP CHOICE **Stary Stalingrad** MINIHOTEL €€
(Отель Старый Сталинград; 385 501; http://hotelstalingrad.pro34.ru; pl Pavshikh Bortsov 2; s/d/ste R2500/3200/6500) Behind the Univermag shops and part of the same building (there's also a *stolovaya* canteen alongside), this modern minihotel has nicely furnished rooms with an individual touch; it's especially worth trying if the larger hotels are full.

Volgograd

Sights

1 Museum of the Defence of Stalingrad D2

Activities, Courses & Tours

Only Body .... (see 17)
Piligrim-Tur .... (see 17)
Volga-Tur .... (see 17)

Sleeping

Gostinitsa Rechnoy Vokzal .... (see 17)
2 Hotel Bank C1
3 Hotel Intourist A3
4 Hotel Volgograd A3
5 Stary Stalingrad A3

Eating

6 Bochka B4
7 Central Market B4
8 Dolya Angelov B4
Grand Café .... (see 4)
9 Kayfe C2
10 Rimini C2
11 Shokoladnitsa B4
12 Superman Shopping Mall B4

Entertainment

13 Klub Amsterdam B3

Transport

14 Airport Bus Stop A4
15 Central Bus Station A1
16 Marshrutka Stop for Volga-Don Canal A4
17 River Station B5

Hotel Bank HOTEL €€
(Отель Банк; ☎742 174; hotelbank@vlink.ru; ul Kommunisticheskaya 40; s R2400-2700, d R2300-2400, ste R3800-6000; ⊖ᯤ) Occupying floors seven, eight and nine in the modern office tower of Sberbank, Hotel Bank offers excellent rooms, with breakfast served in the canteen on the 2nd floor.

Hotel Intourist HOTEL €€
(Гостиница Интурист; ☎364 553; ul Mira 14; s R3000, d R3300-5600, ste R7000-9700; ⊖❄ᯤ) This is a vintage Soviet gem with the level of service matching the bright, welcoming lobby. Rooms are well lit and tasteful, if slightly overpriced.

Eating & Drinking

The **Superman Shopping Mall** (Супермен; Sovetskaya ul 17; ⌚8am-10pm) and the **central market** (Центральный рынок; between Sovetskaya ul & pr Lenina; ⌚7am-7pm) are useful for supplies. The market stocks everything from Astrakhan watermelons to Volga fish.

TOP CHOICE Kayfe CAFÉ, RUSSIAN €€
(Кайфе; pr Lenina 23a; mains R250-425; ⌚9am-6am; 📖) A cosy café that offers everything you might want, be it a large meal or a light snack, tea or coffee, alcohol or water pipe. It's good for breakfast, lunch or especially a predawn chill-out.

Dolya Angelov CAFÉ, MEDITERRANEAN €€
(Доля ангелов; alleya Geroyev 1; mains R250-400; ⌚noon-midnight) This elegant café and restaurant offers delicious soups, pastas, salads and international foods with a Mediterranean swing amid antique furnishings, but it's also an excellent choice simply for coffee, wine or one of the varieties of tea.

Shokoladnitsa CAFÉ €
(Шоколадница; cnr alleya Geroyev & Sovetskaya ul; bagels R170; ⌚10am-midnight; 📖ᯤ) Although its speciality is hot chocolate, this café is also good for bagels as well as wraps, sandwiches and especially soups and light dishes. Wi-fi is good, staff are friendly and in summer it has a marquee.

Grand Café RUSSIAN €€
(Гранд Кафе; ☎408 484; ul Mira 12; meals R250-500; ⌚9am-6am; 📖) Situated on the ground floor of Hotel Volgograd, this is the city's most popular spot to sip a cappuccino and scope out the scene. Part of the premises has been turned into a pizzeria.

Bochka GERMAN €€
(Бочка; ☎919 319; Sovetskaya ul 16; mains R300-550; ⌚11am-midnight; 📖) Basement place with good selection of beers. It draws a business lunch crowd, but it's more fun in the evening, when live music is staged.

Rimini ITALIAN €
(Римини; www.trattoria-rimini.ru; ul Gagarina 9; pizza R200-300, meat mains R350; ⌚noon-midnight) This large, bustling Italian place has neorustic decor and a large menu offering straight-up-and-down Italian pizza, pasta and meat dishes complemented by salads.

Entertainment

Klub Amsterdam NIGHTCLUB
(Клуб Амстердам; Komsomolskaya ul 3; ⌚10pm-5am Wed-Mon) This centrally located club is the most popular in town, with DJs spinning anything from indie to the pop-girls Serebro.

Information

Post office (Главпочтамт; pl Pavshikh Bortsov; per MB R6; ⏲8am-10pm Mon-Fri, 9am-6pm Sat & Sun)

Sberbank (ul Mira 11; ⏲9am-7pm Mon-Fri, to 5.30pm Sat)

Getting There & Away

Tickets can be bought at **TAVS Volga** (ТАВС Волга; ☎381 559; alleya Geroyev 5; ⏲8am-7pm); it's especially useful for picking up bus tickets to Elista and train bookings. For information on boat trips from Volgograd, see the boxed text on p371.

AIR Several airlines fly to Moscow (from R5000, two hours).

BUS For frequent buses to Elista (R450, five hours) head to the **central bus station** (Центральный автовокзал) – a 10-minute walk across the tracks or through the underpass from the train station. Frequent buses leave from the train station square to Astrakhan (R750, 10 hours), Moscow (R1500, 14 hours) and Rostov-on-Don (R700, nine hours).

TRAIN Train connections from Volgograd include the following:

Astrakhan *platskart* R685, 7½ to 11 hours, one or two daily

Moscow *kupe* R4127, 19 hours, almost daily (No 1)

Rostov-on-Don *kupe* R1402, 14 hours, at least daily

Saratov *platskart* R685, 7½ hours, frequent

St Petersburg *kupe* R4130, 36 hours, at least daily (No 79 is the best train)

There are cheaper but slower train connections to Moscow and St Petersburg.

Getting Around

The city centre is accessible on foot. To get to Mamaev Kurgan or the Museum of the Defence of Stalingrad you can take the *skorostnoy tramvay* (high-speed tram), which is a single metro line that runs along or under pr Lenina. To get to the airport, catch *marshrutka* 6 (R15, every 30 minutes) from the stop in front of the TAVS Volga office or at the train station.

ASTRAKHAN REGION

Astrakhan Астрахань

☎8512 / POP 504,000 / ⏲MOSCOW

With its East-meets-West feel, Astrakhan is an unusual provincial capital where a pretty river promenade and city parks are offset by architectural heritage in a shocking state of decay. Once upon a time, its streets saw German pastors mingling with Indian tea traders and Kazakh herdsmen. These days, you can still feel an abrupt change as the striking kremlin, stone mansions and churches of the European and Christian centre give way to Tatar and Persian *sloboda* (suburbs) with their wooden cottages, mosques and quaint courtyards where garlands of drying *vobla* fish flutter in the breeze.

Built in 1558 after Ivan the Terrible defeated the local Tatar khanate, Astrakhan is the successor of two imperial capitals in the area: Saray of the Golden Horde and Itil of the earlier Khazar kaganate, which adopted Judaism as its official religion. Both cities prospered thanks to their location on the Silk Route and by the sea.

Today, however, Astrakhan is first and foremost a jumping-off point for the Volga Delta, whose intricate wetlands are home to hundreds of bird and fish species and the scene of sharp tourist growth.

Sights

Kremlin HISTORICAL BUILDING

The kremlin (Кремль) on top of Zayachy Hill is a peaceful green haven in what can be a hot, dusty city. Its walls and gate towers were built in the 16th century using bricks from the ruins of the Golden Horde's capital Saray, which was located near the present-day village of Selitrennoye up the river from Astrakhan. Highlights of a stroll through the grounds are the various gates, the magnificent **Assumption Cathedral** (Успенский собор; 1698–1720) and its frescoes and the 17th-century **Trinity Cathedral** (Троицкий собор), which was being restored at the time of research.

Dogadin Art Gallery ART GALLERY

(Художественная галерея Догадина; http://agkg.narod.ru; ul Sverdlova 81; admission R120, guided tour R500; ⏲10am-6pm Tue-Sun) The Dogadin Art Gallery has one of the best art collections outside Russia's major cities. Check out the works of Astrakhan-born Boris Kustodiev, who painted lushly coloured semi-folkloric scenes of merchant life. Excursions (guided tours) are in English and German.

Kriushi Quarter NEIGHBOURHOOD

This Kriushi (Крюши) area of former Tatar and Persian suburbs south of the May 1st Canal is still predominantly Muslim, which is reflected in the proliferation of mosques, such as the **White Mosque** (Белая мечеть; ul Zoi Kosmodemyanskoy 41), built in 1810 and the city's oldest; the **Red Mosque** (Красная мечеть; ul Kazanskaya 62); and the **Black Mosque** (Черная мечеть; ul Zoi Kosmodemyanskoy), which was erected by Bukhara merchants in 1816 and destroyed by the Bolsheviks in 1939. It is gradually being restored.

Kriushi is also the location of the beautifully restored **Ioann Zlatoust church** (Церковь Иоанна Златоуста; Donbaskaya ul 61), dating from 1763; the **German Lutheran church** (Немецкая лютеранская церковь; ul Kazanskaya 102); and the **St Ripsime Armenian church** (Армянская церковь св Рипсиме; nab Kanala 1 Maya 120).

Velimir Khlebnikov Museum MUSEUM
(Музей Велимира Хлебникова; www.hlebnikov.ru; ul Sverdlova 53; tours in English/Russian R500/200; ⏲10am-6pm Tue-Sun) Come here for a small collection of portraits, drawings and personal objects from the futurist poet.

Local Studies Museum MUSEUM
(Краеведческий музей; ul Sovetskaya 15) The Local Studies Museum contains treasures excavated from the region. It was closed for renovation at the time of research but should reopen by the time you read this.

Tours

Cezar TOUR COMPANY
(Цезарь; ☎392 951; www.zesar.ru; ul Lenina 20, office 306) Apart from organising lodge-stays in the delta, this highly professional company also does trips to Baskunchak Salt Lake and Bogdo Mountain (R1400 including one meal and all costs), sacred to Buddhists.

Astrintur TOUR COMPANY
(Астринтур; ☎392 984 or 392 406; www.astrintour.ru; ul Lenina 20) This agency is reliable and has a lot of experience with foreign groups. It handles hotel bookings, individual tours and boat trips to the delta. It can also book you into the hotel 'Na Raskatax', one of the floating hotels on the delta, reached from a jetty and – in season – lily-fringed boardwalk.

Sleeping

Hotel 7 Nebo HOTEL €€
(Отель 7 Небо; ☎640 810; www.7nebo-hotel.ru; Krasnaya nab 27; s R2500-3500, d R3200-4500, ste R6000; @📶) This hotel upstairs in a modern office building offers excellent value for clean, parquet-floored rooms in tasteful colours. From the train station, take *marshrutka* 13 and ask for Krasnaya nab.

TOP CHOICE **Hotel Azimut** HOTEL €€
(Гостиница Азимут; ☎326 839; www.azimuthotels.ru; ul Kremlevskaya 4; s R2500-3300, d R3200-3600; 📶🚭@) This excellent business and tourist hotel has some of the best river views in town from the top floors. The downside is that noise filters in from the corridors; if this bothers you ask staff to find you a quieter floor. Take *marshrutka* 1 from the train station to pl Lenina.

Lotus Hotel MINIHOTEL €€€
(Лотус Отель; ☎262 200; http://hotel-lotus.ru; ul Maksima Gorkogo; s R2600-4300, d R4000-5000; @📶🏊) This is a top-quality minihotel with a small pool for sauna-goers. Rooms are modern and spacious.

Hotel Omega MINIHOTEL €€€
(Отель Омега; ☎517 975; www.hotelomega.ru; ul Kirova 1; s/d R3000/4200; ❄@📶🏊) A small and top-quality hotel with five spacious, nicely furnished rooms. It's close to the museums.

ROE TO RUIN – A FISHY BUSINESS

Caviar: the very word evokes glamorous lifestyles, exotic travel and high-kicking parties, and the caviar from the Volga Delta sturgeon is a lucrative commodity. Over its 100-year lifespan a single sturgeon can produce hundreds of kilograms of fish eggs, or roe. But it's in grave danger due to poaching and damage to its habitat. In 2007 Russia introduced a 10-year ban on sturgeon fishing, although catching the caviar-filled fish for the purposes of removing the embryos to the safety of fish farms is allowed. The latter loophole in the law permits the sale of caviar deemed unsuitable for reproduction. This is why the product is available in Russian shops, though at a very high price. It also explains the caviar smugglers and heightened security in town: police regularly check passengers and baggage on buses, planes and trains going out of the region, and bags are frequently searched when you enter Astrakhan bus and train stations.

Astrakhan

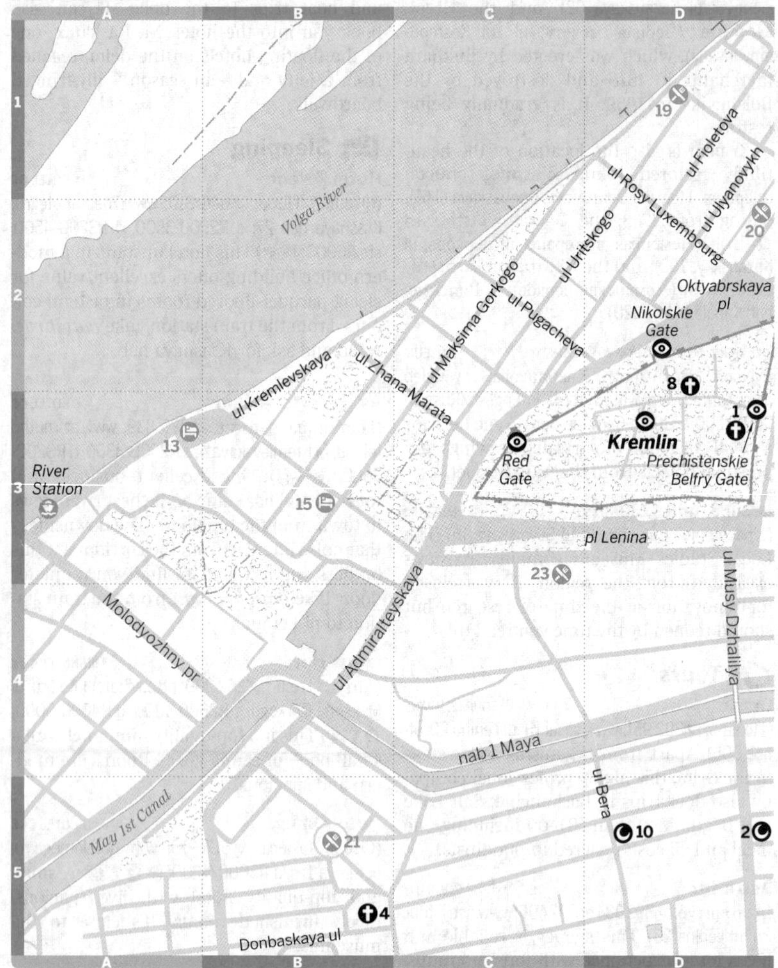

Victoria Palace HOTEL €€

(Гостиница Виктория Палас; ☎394 801; vphotel@astrakhan-dobycha.gazprom.ru; Krasnaya nab; s R2900, d R3800-4200; ❄@📶🏊) A shiny four-star business hotel with 36 rooms and the usual 'business' facilities like a bar, nightclub, sauna and free wi-fi (internet terminals cost R100 per 30 minutes).

Delta Day Spa Hotel HOTEL €€

(Гостиница Дельта; ☎253 821; www.astdayspa.ru; pl Vokzalnaya 1; s R1500-1800, d R2000-4000; 🚭📶) This hotel is close to the train station; it also has a public sauna with a rest room costing R1200 for two hours. Wi-fi is only available in the café.

✕ Eating & Drinking

TOP CHOICE **La Vanile** FRENCH €€

(Ла Ваниле; ul Admiralteyskaya 35/37; mains R350; ⏰9am-11pm Mon-Sat, 11am-11pm Sun; 🚭) Flowerpots abound, water streams down a glass wall and a canary sings favourite French pop tunes, as is appropriate for this French restaurant with both permanent and changing menus. Expect a creative twist on standard dishes, such as duck with walnuts.

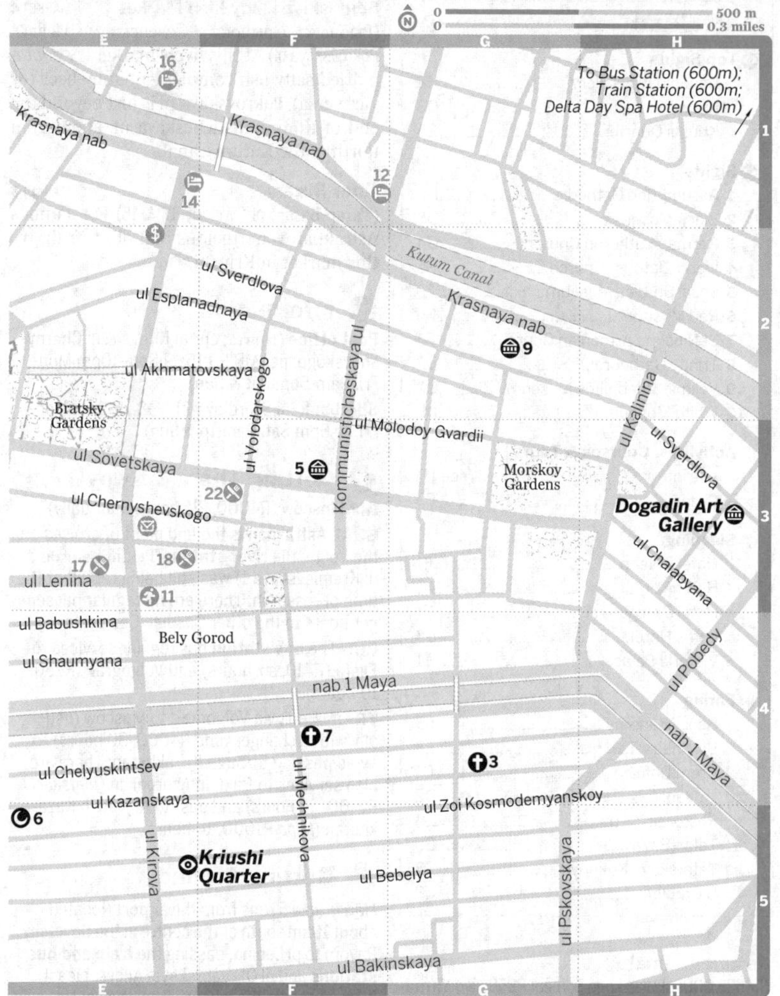

It does good cocktails (R200) but, unsurprisingly, doesn't serve beer.

Tatarskaya Kukhnya TATAR €
(Тартарская Кухня; cnr ul Sovietskogo & ul Volodarskogo; mains R250; ⏰11am-midnight) Owned and run by a friendly Volga Tatar family, this is the best place to try simple regional Tatar cuisine, which relies heavily on simply stewed meats, dumplings and grains, and sweets in scene-setting decor.

Bir Khaus PUB €€
(Бир Хаус; ul Krasnogo Znameni; mains R150-3500; ⏰noon-11pm; 📶📋) The inauspicious entrance gives way to the convivial, neorustic 'Beer House' pub upstairs that serves a competent range of salads and hot snacks (including light seafood dishes), as well as more substantial steaks and sausage dishes. Nonalcoholic cocktails feature on the drinks menu, as well as 'beer cocktails'.

Crem Café CAFÉ €€
(Крем Кафе; ul Uritskogo 5; mains R200-400, salads R250; ⏰11am-11pm; 📶📋) This hookah café is obviously not smoke-free, but ventilation is OK and it does good salads, sushi and meats, with top-of-the-range lamb at around R400. Staff are young and friendly.

Astrakhan

Top Sights

Dogadin Art Gallery H3
Kremlin D3
Kriushi Quarter E5

Sights

1 Assumption Cathedral D3
2 Black Mosque D5
3 German Lutheran Church G4
4 Ioann Zlatoust Church B5
5 Local Studies Museum F3
6 Red Mosque E5
7 St Ripsime Armenian Church F4
8 Trinity Cathedral D2
9 Velimir Khlebnikov Museum G2
10 White Mosque D5

Activities, Courses & Tours

Astrintour .... (see 11)
11 Cezar E3

Sleeping

12 Hotel 7 Nebo F1
13 Hotel Azimut A3
14 Hotel Omega E1
15 Lotus Hotel B3
16 Victoria Palace E1

Eating

17 Beer Academy E3
18 Bir Khaus E3
19 Crem Café D1
20 La Vanile D2
Restoran Yamato .... (see 19)
21 Tatar-Bazar B5
22 Tatarskaya Kukhnya F3
23 U Gamleta C3

Restoran Yamato ASIAN €€
(525 000; ul Uritskogo 5; meal R850;) Yamato has an excellent range of Japanese sushi, wok and pan-Asian dishes that are more ambitious than most. It's also the best place for watching a sunset.

U Gamleta RUSSIAN €€
(У Гамлета; ul Lenina 6a; mains R250-350; noon-11pm) For good Russian fare, enter through the gate here and go left downstairs.

Beer Academy PUB €
(Академия Пива; ul Lenina 7; mains R350-450; 11am-midnight) This convivial place has a great selection of draught beers and an extensive food menu.

Selenskiye Isady Fish Market MARKET €
(Рыбный рынок Селенские Исады; Pokrovskaya pl) At this lively market try *vobla*, a dried salty fish complemented by beer (or vice versa). Pokrovskaya pl is just beyond the end of Kommunisticheskaya ul, about 2km north of the Kutum Canal.

Tatar-Bazar MARKET €
(Татар-Базар; pl Svobody 12 & 15) For famous Astrakhan watermelons and other fruit, try this market in Kriushi.

Information

Post office (Почта; cnr ul Kirova & ul Chernyshevskogo; per MB R3.15; 8am-10pm Mon-Fri, 9am-5pm Sat & Sun)

Sberbank (ul Sverdlova 21; 8.15-6pm Mon-Fri, to 5pm Sat, 9am-1pm Sun)

Getting There & Away

AIR Moscow (R4000, 2½ hours, four daily)

BOAT Astrakhan is the end point of cruises on the Volga; the **river station** (Речной вокзал; ul Kremlevskaya 1) was still being rebuilt at the time of research. There are no regular passenger boats to the other Caspian Sea ports.

BUS The **bus station** has regular services to Elista (R410, six hours) and Volgograd (R750, 10 hours).

TRAIN Book via Volgograd to Moscow (usually with a change; *kupe* R4000, 30 hours) to avoid passing through Kazakhstan. There are also services to Baku in Azerbaijan (*platskart* R2100, 25 hours) and east to Atyrau in Kazakhstan (*kupe* R1000, 14 hours).

Getting Around

Marshrutka 5 runs from the airport (located about 10km south of the centre in the Sovetsky Rayon) to pl Lenina, passing the **train and bus stations** and pl Oktyabrskaya. Allow at least 30 minutes for the journey from the centre. *Marshrutka* 1 goes from the train station to pl Oktyabrskaya and pl Lenina.

Volga Delta Дельта Волги

The Volga Delta is the natural highlight of any trip to the region and, if you are travelling from north to south, you are likely to feel a sense of enormous achievement in reaching the point where this magnificent river flows into the Caspian Sea in Central Asia.

About 70km south of Astrakhan, the river bursts like a firecracker into thousands of streams, creating a unique ecosystem teeming with wildlife. The three symbols of the delta are the Caspian lotus flower (abundant), the sturgeon (critically threatened) and the Caspian flamingo – a semilegendary bird that the average ranger will have seen once in their life, if at all.

The most biologically diverse area is covered by the **Astrakhan Biosphere Reserve**, which you can visit on excursions organised by Astrakhan travel agencies. The rest of the delta is dotted with floating and land-based lodges that mostly specialise in fishing and hunting. These days, though, operators are used to the occasional foreigner drifting down here for the simple pleasure of experiencing this beautiful wetland area and travelling by boat into the *raskaty* (the channels) to watch the birdlife. Although there are many tourist bases along the broader northern arms of the delta, the experience will be richer if you organise a stay deeper in the delta where your companions will be. In addition to the visiting hunters and anglers, local rangers and others from the nearby villages provide a rudimentary infrastructure and protect the park and border zone. Needless to say, even the dirt roads peter out into *raskaty* quickly here, making boat the best means of transport.

The best time to visit is between late July and late September when lotus flowers blossom and there are not so many mosquitoes as in May and June. April and October are major fishing seasons.

REPUBLIC OF KALMYKIA

Elista Элиста

84722 / POP 104,200 / MOSCOW

Prayer drums, red-robed monks, boiled guts and butter tea for lunch… Wait, it's still Europe! Elista is the capital of Kalmykia (Республика Калмыкия), the continent's only Buddhist region and a fragment of Mongolia thrown onto the shores of the Caspian Sea. With its Tibetan-style *khuruls* (temples) and possibly the world's highest density of street sculpture, the otherwise very drab Elista makes for a fascinating if slightly surreal place to visit.

History

Kalmyks are nomads (nowadays at heart rather than in practice), and their history is that of migration, forced and voluntary. They descend from the Oirats, the western branch of Mongolians who embraced Buddhism in the early 17th century and soon after resolved to look for pastures green in the west.

In the last massive nomadic migration in the history of Eurasia, the Oirats traversed thousands of kilometres and ended up on the banks of the Volga, which at that time marked the border of the emerging Russian empire. Moscow welcomed the newcomers, allowing them to retain their way of life in return for guarding the border. But in the

ORGANISING TRIPS TO THE DELTA

Permit & Excursions

With the exception of day trips organised by Procosta, foreigners will need a permit to enter the delta as it is a border zone. This formality takes three to five days and is handled by an agency. Astrintur and Cezar in Astrakhan can organise an excursion and stay in virtually any tourist base or hotel on the delta, including Rybnoye Mesto in Stanya (Станья), situated about 80km south of Astrakhan and a couple of kilometres from the last settlement of any size, Kamyzyak (Камызяк). Requirements for a permit are a copy of your passport's main page and visa and a copy of your migration card. Typically, a package consists of accommodation, an excursion for a couple of hours with a ranger and full pension.

Tourist Bases

Procosta (Astrakhan office: 791 313; www.procosta.ru; ul Kirova 64; per person from R3800 for a day excursion with boat & ranger from Astrakhan, food not included; tw cottage R2000) has wooden cottages, linked by a boardwalk, sleeping two to four people. It is reached by boat from **Rybnoye Mesto** (manager@vipvolga.ru; http://vipvolga.ru; ul Vostochnaya 2, in Kirovsky; per person with full board from R2000). Unless you speak Russian, Rybnoye Mesto is best booked through agencies in Astrakhan; it's a small hub for boat hire and transfers in this part of the delta.

18th century, the Oirats came under pressure from Russian and German settlers encroaching on their lands. One winter's night in 1771 they made their second escape – back to Mongolia. But the ice on the Volga was not strong enough for those on the western bank to cross the river, so 20,000 out of 160,000 families stayed. The flight turned into a disaster, with two-thirds of the people killed by enemies on the way.

Those who remained on the Volga lived quietly and not entirely unhappily until the 1920s when the Bolsheviks destroyed all *khuruls,* arrested most monks and expropriated the cattle. No surprise that during the short-lived German occupation in 1942 some Kalmyks joined Hitler's army. At the same time, thousands of others fought on the Soviet side.

Stalin's reprisal was terrible. On 28 December 1943 all Kalmyks, including party members and policemen, were put in unheated cattle cars and sent to Siberia. When in 1957 Nikita Khrushchev allowed them to return, less than half the prewar population of 93,000 could make it home; the others perished in Gulag camps.

In 1993 the Kalmyks elected their first president – 31-year-old multimillionaire Kirsan Ilyumzhinov – who presided over the republic until 2010 and left his footprint through his two chief fascinations: chess and a predilection for the fictional trickster Ostap Bender. This conflux of chess, fiction and the reality of Kalmyk history lends the steppe republic a rather bizarre edge. The 14th Dalai Lama has visited several times despite Moscow's reluctance to spoil relations with China. Boring it is not.

Ul Lenina is Elista's main axis. The long, narrow stretch of green south of it is alleya Geroyev, which is flanked on the eastern side by the nameless main square where government buildings are located. The website www.rus-trip.ru/content/view/163/2 has a map of town.

Sights

National Museum of the Republic of Kalmykia MUSEUM
(http://museum.kalm.ru; ul Dzhangara 9; admission R60; ⏲9am-6pm Tue-Fri, 10am-4pm Sat & Sun) The new building of the Nikolai Palmov Local Studies Museum offers a perfect space for getting an insight into the Kalmyk people and the republic. Its six rooms are spread over two floors, beginning on the ground floor with one room dedicated to the history of the Kalmyks – complete with a large yurt – and another with excellent displays of Kalmykia's wildlife and fauna. Upstairs one room has changing art exhibitions, while another two rooms focus on Buddhism and WWII respectively. A room should one day be dedicated to the Kalmyk deportations, but this could take some time yet. Descriptions are in Russian only, but someone can help if you ask. Take *marshrutka* 5 and ask the driver to stop at the museum.

Gol-Syume Burkh Bagshin Altn Syume BUDDHIST TEMPLE
(☎40 109; www.buddhisminkalmykia.ru; ul Klykova; ⏲grounds & temple 7.30am-8pm daily, library & museum 10am-6pm Tue-Sun, daily morning prayer 9am) The 'Golden Abode of Buddha Shakyamuni', or New Khurul as it's locally known, was built in 2005 in the Tibetan style. The prayer hall sports an 11m statue of Buddha and the monk's robe of the 14th Dalai Lama; downstairs a small museum depicts the history of Kalmyk Buddhism. Take *marshrutka* 9 or any other going east along ul Lenina.

Geden Sheddup Goichorling BUDDHIST TEMPLE
The Geden Sheddup Goichorling (Sacred Abode of the Gelug School's Theory and Practice) was the first post-communist *khurul* in Kalmykia and consists of two temples and a brick cottage for monks, surrounded by the endless steppe. The large temple (built in 1996) has lavish frescoes but it's usually closed; you can visit by asking at the monks' cottage. Behind the temple stands the pink kiosk-like structure of **Syakyusn-syume** – Kalmykia's oldest temple, dating from the early 1990s.

To get there, take *marshrutka* 15 at the corner of ul Pushkina and ul Gorkogo. Once out of town, ask to stop by the *khurul*.

Chess City NEIGHBOURHOOD
Once a literary fantasy, Chess City was built for the 1998 Chess Olympics and has since seen many a grandmaster. For all the hype, it has an air of surreal suburban bliss clustered on the edge of steppe around the glassy structure of the Chess Palace, and there is virtually nothing else here except the Chess Palace and a large ensemble of cottages. *Marshrutka* 7 plies the route between Hotel Elista and Chess City (R10, 20 minutes, every five minutes). From Chess City, take *marshrutka* 7 back one stop or walk back about 500m to the roundabout, where you find the **Ostap Bender monument**, complete with all the tale's 12 chairs (which you can sit on).

Return Memorial MONUMENT
Located 500m along ul Khrushcheva from the roundabout in the direction away from the centre, the Return Memorial by sculptor Ernst Neizvestny (www.enstudio.com) is a striking memorial to the Kalmyk deportation. A cattle car like those used to transport the Kalmyks to Siberia stands close by.

Alleya Geroyev PARK
This pleasant park stretching along a narrow ravine is the town's main promenade and has the city's largest concentration of sculpture and Buddhist architecture. Enter by crossing ul Lenina from Hotel Elista and walk east (left) towards the main square, taking in along the way the **monument to Basan Gorodovikov**, a Soviet general who led the return of the Kalmyks from exile; the **sculpture of the White Elder** deity (the owner of the Earth in Kalmyk mythology); the Tibetan-style **Altn-Bosh** (Golden Gate) and the **Arbour of Buddha Shakyamuni**; and a thoughtful Lenin hiding in the shade of the **Seven-Tiered Pagoda**, which has a large prayer drum in the middle.

Sleeping

Hotel Elista HOTEL €
(Korpus 1 ☎25 540, Korpus 2 ☎20 470; www.hotelelista.ru; Korpus 1: ul Lenina 241, Korpus 2: ul Lenina 237; Korpus 1 s/d R1600/2200, Korpus 2 s/d R1000/1400; @) This Soviet relic occupies two Stalinesque buildings (Korpus 1 and Korpus 2), which almost behave as separate hotels. Korpus 1 has the better facilities at the moment, with a 24-hour supermarket and a coffee bar; internet computers were being set up there when we visited. Take any *marshrutka* going to the stop Gostinitsa (Гостиница).

Bely Lotos HOTEL €€
(Белый Лотос; ☎34 416; www.hotel-elista.ru; ul Khoninova 7; s/d R2500/3200, ste R5200-7500; ❄) The 14th Dalai Lama stayed here when in town. Tucked away on a quiet street near alleya Geroyev, the White Lotus is professionally run, friendly and simply the best in town.

Chess City HOTEL €€
(☎62 570; www.citychesshotel.ru; City Chess Hall; r R2900-3300, lyux R8800) The reception is inside the Chess Palace, from where guests are led to rows of bungalow cottages. Room prices are for one to two people, but there are more expensive thee- and four-person cottages. The neighbourhood is quiet and suburban, but it's away from everything; apart from the comfortable cottages, there are few advantages to staying here.

Eating & Drinking

Elista's culinary scene has recently been pepped up with some decent choices; this

CHESS & CHAIRS

It's hard to appreciate Elista's Chess City without knowing about Ostap Bender. This young gentleman is the main character in the Soviet satirical classic *The Twelve Chairs*, written in 1933 by Ilya Ilf and Yevgeny Petrov. Although he is a crook who dupes honest and not-so-honest citizens, he somehow appears much more attractive than most of his victims.

The chairs in question once belonged to a semi-deranged aristocrat, Kisa Vorobyaninov, but were expropriated by the Bolsheviks. Kisa confides to Ostap that he had hidden his diamonds in one of them, so together they embark on a journey that takes them all the way down the Volga and through the Caucasus, in pursuit of a touring theatre that purchased the precious furniture to use as props.

At one point they find themselves stranded in a fictional Volga town called Vasyuki where the population is obsessed with chess. Ostap immediately declares himself a chess champion and captivates the Vasyukians with a plan to transform their town into the world chess capital, complete with a grand chess palace, skyscrapers, luxury hotels and zeppelins full of chess fans arriving every minute. It will be a new city called New-Vasyuki (the Russian original uses the English word 'new'), Ostap says. The fraud is uncovered when Ostap accedes to requests to play a simultaneous match with local experts – it turns out he has no idea how chess pieces move, but flees with the collected money.

Unlike Ostap, ex-president Kirsan Ilyumzhinov can play chess, and political chess, too. Not only did he charm the Kalmyks, who elected him their president in 1993 when he had just turned 31, but he also worked his way to the very top of the international chess body (the FIDE), built Chess City (whose semiofficial name is New-Vasyuki) and brought the Chess Olympics to Elista.

is your chance to try Kalmyk food and the delicious pastries. The main staples include meat-filled *berg* (or *berigi*) dumplings, *doutour* (a mixture of intestines, kidneys and liver in a broth), *hasn makhn* (sliced beef with flat pasta) and *dzhomba* (butter tea).

You will find a fair sprinkling of places to eat and drink along ul Ochirova. Also look for a couple of cheap places on ul Gorkogo, behind Hotel Elista towards the market and pedestrian zone.

Orient RUSSIAN, KALMYK €€
(Ориент; cnr ul Lenina & ul Neyman; mains R220-300; 9-3am) This restaurant on the corner of the so-called Arbat pedestrian zone has on its wall pictures of Russia's presidents and prime ministers Putin and Medvedev, who apparently ate here at least once. Expect the usual range of lamb, beef, pork and salmon, but it also does a tasty chicken dish stewed with dried fruits.

Gurman KALMYK, INTERNATIONAL €€
(Гурман; 50 707; ul Ochirova 9; mains R350, Kalmyk dishes R160-200, steaks R450; noon-2am) This elegant restaurant located inside the modern entertainment complex (bowling, cinema, billiards, you name it) offers Kalmyk dishes along with Russian and international cuisine ranging from steaks to sushi.

Esinen CAFÉ €
(Эсинен; ul Lenina 255a; blinchiki R50-60, coffee R50; 9am-9pm) Relaxed Esinen, decked out in cloth wallpaper, has a hint of a Parisian or Viennese coffee house and is perfect for chilling out between sights.

Praha CZECH, BAVARIAN €
(ul Ochirova 5; noon-2am) Another of the Ochirova bunch, with a laid-back beer-hall feel and slightly off-beat edge.

Stereo RUSSIAN, KARAOKE €€
(ul Neyman 1; 11am-2am) Stop by for food, drinks, friendly staff and Russian karaoke; it's on the 4th floor of the corner building.

THE DZHANGARIADA FESTIVAL

The Kalmyk equivalent of the Mongolian Naadam, Dzhangariada (late August or September) is an annual celebration of the Kalmyk epic *Dzhangar* – a 12-song story about life in the blessed land called Bumba. Held in the open steppe (the location is changed every year), it includes wrestling and archery contests and performances by *dzhangarchi* (traditional singers). Few tour agencies are used to handling foreigners, but **Kalmykia Tour** (kalmykiatour@mail.ru; www.kalmykiatour.com) says it can arrange accommodation and local transfers for the festival for about R4000-5000 per day, *excluding* meals and getting there and away. The fee is less for small groups.

Shopping

Teegin Gera BOOKSTORE
(ul Lenina 247; 9am-6pm, closed 2-3pm) This bookstore sells the combined Elista street map and map of the republic (R80); it also has various books on Kalmyk culture and Buddhism.

Information

Few agencies are geared to handling foreigners on excursions. Kalmykia Tour (see the boxed text 'The Dzhangariada Festival') should be able to help with tailor-made excursions.

Internet Kafe Online (ul Lenina 247; per hr R40; 9am-8pm Mon-Sat, to 9pm Sun)

Main post and telephone office (ul Suseyeva 31; 9am-5pm)

Sberbank (ul Gorkogo 13; ul Suseyeva 13) Two central branches with ATMs and currency exchange.

Getting There & Away

AIR Three flights to Moscow – on Sunday, Tuesday and Thursday – is all that keeps Elista airport busy. Airline tickets are available at **Elya** (41 297; ul Lenina 247/2; one way R4650-7750).

BUS The bus station is on the outskirts of town. Elista is approximately the same distance from Volgograd, Astrakhan, Mineralnye Vody (Caucasus) and Stavropol (Caucasus). A trip to any of these takes about five hours and costs around R500. Eurolines (www.touring.de) runs buses from Frankfurt in Germany to Yashalta (one way €160, two days five hours, weekly April to mid-September), western Kalmykia. Currently there are no train services to Kalmykia.

Getting Around

Marshrutka minibuses are the only mode of public transport. Their main hub is in front of Hotel Elista (appearing as Гостиница on signs), from where you can get to any part of town. *Marshrutka* 9 goes to the bus station, *marshrutka* 7 to Chess City.

The Urals

Includes »

Best Places to Eat

» Grill Taverna Montenegro (p387)

» Vkus Stranstvy (p387)

» Dacha (p397)

» Rosy Jane (p397)

» Only (p404)

Best Places to Stay

» Hotel Tsentralny (p395)

» Hotel Bashkortostan (p400)

» Ecopark Zyuratkul (p401)

» Minigostonitsa Vesta (p396)

» Golden Beach (p402)

Why Go?

Marking the border between Europe and Asia, the Ural Mountains (Урал) stretch from the Kara Sea in the north to Kazakhstan in the south. Modest in scale in the south, they nevertheless proved to be rich in resources, and when Russia stumbled onto this Aladdin's cave full of lustrous treasures many centuries ago, the mineral riches filled the coffers and allowed Russia to expand into Siberia beyond.

Today Yekaterinburg, the largest of the Ural Mountains towns, is a bustling centre with interesting sights; it also offers a base for exploring less-visited towns. West of Yekaterinburg, the city of Perm – better known in Soviet times for its Gulag camps and industries – is reinventing itself as a cultural capital with considerable success. Kungur has a spectacular ice cave, and take the time to venture into the countryside between Ufa and Chelyabinsk for hiking, bicycle, rafting or horseback expeditions.

When to Go

Yekaterinburg

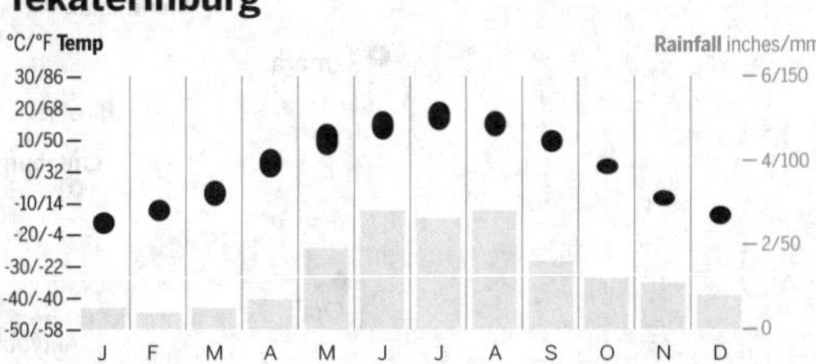

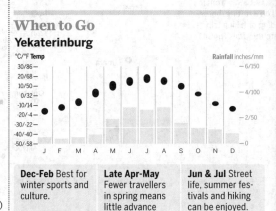

Dec-Feb Best for winter sports and culture.

Late Apr-May Fewer travellers in spring means little advance booking is needed.

Jun & Jul Street life, summer festivals and hiking can be enjoyed.

The Urals Highlights

1. Experience ice and a moment of pitch darkness in Kungur's **ice cave** (p389)
2. Hike into the **Zyuratkul** mountain range or stroll the shoreline of Lake Zyuratkul (p401)
3. Visit **Perm-36**, the former labour camp and today a haunting Gulag memorial (p389)
4. Make sense of the modern at **PERMM**, the new museum of contemporary art in Perm (p386)
5. Trace the historical contours of the murder of Russia's last tsar and his family by visiting Yekaterinburg's **Church upon the Blood** (p391) and **Ganina Yama** (p398)
6. Take an excursion to the top of Nevyansk's **leaning tower** for spectacular views (p398)
7. Get away from it all on a rafting, horse-riding or hiking trip into the Urals (p404)

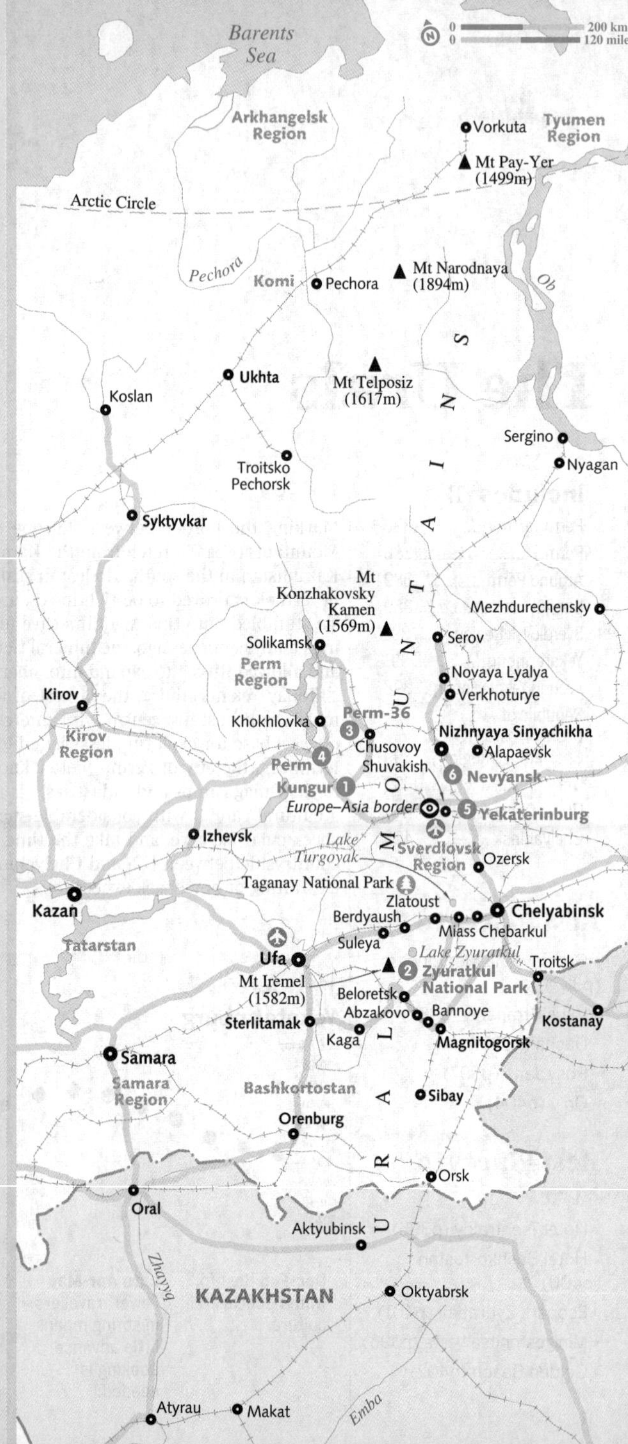

History

The Ural Mountains, running north to south and stretching from the Arctic ice to the Central Asian steppe, are one of the world's oldest mountain chains, the geological consequence of a colossal continental collision that occurred over 300 million years ago. The range marks the borderline of the more recent geographical heirs to these once separate landmasses – Europe and Asia.

Before the Slavs moved in, the region was populated by various Uralic tribes, whose contemporary descendants include the Khanty and Mansi peoples of Western Siberia as well as the Finns and Hungarians of central Europe.

SLAVIC EXPANSION

In the 16th century, the rising Muscovite principality won a series of strategic battles against its tribal foes that finally opened the way for eastward expansion. Russian settlement of the Ural Mountains was led by monks, merchants and Cossacks.

Russia gained control over the lands between Moscow and the Ural Mountains through the work of St Stephan, the bishop of Perm, who built a string of monasteries and converted the native tribes. Seeking to exploit the natural wealth of the taiga, pioneering merchants followed the clergy. They set up markets next to the monasteries, erecting great churches with their profits from the fur trade. Industrial families such as the Demidovs and Stroganovs began establishing factories in the region.

INDUSTRIAL EXPANSION

The discovery of mineral wealth in the Ural Mountains during the reign of Peter the Great led to the first large-scale Russian settlements. Yekaterinburg, founded in 1723 and named for the Empress Catherine I (Yekaterina), wife of Peter the Great, emerged as the region's economic centre. Rich deposits of coal, iron ore and precious stones gave rise to a mining industry, including science and engineering institutes. By the early 19th century the region's metals industry supplied nearly all the iron produced in Russia and exported to European markets. The Statue of Liberty in New York and the roof on London's Houses of Parliament were made from copper and iron from the Ural Mountains.

In 1917 the Russian empire was consumed by the outbreak of revolution and civil war. Red radicals and White loyalists fought back-and-forth battles across the Ural Mountains. Yekaterinburg became the site of one of history's most notorious political murders when Tsar Nicholas, Tsaritsa Alexandra and their children were shot in the middle of the night and disposed of in an abandoned mine.

The region figured prominently in the Soviet Union's rapid industrialisation drive in the 1930s. Some of the world's largest steelworks and industrial complexes were built there, including Uralmash in Sverdlovsk (modern-day Yekaterinburg) and Magnitogorsk in Chelyabinsk.

During WWII more than 700 factories were relocated to the region, beyond the reach of the advancing Nazis. The Ural Mountains became a centre of Soviet weapons manufacturing: Kalashnikov rifles from Izhevsk, T-34 tanks from Nizhny Tagil and Katyusha rockets from Chelyabinsk. During the Cold War, secret cities, identified only by number, were constructed in the region to house the military nuclear and biochemical industries.

THE URALS AFTER COMMUNISM

In the late Soviet period, a Urals-bred construction engineer turned anticommunist crusader toppled the Soviet dictatorship. Boris Yeltsin had gained a reputation as the energetic and populist-leaning communist governor of Sverdlovsk when the reform-minded Mikhail Gorbachev first introduced him to the national political stage, a move that Gorbachev would soon regret.

In his political fights against the old Soviet order and the neocommunists of the post-Soviet transition, the region provided Yeltsin with strong support. Despite the hardships that radical economic reform inflicted on the heavily subsidised industrial sector, Yeltsin scored big election victories in the Ural Mountains cities in the 1991 and 1996 Russian presidential campaigns.

As elsewhere in Russia, the postcommunist transition in the Ural Mountains did not go according to the early optimistic plans. The region suffered the severe collapse of its manufacturing and agricultural sectors. Public employees went without wages. Rocket scientists became taxi drivers. Mafia turf wars were waged over the right to 'protect' the nascent private business sector.

But a gradual economic recovery is obvious today, especially in the larger cities. The Ural Mountains' rich export commodities, especially metals, and the revival of the military industrial sector have helped sustain the region.

PERM TERRITORY

Perm Пермь

☎342 / POP 1 MILLION / ⏰MOSCOW +2HR

The word 'Perm' once meant a mysterious Finno-Ugric land encompassing most of the northwestern Ural Mountains that was slowly colonised by Russians since the early medieval ages. But the city is relatively new, founded by the lieutenants of Peter I in 1723.

It is believed that Chekhov used Perm as the inspiration for the town his Three Sisters were desperate to leave, and Boris Pasternak sent his Doctor Zhivago to a city clearly resembling Perm. It would be hard for these characters to recognise their city today. The neat provincial architecture has been critically diluted by Soviet concrete blocs and post-Soviet glassy structures. Huge military plants were moved here during WWII when the town was called Molotov after the Soviet minister of Molotov cocktail fame.

Today the city is in the throes of reinventing itself as a cultural centre outside Moscow and St Petersburg, having long had a famous ballet school, augmented by some interesting museums. It is also the base from which to visit one of the best wooden architecture museums in Russia, located in Khokhlovka; the famous ice cave in Kungur; and a grim reminder of Soviet-era political persecution – the Perm-36 labour camp.

Sights

A green line runs through the central district connecting the major sights, complemented by signs in Russian and English explaining the history. Perm Tourist has a free, multilingual *Green Line* booklet for self-guided city walks. This is complemented by a red line, focusing on local love stories.

TOP CHOICE Museum of Contemporary Art 'PERMM' ART GALLERY
(Музей современного искусства PERMM; www.permm.ru; ul Ordzhonikidze 2; admission R100; ⏰noon-9pm) The brainchild of Marat Gelman, a prime shaker and mover in Russia's gallery scene, this museum of modern and contemporary art is housed inside the former river station hall on the banks of the Kama River. It forms the centrepiece of Gelman's vision to transform Perm into a cultural hub. The exhibitions are often controversial locally, which probably means the museum fulfils its role as a contemporary art space very successfully. Check out the website for what's on. Trolleybus 1 and bus 3 take you there.

Perm State Art Gallery ART GALLERY
(Художественная галерея; www.sculpture.permonline.ru; Komsomolsky pr 4; Russian/foreigner R120/210; ⏰11am-6pm Tue-Sun) Housed in the grand Cathedral of Christ Transfiguration on the banks of the Kama, the Perm State Art Gallery is renowned for its collection of Permian wooden sculpture. These brightly coloured figures are a product of an uneasy compromise between Christian missionaries and the native Finno-Ugric population. The latter, having been converted, closely identified the Christian saints these sculptures depict with their ancient gods and treated them as such by smearing their lips with the blood of sacrificed animals. There are plans to house the museum in a new building, but the location is yet to be decided; Perm Tourist can tell you more. Take trolleybus 1 to the stop Galereya or trams 3, 4, 7, 12 or 13 to the stop Tsum.

Perm Regional Museum MUSEUM
(Пермский краевой музей; ul Ordzhonikidze 11; admission R100; ⏰10am-6pm Tue-Sun) Located inside the imposing Meshkov House, the regional museum has a moderately interesting collection of household objects, weapons and other cultural relics of the region. It only gets really interesting when you see the small collection of intricate metal castings of the 'Perm animal style' used in the shamanistic practices of ancient Finno-Ugric Permians. More of these metal castings may be on display in the museum branch known as the **Archaeological Collection** (Sibirskaya ul 15; admission R100; ⏰10am-6pm Mon-Fri).

Sergei Diaghilev Museum MUSEUM
(Дом Дягилева; Sibirskaya ul 33; admission by donation; ⏰9am-6pm Mon-Fri, closed 31 May-1 Sep) The Sergei Diaghilev Museum is a small, lovingly curated school museum dedicated to the impresario (1872–1929) who turned Russian ballet into a world-famous brand. Children speaking foreign languages, including English, serve as guides.

Mosque MOSQUE
(Мечеть; ul Osinskaya 5) A lovely mosque that has served local Tatar Muslims since 1902.

Tours

Krasnov TOURS
(Краснов; ☎238 3520; www.uraltourism.ru; ul Borchaninova 4; ⏰10am-6.30pm Mon-Fri, 11am-5pm Sat) Offers active and adventure tourism

such as 19 days of rafting (R22,800) or cross-country skiing in the Urals, beginner Russian courses, river cruises and many more activities. The Russian version of the website has a wider and sometimes less expensive choice.

Perm Tourist Travel Agency TOURS
(Пермь Турист туристическое агентство; ☎218 6999; www.hotel-ural.com/tourist; office 209, ul Lenina 58; ⏰10am-7pm Mon-Fri, 11am-4pm Sat) Inside the Hotel Ural, organises excursions such as to Kungur and Perm-36 (each from R5800), as well as city tours in Perm and Volga river cruises.

Festivals & Events

Kamwa Festival CULTURAL
(www.kamwa.ru) The annual 'ethno-futuristic' Kamwa Festival held in late July to early August in Perm and Khokhlovka brings together ancient ethno-Ugric traditions and modern art, music and fashion.

White Nights CULTURAL
(www.permfest.com) Inaugurated in 2011, the White Nights festival runs through most of June, presenting a month of contemporary music, street art, theatre, readings and interesting side-festival events.

Sleeping

TOP CHOICE **Hotel Edem** HOTEL €€
(☎212 0036; ul Maxima Gorkogo 21b; r R2000-2500;) The six large rooms with double beds in this excellent minihotel are named by their colour scheme – the 'Pink Room', and so on. As with some minihotels, service is friendly but patchy; here you get a kettle, coffee, plates and cutlery as well as a fridge in order to make good use of the 24-hour supermarket across the road if you're on a tight budget.

Hotel Ural HOTEL €€
(Гостиница Урал; ☎218 6262; www.hotel-ural.com; ul Lenina 58; s R2000-2700, d R3500-4300; @) This one-time Soviet monolith rising up in the heart of the city has shed virtually all of its cheap, unrenovated rooms and boasts a shimmering, high-tech lobby and mostly modern rooms at reasonable prices.

Hotel Astor HOTEL €€
(Гостиница Астор; ☎212 2212; www.astorhotel.ru; ul Petropavlovskaya 40; s R2900-5000, d R3400-5500, tr R6000;) Spotless white dominates this hotel's colour scheme. Its reputation among business travellers is high, and rooms are low-allergy.

Hotel Prikamye HOTEL €€
(Гостиница Прикамье; ☎219 8353; www.prikamie-hotel.ru; Komsomolsky pr 27; s R2300-3200, d R3300-3850, ste R4600-4900;) Nicely spruced-up rooms in this former Soviet eyesore make Prikamye a very decent option. Deals are better if you book on the web. Wi-fi is available but expensive.

Hotel New Star HOTEL €€
(☎220 6801; www.newstar-hotel.ru; ul Gazety Zvezda 38b; s/d R3500/5000; @) Modern well-equipped rooms. The R1900 'economy class' singles are attractive for solo travellers but can be noisy. Kids get significant discounts.

Eating & Drinking

TOP CHOICE **Grill Taverna Montenegro** BALKAN €€
(Гриль-Таверна Монтенегро; ul Maxima Gorkogo 28; meals R700; ⏰noon-midnight;) The trompe l'œil village fresco downstairs, upstairs pseudo-portico and outdoor terrace lend nice touches to this excellent restaurant. The Kalmyk lamb kebab is superbly grilled.

Vkus Stranstvy CAFETERIA €
(Вкус странствий; Sibirskaya ul 8; meals R300; ⏰10am-10pm;) With the feel of a midpriced restaurant, the cheerful 'Taste for Travel' neo-*stolovaya* (canteen) serves some of the best cafeteria food in the Ural Mountains.

Zhivago RUSSIAN €€
(Живаго; ☎235 1716; ul Lenina 37; mains R350-600; ⏰9am-midnight) This restaurant for the well heeled and the literary inclined is actually two in one. Pasternak downstairs has a lounge-like, postmodernist café feel, while Zhivago upstairs is a fully fledged formal restaurant. Steaks and several more-expensive dishes cost over R1000.

Kama BREWERY €€
(Кама; www.pivzavodkama.ru; Sibirskaya ul 25; mains R300-600; ⏰noon-2am;) This microbrewery brews several tasty varieties of own-brew. The food, including its vegetarian borsch, is reasonably priced by Russian microbrewery standards. Sometimes good bands perform live here; other times it's a guitar soloist with canned backing.

Entertainment

TOP CHOICE **Labarint** KARAOKE
(Лабаринт; 3rd fl, ul Lenina 88; cover Thu-Sat R300-400, Sun-Wed free; ⏰6pm-6am) This club has 50,000 tunes and everything from Russia's best- and least-known to Western rock

Perm

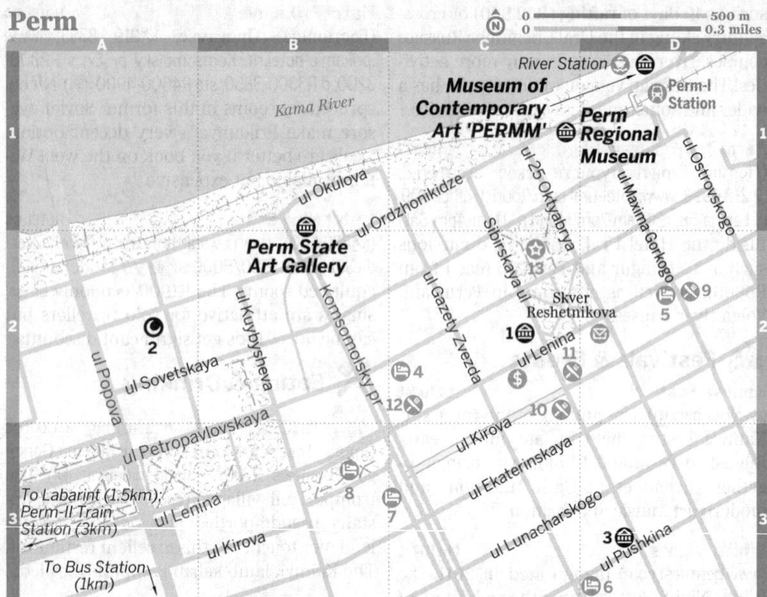

of all types (just write down the title and artist's name if it's not on the list).

Tchaikovsky Theatre of Opera & Ballet THEATRE
(Театр оперы и балета Чайковского; ☎212 5416; www.opera.permonline.ru; ul Petropavlovskaya 25) One of Russia's top ballet schools.

Information

Main post office (Главпочтамт; ul Lenina 29; per hr R45; ⏲8am-10pm Mon-Fri, 9am-6pm Sat & Sun)

Perm Tourist (Пермь Турист; ☎218 6021; www.visitperm.ru; ul Lenina 58; ⏲9am-8pm Mon-Fri, from 10am Sat & Sun; 📶) City and regional information, including the free multilingual *Green Line* booklet explaining sights on a city walk. Hires city bikes (24 hours R550) and has a list of tour operators. Inside the Hotel Ural; use side entrance.

Getting There & Away

Inside the Hotel Ural you will find a **railways booking office** (☎233 0203; ⏲8am-7.30pm Mon-Sat, to 6pm Sun) and an **Aviakassa** (☎233 2509; ⏲8.30am-8pm Mon-Fri, 10am-5pm Sat & Sun).

Air

Several airlines fly to Moscow daily (about R5000, two hours, nine daily). Lufthansa flies to/from Frankfurt four times a week.

Boat

The **river station** (Речной вокзал) is at the eastern end of ul Ordzhonikidze, in front of **Perm-I station**. Boats do short tours of the Kama in the navigation season. Seven- to 14-day cruises down the Kama River to the Volga and continuing to the major towns between Kazan and Astrakhan cost anything from R11,000 for the cheapest class to R58,000 for the most expensive.

Bus

From the **bus station** (Автовокзал; ul Revolyutsii 68) numerous buses go to or via Kungur; there are three buses a day to Khokhlovka (R84, 1½ hours) and two daily buses to Ufa (R569, 11½ hours). Buses to Kazan depart Friday and Saturday (R1300, two weekly, 12 hours).

Train

Perm-II, the city's major train station, 3km southwest of the centre, is on the trans-Siberian route. Many trains travel the route from Moscow, including the *firmeny* train (a premium, long-distance train) called the Kama (*kupe* R4370, 20 hours). Heading east, the next major stop on the trans-Siberian route is Yekaterinburg (*platskart/kupe* R700/1450, six hours). There were no direct trains to Kazan at the time of research. Note that some trains depart from the *gorny trakt* (mountain track) on the north side of Perm-II, as opposed to the *glavny trakt* (main track).

Perm

Top Sights

Museum of Contemporary Art 'PERMM' D1
Perm Regional Museum C1
Perm State Art Gallery B1

Sights

1 Archaeological Collection C2
2 Mosque A2
3 Sergei Diaghilev Museum D3

Activities, Courses & Tours

Perm Tourist Travel Agency .... (see 8)

Sleeping

4 Hotel Astor C2
5 Hotel Edem D2
6 Hotel New Star D3
7 Hotel Prikamye C3
8 Hotel Ural B3

Eating

9 Grill Taverna Montenegro D2
10 Kama C2
11 Vkus Stranstvy C2
12 Zhivago C2

Entertainment

13 Tchaikovsky Theatre of Opera & Ballet C2

Information

Perm Tourist .... (see 8)

Transport

Aviakassa .... (see 8)
Railways Bookings Office .... (see 8)

The disused and crumbling Perm-I station, 1km northeast of the centre, is being restored.

Getting Around

Marshrutka (fixed-route minibus) 1t links the bus station, Perm-II train station and the airport. Bus 42 goes between the bus station and the airport. Tram 4 goes between Perm-II train station and Hotel Ural, and tram 11 connects ul Maxima Gorkogo with the central market (about 400m from the bus station) via ul Petropavlovskaya and ul Lenina.

Around Perm

KHOKHLOVKA ХОХЛОВКА

342

The **Architecture-Ethnography Museum** (299 7181; admission R100; 10am-6pm) is set in the rolling countryside near the village of Khokhlovka, about 45km north of Perm. Its impressive collection of wooden buildings includes two churches dating from the turn of the 18th century. Most of the structures are from the 19th or early 20th centuries, including an old firehouse, a salt-production facility and a Khanty *izba* (traditional wooden cottage). A few buses a day serve Khokhlovka from Perm (R84, one hour), the best ones departing Perm at 9.55am and returning from Khokhlovka at 4.25pm.

PERM-36 ПЕРМЬ-36

Once an ominous island in the Gulag Archipelago, **Perm-36** (www.perm36.ru; admission R50, tours in Russian R500; 10am-5pm Tue-Sun) is now a haunting memorial and museum dedicated to the victims of political repression. The buildings have been preserved in their original condition, with the interior of some re-created to illustrate the conditions under which prisoners lived.

For most of its history since 1946, Perm-36 was a labour camp for dissidents. Countless artists, scientists and intellectuals spent years in the cold, damp cells, many in solitary confinement. They worked at mundane tasks like assembling fasteners and survived on measly portions of bread and gruel.

The admission fee allows you to walk around, but doesn't include a tour (which are by appointment). The museum has an **office** (342-212 612; www.perm36.ru; bul Gagarina 10) in Perm.

The memorial is located in the village of Kuchino, about 25km from the town of Chusovoy, which itself is 100km from Perm. To reach it, take a bus bound for Chusovoy or Lysva (R220, two hours), get off at Tyomnaya station, walk back to find the Kuchino turn-off, then walk another 2.5km to the village. The museum's office in Perm can arrange a taxi for about R3000 and interpreter for R2500 to R3000 per trip.

Kungur Кунгур

34271 / POP 68,000 / MOSCOW +2HR

Between the two regional capitals Perm and Yekaterinburg, Kungur is like cream in a biscuit. Despite the city's rundown appearance, its skyline is graced by a multitude of pretty church cupolas, including the 18th-century **Tikhvinskaya Church** in the centre and the **Transfiguration Church** on the other bank of the Sylva, while the frozen magic of its ice cave draws a steady stream of visitors.

PERM-36: EVEN WALLS HAVE EARS *YAKOV L KLOTS*

'Even walls have ears', goes the Russian saying. At Perm-36, the former camp for political prisoners, the walls have survived...unlike most of those who were kept behind them: dissidents, poets, intelligentsia; ordinary people whose lives had been taken away and silenced. Concrete floors, barred windows, plank beds, aluminium bowls, spoons and mugs, and the barbed wire coiling along the borders of the restricted areas: all outlived the inmates.

Nowadays, representing the camp's daily routine with an existential accuracy, the walls keep the memory of bygone times – of prisoners who were not fated to see their place of detention become a museum, of halls walked by prison guards instead of high-school students.

Before the first prisoners were brought to Perm-36, all of the trees around the grounds were destroyed. The purpose was to prevent convicts from determining in which part of this vast country they had landed. Prisoners were not allowed to leave their cells, so they could not hear the gush of the Chusovaya River, which flowed a few hundred metres from the camp's gate. And the rich local landscape that they might spy through narrow window slits was wiped out.

But the guards were powerless to prevent local birds from flying and singing above the camp barracks. So an inmate – a biologist sentenced to 25 years of 'special regime imprisonment' – identified the bird species by their songs, and determined he was in the Urals.

One can never know for sure what tomorrow is going to be like. Perhaps the darkest side of life in imprisonment is the constant awareness that tomorrow is *not* going to be different from yesterday. The deathly silence that resounds in the damp, dark cells at Perm-36 reminds us of what this place was like yesterday.

Founded in 1663 on the banks of the meandering river, Kungur was a copper-smelting centre during the 17th and 18th centuries. This topic is covered in the **Regional Local Studies Museum** (ul Gogolya 36; admission R20; ⏲10am-5pm Wed-Sun).

The **Kungur Ice Cave** (guided tour R500-600; ⏲10am-4pm) is about 5km out of town. The network of caves stretches for more than 5km, although only about 1.5km are open to explore. The ancient Finno-Ugric inhabitants of the Perm region believed the cave to be the home of a fiery underground creature, and the grottoes are adorned with unique ice formations, frozen waterfalls and underground lakes. You can enter only with one of the guided tours that depart every two hours. Tickets are sold at the box office outside; the number of participants on each tour is limited to 20, so tickets may not be available for the next departure. The cost of the excursion includes admission to a small museum on the site with displays of rocks and fossils. Take enough warm clothes to withstand subzero temperatures in the initial grottoes.

If the cave is your reason for visiting Kungur, you can stay at the popular **Stalagmit Tourist Complex** (☎62 610; www.kungurcave.ru; s incl breakfast R800-1500, d R1400-2500; ⊖), close to the cave entrance; it has excellent rooms, all with their own bathroom (the cheaper ones don't have fridges and TV). The beautiful countryside surrounding Kungur is great for outdoor sports, and bicycles as well as rafts, canoes and cross-country skis can be hired inexpensively at Stalagmit.

In the centre of town, **Hotel Iren** (☎32 270; ul Lenina 30; s without bathroom R500-1400, d R1000, s with bathroom R1300-2500, d R2100) is good value, though it doesn't have a lift. Even the rooms without bathrooms are pleasant enough, and the shared toilets and showers are very clean. Prices include breakfast.

Across the bridge, the riverside café-disco **Tri Medvedya** (ul Vorovskaya 5; mains R150; ⏲24hr) is a good place to eat. Helpful staff can order a taxi for you back to the bus and train stations.

Located on the trans-Siberian route, Kungur is served from Perm by frequent intercity trains (*kupe* R472, 1½ hours), suburban trains (R110, 2¼ hours, four daily) and trains to/from Yekaterinburg (*platskart* R872, four hours). Bus is the best option from Perm, however, with departures every one to two hours; the most convenient leaves Perm at 8.25am or 9.25am and returns from Kungur at 6.40pm or 7.55pm (R181, 2½ hours). Buses to Ufa (R740, one daily) depart at 10am.

In Kungur, the bus and train stations are located alongside each other. Bus 9 (R11, every one to two hours) plies the route between Hotel Iren, the train and bus stations, and the Stalagmit complex.

SVERDLOVSK REGION

Yekaterinburg

Екатеринбург

343 / POP 1.35 MILLION / MOSCOW +2HR

Gem rush, miners' mythology, the execution of the Romanovs, the rise of Yeltsin and gangster feuds of the 1990s – Yekaterinburg is like a piece of conceptual art in which the subtext is perhaps more startling than surface appearances.

Bland on the outside, the political capital of the Ural Mountains is overflowing with history and culture, while its economic growth is manifested in a thriving restaurant scene and, as in many other regional capitals, in atrociously trafficked avenues.

With one of the best international airports in Russia and a couple of agencies experienced in dealing with foreign travellers, Yekaterinburg is a good base camp for exploring the Ural Mountains.

History

Yekaterinburg was founded as a factory-fort in 1723 as part of Peter the Great's push to exploit the Ural region's mineral riches. The city was named after two Catherines: Peter's wife (later Empress Catherine I), and the Russian patron saint of mining.

The city is notorious, however, for being the place where the Bolsheviks murdered Tsar Nicholas II and his family in July 1918. Six years later, the town was renamed Sverdlovsk, after Yakov Sverdlov, a leading Bolshevik who was Vladimir Lenin's right-hand man until his death in the flu epidemic of 1919. The region still bears Sverdlov's name.

WWII turned Sverdlovsk into a major industrial centre, as hundreds of factories were transferred here from vulnerable areas west of the Ural Mountains. The city was closed to foreigners until 1990 because of its many defence plants.

During the late 1970s a civil engineering graduate of the local university, Boris Yeltsin, began to make his political mark, rising to become regional Communist Party boss before being promoted to Moscow in 1985. Several years later he was standing on a tank in Moscow as the leading figure in defending the country against a putsch by old-guard communists. He became the Russian Federation's first president in June 1991.

That year Yekaterinburg took back its original name. After suffering economic depression and Mafia lawlessness in the early 1990s, the city has boomed in recent years and weathered the various crises well.

Sights

TOP CHOICE **Romanov Death Site** CHURCH, MEMORIAL
(Место убийства Романовых; ul Karla Libknekhta & ul Tolmachyova 34; dawn-dusk) On the night of 16 July 1918, Tsar Nicholas II, his wife and children were murdered in the basement of a local engineer's house, known as Dom Ipatyeva (named for its owner, Nikolay Ipatyev). During the Soviet period, the building housed a local museum of atheism, but it was demolished in 1977 by then governor Boris Yeltsin, who feared it would attract monarchist sympathisers.

Today the massive Byzantine-style **Church upon the Blood** (Храм на Крови) dominates this site and is easily the most celebrated of memorials to the Romanovs. Nearby, the pretty wooden **Chapel of the Revered Martyr Grand Princess Yelizaveta Fyodorovna** (9am-5.30pm) honours the imperial family's great-aunt and faithful friend. After her relatives' murders, this pious nun met an even worse end when she was thrown down a mineshaft, poisoned with gas and buried.

Opposite the site are the historic **Rastorguev-Kharitonov mansion** (Усадьба Расторгуев-Харитонова) and the restored **Ascension Church** (Вознесенская церковь; ul Klary Tsetkin 11).

Istorichesky skver PARK
The prettiest and most lively part of Yekaterinburg in summer is the landscaped parkland alongside the City Pond (Gorodskoy prud), where pr Lenina crosses a small dam. This was where Yekaterinburg began back in 1723. The **Monument to the Founders of Yekaterinburg** (Памятник основателям Екатеринбурга) standing nearby depicts founders Vasily Tatishchev and George Wilhelm de Gennin.

Literary Quarter NEIGHBOURHOOD
Situated north of skver Popova, the Literary Quarter features restored wooden houses.

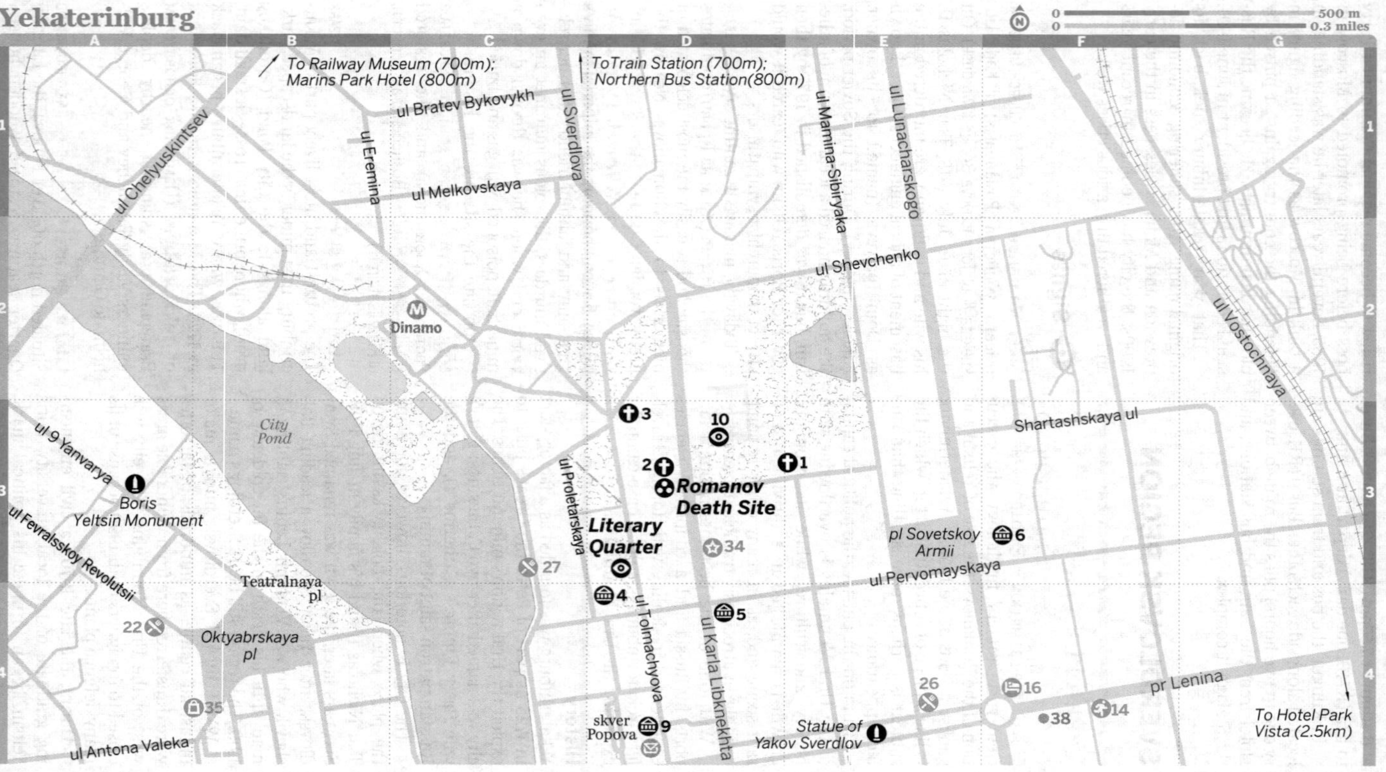
Yekaterinburg
0 500 m
0 0.3 miles
To Railway Museum (700m); Marins Park Hotel (800m)
ToTrain Station (700m); Northern Bus Station(800m)
ul Bratev Bykovykh
ul Sverdlova
ul Mamina-Sibiryaka
ul Lunacharskogo
ul Chelyuskintsev
ul Eremina
ul Melkovskaya
ul Shevchenko
ul Vostochnaya
Dinamo
City Pond
3
10
1
2
Romanov Death Site
Shartashskaya ul
ul 9 Yanvarya
Boris Yeltsin Monument
ul Fevralsskoy Revolutsii
ul Proletarskaya
Literary Quarter
34
pl Sovetskoy Armii
6
27
ul Pervomayskaya
Teatralnaya pl
4
ul Tolmachyova
5
ul Karla Libknekhta
22
Oktyabrskaya pl
26
16
pr Lenina
35
14
38
skver Popova
9
Statue of Yakov Sverdlov
To Hotel Park Vista (2.5km)
ul Antona Valeka

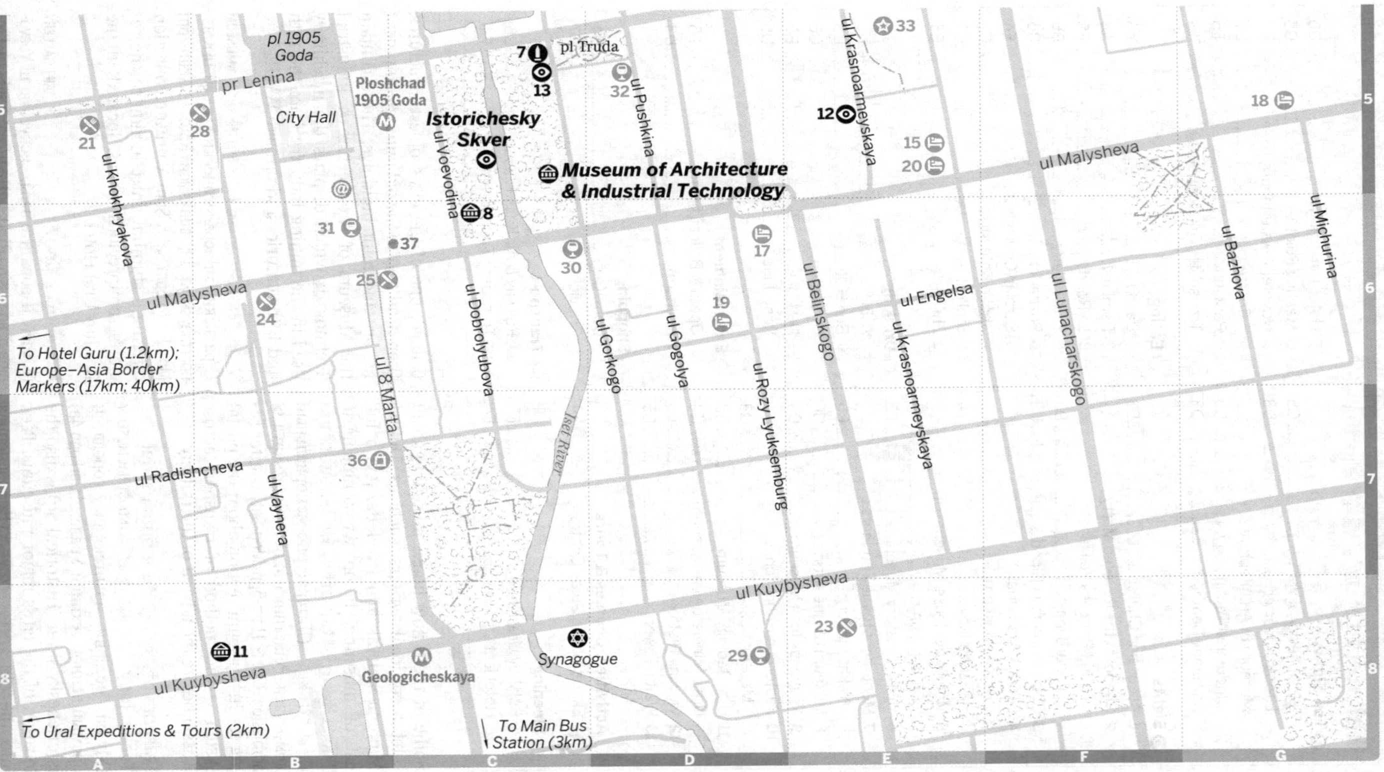
pl 1905 Goda
pr Lenina
Ploshchad 1905 Goda
City Hall
7
pl Truda
13
32
ul Pushkina
33
ul Krasnoarmeyskaya
12
18
15
20
ul Malysheva
Istorichesky Skver
ul Voevodina
Museum of Architecture & Industrial Technology
21
28
ul Khokhryakova
31
8
37
30
17
ul Michurina
ul Bazhova
25
ul Malysheva
24
19
ul Engelsa
ul Dobrolyubova
ul Gorkogo
ul Gogolya
ul Belinskogo
ul Lunacharskogo
To Hotel Guru (1.2km); Europe–Asia Border Markers (17km; 40km)
ul 8 Marta
ul Rozy Lyuksemburg
ul Krasnoarmeyskaya
Iset River
36
ul Radishcheva
ul Vaynera
ul Kuybysheva
23
11
Synagogue
29
Geologicheskaya
ul Kuybysheva
To Ural Expeditions & Tours (2km)
To Main Bus Station (3km)
A
B
C
D
E
F
G
5
6
7
8

Yekaterinburg

Top Sights
- Istorichesky Skver C5
- Literary Quarter D3
- Museum of Architecture & Industrial Technology C5
- Romanov Death Site D3

Sights
1 Ascension Church E3
2 Chapel of the Revered Martyr Grand Princess Yelizaveta Fyodorovna D3
3 Church upon the Blood D3
4 Literary-Memorial House-Museum Reshetnikov D4
5 Metenkov House-Museum of Photography D4
6 Military History Museum F3
7 Monument to the Founders of Yekaterinburg C5
8 Museum of Fine Arts C6
9 Nevyansk Icon Museum D4
10 Rastorguev-Kharitonov Mansion D3
11 Ural Geology Museum B8
Urals Mineralogical Museum ..... (see 15)
12 Viewing Platform E5
13 Water Tower C5

Activities, Courses & Tours
14 Ekaterinburg Guide Centre F4

Sleeping
15 Bolshoy Ural Hotel E5
16 Hotel Iset F4
17 Hotel Tsentralny D6
18 Meeting Point G5
19 Novotel Yekaterinburg Centre D6
20 Park Inn E5
Transhotel Yekaterinburg ..... (see 19)

Eating
21 Dacha A5
22 Demidov A4
23 La Rond E8
24 Paul Bakery B6
25 Pozharka B6
26 Serbian Courtyard E4
Shoko Kofeyniya ..... (see 17)
27 Stolle C3
28 Zhili Byli B5

Drinking
Alibi ..... (see 17)
29 Ben Hall D8
30 Dr Scotch C6
31 New Bar B6
32 Rosy Jane D5

Entertainment
33 Opera & Ballet Theatre E5
34 Philharmonic D3

Shopping
35 Dom Knigi B4
36 Grinvich B7

Transport
37 Railway & Air Kassa C6
38 Transaero Tours Centre F4

Some of them now house museums about celebrated local writers such as Dmitry Mamina-Sibiryak and Pavel Bazhov; a full list of museums is on www.ompu.ur.ru. The **Literary-Memorial House-Museum Reshetnikov** (Литературно-мемориальный дом-музей Решетникова; ul Proletarskaya 6; admission R70; 11am-5pm Mon-Sat) is interesting for its museum section about the postal system – the method of transport across Russia before the advent of the railway.

Museum of Architecture & Industrial Technology INDUSTRIAL MUSEUM
(Музей истории архитектуры города и промышленной техники Урала; ul Gorkogo 4a) Istorichesky skver (Historical Sq) is also the location of the city's major museums. Peek into the old **water tower** (Водонапорная башня), one of the city's oldest structures, then head over to the old mining-equipment factory and mint buildings. These contain the Museum of Architecture & Industrial Technology, which displays the machinery used in the mining industry from the 18th and 19th centuries and through WWII.

Urals Mineralogical Museum MUSEUM
(Уральский минералогический музей; ul Krasnoarmeyskaya 1a; admission R50; 10am-7pm Mon-Fri, to 5pm Sat & Sun) A private collection offering a stunning introduction to the region's semiprecious stones, located in the Bolshoy Ural Hotel.

Museum of Fine Arts ART GALLERY
(Музей изобразительных искусств; ul Voevodina 5; admission R150; 11am-7pm Tue-Sun) The

star exhibit of the Museum of Fine Arts is the elaborate Kasli Iron Pavilion that won prizes in the 1900 Paris Expo.

Ural Geology Museum MUSEUM
(Уральский геологический музей; ul Kuybysheva 39; admission R50; ⏲11am-5pm Mon-Fri) Over 500 minerals from the Ural Mountains region and a collection of meteorites. Enter from ul Khokhryakova inside Urals State Mining University.

Military History Museum MUSEUM
(Военно-исторический музей; ul Pervomayskaya 27; Russian/foreigner R50/100; ⏲9am-4pm Tue-Sat) Well worthwhile for buffs and anyone with a general interest. Has a small piece of Gary Powers' spy plane, shot down in 1960.

Metenkov House-Museum of Photography MUSEUM
(Музей Фотографии; ul Karla Libknekhta 36; admission R100; ⏲10am-6pm) Features evocative photos of old Yekaterinburg.

FREE **Nevyansk Icon Museum** MUSEUM
(Музей Невянская икона; ul Tolmachyova 21; ⏲11am-7pm) Excellent icons from the 17th to the 20th century, from the local Nevyansk school.

Railway Museum RAILWAY MUSEUM
(Железнодорожный музей; ul Chelyuskintsev; admission R75; ⏲noon-5pm Tue-Sat) Housed in the old train station, dating from 1881. Exhibits highlight the history of the railroad in the Urals, including a re-creation of the office of the Soviet-era railway director.

Tours

Ekaterinburg Guide Centre TOURS
(Екатеринбургский центр гидов; ☎359 3708; www.ekaterinburgguide.com; office 12, pr Lenina 52/1) Organises English-language tours of the city and trips into the countryside, including the difficult-to-reach village of Verkhoturie (where Grigory Rasputin started his spiritual journey), as well as hiking and rafting expeditions. Day trips cost anything between R1300 and R7300, depending on numbers. It also books budget dorms from R1150 in a central minihotel.

Ural Expeditions & Tours TOURS
(☎356 5282; http://welcome-ural.ru; ul Posadskaya 23; ⏲9am-6pm Mon-Fri) This group of geologists from the Sverdlovsk Mining Institute leads trekking, rafting and horse-riding trips to all parts of the Ural Mountains, including Taganay and Zyuratkul National Parks. English-speaking guides.

Sleeping

TOP CHOICE **Hotel Tsentralny** HOTEL €€
(Отель Центральный; ☎350 0505; www.hotelcentr.ru; ul Malysheva 74; s R3150-3780, d R4050-5900; ⊜📶) This historical hotel is housed in a grand art nouveau building in the heart of town, with excellent business-class and standard rooms. Eating and nightlife are never far away from here. Trolleybuses 1 and 9 are among the many going there from the train station.

Marins Park Hotel HOTEL €€
(Маринс Парк Отель; ☎214 3000; www.sv-hotel.ru; ul Chelyuskintsev 106; s R1600-2900, d R2300-3900, ste R4400-5100; 📶) Formerly known as the Sverdlovsk, a Soviet disaster zone when it came to hotels, this place has been renovated and is gradually reinventing itself as a modern congress hotel; it retains its chief advantage of being right across the road from the train station.

Hotel Iset HOTEL €€
(Гостиница Исеть; ☎350 0110; www.hoteliset.ru; pr Lenina 69/1; s R3400, d R3800-4800, ste R4500; ⊜📶) If it looks funky from the street, it's because it's shaped like a hammer and sickle when seen from the sky. Inside, curving corridors lead to nicely furnished rooms, though they aren't large. Take any tram going south down ul Lunacharskogo from the station.

Hotel Guru HOTEL €€
(☎228 5070; www.guruhotel.ru; ul Repina 22; s/d R2800/3500; ⊜❄@📶) This is an intriguing option located inside the new building of a dance school of the same name. But before you check in at a weekend, find out if the disco downstairs is operating (which can be annoying). Trolleybuses 3 and 17 from the train station stop nearby at Institut Svyazi.

Hotel Park Vista HOTEL €€
(☎216 4244; hotel@parkvista.ru; ul Vostochnaya 45; s/d R2000/3000; ⊜📶) Rooms are large and the only downsides of this excellent-value minihotel owned by a local metals-cutting company are the minimal service and that breakfast is a couple of wearily fried eggs and a cup of tea in the 24-hour Azeri eatery downstairs. Bring your own coffee. Take tram 21 from the train station to TsPKiO (ЦПКиО).

Novotel Yekaterinburg Centre HOTEL €€
(☎253 5383; http://novotel-ekaterinburg.ru; ul Engelsa 7; s R7000-8000, d R8000-9000;) This excellent new chain hotel in the centre is 20% cheaper on weekdays and offers good deals online through www.hotel.com. The easiest way from the station is *marshrutka* 56 to ul Rozy Lyuksemburg.

Park Inn HOTEL €€
(☎216 6000; www.parkinn.com/hotel-ekaterinburg; ul Mamina-Sibiryaka 98; r R6800-7650;) Offers rooms with cheering colour schemes and all amenities you would expect for the price. Trolleybuses 18 and 19 from the station stop at Dom Kino close by.

Bolshoy Ural Hotel HOTEL €
(Гостиница Большой Урал; ☎350 0143; www.b-ural.ru; ul Krasnoarmeyskaya 1; r without bathroom from R1050, r with bathroom R2300-3500, ste R3800-4200) Occupies an entire city block. The somewhat dour atmosphere is buffered by the prime location. Trolleybus 18 from the station to Dom Kino takes you close.

Transhotel Yekaterinburg HOTEL €€
(☎355 1211; www.transhotel.su; ul Gogolya 15; s R3500-4100, d R4100-5900, ste R6200-6900;) A small and friendly modern hotel behind the Novotel.

Minigostonitsa Vesta APARTMENT €€
(☎219 5488; www.hhotel.ru; reception@hhotel.ru; apt from R2500) Very centrally located apartments in new buildings for short stays of a couple of days or more.

Meeting Point HOSTEL €
(☎8-953-604 1941; www.meetingpoint.hostel.com; apt 73, ul Malysheva 87; 8-bed dm €16; @) Small hostel in the centre of town with registration that's free for guests staying three days

LOCAL KNOWLEDGE

LUBA SUSLYAKOVA'S PLACES

The Yekaterinburg journalist and blogger Luba Suslyakova works on the English-language newspaper *Your Yekaterinburg* and blogs on **Ask Urals** (http://askural.com).

The Romanov Memorial

It's popular with locals, who go there for wedding photos. Russian tourists also like it. Some strong Orthodox believers say they prefer to go to the older churches. Foreigners like it because of the small museum on the ground floor, which gives you a picture of what happened there.

For Russian Pies

Stolle (Штолле, Shtolle; ul Maxima Gorkogo 7a; pirozhki from R200; ⊙10am-midnight) – we have three in Yekaterinburg. The atmosphere is good and they usually play jazz music.

Boris Yeltsin Statue & Memorial Centre

The sculptor **Georgy Frangulyan** is known for his unusual views. He says he saw Yeltsin as a huge piece of stone moving forward, leaving debris behind him. The 'presidential centre' behind it will have a library and a small museum about Yeltsin.

Drinking Spots

Dr Scotch; there's also a new place called **Alibi** (www.alibibar.ru; ul Malysheva 74; ⊙noon-3am Sun-Thu, to 5am Fri & Sat).

Bird's-Eye View

I'd definitely go to the **viewing platform** in the **Antey Shopping Centre** (Смотравая площадка; ul Krasnoarmeyskaya 10; R50; ⊙noon-11.30pm; enter through door on far right).

Somewhere Peaceful

Lake Shartash (Озеро Шарташ), a piece of nature right within the city. It's easy to get there by tram. It's peaceful, you can picnic there, walk around the lake, rent a bicycle.

(To get to Lake Shartash, take tram 8, 13, 15, 23, 32 or A from pr Lenina to stop Kamennie palatki. Follow the sign to Shartashsky Lesopark (Шарташский лесопарк) and climb the stone steps.)

or more. Trolleybus 18 from the train station runs to the Transagenstvo stop nearby.

See **Ekaterinburg Guide Centre** (Екатеринбургский центр гидов; ☎359 3708; www.ekaterinburgguide.com; office 12, ul Lenina 52/1) for another cheap hostel.

Eating

Ulitsa 8 Marta between pr Lenina and ul Malysheva has several popular chain and Western-style places such as Thank God It's Friday and Traveller's Coffee, and ul Vaynera has a moderate choice of eateries.

TOP CHOICE Dacha INTERNATIONAL, RUSSIAN €€€
(Дача; ☎379 3569; pr Lenina 20a; mains R500-800, business lunches R300; ⏰noon-midnight) Each room in this quality restaurant is decorated like a Russian country house, from the casual garden to the more formal dining room. Enjoy unbeatable cuisine and hospitality.

TOP CHOICE Zhili Byli RUSSIAN €
(ul Vaynera 8; mains R250-350; ⏰11am-11pm;) Decorated in the traditional village style of this chain, Zhili Byli serves Russian dishes to the wheeze of saxophones and tinkling lounge music, all totally out of keeping with the fake oak tree, coloured glass windows and peasant costumes that hang around.

La Rond FRENCH, RUSSIAN €€€
(☎359 6222; http://atriumhotel.ru; ul Kuybysheva 44; mains R1000-1600; ⏰lunch & dinner) Located inside the Atrium Palace Hotel, this is an upmarket gourmet act especially popular among its business guests.

Shoko Kofeyniya CAFÉ €€
(www.restoraciya.ru; ul Malysheva 74; mains R400; ⏰8am-2am Mon-Fri, from 6am Sat, 6am-midnight Sun) This upmarket café is the pick of the crop among the cluster of bars and eateries located in and alongside the Hotel Tsentralny building. The hours are useful for chilling out late at night.

Paul Bakery BAKERY €
(ul Malysheva 36; light meals R250-350; ⏰8am-1pm Mon-Fri) This café, entered from ul Vaynera, is great for a quick snack and coffee, ordered from the counter.

Demidov RUSSIAN €€€
(☎371 7344; ul Fevralsskoy Revolutsii 9; mains R350-700; ⏰11-2am) 'Museum' restaurant located in the house where the White Russian leader Kolchak stayed in 1919. Has an outdoor grill.

Pozharka PUB €€
(ul Malysheva 44; mains R350-500; ⏰noon-midnight Sun-Thu, to 2am Fri & Sat) About 40 different beers and food (that gets expensive if you don't choose carefully) as an accompaniment.

Serbian Courtyard SERBIAN €€
(Сербский дворик; ☎350 3457; http://serbskiy-dvorik.blizko.ru; pr Lenina 53; meals R700; ⏰noon-midnight) Best Balkan food in town.

Drinking

TOP CHOICE Rosy Jane PUB €€€
(pr Lenina 34; mains R600-900; ⏰6am-4am) This English-style pub aims at the New Russian drinking and eating crowd, who grace the bar (with or without cigars) and perch at polished wood tables gourmandising on steak and other very well-prepared Russian and international dishes.

Dr Scotch PUB
(ul Malysheva 56a; ⏰noon-2am) Less expensive and more popular than Rosy Jane.

Ben Hall PUB
(☎251 6368; ul Narodnoy Voli 65; mains R350-600; ⏰noon-2am Sun-Thu, to 4am Fri & Sat;) This popular pub hosts local rock bands at weekends, its owner being a well-known musician. Trams 15 and 27 from Operny Teatr or along pr Lenina to Tsirk (Цирк) drop you close by.

New Bar BAR
(ul 8 Marta 8; ⏰10am-2am Mon-Thu & Sun, to 6am Fri & Sat) Art-scene café and cocktail bar on the top floor of Mytny Dvor mall.

Entertainment

Philharmonic CLASSICAL MUSIC
(Филармония; ☎371 4682; www.filarmonia.e-burg.ru; ul Karla Libknekhta 38) Yekaterinburg's top venue for the classical performing arts often hosts visiting directors and soloists, as well as the regular performances of the acclaimed Ural Mountains academic orchestra.

Opera & Ballet Theatre OPERA, BALLET
(Театр оперы и балета; ☎350 8057; www.uralopera.ru; pr Lenina 45a; tickets from R100) The level of professionalism is not quite on a par with the Philharmonic, but the ornate baroque theatre is still a lovely place to see the Russian classics.

Shopping

Grinvich SHOPPING MALL
(ul 8 Marta 46; ⌚10am-10pm) This enormous shopping complex near the ul Vaynera pedestrian zone is an oasis away from the traffic.

Dom Knigi BOOKSTORE
(Дом книги; ul Antona Valeka 12; ⌚10am-8pm)

Information

Main post office (Почтамт; pr Lenina 39; ⌚8am-10pm Mon-Fri, 9am-6pm Sat & Sun) With internet.

Traveller's Coffee (ul 8 Marta 8; ⌚8am-midnight) Free internet on borrowed laptops.

Getting There & Away

Air

The main airport is **Koltsovo** (☎224 2367; www.koltsovo.ru), 15km southeast of the city centre. Frequent services include Moscow, Novosibirsk, Krasnoyarsk, Irkutsk, Khabarovsk, Ufa, St Petersburg, Samara and a host of Black Sea hubs. International services include Frankfurt am Main (Germany), Beijing (China), Prague (Czech Republic), and Almaty and Astana (Kazakhstan). **Transaero Tours Centre** (Трансаэро; ☎365 9165; pr Lenina 50), located inside the City Centre shopping mall, handles bookings for all airlines.

Bus

The main **bus station** (ul 8 Marta 145) is 3km south of the city centre, but most buses pass the **northern bus station** (Автовокзал; Severny avtovokzal), conveniently located by the **train station**. Here you can catch frequent buses to Chelyabinsk (R400, four hours) and Alapaevsk (R260, three hours, three daily). There is also a bus station at the Koltsovo airport serving destinations in the Sverdlovsk region and Chelyabinsk (R400, 3½ hours, five daily).

Train

Yekaterinburg – sometimes still called 'Sverdlovsk' on timetables – is a major rail junction with connections to all stops on the trans-Siberian route. All trains to Moscow stop at either Perm (*platskart/kupe* R700/1450, six hours) or Kazan (*kupe/platskart* R2670/1730, 15 hours). Frequent trains to/from Moscow include the Ural (*kupe* R4520, 27 hours, daily) via Kazan. Heading east, the next major stops are Omsk (*kupe* R2580, 14 hours) and Novosibirsk (*kupe* R4087, 22 hours). You can buy tickets at outlets throughout the city, including the convenient **Railway & Air Kassa** (Железнодорожные и Авиакассы; ☎371 0400; ul Malysheva 31d; ⌚7am-8.30pm).

Getting Around

Bus 1 links the Sverdlovsk-Passazhirskaya train station and Koltsovo airport (one hour) from 6.30am to 11.30pm. *Marshrutka* 26 goes from the airport to metro pl 1905 Goda. *Marshrutka* 39 goes to metro Geologicheskaya.

Many trolleybuses and *marshrutky* (pay on board) run along ul Sverdlova/ul Karla Libknekhta between the train station and pr Lenina. Trams 13, 15 and 18 cover long stretches of pr Lenina. *Marshrutka* 24 runs along ul 8 Marta to the train station and *marshrutka* 57 connects Grinvich shopping centre via ul 8 Marta with the train station.

A single metro line runs between the northeastern suburbs and the city centre, with stops at the train station (Uralskaya), pl 1905 Goda and ul Kuybysheva near the synagogue (Geologicheskaya).

Around Yekaterinburg

GANINA YAMA ГАНИНА ЯМА

After the Romanov family was shot in the cellar of Dom Ipatyeva, their bodies were discarded in the depths of the forests of Ganina Yama, 16km northeast of Yekaterinburg. In their honour, the Orthodox Church has built the exquisite **Monastery of the Holy Martyrs** (☎343-217 9146; www.g-ya.ru) at this pilgrimage site. In 2010 one of the seven chapels burned down but is earmarked for reconstruction. According to the Orthodox Church, this is the final resting place of the Romanov family and is therefore sacred ground.

The nearest train station to Ganina Yama is Shuvakish, served by *elektrichka* (suburban train) from the central station. The monastery owns a bus that runs six times a day between the central station, Shuvakish station and Ganina Yama. Ekaterinburg Guide Centre offers three-hour tours for R1300 to R3500, depending on the number of people.

NEVYANSK & AROUND НЕВЬЯНСК

The small town of Nevyansk is in the heart of the former patrimony of the Demidovs, a family of industrialists who effectively controlled much of the Ural Mountains and who received Peter I's blessing to develop the region. At their most decadent stage, they bought the Italian feudal title of Count San-Donato. The main highlight here is the **Nevyansk Leaning Tower**, an impressive structure flanked by an equally impressive **Saviour-Transfiguration Cathedral**, which would have graced any large city.

The **Nevyansk History and Architecture Museum** (http://museum-nev.ru; pl Revolyutsii 2;

museum R60, Nevyansk tower excursion per group of 1-5 people R1200; ⏲9am-5pm Tue-Sun) is where you buy tickets for worthwhile excursions into the tower. This is the only way to access it and get great views over the landscape.

Seven kilometres from Nevyansk is the lovely Old Believers' village of **Byngi**, where an entrepreneurial German and his Russian wife have converted an *izba* into a **guest-house** (www.semken.eu) in the building itself and erected three yurts in the yard. Excursions, including rides on vintage Ural motorcycles, are available. Ekaterinburg Guide Centre runs seven-hour tours to Nevyansk and the nearby old potters' village of **Tavolgi**. Ask to stop on the way at the village of **Kunary**, where a local blacksmith has turned his wooden *izba* into a masterpiece of naive art.

Elektrichka (R104, 2½ hours, 12 daily) – some of them express trains (R154, 1¾ hours) – run to Nevyansk, most bound for Nizhny Tagil.

NIZHNYAYA SINYACHIKHA & AROUND НИЖНЯЯ СИНЯЧИХА

The pretty village of Nizhnyaya Sinyachikha, about 150km northeast of Yekaterinburg and 12km north of the town of Alapaevsk, is home to an open-air **Architecture Museum** (☎34346-75 118; admission R100; ⏲10am-5pm). Here there are 15 traditional Siberian log buildings, featuring displays of period furniture, tools and domestic articles. The stone cathedral houses a collection of regional folk art, which is one of the best of its kind. This impressive grouping of art and architecture was gathered from around the Ural Mountains and recompiled by the single-handed efforts of Ivan Samoylov, an enthusiastic local historian.

Three buses a day go to Alapaevsk (R260, three hours) from Yekaterinburg.

REPUBLIC OF BASHKORTOSTAN & CHELYABINSK REGION

Ufa Уфа

☎3472 / POP 1.03 MILLION / ⏲MOSCOW +2HR

Ufa is the proud capital of the autonomous republic of Bashkortostan (Республика Башкортостан), home of the Bashkirs, a Muslim Turkic people who dominated most of the southern Ural Mountains before Russian colonisation. Although they're only a third of the republic's population, you can hear their lispy language spoken on the streets of Ufa, in rural areas and on the radio. Substantial hydrocarbon reserves have turned Bashkortostan into something of an oil khanate.

Although Ufa has no major sights, you can spend a pleasant day walking through the streets where wooden cottages are reflected in glass office blocks, before heading out for your hiking, rafting or horseback adventure.

The city fills a 20km-long dumbbell-shaped area of land between the Belaya and Ufa Rivers. The southern lobe contains the city's dynamic centre. The main thoroughfare is ul Lenina, which runs from the centre,

STRADDLING THE CONTINENTS

The Ural Mountains have numerous monuments marking the border between Europe and Asia. Interestingly, the border was thought to be the Don River by the Ancient Greeks, but Yekaterinburg's founder Vasily Tatishchev drew it at the Ural Mountains in the mid-18th century, based on ideas of the day.

One of the more historic monuments is located 40km west of Yekaterinburg near Pervouralsk. It was erected in 1837 to commemorate a visit by Tsar Alexander II, who drank wine there and inadvertently began a favourite pastime of locals – drinking a glass in Europe and another glass in Asia (as if you needed an excuse!). To reach the monument, take a taxi (about R1000 if you order in advance) to Pervouralsk or one of the very frequent buses 150 or 180 from the Severny bus station (R60). They also stop at the Institut Svyazi at ul Repina 15.

In an attempt to make this geographic landmark more accessible to intercontinental travellers, the city has erected a new border marker, more conveniently located just 17km out of Yekaterinburg and looking a little like a mini Eiffel Tower. This one is more kitsch, but a taxi will take you out there for about R500. Ekaterinburg Guide Centre can organise a trip for R1050 to R2950 per person, depending on the number of people.

north to the river station. The train station is at the end of a serpentine road accessed via the northern end of ul Karla Marksa, which runs parallel to ul Lenina two blocks west. Pick up the Ufa City Transport Map (Схема городского транспорта Уфы; R20) from the **Belaya Reka Dom Knigi** (ul Lenina 24; ⌚9.30am-9pm) bookshop, which has all routes and stops and doubles as a useful street map.

Note that ul Zaki Balidi is sometimes called by its old name, ul Frunze.

Sights & Activities

Trading Arcade HISTORICAL BUILDING
(Гостинный Двор; ul Lenina) The focus of appealing ul Lenina is the 19th-century Trading Arcade, set on a fountain-cooled piazza. Behind the renovated facade is a luxuriously marble-lined shopping mall full of boutiques, cafés and carts selling freshly squeezed orange juice. Take any *marshrutka* going to the stop Gostiny Dvor (Гостиний двор).

Nesterov Art Gallery ART GALLERY
(Картинная Галерея Нестерова; ul Gogolya 27; admission R70; ⌚11am-8pm Tue-Sun) This small but interesting gallery contains a fabulous collection of artwork by the Ufa native Mikhail Nesterov and 50 paintings by Ukrainian futurist David Burlyuk, which he left in a Bashkir village when escaping from the Red Army during the Civil War. It's located two blocks west of ul Lenina, on the corner of ul Pushkina.

Bashkortostan National Museum MUSEUM
(Национальный музей Башкортостана; Sovetskaya ul 14; Russian/foreigner R100/250; ⌚10am-6pm Tue-Sat) Housed in a renovated art nouveau building behind the government office, the National Museum has two rooms downstairs dedicated to the natural environment and upstairs rooms to culture. The exhibits on Bashkir history and current events are the most interesting; all descriptions are in Russian only. Walk a few minutes south along ul Lenina from the Trading Arcade to ul Pushkina.

Tengri TOURS
(Тенгри; ☎273 4320; www.tengri.ru; 2nd fl, ul Zentsova 70) Offers a wide range of inexpensive adventure trips in the southern Urals.

Sleeping & Eating

TOP CHOICE **Amaks** HOTEL €€
(☎282 4630; www.amaks-hotels.ru; ul Rikharda Zorge 17; s R2600-3650, d R5100-5700; 📶) This hotel is excellent value and has friendly, professional staff and high standards. It's alongside the bus station; take *marshrutka* 101 from the train station to Yuzhny vokzal (Южний вокзал).

Hotel Bashkortostan HOTEL €€
(Гостиница Башкортостан; ☎279 0000; www.gkbashkortostan.ru; ul Lenina 25-29; s R3700-4400, d R6800-7200, ste R9000-15,000; ❄@📶🏊) This modern complex offers all the facilities you would expect from a business hotel, including bar, restaurant and fitness centre, not to mention the efficient service. A small pool complements the sauna.

Hotel Agidel HOTEL €
(Гостиница Агидель; ☎272 5680; ul Lenina 14; s/d without bathroom from 850/1100, r with bathroom from R1600/3100, renovated r R3950/5700) The selling point here is the superb central location opposite the Trading Arcade. The reception hall looks great, the rooms much less so, especially those not renovated.

Ashkhane Guzel CAFETERIA €
(Ашханэ Гузель; ul Mustaya Karima 11; mains R100; ⌚8am-10pm) Customers buzz like bees around the counter of this popular canteen that offers *belish* (meat pie), *tukmas* (chicken broth) and other Bashkir fare.

Coffee-Time CAFÉ €
(Кофе-Тайм; ul Oktyabrskoy Revolyutsii 3; coffees R95; ⌚24hr) One of Ufa's most popular spots for a coffee break. Jazz music, B&W photos and a menu featuring crêpes instead of bliny give this place European flair. In the evening, the café is often crowded with couples on dates and other fashionable young folk.

Shinok Solokha UKRAINIAN €€
(Шинок солоха; Kommunisticheskaya ul 47; mains R200-300; ⌚noon-11pm) A homely Ukrainian cottage restaurant. One in a row of themed restaurants, including a Czech beer pub.

Tinkoff PUB €€
(Тинкофф; ul Lenina 100; ½ litre beer R160, meals R700; ⌚noon-2am; 📶)

Friendship Shopping Mall FAST FOOD €
(Торговый центр Дружба; ul Zaki Balidi 7; ⌚10am-9pm)

Entertainment

Bashkir Opera & Ballet Theatre THEATRE
(Башкирский театр оперы и балета; ☎272 7712; www.bashopera.ru; ul Lenina 5/1) The thea-

tre where Rudolf Nureyev took his first steps.

Lights of Ufa LIVE MUSIC
(Огни Уфа; www.ogni-ufa.ru; ul 50 let Oktyabrya 19; ⌚11am-2am) Concert hall, disco, sports bar and microbrewery in one. From ul Lenina, take any bus north to 'Dom Pechati'.

Information

Post office (Почтамт; ul Lenina 28; per hr R39; ⌚8am-9pm)

Getting There & Away

The train station is 2km north of the centre at the end of ul Karla Marksa. There are daily trains to Moscow (*kupe* R3457, 27 hours) via Samara (*kupe* R1185, 8½ hours). Trains also go to Ulyanovsk (*kupe* R1265, 14 hours) in the west and Chelyabinsk (*platskart* R850, 9½ hours) in the east. There is an overnight service to Magnitogorsk (*kupe* R1040, nine hours). Air and train tickets are available from the **Aviakassa** (⌚8am-8pm) inside Hotel Bashkortostan.

Getting Around

The handy if convoluted bus 101 route snakes between the train station (climb the high steps outside to the top) and the airport, via the main bus station alongside the Amaks hotel and ul Lenina. *Marshrutka* 234 connects the train station with Gostiny Dvor (R15) via ul Pushkina.

Ufa to Chelyabinsk

It might hearten (or annoy) Australian travellers, but the area west of Chelyabinsk is called Sinegorye – Blue Mountains. Unlike its down-under namesake, it is conifer not eucalyptus forest that makes the low, gently sloped ranges of the southern Ural Mountains look like frozen blue waves. Also blue are the large placid lakes between the mountains, of which the most lauded are Lakes Turgoyak and Zyuratkul. The lakes and two national parks are accessed from stations along the Ufa–Chelyabinsk railway. Most tourist infrastructure gravitates to Chelyabinsk, but foreign or Moscow-based travellers will most likely be coming from the west.

ZYURATKUL NATIONAL PARK
НАЦИОНАЛЬНЫЙ ПАРК ЗЮРАТКУЛЬ
☎35161

This very remote and quietly beautiful part of the Urals, unspoiled by industry and urbanisation, is only beginning to be explored by travellers. It's great for hiking – if you

GETTING TO ZYURATKUL

Getting to the national parks is easy, but for Zyuratkul National Park you need slightly more planning. Coming from Chelyabinsk, take the bus to Satka and then a taxi to Zyuratkul. Travelling from west to east, get off the train at Berdyaush, take a taxi to Zyuratkul and then a taxi back to Satka for the Chelyabinsk bus.

Trains to Berdyaush

The main way from Ufa or Chelyabinsk into Zyuratkul National Park is by long-distance train to Berdyaush (*platskart:* from Ufa R550, 5½ hours; from Chelyabinsk R575, 3¾ hours). The town of Suleya (west of Berdyaush) is also an option.

Marshrutky Between Berdyaush & Satka

There are 13 daily, leaving Berdyaush from the bus station (near the train station) and leaving Satka from the main bus station.

Buses Between Satka & Chelyabinsk

A dozen buses go daily to/from Chelyabinsk (R260, 4½ hours).

Taxis to Lake Zyuratkul

There are no *marshrutky* or buses to the lake, so you need to take a taxi – the best springboard is Berdyaush, but Satka (off the main line) is also good. Taxis from either cost roughly R800 and take about an hour. You need to book an hour or more ahead using Satka-based **taxi companies** (☎8-904-803 1010, 8-922-236 8878). For more taxi contacts, try the **national park headquarters** (☎31 951; www.zuratkul.ru) in Satka, which has a railway station off the main line. **Ecopark Zyuratkul** (☎31 951; www.s-travel.ru) can also book for you (R1000 all up), and the driver will add R100 for park entrance.

climb the Zyuratkul range, swim in a lake, go to a *banya* (hot bath) and sleep in a log house, you may wake up and feel rather like Henry Thoreau at Walden Pond.

The jewel in the crown here is **Zyuratkul National Park** (Russian/foreigner R40/100, taxi R40), dominated by several forest-covered ranges and **Lake Zyuratkul**, which translates from Bashkir as 'heart lake'. It is best observed from the Zyuratkul range nearby – an easy four-hour hike along a boardwalk through the forest and then along the mostly well-marked mountain path, though the *kurum* (path of loose rocks) at the top can be challenging in wet weather. Access is through the wooden arch on the main access road, 100m before the lake and about a 10-minute walk back from Ecopark Zyuratkul.

The most comfortable resort here is **Ecopark Zyuratkul** (☎31 951; www.s-travel.ru; r without bathroom R3200, cottages sleeping 4/5/7 R13,600/17,000/23,850). Stays of less than two nights cost about 20% more. There is little that's truly 'eco' in this realm of manicured lawns, asphalt paths, tennis courts and large modern cottages, but it is a well-run and friendly resort. There's a nice restaurant on the premises and also a couple of new eateries just down the road. It offers a large range of activities, including expeditions into the wilderness of the national park.

A 10-minute walk along the main road curving around the lake shore are the basic but comfortable **Zyuratkul National Park guesthouses** (☎42 901; www.zuratkul.ru; cottages from R500). The phone number connects you to the national park office in Satka. Staff can also organise overnight guided expeditions into the park.

A short walk beyond this is Kitova Pristan, or what locals call **Urals Disneyland** – a mock Russian village in chunky wood with large-scale ships, set on the lake. The local businessman responsible for this anomaly was building another 'Urals Disneyland' in Satka at the time of research.

TAGANAY NATIONAL PARK

НАЦИОНАЛЬНЫЙ ПАРК ТАГАНАЙ

☎3513

Dramatically set in a lake-filled valley, the otherwise gloomy town of Zlatoust serves as the gateway to one of the most popular national parks and hiking, mountain biking and rafting getaways in the Ural Mountains. Taganay National Park is a narrow 52km-long band containing a wide variety of landscapes, from flower-filled meadows to mountain tundra, as well as some of the southern Ural Mountains' notable ridges (Small, Middle and Big Taganay, and Itsyl). The entrance is located on the outskirts of Zlatoust, reached from the train station by *marshrutka* 33. From its final stop, take the road leading towards the forest to a signposted turn.

The **Taganay park headquarters** (☎637 688; www.taganay.com; ul Shishkina 3a) on the other side of town, is also reached by *marshrutka* 33. The park administration can organise a stay at one of the *kordony* (forest lodges) inside the national park and **Taganai Travel's turbaza** (cottage per person from R1000) at the park's entrance, with spartan cottages and *banya* on the premises.

WORTH A TRIP

LAKE TURGOYAK

Although it's not as isolated or as beautiful as Zyuratkul National Park, Lake Turgoyak (http://turgoyak.com), near the factory town of Miass, is surrounded by mountains and provides a tranquil getaway for the locals of Chelyabinsk. One of the prime resorts on the lake is **Golden Beach** (☎3513-298 091; www.goldenbeach.ru; s R3300-5200, d R3800-5700, ste R6700;), which has several large log-house buildings with joyfully polychromic rooms, each with an individual design. It has a Chinese medicine centre on the premises. Room rates start at s/d R1700/2100 in spring and early summer, and there's free wi-fi in the restaurant.

Golden Beach can organise boat trips to St Vera's Island, the location of an ancient site abandoned about 9000 years ago and later used by Old Believers in the 19th century. Expect to pay R2000 individually for a one-hour trip, less in small groups.

Taxi Miass (☎3513-284 949) will take you from Miass to the hotel for about R200 to R250 (no other transport goes there). Miass can be reached by distance trains and regular *elektrichka* (R154, two hours) from Chelyabinsk.

Send an email in English to admin@taganay.ru for more information.

At Zlatoust, **Hotel Bellmont** (☎655 700; www.bellmont.ru; ul Taganayskaya 194a; s R1400-2700, d R2700-3700, ste R4700;) is a nice business-class option.

Zlatoust is served by distance trains on the Ufa–Chelyabinsk route (*platskart* R510, three hours) and *elektrichka* from Chelyabinsk (R225, six daily).

Chelyabinsk Челябинск

☎3512 / POP 1.09 MILLION / MOSCOW +2HR

Industrial, earthy, like many Russian cities in shocking disrepair beyond the main squares and streets, and lacking high-profile sights, Chelyabinsk would at first glance seem to be a place best visited as a springboard rather than as a destination in itself. If you are doing the lakes and cities of the region, however, take the time to stay in this oft-overlooked and underrated city to get a taste of everyday Ural Mountains life.

The central point is pl Revolyutsii on pr Lenina, where a harried-looking Vladimir Ilych heads resolutely 'forward to communism'. North of here, the streets lie in a navigable grid pattern, with the pleasant pedestrian ul Kirova heading north to the River Miass. The bus and train stations are side by side on ul Svobody, 2.5km south of pl Revolyutsii. Hotels have a free transport and street map of town.

Sights

Ulitsa Kirova STREET

Chelyabinsk's highlight is strolling down pedestrianised ul Kirova, paved with cobblestones. Life-sized bronze statues of local personages dot the street – look out for an Asian lad with a camel. The animal is the heraldic symbol of the Chelyabinsk region, signifying its importance as a fortress on the border with Asia.

Local Studies Museum MUSEUM

(ul Truda 100; admission R160; 10am-6pm) At the northern end of ul Kirova, the modern Local Studies Museum uses natural light well to create an attractive exhibition space. Floor 1 has an unspectacular display on 20th-century history and a few household items, but the sections upstairs on the region's prehistory and fauna and flora are very worthwhile. A few explanations are in English.

Fine Arts Gallery ART GALLERY

(ul Truda 92; Russian/foreigner R80/220; 10am-6pm Tue-Sun) Near the Local Studies Museum, with a decent collection of European and Russian paintings and china.

Southern Urals University HISTORICAL BUILDING

(pr Lenina 76) Built in Stalin's wedding-cake design.

Synagogue HISTORICAL BUILDING

(ul Pushkina 6a) Dating from the early 20th century.

Mosque HISTORICAL BUILDING

(ul Yelkina 20) Dating from 1899 and topped with a golden spire.

Sleeping

TOP CHOICE **Parkcity** HOTEL €€

(☎731 2222; www.parkcityhotel.ru; ul Lesoparkovaya 6; s R3800-4500, d R4500-5200, ste R7000-8500;) This place has friendly, efficient staff and, as well as the usual business facilities, bicycles for hire. Ten 'economy class' singles (near the lifts, but nevertheless quiet) cost R2500, and other discounts are available. Wi-fi costs R300. *Marshrutka* 54 runs here from pl Revolyutsii.

Congress Hotel Malakhit HOTEL €€

(☎247 4502; www.hotel74.ru; ul Truda 153; s R2600-3400, d R4000, ste R5300;) The Malakhit recently reinvented itself as a congress hotel, but like its cousin the Yuzhny Ural it has a way to go yet. The cheaper singles get hot but are otherwise fine (ask for a fan), while most other rooms have air conditioning. The foyer's great, but the lifts are stuck somewhere in the Soviet era. It's a 15-minute walk down ul Kirova from pl Revolyutsii or take minibus 18 from the train station.

Yuzhny Ural HOTEL €

(☎263 5808; www.hotel74.ru; pr Lenina 52; s/d without bathroom R800/1500, s with bathroom R2400-3400, d 3400;) The corridors are a disaster zone but are gradually being renovated. In contrast, the rooms are fairly well appointed in this centrally located hotel – give it a year or two and the facelift will be complete. Take any transport going to pl Revolyutsii.

Wall Street MINIHOTEL €€

(☎263 7454; www.wall-street74.ru; ul Kirova 82; r R4000;) Excellent minihotel with large, well-styled rooms, right among the sights and restaurants. Used to foreigners.

WORTH A TRIP

EASTERN BASHKORTOSTAN

The highly industrial city of Magnitogorsk is of limited interest to travellers, but once you leave it you enter eastern Bashkortostan and the southern Ural Mountains, a region where picture-perfect birch groves and large blue lakes fill depressions between gentle grass-covered hills and the mountain ranges. The region is a favourite locally for rafting, horse riding and skiing. **Lake Bannoye** (Yakhty-Kul in Bashkir), located 43km from Magnitogorsk, has the **Sanatorium Yubileyny** (☎3519-254 465; www.bannoe.mmk.ru; s/d incl full board from R2200/3200) and other accommodation options in the village and around the lake.

Twenty kilometres along the road towards Ufa you reach **Abzakovo** (also called Novoabzakovo, and not to be confused with the small village of Abzakovo even further down the road). Novoabzakovo (Новоабзаково) is a high-profile ski resort, and here **Abzakovo Bungalo Club** (☎351-901 0091; www.bungalo.net.ru; Gorny pr 8; s incl breakfast from R2000) is one of the numerous places to stay. Prices are for the summer season and may double in winter.

Beloretsk (Белорецк), another 30km from Novoabzakovo along the road to Ufa, is an access point for several interesting country lodges specialising in horse-riding and rafting trips. **Turbaza Malinovka** (☎34792-43 064, 8-906-370 7150, 8-903-311 9366; www.go-ural.com/malinovka; go@go-ural.com; s/d R1400/1600) is 10km away from Beloretsk (R300 by taxi; call ☎34792-53 350/56 699) under the Malinovaya (Raspberry) mountain and has several log houses sleeping up to about 20 people, plus a two-to-four-person dacha. Use of the sauna is free with the dacha, otherwise it costs from R500 per hour. A range of inexpensive horse-riding, rafting and hiking trips are offered, including an 11- or 12-day combined horse-riding and rafting tour (R13,100 to R16,500).

Transport

Magnitogorsk–Ufa Daily train service (*kupe* R1360, nine hours)

Magnitogorsk–Chelyabinsk Buses every 30 minutes (R500, five hours)

Magnitogorsk–Bannoye *Marshrutky* from train station (R100, 1½ hours, hourly)

Magnitogorsk–Beloretsk Hourly buses (R90, 1½ hours), via Novoabzakovo station

Ufa–Beloretsk The nightly Ufa–Sibay train calls at Beloretsk at 6.25am local time (*platskart* R620, six hours)

Eating & Drinking

TOP CHOICE Uralskiye Pelmeni RUSSIAN €

(pr Lenina 66a; 3-course meals R500, pelmeni R150; ⏱noon-2am) When Russians first crossed the Urals, they were a tribe of porridge-eaters, but through the encounter with Asian tribes they found something that changed their cuisine forever – *pelmeni* (Russian-style ravioli). This two-storey restaurant-cum-disco (often heaving with golden oldies) is all about *pelmeni*.

Only INTERNATIONAL €€

(ul Kirova 94; mains R450-900; ⏱noon-midnight) The summer terrace on the upper floor is the main attraction in this friendly young restaurant – the best vantage point to watch the hustle and bustle on ul Kirova below. The 2nd floor is occupied by Casa Project nightclub (1am to 6am Friday to Sunday) with the 'restaurant at the end of the universe' interior and DJs.

Bon Bon FRENCH €€

(ul Tsvillinga 31; meals R600; ⏱10am-11pm; 🚭📶) Excellent café and restaurant with a summer outdoor deck. Serves wine but not beer.

Entertainment

Rome BAR, CLUB

(ul Truda 105; admission free) Multilevelled, includes a lounge downstairs, lively dance club and a hookah bar upstairs, plus a restaurant with live bands.

Information

Post office (ul Kirova 104; per hr R45; ⏱8am-9pm Mon-Fri, 9am-6pm Sat & Sun)

Getting There & Away

Sputnik (ul Truda 153; ⏲10am-7pm Mon-Fri, 11am-3pm Sat) inside the Congress Hotel Malakhit sells rail and air tickets.

Trains go daily to Moscow (*kupe* R4171, 35 hours) via Ufa (*platskart* R850, 9½ hours) and Samara (*kupe* R2135, 19 hours). Trains 146 and 39 run on odd and even days respectively via Yekaterinburg and Moscow to St Petersburg (*kupe* R6350, two days). Heading east, the choices are limited as most trains cut through Kazakhstan (separate visa required). But if you have a Kazakh visa, there are three daily trains to the capital, Astana (*kupe* R2825, 21 hours).

Several fast trains run daily to Yekaterinburg (*kupe* R600, five hours); the best is the No 142 from Simferopol, departing Chelyabinsk at 10.30am local time (8.30am Moscow time). Frequent buses also run to Yekaterinburg (R400, four hours). Bus is more useful for Magnitogorsk (R500, five hours, every 30 minutes).

Getting Around

The **bus and train stations** are side by side on ul Svobody, 2.5km south of the centre. Bus 18 and tram 3 connect the train station with pl Revolyutsii and run north along ul Tsvillinga. *Marshrutky* 92, 96, 36 and 35 connect pl Revolyutsii with the train station; buses 92, 22 and 56 do the same. Bus 1 goes to the airport from the train station.

Call ☎737 3737 for a **taxi** or get a hotel to call, especially at night from pl Revolyutsii, where the drivers overcharge.

Russian Caucasus

Includes »

Best Places to Eat

» Brigantina (p420)
» Restoran Zamok (p434)
» Shalashi (p431)
» U Zuli (p440)

Best Places to Stay

» Grand Hotel Polyana SAS Lazurnaya (p419)
» Grand Hotel & Spa Rodina (p419)
» Grand Hotel Polyana (p425)
» Solnechnaya Dolina (p439)

Why Go?

In the southwestern corner of Russia lies the Caucasus (Кавказ), an enchanting and ethnically rich region that's home to awe-inspiring mountains, relaxing mineral-spa towns and old-fashioned resorts dotting the sunny shores of the Black Sea.

In the past, few foreign travellers made their way here, discouraged by the conflicts in the breakaway republics of Chechnya and Dagestan. Big changes, however, are in store for the Caucasus, as Sochi and neighbouring towns gear up to host the 2014 Winter Olympics. Fantastic skiing on world-class slopes is just one of many ways to experience the great allure of the region. There's also superb trekking and horse-back riding amid soaring peaks, as well as climbing the granddaddy of them all, Mt Elbrus, Europe's highest mountain. Black Sea resort towns offer coastal intrigue – sun and sea, festive nightlife – while pretty spa towns like Pyatigorsk and Kislovodsk make for some memorable exploring.

When to Go

Sochi

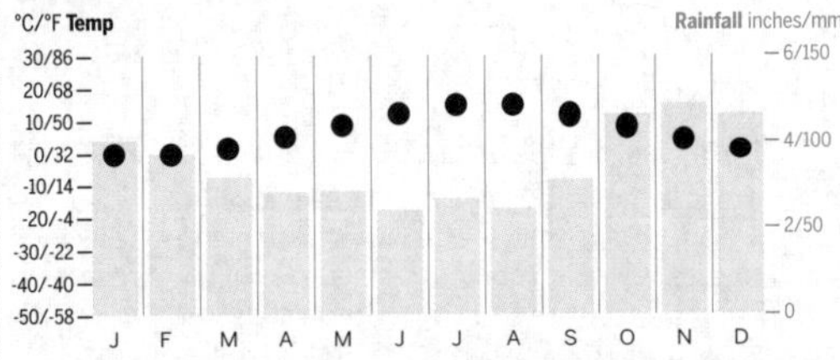

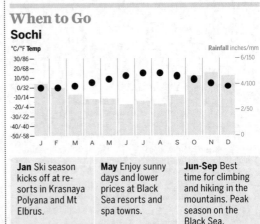

Jan Ski season kicks off at resorts in Krasnaya Polyana and Mt Elbrus.

May Enjoy sunny days and lower prices at Black Sea resorts and spa towns.

Jun-Sep Best time for climbing and hiking in the mountains. Peak season on the Black Sea.

History

The Caucasus has stood at the crossroads of Asian and European cultures since the Bronze Age. The result is an extraordinary mix of races with three main linguistic groups: Caucasian, Indo-European and Turkic. The Caucasus has suffered many invasions and occupations, having been squeezed between rival Roman, Byzantine, Persian, Arab, Ottoman and Russian empires.

LIFE BEFORE THE RUSSIANS

Earliest human traces in the Russian Caucasus date from Neolithic times, when farming was replacing hunting and gathering. The first communities evolved in Dagestan's

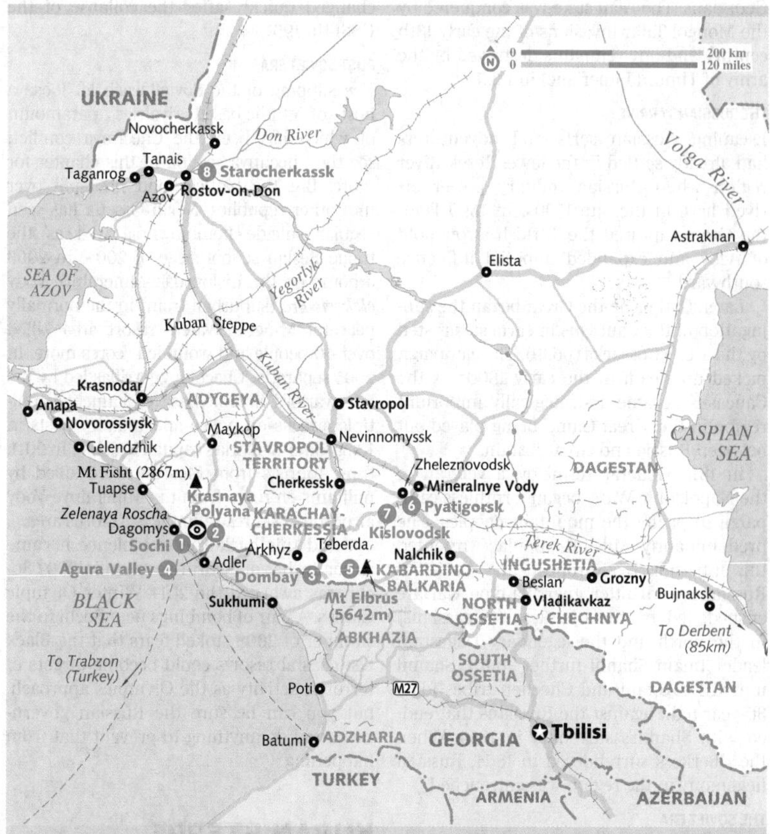

Russian Caucasus Highlights

1. Frolic in the Black Sea followed by dinner and dancing in everlively **Sochi** (p415)
2. Carve up Olympic ski slopes, followed by a *banya* in **Krasnaya Polyana** (p424)
3. Hike or ski amid the dramatic peaks of **Dombay** (p435)
4. Take a walk past waterfalls and up to sublime panoramas in the verdant **Agura Valley** (p422)
5. Reach the summit of Europe's highest peak on **Mt Elbrus** (p443)
6. Stroll the tree-lined streets of peaceful **Pyatigorsk** (p428) followed by a visit to the site where Lermontov perished in a duel
7. Drink the carbonic Narzan spring waters, then take to the pristine hilly slopes of **Kislovodsk** (p432)
8. Absorb the mellow setting and historic buildings of former Don Cossack capital **Starocherkassk** (p411)

valleys around the same time as agriculture developed in West Asia and China, establishing this region as an early cradle of civilisation.

The first dominant state was created by the Alans, ancestors of modern Ossetians. It blossomed during the 10th century AD and at its peak ruled most of the Northern Caucasus. The Alans were Christians, probably having been introduced to the religion by the Georgians. The Alan state was conquered by the Mongol Tatar invasions of the early 13th century and any remnants destroyed by the army of Timur (Tamerlane) in 1395.

THE RUSSIANS ARRIVE

Escaping Russian serfs and adventurers had already settled in the lower Terek River region when Russian military power arrived here in the late 1500s. In 1696 Peter the Great captured the Turkish stronghold of Azov and expanded imperial influence southward.

Later, Catherine the Great began the subjugation of the Caucasus in earnest, assisted by the area's Cossacks (p629). The campaign picked up steam in the early 1800s as the Caucasus became a strategically important region in the 'Great Game' being played out between Russia and Great Britain.

In 1816 General Yermelov, a veteran of the Napoleonic Wars, began a ruthless campaign to pacify the mountain peoples. The predominantly Muslim populace resented this intrusion by European and Christian Russians, and bitter guerrilla-type warfare ensued, led by the Cherkess (Circassians) in the north and the legendary Dagestani leader Imam Shamil further south. Shamil united Dagestani and Chechen tribes for a 30-year fight against the Russians that ended with Shamil's surrender in 1859. When the Cherkess surrendered in 1864, Russian hegemony in the region was entrenched.

THE SOVIET ERA

During the October Revolution, many tribes united to form the Mountain Republic. Independence lasted until 1921 when Soviet forces overran the Caucasus. Soviet policy was to divide and rule by creating small autonomous regions, often combining two totally different nationalities. The Muslim-dominated portion of the Caucasus was split into five autonomous regions: Dagestan, Adygeya, Chechnya, Kabardino-Balkaria and Karachay-Cherkessia.

In 1944 Stalin ordered the mass deportation of Balkar, Chechen, Ingush and Karachay peoples to Central Asia and Siberia, on the pretext of potential collaboration with German forces. Those left behind took over the property and land of the deported. Khrushchev allowed the exiled groups to return in 1957 but without compensation or repossession of their property. The Soviet regime smothered any potential conflict caused by this injustice, but the situation changed quickly after the collapse of the USSR in 1991.

POST-SOVIET ERA

The slipping of the Soviet leash let loose a host of ethnic-based rivalries, paramount of which has been the Chechnya conflict; see the Chechnya section in this chapter for more. But the battleground has spilt over into other republics. North Ossetia has seen regular suicide bombings as well as the tragic Beslan school siege of 2004. In 2003 a bomb on the Kislovodsk–Mineralnye Vody *elektrichka* (suburban train) in the normally peaceful Mineral Waters resort area killed over 40 people and wounded scores more. In 2005 separatist Chechen guerrillas led by the late warlord Shamil Basayev launched multiple attacks on police and military posts in Kabardino-Balkaria's capital, Nalchik. In 2011, three tourists from Moscow were killed by militants en route from the Mineralnye Vody airport to a ski resort in the Mt Elbrus area.

Amid this backdrop of violence it came as somewhat of a surprise when in 2007 Sochi was awarded the 2014 Winter Olympic Games. A pair of bombings near Sochi in the summer of 2008 stoked fears that the Black Sea coastal resorts could become targets of terrorist activity as the Olympics approach, but you can be sure the Russian government will do anything to prevent that from happening.

KUBAN STEPPE

From Rostov-on-Don, the overland routes to the Northern Caucasus and the Black Sea coast cross the intensively cultivated Kuban Steppe (Кубанская Степь), named after its river flowing from Elbrus into the Sea of Azov. This is Cossack country. Two of the main groups, the Don Cossacks and the Kuban Cossacks, fought wars for Russian tsars from bases here and still maintain atamans (chiefs) and armies; the former are headquartered in Novocherkassk, the latter in Krasnodar. A host of Cossack-related tourist attractions make the Kuban Steppe a must-visit for Cossack junkies.

Rostov-on-Don

Ростов-на-Дону

☎863 / POP 1.1 MILLION / ⏲MOSCOW

Rostov-on-Don (simply 'Rostov' to locals) is the gateway to the Northern Caucasus region. It's southern Russia's largest and most cosmopolitan city, as well as an important industrial centre. Passing through the city is the Don River, celebrated in Mikhail Sholokhov's novels of the Civil War, *And Quiet Flows the Don* and *The Don Flows Home to the Sea*. Most foreigners arrive strictly for business reasons, but the pretty surrounding countryside offers a few interesting side trips. If possible, take a boat ride along the Don.

Rostov is mostly on the northern bank of the Don. The main east–west axis is Bolshaya Sadovaya ul; the bus and train stations are at its western end. Parallel to it runs park-lined, pedestrianised Pushkinskaya ul.

Sights & Activities

Regional Museum MUSEUM
(Bolshaya Sadovaya ul 79; adult/child R130/50; ⏲10am-5.30pm Tue-Sun) From the 3rd century BC until the 4th century AD, Greek trading colonies flourished at the mouth of the Don. Rostov's Regional Museum has exhibits from this era, as well as pieces covering the last 1600 years as well. A large display on the 2nd floor is devoted to the Don Cossacks. The highlight is the separate **Gold Museum**, which has a pair of 17th-century Buddhas and other artefacts from Kalmykia. Admission to this is only by guided tour, which costs an extra R600 per group (plus the Gold Museum ticket charge of R120 per person).

Riverside Area PROMENADE
Along the Don, it's a pure carnival atmosphere by night, with sizzling shashlyk stands, outdoor discos, karaoke and cranking music. Just uphill lies eclectic turn-of-the-20th-century architecture in the streets east and south of the **central market** (cnr Budyonovsky pr & ul Stanislavskogo). For a longer stroll, cross Voroshilovsky most to check out the beaches and shashlyk stands on the Don's **left bank** *(levo bereg)*.

River Cruise BOAT TRIPS
For an entertaining slice of local life head to the river embankment and board one of the **party boats** (admission R130-210) for a one-hour disco-infused cruise along the Don. These kick off midmorning and run until 1am, getting more raucous as the day progresses. Prices range – they're highest on weekend evenings.

'CAUCASIAN MALE, HEIGHT...'

Ever wondered why white people are referred to as Caucasian? Well, in 1795 the German ethnologist Johann Blumenbach visited the Caucasus and was impressed by the health and physique of the mountain people. Despite them not being quite white he used the term 'Caucasian' as one of his five great divisions of mankind. In bartending, a Caucasian is a mixed drink also referred to as a White Russian.

Pushkinskaya ulitsa PROMENADE
In park-filled Rostov, Pushkinskaya ul is a standout. This idyllic promenade is blissfully free of traffic and sprinkled with fountains, sculptures, cafés and restaurants, with outdoor seating and music-playing buskers during the summer.

Nativity of the Virgin Cathedral CHURCH
(ul Stanislavskogo 58; ⏲8am-7pm) The lavish, neo-Byzantine Nativity of the Virgin Cathedral, built in 1856, overlooks the central market.

Gorky Park PARK
(Bolshaya Sadovaya ul 55; 👪) Leafy Gorky Park hosts a riotous collection of open-air spots that serve up food, drink and pumping Russian disco. Amusement-park rides and games run late into the night.

Sleeping

Park City Rose HOTEL €€
(☎288 8222; www.hotelparkciti.ru; Shaumyana ul 90; s/d incl breakfast from R2500/R3000; ❄📶) New in 2011, Park City Rose offers professional service and spacious rooms done up in cream and burgundy with dark wood furniture. It has free wi-fi and good breakfasts and sits in a good location one block south of Bolshaya Sadovaya ul.

Don Plaza HOTEL €€€
(☎263 9052; www.don-plaza.ru; Bolshaya Sadovaya ul 115; s/d incl breakfast from

R5050/R5950; ❄@📶) This massive, recently remodelled Soviet-style high-rise has clean, modern rooms with sizeable windows (good views from upper floors) and decent amenities (including free wi-fi), though the price-to-value ratio seems poor. Don Plaza also has English-speaking staff and a first-rate buffet breakfast.

Hotel Rostov HOTEL €€
(☎290 7666; www.rostovhotel.ru; Budyonovsky pr 59; s/d incl breakfast from R2400/2900; ❄@) Full-service, fully renovated business hotel with clean and compact rooms.

Airport Hotel HOTEL €
(☎276 7894; pr Sholokhova 270/1; s/d from R800/1300; ❄) At the airport, you'll find this friendly, functional, budget-friendly hotel. It's an easy 20-minute bus ride into the centre.

Eating & Drinking

Scher Hof RUSSIAN €€
(mains R150-400) Near Gorky Park, Scher Hof makes its own tasty brews (pilsner, amber, lager and weizen), which go nicely with the grilled meats and German-style sausage plates at this upmarket spot. In the summer, the open-air roof deck is a fine spot for a sundowner.

Svinya i Svistok RUSSIAN €€
(ul Universitetskaya 48; mains R200-450; ⏲8am-10pm; 🗐) The downstairs 'Pig and Whistle' aims vaguely for Scottish pub ambience though curious newspaper-covered lamps and a fantastical ceiling add a surreal touch. The menu features Russian standards, grilled meats, trout, salmon and loads of sharing plates, plus European beers on tap.

Zolotoy Kolos CAFÉ €
(Bolshaya Sadovaya ul 43; pizza R110-150; ⏲8am-10pm) This immensely popular café has outdoor tables that are ideal for enjoying pizza, soups, ice cream, desserts and cold beer. It's next to Gorky Park.

Artist Café CAFÉ €
(ul Universitetskaya 44; mains R200-250; 📶) Comfy, body-swallowing sofas and groovy tunes mark this hip café. Certainly adding to Rostov's street cred, its European menu features pasta, veal and fish dishes, all done right.

Yolki Palki RUSSIAN €
(Bolshaya Sadovaya ul 68; all-you-can-eat buffet R280) Amid rustic-country ambience, Yolki Palki spreads a small but stocked buffet of bliny, *zalivnoe* (jellied fish), Ukrainian *salo* (cured pig fat) and other classics, along with a menu of heartier dishes.

Entertainment

Rostov Musical Theatre THEATRE
(Musykalny Teatr; Bolshaya Sadovaya ul 134; ⏲ticket office 10am-7pm) This modern and notable theatre presents ballet and opera between September and June.

Information

Citibank (Sadovaya ul near Kislovodsk) ATM.

Post & telegraph office (Lermontovskaya 116; ⏲8am-6pm)

Sberbank (Beregovaya ul 29; ⏲8am-1pm & 2-7pm Mon-Fri, 9am-2pm Sat) Changes travellers cheques; ATM.

Getting There & Away

Air

Sky Express (www.skyexpress.ru) among other airlines flies to Moscow (from R2800). **Donavia** (www.aeroflot-don.ru) flies to St Petersburg (from R7000) and other Russian and international destinations. Austrian Airlines flies daily to Vienna (return €770) and Lufthansa flies to Frankfurt (return €584, four weekly).

Boat

Don Tour (☎279 7366; www.dontour.ru; Beregovaya ul 23) runs *teplokhody* (passenger boats) to Starocherkassk at 9am on Saturday and Sunday from March to November, returning to Rostov at 5pm (return including food R550 to R590).

Bus

Private bus companies parked in front of the **bus station** (pr Siversa 1) run express trips to the following:

Moscow R1300, 17½ hours
Pyatigorsk R700, 9½ hours
Volgograd R620, 9¼ hours

Public buses serve those destinations plus the following:

Anapa R500, 10 hours, daily
Astrakhan R930, 14 hours, two daily
Krasnodar R320, 5½ hours, three daily

Train

Numerous trains pass through Rostov's **main train station** (pl Privokzalnaya) chugging north to Moscow (*platskart/kupe* from R1800/3800, 17½ to 25 hours) and south to Sochi (*platskart/kupe* from R1020/1760, nine to 15 hours) via Krasnodar. There are also trains to Novorossiysk (*platskart/kupe* from R970/1100, seven to nine hours) and summer trains to Anapa, or change in Krasnodar for either city.

The **local train station** (pr Siversa) is 200m south of the main train station. *Elektrichki* (suburban trains) trundle to Kislovodsk (R630, eight hours, daily at 2.20pm) via Mineralnye Vody, and to Krasnodar (R310, 3¾ hours, two daily).

Getting Around

Bus 7, bus 1 and *marshrutka* 7A shuttle between the airport and the train station via Bolshaya Sadovaya ul (25 minutes).

Around Rostov

To see the various sights around Rostov more efficiently you might consider a tour. Typical tours include Starocherkassk, Azov and the ancient Greek trading colony of Tanais, which has an archaeology museum and excavation; the 'new' Don Cossack capital of Novocherkassk, with its well-regarded Don Cossack museum; and Taganrog, birthplace of Anton Chekhov. Hotels in Rostov can arrange tour guides.

STAROCHERKASSK СТАРОЧЕРКАССК

863 / POP 5100 / MOSCOW

Founded in 1593, flood-prone Starocherkassk was the Don Cossack capital for two centuries before the ataman reluctantly moved to Novocherkassk at the behest of the tsar. Once a fortified town of 20,000, it's now a farming village with a main street restored to near 19th-century appearance.

Allegedly, Peter the Great met a drunken Cossack here sitting on a barrel, wearing only a rifle. This image of a soldier who'd sooner lose his clothes than his gun so impressed the tsar that he commissioned the scene as the Don Cossack army seal.

There are several tourist attractions here, but the real appeal is the town's mellow, old-Russia feel. The village hosts boisterous **Cossack fairs**, with much singing, dancing, horse riding and merrymaking, on the last Sunday of the month from May to September.

All sights are open from 9am to 5pm, with separate admission charges at each site (the churches are free). Most interesting is the **Ataman Palace** (admission R100), formerly the ataman's living quarters. The kitchen building has a display of Cossack weapons while the upstairs floor of the palace is a cultural museum of Cossack Russia. Of particular interest are the displays of Cossack fashion and the bronze relief map of Starocherkassk. Adjacent to the palace is the 1761 **Church of Our Lady of the Don**, which was the private church of the ataman. Within is a magnificent golden iconostasis with rows of saints in pious poses.

In the square at the main street's eastern end, Stepan Razin rallied his followers in 1670 and was later clapped in chains. The **Resurrection Cathedral** here contains a soaring golden iconostasis, a baroque chandelier and an unusual floor of metal tiles. Peter the Great took a special interest in the church, and even helped lay the altar brickwork when he visited in 1709. The adjacent **bell tower**, currently closed for renovations, provides a bird's-eye panorama.

Near the main street's northwest end is the **fortified house** (admission R34) of Kondraty Bulavin, leader of the Peasant War (1707–09). Bulavin lived and died in this solid stone house with 1m-thick walls, iron doors and an elevated basement to stave off flooding.

Boat tours provide a fine way to visit Starocherkassk if you come on a weekend. These typically run on Saturday and Sunday, from May to early October, setting off at 9am and returning at 5pm (from R550). Otherwise, it's *marshrutka* 151 (R34, 50 minutes, six to 12 daily) from pl Karla Marksa, Rostov; last return service is 8pm.

AZOV АЗОВ

86324 / POP 83,000 / MOSCOW

In the 13th century, Genoese merchants established a trading settlement here but in 1471 they were turfed out by the Turks, who built a massive fortress to keep the Russians out of the Black Sea. For more than 200 years this was largely successful until Peter the Great captured the fortress in July 1696.

Today, Azov is a sleepy country town with a large **museum** (ul Moskovskaya 38/40; adult/child R30/10; 10am-6pm Tue-Sun). The prime attraction is a model of Azov Fortress during its initial years in Russian hands, when it contained both mosques and Orthodox churches.

Only a renovated stretch and some embankment remains of **Azov Fortress**. From the top you can sit and watch the busy river port.

Don Tour (www.dontour.ru; Beregovaya ul 23, Rostov) occasionally runs *teplokhody* (passenger boats) to Azov on weekends during the summer, departing 9am and returning 5pm (from R550).

Otherwise take a *marshrutka* from Voroshilovsky pr near Moskovskaya ul (R45, 45 minutes, every 20 minutes).

Krasnodar Краснодар

☎861 / POP 650,000 / ⌚MOSCOW

When Catherine the Great travelled south to tour the lands conquered from the Turks, her lover Potemkin had cheerful facades erected along her route. These hid the mud-splattered hovels that made up the newly founded city bearing her name, Yekaterinodar ('Catherine's gift').

Krasnodar no longer needs those facades, as many of the elegant pre–Bolshevik revolution buildings have been externally restored. Wander east through the backstreets or hop on a rickety tram down ul Kommunarov to enjoy the old houses.

The road from Rostov-on-Don feeds into the northern end of Krasnaya ul, Krasnodar's 2km-long leafy colonnade of a main street. Train and bus stations are to the southeast, just north of the Kuban River, which snakes around the city's southern and western flanks.

Sights

Statue of Catherine the Great MONUMENT
(cnr Postovaya ul & Krasnaya ul) At the foot of Krasnaya ul an elaborate statue of Catherine the Great, with lute-strumming Cossacks and Potemkin at her heels, roosts in an attractive park. There are fine old buildings in the side streets east of here, plus the converted mosque at ul Pushkina 61 and the restored neo-Renaissance facade of ul Kommunarov 8.

Regional Museum MUSEUM
(Gimnazicheskaya ul 67; admission per exhibition R30-60; ⌚10am-6pm Tue-Sun) Archaeological finds and an exhibit on the secret history of the Kuban Cossacks headline the Regional Museum.

Art Museum ART GALLERY
(Krasnaya ul 13; admission per exhibition R50-100; ⌚10am-6pm Tue-Fri, 11am-6pm Sat & Sun) The Art Museum includes a portrait of Catherine the Great apparently concealing a hot-air balloon under her huge dress.

Sleeping

Hotel Intourist HOTEL €€€
(☎255 8897; www.int-krd.ru; Krasnaya ul 109; s/d from R4000/4500; ❄@☎) Fresh from a makeover, this Soviet-era high-rise has bright rooms with oversized windows and sleek bathrooms, and boasts an overall business-class feel despite dashes of colour – like the entrance mosaic of fighting cocks. Friendly reception staff speak English and can arrange airport transfers, airline ticketing and excursions.

Hotel Moskva HOTEL €€
(☎273 9304; www.kit-com.ru; Krasnaya ul 60; s/d incl breakfast from R2900/3100; ❄) Yet another Soviet relic, Moskva has a gloomy, oversized lobby and varied rooms – the cheapest have battered carpets and thin mattresses. Pricier digs are spacious, modern and clean with balconies, but equally overpriced. The hotel is central, and there's an 8th-floor bar with views.

Resting rooms HOSTEL €
(komnaty otdykha; ☎214 7344; dm/d R650/2600) At the train station, the immaculate resting rooms are a fine option if your stay is short.

Eating & Drinking

Krasnaya ul boasts many indoor and outdoor eateries. Self-caterers should head to the central market **Sennoy Bazaar** (ul Budyonnogo; ⌚7am-6pm) or the **Kooperativny Market** (cnr ul Golgolya & Krasnoarmeyskaya ul; ⌚7am-6pm) for rows of fresh fruit, pickled vegetables and dairy products.

Patrick & Mary CAFÉ €
(Krasnaya ul 93; pastries R30-50; ⌚9am-10pm) This delightful little café serves big salads, antipasti, meat- and cheese-filled blintzes, fresh-squeezed orange juice, strong coffee and excellent pastries.

Don Bazillo ITALIAN €€
(Krasnaya ul 109; mains R300-500) This Italian eatery to the side of Hotel Intourist is encouragingly popular among the many Italians who do business in Krasnodar. Excellent menu choices include pizzas, pastas, seafood, rack of lamb and desserts. Intimate atmosphere and friendly service.

Mirage RUSSIAN €
(cnr Kubana nab & ul Gogolya; shashlyk per 100g R100-180) This pleasant café down by the river has tasty shashlyk and salads. You can also just drain a few beers and watch the Kuban River pass patiently by.

Information

There are currency changers and ticketing agents in the main hotels, and ATMs along Krasnaya ul.

Main post office (Rashpilevskaya ul 58)

Telecommunications Centre (Krasnaya ul 118; ⌚8am-11.45pm) Internet access available until 9pm for R40 per hour.

Getting There & Away

Krasnodar's **airport** is 15km east of town. **Kuban Airlines** (www.alk.ru) flies to Sochi (from R2030, two daily), Moscow, St Petersburg, Kaliningrad and other destinations. Numerous airlines serve Moscow (from R3000). Take trolleybus 7 to the airport from the train station (one hour) or a taxi (R600, 30 minutes).

The **bus station** (pl Privokzalnaya) has services to Anapa (R230, 3½ hours, frequent), Novorossiysk (R180, three hours, frequent) and Rostov-on-Don (R340, four to six hours, five daily).

The **train station** (pl Privokzalnaya) serves the following destinations:

Mineralnye Vody R480, six hours, Monday, Thursday and Saturday (*elektrichki*)

Moscow *platskartny/kupe* from R2000/4500, 22 to 31 hours, frequent (passenger)

Novorossiysk R190, 3½ hours, four daily (*elektrichki*)

Rostov-on-Don R310, 3¾ hours, two daily (*elektrichki*)

Sochi R450, five hours, daily at 7.20am (*elektrichki*)

Sochi R830, 5½ to seven hours, frequent (passenger)

BLACK SEA COAST

A narrow coastal strip edges the Black Sea from where rolling hills ascend fairly rapidly into mountains in the southeast and low uplands in the northwest. This is the Black Sea coast (Побережье Чёрного моря), Russia's seaside playground. A long summer from June to October gives rise to pleasant weather, plenty of sunshine and a warm sea. Several resort towns dot the sometimes rugged coast, the best known being Sochi.

The resorts of the optimistically nicknamed 'Russian Riviera' are uniquely Russian, with nary a foreign face to be seen. But that may change as Russia tries to position the Sochi area as a world-class beach and ski destination in the lead-up to the Olympics. Besides mostly pebbly beaches, the region offers terrific walking in the Greater Caucasus foothills and skiing at Krasnaya Polyana in the mountains near Sochi.

Anapa Анапа

☎86133 / POP 57,000 / ⌚MOSCOW

A pleasant sheltered bay, sandy beach and airport make Anapa a popular family resort for Russians from as far away as Siberia. There are pleasant places for strolling among the leafy parks and along the seemingly endless promenade in the town's southwest, set against the distant backdrop of looming sea cliffs. As elsewhere in this part of Russia, foreign travellers are few and far between.

Sputnik (ul Krymskaya 77; ⌚8am-8pm) can handle your plane- and train-ticket bookings.

Sights & Activities

Life in Anapa revolves around the seaside embankment (**Naberezhnaya**), where you'll

THE CIRCASSIAN MASSACRE

Sadly, one of the great tragedies of the 19th century is all but forgotten today and remains unacknowledged by the Russian government. Russian tsars dating back to Peter the Great had long eyed the Caucasus and the strategic access to the Black Sea as keys to imperial expansion. The bloody conquest of the Caucasus kicked off in earnest in 1816, with Russian general Alexey Yermolov using a campaign of terror – plundering and wiping out whole villages – to pacify the mountain peoples.

Despite fierce resistance and years of guerrilla fighting, the Circassians eventually surrendered in 1864. What happened next was the complete ethnic cleansing of all Muslim peoples from the Black Sea coast and surrounding areas. The Circassians were given a choice: to leave the mountains and move to the far-off plains or leave the country. According to 19th-century Russian historian Adolf Berzhe, some 400,000 Circassians were killed, nearly 500,000 forced to flee to Turkey and only 80,000 permitted to settle elsewhere in Russia. Along with those who fled earlier, however, the total estimated number of expelled or slaughtered, according to contemporary historians like Antero Leitzinger, is upwards of 1.5 million, with perhaps hundreds of thousands dying on overloaded ships in transit or in disease-ridden refugee camps after arriving in Turkey. Today's descendants of the Circassians can be found in Turkey, Kosovo, Syria, Jordan and Israel – though you will find no trace of them in the resort towns along the Black Sea, their former ancestral homeland.

find restaurants, bars, nightclubs, an aquapark and excursion hawkers in addition to a few relatively sandy beaches – unusual for the Black Sea (the sand is imported).

Archaeological Museum MUSEUM
(Naberezhnaya 4; adult/child R190/130, excavation only R50/30; ⊙8am-8.30pm) The Archaeological Museum recounts Anapa's history as the walled Greek city of Gorgipaya, founded in the 4th century BC. Behind the museum are some of the excavated foundations.

Sleeping & Eating

Idillia HOTEL €€
(☎59 672; ul Chernimorskaya 14; r incl breakfast from R2100; ❄🏊) The well-located Idillia has simple but bright rooms with wood floors and small but modern bathrooms. The service is friendly and there's a pool and sundeck. Some rooms have balconies. Cash only.

Yason HOTEL €€
(☎31 725; www.anapa-yason.ru; ul Terskaya 52; s/d incl breakfast from R2500/3000; ❄@📶🏊) At Yason, the Greek owners are friendly and the rooms (wi-fi enabled) are spacious and spic and span. Cash only.

Praga RUSSIAN, CZECH €
(ul Gorkogo 2; mains R200-450) Praga serves stews, soups, grilled sausages and other meaty fare amid a rustic old-world interior with big windows and outdoor seating on pedestrian-lined ul Gorkogo. Foreign brews – Krusovice (Czech) and Paulaner (German) – are on hand.

Café Expa CAFÉ €
(ul Lenina 22; pastries R40; ⊙9am-10pm; 📶) Expa is a tiny café serving up good coffees, pastries and tortes. There's free wi-fi and the English-speaking owner always enjoys meeting foreign travellers.

Getting There & Around

Buses run every 30 minutes or so to Novorossiysk (R75, one hour) from the **bus station** (ul Krasnoyazmeyskaya 11). There are frequent buses to Krasnodar (R250, 3½ hours). In the summer buses serve Crimea and all regional centres in the Caucasus.

The **train station** (ul Krestayanskaya) is a 10-minute taxi ride from the centre. Most trains to Anapa are seasonal, including train 247 to Moscow (*platskartny/kupe* from R2200/4800, 30 hours, daily in summer).

S7 (www.s7.ru) has about 10 daily flights to Moscow (from R4500) from Anapa **airport** (AAQ). Aeroflot (www.aeroflot.ru) and UT Air (www.utair.ru) also fly the route. Flights dwindle in the off-season. *Marshrutka* 3 zips to the airport from the bus station (R40, 30 minutes).

Novorossiysk Новороссийск

☎8617 / POP 242,000 / ⊙MOSCOW

Novorossiysk is home to the Russian navy, and war buffs might appreciate the eye-popping range of WWII memorials. Otherwise, there's little of interest in this gritty port, which seems to be stuck in a Soviet time warp. Much of the country's cement production comes from dismantling the surrounding hills.

Sights

Malaya Zemlya MONUMENT
In 1943, a small Soviet landing party heroically held out here for 225 days, forming a bridgehead for the counteroffensive against the occupying Germans. The immense memorial at Malaya Zemlya celebrates their feats. This huge concrete wedge represents a landing ship disgorging a party of soldiers and sailors depicted in chunky bronze. Inside the 'ship' is a walk-through **gallery** (adult/child R50/5; ⊙9am-1pm & 1.30-5.30pm May-Sep, closed Mon Oct-Apr), with plaques of heroes and a recording of a solemn, deep-voiced choir singing patriotic songs. It's a 60-minute walk from the port or a 10-minute cab ride (R150).

Sleeping & Eating

Hotel Novorossiysk HOTEL €€
(☎606 505; www.hotel-novoros.ru; ul Isayeva 2; r from R3600; ❄@📶) Down by the port, this fully renovated hotel has bright, cheerfully furnished rooms, some of which overlook the industrial waterfront. Friendly English-speaking staff.

Hotel Brigantina HOTEL €€
(☎216 373; www.hotelbrigantina.ru; Anapskoe sh 18; s/d from R1700/2500; ❄@) On the main road leading into town, the eight-storey Brigantina has small but well-maintained rooms. It's a 20-minute walk to the port.

Lounge JAPANESE €€
(ul Ledneva 5; meals from R600) Sink into comfy armchairs and enjoy excellent sushi and tropical cocktails in the stylish, Zen-like lounge. It's half a block from the waterfront, with a picture menu.

Aroma CAFÉ €
(ul Novorossiyskoy Respublika 8; mains R150-300; 📶) Aroma is an inviting café with ample pizza, pasta, salad and dessert selections,

plus hot and iced coffees. Outdoor seating and free wi-fi.

Information

The **post office** (ul Sovetov 36; ⏲8am-9pm) has an ATM outside.

Getting There & Away

The fastest way to Sochi is the seasonal hydrofoil *(raketa)* from the **Seaport**, located at the end of ul Novorossiyskoy Respublika. The departure time for the three-hour journey is 8am from mid-June to mid-September (adult/child from R1820/1364). The return trip from Sochi departs at 5pm.

To travel overland direct to Sochi along the coast you must take a bus (R280, eight hours, three daily) from the **bus station** (ul Chekhovskogo). If space is scarce, ride a combination of buses and taxis (teaming up with others who share your predicament) down to Tuapse and pick up a train there. Buses also serve Anapa (R75, one hour, every 30 minutes until 8pm), Gelendzhik (R40, 35 minutes, frequent) and Krasnodar (R190, three hours, frequent).

If you insist on a train to Sochi you must backtrack to Krasnodar. From the **train station** (ul Zhukovskogo) there are four daily *elektrichki* to Krasnodar (R150, 3½ hours). Train 30 is the quickest of several trains to Moscow (*platskart/kupe* from R2400/5900, 24 hours) via Rostov-on-Don.

Sochi Сочи

☎8622 / POP 343,000 (SOCHI PROPER) / ⏲MOSCOW

The gateway to the 'Russian Riviera', Sochi is a sprawling seaside city that's received massive investment for the 2014 Winter Olympics. While the sea is warm and the climate subtropical (among Russia's warmest destinations in winter), the beaches are rocky and grey. This is an obvious disappointment for those seeking Mediterranean shores – though perhaps nothing a little imported sand can't cure.

Sochi has seen the arrival of high-end retailers and a handful of resorts – including the stunning US$45 million Grand Hotel Rodina – in recent years. There are still, however, ever-present vestiges of Sochi's day in the socialist sun as the nexus for Soviet-era rejuvenation and relaxation – courtesy of the unsightly high-rise sanatoriums still littering its shores.

Olympics or not, there has always been a buzz to Sochi. The pedestrian-only sea embankment is packed with restaurants, bars, shops and souvenir stalls, with pumping disco and ballad-singing crooners competing for airtime when the sun goes down. Magnolia- and cypress-filled parks provide a fine setting for a stroll away from the traffic-clogged avenues, while just outside of town you'll find memorable hikes amid waterfalls and sublime views in the Agura Valley. A little further north lie the towering peaks of Krasnaya Polyana, with its top-notch ski resorts.

The high season is early May to late September, with the big crowds arriving in July and August, driving prices up.

Kurortny pr runs the length of Sochi a few blocks from the sea. The train and bus stations are centrally located a few blocks north of Kurortny pr.

Sights & Activities

No matter that they are narrow and stony, Sochi's **beaches** are dressed up with artificial trees, sunbathing loungers, awnings and private changing pavilions to imitate a South Seas ambience. And the Russians love it. The main beaches are along Naberezhnaya and in front of Park Rivera. More private and secluded beaches, including some nude beaches, extend north virtually all the way to Tuapse. To access these beaches, just hop on the Sochi–Tuapse *elektrichka*.

The snow-capped mountains behind Sochi can be appreciated only from a sea cruise, which may carry the bonus of seeing dolphins. One- to two-hour cruises aboard a variety of vessels (yachts, passenger boats, catamarans, speedboats) leave throughout the day from the **sea terminal** (Морской вокзал; cruise per person R300-500).

Town History Museum MUSEUM

(Музей истории города-курорта Сочи; ul Vorovskogo 54; adult/child R100/50; ⏲9am-7.30pm) The Town History Museum delves into Sochi's maritime roots, with the usual sprint through history from Stone Age relics to WWII memorabilia. What shines is the space display, with the Soyuz 9 capsule that returned to Earth in June 1970 after 18 days in orbit. On board were a local lad, engineer Sevastyanov, and his pilot Nikoliev.

Arboretum PARK

(Дендрарий; Kurortny pr; admission adult/child R230/120, cable car R455/230; ⏲park 8am-8pm, cable car 9am-8pm Tue-Sun & 11am-8pm Mon) Sochi's lovely arboretum, with more than 1500 species of trees and shrubs, including

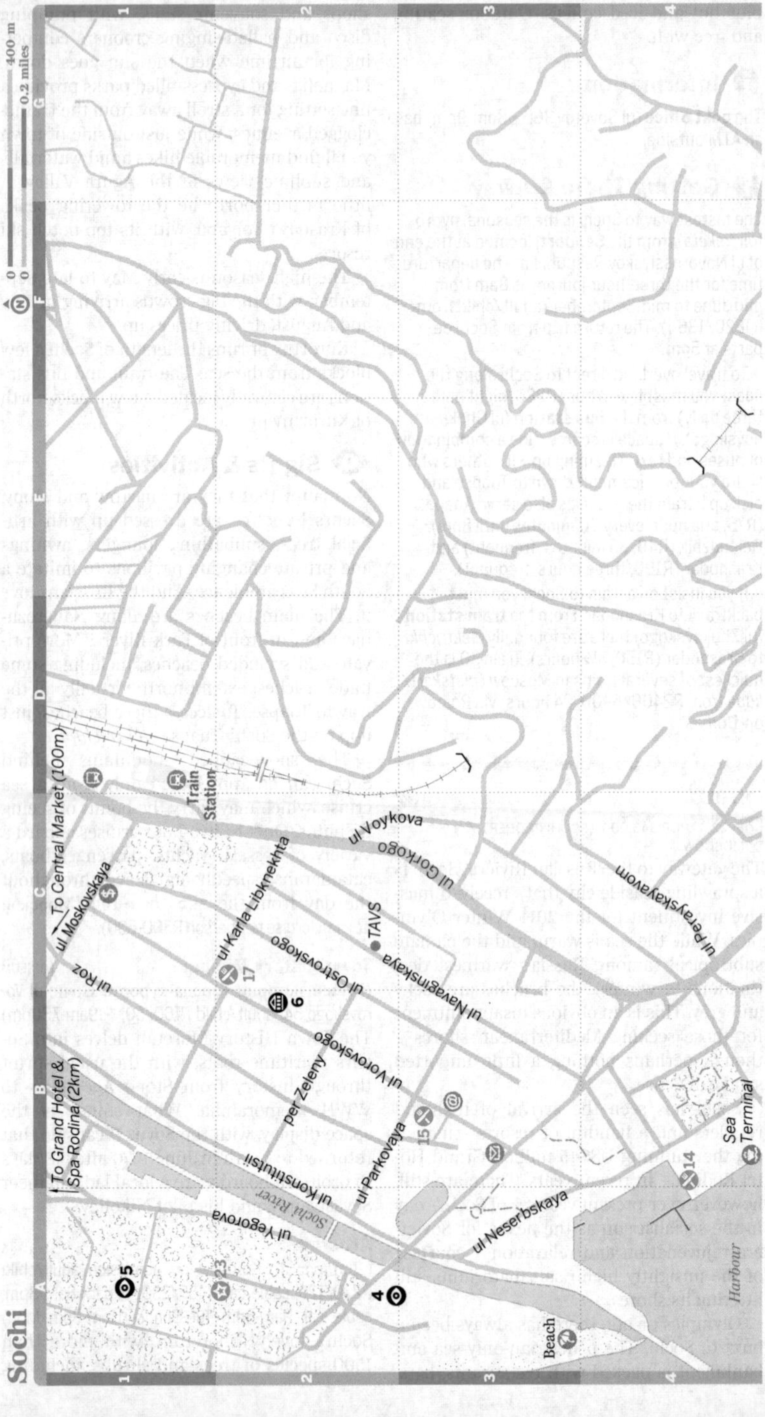

Sochi

0 — 400 m
0 — 0.2 miles

To Grand Hotel & Spa Rodina (2km)
To Central Market (100m)
Train Station
TAVS
Beach
Sea Terminal
Harbour
Sochi River

ul Moskovskaya
ul Roz
ul Karla Libknekhta
ul Voykova
ul Gorkogo
ul Ostrovskogo
ul Navaginskaya
ul Vorovskogo
per Zeleny
ul Konstitutsii
ul Parkovaya
ul Yegorova
ul Neserbskaya
ul Pereyaslavskaya

5, 23, 4, 17, 6, 15, 14

A B C D E F G
1 2 3 4

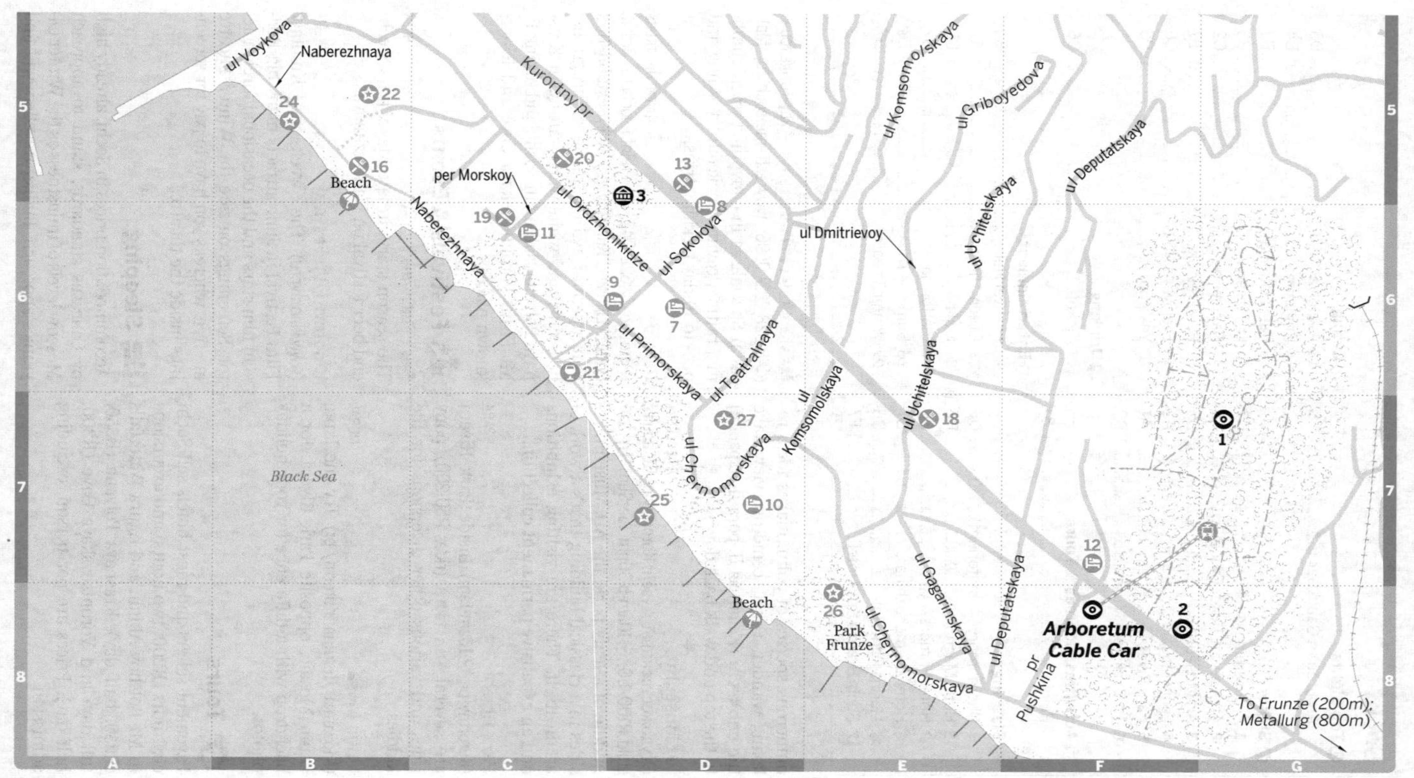

ul Voykova
Naberezhnaya
Beach
per Morskoy
Naberezhnaya
Kurortny pr
ul Ordzhonikidze
ul Sokolova
ul Primorskaya
ul Teatralnaya
ul Komsomolskaya
ul Chernomorskaya
Black Sea
ul Komsomolskaya
ul Griboyedova
ul Deputatskaya
ul Uchitelskaya
ul Dmitrievoy
ul Uchitelskaya
Beach
Park Frunze
ul Chernomorskaya
ul Gagarinskaya
ul Deputatskaya
pr Pushkina
Arboretum
Cable Car
To Frunze (200m);
Metallurg (800m)

Sochi

Top Sights
Arboretum Cable Car F8

Sights
1 Arboretum G7
2 Arboretum Ticket Office F8
3 Art Museum D5
4 Lenin Mosaic A2
5 Park Rivera A1
6 Town History Museum B2

Activities, Courses & Tours
Reinfo .... (see 8)

Sleeping
7 Chernomorye Sanatorium D6
8 Hotel Magnolia D6
9 Hotel Primorskaya D6
10 Hotel Zhemchuzhina D7
11 Marins Park Hotel C6
12 Sochi Breeze Spa Hotel F7

Eating
13 Anatolya D5
14 Brigantina B4
15 Kafe Natasha B3
16 La Pizzeria B5
17 Napoleon C2
18 Perekrestok E7
19 Stolovaya No 17 .... C6
20 Yakamoz C5

Drinking
21 Tinkoff C6

Entertainment
22 Festival Hall B5
23 Green Theatre A2
24 Malibu B5
25 Platforma D7
26 Summer Theatre E8
27 Winter Theatre D7

numerous species of palm, makes for a relaxing wander. For a scenic overview, take the **cable car** (Канатная Дорога Дендрарий) to the top and walk back down.

Art Museum ART GALLERY
(Художественный музей; Kurortny pr 51; adult/child R100/50; 10am-5.30pm Tue-Sun) In the middle of a leafy park, the Art Museum resides in a classical building that's a work of art in itself. There are visiting exhibitions and an expansive permanent collection.

Park Rivera PARK
(Kurortny pr; 10am-1am) Inside Park Rivera are several **fun fairs** (rides R50-200), pony rides and various other diversions for the kiddies.

Lenin Mosaic MURAL
(Мозаика Ленина; Kurortny pr) Try the large Lenin Mosaic, opposite Park Rivera, for a backdrop with a difference for your holiday photos.

Tours

Pavement sellers and most hotels sell Sochi city tours (R200, two hours) and excursions to Mt Bolshoy Akhun and Agura Waterfalls (R250, half day), Krasnaya Polyana (R350, full day) and Vorontsovskaya Cave (R300, half day). Prices are per person, excluding admission.

Masterskaya Priklucheny ADVENTURE TOURS
(8-928-292 0596; www.extreme-sochi.ru; Matsesta) Specialises in canyoning, rock climbing, rafting, caving, backcountry skiing and one- to 10-day trekking trips.

Reinfo ADVENTURE TOURS
(Реинфо; 622 042; www.reinfo-sochi.ru; 3rd fl, Hotel Magnolia, Kurortny pr) Well-established tour operator with a range of programs: heliskiing and white-water rafting in Krasnaya Polyana; sailing in Sochi; and hiking to Mt Fisht, Vorontsovskaya Cave and lesser-known places.

Festivals & Events

Beer Festival BEER
The season starts in late May with a weekend beer festival on Naberezhnaya.

Kinotavr Film Festival CINEMA
(www.kinotavr.ru) The week-long Kinotavr Film Festival in June attracts many big Russian film stars and the occasional foreign actor. Screenings outside the Winter Theatre are free, whereas you have to pay for screenings inside the theatre.

Sleeping

Accommodation prices in Sochi, already high by Caucasus standards, stand to approach Moscow levels of unjustness as the Winter Olympics approach. Budget travellers will find better deals in Adler. Rates increase by about 25% monthly between May and August.

Those looking for complete immersion in Russian culture might consider staying for a week or more in a sanatorium – see the boxed text in this section.

TOP CHOICE **Grand Hotel Polyana SAS Lazurnaya** HOTEL €€€

(☎7095-255 3800; www.radisson.ru/hotel-sochi; Kurortny pr 103; r with breakfast from R8500; ❄@≋) This 25-storey four-star is set in copious grounds with a private beach, inviting pools and oodles of services. All 300 rooms have sea views, internet connections and satellite TV. Pricier rooms have bigger bathrooms, jacuzzis and balconies. The location, about 6km south of the centre, is a drawback.

Grand Hotel & Spa Rodina HOTEL €€€

(☎539 000; www.grandhotelrodina.ru; ul Vinogradnaya 33; r from R15,000; P❄@≋) This sprawling former sanatorium just north of Park Rivera is Sochi's *crème de la crème* in terms of luxury living. Caviar and champagne breakfasts, sprawling gardens with a private beach and just 40 luxurious rooms with terraces – all are part of the charm.

Marins Park Hotel HOTEL €€€

(Маринс Парк Отель; ☎693 000; www.parkhotel-sochi.ru; per Morskoy 2; s/d from R6000/6500; ❄@wifi≋) Through the doors of this high-end hotel with its marble-filled lobby sprinkled with shops, you'll find good service (including English-speaking staff) and cheerily furnished rooms decorated in light pastels, with big windows and blonde-wood trim. Loads of amenities – room service, laundry, travel agent, and, rather bafflingly, two on-site strip clubs.

Hotel Primorskaya HOTEL €

(Гостиница Приморская; ☎620 113; www.hotelprimorskaya.ru; ul Sokolova 1; r incl breakfast from R1200; @wifi) This striking architectural jewel is a 1930s yellow-and-white confection that's in desperate need of an update. Endless corridors link the 382 rooms, all wrapped around an interior courtyard. The rooms are basic but clean and a good value for pricey Sochi. The stylish indoor-outdoor restaurant has free wi-fi for diners and drinkers.

Hotel Magnolia HOTEL €€

(Гостиница Магнолия; ☎620 166; www.sochi-magnolia.ru; Kurortny pr 50; s/d R2800/3600; ❄) Named after the flowering trees fronting this 126-room complex, Magnolia has bright, renovated rooms with balconies, minifridges and modern bathrooms.

Hotel Zhemchuzhina HOTEL €€

(Гостиница Жемчужина; ☎661 188; www.zhem.ru; ul Chernomorskaya 3; s/d incl breakfast from R2900/3400, renovated s/d from R5200/5700; ❄wifi≋) This concrete monstrosity is popular

OLYMPIC FEVER

When Sochi won the 2014 Winter Olympics in 2007 the world uttered a collective 'Say what?' Russians, too, were perplexed. Sochi is to Russia as Miami is to the US: a balmy, ethnically diverse, resort city famous for palm trees – hardly winter sports material, in other words.

Since that surprising victory, the greater Sochi area has undergone a massive transformation, to the tune of nearly US$11 billion. Along with the building of stadiums and new hotels, dozens of infrastructure projects were launched – including new roads, power stations, sewage systems, an upgraded airport and a high-speed rail to connect Krasnaya Polyana with Sochi and Adler. Nearly all of the venues are being built from scratch, which is one reason why it's slated to be the most expensive Winter Olympics in history.

Developers have torn down old hotels and erected scores of new ones. Notoriously clogged Kurortny pr will be widened and new roads put in. The city, already pricey by Russian standards, will go even more upmarket (which particularly worries locals). In short, Sochi is on its way to becoming what Putin hopes will be the face of the new, economically prosperous Russia come 2014. Exactly what that face will look like remains unclear.

Interestingly, Sochi proper will not be hosting any Olympic events. The Olympic Village, main stadium and skating facilities are in the Imeretinskaya Valley, dramatically set on the edge of the Black Sea, around 5km southwest of Adler. The skiing events are slated for Krasnaya Polyana. These two districts are experiencing the most dramatic changes, although Adler – which is where the airport is and an important transport link between Sochi and Krasnaya Polyana – is also seeing big changes.

GOING LOCAL: SANATORIUMS

Sochi is one of several areas in the Caucasus where you'll encounter sanatoriums – those quirky, quintessentially Russian wellness centres that defined tourism in the Soviet era. Sanatoriums grew up around mineral-rich spa towns such as Kislovodsk and Pyatigorsk and seaside resorts like Sochi and Yalta. They tend to be capacious (up to 1000 rooms), towering, concrete and spectacularly unattractive. But in Sochi, at least, there are some exceptions, such as the **Metallurg** (☎672 554; www.metallurg-sochi.ru; Kurortny pr 92; per person per night from R2200), a stately 1930s neoclassical building in a gorgeous compound festooned with statues of Greek gods.

A typical Russian holiday would once have been a month at the sanatorium related to one's profession, such as the Metallurg for metal workers. These days many have morphed fully or partially into hotels catering to holidaying Russian families. A handful even target Russia's superwealthy with luxurious rooms, Asian-style massage parlours and fine dining to complement the requisite medical treatments (which are always included in the price).

Foreigners rarely set foot in these bastions of Russian culture, but if you truly want to go local look no further. Programs are typically 21 days, but one- to two-week stays are possible. If that sounds like too much commitment, a few sanatoriums do accept walk-in guests, but availability for short-term stays is limited.

Other Sanatoriums

Chernomorye Sanatorium (Чёрноморье Санаторий; ☎609 060; www.chernomorye.ru; ul Ordzhonikidze 27; packages per person from R4500; ❄🏊) This centrally located former Ministry of Railways sanatorium is one of the area's most luxurious and aesthetically pleasing.

Dagomys (Дагомыс; ☎521 400; www.dagomys.ru; ul Leningradskaya 7; packages from R8000; ❄@🏊) A towering 2000-bed resort-sanatorium in Dagomys catering to upper-middle-class Russians.

Frunze (Санаторий Фрунзе; ☎672 558; www.frunze.net; Kurortny pr 87; packages per person from R2600) Well-regarded midrange option.

with tour operators and has a swanky lobby and casino but basic, overpriced standard rooms. Wi-fi costs extra.

Sochi Breeze Spa Hotel HOTEL €€
(Сочи Бриз Спа Отель; ☎663 800; www.sochibreeze.ru; Kurortny pr 72; s/d from R3000/3400; ⊖❄@📶) Decent midrange place with pleasant rooms. Wi-fi costs extra.

Eating

Open-air restaurants line the seaside path, Naberezhnaya. You'll also find a few options sprinkled near the beach south of Park Rivera and along per Riversky, the shaded walkway along the Sochi River's west side.

TOP CHOICE Brigantina RUSSIAN, FRENCH €€
(ul Neserbskaya 3; mains R450-1000; ⊙8am-11pm) This pleasant French-owned restaurant enjoys a breezy location overlooking the harbour, with outdoor tables and a big menu of seafood and grilled meats. Mussels (served a variety of ways) and bouillabaisse (fish stew) are highlights. There's excellent gelato too.

Kafe Natasha RUSSIAN €€
(Наташа; ul Vorovskogo 3-1; mains R150-350; ⊙8am-11pm) If you've never tasted *khachapuri* (Georgian cheese bread) then this café is the master creator. The house speciality is the *khachapuri po-adzharski*. A hand-kneaded monster-sized pastry is filled with melted cheese and butter, then an egg's floated in it. Other Georgian specialities like *kharcho* (rice with beef or lamb soup) and *chanakhi* (spicy meat stew in a clay pot) are also available. Service is snail-slow.

Yakamoz TURKISH €€
(Park Kultury; mains R350; ⊙9am-midnight; 📶) In a shaded park setting, you can enjoy kebabs, salads, pizzas and strong Turkish coffee amid gurgling fountains (and pumping disco by night). Find it just off ul Ordzhonikidze.

Anatolya TURKISH €
(Kurortny pr 50; mains R200-400; ⊙9am-midnight) Below Hotel Magnolia, friendly Anatolya has outdoor tables where you can enjoy simple, unfussy fare – kebabs, salads, baklava and other Turkish sweets.

Salkhino CAUCASIAN €€
(☎389 111; Agura Valley; mains R250-600) Near the entrance to Sochi National Park, Salkhino prepares *khashlama* (Caucasian-spiced lamb stew), among many other delectable dishes. There are Kuban dry reds on the wine list along with Georgian and French vintages. In favourable weather sit outdoors in a hut. Reservations recommended.

Stolovaya No 17 CAFETERIA €
(Столовая 17; per Morskoy 3; meals R40-100; ⏲8am-8pm) This wonderful canteen is a relic of Soviet days when long queues waited patiently for a cheap meal. Now there's a kitchen full of babushkas serving tasty dishes at a pick-and-choose counter.

Napoleon CAFÉ €
(ul Vorovskogo 54; pastries R60-120; ⏲9am-9pm) Brigantina's owners also run this charming café with excellent pastries and decent coffee.

La Pizzeria ITALIAN €€
(Ла Пиццерия; Naberezhnaya; pizzas R250-350; 📋) This spot on the sea embankment has a large canopied bar in front and a rustic Italian interior. There's a large range of pizzas and pasta.

Central Market MARKET €
(Рынок; ul Moskovskaya; ⏲6am-6pm) Come to this market for fresh fruit and vegetables. Try fresh pomegranate juice in season and *churchkhela*, tasty sticks of nuts coated with fruit leather.

Perekrestok SUPERMARKET €
(cnr ul Uchitelskaya & Kurortny pr; ⏲24hr) This large supermarket has everything you might need.

Drinking

Tinkoff BREWERY €€
(Тинькофф; Naberezhnaya; meals R250-600) Below the Winter Theatre, this brewery-restaurant rises up from the sea embankment as a three-storey monument to the new Sochi. In summer bands play on the top-floor open terrace.

Entertainment

Pick up the free bimonthly listings magazine *Vybiray* ('Choose') for upcoming events, or keep your eye on the billboards. In the warm months the action is on Naberezhnaya, where party people club-hop and stroll the promenade, beverage in hand.

Platforma NIGHTCLUB
(Naberezhnaya; cover R300-2500; ⏲8pm-late) Sochi's hottest nightclub of the moment juts over the water and offers a range of environments catering to a high-spending VIP crowd. There's a see-through dance floor, beach and aquatic area, several bars and a restaurant.

Malibu NIGHTCLUB
(Naberezhnaya; cover R200-2000; ⏲10pm-4.30am summer) This sprawling open-air spot throbs to the sound of DJ-spun music while the moon casts a silvery path over the ocean. Often draws huge Russian pop acts.

Festival Hall LIVE MUSIC
(Фестивальный зал; ul Ordzhonikidze 5; tickets R300-1000; ⏲box office 1-8pm) Many of Russia's top music acts play in Sochi in summer, and this massive hall, with its open front to the sea embankment below, plays host to many of them.

Winter Theatre LIVE MUSIC
(Зимний театр, Zimny Teatr; pl Teatralnaya; ⏲booking office 10am-7pm) Built in a majestic imperial style, this massive, colonnaded building would add grace to any world capital. Opera, ballet and drama are presented here.

Green Theatre LIVE MUSIC
(Зелёный театр, Zelyony Teatr; Park Rivera) Puts on drama performances and concerts in the summer.

Summer Theatre THEATRE
(Летний театр, Letny Teatr; Park Frunze) True to its name, this architecturally striking neoclassical theatre stages open-air concerts and drama performances during the summer.

Information

Post office (cnr ul Vorovskogo & Kurortny pr)

Sochi Club (www.sochiclub.ru) A perkily written site on Sochi.

TAVS (ТАВС; ☎641 101; www.sochitavs.ru; ul Navaginskaya 16; ⏲8am-8pm) Efficient air and train ticketing agency.

Uralis Bank (ul Moskovskaya 5) Currency exchange and American Express travellers cheques cashed.

YuTK (ЮТК; ul Vorovskogo 6; per hr R30; ⏲8am-8pm) Telephone and internet café.

Getting There & Away

Air

Sochi's **airport** (sochi-airport.com) is at Adler, which is 25km away. There are dozens of domestic flights daily to all the major airports in Moscow. Sky Express (from R2700) followed by S7 offer the best value. In summer there are flights to most other major Russian cities. Austrian Airlines has twice-weekly flights to Vienna (return €721).

Boat

The **sea terminal** has various information kiosks with posted departures. See Novorossiysk in this chapter for information on the hydrofoil there.

TRABZON, TURKEY From May to October, speedy hydrofoils operated by **Olympia** (☎609 617; www.olympia-line.ru) depart Sochi on Wednesdays and Saturdays at 2pm (from R3500, 4½ hours). Returning to Sochi, they depart Trabzon on Tuesdays and Fridays at 1pm. The *Erke* (☎609 617), a slower car ferry (from R4000, 12 hours), makes the journey once a week, but has no fixed schedule.

BATUMI, GEORGIA Currently, foreign travellers are not allowed to enter Georgia through Russia. Check the latest before disembarking. If the situation changes, there are boats travelling daily except Sunday. Hydrofoils sail thrice weekly for Batumi at 10.30am (R3500, 4½ hours, Tuesday, Thursday and Saturday). A passenger ship leaves at 6pm for Batumi (R3000, 12 hours).

Bus

From the **bus station** (Автовокзал; ul Gorkogo 56a), two or three buses per day travel the coastal route to Novorossiysk (R280, eight hours) via Gelendzhik; at least one continues to Anapa.

For other long-distance destinations in the central Northern Caucasus region you're better off on a train, although infrequent buses do serve Rostov-on-Don, Krasnodar and the Mineral Waters area.

Train

The **train station** (ul Gorkogo) has services to the following:

Adler fast/slow R70/30, 30/45 minutes, hourly (*elektrichka*)

Kislovodsk *platskartny/kupe* from R900/1900, 13½ hours, odd-numbered days (train 644)

Krasnodar R450, five hours (*elektrichka*)

Moscow *platskartny/kupe* from R1800/3800, 24 to 37 hours, at least six daily

Rostov-on-Don *platskartny/kupe* from R900/1500, eight to 15 hours

St Petersburg *platskartny/kupe* from R2300/4000, one day 16 hours

Tuapse fast/slow R180/60, 1¾/2½ hours, hourly (*elektrichka*)

Train 644 to Kislovodsk goes via Mineralnye Vody and Pyatigorsk. All Moscow-bound trains go via Krasnodar. The regular *elektrichki* stop frequently at beaches and coastal towns along their route, the fast (*skory*) ones less so.

Getting Around

From the bus station take *marshrutka* or bus 105 (R70, 40 minutes, every 20 minutes) to the airport in Adler. A taxi costs about R600.

Around Sochi

☎8622 / ⊙MOSCOW

The following are part of Greater Sochi, as are the main Olympic sites Krasnaya Polyana and Adler.

ZELENAYA ROSCHA ЗЕЛЁНАЯ РОЩА

Stalin's dacha, **Zelenaya Roscha** (Green Grove; Kurortny pr 120; admission R300; ⊙9am-6pm), dates from 1936. It still functions as a sanatorium, but part of the complex has been preserved and is open to tourists.

It is an amazing place, built to accommodate a small, private man who without remorse caused death and misery to millions of Russians. The depth of the water in Stalin's swimming pool (just 1.5m) and the height of the stair treads, sofas, chairs, tables, bed and even billiards table were fixed to accommodate his small stature (165cm; 5ft 5in). Security was extremely tight: a guard every 15m around the dacha, a secret lift and tunnel down to the sea, and buildings painted green to camouflage them within the forest.

Visitors can see Stalin's private rooms (some original furniture remains), the movie theatre where he checked every film before public release, and his billiards room. Stalin was a lousy player; he played only those he could beat or who were wily enough to lose.

Tours are in Russian but guides speak some English. From Sochi take any Adler-bound bus and get off at the 'Zelenaya Roscha' stop.

AGURA VALLEY АГУРСКОЕ УЩЕЛЬЕ

There's scenic, easy-to-access hiking in this valley beneath **Mt Bolshoy Akhun** (662m), about 7km east of Sochi centre. From the entrance of **Sochi National Park** (admission R80), located east of Matsesta near Salkhino restaurant, a well-marked trail follows the Agura River past three waterfalls.

After one hour the trail forks. The right (southeast) fork leads up to Mt Bolshoy Akhun, topped by a **lookout tower** (admission R80; ⊙10am-6pm Oct-Apr, until 9pm May-Sep). The tower gives commanding views of Sochi, Adler and Mt Fisht.

The left fork leads to the precipitous **Orlinye Skaly** (Eagle Cliffs), with good views of the waterfalls, Mt Bolshoy Akhun and snow-capped peaks in Abkhazia. Also sharing the view is a golden statue of Prometheus waving his broken chains. In Greek mythology Prometheus stole fire from the gods to give to humankind. As a punishment, Zeus had him chained to a Caucasian mountain thought to be Mt Fisht.

There is **rock climbing** to suit all levels around Orlinye Skaly, including some set routes; talk to Masterskaya Priklucheny (p418) in Matsesta. From Orlinye Skaly a rough road continues to Matsesta centre, from where there are frequent *marshrutky* back to Sochi.

Pick up an Agura Valley trail map (R40) at the park entrance. You can do these walks in reverse (ie starting in Matsesta or Mt Bolshoy Akhun) and pay your entrance fee at the park entrance upon concluding your hike.

From Sochi, bus 124 or 125 turns east off pr Kurortny about 750m south of Zelenaya Roscha and drops passengers off at the Sputnik skyscraper. From here the entrance is a 15- to 20-minute walk (1km); follow the road along Agura River until you get to Salkhino restaurant and the entrance beyond. Alternatively, walk from Zelenaya Roscha (about 30 minutes).

Mt Bolshoy Akhun is also serviced by an 11km road, which makes it a popular organised tour from Sochi. A 5½-hour excursion costs R300 and includes a stop at the Agura waterfalls.

MT FISHT ГОРА ФИШТ

This 2687m mountain, one of the highest around Sochi, makes a splendid three- to four-day **trek**. The trek usually starts in Solokhay, about 25km inland from Dagomys. From here, a rough road leads another 20km to the trailhead – you can hike it or hire an expensive jeep. From the trailhead it's 14km to stunning alpine Khmelnovskogo Lake, where you can camp in view of the surreal lunar landscape and spires of Mt Fisht.

You'll need to go with a guide such as Reinfo in Sochi or Masterskaya Priklucheny in Matsesta (p418). Tours start from R7500 per person including food, camping gear, national park permits and transport to Solokhay.

WORTH A TRIP

VORONTSOVSKAYA CAVE

A popular and worthwhile excursion is to **Vorontsovskaya Cave** (Воронцовская Пещера; admission R350; ⏲11am-6pm Tue & Sat winter, 11am-6pm daily summer), inland from Matsesta. It has about 500m of illuminated passage with stalactites and the like. The scenic drive out here from Sochi takes about one hour; a round-trip taxi should cost about R2500 or you could join an organised tour (per person R300).

Adler Адлер

☎8622 / POP 71,000 / ⏲MOSCOW

This Black Sea retreat with its waterfront promenade lacks the nouveau riche affluence and attitude of Sochi. It has long been popular among average Russian holidaymakers, with lower prices for food and lodging. Like other nearby resort towns, the main action is along the seaside promenade (Naberezhnaya), where you'll find restaurants, shops, drink stands and shooting galleries, with a soundtrack provided by heavily amplified ballad singers.

Adler is at the very epicentre of Sochi's Olympification plans and has some serious traffic problems owing to road closures (a necessary evil while a new highway and rail line are added). It is also slated for heavy development to add new high-end resorts before 2014.

Sleeping

There are private rooms galore for rent in Adler, starting from R400. Talk to babushkas in the train station or just stroll the streets knocking on doors that say 'сдаёться' (rooms for rent).

The following options are all near the seaside promenade, a short walk to the bus station.

Chernomor HOTEL €€

(☎404 582; www.hotel-chernomor.ru; ul Prosveshcheniya 25a; rear-facing/seafront r R2500/3500; ❄) A good-value seafront option, the modern, four-storey Chernomor has clean and spacious rooms with wood floors and big windows. The best have seafront balconies hanging over Naberezhnaya.

Fregat-1 HOTEL €€

(☎407 000; ul Karla Marksa 1; r from R2200; ❄📶) An excellent location on Naberezhnaya is only part of the appeal here. The rooms are gigantic, with blue rugs and maroon-hued wooden furniture. Seaside restaurants are just outside the entrance.

Ritza HOTEL €
(☎404 432; ritza-sochi@mail.ru ; ul Prosvesheniya 4a; r from R1500) This small, modern hotel has friendly service and bright, simple rooms. Minuses: foam mattresses and worn carpets. A bit hard to find, it's between ul Prosveshcheniya and Krupskoi, near ul Kirova.

AC HOTEL €€€
(☎410 133; www.ac-hotel.ru; ul Prosveshcheniya 36; d from R5000;) This sleek-looking six-storey hotel has sizeable rooms with clean lines and soft tones, while upper-floor rooms have balconies with sea views. There's a café, restaurant and spa.

Eating

Adler is one place where the good old-fashioned *stolovaya* (canteen) is alive and well. Dozens line the promenade, offering dirt-cheap dining with great views.

Café Radost RUSSIAN €
(ul Karla Marksa 2; shashlyk per 100g R100-200; ⌚10am-2am) In addition to mouth-watering pork, lamb and salmon shashlyk, there's cold Baltika beer on hand and a festive open-air ambience.

Café Tsentralnoe CAFÉ €
(ul Kirova 46; mains R70-300; ⌚8am-midnight;) This pleasant café is halfway between the market and the promenade, with good inexpensive breakfasts (bliny, scrambled eggs), pastas, sandwiches, hearty salads and Russian fare. Free wi-fi.

Café Fregat RUSSIAN €
(ul Karla Marksa; mains R200-400) An open-air spot with tables surrounding a gurgling fountain and live music most nights. Big menu of Western and Russian standards.

Information

Gamehouse (ul Ulyanova 36; per hr R50; ⌚9am-midnight)

Getting There & Away

The **bus station** (ul Lenina) is near the central market, a 12-minute walk to the hotel- and restaurant-lined seaside promenade; pick up frequent buses and *marshrutky* to Sochi (R34, 40 minutes) here or opposite the **train station** (ul Lenina), which is an inconvenient 3km north of the bus station.

All long-distance trains to Sochi continue to and terminate in Adler. A taxi from the airport or bus station to the seaside area should cost R200.

Krasnaya Polyana

Красная Поляна

☎8622 / POP 4,000 / ELEV 550M / ⌚MOSCOW

A scenic road passing through a deep, narrow canyon leads up from Adler to Krasnaya Polyana (Red Valley), a burgeoning ski mecca that will host the 2014 Winter Olympics ski events. The scenery here is simply spectacular, with snow-capped mountains looming above the small mountain settlements and the scent of burning pinewood lingering in the air.

When we visited, cranes and bulldozers were busy creating a world-class ski resort – a far cry from the rustic simplicity of Krasnaya Polyana's original ski area, which once consisted of a handful of single-chair lifts and T-bars.

The first stage in the developers' master plan, Gazprom's elaborate Grand Hotel Polyana ski resort complex on Psekhako Ridge, is already up and running. Although it's primarily a downhill mountain, the Nordic events will be held atop this broad, gently sloping ridge. Roza Khutor Alpine Resort, located up the Mzymta River valley east of Alpika, will be the site of the downhill skiing events. Formerly rustic Alpika, meanwhile, will host freestyle skiing, bobsled and luge racing. Lastly the Karusel resort, between Krasnaya Polyana and Alpika, will stage the ski jumping events. For complete details on what's happening where, visit http://sochi2014.com.

As for the sleepy mountain village of Krasnaya Polyana, it's slowly being transformed as new hotels and restaurants and the cash-seeking developers behind them arrive in town.

In the warmer months Krasnaya Polyana is a popular day excursion from Sochi, with lifts whisking sightseers up to vertiginous heights.

Krasnaya Polyana village is approximately 40km east of Adler along the Mzymta River. A few kilometres east is the small village of Esto-Sadok and, just beyond, Karusel resort. Alpika is another 2km east of Karusel. The turn-off to the Grand Hotel is just east of Karusel.

Sights & Activities

At one time, Krasnaya Polyana played host to a wide range of activities, including heliskiing in the winter and rafting, horse riding and jeep tours in the summer. When last we passed through, none of these activities were available, owing to the enormous construction happening everywhere in preparation for the 2014 Olympics. Enquire at your accommodation for the latest info.

Skiing

Roza Khutor SKI RESORT
(☎419 222; www.rozaski.com; Alpika; lift ticket from R1600; ⏰9am-4pm) This soon-to-be world-class ski complex will be the largest venue for the Sochi Winter Olympics. Currently four lifts are operating, with 38km of open piste, though a staggering 18 lifts (and 80km of piste) will be operating once construction is complete.

Grand Hotel Polyana SKI RESORT
(☎595 595; www.grandhotelpolyana.ru; ul Etonskaya, Esto-Sadok; lift ticket weekdays/weekends from R1000/1200; ⏰9am-11pm) Gazprom's sparkling new resort currently has six lifts and 15 runs (with five more on the way) that cover a range of difficulty levels. Five runs are floodlit for night skiing (from 5pm to 11pm).

Alpika-Service SKI RESORT
(☎439 150; Alpika; lift ticket weekdays/weekends from R1000/1200; ⏰9am-4pm) This complex has a good mix of runs and four ski lifts, covering in total nearly 1700m of vertical drop. The highest run tops out at 2238m.

Gornaya Karusel SKI RESORT
(☎349 111; www.gornaya-karusel.ru; Esto-Sadok; lift ticket R1000; ⏰9am-4pm) Another new resort still in the works, Gornaya Karusel currently has three lifts and nine ski runs, though more are planned. As much work is ongoing here, only 10km of runs are currently open (although 75km of piste will be operating by 2014). Its highest run tops out at 2200m.

Banya

After a day spent skiing or hiking in the mountains, the warm Russian *banya* (bathhouse) makes a great spot to recover.

British Banya BANYA
(☎8-918 607 6611; www.britishbanya.com; per Kosmolsky, Krasanaya Polyana; per person per hr R1000) In Krasnaya Polyana village, British Banya has a beautiful setting against a mountainous backdrop with a round dipping pool and two saunas – all beautifully designed in natural wood and stone. Massages and other treatments are available, plus good teas on hand.

Banya Land BANYA
(☎437 044; www.banya-land.ru; ul Zapovdnaya 94, Krasanaya Polyana; per person per hr R1000) Also in Krasnaya Polyana village, Banya Land is a big complex with five artfully designed spas, including a Russian-style sauna with mosaic tiles, Native American–style sweat lodge and Japanese *o-furo* (traditional wooden tub). Many treatments are available.

Sleeping

Avoid coming on weekends, when prices are higher and there are more crowds on the slopes.

Grand Hotel Polyana HOTEL €€€
(☎595 595; www.grandhotelpolyana.ru; ul Etonskaya, Esto-Sadok; r with breakfast & dinner low season from R9000, high season R12,000; ❄📶🏊👪) Offering Krasnaya Polyana's finest accommodation, the Grand Hotel is Gazprom's crown jewel. The sprawling 400-room resort has spacious, handsomely designed rooms (gold-framed oil paintings on the wall, luxury linens, Bulgari bath products), plus indoor and outdoor pools, tennis courts, spa centre, saunas, restaurants and its own ski slopes right on the grounds.

Chalet Polyana HOTEL €€
(☎439 095; www.chaletpolyana.ru; ul Berezovaya 134, Esto-Sadok; r with breakfast low season from R3000, high season R6000; ❄📶🏊) At the turn-off to Grand Hotel Polyana, this friendly midrange option has attractive rooms done in warm tones, with balconies (some with mountain views). Third- and 4th-floor rooms have peaked roofs and exposed wooden beams, giving it the 'chalet' touch. There's a small spa centre with indoor pool and saunas (free for guests from 9am to 6pm).

Peak Hotel HOTEL €€€
(☎595 999; www.peakhotel.ru; ul Zaschitnikov Kavkaza 77; r with breakfast low season from R5000, high season R6500; ❄📶🏊) Apart from high-class accommodation, this top-end hotel in Krasnaya Polyana village has excellent amenities, including a top-notch restaurant, fitness centre, indoor pool and sauna, and free transfers to the slopes. After skiing, the stylish 24-hour lobby bar with big open fire is a fine place to recharge. Guests can also use the facilities at the Grand Hotel Polyana.

Gala Plaza HOTEL €€
(☎439 141; www.galaplaza.ru; ul Olimpiskaya; s/d incl breakfast low season from R2500/2800, high season R4500/4800; 📶) This modern 40-room hotel within walking distance of Alpika's lifts has spacious, well-appointed rooms painted in warm tones and bathrooms equipped with Italian fixtures. There's also a billiards room and restaurant with fireplace.

Gorny Skit HOSTEL €
(☎437 301; per Achishkhovskaya 8; dm/d low season from R300/1000, high season R500/1500; @📶) There's a bohemian vibe at this small, familial hostel hidden on a quiet street in Krasanaya Polyana village. There are three dorm rooms, sleeping four to eight, and two private doubles. It's a rustic place (not for neat freaks), with shared kitchen and laundry available. The owner is an avid skier with a wealth of info on the area. You can also arrange guided hikes (including multi-day treks) into the mountains.

Hotel Tatyana HOTEL €
(☎439 111; www.tatyana-alpik.ru; Esto-Sadok; r winter/summer incl breakfast from R1800/3600) On the Krasnaya Polyana road, Hotel Tatyana has bright, clean rooms with colourful duvets and a warming fire in the lobby.

Eating

Trikoni RUSSIAN, EUROPEAN €€
(Krasnaya Polyana; mains R300-500; ⏰11am-11pm; 📶) Opposite Peak Hotel on the main road, Trikoni has a diverse menu of Russian and Italian fare (pasta, lasagne, risotto), and local hits like the recommended trout stuffed with vegetables. The all-wood interior conjures classic ski country and there's a deck with mountain views.

Krasnaya Polyana RUSSIAN €
(Esto-Sadok; meals around R350; ⏰10am-7pm) One of the finest *stolovye* in the region adjoins Chalet Polyana and serves tasty borsch (and other soups), smoked trout, fish cakes, fresh berries (in summer) and other delights, with outdoor tables offering mountain views. There's a pricier restaurant upstairs (mains R500 to R1000).

Shopping

Outdoor stalls at the Alpika base area sell rather large hairy Caucasian hats called *papakha,* tacky souvenirs, homemade wine, pickles and honey to the swarms of day visitors.

Information

There are ATMs at all top-end hotels and at the Grand Hotel and Alpika base stations. Ski-hire shops abound at both ski areas and in Krasnaya Polyana village.

Emergency services (☎430 422)

Getting There & Away

From Sochi's bus station, take bus or *marshrutka* 105, which goes to Krasnaya Polyana and continues to Alpika (R70, 1¾ hours, 20 daily). In summer the first one leaves at 6am and the last returns around 7.30pm. These also pass the airport in Adler.

From Adler's bus station, take bus or *marshrutka* 135 (R50, 1¼ hours, 15 daily). These pass Adler's train station.

In the ski season shared taxis lurking around Adler bus station charge about R200 per passenger.

MINERAL WATER SPAS

The central Caucasus rises from the steppe in an eerie landscape studded with dead volcanoes and spouting mineral springs. The curative powers of the springs have attracted unhealthy, hypochondriac or just holiday-minded Russians since the late 18th century, when wounded soldiers appeared to heal more quickly after bathing in them.

Today the healthy outnumber the ailing in the spas, sanatoriums and hotels scattered across the region known as Kavkazskie Mineralnye Vody (Caucasian Mineral Waters, Минеральные Воды). The atmosphere is relaxed, the air is fresh and the walks are lovely. The parks and elegant spa buildings recall the 19th century, when fashionable society trekked from Moscow and St Petersburg to see, be seen and look for a spouse.

Many of the 130-plus springs have fizzled out from lack of maintenance. Those remaining feed fountains in drinking galleries and provide the elixir for sanatorium treatment of muscle, bone, heart, circulation, nervous system, joints and skin problems. For a fee, at some sanatoriums you can experience being plastered with supposedly curative black mud or being blasted by a shock shower.

Pyatigorsk and Kislovodsk are the main resorts and Essentuki and Zheleznovodsk the minor resorts. The main transport hub, Mineralnye Vody, lacks mineral spas of its own despite the name.

Mineral Water Spas

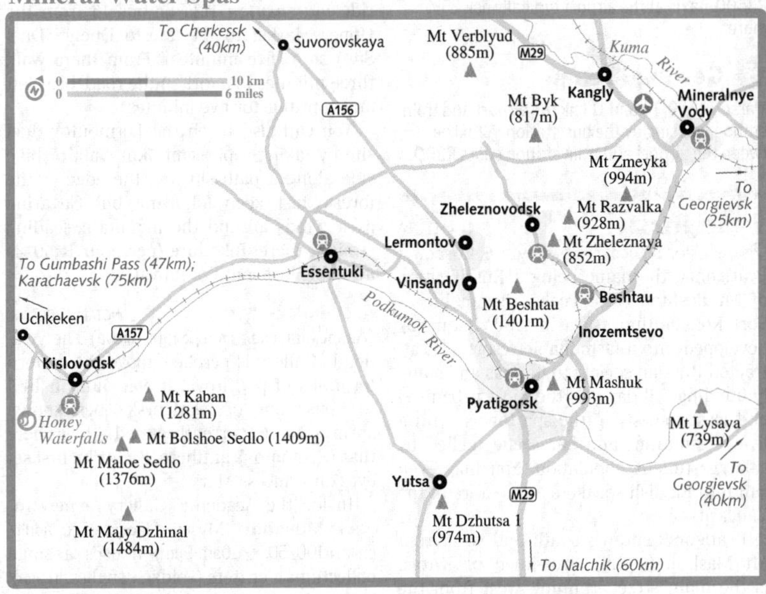

Mineralnye Vody

Минеральные Воды

86531 / POP 75,000 / ELEV 316M / MOSCOW

'Minvody' is the main air-transport hub not only for Mineral Waters but also for skiing and hiking around Mt Elbrus and Dombay.

There's little to divert you in Minvody. If you arrive late and need a bed, the **train station resting rooms** (komnaty otdikha; r from R500) offer reasonably clean, affordable accommodation.

Getting There & Away

During ski season, unscheduled *marshrutky* await planes arriving at Minvody airport and shuttle groups of people straight to the Dombay and Elbrus ski areas (per person R400).

Air

Minvody's recently refurbished **airport** is 2km west of the centre on the M29 Highway. Flights to Moscow are frequent and start at R3900. Try local carrier **KMV** (www.kmvavia.aero) or S7.

Bus

The **bus station** is on the M29 highway, about 1.5km east of the airport. Services run to the following:

Elista R550, eight hours, twice daily
Krasnodar R490, 7½ hours, 10 daily
Moscow R1300, 22 hours, one daily
Nalchik R180, two hours, eight daily
Rostov-on-Don R590, 9½ hours, one daily
Stavropol R250, 3¼ hours, frequent
Teberda R280, six hours, daily at 2.45pm
Vladikavkaz R240, four hours, eight daily

The daily buses to Rostov-on-Don and Moscow come from Pyatigorsk and may be full.

Bus 223 to Pyatigorsk departs every 30 minutes from ul XXII Partsezda near the train station (R30, 45 minutes). For Kislovodsk you are much better off on an *elektrichka*.

Train

Minvody is on the main train line and thus well connected to points north and south. The centrally located **train station** (ul XXII Partsezda) picks up all trains heading to/from Pyatigorsk and Kislovodsk and Nalchik and Vladikavkaz. See those sections later in this chapter for details.

Elektrichki service Kislovodsk (R84, 1¾ hours) via Pyatigorsk (R48, 50 minutes) roughly every 30 minutes until 10pm. There are also *elektrichki* to Krasnodar (R465, six hours, three weekly), Nalchik (R148, three hours, 9.30am and 5.25pm daily) and Vladikavkaz (R198, 4½ hours, daily).

Taxi

Sample taxi prices from the bus station are as follows: Pyatigorsk R500; Kislovodsk R1000;

Nalchik R1800; Terskol/Elbrus R3000; Dombay R3500. Taxis at the airport typically ask 25% more.

Getting Around

Marshrutky 9, 10 and 11 link the airport and train station, passing by the bus station. A taxi between the airport and train station costs R200.

Pyatigorsk Пятигорск

8793 / POP 141,000 / ELEV 510M / MOSCOW

Pyatigorsk, the name being a Russification of Mt Beshtau (Five Peaks), began life as Fort Konstantinovskaya in 1780. It quickly developed into a fashionable resort as it attracted Russian society to its spas and stately buildings. Today it is the most urbanised and least touristy of the spa towns, with a lively restaurant and bar scene fuelled by a large student population. You may even run into English speakers here – rare in the Caucasus.

Pyatigorsk sprawls south and west from Mt Mashuk (993m). Tree-lined pr Kirova is the main street, running west from the Academic Gallery at the foot of Mt Mashuk through the town centre to the train station. To the northwest looms Mt Beshtau (1400m). To the south, the Padkumok River separates the main part of town from the sprawling suburbs.

Sights & Activities

Mt Mashuk MOUNTAIN

There are various sites spread out along the base of Mt Mashuk, some of which require long walks or a taxi to reach.

On the south slope of the mountain, you can join camera-toting crowds as they photograph the natural spring known as **Proval** (bul Gagarina; 9am-5pm), which lies hidden inside a cavern.

Closer to the city centre, a **cable car** (bul Gagarina; one way adult/child R150/75; 10am-5.30pm) whisks you to the top of Mt Mashuk for fresh breezes and a great panorama. The best views of Mt Elbrus are early in the morning.

If you're hoofing it, Mt Mashuk is about a 45-minute climb from the cable-car station.

Lermontov duel site HISTORIC SITE

In a clearing on the forested western flank of Mt Mashuk is a monument marking the **Lermontov duel site** (bul Gagarina). The actual duel site is unknown but is thought to be near the needle-point obelisk that even today is bedecked with flowers. To get here ride *marshrutka* 113a or bus 16 from the Upper Market to the 'Mesto Duely' (Duel Site) stop (five minutes). From there walk three minutes to a fork in the road, bear left and continue for five minutes.

You can also reach the Lermontov duel site by taking a pleasant 5km walk or bike ride along a path skirting the edge of the forest. Just keep following bul Gagarina as it winds around the mountain, leading straight there. Bike hire (per hour R150) is available just south of Proval.

Academic Gallery NOTABLE BUILDING

(Академическая галерея; pr Kirova) The Academic Gallery is perched above the eastern terminus of pr Kirova. It was built in 1851 to house one of Pyatigorsk's best-known springs, No 16 (currently closed). It was here that Lermontov's antihero, Pechorin, first set eyes on Princess Mary.

Inside the Academic Gallery, a new **Insect Museum** (Музей Насекомых; adult/child R100/50; 10am-9pm) houses a small collection of critters (spiders, snakes, frogs), which the proprietor is happy to show you up close. Upstairs is a lovely butterfly collection from around the globe.

Lermontov Museum MUSEUM

(Музей-заповедник Лермонтова; ul Karla Marksa 15; adult/child R100/50; 10am-5pm Wed-Sun) Many Pyatigorsk attractions revolve around larger-than-life writer, poet, painter, cavalry soldier, society beau and duellist Mikhail Lermontov. Chief among these is this museum. Three cottages contain some original furniture, copies of Lermontov's poems, sketches and 19th-century trinkets. Lermontov lived here during his final months.

Lermontov Gallery NOTABLE BUILDING

(Лермонтовская галерея; pr Kirova) Prime attraction is the striking light-blue and beautifully proportioned Lermontov Gallery, built in 1901 in cast iron with stained-glass windows, now a concert hall. Behind are the 1831 **Lermontov Baths** (Лермонтовские бани) and the 1880 **Yermelov Baths** (Ермоловские бани), now a treatment centre.

Drinking Gallery NOTABLE BUILDING

(Питьевая Галерея; pr Kirova; 7-10am, 11am-3pm & 4-7pm) Opposite Lermontov Gallery is a modern drinking gallery, where you can sample the local mineral water (cups are R2 if you need one). The taste is flat and yucky – salty, rotten-egg-flavoured seltzer water comes to mind. It's the sulphur content that's supposedly good for stomach complaints, probably because it kills off anything that's in there.

Park Tsvetnik PARK

The hill rising up behind the Lermontov Gallery is Park Tsvetnik, which forms a 1km-long arc around the eastern end of pr Kirova. Walk around the right side of the Lermontov Gallery and ascend to the park via **Diana's Grotto** (Грот Дианы), a favourite picnic spot of Lermontov. At the top of the hill a network of paths leads to a much-photographed bronze **eagle sculpture** (Скульптура Орла).

Regional Museum MUSEUM

(Краеведческий музей; ul Bernardacci 2; adult/student R100/50; ⏲10am-5.30pm) The 3rd floor of Pyatigorsk's Regional Museum is the most interesting, with colourful costumes, weavings, samovars and photos of ceremonies (weddings, festivals) in the Caucasus. Also look for photos of Pyatigorsk from the 19th and early 20th centuries.

Spa Research Institute NOTABLE BUILDING

(Институт Курортологии; pr Kirova 34) The striking, classical-style Spa Research Institute, built in 1828 and rebuilt in 1955, was once Restoratsiya, the town's first hotel and scene of the balls described in Lermontov's *A Hero of Our Time*.

University NOTABLE BUILDING

(Университет; pr Kirova 36) Adjacent to the drinking gallery is the university, which has some expressive gargoyles and bas-reliefs on its upper facade.

Tours

Full-day group excursions to Dombay (R600, Wednesday, Saturday and Sunday) and Arkhyz (R600, Sunday) are hawked from in front of the university on pr Kirova. These tours involve about eight hours of drive time and just four hours on the ground at your destination. More worthwhile are the shorter afternoon trips to Honey Waterfalls near Kislovodsk (R350 per person, Wednesday and Saturday). There are currently no trips offered to Elbrus, though check the latest upon arrival.

Sleeping

Hotel Intourist HOTEL €€

(Гостиница Интурист; ☎392 222; www.pyatigorskintour.ru; pl Lenina 13; standard r from R1500, renovated from R2500; ❄@📶) A classic Soviet frog turned not-quite prince. The foyer and some rooms have been smartly remodelled and have air-con, while the 'economic class' standards are a fine deal – old wood floors, heavy wood furniture, including desk and armchair and small twin beds. The competent English-speaking service comes with a smile, and many services are on offer. All rooms have balconies and access to free wi-fi. Breakfast costs R250 per person.

Hotel Pyatigorsk HOTEL €€

(Гостиница Пятигорск; ☎390 505; piatigorsk.g@yandex.ru; ul Kraynego 43/1; s/d without bathroom from R830/1610, with bathroom from R1470/2350) Not a pretty place, but it's perfectly located and mercifully cheap. Noise in the courtyard out back can be a problem, but the singles are downright cosy and even those sans bathrooms have basins.

A HERO OF OUR TIME

The Mineral Waters area is haunted by the Romantic writer Mikhail Lermontov, whose tale 'Princess Mary' from his novel *A Hero of Our Time* is set here. In an uncanny echo of the novel's plot, Lermontov was killed in a duel at Pyatigorsk in 1841. The book – short by Russian literary standards – makes a great travelling companion, as does *Lermontov, Tragedy in the Caucasus* by Laurence Kelly, which provides an intriguing background to the man and his society.

Lermontov was banished twice from his native St Petersburg to serve in the army in Pyatigorsk: first, after blaming the tsarist authorities for the death in a duel of another 'troublesome' writer, Pushkin; and second, for himself duelling. Lermontov was challenged once again in Pyatigorsk for jesting about the clothes of one Major Martynov. Lermontov, firing first, aimed into the air but was in return shot through the heart. Many saw his death, like Pushkin's, as orchestrated by the authorities.

Many places in Kislovodsk and Pyatigorsk are linked to the man and his fiction, and a visit to the superb Lermontov Museum in Pyatigorsk is essential.

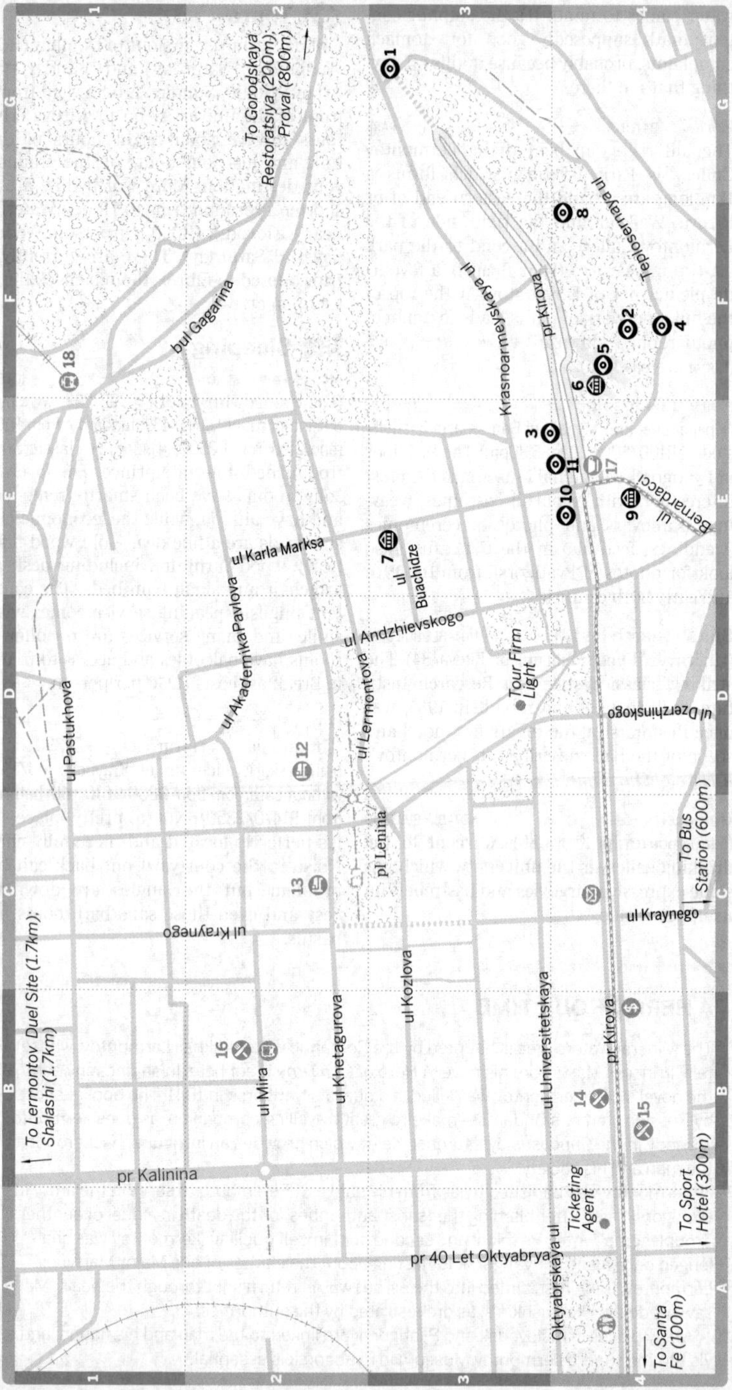

Pyatigorsk

0 — 400 m
0 — 0.2 miles
To Lermontov Duel Site (1.7km); Shalashi (1.7km)
ul Pastukhova
18
pr Kalinina
ul Kraynego
16
ul Mira
13
12
ul AkademikaPavlova
ul Karla Marksa
bul Gagarina
To Gorodskaya Restoratsiya (200m); Proval (800m)
ul Khetagurova
ul Lermontova
pl Lenina
ul Andzhievskogo
7
ul Buachidze
1
ul Kozlova
pr 40 Let Oktyabrya
Krasnoarmeyskaya ul
Tour Firm Light
3
ul Universitetskaya
Oktyabrskaya ul
10
11
pr Kirova
8
Ticketing Agent
14
6
5
17
pr Kirova
9
2
Teplosernaya ul
15
ul Kraynego
ul Dzerzhinskogo
ul Bernardacci
4
To Santa Fe (100m)
To Sport Hotel (300m)
To Bus Station (600m)
A B C D E F G
1 2 3 4

Pyatigorsk

Sport Hotel HOTEL €€
(☎390 639; ul Dunaevskogo 5; r with breakfast R2600; ❄@) This modern glass-and-chrome hotel is set in a football grandstand – but the nonviewing side, so you don't see any matches for free. The rooms are furnished with blonde-wood furniture, oversized windows and bathrooms with big tubs. There's also an on-site bowling alley. Get there via the pedestrian path through Park Kirova.

Resort Bureau APARTMENTS €
(Курортное бюро; ☎393 900, after hr 8-905-443 8519; Yermelov Baths, pr Kirova 21; r from R500, apt from R1200; ⏱9am-3pm Mon-Sat summer) This private accommodation agency can set you up in private apartments.

Eating

Cosmopolitan Pyatigorsk is a great place to discover the various flavours of the Caucasus, Central Asia and the world, for that matter.

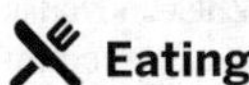
Shalashi CAUCASIAN €€
(Lermontov Duel Site; mains R200-750; ⏱11am-1am) This peaceful Caucasian restaurant, hidden in the forest 50m from the Lermontov duel site, has outdoor seating in round twig huts. The house speciality is Azeri *sadzh* (a sizzling meat dish served in a cast-iron pan with potatoes and onions). The beer is expensive; go with local Stavropol wine or imported Azeri wine instead (from around R80 to 130 a glass).

Gorodskaya Restoratsiya RUSSIAN €€
(bul Gagarina 5; mains R300-600) This excellent restaurant has several elegant dining rooms, plus an outdoor terrace with fine views. Standouts include classic Russian dishes (including game meats prepared from old-fashioned recipes) as well as nicely prepared European fare – gazpacho, ratatouille, risotto, filet mignon and penne with vegetables are among the options.

Art Café Nostalgia RUSSIAN €€
(Арт Кафе Ностальжи; pr Kirova 56; mains R200-500; 📝) On restaurant-lined pr Kirova, Nostalgia has a relaxing outdoor terrace where you can dine on *pelmeni* (Russian-style ravioli), *pirozhki* (pies), trout, salmon and lots of other choices, including vegetarian options. Slow service.

Don Kappuchino ITALIAN €€
(pr Kirova 61; pizzas R210-370; ⏱10.30am-midnight; 📝) Serves good thin-crust pizzas and pastas in a dining room adorned with Italian-themed murals and decor, plus outdoor seating.

Santa Fe INTERNATIONAL €€
(pr Kirova 69; mains R300-500; ⏱10am-midnight; 📝) Stylish café and restaurant with a huge menu (pastas, lasagne, steaks, sushi and over a dozen salads) and pleasant open-air tables.

Upper Market MARKET €
(Верхний рынок, Verkhny Rynok; ul Levanevskogo; ⏱7am-4pm) Here you can gorge on shashlyk

and filling *Balkarsky khichiny* (Balkar-style stuffed flatbread) for under R80.

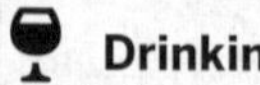

Drinking

Café Tête-à-Tête CAFÉ
(Кафе Тет-а-Тет; 2nd fl, Tsvetnik Exhibition Hall, pr Kirova 23; desserts R80-120; ⏲11am-11pm) A serene perch for a pick-me-up is on the wrap-around balcony of this 2nd-floor café overlooking lively pr Kirova. Inside, you'll find an artwork-filled café and a good selection of coffee, teas, cocktails and desserts.

☆ Entertainment

Lermontov Gallery Concert Hall LIVE MUSIC
(Лермонтовская галерея; tickets R200-500; ticket office ⏲9am-7pm) It's well worth taking in a concert (philharmonic, organ, opera) in Pyatigorsk's architectural highlight. Shows are of good quality and rarely sell out.

ℹ Information

Internet access is available at the **main post office** (Главпочтамт) and the telephone centre for R50 per hour.

Pyatigorsk Intour (☎349 213; tour@pintour.kmv.ru; pl Lenina 13; ⏲10am-6pm) Handy travel agent inside Hotel Intourist.

Sberbank (Сбербанк; pr Kirova 59; ⏲8am-noon & 1-5pm Mon-Sat) Cashes travellers cheques; has an ATM.

Ticketing Agent (Билетная касса; pr Kirova 72; ⏲8.30-1pm & 2-8pm) Useful office, has separate booths for air, bus and train tickets.

Tour Firm Light (Туризм Лайт; ☎333 331; www.light-tour.ru; ul Dzerzhinskogo 41; ⏲10am-6pm Mon-Fri, 11am-3pm Sat) Books accommodation and runs various excursions. Often has an English speaker around.

ℹ Getting There & Away

Pyatigorsk's long-distance **bus station** is south of the centre, along pr Kalinina. There are numerous buses to Nalchik (R120, 1½ hours). The daily bus to Teberda (near Dombay) departs at 3.35pm (R320, four hours).

A better way to Dombay is to buy a one-way trip on a regularly scheduled tour bus (one way R600).

The Pyatigorsk **train station** (Oktyabrskaya ul) has frequent *elektrichki* to both Kislovodsk (R30, one hour) and Mineralnye Vody (R40, 50 minutes).

ℹ Getting Around

Trams 3 and 5 connect the train station with the town centre through pr Kirova. A taxi to Mineralnye Vody airport costs R500.

Zheleznovodsk

Железноводск

☎86532 / POP 29,000 / ⏲MOSCOW

The smallest spa town, Zheleznovodsk (Iron Waters) lies at the foot of Mt Zheleznaya (852m) on the northern side of Mt Beshtau. It's an easy 25-minute trip from Pyatigorsk on *marshrutka* 113 (R23) from the Upper Market.

Get off at the last stop, opposite the train station on the main drag, ul Lenina. In the park near the stop are the red-and-white-striped 1893 **Ostrovsky Baths** (Островские ванны). They've been closed for a while but of particular interest is the Islamic influence – pointed arches, a pseudominaret and decorative Arabic calligraphy.

From here walk 150m back (east) on ul Lenina to the Lenin statue, and turn left on ul Chaykovskogo, following the road uphill into pleasant Kurortny Park that sprawls around the forested Mt Zheleznaya. You'll arrive near the blue-and-white iron-and-glass **Pushkin Gallery** (Пушкинская галерея), now a concert hall with a small shop selling amber jewellery. It's similar to Pyatigorsk's Lermontov Gallery. The path in front is littered with merchants selling fresh fruit, *churchkhela* (tasty sticks of nuts coated with fruit leather), fur coats, books and souvenirs. Nearby, the aptly named **Kafe Park** has outdoor tables and the usual assortment of Russian dishes.

West of here is another Islamic-influenced architectural gem, the blue-and-yellow **Telman Sanatorium**, formerly the Emir of Bukhara's palace.

To see photos of how Zheleznovodsk looked in its heyday, visit the **local museum** (Краеведческий музей; ul Lermontova 3; adult/child R40/10; ⏲9am-6pm Tue-Sun), on the road below Telman Sanatorium.

Marshrutky back to Pyatigorsk (R23, frequent) peter out around 8pm.

Kislovodsk

Кисловодск

☎87937 (5-DIGIT NOS), 8793 (6-DIGIT NOS) / POP 133,000 / ELEV 822M / ⏲MOSCOW

The name means 'Sour Waters', but Pyatigorsk's more subdued cousin has a decidedly sweet vibe. Despite the many tourists and the time-worn sanatoriums scattered about, Kislovodsk remains relaxing to the core. The landscape is green, the many gardens well manicured and the air, at nearly 1km above sea level, is crisp. 'Love affairs that begin at the foot of Mashuk reach happy endings here,' Lermontov wrote.

Pedestrianised Kurortny bul, running north–south from the post office to the Narzan Gallery, is Kislovodsk's main drag and spiritual nerve centre. The train station is just east of Kurortny bul up a smaller pedestrianised street, cobbled ul Karla Marksa. Kurortny Park spreads southeast from Narzan Gallery.

Sights & Activities

Dozens of pleasant, relaxing trails have been carved out of the lush, hilly landscape for the benefit of sanatorium-goers. If serious trekking in the high Caucasus isn't your thing, then the walks here, some of which afford views of Mt Elbrus to the south, might appeal. Pick up a map (R50) of trails in Kurortny Park from kiosks behind the colonnade.

Kurortny Park NATURE RESERVE

Many of the walking trails intersperse the hills, ponds and forests of this huge **park**, which ascends southeast from a plaza behind the semicircular **colonnade** (Колоннада) in the town centre to the peak of Mt Maloe Sedlo (Little Saddle; 1376m). This plaza is a hive of activity in the summer months, drawing street musicians, chess players and numerous stalls hawking some truly bad art.

Just north of here holidaymakers imbibe the waters inside the **Narzan Gallery** (Нарзанная Галерея; cup of water R2; ⏲7-9am, 11am-2pm & 4-7pm). The warm yellow stone of this graceful, well-preserved 1850s building recalls the spa town of Bath, England. Inside, the rich, carbonic Narzan Spring bubbles up inside a glass dome and spits out nearly undrinkable water into several fountains. Never mind the foul taste; if you come here you're obliged to have a cup, so drink up!

On the east edge of the plaza, up some steps, is a **Lermontov statue**. Caged in a grotto below is the **demon** from Lermontov's famous poem, 'The Demon', believed to be his troubled alter ego.

The walking trails materialise south of the plaza. It's a two- to three-hour hike from the colonnade to the top of the so-called Olympic Complex (1200m), where the cable car terminates. On the way you'll pass various cafés, statues and other points of interest. At 1065m you reach the **Krasnoe Solnyshko Hill** (Red Sun Hill), where on a clear day there are great panoramas of the yawning valleys and green plateaus of the pretty surrounding countryside.

From the top there are good views of Mt Maloe Sedlo to the west and, on clear mornings, Mt Elbrus to the south. It's another 45-minute walk to Mt Maloe Sedlo. Trails also lead to Mt Maly Dzhinal (1484m) and Mt Bolshoe Sedlo (1409m); Kislovodsk maps show all the walks, most of which are numbered and signed.

For a speedier ascent, make your way to Ordzhonikidze Sanatorium, then walk 500m to the **cable car** (канатная дорога; one way adult/child R100/50; ⏲10am-1pm & 2-6pm). *Marshrutka* 21 runs to Ordzhonikidze Sanatorium every 20 minutes from Snizhenka Café across from the main post office.

Fortress Museum MUSEUM

(исловодский историко-краеведческий музей "Крепость"; per Mira 11; adult/child R50/20; ⏲10am-6pm) To secure Russia's new southern frontier, Catherine the Great built a line of forts along the Caucasus mountain range. Kislovodsk was one of them, and the Fortress Museum is within the remaining walls of that 1803 fort. The museum traces the city's history. Pushkin, Tolstoy and Lermontov were visitors, and the late dissident writer Solzhenitsyn was born here.

Yaroshenko Museum MUSEUM

(ul Yaroshenko 1; per exhibit adult/child R50/30; ⏲10am-6pm Wed-Mon) This small museum houses the works of the incomparable late-19th-century Russian portraitist Nikolai Yaroshenko, a leading proponent of Russian realism. One room is dedicated to landscapes of the surrounding countryside. Yaroshenko's lovingly cared-for tomb is just outside nearby **St Nicholas Church** (pr Mira), destroyed by the Soviets in 1936 and rebuilt in 1991.

Chaliapin Dacha Literary Museum MUSEUM

(Музей "Дача Шаляпина"; ul Shalyapina; adult/child R30/10; ⏲8.30am-6pm) Fyodor Chaliapin, the legendary Russian opera singer, lived in a palatial wood and stained-glass villa near the train station in 1917, which is now this museum. There are lots of photos of him in various roles, plaster ceilings bursting with cherubs and fruit designs, and a lovely glaze-tiled chimney.

Narzan Baths NOTABLE BUILDING

(Нарзанные ванны; Kurortny bul 4) The main Narzan Baths are in an eye-catching 1903 Indian temple-style building that has been closed for years. Narzan means 'Drink of Brave Warriors' in Turkish.

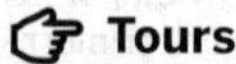

Tours

Excursion bureaus clustered around the south end of Kurortny bul sell trips to Dombay (R600, 6.30am Tuesday, Friday, Saturday and Sunday), Arkhyz (R600), and Honey Waterfalls (R300, 2.30pm daily).

Sleeping

TOP CHOICE Pansionat Beshpagir GUESTHOUSE €
(Пансионат Бешпагир; 22 317; ul K Tsetkin 47; s/d without bathroom R450/900, r with bathroom from R1500) In a quiet, tree-lined neighbourhood away from the mayhem, family-run Pansionat Beshpagir is a three-storey guesthouse that provides excellent value for its simple but clean rooms. A mere R350 extra nets you full board, or you could self-cater in the common kitchen. Rooms are bright with painted wood panelling and well-maintained bathrooms.

Pan Inter HOTEL €€
(28 877; www.hotel-paninter.ru; ul Kurortny 2; s/d incl breakfast from R2500/3500;) Part of a new crop of hotels sprouting along ul Kurortny, modern Pan Inter has small but spotless, well-equipped rooms with a subdued colour scheme and shimmery fabrics. There's a small desk, stocked minibar and modern bathroom. Good free wi-fi throughout.

Pansionat Kurortny HOTEL €€
(22 247; Kurortny bul 12; s/d from R1750/2500) This small, well-located no-frills hotel has varying rooms; the cheapest are small, but with high ceilings, sizeable windows, a fridge and wood floors warmed by throw rugs.

Grand Hotel HOTEL €€
(Гранд Отель; 33 119; www.grandhotel-kmv.ru; Kurortny bul 14; s/d incl breakfast from R2200/3000;) This classy, perfectly located place has a grand entrance staircase, friendly service and well-furnished rooms – complete with spacious bathrooms.

Korona Hotel HOTEL €€€
(Гостинца Корона; 20 396; www.hotel-korona.ru; Kurortny bul 5; ste incl breakfast from R4200;) The six suites here are exquisitely appointed, especially the bathrooms, which are pimped out with jacuzzis, fluffy robes and expensive German fixtures.

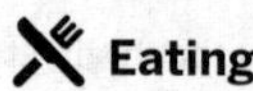

Eating

A good strategy is to stroll Kurortny bul and choose from the many outdoor dining terraces. Service is notoriously slow in Kislovodsk. Many places have live music (synth bands) that adds an air of festivity (plus R50 to R80 cover).

Restoran Zamok GEORGIAN €€
(Ресторан Замок; 34 609; mains R250-500) This modern castle, 7km west of Kislovodsk in the Alikonovka Gorge, trades on a legend about a boy who leapt from the edge of a nearby cliff out of love for a local girl. The girl was supposed to leap too, but thought better of it. The setting is pseudomedieval and the tasty Georgian dishes are beautifully prepared. A taxi there should cost about R100 (but more coming back).

Golden Dragon ASIAN €€
(Золотой Дракон, Zolotoy Drakon; ul Shalyapina 12; mains R200-400;) Tired of shashlyk? Golden Dragon's huge menu of pan-Asian fare makes it a popular spot. The colourful garden-like setting is a fine spot to feast on dumplings, asparagus and mushrooms, sushi, seaweed salad and much more.

Mimino GEORGIAN €€
(Kurortny bul 6; mains R150-350) This lively spot has an outdoor terrace that always draws a crowd. Start off with piping-hot *khachapuri* (cheese bread) and Georgian-style *solyanka* (a spicy soup) before moving onto sizzling kebabs.

Kazan House RUSSIAN €
(ul Kirova 50; shashlyk per 100g R55-100) This shashlyk specialist lies outside the main tourist zone, so it's quieter, better and cheaper than places on Kurortny bul. The *lulya* kebabs (minced-meat sausage cooked on an open flame) are huge. Wash it down with *ayran*, a sour yoghurt-like drink. To get there, head north along Kurortny bul to ul Kirova, turn right and follow this road another 400m as it veers to the left.

Russky Chai RUSSIAN €
(Kurortny bul 12; mains R30-100; 9am-9pm) This colourfully painted café has a small but inexpensive buffet.

Magnit SUPERMARKET €
(pr Mira 14; 9.30am-8pm) This supermarket is 300m south of the colonnade on pr Mira.

☆ Entertainment

Chaliapin Dacha Literary Museum MUSIC
(Музей "Дача Шаляпина"; ul Shalyapina; admission R100-300) An intimate space, the Chaliapin Dacha Literary Museum hosts classical-music concerts on Wednesdays and Fridays at 3pm. A film club also meets here on Saturdays at 3pm (admission R100 to R200).

Circus CIRCUS
(pr Pobedy 12; ⌚noon & 4pm Sat & Sun) Ticket office (Билетные кассы цирка; ul Karla Marksa 1; tickets R150-300) Kislovodsk's circus has a good reputation.

Philharmonia LIVE MUSIC
(Филармония; ul Karla Marksa; tickets R150-1000) Offers concerts in a beautiful baroque and neoclassical auditorium from 1895.

ℹ Information

Main post office (pl Oktyabrskaya)
Narzan Network (pl Oktyabrskaya; per MB R1.50, per hr R30; ⌚10am-8.30pm) Internet access upstairs in the post office.
Sberbank (ul Kuybysheva 51) Cashes travellers cheques and has currency exchange. About 700m north of the post office.

ℹ Getting There & Away

Bus

The **bus station** (ul Promyshlennaya 4) is terribly located 6km north of the centre. Buses head to the following destinations:

Arkhyz R330, five hours, one daily
Cherkessk R152, two hours, six daily
Krasnodar R710, 8½ hours, daily
Nalchik R182, two hours, two daily
Stavropol R320, five hours, nine daily
Vladikavkaz R382, 5½ hours, two daily

Frequent *marshrutky* and shared taxis leave from the train station for Pyatigorsk all day until late evening (R70, one hour).

The easiest way to Dombay is on a regularly scheduled tour bus (R600). Alternatively, head to Cherkessk and transfer there.

Train

From Kislovodsk's attractive **train station** (Vokzalnaya ul) there are services to the following:

Mineralnye Vody R60, 1¾ hours, half-hourly (*elektrichka*)
Moscow *platskartny/kupe* from R2500/R6200, 27 hours, daily (express train 3F)
Moscow *platskartny/kupe* from R1800/R4200, 31 to 36 hours, daily
Pyatigorsk R30, 60 minutes, half-hourly (*elektrichka*)
Rostov-on-Don R420, eight hours, 7.09am (*elektrichka*)
Sochi R1500, 14½ hours, even-numbered days
St Petersburg R4880, two days two hours, daily

Passenger trains also pass through Pyatigorsk on their way to Sochi and St Petersburg.

CENTRAL CAUCASUS

Most visitors to the Russian Caucasus have their sights set firmly on the awesome Greater Caucasus mountains, in the central Caucasus (Центральный Кавказ), Europe's highest by a considerable margin. There are 200 peaks over 4000m, 30 over 4500m and seven over 5000m, including the granddaddy of them all, Mt Elbrus (5642m). Mont Blanc, highest in Western Europe at 4807m, is exceeded by 15 Caucasus peaks.

But the statistics speak nothing of the savage beauty of these mountains. Heading southwest from the Mineral Waters area, the smooth green foothills morph with brutal assertiveness into a virtually impenetrable wall of rock spires, glaciers and daunting cliffs rising hundreds of metres into the air. Seeing photos just won't do; to truly appreciate these awesome mountains one must frolic among them.

The Greater Caucasus mountains are, naturally, an adventure-lover's playground. The two places most visited by foreigners for wonderful skiing, hiking and climbing are Dombay and Elbrus. More experienced and adventurous trekkers and backcountry skiers will find no shortage of less-beaten tracks. Keen hikers and climbers should read *Trekking in the Caucasus* by Yury Kolomiets and Alexey Solovyev.

Dombay & Teberda
Домбай и Теберда

☎87872 / POP 600 / ELEV 1600M / ⌚MOSCOW

Even those well travelled in the world's most stunning wilderness areas can only gape in awe when they first set eyes on Dombay. Wedged into a box canyon at the confluence of three raging mountain rivers, the town is surrounded by a soaring crown of jagged, Matterhorn-like peaks of rock and ice, festooned with glaciers and gushing waterfalls.

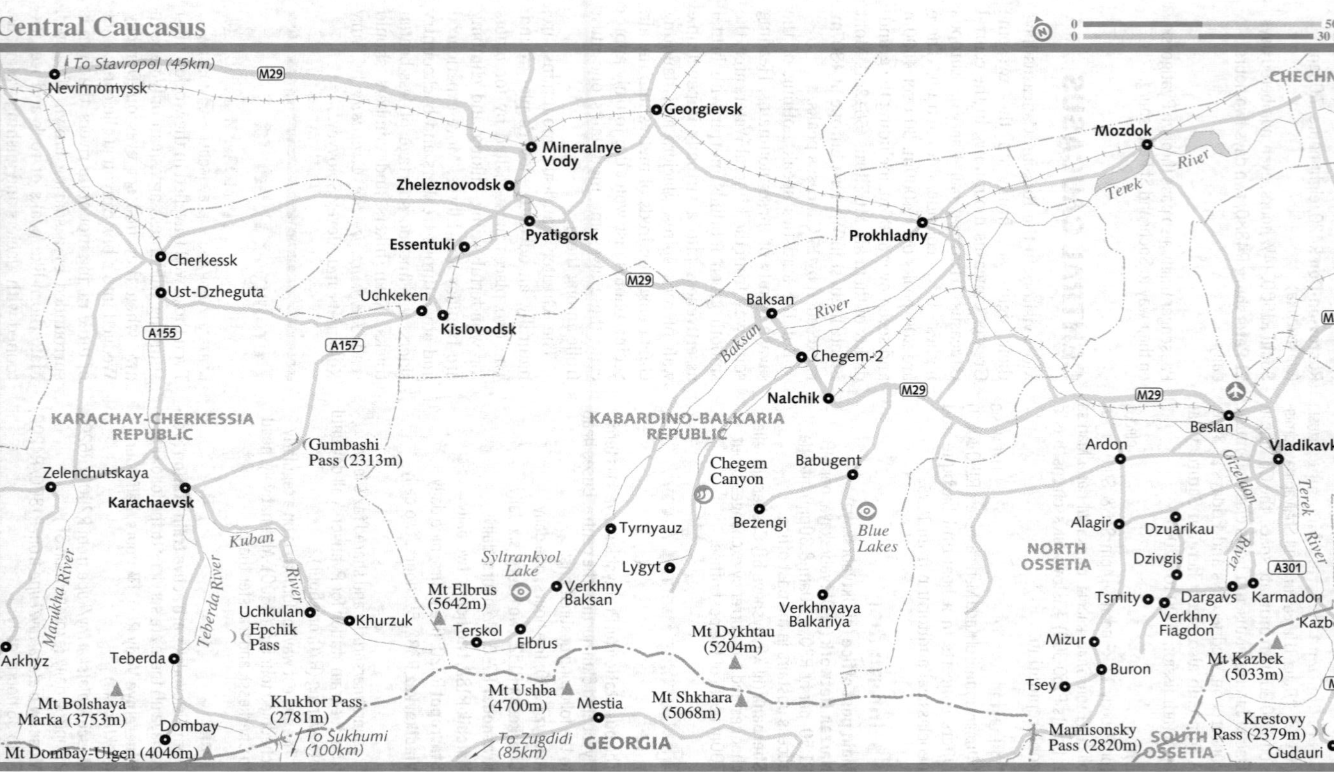

Central Caucasus
0 50 km
0 30 miles
To Stavropol (45km)
Nevinnomyssk
M29
Georgievsk
Mineralnye Vody
Zheleznovodsk
Pyatigorsk
Essentuki
Cherkessk
Ust-Dzheguta
Uchkeken
Kislovodsk
A155
A157
Baksan
Baksan River
Chegem-2
Nalchik
Prokhladny
Mozdok
Terek River
CHECHNYA
KARACHAY-CHERKESSIA REPUBLIC
KABARDINO-BALKARIA REPUBLIC
Gumbashi Pass (2313m)
Zelenchutskaya
Karachaevsk
Kuban River
Teberda River
Marukha River
Arkhyz
Teberda
Mt Bolshaya Marka (3753m)
Dombay
Mt Dombay-Ulgen (4046m)
Uchkulan
Epchik Pass
Khurzuk
Klukhor Pass (2781m)
To Sukhumi (100km)
Mt Elbrus (5642m)
Syltrankyol Lake
Verkhny Baksan
Terskol
Elbrus
Tyrnyauz
Lygyt
Mt Ushba (4700m)
To Zugdidi (85km)
Mestia
GEORGIA
Chegem Canyon
Bezengi
Babugent
Blue Lakes
Verkhnyaya Balkariya
Mt Dykhtau (5204m)
Mt Shkhara (5068m)
Beslan
Ardon
Vladikavkaz
Gizeldon River
Alagir
Dzuarikau
NORTH OSSETIA
Dzivgis
Tsmity
Dargavs
Karmadon
A301
Verkhny Fiagdon
Mizur
Buron
Tsey
Mamisonsky Pass (2820m)
SOUTH OSSETIA
Kazbegi
Mt Kazbek (5033m)
M3
Krestovy Pass (2379m)
Gudauri

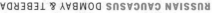

PEOPLE OF THE CENTRAL CAUCASUS

The Dombay and Elbrus areas are a melting pot of various Muslim peoples. They consist, broadly, of highlanders and lowlanders. The highlanders are the Balkar of Kabardino-Balkaria, who live in the Elbrus area, and the Karachay who populate Dombay, Arkhyz and other mountain zones of Karachay-Cherkessia. The Balkar and Karachay speak a similar Turkic tongue and traditionally make their living raising livestock – if you do any trekking around here you might be surprised to encounter Karachay and Balkar tending to their herds and flocks in the most remote reaches of the Greater Caucasus.

The lowlanders are often collectively described as Circassians (by outsiders) or Adygeya (by themselves). All Adygeya speak dialects of an intensely complex language broadly classified as 'Northwest Caucasian'. Dialects include Adygeyan – spoken throughout the Adygeya Republic (not covered here) and by the Circassian (Cherkess in Russian) minority in Karachay-Cherkessia – and Kabardian, spoken by the Kabardian majority in Kabardino-Balkaria. The closely related Abkhaz (spoken mainly in Abkhazia) and Abaza dialects are the other main Northwest Caucasian dialects.

Besides language and history, the Adygeya are united by a flag (three yellow arrows crossed over a green background, symbolising peace) and an unwritten code of etiquette known as *khabza*.

There's only one snag: the town itself, dishevelled and dominated by several brash concrete hotels, is an eyesore. Fortunately, it takes only a brisk walk to be far removed from the incongruous creation of *Homo sovieticus* that is the town proper.

Dombay and its surrounding mountains lie within the **Teberdinsky State Natural Biosphere Reserve**. Most locals belong to the mountain-dwelling Karachay ethnic minority.

New hotels and cafés are being built for an expected increase in the number of visitors as the 2014 Winter Olympics approach. Dombay is a possible backup site for the Olympic ski events should the mountains around Sochi be dry.

Three *ushchelie* (deep valleys) watered by glacier-fed torrents – Alibek from the west, Amanauz from the south and Dombay-Ulgen from the east – meet here to flow north, eventually as the Teberda River. Straddling both sides of the Amanauz River is the village of Dombay. From here two cable cars and several chairlifts ascend the Mussa-Achitara (Horse Thief) ridge to the east.

You'll find good hikes and horse riding in Teberda, 20km north of Dombay.

Sights & Activities

The main activities are skiing in winter and hiking in summer.

Teberdinsky State Natural Biosphere Reserve NATURE RESERVE
(Тебердинский государственный биосферный заповедник; admission R50; ⌚9am-1pm & 2-6pm) This park near the reserve office in Teberda has a small museum with stuffed animals and info on wildlife and geology; it also has stiflingly small pens with deer, foxes, wolves and other local fauna.

Hiking

The following routes require a border permit and additionally may require a nature reserve pass (currently R50, payable at the guard post at the entry to the hike). No guide is needed for Amanauz Valley or Alibek Falls. Other hikes, including Lake Turie, require mountaineering experience or a guide, as they may involve crossing glaciers and torrential rivers. There's also a bear population.

Mussa-Achitara Ridge HIKING
The 3012m-high Mussa-Achitara Ridge provides magnificent skiing, similar to the European Alps, from November until late May. Trails drop an eye-popping 1400 vertical metres from the top to the valley floor. There is bowl skiing up above the treeline as well as some mogul and glade runs for experts, and plenty of intermediate terrain. A brand-new high-speed cable car was added in 2006, and the mountain continues to add lifts and trails.

Several **chairlifts** (Канатно-кресельная дорога) and two **cable cars** (⌚8am-5pm) haul skiers up the mountain. An all-day ski pass costs R900. Most hotels and several shops around town hire out skis and snowboards.

The lifts remain open for sightseeing in the summer months. To reach the top, either

Dombay & Around

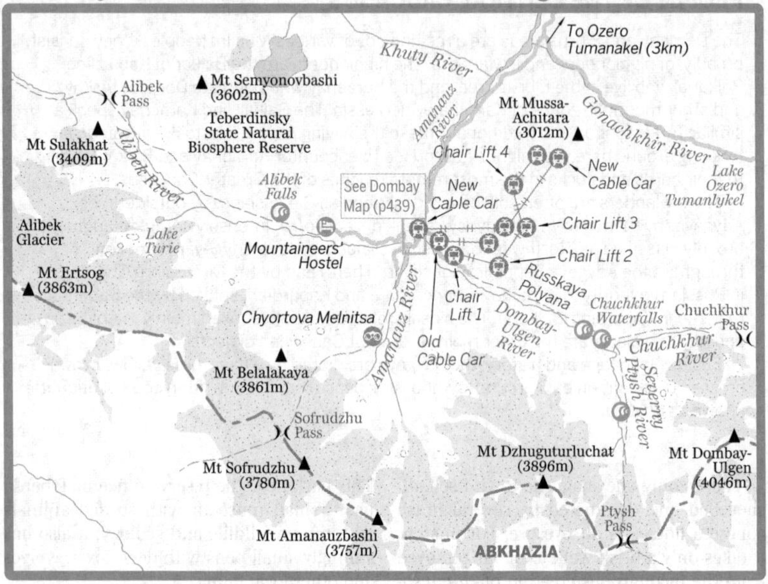

See Dombay Map (p439)

ride the new cable car or take four separate chairlifts, starting with single-chair lift 1 near the Krokus Hotel. Either way it costs R600, round trip, to the top (less if you go only part-way).

Plenty of backcountry terrain exists for freeriders, but take a local guide and beware of avalanches.

Chuchkhur Waterfalls & Ptysh Valley HIKING

It's a scenic, relatively easy walk from the start of chairlift 1 to two fine waterfalls on the Chuchkhur River. First, follow the vehicle track and then branch across the **Russkaya Polyana** clearing and continue to the first set of waterfalls. It takes about two hours (6km) to get here. Twenty minutes downstream from these falls, a path forks south for a steady 2km walk up Severny (North) Ptysh Valley and another waterfall.

Amanauz Valley HIKING

South of town, a short (45-minute, 3km) but tricky walk follows the Amanauz River to **Chyortova Melnitsa** (Devil's Mill), with good views of the **Amanauz Glacier**. Head south out of town past the Dombay housing area and pick up the trail along the river. After negotiating a slippery stream crossing (icy through June) the path dissipates. Head uphill through the woods until the trail materialises again and follow it to the viewpoint.

Alibek Valley HIKING

The dirt road behind Solnechnaya Dolina hotel leads 6km up Alibek Valley to a **mountaineers' hostel**, passing a climbers' cemetery after 2km. From the hostel a trail ascends about two hours to Lake Turie near Alibek Glacier, via dramatic Alibek Falls.

Lakes

There are several pretty lakes in the area that make for a fine swim on a warm summer day. **Ozero Karakel** is located 800m south of Teberdinsky State Natural Biosphere Reserve in Teberda. **Ozero Tumanlykel** is 7km northeast of Dombay, best reached by taxi (around R250).

Longer Hikes & Climbs

The sky is the limit for multiday hikes, but two intriguing options leave from Teberda. One is the three- to five-day trip to Arkhyz over Nazgir Pass. This follows the Mukhinskie Valley west, then veers south toward Mt Bolshaya Marka (3753m) before heading west again over Nazgir Pass (2981m), into the Marukha River valley and onto Arkhyz.

Another three- to four-day route goes east over the even higher Epchik Pass (3006m).

The route then continues to Lozhny Pass before dropping into the village of Uchkulan, just 30km due west of Mt Elbrus. A couple of kilometres east of Uchkulan is Khurzuk. Hard-core mountaineers can use Khurzuk as a base for ascents up the western flank of Mt Elbrus.

Peaks that serious climbers can tackle from Dombay include Sofrudzhu (3780m), Dombay-Ulgen (4046m), Sulakhat (3409m) and Semyonovbashi (3602m) above Alibek Valley. Check www.dombai.info for more information on these and other technical climbs.

One recommended guide who leads hikes in the area is **Rassul** (☎8-928-925 6038).

Horse Riding

Oleg HORSE RIDING
(☎8-960-438 5862, 8-928-388 8872) Horse-trekking guide Oleg operates out of stables located inside the Teberdinsky State Natural Biosphere Reserve in Teberda. He leads full-day rides taking in stunning alpine scenery. You can also do a four-day-return ride over Epchik Pass to Uchkulan (described in the previous section), one of the highest horse treks in the world. It costs R2500 to R3000 per day (food and tents not included). Day trips cost R300 per hour. Oleg can arrange the necessary border permits (easier in Teberda than in Dombay), though you'll need to contact him in advance.

Sleeping

The following are peak summer rates. Rates double or triple in the ski season.

Solnechnaya Dolina HOTEL €
(Гостиница Солнечная Долина, Sunny Valley; ☎58 269; soldol@yandex.ru; s/d from R500/1000;) Built in 1936 as the first hotel in Dombay, the old wing of this picturesque place is made entirely of wood and without nails in the manner of north Russian buildings. New and old rooms alike feature cosy blankets and are redolent of pine. Many rooms have balconies though some lack views, and the cheapest quarters have vintage wallpaper and elderly bathrooms. There's a pool and *banya*.

Hotel Snezhny Bars HOTEL €
(Отель Снежный Барс; ☎58 813, 8-928-923 1734; snezh-bars@yandex.ru; s/d from R600/1200; @) Part of a new crop of modern hotels opening in town, Snezhny Bars has nicely appointed rooms with red-wood furniture, comfy queen-sized beds and balconies with views. Upper-price rooms add more space to the equation. Excellent value.

Hotel Dombay HOTEL €
(Гостиница Домбай; ☎58 225; www.hotel-dombay.ru; s/d R700/1400) This Soviet-style behemoth has recently been spruced up with modern renovated rooms sporting fuzzy

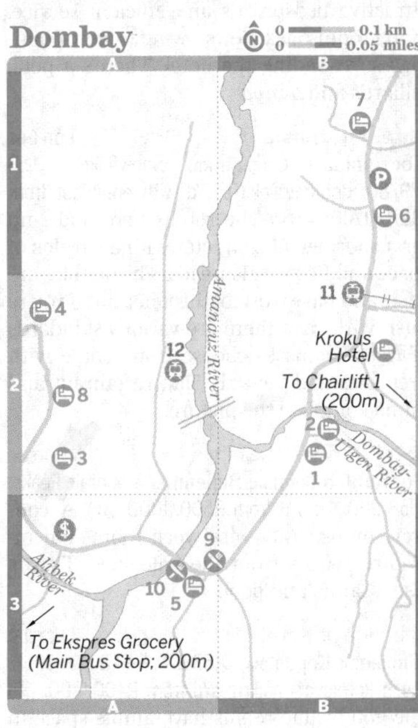

Dombay

Sleeping

1	Grand Hotel	B2
2	Hotel Dombay	B2
3	Hotel Gornye Vershiny	A2
4	Hotel Snezhinka	A2
5	Hotel Snezhny Bars	A3
6	Hotel Uyut	B1
7	Snezhnaya Koroleva	B1
8	Solnechnaya Dolina	A2

Eating

9	Café Kristall	A3
10	U Zuli	A3

Information

	Dombay Tourist	(see 11)
	Rescue Service	(see 11)

Transport

11	New Cable-Car, Base Station	B2
12	Old Cable-Car, Base Station	A2

carpeting (charcoal in hue) and wooden balconies that offer great views over the mountains.

Grand Hotel HOTEL €€
(☎8-928 923 8888; r from R1600; ▣) A newish option in the centre of town, Grand Hotel has modern rooms with red-wood furniture, attractive bedspreads and efficient service. Many rooms lack views owing to new buildings surrounding the hotel. There's a pool, billiards and *banya*.

Hotel Snezhinka HOTEL €€
(Гостиница Снежинка, Snowflake; ☎58 279/80; dombay@ok.ru; s/d with breakfast from R1275/1700; ❄▣) The rooms here make up for a shortage of character with a surplus of space and fuzzy bedspreads. The doubles are basic and have worn bathrooms, but if you're flush with cash there are various standards of *lyux* rooms to choose from, some with fireplaces and jacuzzis. Bar, restaurant and sauna complete the picture.

Hotel Gornye Vershiny HOTEL €
(Гостиница Горные Вершины, Mountain Peaks; ☎58 260/41; s/d from R500/1000; ▣) A concrete monstrosity with worn rooms but incredible vistas from the balconies. There's also a sauna and pool.

Snezhnaya Koroleva HOTEL €
(Снежная Королева; ☎58 370, 8-928 906 5958; snezh_koroleva@mail.ru; s/d from R400/800; ▣) The good-value rooms have ample space to accommodate both you and your ski equipment. There's also a sauna and pool.

Hotel Uyut GUESTHOUSE €
(Гостиница Уют; ☎57 788, 8-928-380 2916; s/d from R400/800) Small, friendly budget option.

Eating

U Zuli RUSSIAN €
(mains R200-500; ⏰10am-midnight) Popular U Zuli draws in Karachay regulars to feast on *zharkoye* (meat, potatoes and spices served in a sizzling cast-iron pan), buttery *khichiny* (flatbread) and other regional specialities in a rustic wood-panelled dining room (with animal skins on the wall). Costumed servers add verve to the place.

Café Kristall RUSSIAN €
(Кафе Кристалл; meals R200-600; ⏰9am-midnight) This place specialises in Karachay cuisine, including *sokhta* (a mammoth sausage-like creation stuffed with minced liver and rice) and *dzhyorme* (smaller Karachay sausage). Specify weight (in grams) to avoid a hefty meal (and bill). Seating is outside on a porch along the river or in the small dining room with refectory tables.

Shopping

The local babushka knitting-circle has stalls all around the village and chairlift stations selling its output of shawls (R300 to R2000), felt Georgian-style hats (R100 to R600), woolly rugs and 'fro-like Caucasian *papakha* hats (R300 to R600).

Information

Border control office (Teberda; ⏰9am-5pm Mon-Fri) Issues border permits.

Dombai Info (www.dombai.info) Infrequently updated but with some nonperishable information and photographs.

Dombay Tourist (☎8-905 422 2383; www.dt-tour.ru) Can organise day and multiday excursions, including hikes, jeep tours and horse riding, plus transfers. Can arrange border permits, but contact them well in advance. On 2nd floor of the new cable-car base station.

Rescue service (Спасательная Служба, Spasatelnaya sluzhba; ☎58 138; ⏰24hr) Emergency help, plus guiding and/or advice on more technical hikes and climbs. On main floor of the new cable-car base station.

Sberbank (Сбербанк; main road; ⏰9am-4pm Mon-Fri) Currency exchange and ATM.

Teberdinsky State Natural Biosphere Reserve Office (☎51 261; Teberda; ⏰9am-5pm Mon-Fri) The nature reserve office issues reserve passes and can arrange guides for hikes originating in Teberda. It's just off the main road on the north edge of Teberda.

BORDER PERMITS

Unfortunately, if you show up to Dombay without a proper *propusk* (permit), you won't be able to do any hiking – or see much beyond the village – which is of course the highlight of visiting this region. Foreigners require border permits for anywhere other than the village environs and Mussa-Achitara Ridge. Permit processing through the border control office in Teberda was one month when last we came through. Plan well in advance and contact a local travel agent, such as **Dombay Tourist** (www.dt-tour.ru) several months before your visit.

Getting There & Away

All buses originate at the **Ekspres grocery** (Экспрес) west of town and pick up passengers in the main **parking lot** (Парковка). Check the latest schedule with staff inside the grocery.

Marshrutky and buses serve the following:

Cherkessk R200, 3½ hours, daily at 8am and 11am

Karachaevsk R100, two hours, five daily

Uchkeken (near Kislovodsk) R290, four hours, daily at 1.30pm

Rostov-on-Don R700, nine hours, daily at 5.20pm

Teberda R40, 25 minutes, all buses pass through

For Arkhyz, the fastest route is to take the daily bus to Zelenchuk (R160, 2½ hours, daily at 9am), where you catch an onward *marshrutka* or a taxi (R500) to Arkhyz.

Additional daily *marshrutky* from Teberda head to Mineralnye Vody via Pyatigorsk (R270, six hours) and Krasnodar (R500, 7½ hours). In ski season frequent *marshrutky* shuttle people straight to Minvody airport (per person R500).

An easier but more expensive method of arriving is on a tour bus from Pyatigorsk (one way R600) or Kislovodsk (one way R600). Unlike public transport, these excursions take you over the 2313m Gumbashi Pass, with sublime views of Mt Elbrus lording it above the whole mountain chain.

Arkhyz Архыз

☎87878 / POP 2000 / ELEV 1450M / MOSCOW

It's no idyllic mountain getaway like Dombay, but experienced trekkers and ski tourers recognise this dusty cowboy town on the banks of the Bolshoy Zelenchuk River as a prime base for excursions into the backcountry. As an almost 100% Karachay village it has also appeal for anybody interested in the culture of these hearty, livestock-raising mountain dwellers.

Talk to guides in Dombay or Pyatigorsk about the many treks around here, including some easy-to-access day hiking around Lunaya Polyana. As in Dombay you'll need a border permit. Apply through travel agencies in Dombay or Pyatigorsk, or through Arkhyz's border control office, 2km south of town.

There are several hikes you can do without a permit. For a short walk (2km each way, 90 minutes return) to **Kazachy Waterfall**, cross the bridge and enter the reserve that's part of the **Teberdinsky State Natural Biosphere Reserve** (admission R50). Take the first path to the left and follow this to the right when it forks, across a meadow and up to the waterfall. It's a popular horse-riding spot.

For a longer hike (8km, roughly three hours return) high above town, follow this popular itinerary, which offers great views, wildflowers and waterfalls at the trail's end: At the main town intersection, instead of turning left through the market stalls and down to the bridge, go right instead, follow the dirt road as it winds around, cross the narrow river and look for the trail going to the left uphill toward the mountain. Follow this trail/cow path for 45 minutes, then at the fork, go right into a pine forest and follow the trail as it links back with the river. After 35 minutes, you'll reach the waterfalls.

Arkhyz's three hotels all offer **rafting** (30-minute trip per person R350), and there are several horse-riding operations around town (R300 per hour), easily arranged through your guesthouse.

Interesting archaeological sites in the area include the ruins of three 1000-year-old Byzantine monasteries. These are located near an observatory on a hill in Nizhny Arkhyz, a 20km taxi ride (R350) north of Arkyz. These can also be visited on an organised tour from Pyatigorsk or Kislovodsk.

Accommodation options include two midrange riverside resorts adjacent to each other on the west bank: **Pansionat Energetik** (☎87937-25 444, 8-928-393 8777; r from R1400), which has bike hire (R200) plus more extensive river frontage (playground, barbecues) than its neighbour **Krasnaya Skala** (☎25 299; r from R1200). Both have decent rooms overlooking the rushing Bolshoy Zelenchuk, with balconies in the upper price range. For budget accommodation, cross the river (to the east bank) for the rustic cabins of **Ogonyok Turbaza** (☎25 270; r from R350). There are several daily *marshrutky* to Cherkessk and Karachaevsk, plus one *marshrutka* daily to Kislovodsk (R300, 4½ hours, 1.30pm). For Dombay, catch the 11.30am *marshrutka* to Teberda (R200) and transfer there.

Nalchik Нальчик

☎86622 / POP 283,000 / ELEV 445 / MOSCOW

The pleasant capital of the Kabardino-Balkaria Republic straddles the rise of the steppes to the foothills of the Caucasus. Apart from a worthwhile museum and side trips to Chegem Valley and some medieval villages, visitors come to Nalchik to reach Mt Elbrus.

Security remains tenuous in Nalchik. In 2005 dozens of people were killed in fighting after Islamic militants took several government buildings, and in 2011 militants attacked a police post and an FSB-owned sanatorium, though no one was killed.

Two parallel streets, pr Lenina and pr Shogentsukova, run southwest through the centre from the train station on Osetinskaya ul.

Sights & Activities

Dolinsk Park PARK

Lush Dolinsk Park is one of Nalchik's highlights. Stroll the long promenade down to the **chairlift** (round-trip R150; 9am-6pm), which ascends over a lake to the Restaurant Sosruko. Climb the staircase inside Sosruko's 'head' for great views of the city and the mountains in the distance. The park also has small green lakes with paddle boats, an amusement park and the scenic Nalchik River, where locals take a dip to cool off on hot days. To get there walk or jump on *marshrutka* 1 heading west along pr Shogentsukova.

Kabardino-Balkaria National Museum MUSEUM

(ul Gorkogo 62; adult/child R50/10; 10am-5.30pm Tue-Sat) The Kabardino-Balkaria National Museum has a good 3D topographical map of the mountains and displays covering the history of the area.

Tours

A kiosk (called Turagenstvo Assol) on the corner of pr Lenina and ul Keshokova hawks semi-regular tours to Chegem Waterfall (per person R350) and the other *ushchelie* (gorges) around Nalchik and North Ossetia (check that restrictions on foreigners entering mountain zones in North Ossetia have been lifted first).

Auto Tour Group TOUR COMPANY

(775 091; www.autotourgroup.ru; 2nd fl, Hotel Rossiya; 9am-6pm) This outfit runs a wide range of full-day tours, including Chegem Waterfall, Blue Lakes, Kurtati Valley, Elbrus and many other destinations. Price per group including English guide run from R2500 to R4000.

Sleeping

Trek HOTEL €€

(720 576; www.trek.web-box.ru; Dolinsk Region, Gorodskoy Park; s/d incl breakfast R2500/3000) Near the chairlift in Dolinsk Park, Trek has spacious and attractive rooms with queen-size beds, sparkling modern bathrooms and oversized windows to take in the surrounding greenery. It's often booked solid by wedding parties on weekends.

Hotel Rossiya HOTEL €

(775 378; pr Lenina 32; s/d without bathroom R700/1000, with bathroom R1800/2500) Right in the middle of town, the five-storey Rossiya has small but nicely renovated rooms with parquet floors and big windows. The cheapest rooms have sinks but not bathrooms (a shower costs R50).

Hotel Alpinist HOTEL €

(423 026; ul Pacheva 34; s/d R600/1000) Hotel Alpinist has no-frills service and rooms with loud rugs and wallpaper, set in an uninspiring concrete edifice in the centre of town.

Eating

Nalchik is a good place to sample spicy Kabardian national dishes such as *zharuma* (fiery sausage stuffed with minced lamb, onion and spices), *gedlibzhe* (a spicy chicken dish) and *geshlubzhe* (a saucy bean dish).

Restaurant Sosruko KABARDIAN €

(720 070; off Profsoyuznaya ul; national dishes R100-200; 10am-late) This architecturally unusual restaurant at the terminus of the chairlift in Dolinsk Park comprises the head of local hero Sosruko with an outstretched arm and hand holding a flame. It's *the* place to try Kabardian national cuisine, including the Sosruko special, a concoction of minced meat, mushrooms and herbs in a pastry pear.

Pizza House ITALIAN €

(427 067; ul Lermontova 5; meals R180-300) Back in the centre this efficient, modern Italian restaurant churns out excellent pizza, pasta and meat dishes and has a salad bar. The front patio is a popular drinking and hookah-smoking spot at night.

Trek RUSSIAN €

(Dolinsk Region, Gorodskoy Park; mains d R220-350) This hotel and restaurant in Dolinsk Park has a pleasant location with outdoor tables beside the rushing Nalchik River. The menu has the usual assortment of grilled meats, fried trout and fresh salads, but slow service.

Central Market MARKET €

(ul Pacheva) Browsing the aisles of fruit and fresh-baked flatbread (R10) to the ubiquitous strains of Caucasian *tanz* (dance) music in the central market is a Nalchik highlight.

Shopping

Adyge Une SOUVENIRS

(Adygeya House; pr Lenina 49; ⏰9am-7pm) This excellent souvenir shop sells all manner of Kabardian and Circassian items, such as hats (R500 to R4000), drinking vessels and jewellery bearing Circassian symbols. It also carries beautifully wrought Dagestani silver jewellery.

Dom Knigy MAPS

(pr Lenina 10; ⏰9am-9pm) This store has a superb selection of Caucasus maps.

Information

Air Communications Agency (☎423 326; ul Lenina 43; ⏰8am-6pm) Air, bus and train ticketing.

Border Control Office (☎916 510; Kabardinskaya ul 192; ⏰9am-6pm Mon-Fri) You can secure border permits here – though the wait time is currently over one month. It's easier to do so in advance through a travel agent in the Elbrus area – though do verify the Elbrus area has reopened (the whole area was off-limits at research time).

Internet Club Pautina (pr Lenina 20; per hr R60, ⏰24hr)

Main post office (pr Shogentsukova 14); Post (⏰8am-8pm); Internet access (1st fl; per hr R60; ⏰8.30am-noon & 1-5.30pm)

Getting There & Away

Buses from long-distance **bus station No 1** (ul Gagarina 124) serve Pyatigorsk (R110, 1¾ hours, 11 daily), Kislovodsk (R162, 2½ hours, two daily) and Terskol (R160, three hours, one daily). Another option to Terskol is to take a *marshrutka* to Tyrnyauz (R120, two hours) and transfer to a Terskol-bound *marshrutka* or taxi there.

The best way to Vladikavkaz is by speedy *marshrutka* (R162, 1½ hours, two daily). For Mineralnye Vody, hope for an open seat on the passing Vladikavkaz–Mineralnye Vody bus (R152, two hours, eight daily) or take a taxi (R1800).

From the **train station** (ul Osetinskaya) there are two daily *elektrichki* to Mineralnye Vody (R120, three hours, 7.26am and 11.36am). Train 061C to Moscow (*platskartny/kupe* from R2100/4700, 36 hours, 4.20pm) passes through Rostov-on-Don (*platskartny/kupe* from R1020/2200, 12½ hours).

Elbrus Area Приэльбрусье

☎86638 / ELEV (TERSKOL) 2085M / ⏰MOSCOW

Mt Elbrus rises imperiously on a northern spur of the Caucasus ridge at the end of the Baksan Valley. Surrounding it and flanking the valley are mountains that are lesser in height but equally awe-inspiring.

The tourist facilities that are littered along the valley floor make this potential Switzerland less attractive. Terskol is a disgrace, with its decrepit and half-built buildings and rusted machines scattered about. But visitors come for the majestic mountains, which provide energetic skiing, exciting hikes and climbing.

Most foreign visitors come for the challenge of climbing Europe's highest peak, but there are dozens of fantastic, less-strenuous hikes in the area, and there's year-round skiing. Day trippers can ride the chairlifts and cable cars for views of Elbrus and the surrounding mountains. Mt Elbrus and its surrounding peaks and towns all lie within the vast **Prielbruse National Park**.

Three villages lining the Baksan Valley make up the area known in Russian as *Prielbruse* (Around Elbrus). Driving in, the first town you'll hit is the bustling ski village of Cheget Polyana, at the base of Mt Cheget. Next is Terskol, the administrative hub. About 3km beyond Terskol the valley ends at Azau, base for the Mt Elbrus cable car and ski area. Mt Elbrus can't be seen from either of these villages – to catch a glimpse, walk up a mountain or jump on any ski lift in Azau or Cheget.

Maps of the Elbrus area are available from stalls at the base of the Cheget and Azau ski lifts.

Sights & Activities

Mt Elbrus MOUNTAIN

Mt Elbrus, enigmatically unusual with two peaks – the western at 5642m and eastern at 5621m – bulges nearly 1000m above anything else in the vicinity. This volcanic cone has upper slopes reputedly coated in ice up to 200m thick; numerous glaciers grind down its flanks and several rivers start here. The name 'Elbrus', meaning 'Two Heads' comes from Persian; in Balkar it's 'Mingi-Tau' (meaning 'thousands', ie very big mountain).

The first (unconfirmed) climb of Mt Elbrus was in 1829 by a Russian expedition with Killar, a lone Circassian hunter hired as

Elbrus Area

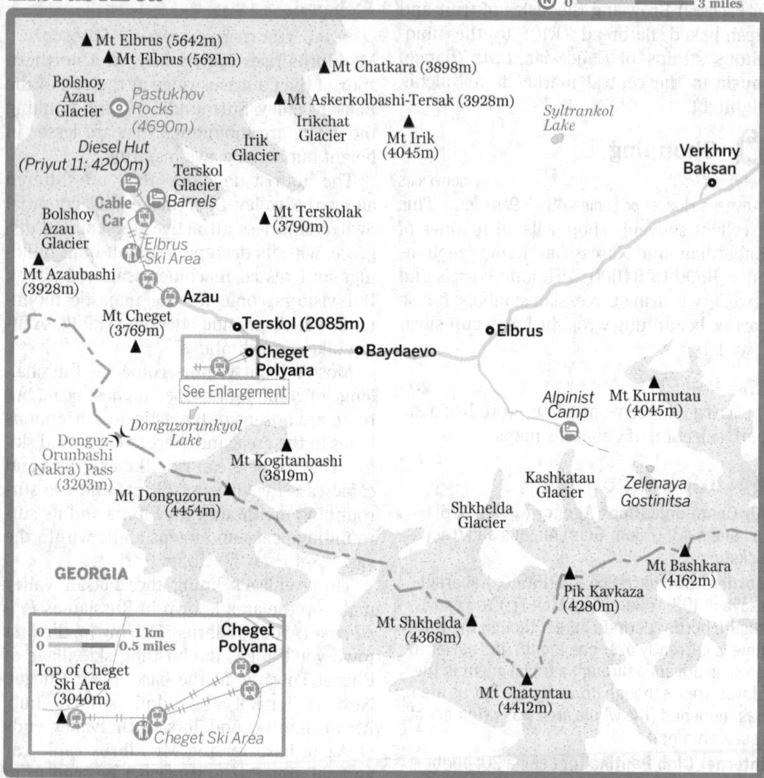

a guide, apparently reaching the peak on his own. The lower eastern peak was officially climbed on 31 July 1868 and the western peak on 28 July 1874, both by British expeditions. For propaganda purposes, in Soviet times there were mass ascents involving hundreds of climbers; a telephone cable was even taken to the top so Comrade Stalin could share the news. Ascent and descent have been done in many ways: by light aircraft, hang-gliders, paragliders, a motorcycle with skis and even in a Land Rover hauled to the top for advertising purposes. Apparently it's still there, some 200m below the summit.

The Climb

The climb up Elbrus is not technically difficult, but it's harder than, say, Mt Kilimanjaro, with which it is often compared. Climbing experience on ice is advisable, and a good degree of fitness is paramount.

The climb itself takes just one long day, but most climbers require at least seven days of training and altitude acclimatisation before attempting the summit. Climbers typically spend a few days in Terskol or Azau before taking the lifts up to spend a few nights in and hike around the **Barrels**, a lodge at 3700m (there are a few more huts up here in case the Barrels is full).

The actual climb starts around 4am from one of two points: the **Diesel Hut** (also called Priyut 11) at 4200m, from where it's a 10- to 12-hour hike to the summit; or the **Pastukhov Rocks** at 4690m, from where it's a seven- to eight-hour hike. Both are accessible by snowcat from the Barrels. Most people start from Pastukhov Rocks. There's obviously a much higher failure rate for climbers starting out from the lower Diesel Hut. Either way, the walk is slow, gradual and gruelling.

One mistake you don't want to make is to take this mountain lightly. As on any 5500m-plus peak, clear weather can turn into thick fog in a matter of hours. On average, about 10 people per year perish on Mt Elbrus. Many victims, fooled by Elbrus' gentle appearance, just start walking up without a guide. Without proper navigational experience it's easy to become disoriented and lose the marked trail, even in fine weather. Off the trail there's a serious risk of falling into a crevasse or never finding your way back. Do the sensible thing and take a guide.

Ascents above 3700m require a permit. These cost US$20 in the past, but fees could rise dramatically in the future.

Skiing

The piste skiing on Elbrus is generally easier than on nearby Cheget, with terrain to suit all levels. The skiing beneath the lower cable car station is good for beginners. The upper cable car (Mir) station services a few steep and challenging runs for experts.

All-year skiing is possible from the uppermost chairlift, which terminates at 3800m. From here snowcats bring advanced skiers a couple of hundred metres further up to the Diesel Hut, from where there are opportunities for off-piste (free-ride) skiing. These run regularly in the peak ski season (per person R600), but must be specially ordered at other times (10-person snowcat R10,000).

An all-day ski pass costs R600 and allows you to ride the cable cars and chairlift but not the gondola, which is run by a separate company. Multiday passes cost less and give you access to Elbrus and Cheget (but not both on the same day). Gear can be hired at any hotel or at numerous ski shops in Azau or Cheget Polyana.

Cable Cars & Chairlift

A new **gondola** (R200; 9am-3.30pm) runs parallel to the **old cable car** (1st stage R160, 2nd stage R250; 9am-3.30pm). This gondola was damaged in the terrorist attack of 2011 but has since been restored. At research time the gondola terminated at the cable car mid-station (2870m), but there are plans to extend it to the upper (Mir) station at 3470m. For now only the old cable car goes from the mid-station to the Mir station; both stations have good cafés.

A **chairlift** (R200; 9am-3pm) continues to 3800m. Both cable cars and the chairlift run year-round except for maintenance during October or November.

Tour buses start arriving at 10am from June to August, and the queues at the cable car base station and mid-station can be brutal – waits of up to two hours are common at weekends. If it looks bad consider just taking the gondola up to the mid-station, which affords exceptional views of Elbrus' twin peaks and, to the southwest, Mts Cheget and Azaubashi.

Mt Cheget MOUNTAIN

Expert skiers relish the moguls, steeps and glades offered by this ski area on the south side of the Baksan Valley. The piste occupies the lower reaches of Mt Cheget (Mt Donguz-Orunbashi; 3769m); two delightfully anachronistic single **chairlifts** (per lift R200; 9am-4pm) haul skiers up to 3040m. There are a couple of T-bars on the back (north) side of the mountain. A day ski pass in season costs R600.

Riding the chairlift up, the raw majesty of the surrounding mountains is quickly revealed. To the west are the smooth milky-white twin humps of Mt Elbrus, to the east the jagged peaks and near-vertical sides of Mt Donguzorun (Mt Donguzorun-Chegetkarabashi; 4454m), with a distinctive glacier shaped like the numeral 7 plastered to its side.

SECURITY WARNING

The Kabardino-Balkaria Republic has seen a flare-up of violence in recent years, with more than 100 terrorist attacks in 2010 – a five-fold increase from 2009. Unfortunately, tourists are now being targeted. Travellers are well advised to assess the latest security risks before visiting this region. In February 2011, three Moscow tourists were killed and two were injured when militants attacked their minibus travelling from the Mineralnye Vody airport to an Elbrus ski resort. The next day a ski lift was blown up and a car bomb was found in Terskol village parked next to a hotel. In response, the FSB (Federal Security Service) closed down the main road into Baksan Valley and at research time there was no access to Terskol, Cheget Polyana or Azau. As a result, we were unable to visit this area and to verify first-hand the information in this section. We have done our best to do an update using local sources in the area, though this section may contain information particularly liable to change.

Hiking

Any walks towards the Georgian border require a border permit. It's easiest to arrange permits in advance through a tour operator. Contact them at least a month before you plan to visit.

In the past, hiking routes to the north and northwest did not require permits, although this situation is likely to change in the future. Inquire locally before setting out. A couple of easy, two- to three-hour walks start on the dirt road behind (north of) the white obelisk in Terskol village. The dirt road's right fork leads up the Terskol Valley to a dramatic view of Mt Elbrus behind the 'hanging' **Terskol Glacier**, dripping over a cliff edge. The left fork follows a 4WD track to an observatory, with wonderful views across the Baksan Valley of Mt Cheget (3769m), Mt Donguzorun (4454m) and Mt Kogutanbashi (3819m).

From the top of Cheget's lower chairlift, it's an easy one-hour walk around the side of Mt Cheget to **Donguzorunkel Lake**. Going further will require a permit.

For a more challenging hike, take a taxi (R600 each way from Terskol, including unlimited wait time) to where the paved road up Adylsu Valley, south of Elbrus village, ends. Here you'll have to go through a checkpoint (permits only). Then strike southeast with the Adylsu River on your right and it's about a one-hour walk along an unsealed road to an **alpinist camp** in sight of the impressive hanging **Shkhelda Glacier**. From here a trail, tricky in spots, leads another two hours up to **Zelenaya Gostinitsa** (Green Hotel), which isn't a hotel but a meadow of sorts, surrounded by impressive peaks, glaciers and a muddy lake.

Tours

Rather than being just folk in offices selling tickets, the agencies listed here are either active tour leaders or providers of specialist services for climbers, skiers and hikers. Most also offer 'light' packages for do-it-yourselfers, which include accommodation and logistical support, but no active tour guiding. English-, German- and French-speaking guides are usually readily available. They can also help with visa and border-permit logistics.

Go-Elbrus ADVENTURE TOURS
(☎78 171; www.go-elbrus.com; Terskol 5-5) The German-Balkar couple in charge here are accomplished free-skiers and mountaineers. Highly recommended for backcountry skiing trips, ski touring, ice climbing, Elbrus climbs and more creative ascents.

Adventure Alternative ADVENTURE TOURS
(☎in UK 44-28708 31258; www.adventurealternative.com) This UK company organises Mt Elbrus climbs.

Pilgrim Tours ADVENTURE TOURS
(☎in Moscow 495-660 3501; www.pilgrim-tours.com; Ostozhenka 41, Moscow) Pilgrim is a large, efficient Moscow-based company that leads Elbrus climbs.

Viktor Yanchenko ADVENTURE TOURS
(☎8-928-225 4623; yanki-viktor@rambler.ru) Contact Viktor for an English-speaking climbing and skiing guide.

Wild Russia ADVENTURE TOURS
(☎in St Petersburg 812-703 3215; www.wildrussia.spb.ru; Fontanka nab 59, St Petersburg) This agency specialises in Mt Elbrus climbs and adventure tours throughout Russia.

Sleeping & Eating

Expect to pay double to triple the listed (June) rates during the peak ski season (late December to early May).

In the winter especially you'll find eating options aplenty on the ski slopes – everything from bundled-up babushkas hawking shashlyk, *khichiny* (stuffed flatbread) and *schorpa* (Balkar soup) to the fire-warmed restaurants at the cable car stations on Elbrus.

Accommodation on Mt Elbrus itself is in the **Barrels** (per person R600), a series of cylindrical huts about 200m beyond the chairlift; and at the **Diesel Hut** (per person R600) at 4200m. Spaces are limited so book through a tour operator.

CHEGET POLYANA

With a clutch of private hotels, slope-side cafés, market stalls and even a legitimate après-ski bar, Cheget Polyana ski area is a more attractive proposition than Terskol, especially during the ski season.

Pansionat Cheget HOTEL €€
(☎71 339; r from R1600, plus breakfast & dinner per person R200) This huge, eight-storey ex-Soviet concrete block is the obvious choice for skiers on a budget as rates include free chairlift passes, transfer to/from Mineralnye Vody airport and daily transfers to Azau. It's timeworn but clean and tidy, and there are views from the upper-floor balconies. The cheap canteen is open to all, as are the ski shop, bank and other services.

Hotel Esen HOTEL €€
(☎71 474; d R1600) This friendly midrange option is notable for its common area with fireplace. No views here but convenient to lifts.

Hotel Ozon-Cheget HOTEL €€
(☎71 453; d from R1800) This somewhat upscale place has LCD TVs but otherwise simple rooms.

Captain Pete's RUSSIAN €€
(mains R150-300) The balcony in view of the ski mountain and Mt Donguzorun is a prime place to sink suds après-ski. Aside from standard Caucasian food, there are European specialities like schnitzel and baked salmon on the (English) menu.

TERSKOL

Terskol has a good selection of accommodation and its central location allows for relatively easy exploration of both Cheget and Azau.

Povorot HOTEL €€
(☎71 499; www.povorot.ru; s/d incl breakfast & dinner from R2660/3240;) This well-run hotel is popular with those who come to climb Mt Elbrus or do hikes in the area. Nicely furnished rooms have beautiful views of the surrounding countryside and there are loads of amenities – sauna, pool and billiards; the hotel can also arrange permits, provide guides, airport transfers and more.

Pansionat Volfram HOTEL €
(☎71 311; r per person R750, plus breakfast & dinner per person R300;) This is Terskol's requisite Soviet-style concrete behemoth. It's much like Pansionat Cheget minus the views, and has Russia's highest-altitude swimming pool and a cheerful *stolovaya*. Rates include lift tickets and free transfer to/from Azau and Cheget in winter.

Kupol Café RUSSIAN €
(mains R200-300) Tasty Balkar and Russian specialities under a strange, sarcophagus-like roof. It stays open late to show big sporting events on its big-screen TV.

AZAU

While not as pleasant as Cheget Polyana, Azau is a better choice for intermediate skiers who want to be closer to Elbrus' gentler groomed slopes. Elbrus climbers also usually end up here for a night or two before moving up to the Barrels.

Hotel Vershina HOTEL €€
(☎71 473; www.hotelvershina.ru; d R4000) A rustic wooden interior gives it a ski-lodge feel and the *banya* adds an authentic Russian touch. Throw in friendly service and it's Azau's best option, even if the rooms are smallish. Walk-in guests may nab a better rate.

Shakherezada Hotel HOTEL €€
(☎71 327, 8-928-937 2815; d with 2 meals from R2500) Cheery rooms barely salvage this otherwise uninspiring option. There's hope, however, in the form of big-time renovations going on when we last visited.

Information

For visa and border permit support, go through one of the tour companies.

Elbrus (www.elbrus.net) Has maps and practical information.

Pansionat Cheget (9am-4.30pm Tue-Sat) Sberbank currency exchange booth and 24-hour ATM in Cheget Polyana.

Post & telephone office (Terskol)

Rescue service (☎71489; Terskol; 24hr) Check in here before setting out for hikes. Look for the letters 'МЧС' on a fence near café Bayramuk on east edge of Terskol.

Turbaza Terskol (Terskol) Currency exchange and ATM in front of a hotel on the main road.

Getting There & Away

There's a bus and two *marshrutky* daily to Nalchik (R160, three hours). Alternatively, take a taxi (R600) or bus (R50, four daily, one hour) to Tyrnyauz and then a frequent *marshrutka* to Nalchik.

Arrange with tour operators running out of Kislovodsk and Pyatigorsk to use their excursions as a means of getting to and from Elbrus. Buses leave from the main road near the post office in Terskol. They do not pass through Cheget Polyana proper.

Getting Around

A taxi costs R120 from Terskol to Azau or Cheget. In ski season plenty of *marshrutky* and free shuttles operate between Cheget and Azau. Otherwise, walk or hitch a ride.

CHECHNYA, DAGESTAN & INGUSHETIA *LEONID RAGOZIN*

Why does Lonely Planet not cover these areas?

Here is Russia's own Iraq and Afghanistan combined. The jihadist insurgency in the northeast Caucasus is like peatbog fire. It might be smouldering deep underground in Chechnya these days, but in adjacent Dagestan and Ingushetia it flares up every now and then. Insurgency apart, the whole area is full of gun-wielding young men who tend to be unpredictable, ie trigger-happy. If you are a journalist or an NGO worker then, hopefully, you are well aware of the risks of travelling here. If not, avoid this minefield of a region.

Why is it dangerous?

Every week brings reports of shootings and bombings in one, two or all three republics. Civilians are regularly killed or injured. Kidnapping has also become a lucrative business, and many foreigners kidnapped during the two Chechen wars were brutally killed after months of torture. As a foreigner, your 'price' is much higher than that of any Russian or local, so even though there has been a substantial decrease in the number of kidnappings, it is still a serious danger.

Who lives there and why are they fighting?

The Chechen, Dagestani, Ingush and other groups in the northwest Caucasus are known in Russia by the common name *gortsy* (highlanders). *Gortsy* found themselves squeezed between two parts of the Russian empire, when Georgia joined it in the early 19th century. Led by Imam Shamil and assisted by Turkey, they fought a long and bloody war against the Russian colonial army, but eventually had to subdue.

At the end of the WWII, Stalin accused the Chechens and the Ingush of collaborating with the enemy and deported the entire people into Central Asia. This trauma was the main reason for the surge of a nationalist movement in the late 1980s. By 1991, the Chechens led by Soviet general Dzhokhar Dudayev achieved defacto independence and forced Russian troops to withdraw. Chechnya evolved into a safe haven for arms dealers, runaway criminals and terrorists.

In 1994, president Boris Yeltsin made an ill-fated attempt to return the republic under Russian control. The ensuing war resulted in yet another embarrassing withdrawal in 1996 amid the international condemnation of atrocities against civilians.

The war resumed in 1999 after a Chechen incursion into Dagestan and a series of apartment-block bombings in Moscow, blamed on the jihadists. This time government troops prevailed. Many rebels swapped sides and one of them – mufti Akhmad Kadyrov – became the new Chechen president.

In the following years, the jihadists carried out numerous terrorist attacks, most notably the seizures of a Moscow theatre and a school in Beslan – both ending in bloodbaths. Akhmad Kadyrov was killed in a bomb attack at a stadium in 2004 and succeeded by his son Ramzan.

How is Chechnya now?

A former rebel, Kremlin-backed Ramzan Kadyrov became president in 2007; in 2011 he began a new 5-year term as Chechen 'head' of government. Credited with bringing stability to Chechnya (the Kremlin officially ceased counterterrorism operations in the region in 2009), Kadyrov has also committed federal funds to rebuilding the republic, especially the capital of Grozny. Diverse groups, from Human Rights Watch

NORTH OSSETIA

A prime destination in Soviet times, North Ossetia has experienced a wave of violence over the last decade owing to its proximity to conflict-strewn Chechnya and Ingushetia. It also lies just north of South Ossetia, the breakaway region of Georgia that led to the war between Russia and Georgia in 2008. As such, visitors are advised against travelling in the region. North Ossetia's capital, Vladikavkaz, has seen its share of terrorist bombings – most recently in 2010, when a deadly car bomb exploded in the central market, killing 18 people and injuring over 160. Just northwest of there is Beslan, which in 2004 was the site of the horrific school siege by Chechen militants, which led to the deaths of 331 people – more than half of them children.

Although much of North Ossetia is off limits to foreigners owing to travel restrictions, you can visit some spectacular sites on an organised tour, easily arranged in Nalchik. Worthwhile destinations include the striking rock fortress of Dzivgis, the old settlement of Tsmiti and an Ossetian city of the dead amid dramatic mountain scenery near the village of Dargavs.

to the European Parliament, claim that regional stability has been purchased at the cost of the murder and torture of dissidents and journalists. Kadyrov vehemently denies any involvement.

On the bright side, the reconstructed Chechen capital is gleaming, as if it has never been flattened by the Russian artillery. Dominating the cityscape is the largest mosque in Europe and a brand-new football stadium where a Ramzan-led team plays an occasional friendly against Brazilian and British football stars and inevitably wins.

Russian laws are largely irrelevant, especially when it comes to gun possession, but elements of Islamic law are very much in force. Alcohol and gambling are banned and women who leave their head uncovered or wear jeans in public are asking for grave trouble. A few of those who defied the rules have been killed in recent years.

What about Ingushetia & Dagestan?

Squeezed out of Chechnya, hardcore rebels found shelter in the neighbouring republics where police brutality, poverty and corruption had created a fertile ground for jihadist ideology.

Operating out of Ingushetia, 'Chechnya's Bin Laden' Shamil Basayev masterminded the Beslan attack before a pinpoint missile strike killed him in 2006. After Beslan, Putin replaced popular Ingush leader Ruslan Aushev with ex-KGB general Murat Zyazikov. The latter's heavy-handed approach put the republic on the brink of a civil war. The authorities defused a seemingly imminent conflict by firing Zyazikov and replacing him with General Yunus-bek Yevkurov, who started emulating Aushev's style of governance and gradually calmed things down despite a series of setbacks and tragedies.

In Dagestan, the insurgency is fuelled by the endless feud between numerous ethnic clans vying for political and economic power. For many young people, radical Islam appears to be the only unifying egalitarian force capable of creating a more just and prudent society. As in Ingushetia, the situation is aggravated by exorbitant unemployment rates.

There's hardly any investment, but €6.5 million was spent in 2011 to create a single job – that of Brazilian football star Roberto Carlos, who joined the local club Anzhi to the utter bewilderment of the international press.

If it becomes safe to travel there, what is there to see?

Dagestan has the largest number of tourist sights of the three regions and is more likely to become a travel destination, although in the rather distant future. The 5000-year-old town of Derbent, listed as a Unesco World Heritage Site, is graced by a magnificent ancient fortress and boasts an interesting multicultural population of Mountain Jews and Lezgians. In more peaceful times hordes of Soviet tourists also used to visit beautiful mountain villages such as Gunib (famous for its silverware), while others preferred to sunbathe on the sandy Caspian beaches.

In Soviet times, Checheno-Ingushetia was popular with hikers, who flocked into the republic to admire medieval clan towers standing amid the graceful mountain landscape and trek over the Itum-Kale district's mountain passes into Georgia. The Ingush castle of Vovnushki came close to being officially declared one of Russia's seven wonders in an internet vote held in 2008.

Further information

Russian journalist Anna Politkovskaya's book *A Dirty War*, and *Chienne de Guerre* by another fearless female war reporter, Anne Niva, are both available in English and are worth reading, as is *Conversation with a Barbarian* by Paul Klebnikov. Politkovskaya and Klebnikov top the list of journalists killed in Russia in recent years.

You may also find useful information on the following websites:

Free Chechnya (www.chechnyafree.ru/en/) Russian government site with tons of information on Chechen life, as well as downloadable Chechen tunes for mobile phones.

Human Rights Watch (www.hrw.org) Remains a vocal defender of people's right to live without fear in the Caucasus.

Institute of War and Peace Reporting (http://iwpr.net/programme/caucasus) London-based institute with a network of stringers in the Caucasus who provide an unbiased and detailed look at recent developments in the region.

Western Siberia

Includes »

Best Places to Eat

» Yermolaev (p455)
» Romanov Restaurant (p457)
» Tamada (p459)
» Perchini (p461)

Best Places to Stay

» Hotel Vostok (p453)
» Hotel Sibir (p457)
» Avenue (p461)
» Toyan (p468)

Why Go?

From unforgettable lakes to underground cafés, the west of this colossal region has much more to offer than snow and ice. In fact, if you come in the summer, you won't even see any of that, with temperatures regularly topping 30°C. But the weather isn't the only surprise waiting for you in Western Siberia (Западная Сибирь).

Expect contrast and extremes, from urban chaos to remote areas where an encounter with a fellow traveller is a real event. An at times surreal mix of Soviet legacies and stunning landscapes, Western Siberia is not the easiest place in which to travel. Visitors need a willingness to rough it, and be able to speak at least rudimentary Russian. But those who make the effort will be rewarded with an insight into the Siberian way of life and – perhaps more importantly – receive a dose of the locals' legendary hospitality.

When to Go

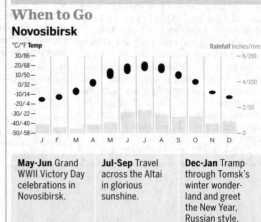

Novosibirsk

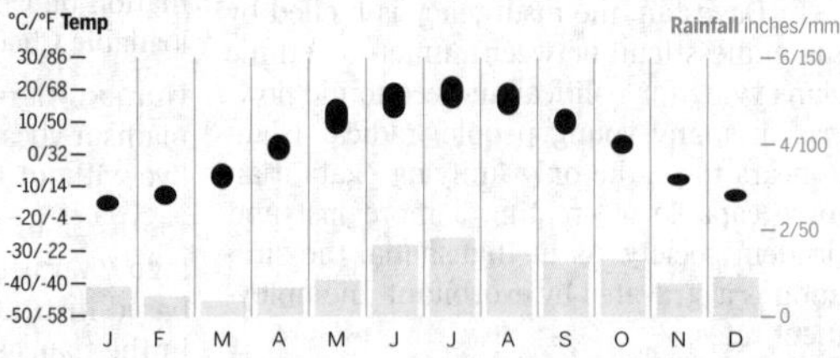

May-Jun Grand WWII Victory Day celebrations in Novosibirsk.

Jul-Sep Travel across the Altai in glorious sunshine.

Dec-Jan Tramp through Tomsk's winter wonderland and greet the New Year, Russian style.

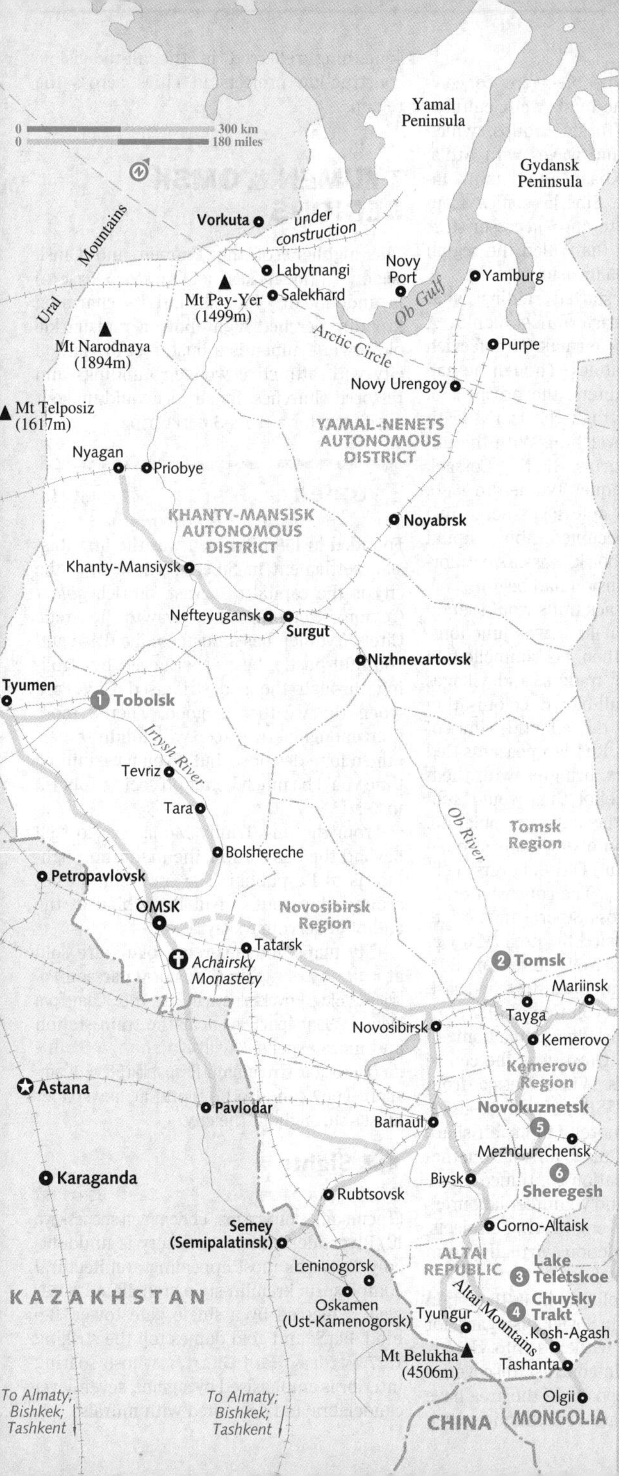

Western Siberia Highlights

1. Explore the dishevelled old town in **Tobolsk** (p456), Siberia's former capital
2. Take a stroll through the student city of **Tomsk** (p464) and its picturesque wooden homes
3. Chill out at placid **Lake Teletskoe**, Western Siberia's answer to Lake Baikal (p479)
4. Drive towards the Mongolian border along the spectacular **Chuysky Trakt** (p484)
5. Pay your respects at the monuments to Soviet worker heroes in **Novokuznetsk** (p488)
6. Check out the ski resort at **Sheregesh**, popular with Russia's skiers and snowboarders (p490)

History

Siberia's early Altai people were conceivably progenitors of the Inuit-Arctic cultures and of the Mongol-Turkic groups, which expanded in westbound waves with Attila, Chinggis (Genghis) Khaan and Timur (Tamerlane). The name Siberia comes from Sibir, a Turkic khanate and successor-state to the Golden Horde that ruled the region following Timur's 1395 invasion.

From 1563, Sibir started raiding what were then Russia's easternmost flanks. A Volga brigand called Yermak Timofeevich was sent to counter-attack. Though he had only 840 Cossack fighters, the prospect of battle seemed better than the tsar's death sentence that hung over him. With the unfair advantage of firearms, the tiny Cossack force managed to conquer Tyumen in 1580, turning Yermak into a Russian hero. Two years later Yermak occupied Sibir's capital Isker, near today's Tobolsk. Russia's extraordinary eastward expansion had begun.

Initially, small Cossack units would set up an *ostrog* (fortress) at key river junctions. Local tribes would then be compelled to supply Muscovite fur traders, and villages slowly developed. Full-blown colonisation only started during the chaotic Time of Troubles (1606–13) as Russian peasants fled east in great numbers, bringing with them the diseases and alcohol that would subsequently decimate the native population. Meanwhile, settler numbers were swollen by exiled prisoners, and Old Believers seeking religious sanctuary. The construction of the first railways across Siberia in the late 19th century transformed the area. Many of today's cities, such as Novosibirsk in 1893, were founded as the rail lines stretched east.

After the October Revolution of 1917, anti-Bolshevik resistance briefly found a home in Western Siberia, and Omsk was the centre of Admiral Kolchak's White Russia from 1918 to 1919. As the USSR grew into a superpower, the area saw more than its fair share of Stalin's notorious Gulag camps. Nonetheless, unforced colonisation continued apace as patriotic workers and volunteer labourers undertook grandiose engineering projects, such as the construction virtually from scratch of Novokuznetsk.

Since the USSR's collapse in 1991, certain settlements built with Soviet disregard for economic logic have withered into gloomy virtual ghost towns. In contrast, discoveries of vast oil and gas deposits in the area have proven Russia's greatest economic asset, something reflected in the all-too-visible construction projects in cities across the region.

TYUMEN & OMSK REGIONS

The highlight of the Tyumen and Omsk regions (Тюменская и Омская Области) is undoubtedly Tobolsk and its charming kremlin, perched high above a ramshackle old town. Tyumen is a bustling Siberian oil city with attractive wooden buildings and restored churches. Its airport could make it a gateway for a cross-Siberia trip.

Tyumen Тюмень

☎3452 / POP 507,000 / ⏰MOSCOW +2HR

Founded in 1586, Tyumen was the first Russian settlement in Siberia. These days the city is the capital of a vast, oil-rich *oblast* (region) stretching all the way to the Arctic Circle. Tyumen has a businesslike drive and youthful bustle, best experienced by strolling through the pedestrianised City Park when the weather is good. There's more than enough here to keep you (mildly) entertained for a day or so, but if you have limited time you'd be much better off seeing Tobolsk instead.

From the fine Trinity Monastery to well beyond the bus station, the main thoroughfare is ul Respubliki. The train station lies around 1km south of ul Respubliki at the end of ul Pervomayskaya.

City maps and bus-route plans are sold at **Knizhny Magazin** (Книжный магазин; Poliklinika Bldg, Privokzalnaya ul 28a; ⏰8.30am-6pm Mon-Sat, 9am-4pm Sun) near the train station and more expensively at **Knizhnaya Stolitsa** (Книжная Столица; ul Respubliki 58; ⏰10am-7pm). They can also be found at newspaper kiosks throughout the city.

Sights

Trinity Monastery MONASTERY

(Троицкий монастырь; ul Kommunisticheskaya 10) Riverside Trinity Monastery is undoubtedly Tyumen's most appealing architectural complex. Its kremlin-style crenellated outer wall is pierced by a single gate tower. Behind, black and gold domes top the striking 1727 **Peter & Paul Church**, whose soaring interior is emphasised by a giant, seven-level candelabra and decorated with murals.

To get to the monastery, walk west out of the city to the end of ul Respubliki or take bus 14 or 30 from the city centre. Both also stop at the nearby 1791 **Krestovozdvizhenskaya Church** (Крестовоздвиженская церковь; ul Lunacharskogo 1). This attractive church is even more photogenic seen across the ferric-brown river from tree-lined Bergovaya ul with its sprinkling of curiously twisted **old wooden houses** (старые деревянные дома, notably numbers 73 and 53). If the weather is good, it's a pleasant 40-minute walk back into the centre of town from the monastery.

City Park PARK
Take a stroll in the City Park (Svetnoi Bulvar) with all the students, new mums and roller skaters. If you get peckish, grab a snack from one of the many fast-food stalls and cafés. The park also contains a big wheel and other fairground attractions.

Znamensky Cathedral CHURCH
(Знаменский собор; ul Semakova 13) With its voluptuously curved baroque towers, the 1786 Znamensky Cathedral is the most memorable of a dozen 'old' churches that have recently come back to life following years of neglect.

Saviour's Church CHURCH
(Спасская церковь; ul Lenina 41) Saviour's Church is structurally similar to Znamensky, but unfortunately lacks the quiet backstreet location.

Archangel Mikhail Church CHURCH
(Храм Михаила Архангела; ul Turgeneva) The attractive Archangel Mikhail Church sits at the top of a hill leading down to streets full of even more old wooden houses.

Fine Arts Museum MUSEUM
(Музей изобразительного искусства; ul Ordzhonikidze 47; admission R270; ⏲10am-6pm Tue-Sun) The Fine Arts Museum has an impressive and eclectic collection, ranging from ornate window frames saved from the city's old wooden houses to tiny, intricately carved bone figures produced by Siberian artists. Also puts on some impressive one-off exhibitions.

Lovers Bridge BRIDGE
(Мост влюблённых; ul Kommunisticheskaya) A short walk from the monastery on the way back into town, Lovers Bridge is a local landmark covered in appropriately romantic graffiti. Some guy called Sasha had just declared his everlasting love for a certain Katya when we were in town (the paint was still wet!).

WWII Monument MONUMENT
(ul Kommunisticheskaya) Opposite Lovers Bridge, this unusual WWII monument features a Soviet woman piercing the heart of a winged reptilian creature. The embodiment of evil, we assume.

Civil War Monument MONUMENT
(Монумент в честь Гражданской войны; ul Respubliki) To the right of Selskhoz Academy (Сельсхоз Академия), this monument is dedicated to locals who died during battles against the Western-backed White Army immediately after the 1917 Bolshevik revolution.

Lenin Statue MONUMENT
(Памятник Ленину; Tsentralnaya pl) Flanked by the sturdy buildings of the Tyumen Oblast **Parliament** (Дом Советов) and the **former House of Soviets** (Бывший Дом Советов), now a local government administrative building, Lenin gazes down on skateboarders in the summer months.

House-Museum of 19th- & 20th-Century History MUSEUM
(Музей истории дома XIX-XX вв; ul Respubliki 18; admission R100; ⏲9.30am-4.30pm Tue-Sun) This museum contains artefacts from Tyumen's past and is housed in the city's finest carved cottage. For more examples of wooden houses, take a walk along ul Turgeneva.

Sleeping

Many hotels in Tyumen will only accept foreigners if they have booked in advance via an officially recognised travel agency. The hotels listed below are willing to accept independent, foreign travellers, and all offer complimentary breakfasts.

TOP CHOICE **Hotel Vostok** HOTEL €€
(Гостиница Восток; ☎205 350; www.vostok-tmn.ru; ul Respubliki 159; s/tw R3150/3350; 📶) This former Soviet monstrosity has seen a massive facelift (inside, at least) and now boasts modern, plush rooms with friendly, helpful staff. Within walking distance of the centre.

Hotel Tura HOTEL €€
(Гостиница Тура; ☎/fax 282 209; www.hotel-tura.ru; ul Melnikayte 103a; s/tw/d R2400/2950/3600) This compact hotel near the Vostok has pleasant, if slightly anonymous, rooms with

Tyumen

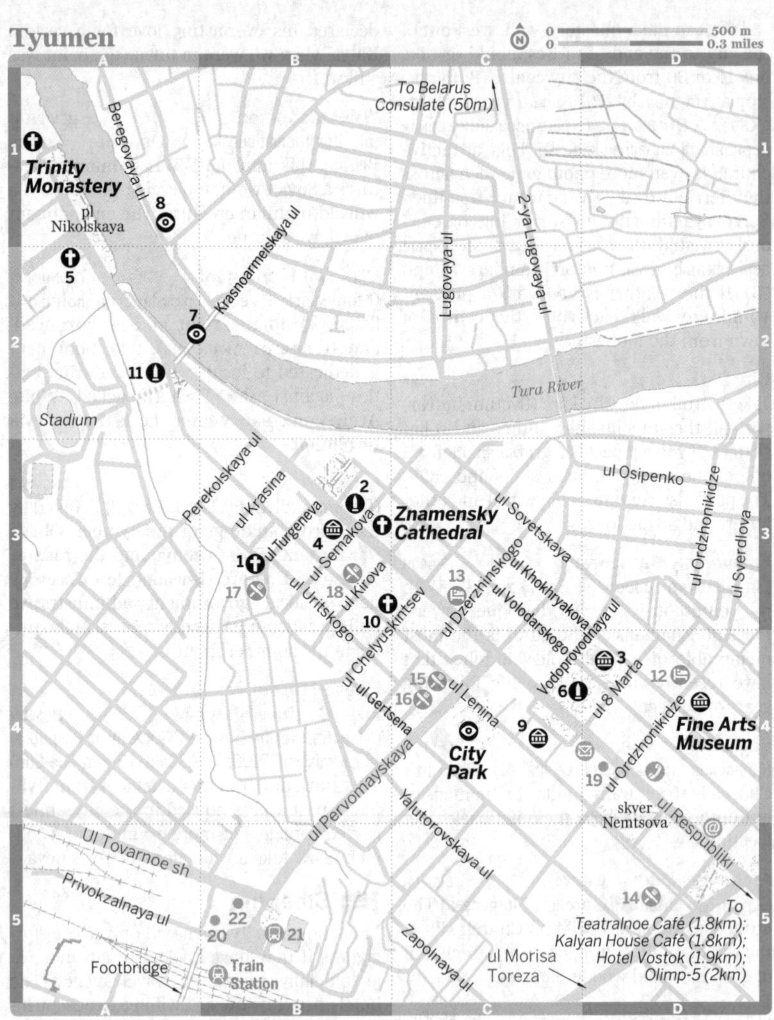

shower booths. Also has a small sports bar (beer R70 to R110).

Hotel Tyumen LUXURY HOTEL €€€
(Гостиница Тюмень; ☎494 040; www.hoteltyumen.ru/en; ul Ordzhonikidze 46; s/d R6500/8700; ❄📶) Tyumen's top hotel offers everything you would expect at a price to match. The complimentary breakfast is one you'll want to linger over.

Prezident Hotel HOTEL €€€
(Президент Отель; ☎/fax 494 747; ul Respubliki 33; s/d/ste R3200/4000/5500; ❄📶) Central and sleek, the Prezident's rooms are fully equipped, but lack a certain charm. If you want to splash out on a hotel, you'd be much better off staying at Hotel Tyumen.

Olimp-5 HOTEL €€
(Олимп-5; ☎273 667; www.olimp5.info/en; ul Respubliki 204; s/d R2300/2900; 📶) This heavily advertised hotel is some way from the centre. Rooms are modest but sufficient and there is free wi-fi in the 1st-floor café. Take bus 15 (25 minutes) from the central market to the Воровского bus stop near a red-and-white Lukoil filling station. From here, it's an obvious five-minute walk down a side street. Or take a taxi for R250.

Tyumen

Top Sights
City Park ... C4
Fine Arts Museum ... D4
Trinity Monastery ... A1
Znamensky Cathedral ... B3

Sights
1 Archangel Mikhail Church ... B3
2 Civil War Monument ... B3
3 Former House of Soviets ... D4
4 House-Museum of 19th- & 20th-Century History ... B3
5 Krestovozdvizhenskaya Church ... A2
6 Lenin Statue ... C4
7 Lovers Bridge ... A2
8 Old Wooden Houses ... A1
9 Parliament ... C4
10 Saviour's Church ... B3
11 WWII Monument ... A2

Sleeping
12 Hotel Tyumen ... D4
13 Prezident Hotel ... C3

Eating
14 Central Market ... D5
15 Cherry Orchard ... C4
16 Malina Bar ... C4
17 Yerevan ... B3
18 Yermolaev ... B3

Information
19 Knizhnaya Stolitsa ... D4
20 Knizhny Magazin ... B5

Transport
Buses to Centre ... (see 5)
21 Buses to Centre from Train Station ... B5
22 UtAir Aerokassa ... B5

Resting rooms HOSTEL €
(комнаты отдыха, komnaty otdykha; s/d from R300/500) Some way from the centre, Tyumen's clean and functional resting rooms are not ideal for the sights.

Eating & Drinking

TOP CHOICE **Yermolaev** RUSSIAN €€
(Ермолаев; www.ermolaev72.ru; ul Kirova 37; meals R450-950; noon-1am) This spacious bar-restaurant is done up in a wooden, rustic style and serves filling traditional Russian meals. The Siberian mushroom soup (R165) is recommended, as is the *kvas* (a drink of fermented rye bread water). Also has a large selection of beers (R100 to R190), including some home-brewed options, plus genuine Cuban cigars (from R1100). Check out the summer garden if the weather is good.

Malina Bar BAR €€
(Малина Бар; ul Pervomayskaya 18; meals R400-800; 24hr; wi-fi) Opposite the City Park, the trendy Malina Bar is popular with a young crowd and their laptops. The eclectic menu runs from Italian food to sushi to pancakes. Also offers a good range of teas, wines, and beers (R120 to R250).

Cherry Orchard CAFÉ €€
(Вишневый Сад; ul Lenina 46; meals R400-800) The flowery Cherry Garden offers pastries, Italian food and sushi along with real English ales (R120 to R250) in a cosy building just down from the City Park.

Kalyan House Café CAFÉ €
(Кальян Хаус; ul Respubliki 155a; meals R300-500; 24hr; wi-fi) Near the Vostok hotel, this spacious café does great breakfasts (R99) and has free wi-fi round-the-clock. Specialises in flavoured water pipes (from R700).

Teatralnoe Café CAFÉ €
(Театральное Кафе; ul Respubliki 36/1; meals R350-550) This refined theatre-themed café features tasty cakes, warming soups and a wide selection of teas and coffee.

Yerevan RUSSIAN, CAUCASIAN €€
(Ереван; ul Turgeneva 19; meals R500-800; menu) Opposite the Archangel Mikhail Church, the Yerevan restaurant is located in a cosy, renovated cellar and offers a choice of Russian, European and south Caucasus food. Worth popping into if you get peckish while walking back into town from Trinity Monastery.

Information

Main post office (Почтамт; ul Respubliki 56; 8am-8pm Mon-Sat, 9am-6pm Sun)

Telephone office (Тюмень Телеком; ul Respubliki 51; per 30min R40; 24hr)

Tyumen.ru (www.tyumen.ru) Has air and railway timetables plus information on local weather, cinema listings etc.

Web Khauz (Хауз; ul Respubliki 61; per hr R70; 11am-8pm) Down the stairs to the left; follow the blue signs.

Getting There & Away

Air

There are five daily flights to Moscow (R6500 to R8800, three hours) and two direct flights a week to St Petersburg (R8600, 3½ hours ,Thursday and Sunday). There are also international connections to Baku (from R12,000, daily) and Munich (from R13,000, Tuesday and Friday). Tickets are sold by **UtAir Aerokassa** (☎453 131; ul Pervomayskaya 58a; ⌚8am-8pm) opposite the train station and by **Transagenststvo** (Трансагентство; ul Respubliki 156; ⌚8am-8pm), which also sells train tickets.

Bus

From the **bus station** (ul Permyakova), 3km east of the centre, seven daily buses to Tobolsk (R450, five hours) travel via Pokrovskoe (R150, 1¾ hours).

Train

Useful overnight rail connections include Omsk (*platskart/kupe* R880/1824, 8½ hours, 10.19pm), Barnaul (R1400/3500, 29 hours, 2.55pm) and Kazan (R1240/3149, 20 hours, 6.24pm). Seven daily trains (4½ hours) serve Tobolsk. The most convenient leaves at 7.10am (R569/1127). The ticket offices are just inside the entrance to the newly renovated **station**, on the right.

Getting Around

Tyumen's **Roshchino Airport** (☎496 450; www.roshino.askar.ru) is 30km west of the centre. Take *marshrutka* 35 (R50, 40 minutes) from outside Transagenststvo, which leaves within 20 minutes of the first passenger getting aboard. Taxis to the city centre cost around R500, depending on your haggling skills.

From the train station, bus 25 serves Hotel Vostok and passes near the bus station – hop off at the Neptun/Stroitel stop, walk a block east and cross the big cloverleaf junction of ul Permyakova and ul Respubliki. Taxis between the bus and train stations cost R150.

Bus 13 from the train station loops around to the **Hotel Neftyanik** (Гостиница Нефтяник); switch to frequent buses 30 or 14 in front of the Prezident Hotel for Trinity Monastery. These follow ul Respubliki westbound but return along ul Lenina.

Tobolsk Тобольск

☎3456 / POP 101,000 / ⌚MOSCOW +2HR

Once Siberia's capital, Tobolsk is one of the region's most historic cities, sporting a magnificent kremlin and a charmingly decrepit old town. Tobolsk is off the trans-Siberian main line but direct overnight trains to both Yekaterinburg and Omsk make getting here straightforward.

The centre of the Russian colonisation of Siberia, Tobolsk was founded in 1587. Its strategic importance started to wane in the 1760s, when it was bypassed by the new Great Siberian Trakt (post road). However, until the early 20th century it remained significant as a centre for both learning and exile. Involuntary guests included Fyodor Dostoevsky en route to exile in Omsk, and deposed Tsar Nicholas II, who spent several doomed months here in 1917.

Buses from the inconvenient train station (some 10km north) give visitors a dismal first impression. Concrete drabness reaches a glum centre around Hotel Slavyanskaya, but don't be put off. Tobolsk's glories begin 3km further south around the splendid kremlin. Immediately beyond and below the kremlin, the old town sinks into the Irtysh's boggy floodplain. The initial view of the old town has been spoiled slightly in recent years by the construction of new office and apartment buildings, but it's still well worth a wander for the views of the kremlin alone.

Sights

Kremlin HISTORICAL BUILDING
(⌚grounds 8am-8pm) Within the tower-studded 18th-century walls of the kremlin are the intriguing but disused **Trading Arches** (Гостиный двор) and the glorious 1686 **St Sofia Cathedral** (Софийский собор). Less eye-catching from the outside, but with splendid arched ceiling murals, is the 1746 **Intercession Cathedral** (Покровский собор). Between the two is a 1799 **bell tower**, built for the Uglich bell, which famously signalled a revolt against Tsar Boris Godunov. The revolt failed; in a mad fury, Godunov ordered the bell to be publicly flogged, detongued and banished to Tobolsk for its treacherous tolling. A tatty copy of the bell is displayed in the **Museum of the Spiritual Cultures of Western Siberia** (admission R50; ⌚10am-4pm Wed-Sun), an otherwise entertaining museum within the elegant Arkhiereysky mansion (Архиерейский дом).

Deputy's Palace MUSEUM
(Дворец наместника; admission R150; ⌚10am-6pm Tue-Sun) Just to the right of the kremlin, this 18th-century former administration building houses a museum detailing Tobolsk's time as the capital of Siberia. It features historical artefacts, paintings and documents. There's some English-language info, but you'll get much more out of it with some Russian.

Fine Art Museum MUSEUM
(Музей изобразительного искусства; ul Oktyabrskaya 1; admission R100, video cameras R200;

10am-6pm Wed-Sun) Built in 1887 for the 300th anniversary of the founding of Tobolsk, the Fine Art Museum has a celebrated collection of WWI-era Russian avant-garde canvases. It also has a newly acquired mammoth skeleton and a display of bone carvings.

FREE **Minsalim Folk Trade** ART GALLERY
(240 909; raznoe72@bk.ru; ul Oktyabrskaya 2; 9am-5pm) Minsalim will happily demonstrate how he turns antler fragments into a range of detailed figures, as well as give visitors the low-down on Tobolsk's history and culture. His son and some members of staff speak English.

Tobolsk Rayon Administration Building HISTORICAL BUILDING
(Административный районный центр Тобольска; ul Mira 10) The less eye-catching Tobolsk Rayon Administration Building was the home-in-exile of the last tsar, and where he was reportedly tortured, before his fateful journey to execution in Yekaterinburg.

Pryamskoy Vzvoz LANDMARK
(Прямской Взвоз) Wooden stairs lead beneath the kremlin's Pryamskoy Vzvoz (gatehouse) to the wonderfully dilapidated old town full of weather-beaten churches and angled wooden homes sinking between muddy lanes.

Mendeleyev Mansion HISTORICAL BUILDING
(Дом Менделеева; ul Mira 9) Near the little 1918 **Victory Chapel** (Часовня Победы), where ul Mira and ul Kirova meet at a small square, is the grand Mendeleyev mansion, which once housed the family of the famous scientist.

Archangel Mikhail Church CHURCH
(Церковь Архангела Михаила; ul Lenina 24) The attractive Archangel Mikhail Church has a colourfully restored interior. The character of Tatiana Larina in Pushkin's epic *Eugene Onegin* is said to have been modelled on Natalya Fonvizina, a Decembrist wife who prayed here.

Zachary & Elisabeth Church CHURCH
(Церковь Захария и Елизаветы; ul Bazarnaya pl) The 1759 Zachary & Elisabeth Church, with its soaring black-tipped spires, is extremely photogenic.

Sleeping & Eating

Tobolsk has seen something of a tourist boom in recent years and now has a number of new or refurbished hotels. All of the hotels listed here – with the exception of the Slavyanskaya and the resting rooms – are perfectly located for the kremlin and offer complimentary breakfasts. Despite increased tourism, there is still no restaurant scene to speak of.

TOP CHOICE **Hotel Sibir** HOTEL €€
(Гостиница Сибирь; 222 390; pl Remezova 1; s/tw/ste R2000/2400/3800) Right across from the kremlin, the Sibir's rooms are comfortable and spacious. Rates include a good breakfast, and the cosy 24-hour restaurant (meals R350 to R600, beer R90 to R130) does a mean fish soup (*pokhlebnaya ribnaya;* R120).

Hotel Georgievskaya HOTEL €€
(Гостиница Георгиевская; 246 614; www.hotel-georgievskaya.ru; ul Lenekaya 35; s/d R2600/3500;) Right behind a Dostoyevsky statue, Hotel Georgievskaya has stylish and plush rooms, as well as a sumptuous restaurant (meals R500 to R850, beer R100 to R175).

Hotel Novy Tobol HOTEL €€
(Гостиница Новый Тобол; 246 614; ul Oktyabrskaya 20; s/d R1500/2000) The badly signposted Tobol has sparse but functional rooms with mostly uninspiring views. It's to the left of Hotel Georgievskaya. There's a bowling alley and a disco on the ground level if you get bored.

Resting rooms HOSTEL €
(Комнаты отдыха, komnaty otdykha; 495 222; train station; 12-/24-hr from R125/250) Clean and friendly. The location is utterly impractical for visiting the city, but ideal if you're arriving late or waiting for an early-morning connection. Cheaper singles are without their own toilet.

Hotel Slavyanskaya HOTEL €€€
(Гостиница Славянская; 399 101; www.slavjanskaya.ru; 9-iy Mikro-Rayon, pr Mendeleeva; s/tw/d from R2200/4400/6000;) Astonishingly well appointed for rural Siberia, the big, modern Slavyanskaya has fully Western-standard comforts. Its only disadvantage is the uninspiring new-town location. Offers internet access for R50 an hour in the lobby.

TOP CHOICE **Romanov Restaurant** RUSSIAN €€€
(Ресторан Романов; 399 104; meals R1000-1500; noon-11pm) Housed in Hotel Slavyanskaya, the Romanov restaurant features succulent 19th-century Russian dishes and is furnished with mock period furniture. Also has a family portrait of Russia's last

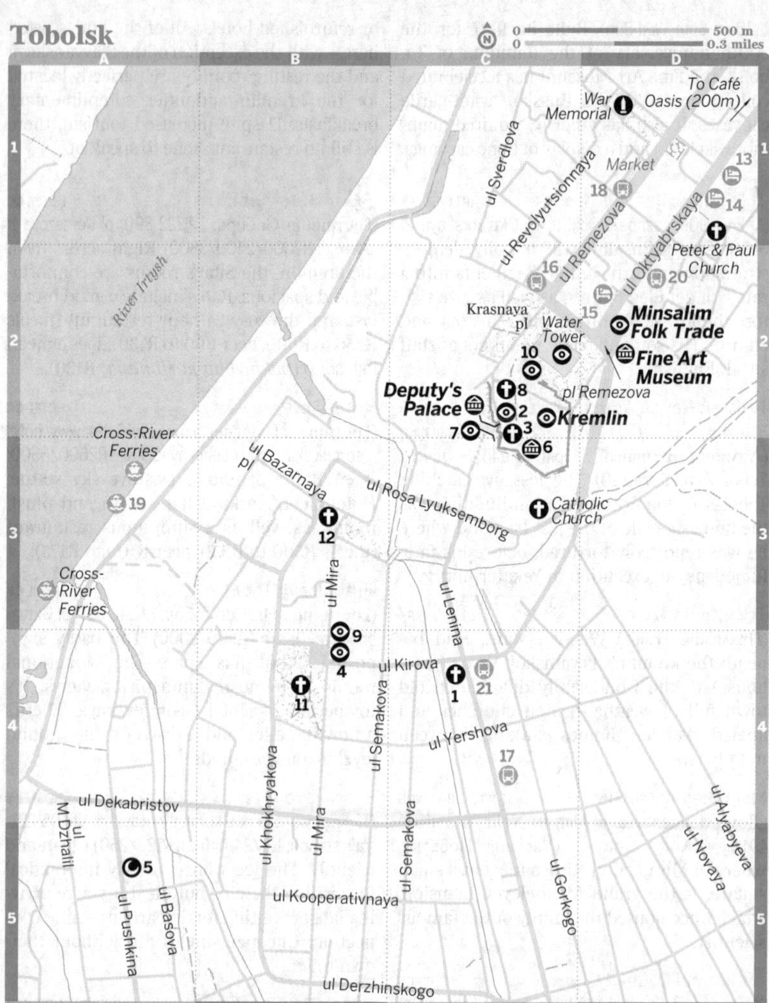

tsar and his family on the ceiling. Dmitry Medvedev visited here shortly after winning Russia's 2008 presidential elections.

Café Oasis CAFÉ €
(Кафе Оазис; ul Oktyabrskaya 44; meals R150-250; ⏲9am-5am) The dark and murky Café Oasis does cheap shashlyk and beers (R60 to R90). Attracts some shady characters as the evening drags on.

ℹ Information

Nashtobolsk.ru (http://Nashtobolsk.ru) Handy info on Tobolsk.

Post office (Почта; Komsomolsky pr 42; ⏲8am-6pm) Has an attached telephone office.

ℹ Getting There & Away

From Tobolsk there are trains at 9.55am and 11.51pm on odd dates to Novosibirsk (*platskart/kupe* R1400/3750 for morning train, R2300/5210 for evening train, both 24 hours). The same train goes to Omsk (R1010/2145, 14 hours).

For Tyumen, over 10 trains a day (*platskart/kupe* R540/1132, four hours) are supplemented by an equal number of daily buses (R450, five hours) via Pokrovskoe (3¼ hours), Rasputin's

Tobolsk

home village. Eight buses per day to various destinations pass Abalak.

Getting Around

Bus 4 and *marshrutka* 20 link the train station, new town and kremlin. Buses 1, 3 and 10 travel past the kremlin and loop around the old town. Bus 1 passes the **mosque** (Мечеть). Taxis from/to the station cost around R200.

Omsk Омск

3812 / POP 1.145 MILLION / MOSCOW +3HR

With its modest sights hidden behind busy roads, this big industrial city is not worth a special detour. You may find it a convenient stopover to break up long journeys.

The trendiest street is **ulitsa Lenina** (Улица Ленина), home to several witty statues including an odd Soviet 1963 'slacker' brass workman and Luba's bench, featuring the wife of a 19th-century city governor reading Pushkin.

If you're looking to kill more time, the **Art Museum** (Омский областной музей изобразительных искусств Врубеля; ul Lenina 23; admission R100; 10am-6pm Tue-Sun) displays a lot of fussy decorative arts. The rectilinear 1862 building, a historical curiosity in itself, was built as the Siberian governor's mansion and hosted passing tsars. In 1918–19, however, the building was home to Admiral Kolchak's counter-revolutionary government. In the gardens behind the museum there is a **war memorial** (Памятник Великой Отечественной войны) and a **Lenin statue** (Памятник Ленину).

Other attractive buildings include the ornate **Drama Theatre** (Омский академический театр драмы; 244 065; www.omskdrama.ru; ul Lenina; cash desk 10am-7pm) and the **Assumption Cathedral** (Успенский собор; pl Lenina), rebuilt after the collapse of the USSR. The Lenin statue that stood nearby was removed in the 2000s – rumour has it a pious official decided the great atheist had no business being anywhere near a house of God.

Sleeping

Hotel Mayak HOTEL €€€
(Гостиница Маяк; /fax 315 431; www.hotel-mayak.ru; ul Lermontova 2; s/tw R2860/4125) In the rounded end of the vaguely ship-shaped art-deco river station, the Mayak has small, stylish rooms with artistic lines and good bathrooms. Popular with Western business travellers. Friendly staff and good complimentary breakfast.

Hotel Turist HOTEL €€
(Отель Турист; 316 419; www.tourist-omsk.ru; ul Broz Tito 2; s/d from R2500/3500) A fairly central address with decent, bright rooms and fine views of the river from upper floors. Complimentary buffet breakfast.

Resting rooms HOSTEL €
(Комнаты Отдыха, komnaty otdykha; train station; s/d R1200/1700) While slightly impractical for the sights, the clean and secure resting rooms should suffice as a base if your time in Omsk is limited. Exit the main station, turn left and find the door before the baggage *kassa* (ticket office).

Eating

TOP CHOICE **Tamada** GEORGIAN €€
(Тамада; ul Gagarina 3; meals R450-800; 10am-midnight;) This extremely friendly, spacious

cellar restaurant serves fine Georgian food amid a setting of fake ponds and vibrant oil paintings. The *khachapuri* (bread baked with cheese filling; R140) and *lobiyo* (spicy red beans stewed in vegetables; R90) are recommended. It's just off ul Lenina in a courtyard. They'll even call a taxi for you when you are ready to – probably reluctantly – leave.

Chashka INTERNATIONAL €€
(Чашка; www.hollcup.ru; 3rd fl, Pyat Zvyozd shopping mall, ul Karla Libknekhta; meals R400-650; 📶) Both cosy and professional, Chashka offers a wide range of dishes from traditional Russian home cooking to reasonably spicy Asian.

Information

Internet Available in the train terminal lobby for R100 per 30 minutes.

Post office (Почтамт; ul Gertsena 1; ⌚8am-7pm Mon-Sat, 10am-5pm Sun)

Getting There & Away

Flight destinations include Moscow (R6500 to R8000, six daily) and St Petersburg (R9400, direct flights on Wednesdays). Numerous air-ticket agencies at the **river station** (Речная станция; pl Bukhgoltsa) sell rail tickets (R150 commission).

There are two trains a day for Tobolsk at 5.54am and 1.24pm (*platskart/kupe* R1300/3100, 13¾ hours), and one a day for Tomsk at 5.42pm (R1450/3900, 14 hours). There are over 15 trains a day to Novosibirsk (R950/2010, 9½ hours).

On a green barge behind the river station is the **Rechflot** (Речфлот; ☎398 563; ⌚9am-7pm) ticket office. Also here is the jetty for hydrofoils to Tevriz via Tara and for ferries cruising the Irtysh River to Salekhard (1st/2nd/3rd class R3750/1750/1300, six days) via Tobolsk (R2100/1000/950, two days) departing roughly three times monthly. Various pleasure cruises depart from a separate jetty near Yubileyny Bridge, notably for Achairsky Monastery (Map p451; R300 return, 4½ hours return, five times daily mid-May to early October).

Getting Around

From the train station, trolleybus 4 and *marshrutka* 335 run along pr Marksa to pl Lenina, past the main post office. Ul Lenina runs parallel to pr Marksa – it's on the left if you are heading into the city. Bus 60 crosses the Irtysh to the **airport** (☎517 570; Inzhenernaya ul 1) while trolleybus 7 or the faster *marshrutka* 366 head for the bus station. Construction began on Omsk's metro system back in 1985, but its opening has been delayed and rescheduled for years.

NOVOSIBIRSK & TOMSK REGIONS

The highlight of the Novosibirsk and Tomsk regions (Новосибирская и Томская области) is the vibrant and attractive student town of Tomsk. Its streets lined with eye-catching wooden houses and boasting a growing number of cafés and restaurants, Tomsk remains one of the – as yet – undiscovered wonders of Siberia.

Novosibirsk Новосибирск

☎383 / POP 1.5 MILLION / ⌚MOSCOW +3HR

It may be the capital of Siberia and Russia's third-biggest city by population size, but there isn't actually very much to see in Novosibirsk. As compensation of sorts, there are a lot of nightclubs and restaurants, and the city has a fairly lively music scene.

Novosibirsk grew up in the 1890s around the Ob River bridge built for the Trans-Siberian Railway. Named Novo-Nikolaevsk until 1925 for the last tsar, it grew rapidly into Siberia's biggest metropolis, a key industrial and transport centre exploiting coalfields to the east and mineral deposits in the Urals.

Despite its daunting scale, Novosibirsk has a manageably simple centre focused on pl Lenina. The city's main axis, Krasny pr, runs through this square linking most points of interest. **Dom Knigi** (Дом книги; Krasny pr 51; ⌚10am-8pm Mon-Sat, to 7pm Sun) has a good range of maps.

Sights

Opera & Ballet Theatre THEATRE
(Театр оперы и балета) Novosibirsk's pl Lenina is dominated by the huge, silver-domed Opera & Ballet Theatre. Bigger than Moscow's Bolshoi, its grand interior alone makes performances one of the city's highlights. In front, wearing a flapping coat, the dashing **Lenin statue** (Памятник Ленину) is flanked by waving partisans vainly trying to direct the chaotic traffic.

Local Studies Museum MUSEUM
(Краеведческий музей; Krasny pr 23; admission R250; ⌚10am-5.30pm Tue-Sun) In an elegant mansion, the Local Studies Museum has Altai shaman coats, cutaway pioneer houses and some splendid religious artefacts.

State Art Museum MUSEUM
(Художественный музей; Krasny pr 5; adult/student R180/100; ⌚10am-5.20pm Tue-Fri, from 11am Sat & Sun) The State Art Museum has an extensive collection including icons, Siberian art and works by celebrated spiritual Russian painter Nikolai Rerikh (Nicholas Roerich).

WWII 'Family' Statues MONUMENTS
Platform 1 at the main train station boasts two WWII 'family' statues depicting a mother and her small daughter and a father and his small son waving off relatives to WWII – it was from this station that many Siberians went directly to the front.

Chapel of St Nicholas CHURCH
(Часовня Святителя Николая; Krasny pr) The pretty little Chapel of St Nicholas was said to mark the geographical centre of Russia when it was built in 1915. Demolished in the 1930s, it was rebuilt in 1993 for Novosibirsk's centenary. Today it is an oasis of calm in the bustling city centre.

Cathedral of the Ascension CHURCH
(Вознесенский собор; ul Sovetskaya 91) The gold-domed 1914 Cathedral of the Ascension has a wonderful, colourful interior with a soaring central space that's unexpected from its fairly squat exterior appearance.

Alexander Nevsky Cathedral CHURCH
(Собор Александра Невского; Krasny pr 1a) The 1898 Alexander Nevsky Cathedral is a red-brick Byzantine-style building with gilded domes and colourful murals.

Monument to First Traffic Light MONUMENT
(cnr ul Serebrennikovskaya & ul Sibrevkoma) This humorous monument is based at the rumoured site of the city's first ever traffic light.

Sleeping

The majority of Novosibirsk hotels are poor value by Siberian standards. On top of this, many will only accept foreigners when booked through a tour agency (incurring booking fees and commission).

TOP CHOICE **Avenue** MINIHOTEL €€
(Авеню; ☎227 0534; www.avenu.vipngs.ru; ul Sovetskaya 57; s/d R3400/3600; 📶) Set in a quiet, leafy residential courtyard, this mini-hotel is by far the best place to stay in Novosibirsk. Just a 10-minute walk away from the centre, all the great-value rooms are spacious, stylish and comfortable. Also has free wi-fi, a sauna for rent (R600 per hour) and a good complimentary breakfast. And staff are friendly to boot!

Hotel Novosibirsk HOTEL €€€
(Гостиница Новосибирск; ☎220 1120; fax 216 517; www.hotel-novosibirsk.ru; Vokzalnaya magistral 1; s/tw/ste R3960/4410/8100) Boasting awesome views of the city centre from its upper floors, this formerly glum Soviet-era tower has been transformed in recent years into a plush modern hotel. An odd pricing scheme means it's possible (we managed it) to get two nights for the price of one if you arrive after midnight for the first night. The complimentary breakfast is tasty and filling.

Resting rooms HOSTEL €
(Комнаты Отдыха, komnaty otdykha; ☎229 2376; 2nd fl, Novosibirsk Glavny station; 12-/24-hr from R550/1100) As clean and pleasant as you could reasonably expect. It's frequently full.

Hotel Tsentralnaya HOTEL €
(Гостиница Центральная; ☎222 3638; fax 227 660; ul Lenina 3; s/tw without bathroom R1300/1600) The cheapest rooms here are depressing cupboard-like hovels, while the more expensive options are no less welcoming. No complimentary breakfast, either. That said, it is centrally located. And relatively cheap. For Novosibirsk, at least.

Eating & Drinking

TOP CHOICE **Perchini** ITALIAN €
(Перчини; www.perchini.ru; Krasny pr 25/1; meals R350-400; ⌚10am-1am; 📶📝) If all the *pelmeni* (Russian-style ravioli) and pancakes are getting you down, visit Perchini. With a choice of seven freshly made pastas to choose from and a range of imaginative sauces, this simple yet effective restaurant is popular with a young, hip crowd. Just behind the Ploshchad Lenina metro station, on the 4th floor.

Tiflis CAUCASIAN €€
(Тифлис; www.tiflisnsk.ru; ul Sovetskaya 65; meals R400-800; 📝) This atmospheric tavern-cavern offers the most authentic Georgian cuisine in town. The filling and delicious *khachapuri po-adzharski* (Georgian cheese bread with a raw egg swimming in the middle) is well worth a try.

Pechki-Lavochki RUSSIAN €
(Печки-Лавочки; ul Frunze 2; meals R250-450) Rustic interior and traditional Russian food at great prices. Try the *kvas*. Can get smoky and noisy in the evenings (beer from R75).

Novosibirsk

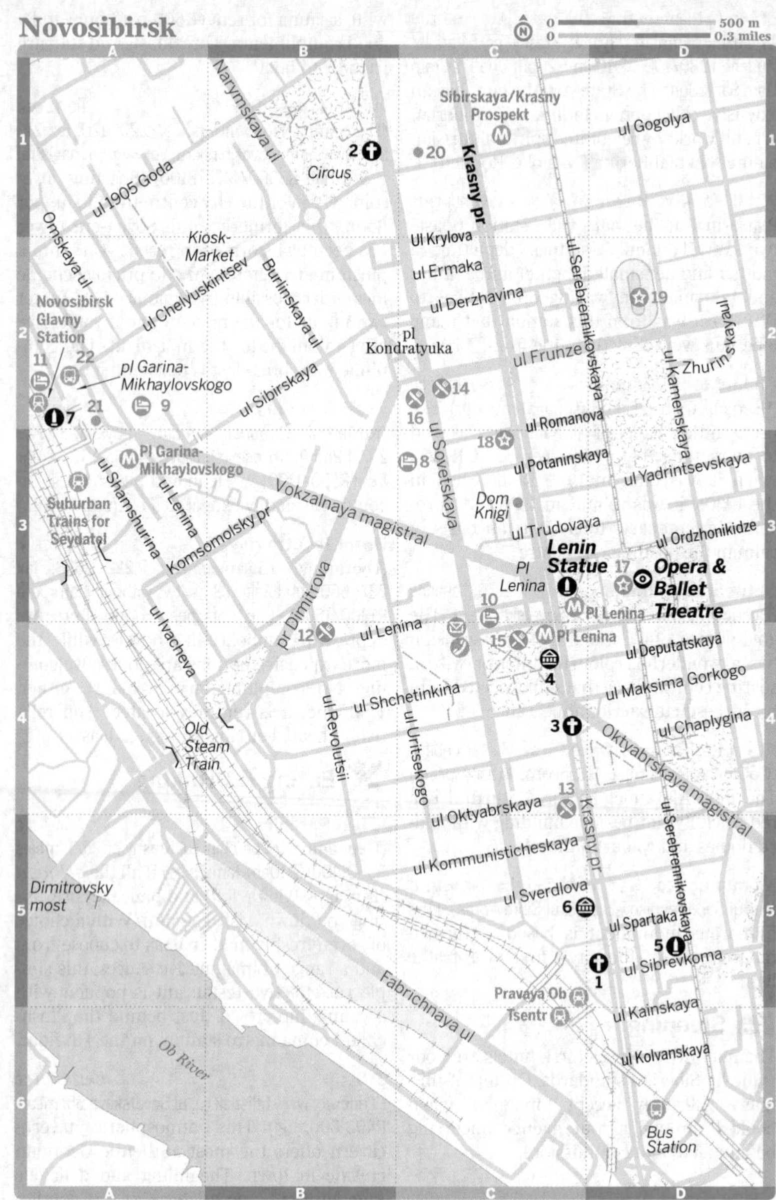

Café Bliss BREAKFAST €

(ul Lenina 20) This modestly named café does great pancakes (from R50) and fresh juices as well as good breakfast deals (R150). A nice way – and place – to start the day.

5Nizza BAR €

(5Ницца; ul Lenina 3; beer R90-150, snacks R70-130; ⏲noon-2am) Sharing its name with a popular Moscow reggae group, this lively bar is on the 1st floor of Hotel Tsentralnaya.

Novosibirsk

Nikolaevskaya Pelmennaya RUSSIAN €
(Николаевская Пельменная; Krasny pr 13; meals R150-210; ⌚10am-11pm) Cheap and simple *pelmeni* with meat and fish fillings in an equally modest café located beneath a sex shop.

Entertainment

Opera & Ballet Theatre THEATRE
(Новосибирский государственный академический театр оперы и балета; ☎227 1537; www.opera-novosibirsk.ru; Krasny pr 36; admission R200-4000; ⌚Oct-Jun) For classical culture don't miss an evening at this gigantic theatre. Ticket prices depend on seats and performances. Morning shows are a lot cheaper.

Spartak Stadium SPORTS
(Стадион Спартак; ☎217 0474; www.fc-sibir.ru; ul Frunze 15) This 12,500-capacity venue is the home of local football team, Sibir. Games are usually played on Saturday, and tickets cost from R200 to R700. Matches are advertised on posters around the city.

Rock City NIGHTCLUB
(Рок Сити; ☎227 0108; www.rockcity.ru; 3rd fl, Krasny pr 37; tickets from R350; ⌚from noon) Novosibirsk's top spot for everything from Latin dancing to heavy-rock concerts. It's above the Old Irish pub.

Information

Main post office (Главпочтамт; ul Lenina 5; ⌚8am-9pm Mon-Fri, to 7pm Sat & Sun)
Telephone office (Междугородный телефонный пункт; ul Sovetskaya 33; ⌚24hr)

Getting There & Away

Air

Novosibirsk's **Tolmachyovo Airport** (☎216 9841; http://en.tolmachevo.ru) is 30km west of the city, off the Omsk road. There are a number of direct daily flights to Moscow (from R6000 to R10,000), as well as five direct flights a week to St Petersburg (from R9000). If you book around four weeks in advance, air tickets from Moscow to Novosibirsk can sometimes cost around R5000 – cheaper than the train. See www.airtickets24.com/en.

Regular international destinations include Beijing, Bangkok, Dubai, Munich, Frankfurt, Prague and Seoul, plus several cities in Central Asia (eg Tashkent, R14,000). The central **Aviakassa** (Авиакасса; ul Gogolya 3; ⌚8.30am-8pm) is one of dozens of places to buy air tickets.

Bus

From the **bus station** (Автовокзал; Krasny pr 4) around 20 daily buses serve both Barnaul (R450, 4¾ hours) and Tomsk (R420, five hours). For roughly double the price, shared taxis shave an hour or more off those times.

Train

The city's huge main train station, **Novosibirsk Glavny** (ul Shamshurina 43), has numerous daily long-distance trains.

For Moscow (48 to 55 hours via Omsk, Tyumen and Yekaterinburg), comfortable train 25 (*platskart/kupe* R5400/12,000, 6.40am, on even-numbered days) is also one of the fastest. The much cheaper 239 (R4600/8400, 5.17am, odd-numbered days) takes six hours longer and isn't quite as comfortable. For Krasnoyarsk, train 12 (R1750/3680, 10.20pm, 11 hours, odd-numbered days) is well timed.

For Altai, there is a daily train to Biysk (R720/1490, 5.45pm, 10 hours) via Barnaul (5½ hours). For Khakassia and Tuva you could take the direct, daily train to Abakan (R1400/3130, 3.26am, 23 hours), or in two overnight hops via Novokuznetsk, for which the best option is train 605 (R767/1141, 10.22pm, eight hours).

Between one and two trains a day run from Novosibirsk to Almaty, the former capital of Kazakhstan (*platskart/kupe* R2470/4000, 40 hours) and two times a week to/from Beijing (R2844/4895, four days and three hours, Monday and Thursday) via Ulaanbaatar, Mongolia.

Getting Around

From the train station, take trolleybus 2 to Severny airport (Тролейбус 2 в Северный аэропорт), *marshrutka* 1122 to Tolmachyovo airport or *marshrutka* 1212 for the bus station via pl Lenina. The metro (trip ticket R12) has a major north–south line running beneath Krasny pr and across the river to ul Studencheskaya and pl Karla Marksa. For the main train station you'll need metro stop Ploshchad Garina-Mikhaylovskogo, which is on a second three-stop line that intersects with the major line at Sibirskaya/Krasny Prospekt. Generally, *marshrutky* are handier within the centre. A **taxi** (☎299 4646) to the airport can be ordered by phone and costs around R500. The journey from the centre takes about 30 to 40 minutes, depending on traffic.

Akademgorodok & Seyatel
Академгородок и Сеятель

Akademgorodok suburbs were elite Soviet academic townships full of research institutes. Attached to most Siberian cities, they attracted scientists by offering special perks and relatively spacious apartments in peaceful surroundings. Nearly 30km south of central Novosibirsk, Siberia's biggest Akademgorodok nestles in taiga close to the beaches of the so-called Ob Sea (in fact a large, narrow lake). The idea is interesting, but the reality is somewhat frustrating for tourists. Although most institutes have 'museums', most are only for invited academics. A potentially brilliant **open-air museum** (ul Benulusku-Bodoni 35) some 4km along the Akademgorodok–Klyuchi road contains a superb Yakutian wooden church and partly restored *ostrog* (fortress) but you can only glimpse them through the high, locked gates.

However, if you feel like lazing around on the beach or wandering in the taiga then you could stay at the cosy and good-value **Zolotaya Dolina** (www.gold-valley.ru; ul Ilyicha 10; s/d R2100/3300). The hotel has no problems with registering foreigners either.

For Seyatel, jump off *marshrutka* 1015 at the *elektrichka* (suburban train) station of the same name, 2km before Akademgorodok beside an interesting **Railway Locomotive Museum** (Музей железнодорожной техники; www.parovoz.com; admission R80; ⏲11am-5pm Sat-Thu).

Marshrutka 1015 (R30, 30 minutes) from Novosibirsk Glavny train station passes the Railway Museum then loops anticlockwise around Akademgorodok. Returning to central Novosibirsk from Seyatel is easier by hourly *elektrichki* (R40) or bus 622. Bus 7 links Akademgorodok with Seyatel station (east of the rail tracks).

Tomsk
Томск

☎3822 / POP 524,000 / ⏲MOSCOW +3HR

Hip and friendly Tomsk is the kind of town where it's no surprise to come across a gigantic and inexplicable Tom Waits poster on the main street (pr Lenina). It's a university city with half a dozen major academic establishments, and around one in every five residents of Tomsk is a student – hence the youthful, intellectual atmosphere.

One of Siberia's oldest cities, Tomsk was founded in 1604 and was a major trade outpost before the founding of Novosibirsk (then Novo-Nikolaevsk) and the subsequent relocation of the trans-Siberian railway line.

Magnificent in snow, but pleasant at any time of the year, Tomsk also boasts endless examples of fine wooden buildings and an animated café and art scene. The city has enjoyed the reputation as the 'cultural capital of Siberia' since the 1960s, when artists, writers and theatre and film directors were invited to take up residence here.

Tomsk is also excellent for strolls: try exploring the numerous side streets that branch off the central pr Lenina to discover some truly memorable buildings and river views.

The bus station and Tomsk 1 (main) train station sit together about 2km southeast of the centre. **Dom Knigi** (Дом книги; pr Komsomolsky 49; ⏲10am-7pm Mon-Fri, 11am-6pm Sat & Sun) sells excellent city maps.

Sights

Ploshchad Lenina HISTORICAL SITE

Central pl Lenina isn't really a square so much as a jumbled collection of beautifully restored historic buildings interspersed with banal Soviet concrete lumps. The frustrated **Lenin statue** (Памятник Ленину), now relegated to a traffic circle, points at the ugly concrete of the Drama Theatre, apparently demanding 'build more like that one'. Fortunately, nobody's listening. The theatre is flanked instead by the splendid 1784 **Epiphany Cathedral** (Богоявленский собор), the **former trading arches** (Бывший Гостиный Двор) and the elegant 1802 Hotel Magistrat. Topped with a golden angel, in a second circle beside Lenin, is the recently rebuilt **Iverskaya Chapel** (Иверская часовня; ⌚10am-6pm), whose celebrated icon is dubbed 'Tomsk's Spiritual Gateway'.

TOP CHOICE **Oppression Museum** MUSEUM
(Музей НКВД; ☎516 133; rear entrance, pr Lenina 44; admission R30; ⌚9am-6pm Mon-Fri) A former NKVD (proto-KGB) prison, this gloomy building is now a memorable Oppression Museum. Tours are recommended, but are only in Russian. Failing that you can just wander round yourself. Look out for the stunning Gulag map, the system of Soviet labour camps depicted as an uncountable mass of red dots across the territory of the former USSR. Outside the museum there are two **monuments to victims of Stalinist repression** – the larger to local victims, the second to Poles slaughtered by Uncle Joe and his cronies.

TOP CHOICE **Chekhov Statue** MONUMENT
On the riverbank, opposite Slavyansky Bazar restaurant, this cheeky Chekhov statue was sculpted in bronze for the 400th anniversary of the city's founding.

WWII Memorial MONUMENT
A Tomsk landmark, this moving mother-and-son monument is at the very southern end of pr Lenina. The beautiful birch tree park (Лагерный сад) here is a local favourite for strolls, not least for its fine views across the Tom River.

University HISTORICAL BUILDING
(Томский Государственный Университет) The classically colonnaded main buildings of the university lie in resplendently leafy grounds, giving Tomsk the sobriquet 'Oxford of Siberia'. There's not much open to the public, but there's nothing to stop you taking a walk around the grounds.

Tomsk Art Gallery ART GALLERY
(Художественный музей; www.artmuseum.tomsk.ru; per Nakhanovicha 5; admission R60; ⌚10am-7.30pm Tue-Sun) Features a wide range of exhibits, from modern art to religious icons.

CHEKHOV ON TOMSK – 'BORING CITY, DULL PEOPLE'

Not everyone falls in love with Tomsk. Playwright Anton Chekhov – who visited the city on his way to Russia's Far East – certainly didn't. 'Tomsk isn't worth a damn,' he wrote in his diary. 'A boring city...with dull people.' He also described it as 'a drunken city' where there were 'no beautiful women at all'. He also complained that a waitress had wiped a spoon 'against her backside' before handing it to him. But then, as legend has it, he did almost drown while crossing the Tom River, so maybe he was feeling grumpy. The city had its revenge though. In 2004, on Tomsk's 400th anniversary, a caricature of the famous writer was unveiled, in the form of a bronze statue entitled 'Anton Pavlovich [the writer's patronymic] through the eyes of a drunk lying in a ditch'.

Atashev Palace HISTORICAL BUILDING
(Краеведческий музей; pr Lenina 75) Built for gold-mining entrepreneur Ivan Atashev in 1842, the Atashev Palace was once used as a church, hence the incongruous steeple tower and wonderful organ hall where concerts are held.

Ulitsa Tatarskaya HISTORICAL AREA
(Деревяные дома, улица Татарская) Contains some fine examples of Tomsk's famed 'wooden-lace' architecture – the carved windows and tracery on old log and timber houses. The street is reached via the steps beside a lovely old house at **prospekt Lenina 56** (пр Ленина 56); shops sell DVDs, seeds and secondhand clothes in its basement.

Ulitsa Gagarina HISTORICAL AREA
Also well worth strolling along – look out for the picturesque **former 'hunter's house'** (Бывший дом охотника) at number 42.

Ulitsa Krasnoarmeyskaya HISTORICAL AREA
Home to some great examples of wooden mansions, including the spired, bright-turquoise **Russian-German House** (Российско-Немецкий Дом; ul Krasnoarmeyskaya 71); the **Dragon House** (Дом Дракона; ul Krasnoarmeyskaya 68), which is home to a clinic; and the fan-gabled **Peacock House** (Дом Павлина; ul Krasnoarmeyskaya 67a). Ul Dzerzhinskogo is worth a look too.

Tomsk

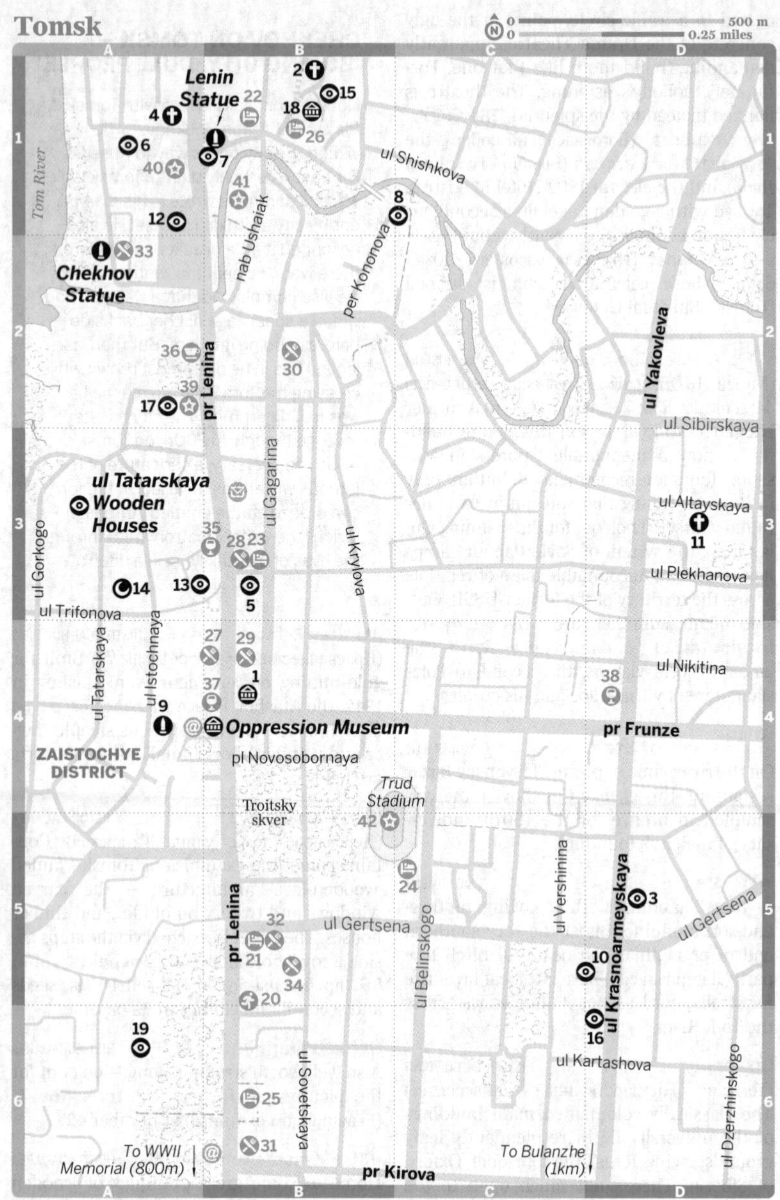

Kirov's House HISTORICAL BUILDING
(Дом Кирова; per Kononova 2) This is where the doomed communist mastermind Sergei Kirov lodged in 1905.

Znameniye bozhyey materi Church CHURCH
(Храм знамения Божьей матери; ul Voykova 14) This attractive church is all the more photogenic for the wooden house that stands alongside it.

Tomsk

Resurrection Hill HISTORICAL AREA

This was the location of Tomsk's original fortress, and the replica of its 'Golden Gate' that stands on it today was built in 2004 for the city's 400th anniversary celebrations.

Tomsk History Museum MUSEUM

(Исторический музей Томска; admission R40; 11am-5pm Tue-Sun) This well-presented museum has resprouted its wooden **lookout tower** (Смотровая башня; admission R35): try to spot the seven historic churches from the top. The stone just outside the museum entrance marks the founding of the city.

Voznesenskaya Church CHURCH

(Вознесенская церковь; ul Oktyabrsky Vzvoz). This Gothic edifice with five gold-tipped black spires has great potential as a Dracula movie set. A truly massive bell hangs in its lurid-pink belfry.

Ozero Beloye Pond POND

(Озеро Белое; ul Bakunina) Popular with mums and kids, students and the odd very optimistic fisherman, this sizeable pond is a good place to chill with a drink and a pie from one of the nearby food stands. On the same street, named after the 19th-century 'father of anarchy' and one-time student in the city, is a **Catholic Church** (Католическая церковь) dating from 1833.

Old Believers' Wooden Church CHURCH

(Деревяная церковь старообрядцев; ul Yakovleva) This cute church is worth a look if you've got any energy left, though its surroundings are relatively uninteresting.

Peter & Paul Cathedral CHURCH

(Петропавловский Собор; ul Altayskaya 47) A Byzantine-style brick cathedral that dates from 1911.

Red Mosque MOSQUE

(Красная Мечеть; ul Tatarskaya 22) This modest mosque, dating from 1904, was used as a vodka factory by the atheist Soviets, but was reopened to worshippers in 1997. The friendly imam is always up for a chat with foreigners.

Tours

Tomskturist TOURS

(Томсктурист; ☎528 179; pr Lenina 59; ⊙9am-7pm Mon-Fri, 11am-4pm Sat) Tomskturist can arrange individual walking tours of the city, with English-, French- and German-speaking guides. It also sells plane and train tickets for a small commission. It's based in a lovely wooden house opposite the university.

Sleeping

TOP CHOICE **Toyan** BOUTIQUE HOTEL €€€

(Тоян; ☎/fax 510 151; www.toyan.ru; ul Obrub 2; s/tw/ste from R3900/5900/6900; 📶) Toyan, built in 2008, is both intensely elegant and laid-back – and well worth splashing out on if your budget will run to it. Rooms are tastefully decorated, somehow managing to be both stylish and homely. The more expensive have great views of central Tomsk. All rooms have wi-fi. The complimentary breakfast isn't bad either!

Bon Apart HOTEL €€€

(Бон Апарт; ☎534 650; www.bon-apart.ru; ul Gertsena 1a; s/tw/ste R3400/4500/5700; ❄) The quiet and professional Bon Apart offers small but plush rooms for reasonable prices. It's centrally located, and the complimentary breakfast in the next-door family restaurant is tasty and satisfying.

Hotel TGU HOSTEL €

(Гостиница ТГУ; ☎534 352; 5th fl, pr Lenina 49; dm/s/tw R600/1000/1500) Uniquely good value, these clean, bright rooms have kettle, fridge and fully equipped new bathrooms (except in the dorms, which share facilities between two triples). Staff are very friendly, to boot. In term-time, reservations are essential (R150 booking fee), but dropping in might work in midsummer. Enter from the rear of the building and climb the stairs to the 5th floor. No lift and no breakfast either. Midnight curfew.

Hotel Siberia HOTEL €€

(Гостиница Сибирь; ☎/fax 527 225; www.hotelsibir.tomsk.ru; pr Lenina 91; s/d/ste R2800/3100/5000) This centrally located old hotel is extremely popular, despite its largely unimaginative singles and doubles. It does, however, offer great suites with real fireplaces for R5500, if you are feeling wealthy. Dinner is available on top of complimentary breakfast for R300 extra, but you'd be better off eating elsewhere.

Hotel Sputnik HOTEL €€

(Гостиница Спутник; ☎526 660; www.sputnik.tomskturist.ru; ul Belinskogo 15; s/d/tw/tr R850/1700/1900/2400; @📶) The winner of Tomsk's first hotel competition in the 1990s, the Sputnik today remains a decent place to stay, let down only by its dodgy plumbing (there was brown sludge coming out of the taps when we stayed) and doors so flimsy that cheers from the nearby stadium could probably knock them down. Complimentary breakfast is hardly worth getting up for. The cheapest singles and doubles have shared toilets. Wi-fi in every room.

Hotel Magistrat HOTEL €€€

(Гостиница Магистрат; ☎511 111; fax 511 200; www.magistrathotel.com; pl Lenina 15; s/d/ste R5500/6500/9500; ❄📶) Behind the palatial 1802 facade, the luxurious rooms are brand new in a comfortable international style though, sadly, without historical idiosyncrasies. English is spoken and the restaurant is lavish.

Resting rooms HOSTEL €

(Комнаты Отдыха, komnaty otdykha; Tomsk I train station; 3hr s/tw R400/R700) Perfectly clean rooms with shared toilets, and shower and TVs. Curfew 1am to 5am.

Eating

TOP CHOICE **Slavyansky Bazar** RUSSIAN €€€

(Славянский Базар; pr Lenina 10; meals R800-1200; 📶) On the bank of the Tom River, Slavyansky Bazar is one of the most upmarket restaurants in the city, housed in a 19th-century building. Black caviar dishes start at R800. Chekhov ate at an earlier incarnation of the present-day establishment in 1890. The food was one of the few things he liked about the city.

TOP CHOICE **Coffee House Leto Café** CAFÉ €

(Кофейная Лето; ul Gagarina 2; meals R300-500; 🖉) One-half of a bright yellow building that also contains a decent sushi restaurant, Bamboo (Бамбук). Sunny and bright and features food with hard-to-get ingredients such as pumpkin, pesto and real feta cheese. Also does real coffee.

Café Fondue CAFÉ €

(Кафе Фондю; ul Belentsa 14; meals R300-500; ⊙noon-1am Sun-Thu, to 2am Fri & Sat) This small and welcoming café was conceived of during the unlikely fondue craze that swept Russia in the mid-2000s. Serves cheese and chocolate fondue options, as well as more traditional Russian and European dishes. Just off pr Lenina 97.

Café Modern EUROPEAN €

(Кафе Модернь; pr Lenina 83; meals R400-600;) An atmospheric café with painstakingly restored plasterwork tracery on the high ceilings and Gustav Klimt prints on the walls. European menu, with large selections of salads, pastries, desserts, teas, wines (from R75 a glass) and beer (R75 to R120).

Vechny Zov RUSSIAN €€

(Вечный Зов; www.vechzov.tomsk.ru; ul Sovetskaya 47; meals R550-900; ⊙noon-4am) Named after a popular Soviet TV serial, this is one of Tomsk's top dining options and boasts a mock Siberian ranch outside and a cosy antique-filled home feel inside.

Obzhorni Ryad RUSSIAN €

(Обжорний Ряд; ul Gertsena 1; meals R250-400; ⊙11am-11pm) Next to the Bon Apart hotel is this good-value family restaurant, whose name translates as Guzzler's Row. The indoor adventure playground means it's great for those with kids, but anyone else might find all the noise distracts from the simple but tasty Russian dishes.

Korchma U Tarasa UKRAINIAN €

(Корчма у Тараса; pr Lenina 51; meals R250-450; ⊙noon-1am) This cheap and friendly café specialises in Ukrainian favourites such as *salo* (salted pig fat; R95 a plate) and borsch (R70). It's a pick-and-mix kind of place, but there's not much for vegetarians.

Inzhir ASIAN €€

(Инжир; pr Kirova 66; meals R400-750) Right opposite the train station, Inzhir (Fig) offers a variety of Eastern food, from Uzbek dumplings to Turkish kebabs. Often full in the evening.

Babulini Pelmeshki RUSSIAN €

(Бабулины Пельмешки; pr Lenina 54; ⊙10am-8pm) The cheap and satisfying *pelmeni* and *vareniki* (dumplings; R50 to R130) in this basement café come with a range of fillings, from lamb and fish to cheese and cherry. Look out for the cardboard cut-out of a babushka on the street.

Drinking

TOP CHOICE **Jazz Café** CAFÉ, BAR

(Кафе Джаз; www.jazz-cafe.tomsk.ru; pr Lenina 46; beer R100-250; ⊙11am-midnight Sun-Thu, noon-2am Fri & Sat;) A hip and literally underground basement hang-out with an extensive drinks and food menu (meals R500 to R700). We liked the vegetarian borsch (R90) and the screenings of old black-and-white films. Live jazz, including frequent US guests, most weekends (cover charge R250 to R400).

Sibirsky Pub PUB

(Сибирский Паб; www.siberian-pub.ru; pl Novosobornaya 2; Guinness per pint R240; ⊙noon-3am) Siberia's first British pub was founded over a century ago by a certain Mr Crawley, an Anglo-Egyptian albino who'd got stuck in Tomsk after touring with a circus freak show. Today's pub is no relation. Bands play live at weekends (cover charge).

Bar House City BAR

(Бар Хаус Сити; pr Lenina 64; beers R80-120; ⊙noon-2am) This popular student hang-out gets extremely lively in term time. Check out the summer garden if the weather is good.

Bulanzhe CAFÉ

(Буланже; 2nd fl, pr Lenina 80; espresso R40; ⊙8am-midnight) Tomsk's answer to Starbucks serves great coffee and stuffed bliny (from R60). There is another branch at ul Krasnoarmeyskaya 107.

People's Bar & Grill BAR

(pr Lenina 54; beer from R90; ⊙noon-2am) Beer, pizza and thumping dance music in a central location. Can get crowded at weekends. Entrance from the rear of pr Lenina.

Entertainment

TOP CHOICE **Tom Tomsk FC** STADIUM

(Томь Томск ФК; ☎527 967; www.football.tomsk.ru; ul Belinskogo 15/1) Trud Stadium is the home of Siberia's top football club. If you're lucky you might catch a game against 2008 UEFA Cup champions Zenit, or one of the big Moscow sides. Tickets cost from R300 upwards. There is also a shop selling Tomsk scarves, T-shirts – and even slippers – attached to the stadium. It's open 11am to 7pm Monday to Friday, and on weekends on home match days.

Human Puppets Theatre 2+ku PUPPET THEATRE

(Театр живых кукол 2+ку; www.2ky.tomsk.ru; Yuzhny per 29; admission from R200) Housed in

TOM TOMSK FOREVER! *MARC BENNETTS*

It's tough being a supporter of FC Tom Tomsk, Europe's most easterly top-flight football team. The side's nearest Premier League opponents are based in Perm, over 2000km away, and a trip to Moscow means either a 4½-hour flight or just over two days on a train.

'It's a hobby, I guess, just like anything else,' Tomsk fan Sergei told me during a visit to the team's 15,000-capacity Trud stadium. 'We all go off together – a group of up to 30 of us usually travel... I gave the recent trip to Chechnya a miss though, only two lads supported the team that day.'

Tomsk almost went under in 2009 after cash-strapped regional authorities cut funding. It took the personal intervention of Vladimir Putin to keep the side afloat. Look out for the billboard featuring the ex-KGB man at the stadium. The words on it read, 'There must be football in Tomsk.'

The side has never seriously challenged for honours, but has been a regular fixture in the Premier League since promotion in 2004. Go along and give them your support if you are in town. They managed a creditable 1-1 draw with 2004 UEFA Cup champions CSKA Moscow when I went along.

a quaint log cabin near the WWII memorial (take ul Savinikh all the way down until you can't go any further), this one-man, homey 'robotic puppet' theatre is a real experience, and one you don't need to understand Russian to appreciate.

Aelita Theatre THEATRE
(Театр Аэлита; ☎516 131; www.aelita.tsk.ru; pr Lenina 78) Eclectic offerings from rock concerts to Indian dance to experimental plays. An adaption of *Clockwork Orange* was on when we visited.

Philharmonia CONCERT HALL
(Филармония; ☎515 965; pl Lenina 1) Classical music and great big-band jazz.

Drama Theatre THEATRE
(Драматический театр; ☎512 223; pl Lenina 4)

Information

Afisha (www.afisha.westsib.ru) Has concert and cinema details.

Main post office (Почтамт; pr Lenina 95; ⏲9am-7.30pm Mon-Fri, 8am-5pm Sat, 9am-5pm Sun) Stamps, but no postcards of Tomsk!

Netcafe (Неткафе; pr Lenina 44; from per hr R19; ⏲24hr) All-night internet access costs R110. Other **branches** at pr Lenina 32 and pr Frunze 57 open 10am to 8pm.

Sent to Siberia (www.senttosiberia.wordpress.com) An American Fulbright scholar's humorous and affectionate account of life in Tomsk.

Tomsk (www.tomsk.ru09.ru) Interactive maps, photos and general info.

Getting There & Away

Air

Bogashevo Airport (☎270 084), 22km southeast of Tomsk, has three flights a day to Moscow (R10,700, 8.40am, 9am and 9.30am), plus some local regional services on **Tomskavia** (Томскавиа; ☎412 466; www.tomskavia.ru; ul Yelizarovkh). The choice is much wider from Novosibirsk's Tolmachyovo Airport, to which there are five direct buses a day (R320, five hours) from Tomsk bus station.

Bus

For Novosibirsk, shared taxis (from R750, 3½ hours) are much faster than buses from the central **bus station** (Автовокзал; R415, 5½ hours, over 15 daily). Buses to Kemerovo leave five times a day (R310, two hours). There are also useful buses to Novokuznetsk (R500, seven hours, four daily) and Barnaul (R530, nine hours, two daily).

Train

From Tomsk I (main) train station there are services on odd-numbered dates at 8.20am to Moscow's Yaroslavsky vokzal (*platskart/kupe* R5491/10,061, 56½ hours). For Omsk, there are two trains on every odd-numbered date. The first leaves at 4.10am (R1276/3288, 15 hours) while the second departs at a more convenient 8.20am (R1868/2968). Trains run to Barnaul on even dates at 4.28pm (R984/1750, 14¾ hours). The same train goes on to Irkutsk (R1800/3165, 34 hours).

Getting Around

For the airport take the rare bus 119 from pl Lenina. Other city *marshrutky* are very frequent. Handy route 7 runs from near the train station, along pr Frunze, up pr Lenina, then east again on ul Pushkina. *Marshrutka* 11 shows you the wooden houses along ul Krasnoarmeyskaya, 29 does the same for ul Tatarskaya via pl Yuzhny, while bus 4 goes west from the train station and then runs north the length of pr Lenina. Hop on and off buses 9, 12 and 17, which all also go along pr Lenina.

ALTAI

Greater Altai (Алтай), bordering on Kazakhstan, China and Mongolia, consists of the Altai Territory and the Altai Republic. The Altai Territory, while pleasant enough, is most noteworthy as a gateway to the wonders of the unforgettable Altai Republic. This sprawling and sparsely populated region is home to over 7000 lakes, snow-capped mountains – including Siberia's highest peak (Mt Belukha, 4506m). The Altai Republic has long been regarded as an area of spiritual and occult significance, and Russian philosopher and painter Nikolai Rerikh (Nicholas Roerich) visited the region in the early 20th century in an attempt to locate the entrance to Shambala, the mythical enlightened land of Tibetan Buddhism. He failed, but you might not…

Altai Culture

Asiatic ethnic-Altai people constitute around 30% of the Altai Republic's 200,000-strong population, and a vastly lower proportion in the heavily Russianised Altai Territory. Despite strong animist undercurrents, most Altai are nominally Christian and villages aren't visually distinct, though some rural Altai homes still incorporate a traditional *ail* (tepee-shaped yurt).

With excessive consumption of alcohol, gentle smiles can turn to unpredictable violence within a bottle. This makes Altai villages such as Ulagan and Balyktuyul somewhat dangerous, especially at night.

Some of the Altai Republic's 5% ethnic Kazakhs are still nomadic herders living in traditional felt yurts, notably around Kosh-Agach. Most Kazakhs are Muslims who are keen on *kumiss* (fermented mare's milk) but don't generally drink vodka, making Kazakh settlements noticeably less hazardous than Altai ones.

Planning

Remnant old areas of Biysk and Barnaul are worth a passing look. After visiting Gorno-Altaisk – the capital of the Altai Republic – for compulsory visa registration, head on for the lakes and mountains. Lake Teletskoe is touted as a 'second Baikal' and is arguably even more picturesque. For glimpses of local culture, rugged valleys, varying scenery and plenty of ancient stones, it's possible to travel down the memorable Chuysky Trakt by bus or chartered car.

However, to get closer to the snow-crested mountaintops you'll have to hike. Generally that requires preparation: compared to Nepal or New Zealand, hiking here requires considerable self-sufficiency. Not even the most popular trails have villages, signs or tea-houses. Sadly, guides and packhorses usually aren't easy to arrange quickly in situ, except

ALTAI TOURS

Travel agencies in Novosibirsk and Barnaul virtually all offer packaged or tailor-made trips to Altai.

Acris (Акрис; ☎218 0001; www.acris.ru; 2nd fl, Krasny pr 35, Novosibirsk; ⏲10am-6pm Mon-Sat) Offers trips to Altai, including Mt Belukha, and can help sort out a range of awkward permits. The staff speak some English.

Ak Tur (☎659 407; www.aktour.ru; pr Lenina 10, Barnaul; ⏲10am-7pm Mon-Sat, to 6pm Sun) Offers Altai rafting, road trips and mountain expeditions. Some English spoken.

Alie Parusa (Алые Паруса; ☎227 1256; www.alparus.ru; ul Trudovaya 12, Novosibirsk; ⏲9am-6pm Mon-Sat) Good for Sheregesh and Altai. Some English spoken.

Altair-Tur (Альтаир-Тур; www.altairtour.ru; ul Sovetskaya 65, Novosibirsk; ⏲10am-7pm Mon-Fri, to 5pm Sat) Specialises in visits to a wide range of destinations, including Altai, Lake Baikal, Mongolia, China and Tibet. English spoken.

Sibir-Altai (Сибирь-Алтай; www.sibalt.ru; office 607a, ul Frunze 5, Novosibirsk; ⏲10am-6pm Mon-Fri, 11am-3pm Sat) Packages Altai trips for local tourists, sold through numerous regional travel agencies. Runs direct weekend buses to Turbaza Katun.

Altai Republic

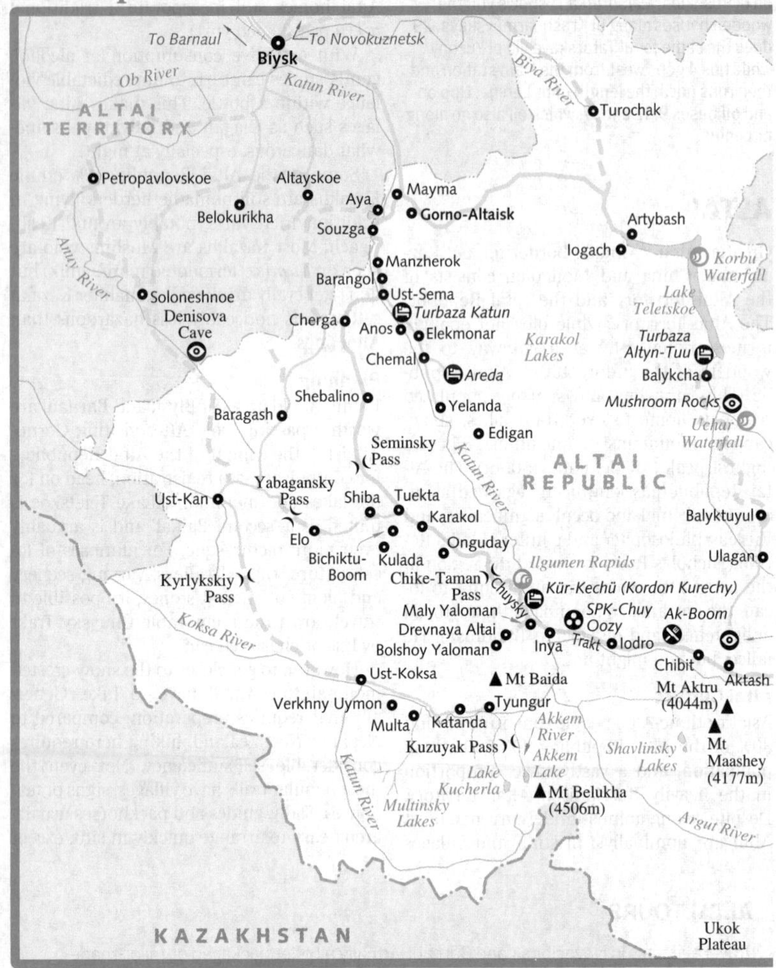

perhaps in Tyungur or Chemal. Tour agencies can help by prearranging various adventure, hiking, rafting or relaxation packages. Consider using them in July and August to book accommodation as demand very often outstrips supply in summer, especially if you want the luxury of a sit-down toilet.

If you are heading to the Mongolian border (further than Kosh-Agach), or to Ust-Koksa or beyond (including Tyungur), you will also need a border permit.

Prices remain low across Altai, one of Russia's poorest regions. For maps, try the Dom Knigi shops in any big city, which sporadically stock 1:200,000 Altai sheets. Ticks are also a real problem in the summer months.

Barnaul Барнаул

3852 / POP 575,000 / MOSCOW +3HR

The capital of the Altai Territory, Barnaul is a fairly prosperous industrial city and has been so almost since its foundation in 1730 as Ust-Barnaulskaya. Though far from the mountains, it hosts the nearest major airport to the Altai Republic and offers just enough cafés and museums to keep you amused between transport connections.

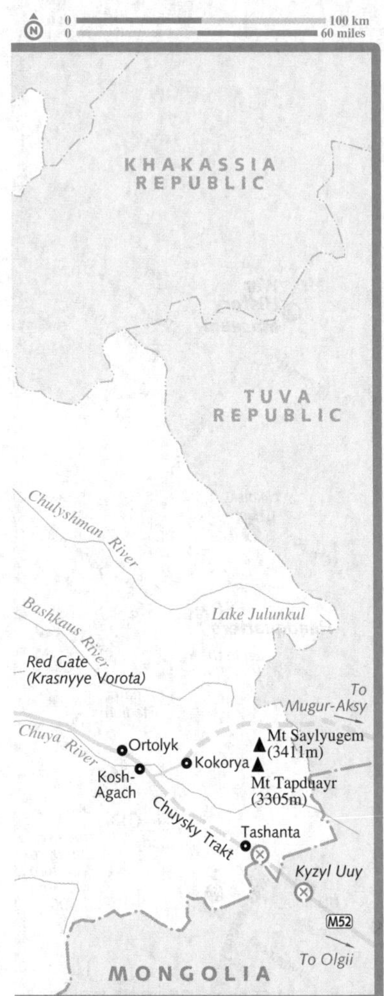

Pr Lenina runs 8km northwest from the river station through pl Sovetov and pl Oktyabrya, paralleled by Sotsialistichesky pr and Krasnoarmeysky pr, which almost meet at pl Pobedy; the bus and train stations are behind the large war memorial here. Both stations and bookshops sell maps of bus and tram routes.

Sights

Altai Arts, Literature & Culture Museum MUSEUM
(Музей истории, литературы, искусства и культуры Алтая; ul Tolstogo 2; www.gmilika.ru; admission R30; 10am-6pm Tue-Sat) The impressively eclectic – not to mention good-value – Altai Arts, Literature & Culture Museum occupies a restored, furnished 1850s mansion. There are some fine icons, Rerikh sketches and an impressive WWII room.

FSB Headquarters NOTABLE BUILDING
(Штаб ФСБ; pr Lenina 30) The city's Federal Security Services (FSB) headquarters is worth a peek. The bearded dude in the courtyard is Felix Dzerzhinsky, Cheka (KGB and FSB forerunner) founder. A much larger monument to Iron Felix was torn down in Moscow as the USSR imploded, and he is a very uncommon face indeed in modern Russia. Be sure to check out the large Soviet-era 'Workers Unite!' mural to Felix's left. Taking photos of the FSB HQ is not advised.

Wooden-Lace Houses NOTABLE BUILDINGS
Rapacious redevelopment has destroyed much of Barnaul's older architecture. Nonetheless, centuries-old remnants are dotted between the shopping malls of pr Lenina's tree-shaded southern end. A few splendid examples include those at **ulitsa Korolenko 96** and **ulitsa Polzunova 31** and 48.

Pokrovsky Church CHURCH
(Покровский собор; ul Nikitina 135-7) This bulbous-domed brick building is the most appealing of the city's many churches and has a fine, gilded interior.

Altai Fine Art Museum MUSEUM
(Алтайский художественный музей; www.ab.ru/~muzei; pr Lenina 88; admission R30; 10am-6pm Tue-Sun) The Altai Fine Art Museum is the best of several galleries in this very cultured city.

War History Museum MUSEUM
(Музей истории войны; Komsomolsky pr 73b; admission R20; 9.30am-5pm Tue-Sat) In an old brick house, the War History Museum is simple and all in Russian but the moving understatement of its Afghanistan and Chechnya memorials is particularly affecting.

Viktor Tsoy Monument MONUMENT
(Sotsialistichesky pr 126) The first official monument in Russia to Soviet New Wave star Viktor Tsoy was unveiled in Barnaul in 2010, despite the fact that the late singer had never even been to the city.

Regional Museum MUSEUM
(Краеведческий музей; www.agkm.ru; ul Polzunova 46; admission R50; 10am-4pm Wed-Sun)

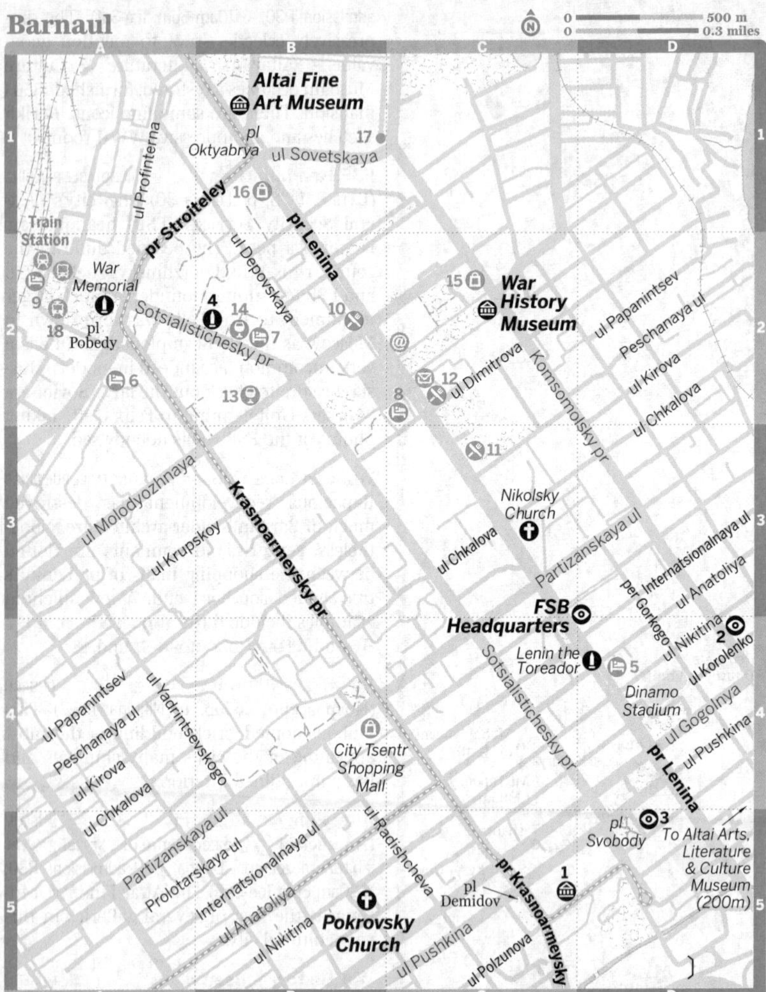

Founded in 1823, the reasonably interesting Regional Museum is Siberia's oldest. Top exhibits include intriguing models of various 18th-century industrial processes.

Sleeping

Complimentary breakfast is included everywhere, unless mentioned.

Hotel Altai HOTEL €

(Гостиница Алтай; ☎239 247; pr Lenina 24; s/tw without bathroom R600/1000, s/tw with bathroom R1200/1800) In an early 1940s building, this good budget choice has certain elements of faded grandeur. It has big nice double rooms, internet in the lobby for R30 an hour and friendly receptionists overly fond of late-night soaps. Nearby is an odd statue of Lenin apparently posing as a bullfighter.

Hotel Barnaul HOTEL €€

(Гостиница Барнаул; ☎626 222; www.barnaulhotel.ru; pl Pobedy 3; s R1750-2200, tw R3100-3800, ste R6000; ❄@) This vast 12-storey block has been thoroughly renovated and is right next to the train and bus stations. They've even got rid of the dodgy Soviet-era lifts. You'll pay extra for a room with a shower cabin though and there is no complimentary breakfast.

Barnaul

Top Sights

	Altai Fine Art Museum	B1
	FSB Headquarters	D3
	Pokrovsky Church	B5
	War History Museum	C2
Sights		
1	Regional Museum	C5
2	Ulitsa Korolenko 96	D4
3	Ulitsa Polzunova 31	D5
4	Viktor Tsoy Monument	B2
Sleeping		
5	Hotel Altai	D4
6	Hotel Barnaul	A2
7	Hotel Siberia	B2
8	Hotel Tsentralnaya	C2
9	Resting Rooms	A2
Eating		
10	Café Vizit	B2
11	Mexico	C3
12	Pechki-Lavochki	C2
Drinking		
13	Carte Blanche	B2
14	Sibirskaya Korona	B2
Shopping		
15	Ekstrim	C2
16	Penaty Bookshop	B1
Transport		
17	Aerokassa	B1
18	Trolleybus 5 to Centre	A2

The free 24-hour computer and internet in the plush lobby is, however, a big plus.

Hotel Tsentralnaya HOTEL €€
(Гостиница Центральная; ☎368 439; www.hotelcentral.ru; pr Lenina 57; s/tw R1400/1800) Slightly cosier than the Barnaul; rooms are, however, slightly cramped. Well renovated, perfectly central and all the rooms have good bathrooms.

Resting rooms HOSTEL €
(Комнаты Отдыха, komnaty otdykha; 12hr d/q R290/220) A decent option at the train station with clean, shared hot showers. No breakfast.

Hotel Siberia HOTEL €€€
(Гостиница Сибирь; ☎624 200; www.siberia-hotel.ru; Sotsialistichesky pr 116; s/d from R4600/5300; ❄📶) This posh business hotel is built almost to international standards. Clean, quiet and comfortable. Great suites available for R7300.

Eating & Drinking

Sibirskaya Korona RESTAURANT, BAR €
(Сибирская Корона; Sotsialistichesky pr 116; meals R300-500) Next door to Hotel Siberia, this popular bar-restaurant does cheap beer (R60 to R100) and all the usual accompanying snacks from dried fish to squid. Also has a range of filling meals, including some good fish dishes.

Pechki-Lavochki RUSSIAN €
(Печки-Лавочки; pr Lenina 24 & 52; meals R250-400) Traditional Russian food served in a rustic setting by waitresses dressed as peasants. The chain is named after a 1972 Soviet road film. Smoky and noisy at weekends.

Café Vizit RUSSIAN €
(Кафе Визит; pr Lenina 63a; meals R300-500) Decent Russian 'home cooking' from pancakes to borsch, and Café Vizit mixes up the menu with the inclusion of some Italian dishes as well. The upstairs restaurant is around 30% more expensive, but you do get spared the blaring pop music.

Carte Blanche CAFÉ €€
(Карта Бланш; ul Molodyozhnaya 26; meals R600-800; ⏰noon-1am) Water pipes, cocktails, live music and imported beers (from R100) make this cosy bar-cum-restaurant popular with a young and lively crowd.

Mexico MEXICAN €€
(Мехико; pr Lenina 44a; meals R400-700) Upmarket Mexican food served with imported beers, including Guinness (R250). Ask if you want your food spicy! Just up from FSB headquarters, so you may hear state secrets being discussed over the decent nachos.

Shopping

Ekstrim OUTDOOR GEAR
(Экстрим; Komsomolsky pr 75; ⏰9am-7pm) Sells climbing, fishing, camping and mountain-bike gear.

Penaty Bookshop BOOKSTORE
(Книжный Магазин Пенаты; pr Lenina 85; ⏰10am-7pm Mon-Sat, to 5pm Sun) Stocks many useful maps, atlases, postcards and Altai picture books.

Information

Internet Kafe Pl@zma (pr Lenina 58; per hr R45; ⏰8am-11pm)

Main post office (Почтамт; pr Lenina 54; ⏲8am-7pm Mon-Sat, to 6pm Sun) The attached telephone office stays open until 10pm.

Getting There & Away

There are four direct flights a day to Moscow (from R9300, 4½ hours). There is much more choice from (relatively) nearby Novosibirsk. Tickets can be bought at the main **Aerokassa** (Централные Аэрокассы; ☎368 181; ul Sovetskaya 4; ⏲8am-7pm Mon-Fri, 8.30am-5pm Sat & Sun).

For Moscow, a train leaves on odd-numbered days at 6.45pm (*platskart/kupe* R3700/8400, 59 hours) and on even dates at 8.55pm (R4100/9200, 56 hours). There are through trains most days to Novokuznetsk (from R700/1000, 6½ hours). Trains to Tomsk leave daily at 12.24pm (R1250/3100, 16 hours).

Buses are better for Novosibirsk (R370, just under five hours, more than 30 daily) and Biysk (R275, three hours, every hour), and the only choice for Gorno-Altaisk (R420, five hours, 10 daily). Shared taxis to Novosibirsk leave from outside the main **bus station** (Автовокзал) and do the journey in 3½ hours (R500).

Getting Around

From the Aerokassa, rare bus 112 runs to Barnaul's airport in the northwestern suburbs. From the **river station** (Речной Вокзал), frequent buses 1 and 10 go straight up pr Lenina, trolleybus 5 connects to the **train station** and the handy bus 43 swings past pl Demidov, turns north up Krasnoarmeysky pr, then passes pl Pobedy (near the bus and train stations) before rejoining pr Lenina at pl Oktyabrya.

Biysk Бийск

☎3854 / POP 236,000 / ⏲MOSCOW +3HR

Friendly Biysk, 160km southeast of Barnaul, is not worth a special detour but its modest attractions may warrant a brief stop en route to or from the Altai Mountains, for which it's the nearest railhead.

One of only three cities created on the orders of Peter the Great (the others were Moscow and St Petersburg!), Biysk was founded in 1709 by a group of 70 Russian soldiers equipped with five cannons. But the fort they set up at the junction of the Biya and Katun Rivers was quickly burnt down by the unimpressed Dzhungarian Mongols. Biysk was reestablished 20km to the east in 1718. Unfortunately, nothing remains from this period.

TICK WARNING

The encephalitis and Lyme disease threat is often underestimated in Siberia (both Western and Eastern). The ticks *(kleshchi)* that spread these nasty diseases are alarmingly plentiful from late April to September. The threat is worst in the taiga, especially in Altai, but ticks have even been found in city parks. Don't panic, but do cover up and be vigilant. Good antitick sprays and creams are available in big cities. It's best to stock up before you arrive in the region. Tick-borne diseases can also be transmitted through milk, so be sure to boil any you buy fresh from local farmers.

Sights

Regional Museum MUSEUM
(Краеведческий музей; www.museum.ru/M1345; ul Lenina 134; admission R20; ⏲10am-4.30pm Wed-Sat) Housed in a grand, if dilapidated, 1912 merchant's house with original art nouveau fittings, this fine museum is home to standing stone idols and petroglyphs. A short walk away is the only **Lenin statue** in Russia dressed in a real Siberian *shanka-ushanka* (winter fur hat with ear flaps). To get here, take northbound bus 23 to the Firsova ex-Department Store (ul Tolstogo 144) and walk a block east, then north. Or take a taxi (R100).

Assumption Church CHURCH
(Успенская церковь; Sovetskaya ul 13) This silver-domed church has a number of interesting 1890s brick edifices for neighbours.

City Theatre THEATRE
(Бийский городской драматический театр; www.biyskdrama.ucoz.ru; ul Sovetskaya 25; admission R150-300) Grand, renovated 1916 theatre.

Tours

Bars Travel TOUR COMPANY
(Барс Трэвел; ☎328 050; www.tbars.narod.ru; Hotel Tsentralnaya) Runs various good-value Altai tours, including helicopter trips.

Sleeping

Hotel Tsentralnaya HOTEL €
(Гостиница Центральная; ☎338 307; Krasnoarmeyskaya ul; s/tw from R600/800) This Soviet-era hotel has been renovated. All rooms have private bathroom with hot showers.

Resting rooms HOSTEL €
(Комнаты Отдыха, komnaty otdykha; dm/s/d R150/250/350) Cheap, clean and secure resting rooms with hot showers (R50).

Hotel Polieks HOTEL €
(Гостиница Полиэкс; ☎236 440; pl 9i Yanvara 3; s/d/tw/tr from R450/600/750/1050) Good value, but far from the old town. Take westbound bus 23 to ul Vasilyeva 46 and walk back past Fortuna grocery.

Eating & Drinking

The café/restaurant scene is extremely basic in Biysk. There's no shortage of beer and shashlyk though.

Café Randevu RUSSIAN €€
(Кафе Рандеву; Sovetskaya ul 4; meals R300-600) Behind a beautifully renovated old-town facade, this midrange café serves decent food and beer in a pleasant atmosphere.

Kavkazskaya Kukhnya RUSSIAN €
(Кавказская Кухна; ul Lenina 314; meals R100-300) Huge portions, cheap Russian beer (R30) and shashlyk. Look for the glistening Sberbank building.

Mirazh RUSSIAN €
(Мираж; ul Sovetskaya 219; meals R150-300) Cheap and simple food and beer (R70 to R90) in equally modest settings.

Information

Post office (Почта; ul Merlina 17; per hr R35; ⊙8.30am-noon & 1-6pm Mon-Fri, 9am-2pm Sat) Erratic internet connections one block south of the bus station.

Getting There & Away

The bus and train stations face each other across a large square at the north end of ul Mitrofanova, 2km west of Hotel Tsentralnaya and 4km from the historic centre. Trains to Novosibirsk leave at 4.26am and 5.55pm (*platskart/kupe* from R750/1100, 11 hours). There are no direct trains to Moscow. Buses leave frequently between 6.30am and 8pm for Gorno-Altaisk (R200, two hours) and Barnaul (R320, three hours). Shared taxis are faster but around twice the price. Handy, if slow, buses rattle across to Novokuznetsk (R420, six to seven hours, three daily).

Gorno-Altaisk

Горно-Алтайск

☎38822 / POP 54,000 / ⊙MOSCOW +3HR

Gorno-Altaisk, the tiny capital of the Altai Republic, was founded in 1830 and immediately saw an influx of missionaries eager to convert local pagan tribes. Today it's a somewhat bland mixture of Soviet-era buildings and newer development running through an attractive valley. From Mayma on the M52, Gorno-Altaisk's main street, Kommunistichesky pr, winds on for 7km before reaching central pl Lenina.

There's no real reason to visit, except to register your visa before going elsewhere in Altai.

Sights

TOP CHOICE **Svyato-Makarevsky Church** CHURCH
(Свято-Макарьевский храм; pr Kommunistichesky 146) Completed in 2006, this attractive wooden church boasts a wonderfully photographic backdrop of rolling lush hills.

WWII Memorial MONUMENT
(Мемориал Великой Отечественной войны; pr Kommunistichesky) This powerful WWII monument is on the outskirts of the city, opposite the Dormostroy hotel.

Lenin Monument MONUMENT
(Памятник Ленину; ul Palkina) Yet another Lenin monument to add to your collection. This one stands guard over the entrance to Hotel Gorny Altai.

Regional Museum MUSEUM
(Краеведческий музей; ul Churos-Gurkina 46) This once-impressive regional museum is undergoing extensive renovation and no one could tell us when it was likely to reopen.

Tours

Altai Info TOUR COMPANY
(Алтай Инфо; ☎26 864; Hotel Gorny Altai; ⊙10am-6pm) Can arrange rafting trips.

Sleeping & Eating

There's further choice in Mayma, Aya and Souzga.

Igman HOTEL €
(Игман; ☎47 242; http://igman.ru; ul Churos-Gurkina; s/d from R800/1100) Just three years old, friendly Igman is at the rear of the bus station and has clean, spacious rooms at reasonable prices. Cheaper rooms have shared showers.

Dormostroy MINIHOTEL €
(Дормострой; ☎62 149; 3rd fl, per Granitny 1; tw R1200) Two cramped but comfy twin rooms with kettle and fridge share a modern toilet and hot shower. You can pay per bed (R600).

REGISTERING YOUR VISA IN GORNO-ALTAISK

It's tedious, and travellers have been known not to bother, but we recommend registering your visa in Gorno-Altaisk if you plan onward travel in the Altai Republic. To do this, go to the **Federal Migration Service office** (Федеральная Миграционная Служба (ФМС); ☎62 012; top fl, Kommunistichesky pr 95; ⏲9am-1pm Mon-Wed & Fri). To find it, walk to your right up Kommunistichesky pr when facing either the bus station or the central Lenin statue. Enter via the stairs at the central doors. Importantly you'll need a *khodataystsvo* – a document from whoever sponsored your visa, listing where in Altai you'll be visiting. Get this before departing as having your sponsors fax it to Gorno-Altaisk can cause days of delays and annoyance. With the letter, registration should only take 15 minutes – assuming you can figure out the Russian forms.

If all that seems like too much hassle, take your documents to **Aguna Travel Agency** (Агуна; ☎22 413; ul Churos-Gurkina 39; ⏲10am-6pm Mon-Sat), where for around R500 the company's friendly staff will sort everything out for you. It's on the street behind the bus station, not far from the Regional Museum.

Two luxurious double rooms with own bathroom go for R2300. It's at the turn-off after pr Kommunistichesky 115.

Hotel Gorny Altai HOTEL €
(Гостиница Горно-Алтай; ☎95 086; ul Palkina 5; s/d R800/1200) This crumbling and somewhat dodgy Soviet slab usually has a room available when all else is full. It's just off pr Kommunistichesky; its more expensive rooms (single/double R1700/2250) have their own toilets and bathrooms.

Venetsiya ITALIAN €
(Венеция; pr Kommunistichesky 68; meals R300-500) Next to the bus station, Venetsiya goes to some effort to re-create a tiny slice of Italy, with fake balconies and themed design. The pasta, pizzas and wine (from R80 a glass) isn't bad either, although the sushi does somewhat spoil the overall effect.

Café Natalya RUSSIAN €
(Кафе Наталья; ul Churos-Gurkina 32; meals R110-170) Daily specials are displayed in the heated cabinet, making point-and-pick an easy option.

Information

The **post office** (Почта; Kommunistichesky pr 61; ⏲9am-6pm Mon-Fri) near the **bus station** (Автовокзал) has an **internet centre** (per hr R60; ⏲9am-9pm Mon-Fri, noon-6pm Sat & Sun). Good city maps are available at street kiosks, as well as in Novosibirsk and Moscow.

Getting There & Away

There's no railway but a **booth** (⏲9am-1pm & 2-5pm) within the bus station sells train tickets.

Buses run to Barnaul (R445, five hours, 12 daily) and Biysk (R175, two hours, 10 daily), and serve most Altai Republic villages at least daily including Tyungur (R640, 1.45pm) and Onguday (R238, 2.40pm). Timetabled minibuses for Kosh-Agach (R650, 7.10am, via Aktash) don't run on Tuesday or Saturday. If passenger numbers are low, you might not get beyond Aktash (R500, eight hours).

Private alternatives leave until mid-morning according to demand. Much faster *marshrutky* usually cost 50% more than buses. Shared taxis are slightly more expensive, but even faster.

Getting Around

From central Gorno-Altaisk virtually all eastbound city buses take Kommunistichesky pr past the bus station, Federal Migration Service office and market. Buses numbered over 100 continue to Mayma.

Around Gorno-Altaisk

MAYMA МАЙМА

Hugging the M52 (ul Lenina) after Gorno-Altaisk, Mayma is Russia's largest village, with a population of 15,000. Despite this, there's nothing at all to see. However, the settlement does have a large market and internet-connected **post office** (per hr R50) right where the road turns off to Gorno-Altaisk. But there's no real reason to stay here – instead, head to nearby Aya. It's here the wonders of the Altai Republic begin for real.

AYA АЯ

☎38537

There is a booming tourist scene south of Mayma concentrated around the small and wobbly wooden bridge at Aya. There are basic but clean rooms above the **Aysky Most Cafe** (s/d R550/750), right before the bridge, which stretches over the rock-dotted Katun River and leads to the picturesque Lake Aya.

Many agencies around the bridge offer **rafting trips** (per hr R300-2000) and horse rides at short notice; handy if you haven't reserved anything more adventurous. In the summer months, right after the bridge, a number of stalls offer reasonably priced trips to Lake Teletskoe and Chemal, among other destinations.

Stalls sell jars of natural honey for around R400 and *sera,* a traditional Siberian 'chewing gum' made from cedar tree resin. There are also numerous outdoor cafés serving the usual shashlyk and beer, as well as a growing number of summer open-air nightclubs.

The grand castle-like building in the middle of the river is the **Korona Altaya Hotel** (Корона Алтая; ☎8-963-500 1058; www.korona-altaya.ru; s/d/ste from R3000/4900/10,000). It's posh and professional, but prices fall by as much as 50% off season. To get there, follow the path after the bridge for around 500m, until you reach the lions. Around 800m or so up the path is the good-value **Tainstvenny Bereg turbaza** (Таинственный Берег; ☎8-906-963 5509; log cabins from R700), whose cosy wooden homes sit on the bank of the Katun. The owners can also arrange rafting trips.

To get to the lake, walk about 1.5km along the road, and take the first left after the souvenir stalls up the steep hill to the path that eventually slopes down to the water. Alternatively, taxis from the bridge charge around R150 for the trip. Entry to the territory of the lake costs R150 in high season, unless you want to skirt some 3km around the fence. Before you head off for the lake, however, a visit to the cute, fairy-tale-themed **Skazka Banya** (per hr R600), some 300m to the left after the suspension bridge, is well recommended.

Lake Aya (Озера Ая), at 280m above sea level, isn't particularly large, but it's an excellent place to relax for a day or two. You can rent a rowing boat for R300 per hour or just take a sedate stroll in the fresh Altai air. Off season is perhaps even more tranquil, as you'll probably have the whole lake almost to yourself.

Overlooking the lake and surrounded by pine trees is the pleasant **Hotel Aya** (Отель Ая; ☎28 103; www.ayahotel.ru; s/d R2500/3100). There is also a good restaurant (meals R300 to R500) on the top floor, which serves Altai honey in ice cream (R100). The live music in the evenings can grate, however, unless you happen to be a fan of keyboard and backing-tape versions of cheesy 1980s rock hits. If the music gets you down, escape to the **banya** (per hr R600). The hotel also offers rafting (from R300) and excursions to the depths of the splendidly named Tush-Kush (Туш-Куш) caves (R4500).

There are even more accommodation options in the village of **Souzga**, which starts some 500m up the main road after Aya bridge. The plush **Na Shumakh** (На Шумах; ☎8-923-641 5575; www.na-shumah.ru; ul Tsentralnaya 53; s/d R2700/3100) has exceedingly cosy rooms with river views. Prices drop 25% from September to April. There are cheaper options across the road at the simple unnamed **homestay** (d R750). Look for signs marked 'Сдаю Дом' and 'Сдаётся Дом' (house for rent) for other similarly priced homestay options.

Souzga *marshrutky* run very rarely from opposite Mayma market. Chemal and Chuysky Trakt buses also pass by. If you have no accommodation booked, consider chartering a taxi from Mayma market to check out various options, saving you very long walks. A taxi to either Aya or Souzga will cost around R300 from Gorno-Altaisk.

Lake Teletskoe & Artybash
Озеро Телецкое и Артыбаш

☎38843 / POP 4500 / ⏲MOSCOW +3HR

Deep, delightful Lake Teletskoe is Altai's serene answer to Lake Baikal, a great place simply to relax and catch your breath. It's also Altai's largest lake. Ridge after forested ridge unfolds as you scuttle along on one of the myriad little pleasure boats that buzz out of Artybash village, the lake's charming tourist hub.

At Lake Teletskoe's westernmost nose, little Iogach village is the main population centre and bus stop. Across the bridge, Artybash is a pretty ribbon of cottages, homestays and minihotels straggling along ul Teletskaya.

Sights & Activities

Korbu Waterfall WATERFALL

From June to September, there are daily lake trips (R400, four hours) to Korbu Waterfall from opposite Stary Zamok One hotel. See the timetable near the boats for details. The falls are hardly memorable but the journey is very beautiful despite the blaring

LAKE TELETSKOE SAFETY

Russia's notoriously poor record on safety matters was highlighted once again in July 2011 when a tourist boat sank on Lake Teletskoe, killing four people. The subsequent investigation revealed that the boat lacked a licence to carry paying passengers. There's no need to be paranoid (after all, dozens of boats use the lake every day), but use your common sense when selecting a boat. Does it appear well maintained? Is the captain drunk? Is it a lot cheaper than other boats?

commentary. Speedboats take the same route for around R750 a head. The lake freezes over in winter and the village transforms into a winter wonderland.

Pioneer Altaya Boat BOAT TRIPS
(Пионер Алтая; ☎8-963-199 5025) This large Soviet-era boat was renovated and brought back into service in 2010. It contains an Altai museum and a café (meals R200 to R300) and offers trips around the lake from R800 a head. Opposite Pensionat Edem at km2.5.

Souvenir Shops SOUVENIRS
The souvenir shops around the start of the bridge sell all manner of interesting items, from Altai honey (R100 a small jar), Altai pop and traditional music, maps of the surrounding area and Altai T-shirts. They even do Russian-Altai phrasebooks (R150).

Sleeping & Eating

Many of the cheaper places open in peak season only. However, all places listed here operate year-round, with reservations highly advisable in July and August. Prices drop by up to 50% off season.

Every second house in Artybash seems to have rooms or huts to rent. Prices start from R400 without any facilities but many places demand minimum groups of three or more guests in summer. Look for signs marked 'Сдаю Дом' and 'Сдаётся Дом' (house for rent). Beyond Turbaza Zolotoe Ozera there are more 'miniresorts'; a wide, grassy free-camping area that gets very noisy on weekends; plus some cheap, very basic hut-camps. Hotel distances given are from the bridge.

There are a few more homestays on the right bank, in the village of Iogach (Иогач). We liked the ones at ul Haberezhnaya 27 and 35a (the lakeside road to the left of the bridge).

Hotel Artybash HOTEL €€
(Гостиница Артыбаш; ☎8-961-709 4242; www.artybash.com; d from R1600) The area's first modern hotel, the good-value Artybash opened in 2009. Big, stylish rooms, some with great views of the Biya River, friendly staff, and the good restaurant (complimentary breakfast) offers some variation from the usual *pelmeni* and noodles. It's just before the bridge, opposite the petrol station.

Stary Zamok Two HOTEL €€
(Старый Замок Два; ☎26 460; www.zamoktel.ru; km1.4; d R2500) This sweetly kitsch little 'castle' has the village's best-value upper-range accommodation. There are shared terraces, lake-view sitting rooms and a dining area. All rooms have toilets and showers. Also has good *banya* for R500 per hour.

Teletskaya 53 GUESTHOUSE €
(Телетская 53; km1; d R400) A very basic homestay run by friendly Sergei, who will lend you one of his many bicycles if you ask nicely. Outside toilet and no mod cons.

Teletskaya 23 GUESTHOUSE €
(Телетская 23; ☎8-963-199 7570; 600m; house per week R6000) For longer stays, or if you just need to stretch out, consider renting this well-equipped wooden house. Prices fall dramatically off season. Worth haggling even in the high season.

Stary Zamok One HOTEL €€
(Старый Замок Один; ☎26 460; 500m; d R2500) This tiny mock-fortress hotel is opposite the departure point for boat trips. Rooms are pleasant and bright. The whole hotel (five rooms) can be rented for R17,000 per 24-hour period. It is owned by the same people who run Stary Zamok Two.

Pensionat Edem HOTEL €€
(☎27 634; www.teleckoe.ru; km2.5; d/tw from R2000/2250) Comfy rooms and organised activities make this a popular choice, though it's set back from the road and lacks any lake views. Overlooks the Pioneer Altaya boat.

Café Yevseich RUSSIAN €
(Кафе Евсеич; meals R100-200) This modest, friendly café serves cheap and filling meals of the meat-and-potatoes variety.

Café Zolotoe Ozero RUSSIAN €
(Кафе Золотое Озеро; ul Naberezhnaya 1; meals R100-200) Even more basic than Yevseich,

this tiny café specialises in microwaved *pelmeni,* pizza and loud pop music from a tinny radio.

Information

Sberbank (Сбербанк; 9.30am-4pm Mon-Sat) Next to the bridge on the Iogach side. Will change dollars and euros.

Getting There & Away

Buses to Gorno-Altaisk leave from the small shop at the end of the bridge on the Iogach side of the river at 7am, 8am and 8.40am (R250, 4½ hours). The 8.40am bus goes on to Barnaul. Check the timetable inside the nearby shop. For taxis to Gorno-Altaisk (R2500), ask at Café Yevseich. From Gorno-Altaisk, the 11.05am bus (R240, 5½ hours) detours via Turochak, where you spend over an hour for lunch. Shared taxis make the journey in less than three hours (R400).

Lake Manzherok

Озера Манжерок

38844 / MOSCOW +3HR

Peaceful Lake Manzherok is 1.5km away from the friendly village of the same name. You could easily spend a couple of days relaxing here before heading deeper into the Altai region.

To get to the lake, take the signposted turn-off (Озера Манжерок), 2500m to the left if heading south out of Manzherok. Go through the tiny village of Ozernoe (Озерное) and take the first left for another 500m or so. It's possible to take a boat on the lake (from R500 a trip). Ask local fishermen or enquire at the nearby Hotel Manzherok.

There is also a ski resort being developed near the lake. Things were still pretty basic when we visited, with the slope only functional from around 1000m. But the ski-lift up Mt Sinyukha operates year-round, and even in snowless months it's well worth the 30-minute ride to the top of the slope (R200). There are stunning views of the lake and the surrounding countryside from the final 2200m viewing platform. You can also dress up like a Mongolian warrior or pose with an eagle for photos, if that's your thing.

Sleeping

There are a number of options, both in as well as around Manzherok and the lake. There are also homestays in Manzherok and Ozernoe from R300. Look out for 'Сдаю

A PART-TIME FIREFIGHTER *MARC BENNETTS*

From his vantage point high above the Altai countryside, ski-lift operator Oleg Trepashkin, aged 44, has a good view of the damage caused by the wildfires that devastate Siberian forests with alarming frequency. 'Look over there,' he tells me. 'It's only May and we've already seen a fire.'

I follow Oleg's finger and make out a black stain – the charred remains of trees – set against the lush green.

'That was just a few weeks ago,' he says. 'And there'll be more. You can bet on it.' Oleg was right: Siberia was hit by massive wildfires later that month.

Apart from his 'day job' hauling holidaymakers up and down the mountain overlooking Lake Manzherok, Oleg is also a voluntary fireman.

The summer of 2010 saw the European part of Russia make the headlines as wildfires encircled Moscow, shrouding the capital in toxic smog. But Siberia and the Far East also suffered. Siberia has seen unprecedented heat waves of late – a few days before my research trip in early May 2011, temperatures rose to around 34°C (93.2°F).

'There's a team of us,' he tells me. 'And we try to get to the fires before they can spread too much. But it's hard work. In the Soviet era things were better organised. Whole factories would be sent out to tackle blazes. There's none of that of course now.'

'I just can't stand by and see our countryside destroyed,' he added. 'And if the authorities can't sort it out...'

While many fires have their roots in the summer heat, a far from insignificant number are caused by holidaymakers leaving bonfires smouldering or being careless with lit cigarettes.

'You know,' Oleg says, sighing, 'most people don't know how to respect the countryside. People from big cities like Novosibirsk are the worst. They come here, thinking they are better than everyone else and throw rubbish everywhere. Then they go home and leave us to clean up the mess.'

Комнату' and 'Сдаётся Дом' signs (room for rent/house for rent). Manzherok's best homestays are at the village's prettier southern edge around km474.

Hotel Manzherok HOTEL €
(Гостиница Манжерок; ☎8-913-992 8888; www.manzherok-hotel.ru; ul Beregovaya 4; d from R1400) The good-value Hotel Manzherok's extremely spacious rooms all have showers and some have breathtaking views of the nearby lake. Staff are friendly and eager to help out with advice etc.

Vityaz CABINS €€
(Витязь; ☎8-905-986 8768; www.vityaz.bem-electronics.ru; log cabins from R1500) The idyllic Vityaz is at km478 on the bank of the river Katun. It's on the right as you head south from Manzherok. It's a 30-minute walk or so from the centre of the village, but its cosy log cabins are worth the trek. Camping is available for R400.

Turkomplex Manzherok HOTEL €€
(Туркомплекс Манжерок; ☎28 399; www.mangerok-altai.ru; dm/s/d from R400/1000/1500) At km469 just before Manzherok, this well-organised holiday centre sits behind a mock-Cossack stockade in a riverbank pine grove. The good-value doubles have private showers and a toilet.

Dva Medveda HOTEL €
(Два Медведа; ☎8-913-690 0777; www.dvamedvedya.ru; s/d/log cabins from R200/800/1500) Great-value log cabins set in attractive grounds just past Vityaz as you head away from Manzherok. Also offers excursions. The name translates as 'Two Bears' – although you won't see even one.

MANZHEROK – THIS IS FRIENDSHIP!

The village of Manzherok found fame in 1966 as the venue for a Soviet–Mongolian youth friendship festival, a big deal for the then-insular USSR. A song was commissioned especially for the occasion and sung by French-born Soviet star Edita Pieha. The result was a catchy pop ditty boasting the chorus 'Manzherok is friendship, our meeting place!' The tune was even accompanied by a video featuring a smiling Pieha and her band dancing around in a snowy forest. Check it out at www.youtube.com/watch?v=egyrzWVaLU8.

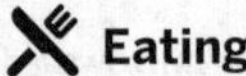

Eating

Uzbekskaya Kukhnya UZBEK €
(Узбекская Кухня; ul Druzhbi 38; meals R200-350; ⏲10am-11pm) An almost exclusively meat-based Uzbek menu ranging from shashlyk to *plov* (meat with rice) is on offer at this modest café on the main road at the southern end of the village. Vegetarians will have to make do with lavash (a soft flatbread), tea and cakes.

Veranda RUSSIAN €
(Веранда; ul Druzhbi 7; meals R150-250; ⏲10am-midnight) More shashlyk, as well as some stodgy Russian 'home cooking'. If you don't find anything to your taste here, you could always buy some food at the useful shop next door.

Information

Post office (per hr R50; ⏲8am-4pm Mon-Fri) Opposite the clearly marked ul Druzhbi 30.

Sberbank (Сбербанк; ul Druzhbi 22) Changes dollars and euros.

Getting There & Away

There are two buses a day from Biysk to Manzherok (R375, four hours, 10.30am, 3.30pm). All go via Gorno-Altaisk, from which it's a two-hour journey (R200). All also go on to Chemal.

Two buses a day from Chemal to Novosibirsk (R850, 10 hours) stop at Manzherok's ul Druzhbi at around 8.40am and 9am. You can also flag them down on the road around the village. Timetables change frequently though and it's worth checking at your hotel. The buses also stop at Gorno-Altaisk and Biysk. Alternatively you could arrange a ride with a local driver. It should cost around R500 to get to Gorno-Altaisk.

Chemal Чемал

☎38841 / POP 9000 / ⏲MOSCOW +3HR

At the attractive junction of the Chemal and Katun Rivers, ever-expanding Chemal is heavily touristed in summer but remains a good base for regional explorations and makes a very pleasant day trip from Gorno-Altaisk, 95km further north. Chemal means 'place of living waters' in the Altai language. You could easily spend a day or two here before heading off for a journey down the Chuysky Trakt. It's also the last outpost of 'civilisation', should you decide to do so.

Chemal's main **bus stop** (ul Pchyolkina 62) is opposite a cute brick **church** (ul Pchyolkina 69a) with a metal-spired wooden tower.

In summer a number of companies have stalls here offering rafting trips from R450 per hour. Walk two blocks south past the central shops and a small park, then turn right to find the **Altaysky Tsentr** (ul Beshpekskaya 6; per person/group R150/300). This comprises three Altai-style wooden *ail*-huts with pointed metal roofs. One is an Altai library, another celebrates Churos-Gurkin's ethnographic work, but most interesting is the traditional 'home' *ail*. Opening hours are whatever the elderly woman who runs it feels like. **Sberbank** (Сбербанк; ⏲9am-4pm Mon-Fri) is near the bus station. The small **Bimtan** (Вимтан; ☎220 20; d per person R500) hotel at number 15 has toilets and showers in its comfortable rooms. There's another unnamed hotel at **number 14** (R400-600) but it's closed off season.

Ul Beshpekskaya becomes ul Sovetskaya and, after 700m, dead-ends at a pedestrian suspension footbridge. This dizzyingly wobbly construction leads across a small canyon to a craggy island in the Katun River on which is perched the tiny wooden **Ioanno Bogoslavski Chapel** (⏲9am-7pm), rebuilt in 2001 to the original 1849 design. Beside it, the rock miraculously shaped like a Madonna and child sculpture is supposedly natural.

A narrow but well-trodden footpath winds high along the Katun riverbank into the **Varota Sartikpayev Canyon**, an important place in Altai mythology. The white pieces of cloth tied to trees here and elsewhere in the region are part of the Altai people's tradition of honouring their ancestors. Despite power lines and summer crowds, views along the canyon remain very pretty. After walking for about 15 minutes you emerge behind a small 1935 dam (GES in Russian, an acronym for hydroelectric scheme) backed by souvenir stalls and open-air cafés. Here you can make 15m **bungee jumps** (pryzhki ve vodu; per jump R300; ⏲10am-1pm & 2-7pm May-Sep) into the frothing outpour waters or 'fly' across on the **kanatnaya doroga** (per ride R300), an amusing elastic-pulley contraption. Both attractions impose 'fines' on anyone who backs out at the last second! You can also try traditional *talkan* Altai tea here (R35). If you follow the path after the dam (entry R100) you come to a big wheel (admission R150), from which there are fine views of the surrounding countryside. There are also more stalls here selling souvenirs and snacks.

WORTH A TRIP

HOLY WATERS & SOUVENIRS

Arzhaan-Su

At km478.7, Arzhaan-Su (Аржан-Су) is a 'holy' cold-water spring at the roadside, shrouded by summer souvenir sellers. The white ribbons tied around trees here (and elsewhere in the region) are part of the Altai tradition of honouring their ancestors. Just across the new suspension bridge is Biryuzovaya Katun, a holiday park with a pool, caves and a café in a bizarre wooden galleon.

Elekmonar

Five kilometres north of Chemal, Elekmonar is the starting point for multiday hikes or horse rides to the seven attractive Karakol Lakes amid picturesque bald mountaintops. The lakes are approximately 30km beyond Elekmonar – start up ul Sadovaya. A sturdy 4WD could get you most of the way. In Elekmonar, very basic homestays are available for around R500 at over a dozen homes, including Sovetskaya ul 53, 107 and 115, as well as Tsentralnaya ul 32, 48 and 61.

Sleeping & Eating

Set in a peaceful garden, the small but cute rooms at friendly **Ludmila Usadba** (☎8-903-956 4814; Zelyonaya Rosha 2; s/d R500/800) are worth considering, even without separate toilets. There is also a *banya* (R500).

Altai Voyazh (Алтай Вояж; ☎22 268; www.karakolaltai.ru; ul Sovetskaya 4; d R1000), opposite the bus station next to Sberbank, is a hikers' hang-out that offers very basic rooms with shared toilets and primitive – but scalding hot! – showers. Camping on the territory costs R300 a night. The hotel also offers a range of reasonably priced rafting and hiking trips.

When you get hungry, you could try visiting the local **greasy spoon** (meals R100-200; ⏲10am-9pm). It's in an unnumbered building four doors down from the main bus stop, on the right. It does greasy pies, greasy potatoes, greasy pasta and some other stuff. You'll have to decipher the handwritten menu to find out what, but it's likely to be greasy. There is another unnamed café (meals R150 to R250) behind the football pitch next to Ludmila Usadba, but it was closed 'for the day' when we were in town.

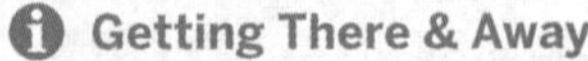

Getting There & Away

Buses run twice a day from Gorno-Altaisk (R270, three hours). The buses back leave at 7.40am and 8am, although times change frequently.

Chuysky Trakt

Чуйский Тракт

While the Chuysky Trakt runs from Biysk, the most interesting stretch of this 600km-long, well-maintained federal highway comes south of Ust-Sema. This section of the road (the M52) offers over 400km of forested mountains, canyons and glimpsed vistas, emerging eventually into peak-rimmed steppe dotted with Kazakh yurts. The views are arguably better driving northbound as the woodlands are less dense on the south-facing slopes, leaving visible the photogenic rocky cliffs.

Transport is incredibly limited, but shared taxis run all the way to Kosh-Agach from Chemal for around R1200 per seat (R5000 per car) and drivers are generally happy enough to make brief stops en route for photos of landscapes, stone idols and petroglyphs. The journey takes around 10 hours if the weather is good. There is little in the way of shops and services, so stock up before you leave. The journey can be extremely hazardous in winter.

DON'T MISS

ALTAI CULTURE

Altai Folk Festival

The **El-Oiyn festival** (www.el-oiyn.narod.ru) attracts some 60,000 people, and guests attend from all over Russia and beyond. The event, whose name translates as Folk Games, involves much horse riding, traditional costumes and merrymaking. It takes place in even-numbered years, on the first weekend in July.

The 'Face' of The Altai

Just beside the slip road for the simple Chuy-Oozy café (meals R100 to R200) at km714.2, very lightly scored roadside petroglyphs depict little antelope figures. But the big sight here, if you can spot it, is the legendary 'rock face' on the left bank of the Katun. If you can't make out its 'features', pop into the café and check out the helpful drawing hanging on a wall. Then go out and have another look. All should now be clear!

ONGUDAY AREA ОНГУДАЙ

☎38845 / POP 5100 / ⏲MOSCOW +3HR

The high and desolate **Seminsky Pass** is topped with a winter sports training centre and some snack kiosks, from which the road descends to **Onguday**. Translating literally as '10 gods' (for the 10 surrounding peaks), the large village isn't especially appealing but its very basic, central **hotel** (☎21 196; ul Erzumasheva 8; dm/tw R350/450) makes a possible base for archaeologists visiting *kurgany* (burial mounds) at Karakol, Tuekta and Shiba. There's a small **museum** (admission R30) dedicated to Altai culture in the school and the Torko Chachak handicraft shop sells Altai felts and fur hats. Just before Onguday, the turn-off at Tuekta leads to the village of Elo, about 30km away, the site for a huge festival celebrating Altai culture.

To Onguday's northwest, a dead-end side road to Kulada village passes some traditional Altai *aily* (tent-like dwellings) and an attractive valley which offers hiking and free-camping possibilities. There are menhirs on the left and right sides as you approach the village, but you'll have to look close to make out the markings. **Kulada** is built around a rocky knob and is a holy place in Burkhanism, a curious but almost extinct Altai religion founded in 1904 by shepherd Chet Chelpan, fusing Orthodox Christianity, Buddhism and folk traditions. There is also a small outdoor **museum** (admission R50) in the village containing a number of well-preserved standing stone idols.

Southeast of Onguday, the Chuysky Trakt crosses the beautiful, serpentine **Chike-Taman Pass**, a deathtrap in winter due to rockfalls and icy roads. The pass is so steep, its name means 'flat sole' in Altai. Locals believed you could see the bottom of the shoe of the person walking ahead of you. The pass descends close to the **Ilgumen Rapids**, which offer challenging rafting (grades 4 to 5) on a five-day adventure to Manzherok. Start by camping at the beautifully positioned **Kur Kechu** (tent sites R100), perched just above the river, 800m east of km681. There are a few summer huts here too from around R400.

In a cliff-ringed curl of river, **Maly Yaloman** has a microclimate allowing local villagers to grow pears, cherries and apples. Up 12km of rough side track, **Bolshoy Yaloman** has several stone idols in fairly good condition. The nearby Drevnaya Altai camp offers tent space for R100. As you enter **Inya** village (km706.4), be sure to keep your eyes open for what may be the most dramatically placed and memorable Lenin statue in Russia. Some 3km before the tiny settlement of **Iodra** (pop 317!), on the left-hand side, stands a stone idol with a well-preserved and somewhat haunting face. Look for the idol's slightly worn sword. Directly opposite there are some faint rock drawings. If driving, watch out for the wild horses and goats that often block the road in this area.

At km712.6, overshadowed by an unsightly pylon, picnic tables and prayer flags tempt you to stop for wonderful views of the meeting of the Chui and Katun Rivers far below. There's another petroglyph group at **Kalbak Tash** crag, a five-minute walk north of km721. The road then snakes scenically through the **Chuya Canyon** to Aktash (km790) with awesome views of snow-capped Mt Aktru to the right.

AKTASH AREA АКТАШ

☎38846 / POP 3400 / ⏰MOSCOW +3HR

This rundown and isolated village, whose name means 'white stone' in the Altai language, commands a dramatic area of craggy valleys. There's nothing at all to see in the village itself, where lazy cows meander down dusty streets. But if you stroll 3km north from the edge of town you'll come to the striking rocky canyon named **Red Gate** (Красные Ворота). As a sight, it doesn't quite deserve the reputation it enjoys locally, but it's worth a look. Some of the graffiti on the rocks was written by soldiers after returning from WWII. (The rest was written by teenagers after too many beers.)

Aktash could make a base for mountain adventures in the lovely Northern Chuysky Range with its challenging mountaineering on **Mt Aktru** (4044m) and **Mt Maashey** (4177m) or for trekking to the **Shavlinsky Lakes** for idyllic mountain views. However, for all of these you will need outside help as in Aktash itself there are no tourist facilities and no waiting guides. Chartering a suitable 4WD to reach Mt Aktru base camp isn't easy, but the trip is lovely if you succeed.

Visa registration (☎23 381; ul Mira 1a; ⏰8am-5pm) is required if you missed registering in Gorno-Altaisk. The local **border post** (☎23 555; ⏰24hr) is at the southern end of ul Pushkina. Turn left after the central WWII memorial.

There's not much accommodation choice here. The central, two-room unnamed **hotel** (☎23 831; ul Pushkina 1; dm R400) is buried within the bowels of a decaying building housing dusty offices. The owners keep irregular hours, so if you really want to stay you may just have to wait around for someone to turn up. The unmarked **Hotel Radioreleyniserkh** (☎23 311; ul Zarechnaya 17; d R150) does have four decent rooms, if you can find the key holder. Try looking in the factory at ul Zarechnaya 15 or asking around. To find it, walk towards the stream from ul Pushkina, cross the bridge and walk straight ahead. Watch out for stray dogs here!

Locals are also willing to put travellers up from R300 a night. Try asking at the two cheap unnamed cafés or the food shop on central ul Molkova, across from the WWII memorial.

Neither Aktash nor Onguday have professional taxis, but shopkeepers can suggest potential drivers. Aktash to Kosh-Agach by car shouldn't cost more than R1500.

KOSH-AGACH AREA КОШ АГАЧ

☎38842 / POP 5500 / ⏰MOSCOW +3HR

Clouds permitting, the best views on the whole Chuysky Trakt are between Aktash and Kosh-Agach. Wide, if distant, panoramas of perennially snow-topped peaks rise formidably behind valleys known somewhat misleadingly as the Kuray and Chuy Steppe (km821 to km840 and km870 onwards). These are interspersed by more great canyons and a colourful mountainside that looks like marbled chocolate pudding (km856). The Kuray Steppe regularly hosts Russia's paragliding championships: see the website of NGO **Triada** (www.triadaclub.com/kurai). At km840 look out for the 'spirit tree' tied with white ribbons.

The road leading to Kosh-Agach sees the greenery start to die out, and the scenery gradually transforms into something resembling a lunar landscape. **Kosh-Agach** means 'two trees' in the Altai language, but – if they ever existed – any trees here would have wilted and died long ago. Some 50km from the Russia–Mongolia border, Kosh-Agach is the driest inhabited place in the Russian Federation, with average rainfalls of under 150mm. It's so dry that potatoes won't grow and have to be brought in from further north.

ALTAI BORDER ZONES

The Altai Republic's border zones with China, Kazakhstan and Mongolia have been under the control of the FSB (formerly the KGB) since 2006. Foreigners are required to submit an application for permission to enter these areas. This is on top of Altai Republic registration. It affects anyone heading beyond Kosh-Agach to the Mongolian border, and anyone travelling further south than, and including, Ust-Koksa.

Applications should be made in Russian and must be submitted by fax to **Aktash** (☎/fax 388-462 3654) at least 10 days before your journey. The application should include passport details (everything, including where and when issued and expiry date), planned route, purpose of journey and home address. Passes are then picked up at the relevant border zone post. The process is extremely complicated and the best way is to use the services of the firm that provided your visa. If you are travelling with an organised group into the border zones, the company will arrange these passes for you, saving you a massive headache. Independent Russian-speaking travellers have, however, been known to receive passes at the FSB HQ in Aktash without applying in advance. Others have simply talked their way into the area. Neither option is something to be relied upon, though.

The town has a strange, end-of-the-world feeling about it, with its shanty-type homes petering out into magical flat steppe just beyond Hotel Tsentralnaya. When the dusty air clears, the nearby mountains appear from nowhere like apparitions. Russians are in the minority here, with Kazakhs and Altai making up something like 90% of the population. Indeed, when the call to prayer sounds from the wooden **Khazret Osman Mosque** (ul Sovetskaya 62), it's easy to forget you are still in Russia.

Central ul Sovetskaya is home to the bus stand and the town's three ultrabasic hotels. **Hotel Tranzit** (Гостиница Транзит; ☎22 682; ul Sovetskaya 50-52; d R400), a friendly but somewhat chaotic crash pad, has five doubles with shared inside toilets and showers. Guests are free to make use of the cooker and fridge. Other hotels are the just-as-elementary **Hotel Shankhai** (Гостиница Шанхай; ul Sovetskaya 63; dm R250) and the grimy **Hotel Bazar** (Гостиница Базар; ul Sovetskaya 61; dm R250), both of which have shared outside toilets. In the event of everywhere being full (as can happen when expeditions are in town), locals will put travellers up for around R300 a night.

Despite posted '24-hour' opening times, most shops and cafés actually close by 6pm. The **Stolovaya** (Столовая; ul Sovetskaya 62a; meals R50-100) has simple Russian fare. **Café Telets** (Кафе Телец) opposite the **post office** (Почтамт) also has the usual stodgy soups and *pelmeni*. There is a handy **supermarket** (⏰10am-10pm) at ul Sovetskaya 61.

If you head out of town towards Mongolia, you'll come across Kosh-Agach's large Soviet-era **welcome sign**, which depicts three stern officials (one Slav, one Kazakh and one Altai) standing next to a hammer and sickle. Well worth a look, if only for the great photo ops.

From the **bus stand** (Такси и маршрутки в Горно-Алтайск; ul Sovetskaya 28), there is a 7am minibus to Gorno-Altaisk (R550, nine hours). Another one usually leaves in the summer at 8am, but check at your hotel. Shared taxis (R800 per seat) offer much better views and leave throughout the morning, depending on demand. It's best to arrange something in advance. For transport to the Mongolian town of Olgii it's best to find a 4WD UAZ vehicle by asking around at the hotels and shops.

UST-KOKSA — УСТЬ-КОКСА

☎38848 / POP 430 / ⏰MOSCOW +3HR

The road to Tyungur branches off the northern Chuysky Trakt at Cherga and crosses a delightfully isolated, mostly forested area via **Baragash**. After the high grasslands of Ust-Kan, there are glimpses of the distant white tops from the **Kyrlykskiy Pass** as the road descends into the Koksa Valley. Though less dramatic than the Chuysky Trakt, the landscape is attractive with bucolic meadows framed by hills and bluffs. Watch out for the seemingly suicidal ground squirrels that sprint from one side of the road to the other as vehicles approach! The locals call the cows that stand in the middle of the road blocking traffic 'freelance traffic cops'.

Ust-Kan has a very basic **hotel** (dm R450) at its bus station, and there is a small **hut-**

camp (d R500) with clean outside toilets and camping for R100 beside the main Tyungur road, 4km east of town near an archaeological cave site.

The valley meets the Katun River at **Ust-Koksa**, which is home to the delightful wooden **Pokrovskoe Church** (ul Nagornaya 31). In the 1930s the many Old Believers of the Koksa and Uymon Valleys offered fierce armed resistance to collectivisation, leading to the almost total destruction of their villages by the Soviet state. Nonetheless, the tiny Verkhny Uymon village has an **Old Believers' Museum** (Музей Старообрядчества), which contains artefacts from their everyday lives. The village also has a small **Nikolai Rerikh House-Museum**. Opening hours vary and entrance costs R40 for both museums.

In Ust-Koksa, the **Nossfera** (8.30am-4pm Mon-Fri) bank behind the hotel changes euros and US dollars. The **Uimonskaya Dolina Hotel** (Sovetskaya ul 71; per person R500), with multicoloured roof, has decent rooms upstairs, let down by a meet-the-neighbours shared squat toilet. Rooms with toilets cost from R1000. **Café Elegiya** (meals R150-300; 10am-midnight) is across the road at ul Sovetskaya 54. The attached supermarket is well stocked and is your last chance to stock up on luxuries before the wilderness begins for real.

Some 10km before Tyungur, the **Dom Okhotnika guesthouse** (22 024; d R1750) has great views and comfortable rooms. It can also organise hiking trips and river trips. Bookings can be made through **Ak Tur** (659 407; www.aktour.ru) in Barnaul.

ALTAI CRIME

The Altai Republic has the second-highest crime levels in Russia. As a retired regional police chief (now forced to work as a taxi driver to make a living) told us, 'It's easier to get away with stuff when you are so far from civilisation.' He was right, of course, but some of the lowest wages and living standards in Russia also play their part. As ever, there's no reason to become unduly alarmed, but it pays to be aware that this is real 'Wild East' territory. Take particular caution in the Aktash and Kosh-Agach regions.

TYUNGUR & MT BELUKHA

ТЮНГУР И ГОРА БЕЛУХА

The tiny village of Tyungur sits in an appealing valley. Although lacking viewpoints itself, it's the normal staging point for treks towards Mt Belukha (4506m), Siberia's highest peak. Surrounding valleys and lakes are among Russia's most spectacular, but access requires strenuous guided hiking.

Tyungur's well-organised **Turbaza Vysotnik** (Турбаза Высотник; 22 024; www.belukha.ru; dm/d from R300/1700, tent space per person R150) is a fantastic place to organise trekking, rafting or ascents of the mighty Mt Belukha. It's just across the tiny suspension bridge from the village itself. Staff are friendly and English-speaking and there's a great café that is the nearest you'll find to an international traveller hang-out in Altai. Almost anything you'll need for mountaineering or treks into the wilderness, including trips to surrounding lakes, is available for hire here, including tents and guides. Bring trekking supplies as Tyungur has minimal groceries.

Ascents of Belukha (grade 3A to 5A) are only for experienced mountaineers but don't require special permits. A two-week package (from around R30,000 per person) available from Turbaza Vysotnik includes guides, food and acclimatisation climbs for individuals or small groups. It also offers trips by raft and horseback to the foot of the mountain for a similar price. If you want to spy Mt Belukha without a full-blown expedition, take a long day hike from Tyungur part-way up Mt Baida.

Before setting off on any of Tyungur's five-to 12-day trekking adventures, be aware that you're heading for real wilderness. Discuss your plans carefully with staff at one of the *turbazy* (camps) in Tyungur, or join an organised group by booking well ahead with one of the many trekking companies, notably those in Barnaul, Novosibirsk, Omsk or beyond. Hiking alone or without a guide is highly discouraged. Renting packhorses for your baggage will make the treks more pleasant and horsemen often double as guides, though none speak any English.

The other accommodation option in Tyungur is **Uch-Sumer** (Уч-Сумер; 29 424; fax 22 872; www.uch-sumer.ru/eng; yurt space/d R500/1400), a five-minute walk to the south-west of the bridge. It's popular with an older crowd, many of them hunters. The hotel rooms all have toilets and showers, and the complimentary breakfast is good. The

ALTAI'S STONE IDOLS

Altai is famous for its standing stone idols. Known locally as *kameniy babi* (most confusingly, given their overwhelmingly masculine forms, 'stone wenches'), the best were carved in human form with moustaches, shown holding a cup that symbolically housed the soul of the dead. Just a few have avoided being carted off to museums. Some examples of varying interest appear beside the Chuysky Trakt and in the depths of Tyungur. There are also many groups of animal-shaped petroglyphs (rock drawings) of debatable origin. These may be fascinating but most are so faint that you might miss the scratches even when you're staring right at them.

owners also offer many tour options, notably hunting around Lake Kucherla and elsewhere in the mountains where they maintain cabins. The old Soviet helicopter on its grounds makes a good place to sit in and read and/or drink beer.

From Gorno-Altaisk a strangely timed 1.45pm bus runs daily to Tyungur (R610, nine hours), arriving just before midnight. It returns at 8am via Ust-Koksa and Ust-Kan. *Marshrutky* run from Gorno-Altaisk to Ust-Koksa (R800) when full, usually two or three times each morning, departing from a corner of the bus station parking area. A taxi from here to Tyungur will cost around R500. Departures are possible as late as 10am southbound, but northbound all will have usually left by 8am.

Taxis plying the Ust-Koksa–Verkhny Uymon route charge from R700 return with waiting time; buses only run twice a week. Turbaza Vysotnik can arrange transfers to Biysk or Gorno-Altaisk. You may also be able to hitch a ride with fellow guests.

KEMEROVO REGION

Although heavily associated with the mining industry of the Kuzbass district, there is more to the Kemerovo region (Кемеровская Область) than endless piles of coal. Novokuznetsk, constructed almost from scratch by Soviet 'shockworkers' (superproductive workers) in the 1930s, is the region's biggest city and boasts a well-laid-out centre with some remarkable Soviet-era monuments dedicated to socialist worker heroes. While worth a brief visit in its own right, Novokuznetsk also makes a convenient stopover point between Abakan and Biysk when overlanding between Altai and Tuva.

Some three hours drive south of Novokuznetsk lie the Gornaya Shoriya mountains, containing the skiing resort of Sheregesh, extremely popular with Russian snowboarders. Even if you don't ski or snowboard, it's still a great place to spend a few days.

Novokuznetsk Новокузнецк

☎3843 / POP 563,000 / ⏰MOSCOW +3HR

Founded on the right bank of the Tom River in 1618, the frequently enlarged Kuznetsk Fortress became one of the most important guardians of imperial Russia's southeastern frontier. The chunky remnants remain one of Novokuznetsk's main attractions. The city's left bank, named Stalinsk until 1961, developed from 1932 as a gigantic steel town and is now the city centre.

An indication of the strength and importance of the local metal plants is that Novokuznetsk supplies 70% of Russia's train tracks. However, they are also mainly responsible for Novokuznetsk being named the third most polluted city in Russia in 2010 (a slight improvement from its previous number two rating).

Novokuznetsk's main sights and hotels are mostly spread around pr Metallurgov, the street that stretches away from you as you come out of the train station. You won't need more than a day here before heading on to Sheregesh. There are good maps available in the kiosk inside the train station and at the **Knizhni Mir** (pr Metallurgov 27; ⏰10am-7pm Mon-Fri, 10am-5pm Sat & Sun) bookshop.

Sights & Activities

Prospekt Metallurgov HISTORICAL AREA

(Пр Металлургов) A good example of the city's 'Brave New 1930s' feel, pr Metallurgov is an easy stroll due north from the cohabiting bus and train stations.

Metallurgists' Garden HISTORICAL SITE

(pr Metallurgov 18) Guarded by two splendidly reverential statues of Soviet-era metalworkers, this pleasant garden contains within its grounds the now empty constructionist building that once housed Siberia's first audio cinema.

Park Gagarina PARK
(pr Metallurgov) Behind Metallurgists' Garden, this oasis of green contains a bust of a jolly-looking Yury Gagarin and Siberia's biggest **Planetarium** (admission R60; ⏲10am-6pm).

Drama Theatre THEATRE
(Новокузнецкий драматический театр; pr Metallurgov 28) Just past the garden, on the right, is the city's grandly colonnaded main theatre, constructed in the early 1960s.

Statue of Vladimir Mayakovsky MONUMENT
Although the doomed writer never actually visited Novokuznetsk, he was so moved by the Soviet project to build a new city that he penned a poem starting with the lines, famous all over Russia, *'Ya znau budet gorod, ya znau sadu svest'* ('I know there will be a city, I know the gardens will bloom'). The statue is opposite pr Metallurgov 39.

Lenin & Gorky Statue MONUMENT
An apparently coal-caked Lenin and Maxim Gorky (founder of socialist realism) discuss – or plot? – something or other, next to the main post office at pr Metallurgov 21.

Former Soviet Builders Club HISTORICAL BUILDING
(ul Ordzhonikidzye 23) Guarded by two more statues of Soviet workers, wielding a hammer and a plasterer's board, the one-time cement workers' club is now used as a cultural centre. Take the first left after the Mayakovsky statue.

Old town HISTORICAL AREA
If you want to visit the sparse remnants of old Kuznetsk, take frequent *marshrutka* 5 from outside the bus station. A taxi straight there will cost about R250. Ask for the 'Ostrog.' Get off at Sovetsky pl and follow the road that leads steeply up beside the beautiful 1792 **Transfiguration Cathedral** (Преображенский собор; ⏲8am-2pm & 4-7pm). On the hilltop, the restored stone ramparts of the **Kuznetsk Fortress** (Острог; www.kuzn-krepost.narod.ru; ul Geologicheskaya; museum admission R100, photography/video R150; ⏲10am-5pm) are massive and topped with cannons but represent only 20% of their 1810 extent.

Sleeping

Complimentary breakfasts are included, except at the resting rooms.

Hotel Gostiny Dvor HOTEL €€€
(Гостиница Гостиный Двор; ☎795 821; www.guest.hotel-el.ru; pr Kirova 34; s/d from R2300/4200) Set in quiet grounds a short walk from Metallurgists' Garden, these bright, good-sized, reasonably priced rooms are in great demand. Book ahead!

Hotel Persona Grata HOTEL €€
(☎390 770; www.persona-nk.ru; pr Kirova 105; s/d from R3200/3900; @ wi-fi) Comfortable hotel with wi-fi and sparklingly clean rooms that are – on the whole – tastefully furnished and large. It's 10 minutes' walk down pr Kirova from Hotel Novokuznetsk.

Hotel Aba HOTEL €€
(Гостиница Аба; ☎424 460; www.aba-hotel.ru; ul Kuybysheva 8; d from R3500; ❄) Rooms in this polite, modern hotel are bright and fairly stylish with clean, modern shower booths and toilets. Soundproofing between rooms is not so great though. It's 1.5km northwest of the station; three huge blocks up pr Kurako then left. There are also saunas for R800 an hour.

Hotel Novokuznetsk HOTEL €€€
(Гостиница Новокузнецк; ☎460 021; www.novokuznetskaya.com; ul Kirova 53; s/d R2500/4400; @) This Soviet-built hotel has seen a facelift in recent years and rooms are decent, if unimaginative. Internet and computer in lobby (R100 per hour). It's on the large traffic circle, two bus stops down the first right turning after Metallurgists' Garden.

Resting rooms HOSTEL €
(Комнаты Отдыха, komnaty otdykha; ☎743 131; main train station; 1-/6-hr R200/700) Clean rooms with TVs, but you'll pay more (R50) for a hot shower.

Eating & Drinking

The majority of restaurants are centred around pr Metallurgov.

Shafran RUSSIAN €
(Шафран; ul Kirova 103; meals R300-450) Next to Hotel Persona Grata, Shafran offers a wide range of good-value sandwiches and soups as well as pizza and *pelmeni*.

Pechki-Lavochki RUSSIAN €
(Печки-Лавочки; ul Kirova 21; meals R250-400) Good, cheap and traditional Russian food served right next to Metallurgists' Garden. Gets busy at lunchtimes with local office workers.

Pivovarnaya BAR €
(Пивоварная; pr Metallurgov 19; meals R350-500) To the left of Hotel Novokuznetsk, this no-nonsense bar-restaurant offers cheap beer (from R70) and filling meals of the meat and spaghetti variant.

Bar-Café BAR €
(ul Bardina 2; meals R130-250; ⌚24hr) A cheap and greasy unnamed bar-café opposite the train station that sells beer (R60 to R100), vodka and the usual *pelmeni* round the clock.

Supermarket SUPERMARKET
(pr Metallurgov 2; ⌚24hr) For self-catering, this large supermarket is conveniently located and cheap.

Information

Main post office (pr Metallurgov 21; ⌚9am-7pm Mon-Fri, 10am-4pm Sat & Sun)

Getting There & Around

There are two flights a day from Novokuznetsk's **Spichenkovo airport** to Moscow (from R10,000, four hours, 6.40am and 7.30 am). To get to the airport, take bus or *marshrutka* 160 from the train station.

Trains run daily to Abakan (*platskart/kupe* R700/1200, 10 hours, 5.55pm). There are up to five trains a day to Novosibirsk, the most convenient of which leaves at 7.17pm (R760/1200, 10 hours). The relatively expensive ski-train to Tashtagol (from which you can reach Sheregesh by bus) departs at 3.42am and 6.20am in season (*platskart/kupe* R863/1430, five hours). Only the first runs off season. There are over 15 buses a day to Tashtagol (R183, 3½ hours). A seat in a taxi will cost you around R500, and will get you there in some two hours.

Two slow, bumpy buses run across lonely, undulating agricultural landscapes to Biysk (R350, five hours) departing at 10.30am and 1.55pm. There are also over 15 buses a day to Tashtagol (R141, four hours) and Barnaul (R214, 4½ hours).

Sheregesh Шерегеш

☎3843 / POP 9600 / ⌚MOSCOW +3HR

Isolated and tiny Sheregesh – or 'Gesh' as many locals call it – is a mining village located in the shade of the Zelyonaya Gora (Green Mountain) peak, the focus of a booming skiing and snowboarding scene in recent years. The mountain is sacred to the local Shortsi people.

The journey here is an added bonus, winding through tiny villages and deserted mountain country roads – not for nothing has Sheregesh been called Russia's 'little Switzerland'. If you arrive out of season, Sheregesh is also a fine place to relax and/or go hiking in the taiga and around the mountain, although many places will be closed.

The main thoroughfare, ul Gagarina, runs from the ski slope through the centre of the village.

Activities

The area's remoteness means that even at the height of the skiing and snowboarding season there are almost no queues for the ski lift (although it can get crowded on 8 March – Women's Day – and during the New Year holidays). The season usually lasts from mid-November to mid-May, although snows start to thin out by March. The Russian national snowboard team trains in the region.

There are as yet no lights on the **Sheregesh ski slope** and so skiing is only allowed until sunset. There are a host of firms offering ski and snowboard rental from R250 an hour at the base of the slopes. Many of these also offer lessons starting from R350 an hour. **Kuba** (☎8-905-947 0499) is one of the oldest companies, but there is very little variation in terms of price or quality. The funicular costs R150 for a return trip. The two-seat ski lift costs R100, but is free from 9am to 9.30am.

From the top of the ski lift at Sheregesh, take a snow motorbike to the nearby giant cross and then on to the unusual *'verbluda'* (camel) rock formation. The ride should cost about R600. With the wind in your face as you speed through the snow, it's hard not to feel a little like James Bond. Hold on tight! The trip lasts about half an hour, with time for photos and clambering about on the rocks.

Tour Academy (☎in Novosibirsk 383-213 8300; touracadem@ngs.ru) is an established company based on the ski slope that can sort out trips to Sheregesh, including transport to and from the village.

Sleeping

The vast majority of hotels are based around the mountain. Prices given here are for the high season and can fall by as much as 40% in off season. Addresses are either non-existent or meaningless. Look out for signs! All hotels listed here offer complimentary breakfasts and all have at least a café. If you don't want to stay in a hotel, locals let out rooms from R500 a night (ask around), but you'll be some distance from the slope.

TOP CHOICE **Ays Club** HOTEL €€
(Айс Клуб; ☎8-923-625 1516; www.ays-club.ru; s/d/ste from R700/1700/2500) One of the first hotels you'll come across as you approach the mountain, friendly Ays is popular with young snowboarders. The rooms are stylish and very spacious and it also has a good café (meals R300 to R500, beer from R80) and club.

Kedrovaya HOTEL €€
(Кедровая; ☎34 715; www.kedr.kuzpress.ru; d from R1500) Kedrovaya is so close to the slope that 'you can walk home without taking off your skis'. The luxury rooms really live up to their name (R2000 to R2500), and all have excellent views of the mountain.

Akvilon HOTEL €€
(Аквилион; ☎8-913-436 4840; www.akvilon-hotel.ru; d/ste R3800/5000;) Grand Akvilon boasts great saunas (R600 per hour) and a swimming pool. It also has an art gallery featuring paintings by Siberian artists. The on-site restaurant (meals R600 to R800) has the widest menu in Sheregesh.

Berloga HOTEL €€
(Берлога; ☎203 040; www.berlogahotel.ru; d/ste from R2400/4200;) This four-floor hotel describes itself as the 'cosiest place' in town and while other establishments might beg to differ, there's no denying the Berloga's attention to detail. Good-quality rooms, some with great views, as well as a swimming pool and a decent restaurant make this an option worth considering. Also offers three-room apartments from R6500.

Olga HOTEL €€
(Ольга; ☎975 975; www.olgahotel.ru; d/ste from R1700/3100) One of the biggest hotels in the area, Olga's economy rooms are decent but uninspiring. Its suites are, however, superb, but pricey. It offers a range of activities throughout the year, from excursions to paintball. Also has a good restaurant (meals R300 to R600, beer from R90).

Eating & Drinking

The restaurant scene is not particularly developed at Sheregesh. Guests generally eat at their hotels, although there is nothing to stop you checking out the food on offer at other places.

While you are in Sheregesh, be sure to try the local wild leek. Local women sell it by the roadside for around R40 a bag. Known as *kabla* locally and *cheremsha* in Russian, its distinctive garlicky taste is one you won't forget in a hurry!

TOP CHOICE **Karitishka** CAFÉ €
(Картишка; meals R200-400) Based at the top of the mountain, this modest café is guarded by a memorable Yeti statue. Awesome views all year-round.

Kurshavel NIGHTCLUB
(Куршавель; meals R300-500) This café and popular nightclub (admission R200) combines sushi with thumping dance music and is right next to the ski lifts. Closed off season.

Tsarskaya Okhota RUSSIAN €€
(Царская Охота; meals R400-600) On the 1st floor of the decent **Gubernskaya hotel** (www.gubernskaya-hotel.ru), Tsarskaya Okhota serves fine European, Russian and South Caucasus dishes.

Korchma UKRAINIAN €
(Корчма; meals R300-500; ⌚11am-1am) Hearty Ukrainian food at reasonable prices, behind the souvenir stalls at the foot of the mountain.

Information

Sberbank (⌚9.30am-6pm) At the base of the ski slope. Decent euro and US dollar rates, considering it has no competition. Also has an ATM.

Sheregesh.ru (www.sheregesh.ru) Has plenty of information on the scene at Sheregesh.

Getting There & Away

Sheregesh is reached by bus or train from the village of Tashtagol. There are regular buses to Tashtagol from Novokuznetsk. From Tashtagol **bus station** (☎334 630), bus 101 takes 30 minutes to reach the last stop in Sheregesh. From here, walk up the hill and turn right at the main road. It's another 45-minute walk to the actual slope and the hotels – walk along the main road and take a right at the first junction. Or take a **taxi** (☎8-960-912 1111) for around R150; definitely recommended if you arrive in the evening. A taxi all the way from Tashtagol to Sheregesh will cost around R350. There is a small and basic hostel above the bus station at Tashtagol if you get stuck. There are over 10 buses a day from Tashtagol to Novokuznetsk (R183, four hours, 6.10am to 8pm).

Eastern Siberia

Includes »

Best Places to Eat

» English School Café (p515)
» Baatarai Urgöö (p552)
» Buddha Bar & Lounge (p515)
» Kochevnik (p533)
» Chingiskhan (p552)

Best Places to Stay

» Baikaler Eco-Hostel (p537)
» Hotel Sayen (p532)
» Derevenka (p538)
» Nikita's Homestead (p542)
» Aldyn Bulak Yurt Hotel (p505)

Why Go?

Endless ice-bound winters, oven-hot summers, a history of imperial exile and Stalinist brutality – Eastern Siberia (Восточная Сибирь) may not sound like everyone's first choice of holiday destination, but there's much more to this vast region than blood-craving mosquitoes and blizzard-lost Gulag camps.

Focus is given to the map by glorious Baikal, the world's deepest lake. Only Siberia could possess such a phenomenon with its crystal waters, mind-boggling stats and a long list of outlandish endemic species. The lake presents a major obstacle to the Trans-Siberian Railway, which cradles Siberia in a string of intriguing cities such as architecturally grand Irkutsk, exotically Asian Ulan-Ude and youthful, oil-rich Krasnoyarsk.

But the trick to enjoying Eastern Siberia is in escaping the cities – hit the Great Baikal Trail, go hunting for Tuvan standing stones or seek out far-flung Buddhist temples in Buryatiya – the possibilities are endless, almost as endless as the immense sweep of geography they occupy.

When to Go

Irkutsk

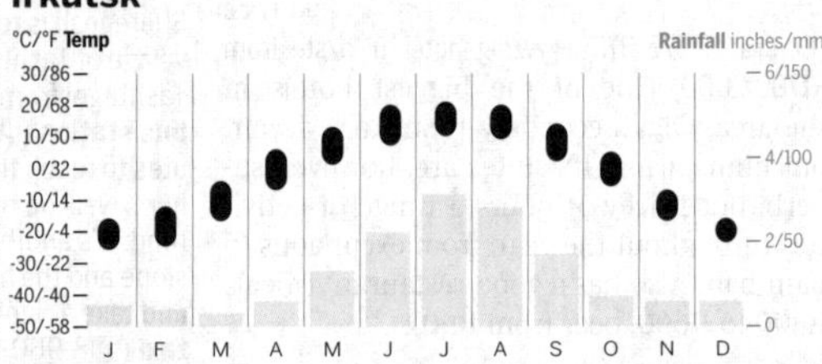

Mar Take a stroll on Lake Baikal when the Siberian winter turns its surface hard as steel.

Jul Get on down at Shushenskoe's Sayan Ring International Ethnic Music Festival.

Sep Watch larch trees around Lake Baikal turn a fiery yellow during the brief autumn.

History

For century after tranquil prehistoric century, Eastern Siberia's indigenous peoples, such as the Evenki (Tungusi) north of Lake Baikal and the Kets of the Yenisey River, lived a peaceful existence in harmony with nature, harvesting game and berries in the thick taiga, fishing the rivers and building their *chumy* (tepees), largely oblivious of the outside world. In the south, horse-riding nomads of the Scythian culture (700 BC–AD 300) thrived in what is now Tuva, leaving behind fields of standing stones and circular *kurgany* (burial mounds) packed with intricately fashioned gold.

Gradually, however, Mongol-Turkic tribes began their expansion north and west, led by fearsome leaders such as Attila the Hun. The Buryats filtered north from Mongolia during the 11th and 12th centuries to assimilate local peoples and become the dominant ethnic group in Eastern Siberia. In the early 13th century, Chinggis (Genghis) Khaan united Mongol tribes across the region and went on to conquer China. Subsequent khans would sweep west across the steppe to sack the great cities of European Russia.

ENTER THE RUSSIANS

With a firm foothold in Western Siberia, small Cossack units began arriving further east in the early 17th century, establishing an *ostrog* (fortress) at river confluence positions such as Krasnoyarsk (1628), Ulan-Ude (1666, originally Verkhneudinsk) and Irkutsk (1651). Traders from European Russia followed and pressed indigenous peoples into supplying sable pelts at bargain prices (a cruel tax called the *yasak*). The Buryats put up some resistance to the European invaders, but were no match for the Russian firearms.

European peasants were the next group to make the treacherous journey from the west, followed by banished prisoners and Old Believers after the religious rift of 1653; the original defensive forts burst like popcorn into ramshackle timber towns. Other Siberian settlers included the influential Decembrists (see p632), who'd failed to pull off a coup in 1825, and political prisoners from the uprisings in Russian-occupied Poland. The end of serfdom in 1861 brought a tsunami of land-hungry peasants escaping the cramped conditions of European Russia.

In the 18th century, Tibetan Buddhism arrived in Buryat settlements east of Lake Baikal and was successfully superimposed onto existing shamanist beliefs. The western Buryats were never converted and shamanism still dominates west of the lake.

THE IMPACT OF THE RAILROADS

Siberia's fur-based economy rapidly diversified and the discovery of gold further encouraged colonisation. Trade with China brought considerable wealth following the treaties of Nerchinsk in 1689 and Kyakhta in 1728. Lucrative tea caravans continued trudging the Siberian post road until put out of business by the Suez Canal and the Trans-Siberian Railway. The railway instantly changed the fortunes of cities, most notably Kyakhta on the border with Mongolia. Once one of the richest towns in all Russia, it plunged into provincial obscurity when the tea trade dried up. In the early 20th century the newly finished line brought yet another influx of Russian settlers east.

Following the 1917 Bolshevik revolution and the outbreak of the Russian Civil War, Siberia declared itself firmly in the White camp under Admiral Kolchak. After much fierce fighting along the Trans-Siberian Railway, Red forces finally took the region in 1919. Kolchak was arrested and executed in Irkutsk in 1920, and the last shots of the civil war were fired in Tuva. From 1920 to 1922, Eastern Siberia was nominally independent with the pro-Lenin Far Eastern Republic centred on Chita.

As the USSR stabilised and Stalin's infamous Gulag camps were created, Siberia reverted to its old role as a land of banishment. Nonetheless, unforced colonisation continued apace, especially after WWII when much heavy industry was shifted east for strategic security. Prisoners, volunteers and Soviets seeking higher pay for working in the east arrived to construct dams and transport infrastructure. The greatest of these projects was the ill-conceived Baikalo–Amurskaya Magistral (BAM) railway stretching over 4200km from Tayshet to Sovetskaya Gavan on the Pacific coast.

POST-SOVIET SIBERIA

Since the end of the USSR in 1991, many towns and villages away from the economic beaten track (such as along the BAM and the Yenisey River) have deteriorated into virtual ghost towns. Others, such as Krasnoyarsk and Irkutsk, have benefited from Russia's new-found economic strength on the back of high oil and gas prices. Lake Baikal is attracting more tourists than ever, and Moscow has declared certain areas on its shores special

Eastern Siberia Highlights

1. Wonder at the craftsmanship of ancient Scythian gold displayed at **Kyzyl's National Museum** (p504)
2. Walk, cycle or hitch a lift across frozen **Lake Baikal** (p524)
3. Admire the ostentatious 19th-century architecture of **Irkutsk** (p525), once known as the 'Paris of Siberia'
4. Be amazed at the uncanny sounds a human voice can make during **Tuvan throat singing** (p505)
5. Mooch with the monks at **Ivolginsk Datsan** (p554) and many other revived Buddhist monasteries around the region
6. Bag up your boots for the **Frolikha Adventure Coastline Trail** (p521), one of Siberia's most exhilarating long-distance hiking routes
7. Get into hot water at **northern Baikal's minispas** (p524) for a spot of r'n'r Siberian-style
8. Take a turn around Baikal's rocky southern shore on the **Circumbaikal Railway** (p540)

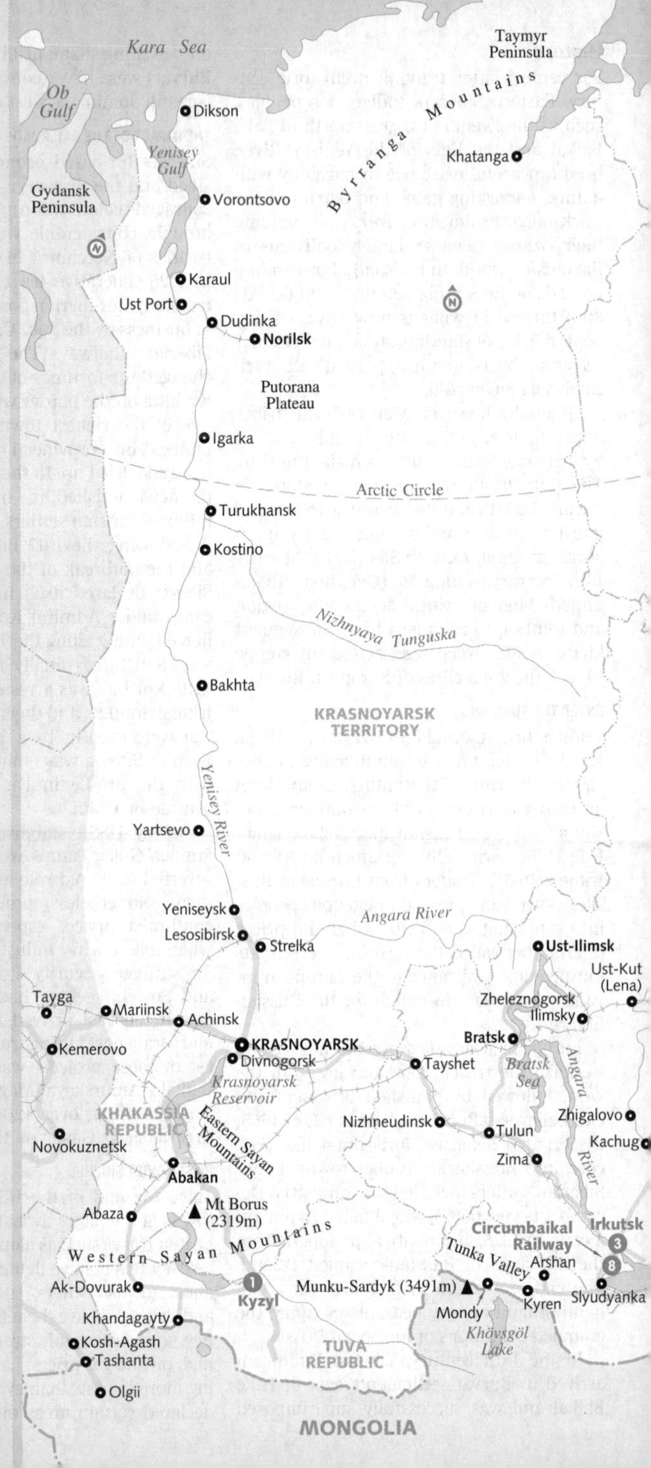

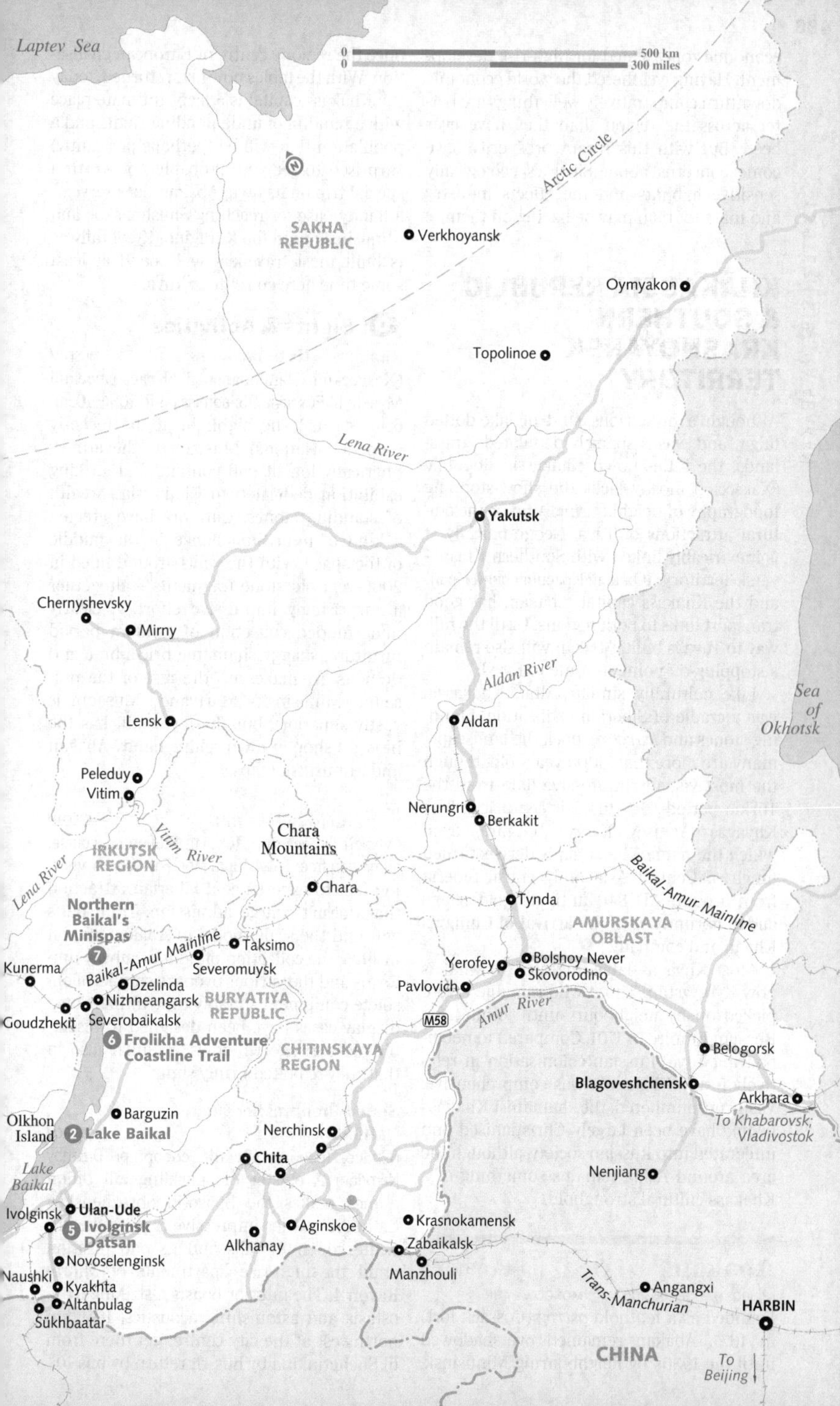

Laptev Sea
0 500 km
0 300 miles
Arctic Circle
SAKHA REPUBLIC
Verkhoyansk
Oymyakon
Topolinoe
Lena River
Yakutsk
Chernyshevsky
Mirny
Aldan River
Sea of Okhotsk
Lensk
Aldan
Peleduy
Vitim
Nerungri
Berkakit
Vitim River
Chara Mountains
IRKUTSK REGION
Lena River
Chara
Baikal-Amur Mainline
Tynda
Northern Baikal's Minispas
7
AMURSKAYA OBLAST
Taksimo
Baikal-Amur Mainline
Severomuysk
Kunerma
Yerofey
Bolshoy Never
Skovorodino
Dzelinda
Pavlovich
Nizhneangarsk
BURYATIYA REPUBLIC
Goudzhekit
Severobaikalsk
Amur River
M58
6 Frolikha Adventure Coastline Trail
CHITINSKAYA REGION
Belogorsk
Blagoveshchensk
Arkhara
To Khabarovsk; Vladivostok
Barguzin
Olkhon Island
2 Lake Baikal
Nerchinsk
Chita
Nenjiang
Lake Baikal
Ivolginsk
Ulan-Ude
5 Ivolginsk Datsan
Aginskoe
Krasnokamensk
Alkhanay
Zabaikalsk
Novoselenginsk
Manzhouli
Naushki
Kyakhta
Altanbulag
Sükhbaatar
Trans-Manchurian
Angangxi
HARBIN
CHINA
To Beijing

economic zones slated for high-rise development. Having weathered the world economic downturn comparatively well, things are better across the region than they have ever been. But with this recent prosperity have come concerns about Siberia's ecologically sensitive habitats and the effects industry and mass tourism may be having on them.

KHAKASSIA REPUBLIC & SOUTHERN KRASNOYARSK TERRITORY

Although a mysterious land of lake-dotted taiga and vast, sparsely-populated grasslands, the little-known Khakassia Republic (Хакассия) mostly lacks the show-stopping topography of neighbouring Altai or the cultural attractions of Tuva. Geographically, it is inextricably linked with Southern Krasnoyarsk Territory (Южный Красноярский Край) and the Khakass capital, Abakan, has good transport links to both regions. Until the railway to Tuva is built, Abakan will also remain a stopping-off point en route to Kyzyl.

Like culturally similar Altai, Khakassia was a cradle of Siberian civilisation. Standing stones and *kurgany* pock the landscape; many are more than 3000 years old, though the most visually impressive date from the Turkic period (6th to 12th centuries). The Khyagas (Yenisey Kyrgyz) empire, from which the name Khakassia is derived, ruled much of Central Asia and central Siberia from around AD 840 until its golden age ended abruptly with the arrival of Chinggis Khaan and company.

Most Khyagas later migrated to what is now Kyrgyzstan. Those who remained were picked on by neighbours until joining the Russian Empire in 1701. Compared to neighbouring Tuva, Russian colonisation in relatively fertile Khakassia was comprehensive. Vastly outnumbered, the shamanist Khakass people have been largely Christianised and integrated into Russian society, although the area around Askiz remains something of a Khakass cultural stronghold.

Abakan Абакан

☎3902 / POP 165,200 / ⏲MOSCOW +4HR

Founded as a foothold *ostrog* (Cossack fort) in 1675, Abakan remained overshadowed until the 1930s by neighbouring Minusinsk, once the region's centre of European civilisation. With the tables now firmly turned, today the Khakass capital is a leafy, intimate place with a handful of undemanding sights and a population that will be (perhaps pleasantly) surprised to see you. Probably not worth a special trip on its own, Abakan does serve as a handy base for reaching Shushenskoe and Minusinsk; until the Kuragino–Kyzyl railway is built most travellers will spend at least some time here en route to Tuva.

Sights & Activities

Khakassia National Museum MUSEUM

(Хакасский Национальный Краеведческий Музей; ul Pushkina 96; admission R100; ⏲10am-6pm Wed-Sun) The highlight at the recently reopened National Museum is the atmospherically low-lit hall containing a striking exhibition dedicated to Khakassia's wealth of standing stones. Curators have erected a kind of mini Stonehenge in the middle of the space, with the walls around lined in 2000-year-old stone fragments – altogether a surprisingly impressive effort. A clearly underfunded collection of random period furniture, shaggy shamanic bric-a-brac and dubious art makes up the rest of the museum (Minusinsk's Martyanov Museum is vastly superior), but the foyer still has the best gift shop in town selling handy Abakan and Minusinsk maps.

FREE **Railway Museum** MUSEUM

(Музей Железной Дороги; Station concourse; admission free; ⏲1-4.45pm Mon-Fri) Worth visiting just to experience a Siberian attraction that doesn't charge admission. Train buffs will find the scale model of Abakan station in 1925, the collection of period railway uniforms and the various oversize chunks of obsolete equipment suitably captivating. Some display cases have been designed to resemble old carriage windows – similar also in that they're bolted firmly shut.

Spaso-Preobrazhenskoy Cathedral CHURCH

(Спасо-Преображенский собор; pr Druzhby Narodov) A cluster of sparkling gilt onion domes makes the Spaso-Preobrazhenskoy Cathedral rather impressive despite the off-white concrete walls and its odd position amid the high-rise apartments of Mikro-Rayon 4. The interior boasts a striking iconostasis and astonishing acoustics. It's 2km northwest of the city centre; get there from ul Shchetinkina by bus 11, return by bus 10.

Abakan

Sights

1 Khakassia National Museum A3
2 Railway Museum A3

Sleeping

3 Hotel Abakan B2
4 Hotel Anzas B3
5 Hotel Khakassia B1
6 Hotel Park-Otel C2
7 Hotel Persona C2

Eating

8 Apelsin B2
9 Central Market D2
10 Kafe Abakan B1
11 Pizza Iceberg B1
12 Stolichny Supermarket B1
13 VSK Bistro A2

Drinking

14 Coffee House B1

Transport

15 Aviakassa A3
16 Bus Station D2
17 Bus to Kyzyl B3
18 Kyzyl bus ticket kiosk B3

Stary Gorod CAFÉ €
(Старый Город; ul Oktyabrskaya 66; ⏲11am-3am Mon-Fri, 7pm-3am Sat & Sun) Knock back some locally brewed beer at the Stary Gorod; unfortunately, it's inexplicably closed most of the weekend.

Getting There & Away

To get here from Abakan, take bus or *marshrutka* 120 (R30, 25 to 40 minutes) direct to old-town Minusinsk. These leave from the left-hand side of the bus station. Buy tickets from the small ticket booth nearby. Catch returning services from opposite the cathedral.

SHUSHENSKOE ШУШЕНСКОЕ

☎39139 / POP 18,500 / ⏲MOSCOW +4HR

As every Soviet schoolkid was once taught, Shushenskoe played host to Lenin for three years of (relatively comfortable) exile. What textbooks didn't reveal was that in 1898 the young atheist was married in Shushenskoe's **Peter & Paul Church** (Церковь Петра и Павла; ul Novaya; ⏲10am-3pm), much to his later embarrassment.

For the 1970 centenary of Lenin's birth, a two-block area of the village centre was reconstructed to look as it had in 1870. These well-kept 'old' Siberian houses now form the **Shushenskoe Ethnographic Museum** (www.shush.ru; ul Novaya 1; admission R120, photography/video R50/150; ⏲10am-6pm). Many are convincingly furnished, and in summer costumed craftsmen sit around carving spoons. It's gently interesting, but as all trips are guided (in Russian) the visit can drag and you're locked into spending over 1½ hours seeing everything. In addition to Lenin's private quarters, other highpoints include the fully stocked late-19th-century shop and a vodka bar, both towards the end of the tour. The ticket-office gift shop sells souvenirs and an interesting English-language guide to Siberia's countless Lenin-related sites.

Away from the museum, there's not a whole lot to see here other than copious amounts of post-Soviet decay. One odd feature is the sheer number of trees – in places it feels as though the town was built in the middle of a forest without clearing the spot first.

The **post office** (ul Polukoltsevaya 5; ⏲8am-1pm & 2-8pm Mon-Fri, 9am-6pm Sat) offers internet and telephone connection and sells rail and air tickets.

In the unlikely event you decide to stay over, **Hotel Turist** (Гостиница Турист; ☎32 841; ul Pushkina 1; s R1060-1290, d R1800) is a fusty Soviet relic with skin-deep renovation in parts.

The only place in town for a sit-down meal is the unexpectedly bright **Kofeynya Sadko** (Кофейня Садко; ul Pervomayskaya 1; mains R120-240; ⏲11am-midnight Sun-Thu, to 2am Fri & Sat), opposite the church, where petite portions of flavoursome food arrive on trendy square plates; waitresses speak some English. As virtually the only source of sustenance for visitors, it's often crammed to the gills. The only other options are the kiosks at the bus station offering oily *chebureki* (fried,

WORTH A TRIP

SALBYK САЛБЫК

This Stonehenge-sized remnant of a 'royal' *kurgan* is Siberia's most impressive ring of **standing stones**. Excavated in 1956, it's in open fields, 5.6km down unsurfaced tracks south of km38 on the Chernogorsk–Sorsk road. About 2km before Salbyk notice the large, grassy dome of the unexcavated **'Princess' kurgan** it once resembled. Taxis from Abakan ask at least R1000 return. Bring buckets of mosquito repellent.

SAYAN RING INTERNATIONAL ETHNIC MUSIC FESTIVAL

In mid-July around 25,000 music fans besiege Shushenskoe during the annual **Sayan Ring International Ethnic Music Festival** (www.festival.sayanring.ru). The week-long folk-music bash attracts ensembles from across Siberia and the occasional overseas act.

meat-filled turnovers), chemical-cheese pizza and 3-in-1 coffee. Bring a picnic.

Buses serve Abakan (R120, 1¾ hours, nine daily), Krasnoyarsk (R788, 10½ hours, three daily) and Kyzyl (R660, eight hours, departures 9am and 6.15pm). While waiting for buses, take time to admire the bus station's spectacular chunk of socialist realism: a gigantic collage celebrating the USSR's achievements, now partially obscured by kiosks.

Usinsky Trakt
Усинский Тракт

Built between 1914 and 1917, the Usinsky Trakt (now the M54 federal highway) is the main road between Minusinsk and Kyzyl in Tuva. Until the Kuragino–Kyzyl railway is completed in 2014, this narrow ribbon of asphalt through the Yergaki Mountains will remain essentially the only route in and out of Tuva for people and goods, most notably Tuva's much-valued coal and other precious minerals. This strategic significance might explain why much of the route is almost Western-standard blacktop and resurfacing and anti-avalanche work continues apace.

Around two hours out of Abakan the road skirts the modest historical township of **Yermakovskoe** and passes the fruit-growing villages of **Grigorevka** and **Chyornaya Recha** before climbing into pretty birch-wood foothills. After a shashlyk (kebab) stop in **Tanzybey** (km560) the route climbs more steeply. A truly magnificent view of the crazy, rough-cut Yergaki range knocks you breathless just before km598, and illustrates just why their Turkic name means 'fingers'. Dramatically impressive views continue to km601 and resume between km609 and km612. Expect heavy snowfalls here as late as early June. A **roadside cross** (km603–4) marks the spot where former Krasnoyarsk governor Alexander Lebed (who negotiated an end to the first Chechen War in 1996) died in 2002 when his helicopter snagged power lines. Walk 1.5km up the steep track towards the radar station above for fabulous views from the ridge.

As the track descends, the scenery morphs through wooded river valleys into Tuva's panoramic roller-coaster grasslands. There's a particularly overzealous police checkpoint at **Shivilig** (km703), which almost serves as passport control between Tuva and Russia proper, but the first real settlement the road bisects within Tuva is **Turan**, an attractive village of old wooden homes largely inhabited by ethnic Russians. A cute little **museum** (ul Druzhby 44) is now the only attraction since the **St Inokent Church** received a tasteless makeover in blue siding. A road barrelling west just before the village heads towards Arzhaan through Tuva's spectacular **Valley of the Kings**. From Turan the road scales one final mountain pass before hurtling down into Kyzyl.

TUVA

Nominally independent before WWII, fascinating Tuva (Тува in Russian, Тыва in Tuvan) is culturally similar to neighbouring Mongolia but with an international cult following all its own. Philatelists remember Tannu Tuva's curiously shaped 1930s postage stamps. World-music aficionados are mesmerised by self-harmonising Tuvan throat singers. And millions of armchair travellers read Ralph Leighton's *Tuva or Bust!*, a nontravel book telling how irrepressible Nobel Prize–winning physicist Richard Feynman failed to reach Soviet-era Kyzyl despite years of trying. Now that visitors are finally allowed in, Leighton's Friends of Tuva (www.fotuva.org) organisation keeps up the inspirational work with an unsurpassed collection of Tuvan resources on its website. With forests, mountains, lakes and vast undulating waves of beautiful, barely populated steppe, Tuva's a place you'll long remember.

History

Controlled from the 6th century by a succession of Turkic empires, in the 1750s Tuva became an outpost of China, against whose rule the much-celebrated Aldan Maadyr (60 Martyrs) rebelled in 1885. Tibetan Buddhism took root during the 19th century, coexisting with older shamanist nature-based beliefs; by the late 1920s one man in 15 in Tuva was a lama.

With the Chinese distracted by a revolution in 1911, Russia stirred up a separatist movement and took Tuva 'under protection' in 1914. The effects of Russia's October Revolution took two years to reach Tuva, climaxing in 1921 when the region was a last bolt-hole of the retreating White Russians, swiftly ejected into Mongolia by 'Red Partisans'. Tuva's prize was renewed independence as the Tuvan Agrarian Republic (Tyva Arat Respublik, TAR), better known to philatelists as Tannu Tuva. However, to communist Russia's chagrin, Prime Minister Donduk's government dared to declare Buddhism the state religion and favoured reunification with Mongolia. Russia's riposte was to install a dependable communist, Solchak Toka, as prime minister, and later to force Tuvans to write their language in the Cyrillic alphabet, creating a cultural divide with Mongolia. Having 'voluntarily' helped Russia during WWII, Tuva's 'reward' was incorporation into the USSR. Russian immigration increased, Buddhism and shamanism were repressed and the seminomadic Tuvans were collectivised; many Tuvans slaughtered their animals in preference to handing them over.

Today, some people have reverted to traditional pastoralism but, unlike in neighbouring Mongolia, yurt camps are often hidden away in the remoter valleys. Buddhist-shamanist beliefs survived the oppressions in better shape. Even avowed atheists still revere local *arzhaan* (sacred springs), offer food to fire spirits and tie prayer ribbons to cairns and holy trees using the colours of the national flag: blue for sky, yellow for Buddhism and white for purity and happiness.

Tuvan Culture

Of the republic's 308,000 people, about two-thirds are ethnic Tuvans; they are Buddhist-shamanist by religion, Mongolian by cultural heritage and Turkic by language. Tuvan Cyrillic has a range of exotic extra vowels and most place names have different Russian and Tuvan variants.

Colourful *khuresh* is a form of Tuvan wrestling similar to Japanese sumo but without the ring, the formality or the huge bellies. Multiple heats (rounds) run simultaneously, each judged by a pair of referees, flamboyantly dressed in national costume. They'll occasionally slap the posteriors of fighters who seem not to be making sufficient effort. Tuvans also love Mongolian-style long-distance horse races but are most widely famed for their *khöömei* throat singers. *Khöömei* is both a general term and the name of a specific style in which low and whistling tones, all from a single throat, somehow harmonise with one another. The troll-like *kargyraa* style sounds like singing through a prolonged burp. *Sygyt* is reminiscent of a wine glass being rung by a wet finger: quaintly odd if you hear a recording but truly astonishing when you hear it coming out of a human mouth. Accompanying instruments often include a Jew's harp, a bowed two-stringed *igil* or a three-stringed *doshpular* (Tuvan banjo). Rhythms often remind listeners of horses galloping across the steppe.

Ironically, it is often easier to get CDs of Tuvan music in the West than in Tuva itself. The biggest throat-singing ensembles are all-star **Chirgilchin**, inventive **Alash** (www.alashensemble.com), Kaigal-ool's **Huun Huur Tu** (www.hhtmusic.com), ethno-rock band **Yat-Kha** (www.yat-kha.ru), **Khögzhümchü** and the girl band **Tuva Kyzy** (www.tyvakyzy.com). Many members of the above bands also perform with the **National Orchestra of Tuva** (www.tuvannationalorchestra.com). Better-known **Kongar-ol Ondar** (www.ondar.com) has collaborated with Frank Zappa and worked on the soundtrack for the Oscar-nominated film *Genghis Blues*.

Learning *khöömei* has become surprisingly popular among foreigners in recent years; see the boxed text later in this chapter for details on experiencing Tuvan music for yourself and how to arrange lessons.

Festivals

Tuva's most dramatic festival is **Naadym**, usually held in mid-August. Vastly less touristy than the Mongolian equivalent, Naadym is your best chance to hear *khöömei* concerts, watch horse races and see *khuresh* wrestling in the flesh. More significant for local families is **Shagaa**, Tuvan New Year (February), the biggest festival of the year, with *sangalyr* (purification ceremonies), including a huge spring cleaning, gift giving, visits to relatives and temple rituals.

Tuvan Food

Almost every rural household keeps a vat of *khoitpak* (fermented sour mare's milk), which tastes like ginger beer with a sediment of finely chopped brie. *Khoitpak* is drunk as is or distilled into alcoholic *araka*. Roast *dalgan* (a cereal, similar to Altai's bran-rich *talkan*) can be added to your salted milky tea or eaten with *oreme* (sour cream). Local cheeses include stringy *byshtag* and rock-hard Kazakh-style *kurut* balls.

Tuvans are said to have learnt from Chinggis Khaan a special way to kill their sheep without wasting any of the animal's blood. Collected with miscellaneous offal in a handy intestine, this blood makes up the local delicacy, *han* sausage. You may be less than disappointed to find that restaurants rarely serve it – not that there are many restaurants anyway! Beyond Kyzyl, truck stops, *pelmeni* (meat ravioli) steamers and temperamental but incredibly cheap village *stolovye* (canteens) are your best hopes for a hot meal unless you're staying with families. Kyzyl residents often take their own supplies when travelling to the provinces.

Dangers & Annoyances

Meeting locals is the key to experiencing Tuva, but be aware that Tuvans are notorious for their reaction to alcohol, becoming disproportionately aggressive, even among friends. Although the situation is improving, travellers should still take extra care wherever they travel in Tuva, making sure to steer well clear of drunks, and avoid drinking vodka with local 'friends'. Wandering Kyzyl's streets after dark without local company is also not recommended.

Information

Tourism Department (www.mert.tuva.ru) Run by the Ministry of Economics (now responsible for tourism), with info on things to see in the regions.

Tuva Online (www.tuvaonline.ru) News from Tuva in English.

Tuvainfo (www.tuvainfo.travel) Recently created government site packed with Tuva-related info.

VisitTuva (www.visittuva.ru) Official tourism site.

Kyzyl Кызыл

39422 / POP 110,000 / MOSCOW +4HR

Fancifully located at the 'centre of Asia', the Tuvan capital is where the vast majority of travellers begin their exploration of this captivating republic. Although the city's Soviet-era concrete lacks any architectural charm, in recent years the purpose-built National Museum and new Cultural Centre have provided attractive focus for those interested in the country's mesmerising traditions. A 25m-tall hilltop Buddha statue, set to dominate the picturesque views across the Yenisey River to the unpopulated north bank, will be the latest landmark to spread some good post-Soviet karma.

In 1914 the imperial authorities decided to construct an administrative capital for their new protectorate from scratch as no other settlement in Tuva was up to the job. It was originally christened Belotsarsk (White Tsarville); the Soviet regime, for obvious reasons, changed the name in 1925 to Kyzyl, a Tuvan word which simply means 'red'.

The key to enjoying Kyzyl (and all of Tuva) is contacting tour companies and Kyzyl-based English-speaking helpers well in advance – up to a month ahead if you're planning to go anywhere near the Mongolian border, an area for which special permits are needed. Arrive in Kyzyl unannounced and you'll see very little of the unique culture Tuva has to offer.

Sights

TOP CHOICE National Museum MUSEUM

(Национальный музей; www.tuvamuseum.ru; ul Titova 30; admission R200, gold exhibition R500; 10am-6pm Wed-Sun) One of Tuva's 'must sees', the National Museum's huge modern home contains the usual arrangements of stuffed animals, WWII artefacts and dusty minerals, as well as more impressive halls dedicated to shamanism, Buddhist art and traditional Tuvan sports. However all of this is just a teasing appetiser before the main course: a single, atmospherically lit and well-guarded room containing kilograms of Scythian gold jewellery, unearthed at Arzhaan I in the Valley of the Kings. The 3000-year-old gold pieces, which can only be seen on a 40-minute Russian-language guided tour (interpreters available or bring your own), are exquisitely displayed against dark blue felt and seem to illuminate the room with their ancient gleam. Look out for the 1.5kg solid-gold torque, never removed by the Scythian emperor, and thousands of millimetrically fashioned sequins, the likes of which modern-day jewellers claim not to have the skills or tools to reproduce.

Centre of Asia Monument MONUMENT

(Памятник "Центр Азии") If you take a map of the world, cut out Asia and balance the continent on a pin, the centre of gravity would be Kyzyl. Well, only if you've used the utterly obscure Gall's stereographic projection. However, that doesn't stop the city from perpetuating the 'Centre of Asia' idea first posited by a mysterious 19th-century English eccentric and still marked with the concrete globe-and-obelisk Centre of Asia Monument on the riverbank, at the end of Komsomolskaya ul. The site provides one of Siberia's best photo opportunities for wedding parties and travellers alike.

Tsechenling Datsan BUDDHIST TEMPLE
(Буддийский храм Цеченлинг; ul Shchetinkina-Kravchenko 1) A short walk east along the riverbank from the Centre of Asia Monument stands the white pagoda-style Buddhist temple Tsechenling Datsan. Brightly coloured prayer flags flutter in the breeze outside, but it's disappointingly plain inside.

Museum of Oppression MUSEUM
(Komsomolskaya ul 5; admission R30; ⏲8am-4pm) The tiny, sorely underfunded Museum of Oppression has touching dog-eared photographs of those who disappeared in the Stalin years. Across the grass is the chest-puffing statue of a Nepokorenny ('undefeated') Aldan Maadyr martyr in his pointy slippers.

Tours

Alash Travel ADVENTURE TOURS
(Алаш Трэвел; ☎21 850; www.terra-tuva.ru; ul Kochetova 60/12) Alash offers full-scale rafting and climbing expeditions and can arrange horse-riding trips between Tuva and Altai. There is, unfortunately, a lack of English speakers in the office.

EcoTuva ADVENTURE TOURS
(Эко-Тува; ☎8-906-998 0700; www.ecotuva.ru) Enthusiastic tour agency offering horseback trips with throat singing and yurt stays, as well as week-long tours coinciding with Naadym.

Sleeping

With a couple of notable exceptions, Kyzyl's limited range of hotels is not much to throat sing about. They're also habitually full, so for a much jollier experience try to arrange a homestay (around R1000) through one of Kyzyl's helpers or tour companies.

TOP CHOICE **Aldyn Bulak Yurt Hotel** YURT €€
(☎20 628; www.tuvatour.travel; km45 Kyzyl–Ak-Dovurak Rd; per yurt R2500-5000, per tepee R1200) Cupped by bare hills at an attractively sacred site by the Yenisey River, the luxury yurts at this upmarket complex have flushing toilets, air-conditioning, hot showers and underfloor heating, while a more authentic experience is provided by basic yurts and five tepees. Order a sheep's head and salty tea in Russia's largest yurt restaurant (pricey), then climb up to the viewing points for spectacular views from the cliffs above the swirling river before paying your respects at the nearby *ovaa* (shamanist holy site) dedicated to *khöömei*. The site is 45km west of Kyzyl, clearly signposted off the main Kyzyl–Ak-Dovurak road. The hotel offers prearranged transfers from Kyzyl for a symbolic R100.

Hotel Buyan Badyrgy HOTEL €€
(Гостиница Буян Бадыргы; ☎56 460; www.badyrgy.ru; ul Moskovskaya 1; s R1200-2500, d R3000-5000; ❄📶) The Tuvan capital's most comfortable place to stay is located a R80 taxi ride from the city centre (or a R13 trip on *marshrutka* 1A heading towards the airport). The 37 standard rooms are clean and often smartly fitted out, but some bathrooms could do with an update. The price-to-quality ratio makes this a traveller favourite and a preferable choice to Kyzyl's hit-and-miss

EXPERIENCING KHÖÖMEI

Without doubt, Tuva's great draw is throat singing, aka *khöömei*. However, finding performances is rather haphazard; perhaps the best place to start is the spanking-new **Cultural Centre** (cnr ul Lenina & ul Internatsionalnaya), a two-storey timber building opened in late 2011 on the site of the old museum. The centre concentrates various aspects of Tuvan culture (throat singing, the National Orchestra, handicrafts, yurt construction) in a single building, with music forming a large part of its activities.

Tuvan-speaking Sean Quirk, manager of the Alash ensemble, can usually arrange a short demonstration of the various styles. For a more hands-on experience, take a throat-singing or *doshpular* lesson with National Orchestra member Evgeny Saryglar. Instruction sometimes takes place in the open air and Evgeny speaks English. Both of these contacts are always in the know about upcoming *khöömei* performances in Kyzyl and beyond. See the information section for details.

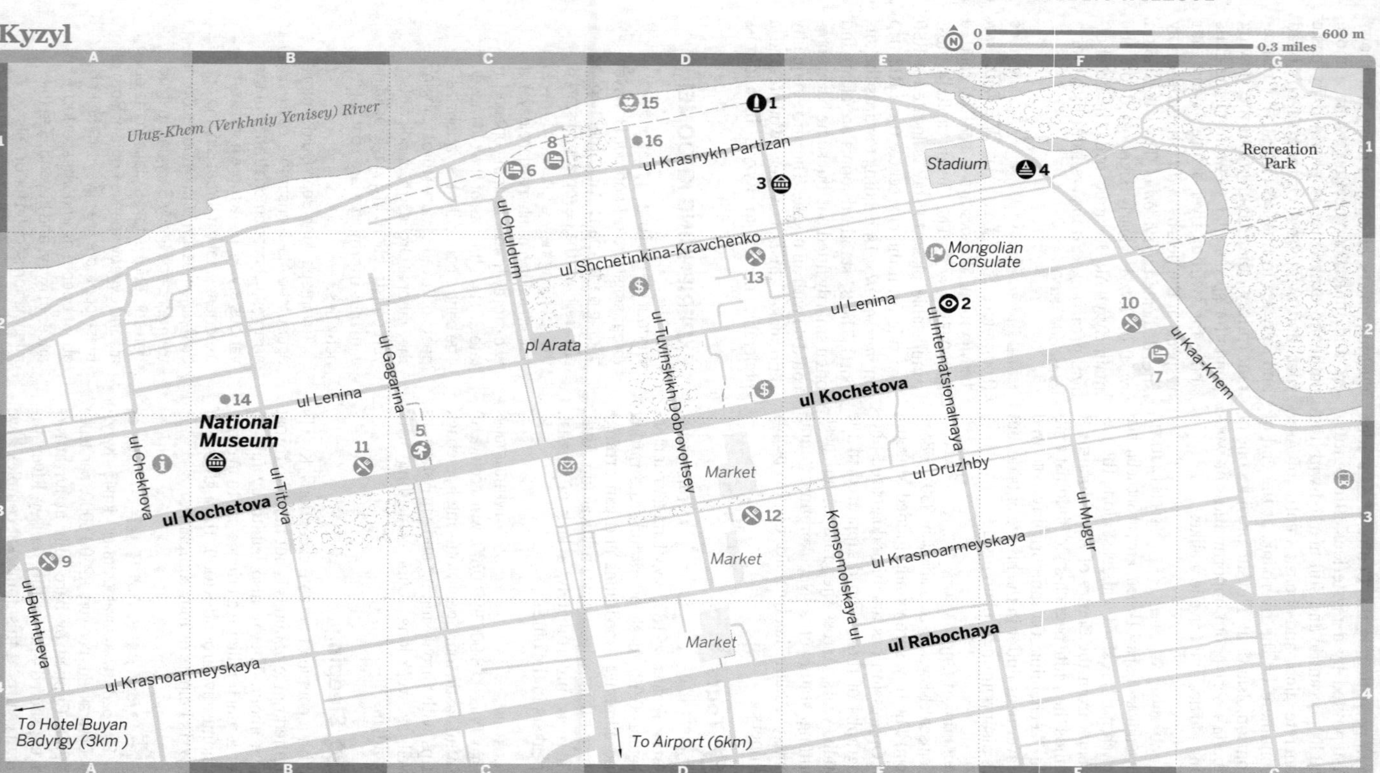
Kyzyl
0
0
600 m
0.3 miles
Recreation Park
ul Kaa-Khem
Stadium
Mongolian Consulate
ul Internatsionalnaya
ul Mugur
ul Druzhby
ul Krasnoarmeyskaya
ul Rabochaya
Komsomolskaya ul
ul Kochetova
ul Lenina
ul Krasnykh Partizan
ul Shchetinkina-Kravchenko
Market
Market
Market
ul Tuvinskikh Dobrovoltsev
To Airport (6km)
pl Arata
ul Chuldum
ul Gagarina
Ulug-Khem (Verkhniy Yenisey) River
ul Lenina
ul Titova
National Museum
ul Kochetova
ul Chekhova
ul Krasnoarmeyskaya
ul Bukhtueva
To Hotel Buyan Badyrgy (3km)

Kyzyl

Top Sights

National Museum B3

Sights

1 Centre of Asia Monument D1
2 Cultural Centre E2
3 Museum of Oppression D1
4 Tsechenling Datsan F1

Activities, Courses & Tours

5 Alash Travel C3

Sleeping

6 Hotel Kottedzh C1
7 Hotel Mongulek F2
8 Hotel Odugen C1

Eating

9 Arlekina Kafe A3
10 Coffee Man F2
11 Kafe Kyzyl B3
12 Kezhik D3
13 Vostorg D2

Information

Tsentr Asii ....(see 8)

Transport

14 Aziya-99 ....B2
15 Boat Quay D1
16 Hydrofoil Ticket Office D1

central hotels. Breakfast is served in the new 4th-floor café and there's a ground-level *stolovaya* (canteen). Booking essential.

Hotel Odugen HOTEL €€

(Гостиница Одуген; ☎32 518; ul Krasnykh Partizan 36; s R2000, tw R3000-3800, ste R5000) This unexpectedly bright Soviet block enjoys a peaceful location and pretty Yenisey views. The 38 en-suite rooms are immaculately kept and some sport real potted plants and microwaves. Small groups could go for the superb-value three-room suite with its contemporary leather furniture, flat-screen TV, water cooler/heater and 21st-century bathroom.

Hotel Kottedzh HOTEL €€

(Гостиница Коттедж; ☎30 503; ul Krasnykh Partizan 38; s R800-3800, tw R1600-2800) As well as an illustrious list of former guests including Boris Yeltsin and the 14th Dalai Lama, this 14-room hotel has cosy rooms and acceptable private bathrooms. The building is slated for renovation, so standards will have been raised, along with prices, by the time you check in. Breakfast is included and reservations are advised as this place is eternally chock-a-block.

Hotel Mongulek HOTEL €€

(Гостиница Монгулек; ☎31 253; ul Kochetova 1; s R900-2000, d R1700-3000) The only rooms to consider here are the five top-floor, two-room *lyux* minisuites with their leatherette sofas, walk-in wardrobes and pleasing views. The Soviet past clings stubbornly to other rooms, though further renovation is planned.

Eating & Drinking

Most hotels have basic eateries while the market on ul Druzhby sells fresh produce and is ringed by several cheap cafés and shashlyk grills.

TOP CHOICE **Vostorg** FAST FOOD €

(Востopr; ul Shchetinkina-Kravchenko 35; mains R30-70; ⏲8am-11pm) Perched above a supermarket of the same name, Kyzyl's best cheap eat is a plasticky no-frills self-service cafeteria where cash-strapped students and office workers fill up for a few roubles on generous platefuls of *pelmeni,* bliny, meatballs, *plov,* pork roast and Ukrainian *holubtsi* (cabbage rolls stuffed with rice and meat). Fresh doughnuts and pastries make this a decent breakfast spot.

Kafe Kyzyl CAFÉ €

(ul Kochetova 62; mains R35-100; ⏲9am-10pm) The walls at this self-service place are stuccoed in reliefs of *kameniy babi* (standing stones), Scythian gold figures from the National Museum and Lowry-style petroglyphs, while the menu is a cookbook index of steppe-dwellers' comfort food with a few Tuvan specialities thrown in. The same people run the excellent Kafe Abakan, though the Kyzyl incarnation is a little more cramped.

Coffee Man CAFÉ €

(ul Kochetova 2; mains R100-250; ⏲10am-11pm) Coffee Man is a romantic Western-style coffee house and the only place in Tuva to serve real espresso as well as pasta, sandwiches and Russian pancakes. Locals complain of long waits for orders – proof that all dishes are made fresh to order as the owners claim.

Kezhik CAFÉ €€

(Кежик; ul Druzhby 151; mains R140-300; ⏲10am-1am) 'Happiness' is the only central café to serve authentic Tuvan fare such as *sogozha* (stuffed grilled liver), *manchi* (mutton ravioli) and the dreaded *han* sausage. Gaudy black-and-gold decor and carefully laid tables lend it a grander ambience than it deserves.

Arlekina Kafe CAFÉ €
(Арлекина; ul Kochetova 99; mains R110-225; ⏲10am-11pm; ❄) Bright colours, Venetian carnival masks and DVDs on a big screen make this the best of Kyzyl's older eateries. Extensive menu and cheap lunch combinations, but often suspiciously empty.

 Information

Aylana Irguit (www.tyvantranslator.com; aashu.dekeyo@gmail.com) Translator with perfect English and many local contacts.

Evgeny Saryglar (ana-saryglar@yandex.ru) Gives throat-singing and *igil* lessons. Have a few introductory sessions via Skype before you arrive.

Post office (ul Kochetova 53; per MB R4; ⏲8am-10pm Mon-Fri, 9am-6pm Sat & Sun) Internet room and telephone office.

Rosbank (Росбанк; ul Tuvinskikh Dobrovoltsev 10; ⏲9am-6pm Mon-Fri) 24-hour ATM accepting almost every kind of card.

Sberbank (Сбербанк; ul Kochetova 34a; ⏲8.30am-7pm Mon-Fri, 11am-4pm Sat) Exchange counter and ATM inside.

Sean Quirk (alashensemble@gmail.com) US-born manager of the Alash ensemble and member of the National Orchestra, Sean is the best person to contact in Kyzyl if you're interested in throat-singing performances.

Tourist office (☎8-913-343 6464; www.visittuva.ru; National Museum grounds; ⏲10am-6pm Wed-Sun Jun-Aug) Recently opened office housed in a summer-only yurt to the left of the National Museum's main entrance as you arrive. English-speaking staff can assist with accommodation and transport and also distribute free maps and leaflets.

Tsentr Asii (Центр Азии; ☎/fax 32 326; Hotel Odugen) Helpful agency that can arrange air tickets and vehicle transfers.

 Getting There & Away

Air

Kyzyl's shockingly up-to-date but sorely underexploited **airport** handles flights to Krasnoyarsk (R3300, three daily) and Novosibirsk (R6640, Tuesday). Handy flights to Irkutsk no longer run, though in 2011 there were plans to relaunch Moscow flights (as there always are). *Marshrutka* 1A (R13) will get you to the airport.

Aziya-99 (Азия-99; ☎22 214; ul Lenina 58; ⏲8am-7pm Mon-Fri, 9am-6pm Sat & Sun), opposite the new museum building, sells air tickets for all flights, including services from Abakan and Krasnoyarsk.

Boat

Summer hydrofoils leave from the **boat quay** and shoot along the Yenisey rapids 285km up to Toora-Khem in Todzha (R2114, 10 hours upstream, seven hours back) on alternate days. Book ahead at the **hydrofoil ticket office** (ul Krasnykh Partizan 28; ⏲9am-4pm). Bring your passport just in case.

Bus

For the spectacularly scenic drive to Abakan, shared taxis (R1000 to R1200 per seat, 5½ hours) are well worth the difference over the grindingly slow buses (R600, nine hours), which depart from the **bus station** three times daily. Abakan-bound shared taxis and others heading to destinations within Tuva congregate in and around the chaotic car park behind Hotel Mongulek, but you'd be well advised to prearrange private transfers (along with accommodation) to places such as Ak-Dovurak and destinations south along the M54.

> **TRAIN TO TUVA?**
>
> Just as Lhasa is now linked to the rest of China, plans to hook Kyzyl up to the Russian railway network are well under way, and the first train should pull into the Tuvan capital sometime in 2014. The fresh set of tracks, laid essentially to ship Tuva's high-quality coal and other natural resources to Russia proper, will join the Krasnoyarsk–Abakan line at Kuragino.
>
> The Kyzyl terminus will probably be constructed on the northern bank of the Yenisey (somewhat inconveniently on the opposite side from the city centre), though no definite plans existed at the time of research. Once the rail link is in place and direct carriages are trundling to Moscow, Krasnoyarsk and other destinations along the Trans-Sib, road transport to/from Abakan is expected to tail off.

Around Kyzyl

On the Yenisey's northern bank, multiple springs gurgle straight from the rocks amid totem poles and trees heavy with prayer flags at cliff-side **Bobry Istochnik** (Beaver Spring). This popular barbecue and picnic spot with picturesque Kyzyl views can only be reached by taxi (at least R1000).

The giant **Kadarchy Herder Statue** surveys the city from a bare hill, five minutes' drive from Kyzyl's southernmost edge. Beyond, prayer rags photogenically deck the **Tos Bulak Spring**, which is the closest *arzhaan* (sacred spring) to the capital. To get a taste for the steppe, consider the relatively easy excursion to mirage-like **Cheder Salt Lake**, 42km. The popular but slightly ramshackle lakeside **Cheder Health Spa** (☎39422-20 130) has basic en-suite rooms, but book well ahead as the summer months see hundreds of locals invade this remote location to take mud cures and cool off in the briny waters.

Isolated amid endless grassy steppe 65km from Kyzyl, **Lake Dus Khol** is crowded with comically mud-blackened vacationers; its waters are so salty that you float Dead Sea style. Larger **Lake Khadyn** nearby is great for summer swimming and camping, though the water is still too salty to drink or use for cooking. To reach both, turn off the M54 at the 840km marker and head 20km along sandy, unsurfaced access tracks; arrange a prepaid private transfer with a Kyzyl agency if you don't fancy putting yourself at the mercy of local taxi drivers.

Following the Ka-Khem (Maly Yenisey) River southeast of Kyzyl, the steppe gives way to agricultural greenery around low-rise **Saryg-Sep**, beyond which an appallingly rutted road continues through woodland to the pretty Old Believers' village of **Erzhey**. Despite the extraordinary inaccessibility, there are several bungalow-hotels and hunting lodges en route and beyond.

From Kyzyl to Erzin

The paved M54 offers a wonderfully varied scenic feast with archetypal Central Asian grassland, then parkland-style rolling woodlands after Balgazyn, thickening to pine forest beyond the two tiny cafés at **Shurmak**. Spot shamanic cairns and prayer-rag ticker tape on passes and herders' yurts in picturesque meadows. The landscape gets starkly drier descending past Samagaltay and **Bay Dagh**, a former camel-breeding centre where memorials commemorate the last scuffles of the civil war in 1921. Between km1023 and km1024, radar posts look down on the junction of a smooth, scenic but unpaved road to Mören, 18km away, passing near holy mountain **Ak-Khayyrakan** (1148m). EcoTuva in Kyzyl can show you its revered spring (whose seasonal flow is aided each summer by multiple shamanic ceremonies) and arrange unforgettable yurt stays with nomadic cattle herders in the glorious valleys beyond.

You'll need permits to continue south into the border zone; with plenty of notice, the head office of the **Ubsunur Basin Biosphere Reserve** (☎39422-53 818; ubsunur@tuva.ru) in Kyzyl can arrange these, as can most Kyzyl agencies.

Sandy tracks continue 20km south of **Erzin** past Dalí-esque rocky outcrops to **Lake Tore Khol**, a popular local picnic spot. Although it's at the edge of the desert zone, herded horses trotting through the shallows give the area a slight feel of the Camargue in France. Across the water is Mongolia, but the border is closed to foreigners. **Tore Khol yurt camp** (per tent R1000) on the banks of

VALLEY OF THE KINGS ДОЛИНА ЦАРЕЙ

This broad grassy vale begins a few kilometres beyond a turning off the M54 highway north of Turan. It's famous in archaeological circles for its pancake-shaped Scythian *kurgany* (burial mounds) named after the village of Arzhaan at the end of the paved road. These have produced the most significant archaeological finds ever made in Tuva, now displayed in Kyzyl's National Museum.

The first roadside *kurgan* is **Arzhaan II**, which lies opposite shimmering Ak Khol (White Lake). During excavations in 2001 archaeologists unearthed some magnificent artefacts in several graves dating from the 7th century BC. Less well-maintained **Arzhaan I**, a little further along the road, is the largest *kurgan* in Tuva. A dig in the early 1970s turned up thousands of gold and silver artefacts plus the graves of two Scythian VIPs, 16 servants and 160 horses, but today only a large disc of clacking stones remains. The valley holds an amazing 700 burial sites and eight large *kurgany* await the archaeologist's trowel. However, digs are unpopular with local villagers and shamans who believe the spirits should be left undisturbed.

the lake can be booked through Kyzyl agencies (p508). To the east of Tore Khol the dunes of the **Tsugeer-Els protected landscape** rise high along the left bank of the Tec Khem River.

Western Tuva

Западная Тува

The route looping round to Abakan from Tuva via Askiz is scenically varied, often beautiful and mesmerisingly vast in scale, though the Chinggis Khaan stone near Ak-Dovurak is virtually the only real 'sight'. While independent travel is feasible, you'll see a lot more in Tuva's west in the company of a local or a guide hired in Kyzyl. Sayan Ring tours in Krasnoyarsk come this way.

KYZYL TO AK-DOVURAK

The spectacularly picturesque and virtually traffic-free grassland route from Kyzyl to Ak-Dovurak is lined with sacred mountains, nomads' yurts and newly raised stupas. Some 80km out of Kyzyl, dramatic **Mt Khayyrakan** (1148m), a spiky ridge blessed by the 14th Dalai Lama in 1992, comes into view but isn't reached until km107. Climb towards the stupa at the base of the mountain from the roadside café where buses make a brief stop. The best place to break the 300km journey is the simple midway **Kafe Aziya** (km145; 8am-11pm), beyond which the conical stand-alone **Mt Syyn-Churee** is scored with almost 200 petroglyphs. The small town of **Chadan** (Chadaana) is attractively dotted with wooden cottages and there's an appealing little **museum** (ul Lenina 33; 9am-4pm Mon-Fri). The town is most famous as Tuva's former spiritual centre, but the once-great **Ustuu Khuree Temple** was utterly devastated in the Soviet era. Lost in peaceful woodlands some 6km south of Chadan and accessed via tracks off the road to Bazhin-Alaak, only sad, chunky stumps of mud wall remain of the original, but a new replica temple now stands nearby. The site hosts a large annual **music festival** (www.ustuhure.ru) in mid-July, embracing everything from *khöömei* to grunge rock. Participants camp in tents and yurts. Ak-Dovurak and Kyzyl-Mazhalik are another hour's drive west.

From **Khandagayty**, where the Mongolian border remains closed to foreigners, a glorious but notoriously tough truck track runs to Kosh-Agach in Altai via Mugur-Aksy, passing the glacier-topped **Mt Mongun-Tayga** (3976m). Bring food, a reliable guide, ample extra fuel and spare parts if you plan a truck or jeep convoy. With many deep fords, this route is impassable after rain. It's much more pleasant on horseback; Alash Travel in Kyzyl can help you organise horses. In ideal conditions it's possible to make the trip by mountain bike in around a week, but getting lost is dangerously easy.

AK-DOVURAK & KYZYL-MAZHALYK

АК-ДОВУРАК И КЫЗЫЛ-МАЖАЛЫК

39441 / MOSCOW +4HR

The world's largest open-pit asbestos mine dominates Ak-Dovurak, Tuva's unlovable second 'city'. Around 10km away, the main attraction is the **Chinggis Khaan stone** (admission R50), a remarkably well-preserved 1.5m-high moustachioed stone idol (*kameny baba* in Russian, *kizhigozher* in Tuvan). To find it, cross the Shui River to **Kyzyl-Mazhalyk** town then drive 8km towards Ayangalty. About 500m after you pass the turn-off to tiny Bizhiktig Khaya village, the stone figure stands all alone in a field, 400m west of the road. To get close, you may have to pay the admission fee. The surrounding meadows are peppered with less prominent standing stones. Ak-Dovurak taxis want at least R500 return.

Long rows of standing stones and Turkic burial sites can be seen by turning onto a dirt track just before the 10km marker on the Teeli road west of Ak-Dovurak. Most still bear fading petroglyphs. Yet more delicately etched ancient stonework is the star attraction at Kyzyl-Mazhalyk's **Regional Museum** (Culture Centre, ul Khomushku Vasily 23; admission by donation), alongside an independence-era newspaper printed in the Tuvan Latin script, a mock-up of a yurt and figures sculpted in soapstone, a tradition practised in the area since Scythian times.

Ak-Dovurak's **Hotel Cheleesh** (21 255; ul Tsentralnaya 6) has cheap, survivable rooms and staff are friendly. It's upstairs in the rear of the building bearing a giant Soviet-era mural. However, homestays with local families are infinitely more enjoyable; these can be arranged through Kyzyl agencies and helpers.

From Kyzyl, sporadic *marshrutky* serve Ak-Dovurak (five to seven hours) via Chadan. However, private transfers arranged through Kyzyl agencies allow you to stop along the way and are much safer. Ak-Dovurak city buses run from the centre of town via the bus station (1.5km) to Kyzyl-Mazhalyk.

WORTH A TRIP

SAY-KHONASH

Located 55km north of Ak-Dovurak, the **Say-Khonash yurt camp** (☎8-923-542 6566, 8-923-383 7109, 8-923-266 8310; www.sai-xonash.com, www.saixonash.wordpress.com; full board R1500) is the quintessential nomadic experience and brings visitors as close to the authentic Tuvan rural lifestyle as they're ever likely to get. The six traditionally furnished yurts sleeping 12 are surrounded by real nomads' dwellings and their assorted animals in a jaw-slackeningly remote location few would ever chance upon. The English-speaking owners (Evgeny and Anay-Khaak) and their extended family give masterclasses in felt production, yurt construction, traditional sheep butchery and Tuvan music, as well as organising multiday horse-riding and hiking trips to fantastically off-the-map locations.

No road, never mind public transport, goes anywhere near this place, so transfers from Kyzyl (or Abakan/Krasnoyarsk) must be arranged in advance.

KRASNOYARSK REGION

Vast and beautiful, the Greenland-shaped Krasnoyarsk region (Красноярский Край) stretches all the way from the Arctic islands of Severnaya Zemlya to a mountainous tip at Mt Borus. Its capital is Krasnoyarsk, a buzzing, forward-looking metropolis and a popular stop for travellers riding the Trans-Siberian Railway.

Krasnoyarsk Красноярск

☎391 / POP 974,000 / ⌚MOSCOW +4HR

Bustling, affluent and backed by attractively jagged foothills, Krasnoyarsk enjoys a more appealing setting than most typically flat Siberian cities. While its architecture isn't particularly inspiring, amid the predominantly unaesthetic concrete of post-WWII industrialisation rise a few outstandingly well-embellished timber mansions and a sprinkling of art nouveau curves. Pleasant river trips, the nearby Stolby Nature Reserve and the region's best concert halls, theatres and museums make Krasnoyarsk an agreeable place to break the long journey between Tomsk (612km west) and Lake Baikal.

The city centre's grid layout is easy to navigate, but there's no central square. The zoo and Stolby Reserve are over 10km west along the Yenisey's south bank.

Sights & Activities

Dotted about Krasnoyarsk are some very fine wooden houses, notably ul Lenina 88 and 67 and ul Karla Marksa 118. There are also many art nouveau facades such as pr Mira 76, ul Lenina 62 and ul Parizhskoy Kommuny 13.

TOP CHOICE **Stolby Nature Reserve** NATURE RESERVE

Arguably Krasnoyarsk's greatest attractions are the fingers and towers of volcanic rock called **stolby**. These poke above the woods in the 17,000-hectare Stolby Nature Reserve (Zapovednik Stolby) south of the Yenisey River. To reach the main concentration of rock formations, you could try to find the track (7km long) near Turbaza Yenisey (bus 50), but there is much easier access via a year-round **chairlift** (Фуникулёр; R160; ⌚Tue-Sun) belonging to the ski resort. From the top, walk for two minutes to a great viewpoint or around 40 minutes to reach the impressive **Takmak Stolby**. Better still is to take a tour with SibTourGuide (p517; priced according to itinerary). Infected ticks are dangerous between May and July and tick protection or predeparture encephalitis jabs are essential at this time.

Regional Museum MUSEUM

(Краеведческий музей; www.kkkm.ru; ul Dubrovinskogo 84; admission R100; ⌚11am-7pm Tue-Sun) Housed in an incongruously attractive 1912 art nouveau Egyptian temple, this is one of Siberia's better museums. Arranged around a Cossack explorer's ship, surprisingly well-presented exhibitions across the two floors examine every facet of the region's past, from Cossacks and gentlemen explorers to the Tunguska explosion and local fauna, prerevolution institutions to religious art. Highlights include the 20th-century 'nostalgia' section on the upper level and the 4m-tall mammoth skeleton looking like something straight off a Hollywood museum movie set. There are touch-screen games for kids throughout and a decent café to look forward to at the end.

Surikov Museum-Estate MUSEUM

(Музей-усадьба Сурикова; ul Lenina 98; admission R59; ⌚10am-5.30pm Tue-Sat) The Surikov Museum-Estate preserves the house, sheds

Central Krasnoyarsk

and vegetable patch of 19th-century painter Vasily Surikov (1848–1916). The heavy-gated garden forms a refreshing oasis of rural Siberia right in the city centre. More of Surikov's work is on show at the old-school **Surikov Art Museum** (Художественный музей Сурикова; ul Parizhskoy Kommuny 20; admission R50; ⏲10am-6pm Tue-Sun).

Bobrovy Log Ski Resort SKI RESORT

(Лыжный курорт Бобровый Лог; www.bobrovylog.ru; ul Sibirskaya 92) Below the stolby the slap and swish of skis and snowboards can be heard at the Bobrovy Log ski resort. Snow cannons keep the slopes going well into May, and in the summer months the Roedelbahn (a kind of downhill forest roller coaster), a pool and regular sports events keep the fun level high. Ask at the English-speaking year-round **information centre** about ski hire, lift passes and other tickets. Bus 37 runs from the train station direct to the resort.

Roev Ruchey Zoo ZOO

(Зоопарк Роев Ручей; www.roev.ru; adult/child R160/30; ⏲9am-9pm) Take bus 50 or 50A to this expanding, relatively humane zoo near the Bobrovy Log Ski Resort to see numerous Siberian species.

Rezanov Statue MONUMENT

(pr Mira) A statue of Nikolai Rezanov, an 18th-century Russian diplomat and nobleman who died in the city in 1807, gazes towards a slightly temporary-looking arch raised in 2003 to mark the site of the first Cossack stronghold.

Resurrection Church CHURCH

(Благовещенская Церковь; ul 9 Yanvarya) The top-heavy but elegant Resurrection Church (1804–22) was decapitated in the 1930s but given a new tower in 1998–99. Its icon-filled interior billows with incense.

Literature Museum MUSEUM

(Литературный Музей; ul Lenina 66; admission R30; ⏲10am-6pm Tue-Sun) This quaint museum

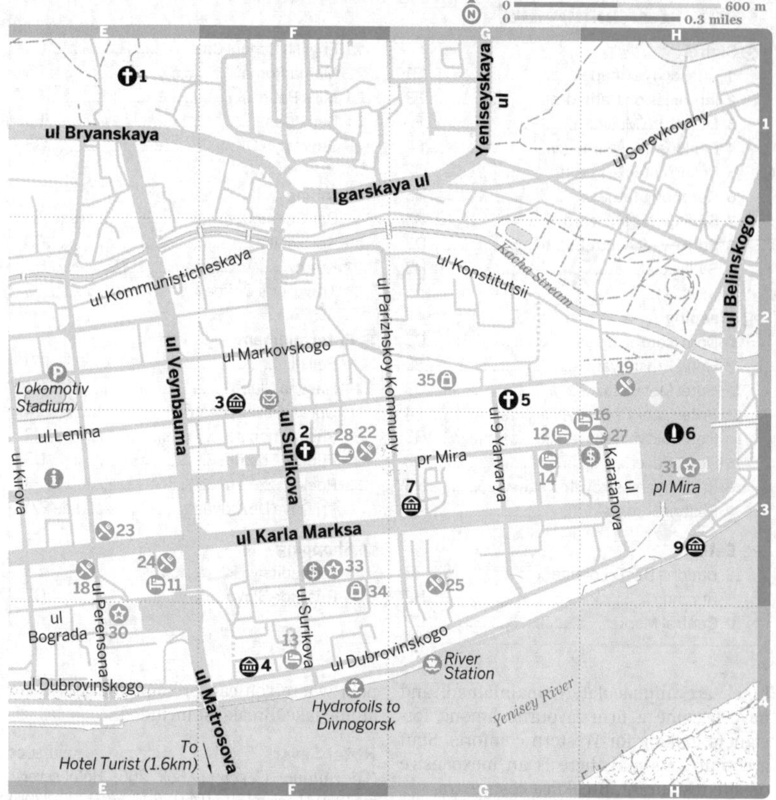

within a glorious 1911 merchant's mansion occasionally hosts classical music performances.

Chasovnya Chapel NOTABLE BUILDING
(Часовня; top of Karaulnaya Hill) For wonderful views climb Karaulnaya Hill to the little chapel which features on the Russian 10-rouble banknote (now slowly being replaced with a coin). At midday there's a deafening one-gun salute here.

SV Nikolai MUSEUM
(СВ Николай; admission R50; ⌚10am-8pm) Permanently docked below an ugly brown-concrete exhibition centre (formerly the Lenin Museum) is the SV *Nikolai,* the ship that transported Vladimir to exile in Shushenskoe.

Intercession Cathedral CHURCH
(Покровский Собор; ul Surikova) This pleasingly small old church dating from 1795 has an interior of unusually glossed and intricately moulded stucco framing haloed saints.

Sleeping

There are plenty of accommodation options in Krasnoyarsk, including a couple of budget choices. Though way out of the centre, there are a couple of small peaceful hotels in the Stolby area (south of the river), relatively handy for skiing and trips to the Stolby Nature Reserve. Use bus 50.

For a great insight into local life take an English-speaking homestay organised by SibTourGuide. Most such homestays are in the high-rise Vyetluzhanka area, which is 20 minutes' drive west of the centre but well served by city buses 91, 49 and 43. Prices include a free station pick-up.

CITY CENTRE

Dom Hotel HOTEL €€€
(☎290 6666; www.dom-hotel24.ru; ul Krasnoy Armii 16a; s/d from R4000/4800; @☎) Centred around a rather characterless courtyard, the 74 light-filled rooms at Krasnoyarsk's newest

Central Krasnoyarsk

Sights

1 Chasovnya Chapel ... E1
2 Intercession Cathedral ... F3
3 Literature Museum ... F2
4 Regional Museum ... F4
5 Resurrection Church ... G2
6 Rezanov Statue ... H3
7 Surikov Art Museum ... G3
8 Surikov Museum-Estate ... D3
9 SV Nikolai ... H3

Sleeping

10 Dom Hotel ... C3
11 Hotel Krasnoyarsk ... E3
12 Hotel Metelitsa ... G3
13 Hotel Ogni Yeniseyya ... F4
14 Hotel Oktyabrskaya ... G3
15 Hotel Sever ... D3
16 Krasnoyarskstroystrategiya ... H3
17 Resting Rooms ... A4

Eating

18 Buddha Bar & Lounge ... E3
19 Burzhuy ... H2
20 Central Market ... D2
21 English School Café ... C3
22 Mama Roma ... F3
23 Miks Patio ... E3
24 Sem Slona ... E3
25 Stolovaya OK ... G3

Drinking

Bar Chemodan ... (see 21)
26 Kofemolka ... C3
27 Krem ... H3
28 Traveller's Coffee ... F3

Entertainment

Bellini ... (see 27)
29 Havana Club ... B4
30 Opera-Ballet Theatre ... E4
31 Philharmonia ... H3
32 Puppet Theatre ... D3
33 Rock-Jazz Kafe ... F3
Tri Dnya Dozhdya ... (see 27)

Shopping

34 Ekspeditsiya ... F3
35 Russkoe Slovo ... G2

hotel are immaculately maintained and have become a firm favourite among foreigners looking for Western comforts. Staff are courteous and there is an inexpensive on-site restaurant. Breakfast costs extra.

Hotel Krasnoyarsk HOTEL €€€
(Гостиница Красноярск; ☎274 9400; www.hotelkrs.ru; ul Uritskogo 94; s/tw from R3860/5320; ❄📶) Every Soviet metropolis has one: a concrete lumpen hotel celebrating the city's name in metre-high lettering. But unlike many of these stale relics, the sprawling eight-storey Krasnoyarsk is well kept with bright corridors, totally rebuilt full-service rooms and English-speaking receptionists. Rates are also decidedly 'post-Soviet' but at least breakfast is included.

Hotel Metelitsa HOTEL €€€
(Гостиница Метелица; ☎227 6060; www.hotel-metelica.ru; pr Mira 14; s/d from R3900/R4900; ❄📶) Intimate, exclusive minihotel of the type favoured by Russia's oil-stained business elite and the ugliest gallery of pop stars you're ever likely to see. Every room is done out differently, some with design-mag flair, and bathrooms are far from bog standard. Staff speak reluctant English and there's a pool where you can pretend you are by an alpine lake. Breakfast included.

Hotel Sever HOTEL €€
(Гостиница Север; ☎662 266; Hotel-sever@mail.ru; ul Lenina 121; s R750-1800, tw R1200-2200) Krasnoyarsk's most central budget option is cheap and friendly with cosmetically improved but loyally Soviet rooms. Pricing has been kept refreshingly straightforward and staff are polite. Breakfast is included in room rates.

Hotel Oktyabrskaya HOTEL €€€
(Гостиница Октябрьская; ☎227 1926; www.hoteloctober.ru; pr Mira 15; s R4000-5300, d R5200-6300) Comfortable and professionally run with rooms approximating Western standards, albeit without air-conditioning. Satellite TV includes CNN and some English is spoken. The trendy lobby area has a stylish juice bar. Includes breakfast.

Hotel Ogni Yeniseyya HOTEL €€
(Гостиница Огни Енисея; ☎227 5262; ul Dubrovinskogo 80; s R750-4600, tw R1350-4350; @📶) One of the last budget options left; there's a vast selection of rooms here, but whatever you plump for, make sure it has Yenisey views.

Krasnoyarskstroystrategiya HOTEL €€
(Гостиница Красноярскстройстратегия; ☎227 6911; pr Mira 12; s R630-2100, tw R1260-2960) The only good thing about this place is the dirt-cheap singles. Otherwise, it's unfriendly with, it must be said, smelly, renovated Soviet rooms in need of rehab. Enter from ul Karatanova, if you dare.

Resting rooms HOSTEL €
(Комнаты Отдыха, komnaty otdykha; ☎248 3820; train station; 12-/24-hr from R320/640) Clean dorm rooms in the train station.

SOUTH OF THE YENISEY

Hotel Turist HOTEL €€
(Гостиница Турист; ☎276 1900; ul Matrasova 2; s R2280, tw R2640) On a busy roundabout directly across the long Yenisey Bridge from the city centre, this 16-storey Soviet monolith has a variety of rooms with toilet and shower. Some are pleasantly renovated.

STOLBY AREA

Snezhnaya Dolina HOTEL €€
(Гостиница Снежиая Долина; ☎269 8110; www.sneg-dolina.ru; per cottage from R5300, s R700-3200, d R1400-3700;) This accommodation complex has a hotel, a minimotel and rows of cosy cottages meaning lots to choose from. There's a swimming pool, a tennis court and a decent restaurant, but the main draw here is the clean air and the proximity to the stolby and ski slopes.

Turbaza Yenisey HOTEL €
(Турбаза Енисей; ☎698 110; ul Sverdlovskaya 140/7; d & tw R700) Despite the name this is a two-storey hotel, not a camp. Good-value renovated rooms are simple but neat and share sparkling-clean showers. Some of the pricier doubles have private facilities. There's a glimpse of the river from the small communal terrace but no café.

Eating

Krasnoyarsk has the highest concentration of eateries of any Eastern Siberian city with new places springing up all the time. However, most newcomers aim to serve the city's moneyed elite with prices and interiors to match. At the other end of the food chain, self-service canteens abound. For more cheap snacks and picnic supplies head for the extensive **central market** (Центральный Рынок; ul Kerchinskogo; ⏲8am-6pm).

TOP CHOICE **English School Café** CAFÉ €€
(www.esc24.ru; ul Lenina 116; mains R70-300; ⏲10am-11pm; @) Every visitor should drop in at this Anglophone sanctuary while in town. While its English-teacher, expat and traveller clientele, wired castle-themed cellar setting, suitably international menu, globalised beer menu, inventive coffees, real porridge and top-notch cooking provide good enough reason to come, there's also the five-minute free (yes free!) call to any number in the world from your table, plus free wi-fi, that might have you looking for ul Lenina 116 sooner rather than later.

Buddha Bar & Lounge TIBETAN, EUROPEAN €
(ul Karla Marksa 127; mains R100-160; ⏲noon-midnight;) This low-lit, incense-infused vegetarian cellar eatery and lounge is a calming place to escape the city-centre blare. Order a plate of exotic Tibetan food (*tsampa*, *momo* and other dishes you won't know) from the English-speaking waitress, then give the bar-top prayer wheel a lazy spin before retreating with a hookah pipe (R400) to the cushioned chill-out lounge where nightly DJs drift chill-out music to a chilled crowd. As if Siberia wasn't chilly enough.

Burzhuy CAFÉ €
(Буржуй; 2nd fl, Metropol bldg, pr Mira 10; pelmeni R52, other mains R40-70; ⏲8am-7pm Mon-Sat, 9am-6pm Sun) Cheap and very popular self-service lunch spot where office workers swap chitchat over plates of *pelmeni* at formica tables. The 'ear bread' comes with several fillings and sauces, or choose from other hot dishes and salads.

Mama Roma ITALIAN €€
(pr Mira 50a; pizzas R200-470, pasta R165-465; ⏲11am-1am;) Herb-infused air wafts temptingly out of one of the best Italian eateries in town, where chequered tablecloths and admirable attempts at pasta, risotto and pizza may make you feel you're in Rome or Naples – but only if you've never been there.

Sem Slona CANTEEN €
(ul Karla Marksa 95; mains R30-70; ⏲24hr) Got a sudden craving for buckwheat at 3am? Then brave the darkened streets and make your way to this all-hours, no-nonsense canteen plating up solid Russian favourites with a growl. The name translates as 'I could eat an elephant' – this being Siberia, a horse just won't do.

Krasnaya Palatka FAST FOOD €
(Красная Поляна; Bobrovy Log ski resort; meals R150; ⏲10am-10pm) Watch skiers slither down the slopes from the huge circular windows at this film-themed self-service cafeteria. The decor is trendy, but the Russian

WORTH A TRIP

YENISEYSK ЕНИСЕЙСК

Using Lesosibirsk overnight trains, historic Yeniseysk makes an engaging two-night, one-day excursion from Krasnoyarsk, 340km away. Founded in 1619, this was once Russia's great fur-trading capital, with world-famous 18th-century August trade fairs (recently revived for tourists), and 10 grand churches punctuating its skyline. Eclipsed by Krasnoyarsk despite a burst of gold-rush prosperity in the 1860s, the town is now a peaceful backwater with an unexpectedly good **Regional Museum** (ul Lenina 106; admission R50; ⌚9am-5pm Mon-Sat), some faded commercial grandeur along ul Lenina and many old houses; over 70 are considered architectural monuments. Most appealing of the surviving churches are the walled 1731 **Spaso-Preobrazhensky Monastery** (ul Raboche-Krestyanskaya 105) and the **Assumption Church** (Uspenskaya tserkov; ul Raboche-Krestyanskaya 116) with its unusual metal floor and splendid antique icons.

To reach Yeniseysk, take the overnight train from Krasnoyarsk to Lesosibirsk (*platskart* R810, 9½ hours). A bus meets the train and takes passengers to Lesosibirsk bus station where they must alight, queue up to buy a ticket and reboard. After that there are at least hourly departures to Yeniseysk throughout the day (R90, 45 minutes). If you don't want to travel back overnight, buses run back to Krasnoyarsk day and night (R519, seven hours, 10 daily).

Further North along the Yenisey

From mid-June to early October, passenger ships slip along the Yenisey River from Krasnoyarsk to Dudinka in the Arctic Circle (4½ days) via Yeniseysk (17 hours) and Igarka (three days two to seven hours). There are three to four sailings per week, most departing early morning. Returning upstream, journeys take 50% longer so most independent travellers choose to fly back to Krasnoyarsk. Foreigners are not allowed beyond Igarka as Dudinka and nearby Norilsk are 'closed' towns. Contact SibTourGuide in Krasnoyarsk for timetables, tickets and round-trip tours. Novosibirsk-based **Acris** (www.acris.ru) can also arrange trips.

and international dishes are unexciting and perhaps appreciated more after a long hike or climb in the stolby.

Miks Patio FAST FOOD €
(Микс Патио; ul Perensona 20; mains R15-42; ⌚10am-10pm) With budget-airline decor, a menu heavy with Slavic comfort food and prompt service, this is the *stolovaya* dragged into the 21st century.

Stolovaya OK CANTEEN €
(Столовая ОК; ul Uritskogo 33; mains R25-40; ⌚10am-6pm Mon-Fri) Well signposted from ul Parizhskoy Komunity, this super-cheap and ultra-basic student canteen keeps both stomachs and wallets happy. Enter from the rear of the building.

Drinking

Traveller's Coffee CAFÉ
(pr Mira 54; ⌚8am-midnight) The tempting aroma of newly milled beans lures you into this trendy coffee house where the circular brown-cream leather tub-seats give the impression you're sitting in a cuppa. Smiley service and sensibly priced milkshakes, muffins and pancakes.

Krem CAFÉ
(pr Mira 10; ⌚24hr) Krasnoyarsk's classiest coffee house has black-and-white photography, dark-wood furniture, a belt-stretching dessert menu and reasonably priced lattes and espressos.

Bar Chemodan PUB
(Бар Чемодан; ul Lenina 116; ⌚noon-midnight Mon-Sat, from 1pm Sun) A wonderfully atmospheric, if fiercely expensive, 1920s-themed pub-restaurant stocking dozens of whiskies. The stair lift outside is for both the disabled and the inebriated.

Kofemolka CAFÉ
(Кофемолка; pr Mira 114; ⌚10am-midnight; wi-fi) Sip roasts from every corner of the bean-growing world amid faux mahogany as dark as the roasts and geometrically patterned screens that divide things up into intimate gossip booths. Long dessert menu.

Entertainment

Opera-Ballet Theatre THEATRE
(Театр оперы и балета; ☎227 8697; www.opera.krasnoyarsk.ru; ul Perensona 2) The architectur-

ally nondescript Opera-Ballet Theatre has two shows a day (11am and 7pm) from October to June.

Philharmonia LIVE MUSIC
(Филармония; ☎227 4930; www.krasfil.ru; pl Mira 2b) The Philharmonia has three concert halls showcasing folk, jazz and classical music.

Puppet Theatre PUPPET THEATRE
(☎211 3162; www.puppet24.ru; ul Lenina 119) Classic Russian puppet shows for both children and adults.

Bellini COCKTAIL BAR, NIGHTCLUB
(www.bellini.bar10.ru; ul Mira 10) Pass the monster Mona Lisa to enter this strikingly white cocktail and sushi bar where DJs spin most nights.

Tri Dnya Dozhdya NIGHTCLUB
(www.3dd.bar10.ru; ul Mira 10) Where Krasnoyarsk's rich, young and beautiful head to pose, drink and dance to top acts.

Havana Club NIGHTCLUB
(Гавана Клуб; ul Bograda 134; ⏲Mon-Thu 8pm-1am, Fri & Sat to 3am) A big nightclub with three dance floors and Moscow DJs.

Rock-Jazz Kafe LIVE MUSIC
(Рок-Джазз Кафе; ul Surikova 12; ⏲4pm-6am Tue-Sun) Entered through a small bar beside the Dublin Irish Pub, this dark venue showcases live bands around an upturned motorcycle from 6pm most days.

Shopping

Ekspeditsiya OUTDOOR GEAR
(ul Uritskogo; ⏲10am-7pm) Source all the equipment you need for a trek into the Siberian wilderness or replace lost or broken camping gear at this small shop.

Russkoe Slovo BOOKSHOP
(Русское Слово; ul Lenina 28; ⏲10am-7pm Mon-Fri, to 3pm Sat) A good central bookshop selling useful public transport plans as well as city and regional maps.

Information

Post office (ul Lenina 62; per hr R38; ⏲8.30am-5.30pm Mon-Fri, to 4.15pm Sat)

Rosbank (pr Mira 7; ⏲9am-6pm Mon-Thu, 9am-4.45pm Fri) Currency exchange and 24hr indoor ATM.

Sayan Ring (☎223 1231; www.sayanring.com; ul 3-ya Krasnodarskaya 14a; ⏲10am-8pm Mon-Fri, 11am-5pm Sat) Specialist agency for Tuva and Khakassia tours.

Sberbank (Сбербанк; ul Surikova 15; ⏲10am-7pm Mon-Sat) Currency exchange window and ATM.

SibTourGuide (☎2512 654; www.sibtourguide.com) Experienced tour guide Anatoly Brewhanov offers personalised hiking trips into the stolby, imaginative tours around Krasnoyarsk and general travel assistance. He also runs a minihostel, provides authentic 'rural experiences' at his dacha, organises cruises along the Yenisey and leads trips to the site of the Tunguska Event, all while maintaining an info-packed website.

Yergaki tourist office (☎227 8637; www.visitsiberia.info; pr Mira 86; ⏲9am-1pm & 2-6pm) Bona fide but little-advertised tourist office with English-speaking staff armed with limited visitor info. Ring the bell to be buzzed in then head to the back of the building, up the stairs and through a grey metal door.

Getting There & Away

Air

From Krasnoyarsk's **Yemelyanovo Airport** you can fly to almost anywhere in Russia. A handful of flights leave from nearby Cheremshanka Airport – check yours isn't one of them.

TSAVS (ЦАВС; www.krascavs.ru; ul Lenina 115; ⏲8am-8pm) is a centrally located one-stop shop for all bus, train and air tickets. Krasnoyarsk has the following flight connections:

Irkutsk from R7000, four weekly
Kyzyl from R3300, three daily
Moscow from R5500, up to 10 daily
Novosibirsk from R1400, daily

Boat

Every few days in summer, passenger boats from Krasnoyarsk's spired **river station** (Речной вокзал) ply the Yenisey to Dudinka (1989km, 4½ to five days) but foreigners may not proceed beyond Igarka. SibTourGuide can arrange tickets.

Summer hydrofoils to Divnogorsk depart up to five times a day, returning an hour later. Buy tickets on board.

Bus

The main **bus station** (Автовокзал; ul Aerovokzalnaya 22) is to the northeast of the city centre and is best reached by buses 49, 53 and 71 from ul Karla Marksa. Destinations include:

Abakan R700, 8¾ hours, frequent
Divnogorsk R54, one hour, frequent
Shushenskoe R788, 10 hours, three daily
Yeniseysk R519, seven hours, 10 daily

Long-distance *marshrutky* also run to Kyzyl (R1700, 11 hours) in Tuva from an unmarked stop behind the Metropol Building.

Train

TSAVS is the most central booking office, though the **station** itself is relatively central and often queue-free. Krasnoyarsk has the following rail connections:

Abakan *platskart/kupe* R970/R2000, 10 hours to 13½ hours, two or three daily
Irkutsk *platskart/kupe* R1400/R3500, 18 hours, up to nine daily
Lesosibirsk (for Yeniseysk) *platskart* R810, 9½ hours, every other day
Moscow *platskart* R3110, *kupe* R6600 to R11,200, two days 16 hours, up to seven daily
Novosibirsk *platskart* R800 to R1250, *kupe* R1360 to R2700, 12 hours, up to 13 daily
Severobaikalsk *platskart* R1660 to R1800, *kupe* R2600 to R4860, one day two to 12½ hours, three daily
Tomsk *platskart/kupe* R1020/2170, 14 hours, every other day

Getting Around

Bus 135 (1¼ hours, hourly) runs from the bus station to Yemelyanovo Airport, 46km northwest of the city. It passes Cheremshanka Airport en route.

Within the city centre, almost all public transport runs eastbound along ul Karla Marksa or pr Mira, returning westbound on ul Lenina. Frequent, if slow, trolleybus 7 trundles from the train station through the city centre via ul Karla Marksa. Useful bus 50 starts beyond the zoo, passes the Turbaza Yenisey and comes through the centre of town, winding on to the bus station.

From June to September, cycle hire is available near the Rezanov Statue (per hour R150).

Divnogorsk Дивногорск

39144 / POP 30,000 / MOSCOW +4HR

From Krasnoyarsk, a popular day trip by bus or summer hydrofoil follows the Yenisey River 27km to Divnogorsk town through a wide, wooded canyon. Some 5km beyond Divnogorsk's jetty is a vast 90m-high **dam**. Turbine-room visits are not permitted, but if you're lucky you might see ships being lifted by a technologically impressive inclined plane to the huge Krasnoyarsk Sea behind. A few kilometres beyond you can observe ice fishing from December to March or, in the summer, boats and yachts can be hired.

The Krasnoyarsk–Divnogorsk road has a panoramic overlook point at km23 and passes quaint **Ovsyanka** village. From the main road walk 100m (crossing the train tracks) to Ovsyanka's cute wooden **St Inokent Chapel** (ul Shchetinkina) then 50m right to find the **house-museum** (ul Shchetinkina 26; admission R50; 10am-6pm Tue-Sun) of famous local writer Victor Astafiev, who died in 2001. Directly opposite in Astafiev's grandma's cottage-compound is the more interesting **Last Bow Museum** (ul Shchetinkina 35; ticket valid for both; 10am-6pm Tue-Sun), giving a taste of rural Siberian life.

Hydrofoils (R250, 45 minutes, up to five daily) depart from Krasnoyarsk's river station and regular *marshrutky* (R54) leave from Krasnoyarsk's bus station. Taxis meet boats on arrival in Divnogorsk and want at least R700 return to shuttle you to a point overlooking the dam. However, it's potentially cheaper, safer and more fun to hire a mountain bike from a stand 200m downstream from the quay. SibTourGuide in Krasnoyarsk offers various tailored excursions in English or will include the Divnogorsk loop as part of its 'Ten-Rouble Tour'.

WESTERN BAM

The official start of the 3100km-long Baikal–Amur Mainline (Baikalo–Amurskaya Magistral, BAM) is Tayshet, but through services from Krasnoyarsk, Moscow and elsewhere mean there's little reason to stop there.

The BAM crosses almost virgin territory that is more impressively mountainous than anything along the Trans-Siberian main line. For most travellers the most popular BAM stop is Severobaikalsk, a hub for visiting north Baikal; further west, Bratsk is famous for its huge dam (if little else). For details on eastern BAM towns Tynda and Komsomolsk-na-Amure, see the Russian Far East chapter.

There are particularly fine mountain views between Kunerma and minispa Goudzhekit, with the line performing a full 180-degree switchback before tunnelling through to Daban. The line between Severobaikalsk and Nizhneangarsk offers flashes of dazzling Lake Baikal views. It then continues to Tynda via Dzelinda, another tiny spa, and the 15km-long Severomuysky Tunnel.

Bratsk Братск

3953 / POP 246,000 / MOSCOW +5HR

Unless you're a fan of BAM or dam, Bratsk is perhaps not worth leaving the 'comfort' of your carriage bunk, though it does neatly

HERO PROJECT OF THE CENTURY

The BAM is an astonishing victory of belief over adversity. This 'other' trans-Siberian line runs from Tayshet (417km east of Krasnoyarsk) around the top of Lake Baikal to Sovetskaya Gavan on the Pacific coast. It was begun in the 1930s to access the timber and minerals of the Lena Basin, and work stopped during WWII. Indeed, the tracks were stripped altogether and reused to lay a relief line to the besieged city of Stalingrad (now Volgograd).

Work effectively started all over again in 1974 when the existing Trans-Siberian Railway was felt to be vulnerable to attack by a potentially hostile China. The route, cut through nameless landscapes of virgin taiga and blasted through anonymous mountains, was built by patriotic volunteers and the BAM was labelled 'Hero Project of the Century' to encourage young people from across the Soviet Union to come and do their bit. Despite this source of free labour, building on permafrost pushed the cost of the project to US$25 billion, some 50 times more than the original Trans-Siberian Railway.

New 'BAM towns' grew with the railway, often populated by builders who decided to stay on. However, the line's opening in 1991 coincided with the collapse of the centrally planned USSR and the region's bright Soviet future never materialised. While Bratsk and Severobaikalsk survived, many other smaller, lonely settlements became virtual ghost towns. Today only a handful of trains a day use the line.

break up the journey from both Irkutsk and Krasnoyarsk to Severobaikalsk. The city's raison d'être is a gigantic **dam** (GES), which drowned the original historic town in the 1960s. New Bratsk is an unnavigable necklace of disconnected concrete 'subcities' and belching industrial zones, with the spirit-crushingly dull Tsentralny area at its heart.

Sights & Activities

Bratsk Dam LANDMARK
(Братская ГЭС) A ferro-concrete symbol of the USSR's efforts to harness the might of Siberia's natural assets, between 1967 and 1971 the Bratsk hydroelectric power station was the world's largest single electricity producer. Slung between high cliffs and somehow holding back the mammoth Bratsk Sea – no one can deny it's a striking spectacle, especially from the window of BAM trains that pass right across the top.

Take any *marshrutka* from Tsentralny to Gidrostroitel, the closest slab of Bratsk to the dam. The only way to access the turbine rooms is through a local tour agency.

Angara Village OPEN-AIR MUSEUM
(admission R100; 10am-5pm Wed-Sun) Some 12km from Tsentralny, this impressive open-air ethnographic museum contains a rare 17th-century wooden watchtower and buildings rescued from submerged old Bratsk. A series of shaman sites and Evenki *chum* (tepee-shaped conical dwellings) lie in the woods behind. Take a taxi or arrange a visit through Taiga Tours.

Sleeping

The following hotels are both in Tsentralny.

Hotel Taiga HOTEL €€
(Гостиница Тайга; 413 979; www.hotel-taiga.ru; ul Mira 35; s R1750-3550, d R2500-5250) The flashiest show in town is this renovated Soviet hulk where cramped rooms are packed with tasteless furniture but have clean 21st-century bathrooms. Some staff speak English, guest visas are registered and there's a decent hotel restaurant. Breakfast is extra.

Hotel Shvedka HOTEL €
(Гостиница Шведка; 412 520; www.hotel-shvedka.ru; ul Mira 25; dm R500, s R700-3000, d R1000-2500) Rooms here range from battered and cheap to well-kept and reasonably priced. Ask to see which you're getting before you commit. On-site tour agency offering Bratsk tours. No breakfast.

Information

Lovely Tour (459 909; www.lovelytour.ru; ul Sovetskaya 3, Tsentralny) Bratsk tours plus plane and train tickets.

Taiga Tours (416 513; www.taiga-tours.ru; 2nd fl, Hotel Taiga) Permits and guides to visit the dam's turbine rooms.

Getting There & Away

For Tsentralny, get off BAM trains at the Anzyobi (Анзеби) station and transfer by bus or *elektrichka*. Bratsk has the following rail connections:

Irkutsk *platskart* R1330, *kupe* R2000 to R3000, 17 hours, daily

Krasnoyarsk *platskart* R1130, *kupe* R1750 to R2500, 13 hours, up to four daily

Moscow *platskart* R4650, *kupe* R7600 to R10,800, three days four hours, even days only

Severobaikalsk *platskart* R1050, *kupe* R1600 to R2260, 14 hours to 17 hours, up to four daily

Irkutsk can also be reached by Western-standard coach (R900, 11 hours) from the Tsentralny **bus station** (ul Yuzhnaya) and summer hydrofoil from a river station in southeast Tsentralny. Check **VSRP** (www.vsrp.ru) for details of the latter.

Severobaikalsk
Северобайкальск

☎30130 / POP 25,500 / ⏲MOSCOW +5HR

Founded as a shack camp for railway workers in the mid-1970s, Severobaikalsk (SB) has grown into the most engaging halt on the BAM, where travellers vacate stuffy railway compartments to stretch legs in the taiga or cool off in Lake Baikal. The town itself is a grid of soulless, earthquake-proof apartment blocks with little in between, but the mountainscape and nameless wildernesses backing the lake quickly lure hikers and adventurers away from the concrete. They discover a land more remote, less peopled and generally more spectacular than Baikal's south, a place where lazy bears and reindeer-herding Evenki still rule in timeless peace, despite the best efforts of *Homo sovieticus*.

Sights & Activities

BAM Museum MUSEUM
(Музей БАМа; ul Mira 2; admission R50; ⏲10am-1pm & 2-6pm Tue-Sat) The town's friendly little museum has exhibits on BAM railway history (workers' medals, grainy black-and-white photos, 'old' BAM tickets), some Buryat artefacts and a few mammoth bones. Around the corner is a small **art gallery** where local artists display their works.

Railway Station NOTABLE BUILDING
(pr 60 let SSSR; ⏲5am-midnight) The epicentre of SB's world is a striking construction with a nostalgically stranded steam locomotive standing guard to the right. The sweeping architectural design of the brave-new-world station resembles a ski jump – thanks to a previous mayor's love of the sport, it's claimed.

Orthodox Church CHURCH
(Leningradsky pr) SB's newest Orthodox church sports two impressive onion domes in gleaming gold and a monster chandelier inside. It stands just beyond the town's gun-toting grey-concrete **war memorial**.

Tours

The following agencies and individuals can help arrange accommodation and backcountry excursions.

Ecoland TOUR COMPANY
(☎22 506; www.ecoland-tour.ru) This award-winning tour agency specialises in horse-riding trips, Baikal boat excursions and trekking.

Maryasov Family TOUR GUIDE
(☎8-924-391 4514; baikalinfo@gmail.com) The English-speaking Maryasov family (Yevgeny and daughters Alyona and Anna) run Severobaikalsk's hostel, information centre and tourism association as well as organising guided treks to Baikalskoe and Lake Frolikha, seal-spotting trips to Ayaya Bay and Evenki-themed excursions to the village of Kholodnoe.

Rashit Yakhin/BAM Tour TOUR GUIDE
(☎21 560; www.gobaikal.com, ul Oktyabrya 16/2) This experienced full-time travel-fixer, guide and ex-BAM worker suffered an immobilising stroke in the mid-1990s rendering his spoken English somewhat hard to follow. Nonetheless, Rashit is quick to reply to emails and is always keen to please. He rents out a brilliant central apartment (R600, negotiable).

Sleeping

TOP CHOICE **Baikal Trail Hostel** HOSTEL €
(☎23 860; www.baikaltrailhostel.com; baikalinfo@gmail.com; ul Studencheskaya 12, apt 16; dm R500; 📶@) Initially set up to house Great Baikal Trail volunteers working in the North Baikal area, this spacious eight-bed apartment-hostel is well equipped with essential backpacker facilities such as kitchen, washing machine and communal climbing frame. It's one of the best places in town to arrange backcountry treks and trips into the wilds around the northern end of Lake Baikal.

Zolotaya Rybka GUESTHOUSE €€
(Золотая Рыбка; ☎21 134; www.baikalgoldenfish.ru; ul Sibirskaya 14; tw R1200-3500) Well signposted from ul Olkhonskaya, SB's best guesthouse maintains immaculate and imaginatively designed rooms in three buildings providing glimpses of Lake Baikal through the trees. There are spotless toilets and showers throughout, guests have access

to kitchens and a cook prepares a restaurant-standard breakfast on request (R300 extra). The owner Oleg runs intriguing taiga trips to visit a self-sufficient family that survives unsupported in the forest north of SB.

Hotel Olymp HOTEL €€
(Гостиница Олимп; ☎239 80; www.hotelolymp.ru; ul Poligrafistov 2b; s & d R1300-2500; 📶) Severobaikalsk's smartest sleep has spotless, cool, airy rooms though the plumbing could be more professionally screwed down. For this price you might expect breakfast and free wi-fi – you get neither. Despite the name you'll be disappointed/relieved to find no Greek theme inside.

Baikal Service GUESTHOUSE €€
(Байкал Сервис; ☎23 912; www.baikaltour.irkutsk.ru; ul Promyshlennaya 19; cottage R3800, s/d R1400/2800) Hidden in a peaceful pine grove at the otherwise unpromising north-east end of town, Baikal Service has three very comfy pine cottages sleeping up to five, and less exciting but well-appointed singles and doubles in a separate guesthouse. Breakfast is included in the rates for the guesthouse but not for the cottages.

Baikal Resort GUESTHOUSE €€
(Дом у Байкала; ☎23 950; www.baikal-kruiz.narod.ru; proezd Neptunsky 3; tw R700-1800) This 'resort' is really just a house and a row of basic cabins in a quiet area, walking distance from the lake. Rooms are spacious and have a clean shower and toilet, but summer-only huts are a bit cramped.

Eating & Drinking

For quick eats – *pozi* (dumplings), shashlyk, *plov* and beer – try the **fast food row** east of the station on pr 60 let SSSR or the greasy spoons around the Torgovy Tsentr. Otherwise, pickings are meagre indeed.

TiTs CAFÉ €
(ТиЦ; Railway Culture Centre, Tsentralny pl; mains R40-70; ⏲11am-5pm & 6pm-1am). Climb the gloss-painted stairs for a return to Soviet-style 1980s dining. The food is basic and cheap, the dinner ladies belligerently unsmiling, the alcohol plentiful and the hand-scrawled menu a challenge even to Russian speakers.

Anyuta CAFÉ €
(Анюта; ul Poligrafistov 3a; mains R90-180; ⏲6pm-2am Tue-Sun) Evening dinner nook housed in a red-brick building amid high-rise blocks at the northern end of town.

VIST Supermarket SUPERMARKET
(ВИСТ) Leningradsky pr 5 (⏲8.30am-9pm) ul Studencheskaya (⏲8.30am-8pm) The town's VIST supermarkets stock a limited range of groceries.

Information

There are ATMs at the railway station, in the Zheleznodorozhnik Culture Centre and at the Leningradsky pr branch of the VIST Supermarket.

Library (Библиотека; Zheleznodorozhnik Culture Centre; ⏲11am-7pm Mon-Thu, to 6pm Fri) Cheap internet access.

Post office (Почта; Leningradsky pr 6; ⏲9am-2pm & 3-7pm Mon-Fri, 9am-2pm Sat).

Sberbank (Сбербанк; per Proletarsky; ⏲9am-6.30pm Mon-Fri, 10am-3pm Sat) ATM and currency exchange counter.

Tourist office (train station forecourt; ⏲9am-6pm Jun-Aug) Yellow-blue kiosk on the train station forecourt providing information on the North Baikal area.

Warm North of Baikal (www.privet-baikal.ru) Website belonging to the local tourism association with tons of information and listings.

Getting There & Away

The **Aviakassa** (Tsentralny pl; ⏲9am-noon & 1-4pm) in the Zheleznodorozhnik Culture Centre

FROLIKHA ADVENTURE COASTLINE TRAIL

The latest instalment in the Great Baikal Trail saga is this incredible, relatively demanding 100km adventure trekking route between the delta of the Verkhnyaya Angara River and the spa hamlet of Khakusy on Baikal's eastern shore. You'll need a boat to find the start of the trail at the mouth of the river, from where it takes eight days to reach the spa village of Khakusy via countless lonely capes and bays, wild camping by the lake all the way. Exhilarating river crossings (including a biggie – the River Frolikha), deserted beaches and show-stopping Baikal vistas punctuate the trail, and from Ayaya Bay a there-back hike to remote Lake Frolikha beckons.

For more information and trail maps, contact Severobaikalsk tour agencies, the Baikal Trail Hostel or Dresden-based **Baikalplan** (www.baikalplan.de).

Severobaikalsk

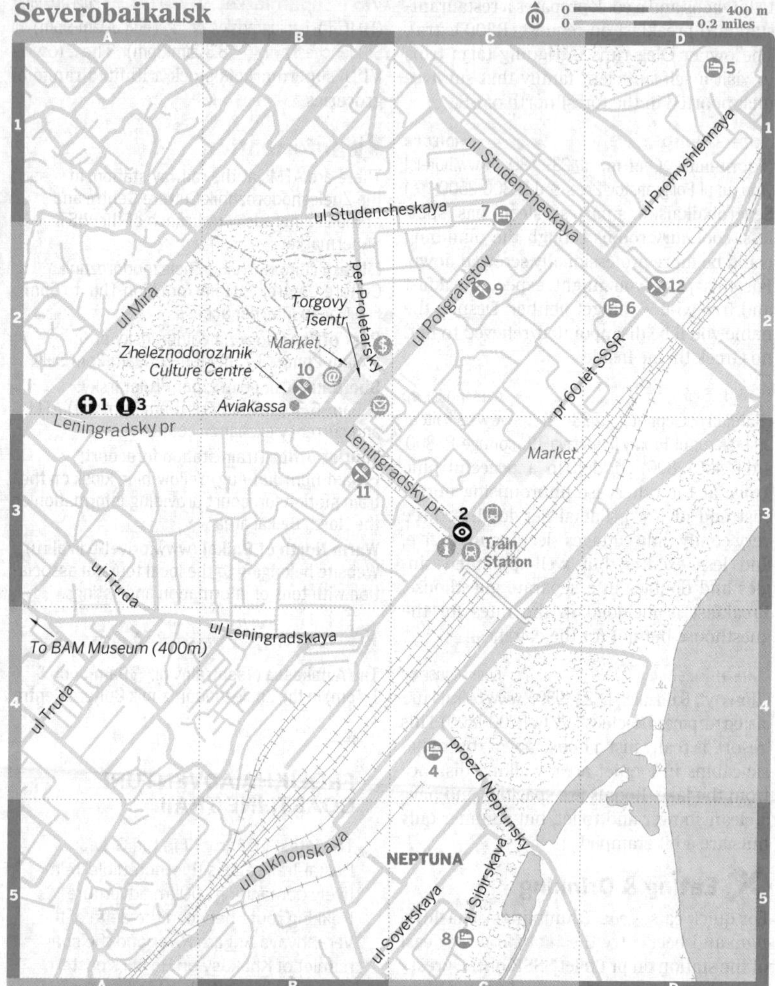

sells tickets for flights from Nizhneangarsk Airport, 30km northeast.

Boat

From late June to late August a hydrofoil service runs the length of Lake Baikal between Nizhneangarsk, Severobaikalsk and Irkutsk via Olkhon Island. Check **VSRP** (www.vsrp.ru) for times and ticket prices.

Bus

Marshrutky cluster outside Severobaikalsk's train station and run to the following destinations:

Baikalskoe R60, 45 minutes, two daily

Goudzhekit R100, 45 minutes, three daily

Nizhneangarsk Airport R37, 50 minutes, half-hourly

Train

Tickets can be bought from the **station** or the Zheleznodorozhnik Culture Centre.

Severobaikalsk has the following rail connections:

Bratsk *platskart* R1050 to R1140, *kupe* R1600 to R2450, 15 hours to 17 hours, up to four daily

Irkutsk *platskart* R2090, *kupe* R3320 to R4700, one day eight to 13 hours, daily

Krasnoyarsk *platskart* R1660 to R1800, *kupe* R2600 to R4860, one to 1½ days, three daily

Moscow *platskart* R5080, *kupe* R8300 to R12,900, three days 20½ hours, daily

Severobaikalsk

Sights
1 Orthodox Church....A2
2 Railway Station....C3
3 War Memorial....A2

Sleeping
4 Baikal Resort....C4
5 Baikal Service....D1
6 Baikal Trail Hostel....D2
7 Hotel Olymp....C1
8 Zolotaya Rybka....C5

Eating
9 Anyuta....C2
10 TiTs....B2
11 VIST Supermarket....B3
12 VIST Supermarket....D2

Tynda *platskart* R1600, *kupe* R3600 to R4400, 26 hours, daily

Around Severobaikalsk

NIZHNEANGARSK НИЖНЕАНГАРСК

30130 / POP 5500 / MOSCOW +5HR

Until the BAM clunked into town, Nizhneangarsk had led an isolated existence for over 300 years, cobbling together its long streets of wooden houses and harvesting Baikal's rich *omul* (a type of fish) stocks. If truth be told, not much changed when the railway arrived, but despite the appearance of now larger Severobaikalsk 30km away, the 5km-long village remains the administrative centre of northern Baikal.

The town's **tourist office** (8-924-354 5092, 47 883; www.sbvizit.ru; ul Rabochaya 125, office 10) is housed in the regional administration building.

The recently relocated **Regional Museum** (ul Pobedy 37; admission R100; 10am-6pm Mon-Fri) chases the history of the region back to the 17th century and includes several Evenki exhibits.

To the east of the town a long spit of land known as **Yarki Island** caps the most northerly point of Lake Baikal and keeps powerful currents and waves out of the fragile habitat of the Verkhnyaya Angara delta. You can walk along its length.

Friendly tour agency **109 Meridian** (8-914-050 5909; sb109m@yandex.ru) runs reasonably priced summer coach excursions to Evenki villages and Baikalskoe, as well as multiday boat trips on Lake Baikal and up the Verkhnyaya Angara River. Staff can arrange permits to land on Baikal's eastern shore and book accommodation in Dzelinda, Goudzhekit and Severobaikalsk. The company also produces a detailed, annually updated Russian-language guidebook to the region *(Poputchik)*.

Few choose to stay over in Nizhneangarsk, but if you do, the timber **Severny Baikal** (47 280; ul Rabochaya 10; tw R1800) has well-appointed standard rooms with attached bathrooms and views across the mudflats towards Baikal. Basic **Baikalsky Bereg** (ul Pobedy 55a; meals R100; 8am-5pm, to 1am summer) has an attractive lakeside location and a hand-written menu of borsch, meatballs and *pelmeni*, while the **airport snack bar** stays open even when there are no flights (which is most of the time).

Scenic low-altitude flights cross Lake Baikal to Ulan-Ude (R5000, four per week) and Irkutsk (R5000, weekly summer only) when weather conditions allow.

Marshrutky (R37, 50 minutes) from Severobaikalsk run every 30 minutes along ul Pobedy then continue along the coast road (ul Rabochaya) to the airport. The last service back to Severobaikalsk is at 6.50pm, and 5.50pm at weekends.

BAIKALSKOE БАЙКАЛЬСКОЕ

This timeless little fishing village of log-built houses 45km south of Severobaikalsk has a jaw-droppingly picturesque lakeside location backed by wooded hills and snow-dusted peaks. Your first stop should be the small, informal **school museum** (admission R100; 10am-4pm) where hands-on exhibits tell the story of the village from the Stone Age to the seal hunts of the 20th century. The only other sight is the wooden **Church of St Inokent**, which strikes a scenic lakeside pose.

Most come to Baikalskoe on a day trip from Severobaikalsk, but if you do want to stay the night, arrange a homestay through helpers in Severobaikalsk. There's no café, just a couple of shops selling basic foodstuffs.

Marshrutky (R60, 45 minutes) leave from outside Severobaikalsk train station every day at 8am and 5pm, returning an hour or so later.

A section of the Great Baikal Trail heads north from the fishing port 20 minutes up a cliff-side path towards the radio mast, from which there are particularly superb views looking back towards the village. Beyond

NORTHERN BAIKAL'S MINISPAS

Seismic activity in the northern Baikal area shakes free lots of thermal springs around which tiny spas have sprouted. These are great places to soothe aching muscles after days of contortion in your BAM carriage bunk, though facilities are pretty basic. Costs are low for accommodation, food and bathing.

Goudzhekit Гоуджекит

Goudzhekit's lonely BAM station is beautifully situated between bald, high peaks that stay dusted with snow until early June. Five minutes' walk to the right, the tiny timber **spa** (⌚7am-3am) has two pools fed by thermal springs whose waters gurgle a soothing 40°C.

There are two basic hotels at the spa, but most visitors just come for the day. Take the *marshrutka* which leaves from in front of Severobaikalsk train station at 9am, noon and 3pm, returning around an hour later.

Dzelinda Дзелинда

Tiny timber Dzelinda is another hot-springs spa on the BAM railway but with a much more appealing forest location than Goudzhekit. Thermal springs keep the outdoor pools at a toasty 44°C even in winter, and when the surrounding hills are thick with snow and the temperature plunges to -35°C, a warm swim can be exhilarating. Guests stay in timber houses, one of which has an intricately carved gable. All meals are provided. Book through Severobaikalsk helpers and tour companies.

Elektrichka 5608 leaves Severobaikalsk at 6.10am, arriving at the Dzelinda halt 92km later at 8.10am. The return service leaves at 7pm. The spa is a short walk from the halt along a newly paved road through the forest.

Khakusy Хакусы

To land at this idyllically isolated hot-spring **turbaza** (holiday camp; www.sbkhakusy.ru) requires permits in summer (available through Severobaikalsk tour companies and hotels), but these are waived in February and March, when it takes about an hour to drive across the ice from Severobaikalsk. Bathing is fun in the snow and frozen steam creates curious ice patterns on the wooden spa buildings. In summer, make sure you book the ferry well in advance as it's a popular trip among Russian holidaymakers. An alternative way to reach Khakusy is along the 100km Frolikha Adventure Coastline Trail (see boxed text p521).

that, Baikalskoe's shamanic **petroglyphs** hide in awkward-to-reach cliff-side locations and can only be found with the help of a knowledgeable local. The well-maintained trail continues another 18 scenic kilometres through beautiful cedar and spruce forests and past photogenic **Boguchan Island** to chilly **Lake Slyudyanskoe**, next to which stands the small **Echo turbaza** (holiday camp) – book through the Maryasov family in Severobaikalsk.

The hike makes for a rewarding day trip and, with the path hugging the lake most of the way, there's little chance of getting lost. From the Echo *turbaza* head along a dirt track through the forest to the Severobaikalsk–Baikalskoe road to hitch a lift, or prearrange transport back to Severobaikalsk. Alternatively some hikers tackle the day the other way round, catching the morning *marshrutka* to Echo *turbaza* then timing the hike to make the 6pm *marshrutka* back to Severobaikalsk.

LAKE BAIKAL

One of the world's oldest geographical features (formed 25 to 30 million years ago), magnificent Lake Baikal (Озеро Байкал) is the highlight of Eastern Siberia for many. Summer travellers enjoy gob-smacking vistas across waters of the deepest blue to soaring mountain ranges on the opposite shore; rarer winter visitors marvel at its powder-white surface, frozen steel-hard and scored with ice roads. Whether they swim in it, drink its water, skirt its southern tip by train, cycle or dog sled over it in winter or just admire it from 2000km of shoreline, most agree that Siberia doesn't get better than this.

Banana-shaped Baikal is 636km from north to south and up to 1637m deep, making it the world's deepest lake. In fact it's not a lake at all, but the world's future fifth sea containing nearly one-fifth of the planet's unfrozen fresh water (more than North America's five Great Lakes combined). Despite some environmental concerns, it's pure enough to drink in most places. Fed by 300 rivers, it's drained by just one, the Angara near Listvyanka.

Foreign tourists typically visit Baikal from Listvyanka via Irkutsk, but approaching via Ulan-Ude (for eastern Baikal) produces more beach fun and Severobaikalsk (on the BAM railway) is best for accessing wilderness trekking routes. Choosing well is important as there's no round-lake road and the northern reaches are in effect cut off by land from the southern shores. Not even the Great Baikal Trail will create a complete loop as some stretches of shoreline are just too remote. Hydrofoil connections are limited to summer services in the south plus the Irkutsk–Olkhon–Nizhneangarsk run. Inexplicably, there are virtually no scheduled boat services linking the east and west shores.

Note that this section also includes the beautiful inland Tunka and Barguzin Valleys as they're accessed via Baikal towns. For Baikal's far northern region see the Western BAM section.

Irkutsk Иркутск

☎3952 / POP 587,000 / ⏰MOSCOW +5HR

The de facto capital of Eastern Siberia, pleasantly historic Irkutsk is by far the most popular stop on the Trans-Siberian Railway between Moscow and all points east. With Lake Baikal a mere 70km away, the city is the best base from which to strike out for the western shoreline. Amid the 19th-century architecture, revived churches, classy eateries and numerous apartment hostels, plentiful English-speaking agencies can help you plan anything from a winter trek across the lake's ice to a short walking tour through the city.

Irkutsk spent the summer of 2011 celebrating its 350th birthday, an event that

BAIKAL'S ENVIRONMENTAL ISSUES

Home to an estimated 60,000 nerpa seals as well as hundreds of endemic species, Lake Baikal is beautiful, pristine and drinkably pure in most areas. As it holds an astonishing 80% of Russia's fresh water, environmentalists are keen to keep things that way. In the 1960s, despite the pressures of the Soviet system, it was the building of Baikal's first (and only) lakeside industrial plant that galvanised Russia's first major green movement. That plant, the Baikalsk Pulp and Paper Mill, continues to pollute air and water in the lake's southern reaches, despite regular promises from the owners to introduce technology that would reduce harmful emissions.

But the ecosystem extends beyond the lake itself. Another challenge includes polluted inflows from the Selenga River, which carries much of Mongolia's untreated waste into the lake. The most contentious of recent worries is the US$16 billion Eastern Siberia oil pipeline which runs from Tayshet to the Pacific coast. Completed in 2009, the route deliberately loops north, avoiding the lakeshore itself. But with a potential 1.6 million barrels of oil flowing daily across the lake's northern water catchment area, an area highly prone to seismic activity, environmentalists fear that a quake-cracked pipeline could gush crude into Baikal's feedwaters. The government decree allowing the project to proceed was signed in December 2004, just days after a huge earthquake caused the disastrous southeast Asian tsunami.

Another ominous development was the July 2008 exploration of the bottom of Lake Baikal by a Russian submarine team (the same group that rather comically planted a Russian flag on the bottom of the Arctic Ocean in 2007). Some claim the team was secretly looking for oil reserves, prompting local environmentalists to fear the worst.

For more information, see the websites of regional ecogroups **Baikal Wave** (www.baikalwave.eu.org), **Baikal Watch** (www.earthisland.org/baikal) and the wonderful **Baikal Web World** (www.bww.irk.ru), which has lots about the wildlife, history and legends of the lake.

Baikal

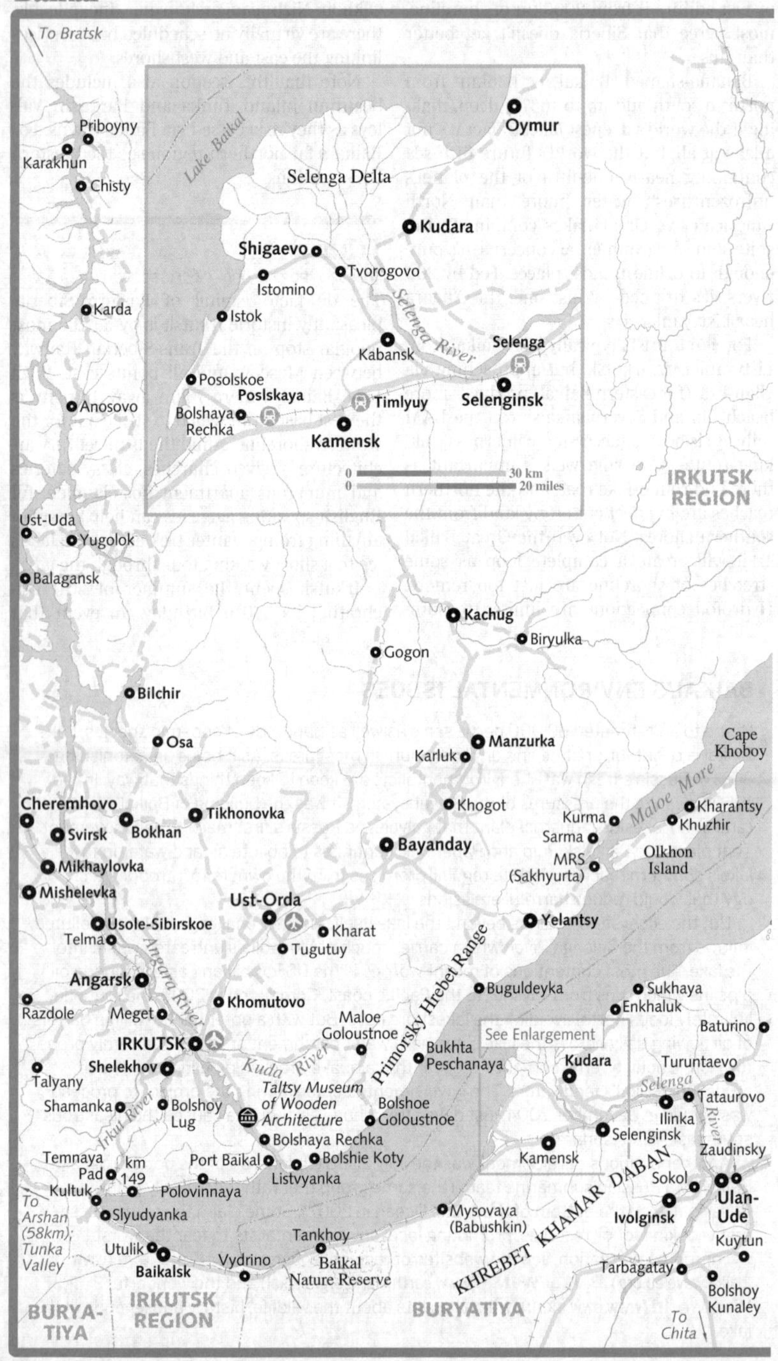
To Bratsk
Lake Baikal
Selenga Delta
Oymur
Kudara
Shigaevo
Tvorogovo
Istomino
Istok
Selenga River
Kabansk
Selenga
Posolskoe
Poslskaya
Timlyuy
Selenginsk
Bolshaya Rechka
Kamensk
0 30 km
0 20 miles
IRKUTSK REGION
Priboyny
Karakhun
Chisty
Karda
Anosovo
Ust-Uda
Yugolok
Balagansk
Kachug
Biryulka
Gogon
Bilchir
Osa
Manzurka
Karluk
Cape Khoboy
Maloe More
Khogot
Kharantsy
Kurma
Khuzhir
Sarma
Olkhon Island
MRS (Sakhyurta)
Cheremhovo
Svirsk
Bokhan
Tikhonovka
Bayanday
Mikhaylovka
Mishelevka
Ust-Orda
Kharat
Yelantsy
Usole-Sibirskoe
Telma
Tugutuy
Angara River
Primorsky Hrebet Range
Angarsk
Buguldeyka
Sukhaya
Enkhaluk
Razdole
Meget
Khomutovo
Maloe Goloustnoe
See Enlargement
Baturino
IRKUTSK
Kuda River
Bukhta Peschanaya
Kudara
Turuntaevo
Shelekhov
Talyany
Taltsy Museum of Wooden Architecture
Selenga River
Tataurovo
Ilinka
Shamanka
Irkut River
Bolshoy Lug
Bolshoe Goloustnoe
Selenginsk
Bolshaya Rechka
Kamensk
Zaudinsky
Temnaya Pad
km 149
Port Baikal
Bolshie Koty
Listvyanka
KHREBET KHAMAR DABAN
Sokol
Kultuk
Polovinnaya
Ulan-Ude
To Arshan (58km); Tunka Valley
Slyudyanka
Mysovaya (Babushkin)
Ivolginsk
Tankhoy
Kuytun
Utulik
Baikalsk
Vydrino
Baikal Nature Reserve
Tarbagatay
Bolshoy Kunaley
BURYA-TIYA
IRKUTSK REGION
BURYATIYA
To Chita

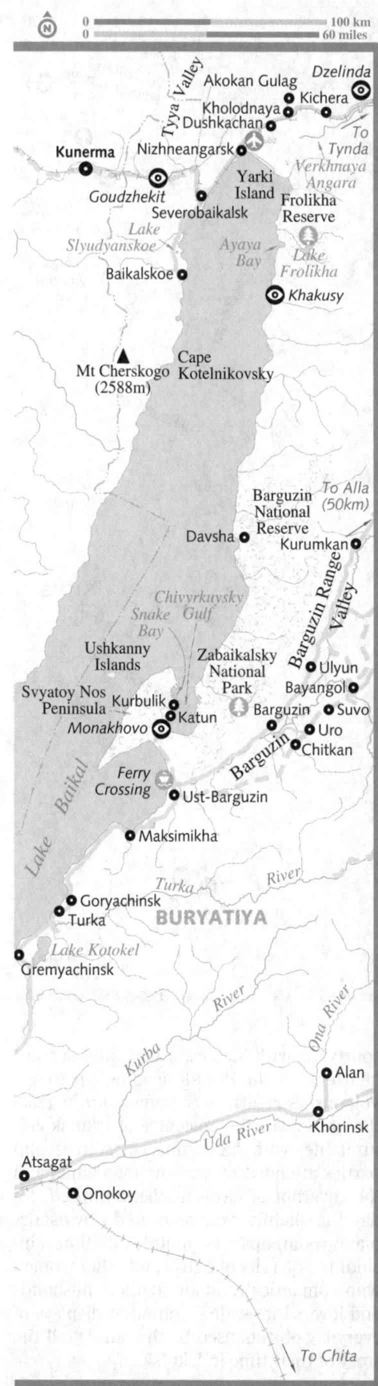

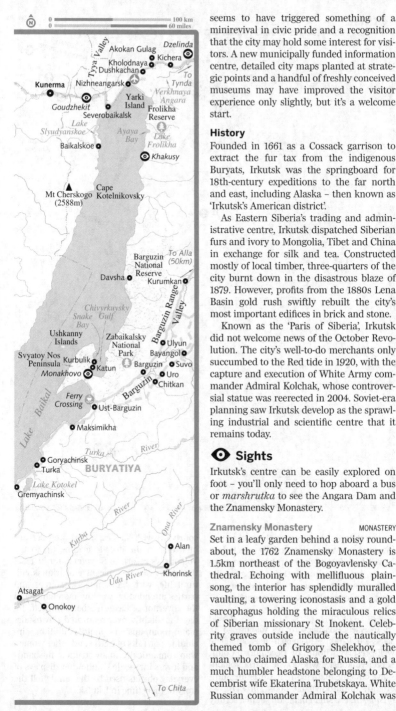

seems to have triggered something of a minirevival in civic pride and a recognition that the city may hold some interest for visitors. A new municipally funded information centre, detailed city maps planted at strategic points and a handful of freshly conceived museums may have improved the visitor experience only slightly, but it's a welcome start.

History

Founded in 1661 as a Cossack garrison to extract the fur tax from the indigenous Buryats, Irkutsk was the springboard for 18th-century expeditions to the far north and east, including Alaska – then known as 'Irkutsk's American district'.

As Eastern Siberia's trading and administrative centre, Irkutsk dispatched Siberian furs and ivory to Mongolia, Tibet and China in exchange for silk and tea. Constructed mostly of local timber, three-quarters of the city burnt down in the disastrous blaze of 1879. However, profits from the 1880s Lena Basin gold rush swiftly rebuilt the city's most important edifices in brick and stone.

Known as the 'Paris of Siberia', Irkutsk did not welcome news of the October Revolution. The city's well-to-do merchants only succumbed to the Red tide in 1920, with the capture and execution of White Army commander Admiral Kolchak, whose controversial statue was reerected in 2004. Soviet-era planning saw Irkutsk develop as the sprawling industrial and scientific centre that it remains today.

Sights

Irkutsk's centre can be easily explored on foot – you'll only need to hop aboard a bus or *marshrutka* to see the Angara Dam and the Znamensky Monastery.

Znamensky Monastery MONASTERY

Set in a leafy garden behind a noisy roundabout, the 1762 Znamensky Monastery is 1.5km northeast of the Bogoyavlensky Cathedral. Echoing with mellifluous plainsong, the interior has splendidly muralled vaulting, a towering iconostasis and a gold sarcophagus holding the miraculous relics of Siberian missionary St Inokent. Celebrity graves outside include the nautically themed tomb of Grigory Shelekhov, the man who claimed Alaska for Russia, and a much humbler headstone belonging to Decembrist wife Ekaterina Trubetskaya. White Russian commander Admiral Kolchak was

Irkutsk

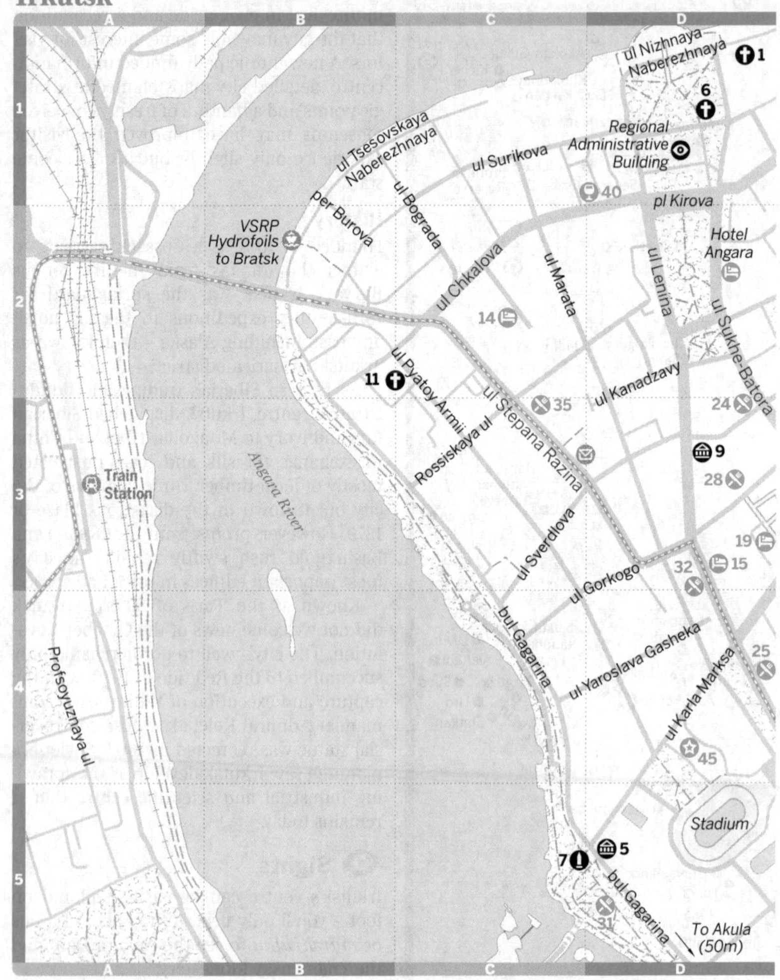

executed by Bolsheviks near the spot where his **statue** was controversially erected in November 2004 at the entrance to the monastery grounds; the plinth is exaggeratedly high enough to prevent die-hard communists from committing acts of vandalism.

Volkonsky House-Museum MUSEUM
(Дом-музей Волконского; per Volkonskogo 10; admission R200; ⏲10am-6pm Tue-Sun). The well-preserved home of Decembrist Count Sergei Volkonsky, whose wife Maria Volkonskaya cuts the main figure in Christine Sutherland's unputdownable book *The Princess of Siberia*, is a small mansion set in a scruffy courtyard with stables, a barn and servant quarters. In the decade leading up to the Volkonskys return to St Petersburg in 1856, the house was the epicentre of Irkutsk cultural life, with balls, musical soirées and parties attended by wealthy merchants and the governor of Eastern Siberia himself. Today the slightly over-renovated downstairs piano room, upstairs photo exhibition – including portraits of Maria and other women who romantically followed their husbands and lovers into exile – and other displays of everyday objects used by the family tell the story of their time in Irkutsk.

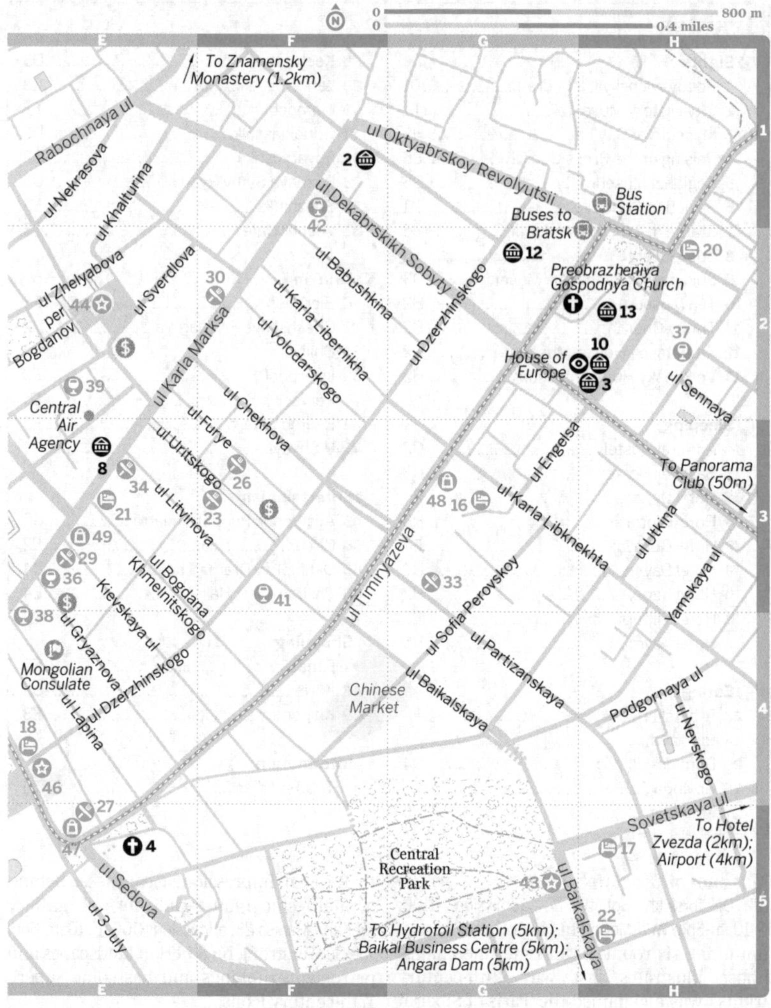

Regional Museum MUSEUM

(Краеведческий Музей; www.museum.irkutsk.ru; ul Karla Marksa 2; admission R200; ⌚10am-7pm) Irkutsk's rapidly ageing Regional Museum is within a fancy 1870s brick building that formerly housed the Siberian Geographical Society, a club of Victorian-style gentlemen explorers. The highlights here are the downstairs ethnographical exhibitions and the nostalgic display of 20th-century junk upstairs, as well as the small gift shop selling birch-bark boxes, jewellery made from Baikal minerals and other interesting souvenirs.

City History Museum MUSEUM

(www.history.irk.ru; ul Frank-Kamenetskogo 16a; admission R150; ⌚10am-6pm Thu-Tue) Relocated in 2011 from its former far-flung location to the interior of one of Irkutsk's most impressive central edifices, the City History Museum is the greatest symbol of the authorities' efforts to perk up the visitor experience. Painstakingly renovated in time for Irkutsk's 350th birthday, this palatial 19th-century school building now houses a comprehensive overview of the city's three and a half centuries, focusing on trade, life of the merchant classes, education, churches and the Trans-Sib.

Irkutsk

Sights

1 Bogoyavlensky Cathedral....D1
2 City History Museum....F1
3 Museum of City Life....H2
4 Raising of the Cross Church....E5
5 Regional Museum....D5
6 Saviour's Church....D1
7 Statue of Tsar Alexander III....C5
8 Sub-Gallery....E3
9 Sukachev Regional Art Museum....D3
10 Tea Museum....H2
11 Trinity Church....B2
12 Trubetskoy House-Museum....G2
13 Volkonsky House-Museum....H2

Sleeping

14 Admiral Hostel....C2
15 Baikaler Hostel....D3
16 Hotel Delta....G3
17 Hotel Gloria....H5
18 Hotel Gornyak....E4
19 Hotel Sayen....D3
20 Hotel Uzory....H2
21 Hotel Viktoria....E3
22 Hotel Yevropa....H5

Eating

23 Arbatski Dvorik....F3
24 Blinnaya....D3
25 Domino....D4
26 Govinda....F3
27 Kafe Elen....E5
28 Kochevnik....D3
29 Lancelot....E3
30 Mamochka....F2
31 Odnoklassniki....D5
32 Povaryoshka....D3
33 Poznaya Sytny Ryad....G3
34 Snezhinka....E3
35 Wiener Café....C3

Drinking

36 Bierhaus....E3
37 Cheshskaya Pivovarnya....H2
38 Chili....E4
39 Liverpool....E2
40 Pervach....D1
41 Ryumochnaya....F3
42 U Shveyka....F1

Entertainment

43 Aystyonok Puppet Theatre....G5
44 Circus....E2
45 Okhlopkov Drama Theatre....D4
46 Philharmonic Hall....E4

Shopping

47 Fanat....E5
48 Karibu....G3
49 Knigomir....E3

Information

Tourist office....(see 10)

Museum of City Life MUSEUM
(ul Dekabrskikh Sobyty 77; admission R100; ⏲10am-6pm Wed-Mon) This brand-new museum filling six rooms of a former merchant's house illustrates just why 19th-century Irkutsk was nicknamed the 'Paris of Siberia'. Changing exhibitions of everyday and decorative items such as lamps, dolls, tableware and porcelain are donated free of charge by the people of Irkutsk and are displayed against a background of period wallpaper, elegant double doors and high ceilings. The new **Tea Museum** opposite (in the same building as the tourist office) is set to open in late 2011.

Sukachev Regional Art Museum ART GALLERY
(Художественный Музей; ul Lenina 5; admission R100; ⏲10am-5.30pm Tue-Sun) The grand old art gallery has a valuable though poorly lit collection ranging from Mongolian *thangkas* (Tibetan Buddhist religious paintings) to Russian Impressionist canvases. Behind a photogenic 1909 facade its **sub-gallery** (ul Karla Marksa 23; admission R100; ⏲10am-6pm Tue-Sun) is strong on Siberian landscapes and petroglyph rubbings and has some superb 17th-century icons.

Raising of the Cross Church CHURCH
(Крестовоздвиженская церковь; Krestovozdvizhenskaya tserkov; ul Sedova 1) The 1758 baroque Raising of the Cross Church has a fine interior of gilt-edged icons and examples of intricate brickwork in a rounded style that's unique to Irkutsk and the Selenga Delta village of Posolskoe.

Kazansky Church CHURCH
(ul Barrikad) The gigantic Kazansky Church is a theme-park-esque confection of salmon-pink walls and fluoro turquoise domes topped with gold baubled crosses. Get off tram 4 two stops northeast of the bus station.

Angara Dam LANDMARK

Some 6km southeast of the centre, the 1956 Angara Dam is 2km long. Its construction raised Lake Baikal by up to 1m and caused environmental problems, most notably the silencing of the so-called singing sands on Baikal's eastern shore. The dam itself is hardly an attraction but moored nearby is the **Angara icebreaker** (admission R150; ⌚10am-8pm). Originally imported in kit form from Newcastle-upon-Tyne to carry Trans-Siberian Railway passengers across Lake Baikal (the trains went on her bigger sister ship *Baikal,* sunk during the Russian Civil War), it's now a less-than-inspiring museum reached by a permanent gangway.

Trubetskoy House-Museum MUSEUM

(Дом-музей Трубецкого; ul Dzerzhinskogo) Dismantled and carted off for renovation in late 2007, Irkutsk's second Decembrist house-museum was expected to make a comeback in late 2011 or 2012. From the outside the restorers seem to have done a cracking job on the pleasingly symmetrical minimansion.

Trinity Church CHURCH

(Троицкий храм; Troitsky khram; ul 5 Armii 8) Restoration work remains half-finished on the 18th-century Trinity Church where Admiral Kolchak was christened and married.

Statue of Tsar Alexander III MONUMENT

(Памятник Александру III) Across the road from the Regional Museum, a recast statue of Tsar Alexander III (a copy of the 1904 original) looks as though he's holding an invisible balloon on a string.

Saviour's Church CHURCH

(Спасская Церковь; Spasskaya tserkov; ⌚8am-8pm) Under heavy renovation at the time of research, this 1706 church has remnants of murals on its facade and until a decade ago housed a museum.

Bogoyavlensky Cathedral CHURCH

(Богоявленский Собор; ul Nizhnaya Naberezhnaya) Much more eye-catching than the Saviour's Church is this fairy-tale ensemble of mini onion domes atop restored salmon, white and green towers. The interior is a fragrant riot of aureoled Byzantine saints with no surface left plain.

Tours

Local tour companies are useful not only for organising excursions but also for booking hotels and most kinds of tickets. All of Irkutsk's hostels can arrange Baikal tours.

Cheap Travel TOUR COMPANY

(☎668 335; www.cheapandtrip.ru) English-speaking travel fanatic Maxim books plane and train tickets for R200 commission, can help out with Mongolian visas and Russian visa registration (R400) and will even find you a bed for the night. The company currently has no base, but is set to operate from 2012 in a new hostel (location to be decided).

Baikaler TOUR COMPANY

(☎336 240; www.baikaler.com) Imaginative Jack Sheremetoff speaks very good English and is well tuned to budget-traveller needs. Original personalised tours, two great hostels and a friendly welcome.

BaikalComplex TOUR COMPANY

(☎461 557; www.baikalcomplex.com) Busy, well-organised operation offering homestays and trips tailored for international travellers.

Baikalinfo TOUR COMPANY

(☎707 012; www.baikalinfo.ru; ul Krasnykh Madiyar 50) Commercial tour company that arranges Baikal tours as well as trips on the Circumbaikal Railway.

Green Express TOUR COMPANY

(☎734 400; www.greenexpress.ru; ul Karla Libknekhta 48) Professional outfit specialising in outdoor activities.

Baikal Discovery TOUR COMPANY

(☎200 550; www.baikal-discovery.com) Adventure tours in the Baikal region and beyond.

BaikalExplorer TOUR COMPANY

(☎8-902-560 2440; www.baikalex.com) Baikal cruises, fishing and diving trips.

Sleeping

Although options are constantly expanding, Irkutsk's accommodation still gets very full in summer. Bookings are generally a very good idea.

The newest swanky places to catch some Zs in Irkutsk will be the Marriott and the Park Inn by Radisson, both under construction at the time of research.

Hostels have sprouted like mushrooms after a rainfall, but lifespans can be short and some are open only in high season. To save you some research time, we've only included a list of the most established backpacker quarters. As across the former USSR, they are ideal for finding English-speaking assistance, arranging tours and meeting fellow travellers.

TOP CHOICE **Baikaler Hostel** HOSTEL €
(☎336 240; apt 11, ul Lenina 9; www.baikaler.com; dm R700; ❄@📶) Run by experienced tour guide Jack Sheremetoff, the super-central Baikaler apartment hostel is Irkutsk's original backpacker haven and still *the* place to meet fellow travellers and organise trips. The spotless, air-conditioned dorms are spacious, but beds are limited and booking ahead from June to September is essential. The entrance is from the rear of the building. Jeff also runs the Baikaler Eco-Hostel in Listvyanka.

Hotel Sayen HOTEL €€€
(☎500 000; www.sayen.ru; ul Karla Marksa 13b; r R7700-13,800; ❄📶) Described by some as the finest luxury sleep east of the Urals, this very central Japanese hotel gets rave reviews and deservedly so. The 24 rooms enjoy design-mag decor, big baths and gadgets galore, going beyond the standards of many Western hotels. The 24-hour room service is a given, there are two top-hole restaurants and a spa is on hand should you feel the urge to have hot stones placed on your back. Possibly about as smart as things will ever get in Irkutsk.

Hotel Viktoria HOTEL €€€
(☎792 879; www.victoryhotel.ru; ul Bogdana Khmelnitskogo 1; s R3500-3800, d R3800-4300; ❄@📶) Just a few steps off ul Karla Marksa, the 30 rooms at this relative newcomer remain stylish and unfrumpy despite the antique-style furniture and flowery wall coverings. If you've been in Russia a while, the courteous staff, baths in every room and online booking could feel almost eccentric.

Admiral Hostel HOSTEL €
(☎742 440; apt 1, ul Cheremkhovsky 6; dm R550; @📶) With its Kolchak-inspired name, this cosy 13-bed apartment hostel has become well-established digs for Trans-Siberian wanderers. The lower bunks sport privacy curtains, staff sell bus tickets to Olkhon Island, there's a free (light) breakfast and you can even get your washing done. Enter from the rear of the building.

Baikal Business Centre HOTEL €€€
(☎259 120; www.bbc.ru; ul Baikalskaya 279; s R3900-6100, tw R5100-6100; ❄📶) If you're in Irkutsk on business, this white and blue-glass tower is where you'll want to unsheathe the company credit card. Rooms are just about international standard, there's a business centre and rates are slashed at weekends – on a winter Saturday you can pay as little as R1800 for a single, a real bargain for this standard.

Baikalhostel HOSTEL €
(☎525 742; www.baikalhostels.com; apt 1, ul Lermontova 136; dm R650; 📶) This German-owned hostel receives rave reviews from travellers, despite the very inconvenient and insalubrious location several kilometres south of the train station; take *marshrutka* 72 from the station to the Mikrochirurgia Glaza stop.

Hotel Yevropa HOTEL €€
(Гостиница Европа; ☎291 515; www.europehotel.ru; ul Baikalskaya 69; s/d from R2900/3700; ❄📶) Behind nine Doric columns immaculate rooms are realistically priced at this gleaming four-star favourite. Reception staff speak English and the Western-style breakfast is reportedly the best in town.

Hotel Zvezda HOTEL €€€
(☎540 000; www.zvezdahotel.ru; ul Yadrintseva 1ж; s/tw R4000/4300, ste R6000-18000; ❄📶) Within a Swiss chalet–style building, rooms here are modern and comfortable, service is pleasant and English is spoken, though you'd expect little less for these room rates. Its atmospheric restaurant specialises in game and exotic meats.

Hotel Gloria HOTEL €€€
(Отель Глория; ☎540 664; www.gloriahotel.org; Sovetskaya ul 58a; s R3500, d R4500-6500; ❄📶) This pastel-beige tower has nine international-class rooms and two bigger suites that have both a bath and shower. English is spoken and there's a decent, if pricey, on-site restaurant.

Hotel Uzory HOTEL €
(Узоры Гостиница; ☎209 239; ul Oktyabrskoy Revolyutsii 17; s/tw R650/1000) Clean, unpretentious rooms with leopard-skin-patterned blankets but communal bathrooms and toilets. It's popular with independent travellers but maintains a tradition of employing Irkutsk's sourest receptionists.

Hotel Delta HOTEL €€€
(Отель Дельта; ☎794 090; www.deltairkutsk.ru; ul Karla Libknekhta 58; s R2950-3850, d R4820-6000; 📶) Bog-standard rooms with little panache, aimed primarily at low-budget business travellers.

Hotel Gornyak HOTEL €€
(Гостиница Горняк; ☎243 754; ul Lenina 24; s R1500-2700, tw R2200-3300) As a last resort

you could try this reasonably presentable if overpriced central hotel, but at the time of research foreigners were being turned away due to visa registration issues. Enter from ul Dzerzhinskogo.

Eating

TOP CHOICE Kochevnik MONGOLIAN €€
(Кочевник; ul Gorkogo 19; mains R200-650; ⌚11.30am-midnight; ⓜ) Take your taste buds to the Mongolian steppe for some yurt-size portions of mutton, lamb and steak as well as filling soups and *buuzy* (dumplings), sluiced down with a bottle from the decent foreign wine list. Smiley service, a picture menu, low prices and an exotically curtained summer terrace make this the most agreeable place to eat in town.

Mamochka CAFÉ €
(ul Karla Marksa 41; mains R80-100, coffee R70-140; ⌚10am-9pm; ⓜ) With its menu of imaginative salads, filling soups and (almost) healthy mains, this is no ordinary point-and-eat canteen. Swab the decks with a Czech, Slovak or German lager then sit back and admire the interior, a mishmash of old newspapers and Soviet bric-a-brac. Great.

Govinda VEGETARIAN €
(2nd fl, ul Furye 4; mains R30-80; ⌚11am-8pm; ❄✍) Irkutsk's only vegie restaurant is a small self-service affair with a half-hearted Indian theme and a menu of soya sausages, basmati rice, spicy soups, mild curries, quorn chilli con carne, imaginative desserts and whole plantations of tea. Extra heat can be added from the chilli bowl on the counter.

Wiener Café CAFÉ €€
(Венское Кафе; ul Stepana Razina 19; mains R80-400; ⌚10am-11pm) Marble-top tables, Parisian bar chairs and a Tyrolean folk ensemble of waitresses make this an entertaining nosh stop. A good mid-morning breakfast option with tempting pastries, real oat porridge and ranks of mouth-watering desserts.

Snezhinka CAFÉ €€
(Снежинка; opposite ul Karla Marksa 25; mains R200-500; ⌚9am-midnight) This cosy belle époque–style café has attentive English-speaking service and regularly wins local awards for its food. It's been around since 1957, making it the city's longest-serving eatery.

Blinnaya RUSSIAN €
(ul Sukhe-Batora 8; mains R25-70; ⌚10am-6pm Mon-Fri, to 4pm Sat) The city centre's cheapest eat is this unrepentantly Soviet canteen where befrilled dinner ladies dispatch plates of filling pancakes, buckwheat *kasha* (porridge), meatballs and pasta, all washed down with plastic cupfuls of over-diluted *kompot* (fruit squash).

Odnoklassniki RUSSIAN €€
(bul Gagarina 13a; mains R150-450; ⌚noon–last customer) The name of this contemporary, purpose-built eatery is a rip-off of the Russian-language equivalent of Friends Reunited, but this is still an enjoyable place to pig out on grilled meat, salads and generous helpings of Slavic stodge. The nostalgic Soviet schooldays theme may be a bit lost on foreigners, but who cares with such a vast drinks menu to peruse on the terrace.

Kafe Elen CAFÉ €€
(ul Timiryazeva; meals R180-350; ⌚9am-11pm Mon-Sat, from 10am Sun; ⊖❄) Bubbling aquariums, rattan furniture, raffia-threaded blinds and lots of potted plants make this a tranquil breakfast and lunch spot as you watch the trams trundle past the church opposite.

Arbatski Dvorik RUSSIAN €€€
(Арбатский Дворик; ul Uritskogo; mains R350-1500; ⌚noon–last customer; 📶ⓜ) This upmarket restaurant is all inside-out, the walls lined with imitation facades, doorways and street lamps. However there's nothing topsy-turvy about the impeccable service and well-crafted menu. Oddly, it's accessed via the gaudy Fiesta fast-food place below.

Lancelot RUSSIAN €€
(Kievskaya ul 2; mains R200-400; ⌚noon-midnight Sun-Wed, to 2am Thu-Sat; ⓜ) Flaming torches lead down through a portcullis into an amusing neomedieval-castle interior. Arthurian-named dishes can be enjoyed at the round table and there's live music at weekends.

Povaryoshka FAST FOOD €
(ul Lenina 32; mains R45-100; ⌚9am-10pm) This new self-service canteen has rural knick-knackery kept high out of clients' reach and a menu of Eurasian standards and half-decent pizzas.

Poznaya Sytny Ryad CAFÉ €
(Позная Сытный Ряд; ul Partizanskaya 9a; pozi R30, other mains R60-180; ⌚10am-11pm) Irkutsk's most appealing cheap *pozi* joint is in a primly faux-rural timber house surrounded by the disarray of the market area.

Domino FAST FOOD €
(Домино; ul Lenina 13a; pizza slices R70; ⊙24hr) Domino has Russian-flavour pizza and vastly superior *bliny* available round the clock.

Drinking

TOP CHOICE Liverpool PUB
(Паб Ливерпуль; ul Sverdlova 28; ⊙noon-3am; 📶) You'll never walk (or drink) alone at Irkutsk's most popular theme pub. The crowds enter through a mocked-up red telephone box to find an interior tiled in Beatles photos and old vinyl LPs and strewn with reminders of northwest England's erstwhile musical prowess. The beer menu is a global affair, the service laid-back and mimicky local rock bands regularly thump and strum for drinkers.

U Shveyka PUB
(У Швейка; ul Karla Marksa 34; ⊙noon-midnight; ❄) This beamed cellar pub serves old-style glass tankards of Czech Pilsner Urquell beer made under licence in Irkutsk. The adjacent beer garden is possibly the city's best and is busy with drinkers from May to late September.

Chili BAR
(Чили; ul Karla Marksa 26; cocktails from R200; ⊙24hr) Aztec-themed nightspot and all-day bar where you can join Irkutsk's moneyed youth on beige couches bathed in flamingo neon for a flashy cocktail or overpriced meals (R250 to R600).

Bierhaus PUB
(ul Gryaznova 1; ⊙noon-2am Mon-Thu, until 4am Fri & Sat, until midnight Sun; 📋) Upmarket Bavarian-style *bierstube* (beer hall with heavy wooden furniture) serving Newcastle Brown and Guinness as well as German beers and sausages. Enter from ul Karla Marksa.

Cheshskaya Pivovarnya PUB
(Чешская Пивоварная; ul Krasnogvardeyskaya 29; ⊙noon-2am Tue-Sat, to midnight Sun & Mon) You'll smell this place before you see it as Irkutsk's unpretentious microbrewery-pub creates its own Pilsner Urquell lager, pumping out a pungent hop aroma in the process.

Pervach PUB
(Первач; ul Chkalova 33; ⊙noon-1am) Pervach is a cosy, stone-and-brick cellar pub, heated by real fires in winter.

Ryumochnaya BAR
(Рюмочная; ul Litvinova 16; ⊙24hr) If low-cost inebriation is your aim, this no-frills bar is your place.

☆ Entertainment

Okhlopkov Drama Theatre THEATRE
(Драматический Театр Охлопкова; ☎200 477; ul Karla Marksa 14) Shakespeare, Russian classics and local playwright Vampilov staged regularly (in Russian) from September to June.

Circus CIRCUS
(Цирк; ☎336 139; ul Zhelyabova; ticket office ⊙10am-7pm) Permanent big top with most performances at weekends.

Aystyonok Puppet Theatre PUPPET THEATRE
(Театр Кукол Аистёнок; ☎205 825; ul Baikalskaya 32) Marionette shows for the kiddies.

Philharmonic Hall LIVE MUSIC
(Филармония; ☎242 968; www.filarmoniya.irk.ru; ul Dzerzhinskogo 2) Historic building staging regular children's shows and musical programs from jazz to classical.

Akula NIGHTCLUB
(www.akula-club.ru; bul Gagarina 9) Nothing subtle about this place – expect top DJs, litres of ethanol-based beverages and public nudity at some point.

Panorama Club NIGHTCLUB
(www.clubpanorama.ru; ul Dekabrskikh Sobyty 102) Four dance floors pounding to different music styles and an international DJ guest list.

Shopping

Fanat OUTDOOR GEAR
(Фанат; ul Timiryazeva; ⊙10am-7pm) Sells Western-brand camping, fishing and skiing equipment, hiking boots and mountain bikes.

Knigomir BOOKSHOP
(Книгомир; ul Karla Marksa 28; ⊙9am-7pm Mon-Sat, 10am-5pm Sun) Best place to source maps of Irkutsk and many other Baikal towns as well as Russian guides, atlases and large souvenir wall maps of Lake Baikal.

Karibu CLOTHING
(ul Timiryazeva 34; ⊙10am-7pm Mon-Sat, noon-5pm Sun) Tiny shop selling beautifully furry *unty* (traditional deerskin cowboy boots) made on-site and typically costing around R10,000. Some English spoken.

Information

Irk.ru (www.irk.ru) Locals city info.
IrkutskOut (www.irkutskout.ru) Practical details including café and restaurant listings.

Moy Bank (Мой Банк; ul Gryaznova 1; ⌚9am-8pm Mon-Fri, 10am-4pm Sat) Exchanges Chinese yuan.

Post office (ul Stepana Razina 23; internet access per hr R50; ⌚8am-10pm Mon-Fri, 9am-6pm Sat & Sun) Internet access.

Sberbank (Сбербанк; ul Uritskogo 19; ⌚9am-7pm Mon-Thu, until 6pm Fri, 10am-5pm Sat & Sun) Currency-exchange window and 24-hour indoor ATM.

Tourist office (☎205 018; www.itsirkutsk.com; ul Dekabrskikh Sobyty 77; ⌚9am-6pm; 📶) Municipally-funded tourist office with English-speaking staff, free wi-fi, free city maps and lots of well-produced brochures and booklets on Irkutsk and Lake Baikal. Located behind the elaborately carved House of Europe.

Travelling to Baikal (www.travellingtobaikal.com) English-language website promoting tourism in Irkutsk and the Baikal area. Lots of listings.

VTB Bank (ВТБ Банк; ul Sverdlova 36; ⌚9.30am-5.30pm Mon-Thu, to 4.30pm Fri) Currency exchange and 24-hour indoor ATMs.

WWW Irkutsk (www.irkutsk.org) Bags of information on every aspect of the city.

ℹ Getting There & Away

Air

Irkutsk's antiquated little 'international' **airport** (www.iktport.ru) is handily placed near the city centre. Foreign destinations include Bangkok (R20,000), Beijing (R10,000 to R20,000), Dushanbe (R20,000) and Tashkent (€250 to €400). **Aeromongolia** (www.aeromongolia.mn) operates twice-weekly flights to Ulaanbaatar while **Yakutia** (www.yakutia.aero) has started useful flights to Munich (R17,400, twice weekly).

For Moscow Domodedovo there are direct flights with **S7 Airlines** (from R7900 daily) and at least two other companies. Irkutsk also enjoys direct air links to many other domestic destinations, with tickets for all services sold through the convenient **Central Air Agency** (Центральная Аэрокасса; ☎201 517; ul Gorkogo 29; ⌚8am-8.30pm, until 7pm winter).

Boat

In summer hydrofoils buzz along the Angara River to Listvyanka (one hour, three daily June to September) and up Lake Baikal to Bolshie Koty (90 minutes, three daily June to September), Olkhon Island (eight hours, three weekly July and August), Ust-Barguzin (11 hours, weekly July and August) and Nizhneangarsk (12 hours, twice weekly July and August). Departures are from the Raketa **hydrofoil station** (Речной Вокзал) beyond the Angara Dam in Solnechny Mikro-Rayon, two minutes' walk from bus 16 stop 'Raketa'. Timetables are posted by the quay. Services in the other direction to Bratsk leave from a separate jetty in the city centre.

All services are operated by **VSRP** (☎356 726; www.vsrp.ru, in English). Check the website for all times and prices.

Bus

From the slowly renovating **bus station** (Автовокзал; ul Oktyabrskoy Revolyutsii) book tickets at least a day ahead in summer for Arshan (R250, four to five hours, four daily), and Listvyanka (R100, 1¼ hours, 11 daily) via Taltsy (R60).

Comfortable coaches for Bratsk (R900, 11 hours, 8pm) leave from a special **ticket booth** opposite the main bus station. Minibuses to Ulan-Ude (R700, seven hours) depart throughout the day but more frequently in late evening from the train station forecourt.

Train

Train tickets can be bought from Cheap Travel (see Tours), the Bratsk bus ticket booth and

FLIGHTS WITHIN RUSSIA FROM IRKUTSK

DESTINATION	COST (R)	FREQUENCY
Bratsk	3000-4000	3 per week
Chita	4500-7000	5 per week
Khabarovsk	7000-10,000	daily
Magadan	12,000-20,000	3 per week
Moscow	from 7900	daily
Novosibirsk	6000-15,000	daily
St Petersburg	15,000	5 per week
Ulan-Ude	2000	3 per week
Vladivostok	8000-12,000	8 per week
Yekaterinburg	8000-12,000	daily

THE EASY WAY TO OLKHON ISLAND

To Khuzhir on Olkhon Island, convenient door-to-door transfers (R700) can be arranged through any of Irkutsk's hostels. Minibuses pick up from any hostel in the morning and drop off passengers at any guesthouse in Khuzhir midafternoon. Hostels sell tickets even to nonguests.

many upmarket hotels. Irkutsk has the following rail connections:

Beijing *kupe* R11,000, two days 22 hours, twice weekly

Chita *platskart/kupe* R1400/3100, 16 hours to 19 hours, up to six daily

Khabarovsk *platskart/kupe* R3600/8400, two days 13 hours, three daily

Krasnoyarsk *platskart/kupe* R1400/3500, 18 hours, up to nine daily

Moscow *platskart* R3500 to R4800, *kupe* R7700 to R12,500, three days three to 15 hours, three daily

Severobaikalsk *platskart* R2100, *kupe* R3300 to R4700, one day 13 hours, daily

Slyudyanka *elektrichka* R70, four hours, four daily

Ulaanbaatar *kupe* R4500, 27 hours, daily

Ulan-Ude *platskart* R875, *kupe* R1300 to R2300, 6½ hours to 8½ hours, up to nine daily

Vladivostok *platskart/kupe* R4400/10,100, two days 22 hours, three daily

Getting Around

Within the central area, walking is usually the best idea as one-way systems make bus routes confusing.

Frequent trolleybus 4 and bus/*marshrutka* 20, 80, 90 and countless others connect the city centre with the airport. A taxi to/from the airport costs around R150 to R200.

From the train station, trams 1, 2 and 4A run to ul Lenina and ul Timiryazeva, 4A continuing on to the bus station. Tram 4 links the central market with the bus station.

Taltsy Museum of Architecture & Ethnography

Архитектурно-этнографический музей Тальцы

About 47km east of Irkutsk, 23km before Listvyanka, **Taltsy** (www.talci.ru; admission R150; ⌚10am-5pm) is an impressive outdoor collection of old Siberian buildings set in a delightful riverside forest. Amid the renovated farmsteads are two chapels, a church, a watermill, some Evenki graves and the eye-catching 17th-century Iliminsk Ostrog watchtower. Listvyanka–Irkutsk buses and *marshrutky* stop on request at Taltsy's entrance (look out for the roadside 'Музей' sign), and the ticket booth is a minute's walk through the forest.

Listvyanka Листвянка

☎3952 / POP 1830 / ⌚MOSCOW +5HR

As the closest lakeside village to Irkutsk, Listvyanka – aka the 'Baikal Riviera' – is the touristy spot to which most travellers are funnelled to dunk their toes in Baikal's pure waters. Having picked at *omul,* admired the hazy views of the Khamar Daban mountains on the opposite shore and huffed their way from one end of the village to the other, most are on a *marshrutka* back to Irkutsk late afternoon. But there's more to Listvyanka than this; others stay longer to hike the Great Baikal Trail, discover more about the lake at the Baikal Museum and chill out at one of Siberia's most eco-friendly sleeps.

If you're looking for beach fun, you're at the wrong address – the eastern shore (Buryatiya) is the place to build sandcastles. However, what the Buryat shore doesn't have is Listvyanka's range of activities: anything from short boat trips to diving and jet-skiing in the summer and ice mountain biking to lake treks and ice sculpting in the winter.

The village extends 4.5km from Rogatka at the mouth of the Angara to the market area. A single road skirts the shore with three valleys running inland where most of Listvyanka's characterful timber dwellings and accommodation options are located. There's no public transport which can mean some very long walks.

Sights & Activities

Sourcing a map at Irkutsk's tourist office before you set off will save a lot of hunting.

Baikal Museum MUSEUM

(ul Akademicheskaya 1, Rogatka; admission R150; ⌚9am-5pm Oct-May, to 7pm Jun-Sep) One of only three museums in the world dedicated solely to a lake, this sometimes overly scientific institution examines the science of Baikal from all angles. Pass quickly by the gruesomely discoloured fish samples and seal embryos in formaldehyde to the tanks containing two frolicsome nerpa seals and the various Baikal fish that you may later encounter on restaurant menus. A new attraction is a minisub simulator which takes you deep down into Baikal's nippy waters; adjoining the building is a park containing over 400 species of plants, some rare or endangered.

Baikal Dog Sledding Centre DOG SLEDDING
(☎8-908-660 5098; www.baikalsled.ru; ul Kulikova 136a) From December to March the centre offers thrilling dog sledding on forest tracks. All kinds of tours are available, from 5km tasters for R1500 per person to multiday trans-Baikal ice expeditions costing over R70,000. Some English spoken.

St Nicholas Church CHURCH
(Krestovka) Listvyanka's small mid-19th-century timber church is dedicated to St Nicholas, who supposedly saved its merchant sponsor from a Baikal shipwreck.

Retro Park ART GALLERY
(Krestovka) This garden near the St Nicholas Church is full of wacky sculpture pieces fashioned from old Soviet-era cars and motorbikes.

Nerpinarium AQUARIUM
(www.baikalnerpa.ru; ul Gorkogo 101A; admission R400; ⏲11am-5pm Tue-Fri, to 6pm Sat & Sun) Thirty-minute seal shows in a silver building resembling an upturned ship next to the Priboy Hotel.

Sleeping

Many Irkutsk tour agents and even some hostels and hotels have their own guesthouse or homestay in Listvyanka. For turn-up-and-hope homestays the best street to try first is ul Chapaeva.

TOP CHOICE **Baikaler Eco-Hostel** HOSTEL €
(☎8-924-839 6520; www.baikaler.com/eco-hostel; ul Chapaeva 77A; dm R300-700, tw R1500-1700; @📶) Located at the far end of ul Chapaeva, this purpose-built hostel provides top-notch digs for backpacker prices, leaving Listvyanka's other flat-footed accommodation in its green wake. From the energy-saving light bulbs and basalt-foam insulation to the solar-heated water and solar-generated electricity, owner Jack Sheremetoff has crafted a low-impact haven with lots of personal touches. Start the day with a bit of sun worship on the yoga deck and breakfast on the forest-facing chill-out area; end it with a scramble up the mini climbing wall and a scrub-down in the *banya* before snuggling up in a hand-made timber bed (no bunks) in an en-suite dorm. Guest kitchen, 24-hour reception and many other features you won't find anywhere else. Booking well ahead is essential.

THE GREAT BAIKAL TRAIL

Inspired largely by the Tahoe Rim Trail (a hiking path encircling Lake Tahoe in California and Nevada), in summer 2003 a small band of enthusiasts began work on the first section of what was grandly named the Great Baikal Trail (GBT; in Russian, Bolshaya Baikalskaya Tropa, BBT). Every summer since has seen hundreds of volunteers flock to Lake Baikal's pebbly shores to bring the GBT organisation's stated aim – the creation of a 2000km-long network of trails encircling the whole of Lake Baikal – closer to fruition. This lofty ambition may still be a far-off dream, but the GBT is nonetheless the first such trail system in all Russia.

These rudimentary bits of infrastructure, the GBT organisation hopes, will attract more low-impact tourists to the region, thus encouraging ecofriendly businesses to flourish and providing an alternative to industrial and mass tourism development. Volunteers and local activists are also involved in raising awareness of environmental issues among local people, visiting schools and fundraising. Nomination as a finalist in National Geographic's 2008 Geotourism Challenge is arguably the GBT's greatest achievement to date and greatly raised its profile in the world of ecotourism.

Many Baikal explorers simply enjoy trekking the 540km of trails created thus far, but every year young and old from around the world join work crews for a few enjoyable weeks of clearing pathways, cutting steps, creating markers and cobbling together footbridges. Those eager to volunteer should visit the **GBT website** (www.greatbaikaltrail.org), or contact Evgenia Nekrasova, GBT's International Volunteer Coordinator (gbt.volunteers@gmail.com).

Derevenka HOTEL €€
(☎8-914-877 5599; www.baikal-derevenka.ru; ul Gornaya 1; s/d R2000/3000, camping pitch R350) On a ridge behind the shore road, cute little wooden huts (named after Baikal's winds) with stove-heaters, private toilets and hot water (but shared showers) offer Listvyanka's most appealing semi-budget choice. Behind the complex is Listvyanka's only official camp site. Rates include breakfast.

U Ozera HOTEL €€
(У Озера; ☎496 777; Irkutsk Hwy km3; d R2500-4000, cottages R3500-5000; 📶) Just 10m from the shoreline, it's not surprising that all nine rooms (doubles only) at this small hotel have wonderful lake views. Rooms are a little too intimate but have balconies where you can stretch out. The cottages sleeping two lack the views but offer more space. Located between Krestovka and Rogatka.

Baikal Dream GUESTHOUSE €€
(☎496 758; ul Chapaeva 69; s R1100-1300, d R1500-2000) Brick-built Baikal Dream offers big bright comfortable rooms with underfloor heated bathrooms but minimalist decor. There's also a common room with leather sofas and TV and a guest kitchen. Eager-to-please owner Nikolai will pick you up from the bus stop and cook you delicious meals. He also guarantees you won't forget his '*banya* experience'. Breakfast included.

Devyaty Val GUESTHOUSE €€
(☎496 814; www.9val.irk.ru; ul Chapaeva 24; d R1800-2200; @🏊) Friendly, family-run guesthouse where the huge, good-value *lyux* rooms with big beds, TV and private shower and toilet in a long timber extension are a big step up from the *polo-lyux*. There's a small indoor pool (R1000 per hour) and rates include breakfast.

Hotel Mayak HOTEL €€€
(☎496 911; www.mayakhotel.ru; ul Gorkogo 85; s/tw R4300/4900; 📶) There were once (now mothballed) plans to transform Listvyanka and other villages on the shores of Lake Baikal into purpose-built resorts with plasticky upmarket hotels like the 'Lighthouse'. The village's most in-your-face hotel has Western-standard rooms, a good restaurant and an unbeatable location near the hydrofoil quay.

Baikal Chalet GUESTHOUSE €€
(☎3952-461 557; www.baikalcomplex.com; ul Gudina 75; tw R2000) The 13 comfortable twin rooms in this timber guesthouse around 800m back from the lake are a good deal. Sister guesthouse in Bolshie Koty offers similar rates and standards. Breakfast included.

Priboy HOTEL €€
(☎496 725; upper fl, ul Gorkogo 101; dm R500, r R2500) Spitting distance from the lake in the port area, this glass-and-steel block of incongruity has cheap, if unappealing, dorms and some basic rooms with shared toilet, shower and dubious taste in wallpaper. A Chinese restaurant occupies the ground level.

Krestovaya pad HOTEL €€€
(☎496 863; www.baikalvip.ru; ul Gornaya 14a; d R3000-6000) Big, brash and quite pricey, this upmarket complex housing very comfortable international-standard pine-clad rooms dominates the hillside above Krestovka.

Green House HOSTEL €
(☎496 707; ul Shtorkmana 3; dm R700) Located right by the market, this one-time guesthouse now touts itself as a hostel. It has a TV room and guest kitchen but ageing communal bathrooms. Bookable through Hostelworld.

Eating

Near the port, the large fish and souvenir market is the best place to buy smoked *omul* and is surrounded by greasy spoons offering cheap *plov* and shashlyk.

Proshly Vek RUSSIAN €€
(ul Lazlo 1; meals R160-520; ⏲noon-midnight; 📋) Listvyanka's most characterful eatery has a nautical theme, a fish-heavy menu and Baikal views. The upper floor is filled with fascinating old junk which you can admire while tucking into *omul* done any which way you please.

Pyaty Okean CAFÉ €€
(ul Gorkogo 59A; mains R150-320; ⏲11am-10pm) The speciality at this lakeside place is Baikal Abyss – fish and potatoes baked in sour cream. Eat indoors or out by the gurgling Cheremshanka stream.

Café Podlemore CAFÉ €
(ul Gorkogo 31; mains R120-160; ⏲9am-midnight; 📋) The Podlemore has porridge and oven-fresh pastries, but rather flummoxed serving staff. Early opening makes it a popular breakfast halt.

Shury Mury CAFÉ €€
(meals R130-400; ⏲10am-11pm) This handy but overpriced café next to the tourist centre boasts a lakeside summer terrace.

SOMETHING FISHY

No trip to Baikal is complete without tasting **omul**, a distant relative of salmon that's delicious when freshly hot-smoked. There are over 50 other varieties of Baikal fish, including perch, black grayling, ugly frilly-nosed bullheads and tasty *sig* (lake herring). While the lake isn't Russia's greatest place for anglers, from February to April it offers the unusual spectacle of **ice fishing**. There are two forms: individuals with immense patience dangle hooked lines through Inuit-style ice holes; elsewhere, especially in shallow waters, whole teams of villagers string long, thin nets beneath the ice and pull out *omul* by the hundred.

You can get beneath the ice yourself with two professional Irkutsk-based scuba-diving outfits: **Three Dimensions** (3952-587 575; www.dive-baikal.ru; ul Fridrikha Engelsa 33, Irkutsk) and **SVAL** (3952-295 051; www.svaldiving.ru; ul Dekabrskikh Sobyty 55, Irkutsk). But the lake's greatest divers are the unique **nerpa seals**. Indigenous to Lake Baikal, they are the only seal in the world to spend its entire existence in a freshwater environment and thrive in many locations on the lake's shore, but usually (and wisely) away from human populations.

Information

ATMs can be found in the Mayak and Baikal hotels.

Post office (ul Gorkogo 49; per hr R50; 8am-1pm & 2-8pm Mon-Fri, 9am-6pm Sat) Internet access.

Tourist office (656 099; hydrofoil quay; 10am-1pm & 2-6pm) Surprisingly useful office handing out free maps as well as providing bus, ferry and hydrofoil timetables and offering imaginative Baikal boat trips. Bike rental available (per hour/day R150/800); some staff speak English.

Getting There & Away

Hourly *marshrutka* 524 (R100, 1¼ hours) leaves for Irkutsk from outside the tourist office (where tickets are bought). The last service departs at 9pm.

From mid-May to late September, hydrofoils stop at Listvyanka between Irkutsk (R320, one hour) and Bolshie Koty (R250, 30 minutes) three times a day.

Year-round a tiny, battered car ferry lumbers across the never-frozen Angara River mouth to Port Baikal from Rogatka.

Port Baikal Порт Байкал

3952 / POP 425 / MOSCOW +5HR

You'd be excused for dismissing Port Baikal as a rusty semi-industrial eyesore when seen from Listvyanka across the unbridged mouth of the Angara River. But the view is misleading. A kilometre southwest of Stanitsa (the port area), Baranchiki is a ramshackle 'real' village with lots of unkempt but authentic Siberian cottages and a couple of handy accommodation options. Awkward ferry connections mean that Port Baikal remains largely uncommercialised, lacking Listvyanka's attractions but also its crowds. It's thus popular with more meditative visitors, but the main draw is that it's both the beginning and terminus of the Circumbaikal Railway.

From 1900 to 1904 the Trans-Siberian Railway tracks from Irkutsk came to an abrupt halt at Port Baikal. They continued on Lake Baikal's far eastern shore at Mysovaya (Babushkin), and the watery gap was plugged by ice-breaking steamships, including the *Angara*, now restored and on view in Irkutsk. Later, the tracks were pushed south and around the lake. This Circumbaikal line required so many impressive tunnels and bridges that it earned the nickname 'The Tsar's Jewelled Buckle'. With the damming of the Angara River in the 1950s, the original Irkutsk–Port Baikal section was submerged and replaced with an Irkutsk–Kultuk shortcut (today's Trans-Siberian). That left poor little Port Baikal to wither away at the dead end of a rarely used but incredibly scenic branch line.

Sleeping & Eating

If the last ferry back to Listvyanka has just left, the B&B is full and the Yakhont seems too expensive, it's always possible to fall back on several basic homestays in Baranchiki. Ask around or look out for 'сдаются комнаты' signs. Apart from the Yakhont restaurant, a couple of poorly stocked grocery kiosks are the only sources of sustenance. Both accommodation options listed here offer meals, and homestays often have a kitchen guests can use.

WORTH A TRIP

CIRCUMBAIKAL RAILWAY
КРУГОБАЙКАЛЬСКАЯ ЖЕЛЕЗНАЯ ДОРОГА

Excruciatingly slow or a great social event? Opinions are mixed, but taking one of the four-per-week Slyudyanka–Port Baikal trains along this scenic, lake-hugging branch line remains a very popular tourist activity. The most picturesque sections of the route are the valley, pebble beach and headland at Polovinnaya (around halfway), and the bridge area at km149. Views are best if you can persuade the driver to let you ride on the front of the locomotive – possible on certain tour packages. Note that most trains *from* Port Baikal travel by night and so are useless for sightseeing.

The old stone tunnels, cliff cuttings and bridges are an attraction even for non-train-buffs who might drive alongside sections of the route on winter ice roads from **Kultuk**. Hiking the entire route or just sections of the peaceful track is also popular and walking a couple of kilometres from Port Baikal leads to some pleasant, if litter-marred, beaches. Or get off an Irkutsk–Slyudyanka *elektrichka* at Temnaya Pad three hours into the journey and hike down the stream valley for about an hour. You should emerge at km149 on the **Circumbaikal track**, from where you can continue by train to Port Baikal if you time things well.

At the time of research, short wooden-seated Matanya trains departed from a side platform at Slyudyanka I station at 1.30pm, four times per week – check timetables carefully. In summer an additional tourist train direct from Irkutsk departs at 7.42am on Saturday. Wonderfully detailed website **Circumbaikal Railway** (http://kbzd.irk.ru/Eng/) has regularly updated timetables plus photographs of virtually every inch of the route.

Irkutsk agencies such as **Krugobaikalsky Ekspress** (☎3952-202 973; www.krugobaikalka.ru) run organised Circumbaikal tours (R1900 including lunch), though some travellers grumble about the rather superfluous 'guides' who tag along for the entire nine-hour trip.

Yakhont HOTEL €€
(☎250 496; www.baikalrest.ru; ul Naberezhnaya 3; s/tw R3000/3100) Port Baikal's top digs could be the Siberian boutique hotel you've been dreaming of. It's a traditionally designed log house decorated with eclectic good taste by the well-travelled English-speaking owners. Guests congregate in the stylish communal kitchen-dining room, above which rooms have perfect Western bathrooms. The large restaurant below the hotel is the village's sole eatery. Advance bookings are essential.

Gostevoy Dom Paradis GUESTHOUSE €
(☎607 450; www.baikal.tk; ul Baikalskaya 12; full board R1450) Cheaper than the Yakhont, this timber guesthouse is set 400m back from the lakeside. Various pine-clad but rather spartan rooms share two Western-style toilets and a shower.

Getting There & Away

The ferry (R70, 20 minutes) to Rogatka near Listvyanka's Baikal Museum runs year-round, four times daily at 8.15am, 11.15am, 4.15pm and 6.15pm (departures at 6.50am, 10.30am, 3.50pm and 5.50pm from Rogatka), but check the schedule beforehand. From mid-June to August there are direct hydrofoils to/from Irkutsk (one hour 10 minutes). All services are operated by **VSRP** (www.vsrp.ru).

Very infrequent trains come via the slow Circumbaikal route from Slyudyanka.

Bolshie Koty Большие Коты

POP 50 / ⌚MOSCOW +5HR

Tiny and roadless, this serene Baikal village is what the great Siberian escape is all about. But things weren't always this quiet; in the 19th century Koty experienced a mini gold rush and boasted soap and candle factories, a glassworks, churches and a school. Today all that's long since over, leaving Irkutsk's nouveau riche to assemble their lakeside dachas in peace.

A section of the Great Baikal Trail runs between Koty and Listvyanka, a fabulous full- or half-day hike (around 20km). Take plenty of food (drink from the lake) as there's none en route.

Three minutes' walk from the hydrofoil quay, the **Lesnaya 7 Hostel** (☎8-904-118 7275; www.lesnaya7.com; ul Lesnaya 7; dm R600-700; ⌚March & May–mid-Oct; @) fills a traditional timber house where showers run hot and the 12 beds are all in double rooms. Booking ahead is essential.

The only way to reach Bolshie Koty (unless you hike from Listvyanka) is aboard one of the three hydrofoils a day from Irkutsk (via Listvyanka). Check **VSRP** (www.vsrp.ru) for times and ticket prices. Winter ice roads briefly unite the village with the outside world.

Ust-Orda Усть-Орда

☎39541 / POP 14,000 / ⌚MOSCOW +5HR

Ust-Orda's smiling Asian faces and low-rise timber skyline come as an enjoyable change from Irkutsk's all-Slav features and 19th-century pomp. This small town 62km northeast of Irkutsk has just a handful of undemanding sights, providing at least a taste of Buryat culture for those not planning a trip to Baikal's Buryat-dominated eastern shore, and a brief introduction for those who are.

The town's trump card is its **Regional Museum** (☎31 402; ul Lenina 6; admission R150; ⌚9am-1pm & 2-5pm Mon-Fri), with three halls of petroglyphs, shamanic knick-knacks and frayed taxidermy. Call ahead to arrange Buryat folk music (R3500 with food) and shamanic rituals (R1000) performed in front of a timber courtyard yurt. Across ul Lenina a **tank** has its gun trained on the museum roof.

The upswept roof of Ust-Orda's pocket-sized **datsan** (Buddhist temple; ul Kalandarashvili), 2km along the Irkutsk road, is hardly noticeable from the main road, its dimensions perhaps reflecting the continuing dominance of shamanism over Buddhism among Buryats on Baikal's western shore. Inside, only a couple of *thangka* (paintings), a few butter lamps and offerings of rice, coins and incense distract the eye.

Behind the cinema on ul Lenina stands the pristine **Trinity Church** (Troitsky khram; ⌚11am-4pm). Beyond the Hotel Baikal, a **Lenin statue** (ul Lenina) has Vladimir Ilych fingering his lapels from a black granite pedestal.

Meals come with a generous dollop of Soviet nostalgia at the classic **Stolovaya Anna** (ul Kalandarashvili; meals R50; ⌚8am-8pm), next to the bus station – almost worth the bus fare on its own. The lace-trimmed dinner ladies, prison canteen decor and, to some extent, the prices are all lodged firmly in the 1980s. **Poznaya Odon** (cnr ul Lenina & ul Kalinina; pozi R30; ⌚11am-8pm) is a simple but well-liked lunch spot among locals, but a better class of Buryat fare is served at the semi-slick **Baikal hotel restaurant** (ul Lenina 24; ⌚noon-2am) where you can tuck into *bukhuler* (mutton or lamb broth), *salamat* (creamy sour porridge) and steaming *pozi* at prettily laid tables. You can also dine nomad-style in the hotel yurt if you call **reception** (☎32 236) beforehand.

Minibuses (R100, one hour) run every 30 minutes to and from Irkutsk bus station. Ust-Orda's tiny terminus is near the museum at the end of ul Lenina. Coming from Irkutsk, ask the driver to drop you off at the *datsan* (Buddhist temple) on the edge of town to save you a 40-minute walk there and back.

Olkhon Island Остров Ольхон

POP 1500 / ⌚MOSCOW +5HR

Halfway up Lake Baikal's western shore and reached by a short ferry journey from Sakhyurta (aka MRS), the serenely beautiful Olkhon Island is a wonderful place from which to view the lake and relax during a tour of Siberia. Considered one of five global poles of shamanic energy by the Buryat people, the 72km-long island's 'capital' is the unlovely village of **Khuzhir** (Хужир), which has seen something of an unlikely tourist boom over the last decade, mainly thanks to the efforts of Nikita's Homestead.

Escaping Khuzhir's dusty, dung-splattered streets is the key to enjoying Olkhon. Every morning tours leave from Khuzhir's guesthouses to the north and south of the island, the most popular a seven-hour bounce in a UAZ minivan to dramatic **Cape Khoboy** at Olkhon's very northern tip, where Baikal seals sometimes bask. Driver-guides cook fish soup for lunch over an open fire, but few speak any English. See the Nikita's Homestead website (www.olkhon.info) for details of this and other excursions. Otherwise, rent

CASH FOR TRASH

At the time of research a small environmental tax (R25) was being levied on all visitors arriving on Olkhon to fund desperately needed refuse collection across the island. Rest assured, this is not a scam.

a bike and strike out on your own. Maps are available from Nikita's but take all food and water with you as there's none outside Khuzhir.

Sights & Activities

The following sights provide minor distraction in Khuzhir.

Museum MUSEUM

(ul Pervomayskaya 24; admission R100; ⏲2-8pm Sun-Fri) Khuzhir's small museum displays a random mix of stuffed animals, Soviet-era junk, local art and the personal possessions of its founder, Nikolai Revyakin, a teacher for five decades at the school next door.

Shaman Rocks LANDMARK

A short walk north of Nikita's, the unmistakable Shaman Rocks are neither huge nor spectacular, but they have become the archetypal Baikal vista found on postcards and travel-guide covers. A long strip of sandy beach lines the Maloe More (Little Sea) east of the rocks.

Sleeping & Eating

Khuzhir has an ever-growing range of places to stay, though the vast majority of independent travellers bunk down at Nikita's Homestead. If all 50 rooms at Nikita's are full, staff can arrange homestays costing around R850 with meals taken at the Homestead canteen (R400 without meals). Booking ahead anywhere in Khuzhir is only necessary during July and August. There's no ATM on the island, so you'll need to bring enough cash to cover your stay.

TOP CHOICE **Nikita's Homestead** GUESTHOUSE €

(www.olkhon.info; ul Kirpichnaya 8; full board per person R900-1150; ⏲reception 8am-11pm) Occupying a sizeable chunk of Khuzhir, this intricately carved timber complex has grown (and continues to grow) into one of Siberia's top traveller hang-outs. The basic rooms in myriad shapes and sizes are attractively decorated with petroglyphs and other ethnic finery and heated by wood-burning stoves – but only a select few have showers (put your name down for the *banya*). The vastly improved organic meals are served three times a day in the large canteen near reception and two other (paid) eateries (French and Uzbek) stand behind. There's a small cycle-hire centre and a packed schedule of excursions and activities, plus staff can register your visa (R350).

U Olgi GUESTHOUSE €

(☎8-908-661 9015; ul Lesnaya 3-1; full board per person R750, without meals R350) This well-liked option has nine rooms, three in a typical village house and six in a purpose-built, pine-fragrant building opposite. New showers and flushing toilets plus scrumptious Siberian fare cooked by Olga herself make this a winner every time. Book through Baikaler in Irkutsk.

Camping Hotel Olkhon HOTEL €€

(Кемпинг-Отель Ольхон; ☎708 885; www.alphatour.ru; ul Baikalskaya 64; summer huts s R900-2100, d R1300-2100, hotel s R2200-3000, d R2700-3500, economy rooms s R300-600, d R600-800, tent pitches R100) This hotel with an enclosure of timber Monopoly houses out back has four standards of accommodation – comfortable hotel rooms, basic cottages, spartan crash-pad cubicles and tent pitches. Full board is an extra R650 and receptionists speak English. It's 200m beyond the shop (to the left) at the top end of the main street (ul Baikalskaya).

Solnechnaya GUESTHOUSE €

(Солнечная; ☎3952-683 216; www.olkhon.com; ul Solnechnaya 14; full board per person R1100-1450; @) No happening scene like at Nikita's, but it's still a pleasant place to stay offering a good range of activities. Accommodation is in two-storey cabins and tiny single-room shacks with verandahs. Enter from ul Solnechnaya or from near the relay station at the top of the hill.

Getting There & Away

The simplest way to reach Olkhon is aboard the morning *marshrutka* that leaves Irkutsk's hostels around 8.30am. Many other services run in July and August but can be impossible to track down in Irkutsk.

With a little warning, agencies or hostels can usually find you a ride in a private car to/from Irkutsk (5½ hours) for R1250 per seat, R5000 for the whole car. Prices include the short ferry ride to/from MRS – from mid-January to March an ice road replaces the ferry. When ice is partly formed or partly melted, the island is completely cut off for motor vehicles, though an ad hoc minihovercraft service is sometimes operated by locals.

In summer a hydrofoil service operates from Irkutsk to Olkhon, dropping passengers near the ferry terminal, from where it's possible to hitch a paid lift into Khuzhir. See **VSRP** (www.vsrp.ru) for times and prices.

Maloe More Малое Море

The relatively warm, shallow waters of the Maloe More (Little Sea) offer a primary do-nothing holiday attraction for Siberians. Main activities here are swimming, hiking to waterfalls and drinking. Dozens of camps, huts and resorts are scattered amid attractive multiple bays backed by alternating woodland and rolling grassland scenery. Since each widely spaced 'resort' is frequently fully booked and hard to access without private transport, you'd be wise to visit Irkutsk agencies first and leaf through their considerable catalogues. Booking something not too far from MRS makes it easier to continue later to Olkhon Island.

From mid-June to late August *marshrutky* run to Kurma (R750, 5½ hours) at 9am via Sarma (R500) from in front of the Hotel Angara in Irkutsk. They return at 2pm the same afternoon. Public buses from Irkutsk serve MRS.

South Baikal & the Tunka Valley

The windows of trans-Siberian trains passing between Irkutsk and Ulan-Ude frame attractive lake vistas along much of Baikal's south coast. Few Westerners are actually tempted off the train along this stretch but if they are, it's usually at Slyudyanka, the best place to start Circumbaikal train rides and a launch pad into the remotely scenic Tunka Valley.

SLYUDYANKA СЛЮДЯНКА

☎39544 / POP 18,500 / ⌚MOSCOW +5HR

Slyudyanka's glittering marble **train station** is a mere five-minute walk from Lake Baikal's scrappy shore. En route you pass a multicoloured timber **church** and, across the tracks, former locomotive workshops host an interesting **museum** (ul Zheleznodorozhnaya 22; admission R50; ⌚11am-5pm Wed-Sun) with archaeological finds, old railway switching boxes and an identification guide to 47 locomotive types. Unfortunately, there is no English. Geology buffs should consider heading to the privately run **Baikal Mineral Museum** (ul Slyudyanaya 36; admission R100; ⌚8am-9pm), which claims to exhibit every mineral known to man. Take any *marshrutka* heading from the bus station up ul Slyudyanskikh Krasnogvardeytsev and ask to be dropped off at the museum.

A popular picnic excursion is to **Cape Shaman**, an easy 4km stroll north towards Kultuk along Baikal's gravelly shore.

With moulting lino, very basic rooms and shared showers, the friendly **Hotel Chayka** (☎54 073; ul Frunze 8a; d R600) charges R300 for 12-hour stays. To get there from the train station, cross the long footbridge and walk two blocks further to a little **bus station** (ul Lenina); from here the hotel is 4km west by very frequent *marshrutka*. A taxi should cost no more than R70. The **Mineral Museum homestay** (☎53 440; ul Slyudyanaya 36; dm R700) is little more than a two-bed garden cottage which the museum curator rents out in the summer months.

At the time of research Slyudyanka had no café or restaurant. The only source of public nourishment was the **Bonus Supermarket** (ul Lenina 116; ⌚9am-10pm) where you can stock up on enough noodles, cheese, bread and instant porridge to keep you going all the way to the Urals.

Elektrichki (R70, four daily) from Irkutsk take four hours to arrive at Slyudyanka 1 station; express trains (*platskart* R540, up to eight daily) take just two to 2½ hours. Slyudyanka is also the usual starting point for the Circumbaikal Railway trip. *Marshrutky* run to Arshan (R170, two hours, at least eight daily) from the bus station.

ARSHAN АРШАН

☎30156 / POP 3600 / ⌚MOSCOW +5HR

Backed by the dramatic, cloud-wreathed peaks of the Eastern Sayan Mountains, the once drowsy Buryat spa village of Arshan has been rudely awoken from its slumber in recent years. The fast-flowing Kyngarga River still murmurs with ice-cold water from elevated valleys above the village, the prayer wheels still twirl at the tranquil little Buddhist temples and cows still blunder through the streets, but Russian-style tourism has intruded into the idyllic scene, bringing 24-hour *banya,* cut-price vodka, pounding stereos and grisly service in its wake. But despite this Arshan is still the best base in the Tunka Valley from which to strike out into the mountains, with some superb hikes accessible on foot from the village.

Arshan in Buryat means 'natural spring' and it's the pleasantly sweet, health-giving mineral water that most Russians come for. The huge **Sayany Spa** stands at the entrance to the village on the main street (ul Traktovaya), which then fires itself 2km straight towards the mountains.

Opposite the spa grounds, the **Dechen Ravzhalin Datsan** has two sparkling new prayer wheels, a miniature stupa and a dazzlingly colourful interior. From here ul Traktovaya then climbs in a parade of shops, derelict Soviet architecture and plasticky cafés and guesthouses towards the bus station, after which it swerves west to the sprawling **Kurort Arshan** resort where you can sample the water for free (pass through the turnstile near the souvenir kiosks). Head up the stream from here to access the mountain footpaths or cross the river and walk 20 minutes through the forest to the dinky little **Bodkhi Dkharma Datsan**, set in an idyllic mountain-backed glade.

Sleeping

Even late at night locals line the bottom end of ul Traktovaya like hitchhikers, brandishing their 'Жильё' (rooms) signs in hope. These usually turn out to be very basic homestays from R300 per bed – check standards before committing. Even if you turn up unannounced you'll have few problems getting a room, even at busy times (July and August). This is probably the way to go in Arshan. Otherwise, try to book ahead at the places listed below.

Yasnaya Polyana GUESTHOUSE €
(Ясная Поляна; ☎8-904-114 7808; ul Traktovaya 109; s/d R350/700) A friendly local English teacher runs this compound of 10 pine cottages, each containing two beds, a table, a stove ring and sometimes a kettle. Otherwise, things are pretty basic with a sun-heated shower (best in the evenings) and outdoor washing facilities. To find it, take the second left on entering the village (at ul Traktovaya 99) and keep going until you see a large unmarked green gate on your left.

Priyut Alpinista GUESTHOUSE
(www.iwf.ru; ul Bratev Domshevikh 8) Long a favourite with backpackers, trekkers and climbers, the 'Mountaineer's Refuge' sadly burnt down in 2008. However, there are plans to rebuild it on the same site, three minutes' walk along ul Pavlova from the bus station. In the meantime, contact the owners of the Arshansky Bor for details of the trips into the mountains that used to run from the Priyut Alpinista.

Arshansky Bor GUESTHOUSE €
(☎8-950-050 6481; ul Bratev Domshevikh 44; dm R350-450) This unmarked pink building is the best budget place to overnight until the Priyut Alpinista is rebuilt. Rooms are dim and spartan, and facilities display the pressures of mass occupation, but there's a large kitchen, a common room and a barbecue area.

Pensionat Vershina GUESTHOUSE €
(☎8-950-388 7590; ul Mikrorayon 22/1; s/d R350/700) Located near the Sayany Spa, this purpose-built two-storey guesthouse has cosy timber rooms with shared showers, free *banya* and a small café.

Monetny Dvor GUESTHOUSE €€
(☎8-904-115 6390; www.arshan-md.ru; ul Traktovaya 89; d from R1000) Brand-new timber-built guesthouse with rooms in a main building and three two-storey cottages. Cycle hire available.

Eating

Eateries are thin on the ground as most Russians prebook full board at the spas. Some of the new cafés at the top of ul Traktovaya are truly dire.

Novy Vek RUSSIAN €€
(Новый Век; ul Traktovaya 4; ⏰10am-2am) For a proper sit-down meal try this restaurant near the Arshan Spa that has recently sprouted a nightclub, entertainment centre and *stolovaya* (canteen).

Zakusochnaya Khamar Daban CANTEEN €
(Закусочная Хамар Дабан; ul Traktovaya; ⏰10am-1am; ❄) Located opposite the Sayan Sanatorium, this pleasant canteen serves up a large menu of Buryat and Russian comfort food and cheap beers.

Getting There & Away

The miniature **bus station** (⏰7.30am-6pm) near the top of ul Traktovaya has the village's only ATM, plus left-luggage lockers. Arshan has the following bus and *marshrutka* connections:

Irkutsk R270 to R350, 11 daily
Slyudyanka R170, two hours, eight daily
Ulan-Ude R610, 11 hours, five daily

BEYOND ARSHAN

From the turn-off for Arshan it's just 9km along the Tunka Valley road to the village of **Zhemchug** (Жемчуг) where, for around R100, you can wallow in a series of hot pools that leave a chalky-green residue on skin and clothes.

Around 25km further along the road, the valley's unkempt, low-rise little 'capital' **Kyren** (Кырен) is home to the **Tunka National Park HQ** (www.tunkapark.ru; ul Lenina

69). Its small onion-topped **church** (ul Kooperativenaya) adds foreground to the photogenic alpine backdrop.

The valley road ends at **Mondy** (Монды) near **Munku-Sardyk** (3491m), the highest mountain in Eastern Siberia and scene of an annual mass ascent (May) marking the beginning of the climbing season. There are provisional plans to open up the nearby Mongolian border to foreigners in 2012, making it feasible to join Russian vodka-and-fishing tourists who already visit Mongolia's appealing Khövsgöl Lake. En route the road passes near **Nilova Pustyn** (Нилова Пустынь), a minor spa where locals voluntarily subject themselves to radioactive radon baths.

Some 190km west beyond Mondy the dumbfoundingly far-flung **Oka Region** has been dubbed 'Tibet in miniature'. The 'capital' **Orlik** (Орлик) is the obvious place to arrange treks and horse-riding trips into some seriously isolated backcountry.

Eastern Baikal

☎30144

Sparsely scattered beach villages of old-fashioned log cottages dot the pretty east Baikal coast. Further north is the dramatic Barguzin Valley, from which Chinggis Khaan's mother, Oilun-Ehe, is said to have originated. Some of the area has been slated for mass-tourism development but little has appeared in the intervening years, save for a mirror-smooth new road which has cut journey times considerably. Ulan-Ude agencies can book basic accommodation along the eastern coast where summer *turbazy* (holiday camps) are popular among Russians seeking sand.

Access to the coast is across a forested pass from Ulan-Ude via tiny **Baturino** village with its elegantly renovated Sretenskaya Church.

After around 2½ hours' drive, the newly paved road first meets Lake Baikal at pretty little **Gremyachinsk** (Гремячинск), a popular trip out of Ulan-Ude for hurried Trans-Siberian travellers with a day to spare. Buses stop at a roadside café from which Gremyachinsk's sandy but litter-strewn beach is a 15-minute walk up ul Komsomolskaya. *Marshrutky* back to Ulan-Ude are often full so consider prebooking your return.

Approximately 5km from Gremyachinsk, at least 10 large tourist camps are strung around **Lake Kotokel**, whose thermal springs keep it warm year-round. At the northern end of the lake rises **Monastyrsky Island**, once home to an isolated hermitage and a church.

The main road offers surprisingly few Baikal views until the fishing port of **Turka**, from where there are pleasant walks to several secluded bays in either direction. Bigger **Goryachinsk** (Горячинск), around 3km from the lake, is centred on a typically institutional hot-springs **kurort** (spa) with cheap cottage homestays in the surrounding village.

Further north through the uninhabited taiga lies the quaint little fishing hamlet of **Maksimikha** (Максимиха) where picturesque Baikal beaches stretch northwest. From here the blacktop bends before zipping through the forest to Ust-Barguzin.

UST-BARGUZIN УСТЬ-БАРГУЗИН

☎30131 / POP 7100 / ⌚MOSCOW +5HR

Low-rise Ust-Barguzin has sandy streets of traditional log homes with blue-and-white carved window frames. These are most attractive towards the northern end of the main street, ul Lenina, where it reaches the Barguzin River **ferry** (runs 8am to 11pm). From here, views are magical towards the high-ridged peaks of the Svyatoy Nos Peninsula. Other than watching the rusting car ferry being towed by a fume-belching motorboat across the fast-flowing Barguzin River, the only other attraction here is the **Banya Museum** (☎91 574; per Bolnichny 9; ⌚by appointment only), displaying four traditional

SELENGA DELTA

Some 300 waterways feed Lake Baikal, but none compare in size and volume to the Selenga River. One of only 80 rivers around the world to form a delta, the Selenga dumps its load of sand (and pollution from Mongolia) on Baikal's eastern shore in a huge fan of islands, reed beds and shallow channels measuring 35km across. Over 200 bird species draw spotters from all over the world; motorboat trips can be arranged through Ulan-Ude agencies. Between birdwatching sessions many bed down in the village of Posolskoe where the Western-standard **Sofiya Hotel** (s/d R1400/1800) shares a lakeside location right beside a beautifully renovated monastery.

timber *bani* lovingly fashioned by national park ranger and guide, Alexander Beketov, who also runs a very comfortable **homestay** (full board per person R1500) at the same address. The Beketovs provide a superb base and run tours to the Barguzin Valley and the national park. Their welcome and home-cooked meals make Ust-Barguzin a preferable base to Barguzin.

Daily *marshrutky* to Ulan-Ude (R500, seven hours) depart around 8am and will pick you up from your accommodation if you book ahead. In July and August a daily hydrofoil links Ust-Barguzin with Irkutsk and Khuzhir on Olkhon Island; check out **VSRP** (www.vsrp.ru) for details. In February and March the ice drive across Lake Baikal to Severobaikalsk takes around five hours.

SVYATOY NOS (HOLY NOSE) PENINSULA ПОЛУОСТРОВ СВЯТОЙ НОС

Rising almost vertically out of shimmering waters, dramatic Svyatoy Nos is one of Lake Baikal's most impressive features. It's within the mostly impenetrable **Zabaikalsky National Park** and joined to Ust-Barguzin by a muddy 20km sandbar that's possible but painful to drive along (there's also a toll). Guides can be hired at the **national park offices** (per Bolnichny 9) in Ust-Barguzin for all-day trek-climbs to the top of the peninsula, more than 1800m above Lake Baikal. The views from the summit are truly awe-inspiring.

Nerpa seals are particularly abundant off the peninsula's west coast around the **Ushkanny Islands**, accessible by charter boat from Ust-Barguzin. Contact Alexander Beketov at the national park headquarters. Prices begin at around R5000.

BARGUZIN & THE BARGUZIN VALLEY БАРГУЗИН И БАРГУЗИНСКАЯ ДОЛИНА

☎30131 / POP 6500 / ⏰MOSCOW +5HR

The road north from Ust-Barguzin emerges from thick forests at Barguzin, a low-rise town of wooden cottages that dates back to 1648. Walking from the bus station you can see its handful of dilapidated historic buildings in about 20 minutes by heading along ul Krasnoarmeyskaya past the cursorily renovated old **church** to pl Lenina. Opposite the quaint little post office, the wooden-colonnaded **former Uezdnogo Bank** (ul Krasnoarmeyskaya 54) was once the grand home of Decembrist Mikhail Kyukhelbeker. Other exiles to make a home in Barguzin were Jews from Poland and European Russia who arrived here in the 1830s and 1860s. The last signs of the Jewish community can be seen in the crumbling old **cemetery** (a block northeast of the church) where crooked Hebrew-inscribed graves stand to the left and Orthodox headstones, including that of Kyukhelbeker himself, to the right.

Hidden in the village school and difficult to access, the small **museum** (☎8-924-391 3126; www.barguzinmuseum.ru; ul Kalinina 51a) has some interesting Decembrist-related exhibits as well as the usual dusty rocks and mammoth bones.

Barguzin's real interest is as a launch pad for visiting the stunningly beautiful Barguzin Valley as it opens out into wide lake-dotted grassland, gloriously edged by a vast Toblerone of mountain peaks. These are most accessibly viewed across the meandering river plain from **Uro** village. Similarly inspiring panoramas continue for miles towards the idyllic village of **Suvo**, overshadowed by rock towers of the **Suvo Saxony** (Suvinskaya Saksoniya), so-called for its similarity to rock formations on the Czech–Saxony border. A few kilometres beyond Suvo the roadside **Bukhe Shulun** (Byk), a huge boulder resembling a bull's hoof, is considered to have miraculous powers. Heading north you'll pass through widely scattered, old-fashioned villages where horse carts and sleighs outnumber cars. Way up on the valley's mountainous west side, **Kurumkan** (411km northeast of Ulan-Ude) has a small but photogenic peak-backed *datsan*. The valley tapers to a point 50km north of Kurumkan at **Alla** where a tiny *kurort* (spa) can accommodate guests in the summer months.

Buy tickets ahead for Ulan-Ude *marshrutky* (R500, eight hours), departing early morning. Other public transport to Ust-Barguzin, Uro and Kurumkan is rare, though there's usually at least one service early morning and in the afternoon. Hitch-hike or arrange a tour through the Beketovs in Ust-Barguzin.

SOUTHERN BURYATIYA & ZABAIKALSKY TERRITORY

Scenically magnificent, southern Buryatiya (Южная Бурятия) crouches on the Mongolian border like a cartographic crab squeezing Lake Baikal with its right pincer. Much of the Baikal region covered earlier also falls within the republic, including Severobaikalsk and the Tunka Valley. For the predeparture lowdown, check out Buryatiya's official English-language **tourism website** (www.baikaltravel.ru) and the **government website** (http://egov-buryatia.ru/eng/), which has English-language tourist information.

The vast, sparsely populated Zabaikalsky Territory (Забайкалский Край) stretches as far east as the wild Chara Mountains on the BAM railway, but in its more accessible southern reaches it's most interesting for the capital (Chita), the Buryat Buddhist culture of Aginskoe and Tsugol, and as an access route to China.

Buryat Culture

Indigenous ethnic Buryats are a Mongol people who comprise around 30% of Buryatiya's population, as well as 65% of the former Agin-Buryat Autonomous District southeast of Chita. Culturally there are two main Buryat groups. During the 19th century, forest-dwelling western Buryats retained their shamanic animist beliefs, while eastern Buryats from the southern steppes mostly converted to Tibetan-style Buddhism, maintaining a thick layer of local superstition. Although virtually every Buryat *datsan* was systematically wrecked during the communists' antireligious mania in the 1930s, today Buryat Buddhism is rebounding. Many (mostly small) *datsany* have been rebuilt and seminaries for training Buddhist monks now operate at Ivolga and Aginskoe.

The Buryat language is Turkic, though very different from Tuvan and Altai. Dialects vary considerably between regions but almost everyone speaks decent, if heavily accented, Russian. Mongolians claim some Buryat dialects resemble their medieval tongue.

Ulan-Ude Улан-Удэ

☎3012 / POP 404,000 / ⏰MOSCOW +5HR

With its smiley Asian features, cosy city centre and fascinating Mongol-Buddhist culture, the Buryat capital is one of Eastern Siberia's most likeable cities. Quietly busy, welcoming and, after Siberia's Russian cities, refreshingly exotic, it's a pleasant place to base yourself for day trips to Buddhist temples and flits to eastern Lake Baikal's gently shelving beaches, easily reachable by bus. For some travellers UU is also a taster for what's to come in Mongolia, to which there are now much improved transport links.

Founded as a Cossack *ostrog* (fort) called Udinsk (later Verkhneudinsk) in 1666, the city prospered as a major stop on the tea-caravan route from China via Troitskosavsk (now Kyakhta). Renamed Ulan-Ude in 1934, it was a closed city until the 1980s due to its secret military plants.

UU's small city centre is easily explored on foot. Divided into two districts, the communist-era upper city is centred around pl Sovetov and the Lenin Head; descend ul Lenina to the partially pedestrianised lower city, the former merchant quarter, half of which still serves as the commercial hub extending from the 19th-century trading rows (pl Revolutsii). Dusty streets of crooked timber dwellings make up the other half.

Sights

Lenin Head MONUMENT

(Голова Ленина; pl Sovetov) Ulan-Ude's main square is awesomely dominated by the world's largest Lenin head, which some maintain looks comically cross-eyed. The 7.7m-high bronze bonce (head) was installed in 1970 to celebrate Lenin's 100th birthday. Oddly, UU's bird population never seems to streak Lenin's bald scalp with their offerings – out of respect for the great man's achievements, claim diehard communists (but perhaps due to the barely visible anti-bird spikes, groan the rest).

Khangalov Museum of Buryat History MUSEUM

(Исторический Музей; Profsoyuznaya ul 29; admission per floor R80, for all floors R180; ⏰11am-7pm Tue-Sun) The historical museum charges per single-room floor and the best of these is Buddiyskoe Iskustvo (3rd floor), displaying *thangkas,* Buddhas and icons salvaged from Buryatiya's monasteries before their Soviet destruction. Note-sheets in English fail to explain the fascinating, gaudy papier mâché models of deities and bodhisattvas rescued from Buryatiya's many prewar *datsany* (temples). Note the home shrine table and the sometimes gory Tibetan medical charts. The less interesting 2nd floor traces Buryat history in maps, documents and artefacts. Spy it for free from the balcony above.

Ethnographic Museum MUSEUM

(Verkhnyaya Berezovka; admission R150; ⏰9.30am-6pm Tue-Fri, 10am-7pm Sat & Sun) In a forest clearing 6km from central Ulan-Ude, this

Ulan-Ude

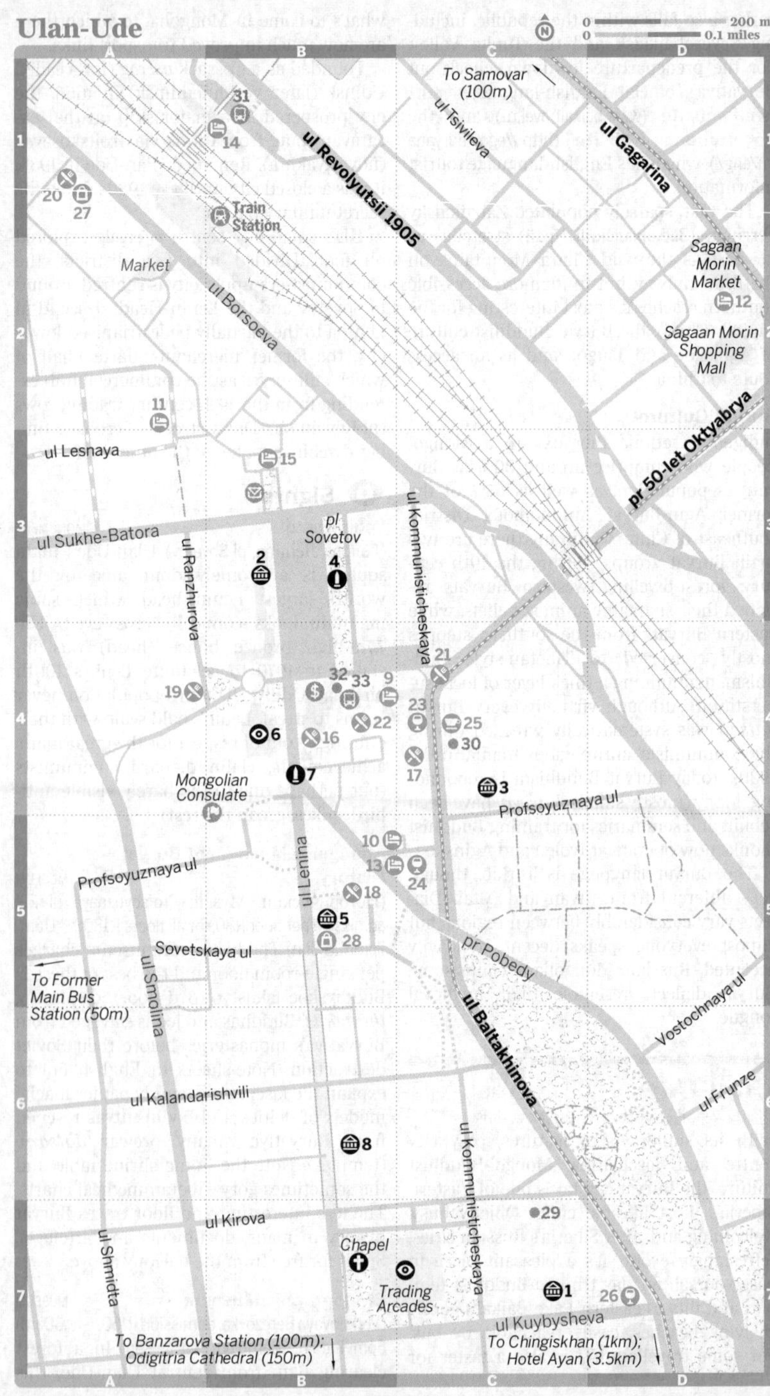
0 200 m
0 0.1 miles
To Samovar (100m)
ul Tsivileva
ul Gagarina
ul Revolyutsii 1905
31
14
20
27
Train Station
Market
ul Borsoeva
Sagaan Morin Market
12
Sagaan Morin Shopping Mall
pr 50-let Oktyabrya
11
ul Lesnaya
15
ul Kommunisticheskaya
ul Sukhe-Batora
pl Sovetov
2
4
ul Ranzhurova
21
19
32
33
9
23
22
25
6
16
30
17
Mongolian Consulate
7
3
Profsoyuznaya ul
10
13
24
Profsoyuznaya ul
ul Lenina
18
5
28
Sovetskaya ul
pr Pobedy
To Former Main Bus Station (50m)
ul Smolina
ul Baltakhinova
Vostochnaya ul
ul Kalandarishvili
ul Frunze
8
ul Kommunisticheskaya
29
ul Kirova
ul Shmidta
Chapel
Trading Arcades
1
26
ul Kuybysheva
To Banzarova Station (100m); Odigitria Cathedral (150m)
To Chingiskhan (1km); Hotel Ayan (3.5km)

Ulan-Ude

Sights
1 Fine Arts Museum ... C7
2 Geological Museum ... B3
3 Khangalov Museum of Buryat History ... C4
4 Lenin Head ... B3
5 Nature Museum ... B5
6 Opera & Ballet Theatre ... B4
7 Triumphal Arch ... B4
8 Ulan-Ude City Museum ... B6

Activities, Courses & Tours
Baikal Naran Tur ... (see 10)
Morin Tur ... (see 12)

Sleeping
9 Hotel Baikal Plaza ... B4
10 Hotel Buryatiya ... B5
11 Hotel Geser ... A2
12 Hotel Sagaan Morin ... D2
13 Hotel Sibir ... B5
14 Resting Rooms ... B1
15 Ulan-Ude Travellers House ... B3

Eating
16 Happyland ... B4
17 King Food ... C4
18 Marusya ... B5
19 Modern Nomads ... A4
20 Nikolayevsky Supermarket ... A1
21 Sputnik Supermarket ... C4
22 Yurt Café ... B4

Drinking
23 Beer Mug ... C4
24 Bochka ... C5
25 Kofeynya Marco Polo ... C4
26 Sky Bar ... D7

Shopping
Baikal Naran Tour Souvenir Kiosk ... (see 10)
27 Ekspeditsiya ... A1
28 Ochir ... B5

Information
29 Buryat-Intour ... C7

Transport
30 Akbes Tur ... C4
31 Buses & Marshrutky to Arshan, Irkutsk and Chita ... B1
32 Central Ticket Office ... B4
33 Marshrutka 37 to Ethnographic Museum ... B4
S7 Airlines ... (see 15)

outdoor collection of local architecture plus some reconstructed burial mounds and the odd stone totem is worth the trip. It's divided into seven areas, each devoted to a different nationality, tribe or ethnic group. There are Hun-era standing stones, Evenki *chumy,* traditional Buryat yurts, timber European townhouses and a whole strip of Old Believers' homesteads, all brimming with period furniture and inhabited by costumed 'locals' giving craft demonstrations. *Marshrutka* 37 from outside the Hotel Baikal Plaza on pl Sovetov passes within 1km and drivers are used to detouring to drop off tourists.

Opera & Ballet Theatre THEATRE
(Театр оперы и балета Бурятии; ☎213 600; ul Lenina 51; www.uuopera.ru; ⏲ticket office 11am-7pm) UU's striking Stalinist-era theatre reopened after lengthy renovation in June 2011 (the first performance was for a group of foreign tourists from the luxury Golden Eagle train). Visitors cannot fail to be impressed by the level of craftsmanship inside, though some might be slightly surprised at the new lick of paint and rub of polish given to all the Soviet symbols, including a couple of smirking Stalins. Next to the building is the 2006 replica of an 1891 **triumphal arch** (Триумфальная арка) honouring the then imperial heir, Nicholas II, the only tsar ever to set foot in Siberia.

Rinpoche Bagsha Datsan BUDDHIST TEMPLE
(ul Dzerzhinskogo) Roosting high above the city's far north, the inside of this new and unexpectedly modern Tibetan temple looks like a kind of Buddhist-themed bus terminal, though the 6m-high gilt Buddha is pretty impressive and if you catch the monks doing their thing with drums, cymbals and chanting the atmosphere can be electric. The real show-stealer here is the panoramic views, the smog-hazed city ringed by rumpled dust-bare peaks. Take *marshrutka* 97 from outside the Hotel Baikal Plaza on pl Sovetov to the last stop (right by the temple entrance).

Ulan-Ude City Museum MUSEUM
(ul Lenina 26; admission R50; ⏲10am-6pm) Occupying the merchant's house where imperial heir Nicholas II stayed in 1891, this small museum

has exhibits examining Verkhneudinsk's role in the tea and fur trades, the huge fairs that took place at the trading arches and several other aspects of the city's past.

Odigitria Cathedral CHURCH

(ul Lenina 2) Built between 1741 and 1785, UU's largest church was also the first stone structure to appear in the city. Used as a museum store from 1929 until the fall of communism, its exterior has been renovated in a chalky white and the domes once again tipped with gold, but the interiors are plain whitewash, awaiting their Byzantine decoration.

Hippodrome HIPPODROME

(Barguzinsky Trakt) This site near the Ethnographic Museum is the venue for major festivals including the Surkharban in early June, the biggest Buryat sporting event of the year featuring archery, wrestling and exhilarating feats of horsemanship. While the hippodrome lies dormant for most of the year, nearby you'll find a pair of attractive *datsany* backed by stupas and trees aflutter with prayer flags. Take *marshrutka* 37 from pl Sovetov.

Nature Museum MUSEUM

(Музей природы Бурятии; ul Lenina 46; admission R100; ⏲10am-6.30pm Wed-Sun) The Nature Museum has taxidermically stuffed animals and a scale model of Lake Baikal showing just how deep it is.

FREE **Geological Museum** MUSEUM

(Геологический Музей Бурятии; ul Lenina 59; ⏲11am-5pm Mon-Fri) This museum displays rocks, crystals and ores from the shores of Lake Baikal as well as art (for sale) made using multihued grit, sand and pebbles.

NATIONAL MUSEUM OF BURYATIYA

Still at the planning stage, the aim of the new National Museum project will be to gather together many of Ulan-Ude's museums and galleries in one purpose-built complex located near the hippodrome in the Verkhnyaya Berezovka suburb. This will create a spectacular repository of the nation's past, and, it must be said, free up some pretty valuable city-centre plots for development. City officials claim it'll all be done and dusted by 2014 – locals are sceptical.

Fine Arts Museum MUSEUM

(Художественный Музей; ul Kuybysheva 29; admission R200; ⏲10am-7pm Tue-Sun) Come here for regularly changing exhibitions as well as permanent displays of Buryat and Russian art.

Tours

Ulan-Ude has many agencies happy to sell you Buryatiya and Baikal tours. The following companies and individuals all speak English and are tuned in to the needs of Western travellers.

TOP CHOICE **Baikal Naran Tour** TOUR COMPANY

(☎215 097; www.baikalnaran.com; info@baikalnaran.com; room 105, Hotel Buryatiya, ul Kommunisticheskaya 47a) There's nothing director Sesegma (aka Svetlana) and charming daughter Naran can't arrange for travellers in Buryatiya. An award-winning tour company and by far the best folks to approach if you want to see the republic's more remote corners, Old Believer villages, the Selenga Delta, the Barguzin Valley and the region's Buddhist and Shamanist heritage.

Denis Sobnakov TOUR GUIDE

(☎8-950-391 6325; www.uuhostel.com; ul Lenina 63) English-speaking Denis runs the city's best hostel as well as fun-packed walking tours of UU and many other Buryatiya-wide trips.

MorinTur TOUR COMPANY

(☎443 647; www.morintour.com; Hotel Sagaan Morin, ul Gagarina 25) Focuses on east Baikal, offering various ice and fishing adventures, a horse-sledge trip, seal watching, rafting in the Barguzin Valley and climbing on Svyatoy Nos (Holy Nose) Peninsula.

Buryat-Intour TOUR COMPANY

(☎216 954; www.buryatintour.ru; ul Kirova 28a) Can arrange birdwatching in the Selenga Delta, monastery visits and city tours. Also sells air tickets.

Firn Travel TOUR COMPANY

(☎555 055; www.firntravel.ru; ul Babushkina 13a) Eastern Baikal tours and activities.

Solongo TOUR COMPANY

(☎8-902-564 7060) Baseless tour company arranging Old Believer tours and city walks.

Sleeping

For years Ulan-Ude has been crying out for a hostel – now it has two excellent budget options, where common rooms buzz with traveller talk and Trans-Sib banter.

Showers can run very cold when the city's central hot water system is turned off for several days (or even weeks) in early summer and autumn for maintenance.

TOP CHOICE **Ulan-Ude Travellers House** HOSTEL €
(☎8-950-391 6325; www.uuhostel.com; ul Lenina 63, apt 18; dm R600; 📶) So central is this brand-new, high-ceilinged apartment hostel, you might even catch a glimpse of Lenin's conk from one of the windows. The 14 beds are divided between two spacious, ethnically themed dorms (Russian and Buryat), there's a small kitchen where a free light breakfast is laid out daily, there's heaps of UU information pasted on the walls and there's a washing machine for guests to use. Exceptionally friendly owner Denis is a professional tour guide, fluent English-speaker and guitar demon – bring your six-string for a common-room jam session. Booking ahead advised.

Hotel Ayan HOTEL €€
(Аян Отель; ☎415 141; www.ayanhotel.ru; ul Babushkina 164; s R1500-2000, tw R1800-4000; ❄📶) The inconvenient location 2km south of the city centre is more than recompensed by pristine international-standard rooms, some with air-conditioning. The cheapest singles are a good deal and every room has its own water heater. There's also a tiny café should you get peckish from all the stair climbing you'll do here – incredibly, this six-storey new-build has no lift.

Hotel Sagaan Morin HOTEL €€€
(Отель Сагаан Морин; ☎444 019; www.sagaan-morin.ru; ul Gagarina 25; s/tw R3000/4200; 📶) The gleaming new 17-storey, 89-room 'White Horse' opened in 2009, replacing its predecessor next door. The switch has promoted the hotel to UU's accommodation premier league with spacious, crisply designed, almost understated rooms, lots of amenities and a 14th-floor restaurant with look-while-you-eat city vistas.

GBT Hostel HOSTEL €
(☎553 470; per Nakhimova 9-2; dm R550, d R1300) A totally different scene from the Travellers House, this homely, freshly-fitted-out hostel occupies a suburban house built by Japanese prisoners of war, 2.5km northeast of the city centre. Two dorms sleep 10 and there's one double as well as a fully equipped kitchen. As the name suggests, the owners are heavily involved in the Great Baikal Trail project and this is one of the best places to get trekking info. Book ahead and arrange a free station pick-up as it's almost impossible to find on your own.

Hotel Baikal Plaza HOTEL €€€
(Гостиница Байкал; ☎210 070; www.baikalplaza.com; ul Erbanova 12; s R3600, tw R4600) The 68 modern, if slightly cramped, rooms were arguably UU's finest offering when first renovated a few years ago, and the central location overlooking the Lenin Head is unrivalled. However, huge price rises in recent years mean this is not the attractive deal it once was.

Hotel Geser HOTEL €€
(Гостиница Гэсэр; ☎216 151; www.geser-hotel.ru; ul Ranzhurova 11; s/tw R2500/3100) Modernisation and realistic prices have made this former Party hang-out a popular option – the only Soviet feature remaining are clacking parquet floors and the odd clunky fridge. Secondhand tobacco pong spoils some rooms but most are decent enough, especially those with rare baths. Rates include breakfast and one or two staff members speak English.

Hotel Sibir HOTEL €€€
(Гостиница Сибирь; ☎297 257; www.hoteltrk.ru; ul Pochtamtskaya 1; s R3000, d R4000; ❄) This futuristic metallic cube stands in stark contrast to the ageing Buryatiya opposite. Welcoming doubles have dark-wood furniture, impeccable bathrooms and flat-screen TVs, but singles are a touch too austere.

Hotel Buryatiya HOTEL €€
(Гостиница Бурятия; ☎211 505; ul Kommunisticheskaya 47a; s & d R1600-4600; @) The mammoth Buryatiya, the former Intourist hotel, has 220 rooms of wildly differing sizes and standards: some are Soviet-era broom cupboards with dodgy plumbing, others are almost palatial with sparkling European bathrooms. One advantage to staying here is the convenience of extra services (internet room, tour companies, souvenir kiosks, ATMs) on the 1st floor – there's even a Buddhist temple!

Resting rooms HOSTEL €
(Комнаты Отдыха, komnaty otdykha; ☎282 696; Ulan-Ude train station; 12-hr/24-hr R600/1200) Well maintained crash pad at the train station.

Eating

For a fascinating insight into traditional Buryat life, Baikal Naran Tour can arrange dinner in a yurt with a local family out in the suburbs of Ulan-Ude.

Baatarai Urgöö BURYAT €€
(Barguzinsky Trakt, Verkhnyaya Berezovka; mains R250-400; ⌚noon-11pm) This large yurt restaurant in the suburb of Verkhnyaya Berezovka is a great lunch spot after a visit to the nearby Ethnographical Museum. Take a seat in the main tent and give your taste buds the Buryat treatment in the form of *buuzy* (aka *pozi,* meat-filled dumplings), *bukhuler* (meat broth), *salamat* (creamy sour porridge) and a mug of milky green tea. Take *marshrutka* 37 from pl Sovetov to the yurt stop.

Chingiskhan ASIAN FUSION €€
(Sun Tower, ul Karla Marksa 25a; mains R250-500; ⌚11am-11.30pm) A huge carved portrait of Chinggis himself offers a stern welcome to this upmarket restaurant, crafted in the shape of a traditional circular yurt. The steppe's bon vivant and conqueror of half the world would no doubt approve of the eclectic Eurasian menu of expertly fused Russian, Buryat and Chinese dishes and the finely tuned feng shui. The restaurant is situated in the Sun Tower, south of the river Uda. Take any tram heading south from the market and alight at the Sayany stop.

Yurt Café BURYAT €
(behind Hotel Baikal Plaza; mains R20-60; ⌚8am-11pm) Three unmarked and interconnecting yurts behind an anonymous grey fence contain the city's liveliest and cheapest nosh spot. A very to-the-point menu lists Buryat dumplings, *shulen* soup, *sharbin* (oily mutton-filled pancakes), bliny, salads, tea and beer – that's it. Stoop through the door, order your food, make a note of your order number and sit down. Waitresses bring out trays in around five minutes. Gets hot in summer and watch out for the wasps!

Samovar UKRAINIAN €€
(Самовар; ul Gagarina 41; mains R90-360; ⌚10am-11pm) Cute basement restaurant with a rural peasant theme (think rag-rug seat covers, spinning wheels and upside-down pots on rickety fences). The menu has a firmly Ukrainian bent, heavy with *salo* (pork fat), *vareniki* (sweet dumplings), *holubtsi* (meat-filled cabbage rolls) and *zapekanka* (cheese cake) but there's plenty of Russian fare in there, too. Filling and tasty lunch menu (R120 to R200).

Marusya RUSSIAN €€
(Маруся; ul Lenina 46; mains R100-280; ⌚10am-10pm) This coy 19th-century dining room with polished samovars, *matryoshka* dolls and waitresses trussed up in pseudo folk costume occupies a corner of the Ulger Theatre. Enjoy inexpensive Russian meals at tightly packed tables to the sound of dreamy 1970s Russian chansons on CD, or flee the Chekhovian pleasantries for the shady terrace.

Modern Nomads MONGOLIAN €€
(ul Ranzhurova 1; mains R70-1000; ⌚11am-11pm Mon-Fri, from noon Sat & Sun; 📋) Clean-cut and very popular Mongolian place, good for a quick snack and a beer or for a full-blown dinner splurge costing thousands. Meat features heavily on the menu, but there are lots of salads with a contemporary twist to choose from, too.

King Food FAST FOOD €
(basement, ul Kommunisticheskaya 43; meals R100-150; ⌚11am-11pm) So-so food, striking pillar-box red-and-jet-black decor and crass Russian MTV; on hot days use the cutlery to slice a hole in the air. On the plus side, it's cheap, clean and conveniently central.

Happyland FAST FOOD €
(ul Lenina 52; mains R100-150; ⌚10.30am-9.30pm, bar to 11pm) This Russian self-service canteen in the cinema foyer is the cheapest source of empty calories in the city centre. It has a popular bar with Baltika 7 and Carlsberg on tap.

Sputnik Supermarket SUPERMARKET
(Супермаркет Спутник; ul Kommunisticheskaya 48; ⌚24hr) A convenient but pricey supermarket stocking foreign groceries. Get there early for real freshly baked croissants.

Nikolayevsky Supermarket SUPERMARKET
(ul Borsoeva 25; ⌚9am-11pm) Another (cheaper) supermarket on the way to the train station from the city centre – handy for buying supplies for long Trans-Sib journeys.

Drinking

Bochka BEER HALL
(ul Kommunisticheskaya 52; ⌚10am-1am) Large timber beer hall serving a range of Russian and international brews to rinse down the succulently smoky shashlyk. The covered terrace is *the* place to do some elbow bending on sultry summer evenings.

Sky Bar CAFÉ
(10th fl, Eurozone Centre, ul Baltakhinova; mains R175-360; ⌚9am-midnight, to 2am Fri & Sat) Perched atop the new glass-and-steel Eurozone Centre (an unwise choice of name if ever there was one), this café-bar has the

best views in all Ulan-Ude with stupendous vistas across the entire city and the hills beyond. Opened in May 2011; the owners were eventually planning to create a more upmarket restaurant here, but whatever the space becomes, the unrivalled views are guaranteed to draw punters.

Beer Mug BAR
(pr 50-let Oktyabrya 8a; 5pm-6am) New and popular nightspot with cheap beer, cocktails, a dance floor but occasional face control.

Kofeynya Marco Polo CAFÉ
(Кофейня Marco Polo; ul Kommunisticheskaya 46; 9am-10.30pm;) This cosy coffee house has a touch of Central European character, great desserts, and wi-fi for R150 per 100MB. Main dishes are pricey.

Shopping

Ochir SOUVENIRS
(Очир; ul Lenina 46; 10am-7pm) Authentic, beautifully hand-painted items such as plates with Buddhist and Buryat motifs, decorated wooden eggs, *matryoshka*/Buryat dolls and Chinggis Khaan key rings. Some items are painted on the premises by the owner.

Baikal Naran Tour souvenir kiosk SOUVENIRS
(room 105, Hotel Buryatiya; ul Kommunisticheskaya 47a) This tiny kiosk in the Baikal Naran Tour office sells authentic Buryat souvenirs such as oriental costumed dolls, shaman drums and colourful felt hats.

Ekspeditsiya OUTDOOR GEAR
(Экспедиция; ul Borsoeva 19; 9am-6pm) The Ulan-Ude branch of Ekspeditsiya offers good-quality sleeping bags, tents and other essential outdoor kit.

Information

There are exchange bureaus and ATMs in the Geser and Buryatiya hotels.

Baikal Bank (Байкал Банк; pl Sovetov 1; 9am-8pm Mon-Fri, 9am-7pm Sat) Most central place for changing dollars and euros.

Post office (ul Lenina 61; 8am-10pm Mon-Fri, 9am-6pm Sat & Sun) Internet access.

UUModa (www.uumoda.ru) Heaps of city listings, all in Russian.

Getting There & Away

Air

UU's ageing **Baikal Airport** (www.airportbaikal.ru), 11km from the city centre, handles surprisingly few flights. Buy tickets at the **Central Ticket Office** (ul Erbanova 14; 9am-1pm & 2-6pm), **S7 Airlines** (ul Sukhe-Batora 63; 9am-7pm) or **Akbes Tur** (Акбес Тур; ul Kommunisticheskaya 46; 9am-8pm, from 9.30am Sun). Ulan-Ude has the following flight connections:

Irkutsk R2500, three weekly

Moscow R10,600 to R17,000, two daily

Nizhneangarsk R4700, four weekly

UU TO UB

There are now three ways to travel from the Buryat capital to Ulaanbaatar. The least comfortable way is by Trans-Mongolian **train**, which takes up to 24 hours to complete the 657km trip and can wait up to 11 hours on the border at Naushki. A much cheaper and convenient way to go is to hop aboard the daily **coach** (R1100, 10 hours), which leaves from a stop near the roundabout behind the Opera & Ballet Theatre. Tickets can be bought from Baikal Naran Tour and the Ulan-Ude Travellers House hostel. If you've got the cash and/or are in a hurry, there are now three **flights** a week from UU to UB with **Eznis Airways** (www.eznisairways.com). One-way tickets cost in the region of R4000.

Bus

Ulan-Ude has three bus stations: the **former main bus station** (Центральный автовокзал; Sovetskaya ul), **Banzarova Station** (Автостанция Банзарова; ul Banzarova) and the new and utterly inconvenient **North Station** (pr Avtomobilistov 3a). For North Station, take bus 30 from pl Sovetov (20 minutes). Buses to destinations on Baikal's eastern shore all take the same route via the resort villages of Gremyachinsk, Turka, Goryachinsk and Maksimikha. The city has the following bus and *marshrutka* connections:

Arshan R610, 11 hours, five daily (Main Station)

Barguzin R500, eight hours, daily (North Station)

Ivolga R30, 40 minutes, many daily (Banzarova Station, *marshrutka* number 130)

Kurumkan R600, 10 hours, daily (North Station)

Kyakhta R250, three hours, many daily (Main Station)

Ust-Barguzin R400, seven hours, daily (North Station)

Additional *marshrutky* to Arshan (R600, six hours), Irkutsk (R700, eight hours) and Chita

(R700, seven hours) run from the courtyard of the train station, departing throughout the day when full but mainly around 9pm.

Train

When travelling to Irkutsk, take a day train for superb views of Lake Baikal.

Ulan-Ude has the following rail connections:

Beijing *kupe* R6000, two days to two days 15 hours, two weekly

Chita *platskart* R970, *kupe* R1500 to R2500, 10 hours to 12 hours, up to six daily

Irkutsk *platskart* R810, *kupe* R1200 to R2000, seven hours, up to nine daily

Ulaanbaatar *kupe* R3000, 18 hours to 24 hours, up to two daily

Getting Around

From pl Sovetov *marshrutky* 28 and 55 run a few times hourly to the airport while *marshrutka* 37 passes the hippodrome, Ethnographic Museum and Baatarai Urgöö restaurant. *Marshrutka* 97 climbs to the Rinpoche Bagsha Datsan. Any ride on public transport costs R14.

Around Ulan-Ude

You could spend a week making day trips out of Ulan-Ude with Buddhist temples, Old Believer villages and forgotten border settlements to explore. The main routes south are the scenic Ulan-Ude–Kyakhta road, which hugs the Selenga River for much of the way, and the Trans-Mongolian Railway, which crosses the border at the unremarkable railway town of Naushki, officially off-limits to foreigners.

IVOLGINSK (IVOLGA) DATSAN
ИВОЛГИНСКИЙ ДАЦАН

Possibly the last person you might expect to have backed the building of a Buddhist temple was Stalin, but in 1946 permission came from the Kremlin to erect a *datsan* in Buryatiya, in gratitude to the locals for their sacrifices during WWII it's often claimed. But instead of reviving the erstwhile centre of Buryat Buddhism at Gusinoe Ozero, the authorities granted a plot of marshy land near the village of Ivolga, 35km from central Ulan-Ude, on which the temple was to be built. The first temple was a modest affair, but today the **datsan** has grown large and is expanding fast. The confident epicentre of Russian Buddhism attracts large numbers of the devout as well as tourists on half-day trips from the Buryat capital.

It was one of only two working Buddhist temples in Soviet days (the other was at Aginskoe); most of what you see today has been built in the last two decades. A clockwise walk around the complex takes in countless monastery faculties, administrative buildings, monks' quarters and temples, but the most elaborate of all is the **Itygel Khambin Temple** honouring the 12th Khambo Lama, whose body was exhumed in 2002. To general astonishment, seven decades after his death his flesh had still not decomposed. Some 'experts' have even attested that the corpse's hair is still growing, albeit extraordinarily slowly. The body is displayed six times a year, attracting pilgrims from across the Buddhist world.

To reach the monastery, first take *marshrutka* 130 (R30, 40 minutes, four hourly) from Ulan-Ude's Banzarova bus station to the last stop in uninteresting Ivolga. There another *marshrutka* (R15, no number, just a picture of the monastery pasted to the front windscreen) waits to shuttle visitors the last few kilometres to the monastery compound. Otherwise contact agencies in Ulan-Ude, which offer private transfers and tours with well-informed guides.

TAMCHINSKY DATSAN
ТАМЧИНСКИЙ ДАЦАН

First founded in 1741, this was Buryatiya's first Buddhist monastery and the mother ship of Russian Buddhism for two centuries. The original complex, 160km south of Ulan-Ude, was destroyed in the 1930s and the modern reconstruction is small scale and surrounded by the slowly dying village of Gusinoe Ozero (30km south of Gusinoozersk). View the newly renovated former school of philosophy, test out the amazing acoustics of the main temple and chat with the mobile-phone-toting head lama who, for a donation, may let you camp in the grounds and eat in the small refectory.

OLD BELIEVERS' VILLAGES

To the south of Ulan-Ude lie several relatively accessible **Old Believers' villages**, most notably Tarbagatay (50km south), with its whitewashed church and small museum, and nearby Desyatnikovo. Turn up unannounced in these places and you'll see precious little; visits involving lots of colourful costumed singing, deliciously hearty homemade food and detailed explanations of the Old Believers' traditions and way of life must be prearranged through Ulan-Ude agencies.

WORTH A TRIP

NOVOSELENGINSK НОВОСЕЛЕНГИНСК

Stockades and wooden houses on broad dust-blown roads give this small, 19th-century town of ten thousand souls a memorable 'Wild East' feel. The town's top attraction is its **Decembrist Museum** (ul Lenina 53; admission R50; ⌚10am-6pm Wed-Sun), which is housed in an unmissable 200-year-old colonnaded minimansion in the town's centre. Lower floors are stocked with 19th-century furnishings, while upstairs are maps and photos relating to the Decembrist exiles and their wives.

Walk a couple of kilometres east of the museum through the town towards the Selenga River to see the isolated ruins of the whitewashed **Spassky Church** on the grassy far bank; this is all that remains of Selenginsk, the original settlement, which was abandoned around 1800 due to frequent floods. You'll also find an unremarkable **obelisk** commemorating Martha Cowie, the wife of a Scottish missionary who spent 22 years here translating the Bible into Mongolian and trying (wholly unsuccessfully) to ween the Buryats off Buddhism.

Marshrutky make the scenic trip from Ulan-Ude (1½ hours, six or seven daily).

To get there, take the 6.37am Naushki train from Ulan-Ude (3½ hours) and alight at Gusinoe Ozero. A train runs back to Ulan-Ude late afternoon or you could hitch a lift to Gusinoozersk at the opposite end of the lake, from where there are regular *marshrutky* back to Ulan-Ude.

ATSAGATSKY DATSAN АЦАГАТСКИЙ ДАЦАН

Once the centre of Buryat Buddhist scholarship with an important scriptorium, this *datsan* was completely destroyed in the 1930s, but has crawled back to life since the fall of communism. The tiny on-site **Ayvan Darzhiev Museum** commemorates the Atsagat monk who became a key counsellor to the 13th Dalai Lama. Photogenically gaudy, the little monastery sits on a lonely grassy knoll and is set back from km54 of the old Chita road – unfortunately there is no convenient public transport. A tour from Ulan-Ude will cost around R5000 for up to three people.

KYAKHTA КЯХТА

☎30142 / POP 19,500 / ⌚MOSCOW +5HR

Formerly called Troitskosavsk, the Kyakhta of two centuries ago was a town of tea-trade millionaires whose grandiose cathedral was reputed to have had solid silver doors embedded with diamonds. By the mid-19th century as many as 5000 cases of tea a day were arriving via Mongolia on a stream of horse or camel caravans, which returned loaded with furs.

This gloriously profitable tea trade was brought to shuddering end with the completion of the Suez Canal and the Trans-Siberian Railway, leaving Kyakhta to wither away into a dust-blown border settlement. Wonderfully preserved by 70 years of communist neglect, the town is dotted with remnants of a wealthier past, which make Kyakhta well worth the trip from Ulan-Ude.

Modern Kyakhta is effectively two towns. The main one is centred around ul Lenina, where the bus terminus sits next to the 1853 trading rows *(ryady gostinye)*. The smaller Sloboda district, 4km to the south, is where you'll find the border post. As this is the border zone, you *must* register your visa as soon as you arrive if you plan to stay the night.

Sights

Kyakhta Museum MUSEUM

(ul Lenina 49; admission R200; ⌚10am-6pm Tue-Sun) Kyakhta's star attraction is its delightfully eccentric museum, perhaps rather comically dubbed the 'Hermitage of the East' by some overzealous locals. It's certainly one of Siberia's fullest museums with room after musty room of exhibits relating to the tea trade, local plants and animals, Buryat traditions, Asian art and Kyakhta's bit part in WWII. Many of the older exhibits were hauled back to Troitskosavsk by 19th-century Russian gentlemen explorers who launched trans-Asian expeditions from the town. English is wholly absent from the building but multilingual guides are sometimes available.

Uspenskaya Church CHURCH

(ul Krupskaya) For years Kyakhta's only working church, this beautiful, late-19th-century building was closed twice during the communist decades (1938 and 1962). Leave a donation for its upkeep.

Voskresenskaya Church CHURCH
(Sloboda) Reopened in 2011 following painstaking restoration, the brilliant white Resurrection Church is the last outpost of European Christianity before Mongolian Buddhism takes over. Take *marshrutka* 1 from ul Lenina.

Trinity Cathedral CHURCH
(ul Lenina) The impressive shell of the 1817 cathedral lies at the heart of the overgrown central park at the end of ul Lenina.

Sleeping & Eating

Hotel Druzhba HOTEL €
(Гостиница Дружба; ☎91 321; ul Krupskaya 8; s R400-1500, d R800-1200) Kyakhta's main hotel has 20 rooms off dim corridors, ageing facilities but welcoming staff. It's beside the Uspenskaya Church, 10 minutes' walk south of ul Lenina.

Hotel Turist HOTEL €
(Гостиница Турист; ☎92 431; ul Lenina 21; dm/s/d R350/350/700) The five basic but well-kept rooms at this centrally located minihotel occupy a 140-year-old former merchant's house. The bathroom is communal and visa registration costs an extra R30.

Letnee Kafe CAFÉ €
(Летнее Кафе; ul Lenina, opposite Hotel Turist; ⏰11am-midnight) No-frills Central Asian shashlyk, *plov* and beer stop on the main drag.

Café Sloboda CAFÉ €
(Кафе Слобода; Sloboda; ⏰11am-11pm) Simple, cheap and clean café located 400m along the road from the Voskresenskaya Church, where the road peels off towards the border crossing.

INTO MONGOLIA

The **Mongolian border** is open to bicycles and vehicles, and some officials speak English. You can't walk across, so pedestrians need to negotiate passage with private drivers. Start asking as close as possible to the front of the chaotic queue: processing takes about an hour, with only a handful of vehicles allowed through at any one time. The going rate is around R300 per passenger across no-man's-land, but it's well worth negotiating a ride all the way to Sükhbaatar train station (around R200 extra) from where there are trains to Ulaanbaatar (*obshchiy/platskart/kupe* T6300/11,800/18,900, nine hours) departing at 9.05pm and 6.25am.

For further information, head to shop.lonelyplanet.com to purchase a downloadable PDF of the Trans-Mongolian chapter from Lonely Planet's *Trans-Siberian Railway* guide.

Getting There & Away

Marshrutky (R250, three hours, leave when full) shuttle between Kyakhta and Ulan-Ude. The Ulan-Ude–Ulaanbaatar bus also takes Kyakhta-bound passengers (R300, 3½ hours) if there are seats. Pay the driver.

Chita Чита

☎3022 / POP 324,000 / ⏰MOSCOW +6HR

Of all Eastern Siberia's major cities, Chita is the least prepared for visitors. Literally put on the map by the noble-blooded Decembrists, one of whom designed its street-grid layout, today there's nothing aristocratic about this regional capital where Soviet symbols still embellish Stalinist facades, shaven-headed conscripts guard pillared military headquarters and Chinese cross-border peddlers lug monster bales past a well-tended Lenin statue. Non-Chinese foreigners are still a rarity here, tourism a thing that happens elsewhere.

Echoes of the Decembrist chapter in Chita's history make the city just worth visiting, and a number of attractive old timber merchants' houses grace its arrow-straight streets. It's also the jumping-off point for two of Russia's best Buddhist temples at Aginskoe and Tsugol.

History

Founded in 1653, Chita developed as a rough-and-tumble silver-mining centre until it was force-fed a dose of urban culture in 1827 by the arrival of more than 80 exiled Decembrist gentlemen-rebels – or more precisely, by the arrival of their wives and lovers who followed, setting up homes on what became known as ul Damskaya (Women's St). That's now the southern end of ul Stolyarova, where sadly only a handful of rotting wooden cottages remains amid soulless concrete apartment towers.

As gateway to the new East Chinese Railway, Chita boomed in the early 20th century, despite flirting with socialism. Following the excitement of 1905, socialists set up a 'Chita Republic' which was brutally crushed within

THE DECEMBRIST WOMEN

Having patently failed to topple tsarist autocracy in December 1825, many prominent 'Decembrist' gentlemen revolutionaries were exiled to Siberia. They're popularly credited with bringing civilisation to the rough-edged local pioneer-convict population. Yet the real heroes were their womenfolk, who cobbled together the vast carriage fares to get themselves to Siberia: in prerailway 1827 the trip from St Petersburg to Irkutsk cost the equivalent of US$200 (about US$10,000 today).

And that was just the start. Pauline Annenkova, the French mistress of one aristocratic prisoner, spent so long awaiting permission to see her lover in Chita that she had time to set up a fashionable dressmakers' shop in Irkutsk. By constantly surveying the prisoners' conditions, the women eventually shamed guards into reducing the brutality of the jail regimes, while their food parcels meant that Decembrists had more hope of surviving the minimal rations of their imprisonment. The Decembrist women came to form a core of civil society and introduced 'European standards of behaviour'. As conditions eventually eased, this formed the basis for a liberal Siberian aristocracy, especially in Chita and Irkutsk where some Decembrists stayed on even after their formal banishment came to an end.

a year. After the 'real' revolutions of 1917, history gets even more exciting and complex. Bolsheviks took over, then lost control to Japanese forces who possibly intercepted part of Admiral Kolchak's famous 'gold train' before retreating east. By 1920 Chita was the capital of the short-lived Far Eastern Republic, a nominally independent, pro-Lenin buffer state whose parliament stood at ul Anokhina 63. The republic was absorbed into Soviet Russia in December 1922 once the Japanese had withdrawn from Russia's east coast. Closed and secretive for much of the Soviet era, today Chita is still very much a military city and once again flooded with Chinese traders.

Sights

TOP CHOICE **Decembrist Museum** MUSEUM
(Музей Декабристов; ul Selenginskaya; admission R100; ⏲10am-6pm Tue-Sun) If you're on the Decembrist trail through Siberia, this small but comprehensive museum is one of the best, though there's not a word of English anywhere. It's housed in the 18th-century **Archangel Michael log church**, an unexpected sight amid the neighbourhood's shambolic apartment blocks. Inextricably linked to the Decembrist story, this was where they came to pray, where Annenkov married his French mistress Pauline and where the Volkonskys buried their daughter Sofia.

The ground-level exhibition begins with the names of all the Decembrists picked out in gold on a green background, followed by interesting items such as the original imperial order sentencing the noble rebels to banishment in Siberia and oils showing their leaders' executions. The 2nd floor looks at the wives who followed their menfolk into the Nerchinsk silver mines and the fates of all the Decembrists once they were allowed to settle where they pleased. It's fascinatingly detailed, but with no Russian you'll flounder.

Kuznetzov Regional Museum MUSEUM
(Краеведческий Музей Кузнецова; ul Babushkina 113; admission R110; ⏲10am-6pm Tue-Sun) The excellent and unusually lively Kuznetzov Regional Museum is housed in an early-20th-century mansion. Beyond the gratuitous stuffed elk, you'll find some pretty interesting local exhibits, including a very thorough examination of the heritage and architectural renaissance of the city and region. There's a decent café on the premises.

Military Museum MUSEUM
(Музей История Войск ЗабВО; ul Lenina 86; admission R80; ⏲9am-1pm & 2-5pm) This dry Russian-language-only museum is only for those with a passion for Eastern Siberia's military history, though it does contain some semi-interesting exhibits on Beketov's Cossacks, the Soviet invasion of Afghanistan and communist repressions. Each of the six floors bristles with weapons, and the museum's collection of **tanks and artillery** can be seen by walking up the passage between the museum and the impressive **Officers' Club** (Дом Офицеров) building next door.

Chita

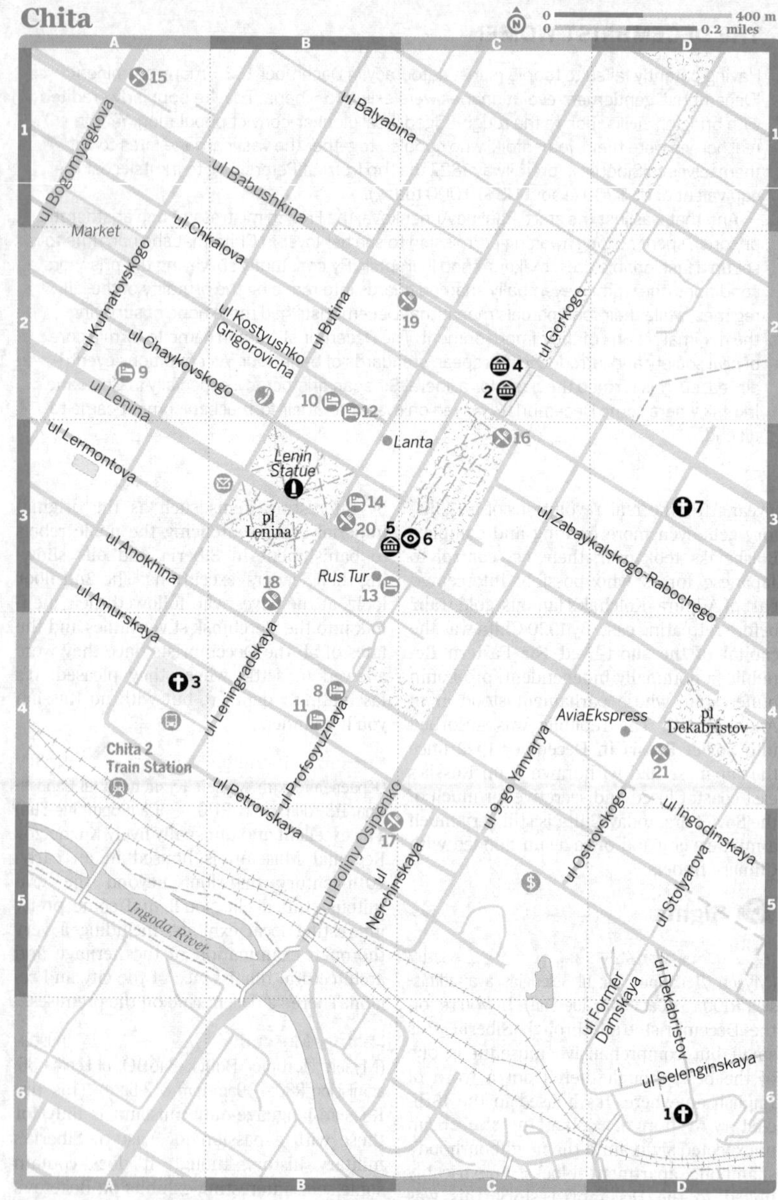

Cathedral CHURCH

(Кафедральный собор; train station forecourt) The train station reflected in its gilt onion domes, Chita's bright turquoise cathedral is the city's most impressive building, though inside it's lamentably plain. The original pre-Stalin cathedral stood on the main square, right on the spot where Lenin now fingers his lapels.

Art Museum ART GALLERY

(Картинная галерея; ul Chkalova 120a; admission R50; ⌚10am-7pm Tue-Sat, to 6pm Sun) The Art

Chita

Sights

Sleeping

Eating

Drinking

Museum shows frequently changing exhibitions by schoolchildren and local artists.

Voskreseniya Church CHURCH
(Свято-Воскресенский храм; ul 9-go Yanvarya) The recent-looking Voskreseniya Church is actually the city's oldest, but was almost burnt to the ground in 1996. Some of the original 19th-century icons are displayed inside.

Sleeping

Chita has little budget accommodation and homestays are nonexistent. Hotels are often full, meaning many travellers who fail to book ahead often have no choice but to check into top-end hotels.

Hotel Vizit HOTEL €€€
(Гостиница Визит; ☎356 945; www.visit-hotel.ru; ul Lenina 93; s/tw R3190/5800; ❄📶) Occupying the 5th floor of an ultramodern smoked-glass tower at the busy intersection of ul Lenina and ul Profsoyuznaya, this is Chita's best luxury offering with relaxing en-suite rooms, English-speaking receptionists and sparkling bathrooms. Some doubles have baths and the air-con provides relief from Chita's superheated summers. It's half-price for stays of between six and 12 hours.

Hotel Montblanc HOTEL €€€
(☎357 272; www.eldonet.ru; ul Kostyushko Grigorovicha 5; s R3150-3450, d R3850-4650; ❄📶) A block away from the main square, this purpose-built business hotel has immaculately snazzy rooms, though at these prices the plumbing could be a touch more professional. The buffet breakfast is served in the Ukraine-themed restaurant and check-out time at reception provides an opportunity to witness just how badly Russian and Chinese businessmen can behave.

Hotel Zabaikale HOTEL €€
(Гостиница Забайкалье; ☎359 819; www.zabaikalie.ru; ul Leningradskaya 36; s from R1900, tw from R3800) Unbeatably located overlooking the main square, and the cheaper renovated rooms at this huge complex are a fairly good deal. The hotel has a huge range of facilities including an air and rail ticket office, a spa, a children's playroom and a gym. Rates include ham-and-egg breakfast in the kitschily grand 2nd-floor restaurant.

Hotel Arkadia HOTEL €€
(Гостиница Аркадия; ☎352 636; www.arkadia.chita.ru; ul Lenina 120; s R1800-2900, tw R2400-4500) The Arkadia is set back from ul Lenina and equipped with 35 bland but comfy rooms and some imaginative plumbing. The foyer has one of Chita's best caffeine halts and is a good place to grab breakfast.

Hotel Chitaavtotrans HOTEL €€
(Гостиница Читаавтотранс; ☎355 011; ul Kostyushko Grigorovicha 7; s/tw R1500/1800) As just about Chita's cheapest digs, the cosmetically improved but cramped rooms here are usually full, so book ahead.

Hotel Dauria HOTEL €€€
(Гостиница Даурия; ☎262 350; ul Profsoyuznaya 17; s from R2000, d from R4000; 📶) Renovated, very comfortable en-suite rooms with semi-stylish furniture make this a characterful choice. Breakfast is included but reservations are essential.

Hotel AChO HOTEL €€
(Гостиница Управления делами Администрации Читинской Области; ☎351 968; ul Profsoyuznaya 19; dm R423-625, s R500-3000, tw R2000-2400) Occupying a fine 1906

brick mansion with many of its architectural features still in place, this hotel sadly sports bare, unlovely, overpriced rooms. Anyone turning up without a booking will be sent packing, even if the hotel is empty.

Eating & Drinking

Eating out ain't high on the list of things to enjoy in Chita, but despite the lack of choice and unimaginative menus, you won't go hungry.

Khmelnaya Korchma UKRAINIAN €€
(Хмельная Корчма; ul Amurskaya 69; mains R150-400; ⊙noon-midnight Mon-Thu & Sun, noon-3am Fri & Sat; ❄) Plastic sunflowers, dangling onion strings, folksy embroidered tea towels and a menu of borsch, *salo* (pork fat), *vareniki* (sweet dumplings) and *holubtsi* (cabbage rolls stuffed with rice) teleport you to rural Ukraine. Live music, liberal helpings and a low-priced lunch menu (R150) arguably make this Chita's best option.

Kafe Kollazh INTERNATIONAL €€
(Кафе Коллаж; ul Bogomyagkova 24; mains R150-400; ⊙noon-midnight; ❄) Unpromising from the outside, this mood-lit and cosy place adorned with spinning wheels, old samovars and dried flowers is one of Chita's better dining spots. The international-themed food is tasty but slightly overpriced.

Shokoladnitsa CAFÉ
(ul Leningradskaya 36; ⊙8am-11pm; 📶) This new central café is good for people-watching from the big windows while sipping a beer or coffee and making full use of the free wi-fi.

Kafe Traktyr RUSSIAN €€
(Кафе Трактыр; ul Chkalova 93; mains R230-460; ⊙noon-2am) Russian home-style cooking is served at heavy wooden tables in this rebuilt wooden-lace cottage, with a quietly upmarket Siberian-retro atmosphere. The summer beer-and-shashlyk tent is a popular drinking spot.

Tsiplyata Tabaka CAFÉ €
(Цыплята Табака; ul Ostrovskogo 20; meals R250; ⊙noon-5pm & 6pm-1am) Judging by the socialist realist reliefs and Brezhnev-era decor, this quirky eatery once had a previous life as something else. Roast chicken priced by weight is the only main course (R47 per 100g).

Poznaya Altargana BURYAT €
(Позная Алтаргана; ul Leningradskaya 5; pozi R30; ⊙10am-midnight Mon-Thu & Sun, to 2am Fri & Sat) If *pozi* are your thing, Poznaya Altargana is your place, but the tasty *plov* and meatballs are an equally filling alternative. There's a larger **branch** at ul Babushkina 121.

Kofeynya Kofe Moll CAFÉ
(Кафе Молл; Hotel Arkadia, ul Lenina 120; ⊙24hr) Occupying half of a hotel lobby, this is one of the few places in town offering true solace to disciples of the bean. It also has a long list of cocktails.

Information

Lanta (Ланта; ☎353 638; www.lanta-chita.ru; ul Leningradskaya 56; ⊙9am-7pm Mon-Fri) Runs limited tours of Chita and Zabaikalsky Region. No English spoken.

Main post office (ul Butina 37; ⊙8am-10pm Mon-Fri, 9am-6pm Sat & Sun) Quaintly spired wooden building on pl Lenina.

Rus Tur (☎264 283; www.rustur.chita.ru; ul Lenina 93, office 410) Can arrange tours to Tsugol (R9000 per car); some English is spoken in the office.

Telephone office (ul Chaykovskogo 22; ⊙8am-8pm) Has an ATM.

VTB Bank (ВТБ Банк; ul Amurskaya 41; ⊙9am-6pm Mon-Fri) Changes US dollars, euros, Chinese yuan and even British pounds.

Getting There & Away

Air

Kadala Airport (www.aerochita.ru) is 15km west of central Chita. Take *marshrutka* 12 or 14. **Avia-Ekspress** (АвиаЭкспресс; ☎325 572; www.aviaexpress.ru; ul Lenina 55; ⊙9am-10pm Mon-Sat) sells tickets for the following flights:

Beijing R10,500, two weekly

Moscow from R12,500, up to three daily

Bus

The only two services you're likely to need are the *marshrutky* to Aginskoe (R250, two hours, hourly) and the long-distance minivans to Ulan-Ude (R700, seven hours). Both leave from a stop on the train station forecourt.

Train

Chita has the following rail connections:

Beijing *kupe* R5500, two days five hours, weekly

MOVING ON?

For tips, recommendations and reviews, head to shop.lonelyplanet.com to purchase a downloadable PDF of the Trans-Manchurian and Beijing chapters from Lonely Planet's *Trans-Siberian Railway* guide.

WORTH A TRIP

NERCHINSK НЕРЧИНСК

Anyone with a knowledge of Russian history will be familiar with the name Nerchinsk. The 1689 Treaty of Nerchinsk recognising Russia's claims to the trans-Baikal region was signed here and 130 years later the Decembrists were sent to work the silver mines around the village. Once one of Eastern Siberia's foremost towns but inexplicably bypassed by the Trans-Siberian Railway just 10km to the south, Nerchinsk leads a forgotten existence with just a few fading reminders of its rich past. If you're looking to break up the long 300km trip from Chita to Blagoveshchensk, hop off here. Most don't.

The only visitable attraction is the **Butin Palace Museum** (ul Sovetskaya 83; admission R100; ⌚10am-1pm & 2-5.30pm Tue-Sat). Mikhail Butin, the local silver baron, built himself this impressive crenellated palace, furnished with what were then claimed to be the world's largest mirrors. He'd bought the mirrors at the 1878 World Fair in Paris and miraculously managed to ship them unscathed all the way to Nerchinsk via the China Sea and up the Amur River. These four mammoth mirrors form the centrepiece of the collection, along with a delightful pair of hobbit-style chairs crafted from polished tangles of birch roots. Three-quarters of the palace, including the grand, triple-arched gateway (demolished in 1970), still stands in ruins.

A block from the museum, the active 1825 **Voskresensky Cathedral** (ul Pogodaeva 85) looks like an opera house from the outside; its interior is plain and whitewashed. Head around the sports pitch with its little silver Lenin to the imposing though now crumbling 1840 **Trading Arches**, slated for desperately needed renovation in the coming years. Nearby is a fine colonnaded pharmacy and the very grand facade of the pink former **Kolobovnikov Store** (ul Shilova 3), now a barnlike Torgovy Tsentr filled with some desultory stalls and kiosks.

About 1km south of the museum, just before the post office and bank, a little pink column-fronted building was once the **Dauriya Hotel** (ul Sovetskaya 32). As locals will proudly tell you, Chekhov stayed here in June 1890. Diagonally across the same junction, the Kozerog shop doubles as a minuscule bus station from where services to Priiskovaya depart.

To reach Nerchinsk, take any train from Chita to Priiskovaya (*platskart* R690, *kupe* R1000 to R1400, six hours) on the trans-Siberian main line, 10km from Nerchinsk. Change there onto local *marshrutky*.

Blagoveshchensk *platskart/kupe* R1300/3050, one day 9½ to 13 hours, two daily

Khabarovsk *platskart* R2700, *kupe* R5500 to R7300, one day 15½ to 17½ hours, up to three daily

Tynda *platskart* R1700, *kupe* R2700 to R3800, 26½ hours, every other day

Ulan-Ude *platskart* R970, *kupe* R1480 to R2570, 11 hours, up to seven daily

Zabaikalsk *platskart* R1170, *kupe* R2500 to R3000, 11½ hours, daily

Around Chita

AGINSKOE АГИНСКОЕ

☎30239 / POP 11,700 / ⌚MOSCOW +6HR

For an intriguing day trip from Chita, take a *marshrutka* (R250, two hours, hourly) to the spruced-up Buryat town of Aginskoe. Scenery en route transforms from patchily forested hills via river valleys into rolling grassy steppe.

Once in Aginskoe, hop straight into a taxi (R100) to visit the beautiful old Buddhist **datsan** (6km west of the centre), a large complex of brightly decorated temples and monastery faculties. Back on the central square, the admirably well-curated **Tsybikov Museum** (ul Komsomolskaya 11; admission R100; ⌚10am-1pm & 2-5.30pm Mon-Fri) takes an in-depth look at the local Buryat culture. Opposite stands the custard-yellow 1905 **St Nicholas Church** whose reconstruction was bankrolled by former Moscow mayor Yury Luzhkov.

Self-service **Kafe Biznes Lanch** (ul Lenina 58; mains R15-50; ⌚9am-10pm Mon-Sat) on the opposite side of the square from the museum has an unpretentious Siberian menu. **Zakusochnaya Yukhen Tug** (ul Tataurova 17a; mains R20-50; ⌚9am-8pm) near the market is a no-frills greasy spoon where tasty goulash, *plov* and salad are piled tall on saucer-size plates. There's a supermarket and an ATM nearby.

TSUGOL ЦУГОЛ

Set just 2km from the 'holy' Onon River, Tsugol village is not particularly pretty but the perfectly proportioned **Tsugol Datsan** is surely the most memorable Buddhist temple in Russia. Built in 1820, it is just four years younger than Aginskoe Datsan and even more photogenic, with gilded Mongolian script-panels, wooden upper facades and tip-tilted roofs on each of its three storeys. The interior is less colourful than the Ivolginsk temple, but clinging to the front is a unique, colourfully painted wrought-iron staircase.

Getting to/from Tsugol is a pain – it lies 13km from Olovyannaya, reachable by a single morning bus (R400, departs 8.30am) from Chita. From Olovyannaya take a taxi (at least R400, more if asked to wait) or hike along the river. On the return journey, you could ask around in Olovyannaya for an unofficial *marshrutka* back to Chita (or Aginskoe) – otherwise it's a long lonely wait for the overnight train (this may be an opportunity to test your hitchhiking skills). Alternatively, contact tour companies in Chita who run (expensive) excursions to Tsugol on request.

Russian Far East

Includes »

Best Places to Eat

» Zima (p585)
» Chochur Muran (p598)
» Tygyn Darkhan (p598)
» Nihon Mitai (p604)
» San Marino (p612)

Best Places to Stay

» Boutique Hotel (p572)
» See You Hostel (p582)
» Biznestsentr (p592)
» Polar Star Hotel (p597)
» Tri Medvedya (p616)

Why Go?

Russia's distant end of the line, the wild wild east, feels likes its own entity. 'Moscow is far' runs the local mantra, and trade and transport connections with Asian neighbours are growing fast.

For those who've not been, the Russian Far East (Дальний Восток) seems impossibly forbidding and it's often mistaken for Siberia (it was considered part of Siberia in precommunist times). The truth is it's bigger, more remote and, in winter, even colder. Areas of snow-capped mountains and taiga, bigger than some European countries, separate former Cossack fort towns, old Gulag camps, decaying Soviet towns along railways heading nowhere special, towns raised on stilts over permafrost and once-closed Soviet ports roaring with new business.

Many travellers skip the Far East entirely, cutting south from Lake Baikal to China – but that's all the better for those who make it. Elbow room is definitely not in short supply.

When to Go

Vladivostok

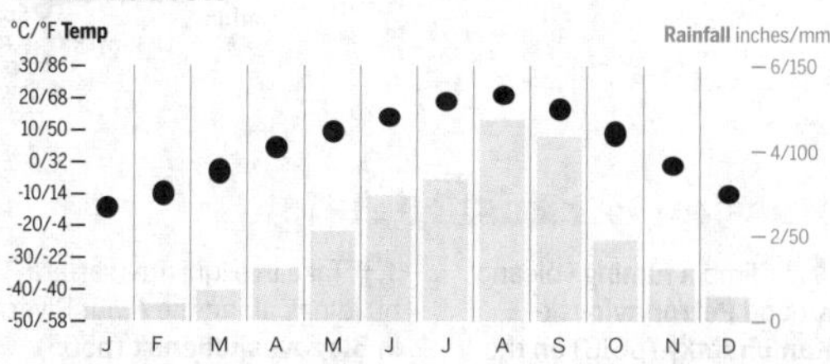

Feb & Mar Still the season for snowy delights, only not dark or slushy.

Jun Essentially midspring, with all the beauty that entails (minus mozzies).

Sep & Oct Better weather and more autumn foliage than anywhere else on earth.

Russian Far East Highlights

1. Climb a fuming volcano around **Petropavlovsk-Kamchatsky** (p613) on the wild Kamchatka Peninsula
2. View sublime Golden Horn Bay in mountain-spiked **Vladivostok** (p575)
3. Go exotic with horsemeat, reindeer and frozen fish meals in fascinating **Yakutsk** (p594)
4. Take in exquisite tsar-era buildings along the Amur River in **Blagoveshchensk** (p565)
5. Splurge on the adventure of a lifetime in the far-flung **Kuril Islands** (p606)
6. Take a party cruise on the Amur River before a night of clubbing in hip **Khabarovsk** (p568)
7. Hike the well-mapped trails of **Bystrinsky Nature Park** (p615) in laid-back Esso, Kamchatka
8. Revisit Soviet power and take a Gulag camp tour at friendly **Komsomolsk-na-Amure** (p590)

History

The Far East is Russia's 'wild east', where hardened Cossacks in the early 17th century – and young Soviets (and Gulag camp prisoners) in the 20th – came to exploit the region's untapped natural resources, such as gold of the Kolyma, diamonds of Sakha and oil off Sakhalin Island. It was just a big chunk of Siberia until the Soviets anointed it a separate administrative entity in the 1920s. Geographers still consider most of the Far East part of Siberia. Yet it has always felt more distant, more challenging, more god-forsaken than points west.

Locally, much ado is made of Anton Chekhov's trip through the Far East to Sakhalin in 1890; of Bolshevik Marshal Vasily Blyukher's victory in the last major battle of the Russian Civil War at Volochaevka outside Khabarovsk; and of Count Nikolay Muravyov-Amursky, the 19th-century governor of Eastern Siberia who did much to open up the Far East and consolidate Russian control of the Left (north) Bank of the Amur River. Less is made of the Russo-Japanese War, which humiliated Russia and ended with Japan taking the southern half of Sakhalin Island in 1905 (see p634); the USSR got it back after WWII.

China and the USSR had their diplomatic bumps too, including an outright battle over an unremarkable river island near Khabarovsk in 1969. In June 2005 Russia and China finally settled a four-decade dispute over their 4300km border by splitting 50-50 the Bolshoy Ussurysky and Tarabarov Islands near the junction of the Amur and Ussuri Rivers, outside Khabarovsk.

EASTERN TRANS-SIBERIAN

Most travellers that make it this far east stick within this region, which extends along the final 40 hours or so of railroad that runs through anonymous villages north of the Chinese border, over the Amur River to lively Khabarovsk, and south through Primorsky Territory, ending at Vladivostok, just 100 miles from the North Korea border.

Natural attractions are generally more rewarding in regions further north, but Khabarovsk and Vladivostok are the region's most lively cities, with sushi bars, big business and plenty of fashionistas pounding summer sidewalks, while Blagoveshchensk has the region's most impressive tsarist architecture.

Chekhov was particularly pleased with his river ride to Blagoveshchensk and Khabarovsk during his famous 1890 trip across Russia. He wrote, 'It is quite beyond my powers to describe the beauties of the banks of the Amur.'

Blagoveshchensk

Благовещенск

☎4162 / POP 210,000 / ⊙MOSCOW +6HR

It's sometimes easy to forget where you are out here – in deepest Asia – until you find a place like this modest border town, 110km south of the Trans-Siberian and across the Amur River from China. The mix of scattered tsarist-era buildings and Chinese tourists walking past Lenin statues is fascinating. On hot days, locals share the river, jumping in from beaches on opposite shores.

The border is peaceful now, but once was tense. In 1900, Cossacks, seeking to avenge European deaths in the Chinese Boxer Rebellion, slaughtered thousands of Chinese people in the city. In the '60s and early '70s, Blagoveshchensk (meaning 'good news') endured round-the-clock propaganda being pumped over the river. One elderly local explained, 'It was awful. Their embankment was lined with pictures of Mao, and we listened to broadcasts – all in Chinese. We were scared.'

Sights & Activities

A good starting point for a wander around is on the riverfront at pl Lenina, where teen skaters take over the Lenin statue steps and tots take over the fountains. From here a short walk west along the pleasant riverside promenade, or along parallel ul Lenina, takes you to yawning pl Pobedy.

Tsarist-Era Buildings HISTORICAL BUILDING

At the regional museum, pick up the darling *Stary Blagoveshchensk* (Old Blagoveshchensk) map (R10, in Russian) to plot your own walking tour of the dozens of glorious tsarist-era buildings on shady backstreets around the centre. The most impressive buildings are on ul Lenina within a few blocks of the museum and on and around nearby pl Pobedy. Anton Chekhov came through Blagoveshchensk during his epic trip through the Far East in 1890 (and headed straight to a Japanese prostitute, as recounted luridly in his later-published letters). A **bust** commemorating Chekhov's visit is on the facade of the lovely Institute of Geology and Wildlife Management building on pl Pobedy.

Amur Regional Museum MUSEUM
(Амурский Облотной Музей; ul Lenina 165; admission R120; ⏲10am-6pm Tue-Sun) A short walk northwest of pl Pobedy, this museum is housed in a former tsarist-era trading house and Soviet-era HQ for the Communist Youth League (Komsomol). Inside are 26 halls, with plenty of interesting photos, 1940s record players and a meteor that fell in 1991 near Tynda. Russian-history buffs will enjoy the model of the 17th-century Cossack fortress in nearby Albazin and a painting depicting the Manchurian invasion of the fort in 1685. This battle swung control of the upper Amur to the Chinese for the next two centuries.

River Cruises BOAT TRIPS
One-hour daytime river cruises (per person R150) and longer evening disco cruises (R240) leave from a pier just east of pl Lenina from mid-May through September.

Sleeping & Eating

Hotel rates include breakfast unless otherwise indicated.

Yubileynaya HOTEL €€
(Юбилейная; ☎370 073; www.bighotel.ru; ul Lenina 108; s/d from R1700/2800; ❄@🛜) This 150-room beast overlooking the river won't win any beauty contests, but the location near pl Lenina is absolutely ideal. Rooms are simple spruced-up Soviet fare, while the international restaurant (mains R150 to R500), festooned with old beer posters, is more 21st-century.

Amur Hotel HOTEL €
(Гостиница Амур; ☎251 113; www.hotelamur.ru; ul Lenina 122; s with/without shower R1500/800, d from P1500; 🛜) The lovely-looking Amur, roughly opposite the Regional Museum, is tsarist on the outside but thoroughly Soviet on the inside, with shoebox-sized rooms, lino floors and narrow beds draped in gold satin. Fancier rooms include air-con and breakfast.

Zeya Hotel HOTEL €€
(Гостиница Зея; ☎539 996; www.hotelzeya.ru; ul Kalinina 8; s/d from R1700/2100; ❄@🛜) Zeya makes a valiant attempt to make Soviet rooms look cheery, but goes a bit over the top with the extra-frilly curtains and bedspreads. Twelve-hour rates available. It's near the river just west of pl Pobedy.

Tsentralnaya Pizzeria PIZZA €€
(Центральная Пиццерия; ul Lenina 115; pizzas R130-270; ❄🛜📝) If you can ignore the overpriced drinks, you'll be quite happy with the thin-crust pizza here, available by the half pie. Neighbouring sister Tsentalnaya Kofeynya focuses on coffee, cocktails and salads.

Khing An CHINESE €€
(Хинг Ан; ul Shevchenko 11; mains R200-400; ⏲10am-midnight; ❄📝) Among the many Chinese restaurants in Blagoveshchensk, this one stands out. On warm days locals amass on the outdoor patio. It's 200m west of pl Lenina.

Getting There & Away

Blagoveshchensk is 110km off the Trans-Siberian, reached via the branch line from Belogorsk. The **train station** is 4km north of the river on ul 50 Let Oktyabrya, the main north–south artery.

Trains heading east backtrack to Belogorsk on their way to Vladivostok (*kupe/platskartny* from R2300/2000, one day eight hours, odd-numbered days) and Khabarovsk (*kupe/platskartny* R2200/1000, 16 hours, even-numbered days). Heading west, trains serve Chita (*kupe/platskartny* R3800/1850, one day 13 hours, daily) and Tynda (*kupe/platskartny* R3400/1400, 16 hours, odd-numbered days).

Additional options are available from Belogorsk to the north or Bureya to the east. *Marshrutky* (fixed-route minibuses) connect Blagoveshchensk's **bus station** (cnr ul 50 let Oktyabrya & ul Krasnoarmeyska) with the train stations in Belogorsk (R250, two hours, almost hourly until early evening) and Bureya (R450, 3½ hours, five daily). Don't miss the awesome mosaic of Soviet *sportsmeny* (athletes) opposite the bus station.

The **River Terminal** (Речной Вокзал; ul Chaykovskogo 1), 500m east of the Druzhba Hotel, sends eight daily boats to Heihe, China (one-way/return R1075/1450, 15 minutes), where there's an evening train to Harbin. You'll need a Chinese visa and a multiple-entry Russian visa to return.

Birobidzhan Биробиджан

☎42622 / POP 80,000 / ⏲MOSCOW +7HR

Quiet and shady, Birobidzhan is the capital of the 36,000-sq-km Jewish Autonomous Region and is a couple of hours shy of Khabarovsk on the Tran-Siberian line (if you're heading east). Its concept has always been a bit more interesting than its reality (as evidenced by the quick influx of Jews coming to 'Stalin's Zion' in the 1930s, then leaving the undeveloped swamp just as quickly). Still, its sleepy provincial feel and riverside setting make it worth a half-day visit – more if the weather's good or if you want to explore the city's Jewish heritage.

The town is quite walkable. The main streets ul Lenina and partially pedestrian ul Sholom-Aleykhema parallel the tracks just a five-minute walk south on ul Gorkogo from the train station. The Bira River is another five minutes along.

History

The Soviet authorities conceived the idea of a homeland for Jews in the Amur region in the late 1920s and founded the Jewish Autonomous Region in 1934 with its capital at Birobidzhan (named for the meeting place of the Bira and Bidzhan Rivers). Most of the Jews came from Belarus and Ukraine, but also from the US, Argentina and even Palestine. The Jewish population never rose above 32,000, and dropped to 17,500 by the end of the 1930s, when growing anti-Semitism led to the ban of Yiddish and synagogues. The Jewish population rose gradually to about 22,000 by 1991, when Russia's Jews began emigrating en masse to Israel. The Jewish population has levelled off at 3000 to 4000 these days.

Sights & Activities

Jewish Birobidzhan CULTURAL HERITAGE
A few vestiges of Birobidzhan's Jewish heritage remain. Note the Hebrew signs on the **train station**, the lively **farmers market** (ul Sholom-Aleykhema) and the **post office** on the riverfront at the southern terminus of ul Gorkogo. On the square in front of the train station a **statue** commemorates Birobidzhan's original Jewish settlers, and on the pedestrian stretch of ul Sholom-Aleykhema is a quirky **statue of Sholem Aleichem** (Памятник Шолом-Алейхему; *Fiddler on the Roof* was based on Aleichem's stories).

A five-minute walk west from the centre on ul Lenina is a complex containing Birobidzhan's Jewish culture centre, **Freid** (Общинный центр Фрейд; ☎41 531, 8-924-642 8731; ul Lenina; ⊙9am-5pm Mon-Fri), and a synagogue with a small **Jewish history museum** (⊙by appointment) inside. Call or ask around for Rabbi Roman Isakovich, who will give you a tour of the complex, talk local history or find you a souvenir yarmulke (skullcap).

Regional Museum MUSEUM
(Краеведческий Музей; ul Lenina 25; admission R100; ⊙10am-6pm Wed-Thu, 9am-5pm Fri-Sun) Next door to Freid, this museum has an excellent exhibit on the arrival of Jewish settlers to Birobidzhan in the 1930s, plus boars and bears and a minidiorama of the Volochaevka civil war battle (akin to Khabarovsk's bigger one, but here blood pours from a 3-D dead guy's head).

Sleeping & Eating

For apartments in the R1500 to R2000 range, call one of the numbers advertising Квартры (apartments) on the building opposite the train station.

Resting rooms HOSTEL €
(Комнаты Отдыха, komnaty otdykha; ☎91 605; Train Station; dm/lyux R600/2000) The simple train-station rooms are probably the best option for a quick visit. There are discounts for 12-hour stays and it's an easy walk from the centre.

Hotel Vostok HOTEL €€
(Гостиница Восток; ☎65 330; ul Sholom-Aleykhema 1; s/d R1800/2600; ❄) Birobidzhan's central hotel has a good location next to the farmers market.

Eating & Drinking

Teatralny SHASHLYK €
(Театральный; pr 60 let SSSR 14; mains R200-300; ❄) An average indoor Chinese restaurant during the cold months, in the warm months its vast outdoor patio near the river is *the* place to eat shashlyki (meat kebabs) and guzzle draught beer (R60). It's behind Birobidzhan's gargantuan Philharmonic Hall.

David Trade Centre RUSSIAN €€
(Торговый Центр Давид; cnr pr 60 let SSSR & ul Gorkogo; mains R150-750) The best overall choice for a bite or a drink on its streetside patio, it offers fine dining, fast food and a happening nightclub (admission R200) all under one roof. It's cater-cornered to the Philharmonic.

Prime Internet Bar BAR €
(Прайм Интернет Бар; pr 60 let SSSR; ⊙24hr; ❄📶) Wi-fi and internet use here are free if you order a drink. It's in front of the Philharmonic.

LIFE IN A SOVIET EXPERIMENT

'How can anyone live here?' is the nagging question from many outsiders who can't fathom enduring life at –50°C in winter. Another one, some argue, is '*Should* anyone be living here?'

The Soviet experiment – of (forcibly) relocating millions to develop the Far East and Siberia – has yielded a bizarre network of disconnected cities across one of the world's most forbidding regions. Russia gets colder as you move east, yet population density never falters. During the Soviet era, populations of cities such as Yakutsk and Khabarovsk rose 1000%; Komsomolsk, meanwhile, grew from an empty riverside meadow into an industrial city of more than a quarter million.

That'd be impressive if productivity and expenses were on par with European Russia. But during winters that can stretch over half a year, productivity suffers and expenses go way up, requiring bail-out subsidies.

Siberian Curse by Fiona Hill and Clifford Gaddy is a fascinating look at Russia's 'temperature per capita'. It suggests that much of Russia is simply too cold and that overpopulated areas in the Far East burden the national economy. Of course the tsars sent the first Russians this far, but the outposts were more strategic – nothing like the mass cities developed later. The authors feel a partial migration to the *materik* (or 'mainland', as locals here sometimes refer to European Russia) needs to be encouraged, with migrant workers in the east during summer (as happens with Canada's north).

If you stop off at purpose-built towns along the Baikal-Amur Mainline (Baikalo-Amurskaya Magistral; BAM), such as Novy Urgal, or make it further north to Magadan (which has lost over a third of its population since the Soviet Union fell), it's tempting to surmise that the whole region is in decline. The truth is far more chequered. Busy Vladivostok will host the high-profile Asia-Pacific Economic Cooperation (APEC) summit in 2012, and Sakhalin Island is running wild in oil revenue. Even remote Yakutsk is seeing a surge in population, due largely to income from diamonds and gold in the area.

One local told us, 'See these mountains, these rivers? Moscow doesn't have anything like this. I was born here and I want to die here.'

Getting There & Away

Coming from the west on the Trans-Siberian, you can easily stop off, have a look and grab a late train or bus for Khabarovsk.

All trans-Siberian trains stop here, but if you're heading to Khabarovsk, it's cheaper on the *elektrichka* (suburban train; R300, three hours, three daily); a *platskartny* seat on other trains runs to R500.

You can also catch *marshrutky* to Khabarovsk (R250, three hours, hourly until 6pm) from beside the train station.

Khabarovsk Хабаровск

4212 / POP 590,000 / MOSCOW +7HR

The Far East's most pleasant surprise – and a welcome break after days of relentless taiga on the train – Khabarovsk boasts a dreamy riverside setting, vibrant nightlife and broad boulevards lined with pretty tsarist-era buildings. Unlike so many places, the city has developed its riverside in the public interest. It has a great strolling area with multicoloured tiles, parks, monuments and walkways. A one-day stop is easily filled looking around.

It's hot in summer, but winter temperatures give it the unglamorous title of 'world's coldest city of over half a million people.' A dazzling display of **ice sculptures** occupy central pl Lenina from January until the spring thaw. Khabarovsk's City Day is a good time to visit – it's 31 May, or the closest Saturday.

History

Khabarovsk was founded in 1858 as a military post by Eastern Siberia's governor-general, Count Nikolai Muravyov (later Muravyov-Amursky), during his campaign to take the Amur back from the Manchus. It was named after the man who got the Russians into trouble with the Manchus in the first place, 17th-century Russian explorer Yerofey Khabarov.

The Trans-Siberian Railway arrived from Vladivostok in 1897. During the Russian Civil War (1920), the town was occupied by Japanese troops. The final Bolshevik victory in the Far East was at Volochaevka, 45km west.

In 1969, Soviet and Chinese soldiers fought a bloody hand-to-hand battle over little Damansky Island in the Ussuri River. Since 1984, tensions have eased. Damansky and several other islands have been handed back to the Chinese.

Sights & Activities

Walking is the main activity in Khabarovsk. Three good spots are the **riverfront**, **Dinamo Park** and **ul Muravyova-Amurskogo** with its impressive turn-of-the-20th-century architecture. Some buildings to look out for on the latter are the striking red-and-black-brick **Far Eastern State Research Library** (Библиотека Дальне-Восточного Иследоьания; ul Muravyova-Amurskogo 1), built from 1900 to 1902; the mint-green Style Moderne (Russian take on art nouveau) **Tsentralny Gastronom** (ul Muravyova-Amurskogo 9), built in 1895 and topped by a statue of Mercury; and the former **House of Pioneers** (Дом Пионеров; Dom Pionerov; ul Muravyova-Amurskogo 17).

No place in the Far East asks more for its museums, so it might be worth just sticking with its best – the newly expanded Territorial Museum.

Khabarovsk Territorial Museum MUSEUM
(ul Shevchenko 11; admission R330; ⏲10am-6pm, closed Mon & last Fri of month) Located in an evocative 1894 red-brick building, this museum contains a far-better-than-average look into native cultures and a full-on panorama of the snowy 1922 civil war battle at Volochaevka – look for the dead dude in a hut minus an arm and note the Trans-Siberian whizzing by to the south of the battle site on Volochaevka Hill. You can actually spot Volochaevka Hill from the train some 30km west of Khabarovsk. Also here is an iconic painting of Count Muravyov-Amursky signing the 1858 Treaty of Aigun, which gave the left bank of the Amur to the Russians. The **new building** has a wing dedicated to the Amur River, with lots of live fish in tanks and some impressive stuffed giant koluga sturgeon. No Gulag coverage, though the nearby prison population was bigger than the city's in the '30s.

Amur River Cruise BOAT TRIPS
(River boat landing; admission day/evening R250/350) Vital to Khabarovsk's rise, the Amur River can be seen on (at times rollicking) party boats. Cruises on the *Moskva-80* depart every two hours from 12.30pm to 12.30am, provided enough customers show up.

Military History Museum MUSEUM
(Военно-исторический музей; ☎326 350; ul Shevchenko 20; admission R150; ⏲10am-5pm Tue-Sun) If you didn't get enough war history in the Territorial Museum, add a stop at this four-room frenzy of battleaxes, guns, knives and busts and photos of moustached heroes of past conflicts. Lined up in the back courtyard are army trucks, cannons, tanks, rockets, a MiG-17 fighter plane and a luxury officers-only rail carriage dating from 1926.

Archaeology Museum MUSEUM
(Музей Археологии; ul Turgeneva 86; admission R220; ⏲10am-6pm Tue-Sun) The highlights of the small Archaeology Museum are the reproductions and diagrams of the wide-eyed figures found at the ancient Sikachi-Alyan petroglyphs.

Far Eastern Art Museum ART GALLERY
(Дальневосточный Художественный Музей; ul Shevchenko 7; admission R240; ⏲10am-7pm Tue-Sun) Lots of religious icons, Japanese porcelain and 19th-century Russian paintings are on display here.

Amur Fish Aquarium AQUARIUM
(Аквариальный Комплекс Рыббы Амура; Amursky bul 13a; admission R180; ⏲11am-5pm Wed-Sun) Spot gilled friends from the nearby Amur in tanks.

Tours

The most popular area tour offered by travel agents is to the interesting Nanai village of **Sikachi-Alyan**, where you can view the Sikachi-Alyan petroglyphs – stone carvings supposedly dating back 12,000 years. Hunting and fishing opportunities abound in the wild and woolly Khabarovsky *kray* (territory).

Dalgeo Tours TOURS
(☎318 829; www.dalgeo.com; ul Turgeneva 78; ⏲10am-7pm Mon-Fri) English-speaking director Olga is the best person to speak to about tours around Khabarovsk, although they get pricey (Baltika brewery tours US$66 per person; tours to Birobidzhan or Sikachi-Alyan are upward of US$250 per person). City walking tours are US$20 per hour.

Sergey Outfitter TOURS
(Велком; ☎735 990; www.sergoutfitter.com; ul Dzerzhinskogo 24; ⏲9am-7pm Mon-Sat) Burly Sergey Khromykh is your man if you are looking to do some hunting or fishing in the vast wilderness of Khabarovsk Territory or elsewhere in the Far East.

Khabarovsk

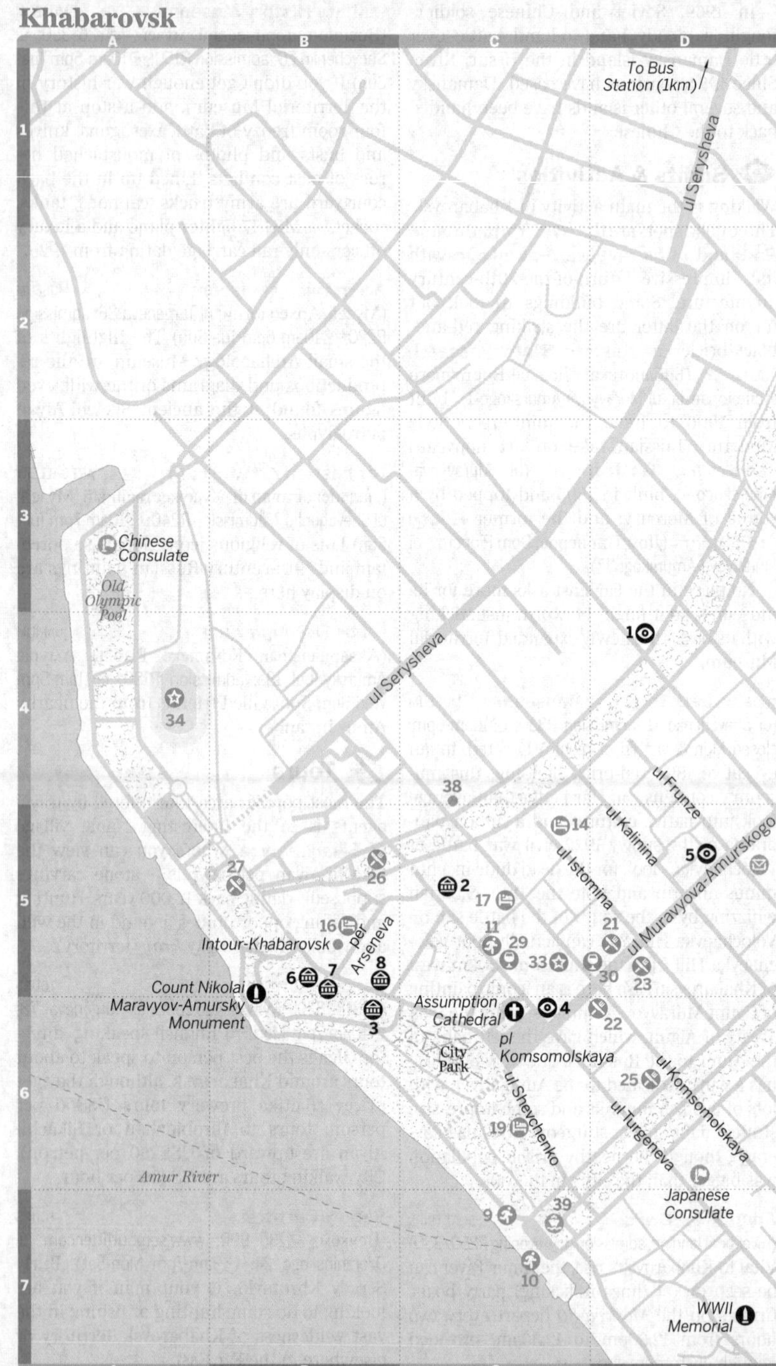

To Bus Station (1km)
ul Serysheva
Chinese Consulate
Old Olympic Pool
34
ul Serysheva
1
38
ul Frunze
14
ul Kalinina
ul Istomina
5
ul Muravyova-Amurskogo
27
26
2
17
16
Intour-Khabarovsk
per Arseneva
11
29
21
6
7
8
33
30
23
Count Nikolai Maravyov-Amursky Monument
3
Assumption Cathedral
4
22
pl Komsomolskaya
City Park
25
ul Komsomolskaya
ul Shevchenko
ul Turgeneva
19
Amur River
Japanese Consulate
9
39
10
WWII Memorial

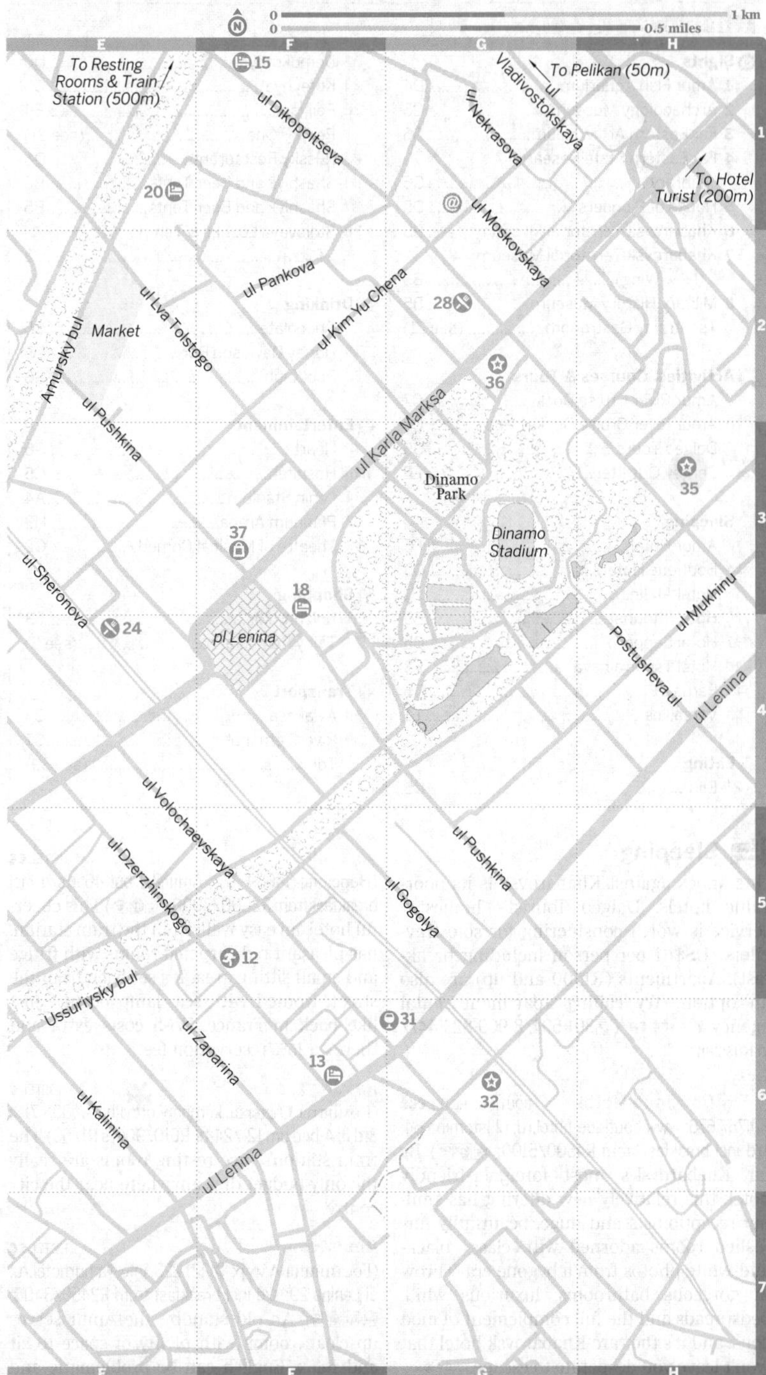
0
1 km
0
0.5 miles
To Resting Rooms & Train Station (500m)
To Pelikan (50m)
To Hotel Turist (200m)
ul Dikopoltseva
ul Vladivostokskaya
ul Nekrasova
ul Moskovskaya
ul Pankova
ul Kim Yu Chena
ul Lva Tolstogo
Market
Amursky bul
ul Pushkina
ul Karla Marksa
Dinamo Park
Dinamo Stadium
ul Sheronova
pl Lenina
ul Mukhinu
Postusheva ul
ul Lenina
ul Volochaevskaya
ul Dzerzhinskogo
ul Gogolya
ul Pushkina
Ussuriysky bul
ul Zaparina
ul Kalinina
ul Lenina
15
20
28
36
35
37
18
24
12
31
13
32

Khabarovsk

Sleeping

One knock against Khabarovsk is its poor-value hotels. Dalgeo Tourist's homestay service is worth considering for solo travellers (US$61 per person including breakfast). Apartments (R1500 and up) are also an option. Try calling apartment rental agency **Kvartira** (☎301 504, 8-909-823 4477, in Russian).

TOP CHOICE **Boutique Hotel** BOUTIQUE HOTEL €€€
(☎767 676; www.boutique-hotel.ru; ul Istomina 64; s/d incl breakfast from R4500/5100; ❄@🛜) By far Khabarovsk's most foreigner-friendly hotel, this relatively new offering has smiling receptionists and huge, beautifully furnished rooms adorned with classy black-and-white photos from a bygone era. Throw in gorgeous bathrooms, luxurious white bedspreads and the full complement of mod cons, and it's the rare Khabarovsk hotel that won't leave you desperate to escape.

Versailles HOTEL €€
(Версаль; ☎659 222; Amursky bul 46a; s/d incl breakfast from R2000/3000; ❄@🛜) This cheerful hotel, an easy walk from the train station, has pleasant red-carpeted rooms with fridge and small sitting area. It's set back from the street, fronted with seal lamp posts – just like back in France. Wi-fi costs extra and there's a 15% reservation fee.

Resting rooms HOSTEL €
(Комнаты Отдыха, komnaty otdykha; ☎383 710; 3rd fl; 4-bed dm 12-/24-hr R610/900, s R1250) The train station's nice resting rooms are really the only budget digs anywhere near the city centre.

Amur Hotel HOTEL €€
(Гостиница Амур; ☎221 223; info@amurhotel.ru; ul Lenina 29; s/d incl breakfast from R2450/3400; ⊖❄@🛜) An old standby, the Amur serves up clean rooms with plenty of space to sit and relax. English can be problematic and

it's a long stroll to the riverfront action, but it's still an excellent choice in this price range. The booking fee is 22%.

Parus HISTORIC HOTEL €€€
(Парус; 327 270; www.hotel-parus.com; ul Shevchenko 5; s/d incl breakfast from R5200/6100;) Part of a century-old brick building near the water, the 80-room Parus sure makes a grand entrance – with chandeliers, iron staircase and reading room. Rooms are also overdone, but sizeable and with expensive Italian furniture and flat-screen TVs.

Hotel Afalina HOTEL €€
(Гостиница Афалина; 211 260; afalina-treld@rambler.ru; ul Dikopoltseva 80; s/d from R3400/3600, 12hr R2200/2500;) Twelve-hour rates and proximity to the train station make this a good choice if you are arriving late into Khabarovsk. Rooms are on the small side but stylish with flat-screen TVs and futuristic shower stalls in the bathroom. English spoken.

Hotel Tsentralnaya HOTEL €€
(Гостиница Центральная; 303 300; ul Pushkina 52; s R1700-2300, d R1900-2500;) It's been years since the staff would let us see a room (maybe they were burned by Paul Theroux when he stayed here while researching *The Great Railway Bazaar*), but you can expect the standard diet of lightly renovated Soviet fare. Half the 200 rooms look over pl Lenina. A booking fee of 25% applies.

Hotel Intourist HOTEL €€
(Гостиница Интурист; 312 313; Amursky bul 2; s/d from R2750/3050;) Teeming with tour groups, this big Bolshevik still breathes as if it's 1975. Service is so-so and the cheaply renovated rooms are closet-sized (but do have remarkable river views on upper floors). You're paying for the prime location and, apparently, the two English TV channels. Wi-fi costs extra and the booking fee is 25%. The entrance is on per Arseneva.

Hotel Sapporo HOTEL €€€
(Гостиница Саппоро; 304 290; www.sapporo-hotel.ru; ul Komsomolskaya 79; s/d incl breakfast from R4300/5000;) Japanese-run mid-range hotel with top-end prices.

Hotel Turist HOTEL €€
(Гостиница Турист; 439 674; www.habtour.ru; ul Karla Marksa 67; s/d/tr incl breakfast R1860/2520/3000;) This Soviet special can often find a roommate for solo travellers looking to split costs; 25% booking fee.

Eating

On nice days, visit the **shashlyk and beer tents** along Amursky bul and at the northern end of the riverside promenade. Expect to pay R200 for a kebab and R80 for a beer. A 2011 law banned beer sales along the spruced-up southern portion of the promenade.

TOP CHOICE **Stolovaya Lozhka & Tempo Pizza** RUSSIAN €
(Столовая Ложка и Темпо Пицца; ul Dikopoltseva 29; meals R200-300; stolovaya 9am-9pm, pizzeria 10am-midnight;) One of a host of upmarket *stolovye* (canteens) that have been cropping up all over Russia, this one boasts an outdoor beer patio and is twinned with a pizzeria selling by the slice (R60 to R90).

Pepper One ITALIAN €
(ul Muravyova-Amurskogo 9; pizzas for 2 R300-400; 10am-2am;) Khabarovsk is famous for its pizzerias and this is one of the best. It has decent pasta and coffee too, plus groovy tunes.

Kofeynya CAFÉ €€
(Кофейня; ul Muravyova-Amurskogo 18; mains R120-350; 8am-midnight;) A snappy little café with wonderful omelettes, bliny (pancakes) and other affordable breakfast fare, along with heartier mains and its trademark coffee.

Russky Restaurant RUSSIAN €€€
(Русский Ресторан; 306 587; Ussuriysky bul 9; mains R300-750; noon-1am;) The kitsch factor at this Russian folk themed restaurant is high but the food is tasty. Traditional music that plays most nights from 8pm cheekily costs R200 per head.

Demokratiya CAFÉ €€
(Демократия; ul Muravyova-Amurskogo 12; mains R150-400; noon-1am;) Join hipsters drinking home brew in this low-lit space. It has good salads and business lunches from R140.

Blin FAST FOOD €
(Блин; Lotus Shopping Centre basement, ul Muravyova-Amurskogo 5; bliny R50-75; 10am-10pm) Locals queue up for the bliny here.

Pelikan SUPERMARKET €
(Пеликан; ul Vladivostokskaya 61; 24hr) There is another **branch** in the Dom Byta shopping centre at ul Sheronova 92.

Drinking

Harley Davidson Bar BAR
(ul Komsomolskaya 88; 24hr;) Features nightly live classic rock, 10 brews on tap, tattooed

bartenders and a looooong wooden bar – the kind you can slide a beer mug down. Weekend after-hours parties are legion.

Pool Club PUB
(ul Lenina 33) More Irish pub than pool bar, this is a great place to warm up for a night out, with an expansive menu of pub grub and suds.

Chocolate CAFÉ, LOUNGE BAR
(ul Turgeneva 74; mains R400-900; ⏲24hr;) A café with a pricey menu of slick international snacks (fajitas, burgers, brownies) by day, it becomes a prime party spot after hours.

☆ Entertainment

Khabarovsk is most definitely a party town, with arguably the best clubs east of the Volga.

Hospital NIGHTCLUB
(Госпиталь; ul Komsomolskaya 79; http://hospitalclub.ru; cover R300-1000; ⏲Fri & Sat) One of Russia's top clubs, with several packed dance chambers and a consistent line-up of top DJ talent from Russia and abroad. YouTube has highlights.

Heart NIGHTCLUB
(ul Sheronova 7; cover R400-600 Fri & Sat, free Thu; ⏲Thu-Sat) Heart is not far behind Hospital in the Far East club hierarchy.

Platinum Arena ICE HOCKEY
(Платинум Арена; ☎233 216; ul Dikopoltseva 12) This is the home arena for Khabarovsk's ice hockey team, the Amur Tigers, a hot ticket from October to March.

Lenin Stadium FOOTBALL
(Стадион Ленина; Riverfront Sports Complex; tickets R150) Home to Khabarovsk's first-division football team, SKA-Energiya.

Theatre of Musical Comedy THEATRE
(Театр Музыкальной Комедии, ☎211 196; ul Karla Marksa 64; tickets R80-800) Funny operettas run from November to April; big musical acts run from May to October. There's also the occasional heavy metal concert (Ronnie James Frickin' Dio started his 2005 tour here).

Shopping

Tainy Remesla SOUVENIRS
(Тайны Ремесла; ul Muravyova-Amurskogo 17; ⏲10am-7pm) This is the best souvenir shop in town, located in the old House of Pioneers building.

Knizhny Mir MAPS
(Книжный Мир; ul Karla Marksa 37; ⏲9am-8pm) Stock up on your Far East maps here; it has the best selection outside of Yakutsk. A compact map of the city centre in English sells for R60.

ℹ Information

Internet Access & Post

Port@l (Порт@л; ul Moskovskaya 7; per hr R75; ⏲10am-10pm)

Post office (Главпочтамт; ul Muravyova-Amurskogo 28; per hr R100; ⏲internet 9am-8pm, post 8am-10pm Mon-Fri, 9am-6pm Sat & Sun)

Medical Services

The Hotel Intourist has a doctor in Room 132.

Travel Agencies

Intour-Khabarovsk (Интур-Хабаровск; ☎312 119; www.intour-khabarovsk.com; Hotel Intourist, Amursky bul 2; ⏲10am-6pm Mon-Fri) Not recommended, but it hands out a good guide to the city in English and an OK free map.

ℹ Getting There & Away

Most travel agents book train or air tickets for a modest commission. The best booking agent is **Aviakasa** (Авиакасса; Amursky bul 5; ⏲8.30am-8pm Mon-Sat, 9am-6pm Sun) because of its generous opening hours.

Air

The **airport** is 7km east of the train station. Airlines have offices at the airport; otherwise, check the company website for more information.

Aeroflot (www.aeroflot.com)
Asiana (www.flyasiana.com)
China Southern (www.csair.com)
Korean Air (www.koreanair.com)
Ir-Aero (www.iraero.ru)
S7 (www.s7.ru)
SAT (www.satairlines.ru)
Transaero (www.transaero.com)
VIM Airlines (www.vim-avia.com)
Vladivostok Air (www.vladavia.ru)
Yakutia Airlines (www.yakutia.aero)

Boat

Between late May and late October, hydrofoils leave five days a week at 7.30am from the **river terminal** (Речной Вокзал; Ussuriysky bul; ⏲8am-7pm) for Komsomolsk-na-Amure (from R800, six hours) and Nikolaevsk-na-Amure (from 4000, 19 hours). There is also a whirlwind of competing boats offering morning and evening departures to nearby Fuyuan, China (one way R350, 90 minutes). A good company is **Tor** (☎584 666).

Bus

The **bus station** (Автовокзал; ul Voronezhskaya 19), 500m north of the train station (go by tram or bus 6), sends hourly buses to Komsomolsk (R430, six hours) and hourly *marshrutky* to Birobidzhan until 6pm.

Train

The **train station** is lovely but there is little in the area grocery wise. Note that almost all trains to Vladivostok are overnight.

Note that the westbound/eastbound 1/2 Rossiya train between Moscow and Vladivostok is significantly more expensive than all other trains, and only slightly faster. The 7/8 train between Novosibirsk and Vladivostok is also relatively expensive.

For Birobidzhan, take any westbound train or a cheaper *elektrichka* (R300, three hours, three daily).

Getting Around

From Khabarovsk's train station, about 3.5km northeast of the waterfront, bus 4 goes to pl Komsomolskaya (board opposite the station and head southeast) and trams 1 and 2 go near pl Lenina.

From the **airport**, 9km east of the centre, trolleybus 1 goes to pl Komsomolskaya along ul Muravyova-Amurskogo and bus 35 goes to the train station (25 minutes) and bus station. A taxi to the centre from the airport is R500; usually R300 or R400 the other way.

Trolleybuses and trams cost R15, *marshrutky* R20 to R30.

GETTING CHINESE VISAS IN THE FAR EAST

Foreigners can get Chinese visas at consulates in **Khabarovsk** (4212-302 590; http://khabarovsk.china-consulate.org; Southern Bldg, Lenin Stadium 1; 11am-1pm Mon, Wed & Fri) and **Vladivostok** (4232-495 037; Hotel Gavan, ul Kyrgina 3; 9.30am-12.30pm Mon, Wed & Thu).

A one-month tourist visa for Europeans costs R900/1500/1800 for one-/three-/five-day processing. Americans pay R4000 (10-day processing only). You'll need a letter of invitation, application form (available on the Khabarovsk Consulate website) and copies of your immigration card, latest hotel registration and Russian visa. Travel agencies in Vladivostok and Khabarovsk may be able to assist with Chinese visas.

Vladivostok Владивосток

4232 / POP 610,000 / MOSCOW + 7HR

At first look, Vladivostok is something like 'Russia's San Francisco' – a real stunner, with pointed mountains springing up above a network of bays, most strikingly the crooked dock-lined Golden Horn Bay (named for its likeness to Istanbul's). Closer up, it can be a little grey, with Soviet housing blocks squeezed between new condos and century-old mansions. But it's a great place to kick off or finish a trans-Siberian trip – however, be warned: leg muscles not used to the ups and downs of hilly streets will get more sore than a butt on the Trans-Siberian.

Big changes arrived in Vladivostok thanks to the 2012 Asian Pacific Economic Conference (APEC). Timing wise, June can often be grey and wet, while September and October are the nicest, sunniest months (another thing Vladivostok has in common with San Francisco). Vladivostok's City Day is 2 July, or the closest Saturday to it.

History

Founded in 1860, Vladivostok (meaning 'To Rule the East') became a naval base in 1872. *Tsarevitch* Nicholas II turned up in 1891 to inaugurate the new Trans-Siberian rail line. By the early 20th century, Vladivostok teemed with merchants, speculators and sailors of every nation in a manner more akin to Shanghai or Hong Kong than to Moscow. Koreans and Chinese, many of whom had built the city, accounted for four out of every five of its citizens.

After the fall of Port Arthur in the Russo-Japanese War of 1904–05, Vladivostok took on an even more crucial strategic role, and when the Bolsheviks seized power in European Russia, Japanese, Americans, French and English poured ashore here to support the tsarist counterattack. Vladivostok held out until 25 October 1922, when Soviet forces finally marched in and took control – it was the last city to fall.

In the years to follow, Stalin deported or shot most of the city's foreign population. Closed from 1958 to 1992, Vladivostok opened up with a bang – literally (Mafia shoot-outs were a part of early business deals) – in the '90s, and is only starting to settle down in recent years.

Sights & Activities

CENTRAL VLADIVOSTOK

On tree-lined streets around the city centre you'll find plenty of tsarist-era buildings from

TRANSPORT CONNECTIONS FROM KHABAROVSK

DESTINATION	MAIN TRAINS SERVING DESTINATION* & FREQUENCY	RAIL PRICE (PLATSKARTNY/KUPE)
Beijing	N/A	N/A
Blagoveshchensk	**35 (odd-numbered days)**, 385 (even-numbered days)	R1000/2200
Irkutsk	1 (odd-numbered days), 7 (even-numbered days), **43 (odd-numbered days)**, 133 (odd-numbered days), 239 (odd-numbered days, summer)	from R3100/7800
Komsomolsk	351 (daily), **667 (daily)**	from R925/1900
Magadan	N/A	N/A
Moscow	1 (odd-numbered days), **43 (odd-numbered days)**, 239 (odd-numbered days, summer)	from R5200/11,000
Neryungri (via Tynda)	325 (daily)	R2000/4000
Petropavlovsk-Kamchatsky	N/A	N/A
Seoul	N/A	N/A
Vladivostok	2 (odd-numbered days), **6 (daily)**, 8 (even-numbered days), 134 (odd-numbered days), 352 (daily), 386 (even-numbered days)	from R1000/2100
Yakutsk	N/A	N/A
Yuzhno-Sakhalinsk	N/A	N/A

*Trains originating in Khabarovsk in bold.

Vladivostok's first crazy incarnation a century past. The main areas for locals to mill about is **pl Bortsov Revolutsii** (on ul Svetlanskaya at the southern end of Okeansky pr) and **Sportivnaya Harbour**, near the west end of ul Fokina (aka 'the Arbat'). There you can find a popular beach and beer and shashlyk stands.

TOP CHOICE Funicular FUNICULAR
(Фуникулёр; ul Pushkinskaya; tickets R6; 7am-8pm) Vladivostok's favourite attraction may just be the smoothest-running operation in the Far East: the well-oiled **funicular railway** makes a fun 60-second ride up a 100m hill every few minutes. At the top, cross ul Sukhanova via the underpass to a great **lookout** over the bay. It's next to a **statue of Saints Cyril and Methodius** (inventors of the Cyrillic alphabet) on the campus of DVGTU.

The base of the funicular is about a 15-minute walk from the centre. Bus 164 goes to/from the top of the funicular from the corner of ul Aleutskaya and ul Svetlanskaya.

Arsenev Regional Museum MUSEUM
(Объединённый Краеведческий Музей Арсеньева; ul Svetlanskaya 20; admission R150; 9.30am-6pm Tue-Sun) Grey-haired ladies keep watch over every Russian museum in existence, but none do it more sweetly than at the interesting Arsenev Regional Museum, which dates from 1890. Exhibits are in Russian only, but it's still enjoyable for non-Russian speakers. On the 1st floor note the stuffed tiger and bear interlocked as if dancing; the 2nd floor is filled with great 19th-century photos of Vlad's early days, including a display of the Brynner family.

Primorsky Picture Gallery ART GALLERY
(Приморская Картинная Галерея; pr Partizanski 12; admission R50; 9am-6pm) Vladivostok's bipolar art museum's **original locale**

RAIL DURATION	AIRLINES SERVING DESTINATION	AIR PRICE (FROM R)	AIR DURATION & FREQUENCY
N/A	Vladivostok Air	5000	3hr, 2 weekly
16hr	Ir-Aero	5000	2hr, 3 weekly
58hr	Ir-Aero, Vladivostok Air	5000	3¾hr, almost daily
10hr	N/A	N/A	N/A
N/A	Ir-Aero, Vladivostok Air, Yakutia Airlines	8500	2½hr, 3 daily
5½ days	Aeroflot, Transaero, VIM Airlines, Vladivostok Air	12,500	8½hr, several daily
35hr	N/A	N/A	N/A
N/A	S7, SAT, Vladivostok Air	7000	2½hr, daily
N/A	Asiana, Vladivostok Air	8000	3hr, almost daily
11-15hr	Vladivostok Air	2500	1¼hr, daily
N/A	Ir-Aero, Vladivostok Air, Yakutia Airlines	13,000	2hr, daily Mon-Sat
N/A	S7, SAT, Vladivostok Air	3500	2hr, 3 daily

(ul Aleutskaya 12) has long been under renovation, but may be open by the time you read this. While most of the impressive collection is in storage, bits and pieces rotate through the annexe east of Park Provotsky. We saw the likes of da Vinci, Botticelli, Goya, Feshin, Kandinsky and Chagall when we dropped by.

S-56 Submarine MUSEUM

(Подводная Лодка С-56; Korabelnaya nab; admission R100; ⏲9am-8pm) Keeping with the aquatic theme, the S-56 submarine is worth a look. The first half is a ho-hum exhibit of badges and photos of men with badges (all in Russian). Keep going: towards the back a periscope provides a green-tinted view of what's going on outside, and you walk through a bunk room with Christmas-coloured torpedoes and an officers' lounge with a framed portrait of Stalin. Outside note the '14', marking the WWII sub's 'kills'.

Vladivostok Fortress Museum MUSEUM

(Музей Владивостокская Крепость; ul Batareynaya 4a; admission R120; ⏲10am-6pm) On the site of an old artillery battery overlooking Sportivnaya Harbour, this museum has cannons outside and a six-room indoor exhibit of photos and many, many guns inside. English explanations. Access is from ul Zapadnaya.

FREE **Artetage** ART GALLERY

(4th fl, ul Aksakovskaya 12; ⏲10am-6pm Tue-Fri, 11am-5pm Sat & Sun) DVGTU's humble modern art showcase has a few intriguing piss-takes at the country's red past, such as a bust of Lenin as a *novy russky* ('new Russian,' aka gangster).

FREE **Arka Art Gallery** ART GALLERY

(ul Svetlanskaya 5; ⏲11am-6pm Tue-Sat) Often interesting rotating exhibits down an alley with great graffiti.

Vladivostok

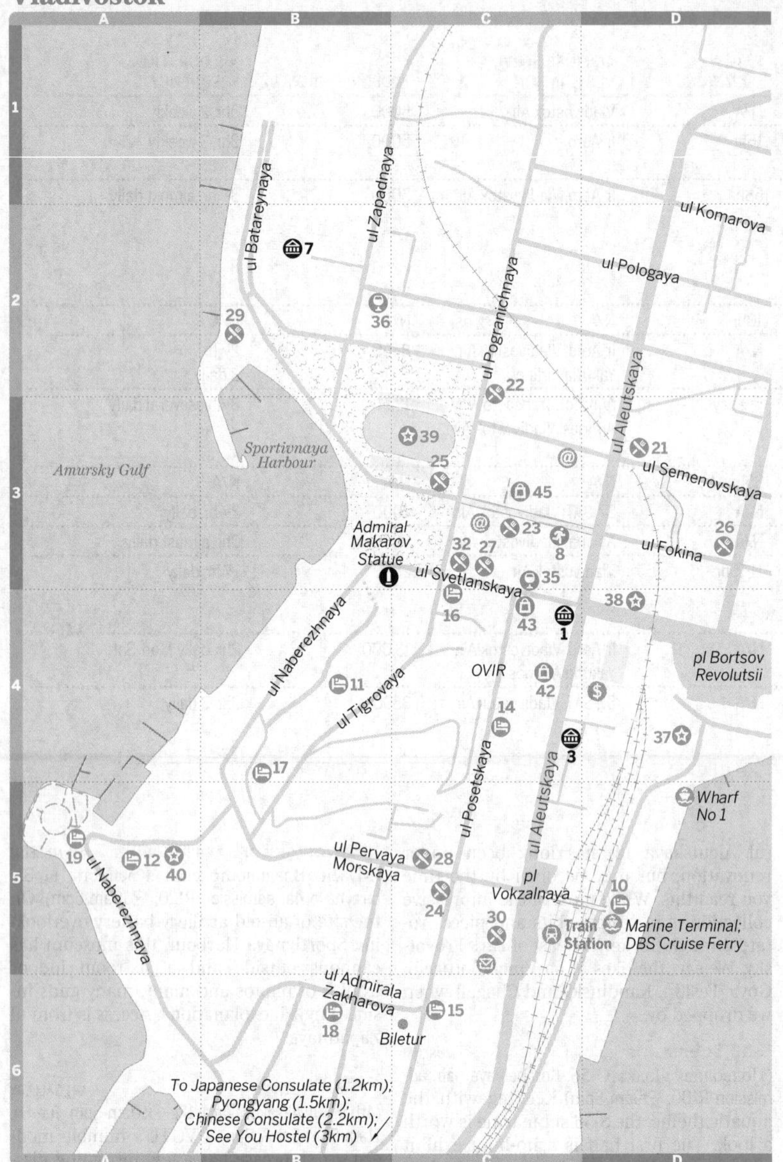

OUTER VLADIVOSTOK

Much of the water facing Vladivostok is quite polluted but it gets cleaner as you go north. Sunbathers can get on a northbound *elektrichka* and hop off at any beach that looks good – try Sedanka, where there are a few resorts with services. You'll find better swimming on Popov or Russky Islands.

Russky Island ISLAND

A fully militarised island for most of the past 150 years, this big island just offshore,

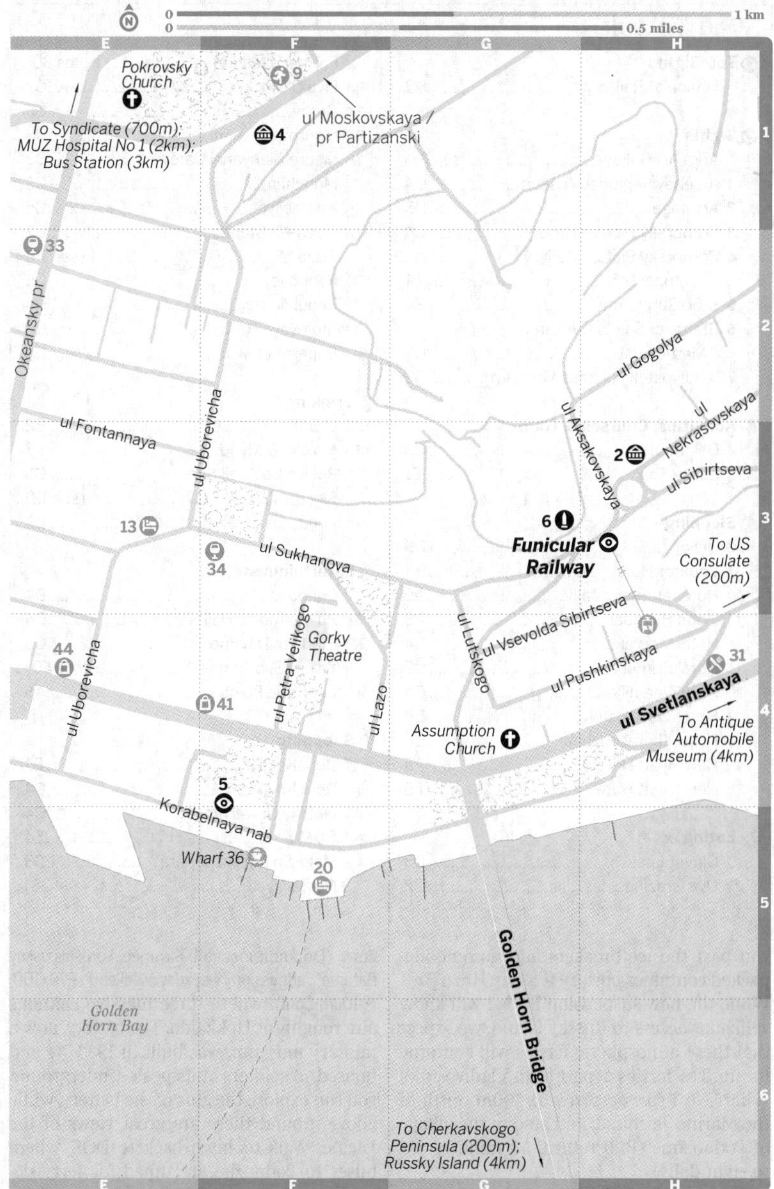

which only opened to foreigners in the early 2000s, has been completely reinvented as a business and – supposedly – tourism zone. The most obvious changes will have occurred near the new bridge's terminus on the island's eastern peninsula. The rest of the island should remain relatively quiet for the time being, despite the newly paved ring road. Voroshilov Battery sells a good map of the island (R50).

One of the highlights has always been the trip out to the island by car ferry, which takes

Vladivostok

Top Sights

Funicular Railway........H3

Sights

Arka Art Gallery........(see 27)
1 Arsenev Regional Museum........C4
2 Artetage........H3
3 Primorsky Picture Gallery........C4
4 Primorsky Picture Gallery (Temporary)........F1
5 S-56 Submarine........F4
6 Statue of Saints Cyril and Methodius........G3
7 Vladivostok Fortress Museum........B2

Activities, Courses & Tours

8 Dalintourist........C3
9 Lucky Tour........F1

Sleeping

10 Dialog........D5
11 Equator Hotel........B4
12 Hotel Amursky Zaliv........A5
13 Hotel Hyundai........E3
14 Hotel Moryak........C4
15 Hotel Primorye........C6
16 Hotel Versailles........C4
17 Hotel Vladivostok........B4
18 Hotel Zhemchuzhina........B6
19 New Hyatt Hotel........A5
20 New Hyatt Hotel........F5

Eating

21 Clover Leaf........D3
22 Dva Gruzina........C2
Farmer's Market........(see 30)
23 Five O'Clock........C3
24 Gutov........C5
25 Mauro Gianvanni........C3
26 Mauro Gianvanni Café........D3
27 München........C3
28 Nostalgiya........C5
29 Open-Air Stands........B2
Pizza M........(see 15)
30 Republic........C5
31 Republic........H4
32 Stolovaya No 1........C3
Supermarket........(see 30)

Drinking

33 El Dorado........E2
34 Moloko & Myod........F3
35 Rock's Cocktail Bar........C3
Sky Bar........(see 13)
36 Zima........B2

Entertainment

37 Cukoo........D4
38 Philharmonic Hall........D4
39 Stadium Dinamo........C3
Yellow Submarine........(see 40)
40 Zabriskie Point........A5

Shopping

41 Dom Knigi........F4
42 Dom Knigi........C4
43 Flotsky Univermag........C4
44 GUM........E4
45 Magazin Kollektsionera........C3
Nostalgiya........(see 28)

you past the ice breakers and automobile-packed container ports of **Golden Horn Bay**. While the new suspension bridge will allow vehicular access to Russky Island, we expect that these atmospheric ferries will continue to run. The ferries depart from Vladivostok's Wharf No 1 *(pervy prichal)*, 100m north of the Marine Terminal, and land in the village of Podnozhne (R90 return, 50 minutes, six to eight daily).

Buses await the ferries in Podnozhne. One goes west to **Rynda**, which has a couple of resorts and the best beaches (just hop out when you see one you like). The other heads east to 'DOF' (Dom Ofitseya Flota). From DOF it's a pleasant 5km walk through the taiga along a newly paved road to Russky Island's main sight, the **Voroshilov Battery** (Ворошиловской Батарее, Voroshilovskoy Bataree; admission weekday/weekend R70/100; ⏲10am-6pm), where three massive cannons aim roughly at Hokkaido. The battery, now a military museum, was built in 1933–34 and housed 75 soldiers at its peak. Underground you can explore the guts of the battery, while above ground there are great views of the Pacific. Walk or hitch back to DOF, where buses to Podnozhe are timed for ferry departures. Podnozhe has an old **monastery** to explore.

Antique Automobile Museum MUSEUM
(Музей Автомотостарины; http://automotomuseum.vl.ru; ul Sakhalinskaya 2a; admission R70; ⏲10am-6pm) If you're a bit of a car (or Soviet) nerd, the Antique Automobile Museum

is an absolute classic. A room full of Sovietmobiles (motorcycles too) from the 1930s to 1970s includes a 1948 M&M-green GAZ-20 'Pobeda' (Victory). If they start selling reproductions of the poster with an acrobat on a motorcycle holding a Stalin flag, send us one, please! Take bus 31 along ul Svetlanskaya and exit after it reaches ul Borisenko's end.

Fort No 7 FORTRESS

(Форт No 7; ☎8-950-282 7373; asomiw@mail.ru; admission 1/2-4/5+ people per person R500/250/150; ⏰10am-6pm Tue-Sun) Attention fort fans: Vladivostok teems with sprawling, rather unique subterranean forts built between the late 19th and early 20th century to ward off potential Japanese (or American) attacks. Sixteen protective forts (including four on Russky Island) and hundreds of artillery batteries and other military objects encircle Vladivostok. The best to visit is the hilltop Fort No 7, 14km north of the centre. It has 1.5km of tunnels, pretty much untouched since the last 400 soldiers stationed here left in 1923, although the NKVD later used it as an execution chamber. Views are good too. Admission includes a tour in Russian with eccentric 'fort commander' Grigory. To get here take bus 59 from the train station, get off at the last stop ('F Zarya'), and walk 20 minutes east on the road leading up the hill (you may have to ask directions). It's not a bad idea to let Grigory know you're coming before you arrive. This and other forts can be visited on a tour with Vladivostok Digger Club (p582).

Popov Island ISLAND

Just beyond Russky Island, Popov Island is better regarded for its beaches and filled with many guesthouses and dachas. You'll probably need to stay overnight if you head out here, as there is usually only one boat per day (R70, 1½ hours), departing from Vladivostok's first wharf. Ask at a travel agent if they can help with accommodation. Day trips are possible on days when there are two trips – check the schedule.

Tours

Vladivostok travel agents run a variety of city and regional tours, but they can get pricey.

FACELIFT FOR VLAD

Vladivostok's infrastructure was torn asunder and rebuilt for the big APEC summit on Russky Island in 2012. A few new developments are sure to catch your eye, starting with two giant suspension bridges: one across Golden Horn Bay to the previously difficult-to-access Cherkavskogo Peninsula, the other spanning more than 1km over the Eastern Bosphorus Strait to Russky Island. They are among the highest suspension bridges in the world – the pylons of the Russky Island bridge are a whopping 321m high.

The Russky Island bridge was just part of a massive development plan for the island that was to continue well beyond APEC. The convention centre used for APEC was slated to become part of the campus of an ambitious new university. The rough ring road around this sleepy island was being paved and widened at the time of research. New resorts and other tourist facilities were slated to follow.

Critics have lambasted the billions being spent on the project, and the island's several thousand residents are generally lukewarm. 'Why do we need this, why are we spending all this money,' wondered Vladivostok resident Yury Shvets, who has family on the island. 'They kicked my aunt off her land to build the new road and gave her nothing in return – just a token. She didn't even have a choice.' Many worry about the toll increased traffic and tourism will have on the island's pristine environment.

Officials retort that upgrades of the city's dilapidated infrastructure will drive economic growth. Other major APEC-related infrastructure projects include the newly expanded airport and the new highway from the airport to the city centre.

Downtown Vladivostok has seen its share of changes, as well. The city's beloved 'Arbat' (walking street), ul Fokina, and the promenade along the waterfront at Sportivnaya Harbour were given flashy upgrades, and all city sidewalks were ripped up and replaced wholesale. Fortunately, this has all been done without detracting too much from the turn-of-the-20th-century elegance of streets such as ul Aleutskaya and ul Svetlanskaya. Indeed, the bridge to Cherkavskogo Peninsula, dubbed the Golden Horn Bridge, adds character to the city, à la San Francisco, with which Vladivostok is often compared.

Heading outside of Vladivostok into Primorsky Territory, the most interesting tour is probably to **Sikhote-Alin Nature Reserve**, home to the Russian-American Siberian (Amur) Tiger project. It's a short flight or an 11-hour drive to Terney, where the 3440-sq-km forested reserve is headquartered. Chances of seeing a tiger are basically nonexistent, but the reserve is thick with birds, seals and other wildlife, and the scenery is incredible. Dalintourist and Lucky Tour run six-day trips here from about €1200 per person (including guide, transport, accommodation and meals) and can be combined with a stay at Lazovsky Nature Reserve east of Nakhodka, home to a population of about 20 tigers.

The Far East is all about its Amur tigers, and at **Gaivoron**, 235km north of Vladivostok, you can see a couple at the Russian Academy of Sciences biological research reserve, run by Dr Victor Yudin and his daughter. Tours by Vladivostok agents include about 90 minutes of tiger time, lunch and a four-hour ride each way. It's not possible to go independently.

Dalintourist TOURS
(☎410 903, 9-914-670 9109; www.dalintourist.ru; ul Fokina 8a; ⏰9am-7pm Mon-Fri, 10am-3pm Sat) Contact English-speaking Evgenya on the 2nd floor for help with area tours and info or to hire English-speaking guides (per hour R450).

Lucky Tour TOURS
(☎449 944; www.luckytour.com; ul Moskovskaya 1; ⏰9.30am-6pm Mon-Fri) Interesting tour to Khasan on the North Korea border; requires several weeks' notice.

Shamor.Info TOURS
(☎499 799; www.trans-siberian.su; ul Svetlanskaya 147; ⏰9am-6pm Mon-Fri) Formerly known as Vizit, covers the basics such as Sikhote-Alin and Gaivoron, and is generally responsive. Speak with Galina.

Vladivostok Digger Club TOURS
(☎552 086; www.vtc.ru/~vladdig; grom-2000@mail.ru) Club head Artur leads hour-long to full-day tours of Fort No 7 and other forts, batteries and the tunnels (some 3.5km long) that link them.

Sleeping

Two five-star **Hyatt hotels** were scheduled to open for APEC – one near the S-57 Submarine at Korabelnaya nab 6 and another on Cape Burny near the Amursky Zaliv hotel.

Apartments *(kvartiry)* and homestays are an option, although registration is usually not available if you go this route. **Dialog** (Диалог; ☎497 909; office 133, Marine Terminal; ⏰9am-8pm) offers studio apartments from R1000 per night and rooms from R500. **Vladivostok Guest House** (vladivostokhostel@yahoo.com) is really more of a homestay and you should get in touch in advance to arrange. **Lyudmila** (lyu-lomakina@yandex.ru) also runs a homestay.

TOP CHOICE **Hotel Primorye** HOTEL €€
(Гостиница Приморье; ☎411 422/582; www.hotelprimorye.ru; ul Posetskaya 20; s/d incl breakfast from R3200/3400, @📶) Considering quality and location, this is Vladivostok's best. Don't be fooled by the 'economy' tag on the cheaper rooms; they are beautifully appointed and have playful details like funny artwork and a clock. The higher-priced superiors offer more space, bigger beds, air-con and views of the warships in Golden Horn Bay. One fuss: rock-hard beds.

Hotel Hyundai HOTEL €€€
(Гостиница Хюндай; ☎402 233; www.hotelhyundai.ru; ul Semenovskaya 29; s/d incl breakfast from R6500/7500; ⊖❄@📶) Big with Asian business travellers, this 12-floor, 335-room tower is perfectly fine – big rooms with writing desk, satellite TV, modern bathroom and some sterling views on higher floors. Service can be clunky – surprising considering the room rates! There's a barber, Korean restaurant, sauna, gym and pool (nonguests R400).

See You Hostel HOSTEL €
(☎487 779; www.seeyouhostel.com; apt 133, ul Krygina 42a; dm R650; @📶) The Far East's only bona fide hostel is hidden in an apartment block near the southern end of the long peninsula running south from the train station. It features 16 beds in several rooms, free wi-fi and laundry at R100 per load. Check website for directions.

Hotel Moryak HOTEL €
(Гостиница Моряк; ☎499 499; www.hotelm.ru; ul Posetskaya 38; s/d from R1500/1700; ⊖❄) Terrific value considering its perfect location, this grey-brick yet cheerful place has an endearing lobby with a stuffed version of the hotel namesake – a sea man. The colourful rooms are compact but shipshape, with thin walls

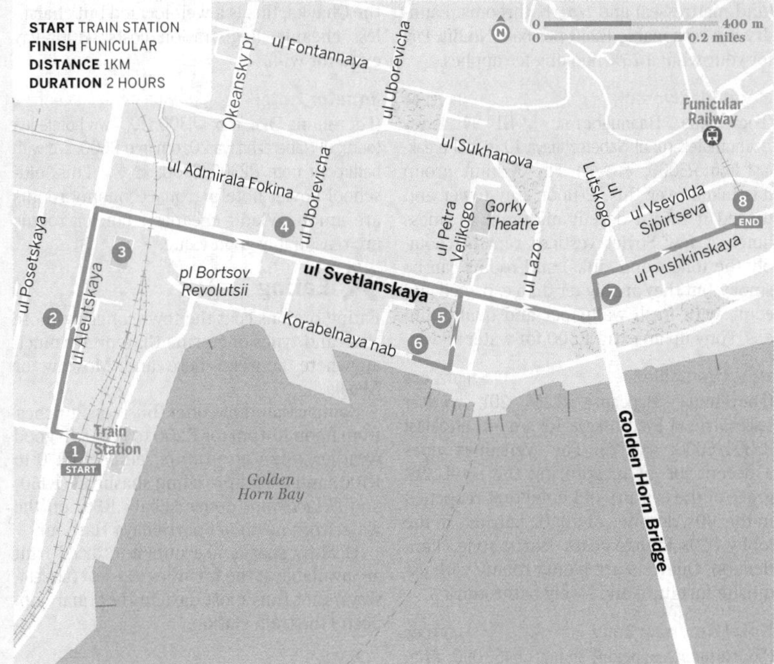

Walking Tour
Vladivostok

This walk passes many of Vladivostok's nicest buildings – look out for many not mentioned here – and finishes with its most famous view, from Eagle's Nest Hill.

Begin at the train station, where at the north end of the main platform a bronze marker indicates the 1 **Trans-Siberian Railway terminus** (reading 9288km, the distance from Moscow). Head up ul Aleutskaya, lined with many impressive buildings from the early 1900s. Half a block down at ul Aleutskaya 15 is 2 **Yul Brynner's house**, where *The King and I* actor was born. It's above the street-side concrete wall, where (ironically?) a small barbershop is now in place.

Continue north before going under the underpass east along ul Svetlanskaya. Towering to the right is the forbidding 3 **White House**, a government building that replaced green gardens for a Soviet HQ in 1983.

Continuing east on ul Svetlanskaya, it's worth popping into the still-going department store 4 **GUM**, with a host of souvenir stands and faded elegance inside. Outside the 1885 building, note the groovy SSSR plaque incongruously attached to the building's original Dresden-inspired facade.

A block east, turn right through a park to the reconstructed 5 **triumphal arch** built originally for *tsarevitch* Nicholas II in 1891 (then destroyed by Soviets and rebuilt by New Russians). Descend the hill to visit the green-and-grey 6 **S-56 submarine** and get an up-close look at the warships on Korabelnaya nab. Check out the memorial behind the submarine that pays tribute to Vladivostok's WWII dead, including 71 Ivanovs by our count.

Return to ul Svetlanskaya, continue east under Golden Horn Bridge and take a left through the courtyard of the petite 7 **Assumption Church**, where you might be lucky enough to hear sublime chanting during evening and morning services. Wind your way up the hill to the base of the 8 **Funicular** and ascend to the top. From here you can return to town by foot or on bus 164, or climb Eagle's Nest Hill for the city's greatest view.

(and mattresses) and *tiny* bathrooms. Laundry is a reasonable R250 per bag. No lift. Pay for your wi-fi; a 25% booking fee applies.

Hotel Vladivostok HOTEL €€
(Гостиница Владивосток; ☎411 941; www.azimuthotels.ru; ul Naberezhnaya 10; d incl breakfast from R3000;) The Azimut group has taken over this 12-floor grey tower and turned it into a decent midrange business hotel. A few Soviet vestiges remain (notably the toilets and sinks) and rooms can be smoky, but they are bigger than expected and come with fresh wallpaper and quality linens. Pony up an extra R500 for water views.

Hotel Versailles HOTEL €€€
(Гостиница Версаль; ☎264 201; www.versailles.vl.ru; ul Svetlanskaya 10; s/d incl breakfast R5300/6000;) The Versailles does a decent job of recapturing the pre-USSR grace of the century-old hotel that reopened in the '90s, despite enigmatic pairings in the lobby ('70s lounge seats, tsarist-style chandeliers). Quarters are plenty roomy with exquisite furniture and lovely bathrooms.

Hotel Amursky Zaliv HOTEL €€
(Гостиница Амурский Залив; ☎462 090; ul Naberezhnaya 9; www.azimuthotels.ru; unrenovated/renovated r from R1800/2900;) Hotel Vladivostok's poor step-sibling is gradually being renovated, so expect a price rise in some rooms. All rooms have balconies overlooking the city beach.

Hotel Zhemchuzhina HOTEL €
(Жемчужина; ☎414 387; ul Bestuzheva 29; www.gemhotel.ru; s/d from R1400/1800;) Formerly the Chayka, this is a well-located but charmless cheapie. Registration costs R100. Pay extra for wi-fi.

Equator Hotel HOTEL €
(Гостиница Экватор; ☎300 110; www.hotelequator.ru; ul Naberezhnaya 20; dm in q R600, s/d with bathroom from R2300/2900;) This old-school Soviet hotel's grotty economy rooms are among Vlad's cheapest; fancier rooms are reasonably good value.

Eating

Eating options coat the town, offering more class and types of cuisine than pretty much anywhere between here and Moscow or Alaska.

Some restaurants offer 'business lunches' from noon to 4pm for R200 to R300. In good weather, **open-air stands** sell beer (R70 to R100) and cook up sizzling shashlyki (R150) and *shawarma* (doner kebab; R80) on the waterfront north of Sportivnaya Harbour.

Healthy snacks like nuts and dried fruit are available at the **farmers market** (ul Aleutskaya) that runs most days in the square opposite the train station.

TOP CHOICE **Pyongyang** KOREAN €€
(Пхенян; Hotel Korona, ul Verkhneportovaya 68b; mains R300-400; noon-midnight;) Staffed by female newcomers from North Korea who periodically break out in karaoke, this DPRK-sponsored establishment is just strange enough to be considered a must-visit. You can pick from a photo menu of excellent food such as *bibimbap* (rice mixed with fried egg, sliced meat, and other stuff) and spicy fried

CAR CITY *ROBERT REID*

It's hard to walk around the centre's traffic-jammed streets without noticing that Vladivostok's gone Texas about cars. You have to have one, the bigger the better. One local with a Bentley stated he wouldn't go to a nearby cinema: 'No parking, and I don't want to walk.' The mass import of Japanese cars with right-hand steering causes some confusion on Russian streets, where cars stick to the right. But the city's so fanatical over the imports that when Yeltsin and later Putin tried to restrict the use of right-hand-steering cars, officials in Vladivostok practically threatened revolution.

Not long ago, locals exchanged old cars in a sketchy park in eastern Vladivostok, but now just enter one of 50 'live auction houses' across town. The auction houses broadcast 30-second internet auctions to bid on used Japanese and Korean cars that arrive a week later. Many of the cars coming will be shipped across Russia; meanwhile, all can be seen, awaiting customs, in multilevel garages along Golden Horn Bay.

For fun, I stopped by an auction house at the Marine Terminal and asked about getting a 1977 Russian Lada. 'Oh, very bad,' the mulleted attendant protested. 'Can't we bid on a Toyota Corolla for you?' Three-year-old Corollas go for US$12,000, plus US$500 shipping and US$3000 customs. I passed. 'Yes,' he said, 'this is a very good business.'

pork with kimchi. The beer is cheap (from R90) and pricier mains serve two.

Stolovaya No 1 CAFETERIA €
(Столовая 1; ul Svetlanskaya 1; meals R150-200; 24hr) Defining '*stolovaya* chic', this is the best cafeteria in all the Far East, with a hip soundtrack, plum location, snazzy bar serving coffee and booze and well-above-average *stolovaya* fare. It gets packed at meal times, but otherwise is a perfect place for a drink in front of the laptop.

Syndicate AMERICAN €€€
(ul Komsomolskaya 11, Ignat Mal; mains R400-1600; noon-2am) Taking over Vladivostok in an Al Capone frenzy, this ultra-1930s themed restaurant – 'Chicago, New York, whatever', per one waitress – has seats next to faux storefronts and a stage that lights up with live music. The speciality is steak – a 350-gram T-bone runs to R1600. Add R300 per person at weekends, when popular band Blues Line plays. It's north of the centre, reachable via any 'Vtornaya Rechna' bus.

Mauro Gianvanni PIZZA €€
(Мауро Джанванни; ul Fokina 16; mains R240-650; noon-midnight) This slick little brick-oven pizzeria – run by an Italian – pumps VH1 videos in the modern interior, though most sit out on the deck when weather behaves. The dozen-plus pizzas are crispy and tasty, probably the best east of the Urals.

Nostalgiya RUSSIAN €€
(Ностальгия; ul Pervaya Morskaya 6/25; mains R200-500; 8am-11pm) This compact, long-running restaurant offers hearty and tasty Russian meals with a little for-the-tsars pomp. Most visitors come for the souvenir shop (big collection of paintings and handicrafts) or a snack at the café.

Dva Gruzina GEORGIAN €€
(Два Грузина; ul Pogranichnaya 12; mains R150-300; 10am-1am) The Georgians are the Italians of the former Soviet Union for their love of wine and food. Sample trademark Georgian *khachapuri* (cheese bread) and rich stews like *chanakhi* and *kharcho,* washed down with wine by the glass (from R60) or beer (from R80). This stretch of ul Pogranichnaya is somewhat of a restaurant row.

Five O'Clock CAFÉ €
(ul Fokina 6; snacks R60-100; 8am-9pm Mon-Sat, 11am-9pm Sun) Vladivostok, take note of this novel idea – coffee, brownies, cakes and quiche (R70), all made daily and sold for less than an espresso costs at most 'cafés'.

Gutov GERMAN €€
(Гутов; ul Posetskaya 23; mains R300-500; noon-midnight, to 2am Sat & Sun) This snazzy beer hall with chunky wood tables serves Bavarian sausages and large Russian meals – mostly meats and fish fillets cooked up with a host of vegetable toppings. 'Business lunch' means gentler pricing of the same dishes.

Pizza M PIZZA €€
(Пицца М; delivery 413 430; Hotel Primorye, ul Posetskaya 20; medium pizzas R260-420; 24hr) Classier than its name might suggest, the M (inside Hotel Primorye) is one of Vlad's coolest hang-outs, with two unique rooms setting their style sights higher than the humble slice. The pizzas are quite good (note: a small is *not* enough for one).

Republic CAFETERIA €
(Республика; meals R150-250; 9am-11pm Sun-Thu, 10am-midnight Fri & Sat) These perfectly respectable twin *stolovye,* one located on ul Aleutskaya, the other on ul Svetlanskaya, draw more than a couple of cheap dates with their tasty Russian dishes, home brew (R80 for a ½ litre) and funky interiors. Both have bars on-site.

Mauro Gianvanni Café ITALIAN €€
(Кафе Мауро Джанванни; Okeansky pr 9; mains R240-500; 11am-midnight, to 2am Fri & Sat) No pizza like in Mauro Gianvanni (the main restaurant), but perfectly cooked pasta served in a basement setting.

München GERMAN €€
(Мюнхен; ul Svetlanskaya 5; mains R180-800) More meaty meals and towers of home brew in a beer-hall setting.

Clover Leaf FAST FOOD €
(cnr ul Semenovskaya & ul Aleutskaya) A convenient mall housing a 24-hour supermarket with a deli, a top-floor beer bar and food court with incredible views.

Supermarket SUPERMARKET €
(Супермаркет; ul Aleutskaya; 24hr) This grocery store is under the Republic restaurant across from the train station.

Drinking

TOP CHOICE **Zima** LOUNGE BAR
(ul Fontannaya 2; drinks from R200; 11am-2am, 24hr Fri & Sun) You'd think a place this swanky would be snobby and grossly

overpriced. Yet Zima dispenses with the *feiskontrol* (face control) and serves up mouth-watering mixed shashlyk and sushi at perfectly normal (for Russia) prices (mains R200 to R500). Oh yeah, and you order on iPads. This all occurs in an elaborate but classy Angkor Wat–themed interior, replete with design surprises (check out the little boy's and girl's rooms). Cocktails and beer are expensive; Leffe on tap makes up for it.

Rock's Cocktail Bar BAR
(ul Svetlanskaya) If you prefer a grungier crowd, this smoky basement dive is for you. Cool kids get dancing – and things often get sloppy – late night, as the DJ pays homage to Kurt, Layne, Zack and other '90s icons.

Moloko & Myod LOUNGE BAR
(Молоко и Мёд; ul Sukhanova 6a; mains R270-320; noon-midnight Sun-Thu, to 3am Fri & Sat;) A busy spot with a trendy street-side terrace shaded by birch trees, 'Milk & Honey' has a daily brunch plus coffee, pricey cocktails and chic chow like crab risotto with asparagus. Blankets warm terrace dwellers on chilly evenings.

El Dorado SPORTS BAR
(Okeansky pr 29; 24hr) You're likely to get into weird conversations with harmless drunks playing online poker, but the 10 TV screens or so will be playing the sport you need (NBA, Premiership, NFL, maybe netball) – best is the viewing room with rows of old airplane seats.

Sky Bar LOUNGE BAR
(12th fl, Hotel Hyundai, ul Semenovskaya 29; 6pm-2am) It attracts its share of high rollers and those looking for their business, but the views are undeniably tremendous.

Entertainment

Stadium Dinamo SPORTS
(Стадион Динамо; ul Pogranichnaya; tickets R150 to R230) The popular local football team, Luch-Energiya, plays games at this bayside stadium from April to November. On other days you can pay R50 to jog on the track.

Zabriskie Point LIVE MUSIC
(Забриский Пойнт; ul Naberezhnaya 9a; cover Tue-Thu & Sun R500, Fri & Sat R700; 9pm-5am Tue-Sun) Attached to the rear of the Hotel Amursky Zaliv, Zabriskie is Vladivostok's main rock and jazz club, drawing an older crowd to view live music acts such as Blues Line. Pricey, but not without character.

Yellow Submarine NIGHTCLUB
(ul Naberezhnaya 9a; cover R100-500) Right next to Zabriskie Point, this thumping club draws a younger crowd to hear a mix of live music and techno-spinning DJs.

Cukoo NIGHTCLUB
(Ку-Ку; Okeansky pr 1a; cover R500; Fri & Sat) One of Vladivostok's poshest clubs, the dance floor here seethes at weekends. Dress to impress to get through the velvet rope.

Philharmonic Hall CLASSICAL MUSIC
(Филармония; ul Svetlanskaya 15) Hosts classical music and jazz performances.

Shopping

And in other news, an explosion of modern malls! It's happened across Vladivostok – often with a confusing network of shops selling similar (but not quite the same) collections of imported clothing.

Magazin Kollektsionera SOUVENIRS
(Магазин Коллекционера; ul Fokina 5/3; 10am-6pm) A retired navy vet, now a spry octogenarian, opened this collection of (mostly) Soviet keepsakes about two decades ago. Super stuff: Soviet cameras, watches, toy soldiers, warship clocks, banners, Stalin paintings – all very reasonably priced.

Flotsky Univermag OUTDOOR GEAR
(Флотский Универмаг; ul Svetlanskaya 11; 10am-7pm Mon-Fri, to 6pm Sat & Sun) For unusual souvenir turf, follow the navy – this outfitter has those cute blue-and-white-striped navy undershirts (R140) and other navy gear, as well as useful travel gear like flashlights, 'Russia' bags, knives, maps and deodorant. Also has an OK map selection.

Nostalgiya SOUVENIRS
(Ностальгия; ul Pervaya Morskaya 6/25; 10am-8pm) Nostalgiya keeps a good range of pricey handicrafts (wood boats from R250 and way up) and many art pieces.

Dom Knigi MAPS
(Дом Книги; ul Aleutskaya 23; 10am-7pm) This store carries compact Vladivostok city-centre maps (R45) and bigger maps of greater Vladivostok and Primorsky Territory, along with postcards and a funny Vladivostok-photo matchbox set (R180). Another **branch** is at ul Svetlanskaya 43.

GUM SOUVENIRS
(ГУМ; ul Svetlanskaya 35; 10am-8pm Mon-Sat, 10am-7pm Sun) This Soviet-style department

store is the Far East's most art deco elegant. Some traditional souvenirs on the 1st floor.

Information

Internet Access, Post & Telephone

Interface (Интерфейс; ul Semenovskaya 8; per hr R70; ⏲24hr)

OS (ОС; ul Fokina 6; per MB R2, per hr R40; ⏲24hr)

Post office (Почта; ul Aleutskaya; per MB R30, per hr R0.80; ⏲8am-10pm Mon-Fri, 9am-6pm Sun) Post, telephone and internet opposite the train station. Watch out – those per MB fees really add up.

Media

Guide to Vladivostok This free ad-based guidebook (half in English) has listings for most tourist-based services. Available at kiosks and bookstores around town.

Vibirai A free Russian-language biweekly entertainment mag available in hotel lobbies and many restaurants.

Vladivostok News (www.vladivostoknews.com)

Vladivostok Guidebook Sound familiar? This English guidebook (R100), found at kiosks and some bookstores, has more listings than the same-named freebie.

Vladivostok Times (www.vladivostoktimes.com)

Medical Services

MUZ Hospital No 1 (МУЗ Больнца 1; ☎453 275; ul Sadovaya 22)

Money

There are currency-exchange desks and ATMs all over town.

Sberbank (Сбербанк; ul Aleutskaya 12; ⏲8.45am-8pm Mon-Sat, 10am-5pm Sun) Accepts travellers cheques (2% commission).

Getting There & Away

Ticket agents all over town sell plane and train tickets, including **Biletur** (Билетур; ☎407 700; ul Posetskaya 17; ⏲8am-7pm Mon-Sat, 9am-6pm Sun).

Air

Vladivostok's airport was undergoing a major expansion at research and should be ready to go by the time you read this, with additional international routes likely and budget flights from Moscow a possibility. Additional international destinations served by Vlad's flagship carrier, **Vladivostok Air** (www.vladivostokavia.ru), include Hanoi (seasonal), Nha Trang, Tokyo, and Niigata, while Transaero runs seasonal flights to Bangkok. See p574 for a list of airline websites.

Boat

DIY travellers can check out the schedule at **Wharf (Prichal) 36** (Korabelnaya nab), 100m east of the S-56 Submarine, where ferries shuttle locals to the port of Slavyanka, 50km south towards the (off-limits) North Korea border. There are usually a couple of hydrofoils per day (R400, one hour) and four weekly car ferries (R130, three hours).

DBS Cruise Ferry (☎302 704; www.parom.su; office 124, Marine Terminal) Sends a passenger-only ferry to Donghae, South Korea (from US$185 one way, 20 hours), continuing on to Sakaiminato, Japan (from US$250 one way, 42 hours), every Wednesday at 3pm.

Bus

Buses to Harbin, China, depart every morning at 6.20am (R2500, eight hours) from the **bus station** (ul Russkaya), 3km north of the centre. There are also frequent departures for Nakhodka (four hours) and other destinations in the Primorsky Territory. Some southbound destinations may be off limits to foreigners without a permit.

Train

Save money by avoiding the No 1 Rossiya train to Moscow.

The Harbin train is a headache, with many stops and a long border check. Departures are at 5.23pm on Mondays and Thursdays, but the first night you only go as far as Ussurinsk, where they detach your car from the 351. You stay overnight in Ussurinsk and depart the next day for the border and Harbin. It's much quicker and easier to take a bus to Harbin. If you're headed to Beijing by train, you'll need to go to Harbin first and transfer there.

Getting Around

To/From the Airport

A rail link connecting the centre with the airport (43km north in Artyom) should be ready by the time you read this.

A taxi booth in the arrivals area charges R1500 for trips to the centre. Outside taxis start higher (up to R2500) and end lower (R1000). Try sharing a ride to reduce costs. Allow at least 90 minutes, although the new highway linking Artyom with Vladivostok will hopefully cut that time in half.

Connecting the train station and airport, bus 107 (R55) runs every 45 to 75 minutes from 8.25am to 8pm. If it's not running, take bus 7 to Artyom's bus station and the frequent 106 from there to Vladivostok's train station.

Local Transport

From in front of the train station, buses 23, 31 and 49 run north on ul Aleutskaya then swing

TRANSPORT CONNECTIONS FROM VLADIVOSTOK

DESTINATION	MAIN TRAINS SERVING DESTINATION & FREQUENCY	RAIL PRICE (R)
Beijing	351 to Ussurinsk (Mon & Thu)	*kupe* 4000 (to Harbin)
Harbin	351 to Ussurinsk (Mon & Thu)	*kupe* 4000
Irkutsk	1 (even-numbered days), 7 (odd-numbered days), 133 (even-numbered days), 239 (even-numbered days, summer)	*platskartny/kupe* from 4000/9000
Khabarovsk	1 (even-numbered days), 5 (daily), 7 (odd-numbered days), 133 (even-numbered days), 351 (daily), 385 (odd-numbered days)	*platskartny/kupe* from 1000/2100
Magadan	N/A	N/A
Moscow	1 (odd-numbered days), 239 (even-numbered days, summer)	*platskartny/kupe* from 6000/13,100
Petropavlovsk-Kamchatsky	N/A	N/A
Seoul	N/A	N/A
Yakutsk	N/A	N/A
Yuzhno-Sakhalinsk	N/A	N/A

east onto ul Svetlanskaya to the head of the bay. For trips of more than 5km, you'll save money ordering a taxi by phone. Try **PrimTaxi** (☎555 555) or the curiously named **Cherepakha** (Turtle; ☎489 948).

Around Vladivostok

The broad, mountainous Primorsky Territory is beloved by locals with cars, who visit the beaches and mountains. You might consider renting a car and doing the same, but note that some areas near the Chinese border require permits. Those without their own wheels lean on pricey tours to get further away. One easy trip to do by public transport is to Nakhodka, where Primorsky's best beaches are a short bus or taxi ride away. Buses and trains to Nakhodka take three to four hours.

Vladivostok's distant airport is in Artyom, a mellow provincial town. Staying out here saves you time, money and sleep if you have an early-morning plane the next day. **Hotel Svetlana** (Гостиница Светлана; ☎307 603; ul Pushkina 39, Artyom; s/d from R1500/2400) offers a very good deal right in the centre of town. **Venice Hotel** (☎307 603; www.venice.far-east.ru; ul Portovaya 39, Artyom; s/d R3500/4000) is a grossly overpriced hotel at the airport.

There are a couple of cafés near the main square in the centre. Bus 7 goes to/from the airport (10 minutes); catch it at the bus station or along the main drag, ul Pushkina.

EASTERN BAM

The eastern half of the Baikal-Amur Mainline (Baikalo-Amurskaya Magistral; BAM), covering 2400km from Khani (where the borders of the Sakha Republic, Zabaikalsky Territory and Amurskaya oblast collide) to Sovetskaya Gavan, is perhaps not as visually stimulating as the more mountainous western half, but is still mesmerising.

The highlights of the eastern BAM are the BAM museum in the unofficial BAM capital, Tynda, and the pastel-coloured pseudotsarist architecture of Komsomolsk-na-Amure, where you can also ski, visit Nanai villages or take a Gulag tour. There's not much between Tynda and Komsomolsk

RAIL DURATION	AIRLINES SERVING DESTINATION	AIR PRICE (FROM R)	AIRDURATION & FREQUENCY
40hr (transfer in Harbin)	China Southern, S7, Vladivostok Air	4500	2½hr, almost daily
40hr	Vladivostok Air	3200	1¼hr, weekly
70hr	S7, Ural Airlines, Vladivostok Air	11,300	4hr, most weekdays
11-15hr	Vladivostok Air	2500	1¼hr, daily
N/A	Vladivostok Air	11,500	3hr, 2 weekly
6 days	Aeroflot, Transaero, Vladivostok Air	4000	10hr, frequent
N/A	S7, Vladivostok Air	9500	3½hr, daily
N/A	Korean Air, Vladivostok Air	11,000	2½hr, daily
N/A	Vladivostok Air, Yakutia Airlines	15,000	3hr, 2 weekly
N/A	S7, Sakhalin Airlines, Vladivostok Air	7000	2hr, daily

besides often lifeless trees, their roots severed by cruel permafrost below, and a slew of rather uninspired Soviet towns created to finish the railroad. Disembark only if you're searching for ghost towns or gold (prospecting is rife in this region). If you do get off, prepare to wait for up to a day for the next train.

A few links cut down to the Trans-Siberian. From Tynda, you can cut down to Skovorodino on the so-called Little BAM, built long before the BAM proper with slave labour in the 1930s. Other links south are at Novy Urgal and Komsomolsk. The end of the line comes near Vanino, where you can catch a ferry to Sakhalin Island.

Tynda Тында

41656 / POP 35,500 / MOSCOW +6HR

The king of the BAM, Tynda is a nondescript BAM HQ flanked by low-lying pine-covered hills. Many stop here, as it's a hub for trains between Severobaikalsk, Komsomolsk-na-Amure and, on the Little BAM, Blagoveshchensk to the south, or, on the in-progress AYaM (Amuro-Yakutskaya Magistral, or Amur-Yakutsk Mainline), Neryungri and Tommot to the north.

Don't expect quaint. Tynda's fully Soviet – there was nothing but a few shacks before BAM centralised its efforts here in 1974. Liven up your visit by arriving during a festival. The **Bakaldin Festival** rotates between several nearby Evenki villages in late May or early June, with traditional song, dance, reindeer rides and plenty of reindeer shashlyki and other native delicacies. March sees the **Reindeer Hunter and Herder Festival**.

Sights & Activities

Besides the BAM Museum, about the only other thing worth checking out in Tynda is the dramatic sledgehammer-wielding **BAM worker statue** at the far eastern end of central ul Krasnaya Presnaya. **Zarya** is a native Evenki village nearby. Bus 105 from the train station goes eight times daily (30 minutes).

Contact feisty adventurer **Alexey Podprugin** (8-914-552 1455; bamland@mail.ru) for kayaking, hiking and cross-country skiing trips.

WHAM BAM, IT'S THE RED ELVIS!

One of the more bizarre tours of all time rolled through Tynda in August 1979 when the 'Red Elvis' – Dean Reed, an American singer turned Marxist – did a 19-day tour on the BAM, immortalised in his song 'BAM' ('Everybody sing along… the towns are here to stay, it's the future of our day!').

His show at Tynda's Festivalnaya Hill drew 25,000 spectators, but didn't kick off the way he wanted: according to one story, told on the priceless website www.deanreed.de, a local refused to let the American use his horse for a dramatic cowboy entrance.

Reed remains virtually unknown in the West – not surprising with songs like 'Wake Up America' and photos of him chumming around with Central American revolutionaries. He died under mysterious circumstances in East Germany in 1986.

Tip: Hours – and hours – of enjoyment can be had YouTubing Dean's videos. You can read more about him in *Comrade Rockstar* by Reggie Nadelson.

BAM Museum MUSEUM

(Музей БАМа; ul Sportivnaya 22; admission R100; ⏲10am-2pm & 3-6pm, to 7pm Sat, closed Sun, Mon & last Thu of month) Tynda's pride and joy has four rooms of BAM relics and photos (no English), but also covers native Evenki culture, WWII, local art, regional wildlife, and medicine (including jarred human organs and foetuses). One section covers the Little BAM and the Gulag prisoners who built it in the 1930s. They lived (and died) in 24 BAM *lagery* ('*bamlag*', or labour camps) between Tynda and Bamovskaya. Photos chronicle the extreme hardships these prisoners endured. Two rooms are dedicated to the big BAM, sections of which were built in the 1930s, 1940s and 1950s before Stalin died and the project was mothballed. Displays cover the period between its relaunch in 1974 and completion in 1984 (although it wasn't made fully operational until 1991). The museum is hard to find: From the Orthodox cathedral walk 400m west, turn left just before the blue building at ul Krasnaya Presnaya 6, and proceed 200m or so.

Sleeping

Resting rooms HOSTEL €

(Комнаты Отдыха, komnaty otdykha; ☎73 297; bed per 6/12/24hr from R350/600/1100) Comfy and clean dorm rooms in the train station. Shower available (R100 for guests and non-guests alike).

Hotel Yunost HOTEL €

(Гостиница Юность; ☎43 534; ul Krasnaya Presnaya 49; 4-bed dm R700, s/d from R820/2400) Faded but fine option in centre; Dervla Murphy recuperated here as related in her book *Through Siberia by Accident.*

Information

Internet access is at **Disly Club** (ul Krasnaya Presnaya 55; per hr R50; ⏲9am-6pm Mon-Sat), in the Rostelekom office between Hotel Yunost and the post office. The train station has an ATM.

Getting There & Away

The **train station** – the city's most striking landmark – is across the Tynda River. A pedestrian bridge leads 1km north to ul Krasnaya Presnaya.

Train 75 heads via BAM to Moscow (*kupe/platskartny* R11,000/4250, five days) on even-numbered days, stopping in Severobaikalsk (*kupe/platskartny* R3100/1400, 26 hours), while train 77 to Novosibirsk (*kupe/platskartny* R7450/2900, two days 19 hours) takes the Little BAM south on odd-numbered days to connect with the Trans-Siberian line at Skovorodino.

For Neryungri (from R520, 5½ hours) take the nightly 326 at 11.52pm, or the 658 at 6.13pm. Train 364 trundles to Komsomolsk daily at 11.26am (*kupe/platskartny* R3110/1400, one day 13 hours), and 325 heads daily to Khabarovsk at 8.13pm via Skovorodino (*kupe/platskartny* R3140/1450, 28½ hours, daily).

Komsomolsk-na-Amure

Комсомольск-на-Амуре

☎4217 / POP 280,000 / ⏲MOSCOW +7HR

After days of taiga and grey Soviet towns, Komsomolsk-na-Amure hits the BAM adventurer like a mini St Petersburg. Komsomolsk was built virtually from scratch by Stalin in the 1930s as a vital cog in the Soviet Union's military industrial complex.

The location was no accident: the city was far removed from potential prying eyes along the Pacific Coast and Chinese border, yet its position along the Amur allowed for relatively easy transport of goods. Imitating the tsars, Stalin erected elaborate neo-Renaissance and neoclassical buildings in the city centre, only festooned with stars, crescents and statues of model Soviet citizens instead of the usual angels and goblins. To build the city he enlisted Communist Youth League (Komsomol – hence the city's name) volunteers as well as Gulag labourers. Around town, factories sprouted up to produce ships, weapons, electricity and, most famously, Sukhoi (Su) fighter jets in a factory that still works today.

Set along a few grand boulevards, the city is worth a night or more if you are getting on or off the BAM. Nearby attractions include ski slopes, Nanai villages and rafting. Just east of the river terminal is a **beach**, which is well attended on nice days.

Sights

Soviet Mosaics — STREET ART

Komsomolsk has a wealth of wonderful murals adorning the sides of apartment blocks and factories. Most were the creation of Khabarovsk-based artist Nikolai Dolbilkin, who lived here in the 1950s and '60s. Among the best are the double triptych **WWII mosaic** (2nd fl, cnr pr Mira & ul Truba) in the central grey *dom kultura* building at Sudostroitel Park; the **nauka (science) mosaic** (pr Lenina) at the Polytechnical Institute, a block east of Hotel Voskhod; and the stunning **electric worker mosaic** (alleya Truda) on the side of the TETs electric station.

Municipal Museum of Regional Studies — MUSEUM

(pr Mira 8; admission R100; ⌚9.30am-5pm Tue-Fri, 10am-5pm Sat & Sun) The several rooms of old photos and knick-knacks show how Komsomolsk rose from the tent camps of original pioneers in 1932 to an industrial Soviet city. It also contains some stylish old fish-skin jackets and other Nanai artefacts.

Memorials — MONUMENT

Just northwest of the river terminal is the impressive **WWII memorial**, which features stoic faces chipped from stone, with nearby pillars marking the years of WWII. Other memorials include a tiny **Gulag victims monument** – an unremarkable jagged piece of rock – in a tiny park next to the city court building on pr Lenina, and a simple **Japanese POW memorial** off pr Mira.

Tours

Nata Tour — TOURS

(Ната Тур; ☎201 067, 8-914-189 1784; www.komsomolsknata.ru; office 110, ul Vasyanina 12; ⌚10am-6pm Mon-Fri) Located in the big grey building

OVERLAND FROM TYNDA TO YAKUTSK

Travellers in Tynda often have their sites on Yakutsk in the Sakha Republic. To get to Yakutsk you must first take a train to **Neryungri**, 5½ hours north. From there you can either fly with Yakutia Airlines (R10,500, 1¾ hours, four weekly), or embark on one of the Far East's classic overland journeys: 15 to 20 bumpy hours in a Russian UAZ jeep or van to cover 810km on the AYaM (Amuro-Yakutskaya Magistral) highway.

Daily departures from the Neryungri train station are timed for the 6.22am arrival of the train from Khabarovsk. Most trips are in 11-passenger vans, but if passengers are lacking you may end up in a four-passenger jeep (as we did). The price varies with the season; it cost us R3500 in early June. It's a pretty trip that cuts over a mountain pass and through tracts of virgin taiga before traversing the Lena by *parom* (car ferry) an hour south of Yakutsk. However, it's extremely rough in patches and incredibly dusty in the warmer months.

Passenger services on the AYaM train line run further north to Aldan (six hours) and Tommot (eight hours), but you'll keep well ahead of the train (and avoid a possible overnight stay in either Aldan or Tommot) by getting a head start from Neryungri. Masochists may prefer the notoriously rickety weekly bus between Yakutsk and Aldan (R2200, at least 16 hours). It departs at 8am from Aldan/Yakutsk on Wednesdays/Tuesdays, requiring that you spend the previous night in Aldan.

The AYaM train line actually extends a couple of hundred kilometres beyond Tommot, although passenger services terminate there. The line is being extended to Nizhny Bestyakh (opposite Yakutsk on the Lena River), and plans are to open the entire route to passenger services. This may happen within the lifetime of this book, but we're not taking bets.

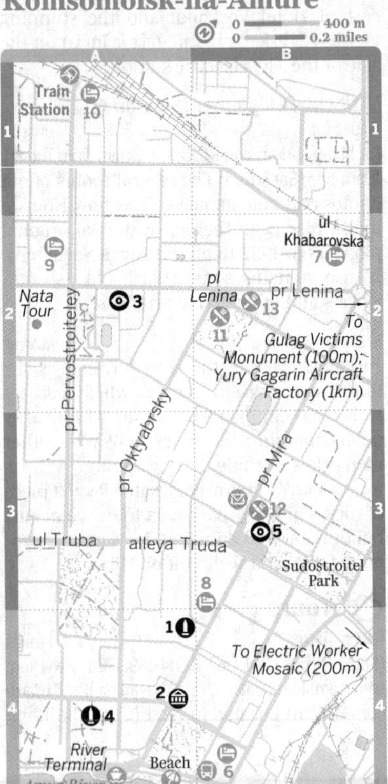

Komsomolsk-na-Amure

Sights

1 Japanese POW Memorial....................A4
2 Municipal Museum of Regional Studies....................A4
3 Nauka(science) Mosaic....................A2
4 WWII Memorial....................A4
5 WWII Mosaic....................B3

Sleeping

6 Biznestsentr....................B4
7 Dacha Khrushcheva....................B2
8 Hotel Amur....................B3
9 Hotel Voskhod....................A2
10 Resting Rooms....................A1

Eating

11 Kofeynya....................B2
12 SSSR....................B3
13 U City Pizza....................B2

in back, this experienced travel service arranges three- to five-hour 'Stalin tours' of city communist sites (including a Gulag camp; R800 to R1500 per person); adventure tours involving fishing, rafting or skiing; and day trips and/or homestays at Verkhnyaya Ekon. White-water rafting trips involve a train ride to Novy Urgal on the BAM. Slower one- to several-day floats can be done closer to Komsomolsk. Tours of the **Yury Gagarin Aircraft Factory**, where the Su jets are built, can also be arranged.

Sleeping

Nata Tour can arrange homestays (R1000 per person including breakfast). Wi-fi requires bling and a booking charge applies unless otherwise stated.

TOP CHOICE Biznestsentr HOTEL €€

(Бизнесцентр; ☎521 522; bc@etc.kna.ru; ul Dzerzhinskogo 3; s/d R2000-4000; ❄@📶) This place is an anomaly in that it's both Komsomolsk's most modern, business-oriented hotel and its cheapest. The rooms are plenty spacious, bathrooms are fresh and English rolls off the tongues of the friendly receptionists. The massive suites, with flat-screen TVs, are fit for Count Muravyov-Amursky himself. No booking charge.

Hotel Amur HOTEL €

(Гостиница Амур; ☎590 984; ruma@kmscom.ru; pr Mira 15; s R500-2350, d R860-2600; ❄📶) A rare budget hotel in the Far East, the Amur has 15 old-fashioned rooms (many with shared toilet and shower) in a lovely 1932 building.

Dacha Krushcheva GUESTHOUSE €€

(Дача Хрущёва; ☎540 659; ul Khabarovska 47; r R2360-3400; ❄) Built for Nikita Khrushchev, this backstreet dacha is a step back in time. The suites could fit a Young Pioneers troupe and all six rooms have 1970s easy chairs to kick back in. Basically, it's the polar opposite of the renovated but cramped Hotel Voskhod.

Hotel Voskhod HOTEL €€

(Гостиница Восход; ☎535 131; pr Pervostroiteley 31; s/d from R2600/3600; ⊖@📶) Eight-storey grey beast with bog-standard Soviet rooms.

Resting rooms HOSTEL €

(Комнаты Отдыха, komnaty otdykha; ☎284 193; train station; s without bathroom R1100, dm in d/tr R910/810) Showers cost R75 at these sparkling-clean resting rooms.

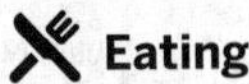

Eating

Kofeynya CAFÉ €€

(Кофейня; ul Oktyabrsky 48; snacks R60-130; 24hr;) Salads and light snacks are on the menu here, along with a diverse coffee selection. There's a built-in internet café (per hr R30).

SSSR RUSSIAN €€

(СССР; alleya Truda 22; mains R150-200; 10am-1am) It's only appropriate that there's an honest-to-Lenin retro-Soviet café in a place like Komsomolsk, innit? All the Russian staples are on the menu, some with names like 'partizan chicken', and the walls are festooned with every type of Soviet kitsch imaginable.

U City Pizza FAST FOOD €

(pr Lenina 19; meals from R150; 10am-11pm) Load up for your BAM ride with pizza by the slice (R70 to R90), bliny, burgers, burritos, salads and other quick eats. It's attached to a one-screen cinema (hence the popcorn smell).

Information

The best internet point is Kofeynya.

Dalsvyaz (Дальсвязь; pr Mira 27; per hr R45; 8am-8.30pm) Internet access in the post office building.

Post office (Почта; pr Mira 27; 8am-10pm Mon-Fri, to 6pm Sat & Sun)

Getting There & Around

From Komsomolsk's pink **train station** (pr Pervostroiteley) the excruciatingly slow 352 leaves daily for Vladivostok (*kupe/platskartny* R2720/1240, 24½ hours). There are also services to Khabarovsk (*kupe/platskartny* from R1900/925, 10 hours).

On the BAM, 363 heads west to Tynda (*kupe/platskartny* R3110/1400, one day 13 hours, daily); to reach Severobaikalsk, change in Tynda. The daily train 351 heads east to Vanino (*kupe/platskartny* R1435/700, 11 hours). The BAM's first/last stop, 'Sovetskaya Gavan-Sortirovka', 15 minutes east of Vanino, is not to be confused with the city of Sovetsakaya Gavan, an hour away from Vanino by bus.

Local and long-distance buses leave from the **bus station** (542 554; 6am-10.30pm) near the river. Buses bound for Khabarovsk (R600, six hours) leave every 90 minutes or so from 7am.

For a DIY adventure, head down the Amur River by hydrofoil to its terminus in Nikolaevsk-na-Amure (from R3320, 12 hours). The boat, which originates in Khabarovsk, leaves five days per week from the **river terminal**). The departure upriver to Khabarovsk is at 1pm (from R800, six hours).

Within the city, handy tram 2 runs from the train station along ul Lenina and pr Mira to the river terminal (R13).

Verkhnyaya Ekon

Верхняя Эконь

Tucked between the Amur River and bear-inhabited hills, this village of 500 (of which half are Nanai) makes a fun day trip from Komsomolsk across the river. Its school has a small **Nanai Museum** (Музей Нанай), with old shaman costumes and plenty of Nanai traditional pieces. It's possible to hike up the mountain.

Three daily buses come from Komsomolsk (R30, 30 minutes), but if you arrange for a taxi you can visit an eerie, unfinished 800m-long BAM tunnel at nearby **Pivan** village (north of the Amur Bridge), with rusted pieces left from the project that was abandoned after WWII broke out.

SAKHA REPUBLIC

Looming like a giant inverted iceberg north of the BAM line, the sprawl of remote Sakha Republic (the country's largest) takes time and effort (or an air ticket) to reach. Life is noticeably different here. The buildings of Yakutsk – a friendly place where Russians are the minority – stand on stilts. Sakha is the correct term for the local ethnic group

BAM ENDS, SAKHALIN BECKONS

BAM completists will end up in the grey Soviet port town of Vanino (actually the BAM ends 15 minutes beyond Vanino, in Sovetskaya Gavan-Sortirovka). From Vanino, there is a theoretically daily 4pm boat (in reality, it leaves when full when the weather allows) to Kholmsk on Sakhalin Island (tickets R1710 to R2850, 18 hours). The information numbers are 8233-66 098/66 516 (in Russian). Call the day before to reserve a seat – they should have a reasonable idea of whether the next day's ship will sail. But no guarantees. Or just go and take your chances.

commonly called by the Evenki name for 'horse people': Yakut. The republic is also known as Yakutia.

The most unrepentant dissidents (including Decembrists and Bolsheviks) were exiled in Sakha. It was a 'jail without doors', as the swamps, mountains, ice and bug-infested forests did a pretty good job of keeping people from going anywhere.

Yakutsk Якутск

☎4112 / POP 215,000 / ⏲MOSCOW +6HR

Talk about bizarre: the world's coldest city stands on stilts (the shifting permafrost collapses buildings otherwise) and is pretty much cut off from the already remote Far East; a dodgy road to the BAM line takes a ferry ride and 24 hours, and airfares can cost R20,000 just to reach Vladivostok! Yet, unlike so many remote Russian cities out here, Yakutsk roars with optimism and gusto. New buildings – some with far more dramatic architecture than you'll see anywhere else in Russia – are popping up all over the city and the population is rising (all the regional gold and diamonds certainly have something to say about why). Brace yourself for weird weather. It's *hot* in June and July (reaching the upper 30s) and freezing in winter (January averages –40°C).

Yakutsk was founded in 1632 as a Cossack fort and later served as a base for expeditions to the Pacific coast. In the late 19th century, Yakutsk became a boozy, bawdy r'n'r centre for the region's increasing number of goldminers. It reclaimed that reputation somewhat in the wild, anything-goes period following the collapse of the Soviet Union.

Sights & Activities

Mammoth Museum and Archaeology & Ethnography Museum MUSEUM
(UGU Bldg, ul Kulakovskogo 48; admission Mammoth/Ethnography museum R200/150; ⏲10am-5pm Mon-Fri, 11am-4pm Sat) All that permafrost in the area has resulted in some of the world's best-preserved mammoth skeletons. You can see some at this excellent two-pack of museums. See if they'll let you glimpse into the Mammoth Museum's refrigerated storage room, which is chock full of mammoth and woolly rhino bones. The Ethnography Museum has one of the Far East's better displays on indigenous peoples.

Regional Museum MUSEUM
(Государственный Музей; pr Lenina 5/2; admission R100; ⏲10am-5pm Tue-Sun) A good place to delve deeper into Sakha culture, it covers local minerals and the region's first Russian settlers to go with the standard Soviet natural history and WWII exhibits. Outside, there's a huge whale skeleton found in 1961.

National Art Museum MUSEUM
(Художественный Музей; ☎335 274; ul Kirova 9; admission R300; ⏲10am-6pm Wed-Sun) Try to look past the (tripled) foreigner admission price at the excellent National Art Museum, as its three floors show off many local customs and much scenery.

Banya BANYA
(Баня; Stary Gorod complex; per hr 1-6 persons R1500; ⏲24hr) A Russian *banya* hidden in the Zastava restaurant; it's not well advertised so ask the staff.

Khomus Museum MUSEUM
(Хомус Музей; ul Kirova 31; admission R150; ⏲10am-1pm & 2-5pm Mon-Fri) *Khomus* (Jew's harps) play a big part in Sakha culture – concerts occur year-round, when performers imitate natural sounds such as a horse neighing. The unexpected (and unfortunately soundtrack-free) Khomus Museum has a collection showcasing international Jew's harp heroes (including local guru Spiridon Shishigin) and old 45s; it sells a Sakha-made harp for R2500.

FREE **Archaeology Museum of Northeast Asia** MUSEUM
(Археологический Музей Северо-Восточной Азии; ul Petrovskogo; ⏲9am-6pm Mon-Fri) Another museum where the story is more interesting than the product, this one is mainly dedicated to artefacts found at Diring Yuriakh, a settlement of ancient humans on the Lena River – thought by some Russian scientists, including museum director and lead site excavator Yury Mochanov, to possibly date back 3 million years. It also has the requisite woolly mammoth skeleton.

Yakut State Literature Museum MUSEUM
(Якутский Государственный Литературный Музей; ul Oktyabrskaya 10; admission R50; ⏲10am-5pm Tue-Sat) Worth a visit if you are into *olonkho* – Unesco-recognised Yakutian oral epics (often accompanied by Jew's harp music). It also has a giant 19th-century bible translated into Sakha and a traditional Yakut winter house known as a *balangan* outside.

Tours

Planet Yakutia TOUR COMPANY
(☎420 522; www.planetyakutia.com; office 409, pr Lenina 4) A remarkably with-it tour company, it can answer just about any Sakha-related question you have and find a way to get you where you need to go. Perfect if you need assistance with sojourns to the remote reaches of the Sakha Republic. Also runs a range of more organised tours, all outlined on its website and in a free glossy brochure. Ask for Sevindzh.

TourService Centre TOUR COMPANY
(☎351 144, 8-924-662 1144; www.yakutiatravel.com; office 66, ul Yaroslavsky 30/1; ⏰9am-6pm Mon-Fri) Experienced English-speaking staff can prearrange Sakha trips or sell Lena Pillars boat trips. They also offer trips to Sakha villages. An English-speaking guide is R1500 per day.

LENA PILLARS ЛЕНСКИЕ СТОЛБЫ
The area's most popular tour is the boat cruise to the 80km-long Lena Pillars (Lenskie Stolby), a 35-million-year-old stretch of Kimberly limestone on the edge of the Lena River, about 220km south of Yakutsk. Jagged spires and picturesque crumbling fronts (almost bricklike) look like ancient ruins if you squint. A laid-back, two-night cruise in a particularly comfy 70-cabin ship costs from R6900, including about five to eight hours at the pillars, a shaman ceremony and the

GETTING OUT THERE IN SAKHA (& BEYOND)

Sakha Republic, cut by the 4265km Lena River (which inspired a certain Vladimir to change his name to Lenin), is bigger than France and, as costs are high even in Yakutsk, getting very far is expensive and requires prearranged transport and guides. But if you have the dosh and the will, Sakha and the neighbouring Chukotka offer the chance to journey to some of the world's last great unexplored places. Winter is generally the best time to travel, as *zimniki* (winter roads) open up and there are no bears and mosquitoes to contend with. Websites http://askyakutia.com and http://askmagadan.com are great resources for travel around here. Tour companies in Yakutsk and elsewhere in the Far East can organise tours to any of the following and ensure you have the required permits.

Topolinoe, 705km northwest of Yakutsk, can be reached by road and is a great place to meet Evenki reindeer herders. Shared taxis go out here sporadically for about R5000 one way per person. You will likely have to change cars 295km southwest of Topolinoe in Khandyga, which has accommodation and a Gulag museum.

Found where the Lena drops into the Arctic Ocean, **Tiksi** (a strategic air-force town in Soviet times, and still a tightly controlled zone) can be reached by air but is best reached on a 14-day cruise from Yakutsk (twice in August). The cruise takes in Sottintsy, the Lena Pillars and several other stops – while plenty of bird-watching opportunities loom, particularly at the delta at the Arctic Ocean. A double cabin costs R75,000 per person. It takes 60 days to secure a permit to Tiksi.

A dream for hardened adventurers, the infamous **Kolyma Highway** – aka the 'road of bones' due to the countless Gulag labourers who froze to death building it – makes for a tough three- or four-day journey 2200km west to **Magadan**, the one-time Gulag town known as 'the Gateway to Hell'. It's possible to try to negotiate a ride with a truck for the trip, or to hire 6WD vehicles going in either direction (at least US$3000 one way). The ride on the frozen Indigirka River is quicker after December; things get slushy and often impassable by May.

It's of course much easier to fly to Magadan. Its cruel weather and cruel past aside, Magadan is pretty and pleasant, with a rather European centre in pastels. The rare visitor can camp at a Gulag, fish or raft on the Arman River, cross-country ski, see birds, hike – or set off on a reverse journey along the Kolyma Hwy to Yakutsk. Contact the excellent **DVS-Tour** (☎4132-623 296, 8-914-852 82 21; www.dvs-tour.ru; ul Lenina 3; ⏰9am-1pm & 2-6pm Mon-Fri) for help with Magadan trips or to arrange Gulag tours.

'Out there' to a region already considered 'out there,' **Chukotka Autonomous Region** brushes its icy nose with Alaska's and is almost solely inhabited by indigenous peoples and a fair share of whales and walruses. The two main access points are Anadyr and Provideniya, where a number of US-based tours come by charter flight via Nome (June to August). Yakutia Airlines has a few weekly flights to Anadyr from Moscow (from R15,000 one way) and Khabarovsk (from R25,500 one way).

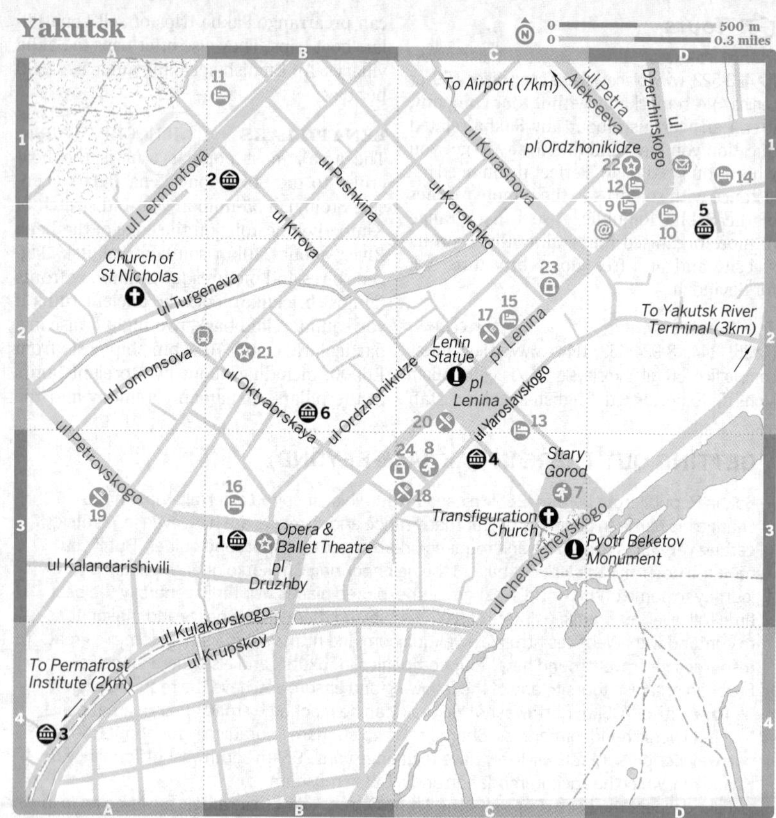

chance to fish or swim. Full meal deals are R3600 extra. Boats leave from Yakutsk once or twice weekly from June to September and should be booked ahead through a travel agent or through the operator, **Alrosa Hotel** (☎4112-423 303; www.alrosa-hotels.ru).

BUOTAMA RIVER

Between the Lena Pillars and Yakutsk, cutting west from the Lena, this narrow tree-lined river is popular for kayaking/rafting camping trips, where you can spot bear and fish in the wild. These start at about R6500 per person per day not including meals.

Festivals & Events

One of Russia's better-kept secrets, the major Sakha festival of **Ysyakh** (tough to pronounce; try 'ehh-sekhh') is celebrated all over the Sakha Republic each year in June. The biggest event occurs in Us Khatyn field near the village of Zhetai, about 20km north of Yakutsk, on the first Saturday and Sunday after the summer solstice. Don't miss the opening, at noon on Saturday, when hundreds of costumed performers, including Chinggis (Genghis) Khaan–like soldiers, reenact battles and people hand out free skewers of horsemeat and offer sips of horse milk.

Stands are filled by Sakha from across the republic, often set up around modern *irasa* (tepees); the rare foreigner is likely to be drawn in for horsemeat and *kumiss* (fermented mare's milk). The 'no alcohol' (other than mildly alcoholic *kumiss*) policy keeps things sober during the day, but it can't be guaranteed later on, when many locals come to greet the dawn – an all-night party for young and old. It's well worth planning your Yakutsk detour around this event.

Packed buses head to/from the festival regularly from pr Lenina in Yakutsk (R50, 45 minutes).

Yakutsk

Sights

Archaeology & Ethnography Museum .... (see 3)
1 Archaeology Museum of Northeast Asia B3
2 Khomus Museum B1
3 Mammoth Museum A4
4 National Art Museum C3
5 Regional Museum D1
6 Yakut State Literature Museum B2

Activities, Courses & Tours

7 Banya C3
Planet Yakutia .... (see 14)
8 TourService Centre C3

Sleeping

9 Hotel Lena D1
10 Hotel Parus D1
11 Hotel Saisary B1
12 Hotel Sterkh D1
13 Hotel Tygyn Darkhan C2
14 Le Grand D1
15 Polar Star Hotel C2
16 Uyut Mini Hotel B3

Eating

17 Bliny C2
18 Jonathan Kofeynya C3
19 Muus Khaya A3
Tamerlyan .... (see 12)
Tygyn Darkhan .... (see 13)
20 Veranda C2

Entertainment

21 Drakon B2
22 Sakha Theatre D1

Shopping

23 Globus C2
24 Sakhabult C3

Sleeping

Travel agencies can set you up with apartments or homestays with full board from R3000 per person per night. Expect a 25% reservation fee at all but the priciest hotels; wi-fi usually requires bling.

TOP CHOICE Le Grand B&B €€€
(☎444 702; www.hotel-legrand.ru; pr Lenina 4; s/d incl breakfast from R3700/4600;) It's not technically a B&B but we'll call it one – it certainly has that warm and inviting B&B feel. Most of the 12 rooms have flat-screen TVs and feathery queen-sized beds that invite entry via flying leap. Cheaper rooms lack air-con and have twin beds.

Polar Star Hotel HOTEL €€€
(Гостиница Полярная Звезда; ☎341 215; pr Lenina 24; s/d incl breakfast from R4950/6800;) In a unique and welcome twist on Russia's 'rip off the foreigner' culture, this top-notch business hotel was giving foreigners a R1000 discount on all rooms when we visited. Too good to last? Probably, but you might as well ask for it. Service can be variable but other than that it's easily Yakutsk's top dawg for high rollers.

Hotel Parus HOTEL €€
(Гостиница Парус; ☎423 727; pr Lenina 7; s/d incl breakfast from R2600/3800, ste R4300;) There's just one single at R2600, and it's a wood-walled gem on the top floor (it was formerly a sauna). The suites are also quite comfy, but standard doubles tribute old-school templates. They can mix-and-match lone wolves with a roommate.

Uyut Mini Hotel HOTEL €
(Уют Мини Гостиница; ☎360 215; ul Petrovskogo 10; dm/d R700/1400) You won't find a much better deal than this place in all the Far East. All rooms are communal doubles or triples that share a clean bathroom. In other cost-saving news, it provides a kitchen for self-caterers and does laundry for R100 per load. No registration, however.

Hotel Lena HOTEL €€
(Гостиница Лена; ☎424 214; www.lena-hotel.ru; pr Lenina 8; s/d from R2800/3800;) If you're a solo traveller pinching pennies the hotel will try to find you a roommate in a double here. It recently upgraded the Soviet-style rooms, but left in the worn-out beds. Free wi-fi!

Hotel Tygyn Darkhan HOTEL €€€
(Гостиница Тыгын Дархан; ☎435 109; www.tygyn.ru; ul Ammosova 9; s/d incl breakfast from R4050/5850;) Just steps from pl Lenina, TD's regular rooms follow a standard Soviet template, but are freshly updated and have modern bathrooms. Rates include

use of the indoor pool, sauna and gym. Still, it's a distant runner-up to Polar Star at the top end.

Hotel Sterkh HOTEL €€
(Гостиница Стерх; ☎421 106; www.sterkh.biz; pr Lenina 8; s/d from R2400/5000, 2-bed dm R2500, r/lyux incl breakfast R2500/3600;) This place has a great location, but it's way too expensive for what you get. Many rooms share showers.

Hotel Saisary HOTEL €
(Гостиница Сайсары; ☎433 401; rynok_sa isary@mail.ru; ul Lermontova 62/2; s/d/tr per person from R1800/1250/1000) Worn rooms, with or without roommates. Take bus 6 or 25 west on pr Lenina.

Eating

TOP CHOICE **Chochur Muran** YAKUT €€
(Чочур Муран; ☎368 014; km7, Vilyusky Trakt; meals R600-1500; noon-midnight;) In a wonderful Cossack-style lodge filled with antiques, massive moose heads and a few mammoth artefacts, Chochur Muran is a must-stop if you are heading out to the nearby Permafrost Kingdom. It's the best place around to try Sakha delicacies like *stroganina* (frozen raw *chyr*, a white fish common in Arctic rivers), *zherebyatiny* (fillet of colt meat) and reindeer. Dog sledding and ice fishing are on offer in winter. Reservations advised.

Tygyn Darkhan YAKUT €€
(Тыгын Дархан Ресторан; Hotel Tygyn Darkhan, ul Ammosova 9; mains R250-500; 7-10am, noon-3pm & 6-11pm;) It's not as atmospheric as Chochur Muran, but it's *the* place to score Sakha specialities in the centre. Try *indigirka* (frozen raw *chyr* and onions – a bit like eating frozen fish in a ball of snow) and Darkhan *pelmeni* (horsemeat dumplings), washed down with a glass of *kumiss* and topped off with whipped cream and foxberries.

Jonathan Kofeynya CAFÉ €€
(ul Yaroslavskogo 26; mains R250-500; 8am-10pm;) This is the only stop in town for your caffeinated, wi-fi-enabled morning. The omelettes (R150), bliny (R180 to R250) and other breakfast eats are more affordable than the rest of the menu.

Tamerlyan MONGOLIAN €€
(Тамерлян; pl Ordzhonikidze; meals from R400; noon-midnight Sun-Wed, to 2am Thu-Sat;) Known for its big salad bar (R69 per 100 grams) and pick-and-watch-cook (then eat)

DON'T MISS

PERMAFROST KINGDOM

Yakutsk's latest and quirkiest attraction allows you to experience Yakutsk's famously frosty climes even at the height of the sweltering summer. At **Permafrost Kingdom** (Царство Вечной Мерзлоты, km7, Vilyusky Trakt; admission R300; 9am-7pm), two neon-lit tunnels burrowed into a permanently frozen hill 13km west of Yakutsk's centre have been filled with dozens of fabulous, never-melting ice sculptures of local pagan gods and a host of more recognisable objects and characters – a sitting Buddha, a pharaoh, Ded Moroz (Russia's Santa Claus), a woolly mammoth and an icy interpretation of Picasso's *Guernica*. There's even an ice luge you can slither down wearing the glistening silver coats and woolly boots they hand out to keep you insulated.

Permafrost affects almost every aspect of life in Yakutsk, obstructing drainage, causing unstilted buildings to bow and then collapse, spontaneously chucking up mounds of earth, and emitting enough methane to possibly alter the earth's climate catastrophically. The Permafrost Kingdom is a great way to get up close and personal with this nebulous and omnipresent beast. In this subterranean permafrost zone, the temperature ranges from –7°C in summer to a balmy (relative to outside temperatures) –20°C in winter. Caves adjacent to the kingdom are used for electricity-free cold storage in the warm months.

True permafrost nerds might check out the **Permafrost Institute** (Институт Мерзлотоведения, ☎334 476; ul Merzlotnaya; individual weekday/weekend R800/1600, group excursion per person weekday/weekend R400/800; by appointment), about 2km west of the city centre. It has a lab that stays a constant –6°C, but high prices make this more of a tour-group option.

Mongolian BBQ (R379 for one trip) indoors, or pork shashlyk (R350) and beer (R160) on its outdoor terrace.

Veranda CAFETERIA €
(Веранда; pr Lenina cnr ul Kirova; meals from R200; 24hr) This conveniently located *stolovaya* has Uzbek dishes to complement the standard Russian fare, plus the cheapest draught beer in town (R120 per ½ litre).

Muus Khaya YAKUT €€
(Муус Хайа; ul Petrovskogo 13; mains R250-500; noon-2am) Another good option for local delicacies. Bowling and billiards on the premises.

Bliny FAST FOOD €
(Блины; pr Lenina 24; bliny R40-90; 9am-3am) This pancake stand is a blessing for budget-minded quick-eaters.

Drinking & Entertainment

Drakon NIGHTCLUB
(Дракон; ul Poyarkova; disco cover R100 Sun-Thu, R300 Fri & Sat) Yakutsk's favourite entertainment complex – for food, disco and home-brewed beer – is just east of the bus station.

Sakha Theatre THEATRE
(Саха Театр; pl Ordzhonikidze) A strikingly modern venue that has theatre and music in the Sakha language; engaging even if you don't get a word of it.

Shopping

A few museums have souvenir shops. The best is at the National Art Museum.

Sakhabult SOUVENIRS
(Сахабулт; pr Lenina 25; 10am-7pm Mon-Fri, 11am-6pm Sat & Sun) Long-running shop where you'll find cool indigenous items like reindeer-skin drums and traditional knives, along with many pelts and much fur. It's pricey if you're looking for big *norka* (mink) hats, but a (real) reindeer Christmas ornament is R250. Good T-shirts too.

Globus MAPS
(Глобус; pr Lenina 18; 9am-6pm Mon-Fri, 10am-4pm Sat) Globus carries topo maps of Sakha and Chukotka, large-scale maps of most Russian regions and a detailed Yakutsk city map. Easily the Far East's best map store.

Information

There are plenty of ATMs around in the top-end hotels and all along pr Lenina.

Telephone & Internet Centre (Телефон и Интернет центр; pr Lenina 10; per hr R70; 8am-8pm)

Getting There & Away

As of this writing, passenger trains from Neryungri go as far north as Tommot in southern Sakha. Our best guess is that the new AYaM passenger train linking Yakutsk with Tommot, Neryungri and Tynda will be ready in 2014.

Air

The **airport**, 6km northeast of the town centre, is well connected to most of Russia but tends to have jacked-up prices. The following are among the many destinations you can fly to:

Khabarovsk from R13,000, 2½ hours
Moscow from R10,000, six hours
Novosibirsk from R16,000, 4½ hours
Vladivostok from R15,000, three hours

Flagship regional carrier **Yakutia Airlines** (www.yakutia.aero) flies to Magadan (from R12,000, two hours) on Tuesdays and serves numerous far-flung destinations in Sakha, including Neryungri (R10,500, 1¾ hours, four weekly) and Tiksi (from R30,000 return, three hours, four weekly). Many air ticket offices line pr Lenina.

Boat

The Yakutsk–Ust-Kut *raketa* (hydrofoil) is long gone. The river ferry service from here only goes as far as Olyokminsk (12 hours), leaving at 5am on even dates from May to October and returning from Olyokminsk at 5am on odd dates. Departures are from the **Yakutsk river terminal** (Речной Вокзал, rechnoy vokzal), 2km northeast of the centre.

Also from the river terminal, you can traverse the Lena by *parom* to Nizhny Bestyakh on the opposite (right) bank (R160, one hour). Departures are every 80 minutes from 7am to 6.20pm. Don't miss the last boat back at 7.40pm.

Private Lena tours go all the way up to Tiksi on the Laptev Sea.

Bus & Taxi

The rough UAZ journey to Neryungri crosses the Lena an hour south of Yakutsk in industrial Mokhsogollakh. Arrange a ride through a travel agent or call 758 888. The unreliable bus to Aldan (R2200, 16 hours) departs Tuesdays at 8am from the Yakutsk **bus station** (Автовокзал; ul Oktyabrskaya 24).

Getting Around

A handy city bus is line 8 (R12), which goes past pr Lenina's hotels on its way between the river terminal and bus station. Bus 4 goes to

THE POLE OF COLD

When thermometers dip further below zero than they go above, and as many as two out of three days of your life are spent slipping on snow, you make some adjustments. In many towns around the Far East, hot-water pipes are elevated above the damaging permafrost. Giant fur coats aren't fashion but (an expensive) necessity, and drivers spring for heated garages and keep their cars running wherever they go during the day. 'If your engine goes off,' one local told us, 'that's it – you have to wait till spring.'

But locals swear that this area – which commonly hits –50°C, and reached –66°C in Yakutsk in 2007 – isn't as bad as outsiders think. For one, transport is easier. Rivers freeze over, offering new 'roads' to reach otherwise isolated areas. 'It's not like kids can't go out and play', one local said. 'It's really not as bad as Moscow, because it's dry here. I don't know how they survive the winters there!'

The unofficial 'pole of cold' is **Oymyakon**, a remote village 650km north of Yakutsk that holds the record as the coldest inhabited spot on earth. Temperatures have been recorded as low as –71°C (in the nearby valleys they go down to –82°C). Besides cold, Oymyakon has a breeding station for reindeer, horses and silver foxes. An annual Pole of Cold Festival, with reindeer races and (outdoor!) concerts, takes place here or in nearby Tomtor in late March.

Yakutsk travel agencies have discovered a market niche in offering trips to Oymyakon and other places in Sakha where the main attraction is extreme cold. An eight-night trip taking in Oymyakon and various other cold places runs to US$3000 per person for groups of four to six people, including transport by Russian UAZ jeeps.

the airport – catch it heading east on pr Lenina. Taxis charge R100 to R150 for rides around the centre. Have a restaurant or hotel call one for you or call ☎429 429.

Around Yakutsk

Yakutsk's city limits can get a little grey and grubby at times, but things get natural – and wild – quickly once you leave town. By just hiring a taxi (about R500 to R700 per hour), you could reach a couple of places; others involve boats.

About 45km south on the road to Pokrovsk, **Orto Doidu** (Орту Дойду; ☎350 373; admission R150; ⏲noon-midnight Wed-Sun) is a nature complex with local animals and shady trails, plus an architectural area with Sakha totems and a *balangan*.

Sottintsy, about 60km north (on the opposite side of the Amur), is home to the **Druzhba Historical Park** – a collection of traditional dwellings. To get here take a bus to Kangalas and cross the Lena River by *parom* to Sottintsy; it's a 2km walk from the riverbank to the park.

Elanka, a two-hour drive south via Mokhsogollakh, has a few rest houses, a small ethnographic museum and fishing on a peaceful patch of the Lena. A beach-side area where ice remains all year, **Bulus** is reached by car ferry from Mokhsogollakh, then a drive south (a three-hour trip).

SAKHALIN ISLAND

El Dorado for oil-struck businessfolk, and 'hell' to Anton Chekhov in 1890 (not to mention the thousands and thousands of prisoners shipped here from the late 19th century), Sakhalin Island (Остров Сахалин) these days is decaying in chunks and booming in others (such as its hub, Yuzhno-Sakhalinsk). It's frequently beautiful too – much of it is filled with a wild terrain of forests, islands of seals, streams full of fish, slopes for skiing and lots and lots of bears – 'much bigger than Kamchatka's', one native assured us. Relatively cheap flights can get you here, but prepare to open the purse strings once you've arrived: Sakhalin is no place for shoestringers.

You'll see more foreigners in Sakhalin than anywhere else in the Far East, but the vast majority are here to do *biznes*. If you're in that boat, definitely make a point of getting out of Yuzhno-Sakhalinsk and exploring Sakhalin's wild side. The main 948km-long island is one of 59 (including the Kuril Islands) that make up the Sakhalinskaya Oblast (Sakhalin Region). Sakhalin's weather is despicable. It was practically snowing in mid-June when we last visited. Summer is brief. August and September are the best months, mosquitoes notwithstanding.

History

The first Japanese settlers came across from Hokkaido in the early 1800s, attracted by marine life so rich that one explorer wrote 'the water looked as though it was boiling'. The island – mistakenly named for an early map reference to 'cliffs on the black river' ('Saghalien-Anaghata' in Mongolian) – already had occupants in the form of the Nivkhi, Oroki and Aino peoples but, just as this didn't give pause to the Japanese, the Russians were equally heedless when they claimed Sakhalin in 1853. Japan agreed to recognise Russian sovereignty in exchange for the rights to the Kuril Islands.

Japan restaked its claim on Sakhalin, seizing the island during the Russo-Japanese War, and got to keep the southern half, which it called Karafuto, under the terms of the Treaty of Portsmouth (1905). In the final days of WWII, though, the Soviet Union staged a successful invasion, and Sakhalin became a highly militarised eastern outpost of the Soviet empire, loaded with aircraft, missiles and guns.

In 1990, Muscovite governor Valentin Fyodorov vowed to create capitalism on the island. He privatised retail trade, but most people soon found themselves poorer. Fyodorov left, head down, in 1993. The demise of the USSR and the influx of thousands of oil-industry internationals succeeded where Fyodorov couldn't.

Yuzhno-Sakhalinsk

Южно-Сахалинск

☎4242 / POP 181,700 / ⌚MOSCOW +7HR

There will be budgets broken. New office towers, hotels and apartment buildings (and sushi bars) are rising – along with prices – all over the oil town's streets (which are still named after Lenin, Marx and other communists). It's quite relaxed, with pleasant tree-lined sidewalks and looming mountains that you can ride chairlifts up and ski or climb down, and a couple of nods to its distant Japanese history.

Sights & Activities

Sakhalin Regional Museum MUSEUM

(Краеведческий музей; Kommunistichesky pr 29; admission R50; ⌚11am-6pm Tue-Sun) The pagoda-roofed Sakhalin Regional Museum has a 21st-century exhibit exploring the Japanese/Soviet overlap of the city's history, typified by the building itself, which served as the home of the Karafuto administration before the Soviets seized the island from the Japanese in 1945. The strong ethnographic section has some unique Aino artefacts and photos from back before the original south Sakhalin inhabitants fled to Japan (check out the photo of the bear ceremony), plus bits on the Nivkhi and the rare Aleuts.

Museum of Sakhalin Island: A Book by AP Chekhov MUSEUM

(Музей острова Сахалин: Книги А П Чехова; ul Kurilskaya 42; admission R30; ⌚11am-6pm Tue-Sat)

CHEKHOV'S SAKHALIN

Perhaps no one will ever really know why, in 1890, Russian literary giant Anton Chekhov left his fame in Moscow and crossed a pre-Trans-Siberian Siberia to come and document the hellish scene of prison life on Sakhalin, which had become a penal colony eight years earlier.

Though cryptic in explaining his move, Chekhov neatly summed up his experiences in the fascinating, if tedious at times, book *Sakhalin Island*, which dryly notes population counts and colourfully describes prisoners chained to wheelbarrows, prisons crawling with cockroaches, freely wandering mass murderers and an overbearing sense of nihilism for many who were banished to the island for life.

Possibly fearing censorship, Chekhov kept a distance from overarching criticism, but wrote to show how a penal system is no way to develop a new region. He summed up, 'If I were a convict, I would try to escape from here, no matter what.'

Chekhov's name now seems forever linked with the island, though many locals seem to shrug their shoulders over the connection. The friendly woman running the Chekhov museum in Aleksandrovsk confessed to us to never having read his work. Another local, fond of the Soviet days, told us, 'He was bourgeoisie! He didn't think about the revolution, only vulgar things like prostitution!'

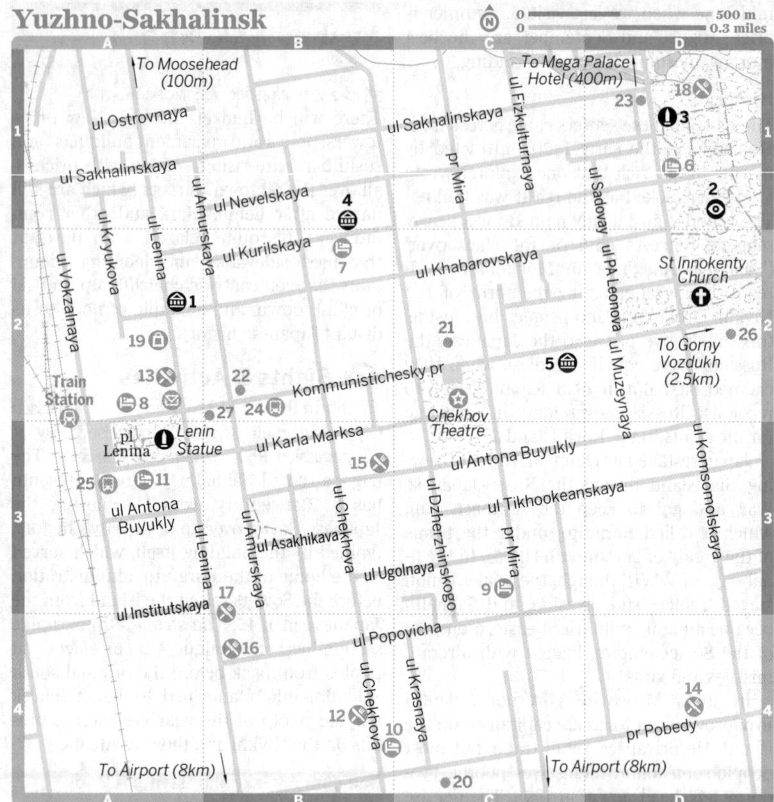

Yes, that's really the name of this two-floor showing of Chekhov's few months on Sakhalin. Look for the photo of Chekhov at a picnic with the Japanese consul and his entourage (looking rather like the bearded Bob Dylan on the *New Morning* album cover). Enrich your visit by purchasing the comprehensive guidebook to the museum (in English!) for R100.

Art Museum ART GALLERY
(Художественный музей; ul Lenina 137; admission R60; ⏰10am-6pm Tue-Sun) This museum has a modest permanent collection of pre-Soviet Russian oils and Korean and Japanese textiles upstairs, and changing exhibits downstairs (fascinating drawings of 19th-century Aino life when we dropped in). Best is getting inside the unique building, a former Japanese bank built in 1935.

Gorny Vozdukh SKIING
(Горный Воздух) 'Mountain Air' ski area looms east of town. A chairlift runs all year (weekends only in summer) and leads up the mountain – another heads down the back side. It's about 300m southeast of the 220-acre **Gagarin Park**, named for a cosmonaut and big with rides, shaded walkways and weekend concerts in summer. The jubilant **Gagarin statue** in the NW portion of the park will thrill lovers of Soviet iconography.

Tours

The Kuril Islands qualify as trip-of-a-lifetime material. Other tours offered by Yuzhno-Sakhalinsk travel agents include seal-infested Moneron Island off Sakhalin's southwest coast, plus shorter hops to points north, such as Tikhaya Bay, about 140km north of Yuzhno-Sakhalinsk (R3000 per person); and 1045m Chekhov Peak, a nice one-day climb in the Sakhalin Mountains not far from Yuzhno. Tikhaya Bay is possible as a DIY tour – just jump on any train heading north to Tikhy.

Yuzhno-Sakhalinsk

Sights

1 Art Museum A2
2 Gagarin Park D1
3 Gagarin Statue D1
4 Museum of Sakhalin Island: A Book by AP Chekhov B1
5 Sakhalin Regional Museum C2

Activities, Courses & Tours

Omega Plus .... (see 8)

Sleeping

6 Gagarin Hotel D1
7 Lotus Hotel B2
8 Moneron A2
9 Pacific Plaza Sakhalin C3
10 Rubin Hotel B4
11 Rybak A3

Eating

12 Cippolini B4
13 Kafe Kolobok A2
14 Nihon Mitai D4
15 Taj Mahal B3
16 Torgovy Kompleks Pervy B4
17 Veranda B3
18 Virazh D1

Drinking

Mishka Pub .... (see 10)

Shopping

19 Ya Maika A2

Information

20 Border Permit & Control Office C4
International SOS Clinic .... (see 21)
21 SakhinCentr C2

Transport

22 Biletur B2
23 Bi-Tomo D1
24 Bus Stop to Airport B2
25 Main Bus Stop A3
26 Sakhalin-Kurily D2
27 SAT B2

Omega Plus TOURS
(☎723 410; www.omega-plus.ru; r 347, ul Kommunistichesky 86; ⌚9am-6pm Mon-Fri, 10am-3pm Sat) The only travel agent in town equipped to handle foreigners, Omega Plus focuses on Japanese heritage tours but also runs various area trips and weeklong trips to the Kurils and Moneron Island. Ask for English-speaking Elena.

Sleeping

In a rare perverse sense of justice, the cheapies have the best location. Don't expect English though. The top-end hotels are tops in the Far East; all have fitness centres, business centres, built-in pubs or clubs and other perks for business travellers. Wi-fi, where available, is not free.

TOP CHOICE **Lotus Hotel** HOTEL €€
(Гостиница Лотус; ☎430 918; www.lotus-hotel.ru; ul Kurilskaya 4a; s/d incl breakfast R2400/3000; ⊖❄📶) While the standard rooms are fine, an extra R300 brings great rewards: an extra room, a kitchenette and small dining area, and even a computer. With free cable internet, these are easily the best value in town. No lift.

Rubin Hotel HOTEL €€€
(Гостиница Рубин; ☎422 212; www.rubinhotel.ru; ul Chekhova 85; s/d incl breakfast from R4500/5000; ❄📶) One of Yuzhno's most popular hotels looks like a polished little Scandinavian motor inn – perfectly run, clean and welcoming. All rooms are essentially serviced apartments with kitchenettes, and include use of the gym and breakfast in the popular Mishka Pub in the basement.

Pacific Plaza Sakhalin HOTEL €€€
(☎455 000; www.sakhalinpacificplaza.ru; pr Mira 172; s/d incl breakfast from R4720/5310; ⊖❄@📶) Inside this eight-floor green-and-grey blob of modernity lurk possibly the Far East's best rooms – extremely attractive, loaded with mod cons and cosy furniture, and with enough space to swing a woolly mammoth.

Gagarin Hotel HOTEL €€
(☎498 400; www.gagarinhotel.ru; ul Komsomolskaya 133; s/d incl breakfast from R3500/4000; ⊖❄@📶) A bit out of the way overlooking the namesake park, this pleasant business hotel capably fills the upper-midrange niche. Rooms are smaller than at the top hotels, but have some style and all the amenities you could ask for, including a gym.

Moneron HOTEL €
(Монерон; ☎723 454; Kommunistichesky pr 86; 2-/3-bed dm R900/600, s/d from R1200/1800; 📶) This sky-blue building facing pl Lenina and the train station is the best cheapie and a fun place to revisit Soviet-style arrangements. Rooms share toilets and each floor has a shared shower (note lack of plural). Stay away from the *lyux* rooms with private bathrooms; there are much better deals elsewhere. There's a 25% booking charge.

Mega Palace Hotel HOTEL €€€
(☎450 450; www.megapalacehotel.com; ul Detskaya 4; r incl breakfast from R4600, ste from R10,000;) Mega Palace bills itself as Yuzhno's most luxurious hotel. It has a point, provided you splurge for the incredibly luxurious suites. It's way out beyond Gagarin Park, so stay elsewhere if you want central location. The trade-off is fresh air and super views of the mountains west of town.

Rybak HOTEL €
(Рыбак; ☎723 768; hotelrybak@mail.ru; ul Karla Marksa 51; 2-/3-bed dm R1000/1200, s/d from R1700/2400;) It might be a baby step up from the Moneron across the square, but prices are higher and *lyux* rooms worse. There's a 25% booking charge.

Eating & Drinking

Business lunches are naturally popular here – think R250 to R350. For shashlyk and beer tents head to the north side of Gagarin Park.

TOP CHOICE **Kafe Kolobok** CAFETERIA €
(Кафе Колобок; ul Lenina 218; meals R200-350; 8am-7pm;) When your budget's stretched and stomach's empty, no one does it like Kolo. A newer take on the old *stolovaya,* it produces piping-hot bliny, *bifshteks* (hamburgers) and those happy breakfast bowls of buckwheat *kasha* (porridge). It's not, however, English friendly: dishes are shown in Russian on a removable-slot board, and frequent lines demand fast orders. If you can't take the pressure, out front an old lady mans a *manti* (Uzbek dumplings) and meat *pirozhki* (pies) cart.

Nihon Mitai JAPANESE €€
(pr Pobedy 28b; mains R250-700; 11am-11pm;) Yuzhno's favourite sushi spot is a bit out of the centre, but the stylish bamboo 2nd-floor dining room is good for soba noodles (R280 to R420) and picking from the sushi conveyor belt after 6pm (about R170 per pair).

Cippolini ITALIAN €€
(SFERA Business Centre, ul Chekhova 78; mains R200-1200; 8:30am-midnight Mon-Fri, 6pm-midnight Sat;) This slick restaurant-bar hauls in the roubles for the R325 set lunch – pizzas get going later. It's also a great place for a coffee on the go. An expat fave.

Mishka Pub PUB €€
(ul Chekhova 85; 6am-midnight;) In the Rubin Hotel's basement, this tiny expat haven is popular for its huge Russian business lunch (noon to 3pm, R250), messy cheeseburgers (R270) and beer later on.

Moosehead PUB €€
(ul Militseyskaya 8b; mains R200-1000; 5am-late Mon-Fri, from noon Sat, from 3pm Sun;) It's not as popular as Mishka, but expats in the know head here for cheaper beer and pub grub, famous seafood chowder (R250) and discount pizza nights. With its big dark-wood bar, it looks more like a pub than Mishka.

Virazh CAFÉ €€
(Вираж; Gagarin Park; noon-2am) This is one of the rare cafés with an outdoor patio in Yuzhno-Sakhalinsk and a go-cart track (R350 per 10 minutes) to boot. Nearby are several fairly ghetto outdoor disco-type places that can be fun in the warm months.

Taj Mahal INDIAN €€
(ul Antona Buyukly 38; veg/meat mains from R250/500; 11.30am-11.30pm;) Stop by the Taj for good Indian curries.

Veranda CAFETERIA €
(Веранда; ul Lenina 219; meals R250-350; 8am-10pm Mon-Fri, 11am-10pm Sat & Sun;) This affordable *stolovaya* has free wi-fi.

Torgovy Kompleks Pervy SUPERMARKET €
(Торговый Комплекс Первый; cnr ul Lenina & ul Popovicha; 24hr) This supermarket also has a deli.

Shopping

Ya Maika SOUVENIRS
(Я Майка; basement, ul Lenina 218; 10am-6.30pm Mon-Sat, 11am-4.30pm Sun) A pretty good little shop with cool dead-fish Sakhalin T-shirts (R650), 'I love Sakhalin' pens (R90) and other stuff that Mum surely asked for. The name is a play on the Russian words for 'T-shirt' and 'Jamaica.'

Information

Border Permit & Control Office
(Сахалинское пограничное управление береговой охраны; www.sakhpubo.ru; pr Pobedy 63a; permit applications 9.30-10.30am & 3.30-4.30pm Mon-Fri) Come here to sort out permits to the Kuril Islands.

Post office (Почта; pl Lenina; per hr R30; internet 8am-8pm, post 8am-10pm Mon-Fri, 9am-6pm Sat & Sun) The internet room is marked 'Dalsvyaz Service Centre'.

SakhinCentr (Сахинцентр; Kommunistichesky pr 32) A one-stop shop for foreigner-geared services: ATMs, banks, an **International**

SOS Clinic (☎462 911, 24hr emergency 474 911) if you're in need of an English-speaking doctor and a kiosk that sells a Yuzhno map for R100.

Getting There & Away

Air

The **airport** is 8km south of the centre. Several airlines, including Sakhalin's flagship carrier **SAT** (CAT; ☎462 288; Kommunistichesky pr 49; ⊙10am-7pm), fly regularly to Khabarovsk (from R3500), Vladivostok (from R7000), Moscow (from R7000) and elsewhere. The competition ensures that prices are quite reasonable.

SAT and Asiana alternate daily flights to Seoul, while Vladivostok Air and/or SAT have flights to Tokyo (two weekly), Sapporo (two weekly), and Beijing (two weekly).

You can buy domestic or international tickets at **Biletur** (Билетур; Kommunistichesky pr 74; ⊙9am-7pm).

Boat

From June to September, once- or twice-weekly ferries run from Korsakov, 40km south of Yuzhno-Sakhalinsk, to Wakkanai on Hokkaido (from R8700, five hours). Book tickets at **Bi-Tomo** (Би-томо; ☎726 889; bitomo@isle.ru; ul Sakhalinskaya 1/1; ⊙9am-6pm).

See p593 for information on boats from the southern Sakhalin port of Kholmsk to Vanino on the mainland. See the boxed text on p606 for information on boats to the Kuril Islands.

Bus

From the **main bus stop** outside the train station you can catch bus 56 for Kholmsk (R270, about 45 minutes) hourly from 8.45am to 9pm, bus 115 to Korsakov (R100, one hour, frequent) half hourly or bus 111 to Aniva (about one hour).

Train

From the **train station**, facing pl Lenina, the fastest train is the 1, which heads north at 8.30pm daily, stopping at Tymovsk (*kupe/platskartny* R2350/1100, 11 hours) and the end of the line, Nogliki (*kupe/platskartny* R2750/1250, 14 hours). The 601 is a slower night train. The 2 train back from Nogliki is a night train. *Elektrichki* go to Bykov (daily, 1½ hours) and Novoderevenskya (two daily, 30 minutes).

Getting Around

Bus 63 leaves for the airport, going east, from the **bus stop** in front of Kino Oktyabr (R15, 30 minutes). A taxi to/from the airport costs about R350.

Kholmsk Холмск

There's really no reason to visit this grotty port, 40km west of Yuzhno, unless you are getting on or off the boat to Vanino. If you get stuck here waiting for the ferry, kill time on the waterfront promenade and, if need be, shack up at **Hotel Kholmsk** (Гостиница Холмск; ☎42433-52 854; ul Sovetskaya 60; s/d R1000/1600). Bus 56 connects Yuzhno with Kholmsk (R180, 45 minutes, hourly).

KAMCHATKA

There are few places in the world that can simultaneously enthral and disappoint quite like Kamchatka (Камчатка). A fickle temptress, it tends to hide its primal beauty behind a veil of thick clouds and fog.

But when the skies finally clear and the powdered snouts of several dozen volcanoes appear through the clouds, all else melts away and you understand that you're in a special place. No matter what you went through to get here, no matter how long you've spent grounded, it was all worth it.

Visitors to Kamchatka are an intriguing mix of outdoorsy types and package tourists. The former have back-country adventure on their mind; the latter want to see Kamchatka's otherworldly geysers, fuming volcanoes and bears the easy way – by helicopter. They're united by deep pockets.

Yet against all odds, Kamchatka has suddenly become viable for independent, relatively budget-conscious travellers. The permit situation has relaxed, allowing visitors to take public transport north to Esso in the heart of the peninsula, where a slick nature park office is busy mapping trails in English and guesthouses hawk beds for less than R1000. Here hot springs abound and you are not far from several volcanoes, including tempestuous Mt Klyuchevskaya (4688m), the tallest active volcano in Eurasia.

The capital, Petropavlovsk-Kamchatsky, may be gritty, but it's in an incredible setting and also has its share of easily accessible activities, including lift skiing into late May and some very doable volcano climbs.

Kamchatka may not be a budget destination yet, but no longer is it strictly the domain of tycoons.

History

The man credited with the discovery of Kamchatka, in 1696, was the half-Cossack, half-Sakha adventurer Vladimir Atlasov, who, like most explorers of the time, was out to find new lands to plunder. He established two forts on the Kamchatka River that became bases for the Russian traders who followed.

The native Koryaks, Chukchi and Itelmeni warred with their new self-appointed overlords, but fared badly and their numbers were greatly diminished. Today, the remnants of the Chukchi nation inhabit the isolated northeast of Kamchatka, while the Koryaks live on the west coast of the peninsula with their territorial capital at Palana.

Kamchatka was long regarded as the least hospitable and remote place in the Russian Empire. In the 19th century, the peninsula became a useful base for exploring Alaska. When Alaska was sold off in 1867, Kamchatka might also have been up for grabs if the Americans had shown enough interest.

During the Cold War, Kamchatka was closed to all outsiders (Russians too) and took on a new strategic importance; foreign interest was definitely no longer welcome. It became a base for military airfields and early-warning radar systems, while the coastline sheltered parts of the Soviet Pacific Fleet.

Getting Around

Locals are fond of repeating that on Kamchatka 'there are no roads, only directions'. You will have a hard time getting 'out there', where the bulk of Kamchatka's glory is (volcano bases, rivers, geysers), without an arranged 6WD truck or helicopter (or several-day hike) – though longer hikes are a possibility too. Regular bus connections go as far north as Esso and Ust-Kamchatsk. The cold months see winter roads *(zimniki)* open up that go further still.

Used by vulcanologists and travellers alike, Mi-2 (capacity: six or eight people) and Mi-8 (capacity: 20 people) helicopters charge by time travelled in the air. The price is high (about R70,000 to R125,000 per hour) and it's risen astronomically over the past several years. Rides are exciting (and loud), with unbelievable views, windows you can open and room to roam about.

WORTH A TRIP

THE KURILS

Spreading northeast of Japan, like stepping stones to Kamchatka, this gorgeous and rugged 56-island chain of 49 active volcanoes, azure-blue lagoons, steaming rivers and boiling lakes is one of the world's great adventures. The Kurils are part of the Pacific 'Ring of Fire' – the islands being the visible tips of an underwater volcanic mountain range. The rare visitors here are treated to dramatic landscapes, isolated coastal communities a world apart from the rest of Russia and seas and skies brimming with marine and bird life.

The three most populous islands, accessible by public boat and/or plane, are Kunashir, Iturup and Shikotan. You can attempt to visit these islands on your own, but secure permits first through a travel agent or from the border control office in Yuzhno-Sakhalinsk. Be prepared to get stuck for a few days because of storms and heavy fog. Late summer and early autumn provide the best chance of stable weather.

SAT (www.satairlines.ru) flies to Yuzhno-Kurilsk on Kunashir Island four times per week, and to Buravestnik, Iturup, three times per week. On the seas, **Sakhalin-Kurily** (Сахалин-Курилы; in Yuzhno-Sakhalinsk ☎4242-762 524; 'Fregat' office, 3rd fl, ul Kommunistichesky 21; ⏲10am-4pm) has a ferry that departs Tuesdays and Fridays from Sakhalin to Kunashir, Shikotan, Iturup and back to Sakhalin. The entire loop takes up to two days. Omega Plus in Yuzhno-Sakhalinsk offers groups of four or more a seven-/eight-day tour to Kunashir or Iturup Island for R33,000 to R47,000 per person, including visa support. Transport is by public boat. Individuals can piggyback on these trips.

More northern islands, many of them uninhabited, can only be visited by private sea craft or on upmarket expeditions such as the 14-day 'Birding the Russian Far East' cruise by **Heritage Expeditions** (www.heritage-expeditions.com), which starts in Kamchatka and finishes on Sakhalin Island. It goes once a year, between May and June (from US$7200 per person).

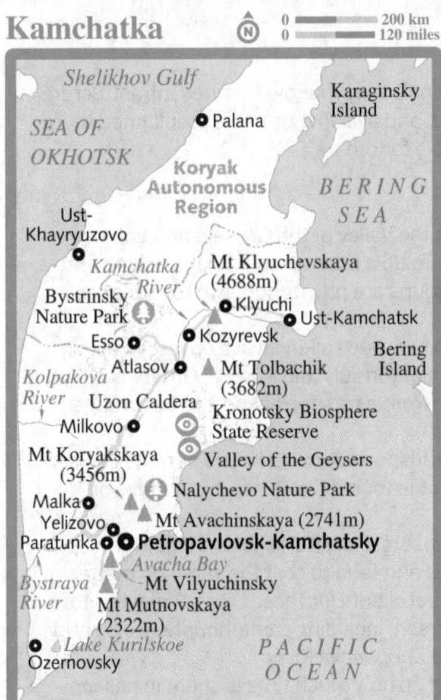

Kamchatka also has its own airline, **Petropavlovsk Kamchatsky Air Enterprise** (www.airport-pkc.ru), which does both scheduled and chartered forays to remote hamlets in the north part of the peninsula, such as Ossora, Palana and Tilichiki on the peninsula, and to Nikolskoye in the Commander Islands, known for its abundant wildlife and seal rookeries. Download the schedule from the website.

Petropavlovsk-Kamchatsky

Петропавловск-Камчатский

☎4152 / POP 195,000 / ⌚MOSCOW +8HR

Some see Petropavlovsk as a necessary evil, a hub to Russia's most beautiful scenery, while others focus on the city's sublime setting, which faces Avacha Bay and is overlooked by two giant volcanoes and surrounded by a long line of snow-capped mountains.

Though it's one of the oldest towns in the Far East, Petropavlovsk's seemingly endless main avenue is lined with mostly grim Soviet block housing, but there are enough attractions to fill a day or two, and the people are quite nice – more outdoorsy and less of that Russian gruffness than elsewhere.

During the Soviet era the town became a sizeable Pacific Fleet submarine base, but its present prosperity is owed completely to the fishing industry, especially its most famous delicacies, salmon and the gargantuan Kamchatka crab (king crab).

Sights & Activities

Avacha Bay BOAT TRIPS

Petropavlovsk's stunningly beautiful bay, with volcanic **Mt Vilyuchinsky** (2173m) visible across the way on most days, is best appreciated on an **Avacha Bay cruise**. Standard three-hour cruises (per person R750) take place most days in summer; book through any travel agency. Better are the more sporadic six-hour tours that reach **Starichkov Island**, a haven for bird life (R3000 per person, including lunch).

Historic Centre NEIGHBOURHOOD

It's worth a wander around the de facto centre of town, where **Lenin** stares out at the bay from pl Lenina. Along the bay is a stone **beach** with great views of Mt Vilyuchinsky, and nearby some cafés serving beer. Looming over the downtown area to the north is **Mt Mishennaya** (382m), an easy climb. Diminutive **Nikolskaya Hill** is to the south near a quaint **wooden chapel** (ul Krasintsev).

Central Market MARKET

(Центральный рынок; ul Leningradskaya) It's not the most practical souvenir, but nothing says you've been to Kamchatka like a kilo of Kamchatka crab. The wonderful, sprawling seafood section of Kamchatka's main market (also known as 'KP Rynok') is full of 30cm crab legs, caviar and different species of whole salmon – worth a look even if you aren't buying. Shelled/unshelled Kamchatka crab legs cost from R1800/700 per kilo.

Kamchatka Regional Unified Museum MUSEUM

(Камчатский краевой объединенный музей; ul Leninskaya 20; admission R150; ⌚10.30am-6pm Wed-Sun) Housed in an attractive half-timbered building overlooking the bay, this museum features an imaginative mix of relics and murals that outline Kamchatka's history, including dioramas of nomadic herders, old cannonballs and flags, photos of the 1975 Tolbachik eruption and maps showing Alaskan expansion.

FREE **Institute of Volcanology** MUSEUM

(Институт вулканологии; ☎997 734, 297 717; bul Piypa 9; admission free, excursion per group R500; ⌚8.30am-5.45pm Mon-Fri) One way to begin a volcano-centric trip is by taking in an expert's lecture accompanied by an excursion

HOW TO SEE KAMCHATKA

While it's getting easier than ever to visit Kamchatka on your own, limited infrastructure, permit requirements and risks like bear attacks and avalanches make preplanned tours mandatory for many places and highly advisable for others.

Tours

Many of Kamchatka's marquee sights, such as the Valley of the Geysers and Lake Kurilskoe, are only available by organised tour. To do a tour doesn't mean packing onto a busload of 50 camera-toting tourists. Some groups are private, just two to four people, and most groups are fewer than 20 people.

Tours range from simple day trips to one- to two-week all-inclusive odysseys taking in several sights or activities. Plan ahead, especially in July and August. Otherwise days can be wasted scrambling for a guide to return from a trip or transport to be arranged from Petropavlovsk.

Tours usually include everything – guides, transport, permits, hotels or tents to sleep in, sleeping bags and food. Most of the high-profile tours involve helicopter rides or 6WD/4WD transport.

Prices for the big day trips – Valley of the Geysers, Lake Kurilskoe and Mt Mutnovskaya – are set by the helicopter companies and tend to cost the same no matter which travel agency you use. Travel agencies pool clients for these tours. A day trip to the Valley of the Geysers costs R27,000 per person, including a one-hour helicopter ride each way, lunch and stops at Uzon Caldera and Zhupanova River.

Prices for longer tours vary wildly depending on how much time is spent in helicopters. A weeklong tour involving some camping and taking in several key sights might cost €2000 to €2500, including a few helicopter rides.

See the Petropavlovsk-Kamchatsky section for recommended tour companies.

DIY Without Guides

DIY travel is more difficult and comes with serious risks. Especially if you're looking to venture into the back country, any misstep can be dangerous, and you're best off having an experienced guide. A couple of local geologists were eaten by bears in 2008, by no means the first bear mauling in these parts. Winter travel eliminates the risk of bear attacks but creates new risks, such as days-long white-outs. This ain't Disneyworld.

With those caveats established, the easiest fully DIY trips around Petropavlovsk include the hike up Mt Avachinskaya and trekking along the well-marked trails from Mt Avachinskaya to Nalychevo Valley. Another option is to head up to Esso, 10 hours north of Petropavlovsk by bus, where Bystrinsky Nature Park has an extensive network of well-marked and well-mapped trails.

While we wouldn't recommend it, we've heard of back-country skiers getting off the Esso bus halfway and heading into the mountains on their own. Others have taken the bus up to Klyuchi near the base of Mt Klyuchevskaya and launched forays into the wilderness from there. Check to see whether you need permits before setting off anywhere.

DIY with Guides

If you're wanting to get more 'out there' than Nalychevo or Esso, another option is simply hiring a local guide and going on a weeklong or longer trek. Some travellers have done so to explore huge pockets of wilderness not featured here.

The Visitor Centre in Yelizovo is the best place to get a freelance guide. Also talk with Chip Levis in Esso for suggestions.

in the small science museum here. Bring your own interpreter. The institute's corridors have some cool photos and displays (some in English!) on the Valley of the Geysers, Uzon Caldera, Mt Klyuchevskaya and other Kamchatka marvels.

Krasnaya Sopka SKIING
(Красная Сопка; ⌚Nov-May) One of several ski areas within the city limits, this one is

noteworthy for incredible views of Avacha Bay. T-bars take you up for R50 per run.

 Tours

All of the following can do the main tours (and many more), offer visa support and help you charter helicopters, planes or 6WD vehicles. The following list is by no means comprehensive – Petropavlovsk has dozens of tour companies, so by all means shop around – but these have shown consistently good service over the years.

Popular tour activities not listed here include rafting and combo rafting/fishing trips, horse riding, dog sledding, snowmobiling, diving and fly fishing for salmon. The following are all run out of Petropavlovsk or Yelizovo, where the helicopter pad is.

Explore Kamchatka TOUR COMPANY
(☎41531-66 601; www.explorekamchatka.com; ul Bolshokova 41, Yelizovo) This place in Yelizovo is run by an Alaskan who promotes alternative destinations (often with more environmentally friendly means, ie no helicopters or 6WD vehicles) and frequently helps visitors with unique requests (eg film crews seeking unique fishing spots). She's a mine of information for independent travellers and runs a great little B&B.

Kamchatintour TOUR COMPANY
(☎271 034; www.kamchatintour.ru; ul Leningradskaya 124b; ⊙10am-6pm Mon-Fri, 9am-7pm daily in summer) This is the most helpful Petropavlovsk agency we've found in terms of preplanning help and responsiveness, although much of its business is with Japanese groups. It can get you to its camp at Mt Avachinskaya on short notice.

Lost World TOUR COMPANY
(☎498 328; www.travelkamchatka.com; room 4, ul Frolova 4/1, Petropavlovsk; ⊙9am-6pm Mon-Fri, daily in summer) This long-running operation has experienced guides (including outdoorsy vulcanologist vets) that specialise in somewhat smaller groups.

VALLEY OF THE GEYSERS ДОЛИНА ГЕЙЗЕРОВ

Kamchatka's most famous attractions lie 200km northeast of Petropavlovsk in the spectacular Valley of the Geysers (Dolina Geyzerov). Discovered in 1941, the 8km-long valley of a few dozen geysers cut through by the Geysernaya River is part of the protected **Kronotsky Biosphere State Reserve**. A 2007 earthquake, contrary to some outside reports, did not destroy the valley, though a few areas were lost.

Around 200 geothermal pressure valves sporadically blast steam, mud and water heavenward. The setting is exquisite and walking tours along a boardwalk take you past some of the more colourful and active geysers.

To get there you must travel by helicopter with a group on a day trip. Arrange through any travel agent. Rising petrol prices only partially explain the gigantic boom in price – from US$250 per person in 2004 to US$800 in 2011. Many visitors feel it's simply too much for what you get.

For an extra R5000 per person, the four- or five-hour trip can be extended with stops at **Zhupanova River** and **Uzon Caldera**, the remains of a 40,000-year-old volcano, now a 10km crater with steamy lakes.

LAKE KURILSKOE ОЗЕРО КУРИЛЬСКОЕ

Kamchatka's 'bear lake' – reached by helicopter – is so popular with the area's bears that, in August and September (when up to three million red salmon come to spawn), visitors can almost get tired of looking at them. The huge lake, formed by an eruption nearly 9000 years ago, is rimmed by volcanoes and home to a couple of lodges. The only trails in the area are bear trails. Don't wander alone: a Japanese photographer was eaten by a bear here in 2000.

Travel agents can set you up with a group flying out here on a day trip for R24,000 per person. Lost World has a 10-day bear/volcano trip that includes a few days around Lake Kurilskoe and a few days around Mt Mutnovskaya for €2650 per person.

MT MUTNOVSKAYA ГОРА МУТНОВСКАЯ

Walking down into an active 4km-wide cone, past boiling mud pools and ice crevices cut by hot vapours of volcanic fumes is like Frodo and Sam's last trek in *The Lord of the Rings*. Kamchatka vulcanologists, who love all of Kamchatka's volcanoes, seem to hold Mt Mutnovskaya (2322m) in special regard – for studying, climbing or simply observing. One said, 'It's easier to reach than the Valley of the Geysers, and much more alive, smoking and bubbling.'

A wild road – handled by 6WD or good 4WD vehicles – reaches the base, but only after snows melt in mid-August (when some

Petropavlovsk-Kamchatsky

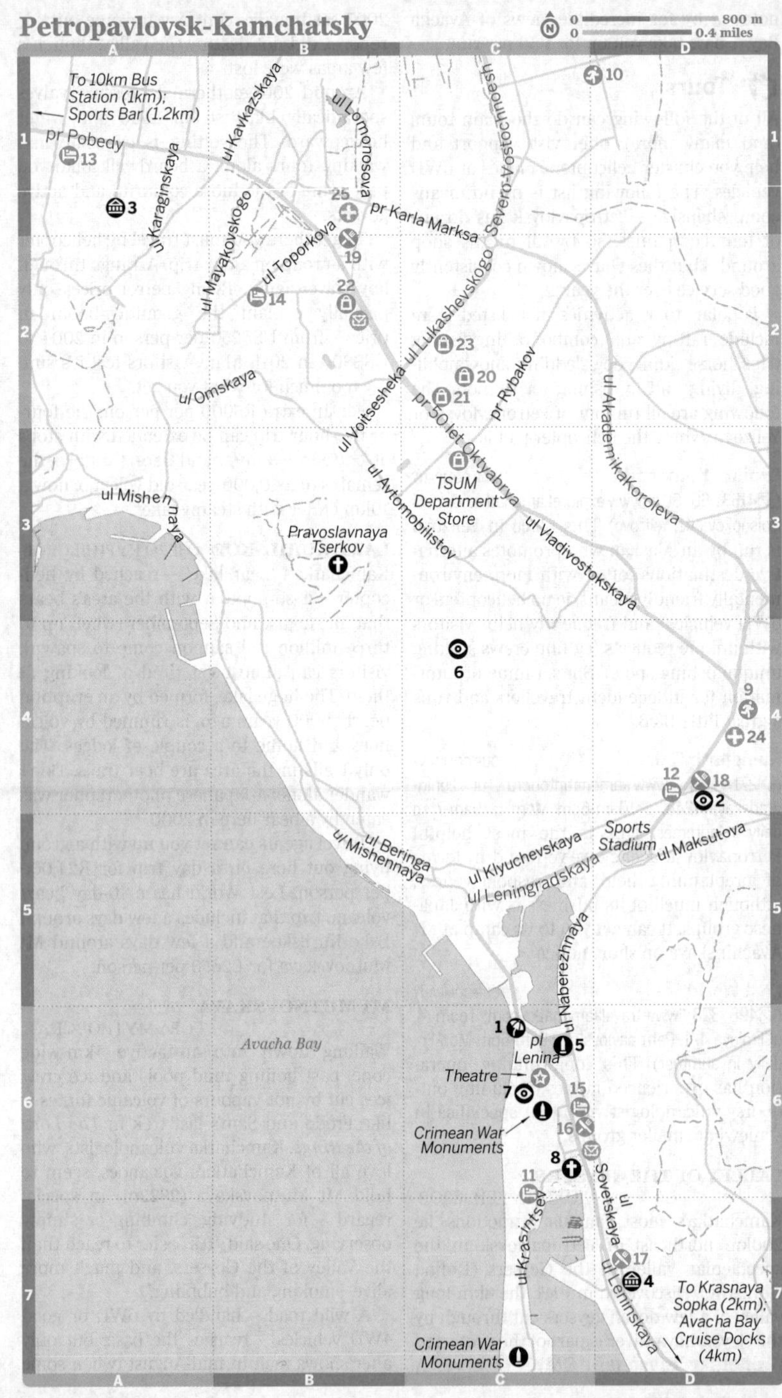

0 800 m
0 0.4 miles
A
B
C
D
To 10km Bus Station (1km); Sports Bar (1.2km)
pr Pobedy
13
3
ul Karaginskaya
ul Kavkazskaya
ul Mayakovskogo
ul Lomonosova
25
19
ul Toporkova
14
22
pr Karla Marksa
Severo-Vostochnoesh
ul Lukashevskogo
10
23
20
21
ul Omskaya
ul Voitsesheka
pr 50-let Oktyabrya
pr Rybakov
ul Akademika Koroleva
TSUM Department Store
ul Avtomobilistov
ul Mishennaya
Pravoslavnaya Tserkov
ul Vladivostokskaya
6
9
24
12
18
2
Sports Stadium
ul Maksutova
ul Klyuchevskaya
ul Leningradskaya
ul Beringa
ul Mishennaya
ul Naberezhnaya
Avacha Bay
1
pl Lenina
5
Theatre
7
15
Crimean War Monuments
16
8
11
ul Krasintsev
ul Sovetskaya
17
4
ul Leninskaya
To Krasnaya Sopka (2km); Avacha Bay Cruise Docks (4km)
Crimean War Monuments

Petropavlovsk-Kamchatsky

Sights

1	Beach	C6
2	Central Market	D4
3	Institute of Volcanology	A1
4	Kamchatka Regional Unified Museum	D7
5	Lenin Statue	C6
6	Mishennaya Hill	C4
7	Nikolskaya Hill	C6
8	Wooden Chapel	C6

Activities, Courses & Tours

9	Kamchatintour	D4
10	Lost World	D1

Sleeping

11	Baza po Priyomu Turistov	C6
12	Hotel Avacha	D4
13	Hotel Edelveis	A1
14	Hotel Geyser	B2
15	Hotel Oktyabrskaya	C6

Eating

16	Bistro	C6
17	Korea House	D7
18	Milk Café	D4
	Molino	(see 21)
19	San Marino	B2
	Yamato	(see 21)
	Yamato	(see 23)

Drinking

	Barraka	(see 21)

Shopping

20	Alpindustriya-Kamchatka	C2
	Central Market	(see 2)
	Galant City Shopping Centre	(see 18)
21	Parus Shopping Centre	C2
22	Planeta Knig	B2
23	Planeta Shopping Centre	C2
	Suveniry i Podarky	(see 2)

Information

24	Hospital	D4
25	Hotel Petropavlovsk Medical Centre	B1

Petropavlovsk agencies offer day trips here). Otherwise, it's an expensive helicopter ride or an 8km to 15km hike (up to four hours one way, though not a difficult climb), depending on accessibility, to reach the cone, where you can hike (or ski) down past boiling mud pools.

It's particularly important to have a guide here. Weather can turn suddenly, and it's easy to get lost. Many tours climb the oval-shaped caldera of nearby **Gorely** (1829m). Base camps here are tent only.

HELISKIING & BACK-COUNTRY SKIING

Heliskiing tours of the mountains and volcanoes that make an arc around Petropavlovsk include unreal experiences such as skiing onto Pacific beaches or into Mt Mutnovskaya's fuming crater.

Tours typically guarantee four days of skiing in a 10-day period to allow for weather inconsistencies – any wind or fog grounds the birds. If the weather cooperates, you can pay (a lot) for extra days of heliskiing. Otherwise, the buffer days are spent snowcat skiing at the base of Mt Avachinskaya or at one of several small ski areas around town, trying out the hot springs, cruising around Avacha Bay or touring wild Pacific beaches. Conditions are most reliable in February and March.

Until recently, Kamchatka was considered a 'budget' heliskiing destination, with packages costing less than half what they cost in Europe, Canada and Alaska. No longer. Tour prices have skyrocketed in line with rising prices for helicopter rides. The three main operators are **Vertikalny Mir** (www.vertikalny-mir.com), **Russian Heliboarding Club** (www.helipro.ru) and **Explore Kamchatka**; other operators usually go through one of the above. Keep in mind that a massive avalanche swept away a helicopter and killed 10 people on a trip in 2010.

Back-country skiing, such as trips into Nalychevo Valley, where there are also hot springs to splash in, is a cheaper alternative. **Fyodor Farberov** (farberovf@mail.ru) is an English-speaking heliskiing and back-country ski guide in Petropavlovsk who charges R4000 per day. He sometimes leads 14-day ski trips to Tolbachik, but there's 'at least 30% bad weather up there – all you can do those days is just camp and survive.'

Sleeping

Petro's hotels are, on balance, putrid value. Staff are friendly enough but you're paying an awful lot for cramped rooms that can't hide from their Soviet past. If you're staying a while ask travel agents about apartment rentals.

Any wi-fi at the following places costs extra. Rates include breakfast unless otherwise noted.

Baza po Priyomu Turistov PENSION €€
(Базз по Приёму Туриистов; ☎258 595; ul Krasintsev 1; dm in d R900, s/d R1500/1800) It's not just because it's cheap that it's our top choice in Petropavlovsk. The rooms really aren't any worse than at Petropavlovsk's 'top-end' hotels (although some rooms lack sinks, so you must brush your teeth in the shower). Flat-screen TVs in some rooms belie that it caters mainly to youth groups. The downtown location is ideal. No registration and no restaurant/breakfast.

Hotel Edelveis HOTEL €€
(Гостиница Эдельвейс; ☎295 000; www.idelveis.com; pr Pobedy 27; 2-bed dm R1700, s/d without bathroom R2500/3400, with bathroom R3400/4500;) Street cred from outside (wrecked cars in dreary hood), rather grandmotherly inside, with old-fashioned but comfy economy rooms and slicker standard rooms. Great English-speaking staff.

Hotel Avacha HOTEL €€€
(Гостиница Авача; ☎427 331; www.avacha-hotel.ru; ul Leningradskaya 61; s/d from R4100/5500; @) Across from the lively Central Market, the rooms here are attractive enough but retain Soviet dimensions, especially the bathrooms. There's a sauna, gym, ATM and air-ticket agency downstairs. The very Russian breakfast is filling.

Hotel Geyser HOTEL €€
(Гостиница Гейзер; ☎258 595; www.geyser-hotel.ru; ul Toporkova 10; s/d R2550/3020; @) Rooms here have sweeping views of Avacha Bay and benefit from a recent renovation, but have some quirks, such as some missing sinks. 'There wasn't room for sinks after the *remont,*' a receptionist explained.

Hotel Oktyabrskaya HOTEL €€€
(Гостиница Октябрьская; ☎412 684; hotelok2@mail.kamchatka.ru; ul Sovetskaya 51; 2-bed dm R2700, s/d from R3300/5400; @) The best thing about this thoroughly Soviet hotel is the big buffet breakfast (R350 if you are walking in). The light renovations hardly justify the price. Its location is good, near the waterfront and museum.

Eating & Drinking

It's a shame the city doesn't have a better selection of restaurants and bars, given how much time tour groups spend waiting around for bad weather to clear.

TOP CHOICE **San Marino** RUSSIAN €€
(Сан Марино; ☎252 481; pr Karla Marksa 29/1; mains R150-750; noon-1am;) Back from a hard trek, San Marino is Petropavlovsk's best splash for an excellent, exotic meal of Kamchatka crab, scallops, moose, *poporotnik* (fern) salad and other wild local delicacies. Prices aren't too bad considering the quality – a salmon steak is R200 and Kamchatka beer just R80.

Milk Café CAFÉ €€
(Милк Кафе; Galant City Mall, ul Leningradskaya; mains R200-400; 11am-10pm;) The town's best pizzas (R280 to R450, good for one or two) are at this bright café, which also has some healthy soups and salads, plus a fine coffee selection. The menu has pictures in lieu of English.

Yamato JAPANESE €€€
(Ямато; meals R400-700; noon-midnight;) Planeta Shopping Centre (ul Lukashevskogo 5); Parus Shopping Centre (4th fl, pr 50 let Oktyabrya 16/1) Yamato's two outlets serve surprisingly tasty sushi amid soothing Japanese-style screens. Set lunches run from R220 to R300, sushi platters are for one R500.

Molino ITALIAN €€
(Молино; Parus Shopping Centre, pr 50 let Oktyabrya 16/1; mains R200-300, pizzas R220-290; 10am-1am) It doesn't have the best pizza in town but it's well located on the central avenue and has reasonably priced beer and good people watching. Pizzas feed one hungry person.

Barraka LOUNGE BAR €€
(Баррака; 4th fl, Parus Shopping Centre, pr 50 let Oktyabrya 16/1; noon-5am) This swanky roof-top lounge in the new Parus Shopping Centre has excellent if pricey sushi, a R250 business lunch and notable after-hours parties. In a very Russian twist, waitresses serve topless on Thursdays.

Sport Bar NIGHTCLUB €€
(Спорт Бар; behind 10km bus station, pr Pobedy; cover R100-500; 10pm-6am Wed-Sun) Many a tour-grouper has spent a boozy evening in this long-running establishment, which despite the billiards tables is more nightclub

than sports bar. It definitely gets jumping on a consistent basis.

Korea House KOREAN €€
(ul Leninskaya 26; meals R400-1000; 11am-11pm;) Ignore high prices – most dishes serve two to three. Local seafood on the menu, imported piranhas in the fish tank.

Bistro CAFETERIA €
(Бистро; ul Sovetskaya 49; meals R150-250; 10am-8pm) Simple cafeteria.

Shopping

Prepurchase Petropavlovsk maps in Vladivostok or Khabarovsk if you can. Local malls carry them for double the price (about R300).

Central Market SOUVENIRS
(Центральный Рынок; ul Leningradskaya) In addition to seafood, the central bazaar has a few good souvenir shops, including **Suveniry i Podarky** (Сувениры и Подарки; 10am-6pm), which among other things has indigenous wood statuettes, furry pendants, amber and other jewellery, and Kamchatka maps.

Alpindustriya-Kamchatka OUTDOOR GEAR
(Алпиндустрия-Камчатка; pr 50 let Oktyabrya 22; 11am-7pm Mon-Fri, to 6pm Sat & Sun) This valuable camping-gear shop rents tents, backpacks, sleeping bags and sleeping mats. It's about 75m off the road, amid housing.

Planeta Knig SOUVENIRS
(Планета Книг; ul Tushkanova; 10am-6pm Mon-Sat) Has some OK souvenirs and a regional map.

Information

Internet Access & Post

Main post office (Главпочтамт; ul Leninskaya 60; per hr R100; internet 10am-7pm Mon-Fri, post 8am-8pm Mon-Fri, 9am-6pm Sat, 9am-4pm Sun)

Post office (Почта; ul Tushkanova 9; per hr R100; 8am-8pm Mon-Fri, 9am-6pm Sat)

Medical Services

Hospital (Больница; 433 936; ul Leningradskaya 114)

Hotel Petropavlovsk Medical Centre (252 075; 2nd fl, pr Karla Marksa 31a; 9am-8pm Mon-Fri)

Rescue Service (410 395)

Money

You can find ATMs at the main post office and in most hotels and shopping centres, including **Parus** (Парус; pr 50 let Oktyabrya) and **Galant City** (Галант; ul Leningradskaya), across from Hotel Avacha.

Getting There & Away

From the Petropavlovsk airport in Yelizovo, 30km northwest, there are at least daily flights to the following destinations:

Khabarovsk from R7000, 2½ hours
Moscow from R8800, nine hours
Novosibirsk from R14,000, seven hours
Vladivostok from R9500, 3½ hours

Yakutia Airlines has a Wednesday flight (Tuesday in the reverse direction) to Magadan (from R11,500). The major hotels and the main post office have ticketing agents. Flights during the peak July/August period sell out months in advance so book ahead.

The big news from the skies when we visited was the possible resumption of sporadic direct flights to Alaska. Vladivostok Air may operate this as a summer-only quasi-charter flight hopping between Petropavlovsk, Anchorage and Tokyo, starting in 2012. (The Tokyo flights were operational in summer 2011.)

From the **'10km bus station'** (Автовокзал; avtovokzal desyaty kilometr; pr Pobedy), buses depart daily at 9am to Esso (R950, nine to 10 hours), and at 8am to Ust-Kamchatsk (R1920, 13 hours) via Klyuchi (R1470, 11 hours).

Getting Around

Kamchatka's 25km central avenue enters the city limits near the 10km bus station as pr Pobedy and changes its name 11 times as it snakes around bayside hills. Dozens of buses (R16) and *marshrutky* (R30) run along its length.

Buses for the airport (R30, 35 minutes) depart from the 10km bus station; take anything marked 'Aeroport' or 'Yelizovo', the town near the airport. From the airport, take any bus signboarded '10km' from the 'Petropavlovsk' stop across from the terminal. Taxis are about R600.

Call 460 160 for the best **taxi** rates around town or to Paratunka/Yelizovo.

Around Petropavlovsk-Kamchatsky

MT AVACHINSKAYA & MT KORYAKSKAYA

Two volcanoes near Petropavlovsk stand side by side 20km north of town (about 35km by road). The bigger and more forbidding one is Mt Koryakskaya (3456m), which takes experienced climbers two days to climb. The smaller one on the east is Mt Avachinskaya, generally included on tours and one of Kamchatka's 'easier' volcanoes to summit (about four to six hours up). Avachinskaya last erupted in 1991, but you can see it smoking daily.

A base-camp complex serves both volcanoes and sees a lot of action, including skiers and snowmobiles into early July; it gets quieter as you climb up. Just below Avachinskaya, the aptly named Camel Mountain is an easy one-hour climb, with lots of Siberian marmots on top and great views of Mt Koryakskaya.

Getting here is problematic. Snow blocks the final few kilometres of the rough access road through mid-July, which means you'll have to walk (or better yet, cross-country ski) the last bit, or hire Kamchatintour's snowcat. After mid-July you can get all the way to the base camp in a 4WD. The Visitor Centre in Yelizovo is the best place to find a driver. Freelance drivers charge R2500 to R3500 per car one way (R4000 to R5000 for round-trip with wait time) to the base camp from Yelizovo; some can guide you up the mountain for an extra R2000 per group. Travel agencies might charge R5000 per car.

Kamchatintour has its own camp at the foot of Avachinskaya and offers a day trip out here for about R3500 per person including lunch and snacks at the camp and a guide.

No permits are required to hike up Avachinskaya.

NALYCHEVO NATURE PARK

One of Kamchatka's most accessible attractions for hearty independent travellers is this nature park encompassing lovely Nalychevo Valley and the 12 volcanoes (four active) that surround it. A trail extends about 40km north from Mt Avachinskaya to the park's main base area, where there are many huts, camping spots, an information centre and, in summer, a handful of rangers who can point out hiking trails leading to hidden hot springs.

Camping is in designated areas or huts that vary wildly in quality. Before heading out, secure a park permit (R500), pick up a crude trail map and reserve a hut (per person R150 to R800) at the **park office** (☎4152-411 710; ul Zaivoko 19) in Yelizovo. GPS coordinates are also available. You might encounter foraging bears from June to September; the park office can brief you on proper precautions.

To get here, follow the instructions to Mt Avachinskaya, then walk. It's about a two-day hike from the Avachinskaya base camp to the park's main base area. You can exit the park via Pinachevo on the park's western boundary, but arrange to be picked up beforehand.

YELIZOVO ЕЛИЗОВО

☎41531 / ⏰MOSCOW +8HR

With an efficient new visitor centre and some reasonable accommodation, this low-key town near the airport is positioning itself as an alternative to Petropavlovsk for independent travellers.

The main attractions are hikes in the surrounding wilderness and the hot springs of nearby Paratunka.

Yelizovo's small **Regional Museum** (Краеведческий Музей; ul Kruchiny 13; admission R100; ⏰10am-6pm Tue-Sat) has ethnographic exhibits, Russian weavings, local art and the requisite stuffed sables and marmots.

The Visitor Centre can arrange apartment rentals in the area for R1300 and up. **Yelizovo B&B** (☎66 601, 8-962-280 7840; www.explorekamchatka.com; 41 Bolshakova ul; r incl breakfast per person R1250), run by an American woman who operates Explore Kamchatka, has three inviting rooms in a bright house, probably the best deal in the Far East. The **Art Hotel** (Арт Гостиница; ☎71 443; www.artotel.ru; ul Kruchiniy 1; r without/with bathroom R2200/2500) is a cheerful place with nice rooms on the main drag in town.

The **Visitor Centre** (☎8-962-282 5265, weekends 8-961-961 8558; www.welcometokamchatka.ru; ul Ryabikov 1a; ⏰10am-5pm Mon-Fri, to 7pm Jul & Aug), on the 2nd floor of the bus station, can point you in the direction of good hikes in the area, find you a trekking guide or help you join an organised tour. It has brochures and a great free glossy map (in Russian) of Nalychevo Nature Park.

The **post office** (Почта; ul Zavoiko 9; ⏰8am-8pm Mon-Fri, 9am-6pm Sat & 9am-2pm Sun) has internet access (R70 per hour). Frequent buses link Yelizovo's bus station with the airport.

PARATUNKA ПАРАТУНКА

Sprawled-out Paratunka (25km south of Yelizovo) is a leafy network of spa resorts set up around natural or pool-like hot springs. Many tours fit in a day here. One of many, **Golubaya Laguna** (Blue Lagoon; ☎124 718) is also a hotel geared to Russian tourists,

NORTHERN KAMCHATKA

Esso and Ust-Kamchatsk are easily reached by public transport. Much of the rest of the north, however, requires a helicopter, plane, 4WD or 6WD.

and has a couple of popular hot pools (with slides and jacuzzi) surrounded by woods.

One worthwhile night out around here is a vodka-downing **Exotic Picnic with a Farmer** (☎8-924-792 3468) aka 'dinner with Sasha', an engaging Muscovite transplant who makes vegetarian meals from wild plants by his dacha, sings folk songs and makes many toasts. For some, it gets too drunken; for others, this researcher included, it's a wonderful night out. It's R1000 to 1500 per person. Most travel agents can arrange this.

Paratunka is served by bus 111 from Petropavlovsk or 110 from Yelizovo.

Esso Эссо

☎41542 / POP 3000 / ⌚MOSCOW +8HR

The totally independent travellers' best destination in Kamchatka, Esso is set snug in a valley of green mountains, with a network of well-mapped hiking trails extending into surrounding Bystrinsky Nature Park, plus hot-spring pools in town and rafting and horse-riding options nearby. It's a quiet, lovely place with the scent of pine, and locals who live in picturesque wooden cottages.

Evenki people migrated here 150 years ago from what is now the Sakha Republic, becoming the distinct Even people in the process. Here they met the local Itelmeni and Koryak people as well as Russians. Although Esso remains a mixed community, the nearby village of Anavgay is mostly Even.

There's no ATM in town. The web may be surfed slowly on a single computer at the **post office** (Почта; ul Lenina; per hr R50; ⌚9am-6pm). The daily bus to Petropavlovsk departs at 9am from in front of the plankwood **ticket office** (ul Mostovaya 9).

Sights & Activities

Bystrinsky Nature Park HIKING

A nature reserve in Russia with trail maps in English and a fully Westernised visitor centre? You'd better believe it. Bystrinsky is a shining exception to the rule of neglected regional and national parks in Russia. Outside the **Esso Visit Centre** (ul Lenina; ⌚8.30am-6pm), a glossy sign in English describes 11 spectacular hikes of 2km to 142km. Inside you'll find extensive trail maps, brochures on this and other protected areas in Kamchatka, helpful English-speaking staff and even some German interns (it's funded by the German foundation Manfied-Hermsen-Stiftung). It gives away a town map as well.

It doesn't have guides but can help you find one and also arrange helicopter or 6WD charters should you wish to venture further to see reindeer herds or climb area volcanoes such as Mt Tolbachik (3682m – not in the park), a place so moonlike the Soviet space program tested its 'moonwalker' vehicle there before sending it out into space.

Before you set off anywhere on your own, have the staff brief you on bear precautions and keep them apprised of your itinerary. And be warned: the easy-sounding 2km hike is a difficult grunt straight up steep Pionerskaya Sopka (Pioneer Hill) just north of town.

FREE **Hot Springs** HOT SPRINGS

Esso is proud of its hot *istochniki* (springs). Most hotels have a simple one, and there's a big, popular public pool in town (admission free), plus more secretive ones around – ask at the Visit Centre.

Ethnographic Museum MUSEUM

(ul Naberezhnaya 14a; admission R100; ⌚10am-6pm Wed-Sun) You can find out much about the history of the area's peoples in this well-kept museum in a charming Cossack-style *izba* (wooden house) set beside the burbling river that flows through Esso. The museum contains some truly memorable old photos. There's a souvenir shop in a separate building.

Rafting RAFTING

Ask about rafting opportunities on the swift **Bystraya River** (its name means 'fast') at Altai guesthouse. Another interesting option is kayaking with **Chip Levis** (www.kamchatkachip.com; kamchatkachip@rambler.ru), a posthippie American who offers small-group trips (of the lesser visited Koserevsk and Kamchatka Rivers) in kayaks he made himself. Chip is going to enjoy the trip as much as you will.

Nulgar DANCE

Esso's folk dance troupe ('Nulgar' means 'strangers' or 'travellers') often plays hour-long concerts for visiting groups. Performances include throat chants and shoulder dances to emulate the sounds and swagger of reindeer. They are set up mainly for tour groups but individuals can join by request.

Reindeer Herds WILDLIFE

A few reindeer herds of 1000 to 2000 heads, managed by nomadic Evens, can be tracked down around Esso and Anavgay. They are reachable by helicopter in the warm months, and possibly by snowmobile during winter. An hour in a helicopter costs R100,000 in these parts. Every late November there's a *zaboy* (slaughter) about 15km from Esso that's easier to reach.

Festivals & Events

Neighbouring Anavgay holds a rollicking **Even New Year** festival during summer solstice, with plenty of dancing and singing into the wee hours.

Sleeping

Esso is the biggest bargain in the Far East for accommodation. All guesthouses listed here arrange meals.

Aleksandra (Александра; mains R80-100; ⌚10am-10pm) and **Minutka** (Минутка; mains R60-100; ⌚10am-8pm) are two simple cafés opposite each other near the museum, or you can self-cater at the small **Supermarket** (Супермаркет; ul Pionerskaya; ⌚8am-10pm).

TOP CHOICE **Tri Medvedya** LODGE €

(Три Медведя; ☎8-924-781 6688; r per person R800) This gorgeous two-storey wooden house has a genuine mountain-lodge feel, with a fireplace, bearskin rugs and cocoon-like beds. Hosts Natalya and Aleksandr cook what they hunt and gather – moose, fern, deer, whatever – and you can dine in a yurt hung with animal skins. No pool but it's near the public hot spring.

Altai GUESTHOUSE €

(Алтай; ☎21 218; ul Mostovaya 12a; r per person R900; ♨) A gingerbread-like house with a small hot pool. The late owner was a pioneer of rafting and other outdoorsy tours, such as horse riding and snowmobiling, in the area. The tours continue to run.

Sychey GUESTHOUSE €

(Сычей; ☎21 294; r per person R600) Visit Centre head Natalya runs this appealing little guesthouse on the well-manicured grounds of her house. It's right next to the public pool.

Paramushir Tur HOTEL €€

(Парамушир Тур; ☎21 442; www.paramushir.ru; s/d incl breakfast from R2000/3600; ♨) This slightly gaudy offering at the base of Pionerskaya Hill is your choice if you need mod cons.

Understand Russia

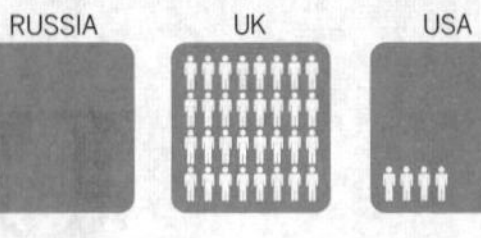

Russia Today

The Ruling Tandem

Under the ruling tandem of President Dmitry Medvedev and Prime Minister Vladimir Putin, Russia is on a roll both in terms of its economy and international standing. Sports fans have their eyes on the country as it hosts first the Winter Olympics in Sochi in 2014 (see p419) and then, four years later, the soccer World Cup. Economic growth is steady at 4% in 2010 and international reserves a very healthy US$537.7 billion as of August 2011 according to the Bank of Russia. *Forbes* magazine says Moscow has more billionaires than any other city in the world. Just strolling any major Russian metropolis (and many minor ones), it's impossible not to notice how much more affluent Russians look compared to a decade ago.

This said, the average Russian lives on a monthly salary of R18,300 (US$650) with some 20 million or so subsisting on less than R5000 a month. A long and consistent list of reports – including those of Transparency International and many commissioned by Russia's government – attests that corruption is rife, with many professions extorting bribes and kickbacks. Russian sociologist Simon Kordonsky lists 'optimizing taxes, winning a tender, getting a building permit, getting a relative care at an "elite" clinic, helping a son avoid the draft, sending a daughter to a good school, getting back a driver's license confiscated by the police, or instigating a police raid on a rival' among the many 'services' a bribe can expedite in Russia.

Russia has proven oil reserves of over 74 billion barrels, most of which are located in Western Siberia. It is even more blessed with natural gas – over 48 trillion cu metres, more than twice the reserves of Iran, the next-largest country.

Crooks & Thieves

Both Medvedev and Putin have declared verbal war on corruption. However, it is 34-year-old lawyer and blogger Alexey Navalny who has become Russia's leading anticorruption crusader. At the end of 2010, he launched **RosPil** (http://rospil.info), a site dedicated to exposing state corruption;

Top Docos

Russia – A Journey with Jonathan Dimbleby (www.dimblebys-russia.co.uk) Covers 16,000km of Russia in a five-episode BBC series; it's a revealing snapshot of a multifaceted country.

My Perestroika (http://myperestroika.com) Robin Hessman's film focuses on five Russians and the effects on their lives of the past 20 tumultuous years.

Disbelief (www.disbelief-film.com) Andrei Nekrasov's emotionally powerful documentary makes the case for state involvement in the Moscow apartment bombings of 1999.

Myths

Regardless of what you may have heard, Russians possess genuine humanity and hospitality that tends to go much deeper than in most Western countries.

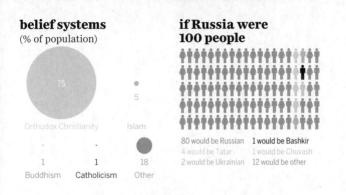

belief systems

(% of population)

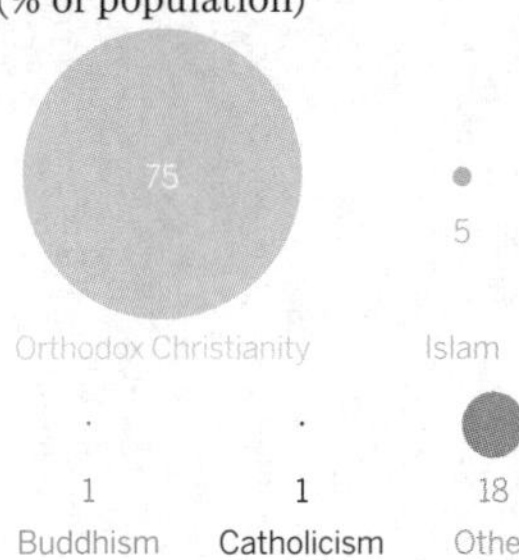

if Russia were 100 people

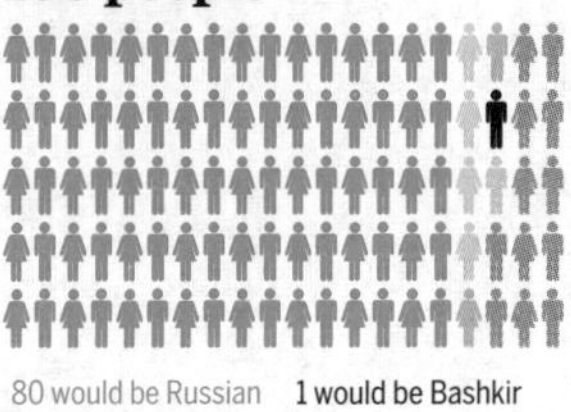

three months later, following reports on the site, suspicious government contracts worth nearly US$7 million had been annulled. Top of the list of wrongdoers according to Navalny is United Russia, the ruling party he has famously rebranded a party of 'crooks and thieves'.

Speaking out this way against the system in Russia has consequences. Reporters Without Borders lists many cases of harassment – judicial and otherwise – that the Russian authorities use to intimidate bloggers and those who dare to speak their mind. Suspicious deaths include Anna Politkovskaya, the human-rights activist and writer gunned down on her doorstep in 2006, and the corruption-investigating lawyer Sergei Magnitsky, who died under suspicious circumstances in a Moscow jail in 2009. Navalny's tearful mother, interviewed for a feature on her son in the *New Yorker* magazine, said 'I'm not ready for my son to become a martyr.'

According to the corruption perception index released by Transparency International in 2010, Russia is the world's most corrupt major economy, ranking 154th out of 178 countries, below Haiti, Pakistan and Zimbabwe.

Russia for Russians!

Another touchy subject is the worrying rise in extreme nationalism in Russia. Sparked by the death of 28-year-old Yegor Sviridov, a fan of Spartak football team, in a brawl with rival soccer supporters from the north Caucasus, 5000 youths went on the rampage through central Moscow in December 2010, shouting 'Russia for Russians!' The youths beat hundreds of people assumed to be foreigners because of the colour of their skin and stabbed to death two Uzbek labourers.

Russia has anything between seven and 12 million immigrants, many from the north Caucasus or former Soviet republics in Central Asia. Reports by the International Labour Organisation and others show that many of them remain undocumented and marginalised in society. Even though in speeches Medvedev refers to Russia as 'our multiethnic nation', *Newsweek* and other media have reported that the Kremlin has

Top Downloads

Russia in Global Affairs (http://eng.globalaffairs.ru) Respected English quarterly with features relating to Russian politics, economy and culture.

Russia Profile (www.russiaprofile.org) Expert analysis of what's going on in the country, including special reports on major topics.

Travel Literature

Lost and Found in Russia Susan Richards charts the effects of events from 1992 to 2008 on people from provincial southern Russia.

Travels in Siberia Ian Frazier's humorous and historically enlightening saga of several trips to Russia since the early 1990s.

Lost Cosmonaut and **Strange Telescopes** Daniel Kalder's books explore some of Russia's quirkiest and least visited locations.

also reached out to far-right and nationalist groups, including the youth groups Nashi and Stal (Steel). In the wake of the December 2010 Moscow riots Putin also met with football fans who had taken part in the riots and visited the grave of Sviridov.

The Next Election

Navalny, who claims to be a pragmatic nationalist, has political ambitions, but he won't be standing for either the national legislative elections in December 2011 or the presidential elections in March 2012. Neither will candidates from the liberal Party of People's Freedom, led by Mikhail Kasyanov, a former prime minister, and Boris Nemtsov, a former deputy prime minister, after it was denied registration by the Russian Justice Ministry.

An investigation by *Newsweek* in August 2011 revealed that many organisers of extreme nationalist groups learned their skills in Kremlin-sponsored youth groups such as Nashi.

Also out of the running is billionaire oligarch Mikhail Prokhorov, who quit his own party, Right Cause, in September 2011. Pointing a finger at Kremlin strategist Vladislav Surkov, the billionaire oligarch was quoted as saying 'real politics are impossible as long as such people rule the political process'.

A few weeks later, Putin made the long-expected announcement that he would run again for president (naming Medvedev as his designated prime minister). In response the much-respected finance minister Alexey Kudrin resigned; fiscally-conservative Kudrin has sharp differences with the ruling tandem over monetary policy. The *Economist* called the Putin-Medvedev deal a 'stitch-up' that 'makes a mockery of any notion of open politics, democratic elections and independent institutions.' Putin is the running favourite to win the election.

Top Fiction

Moscow Noir 14 short stories by contemporary authors.
The Master and Margarita Mikhail Bulgakov's satirical masterpiece.
Snowdrops An edgy morality tale by AD Miller set in modern Russia.

Top Playlist

Leningrad (www.sosimc.ru) Punk rock, Latino, polka and Tom Waits with a strong brass section.
Markscheider Kunst (www.mkunst.ru) Afro-beat-infused music.
Deti Picasso (www.myspace.com/detipicasso) Armenian-Russian folk-rock band.
Zemfira (www.zemfira.ru) A jazz-rock musician who is Russia's Alanis Morissette.
Leonid Fedorov (www.leonidfedorov.ru) Semiabsurd poetry fused with acoustic guitars and hypnotic melodies.

History

Russia's birth is usually identified with the founding of Novgorod in AD 862. Just over a century later Kyivan Rus emerged under Vladimir I. From the early 13th century until 1480 the country was effectively a colony of the Mongols. In the 16th century Ivan the Terrible expanded his domain eastward to the Volga Basin. Between the 17th and 19th centuries Siberia, Central Asia and the Caucasus fell under Russia's sway, creating the huge country it is today.

Intent on modernisation, Peter the Great set up a navy, educational centres and began the construction of St Petersburg in 1703. This grand city on the Baltic became Russia's capital in 1712. Catherine the Great continued Peter's legacy, in the process making Russia a world power by the mid-18th century.

Lack of social reforms and successively autocratic tsars sowed the seeds of a revolutionary movement in the 19th century. This culminated in the 1917 revolution, the literal demise of the Russia's monarchy and the ascendancy of the Bolsheviks under Vladimir Ilych Ulyanov, aka Lenin.

Lenin's successor Josef Stalin, with single-minded brutality, forced Russia's industrialisation. Millions were killed or imprisoned but Stalin also saw the nation through the devastation of WWII, and by the time he died in 1953, the USSR had a full nuclear arsenal and half of Europe as satellite states.

A brief period of cautious reform in the early 1960s under Khrushchev gave way to economic stagnation and growing internal dissent in the 1970s. Mikhail Gorbachev's period of reform, known as *perestroika,* began in 1985, but was too late to save the Soviet system.

In 1991 the USSR collapsed and reformer Boris Yeltsin was elected Russia's first-ever president. Yeltsin led Russia into the roller-coaster world of cut-throat capitalism; prices soared and the rouble crashed, wiping out the meagre savings of the vast majority of the population but also creating the super-rich oligarchs.

TIMELINE

c 30,000 BC

Humans settle in many locations across what would become Russia's vast territory, including Sunghir near Vladimir and along the Aldan River in the Sakha Republic in the Russian Far East.

5th century BC

Greek historian Herodotus writes about the Scythians, who probably originated in the Altai region of Siberia and Mongolia and were feared for their riding and battle skills.

4th century AD

The Huns, a nomadic people from the Altai region, move into eastern Europe. Under their leader Attila their empire stretches from the Ural River to the Rhine.

His successor Vladimir Putin, a steely-faced ex-KGB officer, steered a more careful course between reform and centralisation. The economy boomed off the back of oil and gas exports, securing Putin a two-term presidency, followed by that of his loyal lieutenant Dmitry Medvedev.

In line with common usage, names of pre-1700 rulers in this guide are directly transliterated, anglicised from Peter the Great until 1917, and again transliterated after that – thus Andrei Bogolyubov not Andrew, Vasily III not Basil; but Peter the Great not Pyotr, Catherine the Great not Yekaterina etc.

Formation of the Country

Russian Ancestors: Slavs & Vikings

There is some disagreement about where the Slavs originated, but in the first few centuries AD they expanded rapidly to the east, west and south from the vicinity of present-day northern Ukraine and southern Belarus. These Eastern Slavs were the ancestors of the Russians; they were still spreading eastward across the central-Russian woodland belt in the 9th century. From the Western Slavs came the Poles, Czechs, Slovaks and others. The Southern Slavs became the Serbs, Croats, Slovenes and Bulgarians.

The Slavs' conversion to Christianity in the 9th and 10th centuries was accompanied by the introduction of an alphabet devised by Cyril, a Greek missionary (later St Cyril), which was simplified a few decades later by a fellow missionary, Methodius. The forerunner of Cyrillic, it was based on the Greek alphabet, with a dozen or so additional characters. The Bible was translated into the Southern Slav dialect, which became known as Church Slavonic and is the language of the Russian Orthodox Church's liturgy to this day.

The first Russian state developed out of the trade on river routes across Eastern Slavic areas – between the Baltic and Black Seas and, to a lesser extent, between the Baltic Sea and the Volga River. Vikings from Scandinavia – the Varangians, also called Varyagi by the Slavs – had been nosing east from the Baltic since the 6th century AD, trading and raiding for furs, slaves and amber, and coming into conflict with the Khazars and with Byzantium, the eastern centre of Christianity. To secure their hold on the trade routes, the Vikings made themselves masters of settlements in key areas – places such as Novgorod, Smolensk, Staraya Ladoga and Kyiv (Kiev) in Ukraine. Though by no means united themselves, they created a loose confederation of city-states in the Eastern Slavic areas.

Old Russia Fortresses

- Staraya Ladoga, Leningrad Region
- Smolensk, Smolensk Region
- Pskov, Pskov Region
- Stary Izborsk, Pskov Region
- Rostov kremlin, Golden Ring

Kyivan Rus

In the 9th century, Rurik of Jutland founded the Rurik dynasty, the ruling family of the embryonic Russian state of Kyivan Rus and the dominant rulers in Eastern Slavic areas until the end of the 16th century. Kyivan Rus became a Christian state under Vladimir I, who also introduced the beginnings of a feudal structure to replace clan allegiances. However, some principalities – including Novgorod, Pskov and Vyatka (north of Kazan) – were ruled democratically by popular *vechi* (assemblies).

862

The legendary Varangian (Scandinavian) Rurik of Jutland gains control of Staraya Ladoga and builds the Holmgard settlement near Novgorod. The infant version of Russia is born.

945

Start of the reign of Svyatoslav I, who makes Kyiv the dominant regional power by campaigning against quarrelling Varangian princes and dealing the Khazars a series of fatal blows.

980

Vladimir I, the illegitimate son of Svyatoslav I, slays his half-brother Yaropolk and establishes himself in Kyiv as leader of breakaway Kyivan Rus.

988

Vladimir I persuades the Patriarch of Constantinople to establish an episcopal see – a Church 'branch' – in Kyiv, marking the birth of the Russian Orthodox Church.

Kyiv's supremacy was broken by new invaders from the east – first the Pechenegs, then in 1093 the Polovtsy sacked the city – and by the effects of European crusades from the late 11th century onward, which broke the Arab hold on southern Europe and the Mediterranean, reviving west–east trade routes and making Rus a commercial backwater.

Rus was the name of the dominant Kyivan Viking clan, but it wasn't until the 18th century that the term Russian or Great Russian came to be used exclusively for Eastern Slavs in the north, while those to the south or west were identified as Ukrainians or Belarusians.

The Rise of Rostov-Suzdal

The northern Rus principalities began breaking from Kyiv after about 1050. As Kyiv declined, the Russian population shifted northward and the fertile Rostov-Suzdal region northeast of Moscow began to be developed. Vladimir Monomakh of Kyiv founded the town of Vladimir there in 1108 and gave the Rostov-Suzdal principality to his son Yury Dolgoruky, who is credited with founding the little settlement of Moscow in 1147.

Rostov-Suzdal grew so rich and strong that Yury's son Andrei Bogolyubov tried to use his power to unite the Rus principalities. His troops took Kyiv in 1169, after which he declared Vladimir his capital, even though the church's headquarters remained in Kyiv until 1300. Rostov-Suzdal began to gear up for a challenge against the Bulgars' hold on the Volga–Ural Mountains region. The Bulgar people had originated further east several centuries before and had since converted to Islam. Their capital, Bolgar, was near modern Kazan, on the Volga.

The Golden Horde

Meanwhile, over in the east, a confederation of armies headed by the Mongolian warlord Chinggis (Genghis) Khaan (1167–1227) was busy subduing most of Asia, eventually crossing Russia into Europe to create history's largest land empire. In 1223 Chinggis' forces met the armies of the Russian princes and thrashed them at the Battle of Kalka River. This push into European Russia was cut short by the death of the warlord, but his grandson Batu Khaan returned in 1236 to finish the job, laying waste to Bolgar and Rostov-Suzdal, and annihilating most of the other Russian principalities, including Kyiv, within four years. Novgorod was saved only by spring floods that prevented the invaders from crossing the marshes around the city.

Ex-diplomat Sir Fitzroy Maclean wrote several entertaining, intelligent books on the country. *Holy Russia* is a good, short Russian history, while *All the Russias: The End of an Empire* covers the whole of the former USSR.

Batu and his successors ruled the Golden Horde (one of the khanates into which Chinggis' empire had broken) from Saray on the Volga, near modern Volgograd. At its peak the Golden Horde's territory included most of eastern Europe stretching from the banks of the Dnieper River in the west to deep into Siberia in the east and south to the Caucasus. The Horde's control over its subjects was indirect: although its armies raided them in traditional fashion if they grew uppity, it mainly used collaborative local princes to keep order, provide soldiers and collect taxes.

1093–1108

Vladimir Monomakh takes control of territory bounded by the Volga, Oka and Dvina Rivers, moves his capital to Suzdal and, in 1108, founds Vladimir, thus creating the Vladimir-Suzdal principality.

1147

Vladimir's son, Yury Dolgoruky, builds a wooden fort, the forerunner of Moscow's Kremlin, and invites his allies to a banquet there; he's later considered the city's founder.

1169

Yury's son, Andrei Bogolyubov, sacks Kyiv and moves his court to Vladimir, where he houses the Vladimir *Icon of the Mother of God* in the newly built Assumption Cathedral.

MARTIN MOOS / LONELY PLANET IMAGES ©

» Assumption Cathedral

Alexander Nevsky & the Rise of Moscow

One such 'collaborator' was the Prince of Novgorod, Alexander Nevsky, a Russian hero (and later a saint of the Russian Church) for his resistance to German crusaders and Swedish invaders. In 1252, Batu Khaan put him on the throne as Grand Prince of Vladimir.

Nevsky and his successors acted as intermediaries between the Mongols and other Russian princes. With shrewd diplomacy, the princes of Moscow obtained and hung on to the title of grand prince from the early 14th century while other princes resumed their feuding. The church provided backing to Moscow by moving there from Vladimir in the 1320s and was in turn favoured with exemption from Mongol taxation.

THE RISE, FALL & RISE AGAIN OF THE RUSSIAN ORTHODOX CHURCH

Legend has it that while preaching the gospel, the apostle Andrew paused in what would later become Kyiv (Kiev) and predicted the founding of a Christian city. In AD 988 Vladimir I fulfilled the prophesy by adopting Christianity from Constantinople (Istanbul today), the eastern centre of Christianity in the Middle Ages, effectively starting the Russian Orthodox Church.

The church flourished until 1653 when it was split by the reforms of Patriarch Nikon. Thinking that the church had departed from its roots, Nikon insisted, among other things, that the translation of the Bible be altered to conform with the Greek original and that the sign of the cross be made with three fingers, not two. Even though Nikon was subsequently sacked by Tsar Alexey, his reforms went through and those who refused to accept them became known as Starovery (Old Believers) and were persecuted. Some fled to Siberia or remote parts of Central Asia, where in the 1980s one group was found who had never heard of Vladimir Lenin, electricity or the revolution. Only from 1771 to 1827, from 1905 to 1918, and again recently have Old Believers had real freedom of worship.

Another blow to church power came with the reforms of Peter the Great, who replaced the self-governing patriarchate with a holy synod subordinate to the tsar, who effectively became head of the church. When the Bolsheviks came to power Russia had over 50,000 churches. Atheism was vigorously promoted and Josef Stalin attempted to wipe out religion altogether until 1941, when he decided the war effort needed the patriotism that the church could stir up. Nikita Khrushchev renewed the attack in the 1950s, closing about 12,000 churches. By 1988 fewer than 7000 churches were active.

Since the end of the Soviet Union, the church has seen a huge revival, with around 90% of Russians identifying themselves as Russian Orthodox. New churches are being built and many old churches and monasteries – which had been turned into museums, archive stores and even prisons – have been returned to church hands and are being restored.

13th century

Novgorod joins the emerging Hanseatic League, a federation of city-states that controlled Baltic and North Sea trade, and becomes the League's gateway to the lands east and southeast.

1240

Aged 19, Aleksandr, Prince of Novgorod, defeats the Swedes on the Neva River near present-day St Petersburg, thus earning himself the title 'Nevsky'.

1300

As Kyiv loses its political and economic significance, the headquarters of the Russian Orthodox Church moves to Vladimir. In 1325 Metropolitan Peter moves the episcopal see to Moscow.

1328

The Khan of the Golden Horde appoints Ivan I (Ivan the Moneybags) as Grand Prince of Vladimir with rights to collect taxes from other Russian principalities.

With a new-found Russian confidence, Grand Prince Dmitry put Moscow at the head of a coalition of princes and took on the Mongols, defeating them in the battle of Kulikovo Pole on the Don River in 1380. The Mongols crushed this uprising in a three-year campaign but their days were numbered. Weakened by internal dissension, they fell at the end of the 14th century to the Turkic empire of Timur (Tamerlane), which was based in Samarkand (in present-day Uzbekistan). Yet the Russians, themselves divided as usual, remained vassals until 1480.

Russians often refer to the Mongol invaders as Tatars, when in fact the Tatars were simply one particularly powerful tribe that joined the Mongol bandwagon. The Tatars of Tatarstan actually descended from the Bulgars who are distantly related to the Bulgarians of the Balkans.

Moscow vs Lithuania

Moscow (or Muscovy, as its expanding lands came to be known) was champion of the Russian cause after Kulikovo, though it had rivals, especially Novgorod and Tver. The Grand Duchy of Lithuania also started to expand into old Kyivan Rus lands in the 14th century. In 1386 the Lithuanian ruler Jogaila married the Polish queen Jadwiga and became king of Poland, thus joining two of Europe's most powerful states.

With Jogaila's coronation as Wladyslaw II of Poland, the previously pagan Lithuanian ruling class embraced Catholicism. The Russian Church portrayed the struggle against Lithuania as one against the pope in Rome. After Constantinople (centre of the Greek Orthodox Church) was taken by the Turks in 1453, the metropolitan – head of the Russian Church – declared Moscow the 'third Rome', the true heir of Christianity.

Meanwhile, with the death of Dmitry Donskoy's son Vasily I in 1425, Muscovy suffered a dynastic war. The old Rurikids got the upper hand – ironically with Lithuanian and Tatar help – but it was only with Ivan III's forceful reign from 1462 to 1505 that the other principalities ceased to oppose Muscovy.

Ivan the Great

In 1478 Novgorod was first of the Great Russian principalities to be brought to heel by Ivan III. To secure his power in the city he installed a governor, deported the city's most influential families (thus pioneering a strategy that would be used with increasing severity by Russian rulers right up to Stalin) and ejected the Hanseatic merchants.

The exiles were replaced with Ivan's administrators, whose good performance was rewarded with temporary title to confiscated lands. This new approach to land tenure, called *pomestie* (estate), characterised Ivan's rule. Previously, the boyars (high-ranking nobles) had held land under a *votchina* (system of patrimony) giving them unlimited control and inheritance rights over their lands and the people on them. The freedom to shift allegiance to other princes had given them political clout, too. Now, with few alternative princes left, the influence of the boyars declined in favour of the new landholding civil servants. This increased central control spread to the lower levels of society with the growth of serfdom.

Masha Holl's Russian History (http://history.mashaholl.com) abounds with intriguing details, such as the fact that surnames didn't exist in Russia for most of the Middle Ages.

1382

Led by the Khan Tokhtamysh, the Mongols invade again, slaughtering half of Moscow's population but allowing a supplicant Dmitry to remain Grand Prince of Vladimir.

1389

Vasily I takes over his father Dmitry's titles on his death, without the weakened Khan's approval. He continues unifying the Russian lands and makes an alliance with Lithuania.

1425–62

The 10-year-old Vasily II becomes Prince of Moscow. His long rule is plagued by civil war but also sees the collapse of the Golden Horde into smaller khanates.

1462

Ivan III (Ivan the Great) succeeds his father, Vasily II. He is the first ruler to adopt the title 'tsar' and goes on to reign for 43 years.

NOBLE TITLES

The title 'tsar', from the Latin *caesar,* was sometimes used by Ivan III in his diplomatic relations with the West. Ivan IV was the first ruler to be formally crowned 'Tsar of All Russia'. Peter the Great preferred emperor, though tsar remained in use. In this book we use empress for a female ruler; a tsar's wife who does not become ruler is a *tsaritsa* (in English, tsarina). A tsar's son is a *tsarevitch* and his daughter a *tsarevna*. Boyars were feudal landholders who formed the early Russian aristocracy.

Ivan IV (the Terrible)

Ivan IV's marriage to Anastasia, from the Romanov boyar family, was a happy one – unlike the five that followed her death in 1560, a turning point in his life. Believing her to have been poisoned, Ivan instituted a reign of terror that earned him the sobriquet *grozny* (literally 'awesome' but commonly translated as 'terrible') and nearly destroyed all his earlier good works.

His subsequent career was indeed terrible, though he was admired for upholding Russian interests and tradition. His military victories helped transform Russian into the multiethnic, multireligious state it is today. However, his campaign against the Crimean Tatars nearly ended with the loss of Moscow, and a 24-year war with the Lithuanians, Poles, Swedes and Teutonic Knights to the west also failed to gain any territory for Russia.

In 2008 in a telephone poll conducted by the TV station Rossiya that involved over 50 million people, the medieval prince Alexander Nevsky took top place as the most famous Russian, followed by reformist Prime Minister Pyotr Stolypin, who was assassinated in 1911, and Stalin.

Ivan's growing paranoia led him to launch a savage attack on Novgorod in 1570 that finally snuffed out that city's golden age. An argument about Ivan beating his son's wife (possibly causing her miscarriage) ended with the tsar accidentally killing his heir in 1581 with a blow to the head. Ivan himself died three years later during a game of chess in 1584. The later discovery of high amounts of mercury in his remains indicated that he died from poisoning – possibly by his own hand, as he had habitually used mercury to ease the pain of a fused spine.

The Time of Troubles

Ivan IV's official successor was his mentally enfeebled son Fyodor, who left the actual business of government to his brother-in-law, Boris Godunov, a skilled 'prime minister' who repaired much of the damage done by Ivan. Fyodor died childless in 1598, ending the 700-year Rurikid dynasty, and Boris ruled as tsar for seven more years.

Shortly after Boris's death, a Polish-backed Catholic pretender arrived on the scene claiming to be Dmitry, another son of Ivan the Terrible (who had in fact died in obscure circumstances in Uglich in 1591, possibly murdered on Boris Godunov's orders). This 'False Dmitry' gathered a huge ragtag army as he advanced on Moscow. Boris Godunov's son was lynched and the boyars acclaimed the pretender tsar.

1478

Surrounded by Ivan's armies, Novgorod recognises his rule over their city-state; Yaroslavl, Rostov, Tver and Vyatka similarly fall under Moscow's sway over the next decade.

1480

Ivan's armies face down those of the Tatars who come to extract tributes withheld by Muscovy for four years; this ends the Golden Horde's dominance of Russia.

1505–33

Vasily III annexes the autonomous Russian provinces of Pskov and Ryazan, captures Smolensk from Lithuania and extends Moscow's influence south along the Volga towards Kazan.

1533

Aged three, Ivan IV is proclaimed Grand Prince of Moscow when his father, Vasily III, dies. His mother acts as regent until she dies – possibly poisoned – in 1538.

Thus began the Time of Troubles (the Smuta), a spell of anarchy, dynastic chaos and foreign invasions. At its heart was a struggle between the boyars and central government (the tsar). Peace was restored in 1613 when 16-year-old Mikhail Romanov became tsar, the first of a new dynasty that was to rule until 1917.

The Empire Expands

Peter the Great

Peter I, known as 'the Great' for his commanding 2.24m frame and his equally commanding victory over the Swedes, dragged Russia kicking and screaming into Europe and made the country a major world power.

DEAD SOULS: SERFS IN RUSSIA

Right up to the turn of the 20th century, Russia had serfs: peasants and servants who were tied to their master's estates. The value of those estates was determined not by their size or output but by the number of such indentured souls.

Before the 1500s peasants could work for themselves after meeting their master's needs, and had the right to change homes and jobs during the two weeks around 26 November, St George's Day, when the annual harvest was complete. However, laws introduced by Ivan III in 1497 began to restrict these limited rights to free movement and by 1590 peasants were permanently bound to the lands in which they lived.

Some peasants, of course, still chose to run away, and authority in the countryside collapsed during the Time of Troubles (1606–13), with thousands absconding south to Cossack areas or east to Siberia, where serfdom was unknown. Despairing landlords found support from the government, which cracked down further on peasants' personal freedoms. By 1675 they had lost all land rights and, in a uniquely Russian version of serfdom, could be sold separately from the estates on which they worked – slavery, in effect.

In 1842 Nikolai Gogol, one of Russia's greatest writers, highlighted the trade in serfs, both dead and alive, in his novel *Dead Souls*. The Russian census of 1857 accounted for over 46 million serfs out of a total population of 62.5 million; around half of these were peasants working state lands who were considered free but in reality still had their movements restricted. As serfdom and slavery were being abolished across Europe and in the USA, it became recognised that changes to Russia's system also had to be made if its economy was to compete in the age of industrialisation.

The emancipation of March 1861 immediately set serfs free of their masters, but in reality liberation was a much more drawn-out affair, with some arguing that a form of serfdom survived well into the 20th century. In his book *The Road to Serfdom*, Friedrich Hayek argued that the collective farm system of Soviet Russia, in which workers were tied to specified farms and had their work quotas dictated by central government, amounted to state-sponsored serfdom.

1547

The coronation of Ivan IV (whose military victories and fearsome temper later earn him the name Ivan the Terrible) sees the 16-year-old become 'Tsar of all the Russias'.

NIDAY PICTURE LIBRARY / ALAMY ©

» Ivan IV (the Terrible)

1552

Ivan IV defeats the surviving Tatar khanates of Kazan and, four years later, Astrakhan, thus acquiring for Russia the entire Volga region and a chunk of the Caspian Sea coast.

1580

Yermak Timofeevich and his band of Cossack brigands capture Tyumen from the Turkic khanate Sibir and, two years later, take the capital, Isker, initiating Russia's expansion into Siberia..

Born to Tsar Alexey's second wife, Natalia, in 1672, Peter was an energetic and inquisitive youth who often visited Moscow's European district to learn about the West. Dutch and British ship captains in Arkhangelsk gave him navigation lessons on the White Sea.

The story of Boris Godunov inspired both a play by Alexander Pushkin in 1831 and an opera by Modest Mussorgsky in 1869.

Following his mother's death in 1694 and his half-brother Ivan's in 1696, Peter became Russia's sole ruler and embarked on a modernisation campaign, symbolised by his fact-finding mission to Europe in 1697–98; he was the first Muscovite ruler ever to go there and in the process hired a thousand experts for service in Russia.

Peter's alliance with Prussia and Denmark led to the Great Northern War against Sweden (1700–21). The rout of Charles XII's forces at the Battle of Poltava (1709) heralded Russia's power and the collapse of the Swedish empire. The Treaty of Nystadt (1721) gave Peter control of the Gulf of Finland and the eastern shores of the Baltic Sea. In the midst of all this (in 1707) he put down another peasant rebellion, led by Don Cossack Kondraty Bulavin, and founded his new capital of St Petersburg in 1703.

Peter's Legacy

Peter's lasting legacy was mobilising Russian resources to compete on equal terms with the West. His territorial gains were small, but the strategic Baltic territories added ethnic variety, including a new upper class of German traders and administrators who formed the backbone of Russia's commercial and military expansion.

Benson Bobrick's book *East of the Sun* is a rollicking history of the conquest and settlement of Siberia and the Russian Far East, and is packed with gory details.

Vast sums of money were needed to build St Petersburg, pay a growing civil service, modernise the army and launch naval and commercial fleets. But money was scarce in an economy based on serf labour, so Peter slapped taxes on everything from coffins to beards, including an infamous 'Soul Tax' on all lower-class adult males. The lot of serfs worsened, as they bore the main tax burden.

Even the upper classes had to chip in: aristocrats could serve in either the army or the civil service, or lose their titles and land. Birth counted for little, with state servants being subject to Peter's Table of Ranks, a performance-based ladder of promotion, in which the upper grades conferred hereditary nobility. Some aristocrats lost all they had, while capable state employees of humble origin and thousands of foreigners became Russian nobles.

Female Rulers

Peter died in 1725 without naming a successor. His wife Catherine, a former servant and one-time mistress of the tsar's right-hand man Alexander Menshikov, became the first woman to rule Imperial Russia. In doing so, she blazed a path for other women, including her daughter

1598

Fyodor I dies without producing an heir, ending the 700-year-old Rurikid dynasty. Boris Godunov seizes the throne and proves a capable tsar, instituting educational and social reforms.

1605

Boris's son Fyodor II lasts just three months as tsar before he and his mother are assassinated on the arrival in Moscow of the first False Dmitry.

1606

Vasily Shuysky plots against the False Dmitry, has him killed and becomes tsar until 1610, when he is, in turn, deposed and exiled to Warsaw.

1612

A Russian militia, led by Prince Dmitry Pozharsky, retakes Moscow after three years of occupation by the Poles, a victory commemorated every 4 November by the Day of Unity.

THE COSSACKS

The word 'Cossack' (from the Turkic *kazak*, meaning free man, adventurer or horseman) was originally applied to residual Tatar groups and later to serfs, paupers and dropouts who fled south from Russia, Poland and Lithuania in the 15th century. They organised themselves into self-governing communities in the Don Basin, on the Dnepr River in Ukraine and in the southern Urals. Those in a given region (eg the Don Cossacks) were not just a tribe; the men constituted a *voysko* (army), within which each *stanitsa* (village-regiment) elected an ataman (leader).

Mindful of their skill as fighters, the Russian government treated the Cossacks carefully, offering autonomy in return for military service. Cossacks such as Yermak Timofeevich were the wedge that opened Siberia in the 17th century. By the 19th century there were a dozen Cossack armies from Ukraine to the Russian Far East and, as a group, they numbered 2.5 million people.

The Cossacks were not always cooperative with the Russian state. Three peasant uprisings in the Volga-Don region – 1670, 1707 and 1773 – were Cossack-led. After 1917 the Bolsheviks abolished Cossack institutions, though some cavalry units were revived in WWII. Since 1991 there has been a Cossack revival particularly in the Don region. Cossack regiments have been officially recognised, there is a presidential adviser on Cossacks and some Cossacks demand that the state recognise them as an ethnic group.

Elizabeth and, later, Catherine the Great, who, between them, held on to the top job for the better part of 70 years.

Catherine left day-to-day administration of Russia to a governing body called the Supreme Privy Council, staffed by many of Peter's leading administrators. When the council elected Peter's niece Anna of Courland (a small principality in present-day Latvia) to the throne, with a contract stating that the council had the final say in policy decisions, Anna reacted by disbanding the council.

Anna ruled from 1730 to 1740, appointing a Baltic German baron, Ernst Johann von Bühren, to handle affairs of state. His name was Russified to Biron, but his heavy-handed, corrupt style came to symbolise the German influence on the royal family that had begun with Peter the Great.

During the reign of Peter's daughter, Elizabeth (1741–61), German influence waned and restrictions on the nobility were loosened. Some aristocrats began to dabble in manufacture and trade.

Documents in Russian History (http://academic.shu.edu/russianhistory/index.php/Main_Page) is an online source of primary documents on Russia, including proclamations by the tsars and speeches by Lenin and Stalin.

Catherine II (the Great)

Daughter of a German prince, Catherine came to Russia at the age of 15 to marry Empress Elizabeth's heir apparent, her nephew Peter III.

1613

Sixteen-year-old Mikhail Romanov, a relative of Ivan IV's first wife, is elected tsar by the Assembly of the Land (Zemsky Sobor), starting the Romanov dynasty.

1617–18

Peace treaties are concluded with Sweden and Poland, the latter allowing Mikhail's father Fyodor to return from exile; Fyodor would be Russia's real ruler until his death in 1633.

1645

Under the careful watch of boyar Boris Morozov, 16-year-old Aleksey I becomes tsar. During his reign Russia's territory expands to over 800 million hectares as the conquest of Siberia continues.

1660

Patriarch Nikon's reforms of the Russian Orthodox Church create a schism. He is deposed and many Old Believers flee to Siberia to practise their religion as they see fit.

RUSSIANS IN AMERICA

In 1648 the Cossack Semyon Dezhnev sailed round the northeastern corner of Asia, from the Pacific Ocean into the Arctic. Eighty years later Peter the Great commissioned Vitus Bering, a Danish officer in the Russian navy, to head the Great Northern Expedition, which was ostensibly a scientific survey of Kamchatka (claimed for the tsar in 1697 by the explorer Vladimir Atlasov) and the eastern seaboard. In reality the survey's aim was to expand Russia's Pacific sphere of influence as far south as Japan and across to North America.

On his second expedition Bering succeeded in discovering Alaska, landing in 1741. The Bering Strait separating Alaska from the Russian mainland are named after him. Unfortunately, on the return voyage his ship was wrecked off an island just 250km east of the Kamchatka coast. Bering died on the island and it, too, now carries his name.

Survivors of Bering's crew brought back reports of an abundance of foxes, fur seals and otters inhabiting the islands off the mainland, triggering a fresh wave of fur-inspired expansion. An Irkutsk trader, Grigory Shelekhov, landed on Kodiak Island (in present-day Alaska) in 1784 and, 15 years later, his successor founded Sitka (originally called New Archangel), the capital of Alaska until 1900.

In 1804 the Russians reached Honolulu, and in 1806 Russian ships sailed into San Francisco Bay. Soon afterwards a fortified outpost was established at what is now called Fort Ross, California. Here the imperial flag flew and a marker was buried on which was inscribed 'Land of the Russian Empire'.

Intelligent and ambitious, Catherine learned Russian, embraced the Orthodox Church and devoured the writings of European political philosophers. This was the time of the Enlightenment, when talk of human rights, social contracts and the separation of powers abounded.

The famously lusty Catherine said of her first husband, 'I believe the Crown of Russia attracted me more than his person.' Once empress, she embarked on a program of reforms, though she made it clear that she had no intention of limiting her own authority. A new legal code was drafted, the use of torture limited and religious tolerance supported. But any ideas she might have had of improving the lot of serfs went overboard with the violent peasant rebellion of 1773–74, led by the Don Cossack Yemelyan Pugachev, which spread from the Ural Mountains to the Caspian Sea and along the Volga. Hundreds of thousands of serfs responded to Pugachev's promises to end serfdom and taxation, but were beaten by famine and government armies. Pugachev was executed and Catherine put an end to Cossack autonomy.

In the cultural sphere, Catherine increased the number of schools and colleges and expanded publishing. Her vast collection of paintings forms

Robert K Massie's *Peter the Great – His Life and World* is a good read about one of Russia's most influential rulers, and provides much detail about how he created St Petersburg.

1667
The war between Russia and Poland over modern-day Ukraine and Belarus ends with the Treaty of Andrusovo; Kyiv, Smolensk and lands east of the Dnepr remain under Russian control.

1670–71
Cossack Stepan (Stenka) Razin leads an uprising in the Volga-Don region. His army of 200,000 seizes the entire lower Volga Basin before he is captured and executed in Red Square.

1676–82
Fyodor III's keen intelligence lays the foundations for a more liberal attitude in the Russian court. Civil and military appointments start to be determined by merit rather than nobility.

1682
Aleksey I's 10-year-old son Peter I becomes joint tsar with his chronically ill half-brother Ivan V. Ivan's elder sister, Sophia, acting as regent, holds the real power.

the core of the present-day Hermitage collection. A critical elite gradually developed, alienated from most uneducated Russians, but also increasingly at odds with central authority – a 'split personality' common among future Russian radicals.

Territorial Gains

Catherine's reign saw major expansion at the expense of the weakened Ottoman Turks and Poles, engineered by her 'prime minister' and foremost lover, Grigory Potemkin (Potyomkin). War with the Turks began in 1768, peaked with the naval victory at Çesme and ended with a 1774 treaty giving Russia control of the north coast of the Black Sea, freedom of shipping through the Dardanelles to the Mediterranean and 'protectorship' of Christian interests in the Ottoman Empire – a pretext for later incursions into the Balkans. Crimea was annexed in 1783.

Poland had spent the previous century collapsing into a set of semi-independent units with a figurehead king in Warsaw. Catherine manipulated events with divide-and-rule tactics and even had another former lover, Stanislas Poniatowski, installed as king. Austria and Prussia proposed sharing Poland among the three powers, and in 1772, 1793 and 1795 the country was carved up, ceasing to exist as an independent state until 1918. Eastern Poland and the Grand Duchy of Lithuania – roughly, present-day Lithuania, Belarus and western Ukraine – came under Russian rule.

Alexander I

Catherine was succeeded by her son, Paul I. A mysterious figure in Russian history (often called the Russian Hamlet by Western scholars), he antagonised the gentry with attempts to reimpose compulsory state service and was killed in a coup in 1801.

Paul's son and successor was Catherine's favourite grandson, Alexander I, who had been trained by the best European tutors. He kicked off his reign with several reforms, including an expansion of the school system that brought education within reach of the lower middle classes. But he was soon preoccupied with the wars against Napoleon.

Under the Treaty of Tilsit in 1807, Alexander agreed to be Emperor of the East while Napoleon was declared Emperor of the West. This alliance, however, lasted only until 1810, when Russia's resumption of trade with England provoked the French leader to raise an army of 700,000 to march on Moscow.

1812 & Aftermath

Vastly outnumbered, Russia's army retreated throughout the summer of 1812, scorching the earth in an attempt to deny the French sustenance

Read about the fascinating life of Grigory Potemkin, lover of Catherine the Great and mover and shaker in 18th-century Russia, in Simon Sebag Montefiore's *Prince of Princes: The Life of Potemkin.*

Vincent Cronin's book, *Catherine, Empress of all the Russias,* paints a more sympathetic portrait than usual of a woman traditionally seen as a scheming, power-crazed sexpot.

1689

Following a botched coup, Sophia enters a convent. Peter's mother, Natalia, becomes the power behind the throne. Her death in 1694 leaves her son as effective sole ruler.

1695

Peter sends Russia's first navy down the Don River and captures the Black Sea port of Azov from the Crimean Tatars, vassals of the Ottoman Turks.

1697–98

Travelling incognito, Peter I leads the Grand Embassy diplomatic mission around Europe, learning shipbuilding in Amsterdam and the UK, meeting England's King William III and hiring foreign specialists.

1700–21

Russia battles Sweden for control of the Baltic in the Great Northern War. Sweden, fighting on several fronts, eventually cedes much territory, including Estonia and part of Karelia.

and fighting some successful rearguard actions. In September, with the lack of provisions beginning to affect the French, the Russian general Mikhail Kutuzov fought back at Borodino, 130km outside Moscow. The battle was extremely bloody but inconclusive, with the Russians withdrawing in good order.

Leo Tolstoy's epic novel *War and Peace* (1869) chronicles the impact of the Napoleonic era on Russian society, including the French invasion of the country.

Before the month was out, Napoleon entered a deserted Moscow; the same day, the city began to burn down around him (by whose hand has never been established). Alexander ignored his overtures to negotiate. With winter coming and his supply lines overstretched, Napoleon was forced to retreat. His starving troops were picked off by Russian partisans. Only one in 20 made it back to the relative safety of Poland, and the Russians pursued them all the way to Paris.

Meanwhile Russia was expanding its territory on other fronts. The kingdom of Georgia united with Russia in 1801. After a war with Sweden (1807–09), Alexander became Grand Duke of Finland. Russia argued with Turkey over the Danube principalities of Bessarabia (covering modern Moldova and part of Ukraine) and Wallachia (now in Romania), taking Bessarabia in 1812. Persia ceded northern Azerbaijan a year later and Yerevan (in Armenia) in 1828.

The Road to Revolution

The Decembrists

Named after the month of their ill-fated and disorganised attempt to overthrow the new tsar, Nicholas I, the Decembrists were a secret society of reform-minded young army officers. Alexander Herzen, the 'father of Russian socialism', called them 'a perfect galaxy of brilliant talent, independent character and chivalrous valour.'

The war against Napoleon and the subsequent four-month occupation of Paris exposed these officers to far more liberal ideas than existed in their homeland. On their return to Russia, they formed a couple of secret societies with the general aims of emancipating the serfs and introducing a constitutional monarchy. The officers' chance for action came with the unexpected death of Alexander on 19 November 1825.

Adam Zamoyski's book *1812: Napoleon's Fatal March on Moscow* is packed with graphic detail and individual stories that bring the famous defeat to life.

Alexander's youngest brother, the militaristic Nicholas, was due to be crowned on 26 December. On 14 December a group of officers led 3000 troops into St Petersburg's Senate Square, proclaiming their loyalty instead to Constantine, Alexander's elder brother. However, their leader, Prince Trubetskoy, suffering a last-minute change of heart, was a no-show along with other key figures. The revolt was quickly squashed by troops loyal to Nicholas.

Five of the Decembrists were executed and over 100 – mostly aristocrats and officers – were exiled to Siberia along with their families for

1703

Peter I establishes the Peter and Paul Fortress on Zayachy Island in the Neva River, thus founding Sankt Pieter Burkh (St Petersburg), named after his patron saint.

1712–14

At the behest of Peter I, government institutions begin to move from Moscow, and St Petersburg assumes the administrative and ceremonial role as the Russian capital.

1724

Catherine I (born Martha Elena Scowronska to lowly Latvian peasants), secretly betrothed to Peter I in 1707 and publicly married in 1712, is officially announced as Russia's coruler.

1728

After the death of Peter I and two years of rule by his wife, Catherine, his grandson Peter II shifts the Russian capital back to Moscow.

terms of hard labour, mostly in rural parts of the Chita region. Pardoned by Tsar Alexander II in 1856, many of these exiles chose to stay on in Siberia, their presence having a marked effect on the educational and cultural life in their adopted towns.

The Crimean War

Nicholas I's reign (1825–55) was a time of stagnation and repression under a tsar who claimed: 'I do not rule Russia; 10,000 clerks do.' The social revolutions that were shaking Europe passed Russia by and when the Marquis de Custine visited in 1839 he found a country paralysed by fear. 'What is called public order here is a mournful quiet, a terrifying peace, reminiscent of the tomb,' wrote the French aristocrat in *Empire of the Czar: A Journey Through Eternal Russia*.

There were positive developments, however. The economy grew and grain exports increased. Nicholas detested serfdom, if only because he detested the serf-owning class. As a result, peasants on state lands, nearly half the total, were given title to the land and, in effect, freed.

In foreign policy, Nicholas' meddling in the Balkans was eventually to destroy Russian credibility in Europe. Bad diplomacy led to the Crimean War (1854–56) against the Ottoman Empire, Britain and France, who declared war after Russian troops marched into the Ottoman provinces of Moldavia and Wallachia – ostensibly to protect Christian communities there. At Sevastopol an Anglo-French-Turkish force besieged the Russian naval headquarters. Inept command on both sides led to a bloody, stalemated war.

The publication of nobleman Aleksandr Radishchev's *A Journey from St Petersburg to Moscow* (1790), a passionate attack on the institution serfdom, enraged Catherine the Great; Radishchev's beliefs later inspired the Decembrist revolutionaries.

The 'Great Reforms'

Alexander II saw the Crimean War stir up discontent within Russia and accepted peace on unfavourable terms. The war had revealed the backwardness behind the post-1812 imperial glory and the time for reform had come.

Abolition of serfdom in 1861 opened the way for a market economy, capitalism and an industrial revolution. Railways and factories were built, and cities expanded as peasants left the land. Foreign investment in Russia grew during the 1880s and 1890s, but nothing was done to modernise farming, and very little to help peasants. By 1914, 85% of the Russian population was still rural, but their lot had barely improved in 50 years.

Revolutionary Movements

The reforms raised hopes that were not satisfied. The tsar refused to set up a representative assembly. Peasants were angry at having to pay for land they considered theirs by right. Radical students, known as

1730

The direct male line of the Romanov dynasty ends with Peter II's death. His successor is Anna, Duchess of Courland, daughter of Peter the Great's half-brother and coruler, Ivan V.

1732

Empress Anna reverses the decision of Peter II and moves the capital to St Petersburg, presiding over the recommencement of the city's construction and development.

1740

Twelve days before her death, Empress Anna adopts a two-month-old baby. He becomes Tsar Ivan VI, with his natural mother, Anna Leopoldovna of Mecklenburg, as regent.

1741

Elizabeth, the second-oldest daughter of Peter I and Catherine I, seizes power in a bloodless coup. She creates the most luxurious court in Europe.

narodniki (populists), took to the countryside in the 1870s to rouse the peasants, but the students and the peasants were worlds apart and the campaign failed.

Other populists saw more value in cultivating revolution among the growing urban working class (the proletariat), while yet others turned to terrorism: one secret society, the People's Will, blew up Alexander II in 1881.

Not all opponents of tsarism were radical revolutionaries. Some moderates, well off and with much to lose from a revolution, called themselves liberals and advocated constitutional reform along Western European lines, with universal suffrage and a *duma* (national parliament).

Discontent was sometimes directed at Jews and took the form of violent mass attacks (pogroms). At their height in the 1880s, these were often fanned by the authorities to divert social tension onto a convenient scapegoat.

Geoffrey Hosking's *Russia and the Russians* is a definitive one-volume trot through 1000 years of Russian history by a top scholar.

Rise of Marxism

The more radical revolutionaries were genuinely surprised that there was no uprising after Alexander II's assassination. Most were rounded up and executed or exiled, and the reign of his son Alexander III was marked by repression of revolutionaries and liberals alike. Many revolutionaries fled abroad – including Georgy Plekhanov and Pavel Axelrod, founders of the Russian Social-Democratic Workers Party in 1883, and, in 1899, Vladimir Ulyanov, better known by his later pseudonym, Lenin.

Social democrats in Europe were being elected to parliaments and developing Marxism into 'parliamentary socialism', improving the lot of workers through legislation. But in Russia there was no parliament – and there was an active secret police, to boot. At a meeting of the Socialist International movement in London in 1903, Lenin stood for violent overthrow of the government by a small, committed, well-organised party, while Plekhanov stood for mass membership and cooperation with other political forces.

Lenin won the vote through clever manoeuvring, and his faction came to be known as the Bolsheviks (meaning members of the majority); Plekhanov's faction became the Mensheviks (members of the minority). The Mensheviks actually outnumbered the Bolsheviks in the party, but Lenin clung to the name, for obvious reasons.

Russo-Japanese War

Nicholas II, who succeeded his father, Alexander III, in 1894, was a weak man who commanded less respect than his father, but was equally opposed to representative government.

The most serious blow to his position was a humiliating defeat by Japan when the two countries clashed over their respective 'spheres of

1756

Russia takes on Prussia in the Seven Years' War that engulfs Europe; her armies are victorious at Battle of Gross-Jägersdorf in 1757, but hold off invading Königsberg.

1761

With Russian troops occupying Berlin, Prussia is saved only by Elizabeth's death in 1761 and the ascension to the throne of her pro-German nephew, Peter III.

1762

A coup led by a lover of Catherine II (Catherine the Great) ousts her husband Peter III. Catherine becomes empress and Peter is murdered shortly after.

1768–74

Victories in the Russo-Turkish War, including the decisive Battle of Chesma, expand Russian control in southern Ukraine and give access to two ports on the Black Sea.

influence' in the Far East – Russia's in Manchuria and Japan's in Korea. As in Crimea 50 years before, poor diplomacy led to war. In 1904 Japan attacked the Russian naval base at Port Arthur (near Dalian in present-day China).

Defeat followed defeat for Russia on land and sea. The ultimate disaster came in May 1905, when the entire Baltic fleet, which had sailed halfway around the world to relieve Port Arthur, was sunk in the Tsushima Straits off Japan. In September 1905 Russia signed the Treaty of Portsmouth (New Hampshire), under the terms of which it gave up Port Arthur, Dalny and southern Sakhalin as well as any claims to Korea – but at least retained its preeminent position in Manchuria.

Despite all this, Siberia and the Russian Far East were prospering. From 1886 to 1911, the immigrant population leapt above eight million, thanks partly to ease of access via the new Trans-Siberian Railway. Most immigrants were peasants, who put Siberian agriculture at the head of the class in grain, stock and dairy farming. (Before the October Revolution, Europeans had Siberian butter on their tables.)

1905 Revolution

Unrest across Russia became widespread after the fall of Port Arthur. On 9 January 1905 a priest named Georgy Gapon led a crowd of some 200,000 people – men, women and children – to the Winter Palace in St Petersburg to petition the tsar for better working conditions. Singing 'God Save the Tsar', they were met by imperial guards, who opened fire and killed several hundred. This was Bloody Sunday.

Social democrat activists formed soviets (workers' councils) in St Petersburg and Moscow, which proved remarkably successful: the St Petersburg Soviet, led by Mensheviks under Leon Trotsky, declared a general strike, which brought the country to a standstill in October.

The tsar gave in and general elections were held in April 1906 that created a *duma* with a leftist majority that demanded further reforms. The tsar disbanded it. New elections in 1907 pushed the *duma* further to the left. It was again disbanded, and a new electoral law, limiting the vote to the upper classes and Orthodox Christians, ensured that the third and fourth *duma* were more cooperative with the tsar, who continued to choose the prime minister and cabinet.

The capable prime minister, Pyotr Stolypin, abolished the hated redemption payments in the countryside. Enterprising peasants were now able to buy decent parcels of land, which could be worked efficiently; this led to the creation of a new class of kulak (wealthier peasant) and to a series of good harvests. It also made it easier for peasants to leave their villages, providing a mobile labour force for industry. Russia enjoyed unprecedented economic growth and radical activists lost their following.

PHOTOS

In 1909 Sergei Prokudin-Gorsky set out to shoot all of the 'lands and people living on Russian land' using his own colour photographic technique. View the stunning results at www.prokudin-gorsky.ru/collection.htm.

1773

Emilian Pugachev, a Don Cossack, claims to be the overthrown Peter III and begins a violent peasant uprising, which is subsequently quelled by brute force.

1796

Upon Catherine the Great's death, her son Paul I ascends the throne. One of his first acts as tsar is to decree that women can never again rule Russia.

SCE / IMAGEBROKER ©

» Catherine II (the Great)

1801

Tsar Paul is murdered in his bedroom in the fortress-like Mikhaylovsky Castle. The coup places on the throne Alexander I, who vows to continue the reformist policies of his grandmother.

Still, Stolypin was assassinated in 1911 and the tsarist regime again lost touch with the people. Nicholas became a puppet of his strong-willed, eccentric wife, Alexandra, who herself fell under the spell of the Siberian mystic Rasputin.

The Priest of Sex

Grigory Rasputin was born in the Siberian village of Pokrovskoe in 1869. Never a monk as is sometimes supposed, Rasputin experienced a vision of the Virgin while working in the fields in his mid-20s and left Pokrovskoe to seek enlightenment. On his wanderings he came to believe, as did the contemporary Khlyst (Whip) sect, that sinning (especially through sex), then repenting, could bring people close to God.

In St Petersburg Rasputin's racy brand of redemption, along with his soothing talk, compassion and generosity, made him very popular with some aristocratic women. Eventually, he was summoned by Tsaritsa Alexandra and seemed able, thanks to some kind of hypnotic power, to halt the uncontrollable bleeding of her haemophiliac son, Tsarevitch Alexey, the heir to the throne. As he continued his drunken, lecherous life, replete with orgies, Rasputin's influence on the imperial family grew to the point where he could make or break the careers of ministers and generals. He became increasingly unpopular and many scapegoated him for Russia's disastrous performance in WWI.

REVOLUTION

By turns anecdotal and specific, *A People's Tragedy: The Russian Revolution, 1891-1924* by erudite scholar Orlando Figes paints a vivid picture of this tumultuous period in Russian history.

In 1916 Prince Felix Yusupov and others hatched an assassination plot. According to Yusupov's own account of the murderous affair, this proved to be easier said than done: Rasputin survived poisoning, several shots and a beating, all in one evening at St Petersburg's Yusupov Palace. Apparently he died only when drowned in a nearby river. However, a 2004 BBC documentary uncovered evidence that Rasputin actually died from his bullet wounds, one of which was delivered by a British secret agent working in conjunction with the Russian plotters. For the fascinating background to this version of events read Andrew Cook's *To Kill Rasputin*.

WWI & February Revolution

Russia's involvement with the Balkans made it a main player in the world war that began there in 1914. The Russian campaign went badly from the start. Between 1915 and 1918 the theatre of war was mostly around Russia's western border and often on enemy territory. Much, if not most, of the fighting was with Austro-Hungarians in Galitsia (Halichina in Ukrainian), rather than with the Germans. The latter didn't make major advances into Russian territory until 1918, by which time an estimated two million Russian troops had been killed and Germany controlled Poland and much of the Baltic coast, Belarus and Ukraine.

1807

Following defeats at Austerlitz, north of Vienna, and then at Friedland, in Prussia, Alexander I signs the Treaty of Tilsit with Napoleon, uniting the two sides (in theory) against England.

1810

Russia resumes relations with England, provoking Napoleon into his ill-fated march on Moscow two years later. Muscovites burn two-thirds of the capital rather than see it occupied by the French.

1814

Russian troops briefly occupy Paris after driving Napoleon back across Europe. A 'Holy Alliance' between Russia, Austria and Prussia is the outcome of the Congress of Vienna in 1815.

1817

Alexander I's appointment of the brutal general Alexey Yermolov to subdue the fractious tribes of the Caucasus sows seeds of discontent that continue to have repercussions today.

The tsar responded to antiwar protests by disbanding the *duma* and assuming personal command in the field. At home, the disorganised government failed to introduce rationing, and in February 1917 in Petrograd (the new, 'less German' name for St Petersburg), discontent in the food queues turned to riots, kicking off the February Revolution. Soldiers and police mutinied, refusing to fire on demonstrators. A new Petrograd Soviet of Workers' and Soldiers' Deputies was formed on the 1905 model, and more sprang up elsewhere. The reconvened *duma* ignored an order to disband itself and set up a committee to assume government.

Now there were two alternative power bases in the capital. The soviet was a rallying and debating point for factory workers and soldiers; the *duma* committee attracted the educated and commercial elite. In February the two reached agreement on a provisional government that would demand the tsar's abdication. The tsar tried to return to Petrograd but was blocked by his own troops. On 1 March he abdicated.

October Revolution

The provisional government announced general elections for November 1917 and continued the war despite a collapse of discipline in the army and popular demands for peace. On 3 April Lenin and other exiled Bolsheviks returned to Petrograd via Scandinavia. Though in the minority in the soviets, the Bolsheviks were organised and committed. They won over many with a demand for immediate 'peace, land and bread', and believed the soviets should seize power at once. But a series of violent mass demonstrations in July, inspired by the Bolsheviks, was in the end not fully backed by the soviets and was quelled. Lenin fled to Finland and Alexander Kerensky, a moderate Social Revolutionary, became prime minister.

In September the Russian military chief of staff, General Kornilov, sent cavalry to Petrograd to crush the soviets. Kerensky turned to the left for support against this insubordination, even courting the Bolsheviks, and defeated the counter-revolution. After this, public opinion favoured the Bolsheviks, who took control of the Petrograd Soviet (chaired by Trotsky, who had joined them) and, by extension, all the soviets in the land. Lenin decided it was time to seize power and returned from Finland in October.

During the night of 24 October 1917, Bolshevik workers and soldiers in Petrograd seized government buildings and communication centres, and arrested the provisional government, which was meeting in the Winter Palace. (Kerensky escaped, eventually dying in the USA in 1970.) Soon after, a provisional government was formed, headed by Lenin, with Trotsky as commissar for foreign affairs and the Georgian Josef Stalin as commissar for nationalities, in charge of policy for all non-Russians in the former empire.

Local soviets elsewhere in Russia seized power relatively easily, but the coup in Moscow took six days of fighting. The general elections

Seventeen Moments in Soviet History (www.soviethistory.org) is a well-designed site that covers all the major events and social movements during the life of the USSR in fascinating detail.

1825

Alexander I dies suddenly; reformers assemble in St Petersburg to protest the succession of Nicholas I. The new tsar brutally crushes the Decembrist Revolt, killing hundreds in the process.

1853–56

Russia takes on an alliance of the British, French and the Ottoman Empire in the Crimean War, a conflict that includes the infamous Charge of the Light Brigade.

1855

Nicholas I's successor, Alexander II, starts negotiations to end the Crimean War and realises reform is necessary if Russia is to remain a major European power.

1860

The Treaty of Peking sees China cede to Japan all territory east of the Ussuri and as far south as the Korea border, including the newly established port of Vladivostok.

scheduled for November went ahead with half of Russia's male population voting. Even though 55% chose Kerensky's rural socialist party and only 25% voted for the Bolsheviks, when the Founding Assembly met in January the Bolsheviks disbanded it after its first day in session, thus setting the antidemocratic tone for the coming decades.

Soviet Russia

Civil War

The Soviet government immediately redistributed land to those who worked it, signed an armistice with the Germans in December 1917 and set up its own secret police force, the Cheka. Trotsky, now military commissar, founded the Red Army in January 1918. In March the Bolshevik Party renamed itself the Communist Party and moved the capital to Moscow.

Edmund Wilson's magnum opus, *To the Finland Station* (1940), is the most authoritative account of the development of socialism and communism in Russia.

In September 1918 the Cheka began a systematic program of arrest, torture and execution of anyone opposed to Soviet rule. Those hostile to the Bolsheviks, collectively termed 'Whites', had developed strongholds in the south and east of the country. But they lacked unity, including as they did tsarist stalwarts, landlord-killing social revolutionaries, Czech prisoners of war, Finnish partisans and Japanese troops. The Bolsheviks had the advantage of controlling the heart of Russia, including its war industry and communications. Full-scale civil war broke out in early 1918 and lasted until 1922 when the Red Army was victorious at Volochaevka, west of Khabarovsk.

By 1921 the Communist Party had firmly established one-party rule, thanks to the Red Army and the Cheka, which continued to eliminate opponents. Some opponents escaped, joining an estimated 1.5 million citizens in exile.

War Communism

During the civil war, a system called War Communism subjected every aspect of society to the aim of victory. This meant sweeping nationali-

THE SWITCH IN CALENDARS

Until 1918 Russian dates followed the Julian calendar, which lagged behind the Gregorian calendar (used by pretty much every other country in the world) by 13 days. The new Soviet regime brought Russia into line by following 31 January 1918 with 14 February (skipping 1 to 13 February). This explains why, in Russia history, the revolution was on 25 October 1917 while in the West it occurred on 7 November 1917. The Julian calendar is still used in Russia by the Orthodox Church, which is why Christmas Day is celebrated on 7 January instead of 25 December.

1861
The emancipation of the serfs frees labour to feed the Russian industrial revolution. Workers flood into the capital, leading to overcrowding, poor sanitation, epidemics and societal discontent.

1866
The revolutionary Dmitry Karakozov makes an unsuccessful attempt on the life of Alexander II, the first of several assassination bids; all student groups are banned at St Petersburg University.

1867
Debts from the Crimean War force Russia to sell gold-rich Alaska and the Aleutian Islands to the USA – their only supporter during the conflict – for US$7.2 million.

1877–78
War against the Ottoman Empire results in the liberation of Bulgaria and annulment of the conditions of the Treaty of Paris of 1856 that ended the Crimean War.

LAYING THE LAST TSAR TO REST

After their 1918 execution the bodies of the Romanovs were dumped at Ganina Yama, an abandoned mine 16km from Yekaterinburg. When grenades failed to collapse the main shaft, it was decided to distribute the bodies among various smaller mines and pour acid on them. But the person in charge of the acid fell off his horse and broke his leg, and the truck carrying the bodies became bogged in a swamp.

By now understandably desperate, the disposal team opted to bury the corpses. They tried burning Alexey and Maria in preparation, but realised it would take days to burn all the bodies properly, so the others were just put in a pit and doused with acid. Even then, most of the acid soaked away into the ground – leaving the bones to be uncovered in 1976, a discovery that was kept secret until the remains were finally fully excavated in 1991. A year later the bones of nine people were conclusively identified as Tsar Nicholas II, his wife Tsaritsa Alexandra, three of their four daughters, the imperial doctor and three servants.

Missing were the remains of the imperial couple's only son, Tsarevitch Alexey, and one of their daughters, giving a new lease of life to theories that the youngest daughter, Anastasia, had somehow escaped. In 1994 an official Russian inquiry team managed to piece together the skulls found in the pit, badly damaged by rifle butts, hand grenades and acid. Using plaster models of the faces, DNA tests and dental records, they determined that the three daughters found were Olga, Tatyana – and Anastasia. The missing daughter was Maria, whose remains were unearthed in 2007 and formally identified along with those of her brother Alexey in 2008.

In mid-1998 the imperial remains were given a proper funeral at St Petersburg's SS Peter and Paul Cathedral, to lie alongside their predecessors dating back to Peter the Great. The Orthodox Church later canonised the tsar and his family as martyrs.

sation in all economic sectors and strict administrative control by the Soviet government, which in turn was controlled by the Communist Party.

The Party itself was restructured to reflect Lenin's creed of 'democratic centralism', which held that Party decisions should be obeyed all the way down the line. A new political bureau, the Politburo, was created for Party decision-making, and a new secretariat supervised Party appointments, ensuring that only loyal members were given responsibility.

War Communism was also a form of social engineering to create a classless society. Many 'class enemies' were eliminated by execution or exile, with disastrous economic consequences. Forced food requisitions and hostility towards larger, more efficient farmers, combined with drought and a breakdown of infrastructure, led to the enormous famine of 1920–21, when between four and five million people died.

1881

Terrorists finally get Alexander II. St Petersburg's Church of the Saviour on Spilled Blood is built on the site of the assassination. Alexander III undoes many of his father's reforms.

IZZET KERIBAR / LONELY PLANET IMAGES ©

» Church on Spilled Blood

1882

Jews are subject to harsh legal restrictions in retribution for their alleged role in the assassination of Alexander II. A series of pogroms provokes Jewish migration from Russia.

1883

The revolutionaries Georgy Plekhanov and Pavel Axelrod flee to Switzerland, adopt Marxism and found the Russian Social-Democratic Workers Party. One of their converts is Vladimir Lenin.

The New Economic Policy

Under the New Economic Policy (NEP) adopted in 1921, the state continued to own the 'commanding heights' of the economy – large-scale industry, banks, transport – but allowed private enterprise to reemerge. Farm output improved as the kulaks consolidated their holdings and employed landless peasants as wage earners. Farm surplus was sold to the cities in return for industrial products, giving rise to a new class of traders and small-scale industrialists called nepmen. By the late 1920s, agricultural and industrial production had reached prewar levels.

But the political tide was set the other way. At the 1921 Party congress, Lenin outlawed debate within the Party as 'factionalism', launching the first systematic purge among Party members. The Cheka was reorganised as the GPU (State Political Administration) in 1922, gaining much greater powers to operate outside the law; for the time being it limited itself to targeting political opponents.

Stalin vs Trotsky

In May 1922 Lenin suffered the first of a series of paralysing strokes. After his 1924 death, his embalmed remains were put on display in Moscow and a personality cult was built around him – all orchestrated by Stalin.

But Lenin had failed to name a successor and had expressed a low opinion of 'too rude' Stalin. The charismatic Trotsky, hero of the civil war and second only to Lenin as an architect of the revolution, wanted collectivisation of agriculture – an extension of War Communism – and worldwide revolution. He attacked Party 'bureaucrats' who wished to concentrate on socialism in the Soviet Union.

But even before Lenin's death, the powers that mattered in the Party and soviets had backed a three-man leadership of Zinoviev, Kamenev and Stalin, in which Stalin already pulled the strings. As Party general secretary, he controlled all appointments and had installed his supporters wherever it mattered. His influence grew with a recruiting drive that doubled Party membership to over a million, and in 1927 he succeeded in getting Trotsky, his main rival, expelled.

STALIN

Simon Sebag Montefiore has penned two highly revealing and entertaining books about Russia's most notorious 20th-century leader: *Stalin: The Court of the Red Czar* and *Young Stalin*.

Five-Year Plans & Farm Collectivisation

The first of Stalin's Five-Year Plans, announced in 1928, called for quadrupling the output of heavy industry, such as power stations, mines, steelworks and railways. Agriculture was to be collectivised to get the peasants to fulfil production quotas, which would feed the growing cities and provide food exports to pay for imported heavy machinery.

The forced collectivisation of agriculture destroyed the country's peasantry (still 80% of the population) as a class and as a way of life. Farmers were required to pool their land and resources into *kolkhozy* (collective

1886

Alexander III authorises the building of 7500km of railroad across Siberia between Chelyabinsk and Vladivostok, laying the foundations for the Trans-Siberian Railway.

1895

Lenin commands Russia's first Marxist cell in St Petersburg. He's arrested and sentenced to three years of exile in Shushenskoe where he marries Nadezhda Krupskaya in a church wedding.

1896

Nicholas II's reign is marked by tragedy from the start when a stampede by crowds assembled in Moscow for his coronation results in over 1300 being trampled to death.

1903

The Russian Social-Democratic Workers Party splits into the radical Bolsheviks and the more conservative Mensheviks. The two factions coexist until 1912, when the Bolsheviks set up their own party.

farms), usually consisting of about 75 households and dozens of square kilometres in area, which became their collective property, in return for compulsory quotas of produce. These *kolkhozy* covered two-thirds of all farmland, supported by a network of Machine Tractor Stations that dispensed machinery and advice (political or otherwise).

Farmers who resisted – and most kulaks did, especially in Ukraine and the Volga and Don regions, which had the biggest grain surpluses – were killed or deported to labour camps in the millions. Farmers slaughtered their animals rather than hand them over, leading to the loss of half the national livestock. A drought and continued grain requisitions led to famine in the same three regions in 1932–33, in which millions more people perished. Ukrainians consider this famine, known as *golodomor*, a deliberate act of genocide against them while others say Stalin deliberately orchestrated this tragedy to wipe out opposition.

The Whisperers: Private Life in Stalin's Russia by Orlando Figes is an engrossing account of how ordinary people coped with the daily harsh realities of Soviet life.

SOVIET LIFE

The Gulag

Many new mines and factories were built in Central Asia or Siberia, which was resource-rich but thinly populated. A key labour force was provided by the network of concentration camps begun under Lenin and now called the Gulag, from the initial letters of Glavnoe Upravlenie Lagerey (Main Administration for Camps), which stretched from the north of European Russia through Siberia and Central Asia to Russia's Far East.

The Gulag's inmates – some of whose only 'offence' was to joke about Stalin or steal two spikelets of wheat from a *kolkhoz* field – cut trees, dug canals, laid railway tracks and worked in factories in remote areas, especially Siberia and the Russian Far East. A huge slice of the northeast was set aside exclusively for labour camps, and whole cities such as Komsomolsk-na-Amure and Magadan were developed as Gulag centres.

The Gulag population grew from 30,000 in 1928 to eight million in 1938. The average life expectancy after being sentenced to the Gulag was two years: 90% of inmates died. The Gulag continued well after WWII; Boris Yeltsin announced the release of Russia's 'last 10' political prisoners from a camp near Perm in 1992.

Anne Applebaum, author of the Pulitzer Prize–winning *Gulag: A History*, reckons that at least 18 million people passed through the camp system. Many more suffered, though. Nadezhda Mandelstam, whose husband Osip Mandelstam, a highly regarded poet, was exiled to Siberia in 1934, wrote that a wife considered herself a widow from the moment of her husband's arrest. She was almost right – Osip lasted four years before dying at the Vtoraya Rechka transit camp in Vladivostok.

The Purges

Early camp inmates were often farmers caught up in the collectivisation, but in the 1930s the terror shifted to Party members and other influential

1904–05

In the Russo-Japanese War the Russians lose Port Arthur and see their fleet virtually annihilated. When Japan occupies Sakhalin Island, Russia is forced to sue for peace.

1905

Hundreds of people are killed when troops fire on peaceful protestors presenting a petition to the tsar. Nicholas II is held responsible for the tragedy, dubbed Bloody Sunday.

1906–07

Nicholas II allows elections for a parliament (duma) in 1906 and 1907. Both duma prove to be too left-wing for the tsar so he promptly dissolves them.

1911

Having survived court intrigues, including the wrath of Tsaritsa Alexandra for ordering Rasputin's expulsion from St Petersburg, reforming prime minister Pyotr Stolypin is assassinated while at the theatre in Kyiv.

people not enthusiastic enough about Stalin. A series of show trials were held in Moscow, in which the charges ranged from murder plots and capitalist sympathies to Trotskyist conspiracies. The biggest such trial was in 1938 against 21 leading Bolsheviks, including Party theoretician Bukharin.

Throughout 1937 and 1938, the secret police (now called the NKVD, the People's Commissariat of Internal Affairs) took victims from their homes at night; most were never heard of again. In the non-Russian republics of the USSR, virtually the whole Party apparatus was eliminated on charges of 'bourgeois nationalism'. The bloody purge clawed its way into all sectors and levels of society – even 400 of the Red Army's 700 generals were shot. Its victims are thought to have totalled 8.5 million.

DEATH

Stalin once remarked that the death of one person was tragic, the death of a million 'a statistic': historians conservatively estimate that some 20 million Soviet citizens died as a result of his policies, purges and paranoia.

The German-Soviet Pact

In 1939 Russian offers of a security deal with the UK and France to counter Germany's possible invasion of Poland were met with a lukewarm reception. Under no illusions about Hitler's ultimate intentions, Stalin needed to buy time to prepare his country for war and saw a deal with the Germans as a route to making territorial gains in Poland.

On 23 August 1939 the Soviet and German foreign ministers, Molotov and Ribbentrop, signed a nonaggression pact. A secret protocol stated that any future rearrangement would divide Poland between them; Germany would have a free hand in Lithuania and the Soviet Union in Estonia, Latvia, Finland and Bessarabia, which had been lost to Romania in 1918.

Germany invaded Poland on 1 September; the UK and France declared war on Germany on 3 September. Stalin traded the Polish provinces of Warsaw and Lublin with Hitler for most of Lithuania and the Red Army marched into these territories less than three weeks later. The Soviet gains in Poland, many of which were areas inhabited by non-Polish speakers and had been under Russian control before WWI, were quickly incorporated into the Belarusian and Ukrainian republics of the USSR.

The Great Patriotic War

'Operation Barbarossa', Hitler's secret plan for an invasion of the Soviet Union, began on 22 June 1941. Russia was better prepared, but the disorganised Red Army was no match for the German war machine, which advanced on three fronts. Within four months the Germans had overrun Minsk and Smolensk and were just outside Moscow. They had marched through the Baltic states and most of Ukraine and laid siege to Leningrad. Only an early, severe winter halted the advance.

The Soviet commander, General Zhukov, used the winter to push the Germans back from Moscow. Leningrad held out – and continued to do

1912

The election of a fourth duma coincides with worker strikes. Even so, an exiled Lenin tells an audience in Switzerland that there will be no revolution in his lifetime.

BRENT WINEBRENNER / LONELY PLANET IMAGES ©

» Lenin statue, Kamchatka

1914

WWI kicks off with an unprepared Russia invading Austrian Galicia and German Prussia and immediately suffering defeats. St Petersburg becomes the less Germanic-sounding Petrograd.

February 1917

The February Revolution in Petrograd results in a soviet of Workers' and Soldiers' Deputies as well as a reconvened duma; Nicholas II abdicates on 1 March.

so for 2¼ years, during which over half a million of its civilians died, mainly from hunger.

German atrocities against the local population stiffened resistance. Stalin appealed to old-fashioned patriotism and eased restrictions on the Church, ensuring that the whole country rallied to the cause with incredible endurance. Military goods supplied by the Allies through the northern ports of Murmansk and Arkhangelsk were invaluable in the early days of the war. All Soviet military industry was packed up, moved east of the Ural Mountains and worked by women and Gulag labour.

Stalingrad

Lasting 199 days and claiming something in the order of 1.5 million lives, the Battle for Stalingrad was the longest, deadliest and strategically most decisive of WWII. In spring 1942 Hitler launched Operation Blue to seize the food and fuel resources of the Soviet south, a goal that would require the capture of the city of Stalingrad. Stalin was slow to respond, keeping Soviet forces in the north in fear of another attack on Moscow. In August, German Field Marshal von Paulus launched the offensive; his troops quickly reached the river and entered the city. Victory seemed all but certain.

Harrison Salisbury's *The 900 Days: The Siege of Leningrad* is the most thorough and harrowing account of the city's sufferings in WWII.

The Red Army's brilliant tactician, Marshal Zhukov, was dispatched to organise a desperate defence, street by street, house by house, hand to hand. Neither side flinched and a flood of reinforcements sustained the bloodletting. By November threadbare Soviet forces somehow still held the city. The German armies were overextended and demoralised. Zhukov launched Operation Uranus, a one-million-man counter-offensive that severed German supply lines and isolated the 300,000 Nazi troops.

German efforts to break out of Zhukov's closing snare continued into winter. By the end of January, most of them were killed or taken prisoner. On 2 February 1943 von Paulus surrendered what was left of the encircled German Sixth Army. It was the turning point of the war. The Red Army had driven the Germans out of most of the Soviet Union by the end of the year; it reached Berlin in April 1945.

Stalingrad by Antony Beevor is a superb book based on new access to long-secret archives and concentrates on the human cost of WWII.

The End of WWII

The USSR had borne the brunt of the war. Its total losses, civilian and military, may never be known, but they are thought to have numbered between 25 and 27 million. This compares to wartime deaths of between five and seven million for Germany, 400,000 for Britain and 330,000 for the USA.

Russia's sacrifices meant that the US and British leaders, Roosevelt and Churchill, were obliged to observe Stalin's wishes in the postwar settlement. At Tehran (November 1943) and Yalta (February 1945) the

October 1917

Lenin returns from Finland to lead the Bolshevik coup. Alexander Kerensky's moderate Socialist Party wins the November election, a result ignored by the Bolsheviks.

March 1918

The Treaty of Brest-Litovsk marks Russia's formal exit from WWI and confirms the independence of Belarus, Finland, Ukraine and the Baltic states. The capital is moved to Moscow.

July 1918

Having first been exiled to Tobolsk, Nicholas II, his immediate family and servants are murdered in Yekaterinburg as nationwide civil war between White and Red forces ensues.

1920

Admiral Alexander Kolchak's White Army is defeated by the Red Army at Omsk. Kolchak retreats to Irkutsk where he's captured and shot. The civil war is over two years later.

three agreed each to govern the areas they liberated until free elections could be held.

Soviet troops liberating Eastern Europe propped up local communist movements, which formed 'action committees' that either manipulated the elections or simply seized power when the election results were unfavourable.

The Cold War

Control over Eastern Europe and postwar modernisation of industry, with the aid of German factories and engineers seized as war booty, made the Soviet Union one of the two major world powers. The first postwar Five-Year Plan was military and strategic (more heavy industry); consumer goods and agriculture remained low priorities.

A cold war was shaping up between the communist and capitalist worlds, and in the USSR the new demon became 'cosmopolitanism' – warm feelings towards the West. The first victims were the estimated two million Soviet citizens repatriated by the Allies in 1945 and 1946. Some were former prisoners of war or forced labourers taken by the Germans; others were refugees or people who had taken the chance of war to escape the USSR. They were sent straight to the Gulag in case their stay abroad had contaminated them. Party and government purges continued as Stalin's reign came to resemble that of Ivan the Terrible.

WWII Memorials

- Monument to the Heroic Defenders of Leningrad, St Petersburg
- Mamaev Kurgan, Volgograd
- Park Pobedy, Moscow
- Alyosha, Murmansk

The Khrushchev Thaw

With Stalin's death in 1953, power passed to a combined leadership of five Politburo members. One, Lavrenty Beria, the NKVD boss responsible under Stalin for millions of deaths, was secretly tried and shot (and the NKVD was reorganised as the KGB, the Committee for State Security, which was to remain firmly under Party control). In 1954 another of the Politburo members, Nikita Khrushchev, a pragmatic Ukrainian who had helped carry out 1930s purges, launched the Virgin Lands campaign, bringing vast tracts of Kazakhstan and Central Asia under cultivation. A series of good harvests did his reputation no harm.

During the 20th Party congress in 1956, Khrushchev made a 'secret speech' about crimes committed under Stalin. It was the beginning of de-Stalinisation (also known as the Thaw), marked by the release of millions of Gulag prisoners and a slightly more liberal political and intellectual climate. The congress also approved peaceful coexistence between communist and noncommunist regimes. The Soviet Union, Khrushchev argued, would soon triumph over the 'imperialists' by economic means. Despite the setback of the 1956 Hungarian rebellion, which was put down by Soviet troops, in 1957 he emerged the unchallenged leader of the USSR.

March 1921

Sailors and soldiers at Kronshtadt rebel against the Communists' increasingly dictatorial regime. The rebellion is brutally suppressed as debate with the Communist Party is outlawed.

March 1921

The New Economic Policy (NEP), allowing limited private enterprise alongside state control of large-scale industry and infrastructure, is adopted by the 10th Party Congress and remains until 1927.

1922

Josef Stalin is appointed Communist Party general secretary. The Union of Soviet Socialist Republics (USSR) is founded.

1924

Lenin dies at 53 without designating a successor. Petrograd changes its name to Leningrad in his honour. Power is assumed by a triumvirate of Stalin, Lev Kaminev and Grigory Zinoviev.

Cuban Missile Crisis

A cautious détente between the USSR and the US in the late 1950s was undermined by a series of international crises. In 1961 Berlin was divided by the Wall to stop an exodus from East Germany. In 1962, the USSR supplied its Caribbean ally Cuba with defensive weapons, effectively stationing medium-range missiles with nuclear capability on the doorstep of the US. After some tense calling of bluff that brought the world to the brink of nuclear war, it withdrew the missiles.

A rift also opened between the Soviet Union and China. The two competed for the allegiance of newly independent Third World nations and came into conflict over areas in Central Asia and the Russian Far East that had been conquered by the tsars.

At home, Khrushchev started the mass construction of cheap and ugly apartment blocks – by the end of his reign most people who had lived in communal flats now had their own, but the cityscapes changed forever. The agricultural sector also performed poorly and Khrushchev upset Party colleagues by decentralising economic decision-making. After a disastrous harvest in 1963 forced the Soviet Union to buy wheat from Canada, the Central Committee relieved Khrushchev of his posts in 1964, because of 'advanced age and poor health'. He lived on in obscurity until 1971.

Night of Stone: Death and Memory in Twentieth-Century Russia by Catherine Merridale is an enthralling read, viewing the country's bleak recent history through the prisms of psychology and philosophy.

The Brezhnev Stagnation

The new 'collective' leadership of Leonid Brezhnev (general secretary) and Alexey Kosygin (premier) soon devolved into a one-man show under

WINNING THE SPACE RACE

The Space Race was the phrase used to sum up the Cold War rivalry between the US and the USSR to be the first to send rockets, satellites and people into outer space. Starting with both sides' efforts to develop rocket-delivered weapons during the 1940s, the competition really got going with Soviet advances in the late 1950s. The successful launch of satellite Sputnik I into orbit in 1957 was followed by Yury Gagarin's historic trip in 1961. Two years later Valentina Tereshkova became the first woman in space, and, in 1965, Alexey Leonov was the first person to perform a spacewalk.

NASA, the US space agency, was desperate to regain the initiative. By spending the equivalent of $150 billion in 2010 dollars (18 times the cost of digging the Panama Canal) on its Apollo project, the US managed to put men on the moon by the end of the 1960s. Some 40-odd years later, with the retirement of the US space shuttle Atlantis, the initiative is back with Russia's federal space agency Roscosmos (www.federalspace.ru), the only body now transferring space travellers – be they astronauts or cosmonauts – out to the International Space Station.

For more about the Space Race read *Red Moon Rising: Sputnik and the Rivalries that Ignited the Space Age* by Matthew Brzezinski.

1928
Stalin introduces the first 'Five-Year Plan', a program of centralised economic measures, including farm collectivisation and investment in heavy industry, designed to make the Soviet Union into a superpower.

1929
Expelled from the Communist Party in 1927, Leon Trotsky goes into exile, ending up in Mexico, where an agent of Stalin wielding an ice pick finishes him off in 1940.

1932–33
Famine kills millions as the forced collectivisation of farms slashes grain output and almost halves livestock. Agriculture does not reach precollectivisation levels until 1940.

1934
Leningrad party boss Sergei Kirov is murdered as he leaves his office at the Smolny Institute. The assassination kicks off the Great Purges, ushering in Stalin's reign of terror.

conservative Brezhnev. Khrushchev's administrative reforms were rolled back and the economy stagnated, propped up only by the exploitation of huge Siberian oil and gas reserves.

As repression increased, the 'dissident' movement grew, along with samizdat (underground publications). Prison terms and forced labour did not seem to have the desired effect and, in 1972, the KGB chief, Yury Andropov, introduced new measures that included forced emigration and imprisonment in 'psychiatric institutions'. Among the many deportees was Nobel Prize winner Aleksandr Solzhenitsyn.

The growing government and Party elite, known as nomenklatura (literally, 'list of nominees'), enjoyed lavish lifestyles, with access to goods that were unavailable to the average citizen. So did military leaders and some approved engineers and artists. But the ponderous, overcentralised economy, with its suffocating bureaucracy, was providing fewer and fewer improvements in general living standards. Corruption began to spread in the Party and a cynical malaise seeped through society. Brezhnev was rarely seen in public after his health declined in 1979.

Glastnost

Brezhnev's successor Yury Andropov replaced some officials with young technocrats and proposed campaigns against alcoholism (which was costing the economy dearly) and corruption, later carried out under Gorbachev. He also clamped down on dissidents and increased defence spending.

But the economy continued to decline and Andropov died in February 1984, only 15 months after coming to power. Frail, 72-year-old Konstantin Chernenko, his successor, didn't even last that long. Mikhail Gorbachev, the next incumbent of the top job, understood that radically different policies were needed if the moribund Soviet Union was to survive.

The energetic 54-year-old launched an immediate turnover in the Politburo, bureaucracy and military, replacing many of the Brezhnevite 'old guard' with his own, younger supporters. 'Acceleration' in the economy and *glasnost* (openness) – first manifested in press criticism of poor economic management and past Party failings – were his initial slogans. Management initiative was encouraged, efficiency rewarded and bad practices allowed to be criticised.

ECONOMICS

Red Plenty by Francis Spufford is an ingenious piece of writing – part novel, part social history – that focuses on real people and events from the 1950s to the late 1960s, when it briefly looked like the Soviet economic system was besting that of capitalist economies.

Foreign Affairs

Bloody clampdowns on nationalist rallies in Alma-Ata (now known as Almaty) in 1986, Tbilisi in 1989, and Vilnius and Rīga in early 1991 made an alliance between Gorbachev, the interregional group in the parliament and the Democratic Russia movement impossible.

With the US, however, Gorbachev discontinued the isolationist, confrontational and economically costly policies of his predecessors. At his

1936–38

At the Moscow show trials former senior Communist Party leaders are accused of conspiring to assassinate Stalin and other Soviet leaders, dismember the Soviet Union and restore capitalism.

1939

When talks with Britain and France on a mutual defence treaty fail, Stalin signs a nonaggression pact with Germany, thus laying the ground for Poland's invasion and WWII.

1940

Lithuania, Latvia and Estonia are incorporated into the USSR; along with Moldavia, they bring the total of SSRs up to its final number of 15.

1941

Hitler invades Russia, beginning what is referred to in Russia as the Great Patriotic War. The Red Army is unprepared, and German forces advance rapidly across the country.

first meeting with Ronald Reagan in Geneva in 1985, Gorbachev suggested a 50% cut in long-range nuclear weaponry. By 1987 the two superpowers had agreed to remove all medium-range missiles from Europe, with other significant cuts in arms and troop numbers following. The 'new thinking' also put an end to Russia's military involvement in Afghanistan and led to improved relations with China.

Perestroika & Political Reform

In an effort to tackle the ingrained corruption of the Communist Party, *perestroika* (restructuring) combined limited private enterprise and private property, not unlike Lenin's NEP, with efforts to push decision-making and responsibility out towards the grass roots. New laws were enacted in both these fields in 1988, but their application, understandably, met resistance from the centralised bureaucracy.

Glasnost was supposed to tie in with *perestroika* as a way to encourage new ideas and counter the Brezhnev legacy of cynicism. The release at the end of 1986 of a famous dissident, Nobel Peace Prize winner Andrei Sakharov, from internal exile was the start of a general freeing of political prisoners. Religions were allowed to operate more and more freely.

In 1988 Gorbachev announced a new 'parliament', the Congress of People's Deputies, with two-thirds of its members to be elected directly by the people, thus reducing the power of the bureaucracy and the Party. A year later, the first elections for decades were held and the congress convened, to outspoken debate and national fascination. Though dominated by Party apparatchiki (members), the parliament also contained outspoken critics of the government such as Sakharov and Boris Yeltsin.

Sinatra Doctrine

Gorbachev sprang repeated surprises, including sudden purges of difficult opponents (such as the populist reformer Yeltsin), but the forces unleashed by his opening up of society grew impossible to control. From 1988 onward the reduced threat of repression and the experience of electing even semi-representative assemblies spurred a growing clamour for independence in the Soviet satellite states.

One by one, the Eastern European countries threw off their Soviet puppet regimes in the autumn of 1989; the Berlin Wall fell on 9 November. The Brezhnev Doctrine, Gorbachev's spokesperson said, had given way to the 'Sinatra Doctrine': letting them do it *their* way. The formal reunification of Germany on 3 October 1990 marked the effective end of the Cold War.

In 1990 the three Baltic states of the USSR also declared (or, as they would have it, reaffirmed) their independence – an independence that, for the present, remained more theoretical than real. Before long, most other Soviet republics either followed suit or declared 'sovereignty' – the

AFGHAN WAR

Afgantsy: The Russians in Afghanistan, 1979–1989 by Rodric Braithwaite, a one-time diplomat-turned-historian, takes its title from the term that Russians use for veterans of the ill-fated involvement in Afghanistan.

1942

Time magazine names Stalin Man of the Year, an accolade he'd previously received in 1939. Russia wins the Battle of Stalingrad at a cost of more than a million lives.

1944

In January the 872-day blockade of Leningrad by the Germans is broken. Leningrad has suffered over a million casualties and is proclaimed a hero city.

1945

In the closing days of WWII, with Japan on its knees, the Soviet Union occupies the Japanese territories of southern Sakhalin Island and the Kuril Islands.

1945

The end of WWII sees Soviet forces occupy much of Eastern Europe, leaving Berlin and Vienna divided cities. Winston Churchill refers to an 'iron curtain' coming down across Europe.

precedence of their own laws over the Soviet Union's. Gorbachev's proposal for an ill-defined new federal system for the Soviet Union won few friends.

Rise of Yeltsin

Also in 1990, Yeltsin won chairmanship of the parliament of the giant Russian Republic, which covered three-quarters of the USSR's area and contained more than half its population. Soon after coming to power, Gorbachev had promoted Yeltsin to head the Communist Party in Moscow, but had then dumped him in 1987–88 in the face of opposition to his reforms there from the Party's old guard. By that time, Yeltsin had already declared *perestroika* a failure, and these events produced a lasting personal enmity between the two men. Gorbachev increasingly struggled to hold together the radical reformers and the conservative old guard in the Party.

Robert Service has written celebrated biographies of Lenin, Stalin and Trotsky, as well as the *Penguin History of Modern Russia,* charting the country's history from Nicholas II to Putin.

Once chosen as chairman of the Russian parliament, Yeltsin proceeded to jockey for power with Gorbachev. He seemed already to have concluded that real change was impossible not only under the Communist Party but also within a centrally controlled Soviet Union, the members of which were in any case showing severe centrifugal tendencies. Yeltsin resigned from the Communist Party and his parliament proclaimed the sovereignty of the Russian Republic.

Economic Collapse

In early 1990 Gorbachev persuaded the Communist Party to vote away its own constitutional monopoly on power, and parliament chose him for the newly created post of executive president, which further distanced the organs of government from the Party. But these events made little difference to the crisis into which the USSR was sliding, as what was left of the economy broke down and organised crime and black-marketeering boomed, profiting from a slackening of Soviet law and order.

Gorbachev's Nobel Peace Prize, awarded in the bleak winter of 1990–91 when fuel and food were disappearing from many shops, left the average Soviet citizen literally cold. The army, the security forces and the Party hardliners called with growing confidence for the restoration of law and order to save the country. Foreign Minister Eduard Shevardnadze, long one of Gorbachev's staunchest partners but now under constant old-guard sniping for 'losing Eastern Europe', resigned, warning of impending hardline dictatorship.

The August Coup

In June 1991 Yeltsin was voted president of the Russian Republic in the country's first-ever direct presidential elections. He demanded devolution of power from the Soviet Union to the republics and banned Communist Party cells from government offices and workplaces in Russia.

1947

US president Harry Truman initiates a policy of 'containment' of Soviet influence; a Cold War breaks out between the two rival superpowers that lasts until 1990.

1948

Allied forces occupying western zones of Germany unify their areas, leading to a year-long Soviet blockade of western Berlin. The result is the split of Germany into two states.

1949

Having used espionage to kick-start its nuclear research program, the Soviet Union conducts its first nuclear weapon test (code name First Lightening) in August.

1950

Following a two-month visit to Moscow, Mao and Stalin sign the Sino-Soviet Treaty of Friendship and Alliance, which includes a US$300 million low-interest loan from Russia to China.

On 18 August 1991 a delegation from the 'Committee for the State of Emergency in the USSR' arrived at the Crimean dacha where Gorbachev was taking a holiday and demanded that he declare a state of emergency and transfer power to the vice-president, Gennady Yanayev. A coup was under way but, in Moscow, Yeltsin escaped arrest and went to the White House, seat of the Russian parliament, to rally opposition. Crowds gathered outside the White House, persuaded some of the tank crews (who had been sent to disperse them) to switch sides, and started to build barricades. Yeltsin climbed on a tank to declare the coup illegal and call for a general strike. Troops disobeyed orders and refused to storm the White House.

The following day huge crowds opposed to the coup gathered in Moscow and Leningrad. Kazakhstan rejected the coup and Estonia declared full independence from the Soviet Union. Coup leaders started to quit or fall ill. On 21 August the tanks withdrew; the coup leaders fled and were arrested.

End of the Soviet Union

Yeltsin responded by demanding control of all state property and banning the Communist Party in Russia. Gorbachev resigned as the USSR Party's leader the following day, ordering that the Party's property be transferred to the Soviet parliament.

Even before the coup, Gorbachev had been negotiating a last-ditch bid to save the Soviet Union with proposals for a looser union of independent states. In September the Soviet parliament abolished the centralised Soviet state, vesting power in three temporary governing bodies until a new union treaty could be signed. In the meantime Yeltsin was steadily transferring control over everything that mattered in Russia from Soviet hands into Russian ones.

On 8 December Yeltsin and the leaders of Ukraine and Belarus, meeting near Brest in Belarus, announced that the USSR no longer existed. They proclaimed a new Commonwealth of Independent States (CIS), a vague alliance of fully independent states with no central authority. Russia kicked the Soviet government out of the Kremlin on 19 December. Two days later eight more republics joined the CIS.

With the USSR dead, Gorbachev was a president without a country. He formally resigned on 25 December, the day the white, blue and red Russian flag replaced the Soviet red flag over the Kremlin.

CHORNOBYL

Twenty years after the explosion at the Chornobyl nuclear station in Ukraine, Gorbachev wrote 'even more than my launch of *perestroika*, [Chornobyl] was perhaps the real cause of the collapse of the Soviet Union'.

The Yeltsin Years

Economic Reform & Regional Tensions

Even before Gorbachev's resignation, Yeltsin had announced plans to move to a free-market economy, appointing in November 1991 a

1953

In March Stalin suffers a fatal stroke. Lavrenty Beria takes charge, but in June is arrested, tried for treason and executed. Nikita Khrushchev becomes first secretary.

JONATHAN SMITH / LONELY PLANET IMAGES ©

» Stalin statue, Moscow

1955

In response to the US and Western Europe forming NATO, the Soviet Union gathers together the communist states of Central and Eastern Europe to sign the Warsaw Pact.

1956

Soviet troops crush a Hungarian uprising. Khrushchev makes a 'Secret Speech' denouncing Stalin, thus commencing the de-Stalinisation of the Soviet Union, a period of economic reform and cultural thaw.

reforming government to carry this out. State subsidies were to be phased out, prices freed, government spending cut and state businesses, housing, land and agriculture privatised. Yeltsin became prime minister and defence minister, as well as president as an emergency measure.

With the economy already in chaos, all of Russia's nominally autonomous ethnic regions, some of them rich in natural resources, declared themselves independent republics, leading to fears that Russia might disintegrate as the USSR had just done. These worries were eventually defused, however, by three things: a 1992 treaty between the central government and the republics; a new constitution in 1993, which handed the other regions increased rights; and by changes in the tax system.

Some benefits of economic reform took hold during 1994 in a few big cities, notably Moscow and St Petersburg (the name to which Leningrad had reverted in 1991), where a market economy was taking root and an enterprise culture was developing among the younger generations. At the same time crime and corruption seemed to be spiralling out of control.

YELTSIN

Yeltsin: A Life by Timothy J Colton casts a favourable light on the much maligned former president, who led the destruction of Soviet Communism and the establishment of the Russian Federation.

Conflict with the Old Guard

Yeltsin's 'shock therapy' of economic reforms and plummeting international status put him on a collision course with the parliament, which was dominated by communists and nationalists, both opposed to the course events were taking. Organised crime was also steadily rising and corruption at all levels seemed more prevalent than before.

Yeltsin sacrificed key ministers and compromised on the pace of reform, but the parliament continued to issue resolutions contradicting his presidential decrees. In April 1993 a national referendum gave Yeltsin a big vote of confidence, both in his presidency and in his policies. He began framing a new constitution that would abolish the existing parliament and define more clearly the roles of president and legislature.

Finally, it came down to a trial of strength. In September 1993 Yeltsin dissolved the parliament, which in turn stripped him of all his powers. Yeltsin sent troops to blockade the White House, ordering the members to leave by 4 October. Many did, but on 2 and 3 October the National Salvation Front, an aggressive communist-nationalist group, attempted an insurrection, overwhelming the troops around the White House and attacking Moscow's Ostankino TV centre, where 62 people died. The next day troops stormed the White House, leaving at least 70 members of the public dead.

Reforming the Constitution

Russia's constitution (www.constitution.ru) was adopted by a national referendum in December 1993, the same month elections were held for a new two-house form of parliament. The name of the more influential

1959

US vice-president Richard Nixon's visit to Moscow is followed with a trip by Khrushchev to the US; he brings the idea of the self-service cafeteria back to the USSR.

1962

US–Soviet relations take a turn for the worse during the Cuban Missile Crisis. Russia's climb-down in the Caribbean standoff deals a blow to Khrushchev's authority at home.

1964

A coup against Khrushchev brings Leonid Brezhnev to power. Poet and future Nobel laureate Joseph Brodsky is labelled a 'social parasite' and sent into exile.

1965

Oil begins to flow in Siberia as Prime Minister Alexey Kosygin tries to shift the Soviet economy over to light industry and producing consumer goods. His reforms are stymied by Brezhnev.

lower house, the State Duma (Gosudarstvennaya Duma), consciously echoed that of tsarist Russia's parliaments.

Among the many rights enshrined in the new constitution are those to free trade and competition, private ownership of land and property, freedom of conscience and free movement in and out of Russia. It also bans censorship, torture and the establishment of any official ideology.

However, the constitution does have potential flaws in that the president and the parliament can both make laws and effectively block each other's actions. In practice, the president can usually get his way through issuing presidential decrees. During Yeltsin's turbulent rule this happened often. Putin and Medvedev have worked to ensure a more harmonious relationship with the Duma.

War in Chechnya

Yeltsin's foreign policy reflected the growing mood of conservative nationalism at home. The sudden demise of the Soviet Union had left many Russian citizens stranded in now potentially hostile countries. As the political tide turned against them, some of these Russians returned to the motherland. Under such circumstances the perceived need for a buffer zone between Russia and the outside world became a chief concern – and remains so.

Russian troops intervened in fighting in Tajikistan, Georgia and Moldova as UN-sanctioned peacekeepers, but also with the aim of strengthening Russia's hand in those regions, and by early 1995 Russian forces were stationed in all the other former republics except Estonia and Lithuania.

However, in the Muslim republic of Chechnya, which had declared independence from Russia in 1991, this policy proved particularly disastrous. Attempts to negotiate a settlement or have Chechnya's truculent leader Dzhokhar Dudayev deposed had stalled by the end of 1994.

Yeltsin ordered troops into Chechnya for what was meant to be a quick operation to restore Russian control. But the Chechens fought bitterly and by mid-1995 at least 25,000 people, mostly civilians, were dead, and the Russians had only just gained full control of the destroyed Chechen capital, Grozny. Dudayev was still holding out in southern Chechnya and guerrilla warfare continued unabated. Yeltsin's popularity plummeted and, in the December 1995 elections, communists and nationalists won control of 45% of the Duma.

Anna Politkovskaya's *Putin's Russia* is a searing indictment of the country and its leaders from a fearless journalist who was murdered in 2006 while working on an exposé of Chechnya's Russian-backed leader.

Rise of the Oligarchs

By early 1996, with presidential elections pending, Yeltsin was spending much time hidden away, suffering frequent bouts of various ill-defined sicknesses. When he was seen in public he often appeared to be confused

1972

President Richard Nixon visits Moscow to sign the first Strategic Arms Limitation Treaty, restricting nuclear ballistic weapons and ushering in a period of détente between the two superpowers.

1979

Russia invades Afghanistan to support its Marxist-Leninist regime against US-backed Islamic militants. The conflict drags on for nine years and is considered the Soviet Union's 'Vietnam'.

1980

Because of the invasion of Afghanistan, the US and 61 other nations boycott the Olympic Games held in Moscow. Four years later Soviet teams boycott the Los Angeles Olympics.

1982–84

KGB supremo Yury Andropov is president for 15 months until his death in 1984. His successor, the doddering 72-year-old Konstantin Chernenko, hardly makes an impact before dying 13 months later.

and unstable. As the communists under Gennady Zyuganov seemed set to rise from the dead on a wave of discontent, oligarchs such as media barons Boris Berezovsky and Vladimir Gusinsky and banker and oilman Mikhail Fridman came to the president's aid. The communists were kept off TV, ensuring that the only message the Russian voters received was Yeltsin's.

In the June elections, Zyuganov and a tough-talking ex-general, Alexander Lebed, split the opposition vote, and Yeltsin easily defeated Zyuganov in a run-off in early July. The communists and other opposition parties returned to their grousing in the Duma, while Lebed was handed the poisoned chalice of negotiating an end to the messy Chechen war. Russian troops began withdrawing from Chechnya in late 1996.

In November Yeltsin underwent quintuple heart-bypass surgery. While he recuperated, much of 1997 saw a series of financial shenanigans and deals that were power grabs by the various Russian billionaires and members of Yeltsin's inner circle known as 'the Family'. (Yeltsin himself would later come under investigation by Swiss and Russian authorities. However, following his resignation in 1999, Yeltsin was granted immunity from legal prosecution by his successor, Vladimir Putin.)

OLIGARCHS

The Oligarchs: Wealth and Power in the New Russia by David Hoffman gives a blow-by-blow account of the rise and sometimes fall of the 'robber barons' of modern Russia.

Economic Collapse & Recovery

In the spring of 1998 signs that the Russian economy was in deep trouble were everywhere. Coalminers went on strike in protest at months of unpaid wages, part of more than the US$300 billion owed to workers across the country. This, added to well over US$100 billion in foreign debt, meant that Russia was effectively bankrupt. Yeltsin tried to exert his authority by sacking the government for its bad economic management.

But it was too late. During the summer of 1998 the foreign investors who had propped up Russia's economy fled. On 17 August the rouble was devalued, and in a repeat of scenes that had shaken the West during the Depression of 1929, many Russian banks faltered, leaving their depositors with nothing. The overall economic impact, though, was generally positive.

Following the initial shock, the growing Russian middle class, mostly paid in untaxed cash dollars, suddenly realised that their salaries had increased threefold overnight (if counted in roubles) while prices largely remained the same. This led to a huge boom in consumer goods and services. Luxuries such as restaurants and fitness clubs, previously only for the rich, suddenly became available to many more people. The situation also provided a great opportunity for Russian consumer-goods producers: in 1999 imported products were rapidly being replaced by high-quality local ones.

1985

Mikhail Gorbachev, 54, is elected general secretary of the Communist Party, the first Soviet leader to be born after the revolution. He institutes policies of *perestroika* and *glasnost*.

1989–90

Gorbachev pulls Soviet troops from Afghanistan. He wins the Nobel Peace Prize in 1990, as Germany is reunited and Moscow relinquishes its increasingly enfeebled grip on Eastern European satellites.

1991

A failed coup in August against Gorbachev seals the end of the USSR. On Christmas Day, Gorbachev resigns and Boris Yeltsin takes charge as president of the Russian Federation.

1993

In a clash of wills with the Russian parliament, Yeltsin sends in troops to deal with dissenters at Moscow's White House and Ostankino TV tower.

Moscow Bombings

In September 1999 a series of explosions rocked Moscow, virtually demolishing three apartment blocks and killing nearly 300 people. This unprecedented terrorism in the nation's capital fuelled unease and xenophobia, particularly against Chechens, who were popularly perceived as being responsible. An FSB (Federal Security Service, successor to the KGB) investigation concluded in 2002 that the bombings were masterminded by two non-Chechen Islamists – a view disputed by some, including the FSB operative Alexander Litvinenko, who would later be assassinated by lethal radiation poisoning in London in 2006.

The discovery of similar bombs in the city of Ryazan in September 1999, on top of Chechen incursions into Dagestan, was used by the Kremlin as a justification for launching air attacks on Grozny, the Chechen capital, sparking the second Chechen war. Amnesty International and the Council of Europe criticised both sides in the conflict for 'blatant and sustained' violations of international humanitarian law. Today, the conflict has eased to a controllable simmer under the watch of the Kremlin-friendly Chechen president Ramzan Kadyrov; see p447 for more details.

A History of Russia, by Nicholas Riasanovsky, is one of the best single-volume versions of the whole Russian story through to the end of the Soviet Union.

The Putin Years

Rise of the Siloviki

Yeltsin's appointed successor, Vladimir Putin, swept to victory in the March 2000 presidential elections. The one-time KGB operative and FSB chief boosted military spending, reestablished Kremlin control over the regions and cracked down on the critical media. Despite the increasingly bloody Chechen war, support for Putin remained solid, bearing out the president's own view – one that is frequently endorsed by a cross-section of Russians – that 'Russia needs a strong state power'.

Putin's cooperation with and support for the US-led assault on Afghanistan in the wake of 9/11 initially won him respect in the West. But doubts about the president's tough stance began to mount with the substantial death tolls of hostages that followed sieges at a Moscow theatre in October 2002 and at a school in Beslan in 2004.

Reelected in 2004, Putin's power was consolidated as Russia's global status grew, in direct correlation to the money the country earned off natural gas and oil sales and a booming economy. Behind the scenes an alliance of ex-KGB/FSB operatives, law enforcers and bureaucrats, known as *siloviki* (power people), seemed to be taking control. The most prominent victims of the regime have been oligarchs who have either fled the country or, as in the case of one-time oil billionaire Mikhail Khordorkovsky, had their assets seized and, following trials widely regarded as unfair, sentenced to long stretches in prison.

1994

Russian troops invade the breakaway republic of Chechnya in December. In a brutal two-year campaign the Chechen capital, Grozny, is reduced to rubble and 300,000 people flee their homes.

1996

Poor health doesn't stop Yeltsin from running for, and winning, a second term as president. His election is ensured by assistance from influential business oligarchs.

1999

On New Year's Eve, in a move that catches everyone on the hop, Yeltsin resigns and entrusts the caretaker duties of president to his prime minister, Vladimir Putin.

2002

In October a 700-strong audience at Moscow's Palace of Culture Theatre are taken hostage by around 50 Chechen terrorists. Security forces storm the theatre, resulting in over 100 casualties.

Stoking Russian Nationalism

In 2005 the Kremlin, worried at the prospect of a Ukrainian-style Orange Revolution, supported the founding of the ultranationalist youth group Nashi (meaning Ours), a band of ardent Putin and United Russia supporters who have been compared both to Komsomol (the Soviet youth brigade) and the Hitler Youth.

One of Nashi's stated aims was 'elimination of the regime of oligarchic capitalism.' However, the group has become best known for its aggressive protests against perceived enemies of the Russian state (which have included foreign missions in Russia, such as the UK embassy, and opposition politicians) and for its summer camp held in the forests around Lake Seliger attended by upward of 10,000 youths.

GOVERNING RUSSIA IN THE 21ST CENTURY

The 1993 constitution established a complex system of government for Russia as a federation. This federation is currently made up of 46 *oblasti* (regions), 21 semiautonomous *respubliki* (republics), nine *kraya* (territories), four autonomous *okruga* (districts), one autonomous region (the Jewish Autonomous Oblast) and the federal cities of Moscow and St Petersburg. The republics have their own constitution and legislation; territories, regions, the federal cities and the autonomous districts and region have their own charter and legislation.

This structure is partly a hangover from the old Soviet system of nominally autonomous republics for many minority ethnic groups. After the collapse of the Soviet Union, all these republics declared varying degrees of autonomy from Russia, the most extreme being Chechnya, in the Caucasus, which unilaterally declared full independence.

Yeltsin struck deals with the republics, which largely pacified them, and in the new constitution awarded regions and territories much the same status as republics but declared that federal laws always took precedence over local ones. Putin brought control back to the Kremlin by creating eight large federal districts each with an appointed envoy. He also saw to it that the regions would have federally appointed governors.

The president is the head of state and has broad powers. He or she appoints the key government ministers, including the prime minister (who is effectively the deputy president), interior and defence ministers. The Duma has to approve the president's appointees. Presidential elections are held every four years.

The Duma's upper house, the Federation Council (Sovet Federatsii), has 176 seats occupied by two unelected representatives from each of Russia's administrative districts. Its primary purpose is to approve or reject laws proposed by the lower house, the State Duma, which oversees all legislation. Its 450 members are equally divided between representatives elected from single-member districts and those elected from party lists. Obviously, this gives extra clout to the major parties and efforts to replace this system of representation with a purely proportional system have been shunned. Duma elections are held every four years in the December preceding the presidential elections.

2004

Putin is reelected. Russia's economy booms off the back of buoyant oil and gas prices. In September Chechen terrorists hold 1200 hostages at a school in Beslan, North Ossetia,; there are 344 casualties.

June 2005

China and Russia settle a post-WWII dispute over 2% of their 4300km common border. For the first time, the whole border between the two countries is legally defined.

2007

The assassination of former FSB spy Alexander Litvinenko in London and closure of the British Council offices in St Petersburg and Yekaterinburg see UK–Russia relations reach a new low.

May 2008

Former chairman of Gazprom Dmitry Medvedev succeeds Putin as Russia's third elected president. One of his first acts is to install his predecessor as prime minister.

Russian nationalism also came to the fore in relations with neighbouring Georgia and Ukraine. A six-day war broke out in August 2008 between Russia and Georgia over the breakaway regions of South Ossetia and Abkhazia, which Russia later recognised as independent countries. Russian Foreign Minister Sergei Lavrov was quoted in a radio interview on Ekho Moskvy as saying 'We will do anything not to allow Georgia and Ukraine to join NATO.'

Threats by Russia's largest company, Gazprom, to cut off gas supplies to Ukraine in 2006 and 2008 because of unpaid bills also sent shudders through much of Europe – a quarter of its gas comes from Gazprom and is piped through Ukraine.

Moscow bureau chief of the *Financial Times* Andrew Jack sums up the thorny political, economic and social issues facing the country in *Inside Putin's Russia: Can There Be Reform Without Democracy?*

Medvedev's Presidency

With no credible opponent, the March 2008 election of Dmitry Medvedev, a former chairman of Gazprom, as president was a forgone conclusion. Loyal to Putin ever since they worked together in the early 1990s for the St Petersburg government, Medvedev carried through his election promise of making Putin his prime minister. The official line has been that Putin and Medvedev are a 'ruling tandem'.

At times during his presidency, Medvedev appeared to come out of the shadow of his predecessor. He sacked Moscow's long-serving mayor Yury Luzhkov in September 2010 and, a month later, struck a truce with NATO over a European missile defence shield. However, in August 2011, Putin confirmed that he would run again for the presidency in 2012 and that Medvedev would be his chosen prime minister.

The Cult of Putin

An opinion poll in 2010 by the independent Levada Center found that over 50% of Russians believe a Soviet-style personality cult is being built around Putin. One of the latest apparent manifestations of this cult is 'Putin's Army', a group of shapely young girls whose slick video urging supporters to 'rip it off' (as in their clothes) for Putin has gone viral.

According to the leader of a religious sect in Bolshaya Elnya village in the Nizhny Novgorod Region, Putin is nothing short of a saint. Mother Fotinya claims Putin is the reincarnation of St Paul – or perhaps the founder of the Russian Orthodox Church. In her own past life, Fotinya was a railway worker, jailed for fraud in 1996.

Interviewed on French TV in 2011, Putin was at pains to distance himself from the negative connotations of personality cults, such as mass breaches of law and political repression. 'Even in nightmares I couldn't imagine this ever happening in today's Russia,' the premier said.

In an interview with the BBC on the 20th anniversary of the coup that led to the end of the Soviet Union, Gorbachev pulled no punches in stating his opinion on Putin, saying that under Putin's rule democracy in Russia has been 'castrated'.

Russia: A 1,000-Year Chronicle of the Wild East by Martin Sixsmith presents an epic and very readable sweep of Russia's history. It is also a 50-part radio series for BBC Radio 4.

August 2008

Georgia makes military moves on the autonomous regions of South Ossetia and Abkhazia. A brief war with Russia follows and Georgia is forced to back down.

2009

The global financial crisis hits Russia as the price of crude oil plummets. The economy begins to recover later in the year. US President Obama visits Moscow in July.

2010

The FBI uncovers a spy ring of 10 Russian agents in the US, including the sultry redhead Anna Chapman; they are swapped in Vienna for four US agents.

2011

Following a suicide bomb attack at Moscow's Domodedovo airport that kills 35 and injures over 100, security is beefed up at the country's transport hubs.

The Russian People

Within the Russian Federation, one's 'nationality' refers to one's ethnicity rather than one's passport – and Russia has dozens of nationalities. Despite such enormous cultural variation, there are characteristics that tend to be common across Russian citizens regardless of ethnicity.

While it's true that some Russians can be miserable, uncooperative and guarded in their initial approach to strangers, once you've earned a small crumb of friendship, hospitality typically flows with extraordinary generosity. Visitors can find themselves regaled with stories, drowned in vodka and stuffed full of food. An invitation to a Russian home will typically result in all of this being repeated several times, even when the family can ill afford the expense. This can be especially true outside the big cities, where you'll meet locals determined to share everything they have with you, however meagre their resources.

Russkiy Mir (www.russkiymir.ru) was created by the Russian government in 2007 as an organisation to preserve and promote the Russian language and culture throughout the world.

There's a similar bipolarity in the Russian sense of humour. Unsmiling gloom and fatalistic melancholy remain archetypically Russian, but, as in Britain, this is often used as a foil to a deadpan, sarcastic humour. This can be seen in Russians bandying around the derogatory terms *sovok* and *novy russky* (new Russians) in jokes about themselves. A *sovok* (derived from the word Soviet but also a play on words as it also means 'dust tray') refers to a lazy, uncouth person stuck in the Soviet mindset (it's also used to refer to anything bad that brings back memories of the worst of the USSR), while *novy russky* are considered obscenely rich and lacking in taste.

You'll also see this contradiction in Russians' attitudes towards their country. They love it deeply and will sing the praises of Mother Russia's great contributions to the arts and sciences, its long history and abundant physical attributes, then just as loudly point out its many failures. The extreme side of this patriotism can manifest itself in an unpleasant streak of racism (see p619). Don't let it put you off, and take heart in the knowledge that as much as foreigners may be perplexed about the true nature of the Russian soul, the locals themselves still haven't got it figured out either! As the poet Fyodor Tyutchev said, 'You can't understand Russia with reason…you can only believe in her.'

Mission to Moscow, the blog of a Canadian English teacher in Moscow, has a funny and very perceptive list of 50 facts about Russians: http://atethepaint.blogspot.com/2011/03/50-facts-about-russians.html.

Lifestyle

In the world's biggest country, the life of a Nenets reindeer herder in Siberia is radically different to that of a marketing executive in Moscow or an imam in a Dagestani mountain village. Travel into the countryside and more remote areas of this vast nation and you'll also witness a very different way of living from that experienced in prosperous urban centres such as Moscow and St Petersburg. Sometimes it even can feel like a trip back in time to the USSR – as witnessed in any of the preserved-in-Soviet-formaldehyde towns along the Baikal-Amur Mainline (Baikalo-Amurskaya Magistral; BAM).

This said, some common features of modern life across Russia stand out, such as the Soviet-era flats, the dacha (country home), education and weekly visits to the *banya* (bathhouse). Cohabitation remains less common than in the West, so when young couples get together, they get married just as often as not.

As the economy has improved so too has the average Russian's lifestyle, with more people than ever before owning a car, a computer and a mobile phone, and taking holidays abroad. The lives of Russian teenagers today couldn't be more different from those of their parents, who just a generation ago had to endure shortages of all kinds of goods on top of the ideology of Soviet communism. It's not uncommon to come across young adults who have only the vaguest, if any, idea of who Lenin or Stalin are.

This has to be balanced against the memories of those who knew the former Soviet leaders only too well and are now suffering as the social safety net that the state once provided for them has been largely withdrawn. It's hard not to be moved by the plight of the elderly struggling to get by on pensions of a couple of thousand roubles, for example.

Read the results of studies carried out by the UN Development Programme in Russia (www.undp.ru/?iso=RU) on issues such as poverty reduction, HIV/AIDS and democratic governance.

Apartments & Dachas

For the vast majority of urban Russians, home is within a Soviet-vintage, drab, ugly housing complex. Many of these were built during the late 1950s and early 1960s when Khrushchev was in power, so are known as Khrushchevkas (or sometimes *khrushchoby,* for Khrushchev and *trushchoby,* or slums). Meant to last just a couple of decades, they are very dilapidated on the outside, while the insides, though cramped, are invariably cosy and prettily decorated.

While there's usually a play area for kids in the middle of apartment blocks, they don't typically come with attached gardens. Instead, something like a third of Russian families have a dacha, or small country house. Often little more than a bare-bones hut (but sometimes quite luxurious), these retreats offer Russians refuge from city life, and as such figure prominently in the national psyche. On half-warm weekends, the major cities begin to empty out early on Friday as people head to the country.

One of the most important aspects of dacha life is gardening. Families use this opportunity to grow all manner of vegetables and fruits to eat over the winter. Flowers also play an important part in creating the proper dacha ambience, and even among people who have no need to grow food, the contact with the soil provides an important balm for the Russian soul.

Country Studies (http://country-studies.com/russia) includes a comprehensive series of essays on many aspects of Russian life including social structure, rural life, the family and the role of women.

The Banya

For centuries, travellers to Russia have commented on the particular (and in many people's eyes, peculiar) traditions of the *banya;* the closest

THE URBANISATION OF RUSSIA

Over the last century Russia has also gone from a country of peasants living in countryside villages to a highly urban one with close to three-quarters of its 142.9 million population living in cities and towns. Rural communities are left to wither, with thousands of villages deserted or dying.

The 2010 census had Moscow growing by 10.9% since the last census in 2002. The official population figure is 11.5 million, making it the largest metropolis in Europe, but the city's many illegal and unregistered residents probably puts the real figure as high as 17 million, according to experts. In contrast 6400 villages officially disappeared between the 2002 and 2010 censuses, as their populations dwindled to zero.

English equivalents, 'bathhouse' and 'sauna', don't quite sum it up. To this day, Russians make it an important part of their week, and you can't say you've really been to Russia unless you've visited one.

The main element of the *banya* is the *parilka* (steam room). Here, rocks are heated by a furnace, with water poured onto them using a long-handled ladle. Often a few drops of eucalyptus or pine oil (and sometimes even beer) are added to the water, creating a scent in the burst of scalding steam released into the room. After this, some people stand up, grab hold of a *venik* (a tied bundle of birch branches) and lightly beat themselves, or each other, with it. It does appear sadomasochistic, and there are theories tying the practice to other masochistic elements of Russian culture. Despite the mild sting, the effect is pleasant and cleansing: apparently, the birch leaves (or sometimes oak or, agonisingly, juniper branches) and their secretions help rid the skin of toxins.

Banya Traditions

The *banya* tradition is deeply ingrained in the Russian culture that emerged from the ancient Viking settlement of Novgorod, with the Kyivan Slavs making fun of their northern brothers for all that steamy whipping. In folk traditions, it has been customary for the bride and groom to take separate *bani* with their friends the night before the wedding, with the *banya* itself the bridge to marriage. Husband and wife would also customarily bathe together after the ceremony, and midwives used to administer a steam bath to women during delivery. (It was not uncommon to give a hot birch minimassage to the newborn.) The *banya*, in short, is a place for physical and moral purification. For more about the design and health benefits of the *banya*, see www.rusbanya.com/eng.htm.

There's a trend in the big cities of renovating *bani* or building new ones with sparkling private facilities – all very welcome as many older *bani* are rundown and unappealing.

A scene in a *banya* kicks off the comedy *Irony of Fate* (*Ironiya Sudby ili s Legkim Parom;* 1975) directed by Eldar Ryazanov, a much-loved movie screened on TV every New Year's Eve.

Best Bani

- Sanduny Baths, Moscow
- Coachmen's Baths, St Petersburg
- Goryachie Klyuchi, Suzdal
- Skazka Banya, Aya
- Banya Museum, Ust-Barguzin

Banya Rituals

Follow these tips to blend in with the locals at the *banya:*

- Bring a thermos filled with tea mixed with jam, spices and heaps of sugar. A few bottles of beer and some dried fish also do nicely, although at the better *bani*, food and drink are available.
- Strip down in the sex-segregated changing room, wishing *'Lyogkogo* (pronounced *lyokh*-ka-va) *para!'* to other bathers (meaning something like 'May your steam be easy!'), then head off into the *parilka*.
- After the birch-branch thrashing (best experienced lying down on a bench, with someone else administering the 'beating'), run outside and either plunge into the *basseyn* (ice-cold pool) or take a cold shower.
- Stagger back into the changing room, wishing fellow bathers *'S lyogkim parom!'* (Hope your steam was easy!).
- Wrap yourself in a sheet and discuss world issues before repeating the process – most *banya* aficionados go through the motions about five to 10 times over a two-hour period.

Education

From its beginning as an agrarian society in which literacy was limited to the few in the upper classes, the USSR achieved a literacy rate of 98% – among the best in the world. Russia continues to benefit from this legacy. Russian schools emphasise basics such as reading and mathematics, and the high literacy rate has been maintained. Many students go on to university and men can delay or avoid the compulsory national service by doing so.

Technical subjects such as science and mathematics are valued and bright students are encouraged to specialise in a particular area from a young age. A June 2011 report by the Russian public opinion foundation FOM found that teachers are among the country's worst bribe-takers. Higher education is the most corrupt sphere, with bribes taken for admission to universities, exams and degrees; also corruption in preschools and kindergartens in 2010 grew fourfold, to R13,838 billion (US$495 million), with the average bribe paid for admission being R8025 (US$287).

According to the UN Demographic Yearbook Russia has the highest rate of divorce of any country in the world: for every 1000 people, five are divorced.

Multiethnic Russia

Russia's multiethnic society is the result of the country's development through imperial expansion, forced movements and migration over many thousands of years. On paper, the USSR's divide-and-rule politics promoted awareness of ethnic 'national' identities. However, according to Professor Aviel Roshwald of Georgetown University, the drawing of ethnic boundaries was often arbitrary and designed to make each of the designated groups dependent on the Soviet state for their very identity. With Sovietisation came a heavy dose of Slavic influence. Most native peoples have adopted Russian dress and diet, particularly those who live in the bigger towns and cities.

Russia's constitution gives courts the power to ban groups inciting hatred or intolerant behaviour. Nonetheless, increased nationalism, xenophobia and racism are creating ethnic tensions. On the other hand, attitudes are broadening among younger and more affluent Russians as, for first time in the nation's history, large numbers of people are being exposed to life outside Russia. Under communism people were rarely allowed to venture abroad – now they are doing so in droves. In 2008, 11.3 million Russians took an overseas trip, up from 2.6 million in 1995.

The result, apart from a fad for the exotic – whether it's Turkish pop music or *qalyans* (hookahs) in restaurants – is a greater tolerance and better

The Moscow-based human rights group SOVA Center (www.sova-center.ru), which issues regular reports on racism and xenophobia in Russia, found in 2010 that 38 people died and 377 received injuries as a result of racist and neo-Nazi violence.

WEDDINGS RUSSIAN-STYLE *LEONID RAGOZIN*

During any trip to Russia you can't help but notice the number of people getting hitched, particularly on Friday and Saturday when the registry offices (Zapis Aktov Grazhdanskogo Sostoyaniya, shortened to ZAGS) are open for business. Wedding parties are particularly conspicuous, as they tear around town in convoys of cars making lots of noise and having their photos taken at the official beauty and historical spots. A relatively new tradition (imported from Italy) is for a couple to place a lock inscribed with their names on a bridge and throw away the key into the river below.

Church weddings are fairly common; the Russian Orthodox variety go on for ages, especially for the best friends who have to hold crowns above the heads of the bride and the groom during the whole ceremony. For a marriage to be officially registered, though, all couples need to get a stamp in their passports at a ZAGS. Most ZAGS offices are drab Soviet buildings with a ceremonial hall designed like a modern Protestant church less the crucifix. There are also *dvortsy brakosochetaniy* (purpose-built wedding palaces) – a few are in actual old palaces of extraordinary elegance.

After the couple and two witnesses from both sides sign some papers, the bride and the groom exchange rings (which in the Orthodox tradition are worn on the right hand) and the registrar pronounces them husband and wife. The witnesses each wear a red sash around their shoulders with the word 'witness' written on it in golden letters. The groom's best man takes care of all tips and other payments since it's traditional for the groom not to spend a single *kopek* (smallest unit of Russian currency) during the wedding. Another tradition is that the bride's mother does not attend the wedding ceremony, although she does go to the party.

understanding of other cultures. The country's declining population is also bringing more migrants from nearby countries like Ukraine or the Central Asian republics to Russia to live and work; UN data shows that Russia has the world's second-largest number of immigrants, after the USA.

Tatars

Russia's biggest minority is the Tatars, who are descended from the Mongol-Tatar armies of Chinggis (Genghis) Khaan and his successors, and from earlier Hunnic, Turkic and Finno-Ugric settlers on the middle Volga. From around the 13th century onward, the Tatars started moving out of Siberia towards the European side of Russia, a process that sped up as Cossack forces conquered their way eastward from the 16th century onward.

Today the Tatars are mostly Muslim, and about 2 million of them form nearly half the population of the Tatarstan Republic, the capital of which is Kazan. A couple more million or so Tatars live in other parts of Russia and the Commonwealth of Independent States (CIS). For more details, see Tatarstan on the Internet (www.kcn.ru/tat_en/index.htm).

BASHKIRS

450 Years with Russia! (http://eng.bashkortostan450.ru) is a website that celebrates the 450th anniversary in 2007 of the Bashkirs voluntarily joining the Russian state.

Chuvash & Bashkirs

You'll encounter these minority groups in the middle Volga region. The Chuvash, descendants of Turkic pre-Mongol settlers in the region, are mainly Orthodox Christian and form a majority (around 68% of the population) in the Chuvash Republic, immediately west of the Tatarstan Republic. The capital is Cheboksary (also known as Shupashkar).

The Muslim Bashkirs have Turkic roots. About half of them live in the Republic of Bashkortostan (capital: Ufa), where they are outnumbered by both Russians and Tatars. After the fall of Kazan in 1555, the Bashkirs 'voluntarily' aligned themselves with Russia. But various conflicts and rebellions subsequently broke out and it wasn't until the mid-18th century that Russian troops achieved full pacification of the area.

Finno-Ugric Peoples

In central and Northern European Russia, several major groups of Finno-Ugric peoples are found, distant relatives of the Estonians, Hungarians and Finns:

» the Orthodox or Muslim Mordvins, a quarter of whom live in the Republic of Mordovia (capital: Saransk)

HAVE A BABY FOR RUSSIA

Russia is facing an alarming natural decline in its population, around 0.5% per year. Results of the October 2010 census puts the country's population at 142.9 million, down by 2.3 million since the last census in 2002 and by nearly 3.4 million from a decade ago.

In April 2011 the government announced it would spend R1.5 trillion (US$53 billion) on demographic projects that would raise the birth rate by an ambitious 30% in the next five years. Adding to an already-existing policy of making cash pay-outs of R250,000 (US$8725) to women who have more than two children is a scheme to provide free land to families with three children or more, as well as increased child benefits and more affordable housing for young people. Harking back to a post-WWII Soviet policy, the government will also resume dishing out medals to 'heroic mothers' who pump out babies for Russia.

According to the Russian Health Ministry, in 2008 there were 1.7 million births in Russia and 1.2 million abortions. In 1920 Russia became the first country in the world to legalise abortion and, since then, it has remained the most popular form of birth control, with women allowed to terminate up to the 12th week of pregnancy. According to RIA Novosti 1.2 million Russian women choose to terminate their pregnancies each year and 30,000 of them become sterile, many from the estimated 180,000 illegal abortions. In its investigation the news agency also found several Moscow clinics offering discounts on abortions for International Women's Day.

» the Udmurts or Votyaks, predominantly Orthodox, two-thirds of whom live in Udmurtia (capital: Izhevsk)

» the Mari, with an animist/shamanist religion, nearly half of whom live in Mary-El (capital: Yoshkar-Ola)

» the Komi, who are Orthodox, most of whom live in the Komi Republic (capital: Syktyvkar)

» the Karelians, found in the Republic of Karelia, north of St Petersburg.

Finno-Ugric people are also found in Asian Russia. The Khanty, also known as the Ostyak, were the first indigenous people encountered by 11th-century Novgorodian explorers as they came across the Ural Mountains. Along with the related Mansi or Voguls, many live in the swampy Khanty-Mansisk Autonomous District on the middle Ob River, north of Tobolsk.

Peoples of the Caucasus

The Russian northern Caucasus is a real ethnic jigsaw of at least 19 local nationalities including the Abaza and Adygeya (both also known as the Circassians), Chechens, Kabardians, Lezgians and Ossetians. Several of these peoples have been involved in ethnic conflicts in recent years; see p447 for more details.

Dagestan, which means 'mountain country' in Turkish, is an ethnographic wonder, populated by no fewer than 81 ethnic groups of different origins speaking 30 mostly endemic languages.

Together with the Dagestani, Ingush and other groups in the northwest Caucasus, Chechens are known in Russia by the common name *gortsy* (highlanders). According to Professor John Colarusso from McMaster University, Ontario, and an expert on the region, '*Gortsy* had the reputation of being proud, freedom-loving and unruly subjects. They lived by strict codes of honour and revenge, and clan-oriented blood feuds were well entrenched in their patriarchal societies. These old patterns persist to some extent today.' Most of the *gortsy* are Sunni Muslims, although the Salafist version of Islam has become popular in recent years.

Turkic peoples in the region include the Kumyk and Nogay in Dagestan, and the Karachay and Balkar in the western and central Caucasus.

Both the Unrepresented Nations and Peoples Organization (www.unpo.org; UNPO) and the Red Book of the Peoples of the Russian Empire (www.eki.ee/books/redbook) contain profiles of over 80 different ethnic groups found in the lands currently or once ruled by Russia.

Peoples of Siberia & the Russian Far East

More than 30 indigenous Siberian and Russian Far East peoples now make up less than 5% of the region's total population. The most numerous groups are the ethnic Mongol Buryats, the Yakuts or Sakha, Tuvans, Khakass and Altai. While each of these has a distinct Turkic-rooted language and their 'own' republic within the Russian Federation, only the Tuvans form a local majority.

Among the smaller groups are the Evenki, also called the Tungusi, spread widely but very thinly throughout Siberia. Related tribes include the Evens, scattered around the northeast but found mainly in Kamchatka (p615), and the Nanai in the lower Amur River Basin; it's possible to visit some Nanai villages near Khabarovsk.

The Arctic hunter-herder Nenets (numbering around 35,000) are the most numerous of the 25 'Peoples of the North'. Together with three smaller groups they are called the Samoyed, though the name's not too popular because it means 'self-eater' in Russian – a person who wears himself out physically and psychologically.

The Chukchi and Koryaks are the most numerous of six Palaeo-Siberian peoples of the far northeast, with languages that don't belong in any larger category. Their Stone Age forebears, who crossed the Bering Strait ice to the USA and Greenland, may also be remote ancestors of the Native Americans. Eskimos, Aleuts and the Oroks of Sakhalin Island, who were counted at just 190 in the 1989 census, are also found in the far northeast.

Anna Reid's *The Shaman's Coat* is both a fascinating history of major native peoples of Siberia and the Russian Far East and a lively travelogue.

The Smithsonian National Museum of Natural History in Washington, DC, (www.mnh.si.edu/arctic/features/croads) provides a virtual exhibition on the native peoples of Siberia and Alaska.

Religion

Russia adopted Christianity under Prince Vladimir of Kyiv in 988 after centuries of following animist beliefs. Atheism was promoted by the state during the Soviet decades with all religions viewed, in Karl Marx's famous phrase, as 'opium of the masses'. Since 1997 the Russian Orthodox Church (Russkaya Pravoslavnaya Tserkov; www.mospat.ru) has been legally recognised as the leading faith and has resumed its prolific role in public life, just as it had in tsarist days. However, Russia is also a multi-confessional state with sizeable communities of Muslims, Buddhists and Jews and a constitution enshrining religious freedom.

Russian Orthodox Church

This highly traditional religion is so central to Russian life that understanding something about its history (p624) and practices will enhance any of the inevitable visits you'll make to a Russian Orthodox church.

Patriarch Kirill I of Moscow and All Russia is head of the Church. The patriarch's residence is Moscow's Danilovsky Monastery while the city's senior church is the Cathedral of Christ the Saviour. The Church's senior bishops bear the title metropolitan.

Beautiful Monasteries

» Trinity Monastery of St Sergius, Sergiev Posad

» Pechory Monastery, Pechory

» Solovetsky Transfiguration Monastery, Solovetsky Islands

» Tikhvin Monastery of the Mother of God, Tikhvin

» Valaam Transfiguration Monastery, Valaam

Church-Going Rules

» Working churches are open to everyone.

» As a visitor you should take care not to disturb any devotions or offend sensibilities.

» On entering a church, men bare their heads and women cover theirs.

» Shorts on men and miniskirts on women are considered inappropriate.

» Hands in pockets or crossed legs or arms may attract frowns.

» Photography is usually banned, especially during services; if in doubt, ask permission first.

Decor & Services

Churches are decorated with frescoes, mosaics and icons with the aim of conveying Christian teachings and assisting veneration. Different subjects are assigned traditional places in the church (the Last Judgement, for instance, appears on the western wall). The central focus is always an iconostasis (icon stand), often elaborately decorated. The iconostasis divides the main body of the church from the sanctuary, or altar area, at the eastern end, which is off limits to all but the priest.

Apart from some benches to the sides, there are no chairs or pews in Orthodox churches; people stand during services such as the Divine Liturgy (Bozhestvennaya Liturgia), lasting about two hours, which is held daily any time between 7am and 10am. Most churches also hold services at 5pm or 6pm daily. Some services include an *akafist,* a series of chants to the Virgin or saints.

Services are conducted not in Russian but 'Church Slavonic', the Southern Slavic dialect into which the Bible was first translated for Slavs. Paskha (Easter) is the focus of the Church year, with festive midnight services launching Easter Day.

Other Christian Churches

Russia has small numbers of Roman Catholics, and Lutheran and Baptist Protestants, mostly among the German, Polish and other non-Russian ethnic groups. Communities of Old Believers (p624) still survive in Siberia, where you may also encounter followers of Vissarion, considered by his followers to be a living, modern-day Jesus.

According to a 2007 US government report on religious freedom, Russian courts have tried to use the 1997 religion law (asserting the Orthodox Church's leading role) to ban or impose restrictions on the Pentecostal Church, Jehovah's Witnesses and other minority Christian faiths.

In its 'freedom of conscience' report for 2007 the SOVA Center found that 'nontraditional' religious organisations in Russia faced 'serious difficulties' in relation to the construction of buildings or leasing of facilities.

Islam

Islam is Russia's second-most widely professed religion with experts reckoning on between seven million and nine million people practising the religion. There are many more millions who are Muslims by ethnicity. They are mainly found among the Tatar and Bashkir peoples east of Moscow and a few dozen of the Caucasian ethnic groups. Nearly all are Sunni Muslims, except for some Shi'a in Dagestan. Muslim Kazakhs, a small minority in southeast Altai, are the only long-term Islamic group east of Bashkortostan.

SAINTS

Just as in Catholic countries, children are traditionally named after saints as well as having a given name. Each saint has a 'saint's day' set in the Orthodox calendar. The day of one's namesake saint is celebrated like a second birthday.

CHURCH NAMES

sobor	cathedral	собор
svyatoi	saint	святой
tserkov	church	церковь
khram	church or temple	храм
chasovnaya	chapel	часовня
monastyr	convent or monastery	монастырь
Blagoveshchenskaya	Annunciation	Благовещенская
Borisoglebskaya	Boris & Gleb	Борисоглебская
Nikolskaya	Nicholas	Никольская
Petropavlovskaya	Peter & Paul	Петропавловская
Pokrovskaya	Intercession	Покровская
Preobrazhenswkaya	Transfiguration	Преображенская
Rizopolozhenskaya	Deposition of the Robe	Ризоположенская
Rozhdestvenskaya	Nativity	Рождественская
Troitskaya	Trinity	Троицкая
Uspenskaya	Assumption or Dormition	Успенская
Vladimirskaya	Vladimir	Владимирская
Voskresenskaya	Resurrection	Воскресенская
Voznesenskaya	Ascension	Вознесенская
Znamenskaya	Holy Sign	Знаменская

Muslim history in Russia goes back over 1000 years. In the dying days of tsarist Russia, Muslims even had their own faction in the *duma* (parliament). The Islamic Cultural Centre of Russia, which includes a *madrasa* (college for Islamic learning), opened in Moscow in 1991.

Some Muslim peoples – notably the Chechens and Tatars – have been the most resistant of Russia's minorities to being brought within the Russian national fold since the fall of the Soviet Union, but nationalism has played at least as big a part as religion in this. In an apparent effort to ease tensions between the state and Muslim communities following the war in Chechnya, Russia became a member of the influential Organisation of Islamic Conferences in 2003.

Islam in Russia is fairly secularised – in predominantly Muslim areas you'll find women who are not veiled, for example, although many will wear headscarves; also, the Friday holy day is not a commercial holiday. Few local Muslims seriously abide by Islam's antialcohol rule.

MOSQUES

If you are allowed into a working mosque, take off your shoes (and your socks, if they are dirty!). Women should wear headscarves.

Buddhism

There are around 1.5 million Buddhists in Russia, a figure that has been growing steadily in the years since *glasnost,* when Buddhist organisations became free to reopen temples and monasteries.

The Kalmyks – the largest ethnic group in the Republic of Kalmykia, northwest of the Caspian Sea – are traditionally members of the Gelugpa or 'Yellow Hat' sect of Tibetan Buddhism, whose spiritual leader is the Dalai Lama. They fled from wars in western Mongolia, where Buddhism had reached them not long before, to their present region in the 17th century.

The Gelugpa sect reached eastern Buryatiya and Tuva via Mongolia in the 18th century, but only really took root in the 19th century. As with other religions, Stalin did his best to wipe out Buddhism in the 1930s, destroying hundreds of *datsans* (Buddhist temples) and monasteries and executing or exiling thousands of peaceable *lamas* (Buddhist priests).

Since 1950, Buddhism has been organised under a Buddhist Religious Board based at Ivolginsk. The Dalai Lama has visited Buryatiya, Tuva and Elista, the capital of the Republic of Kalmykia – despite Chinese pressure on the Russian government for them not to grant the Tibetan

ANIMISM & SHAMANISM

Many cultures, from the Finno-Ugric Mari and Udmurts to the nominally Buddhist Mongol Buryats, retain varying degrees of animism. This is often submerged beneath, or accepted in parallel with, other religions. Animism is a primal belief in the presence of spirits or spiritual qualities in objects of the natural world. Peaks and springs are especially revered and their spirits are thanked with token offerings. This explains (especially in Tuva and Altai) the coins, stone cairns, vodka bottles and abundant prayer ribbons that you'll commonly find around holy trees and mountain passes.

Spiritual guidance is through a medium or shaman, a high priest, prophet and doctor in one. Animal skins, trance dances and a special type of drum are typical shamanic tools, though different shamans have different spiritual and medical gifts. Siberian museums exhibit many shamanic outfits. Krasnoyarsk's regional museum shows examples from many different tribal groups. Tuva is the most likely place to encounter practising shamans. Popular among a few New Age groups, another form of religious shamanism emphasises the core philosophical beliefs of ecological balance and respect for nature. Buryat shaman Sarangerel's book, *Riding Windhorses,* is a great general introduction to shamanism.

There are three shamanic school-clinics in Kyzyl, Tuva, but, like visiting a doctor, you'll be expected to have a specific need and there will be fees for the consultation.

leader a visa, as reported by the BBC. For more about Buddhism in Russia see http://buddhist.ru/eng.

Judaism

Jews, who are estimated to number around 200,000 people, are considered an ethnicity within Russia, as well as a religion. Most have been assimilated into Russian culture.

The largest communities are found in Moscow and St Petersburg, both of which have several historic, working synagogues. There's also a small, conservative community of several thousand 'Mountain Jews' (Gorskie Yevrei) living mostly in the Caucasian cities of Nalchik, Pyatigorsk and Derbent. Siberia was once home to large numbers of Jews but now you'll only find noticeable communities in Yekaterinburg and the Jewish Autonomous Region – created during Stalin's era – centred on Birobidzhan.

There are two umbrella organisations of Russian Jewry:

Federation of Jewish Communities of the CIS (www.fjc.ru) supports the Italian-born Berl Lazar as chief rabbi – he is also a member of the Public Chamber of Russia, an oversight committee for government.

Russian-Jewish Congress (www.rjc.ru) recognises Russian-born Adolf Shayevich as their chief rabbi.

Visit *Beyond the Pale: The History of Jews in Russia* (www.friends-partners.org/partners/beyond-the-pale/index.html), an online version of an exhibition on Jewish history, for more about Jews in Russia.

Buddhist Temples

- Ivolginsk Datsan, Buryatiya
- Aginskoe Datsan, Zabaikalsky Territory
- Tsugol Datsan, Zabaikalsky Territory
- Datsan Gunzechoyney, St Petersburg

Performing Arts & Music

The roots of Russian music lie in folk song and dance, and Orthodox Church chants. *Byliny* (epic folk songs of Russia's peasantry) preserved folk culture and lore through celebration of particular events such as great battles or harvests. By late tsarist Russia musical culture had evolved into grand and refined spectacles of ballet and opera created to entertain the nobility of St Petersburg and Moscow. These still delight audiences of all means around the world.

During the Soviet era, theatre companies such as Bolshoi and Kirov (now renamed the Mariinsky) enjoyed the prestige of being considered high Russian culture, protecting them from the dramas being played out in other spheres of the arts as communist ideology took hold. It fell to underground musicians and dramatists to represent and express the stifled hopes and frustrations of the population.

Everyone suffered in the immediate post-Soviet period as state sponsorship dried up, but since Russia's economic resurgence funding has been less of a problem and creativity has been unshackled from party politics. The classics still reign supreme and have found a boost in a reinvigorated Tchaikovsky prize in 2011, the reopening of the Bolshoi's main stage after a protracted period of renovation and the Mariinsky's new second stage, set to open in 2012.

BALLET

For Ballet Lovers Only (www.for-ballet-lovers-only.com) has biographies of leading Bolshoi and Mariinsky dancers, both past and present, as well as a good links section if you want to learn more about Russian ballet.

Dance

Birth of Russian Ballet

First brought to Russia under Tsar Alexey Mikhailovich in the 17th century, ballet in Russia evolved as an offshoot of French dance combined with Russian folk and peasant dance techniques. The result stunned Western Europeans when it was first taken on tour during the late 19th century.

The 'official' beginnings of Russian ballet date to 1738 and the establishment of a school of dance in St Petersburg's Winter Palace, the precursor to the famed Vaganova School of Choreography, by French dance master Jean-Baptiste Landé. Moscow's Bolshoi Theatre dates from 1776. However, the true father of Russian ballet is considered to be Marius Petipa (1818–1910), the French dancer and choreographer who acted first as principal dancer, then premier ballet master, of the Imperial Theatre in St Petersburg. All told, he produced more than 60 full ballets (including Tchaikovsky's *Sleeping Beauty* and *Swan Lake*).

At the turn of the 20th century – Russian ballet's heyday – St Petersburg's Imperial School of Ballet rose to world prominence, producing a wealth of superstars including Vaslav Nijinsky, Anna Pavlova, Mathilda Kshesinskaya, George Balanchine and Michel Fokine. Sergei Diaghilev's Ballets Russes, formed in Paris in 1909 (with most of its members com-

BUYING TICKETS FOR PERFORMANCES & EVENTS

Teatralnye kassy (theatre ticket offices, sometimes kiosks) are found across all sizeable cities, although it's not difficult to buy face-value tickets from the *kassa* (ticket office) at the venue itself, typically open for advance or same-day sales from early afternoon until the start of the evening show. Outside the major cities tickets can start as low as R100 and only the most popular shows tend to sell out completely, so there's usually hope for obtaining same-day seats. In Moscow and St Petersburg, however, competition is much greater – the top venues have 'foreigner pricing' and it can be worth falling back on a hotel service bureau or concierge to get the best tickets, even though that can mean paying a huge premium over face value.

Tickets for both Moscow's Bolshoi and St Petersburg's Mariinsky Theatres can be booked online – this is the best way to ensure that you get the seat you want. For Moscow events, consider booking using a web-based service such as www.parter.ru.

If all else fails, there are usually touts (scalpers): not only professionals but also people with spares. It's standard practice to sell tickets outside the main entrance before starting time. Remember that prices are a free-for-all and you run the risk of obstructed views. Before handing over any money make sure that the ticket actually has the date, performance and section you want.

ing from the Imperial School of Ballet), took Europe by storm. The stage decor was painted by artists such as Alexander Benois.

Soviet Era to Modern Day

During Soviet rule, ballet enjoyed a privileged status, which allowed schools like the Vaganova and companies like the Kirov and Moscow's Bolshoi to maintain lavish productions and high performance standards. At the Bolshoi, Yury Grigorovich emerged as the leading choreographer, with *Spartacus, Ivan the Terrible* and other successes that espoused Soviet moral and artistic values. Meanwhile, many of Soviet ballet's biggest stars emigrated or defected, including Rudolf Nureyev, Mikhail Baryshnikov and Natalia Makarova.

As the Soviet Union collapsed, artistic feuds at the Bolshoi between Grigorovich and his dancers, combined with a loss of state subsidies and the continued financial lure of the West to principal dancers, led to a crisis in the Russian ballet world. Grigorovich resigned in 1995, prompting dancers loyal to him to stage the Bolshoi's first-ever strike. The company ran through a series of artistic directors before finding stability and renewed acclaim under the dynamic direction of Alexey Ratmansky from 2004 to 2008. *Dreams of Japan,* one of the 20-plus ballets that Alexey Ratmansky has choreographed, was awarded a prestigious Golden Mask award in 1998. Under his direction the Bolshoi won Best Foreign Company in 2005 and 2007 from the prestigious Critics' Circle in London.

Natasha's Dance: A Cultural History of Russia by Orlando Figes is an excellent book offering plenty of colourful anecdotes about great Russian writers, artists, composers and architects.

Scandal struck the company again in 2011 when the ballet troupe's director Gennady Yanin was forced to step down following the release on the internet of erotic photos of him. Shortly after, the theatre appointed Bolshoi-alumni Sergei Filin as its new artistic director. The former director of Moscow's second ballet company, the Stanislavsky & Nemirovich-Danchenko, he is considered an innovator.

Meanwhile, in St Petersburg, charismatic Valery Gergiev is secure in his position at the Mariinsky, where he has been artistic director since 1988 and overall director since 1996. The ballet troupe reports to Yury Fateyev, who has pushed the dancers to embrace more than the classical repertoire for which they are most famous, staging ballets by George

Balanchine and Jerome Robbins as well as Ratmansky, whose *Anna Karenina* (based on the Tolstoy novel) premiered in 2010.

Native Folk Dancing & Music

Traditional Russian folk dancing and music is still practised across the country, although your main chance of catching it as a visitor is in cheesy shows in restaurants or at tourist-orientated extravaganzas such as Feel Yourself Russian in St Petersburg. Companies with solid reputations to watch out for include Igor Moiseyev Ballet (www.moiseyev.ru), the Ossipov National Academic Folk Instruments Orchestra of Russia (www.ossipovorchestra.ru/en) and the Pyatnitsky State Academic Russian Folk Choir, all offering repertoires with roots as old as Kyivan Rus, including heroic ballads and the familiar Slavic *trepak* (stamping folk dances).

In Siberia and the Russian Far East, it's also possible to occasionally catch dance and music performances by native peoples. In the Altai, minstrels sing epic ballads, while in Tuva *khöömei* (throat singing) ranges from the ultradeep troll-warbling of *kargyraa* to the superhuman self-harmonising of *sygyt;* see p503 for more details.

Music

Classical

The defining period of Russian classical music was from 1860 to 1900. Mikhail Glinka (1804–57) is considered the father of Russian classical music: he was born in Smolensk, where an annual festival is held in his honour.

As Russian composers (and other artists) struggled to find a national identity, several influential schools formed, from which some of Russia's most famous composers emerged. The Group of Five – Modest Mussorgsky, Nikolai Rimsky-Korsakov, Alexander Borodin, Cesar Kui and Mily Balakirev – believed a radical departure from traditional Western European composition necessary, and looked to *byliny* and folk music for themes. Their main opponent was Anton Rubinstein's conservatively rooted Russian Musical Society, which became the St Petersburg Conservatory in 1861, the first conservatory in Russia. Triumphing in the middle ground was Pyotr Tchaikovsky, who embraced Russian folklore and music as well as the disciplines of the Western European composers.

Following in Tchaikovsky's romantic footsteps were Sergei Rachmaninov (1873–1943) and Igor Stravinsky (1882–1971) – both fled Russia after the revolution. Stravinsky's *The Rite of Spring* – which created a furore at its first performance in Paris – and *The Firebird* were influenced by Russian folk music. Sergei Prokofiev (1891–1953), who also left Soviet

PYOTR TCHAIKOVSKY

The most beloved of all Russian classical composers is arguably Pyotr Tchaikovsky (1840–93). The former lawyer first studied music at the St Petersburg Conservatory, but he later moved to Moscow to teach at the conservatory there. This was where all of his major works were composed, including, in 1880, the magnificent *1812 Overture*.

Among his other famous pieces are the ballets *Swan Lake* (Lebedinoye Ozero), *Sleeping Beauty* (Spyashchaya Krasavitsa) and *The Nutcracker* (Shchelkunchik); the operas *Eugene Onegin* (Yevgeny Onegin) and *Queen of Spades* (Pikovaya Dama), both inspired by the works of Alexander Pushkin; and his final work, the *Pathétique* Symphony No 6. The romantic beauty of these pieces belies the more tragic side of the composer, who led a tortured life as a closeted homosexual. The rumour mill has it that rather than dying of cholera, as reported, he committed suicide by poisoning himself following a 'trial' by his peers about his sexual behaviour. For more about Tchaikovsky go to www.tchaikovsky-research.net.

Russia but returned in 1933, wrote the scores for Sergei Eisenstein's films *Alexander Nevsky* and *Ivan the Terrible,* the ballet *Romeo and Juliet,* and *Peter and the Wolf,* beloved of those who teach music to young children. Even so, he fell foul of the fickle Soviet authorities towards the end of his life and died on the same day as Stalin.

Similarly, the ideological beliefs of Dmitry Shostakovich (1906–75), who wrote brooding, bizarrely dissonant works, as well as accessible traditional classical music, led to him being alternately praised and condemned by the Soviet government. Despite initial official condemnation by Stalin, Shostakovich's Symphony No 7 – the *Leningrad* – brought him honour and international standing when it was performed by the Leningrad Philharmonic during the Siege of Leningrad. The authorities changed their minds again and banned his music in 1948, then 'rehabilitated' him after Stalin's death.

Progressive new music surfaced only slowly in the post-Stalin era, with outside contact limited. Symphony No 1 by Alfred Schnittke (1934–98), probably the most important work of this major experimental modern Russian composer, had to be premiered by its champion, conductor Gennady Rozhdestvensky, in the provincial city of Gorky (now Nizhny Novgorod) in 1974. It was not played in Moscow until 1986.

Opera

Russian opera was born in St Petersburg when Mikhail Glinka's *A Life for the Tsar,* which merged traditional and Western influences, premiered on 9 December 1836. It told the story of peasant Ivan Susanin, who sacrifices himself to save Tsar Mikhail Romanov. He followed this up with another folk-based opera, *Ruslan and Lyudmila* (1842), thus inaugurating the 'New Russian School' of composition.

Another pivotal moment in Russian opera was the 5 December 1890 premiere of Tchaikovsky's *Queen of Spades* at the Mariinsky. Adapted from a tale by Alexander Pushkin, Tchaikovsky's *Queen of Spades* surprised and invigorated the artistic community by successfully merging opera with topical social comment.

Classical opera was performed regularly in the Soviet period and continues to be popular. In March 2005 the Bolshoi premiered its first new opera in 26 years, *Rosenthal's Children* – with music by Leonid Desyatnikov and words by Vladimir Sorokin – to a hail of protests over its plot. The Bolshoi opera company's director is Dmitry Tcherniakov, whose unconventional production of Tchaikovsky's *Eugene Onegin* in 2006 split public opinion in Russia but wowed critics abroad.

Russian opera has produced many singing stars, from Fyodor Chaliapin in the early years of the 20th century to the current diva, soprano Anna Netrebko, who started as a cleaner at the Mariinsky and now commands the stages of top opera houses around the world.

TCHAIKOVSKY

Ken Russell's *The Music Lovers* is a feverishly sensational and at times hysterical biopic about Tchaikovsky with Richard Chamberlain playing the famously closeted composer and Glenda Jackson his entirely unsuitable wife, Nina.

Rock & Pop

The Communist Party was no fan of pop music. Back in the 1960s, the gravel-voiced Vladimir Vysotsky (1938–80) was the dissident voice of the USSR, becoming a star despite being banned from TV, radio and major stages. Denied the chance to record or perform to big audiences, Russian rock groups were forced underground. By the 1970s – the Soviet hippie era – this genre of music had developed a huge following among a disaffected, distrustful youth. Although bands initially imitated their Western counterparts, by the 1980s there was a home-grown sound emerging, and, in Moscow, Leningrad (St Petersburg) and Yekaterinburg, in particular, many influential bands sprung up.

Boris Grebenshikov and his band Akvarium (Aquarium; www.aquariumband.com) from Yekaterinburg are one such influential band, causing a sensation wherever they perform; his folk rock and introspective lyrics became the emotional cry of a generation. At first, all of their music was circulated by illegal tapes known as *magizdat,* passed from listener to listener; concerts – known as *tusovka* (informal parties) – were held in remote halls or people's apartments in city suburbs, and just attending them could be risky. Other top bands of this era include DDT, Nautilus Pompilius, Mashina Vremeni and Bravo, whose lead singer Zhanna Aguzarova became Soviet rock's first female star.

Late-Soviet rock's shining star, though, was Viktor Tsoy, an ethnic Korean born in Leningrad, frontman of the group Kino; the band's classic album is 1988's *Gruppa Krovi* (Blood Group). Tsoy's early death in a 1990 car crash sealed his legendary status. Fans gather on the anniversary of his death (15 August) to this day and play his music. His grave, at the Bogoslovskogo Cemetery in St Petersburg, has been turned into a shrine, much like Jim Morrison's in Paris. There is also the 'Tsoy Wall', covered with Tsoy-related graffiti, on ul Arbat in Moscow.

Directed by Alexey Uchitel in 1988, *Rock* is a revealing documentary about the Leningrad rock scene of the 1980s, featuring legends such as Boris Grebenshikov and Viktor Tsoy.

The ageing diva Alla Pugacheva, a survivor from the 1960s, is still around, although she's become more famous for her torrid love life (married four times and countless affairs) and battles with alcohol.

Music Festivals

Of late rock festivals have become huge business, with events like Rock on the Volga attracting over 240,000 attendees to its June 2011 event near Samara (p363). Afisha Picnic (http://picnic.afisha.ru) held at the Kolomenskoe Museum-Reserve near Moscow, is a leading alternative music fest in the capital, while in St Petersburg the Sergei Kuryokhin International Festival (SKIF) of offbeat music celebrated its 15th anniversary in 2011; it's usually held in mid-May.

Jazz lovers should mark their calendar for Usadba Jazz (www.usadba-jazz.ru), an outdoor festival of both local and international talents that takes places in both Moscow (at the Arkhangelskoe estate) and St Petersburg (on Yelagin Island) in late June or early July.

Theatre

Drama lover Catherine the Great set up the Imperial Theatre Administration and authorised the construction of Moscow's Bolshoi Theatre. During her reign Denis Fonvizin wrote *The Brigadier* (1769) and *The Minor* (1781), satirical comedies that are still performed today.

Dramatists in the 19th century included Alexander Pushkin (see p672), whose drama *Boris Godunov* (1830) was later used as the libretto for the Mussorgsky opera; Nikolai Gogol, whose tragic farce *The Government Inspector* (1836) was said to be a favourite play of Nicholas I; Alexander Griboedov, whose comedy satire *Woe from Wit* was a compulsory work in Russian literature lessons during the Soviet period; and Ivan Turgenev, whose languid *A Month in the Country* (1849) laid the way for the most famous Russian playwright of all: Anton Chekhov (1860–1904).

Go to Russia Profile (http://russiaprofile.org/special_report/39117.html) to download a PDF of a special report on Russia's performing-arts scene that includes essays on rock and pop music, opera and provincial theatre.

Chekhov's *The Seagull, The Three Sisters, The Cherry Orchard* and *Uncle Vanya,* all of which take the angst of the provincial middle class as their theme, owed much of their success to their 'realist' productions at the Moscow Art Theatre by Konstantin Stanislavsky, which aimed to show life as it really was.

Through the Soviet period theatre remained popular, not least because it was one of the few areas of artistic life where a modicum of freedom of expression was permitted. Stalin famously said that although Mikhail Bulgakov's *White Guard* had been written by an enemy, it still deserved to be staged because of the author's outstanding talent. Bulgakov is perhaps the only person dubbed an enemy by Stalin and never

CIRCUS

While Western circuses grow smaller and become scarce, the Russian versions are still like those from childhood stories – prancing horses with acrobats on their backs, snarling lions and tigers, heart-stopping high-wire artists and hilarious clowns. They remain a highly popular form of entertainment.

The Russian circus tradition has roots in medieval travelling minstrels called *skomorokhi*, although the first modern-style circus (a performance within a ring) dates to the reign of Catherine the Great. The country's first permanent circus was established in St Petersburg in 1877 and, in 1927, Moscow's School for Circus Arts became the world's first such training institution. Many cities still have their own troupes and most at least have an arena for visiting companies. Best known is Moscow's Nikulin Circus (p122).

A word of warning: Russian attitudes towards animals are often less 'humane' than in the West, and some sensitive visitors find the acts and off-stage confinement of circus animals upsetting.

persecuted. The avant-garde actor-director Vsevolod Meyerhold was not so fortunate (see p675).

Today both Moscow's and St Petersburg's theatre scene are as lively as those in London and New York. Notable directors include Kama Gingkas, who works with the Moscow Art Theatre, Pyotr Fomenko, who heads up Moscow's Pyotr Fomenko Workshop Theatre, and Lev Dodin at the Maly Drama Theatre in St Petersburg. Gaining an international reputation are brothers Oleg and Vladimir Presnyakov, who write and direct their plays together under the joint name Presnyakov Brothers; they've been praised for their plays' natural-sounding dialogue and sardonic wit. *Terrorism*, their best-known work, has been performed around the world.

Literature & Cinema

Some of the most vivid impressions of Russia have been shaped by the creative works of the country's writers and movie-makers. Although they really only got going in the 19th century, Russian writers wasted little time in carving out a prime place in the world of letters, producing towering classics in the fields of poetry and prose. In the process they have bagged five Nobel Prizes and frequently found themselves in conflict with the Russian establishment.

'Of all the arts, for us the most important is cinema,' said Lenin. Embraced and supported for its propaganda potential during Soviet times, the industry was left to find its own way economically in the post-Soviet world. After a rocky few years, Russian cinema has revived, producing both box-office blockbusters and art-house gems that have charmed critics and audiences at home and abroad.

Literature

The Golden Age

The great collection of works produced during the 19th century has led to it being known as the 'Golden Age' of Russian literature. Alexander Pushkin (1799–1837) is to Russia what Shakespeare is to England. Like fellow poet Mikhail Lermontov (1814–41), author of *A Hero of Our Time,* Pushkin died in a duel widely perceived as engineered by the authorities, who were aggravated by his writing.

Continuing the tradition of literary criticism of the powers that be was the novelist and playwright Nikolai Gogol (1809–52), whose novel *Dead Souls* exposed the widespread corruption in Russian society. Gogol created some of Russian literature's most memorable characters, including Akaki Akakievich, the tragicomic hero of *The Overcoat,* and Major Kovalyev, who chases his errant nose around St Petersburg when the nose makes a break for it in the absurdist short story *The Nose.* His love of the surreal established a pattern in Russian literature that echoes through the works of Daniil Kharms, Mikhail Bulgakov and Viktor Pelevin in the next century.

More radical Russian writers figured in the second half of the 19th century. In *Fathers and Sons,* by Ivan Turgenev (1818–83), the antihero Bazarov became a symbol for the anti-tsarist nihilist movement of the time. Before penning classics such as *Crime and Punishment* and *The Brothers Karamazov,* which deals with questions of morality, faith and salvation, Fyodor Dostoevsky (1821–81) fell foul of the authorities and was exiled for a decade from St Petersburg, first in Siberia and later in what is now Kazakhstan.

Leo Tolstoy (1828–1910) sealed his reputation as one of Russia's greatest writers with his Napoleonic War saga *War and Peace,* and *Anna*

TOLSTOY

The Last Station (2009), based on the novel by Jay Parini, is about the last year of Tolstoy's life. Christopher Plummer, who plays the writer, and Helen Mirren, playing his wife Sofya, were both nominated for Oscars.

PUSHKIN: POET OF PASSION

Born in 1799, the son of nobility with a dollop of African blood in his lineage, Alexander Pushkin grew up in the French-speaking high society of St Petersburg. Before he reached puberty, this precocious youth was using his perfect pitch, sharp wit and flawless sense of timing to hit on court women, diplomats' wives, peasant girls and the like. He and his school friends, many of them also poets, would spend their idle hours, between balls, composing odes and love poems. A child of his time, the Romantic Age, Pushkin was obsessed with obsessions – war, male honour, and beautiful and unattainable women – and he is said to have had a foot fetish. His heroes were Lord Byron and Napoleon.

Pushkin wrote everything from classical odes and sonnets to short stories, plays and fairy tales. He is best loved for his poems in verse, *The Bronze Horseman* and *Eugene Onegin,* in which he nearly answers that eternal question – why do Russians (like to) suffer so much? Politically, he was a hot potato and the tsars exiled him from St Petersburg three times, once to his home estate in Mikhailovskoe and twice to the Caucasus, where his romping with the local beauties and war-loving men added more fuel to his poetic fire. At home in Mikhailovskoe, he is said to have spent long evenings drinking with his childhood nanny. Pushkin himself admitted she told him many of the tales that he then turned into national legends. While on long walks, he would compose aloud. To keep his arm in good shape for duelling, he carried a cane filled with rocks.

In the end, it didn't help. In 1837, Pushkin was mortally wounded in a duel fought over the honour of his wife, the Russian beauty Natalia Goncharova. He lay dying for two days while all of St Petersburg came to pay homage, dramatically directing taxi drivers, 'To Pushkin!' For a riveting account of the duel and the events that preceded it, read Serena Vitale's *Pushkin's Button*.

Karenina, a tragedy about a woman who violates the rigid sexual code of her time. Such was his popularity that his unorthodox beliefs in Christian anarchy and pacifism protected him from reprisals by the government. If you don't have the time or stamina for Tolstoy's *War and Peace,* then sample the master's work in his celebrated novellas *The Death of Ivan Ilyich* and *The Devil.*

The Silver Age

From the end of the 19th century up until the early 1930s, the 'Silver Age' of Russian literature produced more towering talents. First came the rise of the symbolist movement in the Russian arts world. The outstanding figures of this time were philosopher Vladimir Solovyov (1853–1900); writer Andrei Bely (1880–1934), author of *Petersburg,* regarded by Vladimir Nabokov as one of the four greatest novels of the 20th century; and Maxim Gorky (1868–1936), who is considered to be the founder of socialist realism (p675) with his 1907 novel *Mother,* written during a Bolshevik Party fund-raising trip in the USA.

Alexander Blok (1880–1921) was a poet whose sympathy with the revolutions of 1905 and 1917 was praised by the Bolsheviks as an example of an established writer who had seen the light. His tragic poem 'The Twelve', published in 1918, shortly before his death, likens the Bolsheviks to the Twelve Apostles who herald the new world. However, Blok soon grew deeply disenchanted with the revolution, and, in one of his last letters, wrote, 'She did devour me, lousy, snuffling dear Mother Russia, like a sow devouring her piglet.'

Soviet Literature: Part I

The life of poet Anna Akhmatova (1889–1966) was filled with sorrow and loss – her family was imprisoned and killed, her friends exiled, tortured and arrested, her colleagues constantly hounded – but she refused to leave her beloved St Petersburg. Her verses depict the city with realism and monumentalism, particularly her epic *Poem Without a Hero,* where she writes:

> The capital on the Neva
> Having forgotten its greatness
> Like a drunken whore
> Did not know who was taking her.

Other notable Silver Age wordsmiths were the poet Velimir Khlebnikov and the poet and playwright Vladimir Mayakovsky, who, together with other futurists, issued the 1913 'Slap in the Face of Public Taste' manifesto urging fellow writers 'to throw Pushkin out of the steamship of modernity'.

Another key poet of this age, who suffered for his art just like Akhmatova, was Osip Mandelstam (1891–1938), who died in a Stalinist transit camp near Vladivostok. Akhmatova's and Mandelstam's lives are painfully recorded by Nadezhda Mandelstam in her autobiographical *Hope Against Hope.*

The great satirist Mikhail Bulgakov (1891–1940) also found his work, such as *The Master and Margarita* and 'Heart of a Dog', banned for years, as did Daniil Kharms (1905–1942), a writer described in *Russia!* magazine as a 'one-man Monty Python show staged at a labour camp.' Kharms starved to death during the siege of Leningrad in 1942; it would be two decades later that his surreal stories and poems started to see the light of day and began to be circulated in the Soviet underground press.

Although best known abroad for his epic novel *Doctor Zhivago,* Boris Pasternak (1890–1960) is most celebrated in Russia for his poetry. *My Sister Life,* published in 1921, inspired many Russian poets thereafter. *Doctor Zhivago,* first published in an Italian translation in 1957, secured him the Nobel Prize for Literature in 1958, but Pasternak turned it down, fearing that if he left Russia to accept the award he would not be allowed to return.

One writer who managed to keep in favour with the communist authorities was Mikhail Sholokhov (1905–84), with his sagas of revolution and war among the Don Cossacks – *And Quiet Flows the Don* and *The Don Flows Home to the Sea.* He won the Nobel Prize for Literature in 1965.

Made into a movie by David Lean, Boris Pasternak's *Doctor Zhivago* is a richly philosophical novel spanning events from the dying days of tsarist Russia to the birth of the Soviet Union, offering personal insights into the revolution and the Russian Civil War along the way.

Soviet Literature: Part II

The relaxing of state control over the arts during Khrushchev's time saw the emergence of poets like Yevgeny Yevtushenko, who gained international fame in 1961 with *Babi Yar* (which denounced both Nazi and Russian anti-Semitism), as well as another Nobel Prize winner, Aleksandr Solzhenitsyn (p676), who wrote mainly about life in the Gulag system. Some believe the camp experience as related in *Kolyma Tales* by the great literary talent Varlam Shalamov (1907–82) is even more harrowing than that depicted by Solzhenitsyn.

Yet another Nobel Prize winner was the fiercely talented poet Joseph Brodsky (1940–96), spiritual heir to Akhmatova. In 1964 he was tried for 'social parasitism' and exiled to the north of Russia. However, after concerted international protests led by Jean-Paul Sartre, he returned to Leningrad in 1965, only to continue being a thorn in the side of the authorities. Like Solzhenitsyn, Brodsky was exiled to the US in 1972.

Preceding *glasnost* was native Siberian writer Valentin Rasputin, who is best known for his stories decrying the destruction of the land, spirit and traditions of the Russian people. His 1979 novel *Farewell to Matyora* is about a Siberian village flooded when a hydroelectric dam is built.

Post-Soviet Writers

Recent years have witnessed a publishing boom, with the traditional Russian love of books as strong as ever. One of the most popular novelists

THE IMPACT OF SOCIALIST REALISM

In *The Magical Chorus,* an enlightening book about Russian art from Tolstoy to Solzhenitsyn, Solomon Volkov writes 'Lenin, and especially Stalin, understood the usefulness of culture as a political tool, not only inside the country but in the international arena, too, and they wielded the weapon well.'

In 1932 the Communist Party demanded socialist realism: the 'concrete representation of reality in its revolutionary development...in accordance with...ideological training of the workers in the spirit of Socialism.' Henceforth, artists had the all-but-impossible task of conveying the Party line in their works and not falling foul of the notoriously fickle tastes of Stalin in the process.

The composer Dmitry Shostakovich, for example, was officially denounced twice (in 1936 and 1948) and suffered the banning of his compositions. Strongly opposed to socialist realism, theatre director Vsevolod Meyerhold had his theatre closed down; in 1939 he was imprisoned and later tortured and executed as a traitor. He was cleared of all charges in 1955.

Writers were particularly affected, including Vladimir Mayakovsky, who committed suicide, and the poet Anna Akhmatova, whose life was blighted by persecution and tragedy. Many, including Daniil Kharms, had their work driven underground, or were forced to smuggle their manuscripts out to the West for publication, as Boris Pasternak famously did for *Doctor Zhivago*.

is Boris Akunin, whose series of historical detective novels, including *The Winter Queen* and *Turkish Gambit,* feature the foppish Russian Sherlock Holmes, Erast Fandorin.

Among the more challenging contemporary Russian writers who have made their mark are Viktor Yerofeyev, whose erotic novel *Russian Beauty* has been translated into 27 languages, and Tatyana Tolstaya, whose *On the Golden Porch,* a collection of stories about big souls in little Moscow flats, made her an international name when it was published in the West in 1989. Her 2007 novel *The Slynx* is a dystopian fantasy set in a post-nuclear-holocaust world of mutant people, fearsome beasts and totalitarian rulers.

The anthology *Today I Wrote Nothing: The Selected Writings of Daniil Kharms,* translated by Matvei Yankelevich, is worth dipping into to discover the bizarre works of this eccentric absurdist writer.

The prolific science-fiction and pop-culture writer Viktor Pelevin has been compared to the great Mikhail Bulgakov. Several of his novels, including *The Yellow Arrow* and *The Sacred Book of the Werewolf,* have also been widely translated. Vladimir Sorokin established his literary reputation abroad with his novels *The Queue* and *Ice*. In *Day of the Oprichnik,* he describes Russia in the year 2028 as a nationalist country that has shut itself off from the West by building a wall and that is ruled with an iron fist.

Dmitry Bykov is one of the biggest names currently in Russian literary circles; he published a well-regarded biography of Boris Pasternak in 2007. His 2006 novel, *ZhD* (entitled *Living Souls* in its English translation), a satirical, anti-utopian, conspiracy-theory-laden tale of civil war set in near-future Russia, caused furious debate because of its Rus-phobic and anti-Semitic themes. It features on a 2011 list of translated works by Russian authors to look out for: http://rbth.ru/articles/2011/02/24/read_all_about_it_a_new_wave_of_authors_12499.html

Rossica is a glossy journal published by Academia Rossica (http://academia-rossica.org) and featuring the works of top Russian contemporary writers and artists.

Cinema

The Propaganda Years

Even though there were a few Russian films made at the start of the 20th century, it was really under the post-1918 Soviet system that this modern form of storytelling began to flourish. Movies made sense as

RUSSIA'S CONSCIENCE

Few writers' lives sum up the fickle nature of their relationship with the Russian state better than that of Aleksandr Solzhenitsyn (1918–2008). Born in conjunction with the Soviet Union, he was persecuted and exiled by that regime, only to return to a country that considered him, in his latter years, both a crank and its conscience. Embraced by Vladimir Putin (whom Solzhenitsyn praised as 'a good dictator') for his nationalism, staunch belief in Russian Orthodoxy and hatred of the decadent West, the one-time dissident was given what amounted to a state funeral.

Decorated twice with medals for bravery during WWII, the young Solzhenitsyn first fell foul of the authorities in 1945 when he was arrested for anti-Stalin remarks found in letters to a friend. He subsequently served eight years in various camps and three more in enforced exile in Kazakhstan.

Khrushchev allowed the publication in 1962 of Solzhenitsyn's first novel, *One Day in the Life of Ivan Denisovich,* a short tale of Gulag life. The book sealed the writer's reputation and in 1970 he was awarded the Nobel Prize for Literature, although, like Boris Pasternak before him, he did not go to Sweden to receive it for fear that he would not be allowed to reenter the USSR. Even so, he was exiled in 1974, when he went to the USA. He finally returned to Russia in 1994.

To the end Solzhenitsyn remained a controversial figure. He was detested by many Gulag survivors, who accused him of collaborating with prison authorities and who looked suspiciously on the writer's ability to gain sole access to the archives that allowed him to write his best-known work, *The Gulag Archipelago,* which describes conditions at the camps on the Solovetsky Islands, even though he was never imprisoned there himself. In his final book, *200 Years Together,* about the history of Jews in Russia, he laid himself open to accusations of anti-Semitism.

propaganda, so vast resources were pumped into studios to make sure the correct message was being conveyed. Historical dramas about Soviet and Russian victories were fine, resulting in Sergei Eisenstein's *Battleship Potemkin* (1925), a landmark of world cinema, and his *Alexander Nevsky* (1938), which contains one of cinema's great battle scenes. However, Eisenstein's *Ivan the Terrible* (1945), a discreet commentary on Stalinism, fell foul of state sponsors and was banned for many years.

The 1936 hit musical *Circus* was typical of the kind of propaganda movies were forced to carry at the height of Stalinism. The plot concerns an American circus artist hounded out of the US because she has a black baby; she finds both refuge and love, of course, in the Soviet Union. The lead actress, Lyubov Orlova, became the Soviet Union's biggest star of the time. She also headlined *Volga, Volga* (1938), another feel-good movie said to be Stalin's favourite movie.

Mikhail Kalatozov's tragic WWII drama *The Cranes Are Flying* (1957), judged best film at Cannes in 1958, illuminated the sacrifices made by Russians during the Great Patriotic War.

Taking Cinematic Risks

Of later Soviet directors, the dominant figure was Andrei Tarkovsky, whose films include *Andrei Rublyov* (1966), *Solaris* (1972) – the Russian answer to *2001: A Space Odyssey* – and *Stalker* (1979), which summed up the Leonid Brezhnev era pretty well, with its characters wandering, puzzled, through a landscape of clanking trains, rusting metal and overgrown concrete. Tarkovsky died in exile in 1986.

Glasnost brought new excitement in the film industry as film-makers were allowed to reassess Soviet life with unprecedented freedom and as audiences flocked to see previously banned films or the latest exposure of youth culture or Stalinism. Notable were Sergei Solovyov's avant-garde *ASSA* (1987), staring rock-god Viktor Tsoy and the artist Afrika (Sergei Bugaev), and Vasily Pichul's *Little Vera* (1989), for its frank portrayal of a family in chaos (exhausted wife, drunken husband, rebellious daughter) and its sexual content – mild by Western standards but startling to the Soviet audience.

Soviet cinema wasn't all doom, gloom and heavy propaganda. The romantic comedy *Irony of Fate* (1975) has a special place in all Russians' hearts, while a whole genre of 'Easterns' are epitomised by *White Sun of the Desert* (1969), a rollicking adventure set in Turkmenistan during the Russian Civil War of the 1920s. This cult movie, still one of the top-selling DVDs in Russia, is traditionally watched by cosmonauts before blast-off.

Post-Soviet Cinema

By the time Nikita Mikhalkov's *Burnt by the Sun* won the best foreign-language movie Oscar in 1994, Russian film production was suffering. Funding had dried up during the economic chaos of the early 1990s, and audiences couldn't afford to go to the cinema anyway. The industry was back on track by the end of the decade though, with hits like Alexey Balabanov's gangster drama *Brother* (1997) and Alexander Sokurov's *Molokh* (1999). Sokurov's ambitious *Russian Ark* was an international success in 2002, as was Andrei Zvyaginstev's moody thriller *The Return* the following year.

Russian cinema has been on a roll in recent years. Historical dramas such as *Turkish Gambit* (2005) and *The State Counsellor* (2005), both based on novels by Boris Akunin, were big hits. The glossy vampire thriller *Night Watch* (2004) struck box-office gold both at home and abroad, leading to an equally successful sequel, *Day Watch* (2006), and to Kazakhstan-born director Timur Bekmambetov being lured to Hollywood.

An audience favourite at various film festivals has been *Stilyagi* (2008; entitled *Hipsters* for its international release), a musical that casts a romantic eye on fashion-obsessed youths in 1950s Russia. Other art-house movies to look out for include the tragic love story *Euphoria* (2006; http://eng.euphoria-film.com) and *The Island* (2006), directed by Pavel Lungin. It's a bleak but beautiful examination of redemption and forgiveness through the eyes of a self-exiled Russian priest. *How I Ended This Summer* (2010) is a tense thriller about the deadly clash of temperaments between an older and a younger scientist working on an isolated meteorological station off the coast of Chukotka.

Russian Animation

Little known outside of Russia is the country's great contribution to the art of animation. Two years before Disney's *Snow White,* stop-motion animation was used for *New Gulliver* (1935), a communist retelling of *Gulliver's Travels* featuring more than 3000 puppets. And rather than Disney's films, it was actually Lev Atamanov's beautiful *The Snow Queen* (1957), based on the Hans Christian Andersen story, that inspired young Hayao Miyazaki to become the master Japanese animator that he is today.

One of Russia's most respected animators today is Yury Norshteyn, whose masterpiece, *Hedgehog in the Mist* (1975), is very philosophical and full of references to art and literature. The current master of the medium is Alexander Petrov, who paints in oil on glass sheets using his fingertips instead of brushes. He photographs one frame, modifies the picture with his fingers and photographs the next; this painstaking approach takes around a year of work to create just 10 minutes of film. *The Cow* (1989), his first solo work, displays Petrov's trademark montage sequences, in which objects, people and landscapes converge in a psychedelic swirl. Petrov won an Academy Award for *The Old Man and the Sea* (1999), based on the Hemingway novella. He was also nominated in 2007 for the dazzling *My Love,* an animated short set in prerevolutionary Russia.

The excellent blog Animatsiya (http://niffiwan.livejournal.com) includes many clips from recent and past Russian animation films.

OSCAR WINNER

Winning an Academy Award for best foreign-language film, *Moscow Doesn't Believe in Tears* (1980), directed by Vladimir Menshov, charts the course of three provincial gals who make Moscow their home from the 1950s to the 1970s.

Architecture & Visual Art

Until Soviet times most Russians lived in homes made of wood. The *izba* (single-storey log cottage) is still fairly common in the countryside, while some Siberian cities, notably Tomsk, retain fine timber town houses intricately decorated with 'wooden lace'. Stone and brick were usually the preserves of the Church, royalty and nobility.

Up until the 17th century, religious icons were Russia's key art form. Though they were conceived as religious artefacts, it was only in the 20th century that they really came to be seen as 'works of art'. Following an initial flirtation with the avant-garde, Soviet Russia's rulers opted instead to promote the more 'politically correct' socialist realism style of art.

In the post-Soviet world, architects and artists are pretty much free to do as they please. Visual artists, in particular, have done so with relish, both thumbing their noses at the past and present and embracing and rediscovering traditional Russian crafts and artistic inspiration.

Architecture

Early Russian Churches

Early Russian architecture is best viewed in the country's most historic churches, in places such as Veliky Novgorod, Smolensk, Pskov and Vladimir-Suzdal. At their simplest, churches consisted of three aisles, each with an eastern apse (semicircular end), a dome or 'cupola' over the central aisle next to the apse, and high vaulted roofs forming a crucifix shape centred on the dome.

Church architects developed the three-aisle pattern in the 11th and 12th centuries. Roofs then grew steeper to prevent the heavy northern snows collecting and crushing them, and windows grew narrower to keep the cold out. Pskov builders invented the little *kokoshnik* gable, which was semicircular or spade-shaped and was usually found in rows supporting a dome or drum.

Where stone replaced brick, as in Vladimir's Assumption Cathedral, it was often carved into a glorious kaleidoscope of decorative images. Another Vladimir-Suzdal hallmark was the 'blind arcade', a wall decoration resembling a row of arches. The early church-citadel complexes required protection, and thus developed sturdy, fortress-style walls replete with fairy-tale towers – Russia's archetypal kremlins.

In the 16th century, the translation of the northern Russian wooden church features, such as the tent roof and the onion dome on a tall drum, into brick added up to a new, uniquely Russian architecture. St Basil's Cathedral, the Ivan the Great Bell Tower in the Moscow Kremlin and the Ascension Church at Kolomenskoe are three high points of this era.

BOOKS

The classic and comprehensive *A History of Russian Architecture*, by William Craft Brumfield, covers all the major epochs from the stone churches of Kyivan Rus to post-Stalinist industrial buildings.

In the 17th century builders in Moscow added tiers of *kokoshniki,* colourful tiles and brick patterning, to create jolly, merchant-financed churches. Midcentury, Patriarch Nikon outlawed such frippery, but elaboration returned later in the century with Western-influenced Moscow baroque, featuring ornate white detailing on red-brick walls.

Baroque to Classicism

Mainstream baroque reached Russia as Peter the Great opened up the country to Western influences. As the focus was on his new capital, St Petersburg, he banned new stone construction elsewhere to ensure stone supplies. The great Italian architect Bartolomeo Rastrelli created an inspired series of buildings, the style of which merged into rococo, for Empress Elizabeth. Three of the most brilliant were the Winter Palace and Smolny Cathedral, both in St Petersburg, and Catherine Palace at nearby Tsarskoe Selo.

Later in the 18th century, Catherine the Great turned away from rococo 'excess' towards Europe's new wave of classicism, which was an attempt to re-create the ambience of an idealised ancient Rome and Greece, with their mathematical proportions and rows of columns, pediments and domes. Catherine and her successors built waves of grand classical edifices in a bid to make St Petersburg the continent's most imposing capital.

From the simpler classicism of Catherine's reign, exemplified by the Great Palace at Pavlovsk, the more grandiose Russian Empire style was developed under Alexander I, with such buildings as the Admiralty and Kazan Cathedral in St Petersburg. St Isaac's Cathedral, built for Nicholas I, was the last big project of this wave of classicism in St Petersburg. Moscow abounds with Russian Empire–style buildings, as much of the city had to be rebuilt after the fire of 1812.

Wooden Architecture

» Tomsk

» Kizhi Museum Reserve

» Vitoslavlitsy, Veliky Novgorod

» Nizhnyaya Sinyachikha, Sverdlovsk Region

» Museum of Volga People's Architecture & Culture, Nizhny Novgorod

Revivals & Style Moderne

A series of architectural revivals, notably of early Russian styles, began in the late 19th century. The first pseudo-Russian phase produced the state department store GUM, the State History Museum and the Leningradsky vokzal (train station) in Moscow, and the Moskovsky vokzal and the Church of the Saviour on Spilled Blood in St Petersburg.

The early-20th-century neo-Russian movement brought a sturdy classical elegance to architecture across the nation, culminating in the extraordinary Kazansky vokzal in Moscow, which imitates no fewer than seven earlier styles. About the same time, Style Moderne, Russia's take on art nouveau, added wonderful curvaceous flourishes to many buildings right across Russia.

FIGHTING TO PRESERVE THE PAST

In Russia it's down to national and local governments to decide what pieces of architecture warrant preservation. St Petersburg in particular spends millions of roubles on maintaining and renovating its stock of historic buildings. However, the pressure group Zhivoi Gorod (Living City; www.save-spb.ru) claims that the city is more interested in destruction, citing the demolition of hundreds of historically important buildings in recent years. Wanting to preserve the city's historic skyline, Zhivoi Gorod is also firmly against skyscrapers, such as the controversial Okhta Tower, Gazprom's planned headquarters.

The Moscow Architecture Preservation Society (MAPS; www.maps-moscow.com), a pressure group founded by architects, historians, heritage managers and journalists of various nationalities, has been fighting for several years to preserve the capital's architectural heritage. Its research shows over 400 of the city's listed buildings have been demolished since 1989.

Soviet Constructivism

The revolution gave rein to young constructivist architects, who rejected superficial decoration in favour of buildings whose appearance was a direct function of their uses and materials – a new architecture for a new society. They used glass and concrete in uncompromising geometric forms.

Style Moderne Architecture

» Yaroslavsky vokzal, Moscow
» Vitebsky vokzal, St Petersburg
» Singer Building, St Petersburg
» Vyborg

Konstantin Melnikov was probably the most famous constructivist and his own house off ul Arbat in Moscow is one of the most interesting examples of the style; Moscow's *Pravda* and *Izvestia* offices are others. In the 1930s, the constructivists were denounced, and a 400m-high design by perpetrators of yet another revival – monumental classicism – was chosen for Stalin's pet project, a Palace of Soviets in Moscow, which mercifully never got off the ground.

Stalin favoured neoclassical architecture as it echoed ancient Athens, 'the only culture of the past to approach the ideal', according to Anatoly Lunacharsky, the first Soviet commissar of education. The dictator also liked architecture to be on a gigantic scale, underlining the might of the Soviet state. This style reached its apogee in the 'Seven Sisters', seven Gothic-style skyscrapers that sprouted around Moscow soon after WWII.

In 1955, Khrushchev condemned the 'excesses' of Stalin (who had died two years earlier) and disbanded the Soviet Academy of Architecture. After this, architects favoured a bland international modern style – constructivism without the spark, you might say – for prestigious buildings, while no style at all was evident in the drab blocks of cramped flats that sprouted countrywide to house the people.

Contemporary Architecture

Following the demise of the Soviet Union, architectural energies and civic funds initially went into the restoration of decayed churches and monasteries, as well as the rebuilding of structures such as Moscow's Cathedral of Christ the Saviour.

Moscow's 93-storey, 506m Federation Tower (www.federationtower.ru) is set to be the tallest building in Europe when it opens in 2016 as part of the huge Moskva-City development.

As far as contemporary domestic, commercial and cultural buildings are concerned, post-Soviet architects have not been kind to Russia. Featuring bright metals and mirrored glass, these buildings tend to be plopped down in the midst of otherwise unassuming vintage buildings, particularly in Moscow. The oil-rich economy is producing some changes for the better, helping to fund interesting projects in the capital and elsewhere. In St Petersburg, the Mariinsky Theatre's second stage, set to open in 2012, will provide a much-needed contemporary boost to this most classical of Russian cities.

Visual Art

Icons

Originally painted by monks as a spiritual exercise, icons are images intended to aid the veneration of the holy subjects they depict. Some believe that there are some icons that can grant luck and wishes, or even cause miracles.

The beginning of a distinct Russian icon tradition came when artists in Veliky Novgorod started to be influenced by local folk art in their representation of people, producing sharply outlined figures with softer faces and introducing lighter colours, including pale yellows and greens. The earliest outstanding painter was Theophanes the Greek (Feofan Grek in Russian). He lived between 1340 and 1405, working in Byzantium, Novgorod and Moscow, and bringing a new delicacy and grace to the form. His finest works are in the Annunciation Cathedral of the Moscow Kremlin.

Andrei Rublyov, a monk at Sergiev Posad's Trinity Monastery of St Sergius and Moscow's Andronikov Monastery, was 20 years Theophanes' junior and the greatest Russian icon painter. His most famous work is the dreamy *Holy Trinity,* on display in Moscow's Tretyakov Gallery.

The layman Dionysius, the leading late-15th-century icon painter, elongated his figures and refined the use of colour. Sixteenth-century icons grew smaller and more crowded, their figures more realistic and Russian looking. In 17th-century Moscow, Simon Ushakov moved towards Western religious painting with the use of perspective and architectural backgrounds.

See p662 for the typical layout of a church's iconostasis.

Peredvizhniki

The major artistic force of the 19th century were the Peredvizhniki (Wanderers), who saw art as a force for national awareness and social change. The movement gained its name from the touring exhibitions with which the artists widened their audience and was patronised by the industrialists Savva Mamontov – whose Abramtsevo estate near Moscow became an artists colony – and brothers Pavel and Sergei Tretyakov (after whom the Tretyakov Gallery is named). The Peredvizhniki included Vasily Surikov, who painted vivid Russian historical scenes; Nicholas Ghe, with his biblical and historical scenes; the landscape painter Ivan Shishkin; and Ilya Repin, perhaps the best loved of all Russian artists. Repin's work ranged from social criticism *(Barge Haulers on the Volga)* through history *(Zaporizhsky Cossacks Writing a Letter to the Turkish Sultan)* to portraits of the famous.

Isaac Levitan, who revealed the beauty of the Russian landscape, was one of many others associated with the Peredvizhniki. The end-of-century genius Mikhail Vrubel, inspired by sparkling Byzantine and Venetian mosaics, also showed traces of Western influence.

Church Architecture

- » Cathedral of St Sophia, Veliky Novgorod
- » Trinity Cathedral, Pskov
- » St Basil's Cathedral, Moscow
- » Church of the Intercession on the Nerl, Bogolyubovo

Modernism

Around the turn of the 20th century, the Mir Iskusstva (World of Art) movement in St Petersburg, led by Alexander Benois and Sergei Diaghilev under the motto 'art pure and unfettered', opened Russia up to Western innovations such as Impressionism, art nouveau and symbolism. From about 1905, Russian art became a maelstrom of groups, styles and 'isms' as it absorbed decades of European change in just a few years, before it gave birth to its own avant-garde futurist movements.

Natalia Goncharova and Mikhail Larionov were at the centre of the Cézanne-influenced Jack of Diamonds group (with which Vasily Kandinsky was also associated) before developing neoprimitivism, based on popular arts and primitive icons.

In 1915 Kasimir Malevich announced the arrival of suprematism, declaring that his utterly abstract geometrical shapes – with the black square representing the ultimate 'zero form' – finally freed art from having to depict the material world and made it a doorway to higher realities.

The propaganda magazine *USSR in Construction* (1930–41) featured stunning design and photography by Nikolai Troshin, El Lisstsky, Alexander Rodchenko and Varvara Stepanova.

Soviet-Era Art

Futurists turned to the needs of the revolution – education, posters, banners – with enthusiasm, relishing the chance to act on their theories of how art shapes society. But at the end of the 1920s, formalist (abstract) art fell out of favour; the Communist Party wanted socialist realism (see p675). Images of striving workers, heroic soldiers and inspiring leaders took over. Malevich ended up painting portraits (penetrating ones) and doing designs for Red Square parades.

After Stalin, an avant-garde 'conceptualist' underground was allowed to form. Ilya Kabakov painted, or sometimes just arranged, the debris

FOLK & NATIVE ART

An amazing spectrum of richly decorated folk art has evolved in Russia. Perhaps most familiar are the intricately painted, enamelled wood boxes called *palekh*, after the village east of Moscow that's famous for them; and *finift*, luminous enamelled metal miniatures from Rostov-Veliky. From Gzhel, also east of Moscow, came glazed earthenware in the 18th century and its trademark blue-and-white porcelain in the 19th. Gus-Khrustalny, south of Vladimir, maintains a glass-making tradition as old as Russia. Every region also has its own style of embroidery and some specialise in knitted and other fine fabrics.

The most common craft is woodcarving, represented by toys, distaffs (tools for hand-spinning flax) and gingerbread moulds in the museums, and in its most clichéd form by the nested *matryoshka* dolls. Surely the most familiar symbol of Russia, they actually only date from 1890 (see http://russian-crafts.com/nesting-dolls/russian-nesting-dolls.html?sef_rewrite=1 for the history of the *matryoshki* and other crafts). You'll also find the red, black and gold lacquered pine bowls called *khokhloma* overflowing from souvenir shops. Most uniquely Slavic are the 'gingerbread' houses of western and northern Russia and Siberia, with their carved window frames, lintels and trim. The art of carpentry flourished in 17th- and 18th-century houses and churches.

A revived interest in national traditions has recently brought much more good-quality craftwork into the open, and the process has been boosted by the restoration of churches and mosques and their artwork. There has also been a minor resurgence of woodcarving and bone carving. An even more popular craft is *beresta*, using birch bark to make containers and decorative objects, with colours varying according to the age and season of peeling. In Tuva, soapstone carving and traditional leather forming are also being rediscovered.

of everyday life to show the gap between the promises and realities of Soviet existence. Erik Bulatov's 'Sots art' pointed to the devaluation of language by ironically reproducing Soviet slogans or depicting words disappearing over the horizon. In 1962 the authorities set up a show of such 'unofficial' art at the Moscow Manezh; Khrushchev called it 'dog shit' and sent it back underground. In the mid-1970s it resurfaced in the Moscow suburbs, only to be literally bulldozed back down.

VOINA

In 2011, radical art collective Voina (War) won a R400,000 government-sponsored contemporary-art prize for its painting of a 64m-tall penis on a drawbridge in St Petersburg.

Contemporary Art

In the immediate post-Soviet years, a lot of contemporary painters of note abandoned Russia for the West. Today, with increased economic prosperity, many of the most promising young artists are choosing to stay put. Specialist art galleries are listed in the shopping sections of the Moscow and St Petersburg chapters. At these galleries you can find the latest works by Russians in and out of the motherland.

One of the best-known Russian painters today is the religious artist Ilya Glazunov (www.glazunov.ru/EN/index.html), a staunch defender of the Russian Orthodox cultural tradition. Creating more iconoclastic works are the Siberian collective Blue Noses, Voina, Ilya Kabakov, Aleksandr Kosolapov, Mikhail Roginskii and the artist group AES+F (www.aes-group.org), whose multimedia work, such as *The Feast of Trimalchio*, reflects the lust for luxury that is part of modern Russia.

Contemporary art galleries are booming from St Petersburg across to Perm. Prestigious events to mark on your calendar include the Moscow Biennale of Contemporary Art (www.moscowbiennale.ru), the annual commercial gallery show Art Moscow (www.art-moscow.ru) and the Kandinsky Prize (www.kandinsky-prize.ru), an exhibition of up-and-coming Russian artists.

A couple of good online resources for Russia's contemporary art scene are GIF.RU (www.gif.ru/rusart) and Art Guide (www.artguide.ru), which includes details of galleries and art shows in Moscow and St Petersburg.

Food & Drink

Russia's glorious culinary heritage is enriched by influences from the Baltic to the Far East. The country's rich black soil provides an abundance of grains and vegetables that are used in a wonderful range of breads, salads, appetisers and soups that are the highlight of any Russian meal. Its waterways yield a unique range of fish and, as with any cold-climate country, there's a great love of fat-loaded dishes – Russia is no place to go on a diet!

Staples & Specialities

Breakfast

Typical *zavtrak* (breakfast) dishes include bliny (pancakes) with sweet or savoury fillings, various types of *kasha* (porridge) made from buckwheat or other grains, and *syrniki* (cottage-cheese fritters), delicious with jam, sugar and the universal Russian condiment, *smetana* (sour cream). *Khleb* (bread) is freshly baked and comes in a multitude of delicious varieties.

Appetisers & Salads

Whether as the preamble to a meal or something to nibble on between shots of vodka, *zakuski* (appetisers) are a big feature of Russian cuisine. They range from olives to bliny with mushrooms and from *tvorog* (cheese curd) to caviar, and include a multitude of inventive salads. Among the most popular recipes that you'll find on restaurant menus are *salat olivye* (chopped chicken or ham, potatoes, eggs, canned peas and other vegetables mixed with mayonnaise) and *selyodka pod shuboi* (literally 'herrings in fur coats'), a classic from the Soviet era that has slices of herring, beetroot and pickles covered in a creamy sauce.

RECIPES

A Taste of Russia by Darra Goldstein offers over 200 recipes as well as some interesting short essays on local food culture.

A GIFT TO YOUNG HOUSEWIVES *MARA VORHEES*

The most popular cookbook in 19th-century Russia was called *A Gift to Young Housewives*, a collection of favourite recipes and household-management tips. The author, Elena Molokhovets, a housewife herself, was dedicated to her 10 children, to the Orthodox Church and to her inexperienced 'female compatriots' who might need some assistance in keeping their homes running smoothly.

Reprinted 28 times between 1861 and 1914, Molokhovets' bestseller had new recipes and helpful hints added to each new edition. The last edition included literally thousands of recipes, as well as pointers on how to organise an efficient kitchen, set a proper table and clean a cast-iron pot.

Having gone out of print during the Soviet era, Molokhovets' 'gift' was bestowed upon contemporary readers when Joyce Toomre, a culinary historian, translated and reprinted this historical masterpiece. The 1992 version, *Classic Russian Cooking: Elena Molokhovets' A Gift to Young Housewives*, includes Toomre's detailed analysis of mealtimes, menus, ingredients, cooking techniques etc.

Soups

No Russian meal is complete without soup, even in the summer when there are refreshing cold varieties such as *okroshka* (chopped cucumber, potatoes, eggs, meat and herbs in a base of either *kvas,* fermented rye bread water, or *kefir,* drinking yoghurt). *Shchi* (made from cabbage) and *solyanka* (a sometimes flavoursome concoction of pickled vegetables, meat and potato that used to be the staple winter food for the peasantry) are both popular soups that you'll find on menus across the country.

The beetroot soup borsch hails from Ukraine but is now synonymous with Russia throughout the world. It can be served hot or cold and usually with *smetana* poured on top of it. Some borsch is vegetarian (ask for *postny* borsch), although most is made with beef stock.

COOKBOOK

Please to the Table by Anya von Bremzen and John Welchman is nothing if not comprehensive, with over 400 recipes from the Baltics, Central Asia and all points between, plus a wealth of background detail on Russian cuisine.

Main Courses

Traditional Russian cuisine tends to be meaty and quite heavy. Popular dishes include *zharkoye* (hot pot; a meat stew served piping hot in a little jug), *kotleta po kievsky* (chicken Kiev) and shashlyk (meat kebab).

In Siberia, the common Russian dish *myaso po monastirsky* (beef topped with cheese) is often relabelled *myaso po Sibirski* (Siberian meat). Originally from Siberia but now available everywhere are *pelmeni,* pasta dumplings generally stuffed with pork or beef, that are served either heaped on a plate with sour cream, vinegar and butter, or in a stock soup. Variations such as salmon or mushroom *pelmeni* are found on the menus of more chic restaurants.

Central Asian–style dishes are also common, notably *plov* (fried rice with lamb and carrot) and *lagman* (noodles and meat in a soupy broth that gets spicier the further south you go). The range of fish and seafood is enormous, but common staples include *osyetrina* (sturgeon), *shchuka* (pike), *losos* or *syomga* (salmon), *treska* (chub) and *kalmar* (squid).

Desserts & Sweets

The Russian sweet tooth is seriously sweet. Russians love *morozhenoye* (ice cream) with a passion: it's not unusual to see people gobbling dishfuls, even in the freezing weather. Gooey *torty* (cream cakes), often decorated in lurid colours, are also popular. *Pecheniye* (pastries) are eaten at tea time, in the traditional English style.

Locally made chocolate and *konfetki* (sweets) are also excellent and, with their colourful wrappings, make for great presents. Local producers typically use more cocoa, so their chocolate is not as sweet as some non-Russian brands can be. Reputable manufacturers include Krasny Oktyabr (Red October) and Krupskoi.

CAVIAR – IF BUYING, BUY CAREFULLY

While nothing is as evocative of Russian imperial luxury as Beluga caviar, be aware that the sturgeon of the Caspian Sea are facing extinction due to the unsustainable and illegal plunder of their roe (p375). If you do buy some caviar, buy carefully. Purchase caviar only from shops (not on the street or at markets), in sealed jars (not loose) and, most importantly, make sure the jar or tin is sealed with a CITES (Convention on International Trade in Endangered Species) label, an international trade-control measure set up to reduce sturgeon poaching. Under international law, tourists are only permitted to bring home 250g of caviar per person. For more information go to www.cites.org/eng/prog/sturgeon.shtml. Also read *The Philosopher Fish* by eco-journalist Richard Adams Carey, a lively investigation into the life of the endangered sturgeon and the prized caviar it provides, and Vanora Bennett's lyrical *The Taste of Dreams*.

VEGETARIANS & VEGANS

Unless you're in one of the big cities or visiting during Lent, when many restaurants have special nonmeat menus, Russia can be tough on vegetarians. Main dishes are heavy on meat and poultry, vegetables are often boiled to death and even the good vegetable and fish soups are usually made from meat stock.

If you're vegetarian, say so, early and often. You'll see a lot of cucumber and tomato salads, and – if so inclined – will develop an eagle eye for spotting *baklazhan* (eggplant) and dairy dishes. *Zakuski* (appetisers) include quite a lot of meatless ingredients such as eggs and mushrooms. Potatoes *(kartoshka, kartofel, pure)* are usually filed under 'garnish' not 'vegetable'.

A good overview of the Russian vegetarian and vegan scene is found at www.sras.org/vegetarian_in_moscow.

Regional Specialities

From the *koryushki* (freshwater smelt) that are a feature of menus in St Petersburg in early May to the mammoth king crabs of Kamchatka, Russia abounds with regional food specialities. As these two examples illustrate, different varieties of fish and seafood are always worth sampling. Try dried, salty *oblyoma* fish, found in the Volga, or Lake Baikal's delicious *omul,* a cousin of salmon and trout. Russia's Far East doesn't yield many specialist dishes but in the port of Vladivostok you can be sure of the freshness of seafood such as *kalmary* (calamari) and *grebeshki* (scallops).

Honey is used as an ingredient in several dishes and drinks in Western European Russia such as *vzbiten,* the decorated gingerbread made in Tula, a tea with herbs and the alcoholic drink *medovukha.* Cowberries, reindeer and elk meat are ingredients that figure in the cuisine of Northern European Russia. From this region, *lokhikeytto* is a deliciously creamy Karelian salmon and potato soup ideally served with crispy croutons.

The tapestry of peoples and cultures along the Volga River yields several other specialities such as the Finno-Ugric clear dumpling soup *sup s klyutskami* and the dried horsemeat sausage *kasylyk* and *zur balish* meat pie, both from Tatarstan, where *chek chek* (honey-drenched macaroni-shaped pieces of fried dough) are an essential part of any celebration.

In the Altai region of southern Siberia you can masticate on *sera,* a chewing gum made from cedar oil. While around the ski resort of Sheregesh, sample the wild leek with a distinctive garlicky taste known as *kabla* in the local language and *cheremsha* in Russian.

The Buddhist-influenced culinary traditions of the Republic of Kalmykia have brought the Tibetan-style buttery tea known as *dzhomba* to Europe. Further east in Buryatiya, and throughout the Russian Far East, you'll often encounter the steamed, palm-sized dumplings known as *manti, pozi* or *buuzy* and *pyan-se* (a peppery version). Two or three make a good, greasy meal. Siberia is most famous for its *pelmeni* (small ravioli dumplings), and you'll find local variations in all the major cities across the region.

Russian cuisine also borrows enormously from neighbouring countries, most obviously from those around the Caucasus, where shashlyk originated. Across Russia, Georgian restaurants are common, though not all offer a fully Georgian menu.

Other Caucasus dishes we like are *sokhta* (a mammoth sausage stuffed with minced liver and rice), eaten around Dombay; Kabardian food such

RUSSIAN DINING

The Food and Cooking of Russia by Lesley Chamberlain (www.lesleychamberlain.co.uk), based on the author's research in the country during the late 1970s, is full of recipes as well as insights into what shaped Russian dining habits in the 20th century.

as *zharuma* (fiery sausage stuffed with minced lamb, onion and spices), *gedlibzhe* (a spicy chicken dish) and *geshlubzhe,* a saucy bean dish that can be sampled around Nalchik; and the sinfully delicious Ossetian *pirozhki,* pizza-like pies that come in *olibakh* (cheese), *sakharadzhin* (cheese and beet leaves) and *fidzhin* (meat) varieties.

Drinks

Alcoholic Drinks

'Drinking is the joy of the Rus. We cannot live without it' – with these words, Vladimir of Kyiv, the father of the Russian state, is said to have rejected abstinent Islam on his people's behalf in the 10th century.

Vodka is the classic Russian drink, distilled from wheat, rye or, occasionally, potatoes. The word comes from *voda* (pronounced va-*da,* meaning 'water'). The classic recipe for vodka (a 40% alcohol-to-water mixture) was patented in 1894 by Dmitry Mendeleyev, the inventor of the

TABLE SCRAPS FROM HEAVEN *MARA VORHEES*

Described by writer Darra Goldstein as 'heaven's table scraps', the rich, spicy cuisine of the former Soviet republic of Georgia must be sampled while in Russia. Georgian meat and vegetable dishes use ground walnuts or walnut oil as an integral ingredient, yielding a distinctive rich, nutty flavour. Also characteristic of Georgian cuisine is the spice mixture *khmeli-suneli,* which combines coriander, garlic, chillies, pepper and savoury with a saffron substitute made from dried marigold petals.

Grilled meats are among the most beloved items on any Georgian menu. Herbs such as coriander, dill and parsley and things like scallions are often served fresh, with no preparation or sauce, as a palate-cleansing counterpoint to rich dishes. Grapes and pomegranates show up not only as desserts, but also as tart complements to roasted meats. For vegetarians, Georgian eggplant dishes (notably garlic-laced *badrizhani nivrit*), *lobiyo* (spicy beans) and *khachapuri* (cheese bread) are a great blessing. *Khachapuri* comes in three main forms:

» flaky pastry squares (snack versions sold at markets)

» *khachapuri po-imeretinsk* – circles of fresh dough cooked with sour, salty *suluguni* cheese (sold in restaurants)

» *khachapuri po-adzharski* – topped with a raw egg in the crater (mix it rapidly into the melted cheese; sold in restaurants)

Here are a few more Georgian favourites to get you started when faced with an incomprehensible menu:

» *basturma* – marinated, grilled meat; usually beef or lamb

» *bkhali* or *pkhali* – a vegetable purée with herbs and walnuts, most often made with beetroot or spinach

» *buglama* – beef or veal stew with tomatoes, dill and garlic

» *chakhokhbili* – chicken slow-cooked with herbs and vegetables

» *chikhirtmi* – lemony chicken soup

» dolmas – vegetables (often tomatoes, eggplant or grape leaves) stuffed with beef

» *kharcho* – thick, spicy rice and beef or lamb soup

» *khinkali* – dumplings stuffed with lamb or a mixture of beef and pork

» *lavash* – flat bread used to wrap cheese, tomatoes, herbs or meat

» *pakhlava* – a walnut pastry similar to baklava, but made with sour-cream dough

» *satsivi* – walnut, garlic and pomegranate paste, usually used as a chicken stuffing in cold starters

» *shilaplavi* – rice pilaf, often with potatoes.

periodic table. The drink's flavour derives from what's added after distillation, so as well as 'plain' vodka you'll find *klyukovka* (cranberry vodka, one of the most popular kinds), *pertsovka* (pepper vodka), *starka* (vodka flavoured with apple and pear leaves), *limonnaya* (lemon vodka) and *okhotnichya* (meaning 'hunter's vodka', with about a dozen ingredients, including peppers, juniper berries, ginger and cloves).

Among the hundreds of different brands for sale are famous ones, such as Stolichnaya and Smirnoff, as well as ones named after presidents (Putinka, the country's top seller) and banks (Russian Standard). Better labels are Moskovskaya, Flagman, Gzhelka and Zelonaya Marka (meaning 'Green Mark'), which was named after the Stalin-era government agency that regulated vodka quality. For more brands see http://russianvodka.com.

These days beer sales outstrip those of vodka. The local market leader is Baltika (http://eng.baltika.ru), based in St Petersburg and with 11 other breweries across the country, but there are scores of other palatable local brands and a growing sector of microbreweries.

The local wine industry is notable mainly for its saccharine *polusladkoe* (semisweet) or *sladkoe* (sweet) dessert wines. *Bryut* (very dry and only for sparkling wine), *sukhoe* (dry) and *polusukhoe* (semidry) reds can be found; getting a palatable Russian dry white can be pretty tough. Locally produced sparkling wine Shampanskoye is cheap (around R300 a bottle) and popular even though it tastes nothing like champagne. For more information about Russian wines see www.russiawines.com.

Russian brandy is called *konyak* – the finest come from the Caucasus. Winston Churchill reputedly preferred Armenian *konyak* over French Cognac, and although standards vary enormously, local five-star brandies are generally good. Homemade moonshine is known as *samogon;* if you're at all in doubt about the alcohol's provenance, don't drink it – some of this stuff is highly poisonous.

Challenging Russian Eats

- Horsemeat fillets, Sakha Republic
- Dried elk noses and lips, Sakha Republic
- Chewy reindeer cartilage, Kamchatka
- *Khoitpak* (fermented sour milk), Tuva
- *Araka* (distilled version of *khoitpak*), Tuva
- Slabs of *salo* (pig fat), Western European Russia

Drinking Etiquette

Breaking open a can or bottle of beer and drinking it while walking down the street or sitting in a park is pretty common. If you find yourself sharing a table at a bar or restaurant with locals, it's odds-on they'll press you to drink with them. Even people from distant tables, spotting foreigners, may be seized with hospitable urges.

If it's vodka being drunk, they'll want a man to down the shot in one, neat of course; women are usually excused. This can be fun as you toast international friendship and so on, but vodka has a knack of creeping up on you from behind and the consequences can be appalling. It's traditional (and good sense) to eat a little something after each shot.

Refusing a drink can be very difficult, and Russians may continue to insist until they win you over. If you can't quite stand firm, take it in small gulps with copious thanks, while saying how you'd love to indulge but you have to be up early in the morning (or something similar). If you're really not in the mood, one sure-fire method of warding off all offers (as well as making people feel quite awful) is to say *'Ya alkogolik'* (*'Ya alkogolichka'* for women): 'I'm an alcoholic.'

Nonalcoholic Drinks

Russians make tea by brewing an extremely strong pot, pouring small shots of it into glasses, and topping the glasses up with hot water. This was traditionally done from the samovar, a metal urn with an inner tube filled with hot charcoal; modern samovars have electric elements, like a kettle, which is actually what most Russians use to boil water for tea these days. Putting jam in tea instead of sugar is quite common for those who like it a little sweeter.

Starbucks-style cafés serving barista-style coffee are found all across Russia's bigger cities – cappuccino, espresso, latte and mocha are now as much a part of the average Russian lexicon as elsewhere.

The popular nonalcoholic beer *kvas* is made from bread and flavoured with ingredients that can include honey and horseradish. In summer, it's often dispensed on the street from big, wheeled tanks, and it is highly refreshing.

Sok can mean anything from fruit juice (usually in cartons rather than fresh) to heavily diluted fruit squash. *Mors,* made from all types of red berries, is a popular *sok. Napitok* means 'drink' – it's often a cheaper and weaker version of *sok,* maybe with some real fruit thrown in.

If you're buying milk away from big supermarkets check whether it's pasteurised. *Kefir* (yoghurt-like sour milk) is served as a breakfast drink – and is also recommended as a hangover cure. The Bashkirs, the Kazakhs of southernmost Altai and the Sakha people drink *kumiss* (fermented mare's milk).

Where to Eat & Drink

In general, a *kafe* is likely to be cheaper yet often more atmospherically cosy than a *restoran,* many of which are aimed at hosting weddings and banquets more than individual diners. A *kofeynya* is generally an upmarket café, though they often serve great meals too, as will a *pab* (upmarket pub with pricey imported beers) or *traktir* (a tavern, often with 'traditional' Russian decor). A *zakusochnaya* can be anything from a pleasant café to a disreputable bar, but they usually sell cheap beer and have a limited food menu. Occasionally you'll come across *ryumochnaya,* dive bars specialising in vodka shots.

Increasingly common as you head east, a *poznaya* is an unpretentious eatery serving Central Asian food and, most notably, *pozi.* These are meat dumplings that you need to eat very carefully in order to avoid spraying yourself with boiling juices, as an embarrassed Mikhail Gorbachev famously did when visiting Ulan-Ude.

In old Soviet-era hotels and stations the *bufet* serves a range of simple snacks including *buterbrod* (open sandwiches). The *stolovaya* (canteen) is the common person's eatery, often located near stations or in public institutions such as universities. They are invariably cheap. Slide your tray along the counter and point to the food, and the staff will ladle it out. While unappealing, Soviet-style *stolovaya* remain, newer 'chic' versions with very palatable food are also common in cities and towns.

In smaller towns the choice will be far narrower, perhaps limited to standard Russian meals such as *pelmeni* and *kotlety* (cutlets); in villages there may be no hot food available at all (though there's almost always do-it-yourself pot noodles available from kiosks and shops). The choice is particularly abysmal in Tuva (beyond Kyzyl).

WEBSITE

Restaurant.ru (http://en.restoran.ru) carries listings and reviews for places to eat in Moscow, St Petersburg and Sochi in a variety of languages. You can also find recipes.

DRINKING WATER

Dodgy tap water has caused sales of bottled water to proliferate to the point where almost half the water drunk in Russia comes from a bottle. Since 2004, over 2000 licences have been issued to producers of bottled water; not all of it is as pure as it may seem. The Bottled Water Producers Union claim you're likely to be safer drinking water labelled *stolovaya* (purified tap water, which accounts for the vast majority of what's available) rather than *mineralnaya* (mineral water), which doesn't have to meet so many legal requirements for purity. One reliable brand of mineral water is *Narzan*. For those concerned about both the environment and their health, boiling water and using a decent filter are sufficient if you want to drink what comes out of the tap.

Ordering Food

It's always worth asking if a restaurant has an English-language menu. If not, even armed with a dictionary and this book (see p725), it can be difficult to decipher Russian menus (the different styles of printed Cyrillic are a challenge). Russian menus typically follow a standard form: first come *zakuski* (appetisers, often grouped into cold and hot dishes) followed by soups, sometimes listed under *pervye blyuda* (first courses). *Vtorye blyuda* (second courses; mains) are also known as *goryachiye blyuda* (hot courses). They can be divided into *firmenniye blyuda* (house specials, often listed at the front of the menu), *myasniye blyuda* (meat dishes), *ribniye blyuda* (fish dishes), *ptitsa blyuda* (poultry dishes) and *ovoshchniye blyuda* (vegetable dishes).

If the menu leaves you flummoxed, look at what the other diners are eating and point out what takes your fancy to the staff. Service charges are uncommon, except in the ritziest restaurants, but cover charges are frequent after 7pm, especially when there's live music (one would often gladly pay to stop the music). Check if there's a charge by asking, *'Vkhod platny?'*. Leave around 10% tip if the service has been good.

There is no charge for using the *garderob* (cloakroom) so do check in your coat before entering. Not doing so is considered extremely bad form.

It's common to find restaurants serving a set three-course menu *(biznes lunch)* from noon to 4pm, Monday to Friday, costing as little as R150 or R200 (up to R500 in Moscow and St Petersburg).

Celebrating with Food

Food and drink have long played a central role in many Russian celebrations from birthdays to religious holidays. It's traditional, for example, for wedding feasts to stretch on for hours (if not days in some villages) with all the participants generally getting legless.

The most important holiday for the Russian Orthodox Church is Paskha (Easter). Coming after the six-week fast of Lent, when meat and dairy products are foresworn, Easter dishes are rich, exemplified by the traditional cheesecake (also known as *paskha*) and the saffron-flavoured buttery loaf *kulich*. Together with brightly decorated boiled eggs, these are taken in baskets to church to be blessed during the Easter service.

Bliny are the food of choice during the week-long Maslenitsa (Butter Festival), which precedes Lent – it is the equivalent of Mardi Gras elsewhere.

Christmas (which is celebrated on 7 January in the Russian Orthodox calendar) is not as big a festival as New Year's Eve, which is celebrated with a huge feast of *zakuski* and the like. However, it is traditional to eat a sweet rice pudding called *kutya* at Christmas. The same dish is also left as an offering on graves during funerals.

In *A Year of Russian Feasts,* Catherine Cheremeteff Jones recounts how Russia's finest dishes have been preserved and passed down through the feast days of the Russian Orthodox Church.

Most restaurant menus give the weight of portions as well as the price. In most cases, you'll be expected to choose an accompanying 'garnish' (priced separately) of *ris* (rice), various potato dishes or *grechka* (split buckwheat).

Quick Eats

There's plenty of fast food available from both local and international operations, supplemented by street kiosks, vans and cafés with tables. *Pitstsa* (pizza, often microwaved) and shashlyk are common fare, as are bliny and *pelmeni.*

All large cities have Western-style supermarkets and food stores with a large range of Russian and imported goods. You'll generally have to leave all bags in a locker before entering. Many places are open 24 hours.

As well as supermarkets, there are smaller food stores, called *kulinariya,* which sell ready-made food. There are also the ubiquitous food-and-drink kiosks, generally located around parks and markets, on main streets and near train and bus stations – their products are usually poor, but the kiosks are handy and reasonably cheap.

EATING WITH KIDS

In all but the fanciest of restaurants children will be greeted with the warmest of welcomes. Some restaurants also have special children's rooms with toys. Kids' menus are uncommon, but you shouldn't have much problem getting the littl' uns to guzzle bliny or *bifshteks* – a Russian-style hamburger served without bread, and often topped with a fried egg. Also, make sure you check whether the milk is pasteurised – outside of major cities it often isn't. For more information on travelling with children, see p701.

Every sizeable town has a *rynok* (market), where locals sell spare produce from their dacha plots (check the market fringes), while bigger traders offload trucks full of fruit, vegetables, meat, dried goods and dairy products. Take your own shopping bag and go early in the morning for the liveliest scene and best selection; a certain amount of bargaining is acceptable, and it's a good idea to check prices with a trustworthy local first.

Homes, roadside vendors and well-stocked markets are your best bet for tasting the great range of wild mushrooms, *paporotniki* (fern tips), *shishki* (cedar nuts) and various soft fruits (red currants, raspberries) laboriously gathered by locals from the forest.

DILL

If, like British journo Shaun Walker, you think Russians' love of dill has gone too far, join his Facebook group Dillwatch (www.facebook.com/groups/186326061392049) so you can post pictures of the inappropriate use of this green herb.

Habits & Customs

It's traditional for Russians to eat a fairly heavy early-afternoon meal *(obed)* and a lighter evening meal *(uzhin)*. Entering some restaurants, you might feel like you're crashing a big party. Here, the purpose of eating out is less to taste exquisite food than to enjoy a whole evening of socialising and entertainment, with multiple courses, drinking and dancing. Dress is informal in all but top-end places.

While restaurants and cafés are common, dining out for the average Russian is not as common as it is in many other countries – don't be surprised if the choice of places to dine is limited outside of the main cities. If you really want to experience Russia's famous hospitality – not to mention the best cuisine – never pass up the opportunity to eat at a Russian home. Be prepared to find tables groaning with food and hosts who will never be satisfied that you're full, no matter how much you eat or drink.

Landscape & Wildlife

Russia is the world's largest country, covering 13% of the globe. As you'd expect, there's a vast variety of terrain, though a remarkably large proportion is relatively flat. Mountains are comparatively rare, but do reach impressive heights in the Caucasus (where 5642m Mt Elbrus is Europe's highest peak), in the magnificent volcanoes of Kamchatka and in the Altai, Sayan and Yergaki ranges of southern Siberia. Cities and towns are concentrated chiefly across central European Russia and along the ribbon of track that constitutes the Trans-Siberian Railway, thinning out in the frozen north and the southern steppe.

Frozen northern Russia is washed by the Barents, Kara, Laptev and East Siberian Seas. Novaya Zemlya, Europe's fourth-biggest island, is also Russian, as are the islands that make up Franz Josef Land (Zemlya Frantsa-Iosifa). Both stretch to the edge of the permanent Arctic ice cap. South of Finland, Russia opens on the Gulf of Finland, an inlet of the Baltic Sea; St Petersburg stands at the eastern end of this gulf.

East of Ukraine, the Russian Caucasus region commands stretches of the Black Sea and rugged, mountainous borders with Georgia and Azerbaijan. East of the Caucasus, Russia has an oil-rich stretch of Caspian Sea coast, north of which the Kazakhstan border runs up to the Ural Mountains.

Beyond the Urals, Asian Russia covers nearly 14 million sq km. Contrary to popular conception, only the western section of Asian Russia is actually called Siberia (Sibir). From the Amur regions in the south and the Sakha Republic (Yakutia) in the north, it becomes officially known as the Russian Far East (Dalny Vostok). The eastern seaboard is 15,500km long, giving Russia more 'Pacific Rim' than any other country.

The Wild Russia website (www.wild-russia.org) belongs to the US-based Center for Russian Nature Conservation, which assists and promotes nature conservation across Russia and publishes the English-language journal *Russian Conservation News*.

Rivers & Lakes

Though none has the fame of the Nile or the Amazon, six of the world's 20 longest rivers are in Russia. Forming the China–Russia border, the east-flowing Amur (4416km) is nominally longest, along with the Lena (4400km), Yenisey (4090km), Irtysh (4245km) and Ob (3680km), all of which flow north across Siberia, ending up in the Arctic Ocean. In fact, if one were to measure the longest stretch including tributaries (as is frequently done with the Mississippi–Missouri in North America), the Ob–Irtysh would clock up 5410km, and the Angara–Yenisey a phenomenal 5550km. The latter may in fact be the world's longest river if Lake Baikal and the Selenga River (992km) are included, which directly feed into it. Beautiful Lake Baikal itself is the world's deepest, holding nearly one-fifth of all the world's unfrozen fresh water.

Europe's longest river, the Volga (3690km), rises northwest of Moscow and flows via Kazan and Astrakhan into the Caspian Sea, the world's

Beautiful Lakes

- Baikal, Eastern Siberia
- Seliger, Tver Region
- Onega, Karelia

largest lake (371,800 sq km). Lake Onega (9600 sq km) and Lake Ladoga (18,390 sq km), both northeast of St Petersburg, are the biggest lakes in Europe.

Until the 20th century, boats on Russia's rivers offered the most important form of transport. Today, rivers are still economically important, but mostly as sources of hydroelectric power, with dozens of major dams creating vast reservoirs. It's possible to visit Russia's largest hydroelectric dam at Sayano-Shushenskaya on the Yenisey near Sayanogorsk.

Vegetation & Wildlife

To grasp the full extent of Russia's enormous diversity of wildlife, it is useful to understand the three major types of vegetation. In the northernmost extremes, fringed by the Arctic Ocean, is the icy tundra. These bleak, seemingly barren flatlands extend from 60km to 420km south from the coast. They gradually become more amicable to life and build up to taiga – the vast, dense forest that characterises and covers the greater part of Siberia. Finally is the steppe (from *stepi,* meaning plain), the flat or gently rolling band of low grassland – mostly treeless except along riverbanks – which runs intermittently all the way from Mongolia to Hungary.

There are three other distinct vegetative zones: the mountainous Caucasus in southern Russia; the active volcanic region of Kamchatka, in the far northeast of Russia; and Ussuriland, in the extreme Russian southeast, which experiences tropical air and rains. The forests covering this region – and their indigenous animals and vegetation – more closely resemble those of Southeast Asia than anything typically associated with Siberia.

Tundra

Falling almost completely within the Arctic Circle, the tundra is the most inhospitable of Russia's terrains. The ground is permanently frozen (in places recorded to a depth of 1450m) with whole strata of solid ice and just a thin, fragile carpet of delicate lichens, mosses, grasses and flowers lying on top. The few trees and bushes that manage to cling tenaciously to existence are stunted dwarfs, the permafrost refusing to yield to their roots. For nine months of the year the beleaguered greenery is also buried beneath thick snow. When the brief, warming summer comes, the permafrost prevents drainage and the tundra becomes a spongy wetland, pocked with lakes, pools and puddles.

Not surprisingly, wildlife has it hard on the tundra and there are few species that can survive its climate and desolation. Reindeer, however, have few problems and there are thought to be around four million in Russia's tundra regions. They can endure temperatures as low as –50°C and, like the camel, can store food reserves. Reindeer sustain themselves on lichen and grasses, in winter sniffing them out and pawing away the snow cover.

A similar diet sustains the lemming, a small, round, fat rodent fixed in the popular consciousness for its proclivity for launching itself en masse from cliff tops. More amazing is its rate of reproduction. Lemmings can produce five or six litters annually, each comprising five or six young. The young in turn begin reproducing after only two months. With the lemming three-week gestation period, one pair could spawn close to 10,000 lemmings in a 12-month period. In reality, predators and insufficient food keep numbers down.

Other tundra mammals include the Arctic fox, a smaller, furrier cousin of the European fox and a big lemming fan, and the wolf, which, although it prefers the taiga, will range far and wide, drawn by the lure of reindeer meat. Make it as far as the Arctic coast and you could encounter seals, walruses (notably around Chukotka), polar bears and whales.

REINDEER

Roger Took's *Running with Reindeer* is a vivid account of his travels in Russia's Kola Peninsula and the wildlife found there.

PAYING THE ENVIRONMENTAL PRICE FOR OIL & GAS

Environmental groups including Greenpeace Russia (www.greenpeace.org/russia/en) and the Norway-based NGO Bellona (www.bellona.org) are highly critical of Russia's oil and gas industry expanding their operations in the country's delicate Arctic regions.

The delicate tundra ecosystem has been destabilised by the construction of buildings, roads and railways and the extraction of underground resources. Of particular concern is the impact on the low-lying Yamal Peninsula at the mouth of the Ob, which contains some of the world's biggest gas reserves; parts of the peninsula have been crumbling into the sea as the permafrost melts near gas installations. However, Russian gas monopoly Gazprom claims continued development of the on- and offshore Yamal fields is 'crucial for securing Russia's gas production build-up' into the 21st century (see www.gazprom.com/production/projects/mega-yamal).

It's not just in the Arctic that new oil and gas fields are being developed: the Caspian and Baltic Seas and the Sea of Japan around Sakhalin and Kamchatka are also being drilled. Yet, according to Greenpeace Russia, there are almost no sea oil-spill and toxic-pollution prevention and response programs in the country – as demonstrated when an oil tanker sank in the Azov Sea in November 2007, spilling 1300 tonnes of fuel oil and 6100 tonnes of sulphur into the sea, affecting at least 20km of coastline.

Taiga

Russia's taiga is the world's largest forest, covering about 5 million sq km (an area big enough to blanket the whole of India) and accounting for about 25% of the world's wood reserves. Officially the taiga is the dense, moist subarctic coniferous forest that begins where the tundra ends and which is dominated by spruces and firs. Travelling on the Baikal-Amur Mainline (BAM) through the depths of Siberia, two or three days can go by with nothing but the impenetrable and foreboding dark wall of the forest visible outside the train: 'Where it ends,' wrote Chekhov, 'only the migrating birds know.'

Though the conditions are less severe than in the Arctic region, it's still harsh and bitterly cold in winter. The trees commonly found here are pine, larch, spruce and fir. In the coldest (eastern) regions the deciduous larch predominates; by shedding its leaves it cuts down on water loss, and its shallow roots give it the best chance of survival in permafrost conditions.

Due to the permanent shade, the forest-floor vegetation isn't particularly dense (though it is wiry and spring-loaded, making it difficult for humans to move through), but there are a great variety of grasses, moss, lichens, berries and mushrooms. These provide ample nourishment for the animals at the lower end of the food chain that, in turn, become food for others.

Wildlife flourishes here; the indigenous cast includes squirrels, chipmunks (which dine well on pine-cone seeds), voles and lemmings, as well as small carnivores such as polecats, foxes, wolverines and, less commonly, the sable – a weasel-like creature whose luxuriant pelt played such a great role in the early exploration of Siberia.

The most common species of large mammal in the taiga is the elk, a large deer that can measure over 2m at the shoulder and weighs almost as much as a bear. The brown bear itself is also a Siberian inhabitant that you may come across, despite the Russian penchant for hunting it. Other taiga-abiding animals include deer, wolves, lynx and foxes.

FORESTS

Forest.ru (www.forest.ru), a site about Russian forests, their conservation and sustainable usage, has a lot of background and current information in English.

Steppe

From the latitudes of Voronezh and Saratov down into the Kuban area north of the Caucasus and all the way across southwestern Siberia stretch vast areas of flat or gently undulating grasslands know as steppe. Since much of this is on humus-rich *chernozem* (black earth), a large proportion is used to cultivate grain. Where soil is poorer, as in Tuva, the grasslands offer vast open expanses of sheep-mown wilderness, encouraging wildflowers and hikers.

The delta through which the Volga River enters the Caspian is, in contrast to the surrounding area, very rich in flora and fauna. Huge carpets of the pink or white Caspian lotus flower spread across the waters in summer, attracting over 200 species of birds in their millions. Wild boar and 30 other mammal species also roam the land.

The small saygak (a type of antelope), an ancient animal that once grazed all the way from Britain to Alaska, still roams the more arid steppe regions around the northern Caspian Sea. However, the species is under threat of extinction from hunting and the eradication of its traditional habitat.

The Russian Far East, A Reference Guide for Conservation and Development, edited by Josh Newell, gathers work by 90 specialists from Russia, the UK and the US on this fascinating chunk of the country.

Caucasus

The steppe gives way to alpine regions in the Caucasus, a botanist's wonderland with 6000 highly varied plant species, including glorious wildflowers in summer. Among the animals of the Caucasus are the tur (a mountain goat), bezoar (wild goat), endangered mouflon (mountain sheep), chamois (an antelope), brown bear and reintroduced European bison. The lammergeier (bearded vulture), endangered griffon vulture, imperial eagle, peregrine falcon, goshawk and snowcock are among the Caucasus' most spectacular birds. Both types of vulture have been known to attack a live tur.

Kamchatka

The fantastic array of vegetation and wildlife in Kamchatka is a result of the geothermal bubbling, brewing and rumbling that goes on below the peninsula's surface, which manifests itself periodically in the eruption of one of around 30 active volcanoes. The minerals deposited by these eruptions have produced some incredibly fertile earth, which is capable of nurturing giant plants with accelerated growth rates. John Massey Stewart, in his book *The Nature of Russia,* gives the example of the dropwort, normally just a small, unremarkable plant, which in Kamchatka can grow by as much as 10cm in 24 hours and reach a height of up to 4m. In the calderas (craters) of collapsed volcanoes, hot springs and thermal vents maintain a high temperature year-round, creating almost greenhouse-like conditions for plants. Waterfowl and all manner of animals make their way here to shelter from the worst of winter.

The volcanic ash also enriches the peninsula's rivers, leading to far greater spawnings of salmon than experienced anywhere else. And in

PUTIN & THE TIGERS

It's no secret that Vladimir Putin has a thing for tigers. In 2008, on one of his infamous macho-man publicity stunts, the prime minister was pictured fixing a tracking collar to a fully grown female Siberian tiger after having shot her with a tranquilising dart. The same year, for his 56th birthday, Putin was presented with a two-month-old tiger cub: he later donated it to a zoo in Krasnodar Territory.

The International Tiger Conservation Forum (www.tigersummit.ru), a World Bank initiative hosted by Putin in St Petersburg in November 2010, attracted leaders from 13 countries in which tigers are found, including Chinese Premier Wen Jiabao. Lending the event some Hollywood star power was Leonardo DiCaprio who pledged US$1 million towards the initiative that aims to double the number of tigers in the wild from 3200 to 7000 by 2022, the next Chinese Year of the Tiger. Currently, there are estimated to be around 350 wild tigers in Russia.

TOP PARKS & RESERVES

PARK	FEATURES	BEST TIME TO VISIT
Bystrinsky Nature Park (p615)	mountain hikes, volcanoes, reindeer herds	Jul & Aug
Kronotsky Biosphere State Reserve (p609)	volcanoes (11 active cones), geysers, bears, caribou, seals, otters	Jul & Aug
Kurshskaya Kosa National Park (p297)	giant sand dunes, ornithological station, 'dancing forest' of twisted pines	year-round
Prielbruse National Park (p443)	Mt Elbrus, glaciers, waterfalls, bears, chamois, wild goats, enormous range of plant life	skiing year-round; climbing & hiking Jun-Sep
Samara Bend National Park (p366)	Zhiguli Hills, hiking along rocky ledges, grand Volga vistas	Jun-Aug
Sikhote-Alin Nature Reserve (p582)	Manchurian red deer, wild boar, subtropical forests, tigers	Jul & Aug
Stolby Nature Reserve (p511)	volcanic rock pillars	Aug-Apr
Taganay National Park (p402)	some of the southern Ural Mountains' notable ridges (Small, Middle & Big Taganay, Itsyl)	Jul-Sep
Teberdinsky State Natural Biosphere Reserve (p437)	European bison, lynx, bears, chamois, boar & deer in a near-pristine temperate ecosystem	skiing Dec-Apr; climbing & hiking May-Sep
Zyuratkul National Park (p401)	forested ridges, heart-shaped lake	Jul-Sep

thermally warmed pools the salmon also gain weight at a much increased rate. All of which is good news for the region's predatory mammals and large seabirds (and for local fisherfolk). The bears, in particular, benefit and the numerous Kamchatkan brown bears are the biggest of their species in Russia: a fully grown male stands at over 3m and weighs close to a tonne. Other well-fed fish-eaters are the peninsula's sea otters (a protected species), seals and the great sea eagle, one of the world's largest birds of prey, with a 2.5m wingspan. The coastline is particularly favoured by birds, with over 200 recognised species including auks, tufted puffins and swans.

In 2007 the 81,000-hectare Zov Tigra (Roar of the Tiger) National Park was established in Primorsky Territory, partly to monitor and safeguard the local population of Siberian tigers.

Ussuriland

Completely unique, Ussuriland is largely covered by a monsoon forest filled with an exotic array of flora and fauna, many species of which are found nowhere else in Russia. The topography is dominated by the Sikhote-Alin Range, which runs for more than 1000km in a spine parallel to the coast. Unlike the sparsely vegetated woodland floor of the taiga, the forests of Ussuriland have a lush undergrowth, with lianas and vines twined around trunks and draped from branches.

However, it's Ussuriland's animal life that arouses the most interest – not so much the wolves, sables or Asian black bears (tree-climbing, herbivorous cousins to the more common brown bears, also found here), as the Siberian or Amur tiger. The largest of all wild cats, the Siberian tiger can measure up to 3.5m in length. They prey on boar, though they've been observed to hunt and kill bears, livestock and even humans.

Ussuriland is also home to the Amur leopard, a big cat significantly rarer than the tiger, though less impressive and consequently less often mentioned. Around 30 of these leopards roam the lands bordering China and North Korea. Sadly, both the leopard and tiger are under threat from constant poaching by both Chinese and Russian hunters. For more about this beautiful animal see ALTA Amur Leopard Conservation (www.amur-leopard.org).

World Heritage Sites

- Virgin Komi Forests, the Ural Mountains
- Lake Baikal
- Kamchatka's volcanoes
- Altai Mountains
- Western Caucasus
- Curonian Spit
- Central Sikhote-Alin Range
- Uvs Nuur Basin
- Wrangel Island Reserve

State Nature Reserves

According to the Centre for Russian Nature Conservation, Russia has around 101 official nature reserves *(zapovedniki)* and 37 national parks *(natsionalniye parki)*, ranging from the relatively tiny Bryansk Forest (122 sq km) on the border with Ukraine to the enormous 41,692 sq km Great Arctic Nature Reserve in the Taymyr Peninsula, the nation's largest such reserve. These are areas set aside to protect fauna and flora, often habitats of endangered or unique species, where controls are very strict. There are also around 70 *zakazniki* (special-purpose reserves) where protection is limited to specific species or seasons, and many other nature parks.

All these nature reserves – which in total account for around 6% of Russian territory – were once the pride of the Soviet government and were lavished with resources. Scientists had ample funding to study the biological diversity of the reserves and conservation laws were strictly enforced. Now, though, the entire network is in danger of collapse due to a shortage of funds. Some reserves are open to visitors and, unlike in the old days when visitors' ramblings were strictly controlled, today you can sometimes hire the staff to show you around.

Survival Guide

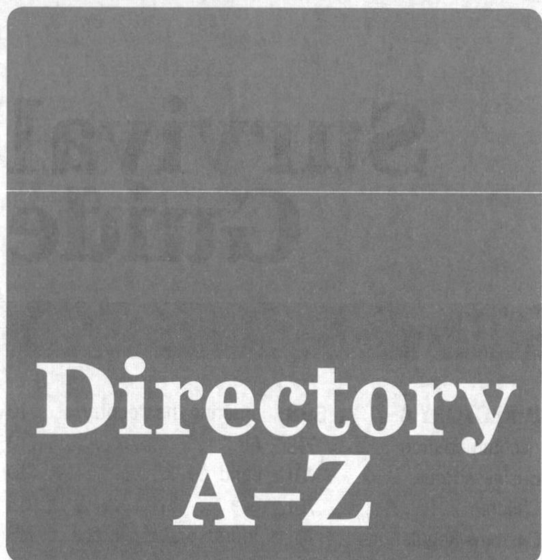

Directory A–Z

Accommodation

Russia offers everything from cosy homestays to five-star luxury hotels. You can generally stay where you like, though a few of the cheapest hotels won't want to register your visa (p21).

The rates quoted for this book are for high season and, unless otherwise mentioned, include private bathroom. Rates generally exclude breakfast. Listings are ordered by preference and price ranges are as follows:

€ <R1500 (R3000 in Moscow & St Petersburg)
€€ R1500 to R4000 (R3000 to R8000 in Moscow & St Petersburg)
€€€ >R4000 (R8000 in Moscow & St Petersburg)

It's a good idea to book a few nights in advance for big cities, but elsewhere it's usually not necessary. Big discounts on rack rates (the ones we list in this guide) can be had for online bookings at sites such as www.booking.com.

Make bookings by email or fax rather than telephone so you get a written copy of your reservation. Some hotels add a booking surcharge *(bron)* which can be up to 50% of the first night's accommodation rate.

If you're looking for cheaper places to stay, head for the smaller towns or consider a homestay or serviced apartment; many travel agencies can arrange these. Occasionally, twin rooms *(potselenye)* are cheaper than singles, but you may end up sharing with a stranger unless you make it clear that you'd prefer single occupancy.

B&B, Homestays & Serviced Apartments

Taking a room in a private home (usually a flat) and sharing with the owners – often referred to as 'bed & breakfast' (B&B) or 'homestay' – gives you a glimpse into how Russians really live. Most places that take in guests are clean and respectable, though rarely large! If you stay in a few you'll be surprised how, despite outward similarities, their owners can make them so different. In the major cities it's also possible to rent serviced apartments by the day or longer.

Moscow and St Petersburg have organisations specifically geared to accommodate foreign visitors in private flats at around €30 to €40 per person, normally with English-speaking hosts, breakfast and other services, such as excursions and extra meals. Many travel agencies and tourism firms in these and other cities, as well as overseas, also offer homestays. The price will depend on things like how far the flat is from the city centre, whether the hosts speak English and whether any meals are provided. Also check whether a homestay or serviced apartment agency can provide visa support and registration and what the costs of this might be.

Camping

Camping in the wild is allowed, except in those areas signposted 'Не разбивать палатку' (No putting up of tents) and/or 'Не разжигать костры' (No campfires). Check with locals if you're in doubt.

Kempingi (organised camp sites) are rare and usually only open from June to September. Unlike Western camp sites, small wooden cabins often take up much of the space, leaving little room for tents. Some *kempingi* are in quite attractive woodland settings, but communal toilets and washrooms are often in poor condition and other facilities few.

Hostels

A hostel movement has yet to emerge across Russia, although you will find them in Irkutsk, Kaliningrad, Moscow, the Solovetsky Islands, St Petersburg, Suzdal, Veliky Novgorod, Vladivostok and Vyborg. For a dorm bed in a Moscow or St Petersburg hostel you can expect to pay R500 to R800.

Hotels

Russian hotels run the gamut from dirt-cheap flophouses to megabuck five-star palaces. Some hotels have one price for Russians and a higher price for foreigners –

HOMESTAY AGENCIES

The following agencies can arrange homestays, mainly in Moscow and St Petersburg, (as can some travel agencies; see individual city listings for details) from as little as US$15 a day, but more commonly it's €30 to €60 depending on location and quality of accommodation.

International Homestay Agency (www.homestayagency.com/homestay/russia.html)

Host Families Association (HOFA; ☎8-901-305 8874; www.hofa.ru)

Worldwide Homestay (www.worldwidehomestay.com/Russia.htm)

this is against Russian law (hence increasingly rare), but in practical terms there is little you can do about it, even if you arrive with Russian friends. In such cases we list the prices hotels charge foreigners.

You can just walk in and get a room on the spot at most hotels. A few hotels aren't registered for foreign guests or will only take you if you've already registered your visa, though these are fairly rare.

Most hotels have a range of rooms at widely differing prices. At older hotels, receptionists may initially offer you the most expensive ones, often feeling, quite genuinely, that cheaper rooms are 'not suitable'. For the budget conscious, there's always a price list displayed (on the wall or in a menu-style booklet on the counter) listing the price for every category. Staff are generally obliging about allowing guests to look around before checking in: ask *'Mozhno li posmotret nomer?'* (May I see the room?).

Not all hotels have genuine single rooms and 'single' prices often refer to single occupancy of a double or twin room. Some hotels, mainly in the bottom and lower-middle ranges, have rooms for three or four people where the price per person is less than a single or double would be. Beds are typically single and where there is a double bed you'll generally pay somewhat more than for a similarly sized twin room.

Hot water supplies are fairly reliable, but since hot water is supplied on a district basis, whole neighbourhoods can be without it for a month or more in summer when the system is shut down for maintenance (the best hotels have their own hot water systems).

A *lyux* room equates to a suite with a sitting room in addition to the bedroom and bathroom. A *polu-lyux* room is somewhat less spacious. Size doesn't always equate to better quality.

In cities and towns, many midrange and top-end hotels catering to businesspeople drop their prices at weekends. There can also be significant seasonal variations, with top prices kicking in over holiday periods such as the first nine days of January and May.

PROCEDURES

When you check in practically all hotels will ask to see your passport – they may then keep it for anywhere up to 24 hours in order to register you with the authorities. Some hotels still operate a system where on each floor a *dezhurnaya* (floor lady) guards the keys for all the rooms in her little kingdom, and from whom you can arrange things like hot water to make tea.

Modern hotels generally have a check-out time (usually noon). However, some places charge by *sutki*, ie for a stay of 24 hours. Check which you've paid for before rushing to pack your bags. If you want to store your luggage somewhere safe for a late departure, arrange it with the *dezhurnaya* or front-desk staff.

BUDGET HOTELS

Rooms may have their own toilet, washbasin or shower, or you may have to use facilities shared by the whole corridor. Some places are clean, if musty, and even include a TV or a huge, Soviet-era fridge in the rooms. Others are decaying, dirty and smelly, and lack decent toilets and washing facilities. Take care with security in some cheap hotels.

A double room with bathroom in a budget hotel in major cities will cost up to R1500 (R3000 in Moscow and St Petersburg). Elsewhere budget hotels can be as cheap R500 a night with shared facilities, although R700 to R1500 is a more realistic minimum.

MIDRANGE HOTELS

The 'minihotel' boom that started in St Petersburg continues to spread across the country, providing options over the old midrange choice of Soviet-era hotels, several of which have been spruced up nicely. Don't always trust the sparkling new facades,

BOOK YOUR STAY ONLINE

For more accommodation reviews by Lonely Planet authors, check out hotels.lonelyplanet.com/russia. You'll find independent reviews, as well as recommendations on the best places to stay. Best of all, you can book online.

however. Sometimes the rooms have not received the same treatment.

Nonetheless, rooms are usually clean, reasonably comfortable with private bathrooms (standards vary greatly) and there will be a restaurant along with a bar or *bufet* (snack bar). These are the most common hotels in cities and you'll pay R1500 to R4000 for a midrange twin (except in Moscow and St Petersburg, where the midrange prices start above R3000).

TOP-END HOTELS

Luxury hotels in the major cities are up to the best international standards, with very comfortable rooms boasting satellite TV, minibars, fawning service, fine restaurants, health clubs and prices to match, from around R4000 upwards. (Prices may be quoted in euros or US dollars and will typically include the 20% VAT – the 5% local tax will sometimes be on top of that.)

In smaller cities and towns, the 'top end' (where it exists) is composed mainly of the very best Soviet-era tourist hotels, along with the occasional former Communist Party hotel or smaller, newer private ventures. Expect to pay upwards from R4000 (R8000 for Moscow and St Petersburg), although you may get better prices through a travel agent and online.

Resting Rooms

Resting rooms *(komnaty otdykha)* are found at all major train stations and several of the smaller ones as well as at a few larger bus stations. Generally, they have basic (but often quite clean) shared accommodation with communal sink and toilet. Some have showers but you'll often pay an extra fee to use them. Sometimes there are single and double rooms and, rarely, more luxurious ones with private bathrooms. The beds can be rented by the hour (from R100), half-day (from R500) or 24-hour (from R1000) period. Some will ask to see your train ticket before allowing you to stay.

Turbazy, Rest Houses & Sanatoriums

To get a feel for the average Russian's holiday, book into a *turbaza*, typically a no-frills holiday camp aimed at outdoor types. Cheap, basic accommodation is usually in spartan multiroom wooden bungalows or *domiky* (small huts). Don't expect indoor plumbing. In the Soviet era, *turbazy* were often owned by a factory or large company for use by its employees. Many became somewhat decrepit, but these days more and more are privatised and have been spruced up. At some, you can arrange boating, skiing, hiking or mountaineering.

Doma otdykha (rest houses) are similar to *turbazy*, although usually more luxurious. In peak seasons it's often essential to book through travel agencies in regional cities as demand can be very high.

Sanatory (sanatoriums) have professional medical staff on hand to treat any illnesses you may have, design your diet and advise on correct rest. Most are ugly concrete eyesores in otherwise attractive rural or coastal settings. Sanatoriums can be spas, sea resorts (there are several good ones in Sochi and the Kaliningrad Region)

ABOUT MUSEUMS (& OTHER TOURIST ATTRACTIONS)

Some major Moscow attractions, such as the Kremlin, State History Museum and St Basil's, have ditched foreigner prices. All adults pay whatever the foreigner price used to be; all students, children and pensioners pay the low price. However, in St Petersburg foreigner prices rule, as they do generally across the country. Higher foreigner fees are said to go towards preserving works of art and cultural treasures that might otherwise receive minimal state funding.

Moscow and St Petersburg apart, non-Russian labels, guides or catalogues in museums are fairly uncommon. If good English labelling at a museum is not mentioned in our reviews, assume that you'll need a dictionary to work out the precise details of what you're seeing – or be prepared to pay an additional fee for a guided tour.

Here are a few more working practices of Russian museums to keep in mind:

» Admittance typically stops one hour before the official closing time.

» If you wish to take photos or film a video there will be a separate fee for this, typically an extra R100 for a still camera and R200 for video camera.

» Once a month many places close for a 'sanitary day', in theory to allow the place to be thoroughly cleaned. Sometimes these special closing days are mentioned in the listings review, but if you specially want to see a museum, it's always best to call ahead to check when it's open.

or resorts where you can get some kind of nontraditional treatment (with *kumiss*, fermented mare's milk, for instance).

Business Hours

Shops generally open between 9am and 11am and stay open until 8pm or 9pm. Banks operate from 9am to 6pm Monday to Friday. Restaurants and bars are generally open from noon to midnight, sometimes with a break between afternoon and evening meals; they'll often work later than their stated hours if the establishment is full. In fact, many simply say that they work *do poslednnogo klienta* (until the last customer leaves). Exceptions to these hours are noted in individual listings in this book.

Children

Russians love children and travelling with them can be fun as long as you have a relaxed attitude and a degree of patience. See p92 and p206 for ideas of how to entertain the little ones in Moscow and St Petersburg respectively. If you're heading for Siberia, Nikita's on Olkhon Island (p542) has a fantastic kids' playground.

Baby changing rooms are uncommon and you wouldn't want to use many public toilets yourself, let alone change your baby's nappy in them. Head back to your hotel or to a modern café or fast-food outlet where the toilets, while typically small, should be clean. Nappies, powdered milk and baby food are widely available except in very rural areas.

There's no shortage of toy shops, but don't expect to find many, if any, English-language kids' publications.

Lonely Planet's *Travel with Children* contains useful advice on how to cope with kids on the road and what to bring to make things go more smoothly.

Customs Regulations

Even though searches beyond the perfunctory are quite rare, clearing customs, especially when you leave Russia by a land border, can be lengthy. Apart from the usual restrictions, bringing in and out large amounts of cash is limited, although the amount at which you have to go through the red channel changes frequently. Currently, visitors are allowed to bring in and take out under US$3000 (or its equivalent) in currency, and goods in value under R65,000, weighing less than 50kg, without making a customs declaration.

The only time it's worth filling in a customs declaration form is if you're bringing into the country major equipment, antiques, art works or musical instruments (including a guitar) that you plan to take out with you – get it stamped in the red channel of customs to avoid any problems leaving Russia with the same goods.

If you plan to export anything vaguely 'arty' – manuscripts, instruments, coins, jewellery, antiques, antiquarian books (anything published pre-1975) – it must be assessed by the **RosOkhranKultura** in Moscow (☎495-628 5089; bldg 2, Kitaygorodsky proezd 7; ⏲10am-5pm Mon-Fri; Ⓜ Kitay-Gorod) or St Petersburg (☎812-571 0302; Malaya Morskaya ul 17; Ⓜ Nevsky Prospekt). Bring your item (or a photograph, if the item is large) and your receipt. The bureaucrats will issue a receipt for tax paid, which you show to customs officers on your way out of the country.

Discount Cards

Full-time students and people aged under 26 can sometimes (but not always) get a substantial discount on admissions – always flash your student card or International Student Identity Card (ISIC) before paying.

Senior citizens also *might* get a discount, but there are no promises: carry your pension card or passport anyway.

Electricity

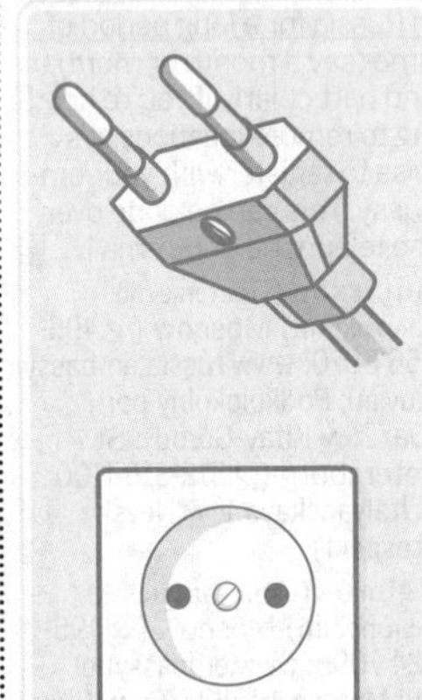

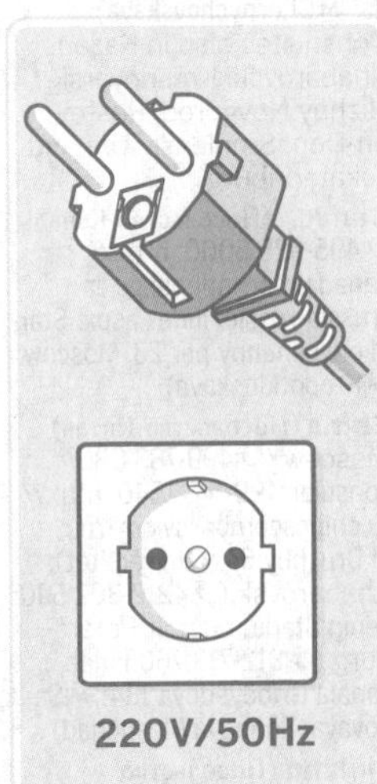

Access electricity (220V, 50Hz AC) with a European plug with two round pins. A few places still have the old 127V system. Some trains and hotel bathrooms have 110V and 220V shaver plugs.

Embassies & Consulates

See www.russianembassy.net for a list of Russian embassies and consulates overseas. If you will be travelling in Russia for a long period of time (say a month or more), and particularly if you're heading to remote locations, it's wise to register with your embassy. This can be done over the telephone or by email.

Australia (Посольство Австралии) Moscow (495-956 6070; www.russia.embassy.gov.au; Podkolokolny per 10a/2; M Kitay-Gorod); St Petersburg (812-315 1100; ul Italyanskaya 1; M Nevsky Prospekt)

Belarus (Консульство Белорусии) Moscow (495-624 7095; www.embassybel.ru; Maroseyka ul 17/6; M Kitay-Gorod); Kaliningrad (4012-214 412; ul Dm Donskogo 35a); St Petersburg (812-274 7212; ul Bonch-Bruevicha 3a; M Chernyshevskaya) Consulates also in Kazan, Khabarovsk, Krasnoyarsk, Nizhny Novgorod, Rostov-on-Don, Smolensk, Ufa and Yekaterinburg.

Canada (Посольство Канады; 495-925 6000; http://canadainternational.gc.ca/russia-russie/index.aspx; Starokonyushenny per 23, Moscow; M Kropotkinskaya)

China (Посольство Китая) Moscow (499-783 0867; consular 499-143 1540; http://ru.chineseembassy.org/rus; ul Druzhby 6; M Universitet); Khabarovsk (4212-302 590; Lenin Stadium 1); St Petersburg (812-713 7605; nab kanala Griboyedova 134; M Sadovaya, Sennaya Ploshchad)

Finland (Посольство Финляндии) Moscow (495-787 4174; www.finland.org.ru; Kropotkinsky per 15/17; M Park Kultury); St Petersburg (812-331 7600; Preobrazhenskaya pl 4; M Chernyshevskaya)

France (Посольство Франции) Moscow (495-937 1500; www.ambafrance-ru.org; ul Bolshaya Yakimanka 45; M Oktyabrskaya); St Petersburg (812-332 2270; nab reki Moyki 15; M Nevsky Prospekt)

Germany (Посольство Германии) Moscow (495-937 9500; www.moskau.diplo.de; Mosfilmovskaya ul 56; M Universitet, then bus 119); St Petersburg (812-320 2400; Furshtatskaya ul 39; M Chernyshevskaya) Consulates also in Kaliningrad, Novosibirsk and Yekaterinburg.

Ireland (Посольство Ирландии; 495-937 5911; www.embassyofireland.ru; Grokholsky per 5, Moscow; M Prospekt Mira)

Japan (Посольство Японии) Moscow (495-229 2550; www.ru.emb-japan.go.jp; Grokholsky per 27; M Arbatskaya); St Petersburg (814 1434; nab reki Moyki 29; M Nevsky Prospekt) Consulates also in Khabarovsk, Vladivostok and Yuzhno-Sakhalinsk.

Latvia (Консульство Латвии) Moscow (495-232 9760; www.am.gov.lv/en/moscow; ul Chapligina 3; M Chistye Prudy); Kaliningrad (4012-706 755; Englesa ul 52a)

Lithuania (Консульство Литвы) Moscow (495-785 8605; http://ru.mfa.lt; Borisoglebsky per 10; M Arbatskaya); Kaliningrad (4012-959 486; Proletarskaya ul 133); St Petersburg (812-327 0230; ul Ryleyeva 37; M Chernyshevskaya)

Mongolia (Посольство Монголии) Moscow (495-290 6792; Borisoglebsky per 11; M Arbartskaya) Moscow Consular Section (Spasopeskovsky per 7/1; M Smolenskaya); Irkutsk (3952-342 145; www.irconsul.angara.ru; ul Lapina 11) Ulan-Ude (3012-211 078; ul Profsoyuznaya 6)

Netherlands (Посольство Голландии; 495-797 2900; www.netherlands-embassy.ru; Kalashny per 6, Moscow; M Arbatskaya)

New Zealand (Посольство Новой Зеландии; 495-956 3579; www.nzembassy.com/russia; Povarskaya ul 44, Moscow; M Arbatskaya)

Norway (Посольство Норвегии; 495-933 1410; www.norvegia.ru; ul Povarskaya 7, Moscow) Consulates also in St Petersburg, Murmansk and Arkhangelsk.

Poland (Посольство Польши) Moscow (495-231 1500; www.moskwa.polemb.net; Klimashkina ul 4; M Belorusskaya); Kaliningrad (4012-976 400; www.kaliningradkg.polemb.net; Kashtanovaya alleya 51)

UK (Посольство Великобритании) Moscow (495-956 7200; http://ukinrussia.fco.gov.uk/en; Smolenskaya nab 10; M Smolenskaya); St Petersburg (812-320 3200; pl Proletarskoy Diktatury 5; M Chernyshevskaya) Consulate also in Yekaterinburg.

Ukraine (Посольство Украины 495-629 9742; www.ukremb.ru; Leontevsky per 18, Moscow; M Pushkinskaya)

USA (Посольство США) Moscow (495-728 5000; http://moscow.usembassy.gov; Bol Devyatinsky per 8; M Barrikadnaya); St Petersburg (812-331 2600; ul Furshtatskaya 15; M Chernyshevskaya) Consulates also in Vladivostok and Yekaterinburg.

Food

Listings in this book are ordered by preference, and prices are based on the cost of a two-course meal with a nonalcoholic drink:

€ <R500

€€ R500 to R1000

€€€ >R1000

For more information about eating and drinking in Russia, see p683.

Gay & Lesbian Travellers

Homosexuality was legalised in Russia in the early 1990s but remains a divisive issue throughout the country. In general this is a conservative country and being gay is frowned upon. See p107 for details about the annual gay pride march in Moscow and the problems surrounding it.

This said, there are active and relatively open gay and lesbian scenes in both Moscow and St Petersburg, although you shouldn't expect anything nearly as prominent as you might find in other major world centres. Away from these two major cities, the gay scene tends to be underground.

For a good overview, visit http://english.gay.ru, which has up-to-date information, good links and a resource for putting you in touch with personal guides for Moscow and St Petersburg. They're also involved in publishing the gay magazine *Kvir*. St Petersburg's **Krilija** (Wings; www.krilija.sp.ru) is Russia's oldest officially registered gay and lesbian community organisation.

Health

» **Insurance** Good emergency medical treatment is not cheap in Russia, so take out a policy that covers you for the worst possible scenario, such as an accident requiring an emergency flight home.

» **Recommended vaccinations** No vaccinations are required for travel to Russia, but the World Health Organization (WHO) recommends that all travellers should be covered for diphtheria, tetanus, measles, mumps, rubella and polio, regardless of their destination. Since most vaccines don't produce immunity until at least two weeks after they're given, visit a physician at least six weeks before departure.

» **Availability and cost of health care** Medical care is readily available across Russia but the quality can vary enormously. The biggest cities and towns have the widest choice of places, with Moscow and St Petersburg well served by sparkling international-style clinics that charge handsomely for their generally excellent and professional service: expect to pay around US$100 for an initial consultation. In remote areas doctors won't usually charge travellers, although it's recommended to give them a present – such as a bottle of Armenian cognac, chocolate or just money. In some cases, medical supplies required in a hospital may need to be bought from a pharmacy and nursing care may be limited. Note that there can be an increased risk of hepatitis B and HIV transmission via poorly sterilised equipment.

» **Infectious diseases** These include rabies, tick-borne encephalitis (a serious risk in rural Russia from May to July), HIV & AIDS, typhoid and hepatitis A. Consider having vaccinations before departure.

» **Environmental hazards** These include altitude sickness in the high mountains of the Caucasus, the Altai and Kamchatka; depending on the season, heat exhaustion and heat stroke or hypothermia and frostbite; stings or bites from insects, leeches and snakes.

» **Water safety** While brushing your teeth with it is OK, assume that tap water isn't safe to drink. Stick to bottled water, boil water for 10 minutes or use water purification tablets or a filter. Do not drink water from rivers or lakes as it may contain bacteria or viruses that can cause diarrhoea or vomiting.

TRAVEL HEALTH WEBSITES

Consult your government's travel health website before departure, if one is available:

Australia www.smartraveller.gov.au

Canada www.hc-sc.gc.ca

UK www.dh.gov.uk

US wwwnc.cdc.gov/travel

Insurance

We strongly recommend taking out travel insurance. Check the small print to see if the policy covers potentially dangerous sporting activities, such as diving or trekking. For medical treatment, some policies pay doctors or hospitals directly but most require you to pay on the spot and claim later (keep all receipts and documentation). Check that the policy covers ambulances or an emergency flight home. Worldwide travel insurance is available at www.lonelyplanet.com/bookings/insurance.do.

Internet Access

The best place to look for internet access is the main post or telephone office, as they often have the cheapest rates (typically around R30 to R40 an hour).

Wireless internet (wi-fi) is common, particularly in Moscow and St Petersburg and other large cities, where many bars, cafés, restaurants and hotels have it. Often access is free (you may have to ask for a password, or *parol*, to get online) or available for the cost of a cup of coffee or via a prepaid card that allows you a set amount of time online. A few hotels have a high-speed link via broadband cables; if so, they can usually provide the connection cords if you don't have one.

To access your home account, you'll need your incoming (POP or IMAP) mail server name, your account name and your password; your ISP or network supervisor will be able to give you these. It is also useful to

PRACTICALITIES

» Russia uses the metric system. Menus often list food and drink servings in grams: a teacup is about 200g, a shot glass 50g. The unit for items sold by the piece, such as eggs, is *shtuka* ('thing' or 'piece') or *sht*.

» TV channels include **Channel 1** (Pervy Kanal; www.1tv.ru), **NTV** (www.ntv.ru), **Rossiya** (www.rutv.ru), Kultura, Sport, **RenTV** (www.ren-tv.com) and **Russia Today** (http://rt.com), an English-language satellite channel. Each region has a number of local channels, while in many hotels you'll have access to CNN and BBC World, plus several more satellite channels in English and other languages.

» Radio is broken into three bands: AM, UKV (66MHz to 77MHz) and FM (100MHz to 107MHz). A Western-made FM radio usually won't go lower than 85MHz.

» Russian DVDs are region code 5.

become familiar with the process for accessing mail from a net-connected machine before you leave home.

Language Courses

English-language publications in Moscow and St Petersburg carry advertisements for Russian-language schools and tutors. The cost of formal coursework varies widely, but one-on-one tutoring can be a bargain – numerous professors and other highly skilled people are anxious to augment their incomes by teaching you Russian.

Another option for learning Russian is through one of the many international universities operating in Moscow and St Petersburg. These are usually affiliated with a school in either Britain or the USA. Or you could take a course through the **Eurolingua Institute** (www.eurolingua.com), which offers homestays combined with language courses.

For specific course recommendations, see p106.

Legal Matters

Avoid contact with the myriad types of police. It's not uncommon for them to bolster their puny incomes by extracting 'fines' from the unaware; you always have the right to insist to be taken to a police station (we don't recommend this) or that the 'fine' be paid the legal way, through Sberbank. If you need police assistance (ie you've been the victim of a robbery or an assault) go to a station with a local for both language and moral support. Be persistent and patient.

If you are arrested, the Russian authorities are obliged to inform your embassy or consulate immediately and allow you to communicate with it without delay. You can't count on the rules being followed, so be polite and respectful towards officials and hopefully things will go far more smoothly for you. In Russian, the phrase 'I'd like to call my embassy' is '*Pozhaluysta, ya khotel by pozvonit v posolstvo moyey strany*'.

Money

The Russian currency is the rouble (рубль), abbreviated as 'ру' or 'р'. There are 100 *kopeks* in a rouble and these come in coin denominations of one (rarely seen), five, 10 and 50. Also issued in coins, roubles come in amounts of one, two, five and 10, with banknotes in values of 10, 50, 100, 500, 1000 and 5000 roubles.

We've listed most prices in this book in roubles (R), with the main exceptions being some (but not all) hotel prices, which may be quoted in US dollars or euros (€).

ATMs

Using a credit card or the debit card you use in ATMs at home, you can obtain cash as you need it – usually in roubles, but sometimes in dollars or euros, too. You're rarely a block or so from an ATM: look for signs that say *bankomat* (БАНКОМАТ).

Credit Cards

These are commonly accepted, but don't rely on them outside of the major cities and towns. Most sizeable cities have banks or exchange bureaus that will give you a cash advance on your credit card, but be prepared for paperwork in Russian.

Exchanging Money

You'll usually get the best exchange rates for US dollars, though euros are increasingly widely accepted and will get good rates, for instance, in Moscow and St Petersburg. British pounds are sometimes accepted in big cities, but the exchange rates are not so good; other currencies incur abysmal rates and are often virtually unchangeable.

Any currency you bring should be pristine: banks and exchange bureaus do not accept old, tatty bills with rips or tears. For US dollars, make certain they are the post-2006 designs printed with large offset portraits.

Carrying around wads of cash isn't the security problem you might imagine – nowadays, there are a lot of Russians with plenty more money on them than you. For security, though, divide your money into three or four stashes hidden out of view about your person.

Every town of any size will have at least one bank (most often Sberbank; www.sbrf.ru) or exchange office – be prepared to fill out a lengthy form and show your passport. Rates are stable but can vary from one establishment to the next, so it's always worth shopping around.

International Transfers

Larger towns and cities will have at least one bank or exchange office that can handle Western Union money wires. Ask at any bank for this information.

Travellers Cheques

These can be difficult to exchange outside the largest cities and the process can be lengthy. Expect to pay 1% to 2% commission. Not all travellers cheques are treated equally by those Russian establishments willing to handle them. In descending order of acceptance, the favourites are American Express (Amex), Thomas Cook and Visa; you'll have little or no luck with other brands. The most likely bank to cash travellers cheques is Sberbank, with branches in all the major cities.

Photography

Any town or city will have several photographic shops where you can download digital snaps to CD and buy memory cards and major brands of print film. Slide film is not widely sold, so bring plenty of rolls with you. The same rare specialist shops that sell slide film will also have a smattering of camera gear by leading brands such as Nikon and Canon.

Photographing People

Use good judgement and discretion when taking photos of people. It's always better to ask first, and if the person doesn't want to be photographed, respect their privacy; older people can be uneasy about being photographed, but a genuine offer to send on a copy can loosen your subject up. In Russian, 'May I take a photograph of you?' is *'Mozhno vas sfotografirovat?'*.

Restrictions

Be very careful about photographing stations (including metro stations), official-looking buildings and any type of military-security structure – if in doubt, don't snap! Travellers, including an author of this book, have been arrested and fined for such innocent behaviour.

Some museums and galleries forbid flash pictures, some ban all photography and most will charge you extra to snap away (typically R100). Some caretakers in historical buildings and churches charge mercilessly for the privilege of using a still or video camera.

Post

The Russian post service is **Pochta Rossia** (www.russianpost.ru). *Pochta* (ПОЧТАМТ) refers to any post office, *glavpochtamt* to a main post office and *mezhdunarodny glavpochtamt* to an international one. The main offices are open from 8am to 8pm or 9pm Monday to Friday, with shorter hours on Saturday and Sunday; in big cities one office will possibly stay open 24 hours a day.

Outward post is slow but fairly reliable; if you want to be certain, use registered post *(zakaznaya pochta)*. Airmail letters take two to three weeks from Moscow and St Petersburg to the UK, longer from other cities and three to four weeks to the USA or Australasia. To send a postcard or letter up to 20g anywhere in the world by air costs R25.

You can address outgoing international mail just as you would in any country (in your own language), though it might help to *precede* the address with the country name in Cyrillic.

In major cities you can usually find the services of at least one of the international express carriers, such as FedEx or DHL.

Incoming mail is so unreliable that many companies, hotels and individuals use private services with addresses in Germany or Finland (a private carrier completes the mail's journey to its Russian destination). Other than this, your *reliable* options for receiving mail in Russia are nil: there's no poste restante, and embassies and consulates won't hold mail for transient visitors.

If sending mail to Russia or trying to receive it, note that addresses should be in reverse order: Russia (Россия), postal code (if known), city, street address, then name.

CYRILLIC COUNTRY NAMES

America (USA)	Америка (США)
Australia	Австралия
Canada	Канада
France	Франция
Germany	Германия
Great Britain	Великобритания
Ireland	Ирландия
New Zealand	Новая Зеландия

Public Holidays

New Year's Day 1 January
Russian Orthodox Christmas Day 7 January
Defender of the Fatherland Day 23 February
International Women's Day 8 March
International Labour Day/ Spring Festival 1 May
Victory Day 9 May (marks the WWII victory over the Germans in 1945)
Russian Independence Day 12 June (marks the day the Russian republic of the USSR proclaimed its sovereignty in June 1991)
Unity Day 4 November

Many businesses are also closed from 1 January to 7 January. Easter Monday is also widely celebrated across Russia.

Safe Travel

Crime

SCAMS

Be wary of officials, such as police (or people posing as police), asking to see your papers or tickets at stations – there's a fair chance they're on the lookout for a bribe and will try to find anything wrong with your documents, or basically hold them ransom. The only course of action is to remain calm and polite and stand your ground. Try to enlist the help of a passer-by to translate (or at least witness what is going on).

Another scam involves the use of devices in ATMs that read credit card and PIN details when you withdraw money from the machines, enabling accounts to be accessed and additional funds withdrawn. In general, it's safest to use ATMs in carefully guarded public places such as major hotels and restaurants.

STREET CRIME

The streets of big cities such as Moscow and St Petersburg are as safe (or as dangerous) as those of New York and London: there are pickpockets, purse-snatchers and all the other crimes (and criminals) endemic to big cities anywhere. The key is to be neither paranoid nor unconcerned – use common sense and try to fit in: shun clothes and accessories that show you're a tourist.

THEFT

Don't leave anything of worth in a car, including sunglasses, CDs and cigarettes. Valuables lying around hotel rooms also tempt providence. At camp sites, watch for items on clothes lines and in cabins. If you stay in a flat, make sure it has a well-bolted steel door.

It's generally safe to leave your belongings unguarded when using the toilets on trains, but you'd be wise to get to know your fellow passengers first.

Dangerous Regions

Check with your government's foreign affairs ministry at home or your embassy in Russia for the latest danger zones. Heading to Chechnya is obviously a dumb idea, as is going to Dagestan, another location of civil unrest and general lawlessness. Certain very isolated villages suffer from the unpredictable side effects of chronic alcoholism, especially in western Tuva where locals are frequently drunk and armed with knives.

In more remote areas of the country specific natural hazards include bears and, in late May to July, potentially fatal tick-borne encephalitis (particularly in Siberia and Ussuriland in the Russian Far East). And if trekking in Kamchatka, remember that many of those volcanoes are volatile.

Racism & Discrimination

Racism is a problem in Russia. Neo-Nazi and skinhead groups are violent and have been linked to many murders, including the fatal stabbing of a nine-year-old Tajik girl in St Petersburg in 2004. In 2008, a skinhead gang led by two teenagers was charged with the racist murders of 20 people in Moscow.

Attacks on Africans and Asians on city streets are not uncommon. Visitors of African, Middle-Eastern and Asian descent should be aware that they may not always receive the warmest of welcomes, though Russian racism seems particularly focused towards Caucasian peoples (ie people from the Caucasus, not white-skinned Europeans).

What is most surprising is that racist attitudes or statements can come from highly educated Russians. Anti-Semitism, which was state-sponsored during Soviet times, is still easily stirred up by right-wing political parties.

It's a good idea to be vigilant on the streets around Hitler's birthday (20 April), when bands of right-wing thugs have been known to roam around spoiling for a fight with anyone who doesn't look Russian.

Transport & Road Safety

Air travel safety is covered on p714. Take care when

> **GOVERNMENT TRAVEL ADVICE**
>
> The following government websites offer travel advisories and information on current hot spots.
>
> **Australian Department of Foreign Affairs** (www.smarttraveller.gov.au)
>
> **British Foreign Office** (www.fco.gov.uk)
>
> **Canadian Department of Foreign Affairs** (www.dfait-maeci.gc.ca)
>
> **US State Department** (http://travel.state.gov)

crossing the road in large cities: some crazy drivers completely ignore traffic lights, while others tear off immediately when the lights change (which can be suddenly), leaving you stranded in the middle of the road.

Telephone

Russian area codes are listed in this book under the relevant section heading. The country code for Russia is ☎7.

Local calls from homes and most hotels are free. To make a long-distance call or to call a mobile from most phones, first dial ☎8, wait for a second dial tone, then dial the area code and phone number. To make an international call dial ☎8, wait for a second dial tone, then dial ☎10, then the country code etc. Some phones are for local calls only and won't give you that second dial tone.

From mobile phones, dial ☎+ and then the country code to place an international call.

Mobile Phones

There are several major networks, all offering pay-as-you-go deals, including the following:

Beeline (www.beeline.ru/index.wbp)
Megafon (www.megafon.ru)
MTS (www.mts.ru)
Skylink (http://skylink.ru)

Reception is available right along the Trans-Siberian Railway and increasingly in rural areas. MTS probably has the widest network, but also the worst reputation for customer service. Our researchers found Beeline to be pretty reliable.

To call a mobile phone from a landline, the line must be enabled to make paid (ie nonlocal) calls. SIMs and phone call–credit top-up cards, available at mobile phone shops and kiosks across cities and towns (you'll usually find them in the airport arrival areas and train stations) and costing as little as R300, can be slotted into your regular mobile phone handset during your stay. Call prices are very low within local networks, but charges for roaming larger regions can mount up; cost-conscious locals switch SIM cards when crossing regional boundaries.

Topping up your credit can be done either via prepaid credit cards bought from kiosks or mobile phone shops or, more commonly, via certain ATMs (look for phone logos on the options panel) and the brightly coloured QIWI Cash-in paypoint machines found in all shopping centres, metro and train stations and the like. Choose your network, input your telephone number and the amount of credit you'd like, insert the cash and it's done, minus a small fee for the transaction. Confirmation of the top-up comes via a text message to your phone.

Pay Phones

Taksofon (ТАКСОФОН, pay phones) are located throughout most cities. They're usually in working order, but don't rely on them. Most take prepaid phonecards. There are several types of card-only phones, and not all cards are interchangeable. Card phones can be used for either domestic or international calls.

Phonecards & Call Centres

Local phonecards (*телефонная карта*) come in a variety of units and are available from shops and kiosks – they can be used to make local, national and international calls.

Sometimes a call centre is better value for international calls – you give the clerk the number you want to call, pay a deposit and then go to the booth you are assigned to make the call. Afterwards, you either pay the difference or collect your change. Such call centres are common in Russian cities and towns – ask for *mezhdunarodny telefon* (международний телефон).

CHANGING TELEPHONE NUMBERS

Russian authorities have an annoying habit of frequently changing telephone numbers, particularly in cities. We've listed the correct phone number as at the time of research, but it's likely that some will change during the lifetime of this book, particularly in cities such as Moscow.

Time

There are nine time zones in Russia; the standard time is calculated from Moscow, which is GMT/UTC plus four hours.

Moscow & St Petersburg	noon
Yekaterinburg & Tyumen	2pm
Novosibirsk	3pm
Krasnoyarsk & Tuva	4pm
Irkutsk & Ulan-Ude	5pm
Chita	6pm
Vladivostok & Sydney	7pm
Magadan & Kamchatka	8pm
San Francisco	midnight
New York	3am
London	8am
Paris & Berlin	9am
Kaliningrad, Helsinki & Minsk	11am

Toilets

Pay toilets are identified by the words платный туалет (*platny tualet*). In any toilet, Ж (*zhensky*) stands for women's, while М (*muzhskoy*) stands for men's.

TRAIN TIME

Right across Russia, timetables for long-distance trains are written according to Moscow time. The only exceptions are those for suburban services that run on local time – but not always, so double-check. Station clocks in most places are also set to Moscow time. In this guide we list how far ahead cities and towns are of Moscow time, eg ⏲Moscow +5hr, meaning five hours ahead of Moscow.

You'll find clusters of temporary plastic toilets in popular public places in cities, although other public toilets are rare and often dingy and uninviting. Toilets in major hotels or cafés are preferable.

In all public toilets, the babushka you pay your R10 to can also provide miserly rations of toilet paper; it's always a good idea to carry your own.

Tourist Information

Tourist offices remain a rarity in Russia. We've located ones in Arkhangelsk, Yelizovo, Esso, Irkutsk, Kaliningrad, Kazan, Kyzyl, Perm, Petrozavodsk, Pskov, St Petersburg, Svetlogorsk, Uglich and Veliky Novgorod.

You're mainly dependent on the moods of hotel receptionists and administrators, service bureaus and travel firms for information. The latter two exist primarily to sell accommodation, excursions and transport – if you don't look like you want to book something, staff may or may not answer questions.

Overseas, travel agencies specialising in Russian travel are your best bet.

Travellers with Disabilities

Disabled travellers are not well catered for in Russia. Many footpaths are in poor condition, hazardous even for the mobile. There are a lack of access ramps and lifts for wheelchairs. However, attitudes are enlightened and things are slowly changing. Major museums such as the Hermitage offer good disabled access. There's even a tour agency specialising in wheelchair-accessible tours in St Petersburg (p205).

Before setting off, get in touch with your national support organisation (preferably with the travel officer, if there is one). The following organisations offer general travel advice:

Nican (☎02-6241 1220, 1800-806 769; www.nican.com.au; Unit 5, 48 Brookes St, Mitchell, ACT 2911) Australia

Mare Nostrum (☎030-4502 6454; www.mare-nostrum.de; Oudenarder Strasse 7, Berlin 13347) Germany

Tourism For All (☎0845-124 9971; www.tourismforall.org.uk; Vitalise, Shap Road Industrial Estate, Shap Rd, Kendal, Cumbria LA9 6NZ) UK

Accessible Journeys (☎800-846 4537; www.disabilitytravel.com; 35 West Sellers Ave, Ridley Park, PA 19078) USA

Mobility International USA (☎541-343 1284; www.miusa.org; ste 343, 132 East Broadway, Eugene, Oregon 97401) USA

Visas

For all about Russian visas see p20. If your trip into or out of Russia involves transit through, or a stay in, another country, such as Belarus, China, Mongolia or Kazakhstan, our advice is to arrange any necessary visa or visas in your home country *before* you enter Russia. For information on obtaining Chinese visas in Khabarovsk and Vladivostok, see p575.

Volunteering

Local enterprises, environmental groups and charities that are trying to improve Russia's environmental and social scorecard are usually on the lookout for volunteers. A good example is the Great Baikal Trail project helping to construct a hiking trail around Lake Baikal (see p537). The US-based School of Russian & Asian Studies (SRAS) has complied an online list of volunteer opportunities in Russia (www.sras.org/volunteer_opportunities_in_russia). Other possibilities:

Cross-Cultural Solutions (www.crossculturalsolutions.org) Runs volunteer programs in a range of social services out of Yaroslavl.

International Cultural Youth Exchange (www.icye.org) Offers a variety of volunteer projects, mostly in Samara.

Language Link Russia (www.jobs.languagelink.ru) Volunteer to work at language centres across the country.

World 4U (www.world4u.ru/english.html) Russian volunteer association.

Women Travellers

Russian women are very independent and, in general, you won't attract attention by travelling alone. That said, it's not uncommon for a woman dining or drinking alone to be mistaken for a prostitute. Sexual harassment on the streets is rare, but a woman alone should certainly avoid ad-hoc taxis at night – have one called for you from a reputable company.

Stereotyping of gender roles remains strong. Russian men will also typically rush

RUSSIAN STREET NAMES

We use the Russian names of all streets and squares in this book to help you when deciphering Cyrillic signs and asking locals the way. To save space, the following abbreviations are used.

bul	bulvar	бульвар	boulevard
nab	naberezhnaya	набережная	embankment
per	pereulok	переулок	side street
pl	ploshchad	площадь	square
pr	prospekt	проспект	avenue
sh	shosse	шоссе	road
ul	ulitsa	улица	street

Please also note that some of the Soviet-era names for streets and places have been changed back to their prerevolutionary names or to new names.

to open doors for you, help you put on your coat, and, on a date, act like a 'traditional' gentleman. (In return, they may be expecting you to act like a traditional lady.)

Russian women dress up and wear lots of make-up on nights out. If you wear casual gear, you might feel uncomfortable at a restaurant, a theatre or the ballet; in rural areas, wearing revealing clothing will probably attract unwanted attention.

Work

Given the large number of unemployed and well-educated Russians, the chances of foreigners finding work in the country are slim. The most likely positions available are as English teachers (look in the *Moscow* and *St Petersburg Times* for ads); your odds for other positions will be slightly increased if you speak fluent Russian.

Bureaucracy also makes starting a business a hassle, but it's certainly possible and you'll encounter several expats who have done so. In the event that you do find work in Russia or are sent there by your company, it would be wise to use a professional relocation firm to navigate the country's thicket of rules and regulations surrounding employment of foreigners. Good websites for expats are www.expat.ru and www.redtape.ru/forum.

Transport

GETTING THERE & AWAY

Entering the Country

Unless you have a transit visa, you can enter the country on a one-way ticket (even if your visa is only good for one day, it's unlikely anyone will ask to see your outgoing ticket), so you have a great deal of flexibility once inside Russia to determine the best way of getting out again.

Air

Airports

Moscow's **Sheremetyevo-2** (airport code SVO; ☎495-232 6565; www.sheremetyevo-airport.ru) and **Domodedovo** (airport code DME; ☎495-933 6666; www.domodedovo.ru) Airports host the bulk of Russia's international flights. There are also many daily international services to St Petersburg's **Pulkovo-2** (airport code LED; ☎812-704 3444; www.pulkovoairport.ru/eng) airport.

Plenty of other cities have direct international connections, including Arkhangelsk, Irkutsk, Kaliningrad, Kazan, Khabarovsk, Krasnodar, Mineralnye Vody, Murmansk, Nizhny Novgorod, Novosibirsk, Perm, Yekaterinburg and Yuzhno-Sakhalinsk.

Tickets

Good deals can be found online and with discount agencies. Use the fares quoted in this book as a guide only. Quoted airfares do not necessarily constitute a recommendation for the carrier.

See the Tours section in Getting There & Away in this chapter (p713) for a list of agencies who specialise in tours to Russia; some may offer discount fares.

Land

Russia borders 13 countries. Popular land approaches include trains and buses from Central and Baltic European countries or on either the trans-Manchurian or trans-Mongolian train routes from China and Mongolia.

Border Crossings

Russia shares borders with Azerbaijan, Belarus, China, Estonia, Finland, Georgia, Kazakhstan, Latvia, Lithuania, Mongolia, North Korea, Norway, Poland and Ukraine; all except Azerbaijan, Georgia and North Korea are open to non-Russian travellers. Before planning a journey into or out of Russia from any of these countries, check out the visa situation for your nationality.

On trains, border crossings are a straightforward but drawn-out affair, with a steady stream of customs and ticket personnel scrutinising your passport and visa. If you're arriving by car or motorcycle, you'll need to show your vehicle registration and insurance papers, and your driving licence, passport and visa. These formalities are usually minimal for Western European citizens.

On the Russian side, chances are your vehicle will be subjected to a cursory inspection by border guards (things will go faster if you open all doors and the boot yourself, and shine a torch for the guards at night). You pass through customs separately from your car, walking through a metal detector and possibly having hand luggage X-rayed.

Train fares for trips to/from Russia listed under individual countries in this section are for a *kupe* (compartment) in a four-berth compartment. Certain routes also offer cheaper *platskartny* (3rd-class open carriage) fares.

Belarus

BUS

There are at least two buses a week from Minsk to Moscow and one a week to St Petersburg.

CAR & MOTORCYCLE

Long queues at border crossings are common. There are six main road routes into Russia from Belarus, the recommended one being the E30 highway that connects Brest and Minsk with Smolensk and finishes up in Moscow.

TRAIN

Minsk is well connected by train with Kaliningrad (from

THINGS CHANGE...

The information in this chapter is particularly vulnerable to change. Check directly with the airline or a travel agent to make sure you understand how a fare (and ticket you may buy) works and be aware of the security requirements for international travel. Shop carefully. The details given in this chapter should be regarded as pointers and are not a substitute for your own careful, up-to-date research.

R3700, 13 hours, two daily), Moscow (R3170, 11 hours, 20 daily), Smolensk (from R2700, four hours, 15 daily) and St Petersburg (R3900, 15 hours, three daily).

China

BUS

The road from Manzhouli to Zabaikalsk in the Chitinskaya Region is open to traffic; it's also possible to cross from Heihe to Blagoveshchensk using a ferry across the Amur River. It's possible to take a bus between Manzhouli and Zabaikalsk, but asking Russians for a ride is usually faster.

TRAIN

The classic way into Russia from China is along the trans-Mongolian and trans-Manchurian rail routes; see p43.

Also see Vladivostok and Khabarovsk for other options on travelling overland to China.

Estonia

The nearest border crossing from Tallinn is at Narva. There are daily trains between Tallinn and Moscow (R6500, 15 hours). By bus you can connect to/from Tallinn with St Petersburg (from R850, 7½ hours, seven daily) and Kaliningrad (R1715, 14 hours, one daily).

Finland

BUS

There are many daily buses between Helsinki and St Petersburg (p224). Also see p328 for routes into and out of Finland from Northern European Russia.

CAR & MOTORCYCLE

Highways cross at the Finnish border posts of Nuijamaa and Vaalimaa (Brusnichnoe and Torfyanovka, respectively, on the Russian side). Fill up with petrol on the Finnish side (preferably before you get to the border petrol station, which is more expensive than others and closes early). Watch carefully for all road signs; a few roads involve tricky curves and signposting is not all it should be. It's best to make this drive during daylight hours.

TRAIN

High-speed Allegro trains (R4100, 3½ hours, four daily) connect St Petersburg and Helsinki. The daily 31/34 Leo Tolstoy service between Moscow and Helsinki (R5320, 13½ hours) also passes through St Petersburg (R3550, 6½ hours).

Kazakhstan

CAR & MOTORCYCLE

Roads into Kazakhstan head east from Astrakhan and south from Samara, Chelyabinsk, Orenburg and Omsk.

TRAIN

There are trains on even days between Moscow and Almaty (R10,300, three days and seven hours) and daily from Astrakhan to Atyrau (R1000, 14 hours) in addition to several services from Siberia.

Latvia

BUS

Rīga is connected by bus to St Petersburg (from R1000, 11 hours) and Kaliningrad (R950, nine hours).

CAR & MOTORCYCLE

The M9 Rīga–Moscow road crosses the border east of Rezekne (Latvia). The A212 road from Rīga leads to Pskov, crossing a corner of Estonia en route.

TRAIN

Overnight trains run daily between Rīga and Moscow (R6300, 16 hours) and St Petersburg (R6300, 13 hours).

Lithuania

BUS

From Kaliningrad there are services to Klaipėda (R445, four hours, two daily) and Vilnius (R920, six hours, one daily).

CAR & MOTORCYCLE

The border crossing points from Kaliningrad into Lithuania are Chernyshevskoe/Kibartay, Sovetsk/Panemune, Pogranichnoe/Ramonishkyay, and Morskoe/Nida.

TRAIN

Services link Vilnius with Kaliningrad (from R1500, six hours, three daily) Moscow (R5000, 15 hours, three daily) and St Petersburg (from R3800, 15¼ hours, two daily). The St Petersburg trains cross Latvia and the Moscow ones cross Belarus, for which you'll need a Belarus visa or transit visa.

Mongolia

BUS

There are direct daily buses between Ulaanbaatar and Ulan-Ude.

CAR & MOTORCYCLE

It's possible to drive between Mongolia and Russia at the Tsagaanuur–Tashanta and Altanbulag–Kyakhta borders. Getting through these borders can be a very slow process; it helps to have written permission from a Mongolian embassy if you wish to bring a vehicle through.

TRAIN

Apart from the trans-Mongolian train connecting Moscow and Beijing, there's a direct train twice a week from Ulaanbaatar to Moscow (R15,200, four days and five hours) as well as a daily service to and from Irkutsk (R4500, 27 hours).

Norway

BUS

See p328 for details of bus connections between Murmansk and Kirkenes.

CAR & MOTORCYCLE

The border crossing is at Storskog/Borisoglebsk on the Kirkenes–Murmansk road. As this is a sensitive border region, no stopping is allowed along the Russian side of this road. Also non-Russian registered vehicles are barred from the Nikel–Zapolyarnye section of the M18 highway between 11pm and 7am and any time on Tuesday, Thursday or Saturday. On those days you will be diverted via Prirechniy, a longer drive involving a rough, unpaved section.

Poland

BUS

There are two daily buses between both Gdansk and Oltshyn and Kaliningrad as well as daily buses to/from Warsaw. See p292 for more details.

CAR & MOTORCYCLE

The main border crossing to/from Kaliningrad is at Bezledy/Bagrationovsk on the A195 highway. Queues here can be very long.

TRAIN

Warsaw is connected with Moscow (R5850, 18 to 21 hours, two daily) and St Petersburg (R6825, 29 hours, daily). The Moscow trains enter Belarus near Brest. The St Petersburg trains leave Poland at Kuznica, which is near Hrodna (Grodno in Russian) in Belarus. Changing the wheels to/from Russia's wider gauge adds three hours to the journey. You'll need a Belarus visa or transit visa.

UK & Europe

Travelling overland by train from the UK or Western Europe takes a minimum of two days and nights.

There are no direct trains from the UK to Russia. The most straightforward route you can take is on the **Eurostar** (www.eurostar.com) to Brussels, and then a two-night direct train to Moscow via Warsaw and Minsk (Belarus). The total cost can be as low as £165 one way. See www.seat61.com/Russia.htm for details of this and other train services to Moscow.

Crossing the Poland–Belarus border at Brest takes several hours while the wheels are changed for the Russian track. All foreigners visiting Belarus need a visa, including those transiting by train – sort this out before arriving in Belarus. To avoid this hassle consider taking the train to St Petersburg from Vilnius in Lithuania, which runs several times a week via Latvia. There are daily connections between Vilnius and Warsaw.

From Moscow and St Petersburg there are also regular international services to European cities including Amsterdam, Berlin, Budapest, Nice, Paris, Prague and Vienna.

For European rail timetables check www.railfaneurope.net, which has links to all of Europe's national railways.

Ukraine

BUS

A handful of weekly buses travel from Kharkiv across the border into Russia on the E95 (M2) road. The official frontier crossing is 40km north of Kharkiv and is near the Russian border town of Zhuravlevka.

CAR & MOTORCYCLE

The main auto route between Kyiv and Moscow starts as the E93 (M20) north of Kyiv, but becomes the M3 when it branches off to the east some 50km south of Chernihiv.

Driving from Ukraine to the Caucasus, the border frontier point is on the E40 (M19) road crossing just before the Russian town of Novoshakhtinsk at the Ukrainian border village of Dovzhansky, about 150km east of Donetsk.

TRAIN

Most major Ukrainian cities have daily services to Moscow, with two border crossings: one used by trains heading to Kyiv, the other by trains passing through Kharkiv.

Trains from Kyiv to Moscow cross at the Ukrainian border town of Seredyna-Buda. The best trains on this route are as follows (specific numbers are southbound/northbound):

Moscow–Kyiv *firmeny* R7800, 9½ hours, 18 daily, 1/2

Moscow–Kyiv R4500, 9½ hours, 18 daily, 3/4

Moscow–Lviv R4700, 23 hours, daily via Kyiv, 73/74

Moscow–Odesa R4900, 23 hours, daily via Kyiv, 23/24

St Petersburg–Kyiv R5300, 24 hours, one daily, 53/54

St Petersburg–Lviv R5400, 37½ hours, three daily, 47/48

St Petersburg–Odesa R6000, 35 hours, one daily, 19/20

Trains on the Moscow–Kharkiv line (all of which pass through Kharkiv) serve the following destinations:

Donetsk R4300, 21 hours, two daily

Dnipropetrovsk R4700, 18 hours, two daily

Kharkiv R3000, 13 hours, about 14 daily via Tula, Oryol and Kursk

Kharkiv (night train) R4500, 19/20 (the Kharkiv)

Sevastopol R5300, 25½ hours, four daily

Simferopol R5700, 26 hours, daily, 67/68 (the Simferopol)

Zaporizhzhya R4900, 18 hours, 19 daily

Many trains travelling between Moscow and the Caucasus go through Kharkiv, including a daily service to Rostov-on-Don (12 hours). There are also daily international trains passing through Ukraine to/from Moscow's Kyivsky vokzal (station). These include the 15/16 Kyiv–Lviv–Chop–Budapest–Belgrade train, with a carriage to Zagreb three times a week.

Sea

Passenger ferries:

» Donghae (Korea) to Vladivostok (p587)

» Helsinki (Finland) to St Petersburg (p224)

» Lappeenranta (Finland) to Vyborg (p279)

» Sakaiminato (Japan) to Vladivostok (p587)

» Stockholm (Sweden) to St Petersburg (p224)

» Tallinn (Estonia) to St Petersburg (p224)

» Trabzon (Turkey) to Sochi (p422)

» Wakkanai (Japan) to Korsakov on Sakhalin (p605)

Tours

Trips to Moscow and St Petersburg are easily organised on your own. But for complex itineraries, having an agency assist in booking transport and accommodation, securing guides, and helping with the visa paperwork is a good idea. For many outdoor activities, such as hiking or rafting, the services of an expert agency or guide are almost always required. Or you may choose to go the whole hog and have everything taken care of on a fully organised tour.

The following agencies and tour companies provide a range of travel services; unless otherwise mentioned they can all help arrange visas and transport tickets within Russia. Numerous, more locally based agencies can provide tours once you're in Russia; see the destination chapters for details. Many work in conjunction with overseas agencies, so if you go to them directly you'll usually pay less.

Australia

Eastern Europe/Russian Travel Centre (☎02-9262 1144; www.eetbtravel.com)

Passport Travel (☎03-9500 0444; www.travelcentre.com.au)

Russian Gateway Tours (☎02-9745 3333; www.russian-gateway.com.au)

Sundowners (☎1300 133 457; www.sundownersoverland.com) Specialises in trans-Siberian packages and tours.

Travel Directors (☎08-9242 4200; www.traveldirectors.com.au) Upmarket trans-Siberian and Russian river cruise tour operator.

China

Monkey Business (☎8610-6591 6519; www.monkeyshrine.com) Tours on the trans-Siberian, trans-Manchurian and trans-Mongolian trains. Their Hong Kong branch is **Moonsky Star Ltd** (☎852-2723 1376).

Germany

Lernidee Reisen (☎030-786 0000; www.lernidee-reisen.de)

Japan

MO Tourist CIS Russian Centre (☎03-5296 5783; www.mo-tourist.co.jp) Can help arrange ferries and flights to Russia.

UK

Go Russia (☎020-3355 7717; www.justgorussia.co.uk) Cultural and adventure holiday specialist.

GW Travel Ltd (☎0161-928 9410; www.gwtravel.co.uk) Offers luxury trans-Siberian tours on the Golden Eagle.

Intourist Travel (☎0844-875 4026; www.intouristuk.com)

Regent Holidays (☎0845-277 3317; www.regent-holidays.co.uk)

The Russia Experience (☎0845-521 2910; www.trans-siberian.co.uk) Experienced and reliable operator that has adventurous programs across the country.

The Russia House (☎020-7403 9922; www.therussiahouse.co.uk) Agency experienced at dealing with

CLIMATE CHANGE & TRAVEL

Every form of transport that relies on carbon-based fuel generates CO_2, the main cause of human-induced climate change. Modern travel is dependent on aeroplanes, which might use less fuel per kilometre per person than most cars but travel much greater distances. The altitude at which aircraft emit gases (including CO_2) and particles also contributes to their climate change impact. Many websites offer 'carbon calculators' that allow people to estimate the carbon emissions generated by their journey and, for those who wish to do so, to offset the impact of the greenhouse gases emitted with contributions to portfolios of climate-friendly initiatives throughout the world. Lonely Planet offsets the carbon footprint of all staff and author travel.

corporate and business travel needs.

Russian Gateway (☎01926-426460; www.russiangateway.co.uk) Small specialist agency that offers mainly city-break packages and river cruises.

Russian National Tourist Office (☎020-7495 7570; www.visitrussia.org.uk) Offers tours across the country.

Travel for the Arts (☎020-8799 8350; www.travelforthearts.co.uk) Specialises in luxury culture-based tours to Russia for people with a specific interest in opera and ballet.

Voyages Jules Verne (☎0845-166 7003; www.vjv.co.uk) Offers a variety of upmarket tours.

USA

Exeter International (☎813-251 5355; www.exeterinternational.com) Specialises in luxury tours to Moscow and St Petersburg.

Go To Russia Travel (☎404-827 0099; www.gotorussia.com) Has offices in Atlanta, San Francisco and Moscow; offers tours and a full range of travel services.

Mir Corporation (☎20-6-624 7289; www.mircorp.com) Award-winning operation with many different tours.

Ouzel Expeditions (☎907-783 2216; www.ouzel.com) Specialises in Kamchatka fishing trips.

Red Star Travel (☎206-522 5995; www.travel2russia.com)

Sokol Tours (☎/fax 724-935 5373; www.sokoltours.com) Tour options include train trips, Tuva and Kamchatka.

Viking Rivers Cruises (☎0800-319 6660; www.vikingrivercruises.com)

VisitRussia.com (☎1800-755 3080; www.visitrussia.com) Can arrange package and customised tours; offices in New York, Moscow and St Petersburg.

World Wise Ecotourism Network (☎206-282 0824; www.traveleastrussia.com) Ecoadventure tour company specialising in the Russian Far East and Siberia.

GETTING AROUND

Getting around Russia is a breeze thanks to a splendid train network and a packed schedule of flights between all major and many minor towns and cities. In the summer months many of the rivers and lakes are navigable and have cruises and ferry operations. For hops between towns there are buses, most often *marshrutky* (fixed-route minibuses).

Don't underestimate the distances involved: Russia is huge. From Yekaterinburg at the western limits of Siberia to Vladivostok on the Pacific coast is about the same distance as from Berlin to New York, while even a relatively short overland hop, such as the one from Irkutsk to its near neighbour Khabarovsk, is still roughly equivalent to the distance from London to Cairo.

Air

Flying in Russia is like the country itself – a unique experience. Flights can be delayed, often for hours and with no or little explanation. Small town airports offer facilities similar to the average bus shelter.

Major Russian airlines allow you to book over the internet. Otherwise, it's no problem buying a ticket at ubiquitous *aviakassa* (ticket offices). Generally speaking, you'll do better booking internal flights once you arrive in Russia, where more flights and flight information are available and where prices may be lower.

Whenever you book airline tickets in Russia you'll need

AIRLINE SAFETY IN RUSSIA

Deadly lapses in Russian airline safety seem to be frighteningly common. The worst crash was in Irkutsk in August 2001, in which 145 people died, prompting the authorities to revoke scores of licences. A string of accidents involving Tupolevs – including ones in April 2010 near Smolensk which killed 96 people, including the Polish president, and in June 2011 near Petrozavodsk, killing 44 – has raised particular concerns about the continued use of these vintage planes.

However, prior to the June 2011 crash, the International Air Transport Association (IATA) had praised the nation's 13 largest carriers for their dedication in striving to meet international safety standards. None of these airlines, which include Aeroflot, Transaero and Rossiya, had recorded an accident involving the loss of life for the past three years.

If you're worried about airline safety, the good news is that for many destinations in Russia, getting there by train or bus is practical and often preferable (if you have the time). Also, on routes between major cities it's possible that you may have a choice of airlines. But in some cases – where you're short of time or where your intended destination doesn't have reliable rail or road connections – you will have no choice but to take a flight.

BUYING AIR TICKETS ONLINE

Online agencies specialising in Russian air tickets with English interfaces include **Anywayanyday** (☎495-363 6164; www.anywayanyday.com) and **Pososhok.ru** (☎495-234 8000; www.pososhok.ru).

Using modern 737s, **Sky Express** (airline code XW; ☎495-580 9360; www.skyexpress.ru/en; hub Vnukovo Airport, Moscow) is a Russian low-cost carrier with service between Moscow and Kaliningrad, Kazan, Murmansk, Perm, Rostov-on-Don, Sochi, St Petersburg, Tyumen and Yekaterinburg.

Primorsky AirAgency (☎4232-407 707; www.airagency.ru), a Vladivostok-based agency with branches in Moscow and St Petersburg, as well as across the Russian Far East, can also quote fares and has English-speaking agents.

to show your passport and visa. Tickets can also be purchased at the airport right up to the departure of the flight and sometimes even if the city centre office says that the plane is full. Return fares are usually double the one-way fares.

It's a good idea to reconfirm your flight at least 24 hours before take-off. Airlines may also bump you if you don't check in at least 60 minutes before departure and can be very strict about charging for checked bags that are overweight, which generally means anything over 20kg.

Have your passport and ticket handy throughout the various security and ticket checks that can occur, right up until you find a seat. Some flights have assigned seats, others do not. On the latter, seating is a free-for-all.

Most internal flights in Moscow use either Domodedovo or Vnukovo airports; if you're connecting to Moscow's Sheremetyevo-2 international airport, allow a few hours to cross town.

Boat

One of the most pleasant ways of travelling around Russia is by river. You can do this either by taking a cruise, which you can book directly with an operator or also through agencies in Russia and overseas, or by using scheduled river passenger services. The season runs from late May through mid-October, but is shorter on some routes.

Moscow, St Petersburg & the Volga

There are numerous cruise boats plying the routes between Moscow and St Petersburg, many stopping at some of the Golden Ring cities on the way. Longer cruises to Northern European Russia and south along the Volga also originate in either of these cities. Some cruises are specifically aimed at foreign tourists; see the Tours section in Getting There & Away in this chapter (p713) for listings of overseas travel companies that can book such trips.

Generally, for lower prices you can also sail on a boat aimed at Russian holidaymakers; note that it was one of these cruises that sank on the Volga near Kazan in July 2011, drowning over 120 people. Other boat operators and agencies:

Cruise Company Orthodox (☎499-943 8560; www.cruise.ru) Also has an office in Rostov-on-Don.

Infoflot (☎495-723 7352; www.infoflot.com) The market leader, with offices in St Petersburg, Samara, Nizhny Novgorod and Kazan.

Mosturflot (☎495-221 7222; www.mosturflot.ru)

Rechflot (☎499-755 8167; www.rechflot.ru)

Rechturflot (☎495-646 8700; www.rtflot.ru)

Solnechny Parus (☎812-327 3525; www.solpar.ru) St Petersburg agency with its own fleet of yachts and motorboats for charter.

Vodohod (☎495-223 9609; www.bestrussiancruises.com)

Northern European Russia

Northern European Russia (including St Petersburg) is well served by various water-borne transport options. Apart from hydrofoil services along the Neva River and the Gulf of Finland from St Petersburg to Petrodvorets, there are also very popular cruises from St Petersburg to Valaam in Lake Ladoga, some continuing on to Lake Onega, Petrozavodsk and Kizhi (p317). Also, from Rabocheostrovsk you can take boats to the Solovetsky Islands (p317).

Black Sea

Between June and September frequent hydrofoils connect the Black Sea ports of Novorossiysk and Sochi.

Siberia & the Russian Far East

Siberia and the Russian Far East have a short navigation season (mid-June to September), with long-distance river transport limited to the Ob and Irtysh Rivers (Omsk–Tara–Tobolsk–Salekhard), the Lena (Ust-Kut–Lensk–Yakutsk) and the Yenisey (Krasnoyarsk–Igarka–Dudinka). You can also make one-day hops by hydrofoil along several sections of these rivers, along the Amur River

(Khabarovsk–Komsomolsk–Nikolaevsk) and across Lake Baikal (Irkutsk–Olkhon–Severobaikalsk–Nizhneangarsk). Other Baikal services are limited to short hops around Irkutsk/Listvyanka and from Sakhyurta to Olkhon unless you charter a boat, most conveniently done in Listvyanka, Nizhneangarsk, Severobaikalsk or Ust-Barguzin. Irkutsk agencies can help.

Ferries from Vanino cross the Tatar Strait to Sakhalin, but it can be murder trying to buy a ticket in the summer months. Although sailings are supposed to take place daily, in reality there is no set schedule. There are also irregular sailings from Korsakov, on Sakhalin, across to Yuzhno-Kurilsk in the Kuril Island chain.

Out of Vladivostok there is a range of ferries to nearby islands and to beach resorts further south along the coast. For the truly adventurous with a month or so to spare, it may be possible to hitch a lift on one of the supply ships that sail out of Nakhodka and Vladivostok up to the Arctic Circle towns of Anadyr and Provideniya.

Beware that boat schedules can change radically from year to year (especially on Lake Baikal) and are published only infuriatingly near to the first sailing of each season.

USEFUL RUSSIAN TERMS FOR BOAT TRAVEL

When buying tickets for a hydrofoil, avoid rows *(ryad)* one to three – spray will obscure your view, and, although enclosed, you'll often get damp.

речной вокзал	*rechnoy vokzal*	river station
ракета, комета, заря	*raketa, kometa, zarya*	river-going hydrofoil
метеор	*meteor*	sea-going hydrofoil
теплоход	*teplokhod*	large passenger boat
катер	*kater*	smaller river or sea boat
корабл	*korabl*	generic word for large ship
лодка	*lodka*	small rowing boat
паром	*parom*	ferry
вверх	*vverkh*	upstream
вниз	*vniz*	downstream
туда	*tuda*	one way
туда и обратно	*tuda i obratno*	return

Bus & Marshrutky

Long-distance buses tend to complement rather than compete with the rail network. They generally serve areas with no railway or routes on which trains are slow, infrequent or overloaded.

Most cities have an intercity bus station (автовокзал, *avtovokzal*). Tickets are sold at the station or on the bus. Fares are normally listed on the timetable and posted on a wall. As often as not you'll get a ticket with a seat assignment, either printed or scribbled on a till receipt. If you have luggage that needs to be stored in the bus baggage compartment then you'll have to pay an extra fare, typically around 10% of the bus fare. We also found in 2011 that some bus stations were applying a small fee for security measures at bus stations to all tickets.

Marshrutky (a Russian diminutive form of *marshrutnoye taksi*, meaning a fixed-route taxi) are minibuses that are sometimes quicker than larger buses and rarely cost much more. Where roads are good and villages frequent, *marshrutky* can be twice as fast as buses and are well worth paying extra for.

Car & Motorcycle

Bearing in mind erratic road quality, lack of adequate signposting, fine-seeking highway police and, in remote areas, the difficulty of obtaining petrol (not to mention spare parts), driving in Russia can be a challenge. But if you've a sense of humour, patience and a decent vehicle, it's an adventurous way to go.

Motorbikes will undergo vigorous scrutiny by border officials and highway police, especially if you're riding anything vaguely flashy. Motorcyclists should also note that while foreign automobile companies now have an established presence in Moscow, St Petersburg and other major cities, you shouldn't count on being able to access any necessary spare parts across the country. A useful general site for motorcyclists, with some information on Russian road conditions, is www.horizonsunlimited.com.

Bringing Your Own Vehicle

You'll need the following if bringing in your own vehicle:

» Your licence

» The vehicle's registration papers

» Third-party insurance valid in Russia
» A customs declaration promising that you will take your vehicle with you when you leave

To minimise hassles, make sure you have all your documents translated into Russian. For more details see www.waytorussia.net/Transport/International/Car.html.

Driving Licence

To legally drive your own or a rented car or motorcycle in Russia you'll need the following:

» To be over 18 years of age
» Have a full driving licence
» Have an International Driving Permit with a Russian translation of your licence, or a certified Russian translation of your full licence (you can certify translations at a Russian embassy or consulate).

Fuel & Spare Parts

Western-style gas (petrol) stations are common. Petrol comes in four main grades and ranges from R25 to R30 per litre. Unleaded gas is available in major cities. *Dizel* (diesel) is also available (around R26 a litre). In the countryside, gas stations are usually not more than 100km apart, but you shouldn't rely on this.

Rental & Hire Cars

Self-drive cars can be rented in all major Russian cities. Depending on where you're going, consider renting a car with a driver – they will at least know the state of local roads and be able to negotiate with traffic police should you be stopped.

Private cars sometimes operate as cabs over long distances and can be a great deal if there's a group of you to share the cost. Since they take the most direct route between cities, the savings in time can be considerable over slow trains and meandering buses. Typically you will find drivers offering this service outside bus terminals. Someone in your party must speak Russian to negotiate a price with the driver which typically works out to about R30 per kilometre.

Select your driver carefully, look over their car and try to assess their sobriety before setting off. Note that you'll always have to pay return mileage if renting 'one way' and that many local drivers want to get home the same night, even if that's at 3am.

Road Conditions

Russian roads are a mixed bag – sometimes smooth, straight dual carriageways, sometimes pot-holed, narrow, winding and choked with the diesel fumes of slow, heavy vehicles. Driving much more than 300km in a day is pretty tiring.

Russian drivers use indicators far less than they should and like to overtake everything on the road – on the inside. They rarely switch on anything more than sidelights – and often not even those – until it's pitch black at night. Some say this is to avoid dazzling others, as, for some reason, dipping headlights is not common practice.

If an oncoming driver is flashing his headlights at you, this usually means to watch out for traffic police ahead.

Road Rules

» Drive on the right.
» Traffic coming from the right generally (but not always) has the right of way.
» Speed limits are generally 60km/h in towns and between 80km/h and 110km/h on highways.
» There may be a 90km/h zone, enforced by speed traps, as you leave a city.
» Children under 12 may not travel in the front seat; seatbelt use is mandatory.
» Motorcycle riders (and passengers) must wear crash helmets.
» The maximum legal blood-alcohol content is 0.03%, a rule that is strictly enforced. Police will first use a breathalyser test to check blood-alcohol levels. You have the legal right to insist on a blood test (which involves the police taking you to a hospital).
» Traffic lights that flicker green are about to change to yellow, then red. You will be pulled over if the police see you going through a yellow light, so drive cautiously.

The GIBDD

Russia's traffic police are officially called the GIBDD (ГИБДД standing for Государственная инспекция безопасности дорожного движения) but still commonly known by their previous acronym: the GAI. The traffic cops are authorised to stop you, issue on-the-spot fines and, worst of all, shoot at your car if you refuse to pull over.

The GIBDD are notorious for hosting speed traps – the Moscow–Brest, Moscow–Oryol and Vyborg–St Petersburg roads have reputations for this. In Moscow and St Petersburg, police are everywhere, stopping cars and collecting 'fines' on the spot.

There are permanent police checkpoints at the boundary of many Russian regions, cities and towns – make sure your car is clean and in good condition to avoid being pulled over. For serious infractions, the GIBDD can confiscate your licence, which you'll have to retrieve from the main station. If your car is taken to a police parking lot, you should try to get it back as soon as possible, since you'll be charged a huge amount for each day that it's kept there.

Get the shield number of the arresting officer. By law, GIBDD officers are not allowed to take any money at all – fines should be paid via Sberbank. However, in reality Russian drivers normally pay the police approximately half the official fine, thus saving money and the time eaten up by Russian bureaucracy, both at the police station and the bank.

Hitching

Hitching is never entirely safe and Lonely Planet doesn't recommend it. Travellers who hitch should understand that they are taking a small but potentially serious risk.

That said, hitching in Russia is a common method of getting around, particularly in the countryside and remote areas not well served by public transport. In cities, hitching rides is called hailing a taxi.

Rides are hailed by standing at the side of the road and flagging passing vehicles with a low, up-and-down wave (not an extended thumb). You are expected to pitch in for petrol; paying what would be the normal bus fare for a long-haul ride is considered appropriate.

Use common sense to keep safe. Avoid hitching at night. Women should exercise extreme caution. Avoid hitching alone and let someone know where you are planning to go.

Local Transport

Most cities have good public transport systems combining bus, trolleybus and tram; the biggest cities also have metro systems. Public transport is very cheap and easy to use, but you'll need to be able to decipher some Cyrillic. Taxis are plentiful.

Boat

In St Petersburg, Moscow and several other cities located on rivers, coasts, lakes or reservoirs, public ferries and water excursions give a different perspective. For details, see Getting Around in the relevant chapters or sections.

Bus, Marshrutky, Trolleybus & Tram

Services are frequent in city centres but more erratic as you move out towards the edges. They can get jam-packed in the late afternoon or on poorly served routes.

A stop is usually marked by a roadside 'A' sign for buses, 'T' for trolleybuses, and ТРАМВАЙ or a 'T' hanging over the road for trams. The fare (R10 to R20) is usually paid to the conductor; if there is no conductor, pass the money to the driver. You will be charged extra if you have a large bag that takes up space.

Within most cities, *marshrutky* double up official bus routes but are more frequent. They will also stop between official bus stops, which can save quite a walk.

Metro

The metro systems of Moscow and St Petersburg are excellent. There are smaller ones in Kazan, Nizhny Novgorod, Novosibirsk, Samara, Vologda and Yekaterinburg. See the Getting Around sections of the relevant city chapters for details on these systems.

Taxi

There are two main types of taxi in Russia: the official ones you order by phone (see city listings for numbers) and 'private' taxis (ie any other vehicle on the road).

Check with locals to determine the average taxi fare in that city at the time of your visit; taxi prices around the country vary widely. Practise saying your destination and the amount you want to pay so that it comes out properly. The better your Russian, the lower the fare (generally). If possible, let a Russian friend negotiate for you: they'll do better than you will.

OFFICIAL TAXIS

Official taxis have a meter that they sometimes use, though you can always negotiate an off-the-meter price. There's a flag fall, and the number on the meter must be multiplied by the multiplier listed on a sign that *should* be on the dashboard or somewhere visible. Extra charges are incurred for radio calls and some night-time calls. Taxis outside of luxury hotels often demand usurious rates although, on the whole, official taxis are around 25% more expensive than private taxis.

PRIVATE TAXIS

To hail a private taxi, stand at the side of the road, extend your arm and wait until something stops. When someone stops for you, state your destination and be prepared to negotiate the fare – fix this before getting in. If the driver's game, they'll ask you to get in *(sadites)*. Consider your safety before doing this.

RISKS & PRECAUTIONS

» Avoid taxis lurking outside foreign-run establishments, luxury hotels, railway stations and airports – they often charge far too much.

» Know your route: be familiar with how to get there and how long it should take.

» Never get into a taxi that has more than one person already in it, especially after dark.

» Keep your fare money in a separate pocket to avoid flashing large wads of cash.

» If you're staying at a private residence, have the taxi stop at the corner nearest your destination, not the exact address.

» Trust your instincts – if a driver looks creepy, take the next car.

Tours

Once in Russia, you'll find many travel agencies specialising in city tours and excursions. Sometimes these are the best way to visit out-of-the-way sights. See the travel agencies listed in the relevant city sections.

Trains

The trains of **Russian Railways** (RZD or РЖД; http://rzd.ru) are generally comfortable and, depending on the class of travel, relatively inexpensive for the distances covered. Every train in Russia has two numbers – one for the eastbound train (even-numbered trains) and one for the westbound (odd-numbered trains).

A handful of new high-speed services aside, trains are rarely speedy but have a remarkable record for punctuality – if you're a minute late for your train, the chances are you'll be left standing on the platform. The fact that RZD managers have a large portion of their pay determined by the timeliness of their trains not only inspires promptness, but also results in the creation of generous schedules. You'll notice this when you find your train stationary for hours in the middle of nowhere only to suddenly start up and roll into the next station right on time.

Buying Tickets

There are a number of options on where to buy, including online. Bookings open 45 days before the date of departure. You'd be wise to buy well in advance over the busy summer months and holiday periods such as New Year and early May, when securing berths at short notice on certain trains can be difficult. Tickets for key trains on the busy Moscow–St Petersburg route can also be difficult to come by, although those with flexible options should be able to find something.

Even if you're told a particular service is sold out, it still may be possible to get on the train by speaking with the chief *provodnitsa* (see p45). Tell her your destination, offer the face ticket price first and move slowly upwards from there. You can usually come to some sort of agreement.

AT THE STATION

You'll be confronted by several ticket windows. Some are special windows reserved exclusively for use by the elderly or infirm, heroes of the Great Patriotic War or members of the armed forces. All will have different operating hours and generally non-English-speaking staff.

The sensible option, especially if there are long queues, is to avail yourself of the service centre (сервис центр) found at most major stations. Here you'll encounter helpful staff who, for a small fee (typically around R200), can book your ticket. They sometimes speak English.

Tickets for suburban trains are often sold at separate windows or from an automatic ticket machine (автомат). A table beside the machine tells you which price zone your destination is in.

AT TRAVEL AGENCIES AND TICKET BUREAUX

In big cities and towns it's possible to buy tickets at special offices and some travel agencies away from the station – individual chapters provide details.

ONLINE

You can buy tickets online directly from RZD and other agencies (see p43) and have the ticket delivered to your home or hotel, or pick it up at an agency or at the train station. RZD has two types of electronic tickets:

» **e-tickets** – these are email vouchers that you print out and exchange for paper tickets at stations in Russia. Some stations (ie those in Moscow, St Petersburg, Irkutsk, Kazan, Nizhny Novgorod, Novosibirsk, Omsk, Rostov-on-Don, Samara, Yekaterinburg and Vladivostok) have dedicated exchange points; at all others you go to the regular booking windows.

» **e-registration** – only available for trains where you board at the initial station of the service, these are 'paperless' tickets; you'll still be sent an email confirmation but there's no need to exchange this for a regular ticket. You show the confirmation email and your passport to the *provodnitsa* on boarding the train.

Long Distances

The regular long-distance service is a *skory poezd* (fast train). It rarely gets up enough speed to really merit the 'fast' label. The best *skory* trains often have names, eg the Rossiya (the Moscow to Vladivostok service) and the Baikal (the Moscow to Irkutsk service). These 'name trains', or *firmeny poezda*, generally have cleaner cars, polite(r) attendants and more convenient arrival and departure hours; they sometimes also have fewer stops, more first-class accommodation and functioning restaurants.

A *passazhirsky poezd* (passenger train) is an inter-city train, found mostly on routes of 1000km or less. Journeys on these can take longer, as the trains clank from one small town to the next. However, they are inexpensive and often well timed to allow an overnight sleep between neighbouring cities. Avoid trains numbered over 900. These are primarily baggage or postal services and are appallingly slow.

Short Distances

A *prigorodny poezd* (suburban train), commonly nicknamed an *elektrichka*, is a local service linking a city with its suburbs or nearby towns, or groups of adjacent towns – they are often useful for day trips, but can be fearfully crowded. There's no need to book ahead for these – just buy your ticket and go. In bigger stations there may be separate time-

READING A TRAIN TIMETABLE

Russian train timetables vary from place to place but generally list a destination; number and category of train; frequency of service; and time of departure and arrival, in Moscow time unless otherwise noted. For services that originate somewhere else, you'll see a starting point and the final destination on the timetable. For example, when catching a train from Yekaterinburg to Irkutsk, the timetable may list Moscow as the point of origin and Irkutsk as the destination. The following are the key points to look out for.

Number

» Номер (*nomer*) The higher the number of a train, the slower it is; anything over 900 is likely to be a mail train.

Category

» Скорый (*Skory*, fast trains)

» Пассажирский (*Passazhirsky*, passenger trains)

» Почтово-багажный (*Pochtovo-bagazhny*, post-cargo trains)

» Пригородный (*Prigorodny*, suburban trains)

There may also be the name of the train, usually in quotation marks, eg 'Россия' ('Rossiya').

Frequency

» ежедневно (*yezhednevno*, daily; abbreviated еж)

» чётные (*chyotnye*, even-numbered dates; abbreviated ч)

» нечётные (*nechyotnye*, odd-numbered dates; abbreviated не)

» отменён (*otmenyon*, cancelled; abbreviated отмен)

Days of the week are listed usually as numbers (where 1 is Monday and 7 Sunday) or as abbreviations of the name of the day (Пон, Вт, Ср, Чт, Пт, С and Вск are, respectively, Monday to Sunday). Remember that time-zone differences can affect these days. So in Chita (Moscow +6hr) a train timetabled at 23.20 on Tuesday actually leaves 5.20am on

tables, in addition to *prigorodny zal* (the usual name for ticket halls) and platforms for these trains.

Timetables

Timetables are posted in stations and are revised twice a year. It's vital to note that the whole Russian rail network runs mostly on Moscow time, so timetables and station clocks from Kaliningrad to Vladivostok will be written in and set to Moscow time. Suburban rail services are the only general exception, which are usually listed in local time; it's best to check this.

Most stations have an information window; expect the attendant to speak only Russian and to give a bare minimum of information. Bigger stations will also have computerised terminals where you can check the timetable.

The boxed text in this section will help you crack the timetable code. Online timetables are available on RZD's website (http://rzd.ru), www.poezda.net and the sites mentioned in the boxed text on p43.

Classes

In all classes of carriage with sleeping accommodation, if you've not already paid for a pack of bed linen and face towels (called *pastil*) in your ticket price, the *provodnitsa* (the female carriage attendant; see p45) will offer it to you for a small charge, typically around R60. In 1st class the bed is usually made up already.

For more details about what each of the different classes of ticket cost see p43.

1ST CLASS/SV

Most often called SV (which is short for *spalny vagon*, or sleeping wagon), 1st-class compartments are also called *myagky* (soft class) or *lyux*. They are the same size as 2nd class but have only two berths, so there's more room and more privacy for double the cost. Some 1st-class compartments also have TVs on which it's possible to watch videos or DVDs supplied by the *provodnitsa* for a small fee (there's nothing to stop you from bringing your own, although they'll need to work on a Russian DVD player). You can also unplug the TV and plug in your computer or other electrical equipment. These carriages

Wednesday. In months with an odd number of days, two odd days follow one another (eg 31 May, 1 June). This throws out trains working on an alternate-day cycle so if travelling near month's end pay special attention to the hard-to-decipher footnotes on a timetable. For example, '27/V – 3/VI ч' means that from 27 May to 3 June the train runs on even dates. On some trains, frequency depends on the time of year, in which case details are usually given in similar abbreviated small print: eg '27/VI – 31/VIII ч; 1/IX – 25/VI 2, 5' means that from 27 June to 31 August the train runs on even dates, while from 1 September to 25 June it runs on Tuesday and Friday.

Arrival & Departure Times

Corresponding trains running in opposite directions on the same route may appear on the same line of the timetable. In this case you may find route entries like время отправления с конечного пункта *(vremya otpravlenia s konechnogo punkta)*, or the time the return train leaves its station of origin. Train times are given in a 24-hour time format, and almost always in Moscow time (Московское время, *Moskovskoye vremya*). But suburban trains are usually marked in local time (местное время, *mestnoe vremya*). From here on it gets tricky (as though the rest wasn't), so don't confuse the following:

- время отправления *(vremya otpravleniya)* Time of departure
- время отправления с начального пункта *(vremya otpravleniya s nachalnogo punkta)* Time of departure from the train's starting point
- время прибытия *(vremya pribytiya)* Time of arrival at the station you're in
- время прибытия на конечный пункт *(vremya pribytiya v konechny punkt)* Time of arrival at the destination
- время в пути *(vremya v puti)* Duration of the journey

Distance

You may sometimes see the растояние *(rastoyaniye)* – distance in kilometres from the point of departure – on the timetable as well. These are rarely accurate and usually refer to the kilometre distance used to calculate the fare.

have the advantage of having only half as many people queuing to use the toilet every morning. A couple of special services between Moscow and St Petersburg and Moscow and Kazan offer luxury SV compartments, each with their own shower and toilet.

2ND CLASS/KUPE

The compartments in a *kupeyny* (2nd class, also called 'compartmentalised' carriage) – commonly shortened to *kupe* – are the standard accommodation on all long-distance trains. These carriages are divided into nine enclosed compartments, each with four reasonably comfortable berths, a fold-down table and just enough room between the bunks to turn around.

In every carriage there's also one half-sized compartment with just two berths. This is usually occupied by the *provodnitsa* or reserved for railway employees; it's where you may end up if you do a deal directly with a *provodnitsa* for a train ticket.

3RD CLASS/PLATSKARTNY

A reserved-place *platskartny* carriage, sometimes also called *zhyostky* ('hard class') and usually abbreviated to *platskart*, is essentially a dorm carriage sleeping 54. The bunks are uncompartmentalised and are arranged in blocks of four down one side of the corridor and in twos on the other, with the lower bunk on the latter side converting to a table and chairs during the day.

Despite the lack of privacy, *platskart* is a deal for one-night journeys. In summer, the lack of compartment walls means they don't become as stuffy as a *kupe*. Many travellers (women in particular) find *platskart* a better option than being cooped up with three (possibly drunken) Russian men. It's also a great way to meet ordinary Russians. *Platskart* tickets cost half to two-thirds the price of a 2nd-class berth.

However, on multiday journeys some *platskart* carriages can begin to resemble a refugee camp, with clothing strung between bunks, a great swapping of bread, fish and jars of tea, and babies sitting on potties while their snot-nosed siblings tear up and down the corridor. Only

HOW TO BUY & READ YOUR TICKET

When buying a ticket in Russia, it's a good idea to arrive at the station or travel agency prepared. If you don't speak Russian, have someone who does write down the following information for you in Cyrillic:

» How many tickets you require

» Your destination

» What class of ticket

» The preferred date of travel and time of day for departure. Use ordinary (Arabic) numerals for the day and Roman numerals for the month.

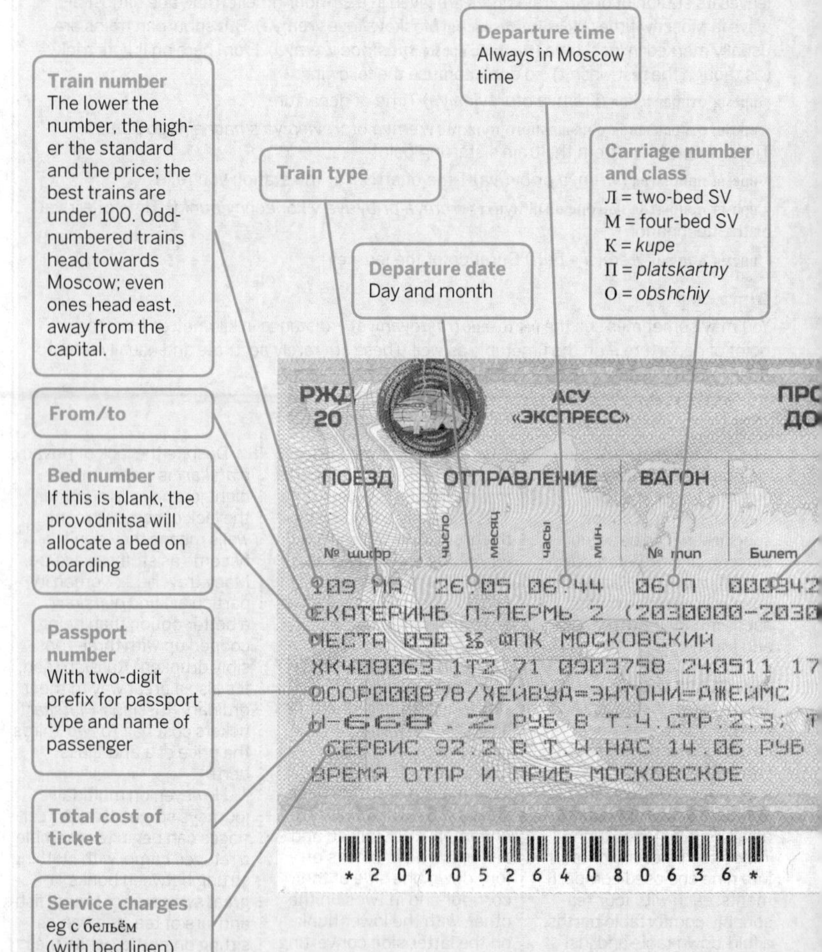

Also bring your passport; you'll be asked for it so that its number and your name can be printed on your ticket. The ticket and passport will be matched up by the *provodnitsa* (female carriage attendant) before you're allowed on the train – make sure the ticket-seller gets these details correct.

Tickets are printed by computer and come with a duplicate. Shortly after you've boarded the train the *provodnitsa* will come around and collect the tickets: sometimes they will take both copies and give you one back just before your final destination; often they will leave you with the copy. It will have been ripped slightly to show it's been used. Hang on to this ticket, especially if you're hopping on and off trains, since it provides evidence of how long you've been in a particular place if you're stopped by police.

Sometimes tickets are also sold with separate chits for insurance in the event of a fatal accident, or for bed linen and meals, but usually these prices appear on the ticket itself. The following is a guide for deciphering your Russian train ticket.

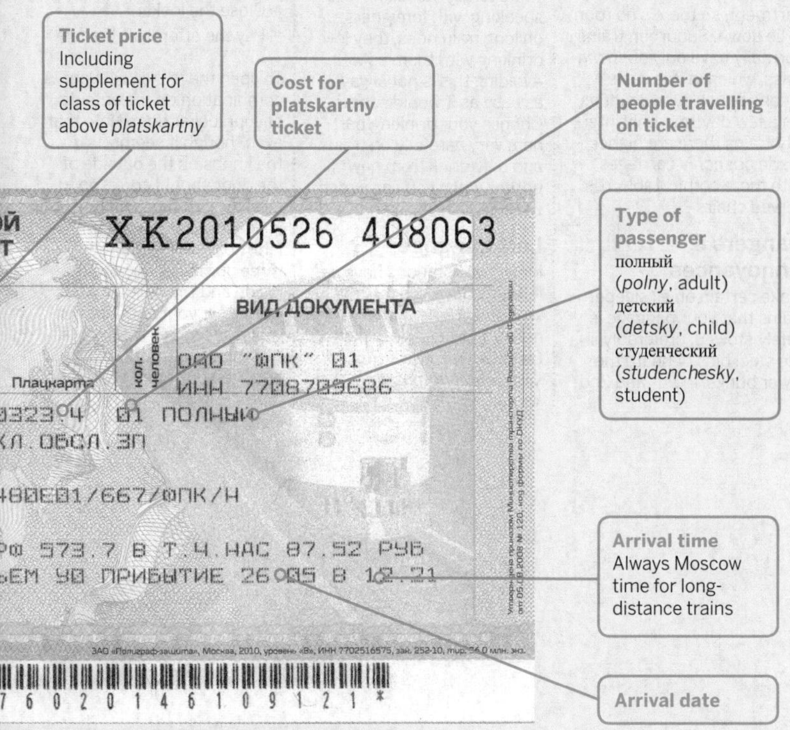

the hardy would want to do Moscow to Vladivostok or a similar nonstop journey this way.

If you do travel *platskart*, it's worth requesting specific numbered seats when booking your ticket. The ones to avoid are 1 to 4, 33 to 38, and 53 and 54, found at each end of the carriage close to the samovar and toilets, where people are constantly coming and going. Also note that 39 to 52 are the doubles with the bunk that converts to a table.

4TH CLASS/OBSHCHIY

Obshchiy (general) is unreserved. On long-distance trains the *obshchiy* carriage looks the same as a *platskartny* one but, when full, eight people are squeezed into each unenclosed compartment, so there's no room to lie down. Suburban trains normally have only *obshchiy* class, which in this case means bench-type seating. On a few daytime-only intercity trains there are higher grade *obshchiy* carriages with more comfortable, reserved chairs.

Dangers & Annoyances

Make certain on all sleeper trains that your baggage is safely stowed, preferably in the steel bins beneath the lower bunks. In 1st- and 2nd-class compartments you can lock the door but remember that it can be unlocked with a rather simple key; on the left side of the door, about three-quarters of the way up, there's a small steel switch that flips up, blocking the door from opening more than a few centimetres. Flip this switch up and make sure to stuff a piece of cork or equivalent in the cavity so it can't be flipped back down by a bent coat hanger.

At station halts it's also a good idea to ask the *provodnitsa* to lock your compartment while you go down to stretch your legs on the platform. In cheaper *platskartny* carriages your unguarded possessions are often safer as there are more people around to keep watch.

Generally, Russians love speaking with foreigners; on long train rides, they love drinking with them as well. Avoiding this is not always as easy as it would seem. Choose your drinking partners very carefully on trains and only drink from new bottles when you can watch the seal being broken.

Left Luggage

Many train stations have a left-luggage room (камера хранения, *kamera khranenia*) or left-luggage lockers (автоматические камеры хранения, *avtomaticheskiye kamery khranenia*). These are generally secure, but make sure you note down the room's opening and closing hours and, if in doubt, establish how long you can leave your stuff. Typical costs are around R100 per bag per day (according to size) or R100 per locker.

Here is how to work the left-luggage lockers (they're generally the same everywhere). Be suspicious of people who offer to help you work them, above all when it comes to selecting your combination.

» Put your stuff in an empty locker.

» Decide on a combination of one Russian letter and three numbers and write it down or remember it.

» Set the combination on the inside of the locker door.

» Close the locker.

» Pay the attendant the fee.

To open the locker, set your combination on the outside of your locker door. Note that even though it seems as if the knobs on the outside of the door should correspond directly with those on the inside, the letter is always the left-most knob, followed by three numbers, on both the inside and the outside. After you've set your combination, wait a second or two for the electrical humming sound and then pull open the locker.

WANT MORE?

For in-depth language information and handy phrases, check out Lonely Planet's *Russian Phrasebook*. You'll find it at **shop .lonelyplanet.com**, or you can buy Lonely Planet's iPhone phrasebooks at the Apple App Store.

Russian belongs to the Slavonic language family and is closely related to Belarusian and Ukrainian. It has more than 150 million speakers within the Russian Federation and is used as a second language in the former republics of the USSR, with a total number of speakers of more than 270 million people.

Russian is written in the Cyrillic alphabet (see the next page), and it's well worth the effort familiarising yourself with it so that you can read maps, timetables, menus and street signs. Otherwise, just read the coloured pronunciation guides given next to each Russian phrase in this chapter as if they were English, and you'll be understood. Most sounds are the same as in English, and the few differences in pronunciation are explained in the alphabet table. The stressed syllables are indicated with italics.

BASICS

Hello.	Здравствуйте.	*zdrast*·vuy·tye
Goodbye.	До свидания.	da svi·*da*·nya
Excuse me.	Простите.	pras·*ti*·tye
Sorry.	Извините.	iz·vi·*ni*·tye
Please.	Пожалуйста.	pa·*zhal*·sta
Thank you.	Спасибо.	spa·*si*·ba
You're welcome.	Пожалуйста.	pa·*zhal*·sta
Yes./No.	Да./Нет.	da/nyet

How are you?
Как дела? — kak di·*la*

Fine. And you?
Хорошо. А у вас? — kha·ra·*sho* a u vas

What's your name?
Как вас зовут? — kak vas za·*vut*

My name is ...
Меня зовут ... — mi·*nya za*·vut ...

Do you speak English?
Вы говорите по-английски? — vi ga·va·*ri*·tye pa·an·*gli*·ski

I don't understand.
Я не понимаю. — ya nye pa·ni·*ma*·yu

ACCOMMODATION

Where's a ...?	Где ...?	gdye ...
boarding house	пансионат	pan·si·a·*nat*
campsite	кемпинг	*kyem*·ping
hotel	гостиница	ga·*sti*·ni·tsa
youth hostel	общежитие	ap·shi·*zhih*·ti·ye

Do you have a ... room?	У вас есть ...?	u vas yest' ...
single	одноместный номер	ad·na·*myest*·nih *no*·mir
double	номер с двуспальней кроватью	*no*·mir z dvu·*spal'*·nyey kra·*va*·tyu

How much is it for ...?	Сколько стоит за ...?	*skol'*·ka *sto*·it za ...
a night	ночь	noch'
two people	двоих	dva·*ikh*

The ... isn't working.	... не работает.	... ne ra·*bo*·ta·yit
heating	Отопление	a·ta·*plye*·ni·ye
hot water	Горячая вода	ga·*rya*·cha·ya va·*da*
light	Свет	svyet

CYRILLIC ALPHABET

Cyrillic	Sound	
А, а	a	as in 'father' (in a stressed syllable); as in 'ago' (in an unstressed syllable)
Б, б	b	as in 'but'
В, в	v	as in 'van'
Г, г	g	as in 'god'
Д, д	d	as in 'dog'
Е, е	ye	as in 'yet' (in a stressed syllable and at the end of a word);
	i	as in 'tin' (in an unstressed syllable)
Ё, ё	yo	as in 'yore' (often printed without dots)
Ж, ж	zh	as the 's' in 'measure'
З, з	z	as in 'zoo'
И, и	i	as the 'ee' in 'meet'
Й, й	y	as in 'boy' (not transliterated after **ы** or **и**)
К, к	k	as in 'kind'
Л, л	l	as in 'lamp'
М, м	m	as in 'mad'
Н, н	n	as in 'not'
О, о	o	as in 'more' (in a stressed syllable);
	a	as in 'hard' (in an unstressed syllable)
П, п	p	as in 'pig'
Р, р	r	as in 'rub' (rolled)
С, с	s	as in 'sing'
Т, т	t	as in 'ten'
У, у	u	as the 'oo' in 'fool'
Ф, ф	f	as in 'fan'
Х, х	kh	as the 'ch' in 'Bach'
Ц, ц	ts	as in 'bits'
Ч, ч	ch	as in 'chin'
Ш, ш	sh	as in 'shop'
Щ, щ	shch	as 'sh-ch' in 'fresh chips'
Ъ, ъ	–	'hard sign' meaning the preceding consonant is pronounced as it's written
Ы, ы	ih	as the 'y' in 'any'
Ь, ь	'	'soft sign' meaning the preceding consonant is pronounced like a faint y
Э, э	e	as in 'end'
Ю, ю	yu	as the 'u' in 'use'
Я, я	ya	as in 'yard' (in a stressed syllable);
	ye	as in 'yearn' (in an unstressed syllable)

DIRECTIONS

Where is ...?
Где ...? gdye ...

What's the address?
Какой адрес? ka·*koy* a·dris

Could you write it down, please?
Запишите, пожалуйста. za·pi·*shih*·tye pa·*zhal*·sta

Can you show me (on the map)?
Покажите мне, пожалуйста (на карте). pa·ka·*zhih*·tye mnye pa·*zhal*·sta (na *kar*·tye)

Turn ...	Поверните ...	pa·vir·*ni*·tye ...
at the corner	за угол	za *u*·gal
at the traffic lights	на светофоре	na svi·ta·*fo*·rye
left	налево	na·*lye*·va
right	направо	na·*pra*·va

behind ...	за ...	za ...
far	далеко	da·li·*ko*
in front of ...	перед ...	*pye*·rit ...
near	близко	*blis*·ka
next to ...	рядом с ...	*rya*·dam s ...
opposite ...	напротив ...	na·*pro*·tif ...
straight ahead	прямо	*prya*·ma

EATING & DRINKING

I'd like to reserve a table for ...	Я бы хотел/хотела заказать столик на ... (m/f)	ya bih khat·*yel*/khat·*ye*·la za·ka·*zat'* *sto*·lik na ...
two people	двоих	dva·*ikh*
eight o'clock	восемь часов	*vo*·sim' chi·*sof*

What would you recommend?
Что вы рекомендуете? shto vih ri·ka·min·*du*·it·ye

What's in that dish?
Что входит в это блюдо? shto *fkho*·dit v e·ta *blyu*·da

That was delicious!
Было очень вкусно! *bih*·la o·chin' *fkus*·na

Please bring the bill.
Принесите, пожалуйста счёт. pri·ni·*sit*·ye pa·*zhal*·sta shot

I don't eat ...	Я не ем ...	ya nye yem ...
eggs	яиц	*ya*·its
fish	рыбы	*rih*·bih
poultry	птицы	*ptit*·sih
red meat	мяса	*mya*·sa

Key Words

bottle	бутылка	bu·*tihl*·ka
bowl	миска	*mis*·ka
breakfast	завтрак	*zaf*·trak
cold	холодный	kha·*lod*·nih
dinner	ужин	*u*·zhihn
dish	блюдо	*blyu*·da
fork	вилка	*vil*·ka
glass	стакан	sta·*kan*
hot (warm)	жаркий	*zhar*·ki
knife	нож	nosh
lunch	обед	ab·*yet*
menu	меню	min·*yu*
plate	тарелка	tar·*yel*·ka
restaurant	ресторан	ris·ta·*ran*
spoon	ложка	*losh*·ka
with/without	с/без	s/byez

Meat & Fish

beef	говядина	gav·*ya*·di·na
caviar	икра	i·*kra*
chicken	курица	*ku*·rit·sa
duck	утка	*ut*·ka
fish	рыба	*rih*·ba
herring	сельдь	syelt'
lamb	баранина	ba·*ra*·ni·na
meat	мясо	*mya*·sa
oyster	устрица	*ust*·rit·sa
pork	свинина	svi·*ni*·na
prawn	креветка	kriv·*yet*·ka
salmon	лососина	la·sa·*si*·na
turkey	индейка	ind·*yey*·ka
veal	телятина	til·*ya*·ti·na

Fruit & Vegetables

apple	яблоко	*yab*·la·ka
bean	фасоль	fa·*sol'*
cabbage	капуста	ka·*pu*·sta
capsicum	перец	*pye*·rits
carrot	морковь	mar·*kof'*
cauliflower	цветная капуста	tsvit·*na*·ya ka·*pu*·sta
cucumber	огурец	a·gur·*yets*
fruit	фрукты	*fruk*·tih
mushroom	гриб	grip
nut	орех	ar·*yekh*
onion	лук	luk
orange	апельсин	a·pil'·*sin*
peach	персик	*pyer*·sik
pear	груша	*gru*·sha
plum	слива	*sli*·va
potato	картошка	kar·*tosh*·ka
spinach	шпинат	shpi·*nat*
tomato	помидор	pa·mi·*dor*
vegetable	овощ	*o*·vash

Signs

Вход	Entrance
Выход	Exit
Открыт	Open
Закрыт	Closed
Справки	Information
Запрещено	Prohibited
Туалет	Toilets
Мужской (М)	Men
Женский (Ж)	Women

Other

bread	хлеб	khlyep
cheese	сыр	sihr
egg	яйцо	yeyt·*so*
honey	мёд	myot
oil	масло	*mas*·la
pasta	паста	*pa*·sta
pepper	перец	*pye*·rits
rice	рис	ris
salt	соль	sol'
sugar	сахар	*sa*·khar
vinegar	уксус	*uk*·sus

Drinks

beer	пиво	*pi*·va
coffee	кофе	*kof*·ye
(orange) juice	(апельсин-овый) сок	(a·pil'·*si*·na·vih) sok
milk	молоко	ma·la·*ko*
tea	чай	chey
(mineral) water	(минеральная) вода	(mi·ni·*ral'*·na·ya) va·*da*
wine	вино	vi·*no*

EMERGENCIES

Help!	Помогите!	pa·ma·*gi*·tye
Call ...!	Вызовите ...!	*vih*·za·vi·tye ...
a doctor	врача	vra·*cha*
the police	милицию	mi·*li*·tsih·yu

Leave me alone!
Приваливай! pri·*va*·li·vai

There's been an accident.
Произошёл несчастный случай. pra·i·za·*shol* ne·*shas*·nih *slu*·chai

I'm lost.
Я заблудился/заблудилась. (m/f) ya za·blu·*dil*·sa/za·blu·*di*·las'

Where are the toilets?
Где здесь туалет? gdye zdyes' tu·al·*yet*

I'm ill.
Я болен/больна. (m/f) ya *bo*·lin/bal'·*na*

It hurts here.
Здесь болит. zdyes' ba·*lit*

I'm allergic to (antibiotics).
У меня алергия на (антибиотики). u min·*ya* a·lir·*gi*·ya na (an·ti·bi·o·ti·ki)

SHOPPING & SERVICES

I need ...
Мне нужно ... mnye *nuzh*·na ...

I'm just looking.
Я просто смотрю. ya *pros*·ta smat·*ryu*

Can I look at it?
Покажите, пожалуйста. pa·ka·*zhih*·tye pa·*zhal*·sta

How much is it?
Сколько стоит? *skol'*·ka *sto*·it

That's too expensive.
Это очень дорого. e·ta o·chen' *do*·ra·ga

There's a mistake in the bill.
Меня обсчитали. min·*ya* ap·shi·*ta*·li

bank	банк	bank
market	рынок	*rih*·nak
post office	почта	*poch*·ta
telephone office	телефонный пункт	ti·li·*fo*·nih punkt

Question Words

What?	Что?	shto
When?	Когда?	kag·*da*
Where?	Где?	gdye
Which?	Какой?	ka·*koy*
Who?	Кто?	kto
Why?	Почему?	pa·chi·*mu*

TIME, DATES & NUMBERS

What time is it?
Который час? ka·*to*·rih chas

It's (10) o'clock.
(Десять) часов. (*dye*·sit') chi·*sof*

morning	утро	*ut*·ra
afternoon	после обеда	*pos*·lye ab·*ye*·da
evening	вечер	*vye*·chir
yesterday	вчера	vchi·*ra*
today	сегодня	si·*vod*·nya
tomorrow	завтра	*zaft*·ra

Monday	понедельник	pa·ni·*dyel'*·nik
Tuesday	вторник	*ftor*·nik
Wednesday	среда	sri·*da*
Thursday	четверг	chit·*vyerk*
Friday	пятница	*pyat*·ni·tsa
Saturday	суббота	su·*bo*·ta
Sunday	воскресенье	vas·kri·*syen*·ye

January	январь	yan·*var'*
February	февраль	fiv·*ral'*
March	март	mart
April	апрель	ap·*ryel'*
May	май	mai
June	июнь	i·*yun'*
July	июль	i·*yul'*
August	август	*av*·gust
September	сентябрь	sin·*tyabr'*
October	октябрь	ak·*tyabr'*
November	ноябрь	na·*yabr'*
December	декабрь	di·*kabr'*

1	один	a·*din*
2	два	dva
3	три	tri
4	четыре	chi·*tih*·ri
5	пять	pyat'
6	шесть	shest'
7	семь	syem'
8	восемь	*vo*·sim'
9	девять	*dye*·vyat'
10	десять	*dye*·syat'
20	двадцать	*dva*·tsat'
30	тридцать	*tri*·tsat'
40	сорок	*so*·rak
50	пятьдесят	pi·dis·*yat*
60	шестдесят	shihs·dis·*yat*
70	семьдесят	*syem'*·dis·yat

80	восемьдесят	*vo*·sim'·di·sit
90	девяносто	di·vi·*no*·sta
100	сто	sto
1000	тысяча	*tih*·si·cha

TRANSPORT

Public Transport

A ... ticket (to Novgorod).	Билет ... (на Новгород).	bil·*yet* ... (na *nov*·ga·rat)
one-way	в один конец	v a·*din* kan·*yets*
return	в оба конца	v *o*·ba kan·*tsa*

bus	автобус	af·*to*·bus
train	поезд	*po*·ist
tram	трамвай	tram·*vai*
trolleybus	троллейбус	tra·*lyey*·bus

first	первый	*pyer*·vih
last	последний	pas·*lyed*·ni
metro token	жетон	zhi·*ton*
platform	платформа	plat·*for*·ma
(bus) stop	остановка	a·sta·*nof*·ka
ticket	билет	bil·*yet*
ticket office	билетная касса	bil·*yet*·na·ya *ka*·sa
timetable	расписание	ras·pi·*sa*·ni·ye

When does it leave?
Когда отправляется? kag·*da* at·prav·*lya*·it·sa

How long does it take to get to ...?
Сколько времени нужно ехать до ...? *skol'*·ka *vrye*·mi·ni *nuzh*·na *ye*·khat' da ...

Does it stop at ...?
Поезд останавливается в ...? *po*·yist a·sta·*nav*·li·va·yit·sa v ...

Please stop here.
Остановитесь здесь, пожалуйста! a·sta·na·*vit*·yes' zdyes' pa·*zhal*·sta

Driving & Cycling

I'd like to hire a ...	Я бы хотел/ хотела взять ... на прокат. (m/f)	ya bih kha·*tyel*/ kha·*tye*·la vzyat' ... na pra·*kat*
4WD	машину с полным приводом	ma·*shih*·nu s *pol*·nihm pri·*vo*·dam
bicycle	велосипед	vi·la·si·*pyet*
car	машину	ma·*shih*·nu
motorbike	мотоцикл	ma·ta·*tsikl*

KEY PATTERNS

To get by in Russian, mix and match these simple patterns with words of your choice:

When's (the next bus)?
Когда (будет следующий автобус)? kag·*da* (*bu*·dit *slye*·du·yu·shi af·*to*·bus)

Where's (the station)?
Где (станция)? gdye (*stant*·sih·ya)

Where can I (buy a padlock)?
Где можно (купить нависной замок)? gdye *mozh*·na (ku·*pit'* na·vis·*noy* za·*mok*)

Do you have (a map)?
Здесь есть (карте)? zdyes' yest' (*kart*·ye)

I'd like (the menu).
Я бы хотел/ хотела (меню). (m/f) ya bih khat·*yel*/ khat·*ye*·la (min·*yu*)

I'd like to (hire a car).
Я бы хотел/ хотела (взять машину). (m/f) ya bih khat·*yel*/ khat·*ye*·la (vzyat' ma·*shih*·nu)

Can I (come in)?
Можно (войти)? mozh·na (vey·ti)

Could you please (write it down)?
(Запишите), пожалуйста. (za·pi·*shiht*·ye) pa·*zhal*·sta

Do I need (a visa)?
Нужна ли (виза)? nuzh·*na* li (*vi*·za)

I need (assistance).
Мне нужна (помощь). mnye nuzh·*na* (*po*·mash)

diesel	дизельное топливо	*di*·zil'·na·ye *to*·pli·va
regular	бензин номер 93	ben·*zin* *no*·mir di·vi·*no*·sta tri
unleaded	очищенный бензин	a·*chi*·shi·nih bin·*zin*

Is this the road to ...?
Эта дорога ведёт в ...? e·ta da·*ro*·ga vid·*yot* f ...

Where's a petrol station?
Где заправка? gdye za·*praf*·ka

Can I park here?
Здесь можно стоять? zdyes' *mozh*·na sta·*yat'*

I need a mechanic.
Мне нужен автомеханик. mnye *nu*·zhihn af·ta·mi·*kha*·nik

The car has broken down.
Машина сломалась. ma·*shih*·na sla·*ma*·las'

I have a flat tyre.
У меня лопнула шина. u min·*ya* lop·*nu*·la *shih*·na

I've run out of petrol.
У меня кончился бензин. u min·*ya* *kon*·chil·sa bin·*zin*

GLOSSARY

You may encounter some of the following terms and abbreviations during your travels in Russia. See also the Language chapter (p725).

aeroport – airport
ail – hexagonal or tepee-shaped yurt
apteka – pharmacy
arzhaan – Tuvan sacred spring
ataman – Cossack leader
aviakassa – air ticket office
avtobus – bus
avtostantsiya – bus stop
avtovokzal – bus terminal
AYaM – Amuro-Yakutskaya Magistral or Amur-Yakutsk Mainline

babushka – literally, 'grandmother', but used generally in Russian society for all old women
BAM – Baikalo-Amurskaya Magistral or Baikal-Amur Mainline, a trans-Siberian rail route
bankomat – automated teller machine (ATM)
banya – bathhouse
bashnya – tower
biblioteka – library
bifshteks – Russian-style hamburger
bilet – ticket
bolnitsa – hospital
bolshoy – big
boyar – high-ranking noble
bufet – snack bar selling cheap cold meats, boiled eggs, salads, bread, pastries etc
bukhta – bay
bulvar – boulevard
buterbrod – open sandwich
byliny – epic songs

chebureki – fried, meat-filled turnovers
chum – tepee-shaped tent made of birch bark
CIS (Commonwealth of Independent States) – an alliance (proclaimed in 1991) of independent states comprising the former USSR republics (less the three Baltic states); Sodruzhestvo Nezavisimykh Gosudarstv (SNG)

dacha – country cottage, summer house
datsan – Buddhist monastery
detsky – child's, children's
dezhurnaya – woman looking after a particular floor of a hotel
dolina – valley
dom – house
duma – parliament
dvorets – palace
dvorets kultury – literally, 'culture palace'; a meeting, social, entertainment, education centre, usually for a group such as railway workers, children etc

elektrichka – suburban train
etazh – floor (storey)

finift – luminous enamelled metal miniatures
firmeny poezda – trains with names (eg Rossiya); these are generally nicer trains
FSB (Federalnaya Sluzhba Bezopasnosti) – the Federal Security Service, the successor to the KGB

garderob – cloakroom
gastronom – speciality food shop
gavan – harbour
gazeta – newspaper
GIBDD (Gosudarsvennaya Inspektsiya po bezopasnosti dorozhnogo dvizheniya) – the State Automobile Inspectorate, aka the traffic police, still commonly known by their previous acronym GAI
glasnost – literally, 'openness'; the free-expression aspect of the Gorbachev reforms
glavpochtamt – main post office
gora – mountain
gorod – city, town
gostinitsa – hotel
gostiny dvor – trading arcade
Gulag (Glavnoe Upravlenie Lagerey) – Main Administration for Camps; the Soviet network of concentration camps
GUM (Gosudarstvenny Univermag) – State Department Store

igil – bowed, two-stringed Tuvan instrument
Intourist – old Soviet State Committee for Tourism, now privatised, split up and in competition with hundreds of other travel agencies
istochnik – mineral spring
izba – traditional, single-storey wooden cottage

kafe – café
kameny baba – standing stone idol
kamera khranenia – left-luggage office
kanal – canal
karta – map
kartofel, **kartoshka** – potatoes
kassa – ticket office, cashier's desk
kater – small ferry
kazak – Cossack
kempingi – organised camp sites; often have small cabins as well as tent sites
KGB (Komitet Gosudarstvennoy Bezopasnosti) – Committee of State Security
khachapuri – Georgian cheese bread
khleb – bread
khokhloma – red, black and gold lacquered pine bowls
khöömei – Tuvan throat singing
khram – church
khuresh – Tuvan style of wrestling

kino – cinema
kleshchi – ticks
kniga – book
kokoshniki – colourful gables and tiles laid in patterns
kolkhoz – collective farm
komnaty otdykha – resting rooms found at all major train stations and several smaller ones
kompot – fruit squash
Komsomol – Communist Youth League
kopek – the smallest, worthless unit of Russian currency
kordony – forest lodges, often found in national parks
korpus – building (ie one of several in a complex)
kray – territory
kremlin – a town's fortified stronghold
kulak – a peasant wealthy enough to own a farm, hire labour and engage in money lending
kupeyny, kupe – 2nd-class compartment on a train
kurgan – burial mound
kurort – spa
kvartira – flat, apartment
kvas – fermented rye bread water

lavra – senior monastery
lyux – a kind of hotel suite, with a sitting room in addition to bedroom and bathroom; a *polu-lyux* suite is the less spacious version

Mafia – anyone who has anything to do with crime, from genuine gangsters to victims of their protection rackets
magazin – shop
maly – small
manezh – riding school
marka – postage stamp or brand, trademark
marshrutka, marshrutnoye taksi – minibus that runs along a fixed route
matryoshka – set of painted wooden dolls within dolls
medovukha – honey ale (mead)
mestnoe vremya – local time
mezhdunarodny – international
mineralnaya voda – mineral water
monastyr – monastery
more – sea
morskoy vokzal – sea terminal
Moskovskoye vremya – Moscow time
most – bridge
muzey – museum; also some palaces, art galleries and nonworking churches
muzhskoy – men's (toilet)
myagky – 1st-class train compartment

naberezhnaya – embankment
Nashi – Ours; ultranationalist youth group
nizhny – lower
nomenklatura – literally, 'list of nominees'; the old government and Communist Party elite
novy – new
novy russky – New Russians

obed – lunch
oblast – region
obshchiy – 4th-class place on a train
okruga – districts
omul – a cousin of salmon and trout, endemic to Lake Baikal
ostrog – fortress
ostrov – island
OVIR (Otdel Viz i Registratsii) – Department of Visas and Registration; now known under the acronym PVU, although outside Moscow OVIR is still likely to be in use
ozero – lake

palekh – enamelled wood boxes
parnyatnik – statue, monument
Paskha – Easter
passazhirsky poezd – intercity stopping train
pelmeni – Russian-style ravioli stuffed with meat
perekhod – underground walkway
perestroika – literally, 're-structuring'; Mikhail Gorbachev's efforts to revive the Soviet economy
pereulok – lane, side street
pirozhki – savoury pies
platskartny, platskart – 3rd-class place on a train
ploshchad – square
pochta – post office
poezd – train
poliklinika – medical centre
polu-lyux – less spacious version of a *lyux*, a hotel suite with a sitting room in addition to the bedroom and bathroom
polyana – glade, clearing
posolstvo – embassy
prichal – landing, pier
prigorodny poezd – suburban train
prigorodny zal – ticket hall
produkty – food store
proezd – passage
prokat – rental
propusk – permit, pass
prospekt – avenue
provodnik (m), provodnitsa (f) – carriage attendant on a train
PVU (Passportno-Vizovoye Upravleniye) – passport and visa department, formerly OVIR (an acronym which is still likely to be in use outside Moscow)

raketa – hydrofoil
rayon – district
rechnoy vokzal – river station
reka – river
remont, na remont – closed for repairs (a sign you see all too often)
restoran – restaurant
Rozhdestvo – Russian Orthodox Christmas
rynok – market

sad – garden
samovar – an urn used to heat water for tea
selo – village
sever – north

shawarma – grilled meat and salad wrapped in flat bread
shashlyk – meat kebab
shosse – highway
shtuka – piece (many items of produce are sold by the piece)
skory poezd – literally, 'fast train'; a long-distance train
sobor – cathedral
soviet – council
sovok – a contraction of *sovokopniy*, meaning communal person and referring to those who were born and lived during the Soviet period
spalny vagon – SV; 1st-class place on a train
spusk – descent, slope
Sputnik – former youth-travel arm of Komsomol; now just one of the bigger tourism agencies
stanitsa – Cossack village
stary – old
stolovaya – canteen, cafeteria
suvenir – souvenir

taiga – northern pine, fir, spruce and larch forest
taksofon – pay telephone
teatr – theatre
teatralnaya kassa – theatre ticket office
thangka – Buddhist religious paintings
traktir – tavern
tramvay – tram
tserkov – church
TsUM (Tsentralny Univermag) – name of a department store
tualet – toilet
tuda i obratno – literally, 'there and back'; return ticket
turbaza – tourist camp

ulitsa – street
univermag, universalny magazin – department store
ushchelie – gorge or valley
uzhin – supper

val – rampart
vareniki – dumplings with a variety of possible fillings
venik – tied bundle of birch branches
verkhny – upper
vkhod – way in, entrance
voda – water
vodny vokzal – ferry terminal
vokzal – station
vostok – east
vykhodnoy den – day off (Saturday, Sunday and holidays)

yantar – amber
yezhednevno – every day, daily
yug – south
yurt – nomad's portable, round tent-house made of felt or skins stretched over a collapsible frame of wood slats

zakaznaya – registered post
zakuski – appetisers
zal – hall, room
zaliv – gulf, bay
zamok – castle, fortress
zapad – west
zapovednik – special purpose (nature) reserve
zavtrak – breakfast
zhensky – women's (toilet)
zhetony – tokens (for metro etc)

behind the scenes

SEND US YOUR FEEDBACK

We love to hear from travellers – your comments keep us on our toes and help make our books better. Our well-travelled team reads every word on what you loved or loathed about this book. Although we cannot reply individually to postal submissions, we always guarantee that your feedback goes straight to the appropriate authors, in time for the next edition. Each person who sends us information is thanked in the next edition – and the most useful submissions are rewarded with a free book.

Visit **lonelyplanet.com/contact** to submit your updates and suggestions or to ask for help. Our award-winning website also features inspirational travel stories, news and discussions.

Note: We may edit, reproduce and incorporate your comments in Lonely Planet products such as guidebooks, websites and digital products, so let us know if you don't want your comments reproduced or your name acknowledged. For a copy of our privacy policy visit lonelyplanet.com/privacy.

OUR READERS

Many thanks to the travellers who used the last edition and wrote to us with helpful hints, useful advice and interesting anecdotes:

Pete Adkins, Charlie Ainsworth, Angela Byrne, Samuel Chan, Priscilla Chan YW, Dr Phil Clendenning, James Cox, Helen Crittenden, Juan Ignacio Cruz, Ben Duncan, Astrid Engelen, Hana Formankova, Gina Green, Toni Grewal, Alexandra Guyot, Arve Hansen, Esther Harper, Ira Hartmann, Dominik Hosters, Marius Huber, Markus Husa, Clive Johnson, Oksana Kaplunenko, Sarah Klinger, Ivana Kuzmova, Jorg Lauberbach, Kate Lomas, Svetlana Lysyakova, Barathi Victoria Magerøy, Petter Magnusson, John Marshall, Dean Moore, Rebecca Nestle, Neena Packing, Leo Paton, Radoslaw Pawlowicki, Jessalyn Peters, Eva Pfarrwaller, Johan Pieterse, Adam Plaskey, Mark Pollard, Andrew Roper, Sabrina, Rene Schreiber, John Soar, Dezheng Tang, Kate Tomlinson, Valentin Torggler, Miikka Tunturi, Michael Tyson, Hans van den Boom, Martin Vegoda, Petra & Robbert Visser, Wataru Yamamoto

AUTHOR THANKS

Simon Richmond

Many thanks to my fellow authors; Sasha, Andrey and Peter; Vyacheslav Bochkov, Ilya Gurevich, Yegor, Mirjana and Neil McGowan; Dmitry Zaytsev, Ksenia, Irina and Artyem Ryzkov; ace Oryol dentist Yelena Savina and husband Alex; Oksana Chernega and her fab team in Veliky Novgorod; Tonny and Donna for holding the forts in Boston and London. A belated thanks to Trans-Siberian Ian Frazier. This book is dedicated to Dora, who made a very different, life-saving Trans-Siberian trip back in 1941.

Marc Bennetts

Thanks to Tanya and Masha the Basha for meeting me in the playground when I came back. Greetings to everyone who helped me on my travels, including above all the many friendly people of Manzherok. Thanks also again to Sayat and Kayrat in Kosh-Agach and Minsalim in Tobolsk. No thanks at all to the Altai's many ticks, but much gratitude to the inventors of amoxicillin.

Greg Bloom

The biggest thanks go to pop, who rolled with me (literally) for four weeks, taking many vodka shots for the team. Dad, you asked for an adventure, you got it! Thanks to predecessor Robert Reid for engaging and passing along many tips. On the road, shouts go out to Daria and Bryan in Khabarovsk, to Leo for various tips, to Misha in Komsomolsk, to Lera and Alyona in Kamchatka and, of course, to my homeboy Christian in Yakutsk.

Marc Di Duca

A huge *dyakuyu* to my Kyiv parents-in-law for taking care of my son Taras while I was away. Thanks to Denis, Marina, Svetlana and Naran in Ulan-Ude, Zhenya in Irkutsk, Maria at Irkutsk tourist office, Yulia in Listvyanka, Svetlana in Irkutsk, Nikita and Natalia in Khuzhir, Anatoly and Oksana in Krasnoyarsk, Sean, Anay-Kaak and Zhenya in Kyzyl, and everyone at the Tuvan Ministry of Finance (Tourism Department). Lastly to my wife Tanya – thank you for all your amazing support throughout.

Anthony Haywood

I'd like to thank the very knowledgeable staff at the Tourist Information Centre of Kazan and Permtourist (Perm), and also Valentina Sorokoletova at the History Museum of the Volga-Don Canal. Very special thanks to Tanya Ryabukhina in Moscow and Tamara Ryabukhina and Gennardy Doronin in Volgograd for their vital assistance and fine companionship. Thanks also to Katya Putina (Perm) and Lyuba Suslyakova (Yekaterinburg). Final thanks go to fellow authors and staff at LP who worked so hard on this book.

Tom Masters

Big thanks to my best friend in St Petersburg, Simon Patterson, for his good-humoured, vodka-soaked company on every trip I make to the city. Thanks also to Grégory Strub, Anna Knutson, Sergey Chernov, Tobin Auber, Gena Bolgolepov, Dima Dzhafarov, Veronika Altukhova, Dima Makarov, Alexei Dmitriev, Jessica Moroz, Chinawoman & Gang and Slava Gusinsky for all their help and company during this research trip. At Lonely Planet many thanks to Simon, Mara, Anna, Imogen and the team in Melbourne for their continued hard work and support.

Leonid Ragozin

I would like to thank my wife, Masha Makeeva, for enduring my absences and accompanying me on some of the Golden Ring trips. Also, many thanks to Simon Richmond for guidance and patience, to Mara Vorhees for writing an excellent chapter for the previous edition, which was very easy to update this time around, and to Ekaterina Koldeyeva for tips on Yaroslavl.

Tamara Sheward

The people to thank would easily fill a *platskart* wagon, when I have but the space of a *kupe* cabin. In brief, hugely grateful vodka-/cognac-clinks to *Barents Observer* journos, Elena in Petrozavodsk, the *morzhi* of Murmansk, Grigori at the Ametist, the human whirlwind Kseniya, Apatity's Alpha-Plus channel for my five minutes of (awkward) fame, Ridel, and Nikolai for the 6am *sto gramma*. Thanks beyond compare go out to the always-awesome Dasha Khyutte and new besties Sergey and Viki. Dušan, my beautiful *blizanac: volim tvoj glava*!

Regis St Louis

Thanks go to Simon, Greg and Leonid for helpful tips on the Caucasus; Vlad and Denis at Wild Russia for Elbrus input; Bruce Talley for Sochi insight; Dmitry Mirzonov for good coffee and a lift to Novorossiysk; and the two babushkas who helped me find my way in Rostov. Thanks to all the great Russians I met on trains, buses and taxis who shared insight into this massive country. Hugs to Cassandra and daughters Magdalena and Genevieve for a warm homecoming.

Mara Vorhees

Moscow with one-year-old twins requires an extra set of thank-yous to everyone who helped the monkeys settle into life in the Russian capital. Our awesome babysitter tops that list – Спасибо дорогая Маша! My regular crew of Muscovite contacts was ever helpful, especially Tim O'Brien and Mirjana Vinsentin. Special thanks to Laura Bridge and Campbell Bethwaite for the 'local knowledge'. And a million kisses to Jerry, Shay and Van for coming along for the ride.

ACKNOWLEDGMENTS

Climate map data adapted from Peel MC, Finlayson BL & McMahon TA (2007) 'Updated World Map of the Köppen-Geiger Climate Classification', *Hydrology and Earth System Sciences*, 11, 163344.

Cover photograph: Church in Sergiev Posad, Gunter Grafenhain / 4Corners Images ©. Many of the images in this guide are available for licensing from Lonely Planet Images: www.lonelyplanetimages.com.

THIS BOOK

This 6th edition of Lonely Planet's *Russia* guidebook was researched and written by Simon Richmond, Marc Bennetts, Greg Bloom, Marc Di Duca, Anthony Haywood, Tom Masters, Leonid Ragozin, Tamara Sheward, Regis St Louis and Mara Vorhees. Mark Elliott and Robert Reid worked on the previous edition. This guidebook was commissioned in Lonely Planet's London office and produced by the following:

Commissioning Editor Anna Tyler
Coordinating Editor Andi Jones
Coordinating Cartographer Valentina Kremenchutskaya
Coordinating Layout Designer Wibowo Rusli
Managing Editors Imogen Bannister, Kirsten Rawlings, Tasmin Waby McNaughtan
Managing Cartographers Adrian Persoglia, Amanda Sierp
Managing Layout Designer Jane Hart
Assisting Editors Janet Austin, Carolyn Bain, Kim Hutchins, Christopher Pitts
Assisting Cartographers Enes Basic, Ildiko Bogdanovits, Katalin Dadi-Racz, Karusha Ganga, Mick Garrett
Cover Research Naomi Parker
Internal Image Research Aude Vauconsant
Illustrator Javier Zarracina
Language Content Branislava Vladisavljevic

Thanks to Elin Berglund, Jo Cooke, Melanie Dankel, Catherine Eldridge, Ryan Evans, Chris Girdler, William Gourlay, Imogen Hall, Briohny Hooper, Yvonne Kirk, Annelies Mertens, Trent Paton, Sally Schafer, Sophie Splatt, Angela Tinson, Gerard Walker, Juan Winata

000 Map pages
000 Photo pages

B

000 Map pages
000 Photo pages

000 Map pages
000 Photo pages

000 Map pages
000 Photo pages

G

000 Map pages
000 Photo pages

I

000 Map pages
000 Photo pages

000 Map pages
000 Photo pages

000 Map pages
000 Photo pages

P

000 Map pages
000 Photo pages

S

000 Map pages
000 Photo pages

000 Map pages
000 Photo pages

U

Y

Z

how to use this book

These symbols will help you find the listings you want:

- Sights
- Beaches
- Activities
- Courses
- Tours
- Festivals & Events
- Sleeping
- Eating
- Drinking
- Entertainment
- Shopping
- Information/ Transport

These symbols give you the vital information for each listing:

- Telephone Numbers
- Opening Hours
- Parking
- Nonsmoking
- Air-Conditioning
- Internet Access
- Wi-Fi Access
- Swimming Pool
- Vegetarian Selection
- English-Language Menu
- Family-Friendly
- Pet-Friendly
- Bus
- Ferry
- Metro
- Subway
- Tram
- Train

Reviews are organised by author preference.

Look out for these icons:

- TOP CHOICE — Our author's recommendation
- FREE — No payment required
- A green or sustainable option

Our authors have nominated these places as demonstrating a strong commitment to sustainability – for example by supporting local communities and producers, operating in an environmentally friendly way, or supporting conservation projects.

Map Legend

Sights
Beach
Buddhist
Castle
Christian
Hindu
Islamic
Jewish
Monument
Museum/Gallery
Ruin
Winery/Vineyard
Zoo
Other Sight

Activities, Courses & Tours
Diving/Snorkelling
Canoeing/Kayaking
Skiing
Surfing
Swimming/Pool
Walking
Windsurfing
Other Activity/ Course/Tour

Sleeping
Sleeping
Camping

Eating
Eating

Drinking
Drinking
Cafe

Entertainment
Entertainment

Shopping
Shopping

Information
Bank
Embassy/ Consulate
Hospital/Medical
Internet
Police
Post Office
Telephone
Toilet
Tourist Information
Other Information

Transport
Airport
Border Crossing
Bus
Cable Car/ Funicular
Cycling
Ferry
Metro
Monorail
Parking
Petrol Station
Taxi
Train/Railway
Tram
Other Transport

Routes
Tollway
Freeway
Primary
Secondary
Tertiary
Lane
Unsealed Road
Plaza/Mall
Steps
Tunnel
Pedestrian Overpass
Walking Tour
Walking Tour Detour
Path

Geographic
Hut/Shelter
Lighthouse
Lookout
Mountain/Volcano
Oasis
Park
Pass
Picnic Area
Waterfall

Population
Capital (National)
Capital (State/Province)
City/Large Town
Town/Village

Boundaries
International
State/Province
Disputed
Regional/Suburb
Marine Park
Cliff
Wall

Hydrography
River, Creek
Intermittent River
Swamp/Mangrove
Reef
Canal
Water
Dry/Salt/ Intermittent Lake
Glacier

Areas
Beach/Desert
Cemetery (Christian)
Cemetery (Other)
Park/Forest
Sportsground
Sight (Building)
Top Sight (Building)

Anthony Haywood

Volga Region, The Urals Anthony was born in the port city of Fremantle, Western Australia, and pulled anchor early on to hitchhike (mostly) through Europe and the USA. He later studied comparative literature in Perth and Russian language in Melbourne. In the 1990s he moved to Germany. Today he works as a freelance writer and journalist and divides his time between Göttingen (Lower Saxony) and Berlin. His book, *Siberia, A Cultural History,* was published in 2010.

Tom Masters

St Petersburg Tom first came to St Petersburg in 1996 while studying Russian at the School of Slavonic & East European Studies in London. He loved the city so much that he came back after graduating and worked as a writer and editor at the *St Petersburg Times*. Since then he's been based in London and Berlin, but returns regularly to Piter to take on documentary work, and to write freelance articles and Lonely Planet guides. You can see more of Tom's work at www.tommasters.net.

Read more about Tom at:
lonelyplanet.com/members/tommasters

Leonid Ragozin

Golden Ring Leonid Ragozin devoted himself to beach dynamics when he studied geology in Moscow. But for want of really nice beaches in Russia, he helped gold miners in Siberia and sold InterRail tickets before embarking on a journalist career. After eight years with the BBC, he became a foreign correspondent for the *Russian Newsweek* – the job that took him to such unlikely destinations as Bhutan and Ecuador. Now back at the BBC, he has plunged into the turbulent sea of TV news.

Tamara Sheward

Northern European Russia After years of freelance travel writing, journalism and authordom, Tamara leapt at the chance to join the Lonely Planet ranks as presenter of LPTV's *Roads Less Travelled: Cambodia*. Following a Lonely Planet stint in Serbia for the *Eastern Europe* guide, Tamara again returned to her Slavic roots to write this book's Northern European Russia chapter. As a result, she now counts Arctic backwater-hopping, raucous *platskart* journeys and drinking in the park among her favourite pastimes, which will no doubt thrill her Russian mother.

Read more about Tamara at:
lonelyplanet.com/members/tamarasheward

Regis St Louis

Russian Caucasus An early fan of Gogol and Dostoevsky, Regis spent his university years in the US and Moscow immersed in the world of Rus, in pursuit of a rather impractical degree in Slavic Languages and Literatures. On this trip into the Caucasus, Regis drank *kvas* copiously, hiked over dramatic mountain peaks and joined in political discussions at a youth conference in Karachay-Cherkessia. A full-time travel writer since 2003, Regis has contributed to more than 30 Lonely Planet titles. He lives in Brooklyn, New York.

Read more about Regis at:
lonelyplanet.com/members/regisstlouis

Mara Vorhees

Moscow Mara has been travelling to Moscow since it was the capital of a different country. The pen-wielding traveller has worked on dozens of Lonely Planet titles, including *Moscow, St Petersburg* and *Trans-Siberian Railway*. When not roaming around Russia, Mara lives in a pink house in Somerville, Massachusetts, with her husband, two kiddies and two kitties. Follow her adventures at www.maravorhees.com.

Read more about Mara at:
lonelyplanet.com/members/mvorhees

OUR STORY

A beat-up old car, a few dollars in the pocket and a sense of adventure. In 1972 that's all Tony and Maureen Wheeler needed for the trip of a lifetime – across Europe and Asia overland to Australia. It took several months, and at the end – broke but inspired – they sat at their kitchen table writing and stapling together their first travel guide, *Across Asia on the Cheap*. Within a week they'd sold 1500 copies. Lonely Planet was born.

Today, Lonely Planet has offices in Melbourne, London and Oakland, with more than 600 staff and writers. We share Tony's belief that 'a great guidebook should do three things: inform, educate and amuse'.

OUR WRITERS

Simon Richmond

Coordinating Author; Western European Russia, Kaliningrad Region After studying Russian history and politics during university, Simon first visited the country in 1994 when he wandered goggle eyed around gorgeous St Petersburg and peeked at Lenin's mummified corpse in Red Square. He's since travelled the breadth of the nation from Kamchatka in the Far East to Kaliningrad in the far west, stopping off at many points between. An award-winning writer and photographer, Simon is the coauthor of Lonely Planet's *Trans-Siberian Railway* editions 1, 2 and 3; *Russia* editions 3, 4 and 5; and many other titles for the company, ranging from Cape Town to Korea. Read more about his travels at www.simonrichmond.com.

Read more about Simon at:
lonelyplanet.com/members/simonrichmond

Marc Bennetts

Western Siberia Marc moved to Russia in 1997 and immediately fell in love with the country's pirate CD markets. Since then, he has written about Russian spies, Chechen football and Soviet psychics for a variety of national newspapers, including the *Guardian* and the *Times*. In 2008 his book *Football Dynamo: Modern Russia and the People's Game* was released. He is currently working on a book about Russia's fascination with the occult. Contact him at marcbennetts@yahoo.com.

Greg Bloom

Russian Far East Greg cut his teeth in the former Soviet Union as a journalist and later editor-in-chief of the *Kyiv Post*. He left Ukraine in 2003 but returns frequently to the region. In the service of Lonely Planet, he has been detained in Uzbekistan, taken a *shlagbaum* to the head in Kyiv, swam in the dying Aral Sea, snowboarded down volcanoes in Kamchatka and hit 100km/h in a Latvian bobsled. These days Greg lives in Cambodia. Read about his trips at www.mytripjournal.com/bloomblogs.

Read more about Greg at:
lonelyplanet.com/members/gbloom4

Marc Di Duca

Eastern Siberia Marc has spent nigh on two decades criss-crossing the former communist world, the last seven of them as a travel guide author. Stints on previous editions of Lonely Planet's *Russia* and *Trans-Siberian Railway* were preceded by other guides to Moscow, St Petersburg and Lake Baikal. Motor boating around the Selenga River Delta, stalking Decembrists across 4 million sq km and munching through perilous amounts of Buryat *pozi* all formed part of research in his beloved Siberia this time round.

Read more about Marc at:
lonelyplanet.com/members/madidu

OVER PAGE MORE WRITERS

Published by Lonely Planet Publications Pty Ltd
ABN 36 005 607 983
6th edition – Mar 2012
ISBN 978 1 74179 579 0

10 9 8 7 6 5 4 3 2 1
Printed in China